MW00812007

Xi Jinping

Xi Jinping

Political Career, Governance, and Leadership,
1953–2018

ALFRED L. CHAN

OXFORD
UNIVERSITY PRESS

OXFORD
UNIVERSITY PRESS

Oxford University Press is a department of the University of Oxford. It furthers
the University's objective of excellence in research, scholarship, and education
by publishing worldwide. Oxford is a registered trade mark of Oxford University
Press in the UK and certain other countries.

Published in the United States of America by Oxford University Press
198 Madison Avenue, New York, NY 10016, United States of America.

© Oxford University Press 2022

All rights reserved. No part of this publication may be reproduced, stored in
a retrieval system, or transmitted, in any form or by any means, without the
prior permission in writing of Oxford University Press, or as expressly permitted
by law, by license, or under terms agreed with the appropriate reproduction
rights organization. Inquiries concerning reproduction outside the scope of the
above should be sent to the Rights Department, Oxford University Press, at the
address above.

You must not circulate this work in any other form
and you must impose this same condition on any acquirer.

Library of Congress Cataloging-in-Publication Data
Names: Chan, Alfred L., author.
Title: Xi Jinping : political career, governance, and leadership, 1953–2018 / Alfred L. Chan.
Other titles: Political career, governance, and leadership, 1953–2018
Description: New York, NY : Oxford University Press, [2022] |
Includes bibliographical references and index.
Identifiers: LCCN 2021056518 (print) | LCCN 2021056519 (ebook) |
ISBN 9780197615225 (hardback) | ISBN 9780197615249 (epub)
Subjects: LCSH: Xi, Jinping. | Presidents—China—Biography. |
Heads of state—China—Biography. | China—Politics and government—2002- |
China—Politics and government—20th century.
Classification: LCC DS779.49.X53 C43 2022 (print) |
LCC DS779.49.X53 (ebook) | DDC 951.06/12092 [B]—dc23/eng/20220103
LC record available at https://lccn.loc.gov/2021056518
LC ebook record available at https://lccn.loc.gov/2021056519

DOI: 10.1093/oso/9780197615225.001.0001

Printed in Canada by Marquis Book Printing

For Michael

Contents

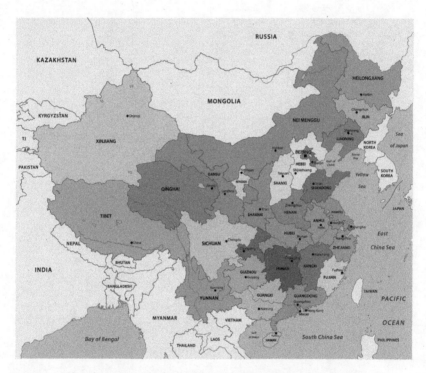

Figure 0.1   China's provincial administrations and neighboring countries

Plate 1. ... with ... ...

Illustrations

Figures

Tables

Acknowledgments

I take great pleasure in expressing here my gratitude to friends, family members, and colleagues who have, in so many ways, sustained my long journey of research and writing over the years.

Amoy Ong, Tony Ma, Roxanna Chan, Lily and Albert Choi, Ivy and Charles Cheung, and Janice and Philip Yeung, in many stimulating discussions, shared with me their firsthand insights about working in China.

Friends Karen McMillan, Patricia Chartier, Fred Berenbaum, Kelly Pykerman (RIP), Esther Bogyo, Lesley Towers, Anna Marie Read, and Patrick O'Neill (RIP) have always been supportive with food and visits, and I thank Charnie Guettel for drawing my attention to the literature on settler colonialism.

I appreciate the long-standing friendship of Ralph Lai, Daniel Dragon, Roland Hoy, Lee Goossens, Eric Tang, James Miller, Billy Newman, Jim Currie, Brian Avery, Michael Ong, Gerald McShane, Judy McKenna, Yakov Lerner, Gilles LeBlanc, J. Kevin Kelliher, and Jack Evans, who have sustained me through dinners and discussions. Gillian Roberts, Ethan Kohn, and their sons Hank and Eli were always pleasant company, and treated me to many dim sum lunches. I relish the fond memories of dear friends the late Yee Nar Lee and Nancy Ing.

I have benefited by the support and good counsel of Gigi and Roland Tong, and thank Zach Child for his assistance at the early stages of research.

I am eternally grateful for the support of my globalized, extended Chan family, for Aunt Tatiana and Kay Chan for enlightening me about China, and for Aunt Helena and my late uncle Desmond Yam and their special appreciation for years of good cheers—Aunt Helena was always there for me, especially when I felt discouraged.

My brothers Davis, Sammy, Ming and their families, and especially Andrew Chan, have been a constant source of encouragement and support. I know that a smile from my mother, who is battling Alzheimer's, is a sign of her confidence in me.

I owe a debt of gratitude to Molly and Jason of the Kato family for their love and companionship, and cherish the loving memory of Billy, Josie, and Joey.

To the members of the Farewell family, John, Mary Rose, Elgin, and especially Julianne, for their thoughtfulness and camaraderie, I'd like to send a big thank you. I relish the affection and support of the late Rose and Harley (Al) Farewell.

The Asian Institute at the Munk Centre on Global Affairs at the University of Toronto provided a stimulating home base for my research and the university library was unceasingly efficient in securing materials for me through interlibrary loans.

I have benefited by numerous discussions with Shu-yun Ma, Margaret Ting, Kam-wing Chan, Joyce Liu, Joan Huang, Kai Yuen Tsui, Ralph Thaxton, and Charles Burton about everything Chinese.

Huron University College colleagues Dianqing Xu, Paul Nesbitt-Larking, Neil Bradford, Jim Crimmins, and Jennifer Mustapha have always been intellectually stimulating, and Jun Fang generously shared his expertise on China and Zhejiang.

I am grateful to Huron University College for granting a two-year leave of absence, and to my students there for their intellectual curiosity, dynamism, and interest in China and politics. I thank the Social Science and Humanities Research Council of Canada for a grant to study the Hu Jintao leadership, although the substance of the project shifted when my research interest moved to this current volume.

Michael Szonyi took time out from his busy schedule to read the manuscript and offer much-needed advice.

I owe a special debt of gratitude to two reviewers for their detailed and valuable comments, which have sharpened my thinking and saved me from embarrassing errors. At Oxford University Press, Holly Mitchell and Katharine Pratt have been patient with my numerous enquries. I thank David McBride for his great help shepherding the project from start to finish, Richard Isomaki for expert copy editing, and Newgen Knowledge Network for an efficient production process.

Of particular importance is my good friend Donald Hickerson, who edited the entire manuscript with patience and care, and to whom I express my deep appreciation.

Last but not least, I am grateful to my best friend and partner Michael Farewell for going through many drafts of the book, for tolerating my constant thinking out aloud, and for sharing his encyclopedic knowledge of history and current events. Without his unwavering support and encouragement, this work would not have been possible. This book is dedicated to him.

Needless to say, I alone am responsible for any or all errors in facts or interpretation in this volume.

Abbreviations

ACC	anticorruption campaign
ADIZ	Air Defense Identification Zone
AIIB	Asian Infrastructure Investment Bank
ASEAN	Association of Southeast Asian Nations
BRI	Belt and Road Initiative
CAC	Cyberspace Administration of China
CAG	Chinese Academy of Governance
CASS	Chinese Academy of Social Sciences
CBIRC	China Banking and Insurance Regulatory Commission
CBRC	China Banking Regulatory Commission
CIRC	China Insurance Regulatory Commission
CC	Central Committee
CCCSM	Central Committee for Comprehensive Social Management
CCDI	Central Commission for Discipline Inspection
CCP	Chinese Communist Party
CDI	Committee for Discipline Inspection
CDRLSG	Comprehensively Deepening Reform Leading Small Group
CEE	Central and Eastern Europe
CFAC	Central Foreign Affairs Commission
CIRC	China Insurance Regulatory Commission
CMC	Central Military Commission
CNSC	Central National Security Commission
COD	Central Organization Department
CPC	County Party Committee
CPLAC	Central Political and Legal Affairs Commission
CPPCC	Chinese People's Political Consultative Conference
CPS	Central Party School
CSRC	China Securities Regulatory Commission
CYL	Chinese Communist Youth League
CYLC	Chinese Communist Youth League Central
DPP	Democratic Progressive Party
FYP	Five-Year Plan
IMF	International Monetary Fund
ISG	innovation in social governance
ISM	innovation in social management
KMT	Kuomintang
LSG	leading small group
MARA	Ministry of Agriculture and Rural Affairs

MEE	Ministry of Ecological Environment
MEM	Ministry of Emergency Management
MEP	Ministry of Environment Protection
MIC	Made in China 2025
MLEP	mass line education practice campaign
MPC	Municipal Party Committee
MPPC	Municipal People's Committee
NAC	National Audit Commission
NDB	New Development Bank
NDRC	National Development and Reform Commission
NPC	National Party Congress
NPeC	National People's Congress
NSC	National Security Commission
NSuC	National Supervisory Commission
OPTC	"one party, two coalitions"
PAP	People's Armed Police
PBOC	People's Bank of China
PBSC	Politburo Standing Committee
PD	Publicity Department
PFTZ	Pilot Free Trade Zone
PLA	People's Liberation Army
PPC	Provincial Party Committee
PRC	People's Republic of China
R2G	Red Second Generation
RMRB	*Renmin ribao* (People's Daily)
SAPRET	State Administration of Press, Publication, Radio, Film, and Television
SASAC	State-Owned Assets Supervisory and Administration Commission
SCS	South China Sea
SCIO	State Council Information Office
SCMP	*South China Morning Post*
SLOC	sea lanes of communication
SME	small and medium enterprise
SMRA	State Market Regulatory Administration
SOE	state-owned enterprise
THAAD	Terminal High Altitude Area Defense
UFWD	United Front Work Department
VASC	village affairs supervisory committee
WMP	wealth management product
WTO	World Trade Organization

1
Introduction

Few contemporary world leaders can boast of such rich, contrasting, and dramatic life experiences as those accumulated by China's paternalistic and authoritarian leader Xi Jinping. Now one of the most influential players on the global stage, Xi is attempting to remake the Chinese political economy, and this is already having a tremendous impact on one-fifth of humankind, and increasingly on the rest of the world. However, Xi's reputation has been controversial and seldom neutral. Foreign opinions on him tend to be negative, and exaggerated discourses have even compared him to Stalin.[1] More realistically, Xi's life history mirrors the trials and tribulations of the history of the People's Republic of China (PRC), and the seismic changes to China over the past sixty-odd years. This includes the breakneck pace of change and development in the post-Mao period, the scope and scale of which find no parallel in human history. As general secretary, Xi has attempted to introduce reforms amid the forces unleashed by rapid development and modernization. Beijing also must contend with a rapidly changing international environment that features more turbulence and uncertainty. The global economy has never been that intertwined and interdependent, but insular tendencies are gaining ground, and a litany of global issues, from poverty to biodiversity loss, and from pollution to climate change, have reached a critical point. Yet China's rise has upset the global balance of power and raised concerns over the emergence of a political and economic juggernaut. At home, Xi attempts to foster more development to catch up with the developed West, and privileges Chinese Communist Party (CCP) leadership to ward off the ever-present forces of instability and disintegration. The governance of China is a complex matter, and Xi's rule exhibits both progressive and regressive features.

Born a princeling to one of the founders of the PRC, Xi's relatively privileged childhood promised unrivaled opportunity, but he was traumatized by the tribulations of the Cultural Revolution (1966–1976). After the cataclysm, he launched his political career during the era of reforms, opening, and globalization. He has lived through both the challenges and the opportunities of rapidly changing times. Xi's princeling status has brought him persecution and suffering, reducing him in turn to a juvenile delinquent, a pauper, and an ordinary peasant performing hard labor and scratching out a living at a bare subsistence level. Through sheer iron determination, he clawed his way back up the political ladder; at times his attempt to shake off his princeling image prompted him to make unusual career choices. In little more than three decades, Xi rose from village branch party secretary to becoming in 2007 heir apparent to the national leadership and then succeeding as general secretary of the CCP in 2012. In between, he governed poverty-stricken hinterlands as well as larger and relatively prosperous provinces and municipalities. He began a second term as general secretary in 2017 and as president in 2018, and barring any accidents he seems determined to stay on for a third five-year term at the 2022–2023 changeover. Some observers suspect that he intends to make himself leader for life.

Several generations of Chinese lived through the trauma of the Cultural Revolution, but the so-called fifth generation (often equated with "lost generation"), of which Xi is a part, suffered disproportionately since they lost the opportunity for formal education during their formative years. Eventually, however, like other leaders of this cohort, Xi ascended step by step up the administrative ladder; but he alone managed to reach the pinnacle of power, the office of general secretary.

During his first term (2012/13–2017/18) as China's paramount leader, Xi had to face up to the dual challenges of a rising nation with ever-increasing economic and military capabilities on the one hand, but with political and systemic vulnerabilities on the other. The policy environment confronting China was becoming increasingly complex and unpredictable, and, as Xi repeatedly asserted, reforms had reached an inflection point. Xi's choice of action was to unleash ambitious and comprehensive plans to reform the political economy, to discipline the state and society, and to assert China's global position. As leader, Xi has accumulated a great deal of power, and he has managed to make himself the "core" of the Party by inserting his theoretical contributions (with his name attached) into the Party and state constitutions. He has privileged his revolutionary heritage, confidence, and sense of mission to unleash numerous widely ambitious and far-reaching projects.

Xi's notion of the "China Dream and Great Rejuvenation" aims to restore China's historical greatness and international stature, and to turn the country into a great power and an innovative economic powerhouse. Like his predecessors in the post-Mao period, he has searched for China's unique path for modernization, development, and prosperity for all. Xi was essentially occupied with those issues confronting most other world leaders—the search for a modern governance model that could reconcile relationships between government, market, and civil society under conditions of intensifying globalization, competition, and technical and climate changes. His new goals were to map out a model of quality and sustainable development. He sought to improve the quality of life, tackle poverty, combat pollution, and improve public services and the social safety net. He attempted to instill greater pride and self-confidence in the Chinese people and to win over their hearts and minds with the aspirational slogan "Awesome

China." And following CCP tradition, Xi set multiple five-year plans to realize these goals.

Unlike his predecessors, however, Xi quickly introduced major dramatic and unprecedented transformations in the party state. After a rapid consolidation of power, he effected a threefold centralization of power in his person, the capital, and the Party. Simultaneously, Xi tried to save the party state by forcing discipline on it through draconian measures, including a sweeping anticorruption campaign. An uber-Leninist, Xi also imposed greater discipline on civil society and other political entities by tightening surveillance, by censorship, and by cracking down on dissent. This earned him the reputation of an authoritarian and even a dictator. He introduced a sweeping reform and reorganization of the judiciary and the military. He pushed development on all policy fronts, and on economic reforms pledged to let market forces "play a decisive role" in the allocation of resources while ensuring that "the government can play its own role more effectively."[2] Xi's first term ended with the most comprehensive restructuring of the party state in the post-Mao reform period.

Externally, Xi's avowed goal was to foster "a more just and rational" new world order and to move China toward "center stage in the world." Abandoning the more cautious foreign policy of his predecessors, he strove to seek a new power relationship with other countries, especially with the United States. Xi's Belt and Road Initiative is an ambitious and colossal venture to connect and enmesh large numbers of Eurasian countries with trade, investment, and infrastructural development. Xi spearheaded globalization and attempted to fight climate change at a time when the United States appeared to be withdrawing into unilateralism, isolationism, and protectionism. Yet Xi's ambition to modernize and strengthen China inevitably deepened security dilemmas with international competitors, especially with the United States, generating mistrust and confrontation.[3]

In describing Xi Jinping as a "Mandela class of person," seasoned Singaporean statesman Lee Kuan Yew might have exaggerated, but he was more accurate when he called Xi an "impressive" leader with "iron in his soul." Lee also noted that Xi's life experiences had hardened him, turning him into a person with emotional stability and an inner sense of purpose who did not allow his personal misfortune or suffering to affect his judgment.[4] One astute analyst painted Xi as a renaissance man, self-assured, self-possessed, and utterly unflappable who is as at home with poverty-stricken farmers in their shacks as with world political and economic leaders in the grand halls at foreign capitals.[5] To others, Xi is not just an authoritarian but also an enemy to democracy. The autocratic party state of Xi, they argued, engages in a relentless attempt to undermine democracy and to spread its own model of development worldwide. This posed an existential threat to specific US interests, the survival of democracy, and the liberal international order. For instance, the 2017 US National Security Strategy branded

China a "revisionist challenger" that "challenge(s) American power, influence, and interests, attempting to erode American security and prosperity."[6] Still other observers portray Xi as bland, colorless, and devoid of charisma. Another oft-used adjective applied to him is pragmatic.[7] Such varied characterizations of Xi are suggestive, although for the sake of a more thorough analysis, it is necessary to interrogate the complexities that make up his personality, life experience, and policy orientation. Xi is indeed a complex person, rich in contrasts, and the nexus of his manifestations of ideology/pragmatism, humility/ambition, and in-security/confidence must be set against situational and relational contexts.

Given the importance of the subject of Xi and China, dozens of academic articles are published every day to satisfy the great demand for information. Numerous prominent academics have already published on Xi.[8] The media, too, are filled with Xi analyses twenty-four hours a day. This book has tremen-dously benefited by the insights contained in existing research, but it differs from it in a couple of aspects. First, this book is the first comprehensive and system-atic exploration, in one convenient volume, of all episodes of Xi's first sixty-five years, with a political career starting at age seventeen. My consideration of Xi's whole career, focusing on governance, leadership, and policymaking, will as well cover his *entire first term* as general secretary, which culminated at the critical Nineteenth Party Congress (October 2017) and Thirteenth National People's Congress (March 2018), where many new decisions and breakthroughs were introduced. I use these two congresses as the endpoints for the analysis, affording a certain historical distance. Chinese developments after 2018 entered a more turbulent stage, with events such as the violent protests in Hong Kong, which ended with the draconian National Security Law, and the international corona-virus crisis, which radically altered the global political economy. The long time frame will provide us with a historical perspective on the larger issues of China's political, economic, and social developments.

Second, this book is an academic study that aims to turn the understanding of China into scientific knowledge, and to integrate China studies with the so-cial science discipline. While common sense and intuition are indispensable for all forms of research, I am inspired by the conceptual schemes, classifications, and theoretical structures drawn from the social sciences. The approach is mul-tidisciplinary, interdisciplinary, and evidence based in order to uncover the patterns and connections underlying the phenomena being explored. Moreover, instead of treating China in isolation, the book is grounded in comparative ana-lyses. It strives for objectivity and balance to describe and explain the Xi era and avoids value judgments, sensational language, and sweeping generalizations. The discussions are backed up by careful citations so that claims can be verified. The detailed notes will indicate introductory texts for general readers, as well as more advanced academic literature for those who wish to probe further.

The book does not rely on one grand theory to explain everything but instead utilizes many middle-range social science theories. The goal is to further our understanding through comparative and contextualized knowledge. For instance, drawing from international relations studies, I refer to the realist, beral, and constructivist paradigms,[9] as well as to the combined utilities of the three levels of analysis—the system, the state, and the individual.[10] I explain China's conflicts with foreign countries in terms of security dilemmas, and Southeast Asia's strategy in coping with China in terms of enmeshment and socialization (constructivist theories). Yet I also try to explain the limitations of some of the major theoretical paradigms. For instance, liberal internationalists tend to argue that economic interdependence fosters cooperation and reduces conflicts, since conflicts tend to hurt both sides. However, there are other intervening variables that must be considered. Nationalism, identity politics, political cultures, and the fear of the loss of control figure prominently in China's relationships with such countries as the United States, Japan, Taiwan, and the Hong Kong Special Administrative Region, even though these entities are economically interdependent on one another.

According to the literature on the sociology of development, modernization, the complex and uneven process by which traditional, rural, and agricultural communities are transformed into more secular, urban, and industrialized societies, generates conflicts, dislocations, and challenges to governance that cannot be overexaggerated. Urbanization, industrialization, and marketization uproot the traditional society by creating new social classes, social and gender norms, migration, and winners and losers that can be very destabilizing. The dislocation and pain generated are especially acute in societies undergoing rapid change, as in China over the past few decades. This is not to say that modernization is a unilinear or irreversible process, since new technologies such as social media can and have reintroduced and reinforced interests in history, religion, and traditional norms and values.[11] From comparative politics, I draw on the notions of rationality, structure, and culture to explain Chinese political behavior as well as how analysts interpret Chinese issues. I refer to the theories of revolutions to explain why Mao launched more "revolutions" even after gaining power in the 1949 revolution. By drawing on the various classifications of corruption (white, gray, and black), I attempt to offer a more nuanced understanding of that phenomenon in China. I refer to organizational and institutional approaches to explain Chinese bureaucratic behavior.

Finally, the theory on governance in turbulent times postulates that rapid technological change, global interdependence, and intensified conflict and divisions have made the governance environment much more complex, volatile, and uncertain. Contemporary policymakers must contend with a dizzying array of "wicked," intractable, and messy problems.[12] I find this resonates with the Chinese experience and explains much of Xi's threat perceptions and policy responses. In all, my analysis goes beyond analogies such as "emperor," dictator, godfather, and the new Mao and provides better contextualization for Xi's thinking and actions. Indeed, the book can be criticized for dabbling in too many social science theories. However, China and Xi are immensely complex subjects, and a variety of angles and analytical and theoretical lenses are appropriate for fostering understanding. One issue in social science in general, and China studies in particular, is the "poor interdisciplinary dialogue."[13] Simply put, in the China field, political scientists tend to focus on the issue of power, policy analysts on the policy process, economists on supply and demand, and sociologists on social stratifications. Some specialists focus on Chinese domestic politics but not Chinese foreign relations, or vice versa. Historians (and many political scientists) provide valuable contexts but seldom engage with social science theories. Each disciplinary approach may illuminate certain aspects of the Chinese reality but obscure others, and I hope that my multi- and interdisciplinary approaches will yield better explanatory value and holistic critical thinking. Additionally, the different perspectives raise awareness on the limitations of knowledge, and the uncertainty and ambiguity surrounding our understanding of the world.

Another assumption that undergirds this book is that scientific knowledge is cumulative. My book is therefore grounded in the large corpus of existing research and debates on China. It attempts to incorporate and synthesize the latest research to reflect on the utilities and limitations of these studies. It does not avoid academic controversies and takes issue with well-established theories on Chinese politics, such as the "one party, two coalitions" thesis and the "Chinese Communist Youth League" faction (*tuanpai*) solidarity argument. Further, I also analyze and classify the assumptions of existing research by China watchers and evaluate the different approaches. This may ruffle some feathers, but my purpose is to stimulate more discussion and to advance knowledge, especially when the social scientific understanding of China is continuously evolving.[14]

Governance and Leadership

Before we begin to examine Xi's governance record, a few words about my framework and assumptions are in order. The term "governance" is a broad and ambiguous one. In general, we use the term to refer to a government's decision-making and implementation, and its management of complexity, especially under the conditions of globalization. Governance is always political since it refers to "the manner in which power is exercised in the management of a country's economic and social resources for development."[15] Good governance is associated with accountability, efficiency, mobilization, and the provision of public goods such as economic growth and the rule of law. It also means the adaptation of the institutions and functions of the state to address the strains of development, such as inequality, imbalances, and environmental challenges. As such, governance is critical to the achievement of society's objectives. It is especially salient in turbulent and rapidly changing times.[16]

On the other hand, leaders are a key to how governments perform. They guide, influence, and modify the behavior of their followers. A competent and committed leadership does not simply manage; it provides high-quality political goods, and governance in this sense denotes "an ongoing process of steering or enhancing the institutional capacity to steer and coordinate."[17] A sound leadership articulates an inspiring vision, motivates people, and ensures the realization of the organizational goals. It can provide high-quality political goods and ensure economic growth and human uplift (or development). It builds a team, trains, and recruits talents for these purposes.

In the developing countries, institutions are weaker, and leaders often must build institutions from scratch. Institutionalization (i.e., the process of infusing formal organization with values beyond the technical requirements of the task at hand) is a lengthy process, and a major challenge is to enable institutions to take root.[18] The handling of weighty matters such as war, peace, stability, economic growth, education, and healthcare is contingent on the skills, competencies, and intention of the leadership. The leaders of developing countries are more responsible for societal outcomes since there is a long tradition of state-controlled development as well as a political culture of dependency. They are expected to tackle simultaneously the tasks of nation-building, the remolding of political cultures, and the forging of a new national identity, much of which is taken for granted in developed countries. Their citizens expect material gains, political freedoms, and economic choices. Consequently, political leadership is tougher in the developing world, especially in an age of intensive globalization. Not only does it have to contend with rapid and unprecedented changes that often bring about serious dislocations, but it has less of a cushion in maintaining the physical well-being of the population. In the matters of governance and policymaking it is confronted by a host of challenges and crises. For instance, developing countries have lower economic and political capabilities, more acute class and ethnic conflicts, greater income disparity across regions, and a lower education and knowledge base. The large proportion of agricultural populations in most developing countries is one manifestation of underdevelopment. Government officials tend to be underpaid, and there are numerous temptations for rent-seeking. Corruption is a perennial problem, and transformational leaders are rare.[19]

Today China is advanced in many respects, but in many respects it is still a developing country. During the first few decades of Xi's political career China was unquestionably poor and undeveloped. For this reason, the literature on governance and policymaking in developing countries provides sound perspectives and contexts for my analysis.

Power and Policy

A distinction has often been drawn between "politics" and "governance," with the former referring to the pursuit of particular interests, the latter to the production of public goods.[20] However, in considering China, I assume that the two are blurred, since decision-making, implementation, and reform there often involve competition and conflict. Further, the issues of power and policy in China are inextricably intertwined. It is a truism that Xi and the CCP strive to preserve a monopoly of political power and suppress all challengers. They resist calls for a single push to a liberal democratic form of government as a panacea to solve all China's problems. Apart from the pursuit of power, the Chinese leadership also uses power as an instrument to fulfill certain goals, such as the modernization of China and its attaining "wealth and power." It strives to spearhead development and change to maintain legitimacy and to provide strong leadership to counter the fear of weakness, instability, and chaos, a fear that is ingrained in the political culture. More specifically, one observer summarizes Xi's goals: preserve party rule and regime unity; sustain economic balance with environmental concerns; maintain peace among border states and project China's maritime power; project economic power in Asia and around the world; and slowly reform certain respects of the postwar rules-based international order to suit its national interests.[21]

Accordingly, the view that Xi is an emperor or dictator who is merely interested in pursuing power for power's sake misses much of the dynamics—the deliberations, conflicts, and change—in Chinese politics. This holds true for views that regard the CCP as just another obsolete elite doomed to collapse or wither away. These views underestimate the extent to which the CCP, a product of history, has adapted itself to changing times, and the extent to which the matters of ideology, organization, and membership have been transformed. For better or worse, in China the CCP is still the only institution serving the functions of nation-state building, interest articulation and aggregation, and socioeconomic transformation. It is also a modernizing elite and a part of society. I concur with China specialists who have urged taking the CCP leadership seriously by "bringing the Party back in."[22]

My analysis of policy is informed by the existing social science literature on decision-making and policymaking. This literature has long dismissed the rational actor model, which assumes that decision-makers have all the necessary information and energy to identify problems, calculate the costs and benefits of each alternative, pick the best decision, and optimize the outcome. In contrast, the "satisficing" model shows that decision-makers often select an alternative that seems good enough, since they do not have full information and cannot pick the best option by extensive calculations of costs and benefits. A related concept is "good-enough governance," which suggests that political and economic development can proceed once certain minimum conditions are met. Given the constraints of time, money, resources, and energy, the long list of institutional and capacity improvements often said to be indispensable for development is unrealistic. Policies for development have to be prioritized according to specific country and historical contexts.[23] In addition, the incrementalism model suggests that policymakers tend to favor a series of small steps and seek marginal improvements rather than drastic and radical measures, even though these improvements rarely completely solve problems. The bureaucratic politics and implementation literature also regard as normal the fact that the decision and policy process is a function of bureaucratic wrangling, competition, and conflict. Further, the concept of pathology of policymaking also highlights such phenomena as inertia, red tape, goal conflict, and goal displacement.[24] Finally, the garbage can model highlights the irrational and chaotic reality of decision-making. In this scenario, organizations often have unclear or disputed goals, and problems and solutions are tossed around like garbage. Decision-makers are disconnected from problems and solutions, since their incentive is to look for work, and the outcome is that choices are looking for problems.[25] These theories are worth mentioning because aspirational official documents and some watchers outside China, explicitly or implicitly, assume that China can and should follow the "rational" tenets and maximize policy outcomes. Others hold an idealized and unrealistic assumption that there are perfect solutions to China's issues, whereas in reality all good things are not achievable at the same time. These policymaking theories alert me to the complexity of the issues I am considering and serve as useful heuristic devices. In the following, several other aspects deserve attention.

First, economists have often drawn attention to policy conflicts, which means that the achievement of one economic objective can only come at the expense of another. They have gone beyond the butter/gun, growth/equity alternatives to account for conflicts such as high employment and high inflation, and economic growth and balance of payments issues. Second, policymaking is about how to deal with sets of constraints and trade-offs. Often, hard choices and balances must be made. Third, the accelerating globalization means that the world is more interconnected, and states are more interdependent on one another. A state's policy is often contingent on other states, and the sources of problems often emanate from without. Economic shocks or pandemics from one part of the world quickly spread to the rest, and the levers of governments are often limited.

Fourth, there is the tendency of policy to generate unintended consequences, and the resolution of certain issues may create new ones in other areas. Fifth, some problems are intractable or can only be mitigated with time. Dubbed "wicked problems," these are complex policy problems where actors and stakeholders disagree on the nature and solution of the issue, where information is insufficient or controversial, and where choices involve the conflicts of values.[26]

In the Chinese context, the various conflicts, constraints, and external determinants are clearly played out in the policymaking process. To cite just a few examples, the promotion of efficiency by favoring coastal development inevitably exacerbates regional inequality, leaving the interior regions behind. Technological advances and automation lead to the loss of jobs and unemployment. To reduce the cost of exports and to make them internationally competitive, China bears the externalities of pollution and environmental decay. Economic development leads to rapid urbanization, which spawns issues such as congestion, pollution, and pressure on social services. A modernizing China brings about new capabilities and defensive/offensive behavior that threatens the security of other states, according to the logic of the security dilemma. The Chinese decision-makers realize that not all problems have solutions, and that many problems are so formidable that they describe them as enduring, large, and intractable (*laodanan*), an expression roughly equivalent to the "wicked problems" referred to in organizational and institutional theory. Reforms in areas such as state-owned enterprises, healthcare, the financial system, migration, and climate change belong to this category. The Chinese are familiar with the management of complexity—when some problems are solved, new ones emerge in an ongoing process with no finality. Exploration along these lines resonates with the notion of governance in China, which privileges its multidirectional, paradoxical, fluid, and open-ended aspects.[27]

Xi's approach during his first term was broadly consistent with that taken by his predecessors during the reform period. Under Xi, strategic planning and initiatives were combined with a series of small steps. Continuous improvements were punctuated by bold policy shifts or even large changes. Policy initiatives could travel from the top down or from the bottom up, and there was a great deal of experimentation and trial and error. There were continuous experiments along such spectrums as centralization/decentralization, government direction/market freedom, and control/relaxation, although the CCP often privileged political and economic stability as necessary preconditions for growth. Achievements in some respects were offset by setbacks in others. All this is consistent with the tenets of incrementalism, or what Lindblom called the "science of muddling through" or "disjointed incrementalism." Incrementalism, however, does not preclude fundamental changes or the neglect of social justice.[28]

Although a seasoned policymaker, Xi was unlikely familiar with social science theories and terminologies, but judging by his constant reference to the new normal, black swans, and gray rhinos, he understood explicitly and implicitly the various aspects of the governance of turbulence as an everyday reality. The public pronouncements of Xi and the CCP tended to exude confidence and to bring forward multiple and ambitious goals as if all values could be achieved at once. But in reality, China's leaders constantly wrestled with attempts to balance various constraints and conflicts.

Specifically, this study of Xi focuses on issues of political career, leadership, and governance. My broad scope, covering Xi's first sixty-five years, allows me to explore not only the historical evolution of the PRC, but also the temporal and spatial dimensions of Xi the leader amid profound political, social, and economic changes. One consideration was to divide this long book into two volumes, but I decided that a single volume with two roughly equal parts makes more sense. Hence, Part I covers the historical and pre-general secretary stage from Xi's birth to age sixty. This part explores, in chronological order, Xi's formative childhood and youth experiences and his entry into Chinese politics while a teenager, as well as his administrative experiences covering all Chinese administrative levels. This enables me to investigate the nature and characteristics of multilevel governance. Such an episodic approach enables me to observe Xi's motivations, performances, and the constraints facing him in specific but changing contexts and the zeitgeist. It allows us to examine Xi's motivations in entering politics and provides psychological insight into his character and personality. I explain how Xi succeeded in climbing to the "top of the greasy pole," whereas others fell by the wayside and even suffered ignominious ends. In addition, this affords us an opportunity to explore the relationship between the individual leaders and the political system, society, and the historical contexts in which leaders rise and fall from power. In his fifty-nine years before becoming general secretary, Xi lived through momentous and radical changes. He experienced extreme highs and lows. The motivations guiding Xi have been a mixture of power, ideology, policy, and expediency, all intertwined. On the other hand, in considering the rise of leaders in China, one often neglected aspect is the institutional role—the active, deliberate, and long-term recruitment and cultivation efforts by the Party Center, together with organs such as the Central Organization Department and the like, to groom potential future leaders to protect and perpetuate CCP rule. Key central and provincial leaders had to be funneled through the small and exclusive pool of the Central Committee with a full and alternate membership of approximately four hundred. Potential national and provincial leaders were groomed by rotation through different administrative posts to gather experience and to gain promotion into the Central Committee. Such a recruitment process is a fascinating subject of study in itself. In any case, the Party's choices were limited and the grooming and selection process long. Furthermore, placements in high political offices were most often a contentious issue affecting different factions and vested interests. The qualities and characteristics of the potential candidates were important for them to get ahead, but so were personal connections, loyalty networks, and affiliations. Inquiry along these lines will allow us to examine the assumptions and values of perspectives on Chinese politics such as power struggle, patron-client, and factional politics. My consideration of Xi's ascendancy will enable us to explore both the formal and the informal aspects of leadership politics. The rise of Xi shows that he was an object of political recruitment and succession, and in turn, Xi and the leadership have continued these functions of recruitment and succession as a significant aspect of rejuvenating the elite and promoting mobility. I will attempt to explain why potential leaders were promoted and others cast aside.

Part II focuses on Xi's first five-year term as general secretary and as president. Because of the complexity of the subject, I depart from the chronological format and explore political and ideological issues in chapter 9, economic and social policies in chapter 10, and military and foreign relations in chapter 11. I return to the sequential format by discussing Xi and policymaking at the critical Nineteenth Party Congress (October 2017) and the Thirteenth National People's Congress (NPeC, March 2018) in chapters 12 and 13. My exploration of all major policy areas, from power consolidation to centralization, from economic reform to social development, and from military reform to foreign relations, enables us to examine the policy process, the conflicts, and the linkages across different policy sectors, and the impact of global interdependency and linkages. The analysis highlights Xi's sense of confidence and his sense of vulnerabilities in China's security. It analyzes the bold and decisive reforms introduced under Xi and their attendant problems and pushbacks. Xi was (and still is) a strong leader, but he operated in conditions of equally strong constraints and resistance. Internationally, Xi also had to contend with a competitive, protean, and uncertain international environment.

In this regard, this book is no mere biography of Xi Jinping even though it is arranged in chronological order. One goal of the book is to utilize the chapters on the different stages of Xi's life experience and career as a series of case studies shedding light on different periods and aspects of China's politics and society since the founding of the People's Republic in 1949, albeit from the perspective of the life history of one important individual. The Roman "cursus honorum," or course of offices, in both the Republic and the Empire, delineates stages of official advancement, each with a distinct institutional locus. Xi's political career followed a similar pattern, which included stints in the central political hierarchy, territorial and local administration, and the military. My mapping of Xi's political career will throw light on major episodes of modern China's development, from the revolutionary upheavals of Mao's time to the seismic changes of the past thirty-odd years. Xi's career spanned the grassroots and the various administrative units, such as the prefectural, county, and provincial levels, as well as the national, and this affords us opportunities to gauge China's developmental experiences through these varied vantage points. Furthermore, I hope to shed light on the unique policy innovations, constraints, achievements, and failures experienced by the regional and local governments, especially in the post-Mao period. This is important because a great deal of the subtlety of vital local issues has often been obscured by studies that focus on China as a whole. I use the NPeC in 2018 as a cutoff point to allow a historical distance for my analysis, but whenever appropriate, I will summarize key developments after that date to give readers a better perspective.

Overall, this study of Xi's grand scheme to restructure China's political economy also shows constraints, contradictions, and pushbacks, especially in foreign policy. Xi's overreach and overcontrol has alienated many people, especially when there is little or no external check on the power of Xi and the CCP. The excessive reliance on hard power could harden the pushbacks and yield diminishing returns. Concerns over Xi's autocratic policy have heightened around the world. The revelations of alleged internment camps for more than one million Uighurs in Xinjiang and the mounting crisis in Hong Kong that cumulated in the oppressive National Security Law in 2020 drew worldwide condemnation. The same year saw the outbreak of the global coronavirus pandemic, which originated from China, engulfing the world with devastating effects on virtually all aspects of life. The pandemic heightened a general sense of trauma and insecurity, which in turn exacerbated xenophobia, racism, and the spread of misinformation and faked news. It exposed the weaknesses and dysfunctionality of institutions worldwide. During crises, states tend to retreat into isolation and discourage connection and cooperation. Additionally, 2020 coincided with election year in the United States and election rhetoric exacerbated Sinophobia, with called for decoupling from Beijing. In the developed economies, unfavorable views on China hiked to 75 percent or higher, and two-thirds of Americans held a negative view of China, and the China-US schism seemed to be deepening to a point of no return.[29]

The lasting impact of the coronavirus pandemic on the world and on China will probably not be entirely clear for years and is outside the scope of this book. However, it does make an objective and sober evaluation of the China experience even more difficult. My focus on Xi's governance record during his first term will pay attention to progressive and regressive features as well as his many blind spots. Domestically, there were reforms, improvements, as well as crackdowns and abuses. Externally, Beijing was assertive in some respects but cooperative in others. In terms of the value of investment and manufacturing, Beijing and

Washington were probably the most interconnected partners in the world, a phenomenon often branded Chinamerica. Chinese industries served the world with abundant and inexpensive manufactured products. Of course, the flip side of the coin of cooperation is the resentment of closeness, interdependency, and the fear of competition. Yet the Manichaean view of China and the world misses the nuances and complexity of what we are trying to grapple with. Also, instead of viewing China's foreign policy as the mere outcome of an authoritarian system, it is more realistic to explore Beijing's external relations in the context of its strategic interaction with stimuli from the outside world. The world can change China as much as China can change the world.

Importantly, reaching back to history gives us a longer perspective to interpret the rise of China and its contemporary implications as well as the many contradictions they demonstrate. My analysis of Xi's first term provides a benchmark to compare the continuities and change during Xi's second and even third term. Individual chapters of this book can be read as a series of case studies. Readers who are interested in the history of Xi's career, regional studies, multilevel governance, and socioeconomic development may focus on Part I. Those who are more interested in Xi's governance record as general secretary, or contemporary political, socioeconomic, military, and foreign relations issues, may focus on Part II.

A Note on the Sources and Citations

Since contemporary sources on Xi Jinping may simultaneously exaggerate, embellish, and underplay his records, I try, as much as possible, to use historical and archival sources that were published contemporaneously with the events I discuss. Internet sources will be cited with web addresses. Books and articles will be listed with the customary citations. However, because of the large numbers of citations, other English sources, such as reports from the *South China Morning Post*, the *New York Times*, and so on, or Chinese sources from the *Renmin ribao* (People's Daily), *Zhongguo jingji xinxiwang*, and so on, that I obtained from the Factiva database will not be cited individually with the phase "Retrieved from Factiva database." Similarly, articles obtained from the China Academic Journals Full-Text Database, which collects more than thirty-five hundred education and social sciences journals, will be listed with full citations including author, name of the journal, issue, date of publication, and page numbers. They will not be individually be cited with the phase "Retrieved from China Academic Journal Full-Text Database." Finally, Chinese concepts and expressions do not always have exact English equivalents, and much can be lost in translation, contributing to misunderstandings and misperceptions. A few cases will be pointed out in this study.

PART I
XI JINPING'S PATH TO THE TOP

2
Childhood and Youth
Privilege and Trauma, 1953–1979

As the son of Xi Zhongxun (1913–2002), a major revolutionary veteran, Xi Jinping is considered a princeling, the offspring of high officials who enjoyed relative privilege and impunity. Yet, like most Chinese who survived the Maoist period, much of Xi's youth was afflicted by hardship and trauma. In 1949 Mao founded the communist regime and unified China after a full century of war, chaos, and disintegration. There was a new sense of purpose for the reconstruction of the country, but the revolutionary impulses that drove the communist conquest were not spent. As theories of comparative revolutions indicate, revolutionaries seldom settle easily into construction after the seizure of power. The habits of violence and struggle, and the fervent desire to transform the old regime with a new ideology, often lead to more radicalism. When the new regime encounters counterrevolution and foreign interventions, the revolution can turn even more violent, fearing for its very survival. The outcome is often alternate "reigns of virtue" and "reigns of terror."[1] This was especially the case with the CCP, which had fought a bitter and projected revolution against internal and external enemies since its founding in 1921. The CCP cooperated with the Guomindang (GMD or Nationalists) during the First United Front (1923–1927) to fight "feudalism and imperialism," but since Jiang Jieshi turned against the communists in 1927, the two continued to duel throughout the early-1930s and during the Sino-Japanese War (1937–1945) despite the nominal cooperation to fight Japanese aggression. After the victory over Japan, the CCP and the GMD were immediately embroiled in a bitter civil war that lasted from 1945 to 1949. As soon as the CCP came to power in 1949, the Korean War (1950–1953) and the onset of the Cold War had turned the United States into an enemy of China, which was isolated by the US nonrecognition, trade embargo, and containment policy. In power, Mao was driven by his sense of volunteerism and utopianism, as well as by his theory of permanent revolution.[2] China was rocked by Mao's grand transformative vision to rapidly catch up with the West and simultaneously revolutionize Chinese culture and society. This led to a series of upheavals including the Three-anti and Five-anti Campaigns, collectivization, and the Great Leap Forward, and culminated in the disastrous Cultural Revolution.[3] Further, scarcity and austerity characterized the entire Maoist period, as most Chinese lived in grinding poverty. At the time of Mao's death in 1976, China's nominal GDP per capita was only US$163,[4] but the chairman did lay down the foundation for industrialization, socioeconomic development, and national independence. Even today, the descendants of the revolution are ultrasensitive to foreign interventions that in turn may radicalize domestic politics.

China's princelings enjoy special access to political power, recruitment, and career mobility. By dint of their ascriptive characteristics and presumed loyalty to the regime, they are well positioned to thrive in a cultural milieu where connections, patron-client relations, and informal politics play important roles. This is especially true for the children of the first generation of revolutionaries, dubbed the *hongerdai*, the Red Second Generation (R2G), who were deemed *miaochungenzheng* (literally, "pure stems and roots" or "pure pedigree"), loyal and trustworthy successors to the revolution. A more subtle classification distinguishes between the "second generation of red communists" and "second generation of officials" (O2G).[5] The former refers to offspring of veteran communist revolutionaries who fought in the communist movement before 1949 and are therefore regarded as founders of the PRC—examples in addition to Xi include Li Peng, Zeng Qinghong, Yu Zhengsheng, Liu Yuan, and Bo Xilai. O2G refers to offspring of high officials who were not communist revolutionaries and includes the sons and daughters of Zhu Rongji, Hu Jintao, Wen Jiabao, Zhou Yongkang, and Guo Boxiong. Yet these are imprecise categories, since the "third generation of red revolutionaries" still enjoy certain allure, even though they are essentially the same as the O2G. In any case, despite norms governing conflicts of interest, nepotism and favoritism have been rampant. The elitist assumption of the Leninist CCP as a vanguard leadership has also encouraged self-perpetuation of the political elite.

However, the privileges of the princelings under Mao need to be put into the context of the Maoist ethos of asceticism and egalitarianism. The Gini coefficient of wealth distribution during the Mao period was .33, and urban necessities were tightly rationed. Even the elite suffered through such calamities as the Great Leap famine of the 1960s, and as a group they experienced numerous political ups and downs. Mao's radical and revolutionary impulses drove him to attack and punish the party-state elite and ultimately to replace them with an entirely new generation of "revolutionary successors," which included Red Guards and Maoist radicals purportedly dedicated to radicalism and mobilization politics. The old elite and their descendants were mercilessly tormented and traumatized during the Cultural Revolution. Consequently, a mixture of revolutionary heritage, privilege, and trauma has left indelible marks on Xi Jinping.

Xi Jinping and His Revolutionary Parents

Xi's father, Xi Zhongxun, was a first-generation Chinese communist revolutionary, a founder and a moderate political leader of the PRC. Xi senior's career was intertwined with the continuous wars and disintegration during most of the twentieth century, before and after the founding of the People's Republic.[6] Xi Zhongxun began as a child activist/soldier/revolutionary and is celebrated for the founding of the communist guerrilla base areas in northwestern China in the 1930s.[7] Born in 1913 into a poor (one source claims relatively prosperous) peasant family in Henan, he fled famine to settle in Shaanxi. Both his parents died when Xi Zhongxun was fifteen, leaving him to look after an extended family of more than a dozen. Xi Zhongxun joined the Chinese Communist Youth League (CYL) at age thirteen in 1926 and was arrested in 1928 by GMD authorities for participating in student demonstrations. He was accepted into the CCP while in prison and, upon his release, joined the peasant movement. In 1930 he joined the GMD's Northwest Army and, after participating in a failed coup attempt from within, joined the communist guerrillas. He then joined Liu Zhidan in 1933 to establish the Shaanxi-Gansu Border Revolutionary Base Area, where the communists seized land from the landlords and distributed it to landless peasants. At the age of twenty-one in 1934, Xi became chairman of the Shanxi-Gansu Border Soviet government formed to resist the GMD's encirclement campaigns.

During a rectification campaign, struggles and disputes within the CCP in 1935 resulted in the jailing of Xi Zhongxun, Liu Zhidan, and Gao Gang. Xi was about to be executed when he was saved by the Long March contingent that reached North Shaanxi. The Northwest Guerrilla Base Area, which gave the marchers refuge, was subsequently transformed into the Yanan Soviet. Mao and the communists spent a decade (1935–1945) in Yanan, where they combined social reforms with resistance against the Japanese, preparing them to take on the GMD during the civil war and to seize power in 1949. Yanan has long since been celebrated as a revolutionary legend and the most creative episode of Chinese communism, and the Yanan spirit is said to have epitomized such Maoist virtues as self-reliance, self-sufficiency, hard work, and struggle.[8] Upon the outbreak of the Sino-Japanese War in 1937, Xi served in various positions, as party secretary, political commissar, principal of the Party School, and an alternate member of the Central Committee. After the Japanese defeat, civil war broke out between the GMD and the CCP, and Xi became secretary of the Northwest Bureau, assisting Peng Dehuai in defeating the GMD forces at the three battles of Xihuachi. He became political commissar of the Northwest Military Region in 1949. After the founding of the People's Republic of China in 1949, he served as minister of propaganda and concurrently as the vice director of the Political Affairs Council's Cultural and Educational Committee, and in 1953, secretary general of the Political Affairs Council. He was elected to the CCP's Eighth Central Committee in 1956. Between 1959 and 1962, he was vice premier and concurrently secretary general of the State Council.

However, from 1962 onward, the political climate tightened, Xi's star began to sink, and he suffered persecution, house arrest, and imprisonment for sixteen years. At the Tenth Plenum of September 1962, when Mao Zedong felt he had to shake up the CCP and society by propounding the slogan "Never forget class struggle," Kang Sheng plotted against and branded Xi the head of an antiparty clique for sponsoring a biographical novel of Liu Zhidan that commemorates the martyr, who died in 1936. In the Alice in Wonderland world of Chinese politics under Mao,[9] the novel was said to be a covert plot to restore the reputation of the disgraced Gao Gang, who was purged in 1954 after a failed plot to succeed Mao while the chairman was ill.[10] Kang Sheng sent Mao a note saying, "It is a new invention to use novels to oppose the Party," and once Mao repeated this statement in the open, it was construed to be Mao's order.[11] Xi Zhongxun was quickly ostracized as an "antiparty" element. Former friends and associates now shunned the Xi family. Only by the intercession of Premier Zhou Enlai was Xi spared the death sentence. In 1963, when Xi was under investigation, he was assigned to the Central Party School for study and "reform." Xi used his spare time cultivating corn and vegetables and told his wife, Qi Xin, that he was resigned to becoming a farmer. He wrote to Mao about his wish, but Mao, through the director of the Central Organization Department, An Ziwen, replied that rural work was too grueling, and it was better to work at a factory. In November 1965, Xi was sent off to the Machinery Works of the Loyang Mine, nominally to become deputy factory director, but in reality, he was to be "reformed" under surveillance. Before Xi left Beijing, Qi Xin took one day off to help him pack and said goodbye, and it would be another seven years before the two met again.

During the Cultural Revolution the disgraced Xi was persecuted anew when marauding Red Guards went on rampages to destroy the "four olds" (culture, custom, habits, and ideas). Responding to Mao's call to become "revolutionary successors," they "smashed" the establishment by attacking the Party and government officials to "seize power." They denounced and "struggled" against all alleged "capitalist roaders" and alleged opponents of Mao, wreaking havoc with violence, beatings, and torture. Although protected by Zhou Enlai, Xi Zhongxun's home was ransacked and his property confiscated by the Red Guards. After being paraded in the streets and "struggled against" in numerous mass criticism sessions, Xi was put into solitary confinement for eight years and not released until May 1975, when he was put to work at another factory in Luoyang.[12] After Mao died in 1976 Xi was rehabilitated at the Third Plenum of the Eleventh Central Committee (December 1978). But already in April 1978, Xi was made first secretary of Guangdong's Provincial People's Congress, as well as its governor, first secretary of its party committee, and political commissar of the Guangdong Military Region, where he played a central role in China's reform and opening. He was also involved in the rehabilitation of those who suffered trumped-up and wrongful charges and persecution during the Cultural Revolution.

In Guangdong, he succeeded in persuading Party Central (a general term that refers to the central party authority in Beijing) to allow the province to spearhead reform and opening and set up Special Economic Zones (SEZs) there, positioning Guangdong as the first window for economic liberalization. Like the rest of China, Guangdong was poor and dilapidated at that time. In 1978, the young Xi Jinping was shocked when he visited Baoan (renamed Shenzhen and now a metropolis of twelve million), a decrepit little town with thousands of abandoned and salinized fields. Waves of impoverished and desperate peasants attempted to flee across the Hong Kong border, but many were arrested and repatriated by the army. The high-rises and the prosperity of Hong Kong were vaguely visible— Hong Kong youths visiting China wore bell-bottoms and carried portable tape recorders, in stark contrast with the shabby locals.[13]

The SEZs were export-manufacturing enclaves intended to attract foreign capital and expertise in exchange for tax incentives, land, labor, and infrastructure. At the beginning, these zones were fiercely resisted by conservative leftists who decried them for being neocolonial enclaves that exploited workers. In 1981 Xi Zhongxun returned to the capital to serve as the secretary of the CCP's Secretariat, taking charge of the day-to-day affairs of the Party such as organization and cadre rejuvenation. He entered the Twelfth Politburo, 1982 to 1987. In 1988, he was elected deputy secretary general of the Standing Committee of the Fifth National People's Congress and later director of the Legal Affairs Committee in charge of the preparation of legislative bills. Formally retired in 1993, Xi died in 2002 at the age of eighty-eight; his funeral was attended by virtually the entire CCP leadership.

Likewise, Xi's mother Qi Xin (b. 1926) grew up in turbulent times. During the Japanese invasion and occupation many young people flocked to the CCP-occupied areas.[14] In 1940, Qi Xin followed her sister to join the CCP's "Resist Japan Political and Military University," which was an organization to train cadres for war resistance. Subsequently she joined the Eighth Route Army and became a child soldier. She married Xi in one of the *yaodong* (common cave dwellings dug out from sides of hills or mountains) near Yanan in April 1944. That summer, as soon as Qi Xin graduated from teachers' college, she was sent to work in the rural grassroots in northern Shaanxi doing such things as land reform, leading a separate life from her husband. According to Qi, in 1947 she took an opportunity to visit Xi Zhongxun, but Xi scolded her for setting a bad example in doing so in such dire times, saying, "If the war lasted another ten years, I'd rather not see you for another decade!" Qi said that instead of being miffed, she was privately proud of her husband's "valor." After 1949, she became a researcher for the rural group of the Northwest Bureau. Qi gave birth to the couple's first child in March 1949 when Xi Zhongxun was attending the Second Plenum at Xipaibao, a historic communist site, after which Xi went with Mao to enter Beijing to form the new government.

At the end of 1952 Qi Xin arrived at Beijing after an absence of fifteen years and was finally reunited with her family. She began studies at the Marxist-Leninist Institute near the Summer Palace, which was far away from their home in east Beijing. She returned only on weekends. Xi Zhongxun was said to have supported her studies and career so that she was spared domestic duties. Their children were sent to boarding schools from kindergarten to primary school, and Xi looked after them over the weekends without a nurse. All four of Xi's children attended the legendary Beihai Kindergarten (nicknamed "cradle for revolutionaries"), an experimental child-care facility created in 1949 and especially designed for the children of revolutionary cadres and soldiers. During the many years of war, children of communist officials had been kept at their home villages, and only after 1949 were they reunited with their parents. The children of central and provincial leaders such as Liu Shaoqi, Chen Yun, Wang Jiaxiang, Bo Yibo, and Mao made up the four hundred students in attendance. Subjects such as language, music, art, dance, and common knowledge were taught, and the school had its own band, healthcare, nutritionist, and doctors. As a "red cradle" for the descendants of leaders and their possible successors, the students could be said to constitute a "red nobility," but the privileges enjoyed were only relative, considering the economic backwardness and the impact of decades of wars and revolution. When Xi Zhongxun was denounced in 1962, Qi Xin was put in an awkward predicament, because party rules dictated that she should "draw the line in the sand," accepting the verdict of the Party, and denounce her husband. Since Qi Xin failed to do this, she was subjected to continuous interrogations and harassment. She volunteered to participate in the "Four Cleans" movement of 1963–1964, and eventually she was driven out of Beijing to a May Seventh Cadre School for labor and re-education for seven years while her three eldest children were left to fend for themselves.[15]

Xi Jinping's Childhood and Youth: Princeling, Pauper, and Peasant

Xi Jinping was born on June 1, 1953.[16] When weaned after ten months, Xi was sent home to be looked after by his father, and Qi Xin returned home once a week. Xi Zhongxun was a devoted but stern and frugal father. His sons wore hand-me-down clothes and shoes from their elder sisters, and once when Xi

Jinping balked at wearing his sister's flower-pattern shoes because of ridicule at school, Xi Zhongxun's prescription was to have them dyed. Xi Zhongxun, like many parents who grew up during hard times, had a habit of reminding his children about how hard peasants worked and why they should not be wasteful. His children were obliged to listen to his many homilies about his revolutionary experiences and the meaning of revolution, and why they must also immerse themselves in the revolution. Xi Jinping once said that he had heard the sermons so many times calluses had formed in his ears.

By most accounts, Xi Zhongxun lived a simple and thrifty life in a typical Beijing *siheyuan* residence, a quadrangular compound of houses surrounding a courtyard. Yet all princelings were entitled to summer at the Beidaihe beach resort and entertainment in the Zhongnanhai government compound, and through these channels encountered senior leaders like Zhou Enlai and Deng Xiaoping. Since Xi senior oversaw propaganda, culture, and education, the children were also acquainted with well-known personalities in these fields.

After finishing primary school, Xi entered another "red aristocracy" boarding school reserved for party and military cadres, the August First School located in the Haidian region of Beijing, originally a Manchu royal residence with a beautiful environment and gardens. Much more than their teachers, the princeling

Figure 2.1 The Xi family in happier times, Beijing, 1960. Front row: Yuanping, Jinping, Anan. Back row: Ganping and Heping (Xi Zhongxun's daughters from an earlier marriage), Qi Xin, Zhongxun, Qiaoqiao. Credit: Zhongguo gongchandang xinwenshe

students were keenly aware of current political issues and personnel changes. Considering themselves an elite, they often did things their own way and failed to take their teachers seriously.[17] However, after Xi Zhongxun was branded "anti-party" and therefore "anti-Mao," the Xi family fortunes plummeted. As Qi Xin was driven out of Beijing, the Xi children were left to fend for themselves in a politically charged environment, their home broken, and their family members scattered. Beginning at age nine, Xi was derided and harassed at the August First School. The saving grace was that Xi was not dismissed from the school, since his father was purged before the onset of the Cultural Revolution, when offspring were still not deemed responsible for the political disgrace of their parents. However, things changed drastically during the frenzy and lawlessness of the Cultural Revolution. Children of those who were found guilty of such "crimes" as being "capitalists" or "counterrevolutionaries," usually by mob justice, were automatically deemed guilty as well by dint of the "bloodline theory." Xi Zhongxun's house was ransacked, and all the Xis were persecuted mercilessly by mass violence. At various stages, Xi was either locked up in "reeducation-through-labor" schools for juvenile delinquents or left homeless. In a 1996 press interview, Xi recalled his harrowing experience with a mixture of anguish and accomplishment:

> In reality I suffered more than most people. During the Cultural Revolution, I was jailed four times. As a "reactionary student," I was castigated at more than a dozen struggle meetings. I suffered hunger and experienced being a beggar. I was infested with fleas when I was in jail. As a fifteen-year-old I had to endure the stigma of being "black material" and had to join a production brigade in northern Shaanxi. In a flash it was seven years there. I was then transformed from among the "five black categories," a "bastard," and a "reactionary student" into a Communist Youth League member, a party member, and then a secretary of the village branch. . . . I became a peasant and learned a whole set of peasant language and was one of the best laborers in the village. This experience has strengthened my belief and self-confidence, making me feel that there is no suffering that cannot be borne in this world.[18]

Like all schools during the Cultural Revolution, the August First was a hotbed of radicalism, but Xi was barred from being a Red Guard because he was branded an "offspring of the black gangs" and a "reactionary student." Xi fought back and angered the "rebels," who ordained that Xi's crime deserved execution by shooting a hundred times over. Xi resisted by nonstop chanting of quotations from Mao well into the night.[19] At the numerous denunciation rallies, victims who hoped for more lenient treatment could recant by scrutinizing the alleged errors made throughout their lives. They also needed to "draw the line" by partaking in the denunciation and even persecution of family and friends. Xi's mother was once compelled to join with the mob to denounce six "capitalist roaders," including her own son. When the hungry Xi escaped home, Qi Xin had to turn him in rather than feeding him,[20] and Xi had to endure a dozen or so mass rallies, large and small. Xi Heping, Xi's half-sister, unable to tolerate similar torment, committed suicide. Such harrowing tribulations were by no means uncommon among officials and their families during the Cultural Revolution. Virtually all top leaders, including Liu Shaoqi, Deng Xiaoping, Peng Dehuai, Zhu De, and Chen Yi, and their families suffered a similar fate. For instance, Bo Yibo was similarly persecuted and imprisoned for fifteen years, and his wife was beaten to death. Bo's son, Bo Xilai, was obliged to join a radical and violent Red Guard group and reportedly denounced and beat his own father, something that was common during the hysteria of the times.

By about 1968, the August First School was disbanded, and Xi and schoolmate Liu Weiping were reassigned to Number 25 Middle School. Liu Weiping was also a princeling since his father Liu Zhen had been an air force deputy commander at the founding of the PRC. Xi was also chums with Nie Weiping, another princeling. The three were pariahs in class because of their "blackest" class background, but eventually the students turned Red Guards at Number 25 Middle School disintegrated into many warring factions.

Finally, Xi was threatened with being packed off to the police and then a juvenile correction establishment. It turned out that the latter was full, and no beds were available. In the summer of 1968, universities and colleges were still closed and factories were not hiring, but high school graduates from 1966 to 1968 had grown to four million. Apart from the destructive activities of the Red Guards, most youths were idle, and that presented Mao with pressing social problems. On December 22, 1968, the *People's Daily* published Mao's clarion call for *zhiqing* (educated youths) to go to the countryside to be re-educated by the poor peasants, take up labor, and help develop the vast hinterland. To escape the fate of juvenile correction, Xi quickly volunteered to be "sent down" to Yanan, and the application was quickly approved, since a harsh internal exile was deemed a "politically correct" endeavor.[21] After just a week, in January 1969, Xi boarded the "East Is Red" train for Xian. Departures of the youths were often boisterously celebratory and tearful occasions; it was considered a great honor to respond to Mao's appeal to be relocated to the poor and remote rural areas to be "re-educated" by the poor, lower peasants. Yet the reality was a prospect of being deported to poor, strange, and underdeveloped areas to possibly settle down for good, perhaps never to see one's family again.

Seven Years at Liangjiahe (Age Fifteen to Twenty-Two) and the *Zhiqing* Experience

By Xi's account, he felt no sorrow, since exile was a better option than juvenile correction and possibly death. He would eventually be assigned to northern Shaanxi and Yanan together with other princelings, including Deng Rong, Deng Xiaoping's daughter, and Luo Diandian, daughter of Luo Ruiqing; altogether a dozen educated youth would serve in the remote village of Liangjiahe. Nationwide, eventually more than seventeen million urban *zhiqing*, mostly Red Guards, were relocated. Formally termed the "Up to the Mountain and Down to the Village Movement," this was one of the largest migrations in human history.[22] On the one hand, Mao intended the movement to be another colossal social experiment to promote rural development by diffusing knowledge and skill. He wanted to use the movement to re-educate urban youth on the realities of rural China, where 85 percent of the Chinese people still lived. Furthermore, the movement was touted as a measure to narrow the three big differences between mental and physical labor, city and countryside, and workers and peasants, and it fit into Mao's grand scheme of tempering a whole generation of "revolutionary successors" to carry forward his notion of a "permanent revolution." On the other hand, the movement was also an expedient to reduce surplus labor in the cities, resolve the unemployment problem, and redirect the radical energy of the Red Guards. While there were numerous variations in their motivations and experiences, most *zhiqing* were "volunteers" (under intense ideological pressure), and most were sent to remote frontier or sparsely populated areas such as the Great North Wilderness in north China or to state farms called "production and construction corps."

The initial idealism and ideological fervor of the *zhiqing*, however, was quickly dispelled by the shock of the drudgery and poverty in the rural areas. Most suffered isolation, deprivation, discrimination, and physical and sexual abuses along with malnutrition, illness, and death. Local peasants regarded them more as intruders, burdens, and extra mouths to feed, especially when state subsidies for their resettlement were meager. Soon many escaped back to the cities in spontaneous waves, but since they had lost their urban *hukou* (household registration),[23] they had to live underground as illegal migrants deprived of the opportunity for education and employment. Others fled later, but virtually all *zhiqing* lost key educational opportunities that would have landed them meaningful employment, especially as they became older. In all, the *zhiqing* formed a unique sociological generation or cohort with shared experiences, identity, and collective memory. Their tribulation is reflected in *zhiqing* literature and the literature of the "wounded." Even today, their tribulations are kept alive in oral histories, memoirs, TV series, literature, and museum exhibits. Yet, ironically, with the passage of time, their memories of

Figure 2.2 Xi Jinping's cave dwelling, recent photo. Credit: Jeremy Koh

harrowing experiences have become mixed with a sense of nostalgia, typified by restaurants with retro decor and food frequented by former *zhiqing* who share and relive their experience.

Initially Xi's goal was to clear his name as a "reactionary student" without any intention of settling down at Liangjiahe. Early on, he fled to his father's ancestral home at Fuping County, which was sixty kilometers away, to seek shelter with relatives. Xi reckoned that these relatives, all poor and therefore belonging to the exalted "five red categories," would give him refuge. Yet it turned out that these relatives dared not shelter him because of the political implications. Since a return to Beijing was not an option, Xi reckoned that Yanan, the holy site of the CCP's revolution, where his father, a native of Shaanxi and a builder of the revolutionary base areas, might still cut some slack for him. Yanan was one of the poorest areas in China. The mountainous terrain was intercepted by gullies, and its arid and infertile yellow earth, like the soil found in the Loess Plateau, was fundamentally unsuitable for cultivation. Lacking electricity, the rural areas outside of Yanan were even more primitive, and the transportation of goods was done by donkey carts or on people's backs. The peasants there scratched out a living by terracing the hillsides by hand and had barely enough to eat. Their dwellings, like those used by the pre-1949 guerrillas, consisted of squalid *yaodong* (caves) halfway up the mountains.

At Yanan, the *zhiqing* were separately assigned to different counties. Xi arrived at Wenan commune, and after a simple welcome ceremony, representatives from the production brigades came to pick up their allotment of students. Xi and fourteen other *zhiqing* were assigned to a small mountainous village about seventy miles from Yanan called Liangjiahe, where a ditch divided two steep mountain slopes, and the two hundred-odd members of the production brigade resided in dim and dusty *yaodong* caves.[24] Xi and six others were assigned No. 1 cave. As was the norm in poor rural areas in China at that time, life was primitive and harsh. An earth trough, straw mat, and a thin cotton quilt served as a bed, a wooden barrel for a toilet. Monthly ration consisted of ten kilograms of coarse grain per person, and starvation was a constant. Villagers were obliged to supplement their diet with husks and wild vegetables.[25]

Xi Jinping arrived in Liangjiahe at age fifteen. Later he recalled the alien environment he was thrust into. The locals looked different and spoke in a different dialect. Treated like an untrustworthy stranger, Xi was aimless, and everything was difficult to get used to. He had no intention of fitting in, treating the place merely as a refuge from the fervor of the Cultural Revolution. On the other hand, the villagers also found it difficult to get accustomed to the *zhiqing*. Apart from some meager state subsidies, the local production brigade had to supply the *zhiqing*, whom they perceived as extra burdens. Villagers had misgivings and prejudices about the *zhiqing* as spoiled and wasteful. One incident illustrates the mistrust: while cleaning up, Xi found half a stale bun and casually fed it to a dog. Rumor spread that the *zhiqing* were so wasteful they fed buns to dogs! This put Xi in a difficult situation, even though there was no mass criticism meeting. By Xi's account, he was lonely and confused. For virtually all sent-down youth, the initial ideological enthusiasm was quickly eclipsed by the shock of the harsh realities and grueling work of rural life, since Chinese agriculture, then and even now, was akin to gardening, with virtually everything done by hand. The *zhiqing* were formed into rows to hoe the land, a strenuous task the urban youth found difficult to get used to, and there were few breaks during the day. Many of the cultivated terraces, created manually, were on mountain slopes, and, as Xi recalled, he was already exhausted at the start of a working day by just climbing up the mountains.

Xi was not too compliant—he refused to work when he was tired. He turned into a heavy smoker, consuming an average of two packs a day, because smoking was the only excuse to slack off; otherwise he was unable to tough it out. To the *zhiqing*, the villagers were uncouth and mostly illiterates. They fretted when villagers wanted to sit on their trough for fear that they carried fleas. Driven by Maoist ideology, the *zhiqing* practiced their own brand of "political correctness." When villagers came to visit, they first inquired about their class backgrounds. If they were designated poor and lower peasants, the *zhiqing* would welcome them for a smoke, but if they carried the "rich peasants" label, they would be driven away. Similarly, desperate peasants panhandling for food would be disparaged as bums or "bad elements" and chased away. In the intensely ideological atmosphere of the time, kindness shown to the "rich peasants" meant not being at one with the people. Yet such behavior by the *zhiqing* was interpreted by the villages as arrogant and nasty. From the villagers' perspective, the rich-peasant label was applied to a peasant simply because he or she owned some goats. As to the alleged bums and beggars, this ditty helps explain: "January is rich, February is poor, and in March and April the peasants are half alive or half dead." This means that during hard times, the grain was reserved for the able-bodied in the household, and old and middle-aged females were obliged to take children out to beg for food.

Eventually, most *zhiqing* at Liangjiahe fled, leaving Xi the only one left behind. After little more than three months (ca. March 1969), Xi could no longer tolerate the exhausting labor, the rural drudgery, and his bad relations with the villagers. Following the example of other *zhiqing*, he sneaked back to Beijing. Once in Beijing Xi was arrested and packed into a reform school, where he stayed for six months. Upon his release (ca. September 1969), Xi was alone, since his two sisters were assigned to Inner Mongolia, and his brother had been deprived of the right to an education. Xi consulted with his maternal uncle and aunt, who were both revolutionaries, but both admonished Xi and urged him to "unite and to rely on the masses." Yet, before Xi had time to make up his mind, he was arrested by police during the regular campaigns to stem "reverse flow population," or vagabonds, before National Day on October 1. This time he was thrown into a hard-labor gang for four to five months to lay sewer pipes in the Haidian region of Beijing.[26] So after almost a year of "labor reform," Xi returned in early 1970 to Liangjiahe, with a new attitude of attempting to fit in, "get close and understand the masses, and receive re-education from the poor, lower, and middle peasants." Armed with this determination, Xi adapted to the flea infestation with agricultural insecticide and the coarse food consisting of husks and wild vegetables.[27]

In Xi's story, in the summer the coarse staple could be mixed with shallots and sesame oil produced locally. A few drops of sesame oil would be regarded as a treat, and there was a period of three months when not even a drop of oil was available.[28] Meat was a luxury barely available a few times a year. Only during the Spring Festival would a couple of pigs be slaughtered by the production team, and everyone would receive a few catties of pork. Once when Xi was rationed meat, he could not wait and ate some raw. Recent accounts by others have painted a more benign picture. For instance, one former production team leader claimed that even the poor peasants tried when they could to give the *zhiqing* corn noodles and dumplings, millet, steamed beans, or boiled vegetables.

Xi learned to sew, but not knit. He read voraciously whatever was available, which during the Cultural Revolution meant subjects that were both heavily politicized and censored. He developed a love of classical essays and poetry. Rural work was strenuous. For instance, a large hamper of pig or cattle manure weighing seventy to eighty *jin* (thirty-five to forty kilograms) had to be carried on the back for several li (one li equals half a kilometer) up zig-zag mountain paths. At the beginning Xi earned only six work points per day, about the same assigned to teenage girls in the village. In general, the *zhiqing* felt that they were derided as inept and therefore discriminated against. Xi gradually learned each activity and became stronger. Two years later, he finally gained ten work points, the highest for the strongest labor. Official reports claimed that in the summer Xi was able to carry wheat up to two hundred *jin* for ten li, a feat commonly regarded as impossible. According to Xi, he took up all forms of agricultural chores almost 365 days a year and rested only when he was sick. In winter, work revolved around irrigation, embankments repair, and livestock tending.[29]

Gradually, Xi became more relaxed with the villagers, who in turn were invited to sit and even sleep on his brick bed. After dinner, curious villagers visited and listened to his stories and asked questions about city life in Beijing, the United States, the food people ate in Beijing, and the best food to eat. They also inquired about classical novels such as *Romance of the Three Kingdoms*, *Dream of the Red Mansions*, and *Water Margin*, from which Xi drew many stories. By 1970, Xi's house became the center of the village, as he had established his credentials and respect to such an extent that even the branch party secretary conferred with him. In turn, Xi worked as a barefoot doctor, a bookkeeper, and an agricultural technician.

In any case, Xi's childhood and youth experience had ignited his political instinct to become an activist. He applied for membership in the CYL but succeeded only after the eighth attempt. After finishing his first application, Xi invited the branch secretary of the production brigade to his *yaodong* and treated him with a dish of fried eggs and two hot steamed buns and inquired about his application. The branch secretary retorted by saying that he had already received a scolding by the commune party secretary for supporting such an outcast. Undaunted, Xi continued to file applications and finally succeeded. A secretary of the commune's CYL, who came to interview Xi and stayed for five days, turned into a good friend. When this secretary became the director of the youth office of the commune, he burned all the "black materials" (negative information) in Xi's dossiers,[30] thereby removing the last hurdle for joining the CYL.

By becoming a member of the CYL, Xi followed in his father's footsteps, and although the organization functioned differently in the 1920s than in the 1970s, it was still a pool of presumably reliable activists from which the Party recruited into its own ranks or to other political posts, such as base-level officials.

Membership required certain advanced political qualifications and presumed "purity." Political recruitment through this channel had already become rather institutionalized prior to the Cultural Revolution, although Mao thought that it had turned into a large bureaucracy and a "new class" of sub-elite biased toward the urban areas and key schools. It was also deemed to be controlled by older cadres jealously guarding the power of judging political qualifications. The Red Guards and leftists wanted to abolish the organization altogether, but it was Mao's intervention that prevented its total disbandment.[31] In any case, Xi's tenacity in getting accepted into the CYL was the first step toward officially beginning his political career.

Figure 2.3 Revisiting Beijing in 1972. Credit: Xinhua

In 1973, Xi wrote a national entrance exam for university, but it was a lost cause since people with his family background were never admitted. By August, as a *zhiqing* activist, he was transferred to Zhaojiahe production brigade by the county CYL secretary, who was himself a *zhiqing* from Beijing, with the intention of mentoring Xi. Xi was put in charge of the "socialist line education movement" to rectify the commune. That campaign removed a party branch secretary, and Xi won the trust of the villagers, who requested that Xi be retained there, but Liangjiahe also requested Xi's return.

Meanwhile, Xi's sister, Xi Qiaoqiao, had been sent in 1969 to a Neimenggu construction corps as the "offspring of a black gang." Reportedly she took with her a plastic Mao statute to show her loyalty. She was assigned to a former labor reform camp where five hundred *zhiqing* were formed into a company, which slept in rooms with two brick beds each accommodating twenty people. In the severely cold climate, they dug ditches knee high in mud, and that led to severe joint disease, tuberculosis, and arthritis. There was only one pot to boil water for several hundred people, and as the water was dirty, dysentery was as widespread as the common cold and flu. Many tried to flee back to the cities or enroll as soldiers, but Qi decided to persevere. After receiving her first wages of ¥5, she resisted buying coarse crackers that cost ¥45 per catty to quench her hunger; instead, she sent it to her brothers, thinking that North Shaanxi was poorer.

In the winter of 1972, Qi Xin received a letter from her sister informing her that their mother was dying, and Qi Xin requested the Party School release her to visit Beijing. Once the request was approved, all the family except Xi Zhongxun attended a reunion in Beijing.[32] At this reunion, the Xis decided to write a letter to Premier Zhou Enlai requesting to see Xi Zhongxun. The request, together with a request to unfreeze his savings account, was approved, although at that time Xi had already been jailed for eight years. Sometime at the end of 1972, Xi Zhongxun was finally allowed to meet his family, but he no longer recognized his own children. Xi Jinping appeared to him to be more like a native Shaanxinese. Upon learning that Xi was already a CYL member, Xi senior encouraged Jinping to apply for party membership, and to stay in northern Shaanxi to continue his "re-education from the poor, lower and middle peasants." From then on, Qi Xin was permitted a yearly return to Beijing to visit her husband and to have a family reunion.

In January 1974, Xi Jinping, age twenty, was finally admitted into the CCP during a surge in recruitment that swelled membership from twenty-eight million in 1973 to thirty-five million in 1977. During this radical period the recruitment criteria tended to favor activists with "red" (political loyalty and moral principles) rather than "expert" (professional competence and expertise) criteria, and popular opinion by the masses also mattered. Party membership, then and now, has been a critical step in career advancement and party recruitment. Unlike the activist and nonparty cadres, membership in the Party assumes certain permanence and growing political responsibility. As a gateway to a political career with significant advancement and power opportunities, it also assumes lifelong political commitment. Indeed, party members can resign or be expelled, and they are not automatically given positions of power, but it has always been assumed that they are Leninist vanguards with special qualities enjoying some political prominence and status.[33]

According to one account, Xi applied for party membership twice—the first time he was rejected because of his father's issues, but the second time, aided by the new policy of "parental issues should not affect offspring," his application was approved. Xi himself said that he had applied ten times. According to Xi, when Liangjiahe requested his return, his last application reached the county party committee for scrutiny. The party secretary there reckoned that it was a challenge for a local cadre to manage Liangjiahe since it was so rife with lineage conflicts. Further, since the Party had not made a "conclusion" (jielun)[34] regarding his father and since Xi was an outsider, he approved the application. Simultaneously, Xi was made the party branch secretary for the Liangjiahe production brigade, whereas the incumbent was made director of the production brigade's "revolutionary committee" (equivalent to village chief, a position subordinate to the branch secretary), only to resume his old position when Xi left.[35] Xi took some pride in noting that he was the first of the twenty-six thousand zhiqing sent to Yanan to become a branch secretary.

With a physical build bigger and stronger than most Chinese—and it being known that no one could defeat him at wrestling—Xi and his strong work ethic soon impressed and won him the support of the villagers. As a leader needed by the villagers, Xi finally felt a sense of belonging. He worked with them to sink wells, build levees, and repair roads. In one sense Xi was lucky: had he been an urban official or worker, he would most likely have been subjected to frequent harassment and persecution. As a leader at Liangjiahe, Xi also had to take charge of mass criticism campaigns and get on the right side of things, but in contrast with the situation in the urban areas and in the factories, these undertakings in the rural areas were more relaxed. There were fewer political taboos than in Beijing. During the many criticism campaigns of the alleged "followers" of disgraced leaders such as Liu Shaoqi and Deng Xiaoping, it was up to Xi to read out and interpret the spirit of central initiatives as reported in the mouthpiece newspaper articles, since the majority of the villagers were illiterate.

Xi granted that his assignment as party branch secretary was benefited by the prestige of his father to a certain extent, even though he was in disgrace. Xi Zhongxun had been "king of the Northwest"—chairman of the soviet at the Shaanxi-Gansu border region at age nineteen—and there was still a certain sentiment for him. Several of his former subordinates still working in Shaanxi might have assisted and even protected Xi Jinping.

As branch secretary, one of Xi's jobs was to mobilize the villagers to build and maintain ditches and dams and sink wells for irrigation and flood control. In one bitterly cold winter, thick ice formed in the river ditches, and if the levees were not reinforced, they would collapse in the spring when snow melted. At one instance, someone had to wade into the icy water to dig and move ice sheets, but when no one moved, Xi took the lead and jumped into the icy water to move the ice sheets, a move that was said to have moved the villagers, who then followed suit. After days of struggle, Xi and the villagers built a dozen or so earth embankments.[36]

Another strenuous winter task Liangjiahe had to endure was to transport sufficient coal for use over the entire year. Coal was delivered by trucks to Wenan commune, and from there it had to be hauled by carts to Liangjiahe. At about three hundred to four hundred catties each, the carts were handled by two people, and it was back-breaking work, especially on hilly slopes. Xi read an article about how villagers in Sichuan's Mianyang Prefecture had utilized biogas generated from human waste as a cheap and easy way to cook and provide light. Xi took time off to go to Sichuan to learn the technique. As Yanan was not connected to a railway, Xi had to take a bus for two days to Xian before taking a train to Sichuan. Several months after his return, biogas was introduced to Liangjiahe, and by 1975, dozens of biogas pools were meeting the villagers' needs for cooking and lighting. This was a first among the villages in Shaanxi, who were said to have been impressed. Even today some villagers still utilize biogas.[37]

Mao's cult of personality was so intense that the entire nation hung on every utterance from the supreme leader. On December 21, 1974, Mao remarked that Xi Zhongxun's case "has been under investigation long enough. It should not be stalled. [I] propose that he be released, with no further action." With this, Xi Zhongxun was finally exonerated. However, Kang Sheng was able to stall the acquittal for five months before informing Xi that the Liu Zhidan novel was a case of "contradictions among the people," but that the "conclusion" made before the Cultural Revolution—that Xi Zhongxun had committed serious error—would still stand. In fact, Mao himself had never read Liu Zhidan's novel, and to morally absolve himself, he added later: "Comrade Zhongxun is a good comrade since he has done a great deal for the Party. What issues does he have! That novel has not even been published, and just one line from me inflated the problem. I was speaking in general terms at the time." With that, in the spring of 1975 the surveillance of Xi Zhongxun was lifted, and his treatment was improved. He was sent to the Luoyang Refractory Materials factory to "recuperate and rest," together with Qi Xin and Qiaoqiao. He would spend another three years there in exile. When Xi's children lacked transportation expenses to visit their father, factory workers and technicians were said to have lent them funds.

Tsinghua University and Career Advancement

During the high tide of the Cultural Revolution in 1966, all universities were closed, and not until the early 1970s did postsecondary institutions begin to accept students, although unified entrance examinations had been abolished. All candidates needed to have three years or more experience as workers, peasants, or soldiers to apply and to be accepted. Quotas were farmed out by the party center to ministries, provinces, and the military so that they in turn could distribute them down the administrative ladder. Among the rural population, mostly *zhiqing* and model laborers were accepted. Although an avid reader, Xi had missed out on his secondary school education. He was keenly aware that higher education was not just necessary for personal enrichment; it was the best avenue for career mobility and for escaping his present predicament. Many *zhiqing*, especially the princelings among them, had already escaped through connections by joining the army, returning to school, or sneaking back to urban areas. For instance, Deng Rong had by 1972 entered Beijing Engineering College, and Luo Diandian was recommended to Shanghai No. 2 Military Medical University. That year, Xi wrote the unified exam but failed. In 1970 less than 1 percent of Chinese received higher education; university acceptance in most regions was less than 0.1 percent of university-age youth. Recommendations and patronage were common; one source claims that from 1972 to 1976, 70 percent of those recommended among the workers-peasants-soldiers were children of cadres or those with political connections. Ironically, this outcome contradicted Mao's goal of favoring the peasants and workers in tertiary education. However, for the tiny minority who were accepted into universities, the educational standard was low since the educational system and teaching had been devastated by the years of chaos when intellectuals were the targets of attack. Much time was devoted to political study (of Marxist-Leninist and Mao Zedong's thought), and scientific research had virtually stopped.[38] The academic requirement for tertiary education was shortened to two or three years. The pedagogical methods and course materials were simplified, with the emphasis placed on practical application for agriculture and industry, politics, and physical labor. Theoretical and scientific research was a major casualty. Teachers were denigrated as "damned intellectuals," and discipline was problematic.[39] Physical labor became an important part of the curriculum. Furthermore, the administration standards were uneven, as many of those admitted into universities had background education ranging from primary school to various levels of secondary school. In many cases university standards were lower than middle schools before the Cultural Revolution.[40] Not until 1977 were competitive university entrance examinations, abolished in 1966, reintroduced.

Even under these circumstances, a turning point for Xi came in 1975 when the prestigious Tsinghua University gave the Yanan region a quota of two. Xi recalled how he yearned for the opportunity for more education, so on his application form, he applied to Tsinghua in all three of his allowable choices. Eventually, the county authorities vouched for Xi when submitting the application to the prefecture, but the Tsinghua recruiters dared not decide, and sought instructions from Tsinghua. Luckily for Xi, in the summer of 1975, a window of opportunity was opened—when leading "leftist" Cultural Revolution stalwarts Chi Qun and Xie Jingyi, who would have blocked Xi's application for ideological considerations, were preoccupied with a campaign to counter an alleged "rightist wind for reversing the verdicts." Liu Bing, a crony of Deng Xiaoping's, oversaw Tsinghua admission, and he approved Xi's application. Luoyang Refractory Materials issued an assurance that Xi Zhongxun's case was one that belonged to "contradictions among the people and should not affect the academic or work career" of his son. Consequently, Xi was accepted into Tsinghua in the first-ever worker-peasant-soldier class. In October 1975, after some emotional farewells, a dozen villagers walked with Xi for sixty li to the county seat and paid for a photograph that cost ¥5.5 (see Figure 2.4).

In the end, as a group the Yanan *zhiqing* eventually did very well in career advancement. Eight of them ended up as provincial officials; two to three hundred

Figure 2.4 Xi Jinping bidding farewell to Liangjiahe villagers in 1975.
Credit: Xinhua

at the bureau/director (*ting ju* 厅局) level; and over three at the division (*chu* 处) level. Others became writers, artists, and entrepreneurs.[41] A prominent member of this group is Wang Qishan (b. 1948), Xi's childhood friend and close associate who has climbed upward to become one of China's leading economic and financial experts. Five years older than Xi, Wang was a *laosanjie* ("old three classes") who managed to complete secondary school before being sent down to Shaanxi. There Wang had to toil on a near starvation diet, as Xi had, but after only two years was lucky enough to be assigned to a Shaanxi museum and then admitted to university to study history as a member of the worker-peasant-soldier category. A princeling by virtue of his marriage to the daughter of Yao Yilin, a veteran revolutionary, vice premier, and Politburo Standing Committee member, Wang has since 2012 been Xi Jinping's right-hand man.[42]

Xi Jinping and the "Lost Generation"

Overall, Xi's experiences place him squarely within the so-called Cultural Revolution generation, or "lost generation," whose members share common characteristics and similar life experiences. It goes without saying that there are large personal variations in the predicaments and experiences of members of this cohort, and furthermore, different analysts define the boundaries of the "lost generation" differently. Here, I use the term to refer to those who were born between 1947 and 1960 and who during their formative years (roughly ages seventeen to twenty-five) lost their opportunity for higher education, since colleges and universities were closed, and entrance examinations were abolished for over a decade.[43]

Members of this cohort experienced their childhood after the establishment of the PRC in 1949, and shared common life and socialization experiences, living through the Great Leap Forward and the subsequent famine (1959–1961). According to Xi, even he, the princeling, was half-starved during the famine years when he was at boarding school, as dinner consisted of mere soup.[44] They were socialized with the Maoist ideals of egalitarianism, altruism, and self-reliance, and they learned from models such as Lei Feng, a model soldier who epitomized the values of selfless sacrifice, devotion to the Party, nationalism, and hatred against class enemies. As adolescents they were inevitably engrossed in the Red Guard movement and were inspired to varying degrees with Maoist radicalism. Many turned into violent Red Guards in response to Mao's call to "make revolution" by destroying the "four olds" and by attacking the establishment, which included the Party, the government, intellectuals, teachers, artists, and writers. Anyone with an above-average knowledge or expertise was regarded as bourgeois (and therefore criminal), and libraries and laboratories were ransacked. Schools and universities were closed to allow students to partake in radical activities and destruction. In the subsequent turmoil created by the "seizing of power," millions were persecuted, and many killed. The education system collapsed when teachers were treated as part of the establishment to be beaten and humiliated, and when intellectuals were treated as enemies of the revolution.

Among the seventeen million youths who were "sent down" to the countryside, most stayed between two and eleven years, losing the opportunity for any further formal education. Another group, also known as the *laosanjie* (old three classes), high school students between 1966 and 1968, missed out on the opportunity for college and university education. In contrast, the *xinsanjie* (new three classes), those students who were enrolled in primary schools between 1966 and 1968 fared even worse, since they skipped secondary education altogether. In the rural areas the youth lived a bare subsistence, but the deprivation was relative, since at that time even urbanites had to contend with a shortage economy with rationing of food and daily necessities.

In any case, most rusticated youths eventually drifted back to the cities, but since about half of them possessed only primary education, they found it difficult to readjust to urban life and were discriminated against. They bore the cost of lost opportunity, especially in the post-Mao period, when knowledge and expertise were deemed more important for rapid modernization and socioeconomic changes. When universities and colleges were finally reopened between 1970 and 1972 after a closure of almost four years, entrance exams to universities were abolished, and the lucky ones were accepted to universities under the worker/peasant/soldier category (like Xi) according to the criteria of "redness"; recommendation by the masses, and grassroots experience rather than academic credentials. This way, a small lucky minority of some 940,000, or 5 percent of the *zhiqing*, were eventually admitted into colleges and universities. A major turning point came when university entrance examinations were reintroduced in 1977, and when some academic credentials were also required alongside "redness." Many "lost generation" youths who wrote entrance exams from 1977 to 1979 (and entered university between 1978 and 1980) are also collectively dubbed the "three new classes" (*xinsanjie*) in contrast with the "old three classes." About five million took the exams, although less than 3 percent were accepted, and despite the fierce competitiveness, academic standards at universities were low after a full decade of disruption. Those who eventually struggled to get to the top were, despite the traumatic experience, motivated into joining the Party and eventually won the rare opportunity to enter university, and their most popular subjects were politics, management, economics, and law.[45] The members of this generation eventually went through adulthood during the gradually liberalizing atmosphere of the 1980s, but because of a substandard education and lost opportunity, they found it difficult to compete with the "fourth generation," those who were born in the 1940s, who had received more proper secondary and university education before the onset of the Cultural Revolution. Nevertheless, all this did not prevent the emergence of prominent writers, artists, and entrepreneurs from this cohort later on. The "lost generation" cohort looked back at past experience with a combination of regret, sorrow, pride, and nostalgia, a sentiment that resonated with a genre of writing called "wounded literature" that recalls the traumatic experience of the Cultural Revolution. Many urbanites among them also participated in the Tiananmen events of 1989.

For the lucky few, many princelings among them, who managed a makeup opportunity for higher education, their credentials would eventually improve their life chances and social mobility. Even a substandard tertiary education eventually stood them in good stead, since by 1983, in reaction to the anti-intellectualism of the Cultural Revolution, a university diploma became a major criterion for promotion. *Zhiqing* who were simultaneously princelings with connections and who had graduated from China's top universities were specially favored. Many of them, in relative terms, even managed to rise politically to the top, as eleven members of the twenty-five-member Politburo of the Seventeenth Central Committee (2007–2012) were members of this "lost generation." The most prominent among them include Wang Qishan, Bo Xilai, Li Yuanchao, Li Keqiang, Wang Yang, Zhang Dejiang, Liu Yunshan, and Xi Jinping.[46] Four members of this category, Li Zhanshu, Wang Huning, Zhao Leji, and Hang Zheng, were inducted in the nineteenth PBSC (2017–2022) (see Table 8.1). Xi, Li Keqiang, Zhang Dejiang, Liu Yunshan, and Wang Qishan were retained in the Politburo of the Eighteenth Central Committee.[47] Ascriptive and achievement criteria helped, and so did the specific circumstances under which they climbed the political ladder, as our analysis of the rise of Xi attests. Other *zhiqing*, princelings or otherwise, have also risen to the top in the private sector and other occupations, and some have developed careers abroad.[48] Notable dissidents include Wei Jingsheng (b. 1950), Ai Weiwei (b. 1957), and Liu Xiaobo (b. 1955), a Nobel laureate. Overall, only a tiny minority of *zhiqing* were princelings, and princelings did not necessarily have rustification experiences, since some were assigned to urban factories. Furthermore, tertiary education was only one attribute for elite advancement, and other paths to the Politburo and the top can flow through the central party or government routes, the provinces, the military, and CYL channels, with or without a degree.

As mentioned, a great deal of his description of their common harrowing experiences comes from Xi's own accounts, although unlike most youths of his cohort he was never a Red Guard because of his "black" background. Looking back, he often tries for balance with some positive slant, blending genuine feelings and nostalgia with rhetoric. Xi says that the *zhiqing* experience was not as miserable as was often portrayed. For him, those seven years were a shattering ordeal, but on the other hand, it was also a transcendental trial of personal development. Xi credits the rustification experience as an opportunity for him to mature and advance. He considers himself a Yanan person, and Yanan was the starting point of a journey where he overcame adversity and where many of his basic orientations were formed. He learned about the real world and the reality of the masses and built up his confidence. Whenever he encountered challenges, he would recall past sufferings and his solidarity with the *zhiqing*. Bewildered and vulnerable upon his arrival, he said, he left at age twenty-two with a firm goal in life and filled with self-confidence.

On the other hand, his close and intimate connection with Yanan, the Mecca of Chinese communism, is clearly good political capital. Xi often labels himself "a son of the yellow earth," claiming that his roots in the high plateau of North Shaanxi have nurtured in him a belief in doing tangible things "for the people." Yanan was a magical land where his father's generation had lived and fought, he said, and he enjoined everyone to promote the Yanan spirit. At the "two sessions"[49] in 2008, Xi stated, "I joined the Party at Yanan, and Yanan raised and cultivated me. Shaanxi is my roots and Yanan is my soul.... I yearn for an opportune time so that I can visit Shaanxi and Yanan and learn from the people in the old regions and the cadres of all levels in Shaanxi." In 1993, as secretary of the Fuzhou Municipal Committee, Xi revisited Liangjiahe for the first time, presenting every household with an alarm clock so that children could be awakened for school. At that time Liangjiahe still lacked power, and he pulled strings so that the village was finally electrified. He spearheaded a donation drive to build a primary school that was completed in five months.

Xi visited Liangjiahe again during the Spring Festival in 2015 when attending a conference on the elimination of poverty in old revolutionary regions such as Yanan where economic development still lagged behind other more prosperous parts of China.[50] In the fall of 2015, it was announced that a forty-five-part TV series on Liangjiahe was planned to promote Xi's ideal of struggle as well as to promote businesses in that area, although this has been criticized as another clumsy attempt by sycophants to promote a cult of Xi in order to serve their vested interests.[51]

In addition, Xi's evaluation of the *zhiqing* experience has been condemned by those who regard the entire experiment as an unmitigated disaster damaging an entire generation and their families. They argue that the movement never achieved the original developmental goals set for it, and the thirty-plus billion yuan to fund it were a total write-off. In addition, these critics maintain, by taking their cues from Xi's positive slant, obsequious writers now laud the movement, representing the fiasco of the era as a brilliant experience, which grossly distorts party history and offends the conscience of the victims.[52]

Conclusion

It has often been observed that one's childhood and youth experiences usually affect, or even determine, one's behavior, personality, and orientation. Adulthood is said to be an extension of these experiences. In this respect a great deal of discussion has taken place on the psychological and personal impacts of the harrowing experiences of the "lost generation" and on their political and policy impact as well, since so many of them have now risen to the top. In general, it is said that members of this group usually possess a pioneering and entrepreneurial spirit, that they are strong and determined, creative and thrifty. By dint of their rustification experience they understand empathy, scarcity, poverty, and the rural condition. To varying degrees, they were socialized by the Maoist ideal of "serve the people." Unlike the single children born since the 1980s and 1990s under the one-child family policy, most of them have siblings with whom they grew up during hard times. Some fought in China's brutal last war with Vietnam in 1979.[53] A more complex view on the political impact of former Red Guards turned politicians argues similarly that the ideals and predicament of the children of senior officials (*gaoganzidi*)[54] are shaped by their rustification experiences, that they are more appreciative of the sentiment of those in the grassroots and possess deep insights into the lives of the poorest. There is a certain princeling solidarity among them too, as well as a certain sense of calling and entitlement. Many have received higher education and are attuned to Western ideas, culture, science, and technology. Now forming the core of·the new power elite, their ultimate premise is unchallenged CCP rule, despite their occasional calls for democracy. They are concerned with corruption as a major issue that could spell the end of the party state. Even though now mostly in their sixties or older, they may still be able to invigorate the Party. However, others allege that many of these former Red Guards were "little Maos," or essentially thugs reveling in cruel and unscrupulous assaults on others during the Cultural Revolution.

Several extremes, or peculiarities, figure prominently in Xi Jinping's childhood and adolescent upbringing: his parents' background as hardened revolutionaries who had gone through decades of struggle, his privileged childhood with early exposure to politics at the top, and his traumatic experience being an object of torment during the height of the Cultural Revolution. This is in addition to his harrowing experience at the edge of starvation and drudgery at the lower depths of China's rural reality. Like other *gaoganzidi* of his generation, he was socialized with Maoist values of nationalism, populism, voluntarism, and struggle. Other Maoist values as embodied in the model soldier Lei Feng included self-reliance, self-sacrifice, and asceticism. Born of privilege as a member of the revolutionary elite, Xi likely harbored a sense of entitlement as well as a sense of mission, obligation, and paternalism. His early youth experience might have contributed to an iron will and determination to change things. It might have afforded him an appreciation of rural and social issues he may not have otherwise had, making him more determined to address issues such as rural poverty and economic backwardness. The hardship suffered might have left a psychological scar on his personality, which features a sense of insecurity, and it is reasonable to assume that he holds an ambivalent attitude toward Mao and Maoist revolution. Yet, in distinction from many princelings and other youths, Xi never was a Red Guard, and in fact, he and his family were victims of Red Guard violence. This might have distinguished him from the excess of the Cultural Revolution and helped his career. And since he has "eaten bitterness" at the base level, he is perceived to have acquired wisdom through suffering. Xi's complex early life experience encompassed many ups and downs. It might have reinforced his fear of chaos and disorder, an aspect of political culture shared by many Chinese. By Xi's own account, he was "fortunate" to be born in an old revolutionary family exposed daily to how the parents dealt with political issues. He conceded that his personal connections did have an impact on his career, although, unlike those who have little contact with power, he has a deeper appreciation of the vicissitudes of political careers that include hardships and humiliations.[55] Hardened by his ordeal, he said, he has developed such tenacity and self-confidence that there is no adversity that he cannot endure.[56]

3
Early Career

Central Military Commission, 1979–1982, and
Zhengding County, 1983–1985 (Age Twenty-Six to
Thirty-Two)

Starting from the Top: Xi Becomes Secretary to the Minister of Defense, Geng Biao

China was changing rapidly when Xi was completing his university studies at Tsinghua between 1976 and 1979. Mao's death in September 1976, and the arrest of the "Gang of Four" only a month after, spelled the end of the Cultural Revolution, and in December 1978 the watershed Third Plenum of the CCP Central Committee ushered in reforms and opening up to the world. Xi Zhongxun was rehabilitated and immediately put in charge of promoting reforms in Guangdong, while his son graduated in April 1979 with a chemical engineering degree from Tsinghua University. This degree was unlikely to be equivalent to a degree as commonly understood, since university education had resumed at a lower base level after almost a decade's disruption. Moreover, Xi was accepted lacking a secondary education as a worker-peasant-soldier student according to the then-prevalent criteria of working experience combined with recommendation by the "masses." But despite the low standard, a degree from Tsinghua was a significant political resource, especially in the context of the massive purge of young radicals recruited during the Cultural Revolution, the dearth of officials with formal education, and the aging leadership. In fact, Tsinghua has long been seen (except during the Cultural Revolution decade) as an incubator for political leaders. So many of its graduates have eventually climbed to the top that some observers label them as the "Tsinghua Clique," a network of technocrats and political elite that has had a lasting impact on Chinese power and politics.

In 1979, upon the recommendation of his mother, the newly graduated Xi landed the strategic position of *mishu*, or confidential secretary, to Geng Biao, Politburo member (1977–1982), deputy premier, secretary general of the Central Military Commission (CMC) (1979–1981) and minister of defense (1981–1982), whose numerous positions straddled all three branches of power. The CMC controlled all military affairs, and as secretary general, Geng Biao assisted the chair in dealing with daily matters.[1] A child worker in a lead-zinc mine, Geng Biao (1909–2000) joined the CYL at age sixteen. In 1926 as a child soldier he led a failed uprising at the mine, and then headed a militia unit after the CCP was crushed by the GMD in 1927. A year later he joined the CCP and the Red Army and fought in the various "encirclement campaigns" launched by the GMD. During the Sino-Japanese War he was reassigned to the Eighth Route Army and tasked with the protection of the Shaan-Gan-Ning border area in northern China. Here Geng Biao began a lifelong comradeship with Xi Zhongxun.[2]

After the formation of the PRC Geng spent almost two decades as ambassador to such countries as Sweden, Pakistan, Burma, and Albania. Returning to China in 1971, he was made head of the CCP's International Liaison Department. After the death of Mao in 1976 he took charge of the CCP's propaganda work, the gist of which was to reverse the Cultural Revolution radicalism of the previous decade. In 1978 he became vice premier managing foreign affairs, military industry, civil aviation, and tourism. In January 1979 he was made concurrently secretary general and a member of the standing committee of the CMC under then-CCP chairman Hua Guofeng. In 1980, Geng was charged by Deng Xiaoping to streamline the People's Liberation Army (PLA), which subsequently was trimmed from 4.5 to 3.5 million.

Observers have assumed that without his princeling background and his father's connections, it would have been impossible for Xi to secure such a plum position at the CMC so soon after university graduation. Furthermore, Xi's degree in chemical engineering was unrelated to military affairs. Xi's ascriptive advantages and connections undoubtedly helped, but his formal education also stood him in good stead.

In the hierarchical and rule-by-man milieu of Chinese informal politics, *mishu*, sometimes referred to as second leaders (*erlingdao*), play an especially strategic and delicate role.[3] Their positions are springboards to higher office through transfer and promotion, and many analysts talk about a *mishu* faction, assuming occupational attributes determinant to group identity. *Mishu* may run the day-to-day affairs of an organization (institutional *mishu*) or individual official (personal *mishu*).[4] Additionally, apart from their normal functions of coordinating operations and processing information as researchers, speechwriters, aides, and gatekeepers, they function like a chief of staff. Behind the scenes they mediate disputes, resolve problems, and act as sounding boards for ideas. They keep their *shouzhang* (superiors) abreast of major domestic and international developments and draft official documents. In a status-conscious society, they manage public appearances and protocol and often look after the personal needs, housing, transport, and health of their superiors. The best of them are presumed to be able to read the minds of their masters.

Often treated as confidants and part of the extended family of the *shouzhang*, *mishu* enjoy high social status, prestige, and power. In public, they operate with the authority of their masters by attending conferences, conducting inspections, and issuing instructions. They interact with *mishu* of other officials by advancing the interests of their masters and by navigating the bureaucracy in circumstances of secrecy. The relationship between the *shouzhang* and the *mishu* can be symbiotic and mutually interdependent, with the latter acting as the alter ego of his *shouzhang*.

At another level the *shouzhang-mishu* relationship can be characterized as a patron-client or principal-agent relationship that drives factional politics. In exchange for their loyalty the *mishu* enjoy career advancement to other parts of officialdom. Often these positions are shortcuts to rapid upward mobility, and promotions can also benefit the *shouzhang* by strengthening the *shouzhang*'s personal ties and connections. Conversely, however, *mishu* of disgraced leaders, whether in a current position or a past position, can be implicated and punished as proxies. Moreover, the strategic position of the *mishu* often provides incentives to abuse the *shouzhang*'s position for private gain and corruption. At any rate, the prevalence of the role of *mishu* as a springboard to political power can be illustrated by the fact that nine out of ten new leaders at various levels in China have had work experience as *mishu*.[5] Many *mishu* of former top leaders such as Mao, Madame Mao, Deng Xiaoping, Chen Yun, Hu Yaobang, Jiang Zemin, and Hu Jintao have gained power and high office. Wen Jiabao and Ling Jihua were former *mishu* as well.[6]

Xi Jinping was the youngest of Geng Biao's three *mishu*, and the two treated one another as father and son. His monthly salary of ¥52 was modest, but he participated in central meetings and decision-making, dealt with regional and foreign affairs, and became familiar with the handling of central documents, confidential or otherwise. Working closely with Geng Biao to inspect the armed forces, draft documents, and oversee Hong Kong, Macau, and Taiwan affairs, he often accompanied Geng Biao to visit foreign countries, including the United States.

Although there is little documentation (such as photographs or records of activities, ranks, etc.) on Xi for this period, Xi's first visit to the United States in May 1980 was eye-opening. Accompanying Geng Biao, Xi visited the Pentagon and the White House (where the Chinese delegation was cordially treated to a showing of the movie *Star Wars II*), and were given a tour of the aircraft carrier *Kitty Hawk*, the very first for Chinese military officials.[7] The United States had formally recognized the PRC in 1978, and the Soviet Union's invasion of Afghanistan in 1979 had led to a convergence of strategic interests between Washington and Beijing. The purpose of Geng's visit was to initiate military contact and to procure defense technology, in exchange for US requests to visit Chinese facilities for supercomputers, ICBMs, and missile development.[8] At that time both sides desired a closer contact between the two militaries, and the United States was considering selling the Chinese civilian and dual-use technology, military equipment, and data. Both sides were also interested in preventing airplane hijacking. As mentioned, China was planning to trim the PLA by one million in 1979, and to eliminate railway soldiers and capital construction corps. Overall, the discussions between China and the United States were so cordial that they were described by US officials as "almost like talking to an ally."[9]

Altogether, Xi's three-year stint as Geng Biao's *mishu* gave him "military" experience. However, in 1982 Xi effected a decisive break in his career path by proposing to return to the "base levels" to "temper" himself. Xi's motivations may have been multiple. One well-established CCP norm is to "go down" to the grassroots level to work among the common people. Xi reiterates often that he has benefited by his seven-year "sent down" experience at Liangjiahe. A regular Xi refrain is that CCP members "must go deep to the base level and strike roots" since the "base level is closest to the masses, and is the best for tempering people."[10] Xi's determination to go down coincided with a similar decision by Liu Yuan (b. 1951), son of Liu Shaoqi and class of 1977 at Capital Normal University (majoring in history). Ideological correctness notwithstanding, the choices of these two were exceptions among the princelings and *laosanjie*, who found their decisions puzzling. In their views, since they had endured such hardship, they deserved restitution, and why shortchange themselves by giving up the urban *hukou* and the privileges of living in the cities?[11]

Xi's self-professed ideological motives have been contradicted by some. One source claims that since Xi's father had been rehabilitated and had become a Politburo member and secretary of the Secretariat, Xi might have felt troubled by the perception of nepotism. Another possible motive is a popular account claiming that Geng Biao had been sidelined during a mini political storm. Consequently, Geng wanted Xi to find another patron because the future did not look bright, and a return to localities might be a better strategic move.[12] But these lines of reasoning cannot be substantiated. Most likely, a combination of idealism, political correctness, and rational choice to burnish his qualifications were factors that motivated Xi. Institutionally, in the 1980s, one norm for the cultivation of "third echelon" (reserve cadres who were around forty years of age who normally had a university education) successors was "sent down" experience. In the reform period, cadres who had worked in the poorest regions often rose to national prominence and into the Politburo.[13] More recently, work experiences in back-country provinces such as Guizhou, Gansu, and Tibet have been given so much credit that they are cynically referred to as "gold-plating"

Figure 3.1 As secretary to Minister of Defense Geng Biao. Credit: Xinhua

(*dujin*). However, it was not readily apparent to Xi in the 1980s that one step backward might propel him forward. In retrospect, since the party, the government, and the military were the three major channels for career advancement, Xi's decision to leave the PLA in favor of the party hierarchy was a witting or unwitting choice that would be critical in propelling him to the top. Geng Biao had urged Xi to acquire grassroots experience by joining a provincial field army, but had Xi heeded that advice, he would likely have ended up becoming a PLA general or a member of the CMC. Such a route was taken by Liu Yuan: after serving as vice governor of Henan he joined the People's Armed Police and the PLA, and was later promoted to full general in 2009 and political commissar of the PLA's Logistics Department in 2010.[14] Liu never entered the CMC and retired at the end of 2015. In the end, Xi's sojourn at the CMC gave him military credentials that are rare among China's "fifth" and "sixth" generations of leaders.

Zhengding, 1982–1985 (Age Thirty to Thirty-Three): A More Modest Restart

Eventually Xi's "sent down" from Beijing did not end in the grassroots—he became deputy secretary of the Zhengding County Party Committee (CPC), Hebei in 1992, and a year later, was promoted to secretary of that committee. At the beginning, the leader of the Prefectural Party Committee told Xi that since he hailed from a big city, it would be better to assign him to a county with "better economic conditions" and "relatively well-off" peasants.[15] Xi said that he preferred to go to poverty-stricken Pingshan County, Hebei, where Xipaipo is located. Xipaibo is a former base area and was headquarters of the Chinese communists when they were driven from Yanan and from where they commanded several military campaigns against the GMD. It is where the CCP held its Second Plenum of the Seventh Central Committee just before entering Beijing to assume power in 1949. Together with Yanan, Jingganshan, and Ruijin, Xipaibo is a most important revolutionary shrine, and Xi was quite aware of the place's ideological significance. However, he was persuaded against going there because it was alleged its factionalism was explosive.[16]

Geographically, Zhengding is located only 240 kilometers south of Beijing and 15 kilometers north of Shijiajiang, the provincial capital of Hebei. An ancient city with many cultural and historical sites, it had the potential to be developed for tourism. At the start of his assignment, Xi encountered several snags. The locals were cynical that the princeling was assigned merely to burnish his credentials and that he would not last more than half a year in a hardship post.[17] However, Xi's princeling confidence and Beijing experience had given him a boldness uncommon among the local officials. First, soon after Xi's arrival he discovered that Zhengding was actually poverty-stricken, belying its reputation as a "relatively prosperous" county. Zhengding was quite fertile and was nationally renowned as a "high yield" (usually measured in output per *mu*) county, but its poverty had been a well-kept secret. In compliance with Mao's dogma of food self-sufficiency ("grain as the key link") and his disdain for commodity production and trade, Zhengding had forced the farmers to devote all resources to grain production at the expense of industry and more marketable crops such as cotton, oil-bearing crops, and vegetables. For instance, a plan to build a chemical factory was vetoed because the site would take away land devoted to grain. Furthermore, ironically, like many other alleged "high yield" units, Zhengding was burdened by a proportionately high state grain procurement rate. Its four hundred thousand inhabitants subsisted on the border of starvation, and grain had to be purchased dearly from out of the county. Xi soon discovered that in 1981 the average annual income was only ¥148 , or forty cents per day. Some peasants had to sell dried potato chips outside of the county rather than inside in order not to lose face.[18] However, county officials were wary of unmasking the charade for fear of reprisals and punishment. Rejecting their concerns, Xi and a deputy CPC leader reported the case to Beijing. Subsequently, in the summer of 1982, the State Council sent out an investigation group, and the outcome was a decision to reduce grain procurement by twenty-eight million *jin*, enabling Zhengding to preliminarily relieve its food shortages. Xi's move was lauded, but he might have sensed the winds of change from the top.

In the early 1980s, some regions in south China were unofficially trying out the large contract (*dabaogan*) system. This allowed groups of peasants to withdraw from the communes and to sign contracts with village governments for the use of land, pledging to pay back part of their produce in return. However, in the absence of a formal central approval, some Zhengding officials were wary of change for fear of charges of "reviving capitalism." Others were dogmatist who felt that the large contract system was a retrogressive step toward the old society. Xi discounted these worries and persuaded the CPC to set up a pilot project in one of the poorer communes, which subsequently doubled its agricultural output value in just one year. Finally, the state constitution of December 1982 formally abolished the communes in favor of household contracts with village governments, although nationally the changeover took another two years to complete, for organizational and ideological reasons. In some places the communes remained. In 1983, Zhengding was the first county in Hebei to formally introduce the household responsibility system with land contracts lasting for five years or longer. This meant the division of the land of the communes and contracting them to farmers who in turn paid a portion of their harvest, in fees or in kind, to the village governments for the usage rights.

The abolition of the communes ended the decree on grain self-sufficiency, and Zhengding peasants quickly diversified into economic crops such as cotton, vegetables, fruits, and flowers, especially on land more suitable for these products. The marketing of this produce enlivened trade, and some peasants began to set up family and service industries to produce industrial raw materials, machine parts, appliance repair, restaurants, and the like. Incentives soared, and rural activities such as irrigation, waterworks, commercial farming, and animal husbandry multiplied. Zhengding finally got rid of its infamous reputation as a "high-yield but poor" county, and its success conformed to a pattern all over the county.[19] Under Xi, the CPC also encouraged the reclamation of land from deserted regions and set up a pilot project to turn over this land to individual households, with contracts lasting thirty years. These longer contracts were subsequently popularized throughout the country, reducing the peasants' reluctance to invest in infrastructural improvement on land still legally owned by the collectives.

At Zhengding, Xi introduced several novel measures to improve the livelihood of the intellectuals. In 1982, Xi proposed three surveys of intellectuals and professionals in various occupations and compiled Zhengding's first talent book. Zhengding advertised nationally to recruit talent to come to Zhengding, a novelty at that time. Second, Xi used his connections in Beijing to invite renowned scholars and experts to act as advisers for his county, attracting luminaries such as mathematician Hua Luogeng, economist Yu Guangyuan, and educator Pan Chengkao.[20]

In 1983, China Central Television (CCTV) was planning to film a TV series based on the beloved classic novel *The Dream of Red Mansions* with a budget for the set of ¥490,000. Xi used his connections to attract the TV production crew to Zhengding by granting a free site for a permanent set which eventually would become a theme park. However, the megaproject was controversial, as many officials worried about the recovery of the needed investment, since the going rate of admissions to scenic spots and temples was only ten cents. However, Xi managed to persuade the CPC to accept the decision. When cost overruns threatened to derail the project, Xi sought help from a friend in Beijing, who persuaded CCTV to invest an additional ¥380,000. Xi also persuaded the secretary of the Shijiazhuang Municipal Party Committee to contribute ¥200,000, and a machinery factory in that municipality to contribute ¥400,000 in the form of shares.[21]

In 1985, tourists to Zhengding broke the half-million mark. The set for the TV series was completed in 1986 at a cost of ¥3.5 million, and the TV series aired in 1987 was a national blockbuster, thereby putting Zhengding on the map. That year 1.3 million visited boosting incomes for various service and hospitality sectors. Tourism and theme parks were novelties at that time, and huge investments in recreations were risky. But thanks to rapid economic growth and pent-up demand, Zhengding quickly recovered its investment, and Xi's initiatives showcased the county as a tourism model. In addition, Xi managed to persuade the provincial authorities to fund ¥1.72 million to refurbish a thousand-year-old temple, turning it into a tourist attraction.

Archival sources laud Xi's work in Zhengding. Several claim that Xi had a record of taking care of retired cadres, helping them resolve problems, and visiting them during holidays. It is said he arranged for a large conference room of the CPC to be transformed into a retired cadre activities room, and the CPC's only 212-style Jeep was assigned to be used by the retirees, something unusual in the 1980s. Retired cadres were given preferential treatment when seeing doctors, special sections in hospitals, and instant refunds for medical expenses. Xi published his first article in the *People's Daily* on the need for middle-aged and young cadres to respect old cadres in December 1984. Other sources claim that Xi's respect for the aged was commended at that time in the *People's Daily* as well as in the provincial Hebei, Jian, and Shijiajian daily newspapers.[22] The issue of retiring cadres and their treatment was salient in the context of the large changeover of the elite in the 1980s. However, some recent propaganda about these past events tend to be clumsy. For example, it is said that at the groundbreaking ceremony for the Changle airport, Xi specifically instructed base-level cadres to remind older cadres to bring sufficient clothes to ward off cold; and that Xi has regularly visited Geng Biao's widow or sent her a greeting card wishing her good health.[23]

In economic development, Xi was cited for the promotion of village and township enterprises in food processing, thereby doubling their value; the revitalizing of the rural economy by allowing cadres to hire workers on contracts to replace life tenure; and the initiation of an economic and social plan. In social affairs, Xi was credited with the refurbishment of many unsafe schools with furniture and playgrounds, and the resolution of salary arrears for private school teachers. In party-building, Xi introduced regulations in 1983 to "oppose bureaucratism, [and] raise efficiency and leadership standards"; and effected a large-scale shakeup of rural party organizations, making their members younger and better educated.[24]

On his personal life, Xi claims that he was frugal throughout the three years in Zhengding. He slept in his office, which was a bed-sitting room with two benches and a wooden board serving as a bed, and a coal stove providing hot water. He ate in community mess halls, and three eggs a day would have meant abundance. Visitors were served with a Zhengding "banquet" consisting of buckwheat cakes, pig head meat, and wontons.[25] Xi rode bicycles within the county seat. A former deputy governor remembers that Xi was shabbily dressed, making him look like kitchen staff. One meal he shared with Xi consisted of two cans of fish and beef, and at that time it was regarded as a treat.[26] Xi's name for the first time was mentioned nationally in an article entitled "The Turnaround at Zhengding" published on page 2 of the June 17, 1984,

Figure 3.2 Receiving the public on a makeshift table at Zhengding, 1983.
Credit: Xinhua

People's Daily, which lauded the Zhengding experience.[27] This was construed as an endorsement from the highest level.

Xi's tenure at Zhengding coincided with a period of rapid improvement in the livelihood of the Chinese. Liberalization of the state's rural and other policies fueled development, but reforms were not always implemented, owing to habit, bureaucratic inertia, and resistance, especially in the context of rigid Maoist conformity.[28] Even mundane consultations with specialists and improved treatment of intellectuals represented a breakthrough from the anti-intellectualism of the Cultural Revolution. Xi's reformist experiences show that he was ready to embrace risky initiatives. And his battles with conservative forces in a backward county were dramatized in a novel entitled *New Star*.[29] Subsequently, the novel was adapted into a popular TV series that has entered Chinese political lore about the struggle between the old and the new.

In retrospect, Xi says that Zhengding allowed him to hone his leadership skills, but his quick placement as head of the Zhengding CPC when he was still shy of thirty years of age was not without controversy. Eyebrows were raised because many cadres who had participated in land reforms in the 1940s and 1950s and who had worked hard for several decades could only be promoted to section-level (*ke*-level) leadership from the bottom.[30] This aside, it is clear that other institutional forces were at work in forwarding Xi's career.

The "Third Echelon": The Party's Plan for Leadership Succession Well into the Twenty-First Century

When Xi was at Zhengding, the CCP decided to launch massive operations toward recruiting, rejuvenating, and training to cultivate thousands of successors to the aging leadership. During the Cultural Revolution regular channels of recruitment had been disrupted or suspended. One reason Mao launched the Cultural Revolution was his dissatisfaction with the party-state bureaucracy, which he thought had turned "revisionist," sabotaging his radical vision. By inciting the Red Guards to cleanse the party state he hoped to purge it of "conservative elements," give real-life combat experiences to a younger generation of "revolutionary successors," and move his revolution forward. In the post-Mao period, many of the younger radicals recruited into the party state by dint of their revolutionary credentials had to be weeded out in favor of those with formal education and expertise. Furthermore, intellectuals who had been persecuted during the Cultural Revolution were once again in favor, although younger talent was scarce due to the decade-long breakdown of the educational system. Xi's young age and educational credentials stood him in good stead.

When the dust of the Cultural Revolution was beginning to settle in February 1980, the Secretariat of the CCP was re-established so that the Politburo would be relieved of daily administrative chores. The average ages of the members of the Politburo Standing Committee (PBSC), the Politburo, and the Secretariat were already 70, 69.6, and 65.8, respectively,[31] when the average life expectancy was just 68 at that time. Consequently, Chen Yun instructed the Secretariat to promote qualified and young cadres who were deemed loyal and technically competent to make up for the antitechnological bias of the Cultural Revolution.

In 1980, Deng Xiaoping and Chen Yun set out the criteria of "more revolutionary, younger, better educated, and more professional" for recruiting a whole generation of cadres, and the rejuvenation at the Twelfth Party Congress of September 1982 saw the election of 112 Central Committee members and alternates (out of a total of 348) under the age of fifty-five. This group would eventually include Jiang Zemin, Li Peng, Qiao Shi, Li Ruihuan, Wang Zhaoguo, Tian Jiyun, Hu Jili, Wei Jianxing, Zhang Wannian, Li Tieying, Song Jian, and Luo Gan, many of whom would eventually rise to the top and into the Politburo. The youngest among this group, Hu Jintao (at age thirty-nine), would eventually become general secretary (2002–2012).[32] Deng's and Chen's principle was enshrined into the 1982 party constitution to institutionalize recruitment. Once the changeover of the central leadership was complete, rejuvenation began at the ministerial and provincial level.

As early as 1980, Central Organization Department (COD) minister Song Renqiong led ten work teams to fan out over the country to inspect middle-aged and younger cadres. These teams identified many potential candidates and winnowed them down to 160 for presentation to Party Central. However, Deng Xiaoping rejected the list, complaining that the candidates were still too old and that few had university education.[33] This is not surprising, since there was still a sociocultural belief that leaders had to be relatively old and experienced. Further, as of 1985, the educational level of the CCP members (numbering over forty million) was still low—those with university education consisting of only 4 percent, secondary school education 13.8 percent, primary education 42.2 percent, and illiterates 10.1 percent.[34]

Deng and Chen ordered the COD to select more middle-aged and younger cadres among the intellectuals. Chen Yun went one step further and proposed a more ambitious scheme of cultivating thousands of "reserve" successors, with the majority around forty years or younger.[35] Following an order by Chen Yun, the COD in March 1982 formed a Youth Cadre Bureau headed by Li Rui, and the provinces and prefectures also formed similar organs. A February 1982 regulation ordered a large group of old cadres to retire to make way for middle-aged and younger ones. One major beneficiary of this was Wang Zhaoguo, who at age forty-one was the youngest person to be elected to the Central Committee.

Once the rejuvenation at the center had made some progress, Party Central in the second half of 1983 turned to the rejuvenation at the provincial and ministry levels to prepare for the eventual advancement to national leadership well into the twenty-first century. The selection criteria were university and secondary school education and age—fifty years or under for provincial-, central-, and ministerial-level posts. The provincial authorities were required to identify cadres age forty-five or below for prefectural, city, or enterprise leadership. In turn, prefectural and city authorities were to identify cadres under forty-five years of age to prepare for county and city/township leadership. This list was subsequently labeled by Hu Yaobang "the third echelon"[36] list, using a military term, although the term was later changed to "reserve cadre." To involve the regional authorities, the COD devised a new and unusual procedure. The preliminary list was to be discussed and passed on by the provincial and ministerial party standing committees. Then the individuals on the list would be vetted by Party Central inspection teams and approved by the COD. Once the list was decided upon, it was to be submitted to the Politburo.

From January to August 1984, the COD dispatched thirty-five inspection teams with a total of six hundred members to fan out and scrutinize candidates for the third echelon. These teams conducted multiple interviews with candidates under the age of fifty and mainly those with a university education. The criteria of "virtue, ability, and innovative reform spirit" were applied. For each candidate, there were also interviews with his or her twenty to thirty superiors, colleagues, and subordinates, but for provincial- or ministerial-level candidates, interviewees could reach one hundred.[37] When this process was completed, the third-echelon list with 632 confirmed candidates was submitted to the Politburo and general secretary Hu Yaobang for approval.[38]

A massive infusion of young blood into the bureaucracy also meant the implementation of mandatory retirement for elderly cadres who hitherto had enjoyed life tenure, but the new retirement policy of 1982 was vague. Many elderly cadres resisted rejuvenation, fearing that they might lose their benefits. The lasting Cultural Revolution impact of prejudice against the intellectuals and factional violence (the young against the old and Red Guards against veteran cadres) had complicated matters. Concerns were also expressed about the fact that princelings, *mishu*, and Tsinghua University graduates might be overrepresented in the third-echelon list.

In the autumn of 1984 the third-echelon reserve list was finalized at one thousand, with twenty each for the thirty provinces (six hundred) and two each for the two hundred ministries and commissions (four hundred).[39] Hu Yaobang ordered that many of these should be assigned to the center and provinces to lower the age of the overall leadership. Other fifty-year-old, capable, and experienced cadres lacking the sufficient education qualifications would be sent to special "culture classes" established by postsecondary institutions for a period of three years. After graduation they would be returned to their original positions. This proposal was accepted by the Secretariat.

According to a former official who worked at the Youth Bureau, various methods of identifying members of the third echelon were tried. For instance, recommendations by senior cadres turned out many young candidates, but they were mostly their *mishu*, chiefs of staff, descendants, and relatives, because they did not know people outside of their immediate circles. But once the procedures were established, generally there was little influence peddling or bribery, even though patronage was not entirely avoided. Most candidates were prefectural-level cadres. The average age of these cadres was forty-three, and 85 percent had a college-level education; 83 percent of them were from "families of laboring masses," 11 percent from "exploited families," and 5 percent from "cadre families, or children of deputy minister level or above." Not all in the list turned out to be capable officials, and some, such as Chen Liangyu, Tian Fengshan, and Chen Tonghai, were later purged for serious malfeasance.[40]

By September 1985, the rejuvenation of the incumbents was "basically complete," and it was anticipated that the central and provincial leadership would be stabilized for five to eight years.[41] Unlike the nomenklatura list, which contains the names of holders of all important party-state posts, the reserve lists were confidential and unbeknownst to the candidates.

The Youth Bureau continued to interview and scrutinize those remaining unassigned on the third-echelon list. Some were sent to Party Central for training; others were rotated among various regional positions, admitted to programs offered by the party schools for training, or were sent abroad as embassy attachés. Some of these programs were short term, but others could last for one or two years. In principle, promotions were to be drawn from this third-echelon list, although there were also exceptions. At the beginning many university graduates were simply recruited into the third-echelon list and then sent to the grass-roots level for more training. In this way, from 1980 to 1986, 12,700 university graduates were sent to the grassroots. After 1986, the method was changed to recruiting those who had already performed well at grassroots units.

During the May 1985 restructuring of top leadership in fifteen provinces/municipalities (China's has thirty-four provincial-level administrations [*shengji xingzhengqu*], which include twenty-three provinces, five autonomous regions, the four municipalities of Beijing, Shanghai, Tianjin, and Chongqing, and two Special Administrative Regions, Macau and Hong Kong; Hainan became a province in 1988 and Chongqing a municipality in 1997), sixty-five from the third-echelon list were made provincial party and government chiefs. Fifteen Provincial Party Committee (PPC) secretaries had an average age of 59.2 and governors 56.4, a lowering of 5.5 and 1.8 years. At the end of 1985, 469,000 younger cadres were promoted to leadership positions at the county level or above, so by 1986, the average age of the leadership contingents for the provinces, prefectures, and counties was lowered from 62, 56, 49 in 1982 to 53, 49, and 44, respectively. Those cadres who had postsecondary education had gone up to 62, 55, and 54 percent, or about 45 percent above the 1982 level.

Hu Jintao, Xi's immediate predecessor as general secretary, was one of the earliest beneficiaries of this policy of recruiting younger cadres. In 1982 (at age thirty-nine) he was plucked from the province of Gansu to enter the Central Committee and become the chair of the All-China Youth Federation, as well as a secretary of the CYL between 1982 and 1984. After being promoted as the first secretary of the CYL 1984–1985, he was made secretary of the Guizhou PPC, a position he served in from 1985 to 1988. He was made secretary of the PPC for the Tibet Autonomous Region between 1988 and 1992. At the Fourteenth Party Congress of 1992, he skipped three steps[42] and was "helicoptered" into the PBSC to be groomed as the transcentury successor for the top post. At fifty years of age he was the personal choice of Deng Xiaoping. During the ten-year process of grooming, he accumulated several key positions and was given several important tasks. He was elected general secretary at the Sixteenth Party Congress of 2002, and he served two terms (see Table 6.1). This set a pattern that was to be repeated by the Xi Jinping succession.

Xi Jinping among the Third Echelon

In 1983, China's provincial leadership was undergoing readjustment. When Li Zhimin led a team inspecting Hebei, the inspectors reviewed Xi as secretary of the Zhengding CPC and found him leading a simple life: lining up for the communal dining halls with the public, and taking his bicycle to inspect the countryside when other officials took cars. In the beginning of 1983, the Young Cadre Bureau's appraisal of Xi was essentially positive, with minor reservations. Xi was said to be young, vigorous, resilient, and enterprising. While some of his policies, such as the building of the *Red Mansions* motion picture sets, were controversial among more conservative cadres, they nevertheless had a certain impact and had stimulated tourism.[43] In 1984, the inspectors descended on Zhengding to interview him again, and Xi was then included in the third-echelon list of one thousand.

As mentioned, Xi Zhongxun was the secretary of the Secretariat from 1981 to 1987, and he managed party personnel affairs such as retirement, rejuvenation, and administrative simplification according to "the four criteria." Hence, it is natural to assume that his position might have an effect on Xi Jinping's promotion.[44] Xi Jinping was among the top 5 percent, but still had to go through the same process as others: recommendation by Hebei PPC, inspection by Central Inspection Group, re-examination by the Young Cadre Bureau of the COD, and collective deliberation of COD directors before being entered onto the list.

The third-echelon list was revised in 1985, 1986, and 1987, and eventually would include leaders like Jiang Zemin, Li Peng, and Li Ruihuan. Years later all members of the PBSC of the Seventeenth and Eighteenth Party Congresses, except two, originated from this list. Xi was selected as the informal heir apparent at the Seventeenth Party Congress and succeeded as general secretary at the Eighteenth. However, the case of Bo Xilai is worth mentioning.[45] Like Xi, Bo, a princeling, was parachuted into the CCP's Central Staff Office right after graduation from university. After a few years Bo bowed to party norms and volunteered to leave Beijing to be hardened at the base level. Bo became a deputy party secretary of Jin County in Liaoning Province, but for unknown reasons, he failed to be selected into the third echelon.[46]

In 1985, Party Central suggested that Xi, a hopeful third-echelon candidate, be promoted into the standing committee of the Hebei PPC, but Gao Yang, the first secretary, strenuously objected on the grounds that Xi was only thirty-two years of age and that his experience had been limited to only a few years in the grassroots. But Beijing could not wait, bypassed the Hebei PPC, and transferred Xi to Fujian.[47] Gao Yang was miffed and raised the issue again several times, saying that this was abnormal and irregular. Prior to this, Gao Yang had clashed with Xi senior when the latter telephoned Gao Yang requesting him to look after Xi the younger. Gao Yang rebuffed the request and later revealed the conversation openly at provincial meetings.[48] Meanwhile, Xi began a new chapter in his career.

4

Seventeen Years in Fujian

Governance and a New Political Economy, 1985–2002
(Age Thirty-Two to Forty-Nine)

After spending his formative years in the underdeveloped hinterland, Xi Jinping was transferred in 1985 to Fujian, a front line in China's opening to the world. Regular rotations among the provinces or regions, or from Beijing to the localities, and vice versa, once every three to five years, were and still are a time-honored method for training officials and upgrading their skills. The seventeen years Xi spent in Fujian were the longest stretch in his career in one province where he served at various administrative levels, advancing slowly but steadily up the hierarchy. Xi's assignment as executive mayor of Xiamen city (1985 to 1988) was clearly a promotion, and his subsequent assignment as secretary of the Ningde Prefectural Party Committee (1988–1990), while often regarded as a setback, was actually an important stepping stone in his career. From 1990 to 1995, Xi served as secretary of Fuzhou Municipal Party Committee (MPC), a rank equivalent to a deputy provincial governor. At age thirty-eight, Xi was one of the youngest to reach this level. From there, Xi advanced to provincial-level politics when he became deputy secretary of the Fujian PPC in 1999, then acting governor, and finally governor of Fujian Province in January 2000. Xi had gained a reputation for being tough on corruption at Ningde. Because of this, he was deemed an efficient administrator and escaped unscathed from the massive Yuanhua smuggling and bribery scandal of 1999–2000, which saw more than three hundred central and regional officials convicted.

In the 1980s and 1990s Fujian was one of the provinces most oriented toward the outside world, with a fast-growing, entrepreneurial, and booming coastal economy. Fujian has long been a strategic frontier because it faces Taiwan across the Taiwan Strait, and was chosen by the post-Mao leadership, together with Guangdong, to be on the front line of China's opening strategy. The Xiamen Special Economic Zone was one of the earliest to receive the privilege to experiment with a market-based economy and to expand foreign trade. Since the 1990s, it has been a major eastern gateway to international economic integration. In addition, six million overseas Chinese trace their ancestral homes here.[1]

Xiamen (June 1985–1988) Special Economic Zone: Opening China

In June 1985, Xi become Xiamen's executive vice mayor and a member of the standing committee of the MPC. A small coastal defense city in a booming and externally oriented area, Xiamen was one of four original Special Economic Zones (SEZs). Xi's transfer from a relatively backward hinterland to an area of reform and opening gave him much greater scope and responsibility. Both personal and institutional factors explain Xi's transprovincial transfer and promotion.[2] During the 1980s, Xi Zhongxun's career path was highly affected by the ups and downs of general secretary Hu Yaobang's political fortunes. A trusted aide and ally of Hu, Xi senior's relation with him was well known, and the Central Organization Department's decision to transfer his son to Xiamen was an outcome of a tacit understanding.[3] When being interviewed in 2000, Xi intimated that the progress of his political career could not be divorced from his family's connections, although the general public tended to see the glamorous side of power and glory rather than the dark side of opprobrium.[4]

As mentioned, Xi left Zhengding because he did not get along with his superior, Gao Yang, allegedly a conservative in protecting the Maoist heritage. Xi Zhongxun loathed Gao Yang and wanted to have nothing to do with him, and he thought that his son did not have much of a prospect if he did not leave Hebei. But why Xiamen? Xi's transfer to Fujian might be related to Xiang Nan, first secretary of the Fujian PPC, and friends with Xi Zhongxun. Like Xi Zhongxun, Xiang Nan was a more liberal reformer and supporter of Hu Yaobang. In the 1980s, both oversaw the most reformist provinces—Xi in Guangdong and Xiang in Fujian—but both suffered exclusion and reprisals by the conservatives. Despite records of rapid growth in development and standards of living, the SEZs fell short of expectations of attracting high technology and foreign exchange, enabling the conservatives to argue that the SEZs were unsocialist, semicapitalist, and neoimperialist enclaves that enabled foreigners to exploit Chinese workers and resources.[5] Xiang Nan was one of the mavericks of the early stage of reform and opening up. When Deng Xiaoping toured the Xiamen SEZ in 1984, Xiang lobbied to expand the SEZ from a mere area of 2.5 square kilometers to the entire span of Xiamen Island, which encompassed 131 square kilometers. Deng consented, and in May 1984, the entire Xiamen Municipality was made an SEZ.[6] Xiang Nan was instrumental in bringing Xi to his own creation, the Xiamen SEZ. It is said that Xi respected Xiang Nan like a father and Xiang wanted to take Xi under his wing to further implement reforms and to act as Xi's patron and protector.[7]

Another source claims that Xi Jinping's transfer to Xiamen was due to his connection with Hu Yaobang under some extenuating circumstances.

Xi's predecessor as vice mayor of Xiamen, An Li, was the daughter of former Central Organization Department chief An Ziwen and the daughter-in-law of Hu Yaobang. In 1983, An Li was the deputy secretary general of the China Food Industry Corporation, and unbeknownst to Hu Yaobang, she approached Xiang Nan for a post in Fujian. Xiang Nan was an old subordinate of Hu Yaobang, and to give face to the latter, Xiang Nan made An Li the deputy mayor of Xiamen. Quickly upon arrival in Xiamen, An Li was given membership in the Party. However, it turned out that An Li was accustomed to the high-living style of a senior cadre and preferred living in a Xiamen hotel rather than more modest accommodations. And she was known to flaunt her connection with Hu Yaobang and make all kinds of demands on Xiang Nan. When her case was brought up at the Party Secretariat by Hu Yaobang's political enemy Hu Qiaomu, the embarrassed Hu Yaobang sternly criticized An Li and faulted Xiang Nan for keeping him in the dark. At the end of 1984, An Li was recalled to Beijing. Hu Yaobang, upon the recommendation of Xiang Nan and with the consent of Xi Zhongxun, picked Xi Jinping to replace her.[8]

Xi Jinping arrived at Xiamen on his thirty-second birthday, on June 1, 1985. When established in 1980, the four SEZs at the time were harbingers of China's reform and opening designed to manufacture goods for export. Geographically situated next to overseas Chinese regions—Shenzhen to Hong Kong, Zhuhai to Macau, and Xiamen to Taiwan, with Shantou equidistant between Hong Kong and Taiwan, their purpose was to attract foreign investment, technology, and managerial expertise by offering favorable policies, low taxes, and other incentives. Joint ventures and partnerships with Chinese enterprises, as well as foreign-owned companies, were to be established. In return, the local governments supplied infrastructure, land, labor, and simplified regulations. Because of ideological constraints and oppositions, these experiments with market mechanisms were carried out in relative isolation since the SEZs were separated from the rest of the country. Right from its small and modest beginning, Xiamen SEZ experimented with reform and opening and enjoyed an influx of Taiwanese capital.[9] Soon, in 1984, early successes of the SEZs prompted the government to extend similar favorable policies to fourteen other coastal cities, and in 1985, to the cities on the Pearl River, Yangtze, and Min River Deltas. By 1992, similar policies were extended nationwide, the goals of the SEZs were deemed accomplished, and the SEZ were special no more.[10]

Xi regards his three years at Xiamen as a most strenuous experience, since it was the first time that he oversaw a city and an SEZ, when he had experience in neither. Among his duties was the relocation of the poor rural residents outside of Xiamen Island. Yet Fujian was much more backward than he had imagined. Xi's first ride from Fuzhou to Xiamen—a distance of 257 kilometers—took eight hours, and Xi was surprised by the narrow roads and poor conditions of transport, as well as by the dilapidated state of Xiamen Island, which betrayed its reputation as a "garden on the sea." The city appeared old and rundown, or in Xi's words, like a "beautiful maiden in a shabby dress."[11]

Soon after he arrived at Xiamen, the overheated national economy prompted an order from the Party Central for retrenchment. In compliance, Xi decided to tread lightly against the wishes of local officials. Originally, they advised him about three aspirations—the development of the Sanduoao port, the refurbishment of the railway, and the establishment of a municipality to replace the district. Xiang Nan, too, had wanted to leverage the reform momentum and build an express highway linking Xiamen with Fuzhou, which would be the first-ever such highway in China. Xiang assigned Xi to take charge, hoping that his connections could boost the fundraising efforts. Xiang was also in favor of loosening control of the state-owned enterprises (SOEs) and giving them more power by initiating a contract system. This was believed to contribute to urban reform and to release productive forces. Because Fujian was economically backward, Xiang Nan was also in favor of promoting township and village enterprises to enliven the economy. He proposed the establishment of a Village and Township Enterprises Bureau at provincial and county levels, a first for the country.

Yet, just when Xi was assuming his new position, Xiang Nan was implicated by the Jin Jiang counterfeit medicine scandal. Although Xiang was not directly involved, his conservative political enemies at the capital—Chen Yun, Wang Zhen, Song Ping, and Hu Qiaomu—launched a media criticism campaign against him. Under pressure, Xiang resigned, and Xi lost his immediate patron. Xi's plan of giving Xiamen a makeover was rejected by the new provincial leadership.[12] The successor to Xiang Nan, Chen Guangyi, was a former subordinate of Song Ping's and was uninterested in the highway, so the plan was shelved and Xi lost an opportunity to promote himself. Affected by the resignation of Xiang Nan and stymied by regional interests, Xi turned to the drafting of a strategic plan for socioeconomic development for Xiamen 1985–2000, and took charge of financial reform and several policies to promote reform and opening.

Xi led a group of officials to Beijing to consult with leading economists and organized a contingent of more than one hundred scholars and officials to research twenty-one topics ranging from strengthening the Taiwan connection to the policy of a free-port-based SEZ. After a year and a half, the first socioeconomic strategic plan for China's SEZs was completed. Its principal goals were to further open up and to engage Taiwan. Specific measures included the opening up of cross-strait financial exchanges to encourage capital flows, turning Xiamen into a vanguard in promoting Beijing's reunification formula of "one country, two systems."[13]

Xi also took charge of implementing the *jihua danlie* (a privilege by which a city is conferred provincial-level status in the state economic plan) by which

Xiamen would bypass the province of Fujian and directly negotiate with the central government on revenue and expenditure sharing so that Xiamen could have its own independent economic policy.[14] By 1993, this privilege was granted to fourteen fast-growing cities.

Xi assumed a low profile so that he could be acceptable to all sides. Having grown up under conditions of his father's political disgrace, he felt it necessary to tread carefully. He had seen the vicissitudes of power, and he might have taken a page from Liu Shaoqi,[15] a Leninist and an organization man, and a prime target of the Cultural Revolution. Liu's treatise, "On the Self Cultivation of a Communist Member," advances an ideal for the party member that eschews heroism, the limelight, and ostentatiousness in favor of plain hard work. In addition, Xi might have subscribed to the traditional career-building strategy of "hide one's capabilities and bide one's time" (*taoguang yanghui*, or literally, shun the limelight and concentrate on self-cultivation and self-development) until an opportune time to advance forward.[16]

At Xiamen, Xi was first married to Ke Xiaoming (aka Ke Lingling) in 1980, the elegant and well-educated polyglot daughter of China's former ambassador to Britain, but a split occurred after three years.[17] According to a Wikileaks source, the couple fought "almost every day," and Ke returned to England after the divorce. With this relationship Xi had had the opportunity to go abroad but declined, preferring to stay in China.[18] Throughout the reform period the two most attractive routes for upward mobility outside of officialdom have been careers overseas or in business. Many *gaoganzidi* and their children have taken either one of these routes and have amassed huge fortunes by privileging their connections. One source speculates that Xi stuck with the Party because he calculated that he commanded neither a foreign language or skills to advance in a foreign country, but this does not explain why Xi did not go into business.

In any case, in September 1987 Xi married Peng Liyuan, a person who had endured similar hardship that Xi could commiserate with. Peng was born in 1962 and raised in a poor village in Shandong during the immediate aftermath of the Great Leap Forward Famine, when material shortages and starvation were still common. Her father was a high school graduate (a rarity in the village) and employed by the government to raise literacy, while her mother was an actress with the local touring drama troupe. Peng spent a great deal of her childhood either on tour with her mother or being strapped on her mother's back while the latter worked in the fields. During the Cultural Revolution Peng's parents suffered persecutions for their "cultural" connections, and Peng's father was packed off to a re-education camp for menial duties such as cleaning latrines. Peng joined the PLA at age eighteen and soon developed her talent in singing folk songs. After studying at the Shandong Arts College, Peng advanced quickly and soon turned into a celebrity folk soprano specializing in ethnic and rural songs of ordinary people. She was promoted to major general and a member of the Eleventh National Committee of the Chinese People's Political Consultative Conference (CPPCC). Peng has frequently performed in uniform and has many fans in the military. Her "laundry song" and many other hit songs often laud the solidarity between the army and the people. Branded a "soldier of the arts," Peng has made numerous entertainment trips to the old revolutionary districts and to impoverished minority districts, and has performed as well at all the defense frontiers. A household name, Peng appears regularly on the extremely popular annual CCTV New Year's gala performance watched by millions during the holidays, belting out popular tunes such as "On the Plain of Hope" and "Image of a Patriot."[19]

Xi and Peng were introduced by a matchmaker, a usual practice during the 1980s when open channels for dating were limited. In contrast to Peng, who was young, popular, glamorous, and a household name, Xi was an unknown official and eight years older. Peng's first impression of Xi was that he was uncouth, rustic, and elderly looking, although "simple and honest." Further, Peng was charmed by Xi's inquiry about the art of singing instead of standard materialist questions such as how much she earned, even though he seemed not to have heard of her. By Xi's own account, before the meeting was over, he had decided that she was the right one. But on the prospect of marriage, Xi warned that his official duties would make him unable to devote himself to family affairs. This sentiment was reciprocal.[20] In an era when jobs were state allocated, it was not unusual for couples to live apart and lead separate lives to pursue different careers, even in different cities.

However, Peng's parents were wary about Xi's princeling status, which for many carried a pejorative association with entitlement and profligacy. Further, they worried that Peng might be marrying above her "station." Xi had to convince them that he was brought up strictly by his father, and that he had suffered rural privation just the way Peng had.[21] On September 1, 1987, Peng and Xi married with a simple ceremony and dinner at home. Afterward, Xi seldom appeared with his wife at public functions, drawing the line by saying, "I am a party member and cadre, and therefore you cannot *zouxue* [literally moonlight, but with a more ominous connotation in Chinese]." They would decline invitations to banquets with big businessmen. Xi did not want Peng to abandon her artistic career, and therefore their married life was more separate than together.[22] Peng was either in Beijing or on tour, while Xi was rotated in his positions from Xiamen, Ningde, Fuzhou, and Zhejiang.[23] Whether Peng and her popularity were an asset to Xi's career can only be speculated, but since Xi has ascended to the top, she plays a prominent public role that is a first in post-1949 China.

The top-level power intrigue in the late 1980s did not appear to affect Xi's career fortunes, and he was transferred to become the secretary of the Ningde

Prefectural Committee in May 1988. In January 1987, the more liberal Hu Yaobang was forced to resign as general secretary in what amounted to a palace coup, and Xi Zhongxun was the only Politburo member who defended Hu. Xi was marginalized, but again he took a stand to oppose the military suppression of the students at Tiananmen in 1989.[24] Upon departure from the Politburo, Xi senior was elected to a more administrative position of vice chair of the Executive Committee of the Seventh NPeC to vet legislative bills. He formally retired in 1993.

According to one source, at that time Xi did not enjoy a good reputation and still had little to show for his efforts. At the Xiamen Provincial People's Congress mayoral election of 1988, he failed to command 50 percent of the votes, and lost out to Zhou Erjun. Hence, he was demoted to become the head of Ningde Prefecture. This source also claims that the Fujianese did not have a good impression of officials, such as Jia Qinglin and Xi Jinping, who were sent from Beijing. Since many Fujian delegates did not vote for Xi during the Central Committee elections at the Fifteenth and Sixteenth Party Congresses of 1997 and 2002, Xi came last as an alternate and second last, respectively.[25] Another source interprets the transfer as a promotion, since, at age thirty-five, Xi became the youngest prefectural party secretary, which the Chinese call a principal (*zheng*, or *yibashou*), as opposed to a deputy position, which carries the most weight. Xi's own version claims that the PPC decision to transfer him to Ningde was

Figure 4.1 Xiamen in 2014. Credit: Alamy

grounded on a recognition of his pioneering spirit in Xiamen. Specifically, Jia Qinglin, then-deputy secretary of the PPC and provincial organization department director, had wanted Xi to turn things around there by using some unconventional methods. This move was said to have been supported by the PPC secretary, Chen Guangyi, and Fujian governor, Wang Zhaoguo. Since Ningde was poorly endowed and was always ranked the worst performer among the province's nine prefectures and municipalities, things could only improve, and Xi was tasked with the challenge of making improvements.[26] However, Xi himself has claimed that after three years as deputy mayor, he had made his mark in reform and in opening up and promoting SEZ construction.

Ningde (May 1988–1990): Combating Poverty and Corruption

In 1988, Xi arrived at the poorer and more backward Ningde Prefecture, its population approximately three million, the least developed and lowest achiever of the eight prefectures and municipalities in Fujian. Ningde was an old revolutionary Soviet base situated directly across from Taiwan.[27] It has 913 kilometers of mostly mountainous coastline and three hundred islands. The terrain was isolated and mountainous, with backward transportation and flatlands making up no more than 4 percent of its total area. It took vehicles four to five hours just to cover 100 kilometers.[28] Not only was Ningde the poorest region of Fujian, but its major economic indicators were declining. Like all coastal areas, Ningde was deprived of state investment during the Maoist period. Mao harbored a strategic fear of invasion from abroad or from Taiwan, preferring to divert investment and human resources away from the coastal areas into the inland areas and to build the Third Front. In 1992, Ningde was designated one of the eighteen poverty regions nationally, and within the prefecture, six out of nine counties were designated poverty counties. Additionally, there were fifty-two "poverty" villages and a total poor population of 775,000, surviving on an average annual income of ¥160. Ningde's average grain ration was lower than the Fujian average, and grain had to be imported from other provinces to the hilly counties, incurring high transportation costs and straining the local budget.[29] On the other hand, Ningde was blessed with a world-class, naturally deepwater port called Sanduao with both strategic and developmental potential, a fact well known to top leaders. For instance, Hu Yaobang and Li Xiannian, accompanied by Xiang Nan, had inspected Ningde in the early 1980s.

Nevertheless, because of their region's backwardness, Ningde officials were said to suffer from an inferiority complex. According to Xi, when Ningde officials attended provincial meetings, they tended to huddle at the back, wary of speaking up. Xi tried to encourage them by the notion that "dripping water can penetrate a rock," a version of Maoist voluntarism that propounds the advantage of the weak and the power of positive thinking, that is, "the foolish old man who moves mountains." Xi added that he had pursued this spirit throughout his life and that, with dogged persistence, things would finally win out.[30] Ningde did indeed require patience and a long-term perspective.

Ningde officials had great expectations for Xi, the son of Xi Zhongxun, thinking that Xi could more easily extract central largesse for big projects. They told Xi that the principal aspirations were the opening of the Sanduao port, the building of the Sanwen railway, and the expansion of Ningde Prefecture into a municipality.[31] Yet Xi's arrival coincided with a period of inflation and an overheated economy, as well as a central government retrenchment policy during 1989 and 1990, which dampened bold initiatives.

Xi had to lower expectations, saying that he could not bring a miracle and that development must be slower. The central policy of retrenchment meant that megaprojects should be avoided. Instead, the focus would be placed on the improvement of trade with Taiwan, foreign trade along the coast, and searching for Ningde's own version of opening up.[32] Their high hopes dashed, Ningde officials thought Xi was a fraud.[33] So Xi had to argue that retrenchment was also an opportunity and that development had to be gradual, again citing the "dripping water" image.

Perhaps Xi's most remarkable accomplishment at Ningde that drew central attention was his prosecution of corruption. Old customs at Ningde dictated that the building of houses, graves, and the taking in of daughters-in-law, that is, marriage,[34] were the three most important life events. Officials in Ningde lacking funds tended to acquire houses by using their power to seize land while simultaneously living in government-supplied housing. At the smaller Ningde city, rows of three- and four-storied houses lined the hilly slopes, conspicuously offending public sensibilities as a sign of the exchange between power and money. As prefectural party secretary, Xi decided to act quickly, and from January to September 1989, investigated more than 2,000 officials. Subsequently 441 were prosecuted, four houses were confiscated, five were demolished, and fines worth ¥700,570 were meted out. The sanctions seem small compared with the scope of the offense, but the case was touted to represent Xi's iron fist to counter corruption, and this reputation spread to Fujian and even nationally.[35]

At the end of the 1980s, a wave of "jumping into the sea"—quitting government jobs to start private businesses—swept the coastal regions. Officials were tempted by lucrative business opportunities to moonlight as well. Xi warned officials and gave them a stark choice—stop using their official positions for private gain or resign if they wanted to go into business.[36]

Xi's "strike hard" campaign, to return purloined houses and to force offenders to pay compensation, reportedly had an impact. He urged the continued prosecution of cadres guilty of corruption, bribery, and feasting and drinking on public funds, in order to build a clean and responsible government.[37] One may also add that such a policy was consistent with national priorities to restore confidence in the regime after the Tiananmen protests and massacre in June 1989. On the protests Xi opined at that time, conflating Marxist and Maoist concepts, that there were needs to accelerate democratization and the rule of law, although it would be a mistake to make democracy absolute by detaching it from its class nature. The "great democracy" of the Cultural Revolution, he said, was nothing but "superstition and stupidity" and a turbulence, and without stability and unity, everything was a nonstarter.[38]

Other measures initiated by Xi were *xiafang* (officials going down to visit complainants) and *zoufang* (officials making the rounds to visit the public at their homes). Theoretically, Chinese citizens who harbor grievances can *shangfang* (which means "visit upper levels") or *xinfang*, "letters and visits" (send letters to or visit higher government offices) to petition for help and/or redress. Xi went one step further by ordering all officials from the prefecture down to the villages to visit the grassroots, carry out investigations, and resolve issues there, without passing the buck upward. This could involve mundane issues such as the unavailability of light bulbs and soap by residents living in remote areas, to more weighty issues such as food and shelter. As well, by 1990, all prefectures and counties had set up specific dates for receiving the public.[39] Xi used the "dripping water" metaphor to argue that persistent baby steps may eventually resolve huge problems. The practices of *xiafang* and *zoufang* were said to have been popularized to the entire Ningde area and then to Fuzhou, where Xi would later become party secretary. Another credit attributed to Xi included the successful experiment of cultivating *Pseudosciaena crocea*, the large yellow croaker, which spawned Ningde's famous fish farms in Sanduao.[40]

Xi's Antipoverty Program: Thatched Huts and Sampan Dwellers

The poor consisted of one-third of Fujian's rural population, many still living in primitive thatched huts under poor conditions, As deputy secretary of the Fujian PPC, Xi was in partial charge of rural affairs. When he learned that villagers at Xiapu still lived in thatched huts, he did some investigative reporting and managed to persuade the PPC to allocate ¥6 million to build one thousand houses, and that went over well with the villagers.[41] In 1997, the provincial government

Figure 4.2 Leading Ningde officials to clear water canals, 1989. Credit" Xinhua

resettled seven hundred thatched-hut dwellers into new homes.[42] Besides, the Ningde coast was still populated by the minority Dan or Tanka people (a less pejorative term is "boat people"), who were not granted access to an education. Most of them resided in small sampans, often with several generations sharing, to eke out a living by fishing and trading in sea products.[43] Xi's antipoverty plan aimed to resettle all sampan dwellers on land by providing housing subsidies and access to long-term employment. Toward this end, the provincial government granted subsidies of ¥500 per person, and the prefectures and municipalities reduced land rent for construction and forestry so that each person could receive the equivalent of more than ¥5,000. Of the 3,676 households (16,706 people) existing in 1997, by 1998 all were resettled in new villages engaging in farming, animal husbandry, water transport, or the processing of aquatic products.[44]

Fujian's minority population of a half million, primarily of the She nationality, is one of the largest in East China. In 1988, most of these minorities lived in the poor northern part of the province, and one hundred thousand of them lived in remote mountainous areas. It was thought necessary that most be relocated, and in the five years after 1994, two thousand households were relocated. In 1997 alone, seven hundred minority households who lived in thatched huts were relocated to new lodgings with full electrification, and access to vehicle transport was provided to 75 percent of them. Clean water was provided to two hundred thousand She people.[45]

When Xi was transferred out of Ningde, a *People's Daily* report entitled "Ningde Has Crossed the Poverty Threshold" was interpreted to be a nod from Party Central to Xi's performance there.[46] In any case, with the departure of Xi, Ningde as an incubator for officialdom was less impressive, being racked by corruption scandals extending all the way up to the provincial level. Hundreds were implicated for involvement in buying and selling of offices (*paoguan maiguan*), smuggling, organized crime, gambling, and shady real estate deals—illustrating a cozy relationship between crime and power that is often labeled the political crime nexus (PCN).[47] The cases of Jin Fusheng (b. 1952) and Chen Shaoyong (b. 1955), both protégés of Jia Qinglin and fast-rising "fifth generation" stars who had risen from the grassroots, also illustrate that the Party's recruitment and grooming efforts can go astray, in contradistinction to Xi's success story. With impeccable credentials, Jin Fusheng[48] was Ningde MPC secretary from 1995 to 2001 before becoming secretary general of the Fujian PPC and propaganda chief. Yet he and his second wife were indicted for pocketing bribes of ¥7.66 million for the sale of offices. Similarly, Jin Fusheng's successor, Chen Shaoyong, Ningde MPC secretary from 2002 to 2005 and later Fujian PPC secretary general, was prosecuted for receiving bribes of ¥8.19 million for favoring businesses and promoting officials. These two cases unearthed wrongdoings, and subsequent dismissals of hundreds of officials earning Ningde the reputation of a "disaster area" for rampant corruption.[49] All this illustrates not only the PCN milieu in which Xi had had to conduct himself but also the prevalent temptation to succumb to systemic corruption in Fujian. Fujian, as we shall see later, was to be racked by further corruption scandals.

By 2017, however, Ningde's GDP per capita, like most places in China, had grown in leaps and bounds to ¥16,147, or a hundred times over that of thirty years ago. Ningde was no longer isolated, boasting 9,449 kilometers of roads, of which 193 kilometers were highways. A nuclear power plant located in Ningde went into operation in 2014, one of nineteen in China and two in Fujian.[50] Ironically, however, as of 2018, Ningde still had six poverty counties out of a total of twenty-three in Fujian, the same number as when Xi began work there in 1988.[51] Partly influenced by international standards, Beijing has continuously upgraded its definition of poverty, but in any case, the issue of poverty is intractable even in a country that is developing as rapidly as China.

Fuzhou Municipality (May 1990–October 1995) and Municipal Politics

After Ningde, Xi received a big promotion, becoming, on May 1, 1990, secretary of the Fuzhou MPC (and chairman of the standing committee of the Fuzhou

MPPC), equivalent in rank to deputy provincial governor. At age thirty-eight, Xi was the youngest deputy provincial governor at that time. Xi had two things going for him: (1) multiple scrutinies by the COD and the Fujian PPC; and (2) the fact that Xi was the only deputy provincial-level official who had accumulated experiences at the village, county, and municipality level and in SEZs, many of them economically backward.[52]

With a population at the time of 5.4 million, Fuzhou was the provincial capital and largest city in Fujian, administratively in charge of eight counties and rural areas. Considered economically and strategically important because of its geographical proximity to Taiwan, it was also one of the fourteen opened cities at that time, and on the front line of Beijing's "united front" tactics toward Taiwan. Yet, in comparison with other opened cities, Fuzhou's competitiveness was much inferior, since it had neither highways nor large ports, and the entire province was served by only two railways.[53]

Fujian, together with Zhejiang and Guangdong, had a large number of private enterprises, and their economies had become mostly externally oriented, thanks to the opening policy. In Fuzhou, foreign capital poured in favoring the private sector, but reform of the SOEs lagged behind. A few SOEs were selected as pilot projects, but because of a fear of accusations of capitalism and stripping of state assets, a joint-stock system was difficult to introduce. In the summer of 1991, Xi gave the go-ahead for the Fuzhou General Construction Company (FGCC) to try out the concept. In February 1992 Xi endorsed the plan to turn FGCC into a joint-stock company to sell shares, and by 1996, it was formally listed on the Shenzhen Stock Exchange. By 2014 FGCC had paid taxes of over ¥20 billion.[54]

However, during the early 1990s, the centrally planned economy still cast a long shadow, with numerous instances of bureaucratic red tape, inertia, and buck-passing, phenomena that still survive today. To do anything, approvals from multiple departments must be sought, even though the outcome can still be uncertain. For instance, up to two hundred stamps were required just to erect a building, from the acquisition of land to the demolition of existing ones.[55] In 1990, just a fortnight after taking office, Xi established a "leadership service receiving week" to resolve a long-standing land dispute that had involved many petition cases. Dissatisfied with government inefficiency, Xi vowed to change the government's work style. He took over the slogan "Will act immediately" (*mashang jiuban*), originally broached in Fuzhou's Mawei economic development zone and demanded that all departments implement this spirit. Subsequently these four Chinese characters were inscribed on a Mawei highway hillside as well as on the Fuzhou Administrative Services Center. This initiative was said to have ushered in a trend for speedy government decisions to facilitate fierce market competition.[56]

In 1992, Deng Xiaoping's southern tour signaled a revival of reform to end the ideological debates over capitalism and socialism and the indecisiveness after the Tiananmen events of 1989. Xi complied with this initiative by taking command and by drafting a twenty-year socioeconomic plan for Fuzhou, setting targets for the next three (1995), eight (2000), and twenty (2010) years (going by the name "3820") in order to catch up with the "four minidragons" (Taiwan, South Korea, Hong Kong, and Singapore). Eventually, all the targets set were said to have been filled ahead of time. Electronics, television picture tubes, auto manufacturing, and aluminum manufacturing, had turned into Fuzhou's major products. The other strategic goals, such as the building of the economic region at the Minjiang Delta, are said to have been basically completed, further accelerating Fuzhou's development.[57] From 1990 to 1995 Fuzhou's GDP is reported to have grown at more than 20 percent annually, exceeding ¥100 billion, ¥200 billion, ¥300 billion, and ¥400 billion in 1990, 1993, 1994, and 1995, respectively.[58] Xi is credited with the resettlement of 3,441 households, or nearly 10,000 shanty dwellers, in Fuzhou's Ceng Xia slums.[59]

On the other hand, a persistent phenomenon in China are the vanity projects (or image or face projects) concocted by regional officials to show off their accomplishments with an eye on burnishing their credentials for promotion. The climate of rapid development and "catching up" often prompts officials to turn to ambitious infrastructural projects such as airports, high-speed railways, new cities, and public squares, though they turn out to be white elephants of dubious utility. Not unexpectedly, these projects have often been wasteful, squandering investment and resources and imposing huge financial burdens on governments.[60] Xi was no exception in this regard. As secretary of Fuzhou MPCs, Xi strongly championed Fuzhou's controversial prestige megaproject, the Changle International Airport, the first modern airport funded entirely by a regional government. When initiated in 1993, the overly ambitious Changle project had already been censured by the then-deputy director of the State Planning Commission (SPC), Chen Tonghai, as a vanity project, and he wanted it stopped. Yet strong arm-twisting by the Fujian and Fuzhou governments overrode the SPC. Continuous expansion and budget overruns inflated the original budget from ¥17 billion to ¥27 billion, or ¥32.28 billion including interest, but political and aspirational factors had gained the upper hand. Although the location of the airport was deemed less than optimal, one justification was that it would match Taiwan's Taoyuan airport to stimulate cross-strait economic development in anticipation of the opening of the "three links" (discussed further in a later section). There was also an aspiration that the airport at the provincial capital match Singapore's Changi airport. But despite such plans, Changle, which opened in 1997, was just one-third the size of Changi. In 1998 then-premier Zhu Rongji, known for his disdain for vanity projects, condemned the project as profligate

because Fujian simply did not have the traffic volume to require two international airports, one in Xiamen and one in Fuzhou. In 2002, China's auditor-
general Li Jinhua accused the project of being a "policy blunder" and a huge
squandering of state resources. The volume of passengers and cargo was only
half of what was projected, or less than one-third of the airport's capacity, and in
just five years' time ¥11 billion had been lost.[61] However, as is often the case with
"white elephants," once a megaproject has proceeded, it costs more to abandon
it than to complete it.[62] By 2006, a restructuring of the facility was said to have
turned things around. Through a state bailout and creative accounting, its debt
had declined year after year, so that even Li Jinhua praised it.[63] In any event, and
lucky fo Xi, rapid economic development and time have changed perspectives,
turning the Changle megaproject into a critical element of Fujian's infrastructure
that has enjoyed a number of expansions.

Xi's other botched project was the solicitation of investment from Hong Kong
real estate tycoon Li Jiacheng (Li Kashing) to rebuild the historic sections of
Fuzhou. Li's initial phase of restoration had demolished many relics to make way
for luxury homes, and Xi took a great deal of flak for the mess.[64] Fortunately,
subsequent remedies and refurbishments were well executed. Another source
also claims that Xi's performance at Fuzhou was unremarkable because his development plan, intended in 1992 to match Fuzhou's economic prowess with
that of Guangzhou by 2000, was unfulfilled. Hence, Xi did not do well in various
elections in Fujian—for instance, in 1988 he lost out to a local candidate in an
election for Xiamen's mayor—although he won the third largest number of votes
as Fujian's delegate to the Fourteenth National Party Congress in 1992.[65]

In military matters, the strengthening of national defense and buildup of
the military was deemed the key to stability, especially after the collapse of
communism in the Soviet Union and Eastern Europe, when people began to
wonder if there was a "future for socialism." As an astute politician, Xi was
adept at connecting with the military, winning him the accolade of being one
of China's hundred best "support the military" models—or one among the top
twenty-six models in Fujian—and a reputation of being a "support the military" secretary. Five days after arriving in Fuzhou, Xi had already visited all
the major military units (ground, navy, and air force) to resolve their concerns.
He commended the military's contributions in areas such as fighting natural disasters and wanted them to assume more prominence during festival
celebrations. He admitted to journalists that special treatment, funding, and
"favoritism" were necessary.[66] In 1991, when Unit 73121 Army was moved
from Lianjiang to Fuzhou, Xi helped them and their family members with
obtaining the urban *hukou* and enrolled their children in quality schools. Xi
authorized the building of a 2.5-kilometer-long road for the relocated troops
that was completed in just a month.[67]

One persistent challenge was how to provide employment for demobilized and retired soldiers. Xi pledged to improve working and living conditions for the military by providing funds for water and electricity supplies and for families with revolutionary martyrs, which was particularly important in the context of high inflation at that time of up to 90 percent. Archives from organizational departments show that former military personnel occupied almost half of the official positions in Fuzhou municipality and county for such portfolios as city construction, industry and commerce, public security, taxation, and foreign trade. In the government reorganization of 2000, when "support the front" offices (government agencies providing logistics support to the military) were either abolished or amalgamated in other provinces, only Fujian retained such offices at the provincial, municipal, and county levels. A 1992 *Liberation Army Daily* claimed that virtually all demobilized soldiers in Fuzhou had all found new employment.[68]

The Xi government also created hog farms (with imported foreign breeds such as the Duroc) for the troops and chicken farms for the navy. Millions were spent to improve equipment, informatization, infrastructure (roads and airport expansion), training of reserves, and everyday benefits for the troops. During the relocation of troops and a naval base, Xi applied preferential policies for land requisition, and resolved issues such as pensions, compensations, and jobs for military families.

In a self-appraisal report of November 1991 Xi claimed that in the year and a half as secretary of Fuzhou MPC, he had worked continuously without taking any holidays. His priority was to improve government efficiency, and once his slogan of "Will act immediately" gained currency, hard work and clean government had become the norm in the city.[69]

Fujian and Provincial Governance, October 1995–September 2002

After six years at Fuzhou in October 1995, Xi was promoted to become deputy secretary of the Fujian PPC following the sacking of several senior Fujian officials. Despite Fujian's success in luring Taiwanese investment, Deng Xiaoping and other reformist leaders were disappointed with the performance of that province and its Xiamen SEZ, which compared unfavorably with Shenzhen.[70] However, Xi's career was on the upswing, as the Politburo and the COD had designated him one of the fifth-generation successors, that is, officials in their forties. Subsequently, Xi was elected as an alternate member of the CC at the Fifteenth Party Congress (1997), making him eligible for further advances at the Sixteenth Party Congress in 2002. In September 1999, Xi was given the concurrent post of acting governor of Fujian, replacing He Guoqiang, who was made secretary of the Chongqing MPC. Zhao Xuemin and Shi Zhaobin were made deputy secretaries of the Fujian PPC to firm up the front-line leadership.[71]

In the staggered pattern of career advancement, alternates to the CC are often groomed for full CC membership, which in turn serves as a conduit for the provincial and national leadership. However, in the post-Mao period, elections to the CC can be quite unpredictable, with the introduction of secret balloting. The Politburo and the COD often apply strong pressure on the delegates in favor of certain candidates, but the outcome of balloting cannot be fully controlled. For example, at the Thirteenth Party Congress, unpopular conservative leftist ideologue Deng Liqun was slated to be inducted into the Politburo, but he was disqualified after failing to be elected to the CC. Humiliated, Deng chose not to be nominated as an alternate, and instead was elected to the Central Advisory Commission.[72]

On the other hand, elected full members of the CC are listed in order of the number of strokes in their surnames, but elected alternates are listed in order of the number of votes they mustered, and therefore their relative popularity can be gauged. At rank 151, Xi finished last.[73] The significance for this poor showing can only be deduced. In the post-Mao period, the number of Politburo and CC members is not fixed and can change from time to time to reflect current needs. The numbers of alternates for the Thirteenth (1987), Fourteenth (1992), and Sixteenth (2002) Central Committees were even, 110, 130, and 158, but at the Fifteenth the number was 151. Things did change at the Seventeenth (2007) and Eighteenth (2012) Party Congresses, where the numbers of alternates were 167 and 171, respectively. Yet China watchers generally agree that the original quota was 150 in 1997, but since the top leadership had miscalculated, to accommodate Xi an additional slot (*ewai zengbu*), the 151st, was added.

Other evidence provides a better context of the conflicting forces at work at that time. First, the top leadership was keen to groom fifth-generation leaders like Xi. Accordingly, Deng Pufang, Deng Xiaoping's son, was elected as alternate member number 150, despite concerns about his dubious business ventures. After the Fifteenth Party Congress, many fifth-generation leaders were promoted to provincial- and ministerial-level posts.[74] Second, there was a great deal of hostility against the princelings, as well as a suspicion that retired elders were trying to privilege their wealth and family connections to promote their offspring.[75] Consequently, some younger princelings were shunned from the CC altogether—they were Liaoning governor Bo Xilai and director of the China Developmental Bank Chen Yuan, sons of elders Bo Yibo and Chen Yun, respectively. Finally, Xi was unknown nationally, and he had to contend with a backlash against the princelings.

In January 2000, Xi at age forty-seven was promoted to become governor of Fujian, the youngest provincial governor at the time, and he remained in that position until a transfer to Zhejiang in 2002. Overall, it took Xi twenty-six years after joining the CCP in 1974—and twenty-one years since working with Geng Biao at the CMC—to finally become a first-in-command of an entire province.[76] One reason for Xi's promotion could be his putative outstanding performance and local recognition, since he was elected at the Fujian People's Congress by large votes.[77] One source said that since Xi assumed the post of secretary of the Fuzhou MPC, the economy of Fuzhou had conspicuously strengthened—GDP and revenue had grown an average of 12.6 percent and 28.5 percent per annum. Since 1991, foreign investment had greatly increased, so that by 1998 approved foreign investment projects totaled more than six thousand, and foreign investment totaled US$6 billion. Subsequent accomplishments in municipal governance, environmental protection, and river, hurricane, and flood management, it was said, owed their origins to policies laid down during Xi's tenure.[78]

In retrospect, this promotion history suggests that his assignment to Ningde was less a demotion than a means for the CCP to prepare him for higher office. Although a provincial governor is a second-ranking position below the PPC secretary, it is not unreasonable to suggest that his promotion was Beijing's attempt to build confidence with Taiwan since he was the son of the eighty-six-year-old Xi Zhongxun, a founder of the PRC.[79] On the other hand, however, Xi's promotion can be interpreted as slow, since it took him nine years to move from a deputy position to the chief position.[80]

As governor and an increasingly important fifth-generation successor to the Politburo, Xi would have been scrutinized continuously by Zhongnanhai, and virtually all his speeches and exchanges with journalists would have been monitored, but that still left room for him to innovate.[81] In the following, we will examine Xi's policy record as a provincial chief.

The Hong Kong Advantage

Hong Kong, one of the four "Asian tigers" or "minidragons," was a major investor in Fujian, and Fujianese are said to comprise one-sixth of Hong Kong's 6.5 million population.[82] As secretary of the Fuzhou MPC Xi visited Hong Kong in August 1991 and again in April 1992, and while there stressed the intimate geographic and personal relationship between Fuzhou, Hong Kong, and Taiwan. As China was backward in many areas, Xi solicited foreign investment in highways, harbors, department stores, real estate, tourism, and banks, as well as in land development in the Fuzhou's outlying islands such as Culu and Langqi.[83] In August 1994, Xi led a trade delegation to Germany and Britain to court European investment. Subsequently a number of agreements were signed for cooperation in the construction of ports, highways, and the Changle International Airport, in addition to partnerships in electronics, machinery, medicine, and automobile parts. Siemens of Germany signed a contract to produce computers, and BP of Britain planned a joint venture factory to produce liquefied petroleum gas for Fuzhou. A contract with a Dutch beer maker planned a brewery and a beer-packaging factory.[84]

In 1997, Hong Kong sovereignty reverted from Britain to China, providing further opportunities for economic cooperation and integration. An economic cooperation promotion committee, a first in the country, was created for this purpose in August 1997. Xi's visit to Hong Kong in 2001 was followed by a "Fujian Festival" in Hong Kong in 2002. Over ten thousand companies, many of them manufacturers, had subsequently migrated to Fujian, attracted by cheaper labor, land, low overhead, and market possibilities. Between 1998 and 2006 Hong Kong invested US$20.8 billion in Fujian, accounting for half of Fujian's total foreign investment. Fujian enterprises were beginning to be listed on the Hong Kong Stock Exchange, and Hong Kong banks entered Fujian. Fujian's strategy was to leverage Hong Kong's advantage as an international free port possessing an advanced regulatory system, highly developed service sectors, especially in finance and trade, and technological expertise in order to develop Fujian.[85]

Taiwan, Friend or Foe?

Another one of the "four minidragons," Taiwan in the 1980s was already enjoying an economic boom and was transitioning into a parliamentary democracy with open elections of both the president and the legislature. Six hundred thousand residents of Taiwan spoke the Fuzhou dialect. In Fuzhou, of the eight counties opened, six were located next to the Taiwan Strait, with the closest being only sixty-eight nautical miles away. Although large numbers of exiled Chinese had relocated to Taiwan after 1949, new values and identities had developed quite distinct from those in China. Apart from geographical proximity and a common cultural heritage—80 percent of Taiwan's population have their ancestral origins in Fujian—the economies of China and Taiwan were both mutually interdependent as well as beneficial to one another. China's gradual opening was providing Taiwan with markets, resources, labor, and investment outlets, while Taiwan was providing investment capital, technology, and managerial expertise. Officials on both sides of the strait were, like Xi Jinping, keenly aware of the potential dividends of trade, cooperation, and direct engagement.[86]

Fujian had actively courted Taiwanese businesses and investment in China by providing infrastructural development and a transport network including the Changle International Airport, the Fuxiazhuang highway, and a number of ports.[87] Xi understood the huge untapped potential, yet mutual nonrecognition since 1949 meant that there were no direct contacts concerning trade, transport, and mail, and these links had to be channeled through a third-party entity like Hong Kong, Macau, or South Korea.[88] Furthermore, the years between 1995 and 2002 were a sensitive and confrontational time in China-Taiwan relations. After its defeat during the civil war, when the GMD (Romanized as Kuomintang, or KMT, in Taiwan) had been exiled to Taiwan, the two sides withheld diplomatic recognition and all forms of contact with one another. Beijing to this day has never given up the right to use force to "reunify" the country. Concurrently, in Taiwan, a separate political-social-economic identity had matured, identification with the mainland had begun to weaken, and Taiwan resented Beijing's diplomatic isolation of the island, which by then was diplomatically recognized only by a couple of dozen countries. To ease tensions, the two sides considered a compromise that recognized that there was only one China, but which enabled them to interpretate what "one China" meant. Often labeled the "1992 Consensus," the compromise has been controversial—the KMT has vouched for its existence, whereas the Democratic Progressive Party (DPP) denies it. The DPP disliked the "one China" part of the formula, whereas Beijing was not keen on the "differing interpretation." Years later, KMT legislator Su Chi admitted he made up the term "1992 Consensus."[89] More concretely, however, Beijing's reunification formula of "one country, two systems," which means the incorporation of Taiwan as one of China's provinces, has never been acceptable to Taiwan. When Taiwanese leaders talked about "reunification," they meant a union of two equals.[90]

The contrasting goals on both sides had exacerbated conflicts. Cross-strait relations became severely strained during the Lee Teng-hui (KMT, 1988–2000) and Chen Shui-bian (DPP, 2000–2008) administrations in response to their proactive "salami tactics" to foster de jure independence or permanent separation. For instance, Lee employed "vacation diplomacy" by making nonstate visits to countries that recognized China and gained entry to the United States to visit his alma mater, Cornell University. And although Taiwan was barely recognized internationally, it attempted to campaign for a return to the United Nations by dispensing largesse. Lee also proclaimed that the cross-strait relationship was actually one between two states, explicitly rejecting the one-China principle.[91]

Beijing reacted fervently to these tactics, and during Taiwan's presidential elections from December 1995 to March 1996 intimidated Taiwan with a military buildup and exercises, and the positioning of over three hundred missiles targeting Taiwan. The United States reacted by sending two aircraft carrier groups near Taiwan waters and the *Nimitz* sailed through the strait.[92] This crisis and brinkmanship were further complicated by the alleged "accidental" NATO bombing of the Chinese embassy in Kosovo in 1999, further weapons sales by the

United States to Taiwan, and the downing of a Chinese military jet in a collision with a US surveillance plane in 2001 near Hainan Island.[93]

At a summer Beidaihe meeting in 1999, the Chinese leadership, alleging that the United States was planning to contain China and to stall its rise, reportedly demanded a timetable for cross-strait reunification to prevent Taiwan from indefinitely stalling reunification. The leadership also called for measures to neutralize proindependence forces in Taiwan and for the PLA to prepare for a local war and another war against the United States.[94] Amid the crisis, Chen Shui-bian of the DPP, which upheld independence in its party platform, was elected Taiwanese president in 2000. Once elected, however, Chen Shui-bian began with a moderate stance pledging "five nos"—no declaration of independence, no change of national title, no inclusion of the two-state theory, no holding of a referendum on independence, and no abolition of the National Unification Guidelines and the National Unification Council. But Beijing, refusing to trust Chen, continued its policy of isolating Taiwan internationally, reaching out to Taiwanese opposition parties to isolate Chen, and pressing for reunification.

Beijing's appointment of Xi as Fujian governor was meant to build confidence as well as to firm up front-line leadership during the crisis,[95] and therefore Xi had to tread a fine line in dealing with potentially explosive situations. On the one hand, he participated in war mobilization drills in Fujian for all eventualities.[96] In 1999, Beijing's saber-rattling saw coastal Fujian and Jinmen Island enter a first-grade mobilization phase. Serving concurrently as first secretary of the Nanjing Military Region, deputy director of the region's National Defense Mobilization Committee, first political commissar of Fujian's Services and Arms, Reserve Artillery Division, and director of Fujian's National Defense Mobilization Committee, Xi participated actively in military planning. For the first time in twenty years, on April 29, 2000, the standing committee of the PPC convened a military affairs meeting to discuss defense mobilization. As governor of a front-line province, Xi was put in charge of specific planning.[97] In May 18–20, 2000, leaders of the Nanjing Military Region along with high officials of five provinces and one municipality congregated at Fuzhou and Xiamen to discuss national defense and mobilization of the reserves.[98] Again, on June 2 and 3, 2001, these officials discussed "war zone" mobilization.[99] Military exercises were conducted by Fujian reserve duty antiaircraft artillery June 6–7, 2001.[100]

On the other hand, Xi tried a conciliatory tone, emphasizing an interdependent relationship and the prospect of the "three links" (the establishment of postal, transportation, and trade) with Taiwan as a means of reconciliation. Elaborating on Jiang Zemin's instruction, "Don't let political differences interfere with the economic cooperation across the strait," Xi stressed the mutual benefits and prosperity for both sides—Fujian was attractive and profitable for Taiwanese investors, and Taiwan had earned US$108 billion since China's opening up. China was already a hinterland for Taiwanese economic development, and with upcoming expansion to central and western China, Taiwan would enjoy even more economic opportunities, especially on the eve of the dual accession to the World Trade Organization (WTO) by China and Taiwan. The prospect for commercial links would be unlimited for Taiwan businesses provided they did not support Taiwanese independence.[101] Under the principle of "one China," Xi said, everything could be discussed. To humor the Taiwanese, Xi added that both sides could emphasize their shared culture and the Minnan dialect, especially when Fujian's feng shui[102] was good for them. To reassure jittery Taiwanese investors, Xi promised to protect their economic interests, to drop the arbitrary fees imposed on them, and to protect their legal rights. As the son of a CCP founder, Xi was generally expected to reflect Beijing's manifestations.[103]

At home, Xi admonished that Fujian must seize the opportunity of Taiwan's economic transformation and attract Taiwanese service industries and high-tech production. At the end of 1999, Fujian had already approved 5,894 Taiwanese enterprises and accepted investment of US$8 billion, an amount second only to Hong Kong investment.[104] The large volume of Taiwanese investment had brought prosperity to Fujian and facilitated in turn Taiwan's ascendance up the production value chain. More benefits would be reaped with the accession of both parties to the WTO. Tourism and various science, technology, cultural, and academic exchanges had intensified, with two hundred thousand to three hundred thousand Taiwanese tourists visiting Fujian annually.[105]

In Taiwan, too, business interests began to exert pressure on their government for more direct Chinese contact, beginning with the "lesser three links" between the Jinmen, Matsu, and Fujian coastal areas. Progress was made in January 2001, when Taiwanese delegations from Jinmen and Matsu sailed directly to Xiamen and Fuzhou to visit graves. A month later, Jinmen residents sailed directly from Xiamen to Jinmen, and these two trips broke the restrictions of fifty-two years. Subsequently, Taiwan residents sailed to Xiamen to explore trade, exhibit products, and conduct arts and cultural exchanges. Such activities broke the impasse with the "lesser three links," and Xi began to argue for the full "three links" (postal, transportation, and trade) since Fujian would be the obvious first choice.[106]

In July 2002, Xi announced that preparation for implementation of the full "three links" was complete. The Mawei port passenger terminal, built for this purpose, was ready, and Fuzhou's Changle airport was ready for more Taiwan traffic, and so were the airports in Xiamen, Fuzhou, Wuyishan, and Jinjiang.[107] At the same time, Xiamen had established the country's first Taiwanese Businessmen Association. By 2002, 7,062 Taiwanese firms had been approved, and Fujian had accumulated Taiwanese investment of US$9.24 billion, or 30 percent of the nation's total.[108] By 2002, Taiwan had become Fujian's largest source of foreign investment and its most important trading partner.

Despite this, Fujian had to contend with fierce competition from Jiangsu and Guangdong for Taiwanese capital. Xi made several plans: (1) to tap the potential and turn Fujian into a center for Taiwanese business by leveraging its labor-intensive and capital-extensive industries; (2) to develop Fujian into a hub for Taiwan tourists, since about 80 percent of Taiwanese were of Fujian origin, and Fujian already enjoyed China's fourth largest tourism income; and (3) to turn Fujian into a food-processing base for Taiwan by banking on the similar climate between the two regions and by learning advanced agricultural techniques and management from Taiwan.[109]

Fujian as a Center for Illegal Emigration and Human Trafficking

Fujianese are often stereotyped as outwardly oriented not only in trade and commerce but also in smuggling. The provincial capital, Fuzhou, was and still is a major center for human trafficking and a departure point for "snake heads," leaders of people-smuggling gangs.[110] Since the ringleaders and vessels frequently came from abroad, human smuggling had become internationalized, polemicized, and a human rights issue. The main destinations for illegal emigrants lured by the illusive prospect of better lives were the United States, Japan, Canada, Britain, and South Korea. China's border police caught 5,151 suspects in 2001 alone. An estimated one hundred thousand Chinese were smuggled out of China each year, and the issue received worldwide attention when in 2000 fifty-eight Fujian migrants were found dead in a container in Dover, England.[111] As deputy governor of Fujian, Xi had to deal with rampant human smuggling along the long Fujian coastline. Xi pledged strict measures to strike against the snake heads, blaming economic disparities between China and the developed countries for the activity, and claiming that many had to pay US$30,000 for being smuggled, whereas such a sum could be better used for starting a small business at home. Xi prescribed education as to the dangers of irregular migration, along with increased patrols, interception, and border security to counter the tide, and sought the cooperation of Interpol, New York police, and overseas Chinese.[112] Again, in 2004, twenty-four illegal migrant workers, mostly from Fujian, drowned while picking cockles at Morecambe Bay, UK, a notoriously dangerous work area because of fast-rising tides and quicksand. Most of these workers had been intimidated by gang-masters into working for low pay under bleak and hazardous conditions.[113] These publicized cases reveal the tip of an iceberg of a "wicked" global problem where the poor in developing countries are lured by the prospect of a better life, joining relatives, and inducement by organized gangs seeking huge profits and cheap labor abroad.

Limited and Service-Oriented Governments

At Fujian, Xi is credited with introducing the new notions of "limited government" and "service-oriented government" in a 1999 government report,[114] and these ideas have been continuously debated and developed. The challenges of the post–September 11, 2001, environment, a slowing down of the global economy, the tense situation with Taiwan, sluggish domestic demand, and the impact of corruption cases (discussed later), in addition to institutional weaknesses, meant that the policy environment at the dawn of the new millennium was more challenging than during the 1997 Asian Financial Crisis. China's accession to the WTO in 2001 had obliged it to conform to external rules such as trade liberalization, transparency, and competition. Many sectors, such as agriculture, manufacturing, and the SOEs, faced the painful prospect of fundamental readjustment, and it was thought that new measures had to be introduced to maintain competitiveness and to provide a sound environment for economic growth. Since changes had to be made to conform to WTO rules, Xi took this opportunity to attempt to transform various levels of governments into service-oriented organizations that focused on economic adjustment, market supervision, and public services. The governments were ordered to clean up their rules and regulations, reduce unnecessary *shenpi* (administrative examination and approval), and promote transparency. They were to take a "people oriented" approach and eliminate bureaucratic issues that fostered "a mountain of documents and an ocean of meetings."[115]

At the 2001 Fujian Forum on nonpublic ownership Xi asserted that the key to the transformation of government functions was to draw the line between what ought and what ought not to be done, so government could become "limited" and focus more on providing efficient public services. Xi chastised governments' overintervention in the enterprises, and their failure to form a new service relationship with society, and officials' ignorance of modern management.[116] Indeed, Xi's much-touted notion of "limited government" referred less to a bias toward free enterprise and government nonintervention than a diminution of the command economy. Often used by the Chinese as a contradistinction to an "omnipotent" and "omnipresent" government that controls everything, the notion speaks to a search for a new role for the government that could bolster social services but not stifle innovation, competitiveness, and job creation.

Since 2001, the Fujian government had revised its laws and regulations involving trade, services, and intellectual property, to conform with WTO principles of nondiscrimination and transparency. This resulted in the aboli-tion of 294 laws or regulations and the revision of 71 others.[117] As governor, Xi relaxed prohibition of foreign investment in areas such as services, trade, high technology, and environment in order to attract international financial groups and multinational corporations. In particular, he strove to attract Taiwanese in-vestment, especially in the electronics industry, to leverage Taiwan's "third wave" of transformation in science and technology.[118] Subsequently, the notion of a service-oriented government was adopted nationally by Zhu Rongji in 2003 and Wen Jiabao in 2004.[119]

Food Safety

The attempt to relax government control in some areas contrasted with the need to bolster the government's regulatory function in areas such as the protection of consumers and the environment. Economic development, which had contrib-uted to a higher living standard and the availability of a large variety of food, had raised the issue of the neglect of food safety. Because of the intense market compe-tition and profit making, in Fujian as in the rest of China, an emerging issue was that food, agricultural and aquatic products, drinking water, rice, and condiments were often contaminated by pesticides, chemical fertilizers, antibiotics, and banned stimulants. Also, the government's control over information and cen-sorship made an independent regulatory regime almost impossible. Regulations were lacking in food processing, storage, and transportation. Counterfeit goods and products (such as vinegar) and unhygienic practices were rampant. The situa-tion was so dire that Xi said that it was "too horrendous to behold." The regulatory regime, cumbersome as it already was, was simply unable to cope with the new free-for-all situation, so food poisoning and poor restaurant hygiene was preva-lent.[120] An egregious example was the use of beta-adrenergic agonists as additives to hog feed to grow lean meat, save on animal feed, and accelerate meat produc-tion. Meat produced with these additives may cause nausea, dizziness, muscle shake, heart palpitation, and high blood pressure in human consumers. Further, illegal slaughtering to evade slaughter taxes and meat inspection meant that the meat of sick and diseased animals found its way to the markets.

After reading two *Xinhua* reports reflecting on the problem in February 2001, Xi launched a campaign and pledged to devote three years to "basically" ensuring food safety, eliminating food poisoning, in the province's twenty-three cities, and for the entire province in five years. The government blamed the large variety of food and agricultural products and the lack of monitoring equipment and regulations for the malaise. Fujian's campaign was a national first; a similar nationwide campaign was not launched until 2004. In June 2002, the Fujian government devoted its tenth five-year plan to ensuring food safety by introducing measures such as tightened inspections of contaminated food and water. Mundane as it was, this was touted as an innovative use of a five-year plan. Henceforth, twenty-three departments coordinated their efforts to form a provincial food safety committee. Xi pledged to import advanced measurement equipment, to set up designated places for slaughtering, and to enter the data on the web to monitor the number of hogs slaughtered.[121]

Fujian's food and drug scandals are more examples of "wicked" problems that would not disappear. In 2005, McDonalds and KFC in China were exposed for using "tony red," a toxic chemical in fried chicken. The most egregious incident was the 2008 scandal involving infant formula contaminated by melamine, an industrial chemical to make fertilizer, which killed six children and sickened three hundred thousand children with kidney stones. Farmers added melamine to pass protein-level testing, then sold it to large dairy companies like Sanlu, a joint venture with New Zealand. Bribed local officials looked the other way, and sensitive information was censored during China's Olympic year. In 2012, the government issued alerts on "gutter oil," reprocessed cooking oil literally recovered from the gutter. Contaminated exports were found in toothpaste, dumplings, and pet food. Public outcries within China led to massive crackdowns on unlicensed food businesses, but even with high-profile firings and heavy sentences for culprits, public confidence over food safety was dismal. In 2012, the central government unveiled a five-year plan to streamline overlapping and contradictory regulations, but the weak regulatory regime continued to be a challenge to governance.[122]

The Yuanhua Smuggling Case in Xiamen and Anticorruption, 1999–2001

Corruption scandals racked Fujian during the reform period. The most notorious and largest corruption scandal to hit China since the founding of the People's Republic, the Yuanhua case implicated hundreds of businesses and government officials in Fujian, involving billions of yuan. Lai Changxing, the kingpin of the Yuanhua Group, was accused, between 1996 and 1999, of smuggling goods worth ¥53 billion (US$6.38 billion), evading taxes of ¥30 billion (US$3.6 billion), and dispensing prodigious bribes that had enriched sixty-four officials with cars and real estate estimated at ¥29 billion (US$5 billion). In addition, Lai was accused of using ¥800 million of bank loans and ¥2 billion from individuals and enterprises to fund his smuggling empire. The large scope of the political-criminal nexus was unprecedented, and the subsequent investigations and trials sent shockwaves throughout the country.[123]

One of eight children and born during the great famine of 1958, Lai was a semiliterate peasant who, through hard work, cunning, and bribery, turned himself into a billionaire. He launched companies in Hong Kong and Xiamen and created a formidable protection umbrella by lavishly bribing officials with cash, assets, and cars (reportedly one hundred Mercedes Benz automobiles).[124] Through monumental profligacy, Lai commanded hundreds of Xiamen SEZ officials in his thrall. His rackets smuggled cigarettes, cars, petroleum, cooking oil, chemicals, equipment, and other goods through the Xiamen SEZ. At one time the Yuanhua Group controlled a sixth of China's oil imports. Lai built a new airport terminal for Xiamen, paid US$4 million for a soccer team, and started construction of the eighty-eight-story Yuanhua International Center. Among Lai's other excesses were the construction of a replica of the Forbidden City and a pleasure palace called the Red Mansion, where he entertained his guests with female employees. Lai's accomplices permeated all levels of party and government, the courts, and the military.

Lai met his Waterloo during the second half of 1999. When then-premier Zhu Rongji was inspecting Fujian, reportedly Lai offered him a half million yuan and a large pearl and invited him as a guest to the Red Mansion. The indignant Zhu then ordered an investigation. Because of the gravity and complexity of the case, in early 2000 Party Central dispatched a 420-person-strong special investigation team assisted by the Departments of Discipline Supervision, Customs, Public Security, Finance, and Taxation, as well as Procurators and Courts. Fujian PPC secretary Chen Mingyi and Governor Xi were summoned to Beijing to face PBSC members Jiang Zemin, Zhu Rongji, Hu Jintao, and Wei Jianxing, head of the Central Commission for Discipline Inspection (CCDI), to account for the scandal, and Premier Zhu Rongji visited Xiamen several times to investigate.[125]

Investigations and a marathon of trials of more than six hundred suspects took place in five cities from August 1999 to April 2001, resulting in three hundred convictions and fourteen death penalties, most of which were commuted to life imprisonment. Those convicted spanned high officials in the Party, government, public security, customs, the military, taxation, and finance in Beijing and Fujian. They included Li Jizhou, deputy minister of the Ministry of Public Security, who was slapped with a death sentence with a two-year reprieve. Among the many leading Xiamen officials convicted were two deputy secretaries of the Xiamen MPC, two deputy mayors, and officials in customs and taxations, the Fujian public security department, harbor affairs, and Bank of China Fujian branches.[126]

Thirty-one suspects were extradited from overseas, but on getting wind of the investigation Lai and his family escaped to Canada, where, for twelve years, he fought extradition and claimed refugee status, since Canada does not have the death penalty and refuses to extradite suspects facing the death penalty in their home countries. China's most wanted fugitive strained China-Canada relations, and it was not until July 2011 that a Canadian federal court upheld Lai's deportation order, after repeated Chinese assurances that he would not be tortured or executed. After Lai's return, Lai was convicted in April 2012 for smuggling and bribing sixty-four officials with cars, cash, and real estate worth more than ¥5 billion. He was sentenced to life imprisonment.[127]

Lai's criminal activities from 1995 to 1999 occurred primarily in Xiamen, and that is where most of the convicted officials came from. Xi left Xiamen in 1988 to become deputy secretary of the Fujian PPC from 1995 to 2002, rising to become acting governor of Fujian in September 1999 and governor in January 2000.[128] He served under Chen Mingyi, Fujian PPC secretary from 1996 to 2000. But this still raises the question of Xi's responsibility and knowledge, and even involvement, given the scope of the crimes, and given Lai's practice of courting favor with the powerful. Rumors have circulated that Xi was a frequent guest at the Red Mansion.[129] Another source claims that because of Xi's web of family connections, he managed to extricate himself from the scrutiny of the CCDI.[130]

As governor of Fujian, Xi apparently was untainted by the Yuanhua scandal, at least in the eyes of the leadership. Xi vowed to cooperate with the central authorities to get to the bottom of this case.[131] After the scandal, Party Central reorganized Fujian's top leadership and sacked Fujian party chief Chen Mingyi, replacing him with Song Defu, head of the Ministry of Personnel. Chen Mingyi was given a sinecure position as chairman of the Fujian CPPCC, in which he served until 2003. He Guoqiang, vice governor and governor from 1996 to 1999 was left unscathed and was even promoted to secretary of the Chongqing MPC. As governor, Xi was tasked with cleaning up the mess and was summoned to Beijing to explain how such prodigious excesses occurred.

One person who was under a cloud with the Yuanhua case was Jia Qinglin, who had worked in Fujian since 1985, first as Fujian governor from 1991 to 1994 and then as secretary of the Fujian PPC from 1993 to 1996. As a protégé of Jiang Zemin, Jia was summoned to Beijing in 1996 to serve in succession as vice mayor, mayor, deputy secretary, and then secretary of the Beijing MPC. At the 2002 Fifteenth Party Congress and the 2007 Sixteenth Party Congress, Jia was promoted to the number four spot of the PBSC and was therefore unassailable. Although Jia Qinglin's tenure in Fujian coincided with Lai's early criminal activities for only a year or so, it has often been assumed that he had either turned a blind eye to Lai's shenanigans or was a discreet beneficiary. In the 1990s Jia's wife, Lin Youfang, was secretary of the Fujian Foreign Trade Party Committee, and rumors swirled that she was complicit in the Yuanhua case and that Premier Zhu Rongji had ordered Jia to divorce his wife in order to distance himself from the scandal.[132] In an interview with Hong Kong's Feng Huang TV on January 26, 2001, however, Lin Youfang denied any plan for divorce, claiming that she never knew Lai or even heard of the Yuanhua Group.[133] Although the denial strained credibility, the next day Xi defended Lin by flatly denying that Lin was in any way involved.[134] The cautious Lai Changxing also avoided questions on whether he knew Lin, and not until six years later admitted that he had met her at a golf club once.[135]

Another person thought to have colluded with Lai was Jia Tingan, a long-term director of Staff Office and *mishu* to Jiang Zemin, making him untouchable. Jia was eventually promoted to be deputy head of the PLA's General Political Department but was eventually convicted for corruption in 2015 when Jiang's ability to shield his protégés was greatly diminished.[136] Back in 2000, fearing that the investigation might further engulf top leadership, Jiang Zemin ordered that the investigation of the smuggling case be completed by the end of February, providing a closure to stabilize the Fujian leadership so that it could focus on Taiwan. Jiang also ordered that no official above the vice-ministerial level should be investigated.[137] All unfinished work such as the prosecution of cases would henceforth be left with the Fujian's disciplinary committee and legal and political departments.[138]

The investment climate was severely tarnished by the Yuanhua case, as foreign investors became wary of investing in a province with a reputation of rampant smuggling and corruption. Both FDI (especially that from Taiwan) and GDP growth were down, out-of-province workers looking for work in Fujian declined, and Fujian workers looked south for work.[139] At a 2001 January Clean Government Work Conference, Xi vowed to prosecute the remaining cases without exception.

The Yuanhua Case and High-Level Maneuvers

A case as profligate as the Yuanhua case was unlikely a merely local phenomenon, and it reflects the complexity of the political corruption axes in reform China. The case is probably intertwined with struggles in national and factional politics. However, as is often the case with factional politics, more theories than hard evidence are available. The following summarizes one version of the events.[140] The Yuanhua case was reported upward to the head of the Central Political and Legal Affairs Committee, Luo Gan, who from 1999 to 2007 was China's top law enforcement and intelligence chief and a member of Li Peng's inner circle. The manifested target of the 420-person special case team was Lai, but Li Peng was banking on the case to bring down Jia Qinglin in order to weaken Jiang.[141] However, Jiang outmaneuvered both Li Peng and Luo Gan. Although Jia Tingan and Jia Qinglin were both complicit in the Yuanhua case, they were members of Jiang's clique, and Jiang was able to protect them and even managed to make Jia Qinglin party chief of Beijing. Furthermore, since Lai's smuggling kingdom relied on military acquiescence and the 420 investigations revealed that many high-level PLA brass (including executive director of the CMC Liu Huaqing, vice chair of the CMC Chi Haotian and vice minister of the PLA Intelligence Department / chief of staff Ji Shengde) had received Lai's bribes, Jiang Zemin used this to force Liu Huaqing to yield military power. In return Jiang did not prosecute Liu and Chi and allowed Liu's offspring to get off scot-free. The only scapegoat was Ji Shengde, only son to vice-premier Ji Pengfei, who was convicted and given a commuted death sentence for taking a bribe worth ¥20 million by a military court. The older Ji protested the sentence in vain and subsequently committed suicide in protest.[142] In this way the involvement of the PLA leadership was swept under the carpet. However, apart from the conviction of Ji Shengde and the suicide of his father, none of the rest can be substantiated.

In any case, Xi took the opportunity of the Yuanhua case investigation to urge a tough crackdown on corruption. During a government teleconference in January 2001, Xi promised no-holds-barred measures to investigate various levels of government, the judiciary, economic ministries, and SOEs. Corruption was broadly defined as bribery, embezzlement, tax and financial fraud, and dereliction of duty involving officials, their spouses, offspring, and relatives. The government would prosecute offenses in public works, asset stripping during SOE reforms, irregularities in the stock market, and the changeover in property rights. Statistics showed that of the 1,993 newly prosecuted cases in Fujian in 2000, 1,196 persons were punished.[143]

The Chen Kai Scandal

Not long after the Yuanhua case, scandal-tainted Fujian was again rocked by the case of Chen Kai, an entertainment and real estate tycoon and the "richest man in Fuzhou" when he was arrested in 2003. Both cases underscored the cozy relationship between organized crime and officials.[144] Organized crime and secret societies have had a long history in China, though they were wiped out under Mao because of tight social controls. During the reform period, the loosening up of control, in addition to issues of unemployment, impoverishment, and inequality, rekindled criminal subcultures and resurrected Mafia-type organizations. By 2005 official estimates put the number of secret societies nationally at 11,300 and a total membership of over twenty million.[145] Fujian was one of the provinces that harbored a thriving organized crime culture, and powerful criminal groups existed in every town and county in Fuzhou, some of which were even controlled by the local governments.[146]

Born in 1962, Chen was a penniless hawker in the 1980s, but in 1991 when gambling became popular, he started a lucrative slot machine business. He needed sites and approvals from public security, and it was rumored that each license required ¥1 million.[147] Chen befriended Xu Li, son of Fuzhou's police chief, Xu Congrong, and later Chen Kai became Xu Congrong's godson. Xu Congrong then packed the judicial and public security systems with people that catered to their interests. When the government banned slot machines in 1995, Chen's were left alone, and other vendors were forced to sell their shares to Chen, who nearly monopolized the business.[148] From 1994, Chen expanded his business empire to encompass entertainment and real estate and bought hotels, saunas, game parlors, and nightclubs.

In 1993 Chen founded a restaurant that catered to the rich and powerful, and in 1998 built the Kaige Music Plaza, which hired more than two hundred women and was frequented by officials. Chen then recruited former criminals to engage in prostitution, gambling, drug trade, tax fraud, and violent crimes. He bribed officials to overlook his illegal activities, obtained illegal state bank loans with kickbacks, and laundered drug money into real estate. The Kaige group then further expanded to a string of karaoke bars, saunas, and slot machine operators. It imported slot machines from the United States and Macau and used its powerful connections to evade customs officials. Chen was even dignified with being made a member of the CPPCC (1999–2003).

Investigations began in 2003 and took more than two years to complete. The entire case was said to have involved ¥3 billion (US$36 million), one-third of which was said to have been recovered. Those investigated included 113 individuals including seventy-six party members and officials. Nanping Intermediate Court meted out sentences to twenty-one underworld criminals. Chen was convicted for running a prostitution ring and gambling syndicate that involved fifty middle-ranking officials. The court alleged that Chen illegally netted ¥12.09 million (US$1.45 million) and ¥150 million (US$18 million) through tax dodging and contract fraud. Chen was convicted for bribing dozens of high officials in charge of the police, and finance and taxation departments. Fifty officials were said to have formed a protective shield and accepted bribes of just under US$1 million. Chen handed out stock to more than two hundred companies, paying retired officials, police, and former convicts handsomely to shield his casinos and brothels. In the end, Chen was slapped with a death sentence for prostitution, life imprisonment for contract fraud and bribery, plus a range of offenses such as tax evasion, gambling, and illegal kidnapping.[149]

Senior officials convicted along with Chen included judges, prosecutors, tax collectors, and public security officers. The top eight convicted included Song Licheng, deputy secretary of the Fuzhou MPC and secretary of the city's Political and Legal Committee; Zhi Dujiang, Fujian Political and Legal Committee member;

Li Kongzhen, deputy bureau chief of the provincial land tax bureau; Liu Yongzhao, deputy mayor of Fuzhou; Zhu Jian, secretary of the Fuqing MPC; Chen Feng, attorney general of the procuratorate of Jinan District; You Lijie, deputy director of the Gulou District Court; and You Kewei, chief of the Gulou Criminal Court.[150]

The Chen Kai scandal was another notorious case after the Yuanhua affair that underlined a cozy relationship between power and money during Xi's tenure in Fujian. By the time the investigation had begun in 2003, Xi was already transferred to Zhejiang, but the question of his role in those events is still a question mark. Chen's Kaige Musical Plaza and Kaixuan Gardens, luxury venues frequented by officials, were located in prime real estate in the Gulou district of Fuzhou, the same areas where the Fujian provincial and Fuzhou municipal party and government offices were situated.[151] It begs the questions of why the shenanigans occurring literally under the nose of the provincial authorities was allowed to fester for so long.

One unsubstantiated view claims that Xi and Chen were closely related and that Xi was transferred to Zhejiang in order to facilitate the arrest of Chen. In addition to Jia Qinglin and Xi Jinping, Luo Gan was a real protector of the corrupt officials.[152] Apart from this, no evidence exists that Xi was related to Chen and had benefited from the latter's largesse. According to investigator Misha Glenny, whistle-blowing on high crime in China is a very risky proposition and therefore rare. However, the ringleaders of a PCN are often objects of jealousy and hostility, especially by officials excluded from their networks. Unless the act of disclosure is supported by someone else, normally in Beijing, who is more powerful than the criminal targeted, the whistle-blower may suffer reprisals, humiliations, and even imprisonment. This is especially the case when the ringleaders enjoy the support of powerful patrons. The ploy is to wait until the PCN is vulnerable to the extent that enemies or law enforcers can move in.[153] This opportunity came in April 2004, when Hu Jintao instructed the CCDI to prosecute the Chen Kai case and dispatched thirty-odd investigators to Fuzhou and dismissed a number of senior anticorruption officials there. An international warrant was issued for officials who had escaped overseas.[154]

Put in comparative perspective, China's reform period from the 1980s onward featured industrialization and rapid socioeconomic transformation reminiscent of America's Gilded Age and the Roaring Twenties, and this laid a new foundation for contemporary China. Money was abundant, regulations were lax and arbitrary, materialism was rampant, and institutions were weak. Entrepreneurial shenanigans were deemed normal at a time when the zeitgeist reflected Deng Xiaoping's dictum "To get rich is glorious." Scams and pyramid schemes abounded. The difference in China was the absence of old money, but Lai Changxing and Chan Kai came close to being the Chinese versions of Jay Gatsby–style bootleggers and rogues.[155]

Economic Planning, Governance, and Globalization

Scandals aside, back in October 1998, Jiang Zemin inspected Jiangsu, Zhejiang, and Fujian and instructed these relatively well-developed coastal regions to lead the way in agricultural modernization. This order was formalized at the Third Plenum of the Fifteenth Party Congress, held in the same month. Fujian complied by mobilizing thirty provincial departments to conduct research and meetings to try out things in ten selected counties. As the newly minted acting governor, Xi led a research group to produce twenty-seven reports on agricultural modernization, which subsequently were published in a book edited by him in February 2001.[156] In December 2001, Xi also published his doctoral dissertation, entitled "A Study on China's Agricultural Marketization" (discussed later), positioning himself as an expert in the field.[157] According to Xi, since Fujian's rural population still consisted of 80 percent of the total, the modernization of agriculture had to contend with issues ranging from weak superstructure to slow urbanization, and from low incomes to large surplus labor. Agricultural modernization was taken to mean the strengthening of policy areas such as marketization, commodification, science and technology, rural industries, and sustained development. Fujian's plan was modest—it would focus on pilot projects until 2005, agricultural modernization in more advanced areas by 2010, and full modernization by 2030.[158]

On agricultural marketization, Xi said that Fujian was already externally oriented, with a high degree of agricultural marketization since its export of agricultural products in 2000 had already reached US$1.71 billion. However, Fujian was a province with a large population and little land—arable land was only 0.036 hectare per capita, or less than half the already meager national average. Although it produced plentiful aquatic products, bamboo shoots, tea, mushrooms, and fruits, much of its food had to be imported from other provinces. The province's food exports suffered from punishing tariffs as well as non-tariff barriers such as quality standards, and its market scale was tiny compared to much smaller, but advanced, countries such as the Netherlands.[159]

As governor, Xi had to wrestle with Fujian's developmental strategy. From 1978 to 2001, GDP growth for both Fujian and Zhejiang was more than 13 percent per annum; whereas Zhejiang had raised its national GDP ranking from twelfth to fourth, Fujian had raised its from twenty-second to eleventh. Yet, Fujian was deemed lagging behind during the Ninth Five-Year Plan (1996–2000), when the five major drivers of the economy—the petrochemical industry, electronic machinery, building materials, forestry, and aqua products, had failed to reach their potential. The technology levels of these factors remained low, and they encountered fierce competition from other localities in China. With the new advances in globalization and China's entry into the WTO, it was inevitable that Fujian needed a new developmental strategy. A leadership consensus was that Fujian would continue to promote its comparative advantage in sectors such as electronic information technology, building materials, and petrochemicals (collectively known as the three pillars) so that their output value could consist of about 5 to 8 percent of GDP by 2005. The government would support established electronic information technology companies such as Xiahua, Shida, and Wanlida, and turn Xiamen and Fuzhou into two major centers of electronic industries. Attention would be lavished on new sectors of finance, insurance, biological industry, and environmental protection technology.[160] Xi said, "Given the conditions of the weakness of the foundation of the state-owned economy, private enterprises and foreign capital have become the prime movers of Fujian's economic development."[161] To improve the business environment, Xi pledged to reduce local government officials by one-half to raise efficiency and to abolish outdated rules and regulations concerning overseas investment. Accordingly, 333 regulations were dropped in 2000, and Fujian approved 26,281 overseas-invested enterprises with a combined investment of US$3.024 billion.[162]

China's accession to the WTO on December 11, 2001, posed both challenges and opportunities since Beijing was obliged to liberalize, compete, and open up its political economy. It had to abolish thousands of tariffs, quotas, and trade barriers to face competition with its SOEs and agricultural sector. In turn, Fujian faced challenges such as economic globalization and intense international competition, although it relished the opportunity to develop its outward-oriented economy and to open up further. As governor, Xi officially played only second fiddle to PPC secretary Song Defu, but at the Seventh Provincial Party Congress in November 2001 he presented on behalf of the PPC a new development strategy for the new millennium. Partly a response to Beijing's modernization plan that aimed to create a "relatively well-off society," the new omnidirectional strategy, entitled "Three Strategic Channels," contained the following measures.[163] The first was to integrate the less developed mountainous and booming coastal areas to narrow the wealth gap since the GDP per capita in the former was only half that of the latter, and the gap was widening because of more rapid growth in the coastal areas. The second was to accelerate economic integration with the Changjiang (Yangtze) River Delta, Pearl River Delta, and Beijing regions by promoting provincial trade, cooperation, and technological exchange. Similar integration would be promoted with Taiwan, Hong Kong, and Macau. Xi broached the notion of a "south China free trade zone" incorporating Hong Kong, a large source of Fujian's FDI with 1.1 million Fujianese among its six million population, many of whom were entrepreneurs.[164] The third was to open up Fujian's economy internationally, to other provinces, and within Fujian itself. Such measures were meant to open new markets, to attract investment, technology, skills, and to accelerate the development of the tertiary industry. The government would transform its management functions to provide services, raise efficiency, improve its guidance role, and encourage urbanization. One significant aspect was the abolition of the restrictions on farmers and out-of-province laborers, allowing them to work in the urban areas. All three measures required the development of transport and telecommunications networks such as roads, highways, railways, ports, internal waterways, and airports. This also entailed the improvement of market mechanisms, investment climate, science and technology, and human resources. Ports at Fuzhou, Xiamen, and Meizhouwan would be integrated to make them more efficient.

In social matters, Xi's schemes were helped by the fulfillment ahead of schedule of various strategic plans implemented by previous administrations. These plans had tripled the GDP and per capita GDP between 1980 and 2000, boosting Fujian's urban disposable income to ¥7,432.[165] Such success had enabled Fujian to extend its welfare benefits. These included the expansion of employment opportunities, augmented payment for social and unemployment insurance, old-age pensions, medical insurance, and special assistance for struggling enterprises.[166] Xi was credited with the implementation of a "minimum livelihood guarantee" (dibao) for urban residents, originally mandated by Beijing in 1998. The supplements benefited families whose average incomes fell below a certain standard or those lacking income or work ability. Eligible families also received favorable assistance in employment, education, and medical care—at rates that were to be updated at least once a year.[167]

The Building of an "Ecological Province"

Embedded in the "Three Strategic Channels" was the twenty-year plan to turn Fujian into an "ecological province."[168] A first among China's provinces, the plan demanded the completion in 2002 of several projects on forest protection, afforestation at river sources, and the creation of model ecological counties.[169] Subsequent decisions earmarked ¥71.6 billion (US$8.63 billion), of which half had to be spent by 2005, to address the issues of high energy consumption, pollution, and the protection of land, forest, and ocean.[170] Xi and Song Defu vowed that Fujian would not take the "pollute first and clean up later" route, pledging to eliminate the "sunset" industries.[171] The raising of environmental concerns onto the agenda after years of obsessive economic growth earned Xi a reputation of being an environmentalist.

After Xi left, a 2017 report claimed that barren mountains in Fujian were green again, and the province had become one of the country's best in terms of water, air, and environmental quality. The forest coverage rate of 66 percent

by 2013 was the highest in China, and Fujian's geographical position along the
Taiwan Strait helped to "diffuse" air pollution.[172] By 2018, with its lush green
mountains and sandy beaches, Fujian's environment was lauded as one of
the greenest in the country. Various indexes of ecological quality, such as in
water and air, ranked it among the best in the country. In a country where only
1 percent of half a billion urban residents breathe air considered safe by EU
standards, Fujian even advertised itself as an attraction for clean-air tourism.
Fujian's standard is, of course, relative: whereas World Health Organization
and US Environmental Protection Agency standards for PM2.5 are 10 and
12 micrograms respectively, Fuzhou and Xiamen's PM2.5 standards of 27
micrograms satisfied China's standards, and the two cities were ranked among
the top ten Chinese cities with the best air quality. Nevertheless, the gains have
been relative, and the intensifying industrialization and urbanization have
made the fight against serious soil and water pollution and the wasteful consumption of energy and resources an ongoing issue.[173]

The Jinjiang Model

In Fujian, Xi encountered a phenomenon that was labeled the "Jinjiang model."[174]
Chinese developmental literature has often highlighted four principal models of
political economy in the reform period, the Sunan, Wenzhou, Zhujiang (Pearl
River), and Jinjiang models.[175] Jinjiang County in south Fujian had witnessed
a robust development of small and medium village and township enterprises
that attracted largely overseas Chinese (especially Taiwanese) capital and foreign technology. Numerous small, family-run businesses and factories began
with very modest means using labor-intensive methods to manufacture light-
processing and counterfeit goods geared for the domestic and export markets.
The strong local commercial culture and kinship ties spawned various forms of
collaborations between private enterprises and cooperative enterprises to raise
capital for trade and manufacture. At the beginning, fearing the label of capitalism, these private start-ups disguised themselves as collective ("wearing the
red hat") or foreign enterprises. Gradually, with more relaxation, the number
of private enterprises and the number of people employed by them increased
exponentially. In 1991, the first-ever national ranking of economic prowess put
Jinjiang fifty-fifth out of one hundred counties, in 1994, fifteenth, and in 2001,
among the top ten. The experiments with the market and free competition soon
turned Jinjiang from an impoverished rural region into a prosperous and competitive one with well-established industries ranging from shoes and textiles
to clothing; and from ceramic building materials, food, and paper products
to umbrellas. These industries in turn promoted commerce. An impressive

economic growth was marked by a sevenfold increase in the GDP in the twenty-two years following 1978 as Jinjiang became Fujian's fastest-growing region.[176]

To comprehend the new phenomenon and its implications on state-market relationships, Xi took many in-depth investigation trips. One source claims that government noninterference is a hallmark of Jinjiang,[177] but this view is inadequate. Successive governments in Jinjiang had encouraged private enterprises by such measures as the lowering of taxes, the provision of credit, and reforms in finance and foreign trade. Infrastructural support came in the form of communication, energy, and industrial parks. And because of the spontaneous nature of these businesses, the government sought to provide guidance on issues such as factory locations, personnel training, management, and technology.[178] Yet rapid development begot issues such as counterfeit goods, shoddy products, poor working conditions, and income inequality. Like many boom areas in China, the influx of rural migrants had swollen to around one million, or about five times Jinjiang's original population. Naturally, this created issues such as the provision of social services, the turning of farmers into urbanites, and the appeasement of farmers whose land had been expropriated. On the other hand, regarding the "minimum livelihood guarantee" for urban residents, Jinjiang went one step ahead and applied it to both the urban and the rural population.

In his many speeches on the Jinjiang model, one of which was published in the *People's Daily*, Xi lauded the feisty entrepreneurial spirit of the locals, saying that the private entrepreneurs had overcome the "constrictions of an ossified planned economy." In this connection, Xi developed further his notion of a "service oriented" government to mean that the government should facilitate market competition by providing such things as capital, infrastructural support, social services, and insurance for SMEs. It should reduce its *shenpi* power and refrain from unnecessary interference in the market.[179] These are major generalizations, but Xi's endorsement of the Jinjiang model was significant at that juncture because the ideological debate over capitalism and socialism was still raging, especially between the neoliberals and the new left at distant opposite ends of the ideological spectrum.

Cadre Integrity and Xi as a "Research-style" Official

One aspect of Xi's exploration of the proper role and function of the government is his frequent lectures on cadre integrity. For instance, in a televised antigraft conference in 2001's lunar new year, he emphasized the importance for cadres to be honest and disciplined and to steer clear of corruption. Officials must take moral education, he said, and lead by example, being honest, or corruption could never be wiped out.[180] Again, in a work report at the Provincial People's Congress on February 7, 2001, Xi reiterated the importance of cadre honesty and clean government, asserting that no officials should accept favors, discounts for company shares, gifts, or cash offerings.[181] He summarized these themes in one of his many articles published in *Qiushi* (the CCP's theoretical journal) entitled "Pay Attention to Official Integrity in Using Power, Be Principled in One's Conduct," in which he echoed injunctions by Hu Jintao at the Sixteenth Party Congress for leading cadres to govern according to law, virtue, and discipline. He discussed official integrity, which he subsumed under Hu's admonition: "For the people, do real work and be clean."[182] In some quarters, Xi's persistent moralizing won him a reputation as a "clean" official, although it is not uncommon for corrupted officials (proven or otherwise) to regularly espouse anticorruption rhetoric.

Often touted as a "research style" official, Xi was already a prolific writer before becoming general secretary, contributing numerous articles to both academic and general journals. A search for articles in the China Academic Journal Full-Text Database authored by Xi between 1995 and 2012 returned 307 items. Discounting government reports, speeches, greetings, duplications, and so on, his essays probably amount to half that number. He edited several books, and his speeches and essays were also collected in book form.[183] For instance, in 1992, Xi published a collection of his speeches and reports while secretary of the Ningde MPC in a book entitled *Overcoming Poverty* (*Baituo Pinkun*), in which he candidly discussed a whole range of issues ranging from surplus rural labor to poverty reduction, from grain supplies to village and township enterprises, and from journalism and education to clean government.[184] Another similar collection of his reports, speeches, and articles was entitled *Do Real Work, Be at the Forefront* (*Ganzai shichu, zouzai gianlie*), published in 2006. From 2003 to 2007, while secretary of the Zhejiang PPC, he contributed a column using the pseudonym Zhe Xin for the *Zhejiang Daily* entitled "New Sayings From Zhejiang." The 232 pieces of opinions, criticisms, endorsements, and sermons were collected in a book first published in 2007.[185] Akin to today's blog posting, these pieces cover a full range of governance issues. While many of his writings might have been written by *mishu*, they do reflect his personal style and knowledge base. Whatever Xi's motivations for this large publication output, what is important is that it raised his profile, helped his brand, and provides a primary source for studying local conditions at that time.

More controversial is the doctoral dissertation published in December 2001, which earned Xi the degree of doctor of law. Xi completed the tome while studying Marxist theory and ideological education part time at the Faculty of Humanities and Social Sciences, Tsinghua University, between 1998 and 2002.[186] Detractors claim that the thesis, entitled "A Study on China's Rural Marketization," has nothing to do with legal studies, that it lacks original research, that it may have been written by another person or group, and that it contains many passages simply lifted from other sources, such as government reports and others' academic writings. They point out that Xi first attended Tsinghua between 1975 and 1979 as a worker-peasant-soldier student, having missed his secondary education, to study chemical engineering, but never achieved a master's degree as a prerequisite for doctoral studies. Critics question as well how he could have enough time to work on a dissertation while he was governing a province of thirty-five million persons. Further allegations claim that Xi may have been helped by Chen Xi, a good university friend of his who was secretary and deputy secretary of Tsinghua's party committee from 1992 to 2002, and who was promoted to deputy minister of education in 2009.[187]

In any case, the originality of the work is perhaps less important than its content. Xi's purpose was to address the issues of how to market agricultural products, raise developmental funds, and deal with rural surplus labor. The independent variable for Xi is the forceful promotion of rural marketization, which he maintains could resolve a whole series of issues such as agricultural modernization, the gap between urban and rural areas, rural surplus labor, inefficiency, and obsolete technology.

Xi concluded his dissertation by demonstrating the work he had already done and touting his research methods as innovative and original, combined as they were with Marxist, comparative, and Western perspectives. Further, he said, since studies by Chinese and foreign academics were "immature," his contribution was a first in China, and that a monograph based on the dissertation had already been published by the People's Publishing House. This monograph cannot be located, but two articles drawing directly from chapter 6 were published in journals.[188] The thesis bibliography lists ninety-seven Chinese and twenty-six English books and articles, but citations are minimal (a dozen in some chapters and none in others), and, as is the norm in China, incorporation of official policy documents seldom includes citations. Overall, Xi's dissertation reads like a policy report due to its many normative recommendations, and like a textbook because of a penchant to list issues in point form.

Generally, in China as in the West, a doctoral dissertation requires extensive independent research and an original contribution to the field of knowledge, although the degree of complexity and quality required varies greatly across disciplines and universities. It normally requires years of full-time work for an extensive collection of empirical data and writing. It is reasonable to suspect that an intense time period for research and writing was unavailable to Xi. In Fujian he had bemoaned the lack of study time because of the hectic work schedule when he lectured officials on the need for theoretical studies. Citing the ancients, he urged that the learning attitude must be serious, scientific, and honest.[189] It is a fact that Chinese officials are supported by a large contingent of aides, advisers, and secretaries whose task is to draft, edit, and write official documents,[190] and since Xi's dissertation incorporates many of these documents, he probably owes quite a debt to these secretaries. One should also remember that academic research had only slowly recovered since the 1980s from the onslaught of the Maoist era.

In my view, the analysis contained in Xi's dissertation could satisfy the standard degree requirements of many English-speaking countries, especially for mature candidates who have had firsthand work experience in their field of research. Its systematic analysis is comparable with academic studies done in the West.[191] As mentioned, in February 2001, Xi had already published an edited volume on agricultural modernization that collected twenty-seven reports by experts, academics, and thirty-odd provincial departments commissioned by the Fujian PPC in 1999.[192] Further, one point omitted by Xi's detractors is that virtually all the provincial examples are illustrated by statistics and policies in Fujian, and that Xi had privileged access to this information as a policymaker. Finally, it is important to note that in the PRC educational system, Marxist theory and ideological education is subsumed under the rubric of legal studies, and that is the reason Xi obtained a doctor of laws degree. Overall, the dissertation contains original analysis quite consistent with Xi's knowledge base, but whether he wrote it all by himself is an open question.

Conclusion

Popular and impressionistic evaluations of Xi's records in Fujian vary. One oft-quoted internet source claims that Xi's plan to match Fuzhou's economy with that of Guangzhou by 2000 was unrealized—the GDP of Guangzhou was ¥2,492 billion, whereas Fuzhou's was only ¥1,003.31 billion, or 40 percent of the former. This, together with the lack of economic innovations and lack of media openness, reflected Xi's failure.[193] Another cynical view deems Xi to be mediocre because of his many failures at Ningde—Xi vowed to cultivate a good cadre team, but after he was promoted to secretary of the Fujian PPC, Ningde was racked by corruption scandals. At Fuzhou, his pet project of Changle International Airport was a vanity project intended to impress for promotion purposes rather than for practical application. Another internet source claims that Xi had actively leveraged his princelings connections as son of Xi Zhongxun to advance his career. He regularly gauged the pulses of the powerful at the capital and strove to squeeze himself into the Tsinghua "faction" to connect with former premier Zhu Rongji, Zhou Xiaochuan, and Wang Qishan. He used his wife's reputation to make connections because virtually all of her performances were attended by members of Party Central and the military.[194]

Still another source claims that while Xi's performance in Fujian was unremarkable, he was nevertheless skillful at employing scams to advance his career. In 1996, in response to a national hygiene inspection campaign, Xi complied by closing virtually all the street vendors. Further, because of his complicity with the Chen Kai scandal, at the end of 1999, some retired cadres petitioned against Xi's promotion as governor.[195]

On the other hand, Yang Yisheng, a former deputy director of Fujian's Government Developmental Research Center, and a close associate of Xi, claimed that he was best in dealing with the big picture, and that his style was more imaginative. He was more earnest with large issues but more relaxed with smaller issues. An amiable person, Xi lacked the arrogance and conceit characteristic of the princelings. For this reason, outsiders often consider him ordinary although, in fact, Fujian under Xi's charge enjoyed a period of rapid economic development.[196]

Wang Jing, president of Xindalu, Fujian's largest and most well-known high-tech business group, recalled how she had benefited by special help for entrepreneurs like her who had little start-up capital.[197] Further, the big ideas developed in Fujian, such as the ecological province, water and soil conservation, the Jinjiang model, limited government, and effective government, were introduced to Zhejiang later on.

It is natural that anecdotal evaluations of Xi's Fujian experience can vary, informed as they are by official propaganda or half-truths arrived at by deduction and intuition. Overall, economic growth in Fuzhou was rapid, although the comparison with Guangzhou was untenable, as the two cities developed under different circumstances. After three decades of reform, Xiamen, Ningde, Fuzhou, and Fujian itself have been completely transformed in many ways.[198] For instance, Fujian's economic growth rate from 1999 to 2006 was 12.58 percent annually.[199] By 2009 Fujian was already crisscrossed by many highways and railways. It was credited for leading the country in implementing the basic livelihood guarantee, comprehensive insurance for rural housing, the elimination of fees for rural schools, and the incorporation of rural migrants in unemployment schemes.[200] As governor, Xi's attempt to elevate the Fujian economy by focusing on the information, machinery, and petrochemical industries[201] appears to have borne fruit. His strategy to apply industrial policy—the targeting of and promotion of sunrise industries and the phasing out of uncompetitive sunset industries—shows that he was inspired by the "developmental state" model even though that term is not used in China.[202] In addition, Xi gained a certain reputation as an "environmentalist" in Fujian.[203]

More significant were the evaluations by Xi's superiors to justify his continuous promotion. A central report presumably prepared just prior to the Sixteenth Party Congress praised him for the streamlining of government, and for redirecting government functions toward providing social services. He was commended for attracting Taiwan investment and for resettling sampan dwellers and slum residents in Ningde and Fuzhou. His persistent hectoring of officials for slothfulness, foot-dragging, and clientelism was compared to those effective policies of Zhu Rongji when the latter was mayor of Shanghai.[204]

According to more recent perspectives, by 2007, the "three pillars" had developed quickly, but the economic structure and high-tech production were still deemed inadequate—Fujian's secondary sector was 49.2 percent of its GDP, or equal to the national average, but its tertiary sector was 40 percent lower than that of the national average and neighbors such as Shanghai, Guangdong, and Zhejiang. The supply of services to consumers and businesses was constrained by resources, social divisions of labor, and the general denigration of the service industry in favor of heavy industry.[205] Fujian would need to further the tertiary sector, modernize agriculture, and develop new information technology, pharmaceuticals, energy, environmental protection, and high-end equipment.[206]

In any case, Xi's steady promotions often raise questions about his links to his father's influence. When asked about the issue while in Fujian, Xi replied, "I cannot say there is entirely no connection, but we cannot say that I depended on him for everything. . . . Frankly, China has not yet established a strict system of selecting officials, and that's why people around the leaders or those familiar to them can be easily selected." He then added, when he became secretary of Liangjiahe party branch, his father was still not rehabilitated and presumably had little influence over his career.[207]

A milestone in China's political succession came during the Sixteenth Party Congress in November 2002, which witnessed the first-ever peaceful transition of power in China since 1949. Reshuffling at the top freed up many spots throughout the hierarchy for personnel advancements before and after the congress. Pre-congress reshuffles saw Xi transferred to Zhejiang in October as deputy governor, acting governor, and deputy secretary of the Zhejiang PPC.[208] Right after the congress, Xi was promoted to become the secretary of the Zhejiang PPC,[209] opening the next chapter in his political life.

5

The Sixteenth Party Congress, 2002, and Governing Zhejiang, 2002–2007 (Age Forty-Nine to Fifty-Four)

The Sixteenth Party Congress and Political Succession

In Chinese political succession, the process of screening, cultivating, and training of cadres is ongoing, but major reshuffles of office intensify immediately before and after each national party congress, which in recent decades have been held every five years. Prior to each national party congress, the localities and provinces hold party congresses to change their leadership personnel by controlled elections. Retirements at the national level according to fixed term and age limits subsequently create vacancies for mobility up the bureaucratic ladder. Nevertheless, the monotonous rituals of party congresses often give the impression that the Chinese political system is regimented and ossified. Beneath the surface and hidden from foreign view, however, party congresses are massive exercises for recruitment, regeneration, and political mobility that promote officials with widely differing skill sets, and this goes far to explain the continuing strength of Chinese authoritarianism.[1]

The Sixteenth Party Congress in 2002 accomplished the first-ever smooth and peaceful transition of power in the People's Republic without purges and bloodshed. History demonstrates that Mao's two designated successors, Liu Shaoqi and Lin Biao, met with ignominious ends. Following Mao's death in 1976, the Gang of Four was forced from power and Mao's putative successor, Hua Guofeng, was soon ousted. Similarly, Deng Xiaoping's two protégés, Hu Yaobang and Zhao Ziyang, were both purged as general secretaries. However, the Sixteenth Party Congress saw the orderly retirement of many top CCP leaders and the promotion of new blood, effecting a generational changeover from the third to the fourth generation of leaders. And in contrast with the previous party congress, princelings gained ground, as many were promoted, especially into the Central Committee.[2]

Specifically, by observing age and term limits, all leaders over seventy years old (except Jiang Zemin) retired from the Politburo, and two-thirds of its twenty-four members were newcomers. Six of seven members of the PBSC retired en masse, and Jiang Zemin resigned as general secretary in favor of fifty-nine-year-old Hu Jintao. This way, "fourth generation" leaders in their early to mid-fifties who had been groomed for succession, like Hu Jintao, Wen Jiabao, and Wu Bangguo, entered the PBSC to replace "third generation" leaders, with Jiang Zemin as its putative core. This reduced the average age of the Politburo to sixty, compared with seventy-two at the Twelfth Party Congress (1982), and sixty-three at the Fifteenth Party Congress (1997) (see Table 8.1).[3]

The membership of the new PBSC was expanded to nine, gaining eight new members, all of whom were promoted from the outgoing Politburo's regular members.[4] These leaders had gained promotion according to the time-honored criteria of "revolutionary dedication," youth, professional expertise, and re-formist spirit, as set out by Deng Xiaoping. In turn, generational turnover at the top created many vacancies and a succession bonanza throughout the party hierarchy, from the top to the bottom.

The contest for political office is often highly intense in all political systems, democratic or authoritarian, and China is no exception. For academics, the analysis of conflicts and cleavages has often been the most fruitful avenue to explore political system dynamics. Conflict and struggle among personal and patronage networks, and the playing out of informal politics, are important elements in political succession, as revealed by official admissions of plots and attempted coups. Alleged cutthroat competitions amid factions often capture the headlines, although in the post-Mao period political succession has been an outcome of consensus and compromise.

The application of the factional politics model to Chinese political succession demonstrates varying degrees of sophistication. Personal connections and bureaucratic politics matter a great deal in China, and the party state has often been meticulous in balancing various interests within its power structures. Informal groups and alliances are often formed according to ascriptive characteristics, common career backgrounds, patron-client relationships, ideology, and institutional interests.[5] Yet identification of faction members and their activities have often been based on static and deterministic criteria, and in the absence of hard evidence, analysts rely on intuition and "slippery speculations"[6] to construct probable scenarios of factional politics. For instance, the major factions most often referred to by observers inside and outside of China are the "Shanghai Gang" (assumed to be led by Jiang Zemin), the *tuanpai* faction, and the princelings. Other groupings often mentioned are the petrochemical faction, Tsinghua faction, Shanxi gang, and so on. Yet it is prudent not to view political groupings as permanent, immutable, and steadfast in their pursuit of their group interests.

For one thing, because of the Party's formal ban on factions, these groups, in order to exist, would have to operate clandestinely. Second, they pale in comparison with the factions existing within, for example, the Liberal Democratic Party of Japan, whereby each faction can legitimately have its own formal leader, staff, fundraising machinery, and even administrative offices. Third, the political careers of many Chinese officials have crisscrossing relationships—princelings have often worked in the Communist Youth League (CYL), and conversely those who have worked in Shanghai are not necessarily Jiang Zemin loyalists. Princelings have often struggled against princelings. As to the evidence of the solidarity of the *tuanpai* as one of the two principal factions in Chinese politics, we will turn to that later. One salient but often ignored factor in succession, as observed before, has been the institutional requirements for the CCP to reproduce itself. This refers to the deliberate grooming of generations of successors to ensure the survival of the institution so that succession takes on the character of a relay and staggered advancement. A party norm, often taken seriously, is for senior leaders to mentor successors through "passing on, assisting, and nurturing" (*chuan, bang, dai*).[7] Formally, succession was also guided by retirement age and two-term limits (until the rules changed in 2018). Further, elections into the PBSC, the Politburo, and the Central Committee are deliberately balanced according to age (old, middle age, and young), seniority, merit, governance experience, and geographical and functional (five lakes and four seas) criteria.

The Ascendancy of Xi Jinping and Li Keqiang

In 2002, just prior to the Sixteenth Party Congress, a book entitled *Disidai* (The Fourth Generation) was published outside China. Armed with a large amount of internal information, the book predicted with almost full accuracy (only one miss) the seven new PBSC members elected at the party congress, although it did not foresee that Jiang Zemin would retain his chairmanship of the CMC. Among the eleven chapters of this book, seven were devoted to the new PBSC members, and two each were devoted to Xi and Li Keqiang, respectively, with the remaining two chapters devoted to other civilian and military leaders. Xi and Li were given pride of place because they, by dint of their age and experience, were tipped to be the front runners for PBSC succession. According to this book, around the time of the Sixteenth Party Congress, discussions in the PBSC on fostering continuity and stability in political succession focused on whether (1) a slate of "fifth generation" leaders should be appointed to the new Politburo; and (2) one younger person should be recruited into the PBSC to represent the core of this cohort by following the Hu Jintao precedent set at the Fourteenth Party Congress. Ideally this person should be under fifty years of age, and chosen from among central ministry officials, provincial party secretaries, or governors. This way, the chosen heir would be under sixty when he took over in 2012, be able to serve two terms until 2022, and would still be under the retirement age of seventy.[8] However, in a Politburo meeting on October 10 Jiang vetoed the idea of promoting a single person into the PBSC to groom as successor designate so far ahead of the 2012 congress.[9] He argued that the qualifications of those under fifty were relatively weak, and that the promising candidates should be further tested by assignments in the Party, the Secretariat, State Council, or some key provinces. Therefore Xi, Li, and Bo all stayed in the provinces. However, five years later, the fifth-generation leaders, or those in their fifties, made great strides at the Seventeenth Party Congress in 2007. In contrast to the Fifteenth Party Congress, where the princelings were sidelined, they made a comeback, as many were elected to the Central Committee either as alternates or as full members. "Fifth generation" princelings who had revolutionary family backgrounds, such as Liao Hui, Yu Zhengsheng, Bo Xilai, Xi Jinping, Jiang Zhuping, Wang Qishan, and Dai Bingguo, were deemed more loyal and reliable. Officially, the new criteria for promotion encompassed the "three represents" ideas (discussed later) and were summarized by thirty-two Chinese characters that translate as "politically astute, firm in belief, good at studying, able to move with the times, principled and truthful, practical and pragmatic."[10] Additional criteria introduced by Jiang Zemin and Hu Jintao included loyalty to party, closeness to the masses, and a "clean governance style."[11] Using these criteria, the head of the COD, Zeng Qinghong, identified Xi (forty-nine years old) and Henan governor Li Keqiang (forty-seven) as the two strongest candidates. Bo Xilai (fifty-three), another princeling and Liaoning governor, was also considered, though he was slightly older.[12] All three would be groomed for and tested, but Bo was never slated for PBSC candidacy (for tabulated summaries of the careers of all three, see Tables 6.1 and 6.2).

As mentioned, as early as the Fifteenth Party Congress of 1997, Xi was taken seriously as a potential candidate for the top to come under scrutiny, and evaluations of him tended to be positive, and he was scandal free. In a pre–Sixteenth Congress reshuffle, Xi was appointed Zhejiang PPC deputy secretary and acting governor in October 2002. He claimed that he was surprised and had expected to be assigned to Shaanxi or a western province because of his past experiences in Shaanxi. For grooming purposes, leaders are often rotated back and forth from poor to rich places, coastal and inland provinces, and the like, but since Xi had already spent much time inland and another seventeen and a half years in Fujian, his assignment to Zhejiang seemed not out of the ordinary. In July 2002, when a journalist asked Xi if he was one of the new generation of leaders to watch for, Xi flushed and almost choked, saying, "I nearly spilt water all down my shirt. Are you trying to give me a fright?" Although Xi's rising political star was apparent and he was slated to enter the Central Committee and perhaps even get a promotion, Xi strove to keep a low profile and to show a lack of ambition. "This is not the time right now to discuss such questions," he was quoted as saying.[13]

According to one account, Xi's greatest advantage was his alleged lack of a clear ideological position, making him appealing to hard-liners and liberals alike. Furthermore, he was well liked by a majority of the old PBSC that included Zhu Rongji, Li Peng, and Li Ruihuan for Xi's alleged thoughtfulness and modesty.[14] At the Sixteenth Party Congress, Xi advanced one rank to become a full member of the CC, qualifying him to take positions at the minister level or above. Bo Xilai, too, was elected a full member, skipping the alternate step. One unverifiable account claims that among the 198 elected to the CC, the seven who had garnered the least votes, in descending order, were Chen Zili, Li Yizong, Xi Jinping, Jia Qinglin, Zhang Gaoli, Li Changchun, and Huang Ju, respectively.[15] Chen Liangyu and Liu Qi were likewise at the bottom, numbered ten and twelve, but Jia Qinglin, Li Changchun, and Huang Ju entered the PBSC, and Chen Liangyu and Liu Qi were put on the Politburo. Soon after the party congress, PPC secretaries in the five provinces of Shandong, Guangdong, Zhejiang, Hebei, and Hainan were changed. With CC membership secured, the forty-nine-year-old Xi, who had already transferred to Zhejiang as PPC deputy secretary in October, was promoted to PPC secretary in November to become the first-in-command, replacing Zhang Dejiang.[16] Xi's transfer to Zhejiang was a big promotion to an office with both a greater scope and greater challenges. As observed, in Fujian, a province with many private enterprises, Xi had articulated ideas about government/business relationships and what he called "limited government" and service-oriented government. Perhaps this experience was deemed appropriate for a neighboring coastal province with similar conditions, since Zhejiang was at the turn of the twenty-first century already synonymous with a political economy dominated, at least in the GDP sense, by private enterprises.[17] Hence, Zhejiang was more complementary to Xi's resume and experience than the Northeast or the interior. Before the reform period, Zhejiang was primarily agricultural, but a boom since 1978 had seen its industrialization and transformation into an economic powerhouse with an average GDP increase of 13.1 percent per annum. Remarkably, private enterprises took off early, during the market reforms of the 1980s, beginning with the manufacturing of small commodities to satisfy the pent-up demands for consumer goods. Industrialization was powered by families engaging in small, light, industrial production. The explosive growth propelled Zhejiang from the twelfth largest provincial economy to the fourth.[18]

Zhejiang was another major step in Xi's grooming as national leader. It was also an opportunity for him to gain experience in the opening of the economy since it was dynamic, outward-oriented, and already China's richest province. As one of the most economically advanced provinces and a national front-runner in many respects, Zhejiang experienced the full impact of rapid industrialization, urbanization, and social change ahead of the rest of the country. Therefore, Beijing tended to view the province as a laboratory to test out central initiatives and expected it to show results.

The other leader chosen to be groomed alongside Xi was Li Keqiang, who would eventually become number two in the CCP hierarchy. Li was originally a farmer from Anhui who spent his early career in the CYL, Hu Jintao's alleged power base, and therefore many analysts regarded him as a protégé of Hu Jintao and a member of the so-called *tuanpai*. Two years younger than Xi, Li was spared the Cultural Revolution persecution experienced by Xi and the princelings because of Li's favorable peasant background. Li was also a *zhiqing* who responded to Mao's call to go down to the countryside, and he was assigned to the legendarily impoverished area of Fengyang County, where he was later promoted as a commune director in 1976. Yet, unlike Xi, who entered university by relying on the status of worker-peasant-soldier, Li wrote the landmark university entrance examination when it was reintroduced in 1977 and was admitted into the prestigious Peking University, where he became a student leader. He graduated with a BA in law in 1982 and subsequently completed a PhD in economics in 1994 under more normal circumstances. On this account, Li's academic credentials were more substantial than Xi's. After graduation Li was assigned to the CYL to be groomed, and for more than a decade he served as a secretary and then as first secretary of the CCYL from 1983 to 1998. However, he failed to be elected as an alternate member of the CC at the Fourteenth Party Congress, although he was made CYL first secretary anyway. This put him again under the direct leadership of Hu Jintao (then a PBSC member in charge of mass organizations such as the CYL, trade unions, and women's associations). At the CYL, Li introduced some reforms but was criticized for failing to foster creativity and earn the trust of the young people.[19]

Li was finally elected to the CC in 1997. To compensate for his lack of regional experience, and with the blessing of Hu Jintao, Li was made deputy secretary of the Henan PPC (later, secretary) and governor of Henan in 1999. At age forty-three, he was then China's youngest provincial governor at a time when Henan, with a population of ninety-three million, was China's most populous, but an economically backward, agricultural province. Serving between 2004 and 2007, Li excelled in mobilization work, but his measures to reduce rural electricity rates and taxes and to address water shortages met with mixed results. He was considered exemplary in promoting Jiang Zemin's Three Stress Campaign, but bad luck haunted him at Henan. He was slow and ineffectual in dealing with a crime wave, bank robberies, a series of fires with large numbers of casualties, and a cotton supply scam. Under his watch, an HIV/AIDS pandemic spread by unhygienic blood collection practices infected hundreds of thousands of rural poor who sold blood for income. He attempted to improve his image by launching an

¥18 million campaign to combat the disease and to start a provincial-level reg-istry of HIV infections. Yet his attempts to close the blood collection stations and to set up cure centers were botched, and he was accused of muzzling the media for reporting the cases. However, he gained a reputation for caring about the dis-advantaged, and the national ranking of Henan's GDP was raised from twenty-eighth to eighteenth in 2004. Aspects of Li's record were regarded a liability, but many issues were deemed not of his own making because of the complex and overwhelming situation. Central support for him was strong, as demonstrated by the large number of central leaders who had inspected Henan.[20]

In 2004, Li was laterally transferred to become secretary of the Liaoning PPC, tasked with the revitalization of the former heavy industrial rust belt. In contrast to agricultural Henan, Liaoning was a former heavy industrial province, under-going deindustrialization and manufacturing decline, where the closing down of SOEs had made 1.78 million workers and miners redundant. In 2005, about 140,000 households did not have a single employed member. Income inequality was acute, and Liaoning had the largest number of urban residents on welfare in the country. Urban disposable income was below the national average, whereas rural disposable incomes were about half of their urban counterparts.

Described as "engaged and well-informed," Li said that the Liaoning public was dissatisfied with education, healthcare, and housing, but it loathed corrup-tion the most. Under Li, corrupt officials were punished as soon as their misde-meanor was discovered to serve as a deterrent. Li also urged strict education, which included prison tours for officials, to deter corruption. Li kept a healthy skepticism regarding official GDP statistics, turning to other variables such as electricity consumption and volume of rail cargo.[21] He gathered his informa-tion through investigative media reports, grassroots tours, the public's letters, and friends from other provinces, and was known to go through a household's garbage to determine its level of poverty. Under Li, provincial legislations were passed only after many revisions. Li attempted to implement the official idea of a nine-year compulsory education, and provided subsidies for the poor, es-pecially rural students, and free tuition for those who majored in education. By the time Li left Liaoning four years later, all Liaoning was covered under pension, social security, and a minimum living standard guarantee, although the standards were low. For instance, the minimum living guarantee in the rural areas was a mere 10 to 40 yuan per month, much lower than the 170 yuan in the cities, and some villagers did not bother to apply because if they did, they would forfeit other forms of assistance that were several times higher. One most notable achievement attributed to Li was government-subsidized apartments provided for 1.2 million workers and miners who dwelled in slums lacking running water, electricity, or heat. Li also pledged to provide a job for every household without an employed member and claimed that that was achieved in 2007. Li was also given credit for utilizing abandoned salt fields along the Liaoning coast to build a highway connecting five major industrial cities that included Dalian and Dandong.[22] Li's background in the CYL system and his legal expertise were considered assets for further promotion, but his more amiable character raised concerns that he might be a weak central leader. If chosen as an heir apparent, he might weaken the authority of Hu as well as that of the new leadership.[23]

Zhejiang in the New Millennium

Often dubbed the "land of fish and rice," eastern coastal Zhejiang was primarily agrarian in the prereform period, since its natural resources were limited for industrialization purposes. Ninety-five percent of its energy needs had to be imported. Its population of forty-six million in 2005, which approximated that of South Korea, was relatively modest by Chinese standards. Geographically, Zhejiang is one of China's smallest provinces with a land mass of one hundred thousand square kilometers, or only 1.06 percent of the country's total. Because of the mountainous terrain—70 percent of Zhejiang consists of mountains, 7 percent rivers and lakes, and 23 percent valleys or flatland—average land per capita was only 0.57 *mu*, or less than half the national average. This geographical constraint is compensated by the natural advantage of a rugged coastline of 6,696 kilometers that harbors more than three thousand islands.[24]

In less than two decades, however, exponential growth had transformed Zhejiang into an economic powerhouse and the richest province and most developed market economy in China. Such success had enabled Zhejiang to weather the 1997 Asian Financial Crisis and to maintain rapid growth rates. Zhejiang boasted the largest number, 203, of the 500 strongest private enterprises nationally, in addition to thousands of commodity-trading markets. It was number one nationally for eight years in a row in terms of private enterprise total production value, sales, and sales of consumption goods. Eighty percent of the capital for urban construction in the major exporting cities of Wenzhou, Taizhou, and Yiwu came from the private sector.[25] Yiwu was reputed to be the world's largest small-commodities wholesale market, supplying retail and "dollar stores" around the world, as well as 80 percent of its Christmas decorations. One company turned into the world's largest drinking straw manufacturer. In 2007, the six hundred thousand medium and small private enterprises comprised 99 percent of the total number of enterprises.[26] The disposable incomes of the urban and rural population were number three and four among China's provinces. Zhejiang transformed itself from an agrarian province with relatively few resources into one with a solid foundation in industry. By the new millennium, prosperous

Zhejiang was already the richest province, and its economy was one of the fastest growing in China.

Zhejiang can also boast a relatively more balanced development than others, since its urban/rural gap has been one of the country's smallest. Per capita GDP and disposable income, in both urban and rural areas, was the highest in China. From 1978 to 2003, Zhejiang's average GDP growth was 13.1 percent per annum, and average GDP per capita soared from ¥331 to US$2,400, conferring on the province middle-income country status (MICS).[27] Total GDP in 2004 exceeded ¥10 trillion yuan, or the fourth largest in the country. By 2005 and 2006, Zhejiang's GDP per capita of US$3,000 and US$4,000 advanced its middle-income status. Zhejiang's rural income was also the highest in the country for a continuous eighteen years.[28] The Engels coefficient for urban areas was 34.4 percent and for rural areas, 35.6 percent.[29]

As an advanced unit, Zhejiang led the country in establishing many firsts. These included a license issued for a market and individual business; a private business group of family factories; a "farmer's city"; a private specialized market; a cooperative share enterprise; a set of regional legislations on private enterprises; and a rural economic cooperative and a limited company.[30]

The export-oriented private sector achieved high levels of both exports and imports. In 2005 the value of imports was already US$30.6 billion and of exports US$76.8 billion.[31] Exports went mostly to the EU, the United States, and Japan. Attractive to foreign companies, Zhejiang already had more than 2,160 foreign

Figure 5.1 Fashion accessories produced in Yiwu on sale, 2011. Credit: Alamy

companies by the middle of the first decade of the twenty-first century, the largest number of any Chinese province.[32] Zhejiang entrepreneurs also went global, and it is reputed that a million of them were operating all over the world. The IMD (Swiss International Institute for Management Development) World Competitiveness Yearbooks of 2005 and 2006, citing criteria such as economic performance, government efficiency, business efficiency, and infrastructure, ranked Zhejiang twentieth and thirty-third, respectively, among the sixty-one most competitive nations or regions surveyed.[33]

The Zhejiang Model in the 1980s and 1990s

Such remarkable achievements have been attributed to a unique path of market economy development in the 1980s and 1990s often labeled the "Zhejiang model."[34] First, unlike other provinces in China where the bulk of businesses were still state-owned, Zhejiang was unburdened by the mammoth and inefficient heavy industrial SOEs that predominated in the Maoist era. Mao, fearing strategic attack in the coastal provinces, preferred to locate heavy industries and investments in the inland areas. The absence of SOE dominance in Zhejiang meant that there was no cumbersome industrial infrastructure to reform when the Maoist centrally planned model was abolished. Rich farmland supported a relatively high living standard. With less reliance on the central government, the province adapted quickly to the new environment.[35]

A second ingredient of the Zhejiang model was that the economy was driven by private capital and private-sector development. Zhejiang relied primarily on domestically generated capital, start-ups, and local talents. As distinct from Guangdong, which relied on foreign investment from neighboring Hong Kong and Macau, Zhejiang's small family businesses started from scratch. A myriad of small and medium enterprises (SMEs) engaged in low-cost production, utilizing low wages and labor-intensive methods to run industries such as textiles, clothing, and shoes, which eventually broke into international markets (and were therefore responsive to fickle market demands).[36] This in turn promoted manufacturing, industrialization, and rural development.[37] By 2005, Zhejiang's urbanization rate was already 55 percent.[38] Zhejiang's vibrant private companies were the main drivers of development, contributing about 75 percent of the provincial GDP, whereas the SOEs' contribution was roughly 20 percent.[39]

Third, the vitality of Zhejiang was driven by the so-called Zhejiang spirit, which featured personal initiative, creativity, competition, and the entrepreneurial energy of risk-bearing and development. It was a bottom-up process that did not rely on government for investment, favorable policy, subsidies, or foreign investment. Since state investment was weak, in the reform period Zhejiang took the lead in developing the "individual economy" and private enterprises, so economic growth had to rely on small enterprises and commodities. Individual households and family enterprises were the motivating force and backbone of the economy.[40]

Fourth, the government did not define its role in terms of interference or noninterference. The "visible hands" promoted private businesses, stressing guidance and services over interference, restrictions, and propaganda. A business-savvy government created a favorable environment for large modern factories while protecting property rights and private initiatives. It decentralized some regulatory powers to a myriad of professional groups, social associations, and self-regulatory organizations to deal with market inadequacies. Apart from providing public goods and services, the governments introduced labor reforms and reform of the *hukou* system.

Fifth, the Zhejiang model is not static, as it is still developing. Economic development has evolved from traditionally intensive production of light industrial products, household goods, and textiles through heavy industries such as chemicals, machinery, electronics, and auto parts into high-tech information technology and modern service industries. The province's brands are now national and even transnational, and production has gradually been integrated into the global production networks, and it is now upgrading to information technology and advanced manufacturing. Zhejiang enterprises have extended their production chains by producing for the domestic market and investing throughout China. It has established a national sales network and has participated in the Great Western Development Strategy, Central China Revival, and the revival of the Northeast industrial bases.

Xi and the Modification of the Zhejiang Model

Going back, when Xi arrived at Zhejiang in 2002 as party chief, the original Zhejiang model was already in a dire need of an overhaul.[41] As an advanced province, Zhejiang was under pressure to show results and to be a pacesetter. Xi visited every county to understand the local conditions and identify sources of the province's growing pains. On the bright side, GDP in 2002 had reached ¥7.67 trillion, up 12.3 percent over that of the past year, and in 2003 exceeded ¥10 trillion, only the fourth province to do so. Many economic indicators bested the national averages. On the downside, the beginning of the reform period privileged rapid growth, but increasingly this was attained by huge and ever-expanding costs. The many bottlenecks in energy supplies slowed down industrial production, the rate of growth slipped to number two nationally, and industrial production in 2005 dropped. Market expansion had generated issues such as poor quality, counterfeit products, and regional protectionism. Further, with the gradual national market integration crossing regional administrative borders, the advantages previously enjoyed by Zhejiang were eroded and businesses were moving out at an alarming rate. The ability of Zhejiang's regional governments to provide favorable policies had diminished. In addition, the time bomb of severe environmental degradation could no longer be ignored.

Several government documents conveyed the worries of the provincial leadership.[42] A special report by the provincial statistical bureau in 2004 noted that industrialization and urbanization had sharply reduced arable land at an alarming rate, that prices for industrial and residential land rose continuously, and that the land-grabbing by some industrial parks amounted to an enclosure movement. Zhejiang depended on other provinces for 95 percent of its energy supplies, and the high-consumption and low-effectiveness model of production had caused a crisis in energy supply, with electricity supply in a critical situation. In the first half of 2004 alone, regular power outages affected more than half of the province's enterprises, with the average outage amounting to 11.32 days per month, leading to huge financial losses and penalties due to delays in fulfilling production contracts. Simultaneously, a more disturbing phenomenon was the high discharge of industrial effluents and environmental pollution. Between 1990 and 2003, the discharge rates for wastewater, waste gas, and solid waste had increased 84.8 percent, 300 percent, and 130 percent, respectively. A larger expenditure on environmental cleanup was required to deal with the intensification of environmental degradation. In 2003 alone, expenditure was raised by 33 percent and reached 2.5 percent of that year's GDP, although it was not possible to calculate an exact cost for the ecological cleanup that was needed. Investment efficiency had also plummeted—the raising of the annual GDP by ¥1 billion during the Seventh Five-Year Plan (FYP), Eighth FYP, and Ninth FYP (1996–2000) required ¥1.78 billion, ¥1.39 billion, and ¥3.71 billion, respectively, but in the first three years of the Tenth Five-Year Plan (2001–2005), the cost had already ballooned to ¥3.38 billion.[43]

The report concluded that such excessive resource consumption was unsustainable in the long run. By focusing on short-term gains and neglecting public services, the government was, it claimed, not performing its function properly, perpetuating the habitual thinking of "first pollute, then clean up." Urgent need was required, it argued, for all levels of government to improve the management of public resources.[44]

Similarly, a white paper on energy use released in 2004 noted that resource-poor Zhejiang's total dependence on imported oil and gas had accelerated, threatening economic development and sustainability. Previously more localized shortages in oil, coal, and electricity were now widespread, and key bottlenecks were more severe in the new century. The huge and mounting demand for electricity had risen to new heights, but there was no awareness of thrift. Demand in 2003 alone had increased by 13.7 percent, and per capita energy and electricity consumption were 40 percent and 80 percent over the national average,[45] almost doubling that during the Ninth FYP, despite rapid economic growth.

Finally, another critique focused on the failure of Zhejiang to establish long-term cooperative relationships. The ability to innovate and to establish brand-name recognition was low, and counterfeit production was pervasive. Regional protectionism made it a challenge to create sales networks. Furthermore, manager job hopping, theft of commercial secrets, and embezzlement of company funds were widespread.[46]

At an economic work conference in December 2004, Xi blamed the accumulated ills on the "rough and ready" (*cufang*, often translated with the word "extensive") style of economic development, which featured high energy consumption, low efficiency, and low-tech production. Industrial enterprises accounted for over 70 percent of total energy consumption, water, and electricity. Xi warned his audience that the Zhejiang economy might not be sustainable and might end up in ruins.[47] Henceforth, the provincial government planned to develop a comprehensive strategy of energy saving, a new growth model of industrialization to raise efficiency and to adjust the economic structure. The strategy pledged to help enterprises to save, and to expand the government's monitoring ability in order to sanction those breaking the rules. The means to this were technological upgrading, and the building of a recycle economy and a resource-saving society. The government pledged to eliminate high-polluting and obsolete technology equipment and promote innovative energy-saving technology in industries such as iron and steel, textiles, construction materials, and petrochemical industries. Finally, the government would redefine its own functions and build regulatory mechanisms to oversee the sustainable use of energy resources.[48] Following the conference, in 2005, measures were quickly devised to begin an overall transformation. Comprehensive developmental plans were devised for eleven key sectors such as automobiles and automobile parts, instruments, and chemicals. This included a plan for the construction of an advanced manufacturing base, specifying key areas, technology, and products to be guided by the government. At year's end, the government drew up a list of "backward manufactures" encompassing nine sectors and 430 types of technology to be eliminated by the withholding of licensing, and various localities were enjoined to facilitate their eradication.[49]

Xi's tenure at Zhejiang from 2002 to 2007 coincided with the duration of the Sixteenth Party Congress and the volleys of national policy initiatives emanating from the center. For instance, the party congress broached broad goals for implementation of the theory of "three represents," the building of a relatively well-off society, the acceleration of socialist modernization, and "socialism with

Chinese characteristics."[50] The SARS crisis during the first half of 2003, among other factors, prompted Chinese leaders to consider a more balanced and inclusive developmental model for both the urban and rural areas aimed at harmonizing human and natural activity. They began to seriously consider new economic indices such as the depletion of land and resources, the gap between urban and rural areas, and degrees of pollution.[51] Furthermore, subsequent Central Committee policy forums also unleashed a number of initiatives: the Third Plenum of October 2003 prescribed the "perfection" of a socialist market economy; the Fourth Plenum of September 2004 prescribed the strengthening of the CCP's governing capacity; the Fifth Plenum of October 2005 advanced the notion of a "new socialist countryside" and set targets for the Eleventh FYP; and the Sixth Plenum of October 2006 instigated the notion of building a "harmonious society."[52] All this promised to reorient China's developmental strategy.

Furthermore, the Eleventh FYP (2006–2010), passed in March 2006 and aiming to realize the "scientific development concept" and the goal of a "harmonious society," churned out a myriad of objectives. For instance, in economic development it would double the 2000 GDP per capita by 2010; improve the quality of economic growth; upgrade the industrial and service structure; and improve enterprise innovation and international competition. In governance, it would reform institutions for a market economy and promote democracy, the legal system, and morals and culture. In social development, it would raise the incomes of urban and rural residents and narrow the gap in living standards; and improve public services such as compulsory education, social security, culture, urban basic pension, and rural cooperative medical care. In environmental protection, it would address the issues of ecological and environmental degradation and emission of pollutants.

Underlying the new plan were the principles of a new and innovative developmental model that featured both quality and sustainable growth, coordinated development of the urban and rural areas, and the building of a harmonious and people-centered society. Significantly, the national planners were prepared to slow down the economic growth rate to 7.5 percent in order to effect more quality growth, upgrade the industrial structure, boost competitiveness, and make resources utilization more efficient. They ordered the reduction of pollutant emission by 10 percent and set targets for the treatment of wastewater and garbage.[53]

Zhejiang as the national front-runner bore the brunt of these new initiatives. Xi duly seconded the new plan by criticizing the "rough and ready" growth model pursued during the Tenth FYP. According to him, the model was characterized as "high investment, consumption, discharge, and low return"; it had promoted rapid economic growth at the expense of resource conservation and environmental protection. Growth was predicated on investment, cheap labor, land, and resources. Needed was more balanced development, structural and production upgrades, innovation, science and technology, and a general transformation of the growth model. Correspondingly, government functions should shift from the reliance on administrative intervention to market transformation.[54]

A notable fact about the policy process in the PRC is that it is often overloaded with numerous and conflicting goals. Typically, central policy initiatives are covered in many documents and touch many bases. The activist party state's continuous piling-on process often makes goal attainment almost impossible, or with diminishing returns. Implementers, subject to multiple pressures, must make strategic choices. They often resort to a variety of strategies such as ritualistic compliance, foot-dragging, buck-passing, and a focus on "image projects," and a great deal of goal displacement has occurred.[55] But perhaps this kind of bureaucratic behavior is unavoidable considering the mammoth task of governing one-fifth of humankind. Operationalization and implementation are, nevertheless, the tasks of the provincial and local authorities, with every administrative level under the center crafting their own slogans-cum-policies, and a great deal of pressure being exerted downward.

Zhejiang was once again caught in the middle when in March 2005, Hu Jintao specifically instructed that Zhejiang should take the lead in realizing his signature projects of building a "relatively well-off society," accelerating "socialist modernization," implementing the scientific development concept, building a harmonious society, and strengthening the Party's advanced quality.[56] This put a great deal of pressure on Zhejiang, and Xi took seriously this assignment both as a personal challenge and as a means to augment his credentials. He and the PPC set a preliminary goal of reaching or surpassing the state targets for turning Zhejiang into a "well off" society by 2010. Xi promoted a slogan, "Do real work and strive to be at the forefront," which eventually would become his motto and the title of one of his books.[57] To surpass state targets and to stay ahead of others is a time-honored means of demonstrating resolve and loyalty to central initiatives. And Xi Jinping complied, either out of expediency or conviction, and in the following we will consider his various policies and activities.

Economic Upgrade and Transformation: The "Five Hundred Billion" Project and the "Double Eight Strategy"

Xi likes to compare his way of doing things with the "dialectics" of balancing two sides. Reform and development of a socialist economy, he has said, require the invisible hands of the market and the visible hands of the government. The function of the government should be "limited," service oriented, and law-abiding. In the context of Zhejiang, this meant that the government should simultaneously reduce its administrative interference but take a more active role in promoting economic growth and transformation. Specifically, Xi set out to reform the *shenpi* system. By 2006, the items subjected to *shenpi* were reduced from 3,251 to 856, one of the smallest in the country. Later, such a large reduction of *shenpi* would figure prominently in Xi's reforms during his first term as general secretary. In Xi's view of economic transformation, the role of government was to prioritize and to encourage entrepreneurship. Toward this end, it should support a mixed economy, reform production rights, expand individual rights and initiatives, strengthen infrastructural support, and preserve economic order. A large investment would be directed to the infrastructure providing efficient support to large, modern factories as well as SMEs.

The "Five Hundred Billion" Project

Toward the above ends, one of Xi's first initiatives was a massive state investment in the economy. In January 2003 Xi broached the notion of five "hundred billion" projects for 2005–2009, which meant ¥100 billion each would be invested in five areas: the economy; informationization; science, education, health, and sports; an ecological environment; and poverty alleviation. Altogether there would be twenty-plus projects, and for each project, at least ¥10 billion would be invested annually and the total would come to more than ¥3 trillion (US$44 billion).[58] The goals of the five hundred-billion projects were to upgrade production and technology to ensure a smooth economic transformation. Another of Xi's signature initiatives was the "Double Eight Strategy."[59] According to Governor Lu Zushan, Zhejiang was approaching a mid-postindustrial stage that required a strategic upgrade and transformation of its economic structure into one featuring new and higher-level technology.[60] Accordingly, Xi employed the "dialectic" metaphor, "Empty the cage and change the bird" (*tenglong huanniao*) and the "phoenix rising from the ashes" (*fenghuang niepan*). This meant retirement of the dead "bird" that did not pay taxes or good wages but was highly polluting in favor of a new one that ate less, laid more eggs, and flew further. This in effect meant letting the low-tech and noncompetitive enterprises go bust in favor of those that were more technologically advanced and more environmentally friendly.

Xi articulated more systematically in July 2003 his "Double Eight Strategy," which attempted to balance the conflicting demands of rapid economic growth and sustainable development. As usual it was meant to be a comprehensive strategy to realize a long list of goals—to improve the socialist market economy, expand the maritime economy, strengthen the rule of law, build credit and efficiency, build a service-oriented government, promote science, education, and culture, and raise the standard of living for both urban and rural areas. It would leverage Zhejiang's advantages in geographic location, industrial structure, and environment to hasten the building of an advanced manufacturing base. Specifically, the strategy aimed to promote state-owned and private production; regional integration with Shanghai and other Changjiang Delta regions; manufacturing and new styles of industrialization; and coordinate urban and rural development. Other goals included the building of an ecological province and a green Zhejiang; oceanic economy; the rule of law; creditworthiness and government efficiency; and science and education to develop talents and culture.

Regional Cooperation and Economic Integration

Such policies resemble "development state" actions, although Xi did not use this term. Xi entertained a vision of cooperating with neighboring provinces Shanghai and Jiangsu to jointly develop the Changjiang River Delta. By promoting government investment and private businesses Xi hoped to leverage Shanghai's prowess in finance, trade, and transport, and Jiangsu's dynamic economy and Taiwanese investment. When he first arrived at Zhejiang, Xi took the initiative of leading a delegation of sixty people to Shanghai to secure an agreement on economic cooperation in March 2002, and subsequently, signed another agreement on economic and technological cooperation with Jiangsu later that month.[61] Dismissing counterarguments as manifestations of bureaucratic interests and local protectionism, Xi did not mind letting Shanghai take the lead in economic integration.[62] For instance, Shanghai, China's most dynamic municipality, lacked a natural deepwater port, and the new Yangshan deepwater container port could only be situated in Hangzhou Bay in Zhejiang's Shengsi County. Intense competition and disputes between the two parties during the construction phase were resolved only when Party Central entrusted Xi to mediate.[63] Xi was willing to let Shanghai take charge of managing Yangshan port, which subsequently began full operation in 2005. Xi's concession enabled the port to be completed, showing him to be a team player and a conciliator in the eyes of the central leadership, even though subsequent disputes over tax income were still at issue after he left Zhejiang.[64] Eventually, Yangshan surpassed Rotterdam and Singapore to become the world's largest cargo port.

Xi's efforts in turning Zhejiang into a province with a strong maritime economy focused on the promotion of the integration of Ningbo, Zhoushan harbor, and islands on the Zhoushan archipelago. Zhoushan Island is China's third largest island after Hainan and Chingming. Xi's plan paved the way for the approval by the State Council of the formation of the Zhoushan Archipelago New Region (ZANR) in 2011, one of ten new state-level regions that enjoyed special favorable policies directed by the State Council, of which Shanghai's Pudong is another.[65] The ZANR was designed to be China's first new maritime economy area and a trade, processing, and transportation hub to rival Singapore and Hong Kong by integrating the economy of the Yangtze Delta. By 2006, the total handling capacity of the Ningbo-Zhoushan port reached 4.2 billion tons, the nation's second largest and the world's third. Zhejiang's maritime economy had an average yearly increase of 19.3 percent, and by 2005 consisted of 8 percent of the provincial GDP. Similarly, Xi promoted the Hangzhou Bay Bridge, the longest bridge in the world at that time.

Private Enterprises, the Pillar of Zhejiang's Economy

Zhejiang has often touted the rapid development of private enterprises as a comparative advantage and a driving force for its economy. The province claims to have followed central policies to assist and promote private enterprises since 1992. Nevertheless, official sources say that it was only in the new century that a preliminary mixed economy, which the Chinese then called a "socialist market economy," was established, especially with China's accession to the WTO in 2001.[66] And it was not until November 2002 that the theory of "three represents" was enshrined in the party constitution. Purportedly the theory meant that the CCP was to represent "advanced productive forces, advanced culture, and the interests of the overwhelming majority"; in effect, it finally affirmed the position of private enterprise in the national economy. With this, the CCP had at long last jettisoned the principle of class conflict and attempted to broaden its support base beyond traditionally favored classes such as the workers and peasants, and to accept into the Party members of other social strata, especially the entrepreneurs and capitalists, who were deemed an important ingredient of the "advanced productive forces" and critical for economic development.

This seemingly innocuous move did not end a long-standing controversy about private enterprise and free markets. Conservative ideologues continued to resist marketization, denigrating it as an unorthodox means and a cynical attack on socialist principles. Other critics saw it as a transparent attempt to solidify the position of an emerging bureaucratic capitalist class and carpetbaggers.[67] Notwithstanding this ideological and policy battle, the development of a private economy was rapid. By 2003, Zhejiang came first nationally in such indexes as the total production value generated by private enterprises, total sales, consumer goods, exports, and the largest number (174) of China's largest 500 private enterprises. Private enterprises reached 282,100 and individual business households 1.56 million, making Zhejiang the number one private enterprise province.[68]

Xi not only signed on to the Sixteenth Party Congress orthodoxy of the "three represents" to embrace private entrepreneurs, but threw his support behind the private economy. He hailed the three hundred thousand private enterprises as Zhejiang's "precious treasure," a key to its economic vitality, and a huge contributor to its reform and modernization. Private enterprises, he said, reflected Zhejiang's brand, dynamism, and potential. To promote them was not an expediency, since in the past Zhejiang had enjoyed a systemic advantage that was now also available to the entire country. Zhejiang was no longer as competitive and must rely on the private economy to revitalize itself. Since competition had become especially intense after WTO accession, Xi promised to open markets for trans-sector, transregion, and transnational boundary exchanges, creating the conditions for private enterprises to prosper. The SMEs, he said, were strong not just in sheer numbers, but in their capacity to innovate in areas of organization, science and technology, and management. The government's role was to ensure free competition, a level playing field in market rules, and continuity assurances for private entrepreneurs. Accordingly, government functions should be oriented toward the provision of services, problem-solving, and the protection of private legal property and workers' rights.[69]

One notable characteristic of Zhejiang's economy is the "cluster" phenomenon, where hundreds and even thousands of enterprises, from small to large, all engage in the production of similar products, from silk ties to socks and from leather to auto accessories. Each cluster has firms that can be called cluster captains and is led by an industrial association that works closely with the local governments. In such a corporatist arrangement, government support takes the form of funds for cluster infrastructure, logistics, and staff training. It provides help resolving issues such as shortages of land and human resources (especially research and development [R & D] and marketing professionals), capital and technology, and lack of brand-name recognition.[70]

Specific measures planned by the government included the revision of a number of laws and regulations to remove barriers to market entry and to simplify regulations. The government pledged financial support, technological transfer, power supplies, and stocks and shares. It vowed to treat SOEs and private businesses equally in privileges such as easy access to cheap bank loans and land. Xi also promised to toughen the protection of private property, even though this was a contentious issue especially opposed by conservatives who, among other things, feared the entrenchment of rights for those who had benefited by stripping state assets.[71] In fact, a national bill on equal protection of private and state property had been hotly debated in the NPeC since 2002, and a constitutional amendment in 2004 specified that "lawful private property was inviolable." But the bill was not passed until October 2007 after seven readings and many setbacks. The law, which held the government accountable for the infringement of citizens' property rights, was hailed as a milestone toward China's transition to a market economy. For others, however, the law was limited and symbolic, because rural land is still "collectively owned," and farmers are forbidden to sell it. This, they argued, discourages investment to boost production.[72]

Nevertheless, Xi's many pronouncements at this time clearly positioned him on the side in favor of the reform of property rights. Xi also fended off conservative criticism that private businesses drove up property value and refused to roll back reforms. To move forward, Xi wanted to expand the private sector and embrace cleaner and more innovative industries. He advocated the relocation of factories, heavy industries, and traditionally labor-intensive manufacturing inland, where land and labor were more abundant. He encouraged privately funded R & D investment, which increased to ¥31.6 billion from ¥5.6 billion in 2003. The number of large private companies had risen from 183 to 203 when he left.[73] By 2013, 139 private companies were listed among the nation's top 500.[74]

Xi tried to demonstrate his support for the private sector by establishing a closer relationship. For example, in 2005 and 2006, Xi participated in the Zhejiang Directors Association and Zhejiang Enterprise Confederation conferences and gave speeches therein. National rankings at the time put Zhejiang at the top in terms of the "rule of law," and number two in terms of marketization after Guangdong. One Chinese observer attributes this to the highly developed private enterprises and more sensible government-market relationship. It claims that private enterprises and society did not require too much government intervention, that the government refrains from acting arbitrarily, and that the level of judicial justice was high. The "rule by law" was also said to be augmented by the encouragement of local initiatives—at Leqing Municipality, people had the right to hear testimony at People's Congresses; Wenling Municipality allowed for popular participation in budgeting; Taizhou Municipality provided a platform for discussion of government policy for out-of-province people.[75] Xi also visited many private enterprises after his arrival in 2002, but Geely was the first. Recognizing that a weak link of Zhejiang's economic structure was its reliance on light industrial products and the lack of brand recognition, he saw Geely as a possible breakthrough from the reliance on small-commodities production.[76]

China's only private auto manufacturer and Zhejiang's only automobile producer, Geely has evolved from its humble origins of manufacturing refrigerator components to building materials, motorcycles, and finally to auto manufacturing. Headquartered in Hangzhou, Geely was outstanding in its performance in R & D and broke into the international market, and subsequently overseas sales accounted for 70 percent of its sales.[77] Government measures to support Geely included the encouragement of taxi companies to use its products and financial backing from state banks. As Xi said, "If we don't give additional strong support to companies like Geely, then whom are we going to support?" Nevertheless, most domestic automakers would have lost money without government subsidies and profits from their international joint ventures. Government subsidies accounted for a large portion of their profits. Geely, which bought Sweden's Volvo from Ford Motors in 2009 and has been listed in Fortune 500 since 2012, would have lost half of its profits without government subsidies. While the company suffers from inefficiency and overcapacity, it does generate tax revenue, create jobs, and help maintain China's foothold in a global industry.[78]

Similarly, Xi bestowed early support on Ma Yun (also known as Jack Ma), founder of Alibaba, soon to become an e-commerce giant and Yahoo's partner in China. In implementing Jiang's policy of bringing the party closer to the entrepreneurs, officials pushed for the formation of party cells in private companies. Under Xi, entrepreneurs were recruited into local People's Congresses as well. From a Western market-centered perspective, this is considered at best corporatism and at worst state control, even though it also gives the entrepreneurs a degree of political participation and influence. From a developmental state perspective, state involvement in East Asian economies is a powerful and persistent force that cannot be wished away. Despite the drawbacks of institutional inertia and an inability to overcome powerful vested interests, state involvement still has life and shows results.[79]

Large private businesses do not seem to be hamstrung by excessive Chinese government interference. As Zong Qinghou, the owner of the Wahaha group, China's biggest seller of bottled water, said, "We didn't have to seek approval for every action we took, such as selecting a site for a factory."[80] By 2019, of China's five hundred largest private companies, with annual revenue of at least ¥18.59 billion (US$2.62 billion), ninety-two came from Zhejiang, more than any other province for the twelfth consecutive year.[81] The strong support lavished on extra-large enterprises, however, did not apply equally to the SMEs and microenterprises, especially in the area of bank loans. By 2006, the number of SMEs in Zhejiang was 45,519, or 99.6 percent of the total number of enterprises, contributing to 84.4 percent of the province's production value, 90.8 percent of its employment, and 85.6 percent of its taxation.[82] Various measures, such as the periodic infusion of billions of yuan earmarked for SMEs, post office loans, various bank loan packages, specialized SME banks, and special favorable policies, were implemented to ease the credit crunch. Yet SMEs sometimes had no choice but to turn to loan sharks, since they often lacked collateral and their loans were often regarded as risky and their modus operandi deemed "nontransparent."[83] Ultimately, the financing of SMEs was a tough nut to crack. SOEs still took the lion's share of bank loans and paid the lowest interest rates.[84]

In 2005, Xi announced a policy to encourage Zhejiang to go outside of the province and to open more. Announcing a new slogan, "Jump out of Zhejiang," he urged companies to invest in other provinces to integrate with Shanghai and the Yangtze Delta economic zone, and to join projects such as the Western Development Strategy, Rise of Central China, and Northeast Revival. Outward investment meant the relocation of traditionally labor-intensive industries such as manufacturing to inland provinces, where land and labor were more abundant, so Zhejiang could attract more innovative businesses. It was hoped that out-of-province trade and investment would bolster Zhejiang's GNP, Xi said, making it bigger than its GDP.[85] Zhejiang could also build out-of-province base areas in grain, energy, and primary resources. Official statistics showed that by 2004, four million Zhejiangese were already doing businesses outside of the province, with an accumulated investment of ¥3 trillion. Of this, half a million were working in Shanghai and the Jiangsu area. To overcome the bottleneck in resources, 1.1 million Zhejiang entrepreneurs had expanded into China's west, with an accumulated investment of ¥1 trillion. Subsequently, one account claimed that in 2004, the total sales by the entrepreneurs operating out of the province exceeded ¥10 trillion, equivalent to Zhejiang's total GDP in 2004. Yet, for detractors who worried about the exodus of private capital, this reflected capital flight. Xi and the PPC tried to calm fears that the exit of these enterprises provided an opportunity for Zhejiang to climb the production-ladder.[86] Xi argued that it was the entrepreneurs' ambition to make it big in other provinces and then return. Although Zhejiang possessed few resources, its large market was the reason it attracted investors.[87]

Xi seemed to be assured by the claim that more than seven hundred thousand Zhejiang entrepreneurs were already doing business outside of China, and of this number, four hundred thousand operated in Europe. Of the 532 major industrial products manufactured in Zhejiang, 56 were ranked first in their categories in the country. Zhejiang's entrepreneurs were ranked the world's most competitive. Xi planned to leverage the sixty-four of the world's top five hundred corporations that had already established enterprises in Zhejiang, in such areas as petrochemicals, textiles, machinery, electronics, information, food, appliances, and light industries, to transform the limitations of Zhejiang's "grassroots" economy. For instance, corporations operating in Zhejiang such as Motorola, Toshiba, and Nokia could be used to upgrade the province's IT production, and Panasonic for the appliance industry.[88]

Zhejiang-Taiwan Relations: The Ups and Downs

Taiwanese capital was an important component of foreign investment in Zhejiang. As Xi had said, cities like Hangzhou, Ningbo, Huzhou, and Jiaxing were first choices among Taiwanese businessmen because of geographical proximity, cultural and ethnic affinity, and economic complementarity. He welcomed economic, technological, and cultural exchanges and made the attraction of Taiwanese capital a priority. By 2006, approximately six thousand Taiwan enterprises had already invested a total of ¥25 billion in Zhejiang. The ever-expanding investments were mutually beneficial, Xi argued, since they could help the Taiwanese economy to transition from more traditional productions into high-tech telecommunications and electronics. Further, China's preferential policies also benefited Taiwanese businesses, resulting in a win-win situation that would improve efficiency and competitiveness for both sides.[89]

Politically, however, Taiwanese president Chen Shui-bian shifted to a proindependence stand in 2003–2004. Amid a Chinese military and missile buildup, Chen was narrowly re-elected in March 2004, although the proindependence Pan Green coalition candidates failed to obtain a parliamentary majority. Beijing threatened Taiwan with an Anti-Secession Law in March 2005 that asserted that a declaration of Taiwan independence would be met with force. Often interpreted as a means of intimidation and intensification of tension, the law did not raise any new threats against Taiwan; it merely recapped previous positions. Further, the law also contained constructive and conciliatory features that included the promotion of mutual understanding and closer economic cooperation, the establishment of direct links of trade, mail and air and shipping services, the protection of rights and interests of Taiwanese in China, and equal status for both parties.[90] In 2006 Chen angered Beijing with the abolition of the National Unification Council, the promotion of nationalist consciousness and education policies, the renaming of government institutions, and the pursuit of recognition of Taiwan as separate from China. When Guomindang elders Lien Chan and James Soong carried out an ice-breaking visit to China in April 2005, Hu Jintao was more conciliatory, offering more economic, cultural, educational, and other benefits.[91] A year later, Lien visited Fuzhou and was received by Xi in Zhejiang, and both pledged a closer relationship. China-Taiwan relations calmed down in 2008 with the election as president of Kuomintang candidate Ma Ying-jeou, who was more reassuring and less confrontational. An era of deeper engagement began.

During his years in Zhejiang Xi served various military posts. As director of the Defense Mobilization Committee of Nanjing Military Region (2002–2003) and first secretary of the Party Committee of the Zhejiang Provincial Military Region, Xi participated in enforcing central military policies and preparing military and economic mobilization plans, air defense, logistical mobilization, and the like. The provincial military region was subject to the dual rule of the Nanjing Military Region and the Zhejiang PPPC and government, and its duties included the management of the reserves and militia, conscription, and border and coastal defense. It can be assumed that Xi shared Beijing's carrot-and-stick approach of encouraging cooperation on the one hand and preparing for war as a threat on the other.

Other more routine military duties, as reflected in his speeches in his capacity as the first secretary of the provincial military region, included the management of national defense and economic development, the development of information warfare, political and national defense education, and the placement of retired soldiers. Like his civilian counterparts, Xi often reiterated the principle of subordination of the military under party control.[92]

Social Governance and Political Development

From a sociology-of-development perspective, modernization and rapid economic growth in China have brought about higher living standards, better infrastructure, communication, and education. However, industrialization and urbanization have also engendered new divisions of labor, social stratification, the emergence of new classes, and new forms of inequality. Massive rural migration to the urban areas has turned farmers and women into factory and office workers. The outcomes have been conflicts, dislocations, and dilution of the traditional way of life that can be alienating for the population.[93] As mentioned, after coming to power in 2002–2003, the Hu Jintao–Wen Jiabao administration began to address issues ranging from social injustice to income inequality, and from social unrest to equitable economic growth. The outcome of this was a whole series of slogans-cum-policies on "people centered" and scientific development, culminating in formal broaching of the notion of a "harmonious society." To address concerns over social stability and tensions, the Fourth Plenum (2004) put forward the notion of "innovation in social management" (ISM) to replace *weiwen* (stability maintenance). *Weiwen* was, and still is, a massive undertaking to control all forms of social unrest attributed to "mass incidents," which include demonstrations, strikes, riots, and petitioning. It employed high-handed methods of surveillance and suppression that eventually led to the growth of a huge and costly security bureaucracy. Yet the "whack-a-mole" approach had been ineffective—the more the government imposed coercive measure to quell disturbances, the more it exacerbated the conflicts.[94] The Hu-Wen leadership began to explore alternative ways to maintain social order. In this vein, in March 2005, Hu Jintao proposed the building of a "socialist harmonious society." The Seventeenth Party Congress (2007) broached the theme format "party committee leadership, government takes responsibility, society coordination, and public participation" as a means to flesh out the notion of ISM. Regional authorities were challenged to find ways to substantiate these initiatives by devising their own policies. As these policy initiatives and propaganda themes continuously evolved, they merged, divided, and snowballed, and regional inputs imparted new layers of meanings and implications to them.[95] Discussions on social participation, public security, censorship, dispute mediation, public services, social safety nets, and workplace safety swirled around.

Beginning in 2004, Xi and the Zhejiang PPC initiated many bundles of policies surrounding slogans such as "Safe Zhejiang," "Rule of Law Zhejiang," and "Harmonious Zhejiang," to boost political stability, social harmony, and living standards. All this was intended to complement economic development and the "Double Eight Strategy," and to improve the governing capability of the party state.[96] As mentioned, Zhejiang's highly developed economy often triggered socioeconomic and political issues much sooner than the rest of China, and the Chinese leadership used it as a laboratory to test policy responses. In Zhejiang as in many parts of China, breakneck development had brought about tremendously complex political, economic, and social changes and a dislocation unprecedented in human history. In a very few years, rapid industrialization and urbanization had radically transformed the socioeconomic structure and challenged the old-style governance system inherited from the Maoist era. Chinese citizens were progressively more aware of their rights, of policy impacts, and of the need for participation. All this fueled an alarming number of social disturbances labeled "mass incidents,"[97] which increased tenfold across China from 8,709 in 1993 to 32,000 in 1999, 60,000 in 2003, 74,000 in 2004, and 87,000 in 2005.[98] Another source indicated that in 2006, there were 60,000 reported cases, and that increased to 80,000 in 2007 and 90,000 in 2009. Ministry of Public Security figures cited by the *China Daily* showed that there were 87,000 mass incidents in 2005, up 6.6 percent over 2004 and 50 percent over 2003.[99] These numbers should probably not be taken literally, as they lump together diverse and complex phenomena that rose and fell in salience according to different time periods. Yet they did pose fundamental challenges to stability and CCP rule, and the types of protests in Zhejiang were more closely related than elsewhere to rapid economic development, industrialization, and modernization.

Workers' protests focused mainly on issues of wages, benefits, pension arrears, and working conditions, and migrant workers protested against additional discriminations. For the farmers, the main issues were land requisitions, demolitions, and resettlements, often forceful and violent, to make way for superstructural projects ranging from highways and high-speed trains to airports, from dams and electrical grids to bridges, and from housing and shopping malls to industrial parks. The same applied to urban renewal efforts that required demolition of old and illegal constructions. Aggrieved farmers resented the forced requisition of land and inadequate compensation, as well as collusion between officials and developers. On the other hand, incentives for local officials, who were evaluated according to the criterion of local economic development, tended to favor business and investment over the farmers and environmental concerns. Bureaucratic land sales and economic growth augmented local financial coffers, which enabled officials to implement central missions and unfunded mandates[100] and to line their pockets. Environmental air, soil, and water pollution generated by modern industrial discharges, dumping of garbage, and ironical cleanup operations, such as garbage incinerations, triggered protests. Further, the large-scale *shangfang* by disgruntled and aggrieved petitioners were interpreted as a sign of instability, especially when petitioners staged angry demonstrations when their demands were not heeded. *Shangfang* activities that reached Beijing often drew a great deal of media attention, which reflected poorly on the ability of the local governments to resolve conflicts.[101]

Of the numerous mass incidents that plagued Zhejiang, several cases in 2005 are emblematic. In 2001, thirteen chemical enterprises were constructed in an industrial park in a heretofore scenic village in Dongyang City. In 2005, villagers there complained that discharges from the industries had killed crops, fruits, and vegetables, caused several cases of deformed babies, and made people's eyes water. Villagers demanded the removal of the industries by attempting to block traffic to the sites. When police attempted to remove the villagers, thirty thousand rioted, leading to forty-eight damaged vehicles and over thirty people injured.[102] In the same year, the newly installed Jingxin Pharmaceutical plant contaminated well water in nearby villages. Rice crops, in addition to snails and frogs, were being killed, and discharged gas and other pollutants were thought to be responsible for various diseases. Nearly ten thousand farmers clashed with the police. At Huzhou, several thousand people clashed with the police over pollution caused by a battery factory.[103]

Estimates on the numbers of mass incidents in Zhejiang are unavailable, but they were likely disproportionately higher than other provinces. A 2004 Chinese Academy of Social Science survey indicated that Zhejiang was the province with the most reported police-investigated cases, and this was complicated by the pull factor for rural migrants (often called the "floating population") because of the advanced economy.[104] Massive migration had flowed primarily from poor to developed coastal provinces, especially to Guangdong, Zhejiang, Shanghai, and Jiangsu, and from rural to urban areas, making for the largest migration in human history. By 2009, the "floating population" nationally was 211 million, and Guangdong and Zhejiang were the top two destinations. In 2002, Zhejiang's massive migrant population was 7.7 million, doubling to 16.7 million by 2007, and reaching 19.4 million in 2009.[105] Since the population of Zhejiang was between 46 and 47 million, the migrant population at times during Xi's tenure consisted of about one-tenth of the national total, hovering from 20 percent to almost 39 percent of the province's population. In some regions of Zhejiang, the number of "floating population" residents was larger than the local population. This huge migrant population posted a formidable challenge to the country's political economy, with Zhejiang bearing the blunt of the problem. Predominantly between the ages of sixteen and forty-five, these migrants contributed greatly toward Zhejiang's economic development, but since they lacked an urban *hukou*, they were denied social services such as education, healthcare, and social insurance. Consigned to second-class citizen status, the floating population suffered from exploitation and deprivation, which in turn complicated social governance and stability.[106]

To overhaul the governance structure, Xi and the PPC decided to channel more public resources to social needs, devoting more than 70 percent of government finance to "people's livelihood." Additionally, they pledged to improve public services, social welfare, and labor dispute resolutions; draw up regulations to protect citizen's rights; reduce the number of *shenpi* and licensing; popularize telecommunication technology to raise government efficiency; solicit public input in policymaking, land requisition, demolition, and relocation; and extend all public services to cover both urban and rural areas. Soon official sources claimed that government had employed information technology to improve its services for the enterprises, the public, and the grassroots, making them more accessible. Community centers equipped with "instructors" were set up in the villages, and a system of public services was created covering both urban and rural areas. The government's initiatives spawned many regional variations and models. For instance, Shangyu municipal government set up service "supermarkets," and Hangzhou set up public bicycles and a "democracy and people's livelihood interactive platform" at Hangzhou, as well a 81890 (homonym with "Dial once and everything will work out") hotline and services for out-of-towners and out-of-town business people.[107] Zhejiang was first in the country to introduce a rudimentary social insurance system covering both urban and rural areas; it enrolled 10.76 million (old-age pensions), 8.55 million (basic medical care), 10.03 million (worker injury), 5.85 million (unemployment), and 5.05 million (maternity), respectively. This put Zhejiang at the forefront since nationally this was not expected to be achieved until 2020. All rural and urban residents were eligible for the minimum living allowance if they fell below a certain income threshold, and 2.8 million farmers who had lost their land through confiscation were included in various security plans.[108]

Another means to resolve conflicts called "grand arbitration" involved people with an administrative and judicial mediation system. Cangnan County established an office for receiving the public, as well as various organizations and "on the spot" venues to solicit public opinion. One stated goal was "harmonious demolitions and resettlements" (clearly an oxymoron), but coercion had been widespread in these practices. Demolitions of squats and evictions of illegal occupiers of land, however, were more conflictual.

Still another innovative model involved Wenling Municipality. There, trade unions in factories manufacturing wool sweaters, pumps, and hats were formed to cooperate with business associations to decide on wage agreements resembling labor contracts. These organizations met every six months to revise wages according to developments in the trades.[109] In addition, from 2005, Wenling Municipality began "participatory budgeting" to expand public participation to incorporate various social forces with government in social management.

In 2003, Xi was the first provincial leader in the country to initiate a practice of regularly going down to the grassroots to receive petitioners. In contrast with the traditional *shangfang* practice, this practice was said to have greatly reduced the number of petitioners. For instance, in 2006, Xi led a team to Jiang district to receive input at local offices for labor, land requisition, social security, grassroots construction, and anticorruption. He received 167 groups and resolved 76 issues.[110] According to aides, in this or other capacities on average Xi spent at least 20 percent of his time at the grassroots and enjoined officers to go down as well. Xi's oft-quoted mantra is, "Those who become county party secretary must visit all the villages; those who are prefectural and municipal party secretaries must visit all townships and cities; the provincial party secretary must visit all counties and municipalities."[111]

Reportedly, Zhejiang had pioneered the establishment of more than thirty thousand service centers engaging a staff of some ninety thousand covering all urban and rural areas. These centers provided multipurpose help such as applications for permits, birth registrations, pension inquiries, postal services, and water supply, so that villagers no longer needed to go out of the villages for these purposes. The experience was touted as a new model for grassroots management.

Xi spoke often on the need to identify new solutions to the issues of the rural migrants or the "floating population," especially in the context of the integration of the urban and rural areas. In July 2004 he endorsed the provision of education to the children of migrants without discrimination, and in April 2005 he underscored the migrants' contribution to economic development and the need to defend their interests against discrimination, to improve their livelihood, and to respect their rights.[112] Chinese elite and the masses are largely aware of these issues. One fundamental resolution of the floating issue was often assumed to be the abolition of the *hukou* system, but this was controversial and easier said than done. The draconian division of the entire country into rural and urban sectors under Mao had resolved some pressures around mass migration to the cities and attending issues such as unemployment and overcrowding, but the system had perpetuated inequality, and the urban/rural gap had spawned a system of discrimination akin to apartheid.[113] In Xi's 2001 doctoral dissertation he had argued that from any of the reforming angles—rural marketization, marketization, and modernization—abolition of the *hukou* system was an "inevitable historical trend." The government must "rationally and boldly confront this reality" and eliminate all socioeconomic inequalities created by *hukou*. But reforms, he cautioned, must be gradual and incremental. Rural migrants, either doing business or working in the cities, who had regular income and urban residency of more than one year should be given priority. The reform should start from smaller towns before extensions to medium-sized and larger cities.[114]

Zhejiang's official policy was integration and inclusiveness for the millions of rural migrants. It was said that services like employment guidance (websites, etc.), low-cost housing, and the abolition of differential fees (between them and the locals) had allowed 96 percent of their children to enjoy the nine-year compulsory education. A 2006 provincial policy to protect the rights of the migrant workers, the first of its kind, was promulgated to address the issues of low wages, wage arrears, social insurance, services, and training. Promises were made to gradually resolve the *hukou* system, to replace the temporary permits with residence permits. The regulation also prohibited the withdrawal of contracted land vacated by the rural migrants. It anticipated that by 2007 the distinction between agricultural and nonagricultural *hukou* would be abolished in favor of a single residence *hukou* so that migrant workers could enjoy the same privileges as urban residents in employment, education, housing, and social insurance.[115]

A most significant development occurred in December 2003 when Haining city announced that it had led the province in abolishing all agricultural and nonagricultural *hukou* distinctions by merging them into resident *hukou*. Freedom of movement would be effected, and the power to approve the transfer, based on criteria of fixed abode, stable jobs, and sources of livelihood, would be decentralized to local police stations.[116] Likewise, Jiaxing Municipality was said to have introduced an integrated urban/rural developmental strategy that culminated in the abolition of the *hukou* system in 2008, the first nationally.[117]

Another variation was in the Yuhuan island county, with a permanent population of four hundred thousand and a floating population of two hundred thousand. In 2007, this county had established the country's first specialized government organization to manage the migrant population, introducing legal education so that migrants would know how to protect their legal rights. This move was touted to be a significantly new orientation that stressed government services rather than a law-and-order approach that relied on the police.[118]

Finally, in November 2003, Xi, in commemoration of Mao's endorsement of Zhejiang's "Fengqiao Experience" during the Socialist Education Movement of 1963, urged the resurrection of that model.[119] Essentially the model admonished local party and governments to resolve conflicts and maintain stability at local levels through prevention, relying on popular mobilization and participation without passing the buck to higher administrative levels.[120] Fengqiao was said to have followed this time-honored method to resolve 96 percent of its disputes at the village and township levels without referrals to the police. Subsequently, a provincial network of mediation committees was entrusted with the resolution of disputes involving labor/capital, medical issues, consumer rights, traffic incidents, and marriage and family issues.[121] Overall, among the various performance rankings of China's provinces, Zhejiang boasted that it was recognized for being the best in areas such as "law and order," services and management for the migrant population, crowd control, internet supervision, and advanced warning for public safety. The province claimed that its resolution rate of criminal cases was number one in the country, and so was the sense of safety felt by its citizens, since the number of various social emergencies was either decreasing or constant.

Environmental Degradation: Issues and Policies

A corollary of rapid economic growth, modernization, and urbanization saw deterioration in the environment. By 2003 GDP per capita in Zhejiang was already more than US$3,000, but environmental decay, garbage, water, and environmental pollution caused by noxious and toxic waste was widespread. For a long time, the sky was gray, the water was black, and virtually all water in the more industrial north of Zhejiang was undrinkable. Rivers were polluted, and garbage piled up everywhere. Regular and accidental discharge of toxic and hazardous chemicals had polluted waterways and underground water. One village was said to have a garbage hill that had existed since the Ming and Qing dynasties. Accordingly, environmental degradation constituted a major social grievance.[122]

In 2003, Zhejiang followed the avowed aspirations of Hainan, Jilin, Heilongjiang, and Fujian to turn themselves into "ecological provinces." In discussing environmental degradation, Xi was optimistic and proactive. He often referred to Kuznets's environmental curve, an inverted U curve delineating the relationship between environmental degradation and economic growth—the more developed the economy, the more severe the pollution, and not until the economy is highly developed can pollution be reduced. In Xi's view, Zhejiang was so economically developed that it was high time it tackled pollution.[123] Elsewhere, Xi referred to the degradation of the environment as an ecological "debt" that, if left unpaid, would be an irresponsible burden to future generations. He argued that pollution was neither "regional nor temporary," as some would think, and that Zhejiang would be willing to spend "real gold and white silver" (i.e., substantially) to pay down the environmental debt.[124] Xi criticized the single-minded pursuit of GDP growth by attracting businesses and investment. Cadres who were ignorant of ecology were unqualified, he averred, and "cadres should protect the environment as they would their eyes."[125] From 2002 onward, some localities sought to seek a balance by beginning to reduce the significance of GDP growth as a criterion for cadre evaluation. In some places, it was eliminated in favor of indicators of "people's livelihood" and social harmony. Proposals were also made to abolish grand rankings of GDP for all counties and municipalities.[126] By 2003, Zhejiang introduced the notions of green GDP (the cost of environmental degradation in development) and ecology promotion as criteria for evaluating economic development. Ecological construction was introduced into the curriculum of party schools and administrative colleges. Reportedly, one Anji County chief turned down a ¥20 million investment project because of its polluting potential.[127]

Xi declared that the narrowing of the quality-of-life gap between the rural and urban areas really hinged on cleaning up the environment. The farmers' major anxieties were over environmental degradation, unsafe drinking water, irrigation, transportation, afforestation, and public hygiene. To resolve these issues, the key was garbage collection and the disposal of wastewater. Subsequently, between 2003 and 2007 the PPC introduced a policy of "Beautiful Villages" with the goal of inaugurating more than one thousand model well-off villages, cleaning up over ten thousand others, and setting up public transportation to the most remote villages. In addition, the Zhejiang provincial government set up a three-year (2004–2007) plan declaring war against environmental pollution, so that by 2007 ecological damage could be brought under control. A first in the country, the plan mandated that all cities above the county level set up wastewater and central garbage management as well as networks of automated surveillance over sources of pollution. Other elements of the plan included the protection of the eight river systems, lakes, water quality, and the marine environment; the unified control of high-polluting industries such as petrochemicals, pharmaceuticals, leather making, dyeing, smelting, and papermaking. The plan required the government to reduce the number of discharge licenses, make environmental legislations and include environmental protection as a criterion of evaluation for officials, and create advanced-warning mechanisms.[128]

In 2005, Xi unveiled another initiative for a recycling economy to reduce, reuse, and decontaminate. The goal was to raise efficiency in resource utilization, turning Zhejiang into a model of sustainable development.[129] By the end of 2007, the Zhejiang government announced that fulfillment of the three-year plan had placed environmental pollution and ecological damages "basically" under control. An amount of ¥33.9 billion (US$5.14 billion) was expended, and 2,419 polluting enterprises were either closed, suspended, or relocated. Such "antibusiness" practices were deemed proper regulatory functions, but, ironically, they often sparked mass protests by entrepreneurs and workers who had lost their means of livelihood.[130] In any event, Zhejiang was ranked number one, scoring 87.1 percent in a national ecological evaluation report, and the fight against pollution continued with another new three-year plan (2008–2011).[131] In 2006, Zhejiang was the first to set up a three-level (province, municipality, and county) risk evaluation system for social policies.[132]

Beijing's national rankings claimed that for four years in a row, between 2004 and 2007, people's sense of security in Zhejiang had risen above 92 percent, and the disposable income for urban residents and the net income for rural residents were first among all provinces. Retirement funds for enterprise staff had gone up year after year, so that it was the highest among China's provinces.[133] Zhejiang reportedly maintained its exalted status as China's safest province up to 2018. There was a "zero increase" in criminal cases, grievance letter cases, and production safety cases. Social safety and harmony had ensured economic development—the main index for social development and urban/rural income remained ranked it first among all provinces for a continuous thirteen and twenty-nine years, respectively. Emergency social responses, social services by governments, and social organizations had largely covered the province. The entire province was divided into 122,800 network cells, with various service groups totaling 245,800.[134] In rural areas where only old people remained, senior centers were formed to provide meals and other services.[135]

Even though internal rankings among the provinces are expected to be relatively fair to avoid dispute, these reports of achievements cannot be accepted at face value. Expressed ideals may not be realized in practice, policies and regulations may not be implemented, and many "image projects" were created just for show. The Chinese people in general concede that this is the case. Most evaluation reports attempted to balance the records of achievements with detailed criticisms of the policy measures and their implementations. For instance, one report blames officials for interpreting social governance in terms of expanding control and police power, relying on high-handed and illegal measures but ignoring justice and fairness. Other reports claimed that officials worked for surface calm and hid issues or used money to buy peace. Further, corruption continued to enable many to amass huge profits and wealth. Social governance policies had fostered perverted interest networks and relationships over which governments had little control and were unable to correct. Officials and citizens alike lacked respect or knowledge of the rule of law. Further, a healthy economic system had not materialized, because of the coexistence of inadequate marketization and excessive marketization. All these reflect the dilemmas confronting a tremendously complex society undergoing unprecedented and rapid change.[136] Nevertheless, the discussion of governance is not merely a top-down process, since demands and inputs from society and the grassroots emanating from the bottom can be significant, and to this we turn to in the following.

Political and "Democratic" Reforms: Local Variations

Not surprisingly, Xi Jinping's notion of democratic reform as articulated in Zhejiang hewed closely to the party line. His main agenda included improvement in the rule of law, intraparty democracy to advance the system of People's Congresses, and multiparty cooperation under the CCP.[137] More specifically, Xi's paternalistic view of "socialist democracy" postulated more citizen self-governance, and changing of government functions from "leadership" or command management, to coordination, guidance, and service provision. Elections were not everything, he often said; instead, they were a necessary but an insufficient condition for democracy since they must be complemented by democratic management and supervision. He granted that the main function of modern democracy was the constraint of power, but the Party must provide the leadership core. Although the democratic consciousness of the masses was rising, he said, the "quality" of the masses could not be elevated at one stroke.[138]

On the other hand, in Zhejiang Xi operated in an environment filled with large numbers of active social organizations such as business associations and unions, especially in economically advanced areas such as Wenzhou and Yiwu. In general, social organizations thrive in regions where the GDP per capita has reached US$3,000, and in 2005, the number of social organizations in Zhejiang had already reached thirty thousand. The social organizations in Zhejiang had facilitated government-society dialogues and contacts between People's Congresses and the public to solicit public opinions. Some would include in the Zhejiang model itself the development of grassroots democracy and the expansion of social space.[139] Business associations and unions regularly carried out negotiations to articulate and defend their interests, often critical of government. For example, social organizations in Wenzhou alone had 703 websites that scrutinized government policies, and they were tolerated. The vitality of these social organizations was palpable. In 2003, Wenzhou's cigarette lighter producers already accounted for 70 percent of the world's production. A watershed occurred when a producers' association representing them won an antidumping suit launched against them by the EU by proving that they were privately owned and receiving no government subsidies. This was China's first victory since accession to the WTO, and subsequently several manufacturers were awarded market economy status by the EU.[140] In Zhejiang, the experience with democratic governance, especially those at Wenling city, has been subsumed by scholars under the rubric of "deliberative democracy."[141] The various local initiatives, in this respect, that explicitly received Xi's blessing, included the following.

The Tangjiadai Experiment

In 2005, Tangjiadai village in Hangzhou was the first to introduce "self- nomina-tion" elections (*zijian haixuan*) to the village committee by which anyone could nominate himself or herself. This replaced the practice of *haitui zhixuan*, which required two procedures: first, candidates would be nominated by the villagers, and those who garnered the most votes would appear on the nomination list; and second, the election would choose from among the nominated. The new prac-tice essentially did away with the nomination procedure, citing high cost and complicated procedures of campaigns and speeches. This new method gained a nationwide reputation and was affirmed by the China-EU Training Program on Village Governance. Subsequently, Xi investigated Xiaogucheng village and endorsed the innovation because he said it would stimulate villagers' participa-tion consciousness and promote grassroots work.[142]

Houchen Village and Village Governance

At Houchen village, Wuyi County, there were messy issues and incessant disputes. From February to June 2004, a pilot project was introduced for improving openness and democratic management. It established the first-ever independent "village affairs supervisory committee" (VASC) elected by villagers to supervise the village government and to open up village affairs. It was tasked not just with ex post facto correction but also preemptive measures.[143] The VASC had power to supervise the implementation of policies, participate in impor-tant meetings, audit finances, and conduct village meetings of representatives. It was also empowered to evaluate the cadres at year end, to impeach incom-petent officials, and to initiate the dismissal of incompetent cadres. Reportedly, the VASC had enabled more independence from upper-level party-government command and more orientation toward local interest. In the nine years following 2004, construction expenditure was closely supervised so that there were zero complaints and *shangfang*. But Chinese commentaries also raised issues of elec-tion irregularities such as vote buying, mobile ballot box security, proxy voting, and unclear voter qualifications. Others were concerned with the unclear delin-eation of official duties, lineage loyalty, the short official terms of three years, and a general lack of experience. The VASCs were said to have instigated conflicts be-tween civil affairs and organizational departments but were unable to deal with issues such as migration of the young out of the villages.[144]

At the beginning the VASCs were opposed by many party branch secretaries, but once provincial leadership had given the green light, they were popularized a year later to 550 villages in Wuyi County. In June 2005, Xi inspected Houchen and gave his stamp of approval.[145] By 2005, village and township draft budgets were discussed by the VASC before being finalized. In 2008, the practice was extended upward to the municipalities. National endorsement came in October 2010 when the NPeC, in revising the organizational legislation for village committees, ordered the formation of VASCs or similar organizations to supervise finance and openness. It prescribed that the village committees must accept "democratic appraisal" of the village representative conference at least once a year, presided over by the VASCs. Members of village committees who were cited twice for incompetence would be dismissed.[146]

Earnest-Talk Meetings

In 1999, at Wenling city's Songmen Township a "rural modernization education seminar," originally meant to be a meeting for officials to lecture the public, was unintentionally transformed into a dialogue between the officials and the public on subjects ranging from agriculture to industry, from social order to education, and from family planning to environmental hygiene. Gradually this format was extended to such issues as village governance, finance, collective property, public works, and electric grids. Private enterprises used these meetings to involve employees, employers, and the trade unions to discuss issues such as wages, working and living conditions, and work training. In 2004, with the assistance of domestic and foreign experts, the MPC of Wenling institutionalized the practice in a directive prescribing "earnest talks" as a mandatory process for decision-making at township governments. Such dialogues were included as a criterion for the evaluation of cadres, linking them directly to the awarding of bonuses for officials.[147] In 2005, Xinhe Township initiated the practice to open up local budgetary planning for inputs and debates so that revised budgets could be passed by the town People's Congresses. From 2008, the practice was extended to the municipality level itself. In 2010, this method was popularized to the entire Wenling Municipality. However, the earnest-talk meetings were a work style existing outside of the party-state system (*tijiwai*) and lacked legal status, so governments were free to accept or reject their outcomes. At locations where social organizations were active, participation was high.[148]

Perhaps it is natural that Zhejiang's entrepreneurs demanded more political participation because of the more developed and marketized economy. Officially, and to a certain extent, public opinion was reflected in multiple channels of participation, which included the People's Congresses, CPPCC, youth federations, industrial and commercial federations, and even membership in the CCP. Using more informal modes of participation, private entrepreneurs and economic and financial groups could use their connections with officials, and even bribery, to get what they wanted. Political scientists have argued that, under certain circumstances, corruption can be a positive means for an otherwise powerless private sector to exert some influence in a state-dominated system.[149] Although the efficacy of political participation in Zhejiang is difficult to gauge, evidence suggests that a certain degree of influence and successful articulation was effected, especially when that coincided with provincial priorities.

From the perspective of the workers, however, the prognosis was not optimistic. For instance, the Zhejiang Federation of Labor had complained that legislation had lagged and that earnest-talk meetings were difficult to implement, inefficient, and suffused with formalism. Workers employed at the SOEs at least received some protection, but workers' rights were clearly deficient in the private enterprises. It is unclear whether there were many incentives for private entrepreneurs to introduce democratic management or worker's control since this was a socialist ideal and not even a global norm as such.[150]

Overall, the preceding practices were small but not insignificant steps toward more political participation. One analyst claims that this reflects a higher quality of governance by the officials and a higher level of rights consciousness among the people, and that the development of Zhejiang democracy was way ahead of anywhere else nationally.[151] Another view maintains that the experiments at Wenling represent a "successful" manifestation of deliberative democracy that was driven by elites interested in blunting social tensions and promoting interest articulations.[152] Still another view sees the earnest-talk meetings as part of a search for "deliberative democracy" to supplement or to replace electoral or interest-competing democracy by dint of its focus on "rational deliberation" and full and orderly political participation.[153] Others count on the proliferation of chambers of commerce and business associations, especially in cities such as Wenzhou, to be heralds of civil society and democracy, although these associations were by and large subservient to and co-opted by the government. Further, a robust civil society requires active participation by other social groups such as workers, migrants, farmers, and environmentalists.[154]

Finally, the extent to which these experiments in "deliberative democracy" could constrain corruption is uncertain. In any case, moralizing and the setting of ethical standards are considered part of the job for Chinese leaders. As an insider, Xi was familiar with the various manifestations of bureaucratic behavior, and his sentiment against the abuse of power was palpable. As in Fujian, or perhaps because of the corruption scandals there, Xi often lectured the cadres on official integrity and on the need to be scrupulous in serving the people. He reminded them often of the importance of being honest and of steering clear of corruption. The cadres were often told to practice self-discipline and immerse themselves in "moral education" to maintain the integrity and advancedness of the Party. If they as leaders did not set an example, social corruption could never be eliminated.[155] As to those cadres guilty of rent-seeking, vying for official positions of power through connections or bribery (*paoguan yaoguan*), or profiteering by offspring and subordinates, they must be resolutely dismissed and penalized.[156] Cadres were enjoined, among other things, to reach out and visit the public.[157] He repeated these themes in one of his many articles on integrity and proper conduct for officials published in *Qiushi*, the CCP's leading theoretical journal. In these homilies Xi took care to echo the Sixteenth Party Congress report of "governance according to law and virtue" and Hu Jintao's injunctions for leaders to pay attention to virtue, discipline, and the harm of greed.[158] One aspect of traditional Chinese political culture, elite rule by example of exemplary conduct, has been incorporated into the Leninist system, and Xi's persistent moralizing had won him a reputation as a "clean" official. Xi was a prolific published writer, even if we assume that aides helped write his speeches.

Rural Development Policies

Statistically Zhejiang in 2011 claimed that its rural and urban incomes were the country's highest for a continuous twenty-six and ten years, respectively.[159] By 2003, GDP per capita in Zhejiang had already reached US$3,000. Behind this national champion status, however, loomed multiple rural challenges as identified by the provincial authorities. The urban/rural gap was one of the smallest in China, but it was expanding, not least because urban living standards were improving faster. Farmers found it difficult to change occupation and to raise income, especially for the middle-aged and older with little education. Modernization of agriculture was a daunting task considering the outflow of resources, the aging of rural labor, reliance on subsidiary production and aging infrastructure, as well as the small scale and low-tech-style of family farming. Rural living conditions were said to have deteriorated rather than improved.

Rapid economic development and the proliferation of village and township enterprises had elevated land values and government rural expenditures, and this raised issues of distribution and investment priorities. Enterprises moving to rural areas meant that valuable farmland was often plowed over to turn into factories and industrial parks. The influx of migrants into local villages often made their numbers exceed that of the local population. Farmers who gave up agriculture in favor of industrial jobs raised a number of issues ranging from social order to public health. The requisition of land, demolition of villages, and resettlement, as mentioned, spawned social conflicts.[160]

In 2003, the PPC and PPPC decided to initiate a comprehensive policy to "build one thousand demonstration villages and fix up (*zhengzhi*) ten thousand villages" by 2007. The method was to pump in billions of yuan to extend urban services to the rural areas, to comprehensively develop urban and rural areas, and to use the cities and industry to promote agriculture and the villages. From 2008 to 2012, a campaign to thoroughly clean up the rural areas through garbage collection and wastewater disposal would be effected. "Fixing up" also included measures to improve the rural infrastructure by introducing paved roads, electrification, road lights, and television and telephone service. It also included environmental measures such as the cleaning up of rivers and lakes, afforestation, garbage removal, building of lavatories, and the introduction of modern hygiene. Thousands of convenience chain stores were to be set up in the towns and villages.[161]

To expand public services, provincial attention was said to have been biased toward rural areas to ensure the establishment of fifteen years of compulsory education, free rural education, professional education for low-income farmers, and rural supply and sale credit cooperatives. A new cooperative medical system was planned, in addition to the introduction of a minimum rural living standard guarantee and a basic livelihood guarantee for farmers who had lost their land. Finally, farmers living in poor and underdeveloped areas would be relocated. When the term "scientific development" came into vogue, the preceding policies would be subsumed under its rubric. For the officials, progress in these areas was made one of the important criteria for annual cadre evaluation.

Ostensibly, at the end of 2007, the five-year project was said to have been completed ahead of schedule so that one-third of the province's villages were comprehensively "fixed up" (*zhengzhi*), and the waste of two-thirds of the province's villages was centrally collected and treated. Huangyan Wucheng was said to have relocated 102,000 households of 363,000 people. Yiwu, a manufacturing center, volunteered to train rural residents, turning surplus labor into secondary and tertiary production. Farmers were said to have lauded the outcome as an equivalent to land reform, the introduction of the household responsibility system, and the reform of taxes and fees.[162] Zhejiang was one of the first provinces to try out the reduction of agricultural tax, which was totally abolished in 2005, a year ahead of its abolition nationally.[163] Overall, however, caution is needed to interpret official accounts of policy outcomes, given the enormity and intractability of rural issues and the flaws of policy design and implementation. The reports of achievements are sometimes actually aspirations, although the numerous rankings of China's regional governments, primarily designed for domestic purposes, do reflect to a certain extent their relative performances. Further, new policies and new policy environments are certain to create new issues and may exacerbate old or unresolved ones.[164]

Zhejiang after Xi Jinping

To gauge Xi's legacy in Zhejiang, one needs to refer to the ongoing discussions of development issues and policymaking occurring long after Xi left Zhejiang in order to see the resiliency of nagging issues and a sense of déjà vu. Despite its exalted status as a national champion and all the efforts at cleaning up, Zhejiang still suffers from deteriorating land and air and increasing water pollution. Before 2000 Hangzhou and other industrial cities such as Wenzhou and Huzhou had on average forty hazy days per annum, but Zhejiang's number of choking and hazy days has risen to twenty times more than it was fifty years ago, from seven in the 1960s to early 1990s up to almost two hundred in the new millennium. The chief cause was a new phenomenon—the ubiquitous reliance on bicycles was giving way to a rapid surge in car ownership, and vehicle exhaust spewed out by the province's 13.38 million vehicles, and industrial fumes comprising dust and sulfuric acid. Diesel vehicles were directly responsible for particularly dangerous fine-particle PM2.5 emissions.[165] The rising middle class quickly embraced the automobile culture, and this has exacerbated the issues of poor air quality and smog in cities.[166] Another often-neglected fact is that foreign countries outsource their polluting industries to China and enjoy the benefits of cheap manufactured products, high living standards, and low inflation, with China bearing the costs of externalities. By ignoring this central linkage, scholars often proffer one-sided analyses.[167] One source estimated that in 2010, China's export sector accounted for 1.8 million tons of PM2.5, with 60 percent of these emissions attributable to manufacturing of exports to the United States and Organization for Economic Cooperation and Development countries.[168] China was also the world's largest importer of waste (including plastic and e-waste) for a quarter of a century, and when it banned further imports in 2018, it created a crisis among developed countries.[169] Heavily polluting textile industries that supply such foreign firms as Zara, H&M, Adidas, Nike, Gap, Guess, and Levi's were accused of discharging large amounts of pollutants.[170] More than 80 percent of the waters of the East China Sea outside Zhejiang had been polluted by sewage and constant industrial discharge by power plants, ship manufacturing docks, and chemical companies and contain hazardous amounts of hydrocarbons, cooper, cadmium, lead, arsenic, and DDT.[171]

Another report cites the case of the Puyang River, which had become so seriously polluted by twenty-two thousand crystal processing factories that the river was black and putrid, and the fear of mass incidents finally prompted provincial

Figure 5.2 Recycling imported electronic waste in Zhejiang, 2006. Credit: Xinhua

authorities to decide in 2013 to clean it up by "acting according to the law"—fourteen thousand factories lacking operating licenses were closed down, and 670,000 square meters of illegal buildings were demolished, and criminal cases were brought against the culprits for polluting the environment.[172] After a string of lead-poisoning scandals, more than 70 percent of lead battery manufacturers were also closed down.[173] However, the planned development of nuclear power in Zhejiang further complicates matters.[174]

High incidences of cancer among villages located near heavy industries finally prompted the government to acknowledge the existence of "cancer villages" in 2013.[175] Large numbers of these villages were located in Zhejiang. For instance, the massive industrial zones and more than three thousand textile factories near Wuli had for decades severely polluted the Qiantang River to satisfy the insatiable worldwide demand for cheap clothing and fashion.[176] To dramatize the issue, a Zhejiang entrepreneur offered ¥200,000 (US$32,000) to dare any environmental officer to swim in the polluted river for twenty minutes.[177] Thus inspired, in 2014, the Zhejiang PPC ordered that all local officials must swim in rivers under their jurisdiction to demonstrate to the citizens that the water quality had improved.[178] An irony is that cleanup efforts and rising living standards drew protests. For instance, a plan to build a waste incinerator in Hangzhou drew a "not in my backyard" (NIMBY) protest by hundreds of locals.[179] A solar panel factory producing silicon wafers in the city of Haining had to be closed down for polluting a nearby river, causing a massive fish-kill.[180]

After Xi left Zhejiang in 2007, provincial officials finally agreed to be measured by the "green GDP" as devised by Beijing, admitting that Zhejiang GDP was at best pale green.[181] The 2008–2009 global financial crisis and subsequent recession led to sluggish overseas demand and rising production costs. Bad debts, bankruptcies, and unemployment mounted. The massive injection of a national stimulus package worth US$586 billion eased the difficulties, but complaints were voiced that SOEs were favored at the expense of the SMEs, which suffered from a lack of credit or very high interest rates, driving them to loan sharks who charged exorbitant interest rates. Investors rushed to real estate and stock markets, creating bubbles. Again, Wenzhou as well as other parts of the province were clamoring for another modification of the "Zhejiang model."[182]

In 2011, the Zhejiang leadership decided to put the brakes on and reduce the growth rate to 9 percent for the next five years. Again, the overdependence on low-end industries, overconsumption of natural resources, and a reliance on low-cost labor were cited as issues. But already there was a sense of déjà vu. Zhejiang was under increasing pressure to conserve energy and to reduce emissions.[183] In 2013, incoming governor Li Qiang complained that Zhejiang's economy was still dependent on low-end, labor-intensive, energy-hogging manufacturers.[184]

An obvious and easy conclusion is that Xi had done little and nothing had changed. But Xi's defenders would say that real change comes only gradually. Under Xi, Zhejiang had advancements in many respects but setbacks in others, and new challenges emerged. Xi's legacy may be vague: had he fashioned, or at least laid a foundation for, a new developmental model for Zhejiang? Perhaps no one could have resolved the perennial and intractable forces unleashed by extremely rapid industrialization and modernization, especially in a five-year stint. And the 2008 global financial crisis and the resultant depression necessitated yet another transformation. Still, Xi's activist agenda was clear, and by giving him a promotion, the party state showed that it was satisfied with his performance, one way or the other.

In his stint at Zhejiang as the first-in-command Xi enjoyed increased authority and personal responsibility for an entire province. Official appraisals to a certain extent reflect his governance record. One appraisal claims that Xi had promoted various slogan-cum-policies such as "Safe Zhejiang," "Green Zhejiang," "Cultural Zhejiang," Rule-by-Law Zhejiang," and "Strong Ocean" province. He had contributed to the Zhejiang model by furthering the works of previous Zhejiang PPC secretaries including Zhang Dejiang, and he was specially credited with the correct positioning of the role of government.[185]

Presiding over Zhejiang during a rapid transformative period in one of China's most highly developed regions, Xi's ambition is reflected in the title of a book collection of his speeches, *Do Real Work, Be at the Forefront*, which subsequently turned into a slogan. Hu Jintao had twice ordered Zhejiang to take the lead to implement his pet projects, such as scientific development and the building of a socialist harmonious society.[186] Xi's overall performance may have received a nod from the general secretary.

Xi was deemed qualified for another promotion by COD chief He Guoqiang, who lauded him for being steadfast in guarding the authority of the center, for transforming the growth model, and in resolving difficult issues in people's livelihood.[187] Deputy chief of the COD Wang Dongming praised Xi for his outstanding work in reform, development, and *weiwen* by uniting with the provincial leadership. Wang also said that Xi was strong in politics but qualified this by saying that Xi showed only a "relatively" (*bijiaoshang*) high level of ideology and policy.[188] In general, robust economic growth continued under Xi's tenure, as Zhejiang's GDP more than doubled.[189] From 2002 to 2008, GDP growth of over 12 percent per year had raised 2007 GDP per capita to nearly US$5,000, and 2008 per capita GDP to more than US$6,000. Zhejiang was said to be almost a "well-off" society.[190] In 2005, national indices ranked Zhejiang highest in the nation for ecology and environment; in 2006, the citizen's sense of safety was 94.77 percent, the highest in the nation; in 2006, the capacity for sustainable development was number four after Shanghai, Beijing and Tianjin; Zhejiang was the first province nationally to realize the overcoming of poverty in all previously poor counties and poor villages and towns. One-third of China's five hundred biggest companies were based in Zhejiang, and thirty had over ¥10 billion in assets. Zhejiang had become a cradle for innovative private enterprises, which included Geely, Alibaba, and Tsingshan Holding.[191]

During the global financial crisis of 2008 and subsequent recession, Zhejiang's economy grew by 10.1 percent and 8.9 percent respectively in 2008 and 2009.[192] In 2013, urban disposable income and rural net income, at ¥37,851 urban and ¥16,106 rural, respectively, per capita were the highest in the country. Rural net income was the highest for twenty-eight consecutive years. Zhejiang's urban/rural income gap ratio of 2.47 (2005), 2.49 (2007), 2.37 (2011), and 2.35 (2013) was one of the smallest and, unlike the other provinces was experiencing a downward trend. The Gini coefficients were .33 and .36 for the urban and rural areas, respectively.[193]

Henry Paulson, a former Goldman Sachs chief executive, reportedly cultivated a personal friendship with Xi in his many visits to China. When Paulson became US Treasury secretary, he visited Xi in Hangzhou before meeting with President Hu Jintao in Beijing. Praising Xi for being "very smart" and "commercial," he added that Xi was "the kind of guy who really knows how to get things over the goal line."[194] Paulson's visit was a conscious decision to identify himself with the promarket reform camp at a time when a fierce debate, exacerbated by the ongoing controversy over the new property law, was raging between the socialists on the one hand and the neoliberals on the other. Paulson's endorsement of Xi, a rising political star, was meant to convey his message that China's future lay with Zhejiang's private-sector-led economy, a can-do government, and "respect for its environment."[195]

Conclusion

Zhejiang is a microcosm of a rapidly industrializing and modernizing China and a bellwether of trends and developments, and perhaps a window for observing the future of China. In the reform period it was transformed from a resource-poor province into an economic powerhouse. With 1.1 percent of the country's territory, it accounted for 6.2 percent of its economy. Official media at the time, and especially since Xi has become general secretary, have highlighted his presumed achievements. Some of the tributes are extravagant, but others more restrained. From our perspective of leadership and governance, Xi's tenure in Zhejiang attempted to implement a whole series of central policy initiatives emanating from the center by fitting them to local conditions. Like most Chinese leaders, Xi can repeat syllogisms ad nauseam. Take just an example: "People are the first ingredient of the concept of scientific development, and development depends on the people and is for the people, and for their comprehensive development."[196] Xi hewed closely to central ideology and initiatives and positioned his province at the forefront but was careful not to brag too much. But he enjoyed a relatively free hand in fashioning specific policies for the complex situations in the province. Xi continued to develop his thinking on reforms and governance and to grapple with a range of issues, from the strict disciplining of the Party to "governance according to law," from anticorruption to rural/urban inequality, and from antipoverty to the *hukou* system. He wrestled with the redefinition of the roles of government and the market.

Although Zhejiang is a small slice of China, much of what Xi articulated there was later applied to the entire country when he rose to the top. Despite the daunting challenges, Zhejiang might have already overcome the constraints of the so-called middle-income trap. According to the World Bank, upper-middle-income economies consist of those countries that have GDP per capita ranging from US$4,000 to US$12,5000, and high-income economies are those that possess GDP per capita above US$12,500 (at constant 2005 US$). By 2017, Zhejiang's nominal GDP per capita had reached US$13,634 (or US$26,255 in PPP terms), and the size of its economy was equivalent to that of the Netherlands;[197] therefore, the province was ready to join the high-income club, according to these definitions. Nevertheless, the notion of the "middle-income trap" and its implications for stagnancy and development are controversial; it is more significant as a heuristic device for policymakers to assess their developmental strategy and to identify drivers for innovative and competitive growth.[198]

Zhejiang was a major stepping stone to the top. Right after Zhejiang Xi was transferred and promoted to Shanghai to play the role of firefighter and to effect damage control. Unsullied by hints of corruption, he was chosen to inspire confidence. As discussed in the following chapter, Shanghai was a further trial for Xi's succession, even though his sojourn there lasted only a few months before he was elevated to be the heir apparent to Hu Jintao.

6

The Shanghai Interlude and Political Succession at the Seventeenth Party Congress, October 2007 (Age Fifty-Four)

The year 2007 was a turning point for Xi Jinping's political career. After governing Zhejiang for five years he was promoted to secretary of the Shanghai Municipal Party Committee (MPC) in March 2007. Then, just shy of seven months later, he was catapulted into the Politburo Standing Committee (PBSC), effectively becoming the heir apparent to be top party leader. Although Politburo membership comes with the Shanghai position, it was not expected that he would move quickly again into the PBSC because in doing so he would be transferred to Beijing and then have to be replaced. Two such promotions in just one year are most likely due to the special circumstances of the time. Xi's tenure at Shanghai was short, but his performance and résumé were deemed by central authorities to be satisfactory when positions were opening up in the PBSC.

The Shanghai Interlude (March to October 2007)

Xi's nomination as secretary of Shanghai MPC was a major promotion because by custom, party chiefs of Beijing, Shanghai, and Tianjin are automatically inducted into the Politburo. For Xi, the glittering metropolis was a different world from the impoverished hinterland and provincial cities where he had worked for almost four decades. From the perspective of factional politics, the Shanghai position was a political prize contested by various factions, especially the *tuanpai*, the princelings, and the "Shanghai Gang." In 2006, corruption scandals had rocked three major municipalities. Beijing deputy mayor Liu Zhehua, Tianjin chief procurator Li Baojin, and Chen Liangyu of Shanghai were censured for corruption. As part of damage control by the Party Center to stabilize the situation, disciplinary inspection commissions of all three municipalities, in addition to that of Chongqing, were reorganized, and their heads were directly nominated and assigned by the Party Center. The party leaders of all three were also reassigned.[1]

A centrally administered municipality with a status equivalent to a province, Shanghai was by the turn of the century already China's largest metropolis, a global financial, economic, and trade center and the world's busiest container port. From 2002 to 2007, Shanghai maintained double-digit growth, with an average annual growth rate of 12.2 percent. Its GDP was more than ¥1 trillion. Of the total population of 13.68 million, 13 million were enrolled in the city's welfare system.[2] Expo 2010 in Shanghai was expected to be an international coming-out party for the metropolis. Xi was picked because of his long experience working in the prosperous coastal areas, a qualification that was deemed more appropriate than work in poorer, internal areas. Private enterprises were the drivers of Fujian's and Zhejiang's economy, but Shanghai's was driven more by foreign capital and large state-owned enterprises. The challenge was perceived to be the dominance by "big government" and weak private enterprises, so it was the Center's hope that Xi might bolster the competitiveness of the private sector.[3]

Beginning July 2006, the Central Commission for Discipline Inspection (CCDI) was already investigating Shanghai's party chief, Chen Liangyu. On September 24, the Politburo approved a CCDI report and dismissed Chen from all party and government posts. Subsequent court trials saw Chen convicted for bribery and abuse of power and sentenced to eighteen years in prison. Chen was accused of using his positions to seek huge bribes, to benefit his family members, and to commit extortion, as well as transferring a stake in a state-owned enterprise to private hands at below-market prices. He was charged for profiting from government fiscal subsidies and deals involving land and property. The biggest charge was that Chen had illicitly helped an unidentified company to obtain financing from the Shanghai social security fund, putting the fund at a huge risk. ¥3.7 billion (US$486 million) was embezzled from highway construction and properties investments. A dozen senior officials and the heads of several major state-owned enterprises implicated by the scandal were sacked.[4]

Corruption was an immediate issue in Chen's downfall, although an additional factor could be Chen's alleged altercation with Premier Wen Jiabao over the Hu-Wen administration's imposition of macroeconomic controls, especially over the real estate sector, which Chen claimed could damage economic growth. Chen is also said to have resisted Hu Jintao's vision of a more regionally balanced socioeconomic growth, and his removal eliminated a policy rival. Further, factional analysts interpret the sacking of Chen as a means for Hu Jintao to weaken the Shanghai Gang.[5]

Who to replace Chen Liangyu with was a contentious and challenging issue, and for six months, the Center wavered, although MPC deputy secretary Han Zheng was made acting secretary. The matter was complicated by the norm that the secretary of the Shanghai PPC must be made a Politburo member. One plausible source claims that the COD, after weighing the concerns of all interested parties, including the elders and highest decision-makers, decided on three candidates: Xi Jinping (Zhejiang), Li Yuanqiao (Jiangsu), and Zhang Gaoli

(Shandong). Opinions were sought and surveys were conducted in these three provinces before deciding on Xi Jinping.[6] This decision came abruptly, as no previous signs were leaked, even during the NPeC and CCPCC conferences in March 2007. But Xi appeared to have provided a perfect résumé, with step-by-step experiences from the grassroots to the provincial level. As observed, Xi had been working in Fujian and Zhejiang from 1985. He was familiar with the economically developed east coast regions, having worked there for twenty-two years. Also, as seen in the chapter on Zhejiang, Xi had in 2003 already initiated the strategy of closely connecting Shanghai and Jiangsu in order to promote integration and development of the Changjiang Delta, deferring to Shanghai's leading role, even at the expense of some of Zhejiang's more immediate interests.[7] Officially, Xi also enjoyed a reputation for being tough on corruption.[8] As a son of Xi Zhongxun he was well connected, or at least well known, in upper echelons.

On March 24, 2007, Party Central announced that Xi would be parachuted into Shanghai to become secretary of the Shanghai MPC, replacing acting secretary Han Zheng. Xi's assumption to the position broke the time-honored tradition of more than two decades of having Shanghai cadres fill the coveted position,[9] reflecting the Center's lack of confidence in local officials and their ability to clean up the mess. Perhaps in choosing an outsider, the Center intended to break the hold of an "independent kingdom." If one takes the perspective of factional struggle, one may say that fierce factional competition resulted in a compromise in choosing Xi. His personal connections were inconspicuous, and he was not linked to the Shanghai Gang, at least in the sense that he had never worked in Shanghai and therefore did not owe his promotions to anyone in that metropolis. He was well positioned to investigate corruption and clean up officialdom.[10]

Henceforth, Xi's selection may be explained by a deliberate effort by the leadership to balance the various forces within the Party to achieve an equilibrium. The rapid expansion and ascendancy of the *tuanpai* had generated unease and possible strain, and by contrast, the Shanghai Gang was perceived to be in decline, with the impact of the Chen Liangyu case its Waterloo. Hu Jintao's strategic choice was to balance the various interests within the Party, and Xi, a princeling, was seen to be a suitable compromise. A factional balance between the Communist Youth League (CYL) and the Shanghai Gang would ameliorate conflict within in the Party and calm fears that any faction had become too predominant. Indeed, a rational choice perspective can assume that Hu had consented to Xi's appointment, calculating that he could preempt his critics, allowing him to then continue promoting the *tuanpai* personnel.[11] In terms of merit, Xi's qualifications on the whole were richer than Li Keqiang's, without disasters like the ones that haunted Li. Hu Jintao needed to balance several networks to achieve an equilibrium, and probably avoid promoting someone seen to have connections to him to avoid charges of nepotism and violation of party discipline.

On the other hand, not surprisingly, official sources on Xi's appointment emphasize process. Once the Chen Liangyu case was revealed, COD director He Guoqiang worked behind the scenes to identify a replacement through investigations and consultation.[12] Originally the new Shanghai chief was to be selected from within the Shanghai PPC standing committee. In January, the COD had already conducted a questionnaire survey regarding the economic and social performance of Shanghai PPC standing committee members among the officials above the bureau level, the delegates to the Shanghai Municipal and District People's Congresses, members of the CPPCC, as well as National People's Congress delegates. Since this group comprised some two thousand members and was deemed too large, only 20 percent were selected to survey. Survey questions covered various issues including healthcare, hygiene, education, law and order, and housing and opinions on the candidates. Eventually, an outsider, Xi was finally chosen since Shanghai officials were by and large perceived to have been tainted by the corruption scandal.[13]

On another hand, the business community, both domestic and international, had wished for someone capable and able to communicate internationally in order to stabilize the situation. Fear of implication by the scandal investigation had stalled large investment projects in real estate, capital construction, and the trading of state-owned assets. Entrepreneurs had hoped for more predictability and stability.[14] The fact that US Treasury secretary Paulson had chosen to visit Xi and Zhejiang on his first official trip to China had left an impression. Those who were familiar with Xi were aware of his family background, career, and his slogan "small government, large society." Zhejiang's booming private entrepreneurship was well known, and Xi's projected image of being a pragmatic and modest team player stuck. For others, Xi appeared to have worked well with Taiwanese business people.[15] His experience working in neighboring coastal provinces and in the integration of the Changjiang Delta put him above officials unfamiliar with these matters.

During the "two sessions" in March 2006, Hu Jintao instructed Shanghai to take the lead in changing its economic model, to raise initiative, to reform and open up, and to construct a socialist harmonious society (the "four forefronts") in order to propel Shanghai into an international economic, finance, trade, and transport center (the "four centers"). It was hoped that apart from economic development, Xi would also pull his weight on issues of livelihood and social justice. Expo 2010 was to be a major event to test his mettle.[16]

Xi's appointment was part of a major reshuffle of six provincial-level leaderships ahead of the impending Seventeenth Party Congress to renew the top leadership. In three days, new party chiefs for Shanghai, Tianjin, Shandong,

Shaanxi, Qinghai, and Zhejiang were installed, of which the first two drew the most attention.[17]

Shanghai under Xi Jinping

Shanghai was widely acknowledged as China's locomotive of economic growth, but Xi's promotion to the metropolis leadership came at a time of stress and uncertainty. The Seventeenth Party Congress was to be convened in just a few months and the Olympics in a year, but in Shanghai the stock market and housing prices were threatening to spin out of control. Personnel changes and shakeup after a major corruption scandal were complicated and sensitive, given the many intricate and crisscrossing networks of vested interests and factional and money/power alliances.[18]

As the center of workers' movements in the 1920s, Shanghai's ideological and symbolic significance was lost on no one. Xi's first public engagement on March 30 was a visit to historic sites of the first and second CCP party congresses, both conveniently located in Shanghai.[19] Xi's bow to historical continuity was to be balanced by modern reality. The next day, Xi visited Pudong, Shanghai's financial and commercial hub, purportedly a microcosm of China's reform and opening, where he pledged to fulfill Hu's instructions to enhance the metropolis's strategic competitiveness. In early April, Xi's research tours were focused on livelihood issues such as employment, healthcare, education, and housing. In various speeches, Xi enjoined the cadres to "wholeheartedly" resolve the preceding issues for the people, especially those in difficulty, starting from the grassroots.[20] Responding to the criticism leveled at the "two sessions" that Shanghai had not allowed other provinces to participate in Expo 2010, Xi visited Pudong several times and openly solicited cooperation and assistance from all ministries, provinces, Hong Kong, and Macau.[21]

The major tasks confronting Xi were to stabilize the political situation, calm public opinion, and reorganize the leadership. The Ninth Shanghai Party Congress in May 2007 presented an opportunity to start anew, but Xi, an outsider, still faced many constraints and had to tread carefully. The Shanghai personnel makeup was an intricate web of patron-client connections. As one source puts it, many of Chen Liangyu's associates, who were clients of top leaders Jiang Zemin, Huang Ju, Wu Bangguo, and Zeng Qinghong and who were promoted by them, could not be touched. The bloodletting had to be limited. For this reason, the MPC standing committee had to retain people like Han Zheng and Shen Hongguang, the latter alleged to be Chen's crony.[22] Further, conflicts over education, healthcare, family planning, and housing policies were intense. Before the Shanghai party congress, Zeng Qinghong and Wen Jiabao had inspected Shanghai, presumably to weigh in on issues of personnel changes and to convey central support to Xi.[23] In any case, Xi pledged to induct middle-age and young cadres into the MPC and the Municipal Commission on Discipline Inspection. Eventually six (out of fifteen) MPC standing committee members aged fifty-eight and above were retired, and four younger officials were inducted into the MPC standing committee, which was reduced to thirteen members.[24] PBSC member and NPeC chairman Wu Bangguo also went to Shanghai to lend support to Xi, declaring that any resisters would be dismissed. Wu affirmed that Xi's assignment was carefully considered and warned that the MPC and the Shanghai government must cease all factional activities. Shanghai officials were quick in extolling Xi's assignment in public, but privately they had, either by design or by habit, set several political and economic traps. First, a couple of days after Xi had assumed the position, members of the standing committee of the MPC, the deputy mayors, and the chair and deputy chairs of the MPC, as well as fifty-eight departments, had written extravagantly to show they "resolutely support" the "correct" decision of Party Central and the new provincial leadership "with Xi Jinping at its head." Shanghai's entire population was said to have passionately welcomed the new party secretary: "Comrade Xi is a long-tested and exceptional leader." Xi reacted by warning against formalism and any flattering activities.[25]

Second, the provincial authorities had arranged a three-story, British-style mansion at Xiangyang Road measuring eight hundred square meters as Xi's residence. Hong Kong media recognized this clearly as a trap, since central regulations prescribed that the residential standard for provincial-level officials was only 250 square meters, whereas for Politburo members the standard was 300 square meters. Xi quickly declined the mansion, suggesting that it should be used as a recuperating center for retired officials or military patients. Third, the municipal authorities supplied Xi with a Mercedes Benz 400 sedan and a Lexus sedan, even though repeated Party Central instructions prescribed that, apart from purposes of receiving and transporting foreign guests, all party and government officials must use Chinese-made vehicles.

Fourth, authorities also transferred a special chef from the Jinjiang Hotel and a professor-level expert on internal medicine from the Second Military University to service Xi, violating the regulation that provincial-level officials cannot be equipped with a professional chef. Politburo members and deputy ministers were allowed a healthcare doctor, but not at the professorial level. Fifth, Xi's position required him to make regular trips to Hangzhou, and authorities had arranged a special train, even though central regulations prescribed that only the president, vice president, the premier, the chairs of the NPeC, the CCPCC, members of the Standing Committee of the Politburo and the vice chair of the CMC were entitled to use a special train. Xi wisely declined the special train, and presumably all the other trappings laid before him. He took a common coach to Hangzhou.[26]

Yet formalism was not to be dispensed with entirely when Xi took care to express loyalty to the Party Center and Hu Jintao. To set the tone for the Seventeenth Party Congress, Hu Jintao had given a speech on June 25 at the Central Party School that was essentially boilerplate to reaffirm the goal to build "socialism with Chinese characteristics" and a "relatively well-off society" by 2020. One significant aspect of the speech was to pave the way for the enshrinement of the notion of "scientific development," purportedly Hu Jintao's theoretical contribution, into the party constitution in the impending congress.[27]

A few days later, Xi devoted a Shanghai MPC standing committee meeting to the study of Hu's speech and his injunctions. Xi vowed to accelerate Hu's "four forefronts" and the "four centers," and to comprehensively promote economic, political, cultural, and social development.[28] Declarations and demonstrations of fidelity to central and leadership initiatives are always good strategy, and Xi played along.[29]

One form of central control over the provinces is the Party Central roving inspections, and two rounds were scheduled before the Seventeenth Party Congress. The first round, lasting about four months and scrutinizing the provincial first-in-commands, had already been completed in the second part of 2006. A second round, which began in March, lasted about two months and focused on inspecting the entire provincial leadership to see if it was working in accord with public wishes and with the principle of "scientific development." Central groups would fan out and, at each place of inspection, the secretary of the MPC would submit reports in the presence of senior provincial officials from the Party, government, and the courts. If the issues involved individual senior provincial leaders, inspection groups would invite them for a "talk" to warn them. Important issues would be reported directly to the Party Central leadership for directions. The second round focused more on the integrity of individual leaders, the awareness of the sense of crisis, public service, and thrift. This round was also meant to deal with feedback from the general public. It tried to weed out those officials suspected of malfeasance from participating in the congress.[30]

Overall, during his tenure in Shanghai, Xi grappled with issues of people's livelihood, development, Expo 2010, and the fight against corruption. Xi was credited with reshuffling the Shanghai leadership, stabilizing the situation, restoring Shanghai's image, and crafting a development blueprint for the coming five years. In 2007 the municipal government had invested ¥30 million to improve the education of the children of migrant workers, and it paid more attention to critical rural issues, consistent with Hu-Wen priorities.

On systemic corruption, Xi urged the MPC members to disclose their individual and household income and property without delay, and he encouraged officials to divulge their illegal economic and financial dealings in order to obtain lenient treatment. The Shanghai government also sponsored a film entitled *The Scourge of Greedy Desire*, a cautionary tale intended to raise consciousness about corruption. In the end, however, the various pilot projects introduced in Shanghai and nationally for the public disclosure of official income and property have gained little ground even up to today. Finally, Xi's reorganization of the standing committee of the MPC incorporated two new members born in the 1960s, Xu Lin and Ding Xuexiang. Ding became Xi's political secretary, and his importance to Xi grew when both moved to Beijing later.

In September, a month before the national party congress, a front-page *People's Daily* article entitled "The Glad Tidings from Shanghai Are a Pleasure to Behold" (*xiting Shanghai xin tao sheng*) showed that Party Central had endorsed the performance of the new Shanghai administration,[31] and it may also have borne Hu Jintao's personal stamp of approval of Xi as his successor. Sensitive China watchers attuned to the esoteric ways of Chinese political communication quickly noted that the Chinese word for "tidings" (涛 tao) is a character in Hu Jintao's name. The article lauded Shanghai for resolutely promoting reforms, Hu's scientific development concept, and the building of a harmonious society. It praised the inclusivity and solidarity of Shanghai's newly minted leadership contingent, saying the "new" Shanghai was no longer selfish and that it had cooperated with neighboring provinces such as Jiangsu and Zhejiang. Shanghai, the article continued, had promoted anticorruption and honesty. Shanghai was said to have paid attention to the needs of the "vulnerable groups" and had looked after the housing needs of low-income households, since there was a palpable improvement in people's housing needs. More importantly, Shanghai had not sacrificed development while attacking corruption.[32]

Apart from being a personal endorsement from the highest levels, the article justified and prepared opinion within the Party for the meteoric rise of Xi to the PBSC in the upcoming congress. Overall, since Xi's regional career has not been explored in contextual detail until this study, existing literature tends to summarily dismiss Xi for being "an unexceptional provincial leader" lacking bold and new ideas.[33] Additionally, while Lam claims that Xi had shown "a relatively high degree of innovative and progressive thinking" at Zhejiang, he nevertheless argues that Xi's background was lackadaisical, dull, and mediocre, and that Xi "appeared to be neither sufficient nor impressive" for the top office.[34] These stereotypes beg the question why the Party picked Xi and pinned its hope on him to bolster and save the regime.

The Politics of Succession at the Seventeenth Party Congress
(October 15–21, 2007)

Xi's appointment as secretary of the Shanghai MPC assured him of Politburo membership, but in less than seven months he was catapulted directly into the PBSC to become one of China's nine top leaders and effectively the heir apparent to the office of general secretary of the Party. In the post-Mao period, the selection of the Politburo and PBSC membership was essentially a top-down affair decided by the outgoing PBSC. It was and still is an outcome of an intense political process of negotiation and compromise among interested parties wherein the realignment of a new top leadership reflects changing distribution and exercise of power and CCP priorities. Party norms have dictated that potential candidates cannot campaign, espouse competing policy platforms, or even express ambition. At the 2006 NPeC, journalists interviewed the three prime candidates of the "fifth generation," Xi Jinping, Jiangsu PPC first secretary Li Yuanchao, and Liaoning PPC first secretary Li Keqiang, on whether they expected that they could advance their careers at the Seventeenth Party Congress. All were evasive, either not giving any answer or saying, "I have not thought about it" or "I will not think about it."[35]

The Seventeenth Party Congress and the follow-up, the Eleventh National People's Congress of March 2008, were the culmination of a national— and contested—reshuffling of party and government leaders that included promotions, resignations, and multidirection transfers (horizontal and vertical, upward and downward, center to regions, coastal to interior, and vice versa) that took more than a year to complete. Examining the rates of turnover, the changing structure of power at the top, and the formal and informal politics involved reveals a great deal about the changing nature, pattern, and process of Chinese politics and leadership transition.

Despite its self-professed claim to be the vanguard of the Chinese people, the CCP leadership is not omnipotent and is subject to a variety of constraints.[36] One of the most striking, but often overlooked, aspects of this leadership is the tiny pool from which top leaders are recruited. In 2020, the CCP had more than ninety million members (seventy-four million in 2007) but its Central Committee (CC) consists of approximately 200 full and 170 alternate members. Virtually all important party, government, and military leaders at the center and the regions are drawn from this CC pool. Hence the CC is China's top elite and a tiny and exclusive percentage of the population, society, and the CCP itself. However, a bigger pool would mean an undesirable dilution of the elitist nature of the leadership. In addition, because of a political culture of status and hierarchy, acceptance for promotion into the elite club of the CC and above involves stringent and long-term grooming and winnowing through many organizational levels, a process known in Chinese as "advancing through incremental and procedural steps" (*xunxu jianjin, anbu jiuban*).[37]

Such a state of limited choices explains the constraints and dilemmas of the top leadership in choosing successors, especially when it fears running up against the danger of aging. Added to this were new rules regarding term and age limits wherein most leading positions in the state apparatus (such as president, premier, vice premier, minister) were limited by the constitution to two terms. At any rate, in June 2007, in preparation for the party congress, the Party Central leadership decided to expand inner-party democracy, inspired by a Vietnamese practice. Hu Jintao presided over a meeting to conduct a straw poll for candidates to be elected to the Politburo. A list of nearly two hundred candidates under sixty-three years old and consisting of cadres at or above the ministerial level and the military region level was supplied to the three hundred-plus voting CC members, alternate members, and other "responsible" comrades to gauge general opinion and to give the delegates a say. A purpose of the poll was to mollify criticisms that the outgoing Politburo appointed its own successors without CC input.[38] Another source says that prior to the Seventeenth Party Congress, the COD organized a preliminary election among provincial-/ministerial-level officials to vote for candidates for the Standing Committee of the Politburo. Consequently, Xi Jinping received the most votes, followed by Li Keqiang, He Guoqiang, and Zhou Yongkang.[39] Such a "democratic" exercise was touted to be an unprecedented move designed to promote "systematization, standardization, and proceduralization" of the succession process. Yet, in reality, this shows an odd understanding of procedural norms, since by the party constitution, it was the duty of the newly elected CC at the Seventeenth Party Congress to elect a new Politburo, and not the business of the outgoing CC to do so.[40]

In any case, Reuters also reported that in early 2007, Xi came first in regional straw polls known as *modi* (literally, trying to fathom the real situation), winning 90 percent of the votes in Shanghai, and also coming out first nationwide.[41] From the perspective of the top leadership, Xi's personal qualifications and attributes were solid. He had a wide range of experience spanning from the grassroots to the top management of two coastal provinces, Fujian, and Zhejiang. In temperament, Xi was not arrogant and extravagant like the *gaoganzidi*. His personal networks had little to do either with the *tuanpai* or the Shanghai Gang. The fact that he was the son of Xi Zhongxun, a founder of the PRC persecuted during the Cultural Revolution, an architect of the opening policy, and a leader close to Deng Xiaoping and Hu Yaobang, also helped.[42] But above all, the key determinant was a perception that Xi was a staunch Leninist best placed to ensure the survival the Party.

The Apex of Power: Politburo Standing Committee

Full members of the newly elected CC, including returning members and neophytes, who were elected on October 21, in turn "elected" the Politburo and its standing committee the next day at the First Plenum of the Seventeenth Party Congress. The candidates were not required to campaign, make speeches, or articulate policy platforms, since the election outcome had been largely predetermined. Unlike election to the CC, where there were 8.3 percent more candidates than positions, there was no chance of losing election to the PBSC (the numbers of candidates and positions are identical), despite talk about adopting such a margin by following the Vietnamese model. In general, advancement into the PBSC is a function of balancing, political contestation, institutional norms and conventions, perceptions of loyalty, reliability, past job records, and connections. However, because of a fixation on rejuvenating the CCP to make it a more effective organization for governance, age had become one of the most important determinants for leadership change.

Prior to the Seventeenth Party Congress virtually all members of the PBSC, Politburo, and Secretariat were in their sixties or seventies, and the average ages of the members of these organizations were sixty-seven, sixty-six, and sixty-five, respectively. Four out of nine PBSC members were expected to retire, and nine out of fifteen remaining Politburo members were expected to be promoted or retired. Likewise, 68 percent of the 356 full and alternate members (and 88 percent of the full members) of the CC were over sixty years old.[43] Once again, the informal retirement age (or cutoff age), which had been set at sixty-eight at the Sixteenth Party Congress, was reapplied at the Seventeenth. Accordingly, Hu Jintao (sixty-five), Wu Bangguo (sixty-six), Jia Qinglin (sixty-seven), Wen Jiabao (sixty-five), and Li Changchun (sixty-three) retained their membership. As expected, Hu Jintao was re-elected general secretary, and Wen Jiabao retained his PBSC seat. Three PBSC members who were born in the 1930s retired—Luo Gan (seventy-two), Wu Guanzheng (sixty-nine), and Zeng Qinghong (sixty-eight) (see Table 8.1). Rejuvenation was a CCP goal, but the strict application of age limits at the top with a staggered scale extending down the administrative ladder was a political issue for those who regarded "rejuvenation" as excessive.[44] There were rumblings among those who felt that strict retirement age limits had harmed their careers.

Before the congress the Politburo complement was compromised by the loss of one PBSC member and one full member—Huang Ju died in June 2007 and Chen Liangyu was dismissed from the Party for corruption in the Shanghai social insurance scandal. These losses deprived the Politburo of members who could have served one more term and two more terms, respectively. The expansion of the PBSC from seven to nine members in 2002 has often been explained as a Jiang Zemin power play to perpetuate his influence and to balance off the new general secretary's power—when Jiang Zemin retired at the Sixteenth Party Congress, he inserted two of his associates into the expanded PBSC, which opened up two slots in the Politburo that were filled again by his cronies, with a net gain of four members for Jiang.[45] Be that as it may, the expanded PBSC provided the opportunity to enlarge the division of power and increase flexibility within a tiny oligarchy. The PBSC had to accept four newcomers. Among these, He Guoqiang (director of the Organizational Department) and Zhou Yongkang (minister of public security) were advanced normally one step from full Politburo membership into the PBSC. However, Xi Jinping (Shanghai party secretary) and Li Keqiang (Liaoning party secretary), who had no Politburo experience, were airlifted from the CC, skipping two steps, into the PBSC.[46]

This unusual practice is what Chinese call "promotion by breaking the rules of orderly progression" (*poge tisheng*). In a status-conscious leadership, this betrays expediency, perhaps even desperation, because of a perceived lack of candidates with the right age, qualifications, and experience. This was made clear at the Eighteenth Party Congress in 2012, when seven out of the nine PBSC members had to be retired. Xi Jinping and Li Keqiang were the only two young enough to stay on for one more term at the Nineteenth Party Congress of 2017 if the retirement age held.

Dual Successors, Dual Tracks

At the first plenum (October 2007), Xi Jinping was assigned the protocol ranking number six in the PBSC. He was appointed executive secretary of the Secretariat and president of the Central Party School, and soon after was named chair of the Central Party Building Leading Small Group (LSG; Hu did that from 1992 to 2002), the Hong Kong and Macau Affairs Leading Small Group, and deputy chair of the Foreign Affairs Leading Small Group. His responsibilities to assist Hu Jintao in party and foreign affairs were clear. Before the end of the year he was also made chair of the Central Olympics Liaison Small Group in charge of the upcoming Olympics in Beijing. At the March 2008 National People's Congress Xi was appointed PRC vice president, taking over from the outgoing political heavyweight Zeng Qinghong. The implicit expectation was that, barring any eventualities, Xi Jinping, the heir presumptive, would succeed Hu Jintao as general secretary. At age 59, he would still be eligible for two five-year terms before normal retirement. In many ways Xi's accent to the PBSC paralleled that of Hu Jintao. At the Fourteenth Party Congress of 1992, Hu was plucked from the CC (and recalled from his formal post in Tibet) directly into the PBSC, skipping three steps as an emergency measure to rejuvenate the gerontocracy.[47] Anointed by Deng Xiaoping as the transcentury successor who was relatively young, he was appointed executive secretary of the Secretariat (1992) and president of the

Central Party School in December 1992. In 1998 Hu was made vice president to give him international visibility and was made vice chair of the CMC at the Fifth Plenum in 2010. Hu's succession as general secretary thus took a full decade to complete. Similarly, Xi's job assignments and activities following the congress suggested that he was tipped to take over as general secretary, most likely as a result of a tacit internal understanding rather than a formal one. However, mindful of the vicissitudes in the fate of heirs apparent in PRC history, the CCP in the post-Deng period no longer officially declares anyone as such in order to keep up a facade of elections and to head off charges of leaders picking their successors. But Xi was now on an accelerated track with his grooming compressed into only five years.

As deputy of the Party Building LSG, Xi directed the Party's eighteen-month campaign to study the "scientific development concept" that began in September 2008. Xi also delivered the keynote speech marking the CCP's eighty-eighth anniversary on June 30, 2008. To give him international exposure, Xi took three high-profile state visits: the first one in June 2008 to Pyongyang, where he met Kim Jong Il, and to Mongolia, Saudi Arabia, Qatar, and Yemen; the second in February 2009 to visit Mexico, Jamaica, Columbia, Venezuela, Brazil, Malta, and Fiji; and a third one to visit Belgium, Germany, Bulgaria, Hungary, and Romania. However, if Xi faltered for any reason, shown some perceived incompetency, or exhibited poor health, things might have changed.

Li Keqiang, on the other hand, was groomed for the premier track. Assigned a protocol rank of number seven on the nine-member PBSC, Li was widely regarded as a protégé of Hu Jintao, with a long personal working relationship between them in the CYL. For this reason, he was assumed by many China watchers to be Hu's first choice for general secretary. Li's heading of China's largest agricultural province, Henan, and the important industrial province of Liaoning were regarded as his most important assets. Like Xi, he was elevated two steps, from the CC directly to PBSC in 2007. After his appointment as Wen Jiabao's deputy in the Finance and Economic LSG, he was put in charge of the formation of five superministries.[48] Elected executive vice premier at the Eleventh NPeC in March 2008, Li was put in charge of the State Council and government and of economic issues, assisting Premier Wen Jiabao. Indeed, Hu and Wen were able to ask PBSC members to take on special tasks outside of their special field of division of responsibility in the PBSC. Li stayed in the latter position until 2013, assisting Premier Wen in economic development, government budgets, land and resources, the environment, and health, while simultaneously being trained for the future premiership.[49] As scheduled, Li succeeded Wen Jiabao as premier. Nevertheless, even after 2018, after Li had worked and cooperated with Xi for a decade, many factional analysts still regarded Li a staunch member of the *tuanpai*, fueling persistent rumors that Xi wanted to get rid of Li.

Xi Jinping Competes with Li Keqiang?

In a 2007 analysis, Cheng Li argues that the intention of picking both Xi Jinping and Li Keqiang was for them to compete with one another in order to introduce some dynamics into elite politics, making it more open. This is a difficult strategy, Li Cheng maintained, because it may well spin out of control and get ugly if social forces were invited to choose between these two leaders who clearly represent conflicting interests.[50] Similarly, Fewsmith also says that Xi and Li were promoted to positions "from which they may compete as successors to Hu Jintao."[51] This line of reasoning is unconvincing.

First, organizationally, as discussed, Xi and Li were promoted into two clearly well-defined tracks at the Seventeenth Party Congress, and subsequent job assignments at the NPeC reinforced this interpretation. The division of labor between the two was clear: Xi Jinping was fed into a party affairs track and Li into a state premier track. As mentioned, the airlifting of both into the PBSC was a matter of expediency, and time was extremely limited for the apprentices to make connections and to establish their authority over the next five years.

Second, the encouragement of competition would have been too disruptive, destabilizing, and unpredictable for the CCP, and it would not serve the overwhelming concern for stability and orderly succession. It is not the style of the cautious Hu Jintao and the CCP to leave a dangling loose end after the grand exercise of the national party congress in 2007. An encouragement for two competitors to fight for the top post was inconsistent with the party discipline of democratic centralism and would encourage others as well to jostle for the top job, in addition to struggling for the remaining Politburo positions. Further, any sort of upset to the strict hierarchical ranking structure of the CCP would be destabilizing.

Third, the pattern of these appointments replicated the precedent of Hu Jintao's own appointment as general secretary, and it can be strongly inferred that Xi was the one intended by the Party to be groomed as successor to Hu Jintao.[52] As we can see in the following, the nature, protocol, and style of Xi's assigned official responsibilities since his assumption as number six in the Politburo also supports this point, which is benefited by hindsight. In the next five years, the CCP continued to groom him and to establish his authority, a subject we will turn to later. As executive secretary of the Secretariat and chair of the Central Party Building LSG, he assisted Hu in running the day-to-day affairs of the party apparatus. In the same capacity he presented the list of Politburo nominations for leading NPeC and State Council positions at the February 2008 Second Plenum, which preceded the Eleventh NPC convened in March.

In any case, with the infusion of this younger blood, the average age of the PBSC was lowered to 62.3 years, or down 4.8 years from the Sixteenth Party

Congress at sixty-seven. This left an age span of fifteen years among the PBSC members—the youngest, Li Keqiang, at age fifty-two, was six years younger than the youngest PBSC member, Li Changchun, on the previous PBSC.

All PBSC members possessed postsecondary degrees, and for the first time high intellectuals (*gaozhi*) with PhDs were also included. In contrast with the Sixteenth PBSC, whose members were uniformly engineers with but one geologist, the new PBSC contained members with more varied and diversified educational backgrounds—seven out of nine had humanities and social sciences backgrounds in such subjects as law, politics, economics, management, and philosophy, including four PhDs and one master's degree. As pointed out by David Shambaugh, a PBSC with such a diverse background may approach policy-making with a more holistic manner, whereas engineers are, by their training, more incremental in their problem-solving.[53] Be that as it may, the education of Chinese leaders should be viewed in context. As pointed out by Li Cheng, most of these degrees were obtained part-time and on the job, and often from party schools. For instance, one can obtain a degree in politics and law without ever studying law.[54] Even decades after the Cultural Revolution, the standard for university education tends to be low, and the fields of humanities and social sciences were still dominated by ideology.

At a brief press conference of the new PBSC, Hu introduced Xi and Li at ages fifty-four and fifty-two as relatively younger leaders, as if age, not other qualifications or background experiences, was the most important issue. Consistent with past practices, public appearance gave no indication of the new leaders' policy orientation and preference, and they appeared mysterious to those outside the elite circle. The new stars avoided media questions and gave no speeches. In response to media queries about the Shanghai corruption scandal, Xi let his aides answer the questions. Even propaganda about their professional background was terse. Discretion was the norm, especially with the media, as newcomers must show no trace of ambition. This makes sense and is fully understandable since succession is based on negotiations and alliances, and the benefits needed to be balanced and the face of all sides to be maintained.

The New Politburo

As mentioned, the anticorruption purge had deprived the Politburo of one possible leader in Chen Liangyu, who, by virtue of his age and position, potentially could have served two more terms. Overall, nine outgoing Politburo members were not re-elected (one died, one was dismissed, and seven had reached the retirement age of sixty-eight). Altogether there were nine newcomers (including Xi Jinping and Li Keqiang, accounting for 36 percent of the Politburo) (see Table 8.1). The average age was sixty-two, and this compares with an average age of sixty for the Sixteenth Politburo and sixty-three at the Fifteenth. Many members were eligible to serve one more term, but only three (apart from Xi Jinping and Li Keqiang) could serve two more terms. They were Liu Yunshan (sixty), Zhang Dejiang (sixty-one), and Yu Zhengsheng (sixty-two).

In terms of origins, background, and past work experiences, there was overall a rough balance between those from the regions, central government, and the military in the Politburo. Many, ten out of twenty-five, were drawn from provinces—from Beijing (both municipal party secretary and mayor), Shanghai, Tianjin, Chongqing, Liaoning, Jiangsu, Xinjiang, Hubei, and Guangdong. The rest hailed from senior party postings and the State Council—Wang Gang (Work Committee of Departments under the CCP CC, Confidential Committee and Security Administration of the CCP CC), Wang Zhaoguo (chair of the All-China Federation of Trade Unions), Hui Liangyu (vice premier, State Council), Liu Yunshan (director, Propaganda Department), Liu Yandong (United Front Work Department), and Bo Xilai (minister of commerce). Two representatives from the military—Guo Boxiong re-elected and Xu Caihou a newcomer—were included by following the pattern of the Sixteenth Party Congress, but none was placed in the PBSC. There was only one woman, Liu Yandong, in the male-dominated Politburo, and one person from a non-Han ethnic minority, the Muslim Hui Liangyu.

The division of labor and the assignment of portfolios were carried out according to expertise and experience, and there was a great deal of continuity. Appointments also reflected an obsession with organization and control. For instance, five out of nine PBSC members were made responsible for organization, propaganda, discipline, and public security. And, as Li Cheng pointed out, despite the importance of the economy, only four PBSC members, President Hu, Premier Wen, Vice President Xi Jinping, and Executive Vice Premier Li Keqiang, were partially or primarily responsible for economic affairs. Among the other sixteen full members of the Politburo, only three were economic decision-makers, whereas six still served as provincial chiefs, and two others oversaw the military.[55] The new Politburo broke with tradition by having no alternate members. My supposition is that elimination of this one unnecessary step was designed to make future fast-track promotions (*poke tisheng*) look less stark or drastic.

Institutionalization of the Chinese Political System and Political Succession?

The conclusion of the Seventeenth Party Congress has generated many reflections on the nature of the Chinese political system that have deepened our understanding of the subject. However, there are also healthy disagreements, and the issue of institutionalization is a good example. In two party congresses the CCP had convened regular party and government meetings and observed institutional rules such as term and age limits for party and state officials. This fact has often been cited as evidence to demonstrate a "more thoroughly institutionalized leadership system," and the transfer of power from Jiang Zemin to Hu Jintao is said to be "a significant step toward the institutionalization of China's politics."[56] Similarly, Jing Huang also argues that the Jiang-Hu transition has contributed to the "growing institutionalization of the political process" and political succession.[57] But this conclusion may be premature.

Three points merit attention. First, the institutionalization of certain aspects of leadership succession is different from the institutionalization of the political system as a whole. The Seventeenth Party Congress had shown that the CCP had accepted certain institutional rules and norms, formal or informal, in political succession that enabled an orderly and deliberate transfer of power. The age sixty-eight retirement norm and two-term limits were observed. Observation also shows that the deliberate grooming of Xi and Li as future successors went smoothly. Second, like many concepts in political science, the notion of political institutionalization is a contested one. Some scholars equate it with democratic-style, multiparty elections and the rule of law, whereas others argue that good governance, nation-building, and self-strengthening by an adaptable leadership are more important aspects of political development.[58] Huntington, on the other hand, defines institutionalization as "a process by which organizations and procedures acquire value and stability," and the level of institutionalization is defined by the "adaptability, complexity, autonomy, and coherence of its organizations and procedures." Leninist parties, in his view, are more adept in dealing with the challenges of modernization and institutionalization.[59]

Third, one appropriate way of measuring political institutionalization is to hold it according to the CCP's manifested values, rules, and procedures as enumerated in the PRC and party constitutions, which include the guarantee of elections; extensive rights for the citizens; freedoms of association, assembly, and religion; and the independence of the judiciary. Here there is a great deal of disparity between theory and practice. The party constitution requires that the Politburo and its Standing Committee are to be directly elected by the CC, but in fact the practice is essentially the opposite. The job-slot system also belies the fact that the Politburo (or for that matter, the CC) was elected because in fact its membership was simply apportioned according to principal bureaucratic and functional interests, or to what the CCP deemed most central to its continued rule, such as ideological control[60] and propaganda. And of course, free and open elections according to the rules set out in the PRC's party and state constitutions would also permit the interplay of informal politics and competition among various interests, but the personnel outcome would, ironically, be more unpredictable. The state constitution also prescribes that the judiciary should be independent. But the judiciary is not only totally subjected to the CCP; it is also accorded very low representation within the party hierarchy. Age and term limits were written into the state constitution, but the CCP has never enshrined these principles in the party constitution. Very little constrains the Politburo oligarchy from changing the job-slot system as it sees fit, so as, for example, to include a public security apparatus or to relax age and term limits according to expediencies. In fact, as we shall see later, the definition of the powers of leaders remain fluid, and age and term limits for the president and vice president were abolished in 2018. In this way, the view that institutionalization in China has in fact been "retarded, uneven and reversible"[61] is closer to the mark. And if institutionalization is viewed as a process, certain norms and procedures are rather institutionalized in Chinese politics whereas others are not. That said, developing countries often must contend with weak institutions since political institutionalization is a lengthy process and institutions must be built from the bottom up. Institution-building efforts by the CCP, such as Xi's efforts to institutionalize corruption control and the functioning of the judiciary, will be discussed later. Overall, even in developed countries political institutionalization is an ongoing process when rules, values, and procedures have become outdated and dysfunctional.[62]

Xi Jinping and the "One Party, Two Coalitions" Thesis: A Critique

Another influential interpretation of Chinese politics is Cheng Li's "one party, two coalitions" thesis, which he has articulated in many publications since 2008. Although the notion has evolved over time, his core assumptions remain intact. A detailed examination of policymaking in China casts serious doubt on the validity of such a formulation. According to Cheng Li, elite politics since the Sixteenth Party Congress was dominated by two coalitions competing for power, influence, and policy preferences. These cooperating coalitions consist of members with two distinct socioeconomic and political backgrounds and geographical regions, as well as distinctive policy initiatives and priorities, although they are complementary to each other in leadership skills and areas of expertise. The "elite coalition" is said to be led by former Party bosses Jiang Zemin and Zeng Qinghong and increasingly by Xi Jinping (assumed to be a protégé of Jiang Zemin), the princelings, and the Shanghai Gang, as well as by entrepreneurs, returnees, foreign-educated Chinese nationals, and urban leaders from coastal regions and major cities. Members of this group are said to share an elite political identity as a "red nobility," and nepotism has ensured rapid promotions in their political careers. Economically, they tend to be liberals supportive of market reforms, efficiency, rapid economic growth, and coastal development. They represent the interests of the entrepreneurs and the middle class and are less concerned with the environment. Politically they are conservatives, especially in matters such as media control and intraparty elections. Generally, this "elite coalition" controls the economic administration, foreign trade and finance, foreign affairs, education, science and technology, military affairs, and public security. Since Xi became general secretary, it is claimed that this coalition has expanded to include the "Shaanxi Gang" as well as Xi's other regional-based political networks in Fujian and Zhejiang.

In stark contrast, the so-called populist coalition is said to be led by Hu Jintao and Wen Jiabao and consists mainly of *tuanpai* officials, that is, those who have "advanced their careers" or "risen through the ranks" of the CYL. Since the CYL is a sprawling organization (membership was seventy-four million in 2006) consisting of the central and numerous regional branches, Li later defined *tuanpai* officials more narrowly as those who had worked at senior levels of the CYL (municipal/prefecture, provincial, and ministerial level or above) between 1982 and 1998, during which time they worked closely with *tuanpai* leaders such as Hu Jintao, Song Defu, and Li Keqiang. This coalition is said to incorporate party functionaries, propaganda organizations, the United Front Work Department, new left intellectuals (critical of market transition and reform and economic liberalization), as well as rural leaders and provincial leaders from inland provinces (except Shaanxi). Members are said to usually be from humble family backgrounds with career experiences at poor inland provinces, who have started from the grassroots and advanced their careers step by step. Supporters of this coalition are said to come from geographically based cliques at inland provinces other than, again, Shaanxi. As such, these members are said to have been socialized with a "people first" policy preference of economic equality, social justice, and more balanced regional development. They allegedly tend to represent the needs of the "common people" as well as such vulnerable social groups as farmers, migrant workers, and the urban poor. In general, this "populist coalition" is claimed to control party organization, propaganda, united-front work, law, party discipline, and provincial leadership.[63]

Referring to the Seventeenth Party Congress in 2007, Cheng Li argues that Li Keqiang and Xi Jinping became the chief representatives of the "populist" and "elitist" coalitions, respectively. Because Li Keqiang hails from a humble family background and advanced his career through the CYL, Hu Jintao's power base, he has been more oriented toward the poor and dispossessed. He has presented himself as a populist and worked in inland provinces and Liaoning. Therefore, Li would likely emphasize policies relating to income distribution and social justice, especially issues in employment, the establishment of a safety net, and public healthcare. On the other hand, according to Li Cheng, "elitist coalition" stalwart Xi Jinping, because of his princeling background, advanced his career by working in the coastal areas of Fujian, Zhejiang, and Shanghai. Therefore, his "elitist" proclivities have represented the interests of entrepreneurs, the emerging middle class, and the rich and the powerful. Xi would most likely continue to accelerate market reforms and efficiency and maintain good relations with foreign countries while trying to resolve problems relating to foreign trade and foreign investment.[64]

Cheng Li has extended his thesis to explain policy changes from the Sixteenth through to the Nineteenth Party Congresses, although this grand thesis has become increasingly unsatisfactory in view of available evidence. While Cheng Li's bold views identify some of the sociopolitical fault lines along which the leadership can be divided, his assumed "coalitions" are made up of competing groups with distinct class backgrounds, careers, values, and policy orientations. These alliances do not approximate the true factions within, to cite a prime example, the Japanese Liberal Democratic Party is officially divided into factions that have their own patrons, offices, budgets, and campaign machines designed to win elections. In order for the party to work as an organization, each faction is given some perks and benefits in terms of top positions and policy input, a state called *habatsu kinko* (factional balance). The CCP formally bans factions but Cheng Li's groups seem to operate overtly and are permanent groupings, notwithstanding the fact that the term "coalition" often denotes temporary alliances. Overall, many of Cheng Li's observations are only hypotheses awaiting empirical testing, particularly his whole range of views about Xi Jinping, which cannot be substantiated by what we have observed about his political career in the previous chapters. As has been shown, although Xi was born in relative privilege, his childhood and adolescence experiences (from age nine to twenty-two) were traumatic, as he was among the many persecuted during the tumult of the Cultural Revolution, losing the opportunity for secondary school education. He then suffered the trauma of toiling in the poorest part of China as a peasant and had to struggle to ascend the bureaucratic ladder. As an official in many poverty-stricken places, from Zhengding to Xiamen, and from Fuzhou to Zhejiang, he had to deal with a wide range of basic governance issues, most of which concerned poverty and underdevelopment. It is unclear how all this would have shaped his "elitist" proclivities as described. Even at relatively prosperous Zhejiang, Xi had to rejig the developmental model and state/market relationships to transform a traditional market into a more modern one, while simultaneously dealing with issues such as rural/urban and regional inequalities, unfair income distribution, pollution, and the like. In this book's next chapter on Xi's governance record between 2007 and 2012, I suggest that the difference between Xi and Li can best be understood by their respective division of labor—Xi put in charge of party affairs and Li of state affairs. As we will discuss in chapters 9 to 13, on his first term as general secretary, Xi was in both words and deeds to spend a great deal of his energy tackling a full range of developmental issues that did not necessarily prioritize market reform, efficiency, rapid economic growth, and entrepreneurial interests, as predicted by the "elite coalitions" preferences. In fact, Xi focused a great deal of his efforts on such issues as poverty reduction, social justice, and environmental improvement.

A comparative review of the life and career experiences of Xi Jinping and Li Keqiang also does not support many of the assumptions of the "one party, two coalitions" thesis (see Table 6.1). Both Xi and Li were sent-down *zhiqing* who toiled at the grassroots for seven and four years, respectively. Unlike the more "privileged" Xi, Li did not suffer the impact of persecution and family break-down during the Cultural Revolution. Nor was Li deprived of a secondary school education. Xi did gain an advantage as a princeling to land a job with the CMC, but he felt obliged to abandon it in favor of a hardship post in impoverished Zhengding. Eventually, both advanced step by step up the administrative ladder. All the provinces they worked in were poor, with Zhejiang slightly more developed than the others. In both words and deeds, both Xi and Li tackled poverty and underdevelopment as one of their core priorities. The notion that their birth background and career paths imparted "elitist" or "populist" policy biases into the two of them cannot be supported. Furthermore, by 2017, Xi and Li had already worked closely together for a decade, and while such working relations may have highs and lows, to still consider them rivals aiming at eliminating one another primarily because of Li's stint with the CYL and his association with Hu Jintao is untenable. Moreover, Hu Jintao also had worked with Xi for five years, helping to groom him as the future general secretary. In short, we are unable to substantiate the "one party, two coalitions" thesis.

A few other observations are in order. First, communist leaders, including those leading the CCP, with similar family origins, ages, and backgrounds can support very different policies and are known to change their political affiliations as needed. It is unclear how and why career backgrounds and attributes would translate directly into permanent factional loyalties subscribing to particular policy preferences and priorities. People change according to circumstances and may develop widely differing mindsets even with virtually identical past experiences.[65] Leaders' affiliations derive from various situational and contextual factors and are clearly capable of evolving. Many of the so-called *tuanpai* leaders have worked at the CYL at the early and middle stages of their careers, either in the regions or at the center, and it is unsure why this particular experience would have left an indelible mark on their connections and policy inclinations for life. Before they were moved into the Politburo they had to work in other capacities for many years and at more senior positions than their CYL stint, and their positions elsewhere as secretaries of PPC were more critical. This is

Table 6.1 The Political Careers of *Tuanpai* Leaders Hu Jintao, Li Keqiang, and Wang Yang in Comparison with That of Xi Jinping

	Year and place of birth; year joined CCP	Family background and youth experience	Education	Early political career	Later political career			
Hu Jintao	1942, Jixi County, Anhui (1964)	Son of a former tea merchant; poor family; worker and technician; father denounced during the Cultural Revolution	Undergraduate & graduate studies, water conservancy engineering, Tsinghua University, 1959–64, 1964–65	R & D, water conservatory engineering, Tsinghua University, political instructor, 1965–68; various positions, Ministry of Water Conversancy, 1968–74	First secretary, CCYL, 1984–85; secretary, CCYL CC, Secretariat 1982–84; secretary, CCYL, Gansu	Secretary, Guizhou PPC, 1985–88	Secretary, Tibet Autonomous Region, 1988–92	PBSC member, 1992–2002; vice president, 1998–2003; vice chair, CMC, 1999–2002	General secretary, 2002–12; vice chair, CMC, 2002–5; chair, CMC, 2005–13
Li Keqiang	1955, Anhui (1976)	Sent-down youth, 1974–76; Party secretary of production brigade, 1976–78	BA in law, 1982; PhD in economics, 1994, Peking University	Various positions in the CYL, incl. positions in the CCYL Secretariat, 1982–98	Governor of Henan, 1998–2003; deputy secretary Henan PPC, 1998–2002	Secretary, Henan PPC, 2002–4	Secretary, Liaoning PPC, 2004–7	PBSC member, 2007–12, executive premier, 2008–13	PBSC member & premier, 2012–17

Continued

Table 6.1 Continued

	Year and place of birth; year joined CCP	Family background and youth experience	Education	Early political career	Later political career				
Wang Yang	1955, Suzhou County, Anhui (1975)	Humble family; manual laborer starting at age seventeen	Degree in public administration, 1979–80; master's in management, University of Science & Technology, 1993–95	Various positions in the regional CYL, 1981–84	Various positions at Anhui and Tongling city, 1984–92	Vice governor, Anhui, 1993–99; member, NDRC, 1999–2003; Deputy Secretary General, State Council, 2003–5	Secretary, Chongqing PPC, 2005–7	Secretary, Guangdong PPC, 2007–12	Member, Politburo, 2012–17; vice premier, 2013–17
Xi Jinping	1953, Fuping County, Shaanxi (1974)	Princeling, sent-down youth, 1969–75; village branch secretary	PhD, part-time, Marxist theory and political education, Tsinghua University, 1998–2002; chemical engineering, Tsinghua University, 1975–79	General Office, CMC, 1979–82	Secretary, Zhengding County PC, 1983–85; executive vice mayor, Xiamen, 1985–88; secretary, Ningde Prefectural PC, 1988–90	Secretary Fuzhou MPC, 1990–96; deputy secretary, Fujian PPC, 1995–2002; governor, Fujian, 2000–2002	Secretary, Shanghai MPC, 2007; secretary, Zhejiang PPC, 2002–7	PBSC member, vice president, 2007–12	General secretary & PBSC member 2012–17

Source: China vitae and Baidu baike.

particularly the case since work experience even at the highest level of the CYL, unlike provincial-level work, has never been a springboard to the Politburo.

Second, a closer examination of the attributes, education, work experience, career advancement patterns, and family backgrounds of the leaders shows that they are crisscrossing, overlapping, and in no way mutually exclusive. For example, many who advanced up the succession ladder through the CYL were princelings, and most members of the fifth generation, princelings or otherwise, shared many formative life experiences (as Cheng Li acknowledges).[66] They endured hard labor and re-education by the peasants in the rural areas during the Cultural Revolution. Like many who aspired to party membership, Xi joined the CYL as an ordinary member to advance his career. Li Keqiang has often been cited as in favor of market reforms, but Xi had also advanced his career in coastal areas of Fujian and Zhejiang and had to cope with the issues of reordering the relationship between the state and the market.

Third, new circumstances and new working relations can also change things. Patrons come and go, and clients can employ strategies of bandwagoning and betrayal to further their careers. A most obvious example is that of the powerful and skillful princeling Zeng Qinghong, who was always regarded as Jiang Zemin's man but apparently served Hu Jintao loyally. By the end of 2017, Xi and Li had already worked together and cooperated for ten years, and Jiang Zemin and Hu Jintao, alleged heads of the "elitist" and "populist" coalitions, had long since retired. There is little to suggest that Xi and Li are now the new heads of such "coalitions."

Fourth, a surer litmus test of whether the main cleavage at the top was based on two competing coalitions is to have case studies of policymaking on specific issues, but that would require further research. Yet no evidence exists whatsoever to demonstrate that such coalitions with unified policy preferences and interests ever actually existed during Hu Jintao's first term or at the Seventeenth Party Congress.

A quick review, as in Table 6.1, of the political careers of the three so-called major *tuanpai* heavyweights shows that the notion of their identity and loyalty to the CYL appears overdrawn. It is plausible that Chinese leaders who have worked in the CYL might share a certain mindset, some organizational solidarity, and even loyalty because of patron-client relationships of mutual support and reciprocity. Hu Jintao might even have preferred to promote leaders who had worked with him in the CCYL (Central Communist Youth League), but it is unclear why the relatively short stint of their CCYL careers would have branded them for life as if it was something immutable. One expects that these leaders would continue their networking and connections building as a continuous process throughout their careers. Xi has clearly cultivated ties and connections in places such as Fujian, Zhejiang, Shanghai, and even Shaanxi, as Cheng Li rightly acknowledges, but it is unclear why *tuanpai* leaders' interests in networking would have been arrested at the CCYL stage. Further, provincial leadership, not CCYL work experience, is the key springboard to national leadership, and all these *tuanpai* leaders were propelled onto the national leadership by virtue of their provincial experiences. Hu Jintao, often branded the head honcho of the *tuanpai*, was a worker and technician with no grassroots administration experience who actually worked primarily with the central CYL for three years, from 1982 to 1985. He then became party chief of the poor provinces Guizhou and Tibet (always regarded as great assets) for a total of seven years before being handpicked by Deng Xiaoping to "helicopter" (skipping two steps) into the PBSC. On the other hand, Li Keqiang spent about a decade in the CCYL from 1982 to 1998, taking six years off to complete his masters and PhD in economics. He then devoted seven and three years, respectively, as Henan and Liaoning party chief before entering the PBSC (2007–2012) as executive premier. Correspondingly, Wang Yang worked in the regional Anhui CYL for three years and then spent another twenty years at the center and provinces before entering the Politburo. In other words, the varied experiences of governing huge provinces with the full range of issues of poverty and underdevelopment, rather than their early-career stint in a youth organization concerned with political recruitment and socialization, are likely the determinants of their evolving identity and orientations. Finally, as China develops, CYL careers in "youth work" have increasingly been regarded as safe , undemanding, and insufficiently challenging for higher-level posts. Promotion within the CYL is regarded as easy, as the organization never handles more weighty issues involving the allocation of personnel and financial resources.[67]

Overall, dichotomous categories seldom can account for the complexity of elite Chinese politics. They are best viewed as ideal types or heuristic devices, since in reality, leaders can and do move between categories. Changes in contextual, situation, and contingent factors must be considered. In the past, politics under Mao were interpreted by a two-line struggle approach that depicts oscillation between two diametrically opposed policy programs and orientations, but as Andrew Nathan has argued in a critique, the options and range of choices in each policy area are always more than two; they are so multiple and complex that they are akin to an array of dials on which fine tuning and different combinations by leaders are always possible.[68] As to the leadership after the Seventeenth Party Congress, the emergence of the fifth-generation leaders who shared a common formative life experience is probably a more remarkable aspect of Chinese elite politics, and we turn to this in the following.

The Emergence of the Fifth (Lost) Generation Leaders

As mentioned, the "fifth" or "lost" generation of Chinese youth born in the 1950s went through many common life experiences of socialization, exile, hard work, and lost educational opportunity. The emergence of a "fifth (lost) generation" of leaders who ran the country for a decade or so was one significant outcome of the

Seventeenth Party Congress. Five years later, in the Eighteenth Politburo (2012–2017), eleven members can be counted as belonging to the fifth generation, and six of these were sent-down youths. At ages fifty-five to sixty-two, they took over the apex of power, forming a unique cohort of leaders with life experiences that will be difficult to replicate. The younger ones among them could serve two or more five-year terms in the party state. In the Nineteenth Politburo, fifth-generation leaders predominated (see Tables 8.1 and 12.5).

Generational analysis is often dependent on subjective criteria, and the notion of the "fifth generation" is not featured in the official Chinese communist lexicon. However, fifth-generation leaders were becoming increasing dominant in the military as well, and this was dubbed the "4968" phenomenon. Because of a strict retirement age limit and a stringent level-by-level promotion schema, especially at the highest reaches of the military, the ten lieutenant generals who were recruited into the Seventeenth CC were treated as tomorrow's stars. These ten were born after 1949, joined the military in about 1968, and had been promoted to positions above the military region level. Subsequently, they were being groomed to become senior generals. Commentators back in 2007 claimed that these officers were tested by the events of the Cultural Revolution and the reform period. Although these officers lacked combat experience, they were nevertheless educated in contemporary military techniques such as informational warfare, and their promotion prospects were bright.[69] As we shall see, this age cohort did take over the military high command by 2018.

Generally, fifth-generation leaders tend to share similar formative adolescent experience that can leave a profound impact on their character and mindset. Having been socialized with the Maoist ideals of hard work, frugality, and struggle, they may harbor a certain appreciation and empathy with lives in the rural hinterland. They had suffered serious hardship and survived, and it is reasonable to assume that they still suffer the psychological effects of their ordeal, that they possess strong personal qualities of adaptability and perseverance.[70] Beyond this, however, it would be unwise to speculate on the values, worldview, and policy inclinations of these leaders as if they are of the same mind, because in fact they are as much divided as the intelligentsia on such issues as democracy, the market economy, nationalism, and globalization.[71] Other factors, such as their most recent career and life experiences, may also loom large as intervening variables in affecting values and choices. Further, many of this cohort were activistic Red Guards, while others, like Xi, were not. Li Yuanchao, for instance, was a Red Guard "general," and Bo Xilai a radical Red Guard. Therefore, Li Cheng's suggestion that the fifth-generation leaders' training in law and politics per se may explain leaders' predilection for "strengthening the country's legal system"[72] may require more substantiation. Further, it is important to remember that the lasting impact of the Cultural Revolution in education remained throughout the 1980s (or longer) and the subjects in "social sciences" were dominated by ideological rhetoric. Political studies, in particular, had been more akin to a study of official ideology.

Similarly, the common observation that the fifth generation distinguishes itself from the previous one (comprised mostly of engineers and hence more technocratic) in its mindset because of its more diverse educational and occupational background must receive further scrutiny. Most fifth-generation leaders received their postgraduate education in the 1980s through part-time or correspondence study while serving as full-time party functionaries, not as apprentice political scientists or practicing junior lawyers. Those fifth-generation leaders who had studied abroad might bring with them a somewhat different mindset, but none of these were inducted into the Politburo until 2017.

In his study of 103 high-ranking fifth-generation leaders, Li Cheng argues that their common characteristics and formative experiences, such as their humble life experiences, hardship endured in the countryside, propensity to study abroad, and social sciences orientation in education, tend to induce in them values of "endurance, adaptability and humility," as well as an interest in learning and sound judgment.[73] Be that as it may, this line of analysis further contradicts his other major thesis, that the very same members in this cohort are now divided, because of their sociopolitical and geographical affiliations, into two polarizing coalitions, the elite and popular, at the apex of power.

Xi Jinping and Bo Xilai: Comparisons and Contrasts of Two Princelings

Among the princelings, both Xi Jinping and Bo Xilai were once considered for the very top, and in many ways their backgrounds and life experiences are almost mirror images of one another.[74] (Biographical sketches for Xi and Bo are in Table 6.1 and Table 6.2, respectively.) They have similar powerful family pedigrees and connections that have driven their political careers. Both belong to the fifth generation of Chinese leaders who were born around 1949, were the products of the new regime, and enjoyed privileged childhoods. Both suffered during the Cultural Revolution and received postsecondary education in the reform period, and their political careers took off in the 1980s. Both were rising stars cultivated and groomed for political succession, and their network of allies, connections, and patrons were similar—Jiang Zemin was said to be a patron of each at one time or the other. Yet their temperaments were very different, and while Xi has risen to the top, Bo has ended up in disgrace and ignominy.

Bo Xilai was a person of pedigree since his father, Bo Yibo, was an illustrious revolutionary hero and Mao's long-serving lieutenant who fought the Guomindang and the Japanese. After 1949, Bo Yibo was one of the PRC's most

Table 6.2 The Political Career of Bo Xilai

Year and place of birth; year joined CCP	Family background and youth experience	Education	Early political career	Later political career			
1949, Shanxi, Dingxiang County (1980)	Princeling; worker, 1972–78; labor camp, 1968–72; worker, hardware repair factory, Beijing No. 2 Light Industry Bureau, 1972–78	Graduate studies, journalism, Chinese Academy of Social Sciences, 1979–82; history, Peking University, 1978–79	Cadre, Research Office of the Secretariat & Party Central Office, 1982–84; secretary & deputy secretary, Jinxian CPC; secretary, Jinzhou Prefectural PC, 1984–88	Member of Liaoning PPC, Dalian MPC, deputy mayor and mayor, Dalian, 1988–2000; deputy secretary, Liaoning MPC, deputy governor, 2000–2001	Deputy secretary, Liaoning MPC, governor, 2001–4	Minister of Commerce, 2004–7	Politburo member; secretary, Chongqing MPC, 2007–12	Dismissed from the CCP, 2012; Sentenced to life imprisonment for bribery, corruption, & abuse of power, 2013

Source: China vitae and Baidu baike.

important planners, and served as minister of finance and vice premier. He also directed such campaigns as the Three-anti and Five-anti Campaigns in the 1950s. Like most veteran CCP officials, however, the elder Bo was persecuted ruthlessly during the Cultural Revolution by the Red Guards as a "revisionist traitor," being dragged to stadiums and factories for kangaroo trials and beatings. He subsequently languished in jail for twelve years. In the reform period he re-emerged as a conservative who favored a slower pace of change, and, working with Deng Xiaoping, he was regarded as one of the most influential "eight elders."[75] Allied with Deng, he had plotted the unlawful ouster of two general secretaries—liberal reformers Hu Yaobang and Zhao Ziyang—during the Tiananmen events of 1989. Hu Yaobang is the leader credited with the large-scale rehabilitation of purged and disgraced cadres, including Bo Yibo and Xi Zhongxun, after the Cultural Revolution, and because Bo turned on Hu, he is often regarded as a backstabber.

Variously described as handsome, suave, and flamboyant, Bo Xilai did possess prodigious charisma that set him apart from his more staid and reserved colleagues, Xi Jinping and Hu Jintao included. Born in the same year as the founding of the PRC, Bo enjoyed a relatively privileged childhood and studied, as did Xi, at the exclusive Beijing Number 4 High School. However, Bo was said to have had a more indulgent childhood, owning luxuries such as a wristwatch, a bicycle, and a radio. In 1967, as a militant Red Guard he was sent to a labor camp for five years. At the end of the Cultural Revolution, Bo made up for lost time and entered Peking University, China's most prestigious, to study history, graduating in 1979. At the age of thirty, he became a CCP member in 1980. After obtaining a master's degree in journalism from the Chinese Academy of Social Science in 1982, his career was set on a fast track, no doubt in part due to his connections and in part due to the Dengist policy of promoting intellectuals, especially the tiny cohort of university graduates. Like Xi, immediately after graduation Bo was recruited into the Party Center, and Bo became a staff member of the CC's General Office and Secretariat, and his career took off when he was made vice mayor and mayor of Dalian in 1989 and 1993, respectively.[76] In 1986, Bo married his second wife, Gu Kailai, a successful lawyer and also daughter of a prominent revolutionary.

Bo's penchant to bask in the limelight also distinguished him from the others. Adept at self-promotion, Bo cultivated this image carefully, often using the public purse strategically for that purpose. Bo's outsized and robust personality seemed a breath of fresh air in Chinese officialdom, endearing him to the media, especially that of the West.[77]

Privately, he was known to be abrasive and ruthless to perceived enemies, often inspiring fear, even among his princeling supporters. His subordinates perceived him to be a demanding and unforgiving boss who always had to have his way. One journalist describes the vainglorious side of him: in his enormous Dalian office, he would, with a press of a button, change the color of water fountains throughout the city or change the music playing in the streets.[78] Bo lived his life always in the fast lane and with excess.

As vice mayor and then mayor for Dalian (1989–2000) Bo showed his capable side, attracting domestic and foreign media attention as a rising political star. He largely succeeded in turning Dalian into the "most beautiful" city in China, and he masterminded a well-known fashion festival in that city, even though fashion was not a major industry there. Making use of the massive central investments to coastal cities, Bo rebuilt Dalian and turned it from a provincial backwater into a modern city "in the image of Hong Kong" that showcased China's economic boom. Flashy projects such as international fashion shows, beer festivals, and the founding of a soccer team (China's best) raised the city's (and Bo's) profile. Bo is four years older than Xi, but at the Fifteenth Party Congress, Bo was shut out of the CC, and Xi barely squeezed in as an alternate member. On the other hand, Bo was upfront in flattering Jiang Zemin—in 1997 a huge billboard portrait of Jiang Zemin was erected in Dalian's city center, the first locality to do so.

In 2001 Bo was made governor of Liaoning (2001 to 2004), presumably due in part to his father's influence. That December, Bo led a sixty-eight-hundred-member delegation to Shenzhen for Liaoning-Guangdong trade talks with foreign, Taiwanese, and Hong Kong business representatives,[79] a swaggering move that no other provincial governor dared to make. As governor he was officially subordinate to the various secretaries of the Liaoning PPC, but he paid scant attention to them. After serving as minister of commerce from 2004 to 2007 he entered the Politburo of the Seventeenth CC, although the death of his father in the same year might have affected his political ambition. He was transferred to become party chief of Chongqing, a bustling municipality with a population of thirty million. Despite his promotion into the Politburo, the transfer to Chongqing was widely seen as a kind of downgrade, as the Hu-Wen team seemed to be bent on removing him from the center of power. Apparently, Bo himself banked on his Chongqing record to bid for a position in the PBSC.

Key differences between Xi and Bo lie in their personalities, sentiments, and cultivated images. Xi has always exhibited and cultivated a staid and easygoing political style that is consistent with a particular ideal of leadership quality, what the Chinese call "hide your capability and bide your time." (See chapter 4.) This style of demeanor requires that leaders and leadership hopefuls be unassuming, deferential, respectful of elders, and not show any sign of ambition. Hu Jintao had perfected this style when he was heir apparent. In some respects an introvert, Xi may have consciously fostered the perception of him as a moderating force, and this may have broadened his appeal.

As we have observed, Xi tended to assume a doer's image when he served in the provinces of Fujian and Zhejiang. In contrast, Bo's popularity and conspicuous governance record may be regarded as an asset, but also raises suspicion and mistrust, and his feisty personality has been perceived as a potentially divisive force. As the Japanese saying goes, "The nail that sticks out gets hammered down," and Bo was probably too much of a highflier for the CCP culture of conformity, hierarchy, and Leninist collective leadership. Bo's transparent efforts to angle for high position drew a sense of uneasiness within the Party.

Yet, the introvert/extrovert, conciliatory/abrasive generalizations should not be overdrawn. These two persons are complicated personalities operating of necessity in response to tremendously complex situations. By 2002, the general perceptions of the images and personalities of Xi and Bo were already well formed. Both were regarded as energetic and able to stand their ground. Xi was regarded as more businesslike, uninterested in ostentatious display or the media limelight. Consistent with what we have described in the previous chapters, he was known to have spent a great deal of time visiting the rural grassroots and factories and showing care for the "vulnerable masses." He was said to be adept at cooperating with his peers and subordinates, treating them with respect, and did not flatter superiors such as Jiang Zemin. He was well liked by Politburo members such as Li Peng, Zhu Rongji, and Li Ruihuan, and had more in common with Hu Jintao and Wen Jiabao in the common touch. Zeng Qinghong treated both men about the same, but Jiang Zemin tended to favor Bo over Xi. In any case, Bo was out of the running for the PBSC because of his more advanced age, and his image of being a gregarious person and a showoff did not help things. However, both Xi and Bo shared one common trait—among the first-generation princelings the two stood out as the only ones who had worked their way step by step up from the grassroots. We will discuss the developments for the two in the next chapter.

7

The Trials of the Heir Apparent and Crisis Management, 2007–2012 (Age Fifty-Four to Fifty-Nine)

Building Authority

The many top official positions assigned to Xi, such as the vice presidency and LSG positions relating to party-building, were essentially the same ones conferred on Hu Jintao when Hu was leader-in-waiting. A pattern of leadership succession can be observed, although officially the CCP never formally acknowledged that Xi was a designated successor, given what had happened to previous leaders-in-waiting. Yet, the grooming process of Xi continued with increasing exposure domestically and internationally. Xi also began to build his authority by establishing his credentials and making connections, but his apprenticeship and probation were now condensed into five years, and he had to learn the ropes quickly. As vice president and the number six person in the Politburo, Xi was entrusted with many major tasks, some of which included potential crisis situations. He had to enforce the collective decisions of the Politburo, but there were also opportunities for personal initiative. One conventional view portrays Xi as another faceless bureaucrat, but in fact he gained confidence gradually and began to assert himself, in contrast with Hu Jintao's apprenticeship, which was marked more by anonymity and deference. Personally, Xi could bank on his princeling status, as well as his own experience and record. Nevertheless, he still had to fend off potential challenges to his succession within the Party.

At the same time, China was plunged into a series of unprecedented new challenges such as the Beijing Olympics of 2008 and the fateful, multiple-anniversary year of 2009, in addition to a host of perennial concerns such as economic growth, social stability, and the personnel changes and contests leading up to the Eighteenth Party Congress in 2012. A further volley of unanticipated challenges, including the global financial crisis and recession of 2008–2012, ethnic unrest in Tibet and Xinjiang, the Jasmine revolutions in 2010 and 2011, had complicated matters. And the Bo Xilai affair dealt a serious blow to the Party's credibility at a critical period of leadership transition. In the end, China weathered the various crises, and Xi completed his succession to the top post.

As executive secretary of the Secretariat, Xi assisted Hu Jintao and the Politburo in running the organizational work and day-to-day affairs of the party apparatus. In this capacity he presented the list of Politburo nominations for leading NPeC and State Council positions at the February 2008 Second Plenum, which preceded the Eleventh NPeC in March. The position of vice president of the PRC, like that of the presidency, is not clearly institutionalized. How big or important a role the vice president plays depends entirely on the general secretary and president (see later). As vice president Xi assisted President Hu Jintao on state affairs, national defense, and military affairs when he became vice chair of the CMC in October 2010. This repeats the pattern of Hu Jintao, when he as heir apparent to succeed Jiang Zemin was given the positions of vice president, secretary of the Secretariat, and, later, vice chair of the CMC. As mentioned, the difference was that the internship period for Hu Jintao lasted ten years, whereas Xi's was compressed into five.

It is customary to refer to Hu Jintao and Xi's positions as "president" and "vice president," but to understand the nature of their formal powers it is necessary to point out that the president (*guojia zhuxi*, which more correctly translates as "state chairman") and vice president in the Chinese political system are far from equivalent to those in presidential-style systems. According to articles 80 and 81 of the constitution, the Chinese president has the power to appoint the premier (the head of the government), represent the Chinese state, conduct China's international activities, and sign treaties when authorized by the NPeC and its Standing Committee, but he has few enumerated administrative or executive powers. Before 1982 the term was translated as "state chairman," and only Mao and Liu Shaoqi had served in that capacity, and the position was formally abolished between 1975 and 1982. In the immediate post-Mao period, the Party's general secretary did not take the concurrent position of president, and this position was occupied by Li Xiannian and later by Yang Shangkun as sinecures for retired elders. However, in 1993, to buttress his power and prestige after the turmoil of the Tiananmen events, Jiang Zemin was made general secretary and president, and when Hu Jintao became general secretary, he also inherited the presidency. Thereafter, the general secretary would inherit the positions of president and chair of the CMC.

Article 82 of China's state constitution stipulates that the vice president assists the president's work, exercising such "functions and powers of the President as the President may entrust to him," and takes the place of the president when the position falls vacant. Consequently, the vice president position did not confer administrative and executive powers on Xi, although in practice the loose degree of institutionalization allows the position to be flexibly used as (1) a sinecure for party elders (Zhu De, Dong Biwu, Ulanhu, and Wang Zhen; (2) a united-front tactic for non-CCP members (Soong Qingling [Madame Sun Yat-sen] and Rong

Yiren); (3) a "superintendent" for the Party, an added position for a powerful member of the PBSC (Zeng Qinghong); and (4) a "lame duck" position for a Politburo member who has gone out of favor (Li Yuanchao, as discussed later). A fifth variation is to utilize the position to groom a presumptive successor (Hu Jintao and Xi Jinping) to give him experience and exposure.[1] In 2018 a sixth variation was devised whose context, characteristics, and implications will be discussed later.

As principal of the Central Party School (CPS), Xi was given the opportunity to get involved in ideology and party-building. The CPS and its two thousand regional counterparts are a chief means for the CCP to maintain and reproduce ideological leadership and conformity. It provides training, education, and in-doctrination for officials moving up the career ladder. Additionally, it is also a laboratory for the transformation of ideology where new ideas and initiatives are tested in various "thought emancipation" exercises for consensus-building. Its large faculty of domestic and foreign instructors consists of a large pool of intellectual expertise, and virtually all senior officials are required to attend courses there from time to time. Accordingly, the CPS is also a huge socialization apparatus where successors presumptive can build connections and authority.[2] Hu Jintao did just that when he led the school from 1993 to 2002, and Xi followed suit and used the position adroitly.

Yet three aspects of Xi's tryout period merit attention. First, Xi's position was still not assured, as potential challenges from other groups or individuals who coveted the position were still a possibility. Overt and tacit oppositions to his promotion might still exist. For instance, Bo Xilai was said to have intimated that he was more qualified than Xi to lead the country and, together with ally Zhou Yongkang, had sneered at Xi's fitness to do so.[3] Second, the tryout was a probationary period to test Xi's ability to handle issues and to enforce the Party's policies, especially when he had little central or international work experience. Further, unlike most PBSC members since the Fifteenth Party Congress who had served as members or alternates of the Politburo or the Secretariat, Xi and Li had done neither.[4] In a system that puts a premium on seniority, dissent over this succession arrangement could not be ruled out. Third, even with support from the top leadership, Xi still needed to establish his authority and to make connections. He had to learn to navigate the complex bureaucracy with its intricate patronage networks and competitions for the prized appointments.

On the other hand, institutional interests to ensure a smooth succession were also at work. One source claims that at a 2008 New Year's Eve Politburo meeting Hu Jintao broached the issue of how to establish the authority of Xi, Li, and the new generation of leaders. Simultaneously, Vice President Zeng Qinghong, Wu Guanzheng, Luo Gan, and Cao Gangchuan did the same at various party and military units to promote the image of the new generation. At organizational life meetings of the Politburo and the CMC, Hu Jintao raised the issue of "passing on, assisting, and nurturing" to help Xi and Li to seize control. Because there were still issues and resistance, Hu warned those who were still fretting or grumbling not to gainsay the succession arrangement and to refrain from sabotage or subversive activities that would affect party unity. This was because both Xi and Li lacked factional support and demonstrated achievements in the Party and the military. Further, this source claims that Xi and Li had expressed on various occasions that they felt heavy pressure and found it difficult to work. After the Seventeenth Party Congress, Hu Jintao, Wu Bangguo, and Wen Jiabao each talked to Liu Qi, Liu Yunshan, Wang Xiaoguo, Zhang Dejiang, Bo Xilai, and others, to demand that they take the central perspective and comply with the central decision. Other central leaders such as He Guoqiang, Li Changchun, and Ling Jihua spoke with regional party secretaries. To counteract dissent among central ministries and regional party committees, the central party leadership had forwarded an Organizational and Propaganda Department statement dated December 26, 2007, which demanded obedience to the new leadership and forbade challenges and urged all to support it with resources and propaganda. To protect the image of Xi and Li, the CCDI Organizational Department destroyed all negative materials submitted on the performances of the two in localities as slanders and libels.[5]

Once installed as dual successors, the grooming of Xi and Li continued, but both were immediately thrown into crisis management mode for several events, anticipated or otherwise. Li assisted Premier Wen on economic issues, but Xi, who was put in charge of party and security issues, had to tackle issues ranging from the Olympics to Xinjiang, and from governance to the economic fallout on social stability.

Governance, Crises, and Authority Issues

The Beijing Olympics (August 2008) among Turbulent Times

Even at the best of times, and even for Western nations, Olympics security and antiterrorism have always been an issue, and the world spectacle has often been politicized and mired in corruption. International Olympics Committee president Jacques Rogge once said that the biggest challenge of an Olympics was security, whose importance exceeded that of the competitions themselves.[6] The Olympics have always had a political dimension, with various interest groups banking on the high-profiled event to push their causes. Moreover, when the spotlight was focused on China, a host of issues ranging from human rights to environment pollution, from Tibet to food safety, and from the jitters of preparation and even the lack of national self-confidence were under international scrutiny. Fears of terrorism and weapons attacks on inland and coastal areas complicated matters. Yet Beijing wanted to have everything perfect, since a successful hosting of the Olympics, China's debutante party as a global power, was deemed to be essential for China's prestige and self-respect.[7]

For Beijing, the stakes were high and time was short, and since the event was a colossal collective effort, Xi bore the foremost responsibility, which tested his ability to cope, especially as he had little experience with the coordination of many central agencies. As director in charge of the nettlesome preparation and security for the Olympics Xi had to work with PBSC member Zhou Yongkang and Politburo members Liu Qi and Liu Yandong. Organizations that had to be coordinated were the General Sports Bureau, the Ministry of Public Security, the Ministry of State Security, People's Armed Police (PAP), the PLA General Chief Department, and the Propaganda Department.

Ahead of the Games, anxieties abounded over international criticism, withdrawals, and even boycotts. First, the Olympic torch relay in Europe, the United States, and elsewhere encountered unanticipated hostility. Aided by Western media and politicians, Tibetan exiles and sympathizers staged many demonstrations to highlight human rights issues in China. Second, unrest in Xinjiang and Tibet led to violent protests and bombings, impacting the security work of the Olympics. Third, in mid-May, a magnitude 7.9 earthquake rocked Sichuan, with the epicenter at Wenchuan. In terms of destruction, socioeconomic impact, and lives affected, the earthquake was one of the most severe in human history. There were eighty-seven thousand fatalities, with over 370,000 injured, 1.5 million houses destroyed, and over six million damaged. An estimated 4.8 million became homeless, and the large number of children killed because of the collapse of shoddily built schools sparked anger and parent protests.[8] But, conversely, the unprecedented devastation and outpouring of relief efforts also in certain ways united the nation in grief. One final Olympics issue was the overblown security measures that spawned numerous complaints about inconveniences for local residents.

Xi never went to stricken Sichuan because of the division of labor but did inspect Shaanxi, where the disaster was less severe. The Central Rescue Command was led by Wen Jiabao, with Li Keqiang as deputy, and Hu Jintao visited the disaster scenes many times to convey sympathy. Peng Liyuan went to Sichuan quickly to boost morale for the PLA troops and the local people, and their sixteen-year-old daughter Mingze volunteered for rescue work and psychological counseling.[9]

Although under great pressure, Xi and the other Chinese leaders knew they could not take any chances. In February Xi inspected the Olympics facilities, and the cautious top leadership met with provincial-level leaders in mid-June, urging them to be better hosts and to guarantee full security. Later in June, President Hu inspected the Olympics facilities and transportation services and reaffirmed a promise to provide smooth transportation and good safety.

Pressure was building when a June 27 Politburo meeting listened to reports on arrangements for the last, critical stage. Hu pledged once again to fulfill China's obligation and create a special, green, and high-quality Olympics. Xi, on another hand, urged self-confidence so that things would turn out well. A month before the beginning of the Games Xi presided over a mobilization rally to review preparations and vowed to ensure safety for the torch relay and the Games. He oversaw test runs of the venues and urged measures to ensure food safety, good air quality, and traffic conditions.[10]

On July 9, Xi told a mobilization rally that security was the most important indicator for a successful Olympics. Beijing had identified terrorism as the biggest threat to the Games, and Xi ordered the intensification of the drilling for security and demanded that provinces surrounding Beijing make contingency plans for security incidents. Xi urged the nation to deploy the same massive drive it had devoted to earthquake relief to hosting the Games.[11] The Chinese media repeated these propaganda themes. In an inspection tour on July 22, Xi stated, in a theoretical formulation (tifa) in slogan form, "A safe Olympics is the precondition for a special and high-standard Olympics; without a safe Olympics, nothing can be achieved."[12]

On several occasions Xi had to comment on the pre-Olympics controversies. Instead of taking a defensive and strident stand, he replied to the media when visiting Qatar on June 25 with a metaphor—if the noisiest birds in a cage with many chattering birds were removed, then things would be much less jolly.[13] Again, on his visit to Hong Kong on July 6, he said, "We have no control over whether people like or dislike a Beijing-operated Olympics. The world is so big that it contains all sorts of people, and this world is always very lively and bustling." Xi linked the immense pressure on Beijing to the challenging path of Chinese development and said, "[We] should not curse heaven and blame others. Once we have set the direction, we must persist in following it through."[14] This response seemed to have appealed to many internet bloggers who instinctively understood the metaphor and who suspected the motivations of Beijing's detractors. Others cited it as an example of tolerance, inclusiveness, and even magnanimity.

In any event, the massive security apparatus deployed for the Olympics was unprecedented in scale in China. Beijing mobilized 150,000 police and military plus 290,000 volunteers to ensure security. Surface-to-air missiles were deployed around the major venues, and hundreds of police checkpoints comprising three rings of security around the capital checked all approaching vehicles. Bag searches were conducted in the subways. At least eighty thousand security guards were assigned to the Games themselves.[15] In the end the megaevent was carried out without major incident. The air pollution issue was partially resolved by a draconian effort to temporarily close down factories in provinces close to Beijing, and 45 percent of vehicles were taken off the roads. Air crews spread bentonite in clouds to prevent rain during the opening ceremonies. China was to win the largest number of gold medals, and the successful conduct of the Olympics and positive reviews made Xi one of the winners.

Of special significance was praise by the military. In an article on how the PLA had supported the Olympics, the director of the PLA's General Political Department, Li Jinai, lauded not only Hu Jintao's strategic decision, but also Xi's effective guidance over the PLA's involvement in both the Summer Olympic and Paralympic Games. Li revealed that since 2004, three hundred thousand members of the PLA and PAP had been involved in an unprecedented scale in planning security, the opening and closing ceremonies, and technical support for up to 114 tasks. The military and the PAP were particularly heavily involved in the Olympics in various antiterrorism and security tasks, which included the safety of foreign guests and dignitaries. In addition, there were sixty-nine hundred PLA and PAP volunteers. Patrol of the air space for all seven military regions of China was conducted during the opening and closing ceremonies for both games, and all levels of military command were put on highest alert. During the games, the PLA deployed more than forty-six thousand servicemen, involving participation of five military regions, the navy, the air force, and fourteen arms of the services, forty-four sets of air defense missiles, sixty-three ships, ninety-eight aircraft, and sixty helicopters.[16]

More than sixty top officials from military regions took command of the security operation, and seventeen hundred senior military officials served on the ground, from changing grass turf at the Bird's Nest to the raising of flags. Troops numbering 118,000 were deployed to clean 210,000 tons of algae plaguing the Olympic venues. This set a precedent for virtually all other megaevents, such as the sixtieth anniversary celebration of the PRC, the security operations of which were said to be as intense as that of the Olympics.[17] In addition, the PLA provided performers, technical assistance, and protections against emergencies and terrorist attacks. The PLA and PAP contributed fourteen thousand officers and men to engage in thirty separate performances and ceremonies, accounting for 70 percent of all performers. That set an activity record for the PLA's security missions and in the number of troops deployed.[18]

Li's piece was interpreted as the military's endorsement of Xi and an expression of loyalty to the succession arrangement. Equally importantly, the piece highlighted the military's role in the Olympics so that it could claim credit for the event's success.

The "6521" Project, *Weiwen* (Stability Maintenance), and
Crisis Management

The Chinese leadership anticipated that 2009 would be a critical year, so the
massive mobilization of Olympics security was resurrected, even augmented, to
prevent and counter social unrest. Political anniversaries are often used by the
Party to glorify and celebrate past events, but Chinese citizens have also used
these commemorations to express dissent, stage protests, and demand policy
changes. Even party congresses and the annual "two sessions" (the CPPCC and
NPeC) have become magnets attracting populist political actions. Particularly,
2009 was marked by a string of anniversaries, such as the sixtieth anniversary of
the founding of the PRC, the fiftieth anniversary of the suppression of the Tibet
uprising, the twentieth anniversary of the June 4 Tiananmen suppression, and
the tenth anniversary of the Falun Gong protests surrounding the party leadership compound of Zhongnanhai. The first digits of these events, 60, 50, 20,
and 10, were nicknamed "6521" to refer to the situation and then specifically
to a *weiwen* taskforce. Other significant events included the twentieth anniversary of the death of Hu Yaobang on April 15 and the ninetieth anniversary of the
May Fourth Movement.[19] A rough estimate by a Tsinghua University professor
claimed that the "mass incidents" had doubled between 2009 and 2010 to more
than 180,000, with a daily average of 500.[20] The top leadership's wariness over
disruption and instability was palpable.

Economically, the global financial tsunami in 2008–2009 was the most formidable crisis that had confronted the Hu-Wen leadership in the new century,
especially coming after five years of continuous growth exceeding 10 percent
per annum. Plummeting exports (a decline of 20 percent) and declines in investment growth (down 33.4 percent) and consumption growth (down 15.1 percent) closed thousands of factories and laid off an estimated ten to twenty million
workers, mostly in coastal and southern areas. Economic growth slowed and
mass incidents swelled, fed by economic hardships and a growing sense of social injustice. Confrontations, demonstrations, and violence occurred daily, led
by workers who complained about such things as owners disappearing without
paying their wages.[21]

In December 2008, three hundred prominent activists put forward a proposal for democratic reform known as Charter 08. *Liaowang*, the authoritative
party journal, issued an unusually stern warning about a high-occurrence period when mass movement might peak. Blaming "hostile forces at home and
abroad," Beijing heightened surveillance at sensitive areas such as financial
centers, tourist spots, entertainment venues, and shopping malls. Tighter control was exercised over the media and the internet, and especially over political
dissidents, human rights activists, and petitioners. The situation was particularly

tense in the capital, where multiple checkpoints were set up on roads leading into Beijing and on its main internal roads.

Accordingly, Xi's involvement in regime security expanded greatly. In early 2009, Xi was put in charge of a 6521 taskforce that included deputies Zhou Yongkang, PBSC member and the head of the CC Central Political and Legal Affairs Commission (CPLAC, or Zhengfawei), and Meng Jianzhu, Ministry of Public Security.[22] The CPLAC is a powerful umbrella organization overseeing law enforcement and domestic security through the nation's courts, procuratorates, and state security offices, as well as the judicial administration that regulates lawyers, legal education, the prison system, and others (see Figure 13.1). During the "two sessions" of 2009, six hundred thousand security personnel were mobilized to ensure security, and Tiananmen was subject to intense surveillance measures. All delegates were urged to restrict their mobility and avoid expressing sensitive opinions. Ministers and high officials avoided the media and left the parliament via special exits. Vice Minister Pan Yu assigned an official spokesperson to respond to questions, and the minister of finance refused to answer any questions after the conference. There were incidents of large groups of petitioners spreading leaflets at Xiushui Street in downtown Beijing, and three petitioners from Xinjiang immolated themselves, but large-scale protests were avoided.[23]

On July 5, deadly rioting broke out in Urumqi, resulting in two hundred deaths and at least sixteen hundred injured, with the Han deaths the majority. A rumor that in a toy factory in faraway Guangdong six Uighur men had raped two Han women set off a brawl wherein two Uighurs were killed. This triggered riots in Urumqi where Uighurs attacked Han civilians, who then turned on the Uighurs for revenge. Vehicles were torched and smashed and other property damaged.[24] Beijing was so alarmed that Hu Jintao had to rush home from a European tour, missing a G8 summit and an appointment with President Obama. The Central Weiwen Leading Small Group (LSG), the Xinjiang Weiwen LSG, and the Antiterrorism LSG were mobilized. As a member of the PBSC and executive secretary of the Secretariat, Xi was put in command to restore order, aided by Zhou Yongkang (head of the Central Weiwen LSG). Zhou, Wang Lequan (Politburo member, secretary of the Xinjiang Autonomous Region, and state counselor), and Meng Jianzhu were tasked to restore order. Security issues had become another test of Xi's judgment and political instinct.[25] Furthermore, the celebration of the sixtieth anniversary of the People's Republic of China on October 1, 2009, was overshadowed by a formidable security challenge. Despite a brave face put on by the leadership, the event was a sullen affair, fortified by a massive mobilization of security forces involving seven hundred thousand personnel. Officials from Beijing, Tianjin, Hebei, Shanxi, Shandong, Liaoning, and Inner Mongolia signed a joint agreement at the capital vowing to build a "security moat" to keep the capital safe. Residents in Beijing were told to watch the military parade and mass pageant on television at home, and only a select number were allowed to participate in the festivities.[26]

Beginning in 2010, the term *weiwen* gained preeminence as an operative word for governance and became an obsession at all levels of government. Increasingly, it involved the massive mobilization and deployment of human and financial resources to maintain stability and to keep a lid on social unrest, often resorting to harsh crackdowns and oppressive measures. It was also a comprehensive call to arms for the party state to promote social stability, employing the *zhengfa* (political and legal) departments, public security, and the courts to deal with social unrest and acts of terrorism. Eventually, an unprecedented surveillance network spanning across China—a country of 9.6 million square kilometers—was formed. Such mobilization was often equipped with state-of-the-art surveillance equipment, high-tech censorship techniques, and sophisticated crime-fighting tools.

For the capital, the spectacle of streams of petitioners was perceived to be a sign of instability and dereliction of duty by the local governments. Therefore, in the name of *weiwen*, tremendous pressure was exerted on local governments to intercept people from conducting *shangfang* to Beijing, to "nip the buds of the sources of instability" and to resolve conflicts at the grassroots.[27] The impact of *weiwen* had been widely debated in the media, in academic exchanges and within the CCP. There seems to be a general awareness that the more the government stressed *weiwen*, peace and stability, the more it was intolerant of the articulation of interests by the masses. The huge price tag for *weiwen* skyrocketed.

A part of Beijing's concern was driven by what was happening internationally. Beginning in December 2010 and extending into the spring of 2011, a cascading wave of mass protests and demonstrations in the Middle East boiled over and toppled governments in Tunisia, Egypt, Libya, and Yemen, despite brutal crackdowns by these regimes. Dubbed the "Jasmine Revolution" or "Arab Spring" by the media, these uprisings also spread to Bahrain, Syria, Algeria, Iraq, Jordon, Kuwait, and Morocco. While the nature and contexts of these upheavals were situation-specific, affecting differently various types of governments encompassing dictatorship, autocracy, and monarchy, they did share some common features. Strikes and marches were motivated by anger over issues ranging from food shortages, poverty, and economic hardship to high unemployment, and from censorship and corruption to oppressive rule. Particularly remarkable was the participation of disaffected youth who were savvy at using social media in communicating and organizing dissent.[28] Such phenomena exacerbated the CCP's worries and raised concern about how to shore up stability before such protests spread to China.

In an unprecedented move, Hu convened three high-level meetings within eight months to discuss the notion of "innovative social governance" (ISG) as a remedy for *weiwen*—the September 29, 2010, regular Politburo study session, a February 19, 2011, provincial leaders' session attended by all nine members of the PBSC, and a May 30, 2011, Politburo meeting. In between, two major decisions were made at the Fifth Plenum (October 15–18, 2010)—the introduction of the notion of ISG and the approval of the Twelfth FYP (2011–2015) setting the agenda for the next five years. According to the official communiqué and further analyses, the CCP determined to make a proactive and strategic shift to deal with risks at home and abroad.

In a nutshell, ISG means that the CCP was finally giving a nod to the role of civil society. This represents an attempt to enhance public services by using nongovernmental organizations (NGOs),[29] to win popular support, and to pay special attention to the welfare of migrant workers. Hu Jintao even asserted that the credibility of the CCP hinged on its ability to find and apply innovative means of governance.

At the February 19 conference, Hu Jintao summoned provincial- and ministerial-level officials to the CCP's party school in Beijing for a five-day symposium on ISG. Acknowledging the issue of social unrest, he repeated the call for improvements and innovations in social governance to achieve greater harmony and stability. Generally, he called for improvement in the mechanism for safeguarding the rights and interests of the people, and the formation of effective institutions to coordinate various interests so that people could express their concerns, settle disputes, and have their rights and interests safeguarded. As Hu Jintao's right-hand man, Xi gave the concluding speech on the last day of the symposium, urging the participants to resolve social issues at their sources, and to improve services and benefits for the general public. He stressed the importance of having the grassroots officials innovate and implement the spirit of ISG.[30]

Eventually China weathered the global financial crisis and subsequent recession lasting until 2012 through measures such as a colossal stimulus package (RMB 4 trillion or US$586 billion) to stimulate domestic demand, currency revaluation, and tax reform. In the process, China augmented its role in the global economy,[31] although the legacy of the crisis persists up to the present. This era spelled the end of the 2003–2007 boom, and the annual growth rate had to be trimmed down to around 7 percent. But the issues of poverty, inequality, income gaps, environmental degradation, workers' and farmers' disputes, and the unemployment that fueled social unrest remained. Nonetheless, most mass incidents in this period were sporadic, local, and incidental. Lacking coordinated plans and organization, involvement by a split elite, or a large-scale organized political opposition, they were unlikely to pose any immediate threat to the regime. In some respects, the ability of various governments to address social grievances had improved. The apparent improvement in people's livelihood, especially in the urban areas, had also weakened protests and dissent. Yet, with the great advances in communications technology, social unrest and popular resistance could spread quickly, and awareness of this has led to an intensification of high-handed security measures.[32]

In any case, the new emphasis on ISG did not mean the negation of the assumptions and methods of *weiwen*; in fact, the two differing approaches to governance had to a great extent merged and perhaps reinforced one another. Little or no information has emerged on how Xi coordinated *weiwen* in the background because of the black box, but the many challenging assignments of preserving regime stability in turbulent times must have provided him an opportunity to establish his credentials. In comparison, a decade previously Hu Jintao, the heir presumptive, was also put in charge of handling potentially explosive issues, such as the "accidental" bombing of the Chinese embassy in 1999 by a US warplane in Yugoslavia, the downing of a US EP-3E spy plane on Hainan Island, and the PLA withdrawal from commercial activities. Eventually the passion generated by the embassy bombing subsided, the captured plane crew was released, and the military disengagement from business was accomplished relatively smoothly, setting the stage for Hu's assumption of chair of the CMC.

The Vice Chair of the CMC Issue

By custom, personnel reshuffles occur at the middle stage of a party congress, in order to leave time to prepare for the next congress and to ensure that the Party's choices will be duly approved by the NPeC and the PLA according to the legislative timetable.[33] Another pattern shows that top leadership changes had occurred at every fourth plenum since the Fifteenth Party Congress, with the lone exception of the Fifth Plenum of 1995. There was therefore a great deal of expectation about Xi's assumption of the CMC vice chairmanship as a logical step in the succession process. It was expected the Second Plenum in February 2008 would recommend a list of appointments to top Chinese posts, some of which had to be formally approved by the NPeC and CPPCC sessions that normally meet in March. If Xi was the heir apparent when he assumed the vice president position, succeeding Zeng Qinghong, he should also be chosen vice chair for the party and state CMC[34] to assist chair Hu Jintao, so that Xi would have sufficient time to familiarize himself with military affairs and to establish connections.[35] As it turned out, Xi was not given the post at the Second Plenum, so it was expected to happen at the Fourth Plenum of September 2009, but that did not occur then either. In the end, Xi was made vice chair of the CMC at the October 2010 Fifth Plenum, as the final appointment for Xi to position himself for the top post.

Before Xi was confirmed as CMC vice chairman, speculations were rife that things had gone wrong, and Xi's succession had become uncertain or even derailed due to opposition and resistance. For instance, the PLA might have argued that Xi needed more experience to become its potential leader. The division of labor and the two-track consensus might have unraveled amid mounting conflict among the factions and between the princelings and the *tuanpai*. Many theories have been put forward.[36] For instance, those taking a factional struggle and balance perspective claim that Hu Jintao and his *tuanpai* sought to overturn Xi in favor of Li Keqiang, who was Hu's client and first choice. Alternatively, Hu was said to stall in order to give Li more time to build up Li's power base. As Hu had now secured more control over the CC, he allegedly wanted to push back princeling allies of former general secretary Jiang Zemin who allegedly included Xi. Further, since princelings were increasingly occupying high command, the theory goes, there was more resistance to Xi as vice chair for fear that the princelings might wield too much influence in the PLA.[37]

Those espousing power maximization theory postulate that Hu Jintao's plan was to delay Xi's promotion so that Hu could retain his chair position of the CMC for a couple of years even after handling power to Xi as general secretary, repeating a pattern experienced by him as heir presumptive, since no term limits or institutionalized rules for the CMC chair existed. According to this view, Hu wanted to ensure his personal imprint in the restructure of the top brass in the military, and to control the assignment of all commanders and vice commanders of the military regions in order to perpetuate his ideas and influence in the PLA. After five years at the helm, Hu felt he had not accomplished what he wanted, and therefore was reluctant to give up power. A variant theory claims that Xi's position was shaky since Xi was less Hu's first choice than a compromise figure to resolve factional struggle within the Party. Now that Hu Jintao had consolidated his power, he might have entertained other thoughts about Xi as the successor.

These are interesting propositions, but in the absence of evidence, other more mundane explanations may be just as plausible. When Hu was made vice chair of the CMC, he had already served many years as vice president, but Xi had served only two, and Xi needed more time to gain experience. Others maintain that, since a confirmation of a successor at the Fourth Plenum was only a precedent and not an institutional requirement and there was no reason why things could not wait until the Fifth Plenum, the fact that Xi was not assigned the position was insignificant, things were on track, and nothing really was wrong. One final explanation pertains to personal choice. This posits that there was a plan to nominate and elect Xi for the position, but on the eve of the Second Plenum, Xi wrote a letter to the elders and other top leaders saying he had not worked at the center for long and was new to many things, and a great deal of energy was needed to familiarize himself with the various tasks, and therefore he was unprepared to take on new duties. Another possible consideration was the annoyance factor—in anticipating personnel changes during the Eighteenth Party

Congress, numerous requests were made for positions, including requests by elders in the PLA on behalf of their clients, so Xi might have requested a deferral in order to stay out of the fray.[38]

Recalling that at the Fourteenth Party Congress of 1992 Hu Jintao was catapulted into the PBSC, and not until seven years later at the Fourth Plenum of the Fifteenth Congress did he acquire the position of vice chair of the CMC, one final explanation is that the CCP was experimenting with a new procedure by expanding "inner-party democracy." As mentioned, the Hu Jintao leadership introduced a straw poll procedure for electing the Seventeenth Politburo, and a similar procedure at the Fourth Plenum in September 2009 to prepare for the Eighteenth Party Congress may explain the delay in conferring the CMC vice chairmanship to Xi.[39]

Personnel conflicts, factional struggles, and power considerations are parts of an equation that are not mutually exclusive, but the relative weight of each factor cannot be ascertained. More mundane explanations could be just as valid, and the decision depended on circumstances and perceptions. Judging by the general gist of our analysis and knowing now the actual outcome, it is probably safe to say that a leadership consensus about grooming and succession had predominated over other secondary issues that were somehow resolved.

As mentioned, the Fourth Plenum was devoted to the issue of strengthening party-building and inner-party democracy, and personnel change was not a priority or even on the agenda. Further, in the four-day plenum, only Hu Jintao and Xi made speeches. Hu read out the lengthy plenum document, and Xi elaborated on the document and described the drafting process, and this is another indication that Xi was on track as the designated successor.[40]

As if right on cue, an interview with Geng Biao's daughters Geng Ying and Geng Yan commemorating the tenth anniversary of their father's death was published in May 2010. The interview included a section lauding Xi. According to these women, their father and Xi Zhongxun were intimate friends and fellow revolutionaries in the guerrilla base areas, and they got along throughout their lives. Geng Biao regarded Xi Jinping as a level-headed and studious youth when he was working as one of his three secretaries. Xi was said to have partaken in many central meetings that involved military, regional, and foreign affairs and was therefore no stranger to the management of central documents and affairs. Since Geng Biao was in charge of Hong Kong, Macau, and Taiwan affairs, it was natural that his secretary, Xi, was familiar with the issues at these places when he took over.[41] As the said interview was published by *China Economic Weekly*, run by the *People's Daily*, it is almost certain that it was meant as an official endorsement of Xi's CMC membership from the highest level. Others could interpret it as princeling solidarity and support. Xi's confirmation as vice chair of the CMC at the Fifth Plenum of October 2010 had therefore consolidated his heir-apparent status. As soon as Xi was appointed vice chair of the CMC, the Pentagon quickly recognized that this marked the "penultimate step" before Xi was to become general secretary and chairman of the CMC, and it mentioned him for the first time in its 2011 annual report on PRC military developments.[42]

Managing Party Affairs

As executive secretary of the Secretariat, president of the Central Party School, and head of the Central LSG for Party Work, Xi was now in charge of the day-to-day supervision of party affairs, allowing him to cultivate and broaden his connections up and down the party hierarchy.[43] As early as 2008, Xi was already in charge of the all-important ideology/policy component and ongoing eighteen-month campaign (September 2008–February 2010) to study and implement Hu Jintao's "scientific development concept."[44] As the chief ideological spokesman of the PRC, Hu's scientific development concept was his signature ideological contribution, on a par with Deng Xiaoping's "reform and opening up" and Jiang Zemin's "three represents." In broaching a new ideological formulation to govern policy decisions, Hu Jintao was fulfilling his function as general secretary to gear ideology and policy according to the changing environment and to justify changes. Simultaneously, Hu Jintao could and did use the campaign to bolster his image and authority as leader. The all-purpose concept, initiated in 2004, speci-fied a new "people first" strategy designed to correct the lopsided emphasis on economic and GDP growth that had favored the coastal areas. It promised to put more emphasis on a more balanced growth pattern paying attention to the "vulnerable groups" and those who had been left behind. Economic advances would be geared toward social welfare, environmental protection, and sustain-able development. Overall, the concept was to be applied broadly to all sectors, from the economy to governance, and from social services to the distribution of resources. For leadership recruitment it meant the recruitment of the "right kind" of people into the Party.[45] The military, too, could refer to the "scientific" part of the formulation to improve science and technology and informationized warfare.[46]

The "scientific development" concept launched a reset of China's develop-mental strategy, and to build consensus and to quell oppositions, the Seventeenth Party Congress of October 2007 mandated a national study campaign to popu-larize and implement the new priorities. After many discussions in the Politburo's "democratic life" meetings, a five-day mobilization conference (September 19–23), during which Hu Jintao detailed the goals and methods, kicked off the colossal campaign. Xi was assigned as head of the Central LSG to oversee im-plementation, although individual PBSC members also inspected campaign progress in the provinces. Numerous sessions at all levels of the Party, including all seventy-two million party members, were involved in the mandatory study of writings by Mao, Deng Xiaoping, Jiang Zemin, and especially the many speeches Hu Jintao gave at various party and military forums. Various authoritative "commentary" articles were published to add substance to the campaign. A parallel campaign was also conducted within the PLA stressing the need to improve people's livelihood and social development, and that these ventures could benefit the PLA in terms of its work style, training, and recruitment.[47]

Although the recession and distress generated by the 2008 global financial crisis complicated matters, the leadership insisted on implementing the original goals of the campaign, but with an added emphasis on maintaining social peace. And despite disagreements about the various goals of the campaign, the economic/social stresses, and opposition from vested interests, the top leadership maintained its cohesion.[48] Undoubtedly, the high profile accorded Xi in the campaign gave him many opportunities to expand his reach and establish his authority within the Party and the PLA, and within society at large. Issues with officialdom, including factionalism and patronage, were among the most nagging problems confronting the party state, and leaders from Jiang to Hu Jintao had repeatedly raised these issues, out of a sense of either obligation or ritual. The "scientific development" campaign gave Xi the opportunity to weigh in, and in 2009 he lashed out at party members with blunt warnings, positioning himself as a stern Leninist disciple.

In March 2009, at a meeting on cultivating and selecting young cadres, Xi charged that their experiences were too one dimensional, and that they were particularly weak in moral compass. Young cadres were now better educated, Xi stated, and many were talented and vigorous, but they were lacking in morality and integrity. Other failings, according to Xi, were their inability to accept people from other circles or to listen to dissenting opinions. Many indulged in eating, drinking, and merrymaking; they lacked decorum, self-discipline, and self-respect, and were shameless in appearing with lovers at public occasions, and in extreme cases, had their mistresses make a scene. Those young cadres were objects of recruitment by various groups of people with ulterior motives, exploiting their lack of experience and moral standards. They lured them using sex and money and turned them into "family slaves."[49]

At various occasions Xi argued that reading and studying were the chief means for officials to become competent and morally upright. For instance, in May 2009, in a Central Party School speech Xi complained that cadres were shallow, unwilling to read or learn, and unable to think for themselves. They grumbled, Xi claimed, that since there were so many hidden rules of the game, the most important way to get ahead was to cultivate connections and not to acquire knowledge. Reading was regarded as counterproductive, making them unable to adapt to "society." Many used their power to seek pleasure and private gains, and Xi concluded that many exposed corrupt officials were mostly those who never read nor studied.[50]

Again, in November 2009, in a speech at Central Party School graduation, Xi castigated party members and cadres for going through the motions in their studies and for failing to apply what they had studied. Since China was now undergoing severe trials in matters of governance and reform amid a challenging external environment, Xi asserted, it was imperative for officials to put a premium on studying in order to raise the standard of governance. They should maintain a high moral standard, live healthily, and cultivate a good disposition. Yet Xi detected a great deal of negligence, ritualistic compliance, and doing things just for show. They became corrupted and criminal because of their lack of discipline and immorality.[51] Needless to say, while Xi may have wanted to drive home several main points, his speeches were laden with multilayers of rhetoric much in the tradition of hectoring of students by a school principal. It is therefore ironic that in May 2010, he gave another speech enjoining officials to rid their speeches and documents of "empty words" and political jargon, and make them shorter and more concise.[52] Top leaders from Mao onward have routinely lectured on bureaucratic evils, and Xi provided few new twists. It is unclear whether these homilies changed anyone's behavior, although they helped to establish Xi's credentials as the person in charge of the important work of party-building.

In this context two measures taken by Xi right at the beginning of 2010 aroused intense speculations. Was Xi in combat mode asserting himself, or did he commit a noticeable faux pas? In January 2010, Xi took the unprecedented move of sending a personal cell-phone greeting, on behalf of the Central Committee, to one million grassroots-level party branch secretaries and *cunguan* (university graduates turned village chiefs). The short message read, "On behalf of the Central Committee of the Party, I am extending my cordial greetings to the nationwide grassroots party secretaries and college graduate village officials." Such a move begs the question of why the often cautious Xi would highlight himself personally.[53] From a simple administrative perspective, Xi's direct contact with grassroots members opened up a new channel of communication in the new information age. The National Cell Phone System of Party Building Work was jointly created by the COD and China Mobile, collecting the cell phone numbers of one million grassroots party secretaries, the chiefs of party organizations and departments of provinces, municipalities, and counties. This was touted as a new and rapid channel of communication by which Party Central could obtain direct feedback from the grassroots.[54] It was also a potential means of ensuring that the letter and spirit of central policies extended all the way to the bottom, bypassing bureaucratic distortion and inertia.

However, Xi's personal greeting could have been construed as a faux pas because the norm has always been that the CCP and Party Central are represented by the general secretary. Central Committee communications have always been issued as "Party Central with so and so as the general secretary" through the Central Staff Office. In issuing a personal message representing the CC, Xi not only could have breached the protocol of collective leadership but exceeded his station.

It is plausible that the message was Xi's preemptive attempt to shore up support, manipulating his resources of direct communication and his areas of responsibility to win over public opinion within the Party, to warn potential "black horses" that the grassroots-level party organizations were Xi's territory. At that time, local leaders competed for attention with their development and governance models, vying to demonstrate political achievements in order to influence opinion within the Party with an eye on jockeying for positions in the upcoming congress. Others might attempt to play the game of "inner-party democracy" (or elections) to compete with Xi and even derail his succession. One source suggests that the tactic of preemptive assault originated from advisers in Xi's office (the so-called *Xiban*). Other commentators defended Xi because he oversaw party affairs, which was his bailiwick. Perhaps because of the controversy Xi did not send similar messages in 2011, 2012, or thereafter.[55]

On the other hand, Party Central convened two meetings at the end of 2009 and the beginning of 2010 at the Great Hall of the People to raise Xi's profile. These meetings attempted to showcase two local leaders embraced by Xi, followed by media campaigns to tout them as national models to be emulated. The first case was that of Wang Boxiang, a former county party secretary for more than thirty years who was praised for hard work and a thrifty and uncorrupted work style. He had reportedly promoted greenhouse vegetable production, treated alkaline soil, and launched industrial projects that had boosted local economic growth, resolving the developmental gap between the north and south of his county.[56] The second case was that of Shen Hao, a Shandong village branch secretary, who was credited with transforming Xiaogang village from poverty into a rich and advanced model through a spirit of honesty and hard work. Normative models are a time-honored method used by the Party to forward an ideal and to inculcate desirable behavior. Xi knew that county and grassroots party secretaries often bore the blunt of mass discontent over corruption and other malfeasances, and his highlighting of models constituted another attempt to improve the behavior of grassroots officials.[57] Indeed, Xi's manifested concern was about the quality of low-level officials, but he could also use the opportunity to stake out his territory and prove his mettle.

Hong Kong and the Assertion of Beijing's Power

Xi's apprenticeship also embroiled him in key issue areas such as Tibet, Xinjiang, and Hong Kong. Returning to Chinese control after a century of British rule in 1997, Hong Kong experienced a unique level of socioeconomic development and political culture. A free port and a major global economic and financial center, Hong Kong enjoys a separate customs territory from the mainland. British rule was not democratic, but Hong Kongers had traditionally enjoyed a large measure of individual rights, civil liberties, and the rule of law. According to Deng Xiaoping's formula of "one country, two systems," Hong Kong is supposed to enjoy a high level of autonomy and freedom. Its semiautonomous status has been intended by the PRC to be an example for Taiwan's reintegration into China. Hong Kong is also an international actor with full membership in international organizations such as the WTO and Asia-Pacific Economic Cooperation, and whose standing is of intense concern to such states as the UK and the United States. How China has been able to manage such a cosmopolitan financial metropolis and a capitalist enclave has always been a test. For Beijing, too many concessions to Hong Kong might encourage mainland Chinese to raise their demands, creating a contagion effect. Beijing often stresses sovereignty and national unity and has treated the Hong Kong government as a subordinate far down the administrative ladder. It is ultrasensitive to any criticism of this that it perceives to be hostile foreign intervention in its domestic issues.[58] For many Hong Kongers, on the other hand, freedom of speech, the rule of law, and, above all, democratic reform are significant issues.

As director of the Central Hong Kong and Macau Liaison Small Group since November 2007, Xi had to handle the delicate relationship as a sort of semidiplomacy with a foreign country. Xi's Hong Kong visit of July 6–8, 2008, a month ahead of the Olympics, as heir apparent and his first to the region as a top leader, gave him an opportunity to introduce himself and make an impression. While the manifest goals were only to cheer on equestrian teams, convey gratitude for the support for the Sichuan earthquake relief, and meet with various social strata, Xi's performance and impact were closely watched on both sides of the border. Unlike his predecessor, Zeng Qinghong, who visited Hong Kong as vice president by meeting with financial and business tycoons, Xi visited middle-class and grassroots families, inquired about their everyday lives, housing prices, mortgages, family expenditures, and work. He was shown shaking hands with people at public housing estates. In his exchanges with families and speeches to officials, there were no grand, rousing rhetoric in the cadenced intonation normally expected of Chinese leaders, which provides ample clues to the audience as to when to applaud. One journalist reported that Xi's placid speeches left the audience bewildered as to when to clap! To some ordinary Hong Kongers who were accustomed to political debates and oratorical flourishes, Xi seemed feeble, perhaps even ordinary, and clumsy, but others found him courteous and approachable.[59]

In his dealings with the Hong Kong government, Xi assumed the deportment of a superior. For the portion of Olympics to be held in Hong Kong, Xi said that he expected the Special Administrative Region to excel in security, equestrian competition, coordination, and food safety. Specifically, he demanded that chief executive Donald Tsang take personal responsibility for preparatory work. Repeating an official line, he wished that all sectors in Hong Kong would focus on development by maintaining prosperity and stability. Apparently dissatisfied with the alleged power of the Hong Kong judiciary, he admonished Hong Kong officials to be more united and cooperative in dealing with issues such as inflation. He urged solidarity within Hong Kong's governance team, "mutual understanding and support among the executive, the legislature, and the judiciary," and "cooperation" of the judiciary with the government in order to forge a harmonious society. This displayed a lack of understanding of the significance of judicial independence and raised eyebrows among many Hong Kongers, especially among the juridical community.

More controversial was Xi's assertion of Beijing's centralizing power over Hong Kong. At a talk with the Hong Kong delegation during the NPeC on March 7, 2010, Xi claimed that China was a unitary state and the currently high level of autonomy enjoyed by Hong Kong was not innate, as it was granted by the party leadership. Stressing the notions that "power lies with the center" and that one must "protect the nation's unity and security" Xi urged all sectors to "rationally" discuss the gradual reform of the Hong Kong political system. Such views were immediately construed as a critique of Hong Kong's Five Constituencies Referendum, and fears were expressed about the resurrection of the Article 23 antisubversion law. Hong Kong's pro-Beijing delegate to the NPeC, Wang Mingang, had said that she would make a motion at the legislature to expedite the codification of Hong Kong's Basic Law Article 23. Article 23 was a national security bill that covered such offenses as treason, attempts to split the Party, the instigating of unrest, subversion, and the stealing of state secrets. Between 2002 and 2004, the Hong Kong government attempted to push through the bill, leading to widespread opposition that culminated in a July 1 protest of a half million people in 2003. The Tung Chee-hua government was forced to back down, and Tung himself resigned as chief executive of the Special Administrative Region a year later. At any rate, even Beijing seemed unwilling to revisit the hot issue at that time, and some interpreted Xi's talk as a general matter of principle. However, the same did not apply to the "Five Constituencies Resignations."

In 2007 China ruled out universal suffrage for election of the chief executive for 2012, and in January 2008, pro-Beijing members got the Legislative Council of Hong Kong to agree to delay the election to 2017. To protest the delay, the League of Social Democrats proposed the "Five Constituencies Resignation" plan in July 2009, by which the democrats would resign, hoping the by-elections would trigger a referendum on universal suffrage. The State Council's Hong Kong and Macau Affairs Office and other Chinese officials denounced this move as contrary to the Basic Law. The democrats interpreted Xi's talk as a warning against Hong Kongers not to support a referendum, which Beijing feared would not only affect Hong Kong, but be an example having an impact on China itself. Others regarded the referendum as consistent with the Basic Law and accused Xi of playing the "one country" (centralizing power) over the "two systems" (autonomy) formula. One legal view argued that the high degree of autonomy was not entirely granted by the central government, because it was a product of a Sino-British negotiation. In this way, the delegation of power could be constrained by international law.[60] In any case, by May, all the democrats who had resigned were duly re-elected.

All major issues on Hong Kong were decided collectively by the Politburo and agencies lower down the bureaucracy, but Xi's visit did reflect his personal style and initiative and showed his shallow understanding of democratic and pluralistic practices.

The Tibet Conundrum

In China's minority provinces such as Tibet and Xinjiang, however, the issues are of a different order. Like Zhejiang and the rest of China, these provinces have been going through the stress and dislocation of rapid modernization and economic development. Massive rural migration to the urban areas, within the provinces and to other parts of China, have turned farmers, nomads, and women into factory and office workers. Social differentiations, such as the emergence of a middle class, have created winners and losers as well as new patters of inequality. New divisions of labor and skills are needed for competition in the marketized economy. Traditional cultural values based on Buddhism (Tibet) and Islam (Xinjiang) are feeling the challenges posed by new social and gender norms. Yet, on the other hand, advances in communications technology and social media have popularized and reinforced interests in tradition and religious values as well.

China-Tibet relations have been complex and intricate stretching back centuries, complicated by foreign interests, rivalry, and intervention by countries such as Britain, India, the United States, and Russia. Like the rest of China, Tibet (population three million and another three million residing outside the province) has gone through the upheavals of Mao's Cultural Revolution, and in the reform period, experienced economic development and the pains of modernization. Tibetans and Tibetan exiles have accused Beijing of reneging on promises of cultural, religious, and even political autonomy and resent an iron-fisted rule, assimilation, and suppression that curbs political, cultural, and religious expressions. After the failed uprising in 1959 the Dalai Lama, Tibet's spiritual leader, fled, and an exile government was formed at Dharamsala in India. Beijing has regularly denounced the Dalai Lama as a dangerous "splittist" or separatist and pressured countries' leaders not to meet with him. For Beijing, Tibet is seen as a matter of core interest, sovereignty, and territorial integrity as well as a source of raw materials producing special highland agricultural products.

Xi senior had close relations with the Tenth Panchen Lama and knew the Dalai Lama. The Dalai Lama recalled that he and Xi senior met when the young monk was in Beijing in 1954 during an extended visit to learn "Chinese and Marxism." Xi senior and he became close friends, and the Dalai Lama gave Xi an expensive watch as a token of trust. According to the Dalai Lama, Xi senior was very friendly, open-minded, and kind. Dalai regarded the latter as a liberal and a dove, who championed the rights of the Tibetans, Uighurs, and other minorities. Xi Zhongxun was also known to be the lone leader who opposed the sacking of Hu Yaobang in 1987 and the military crackdown of Tiananmen of 1989. Such past connections prompted the Dalai Lama to be cautiously optimistic, speculating that Xi might be more moderately open-minded toward Tibet in the same way that Deng Xiaoping had opened up China by introducing market reforms. Other signs that Xi might be inclined to take a more moderate line were that his wife was reputed to be a Buddhist even though this is forbidden for a CCP member and that Xi, when party boss in Zhejiang, went the extra mile to host the first World Buddhist Forum at the provincial capital.[61] All this notwithstanding, there was a great deal of talking past one another. For instance, an earlier office source claimed that Xi senior had told the Dalai Lama that "Tibet is not a nation" and that independence, a "high level of autonomy," or a greater Tibetan autonomous region were both out of the question.[62] However, in 2019, the Dalai Lama let slip that Xi agreed to meet him during a state visit to India in 2014, but the plan was scuttled by the Indian government.[63]

Beijing has banked on the passing of the Dalai Lama as a solution to the political issue, whereas the latter has steered a "middle-way approach" demanding genuine autonomy, not secession, from China, with China still looking after Tibet's foreign policy.[64] Formally retired in 2011, the Dalai Lama was succeeded in power by Lobsang Sangay as "sikyong," a position akin to prime minister, of the exiled Tibetan government. Sangay was re-elected in 2016 and continues to observe the "middle-way approach." However, younger Tibetans, frustrated by the lack of significant change, are becoming somewhat more radical and confrontational and may ultimately demand independence as the way out.[65]

Back in 2008, ahead of the Olympics, Tibetan protests, riots, and self-immolations triggered official crackdowns and attracted international attention. At the time Xi seemed to take a more conciliatory line when he said that Beijing should "have normal hearts" in dealing with the issues. This stood in stark contrast with the strident official rhetoric denouncing the Dalai Lama. Many Chinese viewed the 2008 unrest in Tibet as a Western plot "to demonize Beijing before the Olympics and try to split Tibet from China."

Between 2006 and 2012, two million Tibetans had been resettled to new houses as part of an antipoverty process that Beijing claimed had improved living conditions by providing electricity, water, education, and healthcare as part of the "building a new socialist countryside" policy. Detractors of this massive re-settlement argued that Tibetans had been deprived of their nomadic roots and means of livelihood in an unsustainable policy change whereby Tibetans were deprived of alternatives, consultation, or compensation.[66]

In 2009 another promotional trial of Xi as heir apparent was his attendance at the sixtieth anniversary of Tibet "liberation" as vice president at the head of a fifty-nine-member delegation representing the central government. Director of the Central Liaison Group on Tibet and CPPCC chair Jia Qinglin was absent, and Xi was put in charge. Xi's first important speech (July 19, 2011) regarding Tibet reinforced Beijing's official hard-line position. Repeating standard fare, he vowed to crack down on separatist activities by the Dalai Lama "clique" and "completely destroy any attempt to undermine stability in Tibet and the national unity of the motherland." Essentially, Xi hewed closely to the official discourse on Tibet, lauding the progress ranging from living standards to income, from education to health, and from the social safety net to life expectancy. He vowed to fight separatism, to maintain social stability, to improve people's well-being, and to continue to build a "new socialist countryside." Claiming that the Han Chinese and ethnic minorities were interdependent on one another, he maintained that prosperity and accelerated economic and social development was the key to resolving all issues in Tibet. However, his pledges for ethnic unity and respect for religious beliefs rung hollow.[67]

The day before Xi's speech, the Dalai Lama concluded an eleven-day public event initiating new followers called Kalachakra for World Peace in Washington, DC, from July 6 to 16.[68] On July 16 the Dalai Lama met with President Obama at the White House, and this drew the usual heated reaction from Beijing accusing the United States of interfering with the internal affairs of China, and harming its core interests. The Dalai Lama told Obama that he wished that meetings between his envoy and Chinese authorities could resume after nine failed previous attempts, the latest in January 2010.

Ajia Rinpoche, former vice president of the Buddhist Association of China and former abbot of Kumbum Monastery, one of the six most important sites of the Gelugpa school of Tibetan Buddhism, said in an interview that Tibet's great transformations in superstructure such as railways, bridges, roads, and high-rises were apparent, but the rise in material conditions had not made Tibetans feel blissful. There were language, culture preservation, and environmental protection issues. Xi's assignment to the celebration, he said, was to stress Tibetan stability and development but was also a kind of nostalgia, noting that in the 1950s, Xi senior had worked in Tibet, and was a close friend with the Dalai Lama. In 1994 Anja Rinpoche and the mother of the Panchen Lama had gone together to Shenzhen to visit Xi Zhongxun, who was just recovering from a stroke. He was astonished, he said, to see that Xi referred to the Buddha and held up both hands and asked Rinpoche, as a follower of the Dalai and Panchen Lamas, to grant him a collective blessing. While Xi senior's friendship with the two lamas might have left some impression, Rinpoche did not think that it would affect Xi Jinping much, because CCP policy was already set and would not change because of the change in leadership.[69]

Others had speculated that the Hu Jintao–Xi Jinping team would be obliged to find a solution for Tibet, since iron-fisted rule was unsustainable, and the complimentary policy of pouring billions into Tibet for development and infrastructure (which included a railway connecting Lhasa to other cities in China in 2006) would not buy long-term stability. Initially Hu had good intentions and had sought to make up for his 1989 crackdown by a decree to "protect Tibetan culture," but was shaken when the Dalai Lama used this to accuse China of "cultural genocide."[70] Further, this point of view claims, Xi's personal inclinations at that stage, whether moderate or hard line, counted for little in comparison to the perceived challenges to national unity, sovereignty, and stability, since Xi was still just one cog in the collective leadership. Xi still had to prove his mettle to appease the hard-liners in the Party.[71] In any case, the big picture and systemic factors are more fundamental, and Beijing's Tibet policy changed little during Xi's first term as general secretary.

The Xinjiang Challenge

Like Tibet, Xinjiang poses major challenges to the PRC's national integration efforts, consuming a great deal of the leadership's energy. Xi's apprenticeship inevitably exposed him to such issues. Situated in the northwest, Xinjiang is China's largest province with many mountains and deserts, covering one-sixth of the country's landmass. It shares a border with eight neighboring states and is strategically and economically important since its huge energy resources contain about 30 percent of China's petroleum, natural gas, and coal deposits, and massive pipelines cross its territories from Russia and Afghanistan.[72] With an area three times the size of France (166,500 square kilometers), the province features large regional diversity in topology, natural endowments, customs, and people's incomes. Its population in 2014 consisted of 45 percent Uighurs, 40 percent Han Chinese, 7 percent Kazaks, as well as 47 other nationalities. The Uighurs are a Turkic-speaking Sunni Muslim ethnicity culturally and socially close to others in Central Asian states.[73] In the post-Mao era new issues of national integration and local resentment came to the fore. To neutralize ethnic dissatisfaction, the leadership pledged economic development and modernization, calculating that prosperity would diminish forces of separation. The Great West Developmental Strategy has shown some results, and Xinjiang experienced unprecedented development from 1999 to 2009, with average GDP growth of more than 10 percent, although such figures hide issues such as the uneven distribution of economic benefits.[74] Preferential central treatment included exemption from the one-child policy, affirmative action in university admissions, and quotas in political and administrative positions, but ironically this has enlarged the rift between Hans and the other ethnic groups. This "imposed modernization" ignored cultural tradition and diversity, and the political, economic, and cultural marginalization of the majority Uighurs. Some scholars regard the Uighurs' orientation toward independence and radical Islam as uncertain, although Beijing worries about Taliban incursions, and the East Turkestan Islamic Movement is known for supporting violence against Chinese rule.[75]

Structural and developmental factors, in addition to rigid government policies, have accounted for several major issues and dilemmas.[76] First, uneven economic growth exacerbated the disparity between Xinjiang and the rest of China, which saw the average GDP in Xinjiang 25 percent lower than the national average.[77] Its national ranking for average wages decreased from sixth in 1978 to thirty-third in 2008. The landlocked position has denied it the outward developmental opportunities of the booming coastal provinces. Those rich provinces could afford the largesse of subsidies to their poor families to the tune of ¥10,000, but not in Xinjiang. The lack of subsidies meant that prices of natural gas were more expensive than in Shanghai. Exports of hundreds of thousands of workers to more prosperous parts of China in search of employment, often organized by the government, have improved income, but have also exacerbated ethnic conflicts. Second, rapid economic growth has widened the income gap *within* Xinjiang as well. Policy and investment have been biased toward the north, where all the centers of development were located. Growth has occurred almost entirely in the north and northeast, whereas simultaneously the south was weakened and left out of the economic boom. This situation has been aggravated by a labor and a brain drain from the rural south to the north. Massive subsidies and developmental programs have been seen to have benefited disproportionately Han Chinese and perpetuated inequality. This economic cleavage has been exacerbated by the rural/urban divide. Hans are primarily urban, whereas the other ethnicities are primarily rural—Hans comprising 73 percent of Urumqi's (the provincial capital) population.

Third, massive Han migration has enlarged the Han population from about 6 percent in 1949 to about 40 percent recently. For the indigenous people this meant the loss of land and political independence, and Hans are seen to have dominated the job market and to have depressed traditional handicrafts, industry, and trade. A string of clashes and terrorist attacks such as bombings had been met with suppression and imprisonment, "Strike Hard" campaigns, and Beijing's declaration of war against the "three evils" of "separation, extremism, and terrorism."[78] Beijing's control tightened further after 9/11, when it cooperated with the United States on the "war on terror" and used the Shanghai Cooperative Organization to co-opt Central Asian states to fight the perceived threat of transnational Islamic fundamentalism. Four, the revival of Islam as a religion and way of life, amplified by the spread of the digital and social media, has reinforced a distinctive culture and identity. This occurs in the context of modernizing initiatives that have disrupted traditional cultures and customs. Moreover, the government's policies on education and language and its restrictions on religious practices (such as limits on time fasting, restrictions on mosque attendance to those age eighteen and above, and the requirement for government officials to be secular) have been seen as efforts of assimilation. The official narrative, which was couched in terms of "freedom from religion," actually encouraged religious separation. Fifth, Xinjiang suffers from an arid natural environment of deserts and frequent wind and sandstorms, and green oases comprise only 4.3 percent of the land mass. Serious ecological issues have been aggravated by deforestation and industrial pollution. Further, there have been fears that high-polluting manufacturers are tempted to relocate there into the arms of willing and irresponsible localities anxious to raise their GDP and financial revenues. All of these have contributed to a sense of discrimination, alienation, and marginalization.[79]

Among China's several hundred thousand CCP cadres, the offices in Xinjiang are regarded as hardship posts with low pay and poor working conditions. A major issue has been how to attract good-quality cadres, especially to the grassroots. Despite the large-scale cultivation of minority cadres, some of whose membership has become hereditary, many positions have been left vacant for years. Many cadres feel that they have little real clout in solving problems since powers over finances and resources are centralized. This was the context that confronted Xi when he was dispatched to Xinjiang from June 17 to June 21, 2009, to conduct investigation tours of local communities, enterprises, schools, and oil and chemical projects.[80] Soon after Xi left, on July 5, another deadly riot broke out in Urumqi. Subsequently, security was immensely tightened, and the internet in Xinjiang was blocked for a ten-month period with only partial access ever since.[81]

On the other hand, Beijing's hard-line measures were balanced by an unprecedented and national mobilization effort to render support to Xinjiang.[82] In March 2010, the central government convened a top-level conference on supporting Xinjiang, a first since 1949. From May 17 to 19, 2010, a three-day national work conference presided over by Hu Jintao to discuss Xinjiang unveiled a massive support package, pledging an investment of ¥100 billion every year for a full decade.[83] Hu pledged to spend more in the province to improve public services and to launch major projects to improve living standards, build an eco-friendly environment, fast-track development, and maintain social stability. Wen Jiabao pledged to introduce favorable policies to boost economic and social development. The central government would raise tax revenue for the various regional governments in Xinjiang and grant them more control over the use of natural resources such as natural gas. Reforms could generate an extra ¥8–¥10 billion (US$1.17–$1.46 billion) to Xinjiang's fiscal income, almost a quarter of its total.[84] The goal was to narrow the gap with the rest of China, especially in the poorest areas, as much as possible in a decade and to turn Xinjiang into a moderately well-off society by 2020.

Nineteen relatively well-off provinces and municipalities, including Beijing, Tianjin, Shanghai, Guangdong, Zhejiang, Shenzhen, and Shandong, along with ministries and commissions, and large corporations pledged to assist and partner with the eighty-two counties/townships in Xinjiang and twelve divisions of the Construction Corps with a large number of projects. For instance, Beijing was paired with the Hotan region and pledged ¥73 billion, whereas Guangdong was paired with Kashi (Kashgar) region and pledged ¥96 billion. These nineteen governments were to contribute 0.3 to 0.6 percent of their fiscal revenue from 2011 to 2020 to support Xinjiang development.[85] Naturally, the Chinese government stresses the success of these measures, whereas detractors dismiss them as another colonial ploy.

In April 2010, Xi visited Urumqi for a second time and announced that Wang Lequan (b. 1944), who had served an unusual three terms as Xinjiang party chief for nearly fifteen years (1995–2010) and who was awarded Politburo membership in 2002, was reassigned as deputy secretary of the Central Political and Legal Commission, a move many interpreted as a demotion.[86] Xi, however, heaped praise on Wang, who was known as an "iron fist" and "stability" secretary who had claimed to have already begun shifting an undue emphasis on economic development in favor of more balanced social and environmental development, but that he was just too old to carry on with the project. Wang was replaced by the younger Hunan PPC chief Zhang Chunhua.[87] Overall, on both Tibet and Xinjiang, Xi was aware of the issues and various models of governance, but continued to rely on economic development, assimilation, and forced participation in competitive markets as a panacea for resolving the issues. There was no sign that he and the Chinese leadership had considered other models of integration to tip the balance toward more respect and celebration of the cultural identities of these minorities.

Once Xi became general secretary, two prominent developments merit attention. First, the abolition of the one-child family policy in 2016 was replaced by a policy that allowed all urban couples to have two children and rural couples three. This was noncontroversial with the Han Chinese since small families had become the norm. Yet, when this family-planning policy was extended to the minorities, accompanied by a campaign to popularize contraception and birth control, a great deal of resentment was generated among the Uighurs, accustomed to large families. Second, the Xinjiang government's antipoverty policy saw the creation of a string of vocational and technical training centers for the Uighurs ostensibly designed to improve the skills and job prospects of the disadvantaged.[88] Additionally, the policy was intended to counter terrorism, to deradicalize, and to thwart independence sentiment,[89] especially when the Belt and Road Initiative (discussed later) reinforced the strategic significance of Xinjiang. In 2018, Western headlines claimed that forced labor was used to produce Xinjiang cotton although Beijing countered that production was largely mechanized. Others alleged that more than one million Uighurs were being tracked by big-data and AI technology and detained in the above-mentioned centers.[90] Further allegations claimed that these centers were "concentration camps," where systematic rape, torture, and forced sterilization occurred,[91] and in 2021, the United States formally charged Beijing with genocide,[92] resulting in an international backlash against the latter. Beijing vehemently rejected these accusations. It denounced the United States for exploiting the human rights issue to smear and destabilize China as part of its geostrategy of containment.[93]

Official rhetoric from both sides contains half-truths and exaggerations, and the complexity of the Xinjiang issue can hardly be accounted for by the lone factor of "oppressive state." From a comparative perspective, the overlapping and crisscrossing cleavages in language, culture, religion, ethnicity, urban/rural divide, and socioeconomic status may potentially make the province ungovernable. The situation is comparable to the North Ireland conflict, where the Protestant settlers tend to be richer, urban, and pro-Britain, whereas the Catholic natives tend to be poorer, rural, and proindependence. However, Beijing's record in Xinjiang can scarcely be compared with the blunders and lasting damages

Figure 7.1 Tower, International Bazaar and Mosque, Urumqi, 2017. Credit: Alamy

inflicted on their indigenous populations by settler states such as the United States, Canada, and Australia.[94] Time will tell if Beijing can avoid repeating these calamities. Most indications suggest the Uighur culture and religion is thriving, dynamic, and resilient, being buoyed by the rise of a native middle class, as well as the rapid developments in communications, technology, infrastructure, and the economy. One governance option for Beijing is to implement its own version of Truth and Reconciliation, already adopted by approximately forty countries globally, to promote restorative justice in its minority regions.

Xi Jinping on the Farewell to the Revolutionary Party (September 2008)

In September 2008, Xi acted as the regime's ideological spokesman to deliver an authoritative statement about the CCP. In his capacity as member of the PBSC, secretary of the Secretariat, and principal of the Central Party School, Xi gave a speech reviewing the CCP's record at a ceremony marking the new term of the Central Party School. In excess of twenty thousand Chinese characters, the long speech is just one more example of numerous official wide-ranging expositions.[95] As means of political communication, these are probably rather inefficient, since the readers have to sift through layers of repetition and rhetoric and may in the end not find anything new or insightful. Or they may be simply numbed by a constant barrage of sententious outpourings. Yet this pronouncement was the CCP's latest theoretical formulation (*tifa*) intended to resolve the long-standing debate on whether the CCP was a revolutionary or ruling party. While Xi said that the speech was his own reflections on the nature of the CCP and party management, it was clear it represented a new consensus of the top leadership. Trite as it may appear to outsiders, the notion of whether the CCP ought to remain a revolutionary party or whether it should transform itself into a ruling party had at times been a taboo subject, and a contentious issue within the Party. Right after the dissolution of the Soviet Union in 1991, an academic report chaired by Pan Yu urging the CCP to transform itself from a revolutionary party into a ruling party was submitted to the central party leadership. Again in 2002, another report by Pan Yu on the subject was circulated among China's top leadership, prompting debates among academics. Briefly, adherents to the revolutionary party view argue that the fundamental task for the CCP is to promote social mobilization and to seize political power. Leftists continue to argue, up to today, the notion that a revolutionary party and a ruling party are not mutually exclusive, that revolution is the true nature of any Communist Party worth its name, and that Maoist revolutionary ideals and methods are still applicable today. A revolutionary party, they argue, is key to dealing with a plethora of contemporary issues to ensure the Party's "advancedness" and to oppose corruption. It would forestall a so-called peaceful transition and a return of revisionism and prevent China from collapsing like the Soviet Union and Eastern European communist states. On the other hand, for the liberals, the function of a ruling party is to maintain the system, promote economic growth, and ensure "normal functioning" of the society. Ideologically, the liberal-style party emphasizes class harmony and cooperation, and practically it stresses democracy and consultation, the strengthening of the constitution, the rule of law, checks and balances, judicial independence, and civil service independence.[96]

Xi's speech maintained that the problem was that since assumption of power in 1949, the CCP had not abandoned the role of a "revolutionary party" and that the confusion between the divergent roles of a revolutionary party and a party in power had created conflict and, if not thoroughly resolved, would have a serious impact. Therefore, a final resolution of the issue would facilitate the strengthening of party-building and raise its ruling capability. Implicit in this view was a criticism of Mao, who tended to see the CCP as an "omnipotent party" that should exert control over all facets of society and economy. This ambiguity, Xi argued, must be resolved because the functions of a ruling party are to implement social justice, preserve social order, promote economic growth and development, and ensure state security. While Xi's speech likely represented the central consensus, he had to strike a balance favoring some of the liberals' thinking, but he had to take care not to offend the leftists too much. Although it was lauded as an important theoretical innovation in the theory of party-building, both sides could muster evidence from the speech to vouch for their positions, and Xi did not give the final word. In one aspect, the medium was more significant than the message, since Xi's stature with the Party was raised with this assignment to announce a critical ideological decision that could potentially justify new policies and changes.

In another aspect, the new formulation reflects the ambiguity in CCP ideology and practice. The post-Mao leadership has abandoned key Marxian concepts such as class struggle, revolution, and the dictatorship of the proletariat, and thereby has indefinitely postponed the goal of a classless/stateless communist society. It defines the characteristics of its current stage of development as the "primary stage of socialism" or "socialism with Chinese characteristics" that could last for a century.[97] It has also downplayed Lenin's theory that imperialism (or class struggle reproduced on a global scale) is the logical outcome of monopoly capitalism.[98] Yet it holds on to the Leninist concept of a vanguard party for the proletariat led by a centralized leadership made up of disciplined and professional revolutionaries (more later). Today, the CCP bears little resemblance to a Marxist-Leninist workers' party that advocates revolutions or violent class wars, although this notion seems to have stuck in many circles, and the mere mention of the CCP insinuates secrecy, monolithicity, and malevolence. In Mao's time, CCP membership consisted primarily of peasants, workers, and soldiers, but in the reform period the CCP has broadened its support base by turning itself into a mass party. Today the CCP has a party member in every four households and is broadly representative of the various segments of Chinese society. It attempts to recruit the elites among them and to generate social support.[99] In many respects, the CCP resembles a catch-all or big-tent party with a broad spectrum of beliefs, principles, and backgrounds, and the reaching of a consensus can be a challenge. As shown in Table 7.1, by 2018, CCP membership had already reached ninety million. Workers were around 7 percent; farmers, herders, and fishers around 25 percent; and party/government staff around 7 percent. Various technicians and managers rose from 22 percent in 2010 to about 26 percent in 2018. In the same period, women and minorities gained some ground: women representation went from 18 percent to 24 percent, whereas minorities rose from 5.34 to 6.65 percent of total membership. Those who were under the age of thirty-five were about 20 percent of membership. Those holding junior college degrees rose from 29 to 44 percent. The Chinese leadership banks on the party elite to spearhead development, but as we shall see later, it must contend with the bureaucratic pathologies inherent in such a huge organization.

Table 7.1 Membership in the Chinese Communist Party, by Occupation, Gender, and Education, 2010, 2013, and 2018 (millions)

	Workers	Farmers, herders & fishers	Technical staff	Technical & managerial staff*	Technical & managerial staff in private nonbusiness units*	Managerial staff	Party/government & state agencies	College students	Other occupations	Retirees	Women	Minorities	Education (junior college degree or above)	Below thirty-five years of age	Total
2018	6.51 (7.20%)	25.44 (28.00%)	14.00 (15.45%)	—	—	9.80 (10.82%)	7.56 (8.34%)	1.80 (1.99%)	7.31 (8.07%)	18.15 (20.03%)	24.67 (27.2%)	6.65 (7.3%)	44.94 (49.6%)	22.11 (24.40%)	90.59
2013	7.34 (8.47%)	25.70 (29.65%)	5.01 (5.78%)	—	10.88 (12.55%)	5.07 (5.85%)	7.30 (8.14%)	2.60 (3.00%)	6.87 (7.92%)	15.89 (18.33%)	21.09 (24.30%)	5.95 (6.9%)	36.06 (41.6%)	22.38 (25.81%)	86.69
2010	6.99 (8.70%)	24.43 (30.44%)	—	18.41 (22.94%)	—	—	6.81 (8.48%)	2.54 (3.16%)	6.24 (7.77%)	14.85 (18.50%)	18.03 (22.5%)	5.34 (6.6%)	29.78 (37.1%)	19.51 (24.30%)	80.26

Source: "Zhongguo gongchandang dangyuan" [Members of the Chinese Communist Party], Baidu baike.

* Technical and managerial staff are grouped under different categories in various years. There is only one category for 2010, three for 2013, and two for 2018.

At any rate, more evidence shows Xi's prominent role in managing party affairs. In March 2009, he was assigned as head of a drafting committee to craft another major document on party-building that was approved by the Fourth Plenum in September 2009.[100] Xi, rather than Hu Jintao, gave the keynote speech at a forum recognizing the Party's eighty-eighth anniversary on June 30, 2009.

State/Foreign Visits

The Mexican Outburst 2009

Externally, the grooming process and exposure took Xi to a series of foreign visits to Mexico, Europe, Japan, and the United States. Overall, Xi's apprenticeship in diplomacy went smoothly, although it also generated some controversy. In addition, a different side of the normally staid Xi was revealed during a speech made in Mexico on February 11, 2009, when he met with overseas Chinese. Apparently miffed by persistent foreign criticisms on such issues as human rights, alleged currency manipulation, distortion of the global trading system, and even accusations of being a culprit in causing the 2008 global financial crisis, Xi departed from diplomatic niceties. He snapped, "Some foreigners who have eaten their belly's fill and have nothing better to do are eager to point the finger at us, . . . First, China does not export revolution; second, it does not export famine and poverty; and third, it does not cause headaches. So what more do they want?"[101]

This incident attracted much interest in the international media and triggered a heated debate in China. For many, Xi had lost his cool and was undiplomatic and strident in a way unbefitting leaders of a great power. For others, Xi's outburst struck a responsive chord among the Chinese, especially the "angry youth" (fengqing), for the alleged persistent interference with China's domestic affairs by the biased foreign media. This was particularly the case with allegations that China "caused" the global financial crisis, which many Chinese thought were ploys to discredit China and turn it into a scapegoat, diverting attention from the West's own issues.[102] Some opined that Xi's tough stance was befitting for a stronger China; others noted that the earthy language used was relatively rare in Chinese leaders' communications.

In any case, Xi's views were quickly deleted from websites and news reports in China, and the incident might well have bewildered China's propaganda departments, more used to dealing with scripts than improvisations made by leaders. They did not seem to represent an official position agreed upon by the collective leadership, because mainstream media did not carry such views. Xi's outburst can be variously explained as an utterance of personal frustration over perceived China bashing, a reflection of the views among the Chinese leadership, or a means for Xi to create a nationalist image to garner support at home. To many Chinese, the straight-talking Xi appeared to fit the oft-used Chinese metaphor "needles hiding inside a cotton ball," which refers to an urbane person capable of toughness. In any case, Xi's outburst is mild compared to the raw language common in today's international exchanges, and he has not used such testy language in diplomacy since.

European Visit and Exposure, October 2009

In Europe, Xi was invited to preside over the opening ceremony at the October 2009 Frankfurt Book Fair, as China was the major sponsoring state. Regarded as the most important cultural activity following the Olympics, it was a first for China. Soft power was one notion beginning to be explored by Hu Jintao, and Xi echoed the idea, claiming that "culture is one important component of a state's soft power," which can promote "spiritual communication among different nations."[103] Yet his harping on China's soft power at every stop of his European tour appeared odd, since soft power is by definition something that is inherently attractive and that requires no formal promotion. To show his personal side, he even volunteered his own family vignettes. Yet more intriguing is that Xi presented German chancellor Merkel with a gift of two English volumes on energy resources and information technology penned by the retired Jiang Zemin when he conveyed the latter's greetings. This begs the question why Xi did not bring mementos on behalf of Hu Jintao and Wen Jiabao. It was customary during the Cultural Revolution for Chinese officials to offer Mao's works or his "Quotations" as gifts on foreign visits, and Mao had often presented books (not his own) to foreign visitors, but gifts of books have been rare in the reform period. Jiang studied as an electrical engineer at National Central University and Shanghai Jiaotong University, and after graduation worked in electrical engineering, but he was not known to have done outstanding research in energy and informational technology, and it was unlikely that Jiang's books would offer any insights for the Germans, although they might provide information about China and Chinese policy in these areas.

The fact that Xi played up his relationship with Jiang may mean little, but sensitive China watchers attuned to "Beijingnology" detected a subtext and offered several explanations of the book gifts. The first is that he wanted to show that Jiang was still influential in internal and external affairs. The second is that Xi was a trusted protégé of Jiang and the two have had close connections, since Jiang gave Xi the books and asked him to convey his greetings. Third, and more important, it conveyed that Jiang endorsed Xi's candidacy in the context of political succession and patron-client politics.[104]

One power maximization interpretation is that Xi slighted Hu and stressed his relationship with Jiang because he was unhappy over not being elected to the CMC.[105] While this is speculative, a more plausible and limited explanation is that the event was a signal for Jiang's clients to support Xi and a subtle reminder to Xi's challengers or rivals (such as Bo Xilai) of who Xi's backstage supporter was. In Chinese politics and culture, retired political leaders still carry a great deal of clout, and culturally respect for elders, extended even to political elders, is in general regarded a virtue.

Japan Visit Controversies, December 2009

The fast-track grooming and international exposure of Xi saw him next assigned to a four-country Asian tour in December 2009. The first stop was a three-day visit to Japan, and the highlight was an audience with the seventy-five-year-old Emperor Akihito. Xi's visit received tremendous media attention in Asia, but the meeting with the emperor stoked controversy and even a political storm. Lasting only about twenty minutes, the audience was essentially a symbolic gesture featuring the exchange of diplomatic niceties and pledges to strengthen ties between the two countries. The opposition Democratic Party of Japan (DPJ) had swept to power in a landslide victory in August 2009, breaking nearly complete rule by the Liberal Democratic Party for over fifty years. Xi's visit was the first time DPJ leaders had met Chinese leaders. Evidence suggests that initially Prime Minister Hatoyama attempted to seek a closer relationship with China to counter US influence,[106] and this pivot toward China had warmed up the relationship. In contrast, Tokyo's dispute with the United States over a campaign compromise to resettle the Futenma Marine Air Station airport in Okinawa had somewhat soured United States–Japan relations.

From the Chinese perceptive, Japan had extended the highest honor to Xi, but an unexpected controversy broke out when the Chinese requested the meeting be expedited, breaking the 1995 protocol that formal application for an audience with the emperor required at least one month's notice. The Chinese request came only nineteen days ahead of the meeting. Initially the Imperial Household Agency (IHA) turned down the request, citing the emperor's health issues. Since it was the Japanese cabinet that organized the audience, Hatoyama prevailed upon the grumbling IHA to break the one-month rule. However, objections were raised that the fast-tracking had violated the constitutional role of the emperor as a mere symbol with absolutely no political role; it had pressed the emperor by using him as a political tool, violating Japanese self-respect. The IHA also alleged the political use of the emperor giving preferential treatment to a Chinese leader violated the principle of sovereign equality for big and small countries. The pro-US LDP used the incident to slam Hatoyama's pro-Beijing initiative.[107]

Several hundred right-wing Japanese demonstrators led by the splinter Great Japan Patriotic Party protested the visit, and former prime minister Shinzo Abe claimed that the emperor was exploited for political purposes when he should have remained above political and diplomatic considerations.[108] Xi's visit had become the most serious political incident for Hatoyama. According to Shinzo Abe, when Koizumi visited China, he was served only a set dinner and deemed this a humiliation; he demanded the termination of Xi's visit, accusing Hatoyama of using the emperor as a political pawn.

A personal power struggle perspective assumes that the political competitor and opponent to vice president Xi was Deputy Prime Minister Li Keqiang, and that Xi had manipulated the audience with the Japanese emperor in order to consolidate his position, thereby engulfing the Japanese in China's internal politics, which needless to say would make it unacceptable for the Japanese.[109] In any event, Xi met a number of Japanese leaders from the LDP, the Japanese Communist Party, the New Party, and legislators and Hatoyama from the Democratic Party, before heading to South Korea, Myanmar, and Cambodia.[110] The tour gave Xi international experience with China's neighbors and probably sensitized him to the intricacies of Japanese politics, especially the maneuvers behind democratic opposition and the idea of emperor neutrality. Although Xi's aim was to improve Sino-Japanese relations, the vicissitudes of Japanese electoral politics saw the resignation of Hatoyama, and subsequently his successor, Abe, reverted to a pro–United States stance.

Sino-American Relations and the Two Vice Presidents

Xi's domestic and international profiles were considerably enhanced by US vice president Biden's first visit to Asia, including China, Mongolia, and Japan, in August 2011. Biden's visit was part of a sequence of visits following on the heels of Hu Jintao state's visit to the United States in January 2011 and a projected visit by Xi to the United States. Officially invited by Xi, Biden made in his five-day visit to China the first direct contact between senior US officials and Vice President Xi, who accompanied Biden throughout the entire trip. It was meant to be a get-to-know-you mission to build relationship, trust, and confidence. For the Americans, Xi was tipped to be China's next general secretary, but he was an unknown quality, especially on issues of governing China, international relations, and global economic issues. Biden would learn how economics and politics interact in China and get a feel for how the new cohort of Chinese leaders might manage China.[111]

Sino-American relations have often been characterized as sweet and sour, shorthand for cooperation and conflict. China and the United States were on good terms when they aligned against the Soviet Union in the 1970s and 1980s, and the United States' forward presence in East Asia was regarded as a bedrock of stability for Asia even by the Chinese. Yet the meteoric economic and military rise of China and its perceived challenge to the sole hegemonic power have complicated their increasing economic interdependence. Although mutual benefits can accrue by cooperating to address global issues and to combat global economic crises, the two sides have often been divided by ideology, strategic competition, suspicion, and misunderstanding. More specifically, Biden's visit came immediately after months of bickering in the United States over raising its debt ceiling and a credit downgrade by Standard & Poors. The Chinese media had criticized Washington's "reckless" fiscal policies. As the United States' biggest foreign creditor, Beijing claimed to be concerned with a further weakening or devaluation of the US currency, which might weaken its vast dollar holdings and US Treasury bills, estimated at two-thirds of China's US$3.2 trillion foreign exchange reserves.

On the other hand, the United States was concerned with a wide range of bilateral and global security and economic issues such as the undervaluation of the Chinese currency (which helps make Chinese exports competitive), trade deficits with China, intellectual property piracy, technology theft, censorship, and human rights.[112] The United States was expected to encourage China to boost domestic consumption, which might help American companies doing business there. On international issues the United States was interested in China's cooperation on Sudan, Iran, and North Korea. China, too, wanted the easing of trade restrictions and fairer treatment of Chinese firms, and a halt to US arms sales to Taiwan that might include the Lockheed Martin F-16 C/D fighter jets. On the eve of Biden's visit, the Chinese tabloid *Global Times* published a survey of 7,965 respondents about what they hoped the visit could achieve for China. The findings, more reflective of official views than public opinion, showed demands for the United States to stop its "interference" in the South China Sea, arms sales to Taiwan, criticism of China's human rights record, and support for the Dalai Lama's "secessionist" tactics. They also demanded that the United States safeguard its national debt, resolve trade conflicts, and relax control on the export of high-tech products to China.[113]

At that time, what US officials knew about Xi probably came from a US Beijing Embassy confidential report (dated 2009) disclosed by WikiLeaks. Allegedly the outcome of a private assessment based on various interviews between 2007 and 2009 with a former close friend of Xi and now a US citizen and professor of political science at a US university, this report gives a detailed and plausible portrait of Xi's personality and is worth summarizing here. The seven-page report paints Xi as exceptionally ambitious, calculating, and confident and as someone who had mapped out a career plan with an eye on the top political prize right from day one. His focused drive distinguished him from his more hedonistic peers, and women found him boring. He was reserved and detached and held his cards close to his chest but could be generous and loyal to his friends. He was of "average intelligence" compared to his peer group. He was adept at developing personal networks and he worked the system first by using his father's and then his own connections. A supreme pragmatist and a realist, he was driven not by ideology but by a combination of ambition and self-protection.

The report goes on to state that Xi's princeling pedigree during his formative years shaped his special sense of entitlement regarding princelings as the legitimate heirs to the first-generation revolutionaries. He was therefore elitist in the sense that he believed that rule by a dedicated CCP leadership was the key to stability and national strength. He invested his faith in the system and its career opportunities, and scoffed at the opportunity to emigrate, believing that opportunities like those available to the professor would not be available to him if he had migrated.

The report also maintains that Xi is not corrupt and does not care about money, although he could possibly be corrupted by power. He was cognizant of rampant corruption in Chinese society and is repulsed by its pervasive commercialization, loss of values, dignity, and self-respect. He resents the nouveau riche, and the vices of drugs and prostitution. In power he would attack these evils and the moneyed class. As the only one in his immediate family to have stayed in China—his sister lives in Canada, his ex-wife is in England, his brother lives in Hong Kong, and he has many friends overseas—he was familiar with the West and the United States, on which he has a favorable but detached outlook. He expressed no strong feelings or impressions regarding the United States. Neither did he have any ambition to confront the United States. He understands Taiwan and its people because of his long tenure in Fujian and his ability to attract Taiwan investment.[114]

Sources like this one and the appraisal of Xi must be taken with a grain of salt, but the presentation seems reasonably plausible, and some general predictions, such as Xi's disdain for the money/power corruption nexus, have been borne out. And indeed, Xi's views on the United States and other issues as portrayed are just a snapshot and are still evolving. The report contains some astute observations on Xi's personality, but more weight should be given to the contexts, and different observers, commenting on Xi's performance under other circumstances and contexts, have come up with different conclusions. It is plausible that formative years of relative privilege tend to be quite deterministic, but the trauma Xi suffered during his youth might also have an impact on his personality. Further, many facets of Xi's personality may be opened to various degrees of emphasis. For instance, another confidential US embassy report exposed by WikiLeaks claims that a key feature of Chinese leadership politics is the imperative to protect oneself and one's family from attack after leaving office, and that was why Xi, who had "maintained a non-threatening low profile and had never made enemies," was chosen general secretary by Jiang Zemin and Zeng Qinghong so that the corrupted offspring of those two would not be harassed.[115] One US journalist reporting from Xiamen claimed that Xi's work style in Fujian and Zhejiang Provinces showed him to be "pragmatic, serious, cautious, hard-working, down to earth and low-key." Xi was said to be a problem-solver seemingly uninterested in the trappings of high office.[116]

In any case, during Biden's visit, Premier Wen and Xi expressed confidence in the resilience of the US economy and its capacity for self-repair. Xi warned that "Taiwan and Tibet issues concern China's core interests, and they concern the feelings of 1.3 billion Chinese people. . . . They must be carefully and appropriately handled to avoid interference in and damage to Sino-U.S. relations." Biden reciprocated by saying that the United States fully understands that Tibet and Taiwan are China's core interests, that the United States firmly adheres to the one-China policy, would not support Taiwan independence, and fully recognized that Tibet is an inalienable part of China.[117] Xi repeated that the two largest economies in the world were obliged to work together to restore confidence in international markets, adding that "confidence is more precious than gold."[118]

Hu Jintao referred to Biden as an old friend of China and wished for enhanced cooperation. Citing Obama, Biden reaffirmed a strong commitment to an enduring and positive engagement with China and the world at large. However, Biden did openly broach the issue of human rights in a speech to students in Sichuan, but his common touch and cheerful humor seemed to have endeared himself to the ordinary Chinese.[119] Overall, the visit was a mutual charm mission, but no agreements were signed. Undoubtedly, the visit, as intended, gave Xi more exposure domestically, and he seemed to have demonstrated an ability to hold his own. Foreign media managed to get a closer look at China's heir apparent.

Xi Visits the United States

Just months before becoming general secretary, Xi's five-day reciprocal trip in February 2012 to the United States, with stopovers at Washington, DC, Iowa, and Los Angeles, gave American leaders and public an opportunity to assess the next Chinese leader. Similarly, the domestic media coverage provided an extended opportunity for the Chinese public to size up their little-known leader-in-waiting to see how he handled things on an international stage. In contrast with his predecessor, Hu Jintao, who was formal and uncomfortable, Xi appeared to be confident, relaxed, and personable when meeting US officials. Domestically, the outcome was a surprising hit, at least among Chinese who followed the news, and gave Xi a major exposure opportunity on the international stage.[120] Further, the visit repeated a succession pattern whereby Hu Jintao had visited as vice president in 2002 when he was being groomed for the top position, but the contrast was that this time the Chinese visited with a sense of newfound confidence. Bilateral trade had reached US$503 billion in 2011, and China had become the world's second largest economy just after the United States.[121] Xi's visit also came on the heels of Russia's and China's veto on sanctions against Syria at the UN.

Despite election year rivalry and rhetoric in the United States, Xi received an exceptional reception that included an Oval Office meeting with President Obama reserved only for friendly countries, a reception at the State Department, a nineteen-gun salute at the Pentagon, and no cold-shouldering by Congress. Replying to Republican Sen. John McCain, who raised the issue of human rights, Xi replied, "Your forwardness is well known in China," adding that "China has made tremendous and well-recognized achievements in the field of human rights over the thirty-plus years," and alluding to a well-known advertising catchphrase for electronics, he said, "There is no best, only better."[122] Xi met former US secretaries of state Henry Kissinger and Madeleine Albright, former US treasury secretary Henry Paulson, and US national security advisors Zbigniew Brzezinski, Brent Scowcroft, and Sandy Berger. On Xi's choosing he visited Muscatine, Iowa, to meet with the family that hosted him during his first visit to study hog-raising and farming techniques in 1985. The publicity generated was meant to show his common touch and approachability.

In Los Angeles, Xi took in a game between the Los Angeles Lakers and the Phoenix Suns, since reputedly he was a fan of Kobe Bryant and the Lakers. This played well back home to fans more interested in basketball than politics. Demonstrations by Tibetan, Taiwanese, and Falun Gong sympathizers dogging every stop passed without any disruption, however. Throughout the tour, Xi asserted that Taiwan and Tibet issues concerned China's core interests, reiterating that Taiwan was the most important and sensitive issue in Sino-US relations. Overall, discussions were relatively cordial, and Xi showed some ability to connect with the general public. For instance, at a high school visit he told the students that he liked to read, swim, and watch American basketball, baseball, and football. Several business deals, which included pledges by Beijing to allow US filmmaking industries better access to the Chinese market and to purchase US$4.3 billion of soybeans,[123] were signed, but image-building was likely more important. Overall, like his predecessor, Hu Jintao, Xi's position of vice president was utilized to give him external exposure and experience. After Xi became general secretary and president, the position of vice president reverted to a more ceremonial function, reflecting the fluidity of state positions.

Political Succession Gone Awry: The Bo Xilai Affair

Back home, however, preparations for the transfer of power in 2012 were thrown into confusion by the Bo Xilai affair, demonstrating that the best thought-out plans for recruitment and succession can go awry. This is perhaps rather natural, since competition for political offices are often the most conflictual activities in all political systems, although the contests in liberal democracies are by and large constrained by rules and open elections. In China, the fierce struggle for top office is concealed from public view, although the lurid details of the Bo Xilai affair have yielded certain insights into the process. In contrast to Xi Jinping's successful elevation, Bo, already a Politburo member and one of China's most powerful politicians and front runner for the PBSC on account of his pedigree and seniority, suffered a public and spectacular downfall. Accused of "serious discipline violations," a euphemism for corruption, the flamboyant princeling was purged from the Politburo and sentenced to life imprisonment. The affair was the biggest political shakeup since the Chen Liangyu and Chen Xitong cases in 2006 and 1995, respectively. It threatened to overshadow the once-in-a-decade leadership transition at a critical juncture when seven out of nine PBSC members, including Hu Jintao and Wen Jiabao, had to be replaced.[124] Bo had been in a position to challenge Xi as the presumptive successor, and Xi later claimed that Bo had "engaged in political conspiracy activities." The purge of Bo was preceded by a string of purges of senior political and military officials that the Xi leadership later claimed had attempted a coup (see later).

The affair began with the defection of Wang Lijun (former deputy mayor and police chief of Chongqing, and right-hand man for Bo's famous campaigns against crime), who sought asylum at the US consulate in Chengdu on February 6, 2012. Reportedly Wang had begun to fear for his career after he was reassigned when he informed Bo that corruption investigations had implicated members of Bo's family. Wang claimed that Bo Xilai's wife, Gu Kailai, had poisoned to death English businessman Neil Heywood, a close friend of the Bo family, in November 2011. Allegedly the relationship between Heywood and the Bo family and a guardian to Bo's son, Bo Guagua, turned sour when Heywood tried to extort the Bo family over a multi-million-dollar business deal. When Wang's asylum was turned down, he was apprehended by PAP, which had been ordered by Bo to surround the US consulate. An August 1, 2012, trial of Gu Kailai found her guilty of murder. She did not contest the charge and was handed a suspended death sentence in November 2012. At his September 2012 trial, Wang was given a fifteen-year sentence for "bending the law, defection, abuse of power and bribe taking."

Other accounts claim that Wang also wiretapped phones by CCDI officials in their investigations of bribery charges against Wang when he was police chief at the cities of Jinzhou and Tieling in Liaoning. Allegedly, Wang testified about orders from Bo to wiretap telephone conversations of China's senior leaders, including Hu Jintao and members of the PBSC, to preempt secret investigations of corrupt officials and to apprise Bo of the central leaders' attitude toward him since Bo was keen to gain PBSC membership. When the alleged wiretapping was exposed, Bo was prepared to make Wang a scapegoat, but such a grave misdemeanor was too sensitive to be made public and was seen as a direct challenge to the central authorities, who determined that Bo could not be trusted.[125]

Bo's "Policy Platform": The Chongqing Model

Like Xi and other regional leaders, Bo crafted his own local governance model, and Bo's was dubbed the Chongqing model. He pursued an activist and populist agenda, spending billions to plant trees, invest in massive public housing and infrastructure, lure foreign investment, provide social benefits for the poor, and subsidize education. To address the issue of rural/urban inequality, he initiated a trial reform of the *hukou* system by allowing some rural migrants to gain rights reserved for urban residents. To boost economic development and to reduce the gap between the rich and poor, he used state funds to increase consumption and pay for extensive social services and welfare (even for migrants), such as subsidized public housing for ordinary citizens and building its accompanying infrastructure. One source said that Bo encouraged local officials to debate on live broadcasts to promote transparency and efficiency, and he negotiated directly with striking taxi drivers troubled by high license fees to reach a settlement rather than resorting to a security crackdown.[126] These populist policies appealed to a certain degree to the working class, the poor, and those critical of the growing income disparity.

Other more colorful measures were his two extensive campaigns to "sing the red" and "strike the black" (*changhong dahei*). Singing red and attacking black are common phenomena not unique to Chongqing. The spontaneous singing of revolutionary songs, sometimes accompanied by dancing, is a common sight in China's parks, especially among the middle-aged and the elderly, and strike black essentially means anticrime measures. Beginning in the mid-1980s, sing the red—a revival of Cultural Revolution–era culture and values by the singing of revolutionary songs and sloganeering—had fed nostalgia and captured the popular imagination in some quarters.

Chongqing was unique in these aspects in terms of the mandate and government sponsorship of these activities using government funds.[127] Bo promoted the sing red campaign by advertising and promoting the singing of revolutionary songs, choruses, and communist anthems resurrected from the bygone Maoist era, often in grandiose scale. He promoted and resurrected old communist values of egalitarianism, frugality, and mass line politics. Officials were even sent down to the countryside. On the other hand, strike the black referred to anticorruption drives and sweeping crackdowns on organized crime and the mafia subculture in Chongqing. While certain successes were achieved, the oppressive methods employed were reminiscent of aspects of the Cultural Revolution.

Taken together, the Chongqing model might be considered to be a distinctly new development model (in contrast with the Zhejiang model, for instance) for its emphasis on a greater state involvement and stimulation of the economy to address the issues of inequality and a more equitable distribution of wealth. The populist components of the model may have resonated with a certain nostalgia about the past and gained support within certain elements within the CCP. They also attracted popular support, a mass following, and intellectuals among the new left at various levels of the Party. Well-known new left intellectuals such as Tsinghua professor Cui Zhiyuan joined the Chongqing government, and others, such as Wang Shaoguang, used Chongqing as a base to criticize neoliberalism. For some time, addressing of the income gap and looking after the disadvantaged appeared consistent with the Hu-Wen "people oriented" policy and priorities, and Mao's legacy was so wide-ranging that they were amenable to various selective adaptations.

Yet the massive revival of Mao-era symbols and practices inevitably raised eyebrows, and the high-profile strike-the-black drives were controversial and unorthodox. For some Chinese, this might trigger memories of chaos during the Cultural Revolution. For some central leaders, the flamboyant and populist flair employed by Bo could be deemed his way of campaigning for higher office, something that may have unsettled some central leaders. These leaders viewed these activities with some trepidation, fearing that they might split the leadership, pitting senior leaders against one another.

There was also a dark side to the four-year strike-black campaign launched in 2009. Under Wang, Bo's right-hand man, the conduct of the all-powerful 329 special cases investigation groups were by 2010 reminiscent of those set up during the Cultural Revolution. In what some described as a "red terror," the inspection groups launched large-scale and systematic attacks on the nonstate sector and private entrepreneurs, many of which were accused of being criminal organizations. Wealthy businessmen were accused of ties to organized crime, and their properties were confiscated. There were arbitrary arrests and confinement, torture to exact confessions, prison terms, and death sentences. Hefty fines were used to boost local government financial coffers and local SOEs and to fund social programs. In prosecuting these cases, the officials of the MPC directly commanded the courts, the procuracies, and public security to work in unison rather than independently. Judicial independence and the functions of mutual checks against one another, however insignificant they had been, were abandoned.

Bo might be considered an activist leader, but likely he had his eye on PBSC position or even the number one or two positions slated for Xi Jinping and Li Keqiang in case they somehow faltered. In this context, the Chongqing model was perceived to be a means, a campaign device, or even a frantic attempt to bid for a PBSC position. Bo's prosecution of former deputy police chief Wen Qiang during the strike-black campaign was likely an attempt to discredit the records of his two predecessors as MPC secretaries, Wang Yang and He Guoqiang, both competitors for the PBSC. Bo's main weakness was his age—three years the senior of Xi, he was already sixty-two by 2012, and at most, he could serve only one term in the PBSC or other higher office. Perhaps because of this vulnerability, Bo felt that he needed to work harder, in case he would be shut out from the Politburo altogether.

On one level, the contingency factor of the Wang Lijun affair and what it revealed, rather than the Chongqing model per se, was the main reason for the top leadership and Bo's potential allies to abandon him. For instance, as late as December 6–8, 2010, Xi flew to Chongqing, heaping praise on Bo's achievements in maintaining social order, his "social welfare model and his red revival campaign." Xi endorsed the Chongqing practices of singing red, reading classics, telling tales, and propagating maxims (*zhenyan*),[128] as a means to inculcate ideals and beliefs. Xi also inspected public housing and the resources center for strike-the-black and security forces. A speculation is that he might have been trying to seek an alliance with his princeling rival.[129]

Things changed in 2011, when Hu Jintao ordered the investigation of Wang. According to the *tuanpai* faction solidarity perspective, Wang was a proxy target for Hu to discredit Bo and the Shanghai/princelings faction to dampen their political prospects.[130] In this study, I have cast doubt on the notion of the Shanghai Gang / princeling / *tuanpai* model of factional politics as well as the view that the *tuanpai* is a water-tight clique, with Hu as its head honcho. Other information and interpretations merit attention. These include the scattered reports on the shady side of the strike-black campaign that began to surface in the media.[131] Additionally, an unflattering research report on the strike-the-black style of social management in Chongqing prepared by Ong Zhiwei, a professor at the East China University of Politics and Law, was submitted to the top leadership. Perhaps a last straw for the central leaders was the revelation of Bo's alleged wiretapping of a phone call by a visiting anticorruption minister of supervision, Ma Wen, to Hu Jintao. The die was cast when at the end of the annual NPeC session in March 2012, Wen Jiabao demanded the Chongqing MPC "reflect" on the Wang Lijun affair. Bo was sacked as Chongqing party chief and expelled from the CCP in April for corruption and abuse of power.[132]

Bo's case throws a great deal of light on Chinese succession politics. Bo's purge removed a source of irritation and a potential troublemaker for the top leadership, repeating a pattern of purges that included Chen Xitong, party chief of Beijing in 1995 and Chen Liangyu, Shanghai's party chief, in 2006. All three cases came to light following the exposure of misdemeanors by their subordinates, all three faced charges of corruption and violations of party discipline, and all were prosecuted criminally and given long prison terms. The ouster of Chen Xitong removed a conservative obstacle to Jiang Jemin's consolidation of power, whereas the ouster of Chen Liangyu eliminated an outspoken critic who disputed Wen Jiabao's recentralization of economic policy. For the top leadership, the expulsion of the flamboyant Bo, who had a penchant for playing to the domestic and foreign media, got rid of someone who was unlikely to play by the rule of collective consensus-building that was deemed essential to the oligarchical rule. In the end, despite the havoc wreaked by the Bo affair, the prospect of a smooth leadership transition had actually been enhanced.[133]

Analysts such as Joseph Fewsmith also agree that Bo's conduct might have challenged the rules of consensus-based elite politics. As well, the proper norm for prospective candidates was to maintain a low profile and appearance of adhering to party unity, but Bo appeared to have canvassed for support within the CC by making use of the talk about "inner party" democracy, but this might have introduced a level of persuasion or unpredictability that the top leadership was unprepared to accept. In addition, Bo posed a threat because of his intellectual/policy program that might have gained a measure of populist support.[134] In this vein, one can also argue that there has always been tension and ambiguity in the notion of democratic centralism in all aspects of Chinese politics of which political succession is only the most prominent. In decision-making terms, free and open discussions are mandated before a decision is made (democracy), but once a decision has been made, all party members must abide by that decision (centralism). Centralism means in practice that all major decisions for personnel changes will be made in a top-down manner by the leadership elite, although the democratic aspects allow for party and CC input and spontaneity.

This delicate balance has always been difficult to keep, and Bo, it was decided, had crossed the line. In any case, one major aspect of political succession in a Leninist system is that the demonstrations of ambition, ability, policy initiatives and platforms, campaigning, and so on, so vital to Western electoral processes, are taboo in Chinese succession politics. Had Bo kept a lower profile and had it not been for the Wang Lijun affair, he might have been "re-elected" into the Politburo and even the PBSC by dint of his qualifications.

In any case, Xi had clearly cooperated with the Hu-Wen leadership in the ouster of Bo, pitting one princeling against another at the apex of power.[135] This illustrates that the cleavage in political succession was less a case of the princelings versus the *tuanpai* than of other factors. Xi's speech at the Central Party School, published in the March 16 edition of *Qiushi*, clearly alluded to the Bo affair when it called for the preservation of the purity of the Party in order to oppose all behavior of splitting the Party, to expel corrupt members, and to maintain a humble attitude eschewing "arrogance and impetuosity."[136]

One analyst argues that Bo might have been very difficult to place in the top leadership, and he was deemed a threat because he was different and that his downfall was political rather than criminal. If he became the chair of the NPeC or chair of the CPPCC, he could have used those positions to mobilize public opinion, and it would be difficult to ignore him. Yet, this analyst says, while Bo was the most talented politician of his generation and his exit a huge loss for political life in China, his sidelining made the succession struggle that much easier. Further, he claims, Bo's rough justice and brutality in dealing with the mafia and criminal leaders, violent and vicious themselves, might get China closer to the rule of law and social predictability, and Bo's trial contained not a shred of evidence linking him to the criminal charges.[137]

With the personnel changes since the Eighteenth Party Congress settled, Bo's sensational trial occurred in September 2013—well after Xi Jinping was fully vested as China's top leader. An Intermediate People's Court in Jinan found Bo guilty of accepting bribes from two businessmen in Dalian directly through his wife and son Bo Guagua; for embezzling ¥5 million (US$800,000) of public funds for a construction project at Dalian when he was governor in 2002; and for abusing power by covering up his wife's act of murder. A total of US$3.2 million was pocketed by him. The prosecution's case that a smaller amount of US$21,000 allegedly embezzled for Bo Guagua's foreign travels was judged to be inadmissible for the lack of evidence. Bo's denial of all charges in a fiery defense was rejected, and he was sentenced to life imprisonment.[138] Bo appealed the verdict, but it was rejected by the Shandong Higher People's Court a month later.[139]

CCP and Chinese media presented the case essentially as a judicial or criminal case and an egregious case of the ongoing campaign against corruption. The fallout of the Bo affair can be interpreted in many ways. Put simply, a positive that could be played up was that the CCP's determination to combat corruption was genuine, since "big tigers," and not just "small flies," were punished. On the negative side, the revelation of the seamy side of power politics and its association with a politician of such a high stature inevitably implicated the entire Party. Moreover, re-examination of many of the strike-black cases under Bo had opened up a Pandora's box. Almost five hundred "criminal organizations" had been attacked, and ¥1 trillion was confiscated. Wrongfully adjudicated cases had to be retried or rehabilitated, and a huge amount of confiscated funds and property, much already disposed of, had to be resolved. What to do with those who had been awarded and promoted for contributing to the attack-black campaign was another issue.[140]

The Bo affair was a major crisis and embarrassment that undermined confidence in Beijing on its road to the Eighteenth Party Congress. Additionally, investigations of Bo had brought to light more corruption cases. The congress went ahead without delay with the usual outward demonstrations of solidarity, but once Xi assumed the country's top positions, he quickly took measures to discipline the party state, as we shall see in the next chapter.

8

The Eighteenth Party Congress, November 2012, and Succession Politics

China's once-in-a-decade top leadership transition at the Eighteenth Party Congress in 2012 is remarkable in several respects. In terms of political recruitment, the efforts of the Deng Xiaoping leadership in the 1980s to cultivate a "third echelon" of leadership had come to fruition. Xi Jinping became the first general secretary (called party chairman up to 1982) in twenty-three years, with the exception of the ill-fated Hua Guofeng, to acquire simultaneously the three chief positions of general secretary, chair of the CMC (de facto commander-in-chief of the PLA), and president (at the ensuing National Party Congress in March 2013) right from the start, the implications of which will be discussed later. Li Keqiang was accordingly selected as the second in rank on the PBSC and similarly confirmed as premier. The ascendancy of Xi was the culmination of decades of scrutiny and deliberate grooming. The congress saw the first leadership transition that was not preordained by either of the two founders of the PRC, Mao Zedong and Deng Xiaoping, and only the second orderly and peaceful transition of power for the CCP since coming to power in 1949. This congress continued to rejuvenate and reinvigorate the leadership with new qualifications. New members recruited into the elite CC, Politburo, and the PBSC also marked the entry of "fifth generation" leaders into the apex of power, which paved the way for a near-complete fifth-generation takeover of the entire top leadership posts at the Nineteenth Party Congress of October 2017. Behind the scenes, Xi worked as successor-designate to organize the congress, familiarizing himself with the complex procedures and contentious issues of personnel, power balances, and policy. The transition of power in China in that year coincided with the US presidential elections whereby Barack Obama prevailed over Mitt Romney and won re-election as president, but the nature and characteristics of these transitions cannot be more contrasting. Hence, this chapter serves several purposes. The first is to examine the more empirically observable phenomena: (1) the Chinese policy process and its peculiarities (such as the continuity and overlap in personnel and policies and extensive consultation); (2) Xi's role and how he discharged his duties; and (3) the outcome of personnel changes and characteristics of the new leadership. The second concerns less observable issues of informal politics of internal bargaining and balancing.

In this regard, this chapter attempts to classify and synthesize existing inter-pretations (and their assumptions) by scholars by referring to the comparative politics approach of rationality, structure, and culture.

Political Succession, Chinese Style

It has often been pointed out that political succession at the top in communist-styled countries is an Achilles' heel because the transfer of power is so often a period of intense conflict, uncertainty, and instability. One reason for this is the lack of institutionalization, meaning that there are no widely accepted procedures and rules to change rulers like those of free and open elections. The shoes of the outgoing leaders, especially those whose rule had been buttressed by charismatic and personal authority, are often too big to fill, and even care-fully planned successions have gone badly awry. Well-known cases in the Soviet Union include the struggles between Trotsky and Stalin for the Lenin succession, the struggle between Malenkov and Khrushchev for successor to Stalin, and the succession plot against Khrushchev by Brezhnev and Kosygin.[1] Often, the transfer of charismatic authority takes the form of dynastic succession, as in the cases of North Korea and Cuba. Mao was keenly sensitive to the perils of these experiences, but ironically, his efforts to avoid a succession crisis by designating successors of his own failed miserably, leading to the ignominious endings of Liu Shaoqi and Lin Biao. Liu Shaoqi was purged and persecuted to death during the Cultural Revolution, and Lin Biao was accused of trying to seize power by a coup d'état and died in a plane crash trying to escape to the Soviet Union. Hua Guofeng, Mao's last choice, lasted a couple of years before being elbowed out of power by reformists. In this regard designated successors in communist-style governments face what is called the "successor's dilemma," which may destabi-lize the leadership transition. First, the designated successor may become impa-tient and try to accelerate the departure of the incumbent. Second, he may draw envy from other senior leaders, making disciplined governance more difficult to achieve.[2] Third, he may be trapped by the power dynamics, as the case of Lin Biao demonstrates. Even though Lin was designated successor by Mao, he did not feel secure until he built up his own power base, and in doing so, he incurred the suspicion of the chairman and antagonized other leaders, eventually leading to his downfall.[3]

Even in the reform period, Deng Xiaoping scarcely had better luck, as he had to sacrifice both his protégés and intended successors, Hu Yaobang and Zhao Ziyang, over policy differences and under circumstances beyond his control. Yet this is not to say that a smooth and peaceful transition of power is impos-sible in communist-style countries, as attested by the Vietnamese cases. Nor is it impossible for leadership stability to resume after a profound crisis. By definition, in a "succession struggle" scenario, senior posts are not filled rapidly, incumbents' positions are not perceived as secure, and changes take place in the three top positions of both party and state throughout the first five-year term after the leadership changeover. In a "smooth transition" scenario, the major political posts are rapidly filled, and the new leadership configuration quickly stabilizes.[4] In China, Deng was able to engineer two smooth successions. After the Tiananmen crisis of 1989, which shook the CCP regime to its foundation, Deng managed to pick a leadership team led by Jiang Zemin, who not only served two terms, but also presided over a highly transformative decade amid turbulent challenges such as the 1997 Asian Financial Crisis and China's entry into the WTO. Deng Xiaoping was later able to handpick and groom a transgenerational and transcentury leader in Hu Jintao, who pulled off two terms as general secretary.

Chinese leaders from Mao onward have been mindful of lessons on political succession drawn from the Soviet Union, although Mao's preventive measures gave way to his own penchant to radicalize and destabilize the polity. In the post-Mao period, the leadership has gradually fashioned a succession mechanism that features continuity rather than breaking with the past (see Table 8.1). Unlike situations in liberal democracies where rival parties come to power intending to undo or even obliterate what had been done before, political succession in China, in terms of personnel and policy, has become more a relay race with a staggered promotion pattern. For over thirty years during the reform period, more than one hundred members have inhabited the Politburo, but only a handful have been purged, invariably for corruption, with the lone exceptions of Hu Yaobang and Zhao Ziyang. Advancement into the top leadership has been governed by consensus and compromise, referring to criteria such as age, seniority, retirement years, term limits, merit, and governance experience. It is also guided by balances among age groups (elder, middle, and younger), geographical and functional requirements, and personal networks. Specifically, the two-term limits and retirement age of sixty-eight for top leaders, an informal norm established since 2002, is said to be conducive to stability by preventing personal dictatorship and domination by one faction on the one hand, and by facilitating peaceful exits and the circulation of elites on the other.[5] And as mentioned, the Party and its leaders take special care in recruitment and rejuvenation by cultivating successors through "passing on, assisting, and nurturing." Potential leaders from lower administrative levels are groomed, with seniority and step-by-step promotion (lunzi paibei anbu jiuban) within the party hierarchy becoming a significant criterion for advancement to the top. Leaders are expected to achieve CC membership before advancement to the Politburo, the membership of which is often a prerequisite for advancing

Table 8.1 Politburo Members, Thirteenth through Nineteenth Party Congresses (1982–2017)

Nineteenth (2017–2022)	Eighteenth (2012–2017)	Seventeenth (2007–2012)	Sixteenth (2002–2007)	Fifteenth (1997–2002)	Fourteenth (1992–1997)	Thirteenth (1987–1992)
Politburo Standing Committee						
Xi Jinping 1953	Xi Jinping (5S) 1953	Hu Jintao (4S)* 1942	Hu Jintao 1942	Jiang Zemin 1926	Jiang Zemin 1926	Hu Yaobang 1 915
Li Keqiang 1955	Li Keqiang (5S) 1955	Wu Bangguo (4S)* 1941	Wu Bangguo 1941	Li Peng 1928	Li Peng 1928	Zhao Ziyang 1919
Li Zhanshu 1950	Zhang Dejiang (4J) 1946	Wen Jiabao (4S)* 1942	Wen Jiabao 1942	Zhu Rongji 1928	Qiao Shi 1924	Li Peng 1928
Wang Yang 1955	Yu Zhengsheng (4J) 1945	Jia Qinglin (4S)* 1940	Jia Qinglin 1940	Li Ruihuan 1934	Li Ruihuan 1934	Qiao Shi 1924
Wang Huning 1955	Liu Yunshan (4J) 1947	Li Changchun (4S)* 1944	Zeng Qinghong 1939	Hu Jintao 1942	Zhu Rongji 1928	Hu Qili 1929
Zhao Leji 1957	Wang Qishan (4J) 1948	Xi Jinping (5S) 1953	Huang Ju 1938	Wei Jianxing 1931	Liu Huaqing 1916	Yao Yilin 1927
Han Zheng 1954	Zhang Gaoli (4J) 1946	Li Keqiang (5S) 1955	Wu Guanzheng 1938	Li Lanqing 1932	Hu Jintao 1942	
		He Guoqiang (4S)* 1943	Li Changchun 1944			
		Zhou Yongkang (4S)* 1942	Luo Gan 1935			

The Politburo

Ding Xuexiang 1962	Ma Kai 1946	Wang Gang (4S)* 1942	Wang Lequan 1944	Ding Guangen 1929	Ding Guangen 1929	Wan Li 1916
Wang Chen 1960	Wang Huning 1955	Wang Lequan (4S)* 1944	Wang Zhaoguo 1941	Tian Jiyun 1929	Tian Jiyun 1929	Tian Jiyun 1929
Liu He 1952	Liu Yaodong (4J) 1945	Wang Zhaoguo (4S)* 1941	Hui Liangyu 1944	Li Changchun (4S) 1944	Li Lanqing 1932	Li Tieying 1936
Xu Qiliang 1950	Liu Qibao 1953	Wang Qishan (4J) 1948	Liu Qi 1942	Li Tieying 1936	Li Tieying 1936	Li Ruihuan 1934
Sun Chunlan (f) 1950	Xu Qiliang 1950	Hui Liangyu (4S)* 1944	Liu Yunshan 1947	Wu Bangguo (4S) 1941	Yang Baibing 1920	Li Ximing 1926
Li Xi 1956	Sun Chunlan 1950	Liu Qi (4S)* 1942	Wu Yi (f) 1938	Wu Guanzheng 1938	Wu Bangguo 1941	Yang Rudai 1926
Li Qiang 1959	**Sun Zhengcai** 1963	Liu Yunshan (4J) 1947	Zhang Lichang 1939	Chi Haotian 1926	Zou Jiahua 1926	Yang Shangkun 1907
Hu Chunhua 1963	Li Jianguo 1946	Liu Yandong (4J) (f) 1945	Zhang Dejiang 1946	Zhang Wannian 1928	**Chen Xitong** 1930	Wu Xuequan 1921
Li Hongzhong 1956	Li Yuanchao (5S) 1950	Li Yuanchao (5S) 1950	**Chen Liangyu** 1946	Luo Gan 1935	Jiang Chunyun 1930	Song Ping 1917
Yang Jiechi 1950	Wang Yang (5J) 1955	Wang Yang (5J) 1955	Zhou Yongkang 1942	Jiang Chunyun 1930	Qian Qichen 1928	Hu Yaobang 1915
Yang Xiaodu 1953	Zhang Chunxian 1953	Zhang Gaoli (4J) 1946	Yu Zhengsheng 1945	Jia Qinglin (4S) 1940	Wei Jianxing 1931	Qin Jiwei 1914

Continued

Table 8.1 *Continued*

Thirteenth (1987–1992)	Fourteenth (1992–1997)	Fifteenth (1997–2002)	Sixteenth (2002–2007)	Seventeenth (2007–2012)	Eighteenth (2012–2017)	Nineteenth (2017–2022)
	Xie Fei 1932	Qian Qichen 1928	He Guoqiang 1943	Zhang Dejiang (4J) 1946	Fan Changlong 1947	Zhang Youxia 1950
	Tan Shaowen 1928	Huang Ju 1938	Guo Boxiong 1942	Yu Zhengsheng (4J) 1945	Meng Jianzhu 1947	Chen Xi 1953
	Huang Ju 1938	Wen Jiabao (4S) 1942	Cao Gangchuan 1935	Xu Caihou (4S)* 1943	Zhao Leji 1957	Chen Quanguo 1955
		Xie Fei 1932	Zeng Peiyan 1938	Guo Boxiong (4S)* 1942	Hu Chunhua 1963	Chen Min'er 1960
				Bo Xilai (4J) 1949	Li Zhanshu 1950	Guo Shengkun 1954
					Guo Jinlong 1947	Huang Kunming 1956
					Han Zheng 1954	Cai Qi 1955
Alternate Members of the Politburo						
Ding Guangen 1929	Wen Jiabao 1942	Zeng Qinghong 1939	Wang Gang 1942			
	Wang Hanbie 1935	Wu Yi 1938				

Note: The names of dismissed or purged members are in bold, and they include Hu Yaobang, Zhao Ziyang, Chen Xitong, Chen Liangyu, Xu Caihou, Guo Boxiong, Bo Xilai, and Sun Zhengcai. *the fourteen who retired at the Eighteenth Party Congress in 2012; 5S: "fourth-generation senior"; 4J: "fourth-generation senior"; 5S: "fifth-generation senior"; 5J: "fifth-generation junior."

into the PBSC. Violations of this norm are generally frowned upon, although so-called helicopter promotions skipping rungs on the ladder are not uncommon, especially under expedient situations. Jiang Zemin's promotion as general secretary from the Politburo, and Hu Jintao and Xi Jinping's entry into the PBSC directly from the CC, are good examples. Other criteria for advancement often officially touted include "virtue/ability" and various balances: the former includes loyalty, integrity, expertise, and experience, whereas the latter refers to balances among institutional and geographical interests (what the Chinese call "five lakes and four seas").

In many cases, however, as leaders such as Jiang Zemin, Hu Jintao, and Xi have decried, personnel advancements are often afflicted by the full range of pathologies such as nepotism, corruption, reliance on "guanxi," clamoring for positions (by means even including murder), whereby the opportunistic and mediocre are promoted. In power, officials are often afflicted by "hedonism," "extravagance," scrambling for positions, and abuse of power. And although Leninist-style systems strictly prohibit factionalism, it often thrives.[6] In 2017, the leadership even suggested that the succession process was so intense that an attempted coup took place (see chapter 13). Yet all this is not surprising, as contests for power and position are often intense and conflictual in all political systems. In China, electoral rules are loosely defined and subject to different interpretations, and elections/selections are conducted mostly behind closed doors. Officials often try to present a facade of unity, although the competition for power and position can be quite acute, and China analysts use words such as "battles" and "combat" to describe the internecine struggles behind the scenes. Yet these struggles for positions are not free-for-alls, as they are constrained by precedents, norms, seniority, and hierarchical forms and structures of promotion. A closer look at personnel changes in the Politburo, as illustrated in Table 8.1, shows a large measure of stability of personnel over the twenty-five years between 1992 and 2017 (from the Fourteenth to the Seventeenth Party Congress). Hu Yaobang and Zhao Ziyang, general secretary and acting general secretary for the Thirteenth Party Congress, were purged for their policy differences with Deng Xiaoping. Other notable purges of Politburo members include Chen Xitong, Chen Liangyu, Bo Xilai, Zhou Yongkang, and the generals Guo Boxiong and Xu Caihou, all of whom were charged with crimes of corruption. The rise of Hu Jintao was remarkable; he was helicoptered into the PBSC in 1992 and groomed for general secretary, a position he served for two full terms totaling ten years. Similarly, both Xi Jinping and Li Keqiang were promoted into the PBSC in 2007, succeeding as general secretary and premier in 2012–2013. Both were "re-elected" for a second term in 2017–2018.

Xi and the Eighteenth Party Congress
(November 8–14, 2012)

A major characteristic of the party congresses is that the congress report—deemed a most significant policy document that lays down the theory, policy, and goals to be implemented by the next congress—is drafted by the *outgoing* Politburo. This practice contradicts Western expectation that a newly elected, *incoming* administration will bring its own vision and policies to bear on the government. A great deal of continuity is ensured when the outgoing and incoming leaders collaborate on the congress document, into which both have significant input. Xi's heir-apparent status had already been made explicit when in January 2012 the Politburo decided to formally begin the drafting of the report for the Eighteenth Party Congress in November. Xi was designated the group leader, with Li Keqiang and Liu Yunshan as deputy group leaders, for the leading small group to oversee the drafting.[7] This repeated a pattern whereby Hu Jintao supervised the drafting of the report to the Sixteenth Party Congress in 2001 as a last duty of a designated successor before assuming the top post.[8]

In the following ten months, a draft report was extensively discussed up and down the party hierarchy by party members and nonmembers alike. Hu Jintao, in the first ten months of 2012, convened four PBSC and two Politburo meetings to examine the drafts, and Xi convened eight drafting group meetings for consultations and briefings. In April, Hu spent five and a half days hearing briefs and research reports from thirty-two units. In May, Xi spent two and half days listening to research reports and giving instructions on four key subjects on socioeconomic goals for 2020: the building of a socialist countryside, urbanization, and technological and ecological development. Research teams were dispatched throughout the country to solicit opinions, and repeated consultations with the Politburo, PBSC, and CC, State Council ministries, provinces, and the PLA led to numerous drafts and revisions. For instance, one revision altered the statement that the migrant population should receive "equal voluntary educational opportunities" to read "equal educational opportunities." A new formulation (*tifa*) was added on "the orderly promotion of the transformation of the rural population into an urban population." Amassing sixty-four pages and nearly thirty thousand Chinese characters, the final document represented a consensus within the Party as well as a certain continuity with past policies. It was a strategic plan that summarized the issues and achievements of the past and set goals and measures for the next five or ten years.

Simultaneously, as executive secretary of the Secretariat, Xi was the head of a preparatory group for the Eighteenth Party Congress tasked with the organization of the congress, which included all the major personnel changes in the national leaderships. In determining these positions, Xi undoubtedly gathered a good sense of the ideological and policy views within the Party, as well as an intimate knowledge about personnel issues and changes (see Table 8.3). As the heir apparent, Xi closely supervised the broader succession process himself, although much of the work was carried out within the Party with little or no media coverage. CCP rules do not see a conflict of interest when a successor directs the preparations for a party congress that will "elect" him as a top leader.

On the election of the PBSC and Politburo, a similar straw vote called "democratic recommendation," first used prior to the Seventeenth Party Congress in 2007, was repeated. In May, Party Central convened a conference consisting of more than three hundred CC members, alternate members, and other "responsible" officials to vote for candidates for the PBSC and Politburo. Each conference participant was given a ballot and a name list of nearly two hundred approved candidates.[9] The outcome of the voting was not binding, although it gave the organizers a sense of the opinion on personnel matters.

As to the elections of the delegates to the Eighteenth Party Congress, they were not free or direct in the Western sense, since they were controlled from the top but with a good deal of spontaneous input from the bottom. Election planning began in October 2011. From April to July in 2012, forty electoral districts in the CCP representing four hundred thousand grassroots-level party organizations and eighty-two million party members participated in an electoral process to elect delegates to the NPC. Not merely constituencies representing population and geography, these electoral districts were also meant to represent administrative units; institutions; and occupational and social groups such as women, workers, farmers, and national minorities (see Table 8.2). For instance, along with districts representing China's thirty-three provincial-level administrations, there were others representing institutions such as central party organizations, government ministries and commissions, the PLA, the PAP and central SOEs,[10]

Table 8.2 Official Breakdown of the Characteristics of the Delegates to the Eighteenth Party Congress

Leadership cadres	1578	69.5%
Front-line party members	692	30.5%
Workers (including 26 migrant workers)	169	7.4%
Women	521	23%
National minorities (44 out of 55 national minorities represented)	249	11%

Source: "Renminwang ping: Kejin xingdang zhize, meiyiwei dangdaibiao dushi yimianqi" [Renminwang Commentary: Strive to Fulfill the Duty of Invigorating the Party: Every Party Delegate Is a Standard Bearer], *Renminwang*, November 8, 2012.

Table 8.3 Nomination and Election of the Eighteenth Central Committee and CCDI Members (the "Two Committees")

Dates	Process and procedure
October 2011	The Sixth Plenum decides that the Eighteenth Party Congress will be convened in the second half of 2012.
July 2011 to June 2012	Party Central sends out fifty-nine inspection teams to the thirty-one provinces/municipalities, 130 central government and financial organs, as well as central SOEs located in Beijing; the CMC dispatches nine inspection groups to all major units of the PLA and PAP. The inspection criteria consist of virtue, ability, diligence, achievement, and integrity.
Beginning second half of 2011	The PBSC convenes eleven meetings to listen to reports by the inspection teams. At the end, 727 candidates for the "two committees" are selected.
October 2012	The PBSC selects 532 candidates for the "two committees."
October 22, 2012	The PBSC approves the lists of candidates for the "two committees" and decides to present the lists to the Eighteenth Party Congress for scrutiny.
November 8, 2012	The Eighteenth Party Congress opens.
November 10, 2012	At the second meeting of the Presidium of the congress, Xi Jinping explains the lists. After the candidates presented by the Seventeenth PBSC are approved by the Presidium, they are presented to the congress at large for discussion. Afterward, a preliminary election nominates 224 candidates as full members of the CC, 190 as alternate members of the CC, and 141 for the CCDI.
November 13, 2012	The third meeting of the Presidium passes the candidate lists for the "two committees."
November 14, 2012	The congress at large formally elects the new CC and CCDI.

Source: "Shibada sudi: Xinyijie zhongwei he zhongjiwei danshengji" [Eighteenth Party Congress Express News: The Formation Process for the New CC and CCDI Is Revealed], *Zhongguo xinwenshe*, November 14, 2012.

as well as those representing various occupations in the economy, science and technology, national defense, political and legal affairs, education, propaganda, culture, health, sports, and social management.[11] The election was not a simple bottom-up affair because the central and higher party authorities directly supervised the proceedings according to complex principles of repeated "up-and-down fermentation" and "step-by-step election/selection" (*congshang erxia, shangxia jiehe, fanfu yunniang, zhuji linxuan*). Nominations were carried out by local party branches, and the lists of candidates were winnowed and approved by upper levels. About 15 percent of the nominees were eliminated to give a sense of competition.[12]

Every step of the election process for the delegates, from initial recommendation,[13] nomination, and scrutiny to public input, was supervised and controlled by the COD. Inspection teams jointly formed by the COD and CCDI were dispatched to electoral districts to scrutinize the proceedings and suitability of the delegates. Commissions for inspecting discipline and organizational departments at various levels adopted measures to ensure the discipline and the integrity of the election and to prevent bribery and the solicitation of votes (*lapiao*).[14] Unlike party conventions in the West, potential candidates were forbidden to campaign and to lobby, efforts derided as akin to a corrupt practice of pulling strings to obtain official positions (*paoguan yaoguan*). They were to be evaluated simply by their alleged merits and qualifications. Eventually, 2,270 congress delegates were elected by the provincial congresses. Delegates served a representation function, and within the Party it is a matter of honor and prestige to be elected. More importantly, however, the delegates elected among themselves the CC, and the CC would in turn elect the Politburo and the PBSC, making the congress a gateway to elite leadership. Because of the function of representing various social and occupational groups, not all delegates are expected to have the qualifications to move upward or become serious contenders for higher office. Considerable effort had to be expended to make sure that the political contenders favored by the Party were included ("elected") and perhaps that's one of the reasons why the COD claimed that the workload was unprecedented. The party constitution does not specify that CC members *must* be elected from among the delegates, although that has been the usual practice, and election of a nondelegate outsider to the CC is extremely rare. As to the candidates for the Politburo, their inclusion as delegates of the congress could not be left to chance, and that was why those slated for the Politburo were directly nominated by the Party Central.[15]

At the actual congress, a preparatory meeting on November 7 approved the agenda and elected Xi as secretary general of the Presidium, which directly supervised the congress. Aided by the Central Publicity Department head Liu Yuanshan, COD head Li Yuanchao, and director of the Central Staff Office Li Zhanshu as deputy secretary generals,[16] Xi supervised and coordinated the complicated processes and contentious gatekeeper functions of selecting the elite CC, Politburo, and PBSC.

CCP congresses are fundamentally different from party conventions in Western multiparty democracies. In the latter, each political party holds a convention where rival groups with competing policy platforms and personalities debate and compete for delegate votes on policy questions and candidate selections. Once a leader has been elected, she or he goes on to compete with other political parties in general elections to become president or prime minister and to form governments according to specific rules. CCP congresses, however, are governed by different assumptions and dynamics. In this comparative context, the CCP congress is a party convention and a top party and government leadership election rolled into one.

Of significance was the participation by convention of the seldom-noted fifty-seven unelected "specially invited delegates" who enjoyed equal voting privileges with regular delegates.[17] In nature very similar to the "superdelegate" party elders, leaders, and functionaries at US party conventions, these delegates consisted mostly of party elders, retired former Politburo leaders, and even non-party personnel. Further, these delegates and outgoing Politburo members such as Hu Jintao and Wen Jiabao formed an important part of the executive committee of the Presidium that supervised the proceedings of the party congress. Such long-retired elders as Jiang Zemin, Li Peng, Wan Li, Qiao Shi, Zhu Rongji, Song Ping, Zeng Qinghong, and Luo Gan also figured prominently at the congress. By using their positions to participate in the congress, they played a role completely outside the purview of the party constitution, and by virtue of their connections, prestige, and seniority, they could easily exert strong influence over the elections of the CC and CCDI.

Ages of the delegates ranged from twenty-two to ninety-six. The younger ones were born in the 1980s, and the majority were born in the 1950s. Those who joined the CCP during the reform period consisted of 72.2 percent. A total of 2,122, or 93.5 percent, had university-level education. Workers elected included delegates working in the coal industry, iron and steel, machinery industry, and service sectors such as communication and transport, city government, environmental protection, finance, economics, and commerce, and included twenty-six migrant workers. Among the rural party members, there were grassroots-level cadres, leaders of production cooperatives, teachers, doctors, ordinary farmers, and four university-educated village officials (*cunguan*).[18] Other delegates included model laborers, exemplary moral models, and standouts who had contributed to disaster relief or advanced party affairs, as well as a handful of sports champions and academics. Some individuals had served as delegates for up to four congresses.[19] Altogether, 145 entrepreneurs were elected. Among these, 111 delegates were from the SOEs, the banking and finance system (of which 52 were from the central SOEs and 42 were from the central banking and finance system), and 34 were from nonstate sectors, showing the predominance of the state sector. In the past, a number of entrepreneurs had advanced one step further by being elected as alternate members of the CC at the Sixteenth and Seventeenth Party Congresses, and this was often a reflective of the center's view regarding the nonstate sector.[20]

In contrast with Western-style party conventions, the retiring Hu Jintao presided over the Eighteenth Party Congress from beginning to end. He delivered the important political report that reviewed the record of the past five years and outlined the general direction to be followed in the next. This repeated a pattern whereby in 2002 Hu Jintao was the head of the drafting group that prepared the report that Jiang Zemin delivered at his retirement as general secretary at the Sixteenth Party Congress. Because the report was a collective enterprise hammered out by extensive consultation within the Party and which received numerous drafts and revisions, it was never a personal statement. It represented a consensus of the leadership and was then up to the newly elected Xi leadership to implement. In addition, the congress amended the party constitution to enshrine Hu's theoretical innovation "the scientific outlook on development" and ranked it among the tenets of Marxism-Leninism, Mao Zedong thought, Deng Xiaoping theory, and the "three represents" as the Party's guidelines for action. Amendments to the Party's constitution also pledged to promote ecological progress.[21]

Xi and the New Eighteenth Politburo Standing Committee

At the closing session of the congress on November 14 the delegates elected a new CC (with 205 full members and 171 alternate members) and a CCDI (with 171 members). Since the Party had formally banned factions and factional activities, there was no open campaigning or speeches; instead, the delegates were given brief biographies of candidates as information. At the time, official accounts attempted to advance an image of a unified Party successful in fostering another peaceful and orderly transition of power, suggesting the superiority and efficiency of the Chinese political system, although Western and diaspora media continued to speculate on conflicts, conspiracy, and assassination. Mysteriously, Xi disappeared from public view from September 2 to September 15, missing scheduled meetings with US secretary of state Hillary Clinton, with Singapore prime minister Lee Hsien Loong, and Danish prime minister Helle Thorning-Schmidt, fueling speculation about Xi's physical or political health. Rumors swelled that Xi might have injured his back swimming or playing soccer or might have been the victim of an assassination attempt. One guess was that Xi, embroiled in family and factional conflicts, deliberately withdrew himself to show that he was indispensable so that he could get his way.[22] One recent source claims that Zhou Yongkang, Guo Boxiong, and Xu Caihou conspired to abort Xi's succession by plotting his assassination.[23] Normally such claims could not be authenticated, but during 2017, a series of official pronouncements shattered the strenuously cultivated appearance of a peaceful and orderly leadership transition by revealing a leadership split and even an actual coup attempt to derail Xi' succession (details in chapter 12).

One day after the formal conclusion of the party congress on November 15, the newly minted CC, including members who were just elected the day before, met in its First Plenum to elect the Politburo and the PBSC, and Xi became general secretary. In contrast with Hu Jintao's experience of not being named as chair of the CMC until two years into his first term, Xi was immediately named chair of the CMC, ending months of speculation on whether Hu Jintao would retain the post for himself to extend his power. The plenum was presided over by Xi, and once again, no campaigning or speeches were reported, and therefore what information the delegates had to go by in their choice is unclear, but this is no surprise as it was mostly a preset formality. The composition and members of the Politburo and PBSC had also been predetermined after months of negotiation and bargaining, which is not to say there were no last-minute surprises. At the press conference introducing him as newly elected general secretary, Xi gave a short ten-minute speech referring to future plans and the combating of corruption without giving any specifics. Members of the new PBSC and Politburo were not required to answer questions, as there was no question-and-answer period. The new leadership was revealed, although the party congress was the show of the outgoing leaders. By the same token, Xi did not become president and Li Keqiang the premier until the National People's Congress in the following March, during which retiring premier Wen Jiabao delivered the key government report.

The Apex of Power: The Politburo Standing Committee and the Politburo

The outgoing Hu-Wen team played key roles in determining and shaping the makeup and structure of the new leadership. Seven out of the nine members of the Seventeenth PBSC stepped down according to age retirement rules, and Xi and Li were inducted into the PBSC (see Table 8.4). The downsizing of the number of members in the PBSC from nine to seven by reverting to the pre-2007 norm gave Xi more leverage and authority as "first among equals." In 2007 the PBSC was expanded to nine so Jiang Zemin could exert his influence with two additional members in charge of political and legal matters, and culture and propaganda. As will be seen in the next chapter, Xi used the advantage of a smaller PBSC to dominate policymaking during his first term, although his ambitious reform agenda also relied on his PBSC colleagues to implement. Past PBSC sizes varied, as the size is not specified in the party constitution, ranging generally from five to seven with a high of eleven. The average age of members

Table 8.4 Members of the Eighteenth Politburo, Its Standing Committee, and the Secretariat

	Date of birth	Eighteenth Party Congress Position(s)	Previous position(s)
PBSC			
Xi Jinping	1953.06	General secretary, president, chair CMC	PBSC member; vice president; deputy chair, CMC; principal, Central Party School
Li Keqiang	1955.07	Premier	PBSC member; executive vice premier
Zhang Dejiang	1946.11	Chair, Standing Committee, NPC	Politburo member; vice premier; secretary, Chongqing PPC
Yu Zhengsheng	1945.04	Chair, CPPCC	Politburo member; secretary, Shanghai MPC
Liu Yunshan	1947.07	Principal, Central Party School	Politburo member; director, Central Propaganda Department
Wang Qishan	1948.07	Secretary, CCDI	Politburo member; vice premier
Zhang Gaoli	1946.11	Executive vice premier	Politburo member; secretary, Tianjin MPC
Politburo			
Meng Jianshu	1947.07	Secretary, Political and Law Commission	State councilor; minister, minister of public security
Zhao Leji	1957.03	Secretary, Secretariat; director, Central Organization Department	Secretary, Shaanxi PPC
Liu Qibao	1953.01	Director, Central Propaganda Department	Secretary, Sichuan PPC
Li Zhanshu	1950.08	Director, Central General Office	Secretary, Guizhou PPC
Li Yuanchao	1950.11	Vice president	Politburo member; director, Central Organization Department
Liu Yandong	1945.11	Vice premier	Politburo member; state councilor
Wang Yang	1955.03	Vice premier	Politburo member; secretary, Guangdong PPC

Continued

Table 8.4 *Continued*

	Date of birth	Eighteenth Party Congress Position(s)	Previous position(s)
Ma Kai	1946.06	Vice premier	State councilor; secretary general, State Council
Wang Huning	1955.10	Director, Central Foreign Affairs Office and Office of the Central State Security LSG	Secretary, Secretariat; director, Central Policy Research Office and State Council Economic Research Center
Fan Changlong	1947.05	Vice chair, CMC	Commander, Jinan Military Region
Xu Qiliang	1950.03	Vice chair, CMC	Commander PLA Air Force
Guo Jinlong	1947.07	Secretary, Beijing MPC	Mayor, Beijing
Han Zheng	1954.04	Secretary, Shanghai MPC	Mayor, Shanghai
Sun Chunlan	1950.05	Secretary, Tianjin MPC	Secretary, Fujian PPC
Sun Zhengcai	1963.09	Secretary, Chongqing MPC	Secretary, Jilin PPC
Hu Chunhua	1963.04	Secretary, Guangdong PPC	Secretary, Neimenggu ARPC
Zhang Chunxian	1953.05	Secretary, Uighur ARPC	Secretary, Henan PPC
The Secretariat			
Liu Yunshan	1947.07	Concurrent, see above	
Liu Qibao	1953.01	Concurrent, see above	
Zhao Leji	1957.03	Concurrent, see above	
Li Zhanshu	1950.08	Concurrent, see above	
Du Qinglin	1946.11	Vice chair, CPPCC	
Zhao Hongzhu	1947.07	Deputy executive secretary, CCDI	Secretary, Zhejiang PPC
Yang Jing	1953.12	State councilor; secretary general, State Council	Deputy director, Central United Front Work Department; director, State National Minorities Affairs Committee

Source: "Zhonggong dishibajie zhongyang zhengzhju weiyuan miangdian" [A Name List of the PBSC of the CCP's Eighteenth Central Committee], n.d., http://news.ifeng.com/mainland/special/zhongg ong18da/zhengzhijuweiyuan.shtml, accessed May 3, 2014.

was 63.4. Xi at fifty-nine and Li at fifty-seven would be able to serve two terms, but the other five—all in their midsixties, would have to retire in the Nineteenth Party Congress in 2017, when they would exceed the age of sixty-eight. By then the fifth generation would dominate the PBSC. Among the twenty-five members of the new Politburo, ten were incumbents and fifteen were newcomers. No woman has ever sat on the PBSC, and the Eighteenth PBSC was no exception.[24] As to the wider Politburo, there were two women, Liu Yandong and Sun Chunlan, as compared to only one in the Fifteenth, Sixteenth, and Seventeenth Politburos. The Nineteenth Politburo had one, but there were none in the Thirteenth and Fourteenth Politburos. In a departure from past practices, no ethnic minority member was included.

Fifteen members were born in the eastern regions (60 percent), but none in Guangdong or the southwest (Sichuan, Chongqing Yunnan, and Guizhou). Provincial or municipal leadership experience at China's thirty-three provincial-level units is normally a sine qua non to PBSC and Politburo membership. Six out of seven members of the PBSC had served as provincial chiefs, party secretaries, governors, or mayors, the exception being Liu Yunshan, who began as a journalist, served as a deputy secretary of Inner Mongolia, and had been deputy (1993–2002) and then director (2002–2012) of the Central Propaganda/Publicity Department.[25]

Explaining the Outcome

As much of Chinese politics occurs in a black box, China watchers have used a range of perspectives and educated guesses to describe and explain Chinese elite and succession politics. At the broader level of comparative communism, the variables employed may not completely fit the case of the Xi Jinping succession. For instance, Holmes has postulated a framework of "3Ps + X," with 3Ps referring to power bases, personalities, and policies, and X to special or contingent circumstances.[26] In Xi's case, the selection appeared dominated by a top-down process whereby outgoing leaders called the shots, and campaigning and lobbying had no place. Hence, Xi could not explicitly form alliances to bolster his position or weaken that of other contestants. As well, little is known for certain about the strength of his patronage or the depth of his regional power base, as both are subject to numerous contrasting interpretations. His personality and policies are known important factors, but as their assessment was in the hands of the elders, Xi could not leverage them to argue his own case, assuming that he even wanted to do so. Perhaps the most significant X factor, as we have observed, was the Party's deliberate planning and cultivation that had come to fruition.[27] By 2007 there was already a rough consensus for assigning Xi and Li as the dual informal successors.

Other attempts to describe and explain Chinese succession politics essentially mirror, consciously or unconsciously, implicitly or explicitly, the three approaches and assumptions of comparative politics: the rationality, structure, and culture approaches.[28] Each perspective favors a particular independent variable and set of assumptions, but the more sophisticated analysts pay attention to all three, with the choice of major perspective being a matter of degree of emphasis. These distinctions are heuristic devices to evaluate existing analyses and to clarify the issues under discussion. At the risk of simplification, I briefly discuss and evaluate these three perspectives and how they have been applied to interpret the Chinese experience.

The Rationality / Power Maximization Approach

The rationality approach explains Chinese politics in terms of rational choices by individual political actors. The independent variable is said to be the actors' desire to maximize their self-interests and power, or at least to better themselves economically. They define their self-interests through cost-benefit analyses. Their behavior is determined by their aspiration to perpetuate their power to influence policy, or even to struggle for power for power's sake. Since a struggle for power may feature fierce and cutthroat battles for supremacy, these actors are said to engage in strategic behavior to strengthen themselves and to weaken their rivals or enemy groups. Chinese leaders are said to be motivated primarily by desires to protect their clients and families and to perpetuate their influence, and this applies even to elders who have long retired. Their strategic calculations and behavior typically comprise competition, balancing, alliance-building, and bandwagoning. Yet this school of thought recognizes that rationality is in turn conditioned by institutions, culture, and society, and that maximization behavior is shaped by a range of economic, social, and institutional constraints.

Some analysts taking this approach postulate that Xi and Li were rivals competing for the general secretary position, although, as we have discussed, the two had long settled into the two tracks, one party and one government, assigned to them. Other rational choice perspectives put long-retired general secretaries front and center. In this view, retired elders often try to maximize or preserve their influences by clinging to their offices and titles even into extreme old age. As patrons, they are interested in protecting and promoting former clients and installing protégés in new leaderships. They continue to pull strings with an eye toward ensuring their legacy and a positive historical evaluation. As to Jiang Zemin specifically, his primary interest was to protect his legacy, as well as his two sons and other relatives who had made fortunes, some by questionable means.[29] In this view, Xi's reign would be complicated by having to face the unique challenge of having two former party chiefs breathing down his neck, in addition to retired "third" and "fourth" generation leaders. The notion that retired leaders strive to maximize or preserve their influences, especially in the Chinese context, is plausible but not immutable. For instance, there is no evidence to suggest that Hu Jintao had attempted to exert his influence during Xi's first term [30]

Another variation of the rationality / power maximization approach is contained in Cheng Li's "one party, two coalitions" (OPTC) thesis, which sees the composition of the PBSC as an outcome of a struggle between the two leaders of the "elitist" and the "populist" coalitions. Although the OPTC scenario focuses on "factional" struggles and may fall under system/institutional analysis, its emphasis on the roles of allegedly power-maximizing leaders and their strategic manipulations has a great deal to do with rational choice. For instance, in this view, long-retired Jiang Zemin scored a "landslide victory" by winning six of the seven PBSC seats, those held by Xi, Zhang Dejiang, Yu Zhengsheng, Liu Yunshan, Wang Qishan, and Zhang Gaoli. Accordingly, Hu Jintao was said to have been outmaneuvered, only able to insert one of his *tuanpai* protégés, Li Keqiang, into the PBSC, since both Wang Yang, Guangdong party chief and Li Yuanchao, presumed to be Hu Jintao's capable protégés, were shut out. Both the latter were regarded as sympathetic to reform, and their omission is said to be a victory of the "conservatives." Additionally, another eligible *tuanpai* candidate, Liu Yandong, failed to make it to the PBSC. Further, the reduction of the PBSC from nine to seven is said to be Jiang's tactic to block Hu Jintao's protégés, and Hu lost the battle. In the broader Politburo, however, the Jiang and Hu camps equally divided up the remaining eighteen seats.[31] When Hu was elevated to general secretary in 2002, Jiang Zemin held on to the post of CMC chairman for two more years before yielding the position to Hu. Rational choice China watchers have often interpreted this to be Jiang's unwillingness to give up his formal power, conforming to a pattern of elders' interference in Chinese politics. They predicted that Hu Jintao would imitate Jiang by hanging on to the position of CMC chair, but as it turned out, Hu gave up the position when he retired as general secretary. The OPTC theory, as a grand thesis, may offer huge explanatory value, but as previously argued, my discussion of the political career and policy orientations of Xi Jinping and Li Keqiang finds no support for it. And the notion that the *tuanpai* is a cohesive and powerful force forged by career experience finds no support throughout the analysis in this book.

Another rational choice variation postulates that Jiang, age eighty-six, had exerted his influence in the choice of PBSC membership by shutting out Hu's own choices. He had accomplished the same feat when he retired as general secretary at the generational turnover at the Sixteenth Party Congress in 2002. He stacked the PBSC with five of his allies, Zhang Dejiang, Yu Zhengsheng, Liu Yunshan,

Wang Qishan, and Zhang Gaoli, all said to be conservatives. Therefore, the PBSC was an outcome of machinations of the long-retired Jiang and his crony Zeng Qinghong to limit Hu's associates in the new leadership in order to reduce Hu's residual influence in retirement, prolonging Jiang's influence and promoting his factional followers.[32]

Overall, the realpolitik assumptions of rationality theory are a dominant paradigm because it provides a compelling explanation, especially when so much is unknown about Chinese elite politics and competition. Power cleavages are often the most fruitful avenues in analyzing politics in all political systems. But since the internal behavior of individuals and groups occur in a black box and there is little or no direct evidence of power relations, analysts tend to rely heavily on deduction and intuition to surmise or to reconstruct scenarios. For any one situation, this often leads to a whole range of power struggle analyses of varying quality, which only feeds the Chinese diaspora rumor mills. One may also add that political behavior and outcomes are often counterintuitive. Not all Chinese officials seek to maximize power or do so to the same degree, and political conflicts are often tempered by cooperation and compromise.

Structure/Institutional Approaches

The structure/institutional approach does not dismiss power struggle and maximization as important variables, but it stresses other determinants such as political structures, institutions, and norms that shape and constrain Chinese political behavior. Often these institutions, norms, and rules of the game have been historically generated and determined.[33] The party state is the predominant political structure in China, but within itself, bureaucratic actors and organizations compete with one another, although they are constrained by rules and conventions. Similarly, despite the formal ban on factions, factions and groups thrive and struggle with one another. This is particularly the case with issues such as personnel selection and political succession, but these competitions are constrained by explicit rules such as age restrictions, seniority, merits, term limits, and governance experience. Often, elite behavior is guided by compromise, which often brings about implicit rules to balance among various factional, geographical, and organizational interests to maintain political equilibrium. How this structure reproduces and sustains itself over time is a central concern for the structuralists' analysts.

One key institutional concern among CCP officials is the long-term viability and survival of CCP rule and the maintenance of regime legitimacy. To achieve these goals, there is a great deal of incentive to ensure that the Party maintains discipline, unity, and effectiveness. As Susan Shirk puts it, CCP leaders know that if they do not hang together, they could hang separately.[34] To ensure orderly succession, party leaders take on the cultivation of successors in the form of "passing on, assisting, and nurturing." Adherents of neoinstitutionalism theory argue that institutions such as the CCP are collective actors in their own right, struggling to maintain their own interests and goals through their agencies. The result is that leadership succession and regime renewal in China have displayed a great deal of continuity and stability, so that the outcome of these processes is often predictable.

One variation on the structural approach is the conflict model, which posits that rival factions, patron-client networks, and webs of human relationships struggle and compete for power and interests. In Mao's time, factional struggle tended to be seen as a zero-sum game, as factions struggled to demolish rival factions in a winner-takes-all ("You die, I live") situation. These conflicts can be so intense that violent events and even coups d'état are often attempted, as attested by official admissions and by insiders who have experienced such events firsthand. Another variation of this conflict model, more applicable to the post-Mao period, postulates that in these factions, patron-client networks still struggle for power with one another to maximize their advantage, but since there is no hope of demolishing their opponents and since the continuation of party survival is a prime concern, struggle is constrained, and rival groups even settle for a kind of cooperation and coexistence. In the post-Mao period, their competition has even been governed by an informal code of civility.

The determinants in system/institutional analyses are party norms, age, term limits, merits, experience, and seniority. By referring to these variables, Miller explains the placement of the seven Eighteenth Congress PBSC members:[35] Party rules stipulate that a party congress meet every five years and incumbents serve five-year terms. A norm set up in 2002 that Politburo members reaching the age of sixty-eight retire at the next congress has been consistently observed. These two arrangements created (1) a calculus of retirement and succession dividing Politburo members into cohorts according to their terms of membership and dates of anticipated retirement. For instance, according to the age-sixty-eight norm, Politburo members born between the years 1940 and 1944 were required to retire at the Eighteenth Party Congress because those born in 1940 would be seventy-two in 2012. Those born before 1940 had already retired at the 2007 congress. The arrangements also created (2) a criterion of selection among the pool of eligible candidates whereby the new general secretary would be around sixty years of age and would serve two consecutive terms and then retire. Hu Jintao, born in 1942, became general secretary in 2002 at age sixty, turned sixty-eight in 2010, and retired at the Eighteenth Party Congress. Xi Jinping, on the other hand, was fifty-nine when he succeeded Hu as general secretary at the 2012 congress. The expectation at that time was that, having turned sixty-eight in 2021, he would retire in 2022, barring other contingencies[36] (see Table 8.1).

Using the above criteria, Miller maintains that Politburo members can be divided into two age cohorts, senior and junior. Hence, the "fourth generation" senior cohort (4S) encompasses those born between 1940 and 1944, and the junior cohort (4J) those born between 1945 and 1949 (denoted by the asterisks in Table 8.1). Since the fifth-generation leaders were likely able to serve two terms, they too can be divided into a senior (5S) and a junior (5J) cohort; the former includes those born between 1950 and 1954 and the latter between 1955 and 1959. By referring to generational and cohort analysis, the logic of the memberships of the Eighteenth PBSC and Politburo became clear and straightforward—it was just a matter of seniority! In 2007, fourteen 4Ss from the Seventeenth Politburo retired, as mandated by the age-sixty-eight norm. Of the remaining ten Seventeenth Politburo carryovers, Xi and Li retained their PBSC posts, consistent with the intention of deliberate grooming. Six were 4J and two were 5S and 5J. The rest were new entrants. Five who were promoted to the seven-seat PBSC came from the 4J cohort, although Liu Yandong was an exception, since patriarchy has so far prevented women from entering the apex of power, the PBSC. Li Yuanchao (5S) and Wang Yang (5J) were excluded from the PBSC simply because of their lack of seniority, although it was assumed that they would become eligible for the PBSC at the Nineteenth Party Congress in 2017, when all five of the 4J cohort leaders promoted to the Eighteenth PBSC would retire, according to the age-sixty-eight norm.

Table 8.5 Institutional Representation in the Eighteenth Politburo

Party apparatus	State organ	Regional	Military/security
Liu Yunshan	Zhang Gaoli	Sun Chunlan	Meng Jianshu
Wang Qishan	Ma Kai	Sun Zhengcai	
Liu Qibao	Wang Huning	Zhang Chunxian	Gen. Fan Changlong
Zhao Leji	Liu Yandong	Hu Chunhua	Gen. Xu Qiliang
Li Zhanshu	Li Jianguo	Guo Jinlong	
	Li Yuanchao	Han Zheng	
	Wang Yang		

Source: Alice L. Miller, "The New Party Politburo Leadership," *China Leadership Monitor*, No. 40, Winter 2013, p. 11.

Looking back at the Sixteenth Party Congress in 2002, Miller argues that age and seniority seem to be the most compelling reason accounting for the transition of leadership generations. All eight of the outgoing Fifteenth Politburo not retired were promoted to the Sixteenth PBSC, expanding that body to nine. The logic of seniority is also evident in the protocol ranking of the PBSC since 2002. The four newcomers to the PBSC in 2007 were ranked after the five who retained their seats from the previous PBSC. Similarly in the 2012 lineup, party seniority dictated that premier designate Li Keqiang was listed ahead of Zhang Dejiang, who was appointed NPeC chair in March 2013, reversing the practice of listing the protocol rank of the NPeC chair before the premier in the 2007 PBSC.[37] Returning to the Eighteenth Politburo, Miller also argues that its composition was carefully apportioned among the four major institutional constituencies, the party apparatus, the state organs, the regional authorities, and the military/security apparatus. As shown in Table 8.5, except for the four heads of the four major hierarchies (Xi Jinping, Li Keqiang, Zhang Dejiang, and Yu Zhengsheng), the remaining twenty members of the Politburo are given a division of labor among the four sectors. This careful balance was probably inspired by the Soviet example during the Brezhnev era, the purpose of which was to prevent (1) any one sector overpowering the institutional interest of the others; (2) one single leader, especially the general secretary, asserting dominance over the collective oligarchy.[38]

In this regard, even if one grants that there was intense bargaining and horse-trading that occurred months before the Eighteenth Congress, and notwithstanding the power struggle and maximization perspective, the outcome of the PBSC configuration was not surprising and was fairly predictable, considering the small pool of contenders, the age limits, and the staggered aspect of orderly succession. Henceforth, the prediction games would be popular with the media and academics.[39] Immediately before the congress, more credible outside sources, such as the *South China Morning Post*, correctly projected the makeup of the PBSC,[40] and others missed the mark by only one or two members.[41]

The Cultural Approach

The cultural approach takes culture as an independent variable that shapes political behavior and is therefore relevant to an analysis of political leadership and succession. Culture is explained in terms of values, ideals, traditions, beliefs, and worldviews shared by a community. It also encompasses elements such as symbols and cognitive and affective characteristics. Culturalists are interested in how values are learned, mutually constructed, internalized, and transmitted through socialization, and how various values form into patterns. China's traditional political culture is based on Confucianism and characterized by such values as hierarchy, dependency, paternalism, respect for age and seniority, and conflict avoidance. It follows that political and other relationships would then be molded by deference to authority, "guanxi," patron-client reciprocity, and informal politics. This is further complicated by other more recent strands of political culture, including the Maoist values of populism, voluntarism, and nationalism; the Leninist values of organization and democratic centralism; and the Dengist reform period values of growth and development, not to mention materialist, postmaterialist, and other sociological and philosophical values.[42]

The tremendously complex Chinese political culture demonstrates why cultural explanations are often ambiguous and why the concept of culture is a nebulous one. Elements of Chinese culture are fluid, amorphous, and malleable rather than static, and are frequently contested and subject to change, especially with modern China's expansive contact with the outside world. Given this, one analyst argues, cultural explanations can be persuasive only when structural and institutional factors have been ruled out.[43] This notwithstanding, many of the hypotheses generated by cultural explanations can be empirically tested and demonstrated. In this respect, several most pertinent points can be made. First, because of the respect for age and continuity, long-retired leaders are venerated and allowed to influence and participate in succession outcomes. Elders have regularly attended party congresses and served as Presidium members even though their "factions" were reportedly wiped out. Their contributions, theoretical or policy wise, are formally acknowledged in order to demonstrate continuity in development. Second, the "meritocracy" of the modern Chinese party state owes its origin to the traditional Confucian bureaucracy, and, according to one analyst, it still constitutes a "meritocratic democracy" that is morally desirable and politically stable.[44] Third, the Leninist culture of organization and planning explains the carefully premeditated relay race of the staggered succession pattern. Fourth, Maoist/Leninist notions of democratic centralism and mass line prescribe a high degree of centralism and top-down decision-making but also advocate widespread consultation regarding personnel changes, especially within the Party.[45] Fifth, the traditional patriarchal strand in Confucian culture prevents women from entering the highest levels of politics.

Each of the three approaches has its strengths and weaknesses, and, inevitably, any one approach highlights certain aspects of the complex Chinese reality but neglects others. One perspective explains a certain situation better, but another does better with other situations. These are not watertight or mutually exclusive categories and can be mutually applied to interpret Chinese politics to differing extents. For instance, rationality can be conditioned by institutions and culture, and culture can be a product of social-economic-political forces. Structures impose constraints but human action and agency can make choices and use power to transcend these restrictions and introduce change. In analyses of factions and group competitions, a perceptive analyst may simultaneously resort to all three to try to capture the complexity. Those who resort to the rational choice approach can factor in institutional constraints. The three perspectives can be used as complements to one another through different weights being applied to each for different degrees of emphasis. Often the researcher must make choices regarding which independent variable to pick and what phenomenon to explain. Equally important, it is necessary to clarify the assumptions that undergird the various forms of analyses, and the reasons why conclusions are reached. Overall, in order to capture the complexities of our subjects, our consideration of the application of these three perspectives will also take into consideration the historical, contextual, situational, and contingent factors as well.

Attributes of the New Leadership

The New Politburo

The Eighteenth Party Congress continued to fulfill Deng Xiaoping's ideal of turning the leadership into a "younger, better-educated, and more competent" group. It followed the pattern established in the 1990s to select members around sixty years of age for the Politburo, so the average age of the Politburo was just over sixty-one, as compared with the average age of sixty-two in the 2007 Seventeenth Politburo. In comparison, the average ages on appointment to the Sixteenth, Fifteenth, and Twelfth Politburos were sixty, sixty-three, and seventy-two respectively. In terms of educational credentials, nineteen out of twenty-five had university degrees, and one had a military degree, with the remaining five having diplomas from the Central Party School. In comparison, twenty-three members in the Seventeenth Politburo had university degrees, twenty-two in the Sixteenth Politburo, and seventeen in the Fifteenth Politburo, whereas none of the Twelfth Politburo had degrees.

The new Politburo contained fourteen members with work experience from coastal provinces and eleven from the central provinces, whereas in 2007, ten were from the coastal provinces and fifteen from the central provinces. Both the Seventeenth and Eighteenth Politburos contained no members from the western or interior provinces. In 2002, however, eleven were from the coastal provinces, whereas the rest were from the interior regions. Since the 1990s, the Politburo has been largely civilian. Military experience refers to services in the PLA or work in military bureaucracies: the Sixteenth Politburo featured twenty-one of twenty-five members with no military experience, and the Seventeenth Politburo had twenty-two with no military experience and three with experience (this included Xi, who had worked as an aide to Geng Biao). In the Eighteenth Politburo, the four with military experience included Fang Changlong, Xu Qiliang, Xi, and Zhang Chunxian, who had been a PLA soldier in the early 1970s.

Career-wise, the makeup of the new Politburo was consistent with the trend of the rise of leaders who began their political careers during the Cultural Revolution. In the Eighteenth Politburo, fifteen had joined the CCP during the Cultural Revolution, ten joined after, and three joined before. In the Seventeenth Politburo, twelve had joined the CCP during the Cultural Revolution, three after, and the rest in the early 1960s on the eve of the Cultural Revolution. As to the Sixteenth Politburo, its members had mainly joined the CCP in the decade before the Cultural Revolution.[46]

Two "sixth generation" leaders who were elected to the Politburo in 2012 and who were widely perceived to be star candidates for intense grooming were Hu Chunhua and Sun Zhengcai, both born in 1963 (see Table 8.6). At age forty-nine, both had spent their early childhood during the tumultuous Cultural Revolution. Hu Chunhua, a graduate of Peking University, had worked in Tibet for almost twenty years before becoming provincial party chief at Neimenggu. Sun Zhengcai held a PhD in agriculture and served as Minister of Agriculture and secretaries of the Jilin PPC and Chongqing MPC and was another potential candidate for the very top. Both were widely seen as Hu/Wen's choice for grooming as successors following the Xi Jinping–Li Keqiang succession model. It is fair to assume that their experiences and perspectives might be different from those who joined before. However, Sun was eventually purged for corruption and misdemeanor in September 2017 in a case reminiscent of the Bo Xilai affair five years earlier.[47]

The background characteristics of Politburo members also show a continuous trend of shrinking representation of the technical elite, or those with engineering or hard sciences backgrounds, which had dominated in the 1990s. In the Fifteenth Politburo, sixteen of seventeen degree holders were technocrats, including fourteen engineers, and the Sixteenth Politburo contained seventeen engineers and one geologist among the twenty-two degree holders. This was probably because in the 1950s and early 1960s, technical education was emphasized and deemed more relevant and practical for the purpose of promoting modern economic development. In contrast, the Seventeenth Politburo had twenty-three degree holders, but only eleven were engineers, and two had degrees in the hard sciences and mathematics. The rest consisted of four with degrees in economics, one in political science, and three in the humanities. The Eighteenth Politburo consisted of eighteen university degree holders, with four in engineering, one in mathematics, six in economics, two each in international relations and in Chinese literature, and one each in history and in political science.[48] The large diversity of background in recent Politburos may be more suited to the governance of an increasingly complex society and economy than one that

Table 8.6 The Political Careers of Sun Zhengcai and Hu Chunhua

	Year and place of birth; year joined CCP	Education	Early political career	Later political career				
Sun Zhengcai	1963 Rongcheng City, Shandong (1988)	Masters in agronomy, 1984–87; PhD in agronomy 1995–97, both at China Agricultural University	Various positions at Shunyi district of Beijing, 1997–2002; various positions at Beijing Agricultural & Forestry Institute, 1987–95	Member, Beijing MPC, 2002–6	Minister of agriculture, 2006–9	Secretary, Jilin PPC; chair, Jilin People's Congress, 2009–12	Secretary, Chongqing PPC, 2012–17	Trial for corruption and given life sentence, 2018; dismissed from the CCP, 2017
Hu Chunhua	1963 Wufent County, Hebei (1983)	Secretary, Secretariat, CYLC, 1997–2001; various positions in Tibet, 1983–2006	First secretary, CYL CC, 2007–8	Governor, vice governor, acting governor, Heibei, 2008–9	Secretary, Inner Mongolia APPC, 2009–12	Chairman, Inner Mongolia Autonomous Regional People's Congress, 2010–12	Secretary, Guangdong PPC, 2012–17	PBSC member, 2017–22; vice premier, 2013–23

Source: China Vitae and Baidu baike.

focused on rapid economic growth and technological development. Finally, the Eighteenth Politburo also boasted thirteen members who had advanced post-graduate degrees, following the trend set in 2007. Xi, Li Yuanchao, and Liu Yandong held law degrees, while Li Keqiang holds a doctorate in economics, and two others hold master's degrees. Yet, as discussed before, a caveat is that these university and advanced degrees were acquired under divergent circumstances, and their value and quality must be viewed in context.

The Central Committee

Nominally the CC enjoys great power since the party constitution prescribes that the Politburo and the general secretary are elected by the CC and supervised by it until the next party congress. The practice is, however, quite the opposite. The Politburo tightly controls CC membership, determining its composition, and the CC selectorate has never been permitted freely to perform its mandated function. Nor has the CC been much of a deliberative forum, still less a decision-making body, especially in foreign policy. It meets infrequently and briefly, as its members hold full-time jobs scattered around the country. Unlike its Soviet counterpart, the Chinese CC has no record of individuals making speeches or of making collective resolutions. Unanimous approval of Politburo initiatives is still the norm. For instance, in the Eighteenth CC, the general secretary's report, the report by the Central Commission for Discipline Inspection, and the revision of the party constitution were all approved unanimously. The CC has almost never been able to perform its constitutional function of checking and constraining the Politburo and PBSC through its power of election and oversight.

All the above notwithstanding, the CC is not just a collection of luminaries. It is the national elite par excellence, and election to the CC, as either full or alternate member, would presage assignment for government posts in the upcoming NPeC in the following March. Retiring leaders such as Hu Jintao and Wen Jiabao were no longer re-elected, and the same applied to those who were dismissed from the Party, people such as Bo Xilai, Li Zhijun, and Kang Rixin.

The functions of CC members can be divided into four categories. First, a large portion of the membership is apportioned according to the chief party, government, and military positions they occupy. All front-line leaders, including members of the Politburo, Secretariat, CMC, CCDI, and State Council, heads of ministries and commissions, provincial-level party secretaries (especially those from the four centrally administered municipalities), PLA and military region leaders, and leaders of the PAP, have to be included. This job-slot system turns the CC increasingly into a predictable collection of occupants of key positions, and the expansion of party-state posts deemed entitled to CC membership explains the steady increase in the size of the CC.[49]

Second, another category of CC members is deemed important less because of their CC status but more because of their own professional accomplishment. In the Eighteenth CC, this consisted of chairmen of the board for such SOEs as China Investment Corporation and the Bank of China and central SOEs such as China Aviation Industry Corporation, China National Petroleum Corporation, and China North Industries Corporation. Also, the heads of the China Securities Regulatory Commission, the China Banking Regulatory Commission, and the China Insurance Regulatory Commission are similarly included. Most are also head of the party committee of their organizations, but not always so.

Third, the CC is an important holding pool or funnel of recruitment into higher positions, even into the Politburo, at future party congresses and the gateway to access the highest positions. A section of the CC is known to comprise aspiring candidates to these posts; therefore, once selected, these members are subject to scrutiny, probation, and grooming as future national leaders in future party congresses. Similarly, those elected as alternates can aspire to be promoted as full members of the CC because leaders for the next five, ten, or fifteen years will emerge from there through hierarchical and seniority-based promotion.

Fourth, a number of celebrities, experts, academics, members of social organizations, and role models at grassroots levels are often elected to the CC for symbolic reasons, as they do not hold important political positions, nor are they likely to hold them in the future. In the Eighteenth CC these types of members included the presidents of Nankai University, Shanghai Jiaotong University, and the Chinese Academy of Sciences, and the All-China Federation of Taiwan Compatriots. The lone entrepreneur included was the CEO of Haier Group.

Historically, everyone nominated to the CC was elected because the number of candidates to the CC and the number of available CC positions were identical. Not until the Thirteenth Party Congress of 1987, when the number of nominated candidates exceeded the available posts, were a few percentages of candidates eliminated. At the Eighteenth Party Congress, nineteen candidates (or 9.3 percent) were eliminated this way.[50]

Over half (55.6 percent) of the full members comprised new blood, as 114 out of 205 CC members were newly elected, and only 91 (44.5 percent) were re-elected. Those who were born on or before 1944 were disqualified,[51] making for an average age of 56.1. Among the newly elected, many were simply being promoted a step from being alternate members of the Seventeenth CC, and many could expect to receive promotions to state positions as well. CC members such as Hu Jintao and Wen Jiabao exited because of age and retirement. There were those, like Bo Xilai, Liu Zhijun, and Kang Rixin, who were convicted of corruption and were dismissed both from the Party and from the CC. Others, like Yu Youjun, State Council deputy director, were discharged from the CC but not from the Party, to be under observation for two years. Still others, like Chen Deming, the minister of commerce, failed to be re-elected and ended their political career, presumably because of incompetence. The thirty-three women members elected consisted of a small percentage of 16 percent, whereas the thirty-nine national minorities (19 percent) were better represented than the population proportion of around 8 percent. Former *zhiqing* who had been sent downward to the poorest rural areas, consisted of sixty-five members (or 31.7 percent). There were seven in the Politburo (or 28 percent), four in the PBSC (or 57.1 percent). Members of this cohort, like Xi, saw their formal education interrupted by the Cultural Revolution, and only when entrance examinations to the universities were reintroduced could they return to their formal studies.

In terms of age, of the 205 full members, thirty (15 percent of the total) were born in the 1940s, and they would soon retire from politics. One hundred and sixty-five fifth-generation (80.52 percent of the total) members who were born in the 1950s and had moved level by level from the grassroots now constituted the main force on the political stage. Those nine (4.4 percent) who were born in the 1960s were expected to make their mark for decades to come. Average age was now 56.1.[52]

In terms of education, 95.7 percent had university education, with 65 percent having master's degrees and 14 percent having PhDs. About 37.2 percent had senior specialized technical occupations, and there were fifteen research fellows from the Chinese Academy of Sciences and the Chinese Academy of Engineering. As mentioned, this education level, like the one acquired by Xi, must be viewed in the context of the generally slow recovery of educational standards immediately after the Cultural Revolution, and the majority of the degrees were acquired through the party schools or by correspondence. The correspondence education was designed by the party schools to provide for those who had lost their education opportunities during the Cultural Revolution. From 1985 to its termination in 2008, this program had educated more than three million cadres.[53] A remarkable change was that the education background of 90 percent of the members of the new CC were now in the humanities, economics, law, and political science. Only twenty-one (or 10.2 percent) were educated in the physical sciences and engineering, and this contrasted with the 60 percent of the Seventeenth CC who were trained in water conservancy, chemical industry, metallurgy, prospecting, and machinery industries. As such, the predominance of Tsinghua University (primarily sciences and engineering) graduates was now eroded in favor of graduates from three institutions: Renmin's University, Peking University, and Jilin University.[54]

Military personnel made up forty members, or about the usual norm of 20 percent representation at the CC. Because of a new and stricter rule applied only to the military representatives, that all those who had reached age sixty-three had to resign, the majority of these members belonged to the fifth generation, who grew up during the reform period.[55] Some had experience in China's war against Vietnam in 1979, and most were, like everyone else in the PLA, "shocked and awed" by the open display of the military prowess of the United States during the Gulf War of 1990–1991 when they were serving mostly at battalion and regimental levels.[56]

Alternate members, a reserve pool of candidates for full membership during the current or in future CCs, saw their numbers increased by 4 over the last congress, to 171. A high turnover rate was registered, since the 126 newcomers constituted 74 percent of the total and only 45 from the previous CC were re-elected. Unlike full members of the CC, who are listed in order by the number of strokes in their Chinese surname, the alternates are listed according to the votes they obtained, and therefore their relative ranking in the list gives an idea of their support within the Party. There were twenty-three women and twenty-nine minority alternates. Many of the alternates had master's degrees or above, and several were research fellows such as the renowned geneticist and expert on cell biology He Fuchu and nuclear arms industry expert Zhao Xiangeng. Rising political stars included Zhu Mingguo, deputy secretary of the Guangdong PPC at rank fourteen, who was lauded for his resolution of the Wukan conflict; and "seventh generation" member Liu Jian (b. 1970), secretary of the Aletai DPC in Xinjiang. Labor and "good Samaritan" role model Guo Mingyi was also selected as alternate. Diplomatic, cultural, and sporting groups were represented by China's ambassador to the United States, Zhang Yesui; table tennis coach Cai Zhenghua; deputy director of the State Council's Hong Kong–Macau office Zhang Xiaoming, and, last, the secretary of Guangzhou MPC, Wan Qingliang. At their election, alternate members of the Eighteenth CC were holders of appointments to mostly deputy positions, and it was expected that they would be promoted to principal positions.[57]

Of special interest is the case of Li Xiaopeng (b. 1959), the son of former premier Li Peng and therefore a princeling. An engineer, former entrepreneur, and president of the Huaneng Group and Huaneng Power International, Li had abandoned the nonstate sector and pursued a political career wherein he became acting governor of Shanxi. Li was elected an alternate member but ranked last on the list because he gathered the smallest number of votes. However, he was quickly named to the full governor position in January 2013 and was expected to be groomed for future promotion, considering his age and pedigree, and noting that Xi Jinping had also come last in his election as an alternate at the Fifteenth Party Congress. On the other hand, Liang Wengen, chairman of Sany Heavy

Industry and one of China's richest people, with a net worth of US$8 billion, was tipped to become an alternate but failed to be elected. He had famously declared that his life and property "belonged" to the Party,[58] and this may have been seen as excessively sycophantic by the delegates.

Conclusion

The post-Mao leadership under Deng Xiaoping, learning from the experience in the Mao era, strove to reintroduce collective leadership to prevent any single institutional sector or single leader, in particular the general secretary, from asserting dominance. For example, representatives from the security apparatus and military hierarchy continued to be limited to two or fewer Politburo members, presumably to check the power of the general secretary and prevent him from using the PLA as Mao had done. As well, Hu was no longer described as the "core leader" of the collective leadership, as Deng and Jiang (core leaders of the Fourteenth and Fifteenth CC) had been. Collective leadership since the Hu era was also supposed to maintain a balanced representation of major institutional constituencies such as the party apparatus, PRC government and its state organs, the provinces, and the military/security apparatus.[59] However, there was a trade-off in that it became more difficult to form a consensus in the face of daunting challenges.

Finally, the Eighteenth Party Congress affords another opportunity to revisit the issue of institutionalization. During the 2002/2003, and 2007/2008 party and state congresses, the retirement age of sixty-eight, five-year terms, and the regular convening of plenums were observed according to formal and informal party norms. Such acts have standardized replacement and set a solid precedent, making for a more predictable succession. Furthermore, appointments to the PBSC according to seniority, clearly observable in all three congresses, have undercut factional competition.[60] Although informal politics, rivalry, and conflict were still common and rules could be manipulated (such as the rule regarding the numbers in the PBSC), competition was carried out within consolidated institutional rules and norms of acceptable behavior. Hu's decision to retire concurrently as CMC chair, rather than to copy the precedent of Jiang, is another example. The orderly and deliberate transfer of power was no "trivial achievement."[61] Yet, as I have discussed before, it is probably premature to suggest that this represents the "institutionalization of the Chinese political system." The age-sixty-eight norm has been observed for four party congresses since 2002, although not applied to the general secretary. And as we shall see later, the rules governing party and state positions in China continue to be loosely defined and malleable.[62] As general secretary, Xi tends to play by his own rules, and he abolished terms limits for the president and vice president in 2018. The CCP's steadfast grooming of Hu Jintao and Xi Jinping and entire cohorts of leaders might have contributed to the routinization and stabilization of political succession, but they may have little to do with political institutionalization. In any case, political institutionalization, variously defined, is a matter of process. In countries where commonly accepted norms and rules are embedded in formal structures, contestation and politics are a normal fact of daily life. In developing countries and young organizations, institutionalization tends to be a lengthy process,[63] and this is particularly the case with China, where development is open-ended.

Two potential "sixth generation" successors were identified, although the pattern of prearranged succession was eventually broken. The congress, overshadowed by the Bo Xilai affair and even an alleged attempted coup, completed its major tasks, even though its late convention in November suggested contentiousness below the surface.[64] For Xi, he was ready to give his ambition and ideal full play. During Xi's first term, he introduced new patterns of leadership and policy. To make the analysis manageable, chapter 9 will discuss political and ideological issues; chapter 10 economic and social policies; and chapter 11 military and foreign relations. Because of the vastness of the topic and limited space, I focus on the most significant issues, and readers interested in more specific analysis may find useful references in the notes and the bibliography.

PART II

XI JINPING'S FIRST TERM AS GENERAL SECRETARY

*Governance and Reform in Turbulent Times,
2012–2017 (Age Fifty-Nine to Sixty-Four)*

9

Consolidation of Power, Image-Building, and Disciplining the Party State and Society

Much ink has been spilled on the view that the Xi administration is inherently conservative, self-serving, suspicious, and authoritarian. As a person, Xi is said to be ambitious, vain, and preoccupied with the "aggrandizement of power." Consequently, he has been characterized with a full series of epithets such as emperor, dictator, godfather, and "chairman of everything."[1] While containing elements of truth, these stereotypes also miss the nuances and changing dynamics of Chinese power and politics. Xi's rule contains repressive and progressive elements, and understanding the full complexity of the Xi phenomenon requires context and precision. We presume that the issue of power is best not viewed in isolation, as it is inextricably intertwined with policy and leadership. The ways by which Xi deployed his power, positions, and strategy to further reforms are more readily observable in a study of policy and process. We are also interested in the subjective and objective factors, or the agency and structural (including the external) forces, that shaped governance during Xi's first term. The political/economic/social changes in China can hardly be explained by the dominance of one person alone. I will elaborate this in the following chapters.

When Xi assumed the positions of general secretary, president, and chair of the CMC, he had already accumulated four decades of diverse experience at virtually every administrative level, encompassing the village, county, province, and center. In addition to a five-year grooming period for the top post at the center, he had governed individual provinces with populations larger than most European countries. This gave him intimate knowledge of China's issues, the legacy of previous administrations, the obstacles to reform, and the downsides of bureaucratic power. Additionally, Xi enjoyed certain advantages over his predecessors Jiang Zemin and Hu Jintao, occupying a stronger position than theirs at a similar stage of their careers. Xi's princeling pedigree as a son of a revered revolutionary veteran and PRC elder and a mandate for further reform gave him a certain measure of legitimacy. Xi's travail in the grassroots was perceived to have afforded him insights into the lives of the poorest in China. He inherited a streamlined Politburo Standing Committee (reduced to seven members) and enjoyed a past background of close ties with the military both at the center and in a region.

In contrast, Jiang Zemin had only become general secretary and chair of the CMC as an expedient after the Tiananmen tumult in 1989. He then served for an additional two terms, 1992–97 and 1997–2002. Deng Xiaoping supported Jiang, but Deng essentially called the shots behind the scenes until his death in 1997. Hu Jintao, on the other hand, was lifted from obscurity by Deng into the PBSC in 1992 and groomed for a full decade as a transcentury successor, to become general secretary in 2002, but he did not become chair of the CMC until 2004, when Jiang Zemin vacated the post. In contrast, Xi was not directly endorsed by a paramount leader like Deng, and his apprenticeship was compressed into five years in the PBSC, giving him less time than Hu to make connections. Yet, as observed, Xi had already made his mark as the heir apparent and vice president, and one of his most remarkable credentials was the drafting of a report to the Eighteenth Party Congress, which was a comprehensive policy blueprint to guide policymaking during his first term. The top leadership had also reached a consensus that Xi could deliver on this mandate and the need to recentralize power.[2] Finally, in contrast with rational choice predictions, Hu Jintao and Wen Jiabao retired, showing no evidence of interfering with politics.

In 2016, Xi was officially designated the "core" of the party leadership, and term limits for the presidency were abolished in 2018. Barring issues such as health, a coup, regime collapse, or assassination, he is posed to serve a third or even fourth term. Xi quickly began to realize his ambition with a confidence and boldness conspicuously lacking in his immediate predecessors, Jiang Zemin and Hu Jintao. For better or worse, in just a few years, he designed and implemented a bold and comprehensive program aimed at transforming China's society, culture, ecology, military, and political economy.

The Changing Policy Environment: Turbulence, Complexity, and Challenges

At the beginning of this term, Xi's optimism was tempered by caution and a sense that the policy environment had become more challenging since the last century. He made a huge claim when he said that under his stewardship China finally enjoyed a "bright prospect" of rejuvenating the Chinese nation after 170 years of struggle.[3] Since the humiliating defeat of China during the first Opium War of 1842 is often regarded as the beginning of China's tumultuous entry into the modern age, Xi's suggestion that 2012 marked a watershed seemed to downplay the contributions of his immediate predecessors. Simultaneously, he also conceded that China had made many big mistakes during the first thirty years after 1949, and that the Cultural Revolution was a "big blunder" (*da cuowu*).[4] However, to protect the legitimacy of the Party, Xi did not reject the Maoist heritage in toto, arguing that elements of Maoism could still inspire in times of rapid and dramatic changes.[5]

Factually, when Hu Jintao took over in 2002, China was only the world's seventh largest economy, but by 2012, China's economy had quadrupled to become the second largest and what happened in China began to impact the world. Rapid economic growth had spawned multiple challenges, including high wealth inequality, rapid urbanization, environmental degradation, and internal migration. Ironically, the massive lifting of seven hundred million out of poverty had aggravated these issues, placing heavy demands on energy, housing, healthcare, and social services.[6] The challenge of governance of China had multiplied, but Xi could no longer govern like charismatic leaders such as Mao and Deng.

In this respect, a suitable context can be provided by organizational and institutional theory, which suggests that, worldwide, governance has become more turbulent, as political interactions and demands have become "highly variable, inconsistent, unexpectable or unpredictable." Accelerating globalization has fostered dramatic social, economic, and political changes. In particular, rapid technological changes have made communication and feedback almost instantaneous, rendering problems more complex and interdependent. Public problems are more "wicked" or superwicked, complex, and rife with conflicts. Large-scale public programs produce unintended consequences and negative externalities. The outcome is surprisingly cascading dynamics that reveal the fragilities of institutions. Even in well-ordered and institutionalized states, governance has become more pluralistic, polarized, and volatile. There is a paradoxical dynamic when "a solution may lead a problem to change, cause new problems, or simply have trouble keeping up with the changing nature of problems." To cope with turbulence, reduce complexity, and to ensure institutional survival, organizations tend to adopt one of three different strategies: the reinforcing of existing institutional patterns (path dependence); fundamental institutional change (punctuated equilibrium); or institutional hybridity, recombination, and improvisation (institutional syncretism).[7] In a similar vein, other system theories postulate that contemporary policymakers are increasingly hobbled by the pressure of governing under conditions of crises, emergencies, and contingencies. They can better cope with turbulence by shared learning and divided responsibility, although another view suggests that power concentration and control are required.[8]

It is unclear whether Xi was familiar with organizational and institutional theory, but his various pronouncements strongly resonated with it. Concepts such as a sense of crisis, butterfly effects, black swans, and gray rhinos were regularly invoked in policy discussions. Such contingencies are seen to have been compounded by China's huge size, regional variations, and stage of development.

As Xi has observed, the acceleration of economic globalization, intensified national competition, and a volatile and protean international situation have made reform and development in China an uphill and risky battle.[9] He has maintained that the governing of a huge, diverse country with many levels of development is a tall order in itself, and to deepen reform by rejigging various vested interests and systems constituted a formidable challenge.[10] As mentioned, at Zhejiang he was familiar with the notion of a "middle-income trap" and the challenges of "graduation" from middle-income to high-income status, compared with the climb from low to middle income.[11] Objectively, China's population of 1.35 billion in 2012 was more than twice that of the United States, Japan, Germany, France, and the UK combined. Many of China's fifty-six minorities are located in poorer inland and border regions, and the national income along the eastern coast was still three times that of the inland and western areas. Of the thirty-three provincial-/municipal-level administrations, ten had populations exceeding fifty million. The CCP had eighty-nine million members as of 2017 and 4.5 million party committees and sent 190,000 first secretaries to the rural areas.[12] Xi said that his work experience from the localities to the center had impressed upon him the "incredible diversity of every layer of China." China is so vast that any attempt to collect information or to understand it is a daunting challenge, like "the blind feeling the elephant."[13]

Domestically, Xi and the Chinese policymakers were keenly aware of the encyclopedic range of the challenges confronting China, from corruption to climate change, and from poverty to inequality, from economic slowdown to the need for a new development model.[14] Breakneck development over the past three decades had created immense social and economic changes, new and rising expectations, and unfulfilled policy promises. Post-Mao reforms had exacerbated ideological differences and created winners and losers. The deepening of reforms carried huge stakes and risks, challenging formidable, entrenched institutions and interests in the Party, government, military, the regulators, and the SOEs. One may also add that the leadership had to take responsibility for blunders, such as the Tiananmen massacre and the faulty Three Gorges Dam, committed by previous administrations. Unlike observers who analyze China's issues in isolation, Xi had to grapple with the totality between foreign and domestic issues in policymaking.

In his 2014 book *On Governance,* Xi argued that China was still a developing country marked by a "relatively low level of social and economic development," a weak economic foundation, tremendous diversity, and uneven development. Its aggregate GDP may be the second largest in the world, but in per capita terms, it ranked about eightieth in the world (or two-thirds of the world's average or one-seventh that of the United States). Seventy million people lived under the poverty line, requiring state assistance, and this number came to two hundred million as defined by the World Bank. There were also eighty-five million disabled. As Xi said, China "still has a long way to go" to provide a decent life for its citizens. Furthermore, virtually all Chinese over fifty years old had experienced poverty and the tumult of the Cultural Revolution and even for the younger generations, poverty was not in the distant past. Many Chinese were aware of the huge gap between China and the developed countries, and they were determined to catch up. Although China's economy had continuously grown for three decades, weathering several major crises, the question was how to sustain growth and development. Further, the drastic downturn in China's economic growth rate in 2015 and the complicated global environment showed that China was heading toward uncharted waters, creating a sense of foreboding. Further, as Xi claimed, China's governing capability did not match the intense socioeconomic demands or the need to foster stability and to counter international competition.[15]

Xi argued that China was confronting another crossroads, and new reforms were required in virtually all fronts to propel China forward, or the alternative would be stagnancy, decline, and even collapse. Like many of his peers, he strove to enhance the sources of legitimacy, such as economic performance, nationalism, culture, governance, and democracy (popular support under one-party rule).[16] A China slipping back into poverty, indignity, and the chaos of the recent past was Xi's worst fear. Yet to govern China was such a delicate matter that it was, in Xi's words, like "frying a small fish," requiring caution as if "treading on thin ice, or standing on the edge of an abyss."[17] Paradoxically, he also compared the deepening of reform to a "profound revolution" to rebalance various interests and demands.[18] In fact, many of Xi's policies were rolled out like a steamroller.

Externally, China's strategic environment, according to the 2015 white paper titled "China's Military Strategy,"[19] was marked by multipolarity and economic globalization that was binding countries together. Yet changes in the balance of power, along with intense competition for power and national interests, were becoming the main sources of conflict. The white paper went on to assert the following: foremost among these new realities for China is the United States' "rebalancing" strategy in Asia and its augmented alliance with such countries as Japan. A world war is unlikely, but issues such as terrorism and ethnic, religious, border, and territorial conflicts may spawn local wars. China's comprehensive national strength and capability has increased, as has its international standing, and there is still a strategic opportunity for development. Yet, as a huge developing country, China encounters multiple and complex security threats and the formidable task of maintaining political and social stability. International and regional turmoil are challenging its territorial integrity and development interests, especially in Tibet and Xinjiang. The more China's economy develops, the more its growth is dependent on exogenous factors such as export markets, especially when China is still smarting from the impact of the 2008 global financial crisis.

Growth also means an expansion of China's national and overseas interests, particularly in energy and resources. Issues such as maritime rights, territorial disputes, terrorism, separatism, natural disasters, and pandemics have gained saliency. The international "revolution in military affairs," which has introduced long-range, stealth, and unmanned weapons, has exacerbated competition and conflict in space, cyberspace, and sea lanes of communication. Persistent "hostile" foreign forces, concluded the white paper, had instigated the so-called colored revolutions, popular uprisings around the world that constitute a major threat to China.[20]

Xi's response to these during his first term was multifaceted, and I will highlight five fundamental aspects of his strategies and approaches before turning to several specific areas of policymaking. In the comparative language of organizational theory, Xi and the Party responded to turbulence with strategies that aimed to reinforce existing institutions (path dependence) and more secondarily with some recombination and improvisation (institutional syncretism). The Chinese reality is, indeed, more complex, as we will explore in the following.

Xi Jinping's Strategies and Approaches

Regime Security and the "Overall Security Concept"

Chinese thinkers stretching from the late nineteenth century up to the present yearn for national wealth and power.[21] As well, most Chinese leaders in the reform period have privileged security as a prerequisite for political and social stability, which in turn is considered essential for the cherished goal of modernization and catching up with the West. These leaders have been mindful of the multiple vulnerabilities and the institutional and systemic weaknesses of CCP authoritarian rule. They have repeatedly reminded the nation of a "sense of crisis," the sources of which could be exogenous or endogenous. Beijing has long realized that its soft power is no match for that possessed by the West, leaving it vulnerable to "peaceful evolution" or violent regime change, especially with external encouragement. The Tiananmen massacre of 1989 is deemed a close call. Another dreaded historical lesson was the collapse of communism in the Soviet Union and Eastern Europe in the 1990s. Dissolution of the Soviet Union into fifteen independent states exacerbated worries about Beijing's vulnerability to minority separation in Tibet, Xinjiang, and, to a lesser extent, Inner Mongolia. The Party has assiduously studied the Soviet downfall, and for Xi, one of the key reasons was the loss of the ideological battle. Once the "ideal and faith" in the system has been shaken, Xi told his first Politburo study session in 2013, how could the Party and state last?[22]

In this century, Chinese leaders are particularly wary of incidents like the "color revolutions" and the Arab Spring that could trigger the collapse of the CCP and plunge the entire country into turmoil and disintegration for an indefinite period. Economically, CCP reforms had turned China into an economic juggernaut, but Beijing was keenly aware that such success is still limited and that it might be unsustainable in an age of fierce competition. China's phenomenal growth had been driven by economic globalization, and therefore any restrictions to global markets was viewed as a national security threat.

Xi inherited this line of thinking, stressing regime security and the security of CCP rule. Subsequently, his new notion of "an overall security concept"[23] became an obsession and a red thread running through all of Xi's political, economic, social, and foreign policy programs. He equated the survival of party rule with the broader survival of the Chinese nation, assuming that the CCP is the only organization capable of holding the country together. If the CCP goes, Xi reckoned, China would sink again into another nightmarish scenario of prolonged chaos and disintegration. Like most historically aware Chinese, he could not forget China's "century of humiliation." He and his cohort of current Chinese leaders had experienced the profound extremes of grinding poverty and backwardness and were determined to move forward and to bring China to modernity. By taking a long historical perspective, Xi was mindful of the rise and fall of the various Chinese dynasties and the interregnums of decay, reform, and revival.[24]

Another anxiety of Xi and his colleagues was the "middle income" trap mentioned earlier. Yet reforms deemed vital to head off such a trap had been vigorously resisted by bureaucratic and entrenched interests. This was exacerbated by a fear of a legitimacy crisis by which the Party's right to govern would be questioned by the general public, whose various demands, ranging from economic growth to social stability, and from national strength to government accountability, seemed to be ever increasing.[25] Xi was determined not to repeat the Soviet scenario; as he said, "A big Party was gone just like that. Proportionally, the Soviet Communist Party had more members than we do, but nobody was man enough to stand up and resist."[26] For Xi and the leadership, the numerous "social contradictions" meant that reforms had reached an inflection point, presaging unpredictable and unprecedented outcomes. All of this was aggravated by the shifting international environment, financial crises, resources supply issues, and nontraditional threats such as terrorism, climate change, refugee crises, and internet warfare, to name a few.[27] A sense of fatalism that China could sink by its own size and weight was reflected in Xi's warning: "A smaller sailboat may spin around in the water, but it may rise up again after a few turns, but if the *Titanic* is going to sink, it will sink."[28]

Progressively, China under Xi began to build up a "national security state" to protect its national interests and to foment a "new model of major country relations."[29] In a departure from his predecessors, Xi strove to introduce a comprehensive rather than compartmentalized security arrangement. Xi argued for more proactive and strategic thinking in national defense and diplomacy. To head off the forces of decline, Beijing felt, it must strengthen the military and defense by augmenting reforms. April 15 was designated National Security Education Day, and a mass campaign on antiespionage was launched in 2017.[30] Overall, the fear of an existential threat to the regime fed anxiety and strong-armed tactics. Xi strove to impose tight control over civil society, ideology, and dissent, whereas simultaneously he struggled to improve governance and performance legitimacy by following through with reforms.

It can be argued that the Party's persistent emphasis on crisis and insecurity is a cynical means to exaggerate dangers and to suppress dissent. But from a theoretical standpoint, such a compulsion on national security is not out of the ordinary. First, realist international theorists assert that the international struggle for power under the conditions of anarchy makes the obsession with national security and strong material and military power a prime concern. Second, the reality of modern policymaking is that emergencies and crises are facts of life, and the management of risks constitutes an important aspect of governance. In this situation, decisions have to be made under pressure, although the coordination of multiple actors under conditions of randomness has always been problematic. The Chinese media have often referred to the "butterfly effect" to denote situations when small random events, either inside or outside of the system, may snowball into disasters or even general breakdowns. This likely explains in part Beijing's more assertive pursuit of national security, and the role of Xi as an agent in effecting these changes. Yet, paradoxically, the Chinese leaders' obsession may reflect a deep-seated sense of insecurity and even weakness.

Xi Jinping as an Uber-Leninist

At heart a staunch Leninist, Xi also believes that leadership and organization are vital for system maintenance, rejuvenation, and advancement. As Xi forcefully puts it, "Party, government, military, society, education, east, west, south, north, and central, the Party leads everything."[31] This mantra was duly inserted into the party constitution at the Nineteenth Party Congress. The Party is cast as a disciplined vanguard for overall leadership and decision-making. Lenin, a revolutionary and a paramount leader of early Soviet rule, placed a premium on a disciplined, tightly knit, and centralized Communist Party to provide leadership.

Ideally, this small and elitist vanguard owes its position to a high level of "consciousness" (or a better grasp of objective reality) that is unavailable to the ordinary proletariat. It leads by forming a strong organization according to the principles of democratic centralism—free and open discussion, within limits, before decisions are taken, but everyone is obligated to obey a decision once it is made. Dissenters may reserve their opinions if they do not obstruct implementation or form opposition factions. However, in this formula, Lenin and his successors have, in practice, always privileged centralization and iron discipline over democracy. Correspondingly, Xi has often iterated that party leadership is everything, and organization its main strength.[32] Discipline, for him, has meant the maintenance of strategic steadfastness, confidence, and patience, since Herculean effort is needed to transform society and politics.

For Xi, the Party's role is to guide and direct through centralization of power, unity of purpose, and control of dissent. Like Lenin, Xi is an organizational man dedicated to the maintenance of organizational discipline and authority. With little patience for spontaneity and disorder, his constant fear is that the country will disintegrate into "a loose sheet of sand."[33] Mao's notion of "great democracy," that is, the arousal of spontaneous mass action to openly rectify the mistakes of the Party, is anathema to him. Additionally, Xi is swayed by Lenin's elitist concepts that feature paternalism and tutelage. In this view, leaders act as guides to control ideology, regulate conduct, and improve the quality (*suzhi*) of the Chinese citizenry,[34] supposedly acting in their best interest by providing public goods such as stability and prosperity. The Party accepts loyal remonstrations and criticisms but not adversary censures. This line of thinking resonates with traditional Confucian ideals of a benevolent, hierarchical, and exemplary elite serving social interests and transforming the *suzhi* of the people through education. Xi faults his predecessors for relaxing party rule, and attempts to redouble efforts to reclaim that leadership. By accentuating the principle of party leadership, Xi has reversed the policy of separating the powers and functions of the Party and the state as pushed under the leadership of Deng Xiaoping, Hu Yaobang, and Zhao Ziyang in the 1980s. Effectively Xi has called for the strengthening of party leadership in all aspects of public political life. In an article published immediately after the Nineteenth Party Congress, Xi confidant Wang Qishan made explicit the critique of party-state separation, asserting Xi's "paramount" principle of asserting authority over the "weakening" of party leadership.[35]

This notwithstanding, Xi harbors no illusion about the flaws of the putative exemplary vanguard. On numerous occasions, he poured scorn on party members in scathing terms, accusing them of being (1) a self-serving elite consumed by power and profits, clannish mentality, lacking even a minimum sense of decency; (2) unprincipled and dictatorial in their dealings with the public, abusing their power with impunity; and (3) befuddled, enfeebled, and evasive in their responsibilities. Harsh in his indictment of the misdemeanors of the Party, he accused some top leaders of being "degenerate" and "decadent." Apparently, Xi was exasperated by the signs of institutional decay,[36] but could see no substitute for a hierarchical administration. He has often used the adage "To forge iron one must toughen oneself," highlighting the need for people of discipline and integrity to accomplish great deeds, but his frustrations with the Party have been palpable. Contradicting Mao's adage that "the party line is the way of the benevolent ruler, but discipline is the way of the autocrat" (luxian shi wangdao, jilu shi badao) Xi believes both are indispensable. He determined that draconian measures are mandatory to clean up the Party, to establish it as a meritocratic bureaucracy, and to re-establish its legitimacy as the leadership core of the nation.

Ever the disciplinarian, Xi eventually urged the extension of hard-line measures to deal with popular manifestations, civil society, and public opinion.[37] As a result, the decisive authority he has insisted for the Party has created an atmosphere that is becoming increasingly autocratic and illiberal.

High Degree of Centralism

For Xi, another Leninist tenet is that strong central governance is critical to counter the ever-present forces of decline and disintegration. The report to the Eighteenth Party Congress also reiterated that "centralized leadership of the Party is the source of its strength" that guaranteed "China's economic and social development, ethnic unity and progress, and enduring peace and stability." Chinese state capacity, in terms of the ability to administer, to manage finances, and to foster policy consensus and socioeconomic development, has improved greatly in the reform period. Yet, in the vast bureaucratic structure of China, centrifugal and centripetal forces are two sides of the same coin. The center controls such things as the developmental strategy, resources for regional redistribution, and above all, the power to assign personnel. The far-flung bureaucracy, however, owns the inherent powers of adjustment and resistance. Similarly, central-provincial relationships are marked by the duality of autonomy and independence on the one hand, and centralized control and domination on the other, depending on the context and issue area. Xi's reforms have centralized much decision-making power in the Party, the capital, and in Xi himself, although they also feature some decentralization measures (discussed later). In fact, for all its centralizing pretensions, the Chinese system is not monolithic—in certain respects power is so highly decentralized and diffused that observers have labeled the Chinese system fragmented or disjointed authoritarianism.[38]

Central-provincial relationships vary along a spectrum between localized autonomy and independence, and centralized control and domination, regulated by a wide range of variables.

The upshot is that central policies are often ignored and unimplemented, as reflected by common quips such as "Government decrees do not make it out of Zhongnanhai" and "The upper levels have policies, the lower levels have counterpolicies." The later statement was deemed so weighty that it was written into the report to the Eighteenth Party Congress, and Xi referred repeatedly to it.[39] Xi has often denounced the bureaucracy for "disobeying orders and defying prohibitions" (*youling buxing, youjin buzhi*).[40]

Further, China's multiple governance structure has tremendously complicated policymaking and implementation. First, structurally, the country is governed by a dual-rule principle—vertical rule by the central ministries by function and horizontal rule by regional authorities—which are characterized by the perennial issues of "silos" and dispersed power.[41] Second, the implementation of central policies and guidelines relies on the State Council, the ministries, and a colossal government bureaucracy, as well as tens of thousands of cadres on the ground. Naturally, there is fertile ground for ingrained bureaucratic politics and for fierce competition for influence and resources. Added to this is a maze of overlapping and conflicting regulations issuing from various agencies that complicate matters. Third, like bureaucrats everywhere, the forty-seven million functionaries staffing the party-state apparatus[42] are generally committed to routines and procedures, resisting reforms that may threaten their entrenched interests using a vast repertoire of means such as evasion, foot-dragging, feigned compliance, and subversion of central intentions. In the Chinese context, beneficiaries of the post-Mao reform status quo have in turn resisted reforms that may erode their positions. For instance, entrenched state monopolies, SOEs, and domestic businesses tend to resist expanded liberalization, marketization, and competition that may undermine their power. SOE managers resist bankruptcies, fearing that they will create unemployment and slow down economic growth, a prime criterion for their career advancement. Ideology, propaganda, and associated educational establishments tend to resist the downgrading of ideology and ideological education.

Third, a similar dynamic exists between the center and the local authorities from the province level down. As our discussion of Xi's governance record at different localities shows, Beijing, ever mindful of the vastness and regional variations of the country, often has tried to avoid a one-size-fits-all policy to allow for flexibility and encouragement of local initiative. My discussion of the various development models (for example, the Zhejiang and Chongqing models) reflects this reality. Policies have often been tried out in pilot projects in the provinces before national adoption, but even after that, provinces are often allowed to adjust central policies to suit local conditions. For these reasons, China has been characterized by some as "one of the most decentralized countries in the world,"[43] since local authorities are able to wield great power and influence. Apart from the centrifugal forces inherent in such a large polity, local authorities have developed a vast repertoire of means to evade, obstruct, and distort central intentions to suit their own priorities. This extends down to the smallest village level, where officials can resist reforms that may threaten their turf, revenue sources, and economic activities. For example, many have resisted such central regulations as environmental protection and the curbing of investment. And above all, localities have resisted land reform since the selling of land has become a major source of their income and power. Often, the local authority / moneyed elite nexus constitutes a major source of graft, racketeering, and personal enrichment that in turn has precipitated mass protest and social unrest.

Finally, it is important to note, to prevent the re-emergence of Maoist dictatorial rule, Deng Xiaoping's efforts in institutionalizing collective leadership and checks and balances at the top have created a clearer demarcation of responsibilities. Different Politburo members were put in charge of party, administrative, legal, and military affairs.[44] Yet such efforts to prevent the concentration of power have also created gridlock and indecisive rule and encouraged factionalism.

In all, Xi has operated in a colossal organizational environment rife with competing bureaucratic, regional, societal, and economic interests. All this has been intersected by dense networks of patronage and personal relations by which careers and interests were nurtured. Further, most policy issues have been intertwined with many others, and a change in one area affects many other areas in a situation Xi and the Chinese refer to with the adage "The pulling of one hair affects the entire body." As one authoritative source puts it, the vast challenges of deep reform, as well as the dogged resistance and intrigue, may well defy imagination.[45] In policymaking, China has been dubbed by some a "consultative authoritarian regime" since the center has tended to consult widely before a decision is made. It consults with citizens, experts, think tanks, public opinion, and elsewhere through channels such as opinion polls, online portals, and direct representations.[46] In lawmaking, for example, so many stakeholders have to be mollified that about half the bills fail to be passed within the prescribed five-year period, and 12 percent of the bills take more than ten years to pass.[47] Beijing has to negotiate, incentivize, and compromise with bureaucratic interests, regional officials, SOEs, and private enterprises in a process that takes on the characteristics of a bargaining treadmill.[48] As China develops, these competing interests have become even more complex and entrenched, and policymaking has become more unwieldy. The outcome is that Xi and the Party Center in Beijing do not always get what they want.

Such a situation raised many governance issues, but Xi was helped by a mandate from the top leadership to recentralize power. Upon becoming general secretary, Xi acted quickly to effect a threefold centralization of power, to his person, to the center, and to the Party. Through a series of institutional changes and other means, Xi has accumulated a great deal of power, both formal and informal, in his person. He has worked to boost the power of the center vis-à-vis the provinces in such areas as anticorruption and judicial reform. He has centralized power in the Party in areas such as ideological control and military reform. By stressing the notions of "top-level design" and "comprehensive planning," Xi has pushed central coordination, top-down decision-making, and recentralized power unprecedented in the reform period. And unlike previous general secretaries who focused primarily on ideology and party affairs, Xi has assumed a major role in economic policymaking as well.

Battles to Reformulate Ideology and to Build Soft Power

Xi and his team were wary of the weakness of China's ideological appeal and the allure of Western cultural and democratic values. Reform-period repudiation of radical Maoist ideology gave way to Deng Xiaoping's obsession with economic development and self-enrichment as epitomized in the slogan "To get rich is glorious."[49] The outcome, as seen by Xi, was rampant materialism, a moral vacuum, and even a state of normlessness. Domestically, the party state continued its ubiquitous veneration of Marxist ideology in all official discourses, and Xi often thinks in terms of dialectics. Yet the key Marxist notions of class, class struggle, and a classless society were no longer relevant to the public or even to the Party. The Party may have wanted to keep the notion of Marxism alive as an alternative to capitalism and liberal democracy, but it had been widely deemed inadequate as a unifying ideology, or even a guide for action.

Besides, Beijing viewed with anxiety Western ideology, cultural and social values transmitted through channels such as the mass media, cyberspace, educational exchanges, and foreign NGOs, which it alleged propounded materialism, individualism, and violence. It was uncomfortable with a pluralism of ideas such as neoliberalism and socialist democracy and was incensed with what it labeled "historical nihilism," or the negative views of party history. It loathed academic ideas such as the "end of ideology" or the "end of history," modernization theory, and theories around China's collapse, since they all assume the ultimate triumph of Western-style liberal democracy and capitalism. The regime was especially worried about the effects of these values on the youth, students, and intellectuals.[50] In general terms, Beijing feared the loss of Chinese identity and cultural autonomy, but more importantly, it feared that Western values of freedom and individualism would challenge its socialist values, undermining the Party's ideological control and even the legitimacy of CCP rule.[51] Indeed, even though the West enjoys strong democratic institutions, liberty, and freedom, it struggles constantly with the contradictions between the ideals and practice of liberal and social democracy. For instance, Samuel Barber coined the notion of "McWorld" to denote contemporary Western values that he said are materialistic, conformist, and homogenized. He uses the term "jihad" (meaning struggle, a metaphor he later regretted) to represent the values in the non-Western world that he deems parochial, fundamentalist, ultranationalist, and exclusive. Both "McWorld" and "jihad," Barber argues, are undemocratic or even antidemocratic.[52] The unfortunate fact is that decades after Barber's pronouncements, the "confrontational globalism" and "intolerant tribalism" values of "McWorld" and "jihad" seem to have converged in many parts of the world. Further, it has been argued that the democratic theory and practices of settler states such as the United States, Canada, and Australia have been forged through colonial dispossession, slavery, racism, and the exclusion of the indigenous population, all in the name of "the people." Consequently, the concepts of freedom, popular sovereignty, consent, and equality, as articulated by theorists from J. S. Mill to Alexis de Tocqueville, and from Thomas Jefferson to Walt Whitman, are more byproducts of a metanarrative of domination.[53]

For the Chinese leaders, however, the need to fill the alleged postreform ideological and moral void seemed more urgent. To rebuild more palatable social values, they resorted to Chinese traditional values and nationalism. Confucianism, with its emphasis on paternal benevolence, social harmony, and respect for power and hierarchy, was deemed eminently suitable for authoritarian rule. Whereas Jiang Zemin and Hu Jintao had incorporated Confucian notions such as the "relatively prosperous society," the "harmonious society," and "people-centered development," Xi became the first general secretary to formally endorse the promotion of Confucianism itself,[54] and his speeches and homilies are replete with traditional aphorisms. Formerly, Hu Jintao had raised the issue of fostering China's soft power, defining it as a core national interest and an important capability in international rivalry (*jiliang*), especially in an age of instantaneous and extensive dissemination of information. Yet, after years of effort, China's international attractiveness and ability to influence the realm of ideas has not improved substantially,[55] and the notion of a Beijing consensus has simply vanished. The obstacles, of course, are primarily China's authoritarian political system and its relatively lower level of socioeconomic development. Generally, soft power is the preserve of the rich and developed West, and China cannot hope to match, let alone surpass, the West in this regard even in the long run. In a global assessment of soft power of sixty countries that ranks only the top thirty,

China is placed roughly in the middle, or twenty-seventh in 2018 after a low of thirtieth in 2015 and twenty-eighth in 2016. Beijing is strong in subindexes such as culture (measured by metrics such as art, tourism, and Olympic medals), education and enterprise, but weakest in government subindexes, which encompasses individual freedoms, liberties, and transparencies. This places China in the same league as the Czech Republic (26), Russia (28), and Brazil (29). Unsurprisingly, wealthy democratic countries such as the UK, France, Germany, the United States, and Japan occupy the top ten positions.[56]

Beijing's sense of frustration with the failure to raise its international image and respect commensurate with its economic might was palpable. Xi was especially suspicious of Western soft power and values, fearing that hostile cultural infiltration could threaten China's "ideological safety" and subvert CCP rule.[57]

To counter these trends, Xi proclaimed, "[We should] tell China's story well, spread China's voice, and strengthen [China's] narrative power internationally."[58] Henceforth, while as even the Party had philosophically embraced many elements of Western values such as marketization, freedom, justice, and the rule of law, not to mention Marxism, it felt it necessary to appropriate the narrative and represent values as China's own. In its attempts to construct a counternarrative, the party state tried to leverage China's developmental approach, economic prowess, and traditional cultural values. It sought to reach back to the revolutionary values of Mao as a symbol of commitment to nationalism and populism. It tried to draw inspiration from Chinese history and philosophy to reconceptualize the global social and economic order from a Chinese perspective.[59] However, nationalism can be an instrument as well as an end in itself, and as a diverse, contested, and evolving phenomenon, it takes many forms in China.[60] One study of the ideological leanings expressed online maintains that generally the Chinese are attracted by things Western, although various clusters can be differentiated. The nationalistic clusters range from the more extreme Party Warriors and Flag Wavers to the more moderate China Advocates (who desire China's own developmental path), Industrialists (who want to catch up with the West), and Traditionalists (who seek inspiration from China's past). On government/market relationships, clusters like the Mao Lovers and the Equality Advocates are keen on communist equality and a social welfare state, respectively, whereas the Market Lovers are neoliberals who favor free markets and government noninterference. Other clusters, such as the Democrats, US Lovers, and the Globalists are the most pro-West.[61] Correspondingly, Xi acknowledged his fondness for Western products such as certain Hollywood movies and Russian writers, but he presented himself as a nationalist steeped in the traditions of Chinese culture. In his first term, nationalism and traditional values were promoted to an unprecedented intensity, giving them both defensive and chauvinistic features.

Developmentalism and Performance Legitimacy

Like most Chinese thinkers and politicians since the mid-nineteenth century, Xi was obsessed with economic growth, development, and the resurrection of China as a world power. This was reflected in common maxims like "rich country, strong military," and "wealth and power." Developmentalism, a notion used to describe the driving force of the political economies of "latecomers" such as Japan[62] and Singapore, has long been embraced by China. It is an elite desire to modernize and to catch up with industrialized Western countries in GDP terms and to increase China's international stature. A new twist in the Xi era was the need for economic growth in accelerating conditions of interdependence and globalization. Beijing felt that it could leverage this interconnectedness to its own economic advantage and play a more prominent and direct role in global affairs.

Concurrent with this, the Chinese public, especially the middle class of four hundred million strong, was increasingly aware and exacting in their demands on and expectations from the government. They generally expected social and economic stability, as well as public goods ranging from economic growth to better living standards, and from public services to good governance. They looked to the party state as an ultimate guarantor of national security. Implicitly, this was a social contract that allowed the CCP to monopolize power.[63] The public was progressively less tolerant of social problems such as corruption, unsafe food, and a polluted environment, and many people engaged in collective action to issue their dissent. The regime also sought to justify its right to rule by performance legitimacy, that is, the ability to satisfy the needs and aspirations of the public. However, public demands and expectations were ever-increasing, and the regime had to cope with or balance a number of contradictions, such as the demands for sustained growth and sustained development. The pressures of risk and emergency management were great.

The five factors discussed previously—regime security, Leninism, centralization, ideological development, and developmentalism—are intricately intertwined with one another and together represent the most fundamental drivers of Xi's hard-line approach to policymaking, which in turn is intensified by his personal determination born of years of struggle. His goals were not all new, having been embraced by Jiang Zemin and Hu Jintao with Xi's acquiescence as vice president. But Xi was determined to vigorously push reforms on virtually all fronts. He shared the general sense of vulnerability felt by other Chinese leaders, especially a sense that the Party showed signs of decay, but he was also confident about the prospect of his grand scheme. In a sense he probably knew that his choices were limited—stick with the party leadership or let the country drift into an indefinite period of chaos and disintegration that he abhorred. Like his immediate predecessors, he knew that he could no longer govern like Mao or

Deng, but he quickly developed his own hard-line style to build power and make policy under the new contexts. Xi was not always in control, and his blaring injunctions for the cadres to toe the party line show progressive frustrations.

In many respects, Xi understood that policymaking does not always follow a unilinear routine in the traditional sense that problems can be identified and solved. A great deal of evidence suggests that he grasped the significance of modern policymaking under high stress and uncertainty without explicit reference to complex system theory or chaos theory.[64] Doggedly, he talked about the interdependency of issues, and crises that involved discontinuities, shifts, and jumps. He realized that a modern reality is that problems come in clusters, and that their boundaries shift continuously. And as his many references to the "broken window" effect shows, he appreciated the impact of small disorders and their rippling effects that can precipitate shock and severe system breakdown. For instance, he said in October 2015:

> In the past, we tended to think that the conflicts and problems afflicting the people resulted from a low level of economic development; if only we could develop the economy, and if the people lived a better life, social conflicts and problems would consequently decrease. Now it seems that problems always exist whether the economy is underdeveloped or developed, and that the problems associated with a developed economy are no fewer than those associated with an underdeveloped one—they can even become more complicated.... What calls for special attention is that risks often may not occur alone, but more likely intertwine with each other and form a risk complex. . . . We must strive to defuse risks at [the] source, and prevent small risks from evolving into big ones, individual ones into complex ones, partial ones into regional or systemic ones, economic ones into social and political ones, and global ones into domestic ones.[65]

At the end of his first term, Xi also managed a massive and contentious leadership changeover at the Nineteenth Party Congress in 2017. Inevitably, the ambitious reform agenda encountered setbacks, resistance, and unanticipated outcomes. The process involved improvisations, trial and error, zigzags, and contradictions. Overall, policymaking during Xi's first term operated along several intersecting matrices—Xi asserted party supremacy over other institutions to foster reforms while at the same time launching an onslaught against the Party in order to strengthen it; he strove to centralize party/government control over the economy while simultaneously fostering the play of market forces; and he attempted to constrain power by the rule of law while expanding censorship and thought control. From a Western perspective, these are just some of the contradictions of Xi's rule, although for Xi, this may simply be "dialectics," or the coexistence and contention of many incongruities in reality. Operating under the complex conditions of multiple constraints and opportunities, Xi has had to effect choices through multiple balances.[66]

Conceptualizing Xi's Power

Many China watchers have argued that Xi has acquired unbridled and unchallengeable power. Xi's rule, they say, is a "resurrection of Mao's one-man rule and symbolizes the death of Deng's two most important legacies, the consensus-building 'collective leadership' and orderly power transition mechanism." Others claim that "Emperor Xi" has dominated the PBSC and could rule even without it.[67] These are powerful assertions, but they tend to miss much of the reality of Chinese power and policy.

In comparative terms, Leslie Holmes distinguishes four types of leadership configurations in communist-style countries, although he also cautions that these are ideal types, and in reality, various leaderships fall between categories and move between them over time. The first type is the supreme leader, who is charismatic and usually a leader of the revolutionary takeover. Like Stalin, Mao, and Castro, this leader has more power than all his colleagues and lays claim to being the ultimate interpreter of ideology. He projects an image of superhuman qualities that is buttressed by a full-fledged cult of personality. The second type is the "first among equals" configuration in which the leader dominates decision-making but to a lesser extent than a supreme leader. He may adopt aspects of a personality cult, but other leaders do not venerate him, let alone fear him. Third, the "oligarchy with collectives" variation describes a situation in which there is a broad division of labor within the top leadership, but three to five individuals usually have more say than the others. A fourth type is the "collective leadership" configuration, which most Leninist systems claim as ideal and which presupposes a well-defined division of labor. Individual leaders specializing in certain policy areas such as the economy and foreign relations will bring their expertise to the top body. Members in the top leadership may not be equal in power and status, but they debate as equals across all major areas of decision-making, but this too can be dysfunctional since no one is likely to have deep knowledge over all policy areas.[68]

The extent of Xi's power can best be viewed as a cross between the last three, a consolidated first among equals in a hierarchical collective leadership. As leader of one-fifth of humankind in a one-party system with little or no institutional check on his power, Xi's power can be enormous. In specific respects things may look different. For instance, Xi's relationship with the PBSC and Politburo is probably on a par with that of presidents and prime ministers. During his first term Xi might have much less power than a newly elected prime minister or president who picks her cabinet, since he inherited a Politburo he did not pick. Neither could he remove Politburo members without just cause, such as corruption. Further, many former Xi associates and subordinates like Li Keqiang have come into their own. Liu Yunshan, a leftist who oversaw ideology and propaganda, had often been at odds with Xi.[69] Xi needed advice, information, and support from his colleagues so that they were interdependent with one another in terms of division of labor and expertise. Not all policy ideas have sprung from Xi's head, and he has relied on his colleagues, loyalists or not, for decision-making assistance and policy implementation. Xi did insert supporters into the party-state bureaucracy as well as into the PLA, but that required a consensus in the Politburo.

Indeed, in applying these typologies one needs to examine different contexts, since power is exercised in situational and relational ways. If we consider the vast range of issues and contexts during Xi's first term, Xi's rule is clearly qualitatively different from that of Mao. In the following we will unpack the issues in more detail and depth.

Power, Policies, and Processes

As mentioned, the specific circumstances of Chinese political succession make the "consolidation of power" one of the most important processes for the new general secretary. We take a broader definition of the notion of "consolidation of power" by referring to the processes by which Xi (1) established his legitimacy, built an image, and strengthened his position, and (2) provided leadership in policymaking and reforms according to his ideals and the demands of problem-solving. Specifically, we will discuss Xi's consolidation of power in the following aspects: the centralization of power; ideology discourses and ideological control; image-making; disciplining of the party state; and judicial reform.

The Centralization of Power

Convinced that there was a gridlock in his ambitious reform agenda, Xi effected an overhaul of the party-state decision-making apparatus by a threefold centralizing of power in the capital, in the Party, and ultimately in his own person. As general secretary and chair of the CMC and president, his power spanned the three pillars of party, government, and military. Additionally, several of Xi's former associates were included in the Politburo. Xi's influence was reinforced by acquiring the chairmanship of eight major central decision-making bodies, such as the Central Committee Leading Small Groups (LSGs), and in January 2014 he was named chair of a new Central National Security Commission (CNSC), another high policymaking organ. In April 2016, Xi was referred to as the commander in chief of the CMC Joint Battle Command Center,[70] and things came to a head when at the Sixth Plenum of October 2016 he was formally designated the "core" of the Party.

The Formation of an Informal Power Base

To strengthen his position and to pursue his policy agenda, Xi had to build up his informal power base and neutralize opposing forces. Of necessity, the power configurations at the top had undergone continuous evolution and realignment. Yet Xi also needed the support of other "factions" within a Leninist context, and his challenge was less the aggrandizing of power than the balancing of the interests of various networks. Xi needed to learn to coexist with the holdovers to achieve his ambitious goals. The cooperation and assistance of people outside of his circle as well as in the vast bureaucracy was vital, especially since factional struggle was no longer a zero-sum game. One can also argue that Xi did not need his own faction, and as discussed, the static treatment of the notions of Shanghai Gang, *tuanpai*, Xi faction, or "elite coalition" to denote permanent alliances of interests cannot be substantiated. Instead, Xi had to contend with shifting power networks to stay above the fray or at least appear to be accommodating to all.[71]

A broad, generalized, comparative perspective may help to place Xi's position in context. In Western practices, once elected to the top office, presidents or prime ministers acquire all the power and trappings that come with the office, since it is the act of election that confers legitimacy. With some exceptions (such as the case of a minority government in a parliamentary system), they enjoy the freedom to pick their cabinet and staff their administration. The new British prime minister or US president may appoint some one hundred high-level bureaucrats in the former case, and up to four thousand in the latter (George W. Bush appointed around sixty-five hundred in 2000). When Donald Trump assumed the US presidency in 2017, he was entitled to fill thousands of positions in the executive branch in addition to his cabinet, and only about one-quarter of these required Senate confirmation.[72] In contrast, the CCP general secretary confronts several predicaments. First, he is picked by his predecessors, who as retired elders may continue to pull strings behind the scenes. To maintain his position, he also needs the support of his peers. Second, he does not stand or run for office with his own policy platform, and therefore his policy preferences and inclinations are unknown beforehand. Third, he inherits a Politburo he did not pick, and he must work with other holdovers and new members according to the principles of collective leadership. Fourth, as a party member, he must, in the near term, continue the policy directions laid down by the outgoing Politburo and can only gradually begin to realize his own agenda and policies. These factors explain why he must consolidate his power after assuming the top office. To build his power base he needs to insert his protégés and allies into positions of power while neutralizing his opponents, especially in his first term. Significant changes, initiatives, and political and economic experiments can often come only later, since delicate and sensitive tasks require careful balancing. The irony is that communist states are reputed to have stronger leadership powers than their liberal democratic counterparts. Yet the new Chinese general secretary operates under many constraints, and his powers are ill-defined in official documents such as the party and state constitutions.[73]

During Xi's first term, an informal network of officials who had had past connections with Xi can be identified, although there is no evidence that these officials formed a cohesive policy or loyalty faction. At the Eighteenth Party Congress, Wang Qishan, a princeling and Xi's childhood friend and confidant (see Table 9.1) was inducted into the PBSC, whereas Shaanxi natives and former Xi associates Zhao Leji and Ma Kai were promoted to the Politburo. After the congress, Ding Xuexiang, Xi's former subordinate in Shanghai, was made deputy director of the General Office of the CC. Similarly, some officials who had worked closely with Xi in Zhejiang were promoted into key political positions.[74] At the center, Shu Guozeng, Xi's right-hand man in Zhejiang, was promoted to deputy director of the office of the Central Finance and Economic LSG; Cai Qi to deputy director of the National Security Commission; Huang Kunming to deputy director of the Central Propaganda Department; and Zhong Shaojun, as a colonel, to the office of the CMC. In the regions, Xia Bolong and Li Qiang became secretary of the Zhejiang PPC and governor, respectively. Bayin Chaolu, a Mongolian and the only minority among provincial chiefs, was made secretary of the Jilin PPC. Chen Min'er became secretary of the Guizhou PPC, and Lou Yangsheng deputy secretary of the Shanxi PPC. We will discuss in more detail the careers and background of these officials in chapter 13.

In the PLA, too, Xi used promotions to consolidate power, but also to boost morale after the corruption purges that had netted more than sixty "tigers" (high officials). For instance, in 2015, after the purges of Guo Boxiong and Xu Caihou, Xi promoted a large batch of ten generals to full general rank.[75] In 2017, just prior to the Nineteenth Party Congress, Xi promoted senior officers to command posts covering all five major services. These include two presumed Xi protégés—Han Weiguo, who had worked at the Nanjing Military Region, was appointed commander of the PLA Ground Forces; Ding Laihang, who had worked at Fuzhou, was named commander of the PLA Air Force. Zhou Yaning was made commander of the PLA Rocket Forces, Shen Jinlong commander of the PLA Navy, and Gao Jin commander of the newly established Strategic Support Force.[76] Overall, the Eighteenth PBSC and Politburo membership was stable, with only

Table 9.1 The Political Career of Wang Qishan

Year and place of birth; year joined CCP	Family background	Education	Early career	Early political career	Later political career				
1948, Tianzhen, Shanxi (1983)	Princeling, sent-down zhiqing, 1969–71	History, Northwest University, 1973–76	Researcher, Chinese Academy of Social Sciences, 1979–82; Shaanxi Provincial Museum, 1971–73, 1976–79	Section chief and research fellow, Rural Policy Research Office, Secretariat; deputy director and director, Liaison Office, Rural Development Research Center, State Council, 1982–88	Governor, People's Construction Bank of China, 1994–97; vice governor, People's Banks of China, 1993–94; vice governor, People's Construction Bank of China, 1989–93; general manager, China Rural Trust and Investment Corporation, 1988–89	Secretary, Hainan PPC, 2002–3; director and secretary, Leading Party Member's Group, Office for Economic Reconstructing of the State Council, 2000–2; member, Guangdong PPC, 1997–2000; vice governor, Guangdong, 1998–2000	Deputy secretary, Beijing MPC; acting mayor and mayor; deputy secretary, Leading Party Member's Group of the Organizing Committee for the Nineteenth Olympiad, 2003–7;	Member, CC and Politburo since 2007; vice premier; member, Leading Party Member's Group, State Council; Chair, Organizing Committee for the 2010 Shanghai World Expo 2008–12;	Vice president, 2018–?; secretary, CCDI, vice premier; member, Leading Party Member's Group, State Council; 2012–17

Source: *China vitae* and *Baidu baike*.

one Politburo member, Sun Zhengcai, purged for corruption. No doubt Xi continued to insert his supporters into other positions of power, and he had the most sway in determining the top leadership lineup at the Nineteenth Party Congress. Even then, factional politics and division did not seem to be a major issue at the top, and leaders were replaced according to age and term limits.

With reference to the factional struggle or rational choice perspectives, some China watchers presumed that Li Keqiang belonged to an opposing *tuanpai* whose patron was the retired Hu Jintao. They claimed that Xi's power had eclipsed the power of Li Keqiang and diluted the power of the Politburo, and that Xi had stacked the LSGs with loyalists and supporters in order to undermine and even to eliminate Li in favor of Xi's own protégés.[77] It is clear that Xi has greatly enhanced his personal power, but an examination of available evidence and context shows that the new institutional setup is more complex and informed by institutional requirements. Organizationally, Xi headed the Party, the state, and the military, whereas Li Keqiang directed the State Council and the cabinet, Zhang Dejiang the NPeC, and Yu Zhengsheng the advisory CPPCC (see Figure 9.1). The fascination with Xi's power neglects the interdependence between Xi and Li, and the critical division of labor and functions between the Party and the state. Among many central coordinating organs, Li served as deputy chair after Xi, as in the Comprehensively Deeping Reform LSG and the CNSC. Unlike Western political systems where the cabinet and ministries/departments are both top decision-making and implementation agencies, in China the CCP Politburo makes policies but relies on the State Council (led by Premier Li), which directs twenty-one ministries (including Finance, Foreign Affairs, Education, etc.), three commissions, and the Central Bank, to operationalize and implement the policies. Dubbed the "grand housekeeper" (*daguanjia*) in Chinese, the premier is assisted by four vice premiers, five state councilors, as well as many State Council LSGs to coordinate new initiatives and programs. As the executive branch of the government, the State Council supervises the bureaucracy, executes laws, devises schedules and budgets, and monitors progress at the provincial/municipal level.[78] To compare, Li's power relationship with Xi is reminiscent of that of the "dual executives" in the French system, where the president and prime minister are, respectively, the head of state and the head of government. The French president appoints the prime minister subject to majority approval in the National Assembly, but the constitution is vague and ambiguous about the extent of their powers. Normally the president has greater decision-making power than the prime minister, although the latter commands a great deal of policy latitude, and much depends on personality.[79] In this perspective, Li's policy role has yet to be studied.[80] The State Council and Li have also developed numerous policy initiatives, such as Made in China 2025 and tax cuts to revive manufacturing and help small and medium-sized enterprises, as well as an Internet Plus

Figure 9.1 Structure of the Chinese Communist Party and the People's Republic of China, as of March 2018

Source: Modified from "China's 2017 Communist Party Leadership Structure & Transition," June 2017, US_China Business Council, https://www.uschina.org/sites/default/files/LeadershipRep ort.pdf. Credit: US China Business Council. CCP membership is about 90 million (as of 2020), consisting 6.5% of the population. The Party's Central Military Commission (CMC) and the state's CMC are the same organization.

strategy to promote technical advancement of the economy.[81] Nevertheless, despite the interlocking of personnel—party leaders also serve in state positions—the CCP has often criticized the sprawling state bureaucracy for inefficiency and insubordination. Sensitive observers have often interpreted these criticisms as reflections of Xi's dissatisfaction with Li.[82]

The Leading Small Groups of Party Central

The prominence attributed to the LSGs is a defining characteristic of Xi's reign. Yet the notion that the LSG setup was designed to sideline Premier Li and other Politburo members simplifies a complex reality. In all, Xi acquired the directorships of six or more (out of a total of twenty-three known) CC LSGs, the Party's highest coordinating and decision-making organs (see Table 9.2).[83] These mysterious LSGs are not mentioned in official organizational charts, and they do not have their own nomenklatura since their members are drawn from other party-state organs. Accordingly, the activities of these LSGs are seldom mentioned in public. The more permanent of them have lasted for decades, but others are more ad hoc or temporary. Yet in terms of power, they supersede all party and government organs, including the Central Committee's departments and commissions (such as Organization, Propaganda, and United Front Work) and the government's twenty-five central ministries and other commissions and agencies.[84] One LSG may direct several other CC organs. For instance, the Personnel Affairs LSG may duplicate the work of the COD and the Propaganda and Ideology LSGs may duplicate the work of the Central Propaganda Department.

First, membership in the LSGs is held concurrently by the PBSC and the Politburo, and since the size of the PBSC was reduced from nine to seven, reorganization was necessary. As the highest decision-making bodies whose main functions are to better coordinate central policies, the LSGs are designed to break down vested interests and resolve conflicts by bringing all stakeholders to a single conference table. They address governance and policy challenges that are becoming increasingly complex, especially since the deepening of reform in any policy area always involves changes and resource allocations in many government agencies. The growing numbers of LSGs reflects the professionalizing of the policymaking process, when specialized expertise and institutional interests are all represented.[85] Xi has regularly consulted think tanks and professionals and worked with a team of capable experts on economic policy.[86] Accordingly, members of these LSGs are also drawn from the dozens of central departments, commissions, State Council ministries, and the like.[87] PBSC member Liu Yunshan also led three LSGs, and further, the Comprehensively Deepening Reform LSG (CDRLSG) included members from the Committee on Political and Legal Affairs, the Supreme People's Procuratorate, and the Ministry of Public

Table 9.2 The Central Committee's Leading and Coordinating Small Groups under Xi Jinping (Twenty-Three in Total)

Central Committee Leading Small Group	Director	Deputy director(s)	Number of members	Year formed
Comprehensively Deepening Reform	Xi Jinping	Li Keqiang, Liu Yunshan, Zhang Gaoli	46	2013
Internet Security and Informationization	Xi Jinping	Li Keqiang, Liu Yunshan	25	2014
Foreign Affairs (State Security)	Xi Jinping	Li Yuanqiao	18	1981
CMC Deepening Reform for National Defense and the Military	Xi Jinping	Fan Changlong, Xu Qiliang	3	2014
Finance and Economy	Xi Jinping	Li Keqiang, Zhang Gaoli	29	1980 (1958)
Judicial System Reform	Meng Jianzhu	Wang Xiaowei	N/A	2003
Hong Kong and Macau Affairs	Zhang Dejiang	Li Yuanchao, Yang Jiechi	6	1978
Xinjiang Affairs	Yu Zhengsheng		3	2000
Taiwan Affairs	Xi Jinping	Yu Zhengsheng	14	1980
Tibet Affairs	Yu Zhengsheng		3	2000
Mass Line Education and Implementation	Liu Yunshan	Zhao Yueli, Zhao Hongzhu		2013
Propaganda and Ideology	Liu Yunshan	Liu Qibao, Liu Yandong, Wang Weiguang	14	1988
Party Building	Liu Yunshan	Wang Qishan, Zhao Liji	21	1993
Personnel Affairs	Zhao Leli	Yin Weimin, Li Zhiyong	9	2003
Rural Affairs	Wang Yang	Chen Xiwen, Yuan Chunqing	13	1994

Small Group	Chair		Other Leaders	Year
Anticorruption	Wang Qishan			1998
Roving Discipline Inspection	Wang Qishan		Zhao Leji, Zhao Hongzhu	2009
Stability Maintenance	Meng Jianzhu	9	Yang Jing, Guo Shengkui	1998
United Front Work	Xi Jinping		Sun Chunlan	2015
Supervision and Management of Enterprises and State Assets	Luo Shugang			2011?
Reform and Development of Cultural Affairs	Liu Yandong	16	Liu Qibao	2003
Prevention and Management of Religious Cults	Yang Jing, Guo Shengkui	12	Meng Jianzhu	1999
Safeguarding Maritime Rights	Undisclosed		Undisclosed	2012

Source: "Zhongyang lingdao xiaozu yu 22 ge: Xi Jinping ren 4 xiaozu zuchang" [Among the Twenty-Two Central Leadership Small Groups, Xi Jinping Heads Four of Them], *news.china.com*, July 31, 2015, http://news.china.com.cn/2015-07/31/content_36190622.htm; "Meiti pandian Zhonggong zhongyang 18 ge zongzitou xiaozu Xi Jinping jian 4 zuchang" [According to Media Estimates, among the Eighteen Central Leading Small Groups, Xi Jinping is Chair of Four of Them], *Sohu*, June 23, 2014, http://news.sohu.com/20140623/n401185266.shtml.

Note: This table based on information available as of 2015. Many of these LSGs were institutionalized as formal commissions in 2018.

Security, since about one-quarter of its policy document output was related to judicial reform. It can be assumed that the bigger the group, the more power Xi had, but the flip side was that there were also more refined divisions of labor, specialized bureaucratic responsibilities, and even more dispersion of power. Each LSG commanded a huge policymaking area and workload. For example, the most important, the CDRLSG, with a membership of forty-six, was divided into six subgroups in charge of economic, environmental/ecological, judicial, culture, social, and party-building reforms. By its fourth anniversary at the end of 2017 it had convened thirty-nine conferences and produced more than three hundred policy documents on policies ranging from the protection of property rights, "two child" families, *hukou* reform, and antipoverty to healthcare reform. At the August 2017 meeting, it approved six documents on subjects from agricultural funding and compensation for ecological damage to village governance and judicial reform. Yet complaints were often raised that officials frequently evaded or ignored the LSG's initiatives, faking implementation by "convening more conferences and issuing more documents."[88] The assumption that the chairs always dictated output of the LSGs may be unwarranted.

Second, Premier Li occupied the deputy directorships of at least three of the LSGs, and in addition, he was the director of at least five State Council LSGs and other supraministry organizations such as the ones for science, technology, and education; western development; state information; the revival of the northeast and other former industrial areas; and climate change and remission reduction (see Table 9.3).[89] This reflected Li's position as head of the government, and Xi did not head any of the State Council LSGs. Granted that the State Council LSGs were less powerful than the CC LSGs, they were also charged with important

Table 9.3 State Council Leading Small Groups Headed by Premier Li Keqiang

	Year formed
Climate Change, Energy Conservation, and Remission Reduction	2007
Revival of Old Industrial Bases in the Northeast and other Regions	2003
Development of the Western Regions	2000
Science, Technology, and Education	1998
Informationization	Undisclosed

Source: "Chaobuji jigou di guowuyuan lingdao xiaozu" [The Supraministry Organization: The State Council Leading Small Groups], *Sohu*, http://news.sohu.com/20130722/n382222978.shtml, accessed June2, 2015; "Guowuyuan duoge lingdao xiaozu yu zuzhi jigou renyuan diaozheng" [The Personnel Adjustments in the State Council Leading Small Groups and Other Organizations), *Xinhua*, July 4, 2013, http://news.xinhuanet.com/renshi/2013-07/04/c_124947684.htm.

policy formulation and implementation functions coordinating China's twenty-five ministries and commissions. Further, like the CC LSGs, membership of the State Council LSGs traversed both the party and state systems. For instance, membership of the State Council LSG on Western Development included the deputy directors of the COD and the Central Propaganda Department. The State Council LSG on the Rural Workforce included the deputy directors of the Central Rural Work Office, the Supreme People's Court, and the All-China Federation of Labor, and the secretaries of the of the Communist Youth League and the All-China Federation of Women.[90] Essentially, there appeared to be a great deal of fractionalization of labor and overlap of staff. Third, some of these LSGs, such as finance and economy, political and legal affairs, and foreign affairs, were six decades old. Introduced after the Eighteenth Party Congress were five new LSGs—the CDRLSG, the Internet Security and Informationization LSG, the CMC Deepening Reform for National Defense and the Military LSG, the United Front Work LSG, and the Mass Line Education LSG. Xi took over the directorship of the first four of them, reflecting the priority accorded to these new policy areas.

Last, the process of forming the CDRLSG also illustrates that such a powerful group evolved over a long gestation period according to the demands of circumstances rather than a move simply to aggrandize Xi's personal power. The reference point for the CDRLSG was the Systemic Reform Commission (abbreviated as *tigaiwei*, a State Council organ) formed in the 1980s, which for various reasons was downgraded to a Systemic Reform Office in 1998, and finally abolished in 2003. Later, the Third Plenum of 2003 proposed "perfecting the socialist market economic system," but subsequent implementation was deemed spotty. Further discussions about the establishment of a top organization to oversee reforms did not materialize, presumably due to bureaucratic resistance, especially regarding the power of *shenpi*. As soon as the Eighteenth Party Congress was concluded, a drafting group for structural reform was struck, for which Wang Qishan was a member. This group proposed the establishment of an overarching organization with various proposed titles, such as Reform Commission (abbreviated to *gaigewei*) or System Reform Commission (abbreviated to *tigaiwei*). The drafting group referenced four hundred thousand pieces of internet opinion and concluded that the top ten priorities were almost identical with the ones put forward by it, and among them, there was a felt need to form a reform commission. Such a proposal was supported by influential academics such as Wu Jinglian and Zhang Weiying but opposed by others, citing the concentration of power. Yet the wide-ranging reforms agenda introduced by the Eighteenth Party Congress traversed political, economic, cultural, social, and ecological issues, and it was doubtful if a State Council organ or even several ministries and departments could carry sufficient weight to fulfill this mandate, and the notion was dropped from the State Council reform in 2013.[91] Finally, when the Third Plenum (November 2013) document was drafted, a new proposal to form an overarching leadership organ entitled CDRLSG (abbreviated to *shengaiwei*) was adopted. Similarly, the National Security Committee was proposed during the drafting of the Third Plenum documents, and despite concerns about overconcentration of power in the two organizations, both were approved. As mentioned, the CDRLSG has masterminded a whole series of reforms covering a dizzying array of issues,[92] the most important of which will be discussed subsequently. The notion that Xi as LSG chair diminished the role of Li underestimates the large amount of work, the division of labor, and the expertise that has gone into the work of this LSG.

The other significance of the new LSG setup under Xi is the two aspects of centralization. First, the old and new LSGs formed a high-level but informal decision-making layer whose control extended to six major areas: personnel/organization, propaganda/culture/education, politics/law, finance/economics, foreign affairs/united front, and party-building. Policy areas previously lacking LSG oversight, such as united-front work, were also incorporated. This setup strengthened Beijing's control and further realized Xi's notion of "top-level design" in policymaking.[93] Since matching LSGs were also formed at the provincial and county levels led by the provincial and county party secretaries, who were answerable to their central counterparts, Beijing bolstered vertical control over the horizontal (geographical) authorities.[94]

Second, the LSG arrangement also strengthened party control over the government, the ministries, and commissions and their many entrenched interests. The new layer of LSGs created a separate chain of command independent of the National Development Reform Commission (NDRC), China's superministry of central economic planning, whose bureaucratic interests and penchant for heavy state intervention in the economy were perceived to have threatened ongoing reforms. For example, by deftly using the anticorruption campaign (discussed later), Xi weakened the state-owned oil sector and the political legal apparatus, the latter being deemed a source of corruption.[95] To assert party control over SOE reform, by 2017 the formerly moribund party committees had been re-established in virtually all SOEs, including those operating in Hong Kong, which traditionally downplayed their party connections.[96] The ten million CCP members among forty million working in the SOEs had accounted for eight hundred thousand party committees in the SOEs.[97]

The Politburo Study Sessions

Another institutional means that Xi used to consolidate his power were the Politburo study sessions, which serve to channel expert input and to build consensus (see Table 9.4). Originally set up by Hu Jintao after the Sixteenth Party

Table 9.4 Politburo Study Sessions during Xi Jinping's First (2012–2017) and Second Term (2017–2022) as General Secretary (Listings up to early 2018 only)

Series	Date	Subject	Series	Date	Subject
1	Nov. 17, 2012	Resolutely adhere to socialism with Chinese characteristics and implement the spirit of the Eighteenth Party Congress	12	Dec. 30, 2013	Bolster cultural soft power
2	Dec. 31, 2012	Resolutely promote reform and opening up	13	Feb. 24, 2014	Promote socialist core values and traditional Chinese virtues
3	Jan. 28, 2013	Resolutely adhere to the principles of peaceful development	14	Apr. 25, 2014	Resolutely promote national security and social stability
4	Feb. 23, 2013	Comprehensively promote governance according to law	15	May 26, 2014	Turn market forces into a decisive factor in resource allocation and improve government functions
5	Apr. 19, 2013	Anticorruption and clean government in Chinese history	16	June 30, 2014	Strengthening of the improvement in work style
6	May 24, 2013	Greatly promote ecological civilization	17	Aug. 29, 2014	New trends in global military development and the promotion of innovations in the PLA
7	June 25, 2013	Socialism with Chinese characteristics: theory and practice	18	Oct. 13, 2014	China's governance in history
8	July 30, 2013	The building of a strong maritime power	19	Dec. 5, 2014	Acceleration of the building of the free trade zones
9	Sept. 30, 2013	The implementation of innovation to drive development	20	Jan. 23, 2015	Principles and methods of dialectical materialism
10	Oct. 29, 2013	Acceleration of the promotion of housing guarantee and supply	21	Mar. 24, 2015	Deepening of the reform of the judicial system and the assurance of judicial fairness
11	Dec. 3, 2013	Fundamental principles and methods of historical Materialism	22	Apr. 30, 2015	Unified development of the urban and rural areas

Continued

Table 9.4 *Continued*

Series	Date	Subject	Series	Date	Subject
23	May 29, 2015	Strengthening the system of public security	34	July 26, 2016	Deepening of the reforms in national defense and the PLA
24	Jun. 26, 2015	Strengthening of the legislation on anticorruption	35	Sept. 27, 2016	Reform of the G20 and global governance
25	July 30, 2015	Reflections on the anti-Japan war	36	Oct. 9, 2016	Implementation of the strategy of a strong cyberspace power
26	Sept. 11, 2015	Implementation of the "three disciplines and three steadfastnesses"*	37	Dec. 9, 2106	The rule of law and rule of virtue in Chinese history
27	Oct. 12, 2015	Global system of governance	38	Jan. 22, 2017	Deepening of the supply-side reform
28	Nov. 23, 2015	Fundamental principles of Marxist political economy	39	Feb. 21, 2017	Strengthening and targeting of antipoverty
29	Dec. 30, 2015	History and development of China's patriotism	40	Apr. 25, 2017	The protection of financial security
30	Jan. 29, 2016	Strategic fundamentals of socioeconomic development during the Thirteenth FYP	41	May 26, 2017	Promotion of green development and lifestyle
31	Apr. 29, 2016	The land and maritime silk routes in history	42	July 24, 2017	Promotion of the Reform of the structure of the PLA
32	May 27, 2016	Policy dealing with the aging population in China	43	Sept. 29, 2017	Contemporary Marxism and its impact
33	June 28, 2016	Strict control and purification of party activities			

Second Term					
1	Oct. 27, 2017	Study and implementation of the spirit of the Nineteenth Party Congress	2	Dec. 8, 2017	Implement the big-data national strategy and accelerating the building of digital China

Table 9.4 *Continued*

Series	Date	Subject	Series	Date	Subject
3	Jan. 31, 2018	The building of a modern economic system	5	Apr. 23, 2018	The contemporary significance of the *Communist Manifesto*
4	Feb. 24, 2108	The Chinese constitution and the promotion of comprehensive governance according to law	6	June 29, 2018	The strengthening of the construction of the Party

Source: "Zhonggong zhongyang zhengzhiju juti Xuexi" [The Study Sessions of the Politburo of the Chinese Communist Party], *gongchandangyuanwang*, http://www.12371.cn/special/lnzzjjtxx/.

* "Three disciplines and three steadfastness" refers to the requirements of "being strict with oneself in practicing self-cultivation, using power, and exercising self-discipline" and "being earnest in one's thinking, work, and behavior." This constitutes the themes of an education campaign for party members that began in April 2015.

Congress, these two-hour study sessions are held every forty days and organized by the Party Central Office and the Central Political Research Office (presided over for a long time by Wang Huning).[98] Normally, a couple of presenters are invited, most commonly experts, scholars, and members of research institutions and think tanks, government or otherwise. Members of the Chinese Academy of Social Sciences generally stand at the top of the invitation list, followed by the State Council's Development Research Center. At least half of the lecturers have had overseas experiences and are normally aged forty to fifty-five. For each policy area, the presenters discuss history, issues, and remedies. Once a subject is assigned, the presenters may be given three months to prepare the research, although in one case when the subject was "the correct handling of contractions among the people" (social unrest), the lecturer took three years to complete his report. At the end of each session the general secretary makes an authoritative summary, usually prepared in advance. Reportedly there are heated discussion and questions, but these do not constitute active debate. Occasionally the sessions serve as briefings for the top leadership; for instance, Hu Jintao attended a session on energy resources and strategy in 2005 just prior to his visit to Russia for "oil diplomacy."

The study sessions institutionalize the commissioning of ideas, and the largely academic research tends to cut across bureaucratic lines and is expected to complement the leadership's strategic big picture. Subjects of the sessions reflect the policy priorities and ongoing deliberations for decision-making at that time, and they may presage later policy decisions. The lecture subjects are often published in book form, with related authoritative statements in the *People's Daily* and *Qiushi*. There are also examples of academic lecturers who were recruited into government after their presentations. For instance, Wan Gang, a non-CCP member, was later recruited as minister of science and technology, and Cao Jianming was appointed chief of the Supreme People's Procuratorate and then deputy director of the Standing Committee of the National People's Congress.

During Xi's first term, forty-three study sessions were conducted (see Table 9.4), and many of them took long historical perspectives to examine a range of political/economic/social issues. This included development issues such as innovations, changes in government functions, the rule of law, and free trade zones; foreign relations issues such as soft power, global governance, and maritime security; and social issues such as housing, the aging population, and green development.

The study sessions, whose contents are widely reported by the official media such as *Xinhua* and CCTV, served to consolidate Xi's power in a number of ways. First, the study sessions highlight the role of the general secretary as the paramount leader of the CCP, affording him a platform to articulate and to legitimize his ideal. They tend to advertise policy consensus in what the Chinese call "unification of thinking," especially when the Politburo members are often seen as followers at these sessions. Second, the sessions show that the party state is open and responsive to current issues and accepts fresh outside ideas and expert perspectives on governance. Third, the sessions reflect Xi's ideal of a "learning Party," or learning organization that continuously incorporates new knowledge. They also give the public a sense of the complexity of policy issues and policy design.

The Central National Security Commission

Importantly, Xi achieved something his predecessor failed to do in his consolidating and centralizing of power. The Third Plenum of November 2013 decided to establish the CNSC, which was officially formed in January 2014 with Xi as chair and Li Keqiang and Zhang Dejiang as deputy chairs (see Table 9.5). For many, this constitutes another of Xi's power grabs, although things were more complex and ambiguous.[99] Organizationally accountable to the Politburo, the CNSC was touted as the fifth center of power after the CC, the State Council, the National People's Congress, and the Chinese People's Political Consultative Conference. Yet the operation of the CNSC was shrouded in secrecy, and its first meeting was not held until April 2014, during which Xi discussed his "notion of comprehensive national security." The CNSC might even have been dormant for

Table 9.5 Leadership of the Central National Security Commission

Chair	Xi Jinping
Deputy chairs	Li Keqiang, Zhang Dejiang
Secretariat	Li Zhanshu

several years after that, raising questions about possible bureaucratic and factional resistance.[100]

The origins of the CNSC can be traced to a debate lasting for more than a decade. After Jiang Zemin visited the US National Security Council in 1997, discussion began on the establishment of a similar organization. Several incidents, such as the US bombing of China's Belgrade Embassy in 1999, the Hainan Island EP-3 crisis in 2001, and the riots in Xinjiang in 2009, had shown that Beijing's response was slow. Similarly, when a Chinese antisatellite missile test destroyed a Chinese weather satellite in 2007, the civilian leadership appeared to be informed by the military only after the fact.[101] There was a general perception that institutional fragmentation in security matters had resulted in inefficiency and poor central coordination. Nevertheless, there were concerns that a new CNSC headed by the general secretary (who already headed the CMC) would make him too powerful and would upset collective leadership. Ultimately, the lack of PBSC consensus and bureaucratic resistance, especially from the military, had scuttled the initiative under Jiang Zemin and Hu Jintao.[102]

Modeled on the United States' National Security Council, the new CNSC was intended to be a powerful body to improve coordination, command, and information sharing. Its creation was consistent with Xi's notions of centralized "top-level design" and "big-power diplomacy" to cope with the new reality of Beijing's growing power and global responsibilities. A comprehensive platform, it was argued, would better manage the ever-increasing traditional and nontraditional domestic and foreign security threats (such as terrorism, cyberthreats, and the spread of infectious diseases) that cannot be dealt with by one department or ministry.[103]

Formally, the CNSC is more powerful than the LSGs and even the CMC, and it replaced the National Security LSG and probably superseded the Foreign Affairs LSG, which were essentially the same organization assigned two titles (a common organization practice); they made decisions that were implemented by the State Council Foreign Affairs Office.[104] According to Yun Sun, the former National Security LSG was an ad hoc committee lacking a regular meeting schedule or fixed membership. Further, it was a reactive mechanism for crisis management rather than an active decision-maker on national security affairs. In contrast, the CNSC coordinates among various party LSGs (such as Internet Security and Information, which deals with cyberthreats and hacking) and state and military intelligence organs, thereby breaking the constraints of vertical and horizontal (*tiao-kuai*) controls.

Organizationally, the CNSC encompasses representatives from dozens of party and state organs such as public security, the PAP, the judiciary, the Ministries of State Security and Foreign Affairs, the Office of External Propaganda, and so on, showing a diversity of functions. It bears some resemblance to the US Department of Homeland Security (DHS), which was formed after 9/11. A massive and highly centralized organization, the DHS coordinates a range of functions previously scattered through the federal government. It takes charge of a wide array of security initiatives that have been criticized for being intrusive, but which others deem a necessary evil for protecting liberty and democratic government.[105]

In China the creation of such a powerful organ rekindled concerns among the elite that it might further upset the consensus-based decision-making system and that Xi may have amassed too much personal power. For instance, the CNSC may weaken the powerful Central Political and Legal Affairs Commission, which oversees *weiwen* and social management policy and manages the judiciary by relying on coercive measures against society.[106] Some China watchers have claimed that the CNSC has broken the tradition of subsuming political and legal affairs under collective leadership.

The irony is that after much fanfare heralding the formation of the CNSC, another three years elapsed before a report of a conference was televised on February 20, 2017, revealing some details about its membership. About twelve members from the Politburo and other senior central and provincial leaders attended.[107] On issues supposedly falling under the CNSC's remit, however, such as the evacuation of Chinese nationals from Yemen in March 2015, the Tianjin explosion in April 2015, and the maritime disputes in the South China Sea, there is little evidence of CNSC involvement. The silence and secrecy surrounding the power and operation of the CNSC have raised questions about Xi's consolidation of power.[108] One unconfirmed report claims that state security had been tightly controlled by powerful leaders from the Jiang Zemin faction such as Zeng Qinghong and Zhou Yongkang, and that only after some of the officials in the state security system were purged (for example, Zhou was purged on corruption charges in December 2014) could Xi finally gain control of this area (see Figure 13.1).[109] In any case, the CNSC remained mysterious, and its second open meeting was not convened until April 2018.

The "Core" Issue

From early 2016, the media and provincial chiefs began to hail Xi as the "core" of the Party, and the Sixth Plenum (October 2016) made this official. Since then, the Party has repeatedly called on all members to "closely unite around the CPC Central Committee, with Comrade Xi Jinping as the core," and argued that the Party required a core "to bond the Party together, to unite the people, to tide over challenges and to continue to forge ahead."[110] At a two-day "democratic life" meeting of the Politburo, individual members professed to set an example by reading out self-criticism statements and pledging a loyalty oath to Xi as the "core." The meeting resolved to fully implement the two new regulations on party conduct and discipline, claiming that only with the strictest discipline could the Party ensure that the "red regime" would last from generation to generation.[111]

According to Deng Maosheng, a drafter of the Sixth Plenum documents, the rights of the "core" to discuss and to vote is equivalent to those of other members, and that the task of the "core" was simply to synthesize everyone's opinions before making the final decision (*dingdiao*).[112] Other sources claim that the "core" owns the power of final approval or veto, and the elevated status would enable Xi to wield more influence over the collective leadership, especially with personnel choices for the Nineteenth Party Congress in 2017.[113] Falun Gong sources interpret this to mean that the Xi "core" would deal a devastating blow to the Jiang "core," especially against the three Jiang clients in the PBSC.[114]

Historically, Deng Xiaoping set a precedent by using the term "core" retroactively to refer to Mao and himself. In the immediate aftermath of the Mao era, Deng warned that it would not be a healthy practice for any party or state to place its hope on the prestige and authority of one or two persons, since any change in these persons would bring about instability. On the other hand, Deng also approved of centralized authority and a person as a leadership core.[115] Jiang Zemin was designated the core of the "third generation" at the Fourth Plenum of the Thirteenth Party Congress in June 1989, but Hu Jintao was never given the same accolade. Analysts who take a "power maximization" approach have interpreted this to mean, among other things, that Hu was not given the same degree of prominence and power as Jiang.[116] Yet a simpler contextual explanation is that Jiang was parachuted in as general secretary right after the 1989 Tiananmen crisis. With the constitutionally illegal disposition of Zhao Ziyang (as with Hu Yaobang before him) as general secretary, Jiang required additional help to legitimize his position and authority. Deng Xiaoping explicitly argued for the bolstering of the "third generation" of leadership and that it must have a "core" to stabilize the situation.[117] In this context, it was expedient to confer the title of "core" to Jiang under the condition of perceived weakness and vulnerability. However, the case of Hu Jintao was different, since he assumed power not under a crisis, but in the first-ever peaceful transition of power in the PRC. One source claims that Central Committee delegates had repeatedly advocated the conferment of "core" status to Hu, but Hu had declined repeatedly.[118] This is not implausible, since in terms of temperament, personality, and policy behavior, Hu tended to be more reserved and self-effacing.[119]

If the "core" bestowal did not confer any more formal power to Xi, it did give him greater stature and authority when reforming China's political economy and cleansing the Party and the military.[120] Xi had demanded loyalty and discipline because reforms had entered a "deepwater zone." The "core" designation also paved the way for Xi to take up a third term as general secretary.[121] In the larger scheme of things, the designation of Xi as a "core" tends to be a symbolic affirmation that the buck stops with the general secretary. Xi's power rests less on the formal definitions of his positions than on the situational and conditional contexts. For instance, according to Zhang Zhuoyuan, one of the drafters of the Third Plenum documents, an exceptionally controversial notion was the "letting the market be the decisive force" in the economy, as many argued that the impact of such a formulation was too sweeping. In the end, Xi decided in favor, representing the view of the majority.[122]

During Xi's first term, the media promoted Xi's image with a frequency and intensity unseen since the Mao era. The magnitude of this was further exaggerated by (1) more openness in the reporting of the numerous policy initiatives introduced by the new administration, and (2) ad infinitum repetitions by large numbers of media sources, which included two thousand newspapers and three thousand TV stations. Administratively, every central initiative and policy was reported and elaborated upon by every level of administration, making for torrents of material. The Party's call for the public to swear loyalty to Xi as the "core" has resulted in a torrent of responses. For the average Chinese, however, the publicity and image-building around the new leader hardly suggested a cult of personality but seemed more indicative of an attempt to modernize the Party's public relations in an age of mass social media. Culturally speaking, many Chinese feared that a weak center would mean instability.[123] Therefore, the equation of the Xi case with the cult of personality, the self-glorification and deification of such dictators as Stalin and Mao, or more contemporary North Korean leaders, is likely an inappropriate historical analogy that leaves little room for nuances.[124]

In any event, among the many definitions and redefinitions of goals and strategies for Xi's first term, official publicity settled on a formula entitled the "four comprehensives"—comprehensively build a moderately prosperous society, comprehensively deepen reform, comprehensively govern the nation according to law, and comprehensively strictly govern the Party. Roughly, the various party plenums focused on each individual "comprehensive" (see Table 9.6).

Table 9.6 Policy Agendas and Themes at Central Committee Plenums of the
Eighteenth Party Congress

Central Committee plenum	Policy goal and initiatives
First (November 15, 2012)	Election of the Politburo, its Standing Committee, the Military Affairs Commission, and the CCDI
Second (February 26–28, 2013)	Approval of the slate of state officials proposed by the CCP
Third (November 9–12, 2013)	Deepening of economic reform
Fourth (October 20–23, 2014)	Comprehensive governance according to law
Fifth (October 26–29, 2015)	Approval of the proposal for the Thirteenth Five-Year Plan
Sixth (October 24–27, 2016)	Strict governing of the CCP
Seventh (October 11–14, 2017)	Approval of the CC and CCDI reports to the Nineteenth Party Congress and amendments of the CCP Constitution

Source: "Shibajie zhongyang weiyuanhui lici quanhui: buju sige quanmian" [The Various Plenums of the Eighteenth CC: The Planning of the "Four Comprehensives" Strategy], *Zhongguowang*, October 26, 2016, http://news.china.com.cn/txt/2016-10/26/content_39569476.htm; "*Xinhua* Insight: Plenary Session Offers Glimpse into CPC's Inner Workings," *Xinhua*, November 4, 2016, http://news.xinhuanet.com/english/2016-11/04/c_135805602.htm.

These initiatives in turn unleashed a kaleidoscope of plans and policies of immense and unprecedented scope that had far-reaching impact on Chinese politics, economy, and society. Driven by a sense of vulnerability and urgency, Xi exuded a sense of mission and opportunity, but there were multiple ironies. Xi strove to elevate the leadership role of the vanguard to make it strong again but attacked it mercilessly with a variety of campaigns. He privileged stability but also launched destabilizing attacks on the party state that generated many crises and shook the regime to its foundation. His reforms created so many enemies that China watchers predicted coup and assassination attempts. In the confines of this chapter, I will therefore attempt a general overview of policy and policy-making under Xi.

Image-Making, Public Relations, and Reactions during Xi's First Term
Notwithstanding the "core" designation, Xi was still an unknown to the Chinese public when he became general secretary, especially compared to his celebrity wife. To build his image, the official media released an unprecedented amount of information on every stage of Xi's career. In these materials, Xi was portrayed as

a man of the people who was tireless, decisive, and down to earth and who cared for the poor and the underprivileged. He was depicted as a leader committed to reform and opening up rather than a distant bureaucrat devoid of warmth, an image that had stuck to Hu Jintao outside of China. At the same time, he seemed to have allowed the propaganda establishment to make adulatory references to him, praising his extensive experiences in the localities and his alleged exceptional leadership qualities. The various dimensions of his image-building can be summarized in the following.

First, as soon as the Eighteenth Party Congress was concluded, *Xinhua* departed from the tradition of not advertising the personal information about leaders. It released detailed information regarding the career, family, and experiences of all seven members of the PBSC, and this was reproduced by numerous media sources nationally. These sources highlighted Xi's credentials as heir apparent that were not well known to the general public. For instance, Xi was credited with directing the eighteen-month campaign to study and implement the scientific development concept (2009–2010); the drafting of the report to the Eighteenth Party Congress; the amendment of the party constitution; Taiwan, Hong Kong, and Macao affairs; and the preparations for the Beijing Olympics.

On Xi's childhood and youth, the biographical information acknowledged that Xi had been traumatized by the Cultural Revolution because of the persecution of his father. It added that he had to endure the hard labor of a sent-down youth, missing out on the opportunity for higher education. This mishap, however, had helped Xi acquire a deep understanding of the countryside and a determination to serve the people. The information credited Xi with the foreign experience of visiting more than sixty countries before arriving at Beijing in 2007 and that he had visited more than forty countries when he was vice president. Xi was said to have drawn wisdom from traditional Chinese culture. To head off questions about the well-known power and money nexus, the official information claimed that after Xi became a national leader, Qi Xin ordered his siblings to withdraw from businesses in areas where Xi worked. Xi himself had also forbade good friends and relatives from doing business in places where he worked as a leader.[125] In another departure from precedent, biographical information mentioned Peng Liyuan, and acknowledged that the couple had often been separated by work since their marriage in 1986. The fact that Peng had given hundreds of free performances at poor and remote areas was highlighted.

Second, quirky public relations videos and graphics began to use cartoons to depict the leaders (including Mao) and their policies, although such caricatures heretofore had been regarded as a sign of disrespect and a strict taboo. (See Figure 9.2.) The media began to refer to Xi with a new nickname, *Xi Dada* (Big Daddy Xi), following a practice of officially sanctioned nicknames for former

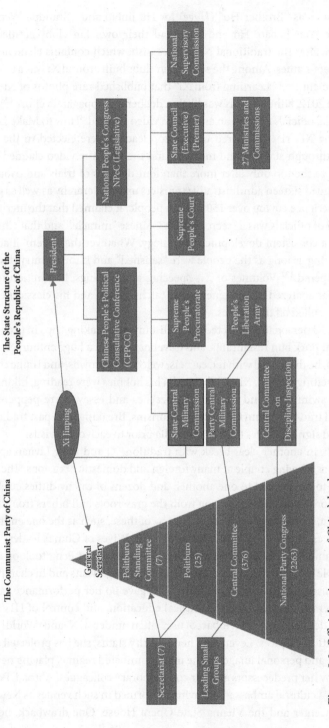

Figure 9.2 Official caricatures of China's leaders

leaders such as "Brother Hu" (*Huge*) for Hu Jintao and "Grandpa Wen" (*Wen yeye*) for Wen Jiabao. Hu and Wen had their own fan clubs entitled *shijin babaofan*, after the traditional New Year's dish, which contains elements of the two leaders' names. Among the several fan clubs built around Xi was a microblog on Weibo entitled "Learning from Xi" that published rare photos of Xi and his family in 2012, although this was likely a deliberate propaganda effort.[126] On social media, officials entered an animation video entitled "How to Make Leaders" explaining Xi's rise compared to how top leaders were elected in the United States ("through stamina and money") and the UK. The video claimed that Xi assented to the top only after more than four decades of trials and tribulations that included sixteen administrative transfers up the hierarchy as well as governance experience coving over 150 million people. It claimed that the meritocratic selection of officials was a "secret" of the Chinese "miracle," and that China had pursued a consistent developmental strategy. Whatever the system, it added, it was working as long as the people were "satisfied" and if the country developed and prospered.[127] Volumes of Xi's speeches and writings, in addition to other tomes that analyzed his statements, his catchphrases, and his classical Chinese allusions, rolled off the presses.

Third, Xi personally projected a populist image by taking trips in taxis, eating lunches at pork bun restaurants, and traveling without a huge entourage. In official visits, he dispensed with red carpets, welcoming crowds, and traffic convoys, thereby setting a trend. Xi told the media his hobbies were reading, hiking, martial arts, swimming, and soccer. His speeches and essays were peppered with slang and traditional and Confucian aphorisms. Breaking with past tradition, he published signed articles for foreign media prior to each of his visits.

Fourth, in another clear break with tradition, Xi and Peng Liyuan appeared together as a loving couple at many foreign and domestic occasions. The couple was said to be devoted to one another, and dozens of catchy ditties celebrating the relationship, some originating from the grassroots and others from the official media, circulated in cyberspace. A few of these, such as the one entitled "Xi Dada Loves Mama Peng," had even gone viral. Wives of China's leaders, except for Madame Mao, tended to stay in the background, but Peng took on a high-profile role as the first lady accompanying Xi's foreign visits and in championing social causes and the fashion industry. She gave up her performance career to devote herself to causes such as musical education, and control of HIV/AIDS, juvenile delinquency, and tobacco use, often under UN and World Health Organization auspices. Leveraging her celebrity status, she has projected a more feminine and personal image for the male-dominated regime, playing new roles dodged by her predecessors and her contemporary colleagues. Abroad, Peng has served as a cultural ambassador, having performed in such venues as New York's Lincoln Center and the Vienna State Opera House. One drawback, however, has been images of Peng singing to the troops immediately after the Tiananmen crackdown.[128]

Internal Tours

To present himself as a legitimate heir of the revolution with a commitment to reforms, Xi traveled extensively to locations linked symbolically to both (see Table 9.7). His first inspection tour in December 2012 was a five-day visit to Shenzhen, loaded with symbolism since the city is synonymous with reform and opening up. As one of the first Special Economic Zones experimenting

Table 9.7 Xi Jinping's Visits to Old Revolutionary Areas

Date	Location	Revolutionary significance
2019 October	Shanghai and Jiaxing	Sites of CCP's First Party Congress in 1921
2019 April	Yudu, Jiangxi	The embarkation point for the Long March in 1934
2017 December	Xuzhou, Jiangsu	Site of the critical Huaihai battle against the Guomindang
2017 June	Liuliang and Xinzhou, Shanxi	Revolutionary base areas
2016 April	Jinzhai, Anhui	Cradle of the Red Army
2016 July	Xiji, Ningxia	A convergence point for Long March forces
2016 February	Jinggangshan, Jiangxi	First revolutionary base area set up by Mao in 1927
2015 June	Zunyi, Guizhou	Mao becomes undisputed leader of the CCP at the Zunyi conference
2015 February	Yanan and Zhaojin, Shaanxi	Shen-Gan-Ning border region where Xi Zhongxun and other revolutionaries establish a revolutionary base in 1933 and the CCP ends its Long March here in 1934
2014 November	Gutian, Fujian	Historic Gutian Party Congress 1929
2013 November	Yimeng, Shangdong	Old revolutionary base area
2013 July	Xibaipo and Zhengding, Hebei	CCP headquarters just before taking power in 1949
2012 December	Fuping, Hebei	Jin-Cha-Ji border base area

Source: "Zhuixun Xi Jinping zongshuji di hongse zuji" [In the Red Footsteps of General Secretary Xi Jinping], *qstheory.cn*, July 14, 2019, http://www.qstheory.cn/zhuanqu/2019-07/14/c_1124751040.htm.

with the introduction of market forces, foreign capital, and technology,[129] Shenzhen had transformed itself from a tiny market town into a metropolis of twelve million. Xi laid a wreath at a statue of Deng Xiaoping at Lotus Hill, reminding everyone of Deng's "southern tour" of 1992. In the aftermath of the Tiananmen incidents, when austerity measures and backlash from the conservatives threatened reforms, Deng had thrown his weight behind the revival of reform by visiting Shenzhen, where he sternly warned: "whoever is opposed to reform and opening up must resign." Xi's Shenzhen tour also drew parallels to his father's reformist role in the SEZs and Guangdong, since both places are disliked by the new left.

Among Xi's dozen or so high-profile visits to remote, rural, and minority regions were trips to former revolutionary base areas that were still underdeveloped. He visited local museums to recall the struggle of the CCP and to highlight the issue of poverty. Apart from positioning himself as an heir of the revolution, he traced the roots and revived revolutionary myths and values such as hard work, frugality, altruism, and struggle. By drawing attention to history, he also hoped to elicit inspirations for reform. For instance, in February 2016 he visited Jinggangshan, where the CCP set up its first revolutionary bases after its crushing defeat by the GMD in 1927. Xi visited Zunyi, where Mao confirmed his position as the supreme leader of the communist movement during the Long March. Just before Xi's visit, four child siblings at Zunyi had committed suicide by drinking pesticide after being abandoned by their migrant worker parents. Xi took this tragic occasion to draw attention to the plight of the sixty million "left behind" children. At Gutian, Fujian, in 2014, Xi reiterated the importance of upholding the cherished spirit of the Red Army, the PLA's predecessor. There he summoned four hundred senior military officials to a conference to urge them to reflect on the case of Xu Caihou, who was dismissed for corruption. Warning the military to obey the Party, he pressed home Mao's refrain, "The Party commands the gun." Xi visited Yanan in February 2015, returning to Liangjiahe for the first time, and while there chaired two conferences on poverty reduction. After Xi's visits, tourists flocked to the historical sites, boosting the already vibrant travel itinerary labeled "red tourism." Following Chinese tradition, during Chinese New Year, Xi has often visited the cradles of the revolution and retired leaders to show solidarity with the local population and to show respect for leadership continuity. Without exception, he paid annual visits to retired leaders such as Jiang Zemin, Hu Jintao, Zhu Rongji, Li Ruihuan, Wu Bangguo, and Wen Jiabao, and lists of those visited are duly published by official media according to strict protocol ranking.[130]

This publicity, although still not quite at Madison Avenue level, represented an attempt to modernize image-building and modify the stiff official propaganda of past eras in an age of social media. Helped by the "personalism" (a particularistic, diffuse authority relationship in a strict hierarchy) aspect of Chinese political culture,[131] the image-building of Xi generated certain spontaneous expressions of goodwill and support. It satisfied to a certain degree the public curiosity about the new leader. Local publicity machines, however, tended to be clumsier. If Xi enjoyed a measure of popularity among the public, the same cannot be said regarding Xi's enemies, such as the losers in his reform campaigns, and victims of some of the Party's oppressive policies.[132] In any case, a 2014 survey on the popularity of ten world leaders, published by the Ash Center for Democratic Governance and Innovation at the Harvard Kennedy School, shows that Xi ranked the highest with 94.8 percent, and 93.8 percent of Chinese expressing confidence in Xi over his handling of domestic and foreign affairs, respectively. In contrast, Pew surveys conducted in 2018 showed a median of 56 percent stating nonconfidence in Xi in doing "the right thing in world affairs." A median of 45 percent held a favorable opinion on China, compared with 43 percent unfavorable.[133] Gallup polls of 2019, however, showed China's median approval rating for its leadership was 34 percent, compared with 31 percent for the United States, 31 percent for Russia, and 39 percent for Germany.[134] The relatively higher scores can be partially explained by the fact that in countries with state-controlled media and censorship, their leaders tend to receive more attention and are ranked high in popularity. In contrast, leaders tend to be ranked lower where the media are more open and critical.[135] Public opinions are snapshots and fluctuate with time. And Western soft power benchmarking seldom takes into account cultural background, political legacy, and the developmental stage of countries, and ideology and values are often embedded in the selection and treatment of data. China's attempt to "tell the Chinese stories well" with its own soft power indexes, such as the China National Image Global Survey, has been barely visible.[136] Foreign and domestic opinions turned more negative on Xi during the second part of his first term as more backlash gathered against his policies, such as the abolition of term limits. Gradually, official publicity had jettisoned cartoons and nicknames, replacing them with images of a confident and powerful international statesman. Even caricatures of Xi as Winnie the Pooh were cleansed from the internet.

Discourses on Ideology and Ideological Control

The China Dream and Great Rejuvenation

Like all Marxist-Leninist systems, the CCP regards its monopolistic control of ideology as a defining characteristic of its system. Ideology consists of a comprehensive set of ideas and beliefs to interpret the world and to delineate the means and ends of the system itself. Apart from being a guide to communication and action, ideology is inherently political because it determines who holds power and how they exercise it. An important function of ideology is to justify and legitimize the party state and its policies. As such, the CCP zealously guards its monopoly in defining ideology and eliminating incompatible ideas. This is often seen to be an essential task and even a matter of survival because, in its evaluation, the Soviet Union fell because of its "stagnant ideology." The CCP's ideology formulations stress the accumulated experiences as well as change and adaptation. Apart from a formal commitment to some aspects of Marxism-Leninism, however, the basic ideological principles can constantly evolve according to new circumstances. Formulations by past administrations, such as the contents of Jiang Zemin's "three represents" and Hu Jintao's "scientific development" have always been incorporated into the latest redefinitions despite the many overlaps.[137]

At a practical level, an important function of the general secretary is to redefine ideology, and this gives him an important means to establish his power and authority. Xi directed the drafting of the Eighteenth Party Congress work report behind the scenes. However, as soon as he was confirmed as general secretary, he quickly used the power of that position to add his imprint on ideology and national goals to expound on his new brand, the "China Dream and Great Rejuvenation," and "core socialist values."

In November 2012, days after becoming general secretary, Xi made his national debut introducing the new formula, the China Dream and Great Rejuvenation, a concept not mentioned in Hu Jintao's report to the Eighteenth Party Congress. He took the newly minted PBSC to visit the "The Chinese Road to Renaissance," an exhibition at the National Museum that depicted nineteenth-century Chinese history as dominated by foreign encroachments in their "scramble for concessions" and the establishment of spheres of influence. According to this narrative, China was repeatedly humiliated in the nineteenth century and by the chaos and disintegration in the twentieth century, turning China into a colony of the Western powers. By taking a long historical perspective, Xi claimed that China had failed to overcome its backwardness and to find a "correct" road until the CCP gained national independence and initiated socialist construction. Currently, a China Dream and Great Rejuvenation was said to be the biggest aspiration of the Chinese nation. The China Dream pledged that China would (a) by 2020, on the eve of the centenary of the founding of the CCP, become "a moderately prosperous society in all aspects" by doubling its 2010 nominal per capita GDP of US$4,524 (US$9,521 in PPP) to about US$10,000; and (b) by 2049, the centenary of the founding of the PRC, be fully modernized, "affluent and prosperous." In this way, China would be transformed from a developing country into a modernized country with advanced culture, economics, politics, society, and ecology. Xi added that China would play a more active role in international affairs to counter global challenges so that it would not be "bullied" again, although the China Dream belongs to the world and not just China.[138]

Indeed, like any ideological or policy statements in China, the ambitious notion is essentially a comprehensive but amorphous wish-list that contains everything thought to be good for China, incorporating all previous ideological formulations, such as Jiang Zemin's "three represents" and "relatively prosperous society," and Hu Jintao's "harmonious society" and "scientific concept of development." Implicitly, the notion also acknowledges the extent to which China has fallen behind the developed countries. Massive propaganda efforts to promote the China Dream have since saturated the public space and spawned spin-offs such as a "strong country" dream, a "strong military" dream, a "strong sports nation" dream, and a "strong aviation" dream, as well as a Henan Dream, Sichuan Dream, Guizhou Dream, and the like. Four interconnected aspects of this formulation, however, deserve attention.

First, the aspiration of the China Dream harks back to Jiang Zemin's report to the Fifteenth Party Congress of 1997 in which he projected that China would double its 2000 GDP by 2010; achieve a more developed economy by the centenary of the founding of the CCP in 2021; and basically achieve modernization by building China into a strong, rich, socialist country with a democratic culture.[139] International Monetary Fund figures show that China's nominal GDP per capital in 2017 was already US$8,643 (US$16,660 in PPP).[140] This probably gave Xi and his team confidence that the 2020 target could be overfulfilled. Further, by 2021 Xi would have entered the ninth year of his tenure, and if China could raise its GDP per capita to US$10,000, its economy would be 40 percent larger than that of the United States if measured in PPP terms.[141]

Second, Xi called for political pragmatism and avoidance of ideological debate that might divide the Party and the nation. Like his predecessors, Xi abandoned an attempt to construct a Mao-style all-pervasive ideology that purported to explain everything. He also abandoned the idea of attainment of a Marxist communist utopia through incessant class struggle. Implicitly he included the Cultural Revolution as part of the decay that the Chinese must transcend to achieve a "rejuvenation," but he suggested that China had already more than recovered from the havoc wrecked by the Chairman. The frequent recounts of Xi's own experience of transcending adversity by rising to the top from the lowest depth in the poorest part of China are used as examples to inspire and resonate with the majority of Chinese who have experienced poverty and hardship.

Third, Xi's vision linked China's development to a grand historical process from modern history to a projected bright future goal of revival promising wealth, a higher standard of living, sustainable growth, and international respect. His notion harks back to various "revivals" and "prosperous" periods in Chinese history that featured growth, peace, and prosperity, as demonstrated by the dynastic cyclical pattern of rise, decline, revival, and collapse.[142] He is confident that China's long-term decline is finally over to be replaced by a period of revival, although he argued that the restoration of past greatness was achievable only with far-reaching reforms and "China's own path" and not just a mere copy of any other system. At this critical juncture, Xi argued, China's destiny was at stake and only the CCP was capable of leading China.

Fourth, Xi tapped into popular nationalism and aspirations and attempted to present his reforms as a key to China's continuous rise so that China could take its place in the world as a major civilization. Xi's formulation is a simple but powerful notion akin to the American Dream (and posited as a counterpoint to it) at a juncture when ordinary Chinese, especially the newly created middle class with its ubermodernistic aspirations, are aware of the huge disparity between China and the developed world, and feel that they should catch up with the latter. By promising wealth and power, and the Party as the only agent capable of nation building and revival of past greatness, Xi hoped that it could inspire the nation and relegitimize the Party's rule. Beijing was following a contemporaneous "make my country great again" trend beginning to sweep the globe from the United States to the UK, and from Turkey to Russia, India, Japan, and elsewhere.[143]

Core Social Values

At another level, one provision of the Eighteenth Party Congress report was the promotion of "core socialist values," a set of twelve moral principles represented in Chinese by twelve four-character principles that include prosperity, democracy, civility, harmony, freedom, equality, justice, rule of law, patriotism, dedication, integrity, and friendliness.[144] In early 2014, Xi belatedly launched a national campaign to promote these values, aiming to turn them into a pervasive moral and ideological foundation to guide morality. These values are said to have derived from traditional Chinese culture to rebuild faith amid concerns that China had "lost its moral compass during its three-decade economic miracle." Xi was quoted: "Core socialist values are the soul of cultural soft power. Basically, the soft power of a nation depends on the vitality, cohesive force and charisma of its core values."[145] As the campaign unfolded, the twelve four-character "core socialist values" have become ubiquitous in the mass media, being memorized by schoolchildren and splashed across walls throughout China. They have been incorporated into such varied things as textbooks, college examinations, stamps, lanterns, songs, and square dance routines.[146]

When addressing the UN General Assembly in September 2015, Xi announced that "peace, development, equity, justice, democracy and freedom are common values of mankind and the lofty goal of the United Nations." Then, in 2017, the State Administration of Press, Publication, Radio, Film, and

Television issued a notice demanding that all television, radio, and internet distributors deliver programs that promote "core socialist values" and eradicate content that celebrates "money worship, hedonism, radical individualism, and feudal thought."[147] Also beginning in 2017, all Chinese moviegoers were obliged to watch propaganda videos on "core socialist values" that featured well-known actors such as Jackie Chan.[148]

Worldwide, even countries with strong soft power feel the need to preserve their own culture and values in an age of globalization and rapid technological change. Canada, for example, has argued that strong cultural values and expressions are vital for maintaining its "sovereignty and sense of identity." To protect the challenges of foreign cultural products, the Canadian government has put in place a raft of policies to ensure a space for itself.[149] In China, previous Chinese general secretaries had propounded ideological campaigns—Jiang Zemin's "three stresses" and Hu Jintao's "eight honors and eight shames" were also designed to combat alleged materialism and normlessness among the population. Consequently, the ideas contained in Xi's "core socialist values" are rehashes of those of his predecessors, with a new rearrangement. The intended functions of the formula were twofold. Domestically, they supplement the notions of the China Dream and rejuvenation to assert Chinese identity and cultural autonomy, bolster confidence, and encourage proper behavior. By appropriating common values as China's own, Beijing hoped to dampen the appeal of the West's narrative of universal values, which may even be weaponized for regime change.[150] Externally, Beijing realized that its severe soft-power deficits were difficult to overcome, and hoped that the "core socialist values" might help project a more benign international image, boosting its global standing and respect. Despite the yearly expenses of billions for such soft power projects as the Confucius Institutes, opinions on Beijing have been predominantly negative in the United States, Europe, and Asia, although opinions are more positive in most of Africa and Latin America. For many foreigners, Beijing relies less on soft power than "sharp power," a manipulative and subversive means that counts on economic coercion such as import/export restrictions and boycotts—to influence foreign governments and societies.[151] In this regard, China is not an exception. From a realpolitik perspective, economic coercion is an age-old means of statecraft employed by all great powers,[152] although Beijing's application of it has often been clumsy.

Overall, the extent to which the Chinese have accepted or internalized the new Xi ideology and values in the public consciousness is difficult to measure. However, one study of Chinese political culture argues that there is a general acceptance of regime ideology. Group solidarity, political trust, regime support, and local participation are generally high.[153] Another study, also based on survey data, argues that most Chinese view democracy in terms of whether the state can provide for the well-being of the people, and in this regard, they believe that China is already somewhat democratic, are satisfied with the current level of democracy, and are optimistic about even higher levels of democracy in the near future.[154] Official ideology and values are often transmitted through a number of channels throughout the party state, such as official newspapers and journals, training at party and cadre schools, and curriculum at universities and schools. Ideological socialization tends to be strict within the Party and lax with the general public, although it is always present in media entertainment and cultural and sporting events.[155] The ideological goals often connote policy implications— the China Dream notion specifies numerical development goals, whereas the "core socialist values" buttressed the "rule of law" campaign (discussed later) and legislation such as the Elderly Rights Law, which requires grown children to attend to the physical and "spiritual needs" of their parents.[156]

Yet ideological campaigns are often parodied and derided by the public, especially on the internet. Conversely, the highlighting of democracy and freedom as "core socialist values" may have heightened the expectations of some, especially the dissidents. In any event, Chinese from across the political spectrum, from conservatives to liberals to the new left, as well as dissidents, will continue to debate the meaning and applicability of the notion.[157]

Tightened Control of Ideology, Dissent, and Expression

Xi's China Dream and "core socialist values" encourage positive standards, but a flip side is his tightened control of ideology, dissent, and the freedom of expression. Ever a disciplinarian obsessed with national security, Xi attempted to force discipline on the party-state apparatus with severe sanctions. Similarly, he imposed tight control on the society, turning this into another repressive aspect of his rule. Xi is wary about the spread of Western ideas and soft power inside China, and especially alarmed by the turbulence generated by the social media-driven revolts during the Arab Spring. Further, he believes that the grand reform enterprise and the benefits of the China Dream can be achieved only through discipline and order led by the Party. Vehement in their rebuke of the party state, Xi and his team nevertheless forbid opposition inspired by Western perspectives, insisting that solutions must be found within the confines of "socialism with Chinese characteristics."

Ideology control, censorship, and the suppression of dissent have always been present under CCP rule, but under Xi, these restrictions have intensified under technologies of instantaneous communications. Party members, intellectuals, entrepreneurs, lawyers, activists, and dissidents were enjoined to toe the political line. Xi asserted Beijing's centralized control, demanded obedience, and forbade anyone "to gainsay the center." In an unprecedented and high-profile move, Xi in 2016 visited three major party-state news organizations, the *People's Daily*,

Xinhua News, and CCTV, on live television. He ordered them to toe the center's line, asserting that their propaganda must be "surnamed" Party, meaning that no divergence from the center was allowed. He explicitly prohibited party members from "improperly criticizing or second-guessing" Beijing's policies.[158]

Early in his tenure, the Xi administration in April 2013 moved to tighten control of ideology by issuing the internal Document No. 9. This document railed against seven ideological taboos, or "political perils": constitutional democracy, universal values, civil society, neoliberalism, Western views of media, historical nihilism, and the questioning of reform and opening.[159] It accused detractors, abetted by hostile Western forces, of exploiting these notions to undermine the Party's leadership. Allegedly, the critics had attempted to use the Western value system to supplant the core values of socialism, the notion of civil society to squeeze out party leadership from local administrations, and the "abstract" principle of freedom of the press to deny the Party's oversight of the media. The matter was complicated by a different version issued one month later to colleges and universities prohibiting them from discussing the seven taboo subjects or "seven unmentionables" (*qibuzhun*) of universal values, freedom of the press, civil society, civil rights, mistakes in party history, the bureaucratic capitalist class, and judicial independence in their teaching and research.[160] Simultaneously, both versions accused critics of resorting to "historical nihilism" and reassessment of history to disparage party leaders and to delegitimize party rule. The gist of the documents shows that the Party was battling on two fronts. On the one hand, the Party reviled liberals or neoliberals who alleged that state intervention and SOE monopolies had strangled efficiency and vitality, and who advocated "market omnipotence," "comprehensive privatization," and political reform. On the other hand, it chided critics from the left who charged that the Party's reforms had gone too far, creating "state capitalism" and a "new bureaucratic capitalist class." My Chinese colleagues have confirmed the gist of the "seven taboos," adding that it created a chilly social climate in academic circles.[161] Officials have neither confirmed nor denied the veracity of the document, and outside observers are uncertain whether the views expressed represented the views of just one faction or the entire Chinese leadership.[162]

In reality, for those who are familiar with Chinese ideological debate, the list of disapproved ideas contains nothing new, since they have been regularly condemned since 1989. And according to the notion of "being internally strict and outwardly relaxed," the documents were directed toward party members rather than the general public or foreign audiences. Exposure of the documents provoked negative responses in the Chinese social media as well as an outpouring of leftist writings supporting them. Finally, in May the Party Central Office ordered the removal of all materials on the internet related to these documents in addition to any "hate speech" attacking it.[163]

In any case, the re-emphasis on the ban of broad subjects was deemed absurd and unimplementable. As one blogger pointed out, one can always circumvent such restrictions by discussing the sins of dictatorship and not universal values, the Taiping Rebellion and not civil society, the Red Second Generation and not bureaucratic capitalism, the predicament of the marginalized masses and not civil rights, and so on.[164] Government officials, journalists, and academics who were party members still felt constrained by the withdrawn documents. Yet serious research on the seven subjects continued.[165] A quick scanning of the China Academic Journals Full-Text Database showed hundreds of articles on the supposedly taboo subjects, although the discussions are generally couched in balanced historical or philosophical terms.

Still, control and censorship took different forms. In 2015, education minister Yuan Guiren told universities to clamp down on the use of foreign textbooks that propound "Western values." Universities were urged to refrain from remarks that "defame the rule of the Communist Party, smear socialism or violate the constitution and laws."[166] In December 2016, Xi at a high-level meeting on tertiary education again called on professors and students to be loyal to the Party and "firmly uphold the correct political direction." Higher education must serve the rule of the Party and "socialism with Chinese characteristics," Xi urged. Universities and colleges, most of them having an institute for Marxism, were enjoined to make political education more interesting and appealing, despite the ineffectiveness of the promotion of Marxist studies.[167] In addition, a social credit system, introduced in 2017, was expected to be implemented in 2020 (discussed later). Overall, the tightening of ideological control over society has stifled dissent, freedom of expression, and academic freedom, which can potentially squelch creativity and initiative.

In addition, beginning in July 2015, an unprecedented campaign to crack down on legal activism netted more than three hundred lawyers and activists from twenty-five provinces who had argued for more freedom of speech and religion, drawing attention to the government's abuse of power. The crackdown, collectively known as "709," was a reference to the date it began, July 9, 2015. Several of those detained were linked to the Beijing law firm Fengrui, which handled human rights and land seizure cases as well as high-profile cases such as the tainted milk scandal in 2008. Most were charged with "harming national security and social stability" for posting online comments and organizing social protests that had allegedly disrupted public order. Eventually, most were released, but others were put in detention. In 2016, several activists were finally summarily tried and given varied sentences. For instance, Fengrui lawyer Wang Yu was released on bail after she, in a video, renounced her legal work, denounced the head of Fengrui Zhou Shifeng as an unqualified lawyer, and stated that "foreign forces" were manipulating Fengrui to undermine the government. Zhai Yanmin, another Fengrui lawyer, was found guilty and given a three-year suspended sentence, which meant that he would be under surveillance and unable to continue his political activities. Lawyer activists Hu Shigen and Zhou Shifeng, both found guilty of subversion, were slapped with jail sentences of seven years each.[168] Such persecution and harassment of lawyers politicized dissent as the "subversion of state power" and contradicted the letter and spirit of the Fourth Plenum. For the Party, legal activism is a red line that cannot be crossed, and the "709" crackdown was used as a deterrent to intimidate those who dared to test the authority of the party state.[169] Predictably, the crackdown was greeted by an international outcry, and the harassment of the legal profession at such a large scale has not been repeated.

On the other hand, public and televised confessions by alleged offenders renouncing their alleged crimes or wrongdoing have become commonplace. Activists, foreign and domestic journalists, and celebrities who had a brush with the law regularly confessed, apparently out of duress or even torture. For instance, celebrities such as the son of movie star Jackie Chan apologized for drug abuse, a Weibo luminary for visiting prostitutes, and others for gambling. An executive of pharmaceutical company GlaxoSmithKline apologized for bribery, and journalist Gao Yu apologized for leaking "Document No. 9." Others apologized for more mundane issues such as posing with the Taiwanese flag. Those formally charged were often freed after such public mea culpas. The Party counted on these public confessions to shame and deter what it considered undesirable behavior, but they had become so routine and contrived that they were often ridiculed. For example, Lin Zuluan, the democratically elected village head at Wukan, was charged with taking bribes. His televised confession was viewed more than seventy-one million times, and many viewers doubted he could receive a fair trial after such a spectacle. On one occasion, thousands of Taiwanese and mainlanders as well mocked the confessions by launching a satirical Facebook event a mock competition to "apologize" to China.[170] These confessions drew international criticism, and clearly contradicted the letter and intent of many aspects of judicial reform.[171] In late 2016, the Supreme Court and the Supreme People's Procuratorate felt obliged to reiterate that the use of violence to obtain evidence must cease, that interviews with suspects must be recorded, and that evidence extracted under torture would be ruled inadmissible.[172] This did not buck the trend of coerced apologies.

Freedom House, a US government-funded human rights NGO, ranked China at the bottom of sixty-five nations in its index of internet freedom.[173] Similarly, Reporters without Borders consistently ranks China 176th out of a total of 180 countries in terms of press freedom, with Vietnam and North Korea ranking 175th and 180th, respectively.[174] To tighten censorship and control, Beijing introduced a slew of laws purportedly for safeguarding "national security" and countering Western infiltration. Several of these laws came into effect in 2017, but they sowed confusion and fear because of their ambiguity. A stringent new law to tighten control over the internet introduced in 2013 prescribed sentences of between three and seven years for libelous posts, spreading rumors, or posting messages leading to mass protests. The Party has always been suspicious of Western NGOs' alleged roles in the "color revolutions," fearing that they could undermine the legitimacy and stability of the one-party state. Beijing was even more wary that foreign agencies or technology companies could help their governments spy on China. It felt vindicated by the public exposure of the Edward Snowden case in 2013; the case revealed the PRISM program operated by the US National Security Agency spied on its citizens and foreign leaders by mining telephone and metadata.[175] A Cyber Security Law that came into effect in June 2017 purportedly to prevent cyberattacks and terrorism required companies to store data within China and empowered officials to carry out security checks of companies in the finance and communication sector. The country's eight hundred million internet users were ordered to register with their real names on social media platforms. As it transpired, the law was so ambiguous that foreign companies were confused, fearing that the latitude enjoyed by the Party would be used against them.[176] Also coming into effect in 2017 was a Film Industry Promotion Law that prohibited films that "endangered" national security, incited ethnic hatred, fostered superstition, and violated religious policies. Since this is China's first firm industry law, movie producers and directors, long subject to the vague censorship rules and caprice of officials, originally were hoping that the law would clarify the gray area of film censorship. As it turned out, the law requires films to eschew "vulgarity" and spread "core socialist values," and for filmmakers to have "moral and artistic integrity." Foreign filmmakers alleged to have "damaged China's national dignity, honor and interests, harmed social stability or hurt national feelings" would be banned. Films sympathetic to the Dalai Lama, such as *Seven Years in Tibet*, featuring Brad Pitt, have long angered censors, and actors who have had a brush with the law for using drugs or soliciting prostitutes have been ostracized. Apart from these legal cases, authorities had censured actors and filmmakers who had supported Hong Kong's Occupy Movement or Taiwan's prodemocracy student movement. The strictures contained in the law were so ambiguously defined that they simply enabled officials to continue their arbitrary ways.[177]

Additionally, a Foreign NGO Management Law that took effect in 2017 required all foreign NGOs (foundations, think tanks, advocacy and charity organizations; estimated number ranges from one thousand to six thousand) to register with the Ministry of Public Security or their local bureau instead of the Ministries of Civil Affairs and Commerce. This change in oversight of foreign NGOs affected such organizations as the International Red Cross, American Bar

Association, World Wildlife Fund, World Economic Forum, Oxfam, and others. The law grants broad powers to the police to question foreign NGO workers, inspect NGO offices, and examine their documents. To register, these NGOs were required to be sponsored by a "professional supervisory unit" or Chinese government organ willing to vouch for them. Some of these NGOs did provide grants for their Chinese counterparts, but increasingly there have been fewer takers. The small exceptions have been NGOs whose expertise and funding coincide with Beijing's priority issues such as rural education, poverty alleviation, or water conservation. Business associations and chambers of commerce fare a little better, but those involved in legal advocacy, political education, labor, and LGBTQ rights found it impossible to find sponsors and to register. Three years after the promulgation of the new law the number of foreign NGOs had been reduced to 420, with another 724 engaging in temporary projects.[178] A few had moved to places such as Hong Kong. Again, the vague wording and the haphazard way by which the law was implemented put the status of other foreign NGOs in limbo. For instance, they were forbidden to engage in "political activities," but a conservative interpretation of this could mean anything. One immediate effect was the closing down of many Chinese NGOs because of the loss of foreign partners or fear of the consequences of cooperation. Little future change in the situation is expected since it is obvious that the law has been issued from the highest level to counter alleged Western influence and threat. The estimated number of China's domestic NGOs ranges from half a million to three million, but the restriction on their foreign counterparts has dealt a blow to civil society in China and its multitrack relationship with the outside world.[179]

During Xi's first term, the internet increased in importance for disseminating information, at the expense of traditional print and television media, which contended with declining ratings and rampancy of rumors and faked stories. New regulations issued in 2017 by the Cyberspace Administration of China required all online service and content providers, including all apps, forums, bloggers, microbloggers, and instant messaging providers, to obtain government licenses. This effectively curbed unofficial reporting of current affairs when the external Great Firewall had already blocked quasi-monopolistic foreign media sites such as Google, Twitter, Facebook, and YouTube.[180] After Xi's tour to several top state media in February 2016 to urge them to toe the party line, a defiant article on free speech published by the respected Caixin website was censored by the Cyberspace Administration of China.[181] In 2016, the *Yanhuang Chunqiu*, a liberal reformist magazine supported by party elders, ceased to function after a hostile takeover by the authorities.[182]

One pushback occurred in March 2016, when a letter on the web signed by "Loyal Communist Party Members" called for Xi's resignation from all party and government posts, citing Xi's various political, social, and economic policies and accusing Xi of centralizing power and fostering a cult of personality. The letter charged that Xi had weakened the power of the state organs and of Premier Li Keqiang, abandoned Deng Xiaoping's low-profile foreign policy to "hide capabilities and bid for time" (more later), mismanaged the economy, resulting in massive layoffs and near economic collapse, and channeled massive foreign exchange reserves to "chaotic" countries with no hope of gain. The anticorruption campaign, the letter alleged, was a mere power struggle that made officials afraid to work.[183] Consequently, twenty persons associated with the letter were detained. Liberal and leftist websites alike were shut down (although later some reopened). These included left-wing websites such as The East Is Red, Utopia, and Mao Flag that had been shuttered since April 2012, right after the Bo Xilai affair.[184]

While this was happening, at a forum in April 2016 on cybersecurity with media, academics, and private companies, Xi urged officials to be patient with and tolerant of "well-intentioned" criticism of the authorities online, but ironically, reactions to his comments were deleted.[185] Yet even after this incident, the government did not refrain from attacking writers and journalists. In June 2016, the CCDI criticized the Propaganda Department for failing to control the media and the internet, or to control ideological teachings at universities. Tian Jin, the deputy director of the State Administration of Press, Publication, Radio, Film, and Television, contributed a piece to the People's Daily stating, "Programs that are hyping trending social hot topics, ridiculing state policies, disseminating wrongful views, advocating extreme views, and sparking conflicts will be severely punished."[186]

The accumulating effects of televised confessions, abductions, surveillance of civil society organs, harassment of human rights lawyers, and the reining in of the media had, by 2017, created a chilly climate and even outright fear. This has generated backlash even by officials working at state-owned publications such as Global Times.[187] But harsh crackdowns combined with contradictory messages continued at the Nineteenth Party Congress in 2017. For instance, crackdowns on foreign media barred the BBC, Financial Times, The Economist, New York Times, and The Guardian from the official ceremony to introduce new leaders at the party congress.

The draconian measures to control ideology and to harass dissidents, disturbing and grotesque as they are, have not established totalitarian uniformity. In evaluating the issue of censorship in China, one large-scale study of the pre-Xi era argues that in general, the leadership allowed the media a full range of negative and positive comments on the government, officials, and policies, but harshly suppressed those criticisms that may foment antiregime collective actions and social mobilization.[188] A more recent study presents a more plausible argument by making a distinction between "solicited" and "unsolicited" critiques of the government. In this view, each year the Chinese state actively encourages public criticism and debate when drafting the hundreds of laws and regulations to gauge public opinion and to satisfy the public. Government policies and legislations formulated with wider consultation are less likely to be repealed and amended. On the other hand, "unsolicited" criticisms of the government and official ideology are more likely to be censored. The practice under Xi is still consistent with the notion of "consultative authoritarianism."[189] No doubt the party state has selectively conditioned public discourse, but not all the boundaries of what is permissible are clearly defined and unchanging. As is often the case in China, dissidents, lawyers, and intellectuals continue to test and push the boundaries of what is permissible. And the dichotomous "control versus resistance" model misses other facets of official-media relations, which feature complex negotiation and mutual adaptations. Critical and investigative journalism has not perished from China.[190] Indeed, many nonconformists still count on a pendulum swing toward a more liberalization phase in the cycles of Chinese politics oscillating between control and relaxation.

Disciplining the Party State

As to the party-state elite, immediately after becoming general secretary, Xi launched two colossal campaigns to tighten Beijing's grip. The first was an anticorruption campaign, and the second was a fifteen-month campaign to rectify the Party through "mass line education." Although these campaigns overlapped with one another, they were organizationally distinct and therefore will be considered separately. Citing the ancients' maxims that "to govern a country one must first fix officialdom," and "benevolent governances [must be] supplemented by punishment," the Leninist Xi relies on the CCP as a leadership core to spearhead development and change.[191] He is also acutely aware of the range of weakness of any vanguard—common bureaucratic pathologies such as evasion, red tape, cronyism, incompetence, abuse of power, and above all, corruption. His long experience managing party organizations and his brush with corruption in Fujian must have left an impression. In his view, collusions between power and money, between power and sex, and the buying and selling of offices had become brazen and shameless, and he said he was "especially distressed" by official extravagance, ostentatious consumption, and competition to show off wealth and influence when there were still so many poor in China. His speeches were replete with indignation over official malfeasance, and he had become progressively outraged with every new revelation of debauchery and revelry. His mission as assigned by the Party was to put the house in order, to revive the CCP leadership, shake it up, and force discipline on it.

Xi and his team also understood that corruption in China had also become globalized—corrupted officials were now intertwined with organized foreign corruption networks, money launderers, and tax havens to stash their ill-gotten gains overseas with their families,[192] and some multinational companies had become party to corrupt practices in China.[193] For instance, the Chinese Academy of Social Sciences estimated that between 1990 and 2011, eighteen thousand corrupt officials fled the country, taking US$129 billion with them.[194] The Panama Papers revealed in 2016 that Hong Kong and China accounted for nearly one-quarter of the 366,000 shell companies in its database.[195]

Corruption, defined simply as the abuse of public power for personal gain, is a complex matter taking many forms in China. Yan Sun's typology distinguishes between embezzlement, bribe-taking, misappropriation, squandering, privilege seeking, illegal earnings, negligence, illegal profiteering, violation of account procedures, smuggling, and moral decadence.[196] Issues such as negligence and moral decadence may not be considered corruption outside of the Chinese context but are considered important in China. Another scholar, Zengke He, distinguishes three types of corruption—white, gray, and black—although the boundaries between them overlap, and the definitions of legality differ from one context to the other. "White" corruption refers to the common social practices of nepotism and favoritism in hiring practices by exploiting guanxi or personal connections. "Gray" corruption refers to the legal, semilegal, or illegal practices by which leaders of party-state organs raise revenue or profit, sometimes for the purposes of improving the welfare of the staff. Other manifestations include extravagance, waste, and luxurious perks for officials. "Black" corruption refers to obviously illegal practices ranging from graft to bribery and from tax evasion and embezzlement to extortion.[197] Political scientists have long argued, counterintuitively, that under certain circumstances, corruption may be beneficial to development. For instance, corruption allows the private sector in a state-dominant system to break the state monopoly in recruitment and promotion, and to exert influence on policymaking by opening up alternative channels of participation.[198] In China, the ambiguity about the boundaries of various forms of corruption has complicated the perception and the extent of corruption. Several major institutional factors that contribute to corruption in China can be identified, although their nature and characteristics have evolved over time. These include party-state domination of the economy; the transition of the centrally planned economy to a partial market economy (which spawned entrepreneurial self-enrichment and corruption); weakness in regulatory policies and institutional inexperience; and the lack of effective and independent checks. Further, rapid economic growth exacerbated corruption since more wealth could now be siphoned off, and an obsession with wealth accumulation, as epitomized by Deng's slogan

"To get rich is glorious," removed moral qualms about making money. Factor in cultural preferences for gift exchange and reliance on personnel connections to get things done, and the result is rampant corruption resulting in everyday abuses that have triggered public outrage.[199]

Mao fought corruption with many campaigns, and among these, the Four Cleans campaign (1963–1966) eventually morphed into the Cultural Revolution. Post-Mao leaders from Deng to Xi have acknowledged and grappled with the issue of corruption as an existential challenge to the regime. During the reform period, several anticorruption campaigns were launched, but there was no agreement as to how and to what extent antigraft efforts should be pushed. Like his predecessors, Xi and his team have repeatedly warned that many ruling parties in the world have lost power because of corruption, and that "winning or losing public support is an issue that concerns the CPC's survival or extinction." The CCP is clearly not the exemplary elite Xi wishes it to be, and Xi has been scathing in his numerous castigations of corruption in China. Corruption is said to have undermined development and retarded the growth of the economy. According to Xi, graft was most rampant in sectors like "mining, resources . . . land and real estate development, infrastructural projects, welfare funds, and research and scientific management." Leaders often encouraged their offspring and relatives to run businesses by exploiting their connections. He was particularly incensed that officials even dared to loot funds designated for poverty relief, rural development, medical insurance, and welfare. They then turned these funds into bribes to purchase official positions, even though these transgressions fetched severe penalties. In developed areas, misappropriations tended to concentrate on construction projects, whereas in poor areas they tended to involve funds allocated for poverty relief. Either way, these phenomena were "hair-raising."[200]

The Anticorruption Campaign (2012–present)

By 2012, the Party had arrived at a consensus that it needed a harsher crackdown on graft, and Xi was given the mandate to mastermind an anticorruption campaign (ACC) of unprecedented scope and velocity designed to reclaim the Party's moral authority. The report to the Eighteenth Party Congress broached the notion of enhancing the "purity" of the Party. It said that party members must purify themselves with the strictest of discipline, since "it takes good iron to make good products." At the first Politburo study session three days after becoming general secretary, Xi drove home his view that the decay within the Party was the source of all problems when he bemoaned: "Matter must be decaying before worms can breed."[201]

Twenty days after Xi assumed the top position, the Politburo approved an "eight-point regulation" that pledged to shake up the Party's work style and to solicit public inputs. The regulation promised to scrap motorcades and traffic controls for leadership trips and welcoming and seeing off ceremonies; it forbade junkets, such as official banquets and commemorative meetings, and luxurious cars and housing for officials. It ordered the reduction of official conferences and official documents. Politburo members were enjoined to take the lead and set an example.[202] On December 6, the sacking of the deputy secretary of the Sichuan PPC was a curtain raiser, but the eight-point regulation itself received scant attention as officials went about their usual ways.[203] In a January 2013 CCDI meeting to mobilize for the ACC, Xi pledged a harsh crackdown to net both "tigers and flies," that is, corrupt officials at both the higher and grassroots levels. Beijing would enforce the ACC directly from Beijing by dispatching inspection teams with full power analogous to the "imperial commissioners" to "shock and awe" (*zhenshe*). It would ratchet up pressure level by level to disarm and to deter, imposing neither limits on nor quotas for the extent of prosecution. Although formally directed only at party members, this campaign would also cover nonparty state officials at every administrative level and the SOEs. Wang Qishan, a respected economic and financial official and a Xi confidant, was chosen to head the CCDI.[204] Without any experience in political security Wang appeared to be an odd choice, but soon it became clear that his long experience in various economic and trade portfolios was an asset in uncovering corruption.[205] Additionally, Wang was a fixer often called upon at short notice to deal with crises. Among Wang's successes were the restructuring of collapsing financial juggernaut Guangdong Enterprises and Guangdong International Trust and Investment Corporation at the height of the Asian Financial Crisis of 1997; the real estate bubble at Hainan in 1995; and the SARS crisis in 2003. As Beijing mayor, Wang was the chair of the Beijing organizing committee for the 2008 Olympics assisting Xi. Under premier Zhu Rongji, Wang managed China's largest bankruptcy restructuring, averting a banking crisis that could have crippled economic growth. In 2009, Wang served as Hu Jintao's special representative at the US-China Strategic and Economic Dialogue.[206] Henry Paulson, who had worked extensively with Wang, described Wang as bold, capable, and charismatic, with a deep understanding of the United States and global markets. Lee Kuan Yew described Wang as an "exceptional talent, very assured and efficient."[207]

Under Wang, the CCDI expanded its original eight offices into ten to comb through the ranks for corrupt officials and patronage networks. Number 1 focused on SOEs, Number 2 on finance organizations, Number 3 on education, science, culture, and health, and Number 4 on all central organizations. The remaining offices managed the provinces geographically: Number 5, southwest; Number 6, north; Number 7, east; Number 8, central south, Number 9, northwest; and Number 10, northeast.[208] The CCDI was given great power to fire and hire and to command local CDIs, thereby freeing it from the grip of local authorities.[209] The CCDI was also empowered to set up bases to inspect all 140-plus central party and state departments, such as the COD, the United Front Work Department, the National People's Congress, and the CPPCC.[210] The public was invited to report the violations of the "eight regulations" through letters, visits, and various "snitch" platforms on the internet. These channels appeared to be popular among the public, although complainants generally had to give their real names, identity card numbers, and addresses.[211]

Overall, the colossal anticorruption campaign was not the show of Xi and the CCDI alone since many other party/state organs participated. For instance, Premier Li Keqiang did his part in coordinating the ACC in denouncing "mediocre, lazy, and lethargic governance." At various State Council conferences on "clean government" in 2015 and 2016, Li warned his audience to better manage public funds and to prevent the stripping of state assets. He urged serious punishments for those who had embezzled "life-saving" funds for poverty reduction, welfare, healthcare, and slum redevelopment. Consistently, he asserted that the key solution for corruption lied with the simplification of administration and the devolution of power. One major task for 2016, he urged, was to draw up comprehensive lists on such subjects as market entry (the related significance of this with marketization will be discussed later) that would clearly delimit the power and responsibilities of local governments. Clearer regulations, he argued, could replace the "hidden rules" of rent-seeking. He also urged the strengthening of incentives by rewarding the good performance of officials, and by "promoting the competent, demoting the mediocre, and eliminating the rotten." According to him, in 2015 alone, the government had abolished 311 regulations and reduced the number of government-fixed prices by 80 percent.[212] In 2017, Li vowed to crack down on corruption by financial institutions involving granting credit, insider trading, insurance fraud, and collusion with big private players. Shortly afterward, the chair of China's Insurance Regulatory Commission was investigated and then charged in April 2018 for bribery.[213] Government officials began to explore the possibilities that free trade treaties, simplified investment procedures, and lower tax rates might be one potential means for reducing corruption.[214]

By June 2013, the CCDI had sent out ten roving inspection teams led by retired ministerial-level officials to the provinces, SOEs, and other units such as the China Grain Reserve Corporation, Ministry of Water Conservancy, China Publishing Group, Export-Import Banks of China, and even Renmin University. The teams gathered evidence on cadre high living and the buying and selling of offices by interviewing hundreds of officials and by setting up public hotlines and email addresses for public tip-offs.[215] The number of roving inspection teams multiplied rapidly, from twenty in 2012, thirty-nine in 2014, eighty-two in 2015, to more than one hundred in 2016. Criminal cases were referred to the country's procurator system. Official numbers show that the number of officials convicted rose year after year, reaching a high of 336,000 in 2015. In addition, in 2015, the CCDI issued a list of one hundred "most wanted" suspects for crimes such as embezzling of public funds, money laundering, bribe-taking, and drug trafficking who had fled overseas to countries such as the United States, Canada, New Zealand, and Australia. Yet, according to Minxin Pei, Beijing deliberately omitted high-ranking officials from the list since that might reveal the "dirt" of the Chinese system to Western intelligence.[216] By 2016, 2,020 economic fugitives, nicknamed "foxes," including 342 officials, were said to have been extradited from seventy countries overseas, and US$1.14 billion of assets were retrieved.[217]

The roving inspection teams and the investigations of Bo Xilai had brought to light more explosive corruption cases at the apex of the leadership. Between 2014 and 2016, retired Seventeenth PBSC member Zhou Yongkang; both military representatives in the Seventeenth Politburo, Guo Boxiong and Xu Caihou; and Ling Jihua, director of the CCP's Central Office, were investigated and met with ignominious downfalls. (See Table 8.1.) Zhou and Guo were also members of the Sixteenth Politburo, and Guo and Xu were the PLA's two most senior military officers after Hu Jintao.

All four were charged with the abuse of power, nepotism, huge bribe-taking, and the indulgence of their family members in corrupt activities to accumulate enormous fortunes. Additionally, Zhou was charged with leaking (unspecified) state secrets and Ling for stealing them. Both were alleged to have traded money for sex. After the four were expelled from the Party, their cases were moved to the judiciary and military courts for trials, and all four were penalized with life imprisonment.

As early as 2014, diaspora media sources began to speculate that Zhou, Bo Xilai, Xu Caihou, and Ling Jihua had constituted a "gang of four" that had plotted to derail Xi's succession, launch Bo Xilai into the PBSC, and make Ling Jihua general secretary.[218] Another bombshell was the conviction of Sun Zhengcai, a sitting member of the Eighteenth Politburo and secretary of the Chongqing PPC, for corruption and serious misdemeanors in 2017–2018. Since these issues related to succession, they will be discussed in chapter 12.

Zhou was a former security chief who had amassed enormous power in the political-legal apparatus under the cover of *weiwen*. Official media alleged that his corruption syndicate included at least thirty-five former associates such as *mishu*, officials from Sichuan, and the petroleum and public security bureaucracies. Further, an SPC report accused Zhou and Bo Xilai of colluding in conspiratorial activities outside of the party organization. The use of such terms as the "*mishu* gang," "petroleum gang," and "Sichuan gang" added fuel to speculations of factional struggle for power. Subsequently, in 2015, an intermediate court in Tianjin found Zhou guilty of most charges and handed down a life sentence.[219] The Zhou case developed further, as we shall see in chapter 12.

On the other hand, Ling Jihua (b. 1956) was a former *zhiqing* and a high-flying "fifth generation" leader. He became Hu Jintao's personal secretary as well as director of the CCP's General Office, which is an extremely important post looking after such matters as central documents, research, the agendas and logistics of central meetings, and the personal needs of the leadership. This strategic position has enabled all its occupants to join the Politburo and even the PBSC during the reform period. Ling rose through the ranks of the CYL and was already head of the Secretariat from 2007 to 2012 and a hopeful for the Eighteenth Politburo or PBSC (Table 9.8). Moreover, he was often regarded as Hu Jintao's closest client and a central figure of the *tuanpai*. However, in 2012, Ling's twenty-four-year-old son and two women were killed when his Ferrari crashed. Ling was subsequently demoted to do united-front work, and his brothers were convicted for corruption.[220] Ling was accused of collaborating with Zhou Yongkang to cover up the news of his son's death and for being complicit in the corruption syndicate in Shanxi Province, where Ling had his power base. The journal *Caixin*, an authoritative source, has intimated that Ling harbored a "certain alliance relation" with the disgraced Zhou Yongkang and Bo Xilai,[221] and a *China Daily* article linked Ling to Zhou Yongkang, Xu Caihou, Bo Xilai, and a "huge corruption network."[222] This charge was denounced as a political/factional maneuver to defame Ling but immediately fueled speculations about a new Gang of Four,[223] although the connections between the four are murky.

Guo Boxiong and Xu Caihou were both vice chairman of the CMC, whereas Guo had served two terms. Both were accused of racking up massive bribes by selling offices in the military. Guo's son Guo Zhenggang was said to have bragged that "more than half" of the officials in the PLA were promoted by his family.[224] Xu Caihou was expelled from the Party, but he died of bladder cancer in March 2015 before a court-martial was held. Henceforth, those generals promoted by Xu and Guo were suspect, and subsequently at least thirty-seven lieutenant generals and major generals, including Guo Zhenggang, a former deputy commissar of the Zhejiang Military Region, were dismissed.[225]

Other fallen "tigers" of corruption included Liu Tienan, deputy director of the NDRC; Su Rong, CPPCC vice chairman; Yang Weize, former party chief for Nanjing; Zhang Kunsheng, former assistant foreign minister; Wang Qingliang, former party secretary of Guangzhou; China Petroleum chief executive Jiang Jiemin; and Song Lin, CEO of the Huayuan Corp.

In the Central Committee and all thirty-two provincial administrations senior officials were purged. By 2015, the numbers were Guangdong (90), Hubei (61), Sichuan (54), Henan (52), Shanxi (50), Fujian (40), Guizhou (38), Hunan (36), Liaoning and Shandong (34), Heilongjiang, Jiangxi, Xinjiang, and Anhui (32), Hainan (30),Yunnan and Hebei (29), Shaanxi (27), Guangxi (23), Jiangsu (20), Jilin (19), Ningxia (17), Chongqing (16), Zhejiang (15), Tianjian, Gansu, and

Table 9.8 The Political Career of Ling Jihua

Year and place of birth; year joined CCP	Family background	Education	Career experience				
1956, Pinglu, Shanxi (1976)	Sent-down youth and worker, 1973–75	MBA, Hunan University, 1994–96; student, political education, China Youth Political College, 1983–85	Deputy director, publicity, CYL CC, 1985–88; staff, Publicity Department, CYL CC, 1979–83; staff, Yucheng Pref PC, Shanxi, 1978–79; cadre, CYL Pinglu County Committee, 1975–78	Director general, publicity, CYL CC, 1994–95; director, deputy general director, General Office, CYL CC, editor-in-chief, Youth League Journal, 1988–94	Deputy director, Party Central Office, deputy director, General Office of the Committee for the Reform of Central Departments, 2003–7; staff and deputy director, Research Office, Party Central Office, 1995–2003	Vice chairman, CPPCC, 2013–15; head, United Front Work Department, 2012–14; director, General Office, 2007–12	Member, Eighteenth CC, 2012–17, expelled from party for corruption

Source: China vitae and Baidu baike.

Inner Mongolia (14), Shanghai (8), Beijing (8), Tibet (7), and Qinghai (6).[226] By 2017, sixty-seven more officials at the provincial-ministerial level were snared, and nine of them who had accepted bribes over ¥1 billion (US$14.7 million) were given death sentences, suspended death sentences, or life imprisonment.[227]

A major political earthquake occurred in Shanxi, a leading coal-producing province, when the CCDI investigators uncovered intricate syndicates of graft and racketeering permeating virtually all administrative levels. Between 2013 and 2014, about 129 senior Shanxi officials were sacked or reassigned, including the provincial party secretary, Yuan Chunqing. More than thirty thousand other officials, about half of them were village cadres, were punished. Subsequently, the Shanxi leadership was reorganized, leaving three hundred official vacancies in various provincial departments. Those who had turned themselves in and who returned the spoils were dealt with more leniently.[228]

Within the PLA, various disciplinary inspection organs had received petitions and complaints for forty thousand cases, registered four thousand cases, and punished thirteen thousand individuals, including more than one hundred army commander-level officials. These officials were accused of a range of crimes from bribery to nepotism; from buying and selling of offices and party memberships, to extortion of money and assets from ordinary soldiers; from interfering with local affairs to the embezzling and withholding of materials and funds for the grassroots.[229]

Xi was increasingly exasperated when roving teams uncovered ever more lurid details about corrupt officials, their resistance, and counterstrategies. According to him, many graft cases had been ignored or covered up, and new officials tried to bury transgressions of former incumbents. Corrupt officials had colluded with entrepreneurs and formed horizontal and vertical cabals for mutual protection.[230] The "total collapse" (*tafang*) form of corruption incorporated intricate webs of officials spanning various levels of government dealing in high stakes. The officials, Xi railed, had turned public coffers into their private property, converting directors of finance departments into their own "family accountants." Xi then declared that antigraft would have to be a long-term endeavor. In time, the ACC was turned inward against graft busters within the CCDI itself, and in 2014 alone, 1,575 from the CCDI system were convicted.[231]

The "Mass Line Education and Practice" Campaign for the CCP

In tandem with the ACC a fifteen-month "Mass Line Education and Practice Campaign" (MLEP) was launched in mid-2013 at the Nineteenth Politburo meeting to cleanse the Party from top to bottom. Specifically, Xi declared that the main goals were to improve the Party's work style, attitude, and behavior. Apparently repulsed by a culture of malfeasance by party members, he issued a long litany of misdemeanors that he subsumed under the overlapping "four winds" of formalism, bureaucratism, hedonism, and extravagance and deca-dence (*shemi*, often translated as "wastefulness"). For Xi, formalism covers such matters as ritualistic and feigned compliance, fraud and forgery, and window dressing. Bureaucratism refers to haughtiness toward the public; clientelism; red tape; and dereliction of duty. Hedonism refers to vainglory, pleasure seeking, sloth, and apathy. Extravagance and decadence refer to high living on public funds, self-congratulatory celebrations, luxurious offices, vehicles, foreign travels, and conspicuous consumption in foreign casinos.[232]

According to Xi, party members often refused to implement the Party's poli-cies or inclined to subvert them. Party superiors were arrogant and arbitrary, and subordinates were groveling. Party units were either disorganized like a "loose sheet of sand" or were split into competing fiefdoms and cliques bedeviled by constant infighting. Party members were said to be obsessed with the cultivation of patron-client relationships, ingratiating themselves to powerful patrons. They were preoccupied with figuring out who belonged to which clique and who had been promoted by whom. In recruitment, unqualified and "tainted" (suspected of wrongdoings) ones were often promoted. As Xi said, "Only underlings who curry favors and dole out gifts get promoted; those who fail to do so either are demoted or remain in their positions." Worst, some cadres were said to believe in "ghosts and gods" and relied on fortune telling to solve problems. A prevalent "nice guy" mentality among the cadres meant that they refused to criticize errors or take on responsibilities. They muddled along and "turned small problems into big ones, and big problems into dreadful troubles." The "most frightening" fact, Xi bemoaned, was that these officials were popular and got on well with others. Further, local disciplinary inspection committees turned a blind eye to corrupted practices of their firsts-in-command.

Xi chided "naked officials" who stashed their families and fortunes overseas, spending money like "dust" on luxurious mansions and cars, and who were al-ways ready to elope. Others were said to have treated directors of financial departments as their own family accountants when dipping into public coffers. Toward the public, party members had behaved essentially as local bullies who pilfered and embezzled their monies and properties as if it was their inherent right to do so. Driven by greed, they concocted false and erroneous court cases that framed innocent people. Xi was moved to concede that the "broken-glass effect" had made all the above a norm within the Party. Furthermore, the ACC officials resisted and obstructed central inspections, and gainsaid central prin-ciples. An exasperated Xi exclaimed, "Power corrupts, and absolute power corrupts absolutely!"[233] For him, only when these problems had been brought under control could others be dealt with more easily.

A January 2013 Politburo meeting made the decision to tighten admission to the Party and to dismiss a multitude of unqualified members. Various attempts were introduced to improve the quality of party members and control the numerical growth. Subsequently, the annual increase in the total numbers of new party members dropped continuously, from a high of 2.5 percent in 2012 to 1.1 percent in 2014, 0.7 percent in 2016, and 0.1 percent in 2017, before rising to 1.2 percent in 2018.[234] Xi ordered the revitalization of the moribund party life meetings whereby party members engage in criticism and self-criticism to uncover problems. New regulations prescribed that all government economic, cultural, and social organs with three party members or more in leadership must form a party cell. Party members were enjoined to reconnect with the people through public service and volunteer work. The "eight-point regulations" from the ACC were incorporated as one of the guiding principles of the campaign.

When inspecting Hebei in July 2013 Xi scornfully ordered the officials to self-reflect by "looking into the mirror, tidying their appearance, taking a bath, and curing their sickness." He demanded "open door" rectifications that allowed the public and mass organizations to participate in criticizing the Party. During the first phase of the campaign, from June 2013 to January 2014, the targets of scrutiny were officers and organizations at the county (*chu*) level or above. During the second phase, January to October 2014, the targets shifted to officials at the county and base levels. At the top, each PBSC member was tasked with connecting with one province and one county in order to set examples on how to pursue the MLEP. Xi volunteered to go to Hebei, probably so he could visit old haunts such as Zhengding, Pingshan, and Shijiajiang to scrutinize activities there. As noted, Xi had offered to work at the revolutionary shrine Xipaibo in 1981 but was advised against the idea. A revisit to Zhengding would also allow him to see how things had developed there. At these localities he collected information on living conditions, rural and urban services, and social welfare. He admonished officials there to study central documents and speeches; carry out criticism and self- criticism; and identify their policy errors and solve them one by one within set time limits. He urged open-door rectifications involving the public, demanding provincial leaders improve their work styles and advance the quality of development and the environment.[235]

After Hebei, Xi went to Henan's Lankao County to assess the damage of the "four winds." While there, he resurrected a county official model from the 1960s named Jiao Yulu who was said to have encompassed the ethos of hard work and asceticism. He urged the officials there to overcome poverty, and a few years later, the Lankao County model would become a national showcase for poverty reduction closely associated with Xi.[236] Within three years 138,867 party officials were punished for violations of the "eight-point regulations" (see Table 9.9).

According to most accounts, official banqueting and entertainment had been reduced, and official sources also claimed reductions in vices such as the number of meetings, plan fulfillment celebrations, and land requisitions for official use.

Table 9.9 Numbers of Party Officials Punished during the Mass Line Education and Practice Campaign

Administrative Level	Numbers
Province	7
Prefectural	678
County	7,389
Township	130,793
Total	138,867

Source: "Baxiang guiding, rang dangfeng zhengfeng weizhi yixin" [Eight Regulations That Have Invigorated Party and Governance Style], *Zhongguo xinwenwang*, December 4, 2015, http://fanfu.people.com.cn/n/2015/1204/c64371-27890716.html.

The same was claimed for expensive government cars, overseas trips, clubs, and "cadre training."[237] Many vanity projects were either deferred or abolished, and the number of *shenpi* was reduced. Chinese and Western media simultaneously reported plummeting sales in luxury goods and services, in banqueting facilities and flowers, and this has even affected the global luxury market. At the conclusion of the MLEP campaign, Xi expressed satisfaction over improved efficiency and openness, although he was aware that the issues could not be fundamentally settled. In the short run, lavish banqueting had gone underground (canteens were transformed into five-star restaurants) or moved to rural hideouts, and gifts were dispensed by e-cards, red envelopes, or internet transactions. In other areas, officials laid low, resisting new projects that involved money, leading to policy gridlocks. Since incentives to motivate them were lacking, official inaction and foot-dragging became an issue. Several unsubstantiated media reports indicated that Jiang Zemin and Hu Jintao, fearing the demoralizing effect of the ACC, urged Xi to tone down the campaign in 2014,[238] but Xi was determined to push ahead.

Breaking with tradition, state media and TV networks widely publicized crackdowns on corrupt officials, with many of them publicly confessing and sobbing with remorse on camera. One very popular TV series (with fifty-five episodes), entitled *In the Name of the People*, on the ACC premiered in 2017, funded by the Supreme People's Procuratorate. Often compared to the TV series *House of Cards*, it chronicled power struggles within the Party as well as the seamy side of Chinese politics, such as sabotage by local officials, collusion between money and power, and even fake police.[239] Xi reckoned that the situation was complex and formidable and required an ongoing "protracted war" to stem the resurgence of extravagant image projects. Suspects who were party members were subjected to *shangqui*—a coercive interrogation method whereby suspects are kept incommunicado and forced to engage in self-criticism under tremendous duress. They were always penalized by expulsion from the Party and prosecution in the courts that usually resulted in imprisonment. One official source claims that from January to November 2016, 35,800 cases of "eight-point regulations" violations involving 50,800 party members were investigated, and 37,000 were punished. Xi ordered that all central investigations be repeated for a second time to net those who escaped scrutiny, and this has become a standard operating procedure ever since.[240]

By 2017, Xi and the CCDI pledged to pursue antigraft with no slowdown despite the destabilizing effect.[241] Among the sixty-seven highest officials, at least nine had received bribes over ¥1 billion (US$14 million) each, with the highest records reaching ¥2.5 and ¥1.4 billion (US$35 and 19.6 million). The death penalty, suspended death penalty, or life imprisonment was meted out for these offenders.[242] Altogether the central roving inspection teams had concluded twelve rounds of inspections with 160 inspections covering 277 localities and units. Repeated inspections of specific units for a second time often apprehended those missed during the first round.[243] By October 2017, Chinese officials claimed the following: 440 officials among the central nomenklatura were investigated and punished. Among those punished were forty members and alternate members of the Central Committee. More than one million corruption cases were investigated, and more than two million party members and cadres were punished; of these were about 1,343,000 party members and cadres at or above the township level, and 648,000 party members and cadres in the rural areas (a total of nearly two million cadres) (see Table 9.10). The "Sky Net" and "Fox Hunt" operations had extradited 3,453 fugitives from more than ninety countries and ¥9.51 billion (US$1.3 billion) were retrieved; forty-eight out of a list of one hundred "most wanted" suspects had been returned to China.[244] In addition, seventy-nine hundred officials in the CCDI and CDI, the overseers of the campaign, were disciplined; 160,000 cases of violating the "eight-point regulations" were investigated, and 136,100 were punished. In 2016, fifty-seven thousand party members turned themselves in and confessed wrongdoing; and 160,000 public complaints were received by the eleventh round of inspections, and 110,000 complaints against the SOEs were received.[245]

In addition, to combat transnational corporate corruption, foreign firms that offered bribes to increase market share or to boost sales were targeted. For instance, Nestle was investigated and fined for bribing Chinese hospital staff to exclusively use its milk formulas for newborns. GlaxoSmithKline was slapped with a fine of US$496 million for ordering its subordinates to pay bribes to boost sales.

Table 9.10 Numbers of Officials and Party Members Convicted during the Anticorruption Campaign, 2013–2017

Administrative level	Numbers
Central level (party and military nomenklatura)	440
Bureau-director (ting ju厅局)	8,900+
County-division (xian chu县处)	63,000
Township-section (xiang ke乡科)	278,000
Rural party cadres	650,000
Total	1,537,000+

Source: Since official statistics were published at various points of the ACC, many different figures were circulated. Even the various numbers published in October 2017 do not always add up, although most important figures are consistent with one another. These numbers come from the most authoritative sources, such as "Bajie zhongyang jilu jiancha weiyuanhui xiang zhongguo gongchandang di shijiuci quanguo daibiao dahui di gongzuo baogao" [The CCDI's Work Report to the CCP's Nineteenth Party Congress], *Xinhua*, October 29, 2017, http://www.xinhuanet.com/politics/2017-10/29/c_1121873 020.ht; "Fanfu 5 nian, 40 wei shibajie zhongyang weiyuan, houbu weiyuan bei chachu" [Five Years of Anticorruption: Forty Members and Alternates of the Central Committee Have Been Convicted], *Ifeng*, October 11, 2017, http://news.ifeng.com/a/20171011/52581102_0.shtml; "China's Anti-graft Drive Wins People's Trust," *Xinhua*, October 7, 2017, http://www.chinadaily.com.cn/china/2017-10/ 08/content_32973939.htm; "Xi Jinping shoujiu fanfu zuo 3 nian zongjie, chengji yilan" [Xi Jinping Makes a First Recap of Anticorruption: A Review of the Achievements], *Zhongguo qingnianwang*, January 17, 2017, http://news.ifeng.com/a/20160117/47105444_0.shtml.

Correspondingly, the US Securities and Exchange Commission imposed a deferred fine of US$20 million on GlaxoSmithKline but slapped a US$264 million fine on JPMorgan for hiring Chinese princelings to boost business. This added to the list of household names such as IBM, Daimler, Pfizer, Avon, and Morgan Stanley that have been punished for corruption in recent years.[246]

Ironically, all this was complicated by revelations of fortunes amassed by relatives of Xi and other top leaders. In 2012, an investigation by *Bloomberg News* showed that Xi's sister Qi Qiaoqiao and her husband Deng Jiagui owned business interests in minerals, rare earth, real estate, and mobile phones worth hundreds of millions, although no assets could be traced back to Xi.[247] Similarly, an investigation by the *New York Times* claimed that relatives and members of Wen Jiabao's extended family controlled assets worth at least US$2.7 billion.[248] This revealed a pattern of relatives of China's top elites who have exploited their political connections to amass fortunes during decades of exponential economic growth. Many in this group had suffered poverty and deprivation but had returned with a vengeance to the Chinese equivalent of a Gilded Age. Other entrepreneurs who have joined the large contingent of millionaires and billionaires were formally workers, farmers, and teachers,[249] but those who are related to the political elite incur more suspicion. For instance, Qi Qiaoqiao worked as a director with the PAP when her father was rehabilitated, and then retired to care for her father until he died in 2002. She then earned an MBA degree in 2006 while building up a huge fortune with her husband. After the *Bloomberg* revelations, many of Xi's relatives allegedly sold off their assets.[250] Yet the publication of the Panama Papers in April 2016 dropped another bombshell by revealing that Deng Jiaqiu and relatives of Politburo members such as Liu Yunshan and Zhang Gaoli and retired members such as Jia Qinglin, Zeng Qinghong, Li Peng, Hu Yaobang, and Bo Xilai (Gu Kailai) owned offshore companies.[251] Although the Panama Papers did not necessarily prove corruption, they were certainly embarrassing for Xi and his team, especially amid the ACC, and therefore information on the subject has been censored in China. Furthermore, in 2017, Guo Wengui, a Chinese property tycoon now living in New York who had been connected with China's intelligence apparatus, alleged corruption among China's top leaders with lurid details in a series of tweets, YouTube videos, and Western media interviews. Guo also accused Wang Qishan and his relatives of being "incredibly corrupt," claiming that Wang's family members control one of China's largest conglomerates and that Wang was being investigated himself.[252] In turn, Guo was wanted in China via Interpol for fraud, money laundering, and rape, being implicated by the corruption purge of Ma Jian, former deputy minister at the Ministry of State Security. Guo's rambling and largely unsubstantiated exposé drew ire from Beijing and cast doubt on Wang's spotless image, but ultimately it did not weaken Wang's position, as we will see later.[253]

Outcome and Perspectives

Taken together, the magnitude and velocity of the ACC and the MLEP amounted to a political earthquake, although the latter was concluded in October 2014 and the former is still ongoing. The two campaigns punished a large number of officials and struck fear that reverberated throughout the entire elite system. Some officials committed suicide out of shame. The campaign atmosphere imposed some constraints over the daily lives of officials, resulting in a drastic decrease in official gift giving and junkets. Merrill Lynch estimated that it had cost China 1.5 percent in its GDP.[254] In their division of labor, Xi relied primarily on moral suasion, shame, and punishment to deter corruption, whereas Li Keqiang and the economists emphasized levers like changing the incentive structure by eliminating regulations and *shenpi* that encouraged corruption. Additionally, Xi and the CCP were determined to control and prosecute the antigraft campaigns strictly on their own terms. Activists who pushed for more transparency by officials to declare their assets were arrested. Further, the expanding reach of the surveillance and security apparatus, and the extralegal methods of the CCDI, had created a chilling effect on academic, religious, and mass organizations.[255]

The intended and unintended significance and outcome of the ACC and MLEP are complex. They can be interpreted essentially as, first, Xi's means to discipline the Party's rank and file in order to restore the legitimacy and reputation of the Party; second, as measures to push forward Xi's agenda of neutralizing bureaucratic and widespread resistance to his market reform initiatives; third, as a means to complement Xi's centralization of power, showing him to be a strong man in charge; and fourth, as Xi's means of removing adversaries to facilitate his consolidation of power with an eye on his second term, especially in view of the impending personnel reshuffle before the Nineteenth Party Congress of 2017. Xi may have gained by convicting many real and potential enemies. The campaign reflects the intensity of the power struggle to eliminate rivals, both political and ideological, and diminish the influence of elders such as Jiang Zemin, uniquely a Chinese succession issue. Further, the ACC and MLEP have created legions of enemies for Xi. Officials whose privileges have been removed and whose new reality is strict discipline were either demoralized or revengeful. The attack on the ingrained patronage system is a dangerous maneuver. Xi was aware of these outcomes, and yet, as Wang Qishan maintained, it was better to offend thousands than to offend 1.3 billion, a statement that harkened back to Xi's earlier endeavor in Fujian.

Some China watchers claim that the targets of these investigations were selective, since members of three groups—the "red second generation" (R2G), the sitting Politburo, and retired elders—were declared off limits. Other reports have claimed that many of the R2G, who controlled key SOEs and private companies, had been busy shedding assets. In addition, the strong personal authority established by Xi could deter elders such as Jiang Zemin from interfering with his initiatives, but there was no guarantee.[256] However, the purge of Sun Zhengcai, a sitting member of the Politburo, broke the second taboo. In the final analysis, Xi believed that draconian measures were required to save the vanguard, even though he understood corruption cannot be totally eliminated in any society.

For others, the ACC and MLEP have met with a degree of public approval and a heightened sense of efficacy. For the public, the ACC is in general popular; many regard the openness with which the campaign was conducted may have created a deterrence effect, although concerns were raised that public confessions by officials might have been extracted under duress, violating their rights to a fair trial. Netizens mocked the public confessions made by the officials, deeming them forced and not genuine. Further, within the Party, many argued that the ACC was unsustainable and should be terminated, since it had shaken the foundation of CCP rule, and no endgame was in sight. Others saw corruption as a kind of original sin for the Party, since in their view the "state will collapse if the Party does not tackle corruption, but the Party will collapse if the anticorruption push is too hard."[257]

Some China watchers have observed a degree of policy paralysis, since alienated officials lay low or resist passively, refusing to take initiatives or to deal with investment projects. To appear squeakily clean, they turned down banquet invitations and gifts, avoiding even legitimate contact with business people, making necessary communication impossible. Even honest officials have become wary of innovations and of spending public funds, fearing that things might go wrong.[258] A systemic incentive for graft was and still is fostered by the huge disparity in income between private and public sectors—officials' salaries and benefits are minuscule compared to those of entrepreneurs, but officials wield great powers over all aspects of the economy.[259] In any case, the ACC and MLEP produced dozens of regulations for the Party on honesty and integrity, self-discipline, roving inspections, and disciplinary punishment. According to Xi, previous regulations were mostly window dressing since they dealt mostly with principles, but the new regulations contain more detailed specifications intended to institutionalize anticorruption. For instance, among the 178 articles contained in the new regulations on disciplinary punishment, around 70 were drawn directly from state laws such as the criminal code.[260] In 2016, the ACC was extended to the base level to combat grassroots corruption by tackling the "flies" that Beijing thought might be more damaging than the "tigers" since their impacts on the lives of ordinary people were more extensive and immediate. The inspection teams unearthed a phenomenon dubbed "low officials, huge graft" (*xiaoguan jutan*), which referred to grassroots officials such as village cadres who have embezzled housing and welfare funds designated for the extreme poor, the disabled, and orphans, appropriating amounts as low as ¥20 and totaling millions of yuan. Hence, the focus of the ACC in 2016 was shifted to such things as land requisitions, the misappropriation of rural subsidies, welfare for the poor, and minimum income guarantees.[261]

In a July 2016 speech to commemorate the anniversary of the CCP, Xi again reiterated the view that the greatest threat to the CCP was corruption and urged the prosecution of the ACC to new heights without an end or upper limits,[262] raising the specter that even more high officials would be netted in the future.[263] At the first G20 meeting held in China (Hangzhou) in September 2016, Xi announced that G20 members had agreed on the principles of fugitive repatriation and asset recovery, on the setting up of a research center on the subject in China, and an action plan for anticorruption for 2017–2018.[264] Subsequently, the research center, designed to be an international cooperation platform for the exchange of expertise in such issues as transnational corruption, extradition, comparative legislations, and investment immigration, was formed in Beijing.[265]

Melanie Manion, an expert on China's corruption, argues that the ACC is distinct from previous anticorruption efforts in that it features institutionalization and credible commitments to good governance. It has been the longest campaign with the most far-reaching impact. The effective enhancement of the power of the CCDI streamlined or severed dual rule at the expense of horizontal leadership by the local authorities. Most importantly, the campaign has significantly reduced rent-seeking opportunities, as thousands (or tens of thousands at the local levels) of *shenpi* required for doing business ten years ago have been abolished compared.[266] Reforms and the removal of structural incentives may also have an impact on corruption. As intractable as the corruption issue seems, back in the 1980s, the two-track system was the major source of corruption—officials secured key goods and commodities at low official prices and sold them at higher market prices to make big profits—but once the prices for those key goods had been marketized, the opportunities for graft were eliminated. Public offices became unattractive, and officials abandoned their jobs and moved massively into the private sector in a phenomenon dubbed "jumping into the sea."

Despite the prevailing evidence and perception that corruption was rampant, China has not been at the bottom globally in terms of corruption according to Transparency International, which ranked China in the middle (79 out of 176) in 2016, sharing the same ranking with the nominally democratic countries of India (79) and Brazil (79), and well ahead of countries like Indonesia (90), Argentina (95), the Philippines (101), Mexico (123), and Russia (131).[267] Another source postulates that China's corruption does not match Gilded Age America, and that China is now taking similar measures to the United States in 1900, when citizens demanded cleaner government. The "life cycle" theory of corruption shows that corruption tends to rise at an early stage of development and then declines as a country reaches advanced economy status.[268] From such perspectives, corruption in China appears to be a typical middle-income country issue that in China is closely intertwined with the political system of a one-party state and rapid social economic development. Furthermore, *The Economist*'s 2016 Crony-Capitalism Index, which calculates billionaire wealth as a percentage of GDP, ranks China number 11 among twenty-two countries, placing below, for example, Malaysia (1), Russia (2), Singapore (4), Philippines (5), and above the UK (14), US (15), Argentina (16), and Thailand (17). China's crony wealth, at 3 percent of GDP, is at par with that of Turkey, India, and Taiwan.[269] Both the Transparency International and *Economist* indices are rough indicators, each with methodological flaws, and they might only provide cold comfort to Xi. In any case, counterintuitively, corruption in China has not retarded investment, economic growth, and development because local officials have a great deal of incentive to promote growth in spite of rampant corruption, especially when they enjoy a great deal of policy flexibility. In one recent study, the author argues that what she labeled "access money," or the elite exchange of power and profit, is universal. Whereas in the developed countries, such practices have long been institutionalized and legalized, in China the exercise of money politics is still crude and personal.[270]

In any case, the ongoing campaign continues in Xi's second term, although the incidences of public shaming have subsided. The massive publicity on corruption in the official and social media might have served an educational purpose.[271] For instance, books on corruption fill large bookshelves in China's huge bookstores called "book cities" (see Figure 9.3). The relationship between authoritarianism and corruption control in China is still an open question, and for Xi, it is not unreasonable to expect that many enemies are waiting to exact revenge for his efforts when he makes a mistake or weakens in power.

The Shakeup in the Communist Youth League

A corollary to the disciplining of the party state was Xi's attack on the CYL and its subsequent shakeup. As mentioned, the CYL serves as a socialization organization and a recruitment device for the Party to attract reliable activists, or a "reserve army." The organization provides ideological training and social services for youths from age fourteen to age twenty-eight. CYL membership helps young activists acquire early political qualifications, and it has often been regarded as a passport to party membership and upward mobility. Furthermore, officials who

Figure 9.3 Two shelves of books on clean governance and corruption in a Beijing bookstore (taken by author)

run the CYL doing "youth work" have been regularly recruited into all levels of the party state. In the 1980s, especially, the CYL under Hu Yaobang played a prominent role in regularly recruiting CYL officials to form a "third echelon" that addressed the shortage of young talent. Hu Jintao, Li Keqiang, and Li Yuanchao are examples of officials who ascended to the top through the CYL stepping stone. By 2013, the CYL had ballooned into a huge organization consisting of ninety million members with a staff of 190,000 serving 3.6 million local chapters.

Because the CYL is a mass organization, its members and officials are considered populists close to the grassroots, and the CYL itself was considered upright, especially because CYL officials seldom handle economic and financial resources. Yet CYL officials have often been criticized for incompetence and mediocrity because their work is deemed unchallenging, unskilled, and narrowly focused. Seldom did they have expertise in economics, foreign trade, finance, and banking. One perceived shortcoming of the CYL organizations was that it was weak in rural areas. A more disparaging view sees the CYL as a career fast-track for ambitious young cadres.[272]

Since 2013, the roving teams of the ACC and MLFP dispatched to inspect the implementation of the "eight regulations" have uncovered numerous corruption issues with the CYL as well as other mass organizations such as trade unions and women's federations. For instance, one CYL branch secretary in Beijing was convicted for embezzling ¥90,000 intended for a major event. Another county CYL committee was convicted for divvying up ¥200,000 of subsidies among its five members. This was in addition to the embezzlement of ¥540,000 from the CYL administration budget to pay for gifts and bribes for their superiors to enhance their promotion prospects.[273]

The prosecution of corrupt CYL officials was not new under Xi, but in the context of the ACC and the MLFP, it intensified. Xi repeatedly lambasted the CYL, and a collection of excerpts of his speeches on the CYL from 2012 to 2017, many revealed for the first time, was published in 2017. Xi castigated the CYL for being a slogan-touting "hollow shell" that was bureaucratic, arrogant, ill-informed, elitist, and hedonistic (jiguanhua, xingzhenghua, guizuhua, yulehua). Inefficient and incompetent, the CYL was said to have failed to connect with the young people or to mobilize the public, and in fact was suffering from various stages of paralysis. Xi charged CYL officials with harboring the illusion that they could use the organization as a springboard to high offices. To atone for their sins and to maintain its "advancedness," it must experience hardship and reorient itself toward vulnerable groups such as the rural poor, migrants, the disabled, and women and children left behind in the countryside.[274] Xi wanted to streamline the CYL leadership, and in 2016 its budget was slashed by half, and its leaders were increasingly marginalized.[275]

As mentioned, the "one party, two coalitions" theory contends that the principal leadership and policy cleavage is between the "elite" and "populist" coalitions. By extension, this view claims that Xi's onslaught against the CYL was a calculated move to weaken the rival *tuanpai*, its "leaders" such as Li Keqiang, and its patronage network so that Xi could fast-track his own supporters. The purge of a major *tuanpai* leader Ling Jihua, who was Hu Jintao's former chief of staff, for corruption was said to be another move in this factional struggle (see Table 9.8). As the director of the Party Central Office from 2007 to 2012, Ling was assumed to have accepted bribes for promotion, but it is doubtful that he did so by promoting only those with CYL work experience to form a "faction." As argued, the assumption that the CYL is a cohesive and powerful faction competing with a hypothetical "elite" coalition cannot be substantiated. In context, Xi's attack on the CYL can best be explained by his attempt to force discipline on the party state as a whole. Similarly, Xi had also chastised other mass organizations such as trade unions and women's federations, blaming them for behaving like the apolitical "rich ladies" clubs in the West. Foremost, Xi wanted them to toe the Party's political line, tighten their organizations, and keep corruption under control. Otherwise, Xi said, they would be no different from other social organizations.[276]

Judicial Reform and "Comprehensively Govern the Country According to Law"

The last leg of Xi's disciplining the party state involved judicial reform.[277] Chinese leaders from Deng Xiaoping onward have repeatedly called for the rule of law not merely to counter the lawlessness during the Cultural Revolution, but as a means to foster economic and social development. Law is regarded as essential in foreign dealings, especially in trade, commerce, and investment.[278] The reform period saw the establishment of a vast judicial infrastructure and the promulgation of thousands of laws and regulations. Yet the Party has always been ambivalent about the rule of law and prioritized political and social stability, and especially party leadership as a precondition. Consequently, old and new issues piled up. The Xi administration wanted to push forward judicial reform as another front to improve governance, to combat corruption, and to restore legitimacy. Hence the rallying cries to promote law-based governance, to safeguard people's rights, and to encourage people to resolve social conflicts through legal procedures and to become law-abiding citizens.[279]

Immediately before Xi became general secretary, various initiatives to promote law-based governance included the white paper on judicial reform of October 2012 and a reform plan by the Supreme People's Court. In December 2012, on the thirtieth anniversary of the 1982 constitution, Xi called for the upholding of the constitution and the protection of the people's political, economic, social, and cultural rights.[280] Since the Party leads the country, Xi stated, it must act in the confines of law. Soon it became clear that Xi would become the first general secretary to personally take charge of judicial reform.[281]

As with party-state problems, Xi took a dim view of problems in the judiciary. He was wary of well-known issues such as inefficiency, unfair trials, wrongful convictions, and local political interference and protectionism. He intimated that the local government-judiciary nexus was a key source of corruption since local authorities hired and fired judges, so that the latter were beholden to their paymasters. Corrupted judges and prosecutors, according to Xi, manipulated cases in exchange for money and favors, and the state of lawlessness in many places made for a "terrible mess." Vested local interests encouraged land expropriation and abused power with impunity. Culturally, China also lacked an ethos of legality among officials and the public. All this contributed to popular resentment and social instability, as reflected in the large number of petitions and mass incidents.[282] In 2013, the judiciary began to review cases of trumped-up charges and wrongful convictions, exonerating those proven to be innocent, a process the Chinese call "rectifying mistakes" (jiucuo).The Supreme People's Court published a regulation on the prevention of wrongful criminal convictions that highlighted the rarely used notion of the presumption of innocence.[283] But these judicial reviews must have encountered resistance, judging by the tone of what Xi told a political legal work conference in January 2014: "Stop worrying about the harm and blowback that the current rectification of mistakes may bring us. We know about the unjust, false, and wrong cases. Let's worry more about the harm and impact these cases have exacted on the people and on the credibility of our judiciary work. The rectification of mistakes—it's better late than never."[284] The Supreme People's Court and the Supreme People's Procuratorate also declared that those responsible for wrongful convictions, especially in cases involving torture to extract confessions, revenge, and the abuse of law for personal gain, must be prosecuted.[285] Inevitably, as the redress campaign unfolded nationally, the CPLC had to reopen many of its cases, as admitted by its chief, Meng Jianzhu.[286]

The Third Plenum (November 2013) dealt primarily with economic issues, but it also pledged to deepen judicial reform, to abolish the "reeducation-through-labor" system, and to accelerate the building of a "just, efficient and authoritative socialist judicial system." All this culminated in the Fourth Plenum (October 2014), the first-ever plenum devoted entirely to the issue of judicial reform and the "rule of law," "clean governance," and "law-based governance."[287] The guidelines for this unprecedented plenum dedicated to realizing "comprehensive governing according to law" can be summarized in the following.

First, to improve judicial autonomy, the plenum decided to set up pilot projects to create circuit courts under the SPC. It also decided to make the local courts more independent from the control of local authorities by severing the connection between local judges and local governments, preventing the latter from interfering to serve their own interests. Second, to improve accountability, the plenum decided to record all interventions by party officials, investigate party and government officials who interfere with the judiciary, and sanction the guilty ones with dismissals and criminal punishment. The principle of "upholding of the rule of law" would be included as a criterion for evaluating officials for promotion or demotion. A lifelong accountability system for major decisions would be installed to ensure quality and to hold judges accountable for erroneous rulings during their lifetimes.[288] The plenum decided to explore the establishment of courts and procuratorates whose jurisdictions would extend beyond administrative divisions in order to control local protectionism. It promised to explore a system of procuratorates handling public interest litigation in addition to consumer protection and environmental issues.

Third, to improve the quality and efficiency of the judiciary, the plenum decided to build a contingent of highly competent legal officials by stressing the professional training of lawmakers, judges, and lawyers. Official elaborations, citing Bacon and Rousseau about the need to foster justice and trust in law, asserted the reliance on guanxi must end, from getting an education to writing a civil service examination, and from setting up a business to buying a lodging and finding employment. They declared that if law and justice were not taken seriously and if the public had no means to express grievances, social turmoil would result.[289]

Fourth, to ensure that "power could be put in a cage," the plenum asserted that the party state must exercise its powers within the confines of the constitution and the law. As the country's vanguard, the Party was urged to govern according to the constitution, ensuring the observation of its own rules and regulations. The latter would be strengthened to ensure exemplary conduct. The "firsts-in-command" in the Party were enjoined to curb cadre privilege and to encourage transparency, ensuring that they would not override the law by fiat, placing their power above law and bending the law for private gains.

Implementation and Policy Development

The Fourth Plenum mandate set off a raft of activities by the Supreme People's Court, Supreme Procuratorate, and the Ministries of Public Security and Justice, resulting in a torrent of documents and white papers on judicial reform, poverty reduction, and human rights. The significance and complexity of judicial reforms is attested to by the fact that under the CDRLSG there were six specialized subgroups to study judicial issues, and of the thirty-eight plenary sessions held by it during the Eighteenth Party Congress session, twenty-five were devoted to judicial reforms. By the beginning of 2018, fifty documents were passed, covering many sensitive policy issues.[290] The SPC had also formed a leading group headed by Chief Justice Zhou Qiang to handle judicial reform and all high courts also formed a leading group to do so.[291]

One first step was the insistence that all reforms had to be based on law, even for pilot projects. That meant the jettisoning of the normal practice of party decisions being implemented with or without legislative approval. For instance, although the Eighteenth Party Congress approved the building of the Pilot Special Trading Zones, none were allowed until the Standing Committee of the NPeC formally authorized them in August 2013. Second, when the policy of allowing families a second child (providing that one parent was a single child) was approved by the Party, the policy was not enforced until the NPeC Standing Committee revised the law. Similarly, when the Fifth Plenum (October 2015) announced the application of the "second child" policy to all families, it was not implemented until corresponding legislation was introduced. Third, in March 2015, the NPeC approved revised legislation on taxation by which the legislature would regain the power over the government to determine the kinds of taxes, who would pay, and how much would be determined by the NPeC. Prior to that, only three out of the eighteen kinds of taxation had ever been formally approved by NPeC legislations.[292]

To be sure, the Party was deemed the guardian over the judicial system and reform, but the Party is not monolithic, and control was somewhat elastic. The experimental and often open-ended policy process meant that implementation often resulted in a diversity of approaches, improvisations, and details unanticipated by the Party Center. Pilot projects were adjusted, and local adaptations and initiatives were incorporated. And there was still much room for bureaucratic input, maneuvering, and contention.

According to official information, such as the white papers on judicial reform issued in 2016 and an updated version issued in 2017,[293] the SPC imposed vertical control of the judicial system by establishing six circuit courts (directly answerable to it). Each of these circuit courts covers several provinces, to adjudicate administrative and transregional civil and commercial cases. For instance, the No. 1 Circuit Court, located in Shenzhen, covers Guangdong, Guangxi, and Hainan; the No. 2 Circuit Court located in Shenyang covers Liaoning, Jilin, and Heilongjiang; whereas the Supreme Court looks after cases from Beijing, Tianjin, Hebei, Shandong, and Inner Mongolia. The central government removed the power over personnel, finance, and resources from the local authorities and assigned them to the provinces. Both the central and provincial governments set aside budgets for the judiciary so that it would no longer be funded by local authorities. Two transregional people's courts, Beijing's No. 4 Intermediate People's Court and Shanghai's No. 3 Intermediate People's Court, were set up to adjudicate administrative cases allowing plaintiffs to sue the government over local interest cases. These cases involve building demolition, redevelopment, environmental protection, food and drug safety, red tape, and failure to follow procedures. In 2015, for instance, the Beijing court heard 1,440 cases, and the government lost in 18.6 percent of them. Intellectual rights courts were established in Beijing, Shanghai, and Guangzhou.[294]

To address the issue of "difficulty in case filing," the SPC initiated a case-filing system that required all lawsuits be handled by the courts. It also introduced electronic case filing, online submission of documents, fee payments, and so on, to improve efficiency. Subsequently, it was said that 16.3 million cases were filed in 2016, a 12.48 percent increase over the year before. Ninety-five percent of these cases were filed at a convenient central filing registry or online. More than twenty-three hundred litigation centers were set up. The SPC is said to have set up data-sharing platforms with various superior courts regarding *xinfang*, and the promotion of electronic and long-distance video resulted in *xinfang* in 1.6 million instances.[295]

A national rectification campaign cleared 1,845 cases and released 4,459 suspects who were in custody for more than three years without trial. Similarly, 3,541 individuals in custody for less than three years, 926 individuals from five to eight years, and two for eight years or longer were released. By 2015, nationally only six were said to be still under custody. Between 2013 and 2016, the courts acquitted 3,718 defendants, and the overturning of the tragic Nie Shubin unjust execution case from 1995 (by the No. 2 Circuit Court) attracted national attention and was hailed as a milestone.[296] In the same period, the courts accepted 16,889 cases of state compensation with a payout of ¥699 million (US$101 million), and the abolition of the reeducation-through-labor system was completed, with the transfer of personnel and facilities to other causes. In the same period, over five million legal cases had been processed, 95 percent of local governments had included legal aid in their budgets, and twenty-eight million had received legal consultation.

In September 2016, a National Human Rights Action Plan (2016–2020) promised to guarantee a long list of rights, including minimum living standards, social security, health and education provision, political rights, fair trials, and freedom for religious beliefs, as well as rights for ethnic minorities, women, the elderly, and the disabled. It pledged to fulfill Beijing's obligation to international conventions such as the International Covenant on Economic, Social, and Cultural Rights, which China had signed and ratified, although no mention was made of the International Covenant on Political and Civil Rights, which China signed but did not ratify.[297]

To promote "transparency and accessibility," the SPC claimed that 419 courts had opened online mediation platforms staffed by 2,390 online mediators. In addition, the courts set up nearly twenty thousand special mediation organizations with more than sixty thousand mediators. The SPC established four platforms to foster transparency in the judicial process, judicial documents, execution information, and court hearings, making them open to the public. China Judgments Online is said to have posted more that twenty-six million written judgments and received 5.5 billion visits, making it the largest document platform in the world.[298]

Other alleged improvements include regulations to standardize penalties, to protect lawyers' rights to practice, and to forbid individuals and administrative and social organizations from interfering with the adjudication of judges. Databases on interference with courts would be set up at every administrative level. Still other measures included the upholding of the presumption of innocence, the tightening of procedures to exclude illegally obtained evidence, and the installation of recording devices in interrogation rooms to prevent torture. A new Anti-Domestic Violence Law was passed in 2015. The authorities pledged to apply strict control of the death penalty and the reduction of the number of crimes punishable by it. Going back, in 2005, the SPC captured the power to approve all cases of death penalty from the localities, and the sixty-eight crimes punishable by the death penalty were reduced to fifty-five in 2011. The 2015 reform removed the death penalty for nine more crimes, including smuggling of arms, ammunitions, or nuclear materials; counterfeiting currency; and the organization of prostitution and coercion of others into prostitution.[299] Despite this, it has been estimated that China still executed more than one thousand in 2016.

A review of the credentials of judges, which required judges to have formal legal education and to have been promoted from base-level courts through merit, saw 110,000 of them qualified to form an elite core. Because of the weak foundation of the judicial system and the disruption of the Cultural Revolution, during the reform period, demobilized soldiers, party/government officials from public security, and the PLA with no formal legal background and inexperienced recent law school graduates were recruited as judges. Poorly paid, they were widely perceived to be inept and corrupt, and resignations were an issue.[300] Efforts, rhetorical or real, have often been expended to address the long-standing issue,[301] and Xi's initiative represented the latest effort to make judges "qualified."[302] Further, a two-year pilot reform to select juries randomly rather than having them chosen through recommendations by local authorities was extended in 2017.[303] More recent rules have attempted to apply the arm's length principle in order to cut the political-legal committees' control over the judiciary to foster more judiciary autonomy and professionalism.

Implementation of such an ambitious and massive undertaking is bound to be a long and uneven process, and extravagant official claims of success cannot be accepted at face value. At one level, a primary goal of judicial reform was to break down the local government-court nexus and to reduce the power of local authorities to resist reforms.[304] But it has been argued that the measures to constrain local interferences with the judiciary may still be insufficient. There were also unexpected outcomes. For instance, evidence suggests that the reforms have not been able to buck the trend of judges resigning because of work pressure, low pay, poor promotional prospects, and the lack of community respect. As well, the quota system to refine the quality of judges has generated resentment by those not selected.

At a broad level, some analysts have distinguished between the "rule of law" and the "rule by law," the former referring to constitutionalism to restrict state power and encroachment on the rights of individuals, putting the emphasis on civil and political rights, an independent judiciary, and the legal profession. The latter assumes that the citizens are objects of law, and that law is a tool of governance rather than a means to restrict state actions. At best, this means governance according to the letter of the law as executed by the judiciary. It follows that since the CCP monopolizes all political power, there is an inherent contradiction in the claim for "law-based governance" and a politicized judiciary. "Rule by law" will always be the defining characteristic of the Chinese judicial system.[305]

At a more practical level, the Party had certain incentives to use law to address grievances and distrust of the party state, and to maintain stability and predictability. The regime needed to use law to further economic development and foreign policy goals, especially with the myriad of legal cases arising from China's hugely expanded foreign relations and initiatives such as the Belt and Road Initiative.[306] One example is the rapid development of the patent and intellectual property protection regime.[307]

In China as in other countries, judicial reforms are contested, and Chinese political culture and public opinion seem to favor heavy penalties and capital punishment and the Party has vowed to build a stronger, more independent, and more professional judiciary to buttress party-cleansing and anticorruption efforts. In 2016, Xi summarized in instrumental terms his goals for judicial reform: he urged the political and legal affairs departments to prevent and contain risks, to safeguard national security and social stability, and to promote social fairness and justice.[308] The reform initiatives under Xi seemed to be adept at problem identification, and the educational value of such practices may prove valuable in raising the awareness of the rule of law. At a minimum, Xi's efforts attempted to remind the Party that it was not above the law, and they reflect an ideal of a kind of rule of law that sees party-state officials operate within the law without challenging party leadership. Chinese society today cannot be compared to the lawlessness of only a few decades ago.

That said, it is natural for dissidents and victims of persecution to assume that all legal reforms were mere lies or window dressing to soothe public concerns over the violations of individual rights.[309] Jerome Cohen, a distinguished scholar on Chinese law, focusing on the suppression of human rights lawyers, argues that the reform spirit died with Xi, and repression reigns in criminal, civil, and political cases.[310] A more optimistic view maintains that Xi was aiming at governance according to the letter of law by encouraging officials and citizens alike to abide by rules and regulations. Xi factored in notions of justice and fairness, while shunning Western notions of judicial review, independence, and the separation of powers. His aim is to create a robust legal system that will effectively govern Chinese political and social life without challenging the Party's core policies. Moreover, Chinese judicial and legal professionals have been developing at a steady pace, and that may bode well for the "rule of law" in future.[311]

As mentioned, developing countries must contend with generally weak institutions that have to be built from the bottom up, and evaluations of China's judicial system vary greatly according to perspectives and expectations. In comparison with well-established legal systems in the West, the Chinese counterpart is still at a low level of development; it works for "run of the mill" cases but is weak in curbing government power or protecting fundamental rights. Further, as observed, the legal system has never been allowed to challenge the Party's monopoly on power and its definition of ideology. Xi's reforms are just another step in the "long march" toward the "rule of law."[312]

10

Economic Revival, Social Development, and the Search for a New Development Model

The Xi-Li Team and Economic Issues

Economic issues under Xi Jinping's leadership shared a great deal of continuity with the Hu-Wen era. But because of rapid changes, some perennial issues took on greater urgency. Growth required reforms and restructuring, altering the political economy and distribution of powers. Despite many zigzags, immediate post-Mao reforms were essentially wrestling with the legacy of the Soviet and Maoist models. These reforms resulted in double-digit growth over almost three decades and turned China into the second largest economy in the world. However, the global financial crisis of 2008, triggered by a massive subprime mortgage default in the United States, obliged Beijing to inject ¥4 trillion (US$600 billion) into the economy to boost employment. The outcome was a massive debt load, mostly sustained by SOEs and local governments, which had boosted the country's debt-to-GDP ratio to 250 percent by 2017. The struggle to repay the debt led to productivity loss, dependence on credit to fuel growth, and fear of a sudden hard landing.[1] Global recovery from this crisis was slow, resulting in decreasing demand for Chinese exports. The new realities exacerbated the structural problems in the Chinese economy.

China's economy grew rapidly in 2013 and 2014, but various factors, such as global insecurity and sagging oil and commodity prices, had reduced demand for Chinese exports and shrunk manufacturing, which was compounded by the bursting of a big stock market bubble in 2015 and 2016. A precipitous drop in the growth rate from decades of double-digit growth to 6.9 percent in 2015, the slowest in twenty-five years, spooked many Chinese and begot all kinds of recriminations, even though the drop had long been anticipated by Chinese officials.[2] Externally, intense competition came not just from manufacturing powers such as the United States, Germany, and Japan, but also from emerging economies such as India, Brazil, and Vietnam. The many uncertainties in Europe, notably the sovereign debt crisis and Brexit, posed a risk of global recession. Complaints about China's alleged unfair trade, closed market, and protectionism persisted. A rising chorus of international protectionism, unilateralism, and nativism intensified, especially with the presidency of Donald Trump. The wrangling had evolved into a trade and a technological war, and even attempts at decoupling. Many factories relocated to Southeast Asia.

The Xi administration felt an urgent need to identify and foster new drivers of economic growth to sustain development and to avert an economic slowdown. Three fundamental aspects were identified. First, it aimed to transform an economy driven by investment to one sustained by consumption, service, and domestic demand; to climb the higher-value chain by shifting from low-cost, low-valued-added production to high-valued-added goods; and to upgrade its manufacturing by reducing energy consumption, material consumption, and industrial pollution.

Second, it aimed to raise efficiency by constantly rejigging government/ market relationships and to transform the functions of the government. It found it necessary to leverage the benefits of market forces to enliven all sectors of the economy, including the private sector. Third, it banked on its technological advances in the profound Fourth Industrial Revolution (4IR), which fuses the digital, physical, and biological worlds, to enhance governance, drive growth, and address social and economic challenges. With tremendous investment in infrastructure, skills, and R & D, China was already a global leader in 4IR technology, such as AI, robotics, and virtual reality by about 2010, and this should help it upgrade and innovate.

Xi oversaw a similar transformation in Zhejiang that maintained stability and boosted economic growth against the forces of social dislocation, albeit at a smaller scale. This might have strengthened Xi's confidence that nationally, goals of economic transformation could be reached. In 2013, Xi called for innovative and sustained growth for both China and the global economy. He declared that growth driven by stimulating policies and "large-scale direct government intervention" could "only treat the symptoms but not the disease," and growth at the cost of high energy consumption and pollution was "even less sustainable."[3] The much-touted market reforms, Xi maintained, were still incomplete since the balance between what he called the visible hand and the invisible hand, that is, between government regulations and market allocation of resources, was still askew. What was needed, he declared, was a relationship whereby the "market can play a decisive role in allocating resources and the government can play its own role more effectively."[4] Since the market was still immature, it was necessary to cut the government's interference in resource allocation and microeconomic activities. As he avowed,

The government should refrain from getting involved in the economic activities the market can regulate effectively, and let the market do what the government is not supposed to do, so that the market can play its role of maximizing

the effectiveness and efficiency of resource allocation, and enterprises and individuals can have more room to develop the economy and create wealth with
vigor and vitality.[5]

In general, Xi was upbeat that the Chinese economy could grow relatively
rapidly, although at a slower and more sustainable rate than before. The focus
of growth should be shifted to quality, efficiency, recycling, and low carbon development, avoiding the simplistic use of GDP growth rate as an indicator of
accomplishment.[6]

All these general principles informed economic policies during Xi's first term.
Henceforth, major landmarks, such as the Third Plenum of November 2013, the
Thirteenth Five-Year Plan (FYP, 2016–2020) in March 2016, and the advancement of the notion of supply-side structural reform, broached in 2016, unleashed
hundreds of reform measures covering every facet of China's political economy.
The Third Plenum (November 9–12, 2013) alone put forth an ambitious program involving sixty areas and 336 specific policy initiatives to deepen reform
and to effect comprehensive changes by 2020. It pledged to promote a more efficient, equal, and sustainable economic development; the rule of law, people's
democracy, and socialist culture; and social reform for social fairness and justice
and ecological progress.[7] Reforms would enhance market forces in the allocating
of resources," strike an appropriate balance between the government and the
market, and reduce excessive government interference. The assumption was that
the government had interfered too much and controlled too many resources. Yet
it had failed to provide adequate public services, ensure fair market competition,
and promote the private sector.

Traditionally, third plenums always deal with economic reforms: Premier
Wen Jiabao had directed the drafting of the key document for the Sixteenth
CC, and Vice Premier Hu Liangyu and Secretary of the Central Office Wang
Huning for the Seventeenth CC, respectively. Breaking with tradition, Xi
took personal charge of the drafting of the key document. Normally twenty to
thirty members were involved in the drafting. This time, however, more than
sixty members were enlisted, including party/government/military officials
and academics from the Chinese Academy of Social Sciences. The expansion
of the drafting arena, the two hundred days devoted to it, and the numerous
consultations and revisions up and down the administration ladder suggest
that strong disagreements over weighty issues were involved. Xi personally
chaired three PBSC and two Politburo meetings to discuss the document, and
afterward Politburo members fanned out across the country to solicit feedback inside and outside of the Party, including that of retired party elders.
The Third Plenum document was still being revised the night before passage
on November 20. According to Zhang Zhuoyuan, a member of the drafting

committee, the most outstanding challenge was how to overcome resistance by vested interests. One subtle but contentious issue, for example, was whether the word "sacred" should be omitted from the draft, which repeated a line from the constitution: "The property rights of the public sector are sacred and inviolable, as are those of the nonpublic sector."[8]

The Fifth Plenum (October 26–29, 2015) finalized the details of the Thirteenth FYP, and its decisions included scrapping the one-child policy in favor of a two-child family and the extension of old-age insurance to China's entire elderly population.[9] In its turn, the government promulgated the FYP in March 2016, formalizing and incorporating previous economic and social reform decisions, and fleshing out the plan with more specific targets and measures.[10] Xi and his team realized that economic reforms were holistic undertakings that involved balancing multiple factors and making trade-offs that affect the entire spectrum of employment, social cohesion, the environment, and the way China is governed.

Eventually, two centenary goals were defined more specifically. It was decided that the economy needed to grow at an average medium-high annual rate of at least 6.5 percent to 7 percent during the Thirteenth FYP period to ensure relatively full employment and to double the size of the economy and per capita income by 2020 from 2010 levels. The hope was that aggregate economic output would exceed ¥90 trillion (US$13.8 trillion) and per capita GDP would be US$10,000 by 2020, or one-third that of the United States. The drivers of growth were designated to be advanced technological innovation, energy efficiency, and productivity, innovation, and efficiency in production. Simultaneously, a multitude of goals to be achieved included progress in urbanization; agricultural modernization; the narrowing of the gap between urban and rural areas and between regions; green development; environmental protection; rising living standards; and rising health standards, with a one-year increase in average life expectancy. In the process, fifty million jobs would be created, thirteen million in 2016 alone.

Overall, these measures, deemed essential for preventing China from falling into the "middle-income trap," were a tall order by any standard. The Xi-Li administration realized that such an upgrade involved tough challenges and painful adjustment. Externally, a global economic downturn, weak trade, and fluctuations in financial and commodity markets had exerted downward pressure on the Chinese economy. Internally, reforms always have to contend with bureaucratic resistance, and battles between promarket (liberal) and progovernment interference forces. The huge subject of economic reforms cannot be detailed here, and in the following I will focus on several key aspects: supply-side restructuring reform, technological advances, Made in China 2025, the Pilot Free Trade Zones, and the new digital economy.

Supply-Side Structural Reform, a New and Evolving Official Line

By November 2015, official discussions of economic reforms culminated in a package of policies labeled "supply-side reform" put forward by the Finance and Economic LSG. This was a new strategic orientation calling for strengthening of supply-side structural reform to boost productivity. According to the official discourse, for more than a decade discussions were centered on domestic consumption and services as the new engine for growth, but it was soon realized that these factors were insufficient to propel growth. On the demand side, the three major drivers of economic growth were investment, exports, and consumption. When the effectiveness of these waned, a new approach was to resort to the supply side of increasing efficiency in production factors such as funding, resources, skilled workers, equipment, and technologies. Productivity could be boosted by improving supply-side competitiveness. This involved the trimming of excess industrial capacity; reduction of inventories and production costs; improvement in the supply of goods and services; reform of the state-owned enterprises; and the energizing of the private sector. Overcapacity was said to have impeded growth and even distorted global markets. The improvement of distribution of goods and services was deemed necessary, particularly considering the huge regional variations in China, where there was oversupply in some areas but undersupply in other areas. For example, despite the proliferation of shopping malls and cinemas in some cities, other cities still did not have any of them.[11]

Officials were keen to distinguish the Chinese notion of "supply-side economics" from the Reagan and Thatcher version, which privileged tax cuts, privatization, and deregulation to boost the supply of goods and services.[12] Xi said that his version of "supply-side structural reform" called for a structural overhaul reducing supply that would bring down debt and promote efficiency, since industrial overcapacity was deemed the Achilles' heel of the Chinese economy. Two factors contributed to debt and overcapacity. First, 2001–2005 was a golden age for the Chinese economy, but the ¥4 trillion stimulus package to cope with the 2008 financial crisis had cast a long shadow. It created jobs and stabilized the economy by investing heavily in infrastructure projects such as highways and railways. China rode out the crisis and stimulated demand for construction materials such as steel and cement. However, this in turn created overcapacity, a real estate bubble, and a huge increase in debt, especially among the localities. Second, local officials, who were promoted by the criterion of GDP growth, competed fiercely to expand manufacturing facilities by offering subsidies, cheap loans, and land, encouraging companies to expand by taking on excess debt. Consequently, the fear was that a combination of economic slowdown, excess production, and rising debt might precipitate a massive wave of bankruptcies and bad loans that could trigger an economic blowout and massive social and political upheaval.[13]

Xi's solution was supply-side reform that would ultimately allow "the market to play a decisive role," ensuring the long-term vitality of the economy. To achieve this, the measures were construed to be tax cuts, regulation simplification, and the forced restructuring or closing of "zombie companies," or debt-ridden SOEs that perpetuated overcapacity. Reforms would reduce ineffective supply, increase effective supply, and align supply more closely with demand. Other components of this strategy consisted of a rapid overhaul of government functions, and reforms in pricing, taxation, finance, and pensions.[14] The specifics included the following. First, since overcapacity was said to be a major obstacle to sustained growth, a policy priority was to cut production and inventory in steel, coal, aluminum, cement, chemicals, refining, and shipbuilding. In view of huge numbers of unsold homes, subdued global demand, and mounting government debt, a strategy was to deleverage and cut costs. In 2016, the targets for cutting steel and coal production by 45 million and 250 million tons were accomplished, but evidence suggested that illegal steel capacity expansion continued, and idle factories quickly resumed production once prices rebounded.[15] Beijing vowed to continue to extend its campaign against overcapacity in other sectors such as glass and shipping.[16] It decided that in 2016 and 2017, it would trim 10 percent of the production capacity for steel and coal, and in 2016 alone, a massive 1.8 million workers were laid off in these bloated industries. To alleviate pain and the prospect of social instability, ¥100 billion (US$15.3 billion) was expended to help these workers to re-establish or relocate.[17]

Second, the reform of the SOEs is a good example of a "superwicked problem." During the Mao years, the centrally commanded economy relied on the SOEs to run everything from banking to transport, and from manufacturing to commerce, employing virtually all urban workers. Unlike Western firms with profit maximization as their raison d'être, the SOEs provided workers with the "iron rice bowl," which meant lifetime employment and a full range of social and welfare benefits. Ran by administrative fiat and unresponsive to market signals, the SOEs were deemed inefficient, overstaffed, and unprofitable. Reforms introduced in the late 1990s by then premier Zhu Rongji had privatized all but the largest SOEs by dismissing 45 million workers (out of a total of 110 million). By 2012, the SOEs had shred most responsibilities such as housing and healthcare for their employees, but they nevertheless still served social functions such as running schools, hospitals, retirement homes, and firefighting.[18] Their importance in the economy is underlined by the fact that as of 2018 they still accounted for one-third to one-half of China's economy. However, under Xi, not all SOEs were drags on the economy, as many have become profitable—they are assets rather than burdens, and their investment capacity is needed for high-tech development.[19] Of the 104 central SOEs and 43,000 at various administrative levels, some dealt in strategic industries such as banking and telecommunications. Others have become the world's largest companies in their fields with many global subsidiaries. Therefore, instead of treating all SOEs uniformly, Beijing's policy starting from 2016 was to encourage bigger and competitive SOEs to streamline themselves into efficient national champions in the global markets rather than just cash cows for cadres. This informed Xi's maxim of "stronger, better, and bigger, without any reservations."[20]

SOEs producing public goods and services were enticed to incorporate market rules to control costs and to increase production quality. Zombie companies in the saturated industrial sectors, on the other hand, would be subject to merger, upgrading, privatization, employee-shareholding, and bankruptcy. Government subsidies to the SOEs would be rechanneled toward profitable manufacturing. Keenly aware that the SOE reform would be a painful process that carried social costs, the Xi administration cautioned that it should be carried out "proactively but prudently." Specifically, the Third Plenum ordered the SOEs to tighten financial discipline and pay higher dividends to the state, at rates from 5 to 15 percent immediately, up to 30 percent by 2020. It also pushed for interest-rate liberalization and new online investment vehicles, and pressured state-owned banks to liberalize interest rates. The restructuring of 345 zombie enterprises was scheduled to be completed in 2019.[21]

Third, the streamlining of administration would deregulate prices for goods and services in competitive sectors, abolish more *shenpi*, improve delivery of government services, and decentralize more powers and responsibilities to local governments. It would also redefine and more specifically demarcate power and expenditure responsibilities between the central and local governments. Some tax income would be devolved to local authorities, who were also allowed to secure financing through bond issuance to address nagging problems of local indebtedness. A ¥10 trillion (US$152 billion) pool of local government bonds was created for future market development."[22] To encourage foreign investment and technology, the government planned to liberalize education, construction, design, accounting, and auditing. It would introduce modern property rights for investors to protect their investments, a unified foreign and domestic investment system to govern all legally established companies under the same laws and regulations, commit to a free-floating renminbi, and reduce capital controls by 2020.

Fourth, the government pledged greater support for the private sector to stimulate investment and innovation by removing red tape, regulations, and hidden barriers; tax burdens; and restrictions on entry to markets such as electricity, telecommunications, finance, and transport, affording private enterprises equal treatment with SOEs in project approvals, financing, and land availability. Proactively, the government would encourage private capital to invest in state-dominated sectors such as banking, insurance, and internet finance; reform the regulatory environment, allowing a bigger role for the nonstate sector; and draw up a negative list for market access so that any businesses not included on the list would be allowed private investment.

Fifth, the supply-side reform was designed to dovetail with reforms in other areas such as pollution control, family planning, and the *hukou* system. In 2015 China declared a "war" on pollution, as choking smog, contaminated water, and solid waste had persistently stroked public anger. As the world's factory churning out manufacturing products (including 90 percent of the world's electronics and personal computers and 70 percent of its cell phones) China had shouldered the outsourced industrial pollution. For decades, China had accepted garbage from the West that included plastic and e-waste presumably for recycling, and this practice was not halted until 2018. In 2015 Xi and Obama found sufficient common ground to agree on the Paris Agreement on climate change, which was signed by all two hundred countries, pledging to keep global temperature increases "well below" 2°C and to pursue efforts to limit it to 1.5°C above preindustrial levels. This represented a major advance beyond the earlier Copenhagen meeting, when China and other nations refused an agreement. Still, the Paris Agreement allows nations to formulate their own plans, and target compliance is voluntary.[23] In contrast, however, the Thirteenth FYP contains several mandatory targets, which include an increase of nonfossil fuel use to 15 percent of total, the reduction of energy consumption by15 percent, and the cutting of PM2.5 levels by 18 percent. Other target cuts included water consumption, energy consumption, and carbon dioxide emissions per unit of GDP by 23 percent, 15 percent, and 18 percent, respectively. Carbon-trading platforms and a green tax were also included. Beijing also hoped that the two-child policy would add two million more children and increase consumption by ¥70 billion (US$10.64 billion). The abolition of the *hukou* system was expected to boost urbanization and increase supply by adding one hundred million to the urban areas. Similarly, the experiment with rural land-use rights promised the use of rural land for market dividend.[24]

Finally, China's new international initiatives, such as the Belt and Road Initiative to boost economic integration, investment and trade, and cultural exchanges across continents were expected to be an integral part of the supply-side reform. We will return to this later.

Official accounts of achievements since the Third Plenum were mixed. One 2014 source said that implementation of thirty-one of the sixty tasks detailed by the Third Plenum had begun, although the progress was slow.[25] On the last day of 2015, Xi Jinping told the CPPCC that the LSG on Deepening Reform had "basically" completed 101 key reform tasks. Other sources claimed that five private banks were formed; liberalization of interest rates had begun; and the upper limits on interest rates for savings held over one year had already been liberalized. In price reform, prices had been decentralized for 80 percent of those commodities still determined by the government. A breakthrough in business license reform separated business licenses from administrative permits. Companies might begin operation immediately after receiving business licenses, and in cases where *shenpi* was still required, companies were allowed to begin operation while waiting. Such simplification was said to have accelerated the registration of private companies.[26] Finally, the biggest tax overhaul in more than two decades created value-added taxes in construction, property, finance, and consumer services to replace revenue-based levies. This cut taxes by ¥320 billion in 2014 and the projected cut for 2016 was another ¥500 billion (US$77 billion). Such a tax cut was intended to encourage factories to upgrade and innovate, and benefit the service sector, which in 2015 made up half of the GDP for the first time.[27]

However, unsurprisingly, many departments and localities resisted the central policies and stalled implementation or pursued only those that were favorable to them. They resorted to the whole range of bureaucratic repertoire to protect their vested interests. For instance, the *yangqi* (央企, or enterprises directed by the central government) and the local governments resisted SOE restructuring and defied the transfer of profits, dismissing the policy as too ambitious. Central guidelines prescribed that, by 2020, the SOEs should transfer 30 percent of their profits upward, but at the beginning of 2014, only Beijing, Hunan, Anhui, and Ningxia had made plans to implement the measure. Most other provinces were equivocal, agreeing to raise transfers only gradually. Some provinces ignored SOE reforms altogether.[28]

Similarly, Beijing's plan to restructure the SOEs by "mixed ownership companies" by merger and privatization were opposed by some ministries and commissions, which cited the danger of stripping of state-owned assets. The Third Plenum specified that monopolies should be gradually opened up, but progress was slow. For instance, in 2015, Sinopec claimed a breakthrough in that it had restructured by allowing twenty-five domestic and foreign investors to hold 30 percent of its equity, but that was an exaggeration.[29] One nagging issue was how party committees could strengthen without interfering with boards of directors. The Third Plenum proposed SOE reform, but it took another twenty-two months before the State Council readied a resolution, which delayed the original goal of achieving a mixed system of ownership by 2020, saying that it should not be subjected to "a fixed timetable."[30]

Local governments and banks whose interests were closely aligned with the "zombie enterprises" were reluctant to close them down. Relying on these SOEs for revenue, employment, and personal interests, they feared the impact of SOE closing on the economy and social stability. Others resisted passively. For instance, a new State Council order demanded the merger of the "three insurances"—urban worker's basic medical insurance, urban resident's basic medical insurance, and rural cooperative healthcare, by June 2013, but by 2015, only a few places such as Shandong had started the process. Other localities simply refused to comply.[31]

On the reduction of steel and coal overcapacity, many money-losing SOEs invented ingenious means to stall restructuring or prevent closure. Unwilling to cut production, they relied on borrowing and cooked financial data to stay afloat. In one case, one iron and steel company claimed a profit of ¥20 billion even though this was accomplished by selling its assets. Another such SOE claimed a profit of ¥50 million, although it had lost over ¥1 billion.[32] All this prompted the State Council to send ten roving teams to the provinces and municipalities to enforce overcapacity reduction.[33]

Resistance also hindered the progress in the reform of property taxes even though that could provide a stable source of finance for local authorities. Inspections showed that regional officials often owned two or three residences, and they therefore argued that property tax should be levied only on the fourth. Consequently, registration of real estate was much delayed.[34] In terms of *shenpi*, since 2012, the State Council had abolished six hundred items, but by 2015, none were actually reduced at the provincial level, where the authorities claimed ignorance of central policies.[35] An irony occurred in Hebei, a major steel producer and a highly polluted province. Hebei officials were threatened with dismissal if new steel mills or closed factories were reopened.[36] Yet Hebei city Baoding, which was seriously polluted, housed hundreds of companies producing solar panels and wind turbines for the domestic and foreign markets.[37]

By 2015, there was a realization that multiple and formidable challenges confronted the implementing of the 336 measures, but that the main obstacles to economic reform had nothing to do with economics and everything to do with "the government, the ruling party," and political reform.[38]

Supply-Side Structural Reform, Implementation Issues and Xi Jinping's Intervention

Meanwhile, various factors in 2015, such as the sagging prices of oil and commodities, reduced demands for Chinese exports, and a contracting manufacturing sector, all conspired to slow economic growth in China. Then a stock market crash was botched by the government. All this strengthened the case of powerful vested interests and exacerbated theoretical differences, while debt-fueled growth showed signs of making a comeback. Fearing a decline in economic growth, even the government seemed to have missed Xi's reform message and resisted the abandonment of fiscal and monetary stimulus, flooding the economy with credit, especially in the first quarter of 2016. The Central Bank reopened the credit taps, hoping to resume borrowing-boosted growth that might have bene-fited the SOEs but delayed long-term restructuring.

In response, Xi repeatedly warned the ministries and local governments. In a speech made in January 2016, he reiterated the determination to push through long-term reforms even at the expense of lower short-term growth. He insisted the ministries and local governments not repeat their mistakes of being lured into projects, investments, and financial ventures simply for the sake of quick money.[39] Apparently, Xi was miffed that in the first quarter of 2016 alone, the Chinese government had unleashed ¥4.6 trillion (US$697 billion) in bank credit, exceeding even the stimulus package of 2009.[40] Such a huge bailout might have compensated for sagging private investment, boosted the stock market, and created a property boom, but it also exacerbated the issues of capital outflows, nonperforming loans, debt, and pollution, or the same structural challenges the leadership had been attempting to correct.[41]

In May, an anonymous *RMRB* article by an "authoritative person," presented in a question-and-answer format, blasted those in the government who had tried to stimulate growth by debt and at the expense of reform. Dashing expectations, the "authoritative person" warned that future economic growth would be L-shaped, leveling off with no rebounds and would last for a long time, not just one or two years. This "authoritative person" lauded that some central ministries, provinces, and SOEs had kept the ball rolling with fact-findings and measures. It named provinces such as Guangdong, Chongqing, Jiangsu, Zhejiang, and Shanxi with approval, but insinuated that other units were laggards. The Thirteenth Finance and Economic LSG meeting of May 2016 also complained that in various places things were essentially stalled.[42]

Xi's comments reflected personal frustration with the situation.[43] A meeting of the CDRLSG in June 2016 declared that reforms were a "revolution" that attacked the beneficiaries of the existing system, and could not be accomplished without draconian measures and pain.[44] On June 28, the Politburo passed a reg-ulation on official accountability ordering the local party committees to take charge or else face sanctions.[45]

Speculation was rife regarding the identity of this "authoritative person." Essentially it could be Xi, his team, or a group led by Xi's right-hand eco-nomic adviser, Liu He. The warning criticizing the heavy reliance on credit to drive growth has been interpreted as Xi's rebuke of Premier Li, fueling the per-sistent rumor that Li pushed for short-term stimulus to sustain a high growth rate, and predictions that he would be replaced in 2017.[46] Others claimed that the CDRLSG had sidelined Premier Li and that Xi had seized complete control.

Other analysts interpreted this to mean a split between the north and the south, or the government bureaucracy and the Party (the central government compound is located in the north part of Zhongnanhai, whereas the party compound is located in the south) so that Xi then had to resort to steamroller tactics to force the Party to embrace his slogan-cum-policy. A more plausible view is that the rebuke was directed at officials and interest groups further down the hierarchy,[47] given Li's pronouncements supporting the various elements of Xi's "supply-side structural reform."[48]

In addition, dissenting views were articulated by nine prominent economists, contradicting the views of the "authoritative person." Although different in their emphasis, the nine were united in dissenting with the official view, which they derided as a form of neoliberalism that, they argued, had created harmful effects as applied to Latin America, Eastern Europe, and Europe. They argued that the economic downturn was due to cyclical and external factors, and to deal with a downward pressure on the economy, a more appropriate policy choice was government interference with a macroeconomic policy and not contraction. To lead China out of the vicious circle while at the same time resolving the overcapacity and debt problem required, they claimed, more superstructure investment. Some among these economists argued that government contraction itself was the cause of shrinkage of demand. Others contested Xi's view on L-shape development as either too pessimistic or too optimistic.[49]

Technological Advances

A more upbeat situation occurred in the technological field.[50] In just a few years under Xi, technology in China had advanced in leaps and bounds by leveraging the various aspects of the 4IR, AI, 5G, nanotechnology, biotechnology, robotics, the internet of things, and quantum computing. Significant advances had also been made in biotech and green energy. More practical applications included face recognition, smart city management, drones, and mobile payment. In many respects China had become a global technology leader, despite concerns about the obstacles for development and the alleged inability of the Chinese system to innovate and compete. The new technologies spawned new products and business models upgrading traditional industries. Chinese companies were going global.

By 2018, R & D expenditures reached ¥1.96 trillion (US$275 billion), capping three years of continuous rise and overtaking those of Europe. Private businesses contributed to this sum, with the rest by the government.[51] In the same year China's 4.19 million people working in R & D continued to be the world's largest for the sixth year. China also ranked first in the world for patent applications for eight consecutive years, and second in terms of the number of science essays and

their citation frequency. Not necessarily a reliable indicator of high-quality innovation or prediction of market transformation, these figures show China as the
undisputed world leader in intellectual property filings. As Beijing transformed
from being a net importer of ideas to a net innovator, the incentive to protect intellectual property became stronger.[52] Elsewhere, there were breakthroughs in
fields such as quantum sciences and lunar exploration engineering.[53] In the same
year, more than fifty technology, media, and telecommunications companies, including Xiaomi and China Tower Company, launched IPOs with a combined
market capitalizations of over US$200 billion.

As well, in 2018, China started 5G trials in more than a dozen cities to be ready
for 2019 commercial applications,[54] and harbingers of 5G can reap disproportionate advantage in economic activity and job growth. Similarly, breakthroughs
in AI can exert enormous impact on competitiveness, economic development,
and the nature of work. Investment in AI totaled US$7.4 billion, or 60 percent
of global total, and private tech giants Baidu, Alibaba, and Tencent (collectively
known as BAT) heavily invested in AI, including areas previously dominated by
US companies. A 2017 State Council plan aimed to turn China into an AI leader
by 2030.

The remarkable advances are an outcome of government/business initiatives
and cooperation. Xi's government prioritized innovation-driven development
and continuously pushed for reforms in its scientific and technological system.
The government actively supported innovation and investment in human capital,
infrastructure, transport, logistics, and education (such as nine-year compulsory
education). In turn, private companies such as BAT had been innovative and responsive, helped by the protectionist measure of banning Google, Facebook, and
Twitter. Of the twenty largest internet companies in the world, nine are based in
China, ten in the United States, and one in Canada. All this is facilitated by the
huge economies of scale of a China market of over one billion customers. China
boasts eight hundred million internet users, most of whom own smartphones,
in addition to 282 million digital natives (users below twenty-five years of age).

State involvement included such state-led policies as Made In China 2025 and
the New Generation of Artificial Intelligence Development Plan. To popularize
the digital economy, the government in 2018 ordered the three big state-owned
telecom companies, China Telecom, China Unicom, and China Mobile, to slash
the cost of mobile data by 30 percent to make exchanges more affordable for the
general public. Similarly, a 2017 State Council plan aimed to turn China into
a global AI leader by 2030 pumped funds into research. It anticipated that AI
would support everything from agriculture and medicine to manufacturing, and
from security surveillance to weapons engineering.[55]

All this created new momentum and drivers for economic development. The
vast amount of data gathered gave China an edge on the tech race, supercharging

China's ability in fintech and AI. New technologies added tremendously to virtually all aspects of Chinese life, from improving energy efficiency and health standards to the combating of pollution, from fighting crime and terrorism to the mitigation of social issues. China was moving up the value chain.

Yet there is also a downside and challenges. For instance, internet penetration rates in China were only 60 percent, compared with 89 percent in the United States. Often, government officials cautioned that few breakthroughs had been achieved. For individuals, high-tech innovations may translate into more large-scale surveillance and erosion of privacy. For the government, large spending may ultimately lead to excessive capacity, duplication, and waste. Internationally, Chinese technological advances have shifted global economic and military power and invited pushbacks and counterbalances. These are reminiscent of the "Japan bashing" of the 1980s, when Japanese economic power grew with its technological advances in electronics, automobiles, and superconductors.[56] Meanwhile, Beijing's Made in China 2025 stirred international controversy.

Made in China 2025 Ten-Year Plan

MIC is a state-led industry policy to promote growth by upgrading Chinese manufacturing and high-tech industries and to lessen dependence on technical imports. Responding to Xi's "innovation-driven development" and "indigenous innovation," four central ministries, including the Ministry of Industry and Information Technology, devised MIC under Premier Li, and it was rolled out by the State Council in May 2015. Xi's government recognized that for China to maintain competitiveness, it was unsustainable for China to remain the world's shop floor, producing low-cost, low-value-added, and labor-intensive goods. The imperative was to move up the manufacturing value chain and to lessen reliance on a low-cost strategy and imported components. Otherwise, the alternative was stagnancy and even decline, falling living standards, unemployment, and perpetuation of rampant pollution, to name a few important consequences.[57]

China's heavy technology dependence on imports, especially from the United States, is a major bottleneck. For instance, up to 2018 the country could produce supercomputer chips of fourteen nanometers, whereas the more advanced electronic equipment and telecommunication networks require seven-nanometer chips. The know-how of producing the latter requires decades of experience, and Beijing is not expected to acquire the expertise until 2023 at the earliest. Meanwhile, it consumed about 41 percent of the world's total in semiconductors, but manufactured only 30 percent of the chips it needed.[58] Reliance on other foreign high-tech goods was more than 50 percent and in some respects, and total dependence in others, such as high-level digital control systems and high-level hydraulic components. Even the most advanced factories relied on labor-intensive assembly lines.[59] In 2018, China' biggest import value was US$320 billion worth of semiconductors, exceeding its import value of US$240 billion for crude oil. There were also other bottlenecks in high-tech research and critical component development. Fear of vulnerabilities was amply realized when the telecom giant ZTE was crippled by the US ban on its products.[60]

Partially inspired by a precedent in Germany's "Industry 4.0" initiative, MIC highlights information technology and advanced robotics to apply to sectors such as aerospace, ocean and railway equipment, energy-saving vehicles, medicine, and agricultural machinery. More specific sectors included electric cars, next-generation IT and telecommunication, and AI. MIC set targets to raise domestic content in core technologies to 40 percent by 2020 and 70 percent by 2025, achieving self-sufficiency by 2049. The Ministry of Industry, Information, and Technology would invest ¥300 billion (US$45 billion) for this purpose during 2016–2020.[61] Forty national and forty-eight provincial innovation centers would be created to develop technology for smart manufacturing and equipment. If successful, China would become self-sufficient in core technologies and catch up and surpass global technological powers. It would become a major if not dominant technical powerhouse and manufacturing power more capable of challenging US dominance.

Beijing's announcement of MIC immediately provoked intense international hostility and pushbacks. Exporters of high-tech products in the United States and Europe were deeply suspicious of Chinese ambition. The MIC plan exacerbated complaints such as discrimination against foreign investment, forced technological transfers, intellectual property thefts, and cyberespionage. In economics, critics claimed that Chinese self-sufficiency would distort global markets, hurt foreign companies, and devastate exporters such as South Korea, Germany, and Taiwan. Government subsidies would enhance unfair practices and lead to overproduction and dumping of cheap products. The exclusion of foreign participation in the Chinese market amounted to a kind of high-tech mercantilism. In strategic and security aspects, critics feared that MIC was China's bid for technical dominance to seize advanced technology such as semiconductors. They claimed that SOE development on facial recognition software, 3D printers, and virtual reality systems threatened Western security. Others feared that China could control entire supply chains in raw materials such as cobalt, indispensable for most modern electronics. A White House report alleged that MIC was an existential threat not only for "the U.S. economy but also the global innovation system as a whole."[62]

Beijing defended itself by pointing out that it was still a developing country in terms of a GDP per capita of about US$8,000 compared with the US figure of US$56,000. It needed development and had a long way to catch up with the developed world. By adopting measures such as MIC it was just following the well-trodden path of developed countries. Yet, facing tremendous pressure from the United States and EU trading partners, the Chinese government toned down its rhetoric, as Premier Li failed to mention MIC in his government report of 2018. Government officials since then have downplayed the MIC goals as aspirational rather than real, although the incentive was to push ahead. In any case, like most Chinese industrial policy, MIC was neither consistent nor comprehensive. Another reality is that there are no short-cuts to technology developments, and self-sufficiency in every part of the manufacturing process is unrealistic. In any event, the MIC storm exemplified a classic case of the "security dilemma" as discussed in chapter 1. For China's competitors, it is always important to maintain an edge, to curb, and to hedge. It is prudent to do more than necessary in the hedging, and there is no happy medium. Factor in the ideological and systemic differences between China and the West, the potential for competition and rivalry tends to be great. We will return to this in the section on China's foreign relations.

Pilot Free Trade Zones

Another plank of the Xi administration's efforts to fashion a new development model was the Pilot Free Trade Zones (PFTZs). Much like the SEZs Xi worked on in the 1980s, the PFTZs were experiments with further reform, opening up, and free-market forces. These zones promised trade and investment liberalization by removing restrictions on foreign capital, technology, personnel, and commodity production. There would be gradual abolishment of tariffs and nontariff barriers, as well as the opening up of formally restricted service sectors such as finance, commerce, culture, entertainment, education, and healthcare. Other measures included tax and foreign exchange incentives, import duty exemptions, and reductions of government red tape.

The multiple purposes and goals set for the PFTZs were to attract foreign investment, advance technology, and managerial expertise by expanding trade, export, and entrepôt trade. The PFTZs would be sites for experiments in the transformation of government functions, decentralization, and institutional innovations. To leverage the tremendous diversity of China and regional comparative advantage, the regional zones were located geographically near ports, transportation hubs, and border areas to perform different functions. By opening markets and developing new investment opportunities, these zones were expected to complement the massive Belt and Road Initiative. Eventually the zones could help boost Chinese income, consumption, and employment. A corollary effect was to address persistent complaints about China's closed market, unfair trade, and red tape.

The first PFTZ was formed in Shanghai in 2013, followed quickly by eleven more in Guangdong, Fujian, Shaanxi, Sichuan, Shanghai, Tianjin, Liaoning, Zhejiang, Henan, Hubei, Chongqing, Heilongjiang, Hebei, Shandong, Jiangsu, Guanxi, Yunnan, and the entire Hainan Island. Initially, the plan was that foreign yuan accounts opened in the PFTZs would be used for payments and exchange free of domestic restrictions. Yet, as with all bold initiatives, the initial optimism has been marred by skepticism and concerns by Chinese and foreigners. Critics fear that the PFTZs may reduce tax revenues for the local governments or provide them with pretexts for creating vanity projects. One major setback came with the stock market turmoil of 2015/2016, when Beijing had to impose tight controls to stem capital flights and to stabilize the yuan. By March 2018, the escalating trade tensions with Washington made matters worse.[63] Individual reports have claimed investor withdrawals and a proliferation of zombie accounts. Others report that the PFTZs were near collapse or not living up to the hype.

Counsels for careful rethinking came from all directions. Some suggested that the zones require more central and local coordination. Others suggested that instead of fenced-off areas with preferential policies, Beijing should open up entire sectors nationally. Overall, reports on the outcomes were conflicting. Official figures claimed that in the first half of 2019, the twelve PFTZs had attracted US$10 billion, accounting for 14 percent of the country's total.[64] The Shanghai PFTZ in 2019 doubled in size and had become home to fifty thousand companies, about half foreign and half domestic.[65] It continued to liberalize, attracting high-tech industries, which included Tesla's first overseas factory. And despite the mixed outcomes, Beijing decided to push ahead and in August 2019 approved six more PFTZs, each tasked with special functions. For instance, the PFTZ at Shandong was tasked with overseeing the marine industries and cooperation with Japan and South Korea; the Jiangsu PFTZ with cooperating with the Yangtze River economic regions; the Heilongjiang PFTZ with cooperating with Russia and revitalizing the Northeast; the Hebei PFTZ with coordinating the Beijing, Tianjin, and Hebei region; the Yunnan PFTZ trade corridor with connecting with South and Southeast Asia; and the Guangxi PFTZ with the land sea trade corridor with ASEAN countries. Future projections include the integration with the Greater Bay Area, which incorporates Hong Kong, Macau, Guangzhou, Shenzhen, and various other south China cities into an integrated economic and business hub.

It is too early to give a definitive evaluation of the PFTZs and whether they will eventually replicate previous successes such as the Shenzhen SEZ and the Pudong financial hub in Shanghai. Observers who favor a big-bang liberalization find the experiment timid and contradictory. Others have already dismissed them as failures. Beijing implements reforms at its own pace and extent by taking a cautious, incrementalist and experimental stance. It responds to various domestic constituencies and occasionally to diverse foreign interests and demands. The pilot plan is immense with huge local variations, and it was certain that some zones would do better than others. It is conceivable that these zones may be energized by China's twenty or so free trade areas encompassing thirty-two countries or regions, including South Korea, Australia, Taiwan, and Singapore, and the most important of which are the ones with Hong Kong and Macau. The negotiation of Regional Comprehensive Economic Partnerships (RCEP), which began in 2012, came to fruition when fifteen nations (ASEAN and China, Japan, South Korea, Australia, and New Zealand) approved it in 2020. China was the driving force for this free trade agreement, which has succeeded despite a climate of protectionism and populism and a pullout by India. And although RCEP is less comprehensive than the Trans-Pacific Partnership and the United States–Mexico-Canada Agreement in matters such as e-commerce, labor, and environment protection, it nevertheless signifies the imperative and willingness for regional economic cooperation. RCEP is the world's largest trade bloc, with 45 percent of its population and represents one-third of global GDP. The US pullout of the TPP means that it is now excluded from both the RCEP and the Comprehensive and Progressive Agreement for Trans-Pacific Partnership.[66]

The New Digital Economy, E-commerce, and E-banking

Xi's first term also witnessed the unexpected and rapid rise of the digital economy, which quickly evolved into a new driver of the Chinese economy. Xi's government realized the power of the internet, big data, and cloud computing, and their potential to stimulate growth and domestic consumption and manage debt. Automation also promised to raise production efficiency and quality. Hopes were raised that the digital economy could offset the decline of traditional sectors such as steel and aluminum. In contrast with capital and labor, digitalization was a new factor of production, capable of boosting production growth and efficiency.

The new digital economy was driven by the exponential growth of cash-rich, competitive, and innovative internet giants such as BAT. Baidu, China's largest search engine, whose revenue source is advertising, invests in future technologies such as self-driving cars. Alibaba, a huge conglomerate, focused on cloud computing, e-commerce business, online retail, as well as digital entertainment and payment. Tencent, the world's largest gaming company by revenue, owned instant messaging and the social media app WeChat (used by 1 billion users). Collectively these giants owned millions of small companies, and they have created more than thirty million jobs over the past decade.

Among the many government measures to promote the digital economy was the 2015 Internet + Action plan to encourage internet companies to integrate with the economy. Helped by the continuous rise in R & D investment, the tech boom had taken off in just a few years. The value of the digital economy rose rapidly from 15 percent to 35 percent of GDP from 2008 to 2018, when it was worth US$4.3 trillion.[67] The rate of digitization was especially high in e-commerce and fintech, especially in coastal regions. China was emerging as a leading global investor. The booming digital economy created new institutions and a new business and consumer culture, providing a wide range of technology products and services such as sharing. Notable advances, including 5G technology introduced in 2019, AI, big data, and other technologies, will likely continually revolutionize the digital economy.

However, no matter the various definitions of the extent of digitalization, China has been consistently placed in the middle range globally. R & D investment of 2.19 percent of its GDP also places China behind the OECD average of 2.37 percent. However, China led in some respects: e-commerce consists of 40 percent of global transactions, whereas fintech occupies 70 percent of total global valuations.[68] By 2018, online retail surpassed the United States, with US$1.253 trillion in volume.

E-commerce, too, was fast becoming a key new engine of economic growth, transforming retail, wholesale, finance, and manufacturing services. Online retail, in particular, was tremendously innovative. Essentially, China had effected a mobile payment revolution, an all-in-one platform encompassing social messaging, mobile payments, and in-app programs. Digital payment accompanied the use of robot and drone delivery, especially in rural areas.[69]

For businesses, e-commerce technology created a new business environment that lowered entry barriers, transaction costs, and information asymmetry. It encouraged small businesses and new entrants to participate in online markets and gain instant access to a large pool of consumers. To open a business, one needed only to set up an account and a phone-scannable QR code. Taobao Marketplace facilitated consumer-to-consumer retail by providing a platform for small businesses and individual entrepreneurs to open online stores. Various social credit scores later evolved into a social credit system (more later) that evaluated individuals and businesses, providing a much-needed sense of security and trust, plus a healthy business environment. For rural areas and hence the poor, the rapid e-commerce development had special implications. It facilitated the marketing and selling of agricultural products and local specialties and integrated rural areas into a national market. Returned migrants with expertise often took to e-commerce. All this fostered an entrepreneurial spirit, encouraging the exploration of niche markets such as local agricultural products and e-tailors to meet consumer demands. Even rural residents had incentives to become entrepreneurs.[70]

For consumers, the e-commerce boom meant more convenience and variety and the formation of a new consumer culture with more public knowledge, economic benefits, convenience, and variety. Consumers, especially the young, no longer needed cash or wallets, and China bypassed the credit card generation in its march toward the cashless society.

The rapid growth of e-commerce can be attributed to a convergence between large and small businesses. At the top, an oligarch of internet giants such as Alibaba and JD provided e-commerce platforms and payment infrastructure. Tencent's WeChat Pay (with a whopping nine hundred million users) and Alibaba's Alipay mobile payment apps dominated the scene. At the bottom, there was a boon for small producers and businesses. Millions of small firms operating with low profit margins competed fiercely, but despite the eliminations, there was rapid aggregate growth. This market was especially attractive to the young.[71]

By 2018 total e-commerce trade had reached ¥32 trillion (US$5 trillion), or 40 percent of the world total. Cashless payments through the country's 1.3 billion mobile phones had become ubiquitous in markets, restaurants, shopping malls, even among street vendors and performers, temple donations, and panhandlers.[72] The facial recognition technology, which dispensed with mobile phones and passwords, was common in supermarkets, immigration processes, other exchanges, and monitoring student attendance. Overall, e-commerce contributed to 5 percent of total employment.[73]

Under Alibaba's auspices, the development of clusters of e-commerce villages was rapid. The villages with e-commerce sales reaching ¥10 million (US$1.5 million) were dubbed "Taobao villages." In 2013, Alibaba had only 20 Taobao villages, but their numbers by 2018 had risen to 3,202 and to 4,310 in 2019. Online shops surged by tenfold to six hundred thousand in 2018. There were even Taobao towns, defined as towns that contain three Taobao villages.

The upshot of e-commerce development was job creation, higher household consumption, and enrichment of the poor. Living standards and employment at Taobao villages noticeably improved. E-commerce showed an impact in poverty reduction and in benefiting vulnerable groups such as women and youth with limited job opportunities. From an economic and social standpoint, many regarded it as a virtuous circle.[74]

In the matter of e-banking, technology facilitated the processing of vast amounts of information to boost small business lending. Online banking and lending saw explosive growth.[75] Armed with metadata and AI on payment systems, social media, and other sources collected by the internet behemoths, mobile banks operated by these same titans could instantly check creditworthiness and make loan decisions, with a minuscule default rate at 1 percent and operating cost of a few yuan per loan. All lenders had to do was a few taps on a smartphone.

The services provided by Alibaba's MyBank, Tencent, and Ping An eased a bottleneck for China's small businesses, which traditionally found it difficult to obtain loans from state banks, which favor SOEs. These small businesses had been disproportionately squeezed by economic downturns and government crackdowns on shadow banking. China's small businesses employ 80 percent of its workers and account for 60 percent of China's GDP and 50 percent of tax revenue,[76] and readily available credit mitigated a "wicked problem."

Founded in 2015, MyBank had lent ¥2 trillion (US$290 billion) to sixteen million small companies.[77] MyBank introduced the lending procedure 3-1-0 (three minutes for lenders to input an application, one second for AI to decide whether to grant the loans, and zero staff requirements), and its mobile bank units extended to rural areas.[78] The tremendous success of e-banking even forced state banks to compete. Yet despite the great advances, even in 2018, about two-thirds of China's eighty million small businesses lacked access to loans, and therefore there was a huge space for e-banking to grow.

The advantages of digitization and e-commerce were obvious, but there was also a downside. First was the fear of the loss of jobs. One estimate pointed out that 77 percent of employment in China was susceptible to automation job loss. Most vulnerable were industry jobs that employed low-skilled workers. Others predicted labor market polarization—rising wages and employment for high- and low-skilled labor at the expense of those in the middle. Second, fintech created many challenges for regulators and supervisions and might precipitate financial instability. The readily available online loans might spawn financial risks, large household debts, and crises. Third, there was the natural concern over privacy, data security, and government surveillance, and we will discuss this later.

Overall, the negative impact of these technological advances was likely to be neutralized in the economic realm. The Chinese government was well placed to shift the economy toward the service sector and to create millions of jobs. On the other hand, digitalization in China was still lagging other developed countries in many respects. In 2018, China ranked 34th among 193 countries in terms of availability of online sources and 65th in the overall E Government Development Index, and therefore there was still room for improvement.[79] China's robot intensity in the industrial sector was only 5 percent, compared with 18 percent in the United States and 60 percent in S. Korea. Only 10 percent of businesses had patented technology within China, compared with 39 percent in the United States, and that means China must improve technological innovation.[80]

Much can be done by the government to maximize the benefits and to minimize the drawbacks of e-commerce by strengthening regulations over oligopoly and protecting personal privacy and consumers. It can (a) improve social safety nets and strengthen retraining; (b) harness digitization to enhance government efficiency; (c) continue to promote infrastructural development such as ICT education, especially in rural areas, and (d) contribute globally to standards in cybersecurity, digital standards, and governance. Growth normally slows down when countries attain middle-class income, but China's burgeoning new middle class provides an enormous source of customers for digital and internet services. Even with the aging population, China still possesses a vast market where tech start-ups can bloom.

The Economy during Xi's First Term

Overall, the ongoing reform measures adopted at the Third Plenum and in the Thirteenth FYP pressed many of the right buttons,[81] but long-term implementation has been a major issue. Xi faced formidable, entrenched resistance and had to devote a great deal of energy to neutralizing opposition to reforms. In terms of debates, liberal economists tended to argue for more market-opening policies, less government intervention, and bold reform of the SOEs. More statist views argued for the dirigisme role for the government and subsidies to strategic industries. Foreign interests, too, continue to exert pressure on the Chinese government to change. Similarly, foreign evaluations of economic reform under Xi vary widely depending on perspectives and methods, but generally they can be subsumed under two schools. According to the first school, there are paradoxes in using a Leninist system to drive free-market reform and to promote economic freedom. Xi's obsession with strict party-state control conflicted with his desire to shrink government and to weaken the SOEs. Similarly, the obsession with "stability" impeded both free-market reform and the reduction of the political allocation of capital. Referring to a popular catchphrase, "State enterprises advanced and the private sector retreated," adherents of this school alleged that the inefficient state sector continued to dominate at the expense of the competitive and vibrant private sector, and this would presage periodic recessions.[82] One NGO that monitors Third Plenum goals in terms of ten categories claims that backsliding, timidity, and stagnancy, especially in SOE reform, were the norm.[83]

According to the second school, a competent albeit authoritarian leadership has managed to mobilize economic and social resources to impose order, structural change, and unity of purpose. The Chinese market is still distorted and wasteful, but strong market forces are at play, aided by the robust private enterprises. The boundaries between SOEs and private enterprises continue to blur with "mixed ownership," and they draw capital from one another in a mutually beneficial fashion.[84] Additionally, a 2017 OECD report on the structural reform of G20 countries generally gave high marks to Chinese reforms under

Xi. The report noted that Beijing had high per capita income growth, labor productivity, investment, and spending in education and R & D. Inequality, measured by the Gini index, had decreased since 2007, and the rural and urban gap had narrowed. China's trade barriers remained high, although the PFTZs had facilitated trade. The simplification of administrative procedures had significantly lowered the regulatory barriers, especially for entrants, increasing overall efficiency.[85]

In any case, Beijing was willing to accept a slowing down of the economy by making difficult choices to avoid a "hard landing." A restraint monetary policy had reduced financial risks through deleveraging, and a more active fiscal policy had resisted the temptation of resorting to large stimulus measures. In encouraging FDI, China eased restrictions with a negative list, and a single window system simplified trade inspections, declaration, taxes, and other procedures. This partly explains why the World Bank's Ease of Doing Business index, which measures how the regulatory environment is conducive to business operations, has moved China up from seventy-eighth in 2017 to forty-sixth in 2018 and thirty-first in 2019. In March 2019, the NPeC passed a new foreign investment law to address foreign complaints such as forced technology transfer, and announced tax cuts of US$298 billion to help the private sector.[86]

For foreign firms, these measures hardly suggest promarket reforms, especially when China's financial and energy sectors are mostly closed.[87] For other observers, however, market reforms and transitions incurred huge social and political costs, and a strong leadership is indispensable. It takes time to let society adjust and to implement tough choices. Strong pushes often trigger pushbacks in a process that defies linearity; often two steps forward are followed by one or more steps backward. Further, Xi had to wait until after the Nineteenth Party Congress, when he could muster sufficient influence to overcome entrenched resistance, even assuming that his commitment to economic reform was genuine.[88] All this has been complicated by the technology and trade conflicts with the United States and the Covid-19 pandemic crisis.

Rapidly Changing Society and Social Issues

By the first decade of this century, the breakneck pace of economic growth, industrialization, urbanization, and modernization had transformed Chinese society beyond recognition. The society structured around work units (*danwei*) by Maoist egalitarianism had rapidly differentiated into classes, with their distinct class interests and consciousness. Chinese society was more divided by cleavages on regional, linguistic, and ethic lines and featured a public with growing awareness and assertiveness unseen just five or ten years before.

Although drug abuse, gun violence, and racial tensions were not major challenges, the gaps between rural and urban areas, the rich and the poor, and occupations and regions had grown bigger rather than narrowing. Social problems and unrest had mounted in areas ranging from food security to employment, social security to public security, housing to ecological environment, and healthcare to the administration of justice. Ironically, some beneficiaries of previous reforms resisted further changes. Even before the Eighteenth Party Congress, the pressure for more reform, which was building up, was keenly felt by the top leadership, and economic slowdown was also making social issues more urgent.[89]

Further, many pledges made by the Hu Jintao administration on healthcare, education, social insurance, services still had to be fulfilled.[90] General decisions made at the Third Plenum, Fifth Plenum, and the Thirteenth FYP had pledged such things as a medium-high rate of economic growth, environmental protection, promotion of entrepreneurship, improved working conditions, technological innovation, decentralization, reduction of government intervention, and anticorruption. More specific promises made at the Fifth Plenum and the Thirteenth FYP included the following: all couples are allowed to have two children; poverty reduction, especially in poor counties; improved services for women, children, and the elderly (the "left-behinds") in rural areas; free secondary and vocational education; universal old-age insurance; a basic health service system and modern hospitals in both the urban and rural areas; and property rights for farmers.[91]

But, as most social issues are intertwined with other issue areas, political and otherwise, any change in the status quo ultimately affects many other values and interests. Therefore, social policies were subject to intense debate within and outside of the Party. Organizationally, all central social policies had to be fleshed out by every ministry, regulator, region, and locality, each making their own subplans. Invariably, these implementation agents have their own agendas, and during the endless and continuous cycles of policy coordination, adaptation, evaluation, and adjustment, central intentions can be thwarted or watered down.

Poverty Alleviation

It has been suggested that without a strong and persistent central commitment to poverty reduction, the millions who have been lifted out of poverty may slide back into destitution and despair.[92] As mentioned, Xi as general secretary made it a personal mission to combat poverty. Despite its many flaws, the massive anti-poverty program in the reform period was an ongoing success, lifting more than eight hundred million Chinese—or one-tenth of the world's population—out of poverty through government policies and popular initiatives. By Beijing's standard, China had almost wiped out urban poverty.[93] Rural poor were officially defined as those individuals who earned an annual income of less than ¥2,800 (US$427). According to this measure, which factored in the cost of living, there were 98.9 million poor in 2013, but this number was reduced to 43.4 million by 2016. According to official figures, 16.5, 12.3, 14.4, and 12.4 million people rose from poverty in 2013, 2014, 2015, and 2016, respectively. This figure was estimated to be no less than 10 million in 2017, so that the remaining poor would be 30 million.[94] Official statistics cited a marginal reduction of the Gini coefficient from a peak of .491 in 2008 to .462 in 2015, though rising to .468 in 2018.[95]

Xi, who experienced near-starvation firsthand, claimed that he had confronted the poverty problem throughout his career, expending most of his energy on this issue. China suffers very low ratios of resources to population: it accounts for 20 percent of the world's population but has only 7 percent of global arable land. Per capita shares of farmland, forests, and water are merely 28, 15, and 33 percent of the global average. The energy resources, especially hydrocarbon, are similarly low.[96] The terraced fields so common in China's countryside and in Xi's youthful experience are indeed desperate means to eke out by hand tiny plots of arable land on the side of mountains. Many of the poverty-stricken areas were located in remote and isolated areas, primarily in central and western China, where the population was still unable to migrate. These areas included much of the "old revolutionary" base areas, especially in Yanan, where Xi and his father spent much of their careers.

In 2015, Xi and his team put forward the ambitious goal of ending absolute poverty by 2020, touting it as the most challenging aspect of achieving a "moderately prosperous society." With decades of domestic experience of fighting poverty and assistance by international agencies such as the World Bank, United Nations Development Programme, UN Food and Agricultural Organization, and Asia Development Bank, the Chinese had refined the multipronged anti-poverty projects by registering and targeting families and even individuals for specific assistance.

Generally, Beijing adopted a multipronged strategy. The first was to develop industry, tourism, and e-commerce to enliven the local economy. The second was to relocate population from remote and hazardous areas susceptible to landslides and earthquakes. The third was to provide basic education, occupational training, health, and social services, especially for the elderly and the infirm.[97]

During his first term, Xi made some thirty inspection tours to research the poverty issue, and in 2014, the government dispatched eight hundred thousand cadres to identify 128,000 improvised villages and 89.62 million poor people. The cadres set up profiles of the poor before tailoring improvement measures ranging from the provision of education, healthcare, and financial services to ecological upgrading, industrial development, job training, resettlement, and e-commerce for farmers. Those unable to work were provided with *dibao*, or a subsistence guarantee. From 2013 to 2017, the government budgeted ¥196 billion (US$30.2 billion) for poverty reduction, and other financial institutions contributed another ¥283.3 billion (US$43 billion) in small loans to eight million families. The Xi administration also upgraded the program by which the nine developed provinces (Beijing, Shanghai, Shenzhen, etc.) pledged assistance to their paired twelve provinces in the west. A total of 320 units of the central government and the Party were entrusted with the task of lifting 592 counties out of poverty. Symbolically, October 17 was designated a Day for the Eradication of Poverty.

These final steps were judged to be the most difficult, as many of the remaining poor were either geographically hard to reach or were jobless because of physical or mental disabilities. Officials also acknowledged the issues of tokenism and corruption. For instance, the massive injection of funds for poverty alleviation also created more rent-seeking opportunities—over half of the complaints submitted to the CCDI pertained to fraud and misappropriation of funds intended for poverty programs. Further challenges included the tackling of inequality, better jobs, access to better services, and the prevention of a new generation from sinking back to poverty. A return to the Maoist egalitarianism of thirty years previously was unthinkable, and even though all agreed basic poverty could be addressed, there would still be relative poverty, leaving a great deal to be done.[98] So despite official pledges to eliminate poverty by 2020, Xi understood that the struggle against poverty would be an unending process.

Lankao County, which is closely associated with Xi, became a national showcase for poverty alleviation. In 2017, it declared that it was the first county in Henan to have shaken off its status as a poverty county, since the poverty rate there had dropped from 12 percent in 2014 to under 2 percent. Cai Songtao, the secretary of the county party committee, claimed that per capita disposable income had doubled between 2013 and 2016. The county pledged to wipe out poverty altogether by 2020. Lankao is located near the flood-prone Yellow River, and its local leader in the 1960s, named Jiao Yulu, was said to have worked himself to death by helping the farmers overcome flooding, wind, sand, and salinization. In 2014, all PBSC members were paired with a poor locality, and Xi's choice was Lankao. The Lankao model and the Jiao Yulu "spirit" have since become one of his favorite models.[99] One source claims that while Lankao had changed tremendously, areas within it were still dilapidated. The official definition of rural poverty, at annual income of less than ¥2,800, was very low, whereas Lankao's US$460 was still below the International Poverty Line as defined by the World Bank's US$694 in PPP terms.[100]

Another case that illustrates the Xi administration's antipoverty program pertains to Guizhou. A relatively small, remote, and rural province with a large ethnic minority population, Guizhou was one of China's poorest provinces, but it had been used as a traditional cultivation ground for potential top leaders, making it an important rung in the political ladder. Rapid developments there had turned it into a showcase of antipoverty programs and the promise of rural development. Going back, Hu Jintao was secretary of the Guizhou PPC from 1985 to 1988. Li Zhanshu, who is considered one of Xi's closest allies, served there between 2010 and 2012 as secretary of the PPC. Chen Min'er, another Xi protégé, was deputy and then secretary of the PPC from 2012 to 2017 before being promoted as secretary of the Chongqing MPC. Guizhou was touted as a role model in the "battle against poverty." It was lauded for poverty reduction, grassroots party-building, and the enforcement of party discipline, all key priorities of Xi's government. Officials claimed that seven million out of a population of thirty-six million were lifted above the poverty line between 2012 and 2016, and they pledged to lift another one million in 2017. In 2016, Guizhou was said to have achieved the second-highest growth rate among the thirty-two provinces, although its GDP was still one of the lowest. During his tenure, Chen Min'er brought nontraditional industries to the province, as he encouraged tech giants Apple, Alibaba, and Tencent to invest in data infrastructure for the establishment of a "big data" hub. Similarly, Fast, the world's largest single-dish telescope, was constructed in the province, and it has since announced the discovery of two pulsars thousands of light years from Earth. Chen was also credited for promoting e-commerce so that poor and isolated farmers could sell their products more easily.[101]

One further example on the transformation of a poor rural backwater and a Xi signature project is the Xiongan smart city project, which began in 2017. Located just one hundred kilometers southwest of Beijing, it is designed to relieve overcrowding in Beijing by relocating universities, hospitals, and businesses. Built from scratch, Xiongan will be a city of about five million (smaller by Chinese standards) featuring a more human scale, with narrow streets rather than the grand avenues that dot the capital. The infrastructure would be integrated with satellite information, sensor recognition, a 5G network, and supercomputing. Xiongan is expected to become an ecological, sustainable finance- and innovation-driven hub. All housing would be state-owned and provided to employees at subsidized rates in order to avoid real estate trading. Chen Gang, a former official of Guizhou experienced with big-data projects, was appointed by Xi to head the modern project. In the attempt to strengthen Beijing's leadership in AI, the internet of things, and 5G networks, the success or failure Xiongan will have an important impact on the credibility of the general secretary.[102]

The Aging Crisis

The size and the rate of growth of China's elderly population is larger and faster than most countries in the world. By international standards, a country is considered an "aging society" when 10 percent or more of its population are aged sixty or above. Already at the end of 2016, 16.7 percent of China's population, or 230.8 million, were aged sixty or above.[103] Often described as a time bomb, this rapid aging process is expected to shrink the labor pool and productivity but raise manufacturing wages and social security expenditure on pensions and healthcare. The decline in labor supply could erode China's labor advantage and reduce economic growth rate by 0.5 to 0.75 percent per year between 2020 and 2050. Chinese policymakers have responded to this by upgrading the industrial base, introducing robotics into manufacturing, and relocating businesses overseas.[104] China's low retirement age—fifty-five for female and sixty for male white-collar workers and civil servants—allows the government some leeway, but the raising of the retirement age is immensely unpopular. Another major remedy was the relaxation of the one-child family policy in favor of the new two-child policy beginning in 2016. Although officials claimed that the one-child family policy had cut four hundred million births at a time when a larger population was deemed unsustainable, the draconian one-child policy, as is well known, led to all forms of rights abuses such as forced abortions, sterilization, and even a skewed gender balance. Therefore, the comprehensive two-child policy was expected to be popular, and China's family planning agency projected a yearly increase of three million babies, pushing the total growth to twenty million. Yet, counterintuitively, a baby boom did not materialize, especially in the urban areas, due to a host of factors such as financial pressure, limited living space, lack of services, and lifestyle changes. The rule of a one-child family, originally imposed by the government, had now become a social norm. In 2016, births rose briefly to 17.86 million, but then declined continuously for three years to 14.65 million in 2019. This posed serious challenges for economic growth and the ability to support the aging population.[105] Hence, Beijing realized that it had to address the issue of a shrinking labor pool by promoting labor mobility, urbanization, and "orderly" rural migration and by improving the quality and efficiency of the labor force. We turn to this in the following.

Urbanization, the *Hukou* System, and Land Reform

The tackling of the demographic shortfall invariably involved another complex bundle of interconnected issues encompassing urbanization, the *hukou* system, and land reform, topics that had been subjected to fierce debate within and outside of the Party.[106] Urbanization had often been touted as a driver for continuous economic growth and poverty reduction. The assumption was that the contribution to the GDP by farmers scratching out a living on tiny, isolated farms amounted to zero until they were transformed into urban workers and consumers. China's urbanization rate of 51 percent was projected to be 75 percent by 2040, and this constant growth was expected to fuel demand for infrastructure such as roads, housing, utilities, and communication. Therefore, urbanization, together with entrepreneurship, were envisioned to be the driver of a vigorous economy for "at least another generation."[107] Yet the *hukou* system in the 1950s mandated that all Chinese must register under a rural or an urban household, and peasants were strictly forbidden to migrate to the cities. The purpose was to prevent uncontrolled migration to the cities that could create massive unemployment, shantytowns, and unbearable pressure on limited urban services. Between 1949 and 1956, rural migration, driven by the pull factors of jobs and opportunities and push factors of poverty, joblessness, and the effects of collectivization, saw China's urban population swell from 10.6 percent to 14.6 percent of the total population. This represented a net gain of 34.6 million, of which 19.8 million were rural migrants.[108] The *hukou* system acted as an expedient to stem a massive rural exodus. Generally, urbanites enjoyed better social services (such as free education, healthcare, and subsidized housing) and job opportunities, even though their daily necessities were rationed during the entire Maoist period. The farmers were restricted to the countryside to produce raw materials and food for the urban areas in order to fuel industrialization, in what can be called "primitive capital accumulation" under the conditions of severe economic backwardness. Industrialization was carried out by the severe exploitation of the countryside, but some economists have argued that this is an inevitable trade-off for any underdeveloped country that wants to industrialize. Mao was indeed aware of this dilemma, but despite his rhetoric and efforts to narrow the rural/urban gap, the divide grew even wider with industrialization. During the reform period, when residence control was relaxed, an estimated three hundred million peasants, almost all surplus labor, were uprooted and drawn to the cities to take up employment in manufacture, construction, and menial work. Often called the floating population, these migrants contributed greatly to the economic boom, and many had to leave their families back home. However, they and their offspring who had grown up in the cities[109] were ineligible for urban social services such as healthcare, education, housing, and welfare, earning a lower income in a situation reminiscent of apartheid. Nevertheless, a movement of such an epic scale toward a new working class is bound to create dislocation, alienation, and deprivation, posing issues of governance that cannot be exaggerated.

The magnitude of the migrant population in Zhejiang has been discussed in chapter 5. And as mentioned in chapter 4, Xi argued in his 2001 doctoral dissertation that the abolition of the *hukou* system was a historical inevitability and so were the socioeconomic inequalities generated by it. Settling years of debate, the Third Plenum decided formally to end the system by abolishing the rural and urban *hukou*, replacing them with residence, family, or collective *hukou*.[110] Abolition also meant more social equality and justice. Beijing anticipated that another one hundred million rural migrants would permanently settle in urban areas by 2020, so that China's population would be 60 percent urban, when the percentage was 56 percent in 2015.[111] Such a massive migration was expected to boost productivity as farmers took urban manufacturing and service employment and boosted consumption, especially in western, southwestern, and central China. Established or well-to-do migrants were expected to take up unsold urban residential units to offset real estate and other overcapacity.

According to the new regulations, those who satisfied certain requirements, such as urban employment, years living in a city, and past contributions to social security, could apply for an urban *hukou*. In general, application was easiest in towns or smaller cities, more difficult in medium-sized cities, and stricter in megacities with populations over five million. In most desirable but crowed megacities such as Beijing, Shanghai, and Shenzhen, where one-third of the population already consisted of nonurban *hukou* holders, application standards were prohibitive.[112] Further, even megacities like Beijing contained rural hinterlands whose inhabitants held rural *hukou*, and in 2016, Beijing finally abolished the distinction.[113]

Overall, the progress of *hukou* reform was slow for the following reasons. First, as with implementation of any central policy, there were huge regional variations, since localities were allowed to adapt the policy to local conditions. Local governments tended to be stricter in applying central guidelines, especially when they were difficult to enforce. Second, local authorities had a great deal of incentive to oppose the policy, fearing that the universalizing of social services and welfare would place huge and unsustainable fiscal burdens on them. Local authorities were responsible for 80 percent of their expenditure, but received only half of this from taxation, the rest made up of either extrabudgetary funds, VAT income, or in some cases up to 74 percent from the sale of illegally seized land. Central government tax cuts often exacerbated the issue. Third, the urban populations were reluctant to accept changes, fearing that the limited funding for social services would be spread thin. Fourth, increased urbanization also meant a full range of issues from urban sprawl to farmland reduction and increased pollution, and from traffic congestion to public safety, overcrowding, and overtaxed power supplies. Fifth, counterintuitively, some farmers were unenthusiastic about urban migration, especially to smaller cities. One CASS survey of farmers in China's central-west found that 50 percent of farmers did not plan to settle in urban areas: 20 percent said they were too old to move; 18 percent wanted to stay put to take care of their parents and children; 10 percent preferred farm work; 9 percent said urban life was unfamiliar. Even rural migrants already settled in urban areas planned to return to their rural homes after a certain age.[114] Other famers who enjoyed subsidies and income from leasing their land had little incentive to migrate.[115] Still others were deterred by the high cost of urban living.

One fundamental obstacle to migration was the farmers' fear of the relinquishment of their rights to rural land, which they regarded as a form of long-term security to hedge against the precarious nature of urban employment. One source claims that 70 percent of rural migrants desired to stay in the cities but refused to give up their land rights conferred by the rural *hukou*.[116] For the regime, too, it was a form of safety valve, since during the 2008 global financial crisis, twenty million laid-off workers returned to their rural roots to ride out the crisis. Meanwhile, a great deal of the migrants' land sat idle back home, constituting a drawback to economic growth.

In this manner, *hukou* reform hinged on the sensitive issue of land reform. In cities, land is state-owned, and in the urban areas, "collectively" owned. In the countryside, the household responsibility system enables farmers to obtain land-use rights by negotiating contracts with village governments for a period of up to thirty years. If the farmers were allowed to transfer, rent out, and mortgage their land-use rights over the rural construction land, they would be more willing to swap rural *hukou* for urban ones, since they would have some capital to support them financially to establish in the cities. They might even buy up excess urban residential units. The Xi administration hoped to create a land transfer market to encourage farmers to relinquish their land. Such experiments had already been introduced in Chongqing under Bo Xilai beginning in 2007, whereby farmers were allowed to directly sell land credits (*dipiao*) to urban developers for cash. This ideally would bypass the land grabs and expropriation by local authorities that had been a major source of social unrest.[117]

Yet implementation of land reform was complex. Local governments controlled the collective assets and needed to issue land certificates confirming the farmers' rights over the plots of contracted land, but this progressed only slowly. By the end of 2015, millions still had not received their certificates, although a promise was made to complete certification by the end of 2017. Land reform required fiscal and tax reform policies to give more power to local governments to raise revenue, and, as noted, this was still in transition. Another remedy was to allow the percentage of VAT retained by the localities to rise from 30 to 50 percent. Many regional experiments had been introduced but there was as yet no national model or consensus. Furthermore, an additional problem had been the phenomenon of counterurbanization, whereby urban residents buy up rural land to build houses, threatening the national red-line minimum 120 million hectares for farmland in both the rural and urban areas. There was also the concern that full marketization of land might enable the wealthy urbanites to accumulate large tracts of land, undermining the revenue of local governments and expanding the rural-urban gap even further. These are complex and contentious issues and will take years to resolve.[118]

The Social Credit System (SocCS)

Apart from the *hukou* and land reform, the process of creating a SocCS follows an experimental and incrementalist path that was open-ended. In this regard, this process was suffused with Chinese characteristics; it also shared policy challenges and uncertainties with developed countries. The Eighteenth Party Congress of 2012 called for the promotion of honesty and integrity in politics, economics, society, and the judiciary. This was echoed by subsequent documents that sought to improve trust, security, and civic mindedness through rewards and sanctions. Xi said that "a feeling of security is the best gift a country can give its people." In 2014, the State Council formally promulgated a comprehensive plan for a SocCS to govern political, social, and economic lives.[119] However, designed to be fully functional by 2020, the SocCS was surrounded by a great deal of conflicting misinformation and uncertainty.

The new policy for creating a SocCS was intended to address a host of issues, the fundamental of which was the generally perceived lack of trust and integrity in Chinese society. The Cultural Revolution had left a heritage of violent conflict with people denouncing one another, but the transfer to a market economy had generated a free-for-all mentality that was exacerbated by new forms of inequality. Pervasive fraud and deception appeared to be a fact of life. The Chinese were confronted by a huge array of issues such as counterfeit and shoddy goods, commercial fraud, online scams, and pyramid schemes. There were numerous scandals in food and product safety, and in the pharmaceutical industry (see chapter 5 on Zhejiang). Academic fraud included plagiarism and faked credentials, whereas economic misconduct involved tax evasion, white-collar crime, loan defaults, and refusals to pay fines. One common form of extortion was dubbed "smashing of porcelain" (*pengci*), an example of which is when a person hurls himself into traffic in order to claim damage compensation. Often the culprits get away with no consequences for their misdemeanors, but these often result in social incidents.[120]

It is unlikely that antisocial and deviant behavior in China was more pervasive than in other countries, but the underdeveloped regulatory regime clearly lacked the suitable infrastructure, standards, and expertise to control it. The Chinese were inspired by the West's stronger social credit infrastructure with its numerous formal and informal ratings. Such things as banking and financial credit, and even ratings for doctors, professors, Uber, and restaurants, had guided decisions on loans, mortgages, and consumer choices. In contrast, China rose from penury to relative prosperity in a short period of time, lacking a well-established credit history. By 2011, only one-third of the Chinese population held bank accounts.[121]

Official discourse claimed that a modern and orderly market economy required social trust and confidence. A SocCS, the government hoped, would reduce transaction costs, economic risks, and social problems and raise the reputation of national brands. Trust in governance, commerce, society, and the judiciary would help reduce government intervention and strengthen the rule of law. And as mentioned, China had already benefited by a myriad of credit scores in the private sector. The advantage in e-banking was most apparent—it had facilitated the lending to hundreds of millions of small businesses and loans to consumers. Accordingly, the government felt that it had a role to play.

At the beginning, the Party projected that all units in government, business, social organizations, and even the judiciary would create their own credit information-sharing platforms in real time. Government officials would be assessed on the extent to which they implemented central orders, remained politically loyal, and were effective and corruption-free. It was anticipated that the construction of the SocCS network would be helped by metadata collected by web giants such as BAT, which in turn was aided by Western companies such as IBM and Google and the OpenPower Foundation. The millions of facial recognition surveillance cameras installed for social management would also be a major source of data.[122]

In 2015, the Bank of China authorized eight credit-scoring companies such as Ant Financial's Sesame Credit to collect consumer credit scores. The intention was to make use of the massive data from financial services such as Alipay, with its seven-hundred-million-user base to construct a database.[123] Yet by 2017 the government decided against having these eight companies become official representatives over concerns of conflicts of interest. Consequently, the task was left to local governments and private businesses to mine metadata on social media connections, behavior, and buying histories to calculate individual scores. The outcome was tremendous variations in the measuring and monitoring of creditworthiness as well as antisocial and selfish behavior. The most common were the black and red scores designed to punish or reward.

· For businesses, all credit information about them gathered from different sources would be incorporated into a centralized platform called Internet + Monitoring, and individual businesses would be ranked according to the matrix excellent, good, fair, or poor.[124] Businesses could be ranked poor and put on a blacklist for a series of offenses, including the endangering of people's lives, health and safety, unfair competition, false advertising, and pollution. Other punishable transgressions encompassed bribery, tax evasion, refusal to perform statutory and defense obligations, and disobedience of a court judgment or ad-ministrative decision.[125] Businesses that were deemed to have committed less se-rious offenses would be put on a monitoring list.

Sanctions for offending businesses included naming and shaming; exclu-sion from preferential tax and financial subsidies and government procurement and bidding; and denial of project approvals and permits. Businesses with poor scores were subjected to more frequent government inspections, audits, and su-pervision. Managers and other senior management associated with companies on the blacklist might also be held liable.

On the other hand, businesses that paid taxes on time, held requisite licenses, obeyed environment regulations, and observed production quality were eligible for the red list. The same applied to businesses that partook in initiatives such as social responsibility activities, poverty reduction, and environmental protec-tion. Rewards included green channels for processing taxes, priority in customs clearing, and license application, streamlined administrative procedures, and fast-tracked approvals. By the fall of 2019, the NDRC announced that thirty-three million companies had been appraised and rated with the results being shared provincially.[126]

For individuals, they were assigned a starting capital of one thousand points, from which points could be added or subtracted. Points were deducted for infractions such as the failure to pay court fines, default on debts, illegal dumping of garbage, and spreading fake news. Even more minor misconducts such as jaywalking, spitting and littering, disobeying traffic rules, and spending too much time on video games could result in low scores. Similarly, more political acts, such as a villager's petitioning at the upper government echelon without going through the village head, could be regarded as a misconduct. Individuals with low scores were barred from buying luxury goods and even booking hotel rooms. Others were disqualified from jobs in government, SOEs, and big banks. Cases were reported that individuals with low scores had their children prevented from entering universities or private schools. In one report, individuals even had messages inserted on their cell phones announcing their untrustworthiness. In Beijing, the face and ID of alleged transgressors were posted on public electronic billboards. Official figures showed that by 2019, five million had been denied high-speed train trips and seventeen million barred from flights.[127]

Individuals could earn points through good deeds such as giving blood, volunteering, and making charitable donations. Those who possessed high scores were rewarded by perks such as lower utility bills, discounts in services, and pri-ority acceptance to hospitals. Theoretically, individuals could get off the blacklist and restore points by remedial measures such as repaying debts, but there was a great deal of uncertainty as to how credits were assigned and by whom.

Anecdotal evidence showed that the general public welcomed the SocCS as a rational project to boost morality. The trust and pride in technology was high, and concerns with privacy low. The SocCS was thought to have provided a better sense of security and certainty, resulting in a noticeable improvement in social behavior as in the case of cars beginning to stop at crosswalks. People treated high scores as an asset by using them in online dating services and job applications. One study shows that the SocCS elicited a high degree of approval, especially among the older, wealthier, better-educated, and urban citizens. These people perceived the SocCS as a means of technical progress that could generate more law-abiding behavior by closing institutional and regulatory gaps. However, this study also suggested public opinion could change, depending on perceptions on whether rewards and punishments were balanced, and on whether the scores were perceived to be calculated impartially.[128] Yet there were also outcries against tech corporations as in the case where one company unveiled an app that utilized AI to allow users to swap faces with media celebrities, or when the Baidu founder claimed that Chinese were willing to trade "privacy for convenience." Both Baidu and Sesame Credit were sued for embedding individual information in their scoring system without consent.[129] When a passenger was murdered in a ride with Didi, China's equivalent of Uber, the Chinese government accused that company of not sharing passenger and vehicle data with it.[130]

Foreign criticisms, and sometimes domestic feedback, however, were severe. The program had often been described as Orwellian, turning China into a "digital dictatorship" or a "dystopian nightmare straight out of the Black Mirror." Critics were troubled by the nontransparent ways by which scores were determined, the infringement on privacy, and the quashing of free speech and dissent, especially in Xinjiang. A nightmarish scenario was the formation of a permanent central and mandatory record similar to the Maoist dossier kept for all citizens. The potential for abuse was enormous.[131]

In any case, by 2018 (and even 2020) the SocCS was still in the pilot stage with a hodgepodge of commercial and government-run experiments. Numerous regional variations existed, lacking one unified and coordinated system. However, the original thinking of constraining all political organizations with credit scores remained unfulfilled. What was happening in China reflected a global trend of governments and companies attempting to manipulate surveillance technology to penetrate the everyday lives of citizens to predict and even change their behavior. The metadata collection by Silicon Valley corporations goes beyond the normal use of such things as credit ratings for insurance and mortgages.[132] This has triggered debates over the great concentration of power, knowledge, and wealth in "behavioral futures markets" where citizen behavior is modified, bought and sold. Pushbacks have been launched against government surveillance programs such as PRISM, governments requisition for metadata from tech giants, and the legality of metadata and surveillance.[133] Similarly, public outcry took place over the Facebook / Cambridge Analytica scandal for harvesting metadata to manipulate voters on a global scale.

China's SocCS reflects a controversial issue confronting all countries, developed or developing. Generally, governments are tempted to use technology to foster innovation and competitiveness while maintaining order and stability. Tech corporations jealously guard their autonomy to collect and to manipulate encrypted metadata, resisting regulations that they say can jeopardize global information flow, internet transactions, and cooperation, and even erect harmful trade barriers. Citizens are increasingly concerned with their privacy and data hacks involving hundreds of millions, although the ordinary citizens in China as in the West are largely unaware of the extent to which their personal data have been manipulated.

In China the proposed SocCS tips the balance toward the government and tech companies, although the latter may potentially be subject to stricter regulations. State digital surveillance can further erode individual liberty and freedom. A centralized and comprehensive SocCS contradicts the goal of a more limited government, and it is uncertain whether the system would revert to its decentralized origins. However, while many in China have argued for the speedy completion of the SocCS, others have called for caution. The latter voice argues that the definitions of creditworthiness and punishments are so broad and vague that both are subject to widespread abuse. Confusion exists regarding the boundary between issues of civil and criminal law, and a centralized national legislation is a blunt instrument to deal with credit issues.[134]

In 2018, Beijing announced that it would embrace Europe's new General Data Protection Regulation in implementing the SocCS, and will require the data of its citizens to be held onshore.[135] New legislations and data protection guidelines were issued in 2019, setting standards for personal data protection and beginning to build a framework for individual data rights and protection. The rational choice approach tends to interpret the SocCS as the CCP's attempt at political control or its blatant attempt to uphold and expand its power. In reality, the situation is more complex, and the final outcome of the SocCS remains to be seen.

The State of Socioeconomic Development

Like Xi, Li Keqiang, premier since 2013, shared the responsibility of taking charge of the US$12 trillion economy and grappling with the remaining legacy of the 2008 financial crisis. The persistent rumors that Xi intended to get rid of Li because Li was the head of the *tuanpai* and that Xi ran an one-man show are informed by faulty assumptions. Together the two had to cope with issues such as

property market bubbles, mounting financial risks, unbalanced industrial structure, and worsening environmental pollution. Li's reluctance to use stimulus to
back economic reform and his efforts to promote market-oriented reforms and
to reduce high leverage ratios, often dubbed "Likonomics," were consistent with
Xi's priorities. So were his consistent pushes to reduce regulations, to encourage
business and entrepreneurship, to create jobs, and to revitalize the economy.
Other Li initiatives such as the policies to harness internet technology for economic growth, to develop bullet-train technology, and the Made in China 2025
plan represented a leadership consensus. Even the Shanghai PFTZ, established
in 2013, was an outcome of a collective decision. Since 2013, Li has announced
70 percent tax cuts for medium and small companies and the reduction of income taxes by ¥70 billion. Government policies to replace business taxes with
value-added tax have cut business taxes for business owners by an estimated of
¥1.7 trillion (US$26 billion) since 2016.[136] Yet in 2015 a stock market collapse
wiped out US$3 to $5 trillion off the value of mainland shares, despite repeated
government interventions. This sent shock waves around the world, highlighting
the weaknesses of China's lax and fragmented regulatory system, which featured collusion between tycoons and officials. After the market meltdown, two
senior officials from the China Securities Regulatory Commission were accused of colluding with speculators to undermine the government's stabilization
efforts, and the chair of the China Insurance Regulatory Commission (CIRC)
was also placed under criminal investigation. In February 2018, the CIRC in turn
seized control of Anbang Insurance Group and charged its former chairman Wu
Xiaohui, who is married to the granddaughter of Deng Xiaoping (and there a
R2G) and well connected with powerful families, with fraud.[137] The persistent
rumors that disagreements between Xi and Li had driven a wedge between them
and that Xi has wanted to dismiss Li have not come to pass.

In 2017, Li Keqiang and Chinese officials assured the world that China's debt
level had improved and was under control, market confidence was rising, and economic recovery was of high quality. They argued that economic fundamentals
and growth potential were sound, and this could kick off another boom cycle. On
the other hand, perhaps to manage expectations, they also stuck with the notion
that economic growth would be L-shaped, meaning that development would
level off instead of ascending.[138] In any case, World Bank figures show that China
had accomplished all the Millennium Development Goals (MDGs) by 2015, and
contributed greatly to global MDGs.[139] Another optimistic OECD short-run appraisal projected continuous economic growth, thanks to early fiscal and monetary stimulus, as well as to regional development initiatives such as the Belt and
Road Initiative and the Beijing-Heibei-Tianjin corridor. Monetary policy was
appropriate to counter financial risks, although reforms such as the reduction of
the cost of doing business and improved corporate governance were needed to

advance income per capita. The report added that higher value-added production would require better quality and relevance in innovation, as lower-skilled jobs were moving to low-cost countries.[140] Available World Bank estimates show that China's Gini coefficient consecutively dropped from 4.37 in 2010 to 3.85 in 2016. This contrasts with US National Bureau of Statistics figures of 4.81 for 2010, falling to 4.62 in 2015, and then rising to 4.68 in 2018.[141]

Summing up of the economic and social achievements for 2013 to 2018, Li Keqiang's government report to the 2018 NPeC claimed that annual growth was 7.1 percent and GDP had risen from ¥54 trillion (US$8.5 trillion) to ¥82.7 trillion (US$13 trillion). More than 68 million people had risen from poverty and 1.35 billion were covered by basic medical insurance. Personal income had risen by an annual average of 7.4 percent, as sixty-six million urban jobs were created. Energy and water consumption per unit of GDP had been reduced by 20 percent, the number of days with heavy air pollution in key cities had been cut by half, and the release of major pollutants had declined. China now had the world's largest "middle-income group."[142] As usual, official figures like these cannot be accepted at face value, but even with the factoring in of caveats, the outcome is impressive. UNDP's Human Development Index value for China registers a continuous rise from .591 in 2000 to .702 in 2010 and .758 in 2018 (a .750 value is considered high HDI).[143]

In the longer run, whether China can achieve quality and sustainable growth and address issues of inequality, employment, and ease social tensions, or whether it will end up with a debt-fueled path to disaster and social upheaval is a hotly debated subject. The Covid-19 crisis of 2020 further slowed Chinese growth rates to their lowest in nearly forty years. Whether Beijing will escape the much-feared but controversial "middle-income trap" will depend on a number of factors and will not be known in the short run.

11

Modernizing the Military and Recalibrating Foreign Relations

Military Reform

One avowed goal of Xi Jinping's China Dream is to build a strong national defense and a powerful military force to project Chinese power internationally, to enforce its territorial claims, and to defend its far-flung interests. Furthermore, the military, treated as the Party's army, is seen as one vital element for securing national and regime security. For similar reasons, the Jiang Zemin and Hu Jintao administrations rejected arguments for the "nationalization" (*guojiahua*) of the People's Liberation Army, which meant placing the military under state control. The ideal military for Xi would be one that is loyal to the Party, capable of winning wars, exemplary in conduct, and capable of carrying out modern joint operations. At a November 2012 meeting of the Party's Central Military Commission, one day after Xi was anointed general secretary, Hu Jintao endorsed Xi as "a competent general secretary and CMC chairman," praising his experience and his ability to lead. In return, Xi lauded Hu for his full retirement by yielding the chairmanship of the CMC and said this "shows his foresight as a Marxist statesman and strategist, and his broad mind and noble character." Soon after, Xi launched an unprecedented restructuring of national defense and the military, the most sweeping since 1949.[1] If successful, the Thirteenth Five-Year Military Development Plan (2016–2020) could significantly increase the joint force combat capabilities of the PLA and transform it into a smaller, leaner, and more modern force. A complete mechanization of all forces was expected to turn them into a world-class military capable of informationized warfare, which was considered paramount in the expansion of military effectiveness. As such, the PLA was expected to protect shipping lanes and resource supplies and present a challenge to US military dominance in Asia. Priorities included the restructuring of the various services as well as advances in weaponry, logistics, information technology, combat training, and international military cooperation. The CMC with Xi at its head would assume overall control of the PLA, the People's Armed Police (PAP), the militia, the reserves, and battle zone commands.[2]

Despite the many post-Mao reforms, the organizational structure of the PLA still reflected Soviet designs for defense in the 1950s. The revolutionary heritage of the PLA meant that it was dominated by overstaffed ground forces. As such, the land forces were an entrenched interest, making up 70 percent of military personnel and a majority representation in the CMC. As a corporate group, the PLA was known to be ultranationalistic, hawkish, riddled with corruption, and often resistant of party control. Hu Jintao had allegedly struggled with the PLA but never gained full control.[3]

Furthermore, for Xi, the division of the PLA into geographical and functional command was incompatible with modern needs for coordination and joint operations. The command structure consisted of four powerful multifunction military headquarters: the General Staff Department, General Political Department, General Logistics Department, and General Armaments Department. And the country was divided into seven geographical military regions that traditionally enjoyed a degree of autonomy, with each having its own schools, hospitals, hotels, newspapers, and even money-making enterprises.[4] (See Figure 11.1.) Bureaucratic politics and interservice rivalry had long ensured that each unit operated as if it were a separate fiefdom. Accordingly, Xi's far-reaching military reforms, rolled out in 2016, launched an unprecedented assault on the many centers of vested interests. He located centralized control of the PLA in the CMC, where he was chair, and reasserted party control over the PLA by prioritizing political work and

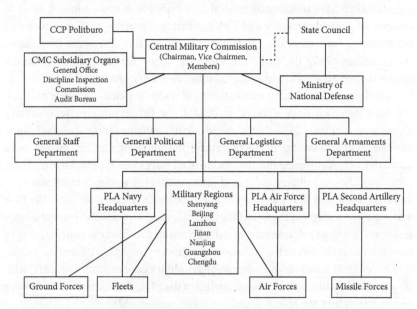

Figure 11.1 PLA structure prior to reforms

Source: Phillip C. Saunders and Joel Wuthnow, "China's Goldwater-Nichols? Assessing PLA Organizational Reforms," *Strategic Forum*, No. 294, April 5, 2016.

absolute obedience to the Party. The reforms aimed to transfer political weight from the ground forces to the naval, air, and missile forces and give other services more say in budgets and operations. Key aspects of the reforms can be summarized in the following.

First, the reforms demobilized some 300,000 of the PLA's 2.3 million troops, many from the ground forces. In the post-Mao period Deng Xiaoping, Jiang Zemin, and Hu Jintao had trimmed the 4 to 4.5 million strong PLA by 1 million, 500,000, and 200,000, respectively, but further demobilization had been a hot potato since massive layoffs meant more jobs had to be found for ex-servicemen. Already there were six million veterans on welfare, and many of the disgruntled ones had staged protests and demonstrations. One government remedy was to order SOEs to reserve 5 percent of their new jobs for veterans, and the March 2016 NPeC session promised to spend ¥39.8 billion (US$6.1 billion) in that year for demobilized troops, a 15 percent increase over 2015.[5]

Second, reorganization of the PLA enabled Xi to increase his oversight. In January 2016, the four departmental pillars of the PLA were dismantled and their responsibilities were divided among fifteen new but less powerful agencies directly under the CMC. These new agencies took charge of responsibilities such as political work, politics and law, equipment, training, mobilization, discipline inspection, and strategic planning.[6] (See Figure 11.2.) Among these new organs, the power to enforce party discipline was transferred from the dissolved General Political Department to a more independent Discipline Inspection Commission, directly under the CMC. Similarly, the Political and Legal Affairs Commission was entrusted with overseeing "governance according to law" and regulations over the military court system.

Third, in February 2016, the seven military regions were reorganized into five theater commands (eastern, southern, western, northern, and central) with more integrated operational control over air, naval, ground, and conventional missile forces in their areas. This was designed to improve response effectiveness and the ability to project power outward. While many reorganized functions had been removed from army control, Xi appeared to have forged a compromise by appointing army officers to head these new theater commands. He also established a new Army General Command at the same level as the navy and air force and promoted the Second Artillery Force under a new name—the PLA Rocket Force—to a full-service equivalent to the army, navy, and air force. The reforms also established the PLA Strategic Support Force, tasked to merge capabilities in space, cyber, and electronic warfare to provide C4ISR (command, control, communications, computers, intelligence, surveillance, and reconnaissance) support directly to field commanders. Separately, a Joint Logistic Support Force was created to offer large-scale military operations for all services within the theater commands.[7]

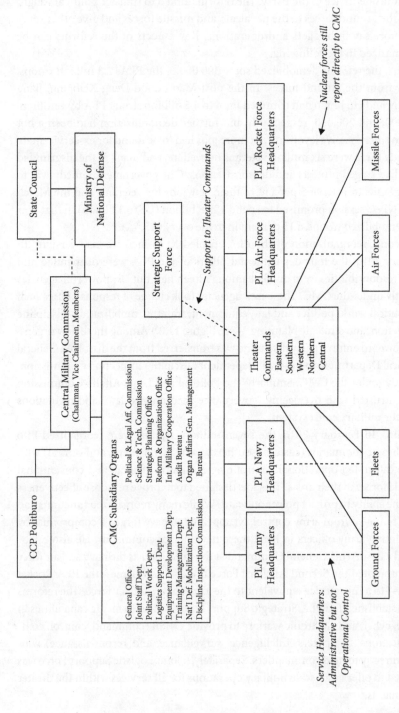

Figure 11.2 PLA structure after reforms

Source: Phillip C. Saunders and Joel Wuthnow, "China's Goldwater-Nichols? Assessing PLA Organizational Reforms," *Strategic Forum*, No. 294, April 5, 2016.

CCP Politburo

State Council

Ministry of National Defense

Central Military Commission
(Chairman, Vice Chairmen, Members)

Strategic Support Force

Support to Theater Commands

Nuclear forces still report directly to CMC

CMC Subsidiary Organs

General Office
Joint Staff Dept.
Political Work Dept.
Logistics Support Dept.
Equipment Development Dept.
Training Management Dept.
Nat'l Def. Mobilization Dept.
Discipline Inspection Commission

Political & Legal Aff. Commission
Science & Tech. Commission
Strategic Planning Office
Reform & Organization Office
Int. Military Cooperation Office
Audit Bureau
Organ Affairs Gen. Management Bureau

PLA Army Headquarters

PLA Navy Headquarters

PLA Air Force Headquarters

PLA Rocket Force Headquarters

Theater Commands
Eastern
Southern
Western
Northern
Central

Ground Forces

Fleets

Air Forces

Missile Forces

Service Headquarters: Administrative but not Operational Control

Fourth, the ACC was extended into the military, where corruption, graft, and buying and selling of offices had become endemic. For instance, a general-ship was alleged to cost ¥10 million (US$1.5 million). A great deal of graft was attributed to corruption rings formed by disgraced generals Xu Caihou and Guo Boxiong, both of whom had been promoted by Jiang Zemin. For the first time, Xi established a standing anticorruption force for the military, and fifteen in-spection teams, after a two-day training session, were dispatched to all fifteen departments and five theater commands to "purify" the PLA. Simultaneously, the PLA set up a hotline and a mailbox to receive complaints of corruption and misconduct. Xi vowed to grant more authority and independence to inspectors and to tighten the military's control over land and housing.[8] By 2017, more than fifty senior PLA "tigers" had been convicted for corruption.[9] Potentially, the ACC could help rebuild the Party's and the military's image, but Xi could also use it as a weapon against his opponents, to neutralize opposition to reform and disrupt personal networks.

This purging and reorganization of the officer corps under Xi was probably the largest since after the fall of Lin Biao in 1971.[10] Deng drastically trimmed the PLA down, but he did not purge its leadership since rampant corruption was less a major issue in the 1980s, in part because less money and resources were floating around. Mao had rehabilitated Deng Xiaoping in 1973, banking on the latter's prestige and influence to help control the ballooning power of the military, an unanticipated outcome of the Cultural Revolution. Deng promptly reshuffled the commanders in all military regions, separating them from their traditional power bases.[11] On the other hand, neither the Jiang Zemin nor the Hu Jintao administrations had attempted to confront the military in such a manner since both lacked military experience and had relatively little leverage over military leadership, even though Jiang did persuade the PLA to offload its huge business empire. Xi has taken a page from Deng in what is seen as a very risky move. His newly assumed personalized control, his experience, and his pedigree as the son of Xi Zhongxun gave him more confidence to shake up the military establish-ment. Further, Xi employed tools and tactics that consisted of sticks and carrots. For instance, he used the threat of corruption investigations, especially referring to the cases of CMC vice chairman Guo Boxiong and Xu Caihou, to neutralize reform opponents. As for carrots, senior PLA officers who were reassigned or relocated could keep their original ranks and grades. Xi wrapped military reforms in the larger reform agenda and used promotions and assignments to win support for reform. In addition, while the anticorruption activities of the ACC might threaten some, it might also appeal to others within the PLA who saw malfeasance as a key barrier to military modernization,[12] not to mention their own promotion prospects.

Certain aspects of Chinese military reforms have been compared to the Goldwater-Nichols restructuring in the United States, which introduced a joint command and control (C2) structure by which authority flows from the president and secretary of defense to regional commanders. One difference, of course, is that a primary responsibility of the PLA is to defend party rule and that political officers and party committees continue to have authority over key functions of the commanders.[13] In April 2016, Xi became commander in chief of the newly established CMC Joint Command Headquarters when he inspected that organization dressed in a military camouflage uniform—a first for a Chinese president and the second time for Xi in a public appearance. The CMC Joint Command Headquarters is similar to the Pentagon's Military Command Center, and various measures have moved Xi closer to the equivalent of a US-style commander in chief.[14]

The PLA and the PAP Are Ordered to Withdraw from Business Ventures

Another Xi initiative had to do with the nagging issue of the PLA's involvement in commercial activities. At the beginning of the market reform period, all organizations were urged by the Party, somewhat naively, to develop entrepreneurial spirit, and the PLA was encouraged to run businesses to supplement its budget. By privileging its control over real estate, communications, logistics, and the like, the PLA soon developed into a business empire controlling companies ranging from airlines to hotel chains, from nightclubs to pig farms, and from real estate to theme parks. This created huge implications for the functioning of the PLA and the corruption it could inspire.[15] Jiang Zemin forced the PLA to abandon its core business empire in 1998, but made exceptions on such things as the provision of social services, professional training, and the leasing of resources to raise revenue. Yet this again gradually evolved into sources of corruption and criminality that served local and vested interests, even cabals. The profit-making ethos of the PLA was said to have distorted market competition, fostering an unhealthy business environment that misallocated resources. Some military units, it was said, had expended all their energy and resources on making profits rather than meeting military goals. The Jiang Zemin and Hu Jintao administrations had attempted to deal with the issue, but to no avail. In 2015, Xi and the CMC felt sufficiently confident that it ordered the PLA and the PAP to completely withdraw from involvement in businesses and social services. Yet such an endeavor was a formidable challenge involving personnel changes, contract cancellations, and debt resolution. The PLA's withdrawal from social services, such as the civilian healthcare in military hospitals, required the collaboration of various levels of government. Although the Party prohibited all new PLA commercial projects and contracts, collectively termed "remunerated services" (*youchang fuwu*), the terminations of existing ones were allowed to proceed gradually and be preceded by pilot projects.[16] Because of the complexity of the task, the plan was to accomplish full withdrawal in a two-step process to be completed in 2018. The first dealt with such services as kindergartens, news publications, culture and physical education programs, communications, personnel training, and maintenance. The second tackled real estate, agricultural production, hospitality facilities, medical services, and scientific research.[17] By October 2017, a PLA source claimed, some eighty-five thousand entities, or 80 percent of the total, had been terminated, although huge regional variations existed.[18] By this reform Xi aimed to foster functional differentiation into the PLA to make it more effective. This was another step in separating the PLA from civilian activities and breaking the long Chinese tradition of military involvement in the civilian sphere. Such a move could even gain support from the PLA because military involvement in civilian activities such as business adventures tends to be detrimental to professionalism and esprit de corps. As long as the civilian government is relatively stable and well run, and the corporate interests of the military such as budgetary allocation are satisfied, the motivation for interfering in civilian politics tends to be low.[19]

However, the intense pressure exerted on the PLA, the trimming of the power of many generals, and reduced opportunity for rent-seeking and graft generated resentment to such a powerful extent that speculation was rife that Xi might be the object of a military coup. Further, continued ground force dominance, interservice rivalry, resistance to political education, and a lack of combat experience posed challenges to reforms. The new system will need years of adjustment and joint exercises to fully set up. Last but not least, all military reform depends on the ability of Xi to supervise their fulfillment and to command loyalty in those tasked with carrying it out.[20] By 2018, Xi felt that he was sufficiently confident to advance another step, as we shall see in chapter 13.

Foreign Relations under Xi: Interdependence and Its Discontents, Competition, and Conflict

In the early reform period of the 1980s and 1990s, Deng Xiaoping stuck with the dictum "Hide one's capability and bid one's time, while making some accomplishments" (*taoguang yanghui, yousuo zuowei*), which prescribed an essentially reactive, low-profile, and passive foreign policy. China focused exclusively on economic development by fostering a stable international environment to facilitate it, avoiding international complications. The preoccupation was domestic issues and regime survival, especially since the close call of the Tiananmen events. Externally, Beijing put up with US hegemony and tried to cultivate a good-neighbor policy, for instance, by settling most of its border disputes even at the cost of making territorial concessions.[21] Yet when it came to Japan and Taiwan, it was uncompromising.[22] Things began to change in the first decade of this century when China was increasingly integrated into the global economy, with Beijing stressing the "do something significant" part of the formula. Dramatic economic growth also boosted China's share of global GDP from 1.27 percent in 1980 to 10.66 percent in 2013.[23]

The CCP is obsessed with preserving regime security and survival within a protean international environment where turbulence, randomness, and crises are a fact of life. It is ultrasensitive to the issue of sovereignty and Western pressure. Xi inherited this mindset and was even more intolerant of what he perceived to be China bashing. Xi proposed to enhance national security with the "overall security concept," and consequently, a striking aspect of foreign policy during Xi's first term was Xi's omnidimensional, activist, and deep engagement with the world. China's economic power had grown tremendously, but so had the global pushbacks. One study of Xi's operational code in foreign affairs postulates that Xi was more optimistic, stronger, and more decisive than his predecessor, Hu Jintao, although both preferred cooperative rather than conflictual means.[24] Yet, in reality, Xi's foreign policy has been more muscular and forward, and this has generated a great deal of mistrust and opposition, which in turn has hardened Xi's position. There is currently a large body of literature on China's international relations from different angles,[25] and in the following I focus on Xi and the issues of competition, conflict, continuity, and change. The analysis will engage theoretical lenses drawn from studies of foreign policy and international relations.

One indication of Xi's activism was his extensive foreign travels to connect with foreign countries with large trade and investment opportunities. In contrast to his predecessors, Xi in his first term was a globetrotter and China's most-traveled leader since 1949. Hu Jintao visited only seven countries during his decade as president and general secretary.[26] In his first four years as general secretary, Xi spent 154 days (or on average one month a year) on twenty-four foreign tours, the longest of which lasted eleven days.[27] At home, he received a steady stream of 165 political leaders. In 2015 alone, he spent forty-two days on eight trips overseas visiting fourteen countries and attending nine international conferences. This compares with Obama (eleven countries), Putin (fourteen), and François Hollande (more than fifty countries) in the same year.[28] In 2016, Xi hosted the first-ever G20 meeting in China at Hangzhou, showcasing him as a major figure on the global stage. Xi attended international conferences such as APEC,

Shanghai Cooperation Organization, and the Sochi Winter Olympics. The diversity and frequency of his first-term tours is reflected in his four visits to Russia, two to the United States, two to South Africa, one to the UK, almost all Central Asian states, Latin America, South Asia, Australia, New Zealand, Fiji, Maldives, and Trinidad and Tobago, with notable exceptions being North Korea and Japan (see Table 11.1).

Since these trips make great demands on leaders' energy and resources, they reflect Xi's geopolitical priorities and his attempts to build multilateral connections and gain political influence to match China's economic power. These trips often resulted in numerous signed agreements on trade, energy, agriculture, cybersecurity, technology, and security. For instance, in 2015 Xi signed US$130 billion worth of business deals that included a US$7 billion agreement to buy seventy Airbus planes, a US$5 billion deal to build a high-speed bullet train linking the Los Angeles area with Las Vegas, and a US$3 billion deal to build "ecological parks" in Wales. And in 2017 Donald Trump's visit to Beijing racked up US$253 billion in trade deals ranging from shale gas to telecom chips, and from Boeing planes to Tesla cars.[29] Even though not all agreements were subsequently honored, Xi's trips did have a palpable impact on cooperation and confidence building. On many of these trips, Xi was accompanied by his wife, appearing as China's "first lady," whose glamour and fashion sense was intended to project a softer and more human face of China. Additionally, Xi's international exposure also served a domestic publicity benefit, showcasing Xi's high international profile, a leader enjoying his prestige amid friendly foreign receptions.[30]

Another indication of activist diplomacy is the building of international institutions. Up to 2013, only one international organization, the Shanghai Cooperation Organization, was headquartered in China. Xi's attempt to change this resulted in his many signature projects, including the Belt and Road Initiative, the Asian Infrastructural Investment Bank, and the BRIC Development Bank. The nature and impact of Xi's active diplomacy are best viewed in several contexts. First, from a theoretical and systems perspective, Beijing's inexorable economic and military rise and the imperatives of sustaining economic development meant that it encountered heightened "security dilemmas" with virtually all its neighbors in addition to the superpower, the United States. China expanded its capabilities and global reach, upset the existing balance of power, and invited counterbalancing efforts. Additionally, power transition theory, or offensive realism, also postulates that an emerging power with rising capabilities is tempted to challenge the hegemonic power and to reshape the system's rules and institutions. In turn, the hegemon will attempt a preemptive strike to short-circuit the newcomer, and this makes for a highly unstable and violent international

Table 11.1 Xi Jinping's Major Foreign Visits

2013	
March	Russia, Tanzania, South Africa, Congo, BRIC Summit (Durbin)
June	Trinidad and Tobago, Costa Rica, Mexico, United States (informal meeting with Obama)
September	Turkmenistan, Kazakhstan, Kyrgyzstan, Uzbekistan, G20 (St. Petersburg)
October	Indonesia, Malaysia, APEC (Bali)
2014	
February	Winter Olympics (Sochi)
March	South Korea, Brazil, Argentina, Venezuela, Cuba
August	Mongolia
September	Tajikistan, Maldives, Sri Lanka, India
November	Australia, New Zealand, Fiji, G20 summit (Brisbane)
2015	
April	Pakistan, Indonesia, Bandung Conference (Jakarta)
May	Kazakhstan, Russia, Belarus
July	BRIC summit (Ufa)
September	United States: Seattle, Washington, DC, United Nations
October	United Kingdom
November	Vietnam, Singapore, Paris Climate Summit (Paris), G20 (Antalya), APEC (Manila)
December	Zimbabwe, South Africa
2016	
January	Saudi Arabia, Egypt, Iran
March/April	Czech Republic, United States
June	Serbia, Belgrade, Uzbekistan, Tashkent
October	Cambodia, Bangladesh, India
November	Italy, Ecuador, Peru, Chile, Spain
2017	
January	Switzerland
April	Finland, United States
June	Kazakhstan
July	Hong Kong, Russia
August	Germany
November	Vietnam, Laos
2018	
June	South Africa
July	United Arab Emirates, Senegal, Rwanda, South Africa, Mauritius
September	Russia

Source: China vitae.

system.[31] Another paradox is that as Beijing's power grows, the international society also demands that it become a "responsible stakeholder" that contributes to international public goods and addresses urgent global issues such as climate change, growth and inequality, terrorism, peacekeeping, and international security. Yet Beijing's involvement in the economic development of the developing countries has exacerbated suspicion and mistrust, since economic power could translate into political influence that challenges the existing status quo of Pax Americana. Real-world situations are indeed more complex, but the preceding discussion provides an appropriate context for our consideration of China's new foreign relations under Xi.

Second, from a regional perspective, China's security environment in Asia has always been a complex and evolving multilevel game since it occupies a unique geopolitical position of being surrounded by fourteen neighboring states and eighteen thousand kilometers of maritime borders. This is complicated by historical and ideological struggles, enmities, and memories. In an important sense, even today the Cold War is not over in East Asia. Ideological rivalry and historical confrontation between "communism" and capitalism are still salient and are partially reflected in competing partnership/alliance structures with China and the United States at their heads. China and the Koreas, divided during the Cold War, must contend with the complex issues of reunification, complicated by the forward deployment of US forces in Asia. Japan and Russia did not conclude a peace treaty after the Second World War, and various territorial disputes between China, Japan, Korea, and Russia have kept up the tension. Some of the world's largest militaries and nuclear powers inhabit East Asia.

Third, paradoxically, China's economic ascendency has also magnified its own sense of vulnerabilities. Since becoming the world's largest manufacturer, exporter, and recipient of foreign direct investment, its second largest importer, third largest foreign investor, and the largest trading partner with over 180 countries, the issues of protecting its foreign markets and outward investments have become more salient. Further, as the world's largest consumer of energy, Beijing is heavily dependent on foreign energy and natural resources. For instance, as of 2018, its dependence on imported oil and natural gas was at 70 percent and 44 percent; iron ore and copper were about 73 percent; and chrome and cobalt at about 90 percent. This trend was expected to continue for a long time.[32] Such dependence made Beijing vulnerable to shifts in supply, protectionism, sanctions, and export controls. It was therefore more sensitive to the issues of strategic sea lanes of communication (SLOC), personnel and assets abroad, and especially maritime rights and interests. In the following space, I will elaborate on these themes by considering Xi's evolving thinking on foreign relations and how they have impacted China's various bilateral relations in terms of cooperation, conflict, and competition.

Xi's Quasi Foreign Policy Doctrine: The China Solution/ Proposition

Since Beijing had not spelled out a specific foreign policy doctrine, Xi followed Chinese tradition by employing a plethora of catchphrases and slogans to communicate broad themes with the Chinese public and foreign audiences. Beijing also used these notions to stake claims and to sell its policy. In general, as is the case with all metanarratives of states, Xi's open and private pronouncements of calculations and motivations of China's foreign relations veered between realism and liberalism/globalism, although they were most often couched in terms of the latter, depending on the audience and context. Accordingly, officially Beijing asserted its desire for a peaceful and secure international order to grow its economy. At different occasions, Xi invoked ideas such as "community of shared human destiny," "community of shared Asian destiny," "upholding justice while pursuing shared interests" in "global governance," and so on, which were later subsumed under the umbrella concept of "Xi Jinping's Thought on Diplomacy."[33] Underlining these ideas was Beijing's nod to liberal norms such as common interests, mutual benefits, win-win cooperation, and international peace and development. Xi reckoned that China could leverage more influence in economic leadership, providing for the international public good by enhancing interdependency. He opined that the world must pull together like a flock of geese to embrace economic globalization and to counter global challenges such as wars, conflicts, inequality, terrorism, refugees, and migrants.[34]

On the other hand, however, Xi did not refrain from articulating realistic notions such as acquiring wealth and power, as mentioned. China's "core interests" were broadly defined as (1) state sovereignty; (2) national security; (3) territorial integrity; (4) national reunification; (5) maintenance of China's political system and social stability; and (6) the safeguarding of sustainable economic and social development. Xi was most adamant regarding China's sovereignty when he asserted: "We absolutely will not permit any person, any organization, any political party—at any time, in any form—to separate any piece of Chinese territory from China," and "No one should expect us to swallow the bitter fruit of damage to our sovereignty, security and development interests."[35] Frequently mentioned goals of building a "strong national defense and powerful armed forces" were rather conventional. His notion of "preparing for the worst in order to achieve the best" was consistent with the realist tenet of hedging, that is, to do more than necessary to ensure national security since the latter is something that cannot always be assured. Xi's other notions, such as active defense, preparation for military struggle, and bottom-line thinking (*dixian siwei*)[36] were simple realpolitik.[37] In this context Xi understood that China was essentially facing a new security dilemma when he remarked, "The more China develops and strengthens, the greater the resistance and pressure and the external risks."[38]

One China watcher argues that these slogans, repeated ad nauseam by official publicity, tended to be banal and unoriginal and merely provide opportunities for subordinates to praise them in order to ingratiate themselves with the leaders.[39] In my view, these scattered notions were meant to convey Beijing's evolving intentions, and by 2017 they coalesced in the idea of the China Solution/Proposition (*zhongguo fangan*), which featured a set of principles and beliefs that approximated a doctrine. Beginning in 2014, Xi used the term to denote Beijing's contributions to issues ranging from global governance to multilateralism, from climate change to reducing poverty, and from cyberspace governance to development in the global South. Some foreigners were quick to interpret *zhongguo fangan* to mean Beijing's chauvinistic declaration to turn itself into a global hegemon, export its one-party authoritarian system, or even reshape the global order in its own image.[40] Things were not helped by the fact that the Chinese words *fang an*, which mean a proposal, proposition, or suggestion, connotes a weaker meaning than a "solution," for which no Chinese noun equivalent exists. Because of the ambiguity, a great deal has been lost in translation. Even official Chinese publications have used the word "solution" in the oft-cited claim that the CCP and Chinese are "fully confident in offering a China *solution* to humanity's search for better social systems"—even though at other places, a more accurate translation turns this phase into "fully confident of offering Chinese *input* [italics mine] to the global exploration of better social systems."[41]

In any case, several dimensions of the solution/proposition concept can be summarized.[42] First, China would position itself as a defender of the liberal global trading system against protectionism and isolation since its export-led industrial development relied on global development and since it was a foremost beneficiary of economic globalization. Economic globalization, Beijing reckoned, was not bad, although it needed effective guidance to promote innovation, inclusivity, fairness, and benefits for all.

Second, China would shoulder more international responsibilities since it now had the capability to do so. Since more participation means more influence, Beijing would no longer remain a spectator and a subordinate, and it would endeavor to have a voice (*huayuquan*) and uphold certain global norms. It would continue to open its market for investment and imports. With more confidence, China would engage in great power diplomacy to become a pillar of multilateralism, making the existing global order work for its purposes.

Third, China would insist on multiple and open-ended roads to development, because the complexities of global issues and liberal democracy could not be one size that fits all. Xi rejected Fukuyama's "end of history" notion, arguing for alternative and complementary approaches, noting that the liberal democratic experimentation in Iraq, Afghanistan, the Middle East, and Africa had not enabled them to overcome the "middle-income trap"; instead, it had caused these areas to be torn apart by religious, sectoral, and regional conflicts. Beijing dismissed these experiments as hegemonic attempts to impose a Western-style government, and it pledged that it would not export its own political system.

Fourth, Beijing would enhance its global role through primarily economic means and seek to champion green and low-carbon development. It would present itself as a peaceful, anti-imperialist, nonhegemonic, and nonallied powerhouse. As the latest "trading state"[43] that eschews military dominance over other countries, China would focus on trade, investment, and cooperation, serving as an engine for global economic development. If the world united like a flock of geese, it would "fly through wind and rain for a long time." For these reasons, Xi alleged, the *zhongguo fangan* could become a global proposition.[44]

There are several perspectives from which to view Xi's foreign policy quasi doctrine. Some argue that since Beijing is a foremost beneficiary of the liberal global order, it has a vested interest in preserving and gaining in it rather than trying to foster an alternative, as Beijing had attempted to do in the past. Skeptics were quick to point out the distance between Chinese rhetoric and reality, claiming that the formulation was just Beijing's self-serving and mercantilist way of attempting to gain influence. Others doubt that Beijing has enough soft power to influence global events. Still others argue that it would be natural for China to become stronger and more powerful, but it would face multiple new security dilemmas. In the following, however, we turn to the specifics of foreign policy during Xi's first term and the extent to which it throws light on these issues. We explore the gap between aspirations and practice, the nature of cooperation and conflict, and the issues of continuity and change. We begin with discussion of China's relations with Hong Kong and Taiwan; these regions are not foreign countries, but the former enjoys certain autonomy, and the latter enjoys de facto independence, with its own political/social/economic systems.

Hong Kong: The Tightening of the Screws

Beijing's predicament is keenly demonstrated in Hong Kong and Taiwan, China's backyard.[45] Tight economic interdependence and integration has brought about economic booms in all parts of Greater China. China is now the largest trading partner for both Hong Kong and Taiwan, but Beijing's mix of preferential policies and hard-line control tactics has not been able to win the hearts and minds of the people in these areas. In fact, in contrast to the tenets of liberal international theory, the closer the economic interdependence, the more fear there is about excessive Chinese control and influence by people in Hong Kong and

Taiwan. This, along with the conflict of political cultures and identity politics, was the major factor in the centrifugal tendencies leading to clashes that culminated in the Umbrella and Sunflower Movements of 2014. In the 1960s and 1970s, when China was suffering from totalitarian rule, Hong Kong and Taiwan began their rapid industrialization and economic takeoff. Under British colonial rule, Hong Kong was a not a democracy, but traditionally it enjoyed a free press, freedoms of speech and association, and large measures of individual liberties. Taiwan started to democratize in the 1980s. Consequently, the political cultures of the three places began to diverge, with the mainlanders more inclined toward patrimonialism and personal control, and Hong Kongers and Taiwanese more oriented toward political pluralism, accountability, and transparency.[46] As mentioned, most mainlanders interpreted democracy in terms of a strong state that could satisfy the well-being of the people and were optimistic that China was already democratic and increasingly so.[47] In contrast, Hong Kong and Taiwan residents tend to attach more salience to the restraint of government power, competitive elections, and the protection of individual rights. Additionally, the young in these two regions came to differentiate themselves from the mainlanders, with fewer and fewer regarding themselves as Mainland Chinese first and foremost. In all, differences in history, culture, and political/socioeconomic systems conspire to create general conflicts, despite the tightly coupled economic interdependence.

Hong Kong had been promised a high degree of autonomy after its reversion back to Chinese rule in 1997 under the "one country, two systems" formula. The region had been important to China in many respects, and Hong Kong also clung to its interdependent relationship with the mainland for its economic well-being and competitiveness, especially when Hong Kong depended on the mainland for water, food, and hinterland development.

By the turn of the century, Hong Kong had already transformed itself into a global financial and trade hub, and a big market for equity, services, and debt financing. Once Asia's freest city, the metropolis enjoyed the advantages of having a free port and a world-class competitive tax regime and legal system. Although the size of Hong Kong's economy was only 2.7 percent that of the mainland (down from 18.4 percent in 1997), it punched above its weight. WTO membership also granted it favorable status as a separate customs territory from the mainland.[48] For China, the city was a conduit of inflowing and outflowing capital, and exports and imports. Mainland companies gained access to global capital and unlimited access to the US dollar, and international companies used Hong Kong as a launch pad into China. For the Red Second Generation, Hong Kong was a place to stash their wealth or to launder their money.

Trade between the two partners reached US$305.3 billion in 2016, with Hong Kong China's fourth largest trading partner and third largest export market.[49]

China made many concessions to Hong Kong, for example, by fostering free trade and preferential Hong Kong access to the Chinese market through the Closer Economic Partnership Arrangements of 2003 and its many subsequent "supplements," the latest of which was signed in August 2013. Beijing's Thirteenth Five-Year Plan (2016–2020) envisaged closer political and economic integration with a megapolis called the Greater Bay Area incorporating Guangdong, Hong Kong, and Macao. This region of 70 million people would become a major innovation cluster privileging Hong Kong's financial expertise, Shenzhen's technical prowess, and Macau's recreational facilities. One aim is to facilitate mobility of people and resources, but the plan is vague about how to deal with the challenges of different customs, legal systems, and public services.[50]

Yet, increasingly, Hong Kongers have become resentful of the expanding Chinese control and interference, especially of the news media, which they think is limiting their freedom and autonomy.[51] While Hong Kong chief executive Leung Chun-ying and his government (2012–2017) were treated by Beijing as subordinates way down the administrative hierarchy, in Hong Kong they were often regarded, especially by the "pan-democrats," as dysfunctional puppets catering to Beijing's dictate. The "Occupy Central" movement of autumn of 2014 and other disturbances were directed at the Chinese government's overbearing attitude, although other factors, such as income inequality and polarization, sky-high housing prices and the high cost of living, and increased mainlander immigration were contributing factors.[52] The growing animosity even extended to the issue of language—although Hong Kongers are Chinese, their dialect is mainly Cantonese, and they still use the traditionally complicated written characters long abandoned in the mainland. Many Hong Kongers also suspected a collusion between Hong Kong's pro-mainland financial and business elite with Beijing.

The aspiration of Hong Kongers for direct elections through universal suffrage for their chief executive in 2017 was hobbled by Beijing's insisting that this officer must be elected from a list of candidates approved by Beijing. Under this constraint, it was predictable that a pro-Beijing candidate, Carrie Lam, would be elected chief executive. In stark contrast with the mainland, the Hong Kong government's economic policy of "positive noninterference" meant that government spending was a mere 14 percent of its GDP. This laissez-faire approach had consistently placed the region on the top two spots of the Heritage Foundation's yearly economic freedom index, but the outcome was a huge gap between the ultrarich and the poor, the latter consisting of residents of subdivided apartments, low-income workers, women, children, and the elderly. In 2018, the Gini coefficient peaked at .539, but successive governments lacked a coherent strategy to address inequality and to maintain the region's competitiveness in the technological age.[53]

In 2015, Hong Kongers reacted strongly when several Hong Kong book publishers who published on topics deemed sensitive by CCP authorities were abducted to China, where they were forced to recant in public confessions. Books published in Hong Kong often tackle the seamy side of Chinese politics, and, apart from serious research, there was also a great deal of thinly sourced yellow journalism and scandal-mongering books, including fictionalized biographies and tales of the private sex lives of leaders.[54] The sensational and titillating varieties, which thrived in Hong Kong because of the freedoms of speech and the press, were in turn popular (through smuggling) in media-controlled China. The kidnappings were suspected to be the work of zealous local officials in Guangdong, but they raised concerns over Chinese security officers operating outside of their jurisdiction. This raised more doubts about the autonomy guaranteed to Hong Kong, and a frustrated minority that called themselves "Hong Kong Indigenous" began to advocate independence.

On the other hand, Beijing continued to foster good economic relationships, an example being the Shanghai and Hong Kong Stock Connect Scheme, which was intended to allow investors to access stocks on either side of the border, to help full convertibility of the yuan, and to open China's capital market.[55] In a July 2017 visit to Hong Kong marking the twentieth anniversary of the city's return to China, Xi urged the local leadership to place national interest above all, and personally approved a visit by the Chinese navy's only aircraft carrier, the *Liaoning*, to underline the city's strategic and defense importance.[56] Yet agitation for true universal suffrage to elect Hong Kong's chief executive and legislature continued apace. Xi understood that the status quo was vital to China as a whole, but increasingly he grew intolerant of the democratic demands in Hong Kong. Fearing the contagious effect of the democracy movement on the mainland, he calculated that Beijing's control over the city outweighed the benefits the city could provide.[57]

In 2019, the underlying tensions exploded when the Hong Kong government introduced an extradition bill allowing suspects to be extradited to the mainland for trial. The bill stroked fear of more mainland control, and although it was eventually withdrawn, it sparked massive demonstrations, guerrilla-style street battles, and police crackdowns for six months. Beijing was deeply anxious about the possible making of a colored revolution in Hong Kong and its contagion effects on the mainland. Eventually, the protests died down with the outbreak of the Covid-19 pandemic in early 2020. However, in July, Beijing took the unprecedented step of imposing a sweeping, oppressive, but vaguely worded National Security Law that criminalized any activity that could be labeled subversion and secession. Article 38 of the law even extended extraterritorial jurisdiction over all non-Chinese citizens worldwide.[58] In one stroke, Beijing had crushed dissent and deprived the Hong Kong people of their unique political freedoms and

Figure 11.3 Hong Kong Protest, January 2020. Many banners read "Five Demands and Not One Less." The five demands are: universal suffrage for Hong Kong's Legislative Council and Chief Executive; retraction of the designation of protestors as rioters; an independent inquiry into alleged police brutality; amnesty for arrested protestors; and withdrawal of the extradition bill. Credit: Alamy

autonomy.[59] So draconian has been the effect of the law that political identities in Hong Kong were beginning to be reshaped,[60] and a new political structure has been imposed from Beijing.

Taiwan: Cooperation, Conflict, and War?

As mentioned in chapter 5, China enjoyed a honeymoon period during the term of Kuomintang president Ma Ying-jeou that saw the formal promulgation of the "three links" in 2008, something for which Xi's work in Fujian and Zhejiang can claim some credit. Since then cross-strait relations have dramatically developed, spurred on by economic complementarity—China has provided land, labor, raw materials, whereas Taiwan has provided capital, technology, and expertise. In 2010 Beijing and Taipei signed twenty-three economic agreements collectively known as the Economic Cooperation Framework Agreement. Rapid economic integration was already striking in the first decade of the century, when seventy thousand Taiwanese companies were operating in China, and by 2018 about two to three million Taiwanese, consisting of business persons, workers, students, and their families, resided in China. Cross-strait trade ballooned to almost US$200 billion in 2014 and 179.6 billion in 2016, when Taiwan became China's seventh largest trading partner and sixth biggest source of imports.[61] China was Taiwan's largest trading partner, taking more than 30 percent of the island's exports.[62] Taiwanese businesses and large corporations relied on the relationship to further Taiwan's economic growth and competitiveness, and Taiwanese investment contributed greatly to China's manufacturing industry. Xi and Ma's meeting in November 2015 in Singapore was an unprecedented first between leaders of both parties since 1949.

Xi reiterated the rhetoric of absolute sovereignty over the island, claiming that "a country that is split cannot make great progress." The long-standing Beijing position is that China reserves the right to use force against Taiwan if the latter declares independence. Specifically, the Anti-Secession Law of 2005 stipulates that peaceful reunification best serves the interests of both parties, and only when that island attempts to secede from China will Beijing employ "nonpeaceful means" to protect China's sovereignty.[63] In Taiwan, however, Taiwanese identity has grown stronger. Between 2012 and 2018, just below 60 percent of the population identified themselves as Taiwanese, and only around 40 percent considered themselves both Chinese and Taiwanese. Around 60 to 70 percent of Taiwanese considered Taiwan and China to be two separate states, and only 20 to 30 percent considered the two regions to be the same country.[64] Yet, ironically, surveys had consistently (2005–2017) shown no appetite for either reunification or independence—over half of the population of twenty-three million preferred the status quo or the middle ground.[65]

Yet, for many average Taiwanese, the ever-closer economic integration and exchange has threatened their self-identity and autonomy. A proposed services sector agreement between the two parties triggered the 2014 Sunflower protest movement led by students and civil society groups opposed to the perceived increasing political influence from Beijing.[66] Consequently, the mainland-friendly KMT was soundly defeated in the January 2016 elections, losing its legislative majority for the first time when DPP leader Tsai Ing-wen was elected president.

One of Beijing's formulas for reunification, "one country, two systems," which means the surrendering of Taiwan's sovereignty in exchange for autonomy under Chinese rule, is deeply unpopular on the island. Tsai went one step further to disavow the "1992 Consensus"—a vague agreement acknowledging that both sides of the strait constitute one China with different interpretations—which was revealed to be a fabrication by a KMT legislator. In fact, Beijing disliked the "different interpretations" aspect, and the DPP disliked the "one China" part of the formula.[67] However, Tsai did not concede to the demand of the "deep green," or the separatist wing of the DPP, for de jure independence.[68] Consistently, she urged Beijing to settle their differences peacefully as equals, and to respect

Taiwan's democratic system. In reaction, Xi rehashed the view that reunification under the "one country, two systems" formula could not be postponed indefinitely. By simple reflex, Beijing reimposed coercive measures that included the suspension of all diplomatic exchanges; restriction of Chinese tourists to Taiwan; and the blocking of Taipei's informal membership at international organizations such as the International Civil Aviation Organization and World Health Organization.

Beijing hawks (mainly in the military) such as retired lieutenant general Wang Hongguang, alleging the "irreversibility" of the Taiwanese independence movement, called for military "reunification," which he claimed could be accomplished "in less than three days."[69] Such outlandish views appearing in government-owned tabloid *Global Times* were directed to the general public to stroke nationalism, to ramp up pressure against Beijing's adversaries, and to shape public opinion. Not necessarily representative of the top leadership, these views often gave vent to its more conservative segment, especially the ultranationalistic PLA. Military planners in the PLA, knowing that Beijing had gained ground vis-à-vis the Taiwan military, often vouched for its ability to overwhelm Taiwan. Beijing applied military pressure by allowing warships to sail near Taiwan's shore and bombers to circle the island. Diplomatic offensive reduced the number of countries that recognized Taiwan to sixteen plus the Vatican.

In contrast, Xi's pronouncements on Taiwan differed in tone and intensity depending on the context and audience. For instance, in a 2018 meeting with Lien Chan, former chairman of mainland-friendly KMT, Xi said that Beijing and Taipei should show empathy and not allow disagreements to hold back regular exchange and cooperation. Xi signaled that Beijing's wrath was directed at the proindependence advocates and not at the Taiwanese public at large.[70] Even during the Coronavirus pandemic, retired general Qiao Liang, a China hawk, argued against the view that Beijing should use the strategic window to forcefully recapture Taiwan, dismissing it as counterproductive and detrimental to the goal of national rejuvenation.[71]

The United States, a major factor in China-Taiwan relations, is Taiwan's informal security ally. A part of its geostrategic interest in Asia is to prevent Beijing from gaining control of Taiwan as a gateway to the Pacific and a conduit to the South China Sea. It sold arms to Taiwan except advanced combat aircraft, but there was ambiguity over whether it would defend Taiwan against a military invasion. Taiwan's fear of abandonment was exacerbated by Trump's erratic and improvisational style, his American First principle, and his distaste for allies. Trump was quoted as having compared Taiwan to the tip of his Sharpie marker and China to his desk in the Oval Office.[72]

Although it is impossible to predict under what circumstance Beijing would resort to war to subdue the island, essentially there are two scenarios, despite the numerous speculations about Xi's intentions. The first postulates that Xi would likely attempt to take the island by force should the latter declare independence. The China Dream and rejuvenation require a unified China, and Xi views reunification as a fulfillment of his personal ambition and legacy. Beijing is more confident of its newfound military and economic capabilities and is more willing to take risks. Reunification by force could distract from domestic issues such as economic decline, domestic unrests, natural disasters, unemployment, and even pandemic crisis. On the other hand, a second scenario foresees a slim chance of Xi taking military action against Taiwan. First, even though Beijing possesses superior military capability, it is not sufficient to overcome Taiwanese resistance, especially with the latter equipped with US weaponry (Taiwan bought more than US$23 billion worth between 2007 and 2018). Second, Beijing's invasion of Taiwan would inflict bloodshed and great harm to both parties. It could destabilize the entire East Asia region and even the world, and the catastrophic outcome could dash the desire on both sides for a peaceful and stable environment to grow their economies. And it could even torpedo Xi's China Dream and Rejuvenation. Even if Beijing succeeded in militarily conquering Taiwan, it is unsure how it could govern a resentful and revengeful population. Third, Beijing's invasion of Taiwan would spark international pushbacks, sanctions, and even interventions at a time when Beijing- US relations are at their nadir.[73] With Beijing and Taiwan weakened, the beneficiary would be a third party.

In this regard, the theoretical lenses supplied by international relations analysis may help to explore two other dimensions. The first one is pessimistic. It is informed by the view that war often occurs as an outcome of misperception, miscalculations, bureaucratic politics, and gambler's syndrome.[74] Even though both Beijing and Taipei strive to avoid conflict, they may eventually stumble into war. The "rational" actor model of decision-making, which assumes that leaders can examine all available alternatives and calculate the cost and benefits before deciding, has not always been established in practice. Beijing's relentless pressure applied on Taiwan resembles a game of chicken that aggravates the prospect of war. The second is more optimistic. Beijing and Xi may realize the futility of the use of force in an interdependent relationship. International relations theorists have postulated that the use of force is a blunt instrument to achieve state goals compared with more cost-effective and predictable instruments of statecraft such as diplomacy, inducement, and soft power; the use of force will bring a loss-loss situation with no winners and may signify a failure in foreign policy right from the beginning. Further, although conventional wisdom presupposes that a strong military power will prevail over the weak, in international conflicts there are many cases of David versus Goliath where the strong do not often prevail. The United States' and the Soviet Union's experiences in Afghanistan, and the former's quagmires in Vietnam,

Korea, and even Cuba, are good examples.[75] CCP members may also remember that its weak predecessors managed to overwhelm the much stronger Guomindang during the civil war with guerrilla tactics, resorting to positional warfare only toward the end. Evidence exists to show that Xi may realize the futility of the use of force in an interdependent relationship. At the 2015 Boao Forum Xi declared, "History has taught us that no country that tried to achieve its goal with force ever succeeded."[76] Elsewhere he also said, "Willful threat or use of force should be rejected. . . . Flexing military muscles only reveals the lack of moral ground or vision rather than reflecting one's strength."[77] It is easy to dismiss such talk as mere rhetoric, but given Xi's experiences dealing with Taiwan and his frequent consultation with academics and think tanks, it is conceivable that he is capable of grasping a simple logic. One may also add that the specter of Chinese killing other Chinese in another bloody civil war is an anathema for both the CCP and the KMT. Yet it is still unclear as to what extent some Chinese officials have learned from their experience, as they are still conditioned by other factors, such as their willful nationalism, bureaucratic positions, and misperceptions of the other side.

Despite the dismal approval rating of Tsai in 2018 and the DPP's crushing defeat in the local elections in the same year, Tsai managed re-election as president, and the DPP retained its legislature majority in January 2020. This represented the DPP's fourth win in six elections since 2000, demonstrating a pattern in which the more saber-rattling from Beijing, the more public opinion rallied around the DPP. The Trump administration also authorized a US$8 billion sale of F-16 fighter jets in 2019, a first in almost thirty years. Taiwan also appeared to be a beneficiary of the China-US trade war when US companies placed billions of dollars of orders with Taiwan as an alternative to mainland suppliers.[78]

It was not until January 2019 that Xi gave his major policy speech on Taiwan that repeated the goal of peaceful reunification, although significantly he indicated no timetable for it. In a more moderate tone, Xi urged the exploration of how the "two systems" aspect of the "one country, two systems" formula could be operationalized. The Taiwanese were essentially Chinese, Xi maintained, and Chinese should not fight Chinese. Since blood was thicker than water, there were no hang-ups on both sides that could not be resolved.[79] For Tsai, however, such assurances were a nonstarter, and she warned Beijing of accidental conflicts. Beijing had intended to use the formula "one country, two systems" as applied to Hong Kong as an inducement for the Taiwanese to reunify, but the harsh crushing of the autonomy in Hong Kong had removed the last vestige of trust in such a promise. Overall, the PRC has been claiming to retake Taiwan under various formulas since 1949, but the centennial of the founding of the CCP in 2021 was indeed too soon, and the centennial of the founding of the PRC in 2049 is still far off, and a volatile stalemate will likely continue.

Overall, events and reactions around the time of Xi's first term again demonstrate the blind spots of Beijing's hard-line control policy toward the two territories, especially in the control of antimainland sentiment.[80] Xi and the CCP were amateurs when it came to the complexities of pluralism and multiparty democratic or semidemocratic politics. They might have fallen for their own propaganda. The overreliance on control, harassment, and hard power, rather than soft power or smart power, may bring diminishing returns. With Hong Kong and Taiwan, Xi and the Chinese leadership still need to fashion a more nuanced policy apart from the economic inducements and forceful reactions.

China and the United States: From Obama to Trump

From a systems perspective, the rise of China on the world stage, which necessitates an expansion of its security interest commensurate with its new role and position, has created a classic security dilemma with the lone superpower. Beijing's rise has upset the balance of power, threatened the preponderant power, and invited a counterbalance. Subsequently, the US "pivot to Asia," along with increased troop deployment and allied war drills, has created pressure on China's periphery and constrained China's strategic space.[81] All this could even produce a Thucydides Trap, wherein two competing great powers view their contestation as a zero-sum game, making war inevitable.[82] Today, of course, the global environment is much more complicated, and simple historical analogies miss a great deal of the nuances. First, the Thucydides Trap is a variant of system-level analysis that ignores the fact that China and the United States are not the only two major players in the multipolar system, like Sparta and Athens in the ancient world. Second, all contemporary states are inextricably intertwined, interdependent with one another through economic globalization, and wars and conflict tend to bring damage to all. Third, many states are nuclear powers with the capabilities of destroying one another: even a poverty-stricken North Korea can exert tremendous influence if power is interpreted in relational and situational terms. Fourth, the historical analogy ignores the specifics of state interactions and the role of the different perceptions and choices of individual leaders, which is the subject of state-level and individual-level analyses, as we shall see later.

A major incompleteness of the Thucydides Trap theory is the neglect of the fact that the economic and military capabilities between China and the United States are vastly asymmetrical.[83] China may be the world's largest manufacturer, largest exporter/importer, and a superstructural powerhouse that enjoys several pockets of advantages, such as electronics, e-commerce market, and a PLA two million strong, but its material power is no match with that of the United States. A few examples will illustrate this point. The United States owns the world's largest concentration of capital and technology, and its wealth and global reach will prevail for at least the next generation. It enjoys energy and food security unmatched by China. Geostrategically, the United States is bordered by allies and oceans, whereas Beijing is surrounded in a crowed neighborhood. The US dollar is the global currency, dominating the world's reserves and transactions, and the renminbi is inconvertible. As the largest military spender in the world, the United States regularly outspends the next eight largest-spending countries combined. In 2018, total global military spending was US$1,822 billion and the United States' share was US$649 billion, or 3.2 percent of its GDP. China, the second largest spender in the world, spent $250 billion, or 1.9 percent of its GDP, a proportion consistent since 2013.[84] As the world's largest arms exporter, US sales to ninety-six states consisted of 36 percent, compared with China's 5.5 percent, of global total between 2015 and 2019.[85] US arms and weapons sales can quickly change the regional balance of power, especially in Asia. In that continent, the US alliance structure labeled "hub and spokes" encompasses Japan, South Korea, the Philippines, Taiwan, and Australia. And the "five eyes" surveillance alliance among the United States, UK, Canada, Australia, and New Zealand created after World War II is now broadening its functions to target China. Conversely, Beijing formally disavows alliances; therefore, only Pakistan, and in an ambiguous way North Korea, can be considered loose allies. The United States' roughly eight hundred military bases located in more than seventy countries,[86] especially the ones situated in Asia, fueled Beijing's fear of a strategic encirclement. China founded its lone foreign military base in Djibouti by following the footsteps of the United States, France, Japan, and Italy. As the United States' largest forward-deployed fleet, the Seventh Fleet dominates the Pacific and the Indian Ocean. As of 2018, China had one obsolete aircraft carrier, whereas Washington has twenty, almost half of the world's total. China has 270 warheads, compared to Russia's 7,010 and the United States 6,550.[87] Beijing's space navigation network relied on US-owned Global Positioning System until 2020, when it completed its own BeiDou system. Yet, despite the asymmetry in hard power, the realist assumption of US security dictates that it must hedge against China's rise.

At the state level, the United States' long-standing concerns with China include trade deficits, currency manipulation, violation of intellectual rights, cyberattacks, human rights violations, and hard-line policies toward Taiwan and Japan. The United States desires less fettered access to the Chinese market to compete for trade and investment. The Xi leadership is perceived to be harboring a "might is right" mentality when dealing with medium and small states.[88] Chinese assertiveness in the South China Sea (SCS) is often regarded by the United States as a salami-slicing tactic to gain strategic dominance of the region. "Freedom of navigation and overflight" operations have been used by the United States to challenge the Chinese claims, since the United States has not ratified the UN Convention of the Law of the Sea (UNCLOS). Rhetoric during the US 2016 election year and the election of a new president exacerbated such resentments.

On the other hand, Beijing has felt that it is often ostracized for simply having a different political system. In its perspective, the United States uses "human rights politics"[89] to assume a moral high ground to hector the Chinese regime, weaponizing compassion and treating it as a convenient whipping boy to justify its own power prerogatives. Undue attention, China says, has been focused on censorship, reproductive rights, religious and ethnic minorities, and a small group of dissidents, to delegitimize the regime. The United States is accused of interference in China's internal affairs, ignoring great progress in improving the lives of its population and failing to understand China in context. Ulterior motives would be to remold China in the US image, changing its political economy to adopt US-style governmental institutions.[90] To counter the US State Department's annual human rights reports criticizing China, ranging from suppression of freedom of expression to crackdowns on dissidents to extralegal practices, the Chinese government now issues its own human rights reports on the United States, highlighting such issues as income inequality, gun violence, systemic racism, police brutality against African Americans, money politics, and civilian casualties in Iraq and Afghanistan.[91] In these reports and elsewhere, China often uses code words such as "hegemonism" and "neointerventionism" to represent the United States.

It is important to note, though, that the United States is not a unitary actor, and its interest groups often attempt to exert influence on China from different perspectives. Some big businesses prioritize opportunity for trade and investment, although others fear competition. Strategists are more anxious about how to contain China and stall its rise. Grassroots and religious groups and NGOs are more concerned with issues such as religious freedom, arms exports, and minority and human rights.[92] Yet the fact of interdependency makes cooperation imperative, and global issues likewise require joint efforts by the world's two largest economies, China accounting for 12 percent and the United States 24 percent of the world's GDP. Cheap imports from China have helped maintain the high US living standard, satisfied large consumer demands, created jobs, and kept inflation low, whereas China's continuous modernization requires the legendary US market and investment capacity. US businesses and competitiveness depend on the China market and on the supply chain of manufacturing in China. So intertwined and interdependent with one another, the partnership has been dubbed "Chinamerica." Yet the interdependence is asymmetrical—the United States is much less dependent on China than the other way around. In 2015 and 2016, US trade with China totaled US$659 billion and US$648 billion, with trade deficits of US$336 and US$310 billion, respectively.[93] China was the largest supplier of goods to the United States. The large amount of US Treasury bills Beijing holds means that it is heavily dependent on a healthy US economy.[94]

Under Xi, cooperation with the Obama administration ranged from the Paris Climate Change Agreement of 2016, an Iranian nuclear deal, and UN sanctions on North Korea. By 2018, Beijing accounted for 45 percent of global renewables investments but still 28 percent of carbon emission (compared with 15 percent for the United States).[95] Potentially, a proposed Bilateral Investment Treaty would allow China's global companies to better access the coveted US market, and the United States to play a major role in China's economic reform and restructuring. Xi demanded a "new model of great power relation" with the United States, to replace conflict and confrontation with mutual respect, parity, win-win cooperation, and more geostrategic space. Xi and Obama agreed that the structural stress between the two states did not constitute a Thucydides Trap, unless they were to repeatedly make strategic miscalculations.[96] During Xi's first state visit to the United States as president in September 2015, both sides pledged cooperation in military relations, nuclear security, ocean conservation, cybersecurity, counter-terrorism, and people-to-people exchange.[97] To counter criticisms about China's human rights record, Xi gave the standard relativistic line that China could do more to make improvements, just as all countries can; that countries develop

Figure 11.4 With Michelle and Barack Obama and Peng Liyuan at the White House, September 2015. Credit: Alamy

differently; that these differences ought to be respected; and that human rights are just one aspect among many in any bilateral relationship. Reforms to achieve social equity and justice serve to advance human rights in China, Xi alleged, and he promised to cooperate by conducting human rights dialogue and expanding consensus. Xi further pledged not to pursue militarization in the SCS.[98] In an established pattern in Xi's foreign visits, he signed large business agreements with US companies such as Cisco and Boeing; the agreement with the latter pledging to buy three hundred aircraft worth US$38 billion.[99]

However, the more cordial diplomacy between Xi and Obama broke down when Donald Trump assumed the presidency in 2017. Trump's erratic and abrasive style drove US relationships with China (and some US allies) to a nadir, although it also provided opportunities to Beijing. Trump's election rhetoric accused China of being a mercantilist state practicing currency manipulation, racking up huge trade surpluses, creating the "hoax" of climate change, stealing and "raping" America of jobs. Trump threatened to slap a 40 percent duty on Chinese imports, and his acceptance of a telephone congratulation from the Taiwanese president mentioning "close economic and security ties" rattled Beijing.[100] Trump's own mercantilist and isolationist standpoint contrasted with Xi's globalist orientation and might afford China the opportunity to step up as a world leader of internationalism, free trade, and action against climate change. At the G20 conference at Hangzhou, the World Economic Forum at Davos (January 2017), and the Belt and Road Initiative Forum in Beijing (May 2017), Xi broadened and refined his definition of China's global role as a peaceful, nonhegemonic, and a free trade champion. As the first Chinese leader to appear at Davos, Xi took several sideswipes at Trump, by remarking, "Pursuing protectionism is like locking oneself in a dark room. While wind and rain may be kept outside, that dark room will also block light and air." Xi also reassured other leaders, such as France's new president Emmanuel Macron, of China's commitment to defend the Paris Agreement on Climate Change.

Trump's pullout from the Trans-Pacific Partnership (TPP) alleviated Beijing's worry that it was a means designed by Obama to isolate and even contain China. The watered-down TPP somewhat weakened the US alliance pressure against China, giving Beijing more influence to push its Regional Comprehensive Economic Partnership. Trump's threats against established institutions, his "America first" doctrine, and his denigrations of NATO, WTO, NAFTA, and other alliances suggested a declining commitment to multilateralism and abdication of global involvement, giving further impetus to Xi's ambitious outward reach. Not all of Trump's various threats came to pass, and he claimed "great chemistry" with Xi at their first meeting at Mar-a-Lago in April 2017, and the Chinese were reassured when Trump declared that Beijing was not a currency manipulator, a statement later withdrawn. Nonetheless, Beijing's calculation that Trump's disruptive energy would spawn foreign and domestic turmoil that would absorb much of the energy of the president in a divided America did not come to pass.

Beginning in 2018, Trump progressively escalated a trade war with China by slapping tariffs totaling US$550 billion on Chinese products, and Beijing retaliated with US$185 billion tariffs on US exports. After multiple negotiations with the Chinese side led by Liu He, Xi's confidant, a tentative truce was reached in January 2020 entitled "Phase One Deal," by which both sides pledged to roll back tariffs and hike trade. Beijing promised to hike US imports by US$200 billion above 2017 levels, and both sides decided to continue dialogue on improving intellectual property rights, technological transfers, and currency practices.[101] This still left the bulk of the US tariffs on US$360 billion of Chinese goods unsettled. On the other hand, the US defense establishment pinpointed China as its top strategic competitor, which intended to displace the United States from the Asia-Pacific and "preferably from the global stage."[102] Trump, however, was obsessed with re-election, and he used relentless China bashing as a means to rouse his base. Ironically, he also in private pleaded with Xi to help him win by purchasing more soybeans.[103] Trump gave up the pretense of moral leadership,[104] but his aides continued to use "human rights" politics to discredit Beijing. Simultaneously, Trump initiated a multipronged technology war on Beijing that blacklisted Huawei, the world's largest telecommunications equipment manufacturer and leader in 5G networks. This restricted all US businesses from selling goods, especially microchips, to the company, and compelled US allies to exclude Huawei from their 5G networks. Huawei's top executive, Meng Wenzhou, was arrested in Canada at the request of the United States. One American concern was Beijing's national security law that requires private companies to surrender information to the government, although Washington has provided little evidence for specific collusions. Further, the United States ratcheted up more pressure on Beijing by forbidding Taiwan's TSMC, one of the world's largest chip makers, to supply Beijing, although Trump had not entirely conceded to the China hawks in his administration.[105] The latter had urged for more drastic hedging measures, even "decoupling" from China, but the supply and demand chains were so intertwined that it is uncertain if it could be achieved and at what cost. With the outbreak of the global coronavirus pandemic, Sino-US relations fell to a nadir.

Overall, system-level, state-level, and individual-level factors will continue to shape the contours of Sino-American relationships, and it is reasonable to conceptualize the nature and changes of the relationships to occur on a spectrum spanning from war to detente. In between, there are scenarios of cold war, conflict, cooperation, rapprochement, peaceful coexistence, as well as many different configurations. One recent study argues that the conflicts between China and the United States have more to do with a clash over ego and self-esteem than a competition over power and interests. A better mutual understanding of one another's cultures and motivations will greatly improve the chances of accommodation.[106] In comparative terms, Washington exerts its power evenly through military, economic, ideological, and technological strengths, whereas Beijing privileges economic and technological relationships in gaining influence. Elite and mass agreement on green development and fighting climate change is well established in China, whereas such a consensus is still lacking in the United States. Given the contrasts in historical development, ideology, political/social/economic systems, and global power positions, whether the two can find a middle way to relate to one another remains to be seen.

China and Japan: The Ice That Won't Melt

The China Japan relationship entered a "honeymoon period" during the 1970s and 1980s when the two countries privileged their natural economic complementarity and interdependency. China sought Japanese capital, technology, and investment, whereas Japan benefited from the Chinese market, labor, and resources. Japan, a close neighbor and US ally, had reached its economic and technological apogee, and China was just beginning to catch up. In security the two sides found a common foe in the Soviet Union. Japanese aid in the form of loans from 1978 to 2008 had aided tremendously China's modernization efforts.[107] Yet during the post–Cold War period, the Sino-Japanese relationship, which some describe as "the ice that won't melt," has fluctuated widely.[108] Economic interdependence, however, continues. China is Japan's largest trading partner, while Japan's is among China's top five largest partners, and bilateral trade reached US$344 billion in 2014 and US$303.3 in 2015.[109] As China's economy developed, Japanese investment increasingly turned to the manufacturing and service industries such as chemicals, machinery, automobiles, finance, insurance, and retail. By 2014, about twenty-three thousand Japanese companies operated in China, and accumulated Japanese investment amounted to US$99 billion.[110] However, in contrast to the expectations of liberal theorists, this has not prevented conflict and rivalry generated by security dilemmas and systemic factors such as strategic and alliance competition, ideology, and military/naval modernization on both sides.[111] Japan, like China, depends on SLOC as an essential lifeline for both trade and natural resources. To hedge against China's ascendency, Japan has augmented its alliance with the United States since the 1990s, instituted theater missile defense systems, and gradually moved toward the further dilution, if not abrogation, of Article 9 of the "Peace Constitution," which specifies that Japan renounces the right of belligerency in settling disputes and the right to keep a military force. Consequently, Japan has effectively rearmed, with the world's eighth largest military budget and a host of military hardware, although it has not yet become a "normal country" that looks after its own defense.[112] Tokyo re-established a Ministry of Defense in 2007, and new security and collective defense laws introduced in 2016 allowed it to defend its allies abroad.[113] Other subsequent legislation has allowed Japan to provide rear logistical support to allies, to respond to "gray zone" infringements of Japanese territories and airspace, and to sell weapons overseas.[114] New strategic realities, and Japan's response, have revived decades-old grievances and mistrust and fueled popular nationalism on both sides.

All this was aggravated by a bitter territorial dispute over Japan's occupation of the uninhabited Senkaku/Diaoyu Islands, which are located in areas believed to contain fisheries and potential rich mineral resources, oil, and gas. This dispute forms a dispute pattern in Asia where Russia occupies the South Kuriles / Northern Territories claimed by Japan, and where China occupies the seven island groups (including the Spratly/Nansha or the Paracels/Xisha) claimed by the Philippines, Vietnam, Malaysia, and Indonesia in the SCS. Such a pattern gives credence to the aphorisms "Possession is nine-tenths of the [international] law" and "Might makes right." As to the Senkaku/Diaoyu Islands, many Chinese, including the Taiwanese government, believe that because the islands were taken by Japan from China after the Sino-Japanese War of 1894–1895, they should have been returned at the end of World War II after Japan's defeat. Yet the issue did not come to the fore until the 1980s, when resources and economic growth became more salient. Since then, airplanes, fishing vessels, and coast guards from both sides have continuously tailed one another in a cat-and-mouse game, while a communications mechanism to avoid an unintended clash is still nonexistent.[115]

General historical enmity and inflammatory events, such as the biased Japanese textbook controversy and visits to the Yasukuni shrine war memorials by Japanese politicians and Prime Ministers Koizumi and Abe, revived Chinese memories of Japan's brutal invasion and occupation that lasted eight years, causing an estimated twenty million deaths, fifteen million wounded, and ninety million refugees. For many Chinese, Japan, in contrast with Germany, has been unwilling to come clean about its wartime atrocities such as the Nanjing Massacre and enslavement of "comfort women." They see Koizumi's and Abe's efforts as a cynical salami tactic to manipulate public opinion, especially the pacifist strand, in order to remilitarize Japan and abrogate Article 9.[116] However, in neither China nor Japan is there a unitary set of views on all issues. In general, Japanese conservatives have argued that they have apologized repeatedly over the war, while others argue that since Japan was the only country that suffered an atomic attack, it was unnecessary for the defeated country to apologize.

Others suggested that the Chinese have used the politics of apology merely to shame Japan, and that Chinese distort history too. Japanese prime ministers and politicians argue that they attend the Yasukuni shrine only to pray for world peace.[117] On the other hand, Japanese progressives opt for a more reconciliatory and confessional stand.[118]

Xi's father spent many years of his career in the anti-Japanese battles, and Xi was socialized with memories of hardship and suffering during the Sino-Japanese War. Unlike his two predecessors, Xi has yet to visit Japan, despite two frosty encounters on the sidelines of international gatherings. In November 2013, Beijing announced the establishment of the East China Sea Air Defense Identification Zone (ADIZ), which covers the disputed Senkaku/Diaoyu Islands and which overlapped Japan's own ADIZ established in 1969.[119] Tension heightened, and there were records of aircraft scrambling as the United States and Japan opposed the new ADIZ. Japan has its own interest in securing the SLOC and has supported US efforts to challenge Beijing's island building in the SCS. In 2015, Xi presided over a grand military parade to mark the seventieth anniversary of the victory in the anti-Japan war and the "World Anti-Fascist War," a first-ever commemoration of its kind in China.[120] This tension damaged economic ties, even though neither side could afford an escalation, as China required stable economic growth, and Japan needed the same to revive a sagging economy. Popular nationalism on both sides is complicated, but in the short and medium term both governments probably saw the political benefits of a certain degree of tension for mustering nationalistic support for their respective agendas.[121] Yet, for China, the encouragement of popular nationalism against Japan might prove to be a double-edged sword, as when anti-Japanese sentiment swelled in 2003, leading to anti-Japanese riots and demonstrations. Beijing might be constrained in its policy with Japan since any official conciliation or concession could be regarded as weak and unpatriotic and could raise questions about the Party's legitimate right to rule. However, Sino-Japanese relations warmed somewhat with Li Keqiang's visit in May 2018 (a first by a Chinese premier in eight years) and Shinzo Abe's first official visit to China (a first by a Japanese prime minister in seven years) accompanied by more than one thousand Japanese business people in October 2018.

For Tokyo, Trump's rhetoric about trade wars and tariffs ignited a perennial fear of US abandonment and *gaiatsu* (US pressure). Driven together by their concerns over Trump's protectionist and unpredictable policies, the two sides at the latter meeting pledged to cooperate more closely on trade, investment, and environmental and Asian security, and agreed to a US$29 billion currency swap for financial emergencies.[122] Sufficient goodwill was generated that in 2019, the two sides agreed on a state visit by Xi to Japan in April 2020, but that was canceled because of the coronavirus pandemic. In addition, the TPP, abandoned by the United States, was ratified by enough numbers to begin operation in December 2018. The UK and several other countries had signaled a willingness to join. This development invigorated another pan-Asian trade liberalization deal, the Regional Comprehensive Economic Partnership, which includes China.[123] However, Sino-Japanese relations were complicated by the US approval of the sale of 105 F-35 stealth fighters to Tokyo at a cost of US$23 billion in July 2020. Such a sale would enable Japan to have the largest fleet of F-35s among all US allies, the UK included.[124] The sale also put pressure on Beijing's calculations in Asia and might even trigger an arms race in that region, since interested buyers included South Korea, Australia, and even Taiwan. Overall, deep economic interdependency for both parties has not been sufficient to overcome political and strategic antagonism.

China Russia Relationship: An Asymmetrical Interdependence or a Marriage of Convenience?

The security dilemma between China and Russia plays out in a different context than that with Japan. The relationship between the two has swung from one extreme to the other, and Sino-Russian relations have often shifted according to the logic of a strategic triangle also involving the United States. Despite the rhetoric about a strategic partnership, Russia and China are not natural allies since suspicions and competition have often permeated the relationship. For both, the United States has always been a preferable partner except when circumstances have made that impossible. Russia has often been torn between its orientation to Europe or to the Asia-Pacific, but ultimately Europe has often been seen as the safest orientation.[125] Yet events such as Russia's annexation of the Crimea in January 2014 and interference in Ukraine, with the subsequent international sanctions and boycott, created diplomatic isolation for Russia, pushing it toward China.[126] The imperative of countering US influence forced both to stress their common interests and downplay their differences. As one Chinese official put it, "China used to play the supporting role in cooperation with the US. . . . It is now joining hands with Russia in playing a more important role in global governance."[127] This new rapprochement has been strengthened by a strong personal relationship between Xi and Putin, who share a similar apparatchik background, policy environment, perceptions of challenges, historical memory of the Second World War, and an authoritarian style of government. Xi made a strong point by making his first overseas trip as general secretary to Russia in 2013, and subsequently he and Putin have met more than twenty times at bilateral and multilateral gatherings.[128] Both are suspicious of the color revolutions encouraged by the West, resentful of Western dominance and normative power, and interested in fomenting multipolarity.

The new, closer relationship facilitated the finalization of trade deals in energy, infrastructure, technology, and innovation, projects that had been in the air for decades. For instance, the two sides approved an oil and gas pipeline worth US$400 billion in 2014. Russia relaxed its export of more sophisticated weapon sales, such as 24 Sukhoi jets, which could tip the balance of power in Asia in China's favor. Beijing and Moscow cooperated on Syria and Iran and pledged more cooperation and less competition in Central Asia. Although Beijing has traditionally propounded the supremacy of state sovereignty, it refrained from criticizing Russia and abstained from UN resolutions to condemn Russia's 2014 annexation of Crimea and activities in Ukraine. This abstention was chosen in spite of Chinese legal scholars' views that such actions were a clear violation of international law that could pose troubling repercussions for China's control over restive regions such as Xinjiang and Tibet. By 2018, China had backed Russia with six vetoes (out of an all-time total of thirteen) at the UN to block Western sanctions against Syria's Bashar al-Assad.[129] Beijing was motivated by perceived self-interest in supporting Russia as a friend, although it had always been skeptical about military intervention and foreign interference in sovereign countries.[130]

Russia relaxed constraints against Chinese investment in sensitive infrastructural natural resources projects, and even Russian complaints about massive Chinese migration in the Russian Pacific Far East eased, especially when the Chinese found making a living in Russia less attractive. They launched joint military training and exercises in the Sea of Japan as well as one in the SCS. A consensus was reached regarding the Asian Infrastructure Investment Bank, the New Development Bank, and the Belt and Road Initiative, even though some of these might traverse Russia's traditional spheres of influence. In return, Beijing supported the Eurasian Economic Union, Putin's pet project. The two sides also cooperated in forums such as the Shanghai Cooperation Organization and the BRIC grouping. But overall, the relationship has been more a marriage of convenience, with Russia occupying a position of weakness and isolation and China occupying a position of strength and enjoying the upper hand. China is still Russia's largest trading partner, but Russia was only China's ninth largest trading partner in 2014, declining to sixteenth in 2015. Russia badly needed investment and cross-border trade to augment its rundown infrastructure and to alleviate the pains inflicted by sanctions and plummeting oil prices. However, the hope that Chinese investment might make up the lost income from the West has remained unfulfilled. Further, the interdependence between the two is asymmetrical, linking together a stagnant and declining former superpower and a rising and reformist China. Russia depends on earnings from hydrocarbon sales for more than 60 percent of the government revenue, conferring on it many of the characteristics of a rentier state. Plummeting oil and commodity prices, weakness of the ruble and the economy, and Russia's pariah international status make it a partner with less influence, although both sides are keen to save face with one another and a semblance of an equal relationship. Even their potential rivalry in Central Asia is more muted.

In the short run, the new realignment, especially in strategic terms, has been firm. Official sources play up the "unprecedented" meeting of minds and the convergence of core interests, commitment, and trust. China has boosted trade with Russia especially in energy and agriculture. Russia has overtaken Saudi Arabia as the main crude supplier to China, bypassing the Malacca Strait choke point. The launch of an eighteen-hundred-mile pipeline in 2019 between the two countries further cemented this relationship. A perceived mutual strategic advantage and expediency has kept the two together for the time being.

China and the Divided Koreas: Uneasy Interdependence

With North Korea, China has a unique form of (inter)dependence and power politics. The two have been traditionally ideological allies, and China is often regarded as the only state that has some sway with the reclusive country. North Korea is dependent on China for approximately 90 percent of its energy and 60 percent of its food. China is North Korea's only ally and economic backer.[131] China accounts for 70 percent of North Korea's total trade volume, but counterintuitively, Beijing has been unable to exert much political influence on Pyongyang. Increasingly Beijing has been impatient and frustrated by the unpredictable and impetuous Kim Jong-un, who succeeded his father in 2011. Since 2006 North Korea has inflamed regional tension with a number of nuclear and missile tests and has progressively alienated Beijing and provoked debate in China about the worthiness of such an ally. Beijing finally and only halfheartedly agreed to participate in UN Resolution 1718 to apply sanctions against the reclusive regime after its fourth nuclear test in January 2016, providing that the sanctions applied only to luxury goods and not to tough general economic penalties.[132] Pyongyang further escalated tension by testing an ICBM that appeared capable of reaching Alaska and Hawaii in July 2017, followed by the firing of a missile across Japan and the detonation of a hydrogen bomb in September.[133] Xi has repeatedly expressed his preference for a nuclear-free Korean peninsula. Nevertheless, Beijing's ability to restrain Pyongyang and to pressure it to abandon its nuclear weapons has been limited.[134] For Pyongyang, nuclear weapons are a critical means for regime survival, whereas Beijing's dilemma can be explained in the following. First, Beijing needs North Korea as a valuable buffer to balance against and to constrain the United States and Japan.

Second, Beijing's interest is served by propping up the North Korean regime to prevent a collapse that could destabilize the Korean peninsula and create a flood of refugees into China. Third, Beijing wants to avoid Korean reunification, which would result in a strong and unified Korea aligned with the United States. Fourth, China has been reluctant to apply pressure, power, and sanctions to an erstwhile historical and ideological ally.[135]

The beginning of Xi's term saw China–North Korea relations noticeably soured. Xi had not visited Pyongyang, met Kim Jung-un, or invited him to visit China. In 2018, events developed quickly and dramatically when North Korean missile tests showed that its ICBMs were now capable of reaching the US mainland, and in April North and South Korean leaders met in a historical meeting to discuss an end to the Korean War and the "denuclearization" of the Korean peninsula, although no details were negotiated. The United States and North Korea continued their saber-rattling until Trump agreed to meet Kim at a summit in Singapore on June 12. At this meeting Trump offered Kim "security guarantees," whereas Kim pledged to "work toward denuclearization" without spelling out any specifics. After the summit, Trump told the American people that a North Korea nuclear risk "no longer existed," and that joint military exercises between South Korea and the United States had been called off. Before the summit Kim went to Beijing twice to consult with Xi and paid another visit after the summit. China took the opportunity then to ease its sanctions against North Korea, although Trump backed renewing them, citing North Korea as an "extraordinary threat."[136] However, even as the world's last totalitarian and autarkic regime, North Korea was not unchanging. It has promoted experiments in decollectivization, family farming and SEZs, and SOE reform that allow factory directors to acquire raw materials and sell their products in the market. These measures were similar to those introduced in China in the early 1980s, but there has been no indication that Pyongyang plans to go as far as China.[137] Xi finally visited Pyongyang in June 2019 to discuss issues such as denuclearization and sanctions.

On the other hand, Beijing and South Korea relations fluctuated in different dynamics. Seoul depends on the United States for security, especially against North Korean threats, but in economics, it is heavily dependent on exports (its trade-to-GDP ratio was 103.2) and especially on China, its largest trading partner. South Korea's exports and imports with China constituted 26 percent and 16 percent of its total, whereas it took in only 4.1 percent of China's total exports and supplied 9.4 percent of China's total imports.[138] Xi and South Korean president Park Geun-hye met many times and exhibited a personal rapport. China and South Korean economic relations were deepening, with two-way trade forty-five times greater than that with Pyongyang. In an apparent snub to North Korea, Xi visited South Korea in July 2014, and, while there, Xi and Park

Geun-hye urged Pyongyang to denuclearize and to resume the Six Party Talks, on hold since 2005.[139] Beijing's quandary was that North Korea had shown no intention of toning down its weapons program to reduce tension. It blamed the "mutual distrust and hostility" between the United States and North Korea for the tension in the peninsula.[140]

However, when in early 2017 Seoul installed a Terminal High Attitude Defense (THAAD), an anti-ballistic missile system designed to counter North Korea's missile and nuclear capability, it drove a wedge between Beijing and Seoul. THAAD was considered by Beijing to be a strategic gain for the United States and a threat to its missile capability, and the system's electronic warfare countermeasures were believed to allow the United States to spy on Beijing's weapons and defense programs. Beijing unofficially boycotted South Korea on everything from tourism to retail, from boy bands, TV, and films, and to automobiles. Chinese riots destroyed some South Korean retail businesses, seriously damaging the Lotte chain. Consequently, the newly elected South Korean president, Moon Jae-in suspended further THAAD deployment.[141] Beijing-Seoul relations were on the mend when Moon visited China officially in December 2017, reassuring Beijing with the "three nos policy"—no additional deployment of THAAD batteries, no missile defense system with the United States, and no alliance with United States or Japan. Reconciliation between the two countries took one step further amid Beijing's trade war with the United States.[142]

China and Europe

Strategically, both China and Europe desire to contain US dominance and to foster multipolarity, but with different degrees of emphasis as ultimately the United States is more important to Europe than China. Mutual security concerns between Beijing and Europe are relatively secondary because of the geopolitical distance, but the European Union (EU) has always encouraged China to contribute to the stability in the Korean peninsula and East Asia, and to cooperate with issues such as terrorism, piracy, immigration, and stabilization in Afghanistan, Africa, the Middle East, and Ukraine. China and Europe have shared common concerns over issues such as climate change, infectious disease control, and environmental pollution, and in these respects there have been talks regarding a "comprehensive strategic partnership."[143] In terms of strategy, the concerns of both parties are regional. Beijing focuses mainly on the Asia-Pacific with an eye on expanding its power and influence to challenge US hegemony, whereas Brussels is more concerned with Russian assertiveness, the Ukraine, and the unprecedented migration crisis.[144] Apart from this, economic relations have been paramount, although full development of its potential has been unfulfilled, and significant obstacles to better relations persist. Beijing has desired to have unhampered access to EU markets, to obtain Market Economy Status and an EU free trade agreement, and an end to the arms embargo imposed since the Tiananmen events in 1989. Yet it has been frustrated on all these fronts.

Beijing also considers any official European contact with the Dalai Lama an interference with its domestic affairs. Conversely, the EU is interested in better access to China's market and limitation of Chinese exports, which it has considered to be subsidized and EU job killing. China's biggest trading partner, the EU has complained about a huge trade deficit that in 2015 amounted to €180 billion, fueling EU charges of mercantilism and unfair trade practices. The EU desires more investment from China and more business opportunities in China, urging the Chinese to deregulate and to liberalize in order to remove barriers and high entry requirements for technological transfers and joint ventures. There is also a normative element in the EU concerning China's human rights issues and a resolution of the SCS disputes by peaceful means.[145] Beijing attempted to reverse the arms embargo by exploiting occasional weakening of the will to enforce it. However, US persistence has prevailed, arguing that military technology transfers will increase China's military capabilities and upset the balance with Japan and Taiwan. EU members have demanded conditions for lifting the embargo, such as the improvement of human rights in China, but they have often been divided, with France most flexible and Germany the more persistent. Nonetheless, leaked information shows that the EU had €400 million in defense exports to China in 2003 and sold other military-grade submarine and radar technology later on.[146] Further, the EU's lofty rhetoric of promoting democracy and human rights is often unmatched in practice, displaying a certain hypocrisy and double standards.[147]

During Xi's first term the EU was China's largest trading partner and China was the EU's second largest trading partner after the United States. China's production saturation, overcapacity, and change in its economic model provided both challenges and opportunities for the EU. A Bilateral Investment Treaty had been under negotiation since 2014, and the EU has insisted on its successful completion before free trade agreement talks could begin. A series of events, such as the financial crisis of 2009, the subsequent Eurozone crisis of 2011, rifts between richer and poorer members, the refugee crisis, and the 2016 Brexit vote, dealt a heavy blow to the organization's unity. The EU's ability to speak in one voice has been hampered by members' divergent interests.

Notably, Beijing made inroads with the UK's Cameron government, which approved the controversial Hinckley Point nuclear power station, Britain's first in a generation, in addition to plans for a high-speed rail link and a joint space research program. Xi's October 2015 visit to the UK was hosted in grand style by Queen Elizabeth II, and deals amounting to US$56 billion were signed. Yet the British referendum in favor of Brexit and the subsequent resignation of Cameron somewhat threatened this "golden relationship." The UK was the largest recipient of Chinese investment in the EU, but the Brexit vote and subsequent change of government might mean the loss of an ally who favored Market Economy Status for China. Brexit has also meant that China may lose an important access point to the EU, and it suffered a setback to the internationalization of the renminbi since London is the only place to conduct offshore transactions.[148] With Brexit, the UK's economic importance could wane for the Chinese, but on the other hand, the UK would have to strengthen relations with other parts of the world, and that might include China. One indication of this was the final approval of the Hinckley project by Teresa May's administration after its initial doubts.

One of Xi's strategies was to connect the EU more closely to his Belt and Road Initiative, potentially linking East Asia with Western Europe via a mammoth infrastructure network of rails, roads, ports, energy, finance, and telecommunication installations, and he paid special attention to the Central and Eastern Europe (CEE) countries that he visited in two trips in 2016 alone, including the Czech Republic, Serbia (not an EU member), and Poland.[149] Beijing saw the CEE countries as more receptive to Beijing's geopolitical and economic influence and lobbying for Market Economy Status in the WTO. On their part, the CEE countries entertained hopes of new sources of finance and investment apart from their traditional sources, such as Germany and France, despite concerns about Beijing's "divide and conquer" strategy and the prospect that Chinese promises might not necessarily come to fruition.[150] In any case, EU disunity was again tested when Greece, with early acquiescence from Hungary, blocked an EU statement at the UN Human Rights Council criticizing China's crackdown on human rights lawyers.[151]

Overall, despite the growing economic interdependence between the two parties, the differences in political values, geopolitical interests, and ideals of a global order have rendered the "comprehensive strategic partnership" shallow and limited. Increasingly, Beijing tends to see the EU as weak, politically fragmented, and militarily inconsequential.[152] By 2018, however, a convergence of interests between China and the EU seemed to have materialized in the pushbacks against Trump's global trade offensive, abrogation of the 2015 Iran nuclear deal, and sanctions against Iran.[153] At the end of 2020, the two sides agreed to sign a Comprehensive Agreements on Investments to remove barriers to foreign investment in China, but when the EU imposed sanctions on Beijing, the first in thirty years, over alleged atrocities committed in Xinjiang, a tit-for-tat reprisal ensued.

China and Southeast Asia: Cooperation amid Conflict

One outstanding strategic reality is that more than half of global trade, estimated at US$5 trillion annually, transits through the crucial SCS—especially through the chokepoint of the Malacca Strait, and the area's extensive SLOC are lifelines to other major economies such as Japan, South Korea, and China. Recent figures show the real trade value is more like US$3.4 trillion, but this still constitutes more than 64 percent of China's maritime trade (including oil and resources), or 42 percent of Japan's.[154] US trade is less reliant on the SCS, with only 14 percent of its maritime trade transiting this area,[155] but the United States' definition of security necessitates a strong presence. The SCS is also a rich fishery area and is believed to have huge deposits of oil and natural gas.[156] Under Xi China has progressively asserted disputed territorial rights in a starkly realist manner at the same time that its economic interdependence with ASEAN has been deepening.

China ranked in 2014 among the top three trading partners of all ASEAN countries and ASEAN's largest external trading partner, with trade volume reaching US$480 billion that year, bringing enormous economic benefits to both parties. Economic integration has progressed quickly, turning the ASEAN-China Free Trade Area in effect since 2010 into the world's largest, comprising 1.9 billion consumers and US$588 billion in annual trade. Overall, ASEAN countries have attempted an evenhanded hedging toward both the United States and China, avoiding falling into the exclusive sphere of influence of either. To constrain Beijing, ASEAN has resorted to a complex strategy of enmeshing, socializing, and balancing, depending on the context, but the SCS territorial dispute remains a major bone of contention.[157]

On the other hand, a security dilemma created by the ascendency of China has been keenly felt in Southeast Asia. Beijing's economic and industrial prowess has reshaped the political economy of Southeast Asia, a locus of strategic competition between China and the United States, both of which have had long-standing and complex relations in this region.[158] However, China's ambitions, maritime interests, and growing power capabilities have motivated it to stake a claim over the SCS as a core national interest. Although in 2002 China and ASEAN signed a code of conduct pledging dialogue, negotiation, and collective exploration in the SCS, China under Xi began large-scale dredging to create islands out of submerged atolls in the Spratley/Nanshi and Paracel/Xisha Islands, which are also claimed by Vietnam, Malaysia, Brunei, the Philippines, and Taiwan. All five of these claimants have occupied some seventy-nine disputed reefs and islets especially around the Spratleys and Paracel: China (twenty-seven), Vietnam (fifty-one), the Philippines (nine),

Malaysia (nine), and Taiwan (two). Xi reneged on a promise to Obama not to militarize the islets by installing runways and fighter jets there, but Beijing argued that the United States had long militarized the region by its naval presence.[159] Overall, Vietnam has created 120 acres of new land, whereas China almost 3,000 acres, and Vietnam's work has also been less environmentally destructive.[160] In addition, both Beijing and the Philippines also claim sovereignty over the Scarborough Shoal.

Throughout the dispute, Xi has maintained China's claim to the SCS as a core interest. This is reminiscent of America's Monroe Doctrine, although China is not the only interested party in the region, and the US presence is ubiquitous. Both Beijing and Taiwan claim sovereignty over the island groups in the entire SCS bound by the "nine-dash line," which includes the Paracel/Xisha and Spratley/Nansha Islands. (See Figure 11.5.) Taiwan's claim, which is based on history, discovery, and settlement, predates that of the PRC. Its case is buttressed by maps issued in 1935 and 1947 showing the vast U-shaped areas as Chinese territory, and by Taiwan's occupation of the Taiping Island (Itu Aba) and the Dongsha Island (Pratas) in the 1950's. Yet unlike Beijing, Taipei lacks diplomatic clout and recognition, and therefore it pursues it claim by stressing cooperation and joint development.[161]

Still, much ambiguity surrounds the nine-dash line, and recently China clarified that its sovereignty claims are over the SCS islands and their adjacent waters, not over the entire SCS.[162] In 2013, the Philippines brought a case under the UNCLOS that was adjudicated by the Permanent Court of Arbitration at The Hague, since both China and the Philippines (and not the United States) are signatories of the convention. China boycotted the proceedings, and in 2016, the tribunal ruled against China and Taiwan, denying that they have historical or sovereign rights over the SCS based on the nine-dash line. The ruling was no more than a moral victory for the Philippines, as China and other permanent members of the UN Security Council, despite their numerous signatures on treaties and much-touted adherence to international law, routinely refuse to respect rulings by such tribunals such as the Court of Arbitration or even the much higher International Court of Justice. Predictably, both Beijing and Taipei rejected the ruling as null and void, and the former asked the newly elected government in the Philippines to disregard the ruling. Xi held out an offer for negotiation, especially with newly elected Philippines president Rodrigo Duterte.[163] The latter, offended by US criticism of his bloody war on drugs, decided to pivot to China, and after visiting Beijing, secured promises of deals worth US$24 billion for railways, ports, energy, and mining.[164] Duterte reportedly entertained a grandiose vision of a "new world order" where the Philippines allied with China and Russia "against the world"; however, his military and defense establishment

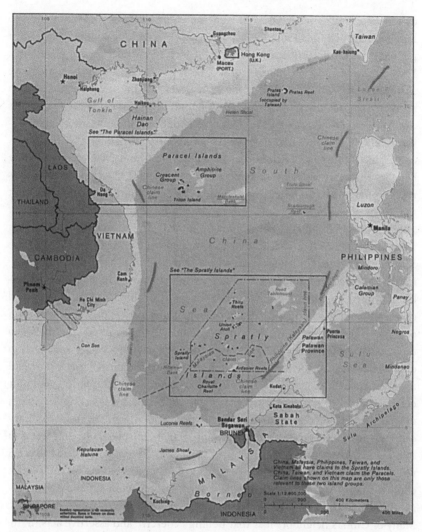

Figure 11.5 The nine-dash lines and China's claims in the South China Sea.
Credit: Perry-Castañeda Library Map Collection

tends to be traditional and American-aligned, especially in regard to new territorial disputes over the Benham Rise with China.[165]

It has been difficult for ASEAN to speak with one voice because of its consensus-based decision principle, and Beijing can effectively exploit this by winning over just one member. ASEAN comprises an assortment of mostly small and medium-sized countries with great variations in levels of development, ranging from poor and undeveloped Laos and Cambodia to highly developed Singapore to vast and sprawling Indonesia, the fourth most populous nation in the world. Further, the strategic landscapes of Cambodia, Laos, Myanmar, and Vietnam, by dint of their geography and history, are more susceptible to Chinese influence. The more developed maritime countries, such as Malaysia and Indonesia, enjoy more options.[166] Further, the ten countries can be classified into three groups according to their different orientations toward Beijing: US allies (the Philippines before 2016 and Thailand), the China-constrained countries (Cambodia, Laos, Vietnam, and Myanmar), and the hedgers (Indonesia, Malaysia, Singapore, and Brunei). Each of these groups reacts differently to Beijing.[167] A divided ASEAN could only express a joint statement of "serious concern" over the outcome of the Permanent Court of Arbitration without mentioning China by name.[168] In February 2016, President Obama hosted ASEAN leaders at his government's Sunnylands Estate in Rancho Mirage, California, the same venue where he met Xi in a "shirt-sleeve summit" in 2013, to discuss economic and strategic issues; a summit that failed to formulate a unified position on the SCS.[169] In May 2017, China and ASEAN agreed on a draft code of conduct for further negotiations toward peaceful resolution of territorial disputes in the SCS. This updated the code of conduct between the two parties signed in 2002; however, this did not slow China's construction of artificial islands, and a Chinese defense newspaper reported that China had installed rocket launchers on the disputed Fiery Cross Reef, purportedly for defense purposes.[170] The United States has countered by asserting "Freedom of Navigation," increasing military presence, and organizing joint military exercises including aircraft carrier groups near the disputed areas. It has also stepped up fighter sorties along China's coast. A 2020 report intimated that US military analysts have suggested Beijing's military installations on the islands could simply be wiped out by a missile strike.[171] Here diplomacy and power politics continue amid deepening interdependency,[172] and the standoff continues. Many of China's neighbors fear that Beijing's coercive and assertive acts in the SCS will eventually result in a fait accompli.[173] To balance China's rising military presence with potential huge economic infrastructural benefit—much of which emanates from the Belt and Road Initiative—ASEAN's strategy is continued enmeshment and socialization, as demonstrated by its ratifying of the RCEP in 2020. Individual countries, however, will have their own emphasis. For instance, Vietnam enters into "comprehensive partnerships" with both Beijing and Washington, while turning to Japan for defense and financial and security support. Indonesia, on the other hand, privileges economic cooperation with Beijing and downplays the SCS dispute.[174] Significantly, Taiwan's position aligns with that of the PRC.

Beijing's Economic and Financial Power, Mega International Projects, and the Building of International Institutions

The Belt and Road Initiative

Xi's most radical departure from the previous administration is his ambitious plans to leverage Beijing's economic and financial power by forming mega international projects and institutions headquartered in China. This way, Xi has hoped to enmesh China's neighbors and the world, and project Chinese power and prestige rivaling that of the West, especially the United States. Domestically, these high-profile projects render many opportunities for Xi to enhance his prestige and personal power. Fast becoming his signature project is the gargantuan Belt and Road Initiative (BRI), initiated by the Xi administration in 2013 and formally approved in 2015, which consists of the Silk Road Economic Belt and 21st Century Maritime Silk Road.[175] Both are designed to revive ancient land and maritime trade routes spanning large swaths of Asia, Africa, and Europe and connecting more than sixty states.[176] Such a project harkens back to historical times when China was in extensive commercial, cultural, and diplomatic exchanges with these countries, creating tremendous wealth and cultural fusion.[177] (See Figure 11.6.)

To promote this "project of the century," Xi has traveled extensively to countries in Asia, Europe, and Africa and pledged to provide a big push for many much-needed infrastructural projects. The Asia Development Bank has warned that if Asia's US$26 trillion infrastructural gap is not filled by 2030, it will threaten the growth of its fastest economies, and a World Bank study shows that every US$1 billion of infrastructure investment can create one hundred thousand jobs.[178] Hence, Beijing touted the BRI as a vastly scaled new development paradigm to build interconnectivity, promising a cumulative investment of US$4 trillion, an amount twelve times larger than the Marshall Plan (worth US$130 billion in current dollars), even adjusted for inflation.

Xi's numerous statements about the BRI have been couched entirely in the language of idealism, cooperation, and mutual benefit, as summarized in his speech at the opening of the Belt and Road Forum in May 2017. Xi claimed that the anticipated trade and infrastructural networks in Eurasia and surrounding areas would be a key driver for more inclusive and balanced global development. It would narrow the rich/poor gap, create jobs, promote industry and development, and foster stability by fighting social unrest and terrorism. In addition, by connecting civilizations, the initiative would encourage win-win cooperation, an opening up, innovation, green and sustainable development, and peaceful governance. For the world, the project promised mutual benefits by stimulating regional and economic development, providing investment in infrastructural

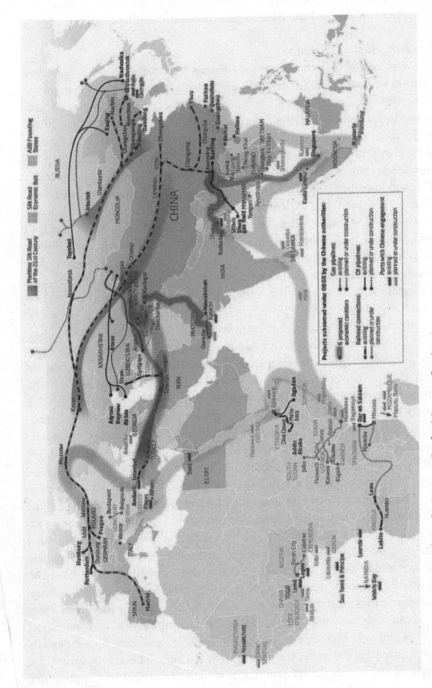

Figure 11.6 The Belt and Road Initiative. Credit: Mercator Institute

development, and help in stabilize Afghanistan and the Middle East to counter terrorism.

Xi claimed that China was not reinventing the wheel because the project complemented the development strategies of countries involved and leveraged their comparative strengths. The BRI promised to connect trade, finance, and infrastructure policies of such national and regional strategies as the Eurasian Economic Union of Russia; the Master Plan on ASEAN Connectivity; the Bright Road Initiative of Kazakhstan; the Middle Corridor initiative of Turkey; the Development Road of Mongolia; the Two Corridors; the One Economic Circle initiative of Vietnam; the Northern Powerhouse Imative of the UK, and the Amber Road Initiative of Poland. Xi argued that it would satisfy surging demands for infrastructural construction, and cooperation would integrate markets and enhance efficiency, satisfying mutual interests in a win-win manner. Finally, Xi pledged that China would neither interfere with the internal affairs of participating countries nor impose China's model of development on them.[179]

Early projects proposed included the following:

- A gas pipeline from the Bay of Bengal through Myanmar to southwest China
- A rail link between Beijing and Duisburg, Germany
- A huge hydropower plant in Pakistan
- A three-thousand-kilometer high-speed railway linking Kunming with Singapore
- Bullet trains budgeted at US$3 billion from Belgrade to Budapest
- A network of rails, roads, and pipelines linking Xian with Belgium
- 12,800 kilometers of cargo rail linking Yiwu in central Zhejiang and Madrid
- A US$46 billion economic corridor of pipelines, railroads, and bridges through Pakistan
- A network of rails, roads, and bridges linking fifty-four African countries

The project gathered steam, and official figures claim that by 2017, nine hundred projects worth US$890 billion were underway. It is China's most ambitious project to foster international cooperation, interdependence, and economic integration. Initially bankrolled by US$40 billion drawn largely from China's huge foreign exchange reserve, the project began to attract foreign investors as well. Some observers expected windfall opportunities for foreign companies, investors, and multinational corporations acting as partners in joint ventures, and this was especially true for multinationals such as GE, Honeywell, Siemens, ABB, and the Tencent Group that are already well connected in China.[180]

To deal with the tremendous complexity of these projects, a leading small group led by PBSC member Zhang Gaoli was formed to take charge. Beijing has played up the cooperative and liberal win-win aspects of the project and downplayed its power implications. Eschewing the term "strategy" in favor of "initiative" to describe the project, it also rejected comparison with the Marshall Plan, claiming that it is all-inclusive and does not cater to one ideological camp or the other. By 2017, Xi reported that already there was construction headway on a Jakarta-Bandung high-speed railway; a China-Laos railway; an Addis Ababa–Djibouti railway; a Hungary-Serbia railway; an upgrade of Gwadar and Piraeus ports; many projects in the China-Pakistan Economic Corridor; the China-Mongolia-Russia Economic Corridor; and the New Eurasian Continental Bridge Economic Corridor.[181]

For China itself, supporters of the initiative have argued that it could yield numerous benefits:

> Stimulate, rebalance, and upgrade the domestic economy and reduce reliance on domestic infrastructural investment
>
> Expedite the transition to a more consumer-driven economy
>
> Export or relocate overcapacity and manufacturing, especially in steel, cement, and aluminum, amid concerns over rising domestic costs and environmental degradation
>
> Spur regional development by enhancing and developing China's border and landlocked regions such as Xinjiang
>
> Bolster SOE capabilities and encourage Chinese capital, enterprises, technique, and capacity to go global (China was divided into five regions to boost local initiatives, to connect with cross-border exchanges, and to encourage central-local cooperation)[182]
>
> Open up land routes of resource supplies away from the choke point of the Malacca Strait
>
> Promote the use of the renminbi as an international currency.[183]

All of the above were expected to speed up restructuring and create jobs, which is deemed critical in realizing "two centennary" goals of the China Dream. Externally, it could reinforce diplomatic ties and counter terrorism, while significantly increasing Beijing's stake and prestige in the international system and even confer a leadership role for a new global order in a post-Trump and post-Brexit era.

On the other hand, Chinese officials and experts had extensively discussed the numerous practical challenges to an initiative of such immense proportions.[184] The first was a fear of overreach and dispersal of energy and resources since the projects cover such a vast and unwieldy area. The second was a concern that the rush to initiate hundreds of projects could be a form of "blind" development and investment that would breed all sorts of white elephants, waste, and duplications. China could simply be exporting its past negative experiences of

megaproject mania to the world. The third was a worry about the huge complexity of dealing with a myriad of cultures of which the Chinese managers knew
very little. Chinese SOEs and companies tended to have few ties with the locals
and little understanding of local customs and political economy. Further, many
of the targeted countries had underdeveloped market economies and administrative capabilities lacking the capacity to cooperate. The fourth was the fear of a
tremendous financial risk, low returns on investments, or even the complete loss
of returns. The fifth was an anxiety about overreliance on SOEs as the backbone
force, whereas private companies and market involvement were insufficiently involved. And the list goes on.[185]

In any case, the issue of management and coordination of thousands of
projects has challenged the organizational ability of the Chinese administration, since the BRI traverses regions and countries with vast and diverse political and economic conditions, not to mention numerous regional conflicts and
instability. In Africa, there have been long-standing concerns that Chinese infrastructural projects and exported Chinese labor working on them have nega-
tively impacted the local economies. A fear of Chinese influence prompted the
Thai government to forgo Chinese financing in favor of its own less ambitious
rail network. A joint venture with state-run Indonesian enterprises encountered
technical issues and mounting costs.[186] In Malaysia, Chinese investments were
entangled in local ethnic politics and cronyism.[187] Apart from these snags, however, Chinese capital investment seems welcome in most developing countries
that are experiencing slower growth. Iran, for instance, has been most open to
Chinese infrastructural projects for its aspiration to become a trading hub between Europe and China.[188] One interlocutor told the author that Chinese SOEs
have employed the services of companies such as Delloitte and KPMG that have
expertise and preexisting offices in countries where the SOEs intend to invest. At
home, it was expected that bureaucratic and regional conflict and competition
over funds and resources would intensify, but Xi and his team have understood
that this is a normal manifestation of politics.

A mammoth project with China at its helm has elicited realpolitik concerns
in other countries over the sensitive issue of increasing Chinese influence. The
following are a few highlights. First, the project has been viewed as a conspiracy,
a Trojan horse, and a unilateral measure to promote Chinese geopolitical power
and influence, raising suspicion and tension among states involved, especially
in view of Beijing's assertive stand in the SCS. Fears have been expressed that
the project is a way to export and dump excess manufactured goods and overcapacity. Opponents of the project in India have seen it as a "string of pearls"
strategy to encircle India.[189] Second, the project has been interpreted to be a direct geopolitical challenge to the United States and its traditional conceptuali-
zation of world trade, as well as a rival to the Washington-centered TPP (which

Trump subsequently annulled) and Transatlantic Trade and Investment partnership. Third, the project was expected to eventually erode some of Russia's traditional spheres of influence, especially in Central Asia. However, Russia has shown a willingness to cooperate with the project, and Central Asian countries have not necessarily pivoted to Beijing,[190] but the prospect of future rivalry cannot be ruled out. Finally, a neglected aspect is what can be labeled "third party" security dilemma. For instance, the massive Chinese investment in Pakistan, such as the Gwadar port, potentially can foster Pakistani economic developments that in turn could exacerbate the security dilemma between India and Pakistan. In the same vein, the prospect of economic developments in various areas covered in the BRI may eventually upset the various power balances in these regions and trigger new strategic reshuffles.

By 2018, various issues and setbacks became clear. There were multiple project delays and heavy losses in Chinese investment. Furthermore, fear and suspicion of Chinese influence persisted, and Beijing was charged with alleged neglect of other countries' sovereignty, disproportionate profits reaped by Chinese enterprises, and creation of a debt trap for participating countries. India expressed fears that the large Chinese investment in Nepal could reduce its own influence there. Such criticisms and pushbacks by rivals prompted Beijing to consider slowdowns and modifications.[191] Yet the momentum continued, and by the end of 2019, six years after the initiation of the BRI, Beijing announced that 136 countries and thirty international organizations had signed a total of 198 cooperation agreements, with Italy the only G7 member joining. Five free trade agreements and eighty-two trade cooperation zones with BRI economies have materialized, and the cumulative trade volume between China and other members had exceeded US$7.5 trillion. New aspects of cooperation include e-commerce and technology transfer, as well as discussions on intellectual property, tax, agriculture, and law.[192] A World Bank report concurs that the BRI can significantly boost development and reduce poverty in dozens of developing countries, providing that they implement reforms, increase transparency, improve debt sustainability, and strengthen environmental standards and social safety nets.[193] In 2020, the global coronavirus pandemic seriously disrupted global economic and diplomatic exchanges, but Beijing proposed public health cooperation within the BRI infrastructure.

The Asia Infrastructural Investment Bank, BRICS New Development Bank, and the Silk Road Fund

Working in tandem with the BRI are new financial organizations initiated by Xi such as the Asia Infrastructural Investment Bank (AIIB), BRICS New Development Bank, Shanghai Cooperation Organization Development Bank, and the Silk Road Fund. Both the AIIB and the New Development Bank, headquartered in Beijing and Shanghai, respectively, began lending in 2016. Formally established in 2015, the AIIB consisted of fifty-seven founding members drawn mostly from Asia and Europe. Many US allies in Europe and Asia ignored US pressure and joined, whereas African and Latin American countries expressed great interest, especially after the market turmoil generated by Brexit, and this boosted total membership to seventy. In part designed to address the aforementioned huge infrastructural gaps in Asia, the AIIB was seen to be a remedy for frustrations with the stymied reforms by existing global institutions that were to give emerging powers a say, and with the slow-moving and excessively bureaucratic ways associated with the World Bank and the Asian Development Bank.[194]

The AIIB offered its first loans in 2016 to the tune of US$10 billion per year. These new international financial institutions, bankrolled by Chinese banks and companies, have supported megaprojects such as the BRI, and have encouraged Beijing's hopes to find its own niche to exert influence. Chinese officials claim that they have a better understanding of the needs of the developing South and that the new initiatives will complement the international finance system given Beijing's experience in economic development. Increased trade and economic interaction with the world will give China more experience in global economic governance, they say, and boost its relations with other counties such as Russia.

On the other hand, as with the BRI, foreign powers have expressed various concerns with the AIIB. First, there is the fear that Beijing will advance its economic and geostrategic influence and challenge the Bretton Woods system dominated by the United States and the West, since Beijing holds an effective veto in AIIB decision-making, holding 26 percent of the voting shares. Others are concerned that it will fragment global governance by creating two competing blocks of economic influence,[195] although Trump's proposed reduced contribution to the World Bank and the IMF and his distaste for multilateralism complicated matters. Second, questions have been raised on whether the AIIB would adhere to international governance standards and honor its clean and green motto, despite its explicit commitment to observe the Paris Climate Agreement and the UN's Sustainable Development Goals. Third, the AIIB lacks experience and knowledge in project selection and in resisting capture by borrowing countries. Critics have pointed out that, in the past, Chinese lending practices had been opaque and problematic since the China Development Bank had rendered financial support to Sudan and Venezuela in exchange for oil exports, apparently indifferent to human rights violations there. For these reasons and others, such as strategic considerations, the United States and Japan still refuse to join, although Japan's position is softening.[196]

Later interpretations of AIIB practices tend to be more favorable.[197] Despite the soft power gain for Beijing, the AIIB does not appear to be a Chinese government-controlled institution, and it has developed into a complement to the multilateral order rather than a counterweight to it. Its board of governors includes a representative from every member country, and as more countries have joined, Beijing's 26 percent voting share is short of the three-quarters vote required for changing governing rules and approving major funding projects.[198] AIIB has set high environmental and social standards commensurate with international practices. Among the twelve current development projects, such as the US$600 million Trans-Anatolian Natural Gas Pipeline connecting Azerbaijan with Turkey and Europe, most have been cofinanced with partners such as the World Bank, the Asian Development Bank, and the European Investment Bank. Thus, the AIIB has an incentive to cooperate widely to reduce risk and to learn from the best practices of other institutions.[199] By 2019, membership in the organization increased to one hundred. In the long run, in the process of challenging the inadequacies of the global banking system, Beijing may also be socialized to its manifested ideals.

Another initiative under Xi is membership in the New Development Bank (NDB) operated by BRIC countries. Each member country contributes one-fifth of the share of the bank and therefore enjoys an equal voting share in decision-making. Beijing has taken pains to emphasize the NDB will complement south-south cooperation and practice equity in power-sharing and sustainable development attuned to the developmental needs of developing nations. In contrast with the World Bank and the IMF, the NDB dispenses with political conditionalities and "structural adjustment," declaring that it favors projects that respect the environment, local communities, and civil society engagement. It also promises to help meet the huge unfulfilled demands for infrastructure. As a multilateral institution, the NDB may deflect some of the criticisms leveled at China for its investment projects in Africa, for neglecting environment standards and for failing to improve the living standards of the local population.[200] If successful, the NDB will likely inject fresh thinking into developmental practices.

Outside concerns expressed about the NDB are similar to those regarding the BRI and AIIB. First, there is the possibility of dominance by China and tensions among member states with such heterogeneity and geopolitical differences. Second, the remit of the NDB may overlap with infrastructural projects supported by the AIIB, the Asia Development Bank, and the "new gold fund" that spearhead the BRI project. Third, there is the question whether the NDB will respect international labor, social, and environmental standards. Last, when the initial seed capital provided by the member states is exhausted, the NDB will have to turn to the financial market to raise funding and therefore will have to command confidence. If China, which has a larger GDP than the other four BRICs combined, is seen to dominate the bank, it will make investors suspicious.[201] Naturally, Beijing has downplayed potential competition with the World Bank and the IMF and highlighted cooperation and complementarity, which are sup-posed to allow developing countries to share greater influence. The NDB, it is argued, will address the long-standing frustration with the dominance by the world's wealthiest countries, which have consistently refused to increase voting shares for the developing countries. Since its founding, the NDB has approved approximately sixty projects worth US$18 billion in sectors like energy, trans-portation, urban development, and environmental protection.[202]

China's UN Policy, Peacekeeping, and Foreign Aid

Xi's more activist diplomacy also showed in the UN, where it already headed four out of fifteen specialized agencies, compared with one for the United States.[203] In 2015, Xi pledged to supply the UN a permanent peacekeeping force of eight thousand troops for the latter's plan to form a standby force of fifteen thousand, and to donate US$100 million to the African Union. Xi also pledged to train two thousand peacekeepers from other countries, donate a US$1 billion "peace and development fund," and to launch ten minesweeping programs. Xi maintained that Africa had the greatest need for peacekeeping in the long run, and Xi's an-nouncement marked a watershed in China's role as a global security provider. Such activism, however, has been viewed as Beijing's efforts to exert its influence at the expense of the United States.[204] Previously, Beijing had been reluctant to vote for UN peacekeeping resolutions, especially the nonconsensual ones. It was wary that the "interference" in the internal affairs of other states might set a prec-edent to question its sovereignty over areas such as Tibet and Xinjiang. A combi-nation of factors, however, such as the desire to protect its national interests and gain real-world military experience, and to secure its reputation and prestige, changed its approach.[205] Beijing's annual contribution to the UN regular budget rose steadily to 7.9 percent between 2016 and 2018, and to 12.0 percent between 2019 and 2021, making it the second largest contributor. China's contribution to the UN peacekeeping budget (total US$7.87 billion for 2016–2017) rose from 6.6 percent in 2015 to 10.2 percent between 2016 and 2018, surpassing Japan for the first time as the second largest contributor after the United States.[206] As the largest contributor of troops among the UN Security Council's permanent members, China has deployed more than three thousand peacekeepers in ten missions worldwide, including South Sudan, Lebanon, and Mali.[207]

In September 2017, Beijing reported that it had completed the registra-tion of eight thousand permanent troops and set up nineteen peacekeeping standby units of six services—infantry, transportation, guards, quick re-sponse, and helicopter units. The opening of China's first overseas military base in Djibouti was said to have facilitated "logistic purposes" for antipiracy, peacekeeping, and humanitarian relief operations. By early 2018, there were twenty-five hundred Chinese peacekeepers in action, and Beijing claimed that it had already trained eleven hundred foreign troops and planned to train nine hundred more by 2020.[208]

Rapidly becoming a leading global financier, China contributes more to the "hardware" of economic development, to energy generation, transport, industry, mining, and construction, than to its "software" of education, health, and governance.[209] Generally, foreign aid is considered a normal means of statecraft serving the interests of the donor states. Seldom motivated by altruism, it is most often an outcome of geostrategic, diplomatic, and economic considerations. Its benefits for recipients have often been questionable. However, in China as well as in Western countries, the general public tends to regard foreign aid contributions as if they are free gifts. This accounts for the often-contradictory official narratives intended for different audiences—an emphasis on how foreign aid benefits the donors' domestic businesses, stakeholders, and public, and a focus on altruism and mutual benefits for foreign consumption.

One irony is that poor and "self-sufficient" China under Mao actually dispensed generous and meaningful aid, for strategic and reputational purposes, whereas in the post-Mao period China was a major international recipient until 2008. Another irony is that the conduct of Chinese foreign aid is opaque, and information is so scarce that not until a major research report published by AIDDATA in 2017 did a clearer picture emerge. AIDDATA estimated that between 2000 and 2014 China dispensed US$354.4 billion of foreign aid, second to the US$394.6 in the same period, to 139 countries in Africa, the Middle East, Asia, Latin America, the Caribbean, and Central and Eastern Europe. Starting from a low base of US$1.32 billion in Official Development Assistance in 2000, China's foreign aid expanded tenfold to US$13.77 billion a decade later in 2010, becoming the fourth largest donor after the US, UK, and Germany.[210]

Like most foreign aid narratives, the Chinese official pronouncements variously emphasize mutual benefits, nonintervention in internal affairs of recipients, lack of conditionalities, and south-south cooperation. Occasionally, however, to reassure a domestic public skeptical about why a middle-income country like China should dispense foreign aid, Chinese officials starkly emphasizes the realpolitik benefits and control of donors. For example, one official source declared that "fundamentally, foreign aid enables China to find new markets for its surplus capital, production capability, and labor. If we do not fight for such footholds, others will do so."[211] On the other hand, foreign critics and rivals have labeled China a "rogue donor" for (1) extracting natural resources and creating dependency; (2) being indifferent to authoritarian and dictatorial regimes and propping up corrupt regimes; (3) creating high-cost, low-return "white elephant" projects; (4) serving Chinese national interests and strategic advantages first; and (5) undermining effectiveness of Western assistance.[212]

AIDDATA estimates that less than 25 percent of China's official financing qualifies as Official Development Assistance (ODA), foreign aid in the strict sense, which requires a development intent and a minimum concessionality level of 25 percent or higher of the grant element. Other documented financial outlays that do not meet these criteria are classified as Other Official Flows (OOF). Further, 16 percent of China's total foreign assistance is termed Vague Official Finance, which does not fall in either category because of a lack of official information. Overall, much of China's foreign assistance has consisted of export credits and market-rate or close-to-market-rate loans. Furthermore, China's net ODA, or the ratio of ODA to a donor's gross national income, is much lower than other major donors such as Japan and the United States, or even minuscule compared to the aid dispensed during Mao's era.

In spite of all this, AIDDATA concluded that Chinese aid, similar to OECD Development Assistance Committee aid and in contrast with World Bank aid, does boost recipients' economic growth both nationally and locally, and that it does not inhibit the economic growth effects of Western assistance. There was, however, no evidence that OOF aid improves economic growth outcomes. In the future, if the sectoral and distribution composition of Chinese aid changes over time and moves toward increased ODA, especially possible with the gradual unfolding of the BRI project, Beijing's impact can potentially be greater.

Conclusion

Globalization and economic interdependence have yielded multiple benefits for China and the world. They have accelerated Chinese economic growth and integrated its economy into the global supply-and-demand chain. In addition, IMF statistics show that between 2013 and 2018 China had been the global growth engine accounting for 28 percent (with the United States and India at 12 percent each) of all growth worldwide. China pulled along other smaller economies in its train by importing raw materials and supplying manufactured products and outward investment.[213] As a foremost beneficiary of the liberal international order despite a few qualms, Beijing has incentive for the status quo to continue. However, the economic and military rise of China and the imperatives of sustaining growth and national and resource security meant heightened security dilemmas between Beijing and the world. To be sure, even during the Hu Jintao era Beijing had begun to expand its international influence and "strategic hedging,"[214] which incorporated an interest in the SCS. China's neighbors were aware of the challenge of the rise of China and the perceived "China threat." Xi's redoubled efforts and ambiguous goals to boost economic development and modernization, to rise up the value chain, in the logic of security dilemma, have exacerbated the fear of the Chinese juggernaut. They have further upset the balance of power and generated mistrust and pushbacks, especially from the dominant power the United States. Xi's notion of a China solution/proposition stroke fear of Beijing's ambition to export its authoritarian model. And China's handling of domestic terrorism, subversion, and secession has been politicized, especially its oppressive measures in Xinjiang.

Several points deserve mention. First, the world had always dealt with China when it was weak, but the new reality of a rising China presided over by a strongman and a strategic thinker is doubly threatening for many. In many circles the mistrust of Beijing turned into China bashing that is reminiscent of the vehement Japan bashing in the 1980s, when Japan expanded its economic and technical power worldwide, bringing with it charges of mercantilism, a closed market, and unfair trade. The pattern is now being repeated, with the added dimensions that China's economic and technological capabilities are complemented by its political and military capabilities and therefore even more threatening. And unlike Japan, which is a liberal democracy and a US ally, China is an authoritarian state subscribing to socialist ideology. Beijing is often seen to be a bully and a usurper, and many states react by hedging, counterbalancing, and even containment.

Second, Trump's administration exerted an unprecedented impact on global politics. His mercantilist and unilateral inclinations alienated allies and adversaries alike. His primary goal was to stay in power and to win the next election, and he saw no intrinsic value in international cooperation or agreement. Diplomacy was reduced to coercion, threats, confrontation, and brinkmanship. Yet, lacking any game plan or strategy, he stumbled along with improvisations and flip-flops, allowing his advisers to cater to his impulses. Sino-American relations sunk to a new nadir, even though economic warfare and partial delinking could damage both sides and cause collateral damages worldwide.

Third, Xi's first term began with ambitious plans for growth and development extending overseas, apparently without anticipating that megaprojects such as Made in China 2025 and the BRI could be interpreted as threatening to its neighbors and trade partners. Beijing expected that "liberal" trade, investment, and infrastructural projects would enmesh with win-win outcomes. Even though it was vigilant about a protean and turbulent international condition, it did not expect a chorus of external hostilities and pushbacks. While confronting multiple security dilemmas and mistrust, Beijing's and Xi's perception of a hostile and fiercely competitive international environment heightened. They were even more sensitive to issues of regime security, sovereignty, and external shocks.

During Xi's second term, the 2020 outbreak of the coronavirus pandemic originating from Wuhan not only put Beijing on the defensive, but had a devastating socioeconomic and political impact globally. Most essential services were at a standstill, damaging the global economy, employment, and income. International relations were more strained and uncertain. Despite early missteps Beijing dealt relatively effectively with the pandemic by privileging its centralized and organizational prowess. However, US election year rhetoric made China bashing a central theme, and China–United States tit-for-tat made the anarchic aspect of international relations more pronounced. Some China observers have argued that the American retreat from global leadership has created a vacuum for China to step into, but this ignores the encyclopedic range of domestic issues and Beijing's general lack of soft power. China's hard-line crackdowns in Xinjiang and Hong Kong have further eroded Beijing's normative appeal. Meanwhile, urgent global issues, such as climate change, ecological disasters, species extinction, and nuclear proliferation, remain untackled. Ordinarily, the security dilemma may not be an inescapable reality, providing that states seek to understand one another's motives and intentions, but in the absence of political will to cooperate and compromise, the dilemma may well become a self-fulfilling prophecy.

12

Power, Policy, and Political Succession

The Nineteenth Party Congress, October 2017
(Age Sixty-Four)

Xi Jinping's packed five-year policymaking agenda came to a head at the Nineteenth Party Congress of October 18–24, 2017, which marked a milestone in the continuous evolution of party ideology and policy. Xi was already designated the "core" of the Party; he dominated decision-making and had effected a massive restructuring of the PLA. The congress was a triumph for Xi personally, denoting another high point in his career. Unlike during the Eighteenth Party Congress, when he worked behind the scenes as the successor apparent, he was now in a strong position to cement his hold and show his personal control over personnel assignments, policy direction, and his vision for China. In addition to taking stock of policymaking during the past five years and supplying a road map for the next five, the Congress broached a remarkably ambitious vision spanning the next thirty years. Salient themes of the Congress reflected Xi's motivations and methods that, as discussed in chapter 9, included a sort of uber-Leninism, discipline, paternalism, and centralization of power in Xi's person and in the Party. In addition, the congress reaffirmed lofty ideals of development, growth, rejuvenation, and a better quality of life. It also finalized top-level personnel changes, revealing the nature of the redistribution of power, policy choices, and political succession. Since the congress was expected to confirm Xi's second term with no change in the general secretary office, attention turned to the identification of a successor or successors in the pattern of the previous Hu Jintao and Xi/Li successions, although this did not happen. Overall, the Party appeared to have rallied around Xi, giving him greater control.

Drafting Process of the Report to the Congress

While the report to the party congress bears Xi Jinping's indelible imprint, it is unlikely that it was simply an elaborate rubber-stamping process or a one-man show. As a summation of policy initiatives of the previous five years and policy directions for the next five, the drafting process took ten months, beginning January 13, when Xi convened a drafting team. Drafting groups consisted of Xi, as the group leader, and outgoing PBSC members Liu Yunshan, Wang Qishan, and Zhang Gaoli serving as deputy group leaders. Five other aides who took charge of the day-to-day drafting were Yang Weimin, deputy director of the Office of the Finance and Economic Affairs LSG, Qu Qingshan, director of the Central Party History Research Institute, Gao Xuanmin, deputy director of the COD, Han Jun, director of the staff office of the Rural Work LSG, and Jiang Jinquan, a member of the CCDI.[1] Expertise of the chief drafters spanned economics, rural affairs, and party history. Qu was one of Xi's most trusted advisers and, as first person in his office to be elected to the CC, was expected to advance in his career. Yang had been a deputy of Liu He, another trusted adviser of Xi.

Dealing with the many policy bundles required a great deal of division of labor, in addition to the great need for information, expertise, input, and feedback. The drafting group solicited opinions from regional governments, think tanks, interest groups, mass associations, and officials and individuals at the grassroots. It consulted up and down the party-state apparatus, performing political communication and socialization functions whereby interests were articulated and aggregated. Conflicts and disagreements had to be reconciled so that the entire Party could be on the same page, a process the Chinese call "unification of thinking." Outgoing Politburo leaders governed the extensive consultation process, but there was an input role for retired elders as well. The extensive drafting process featured countless meetings and seminars that produced dozens of research reports. The report itself underwent numerous revisions, but the outcome represented a consensus showing the priorities of the Party (see Table 12.1).

Xi Reports to the Congress

On the opening day of the congress, Xi delivered a marathon three-and-a-half-hour oral report consisting of some thirty thousand words and sixty-eight pages. Indeed, the report could have been edited down by one-half without losing its essence, but it did provide a comprehensive outline of the complex policies and initiatives to be expected during Xi's second term. Familiar themes were intertwined with some new additions, and occasionally the generalizations were balanced by announcements of more specific decisions, such as the abolition of the *shuanggui*[2] system and the extension of current rural contracts by another thirty years.

In the revised party constitution, the tongue-twisting new formulation "Xi Jinping Thought on Socialism with Chinese Characteristics for a New Era" was inserted as a new doctrine, raising Xi almost to par with Mao Zedong and Deng Xiaoping in terms of theoretical contributions. Carefully calibrated, the revised party constitution mentions Xi eleven times, compared with thirteen times and

Table 12.1 Drafting Process of the Nineteenth Party Congress Report in 2017

Dates	Process
January 13	First meeting of the drafting group led by Xi with outgoing leaders Liu Yunshan, Wang Qishan, and Zhang Gaoli serving as deputy group leaders.
January 17	Party Central solicits opinion from party, government, and military units.
February (no specific dates)	Nine research teams dispatched to sixteen provinces to discuss the draft; sixty-five meetings are convened.
February 20– March 31	Eighty research teams formed by fifty-nine responsible units are dispatched to 1,817 grassroots units and convene 1,501 meetings involving 21,532 persons; eighty research reports on specific subjects are produced.
May	Twenty-five high-level think tanks produce sixty-five reports on major theoretical and practical issues.
July 13–24	Xi chairs two PBSC meetings and one Politburo meeting to scrutinize a draft report.
July 26	Xi gives an important speech at study session attended by main leaders at the provincial and ministerial levels.
August 5	Party Central solicits opinions on a draft report from party, government, military, and mass organizations.
Prior to August 25	Feedback is received from 4,700 individuals and 118 written reports; thirty-three items of feedback from party leaders and retired elders is received.
August 21–25	Xi convenes five meetings to hear revision proposals from leaders of Party and government from thirty-one provinces, PLA units, and the CMC.
August 30	Xi convenes meeting to hear opinions from representatives of democratic parties, All-China Industrial and Commercial Federation, and persons with no party affiliations; these participants present ten written proposals.
October 11	At the opening of the Seventh Plenum, the drafting group hears speeches from ten groups from the CC, four groups from the CCDI, and revises the draft report.
October 14	The Seventh Plenum approves the draft report to the Nineteenth Party Congress.
October 18	Draft report is distributed to the 2,300 delegates of the Nineteenth Party Congress; Xi reads the report.

Source: "Jianfu lishi zhongren, kaichuang fuxing weiye—xinyijie zhongyang weiyuanhui he zhonggong zhongyang jilu jiancha weiyuanhui danshengji" [Shouldering the Historical Mission and Launching the Grand Enterprise—the Birth of the First Central Committee and CCDI], *Xinhua*, October 24, 2017, http://news.xinhuanet.com/politics/2017-10/24/c_1121850995.htm; "5 men, 10 Months and 1 Long Speech: the Cadres behind Xi Jinping's Marathon Address," *SCMP*, October 29, 2017.

twelve times for Mao and Deng, whereas Jiang and Hu were mentioned only once each. In previous constitutions, only the doctrines of Mao Zedong's thought and Deng Xiaoping's theory were referred to by name, with Deng's name added posthumously. Xi's contribution was highlighted by the fact that Jiang Zemin's and Hu Jintao's theoretical formulation, the "three represents" and "scientific development," were inserted without their names attached. Furthermore, the revisions incorporated many of Xi's policy slogans, and the study and implementation of "Xi's thought" has become obligatory for party members and the military.[3]

The congress report stressed that the Party should always be the "backbone of the nation" and its "leadership core," asserting categorically the principle that "the Party, government, military, society, and education; east, west, south, north, and central—the Party leads everything."[4] Accordingly, the Party would uphold the authority and centralized and unified leadership of Party Central. On the other hand, it would impose strict discipline and oversight of itself, purify itself, and maintain its "advancedness" and competence. It would resolutely correct misconduct and show zero tolerance for corruption by continuing the anticorruption campaign. In terms of recruitment, the Party would attract more young reserve cadres, especially those who work the front lines under harsh conditions. It would engage more women cadres, ethnic minorities, and nonparty cadres. The public was encouraged to take part in "orderly" political participation to further "consultative democracy." In a new dialectic twist, Xi declared a plan to decentralize decision-making powers to provincial, prefectural, and county governments, and to merge party and government bodies with "similar functions" to operate from one office while "keeping separate identities." This notion was operationalized at the following NPeC, as we shall see later.

Xi reasserted that the "principal contradiction" confronting China was between the "unbalanced and inadequate development" and the "people's ever-growing needs for a better life," and insisted that development was the Party's top priority. The focus, however, should be shifted from rapid growth to more high-quality development. Consequently, the customary GDP growth numbers were omitted. Instead, the Party pledged to achieve common prosperity in two stages: (1) from 2020 to 2035, to realize socialist modernization on the basis of a relatively well-off society; (2) from 2035 to 2050, to turn China into a "great modern socialist country that is prosperous, strong, democratic, culturally advanced, harmonious, and beautiful."

Aspects of the paternalistic style of governance were reflected in the avowed goals to enhance "social etiquette and civility," public awareness of the rule of law, people's political awareness and moral standards, fine taste and style (by rejecting "vulgarity and kitsch" in arts and literature), and virtues through education.[5] The report promised to launch a civic morality campaign to raise public ethical standards, enhancing work ethics, family virtues, and personal integrity.

In terms of social/economic development, the report claimed that in the previous five years, sixty million had been lifted out of poverty, and the poverty rate had dropped from 10.2 to less than 4 percent of the population. In the same period over thirteen million jobs had been created each year. The new goal was to lift all rural poor out of poverty by 2020. The urbanization rate had been 1.2 percent per annum, adding more than eighty million to the urban population. Another goal was to create a sustainable, multitiered social security system, covering the entire population, urban and rural. The report repeated the pledge of deepening reform so that the market could play a decisive role in resource allocation and the government could play its role better, fostering a new industrialization merging IT application, urbanization, and agricultural modernization. Pledges were made to expedite the creation of a modern public finance system; redefine the fiscal relationship between the central and local government; move Chinese industries up to the medium-high end of the global value chain; and foster a number of world-class advanced manufacturing clusters.

The report vowed to continue a war against pollution, saying that any harm inflicted on nature would eventually be rectified. It pledged to fight climate change by continuing with a green, low-carbon, and recycling style of development. On the military, the report called for the building of a word-class force that would obey the Party's command, would fight and win, and would maintain excellent personal conduct. Both the military and national defense would be "mechanized" by 2020 and "modernized" by 2035. In external relations, the report pronounced a mixture of self-affirmative, realist, and liberal elements. It sought to encourage the Chinese to profess self-confidence in their own "system, developmental path, theory, and culture" (the "Four Self-Confidences") and asserted that their road to greatness would be "different from that of traditional great powers." Externally, it pledged that China would continue to be a responsible power, participate in the reform of global governance, and foster "a community with a shared destiny for mankind." All this tallied with contemporary propaganda themes of an "awesome China," a country that had risen and was ready to take on new roles. On the other hand, Xi recounted uncertainties and destabilizing factors, such as flaccid global economic growth, a widening gap between rich and poor countries, climate change, and the spread of ungovernable hotspots, terrorism, cybersecurity attacks, and infectious diseases. Consequently, China would (1) staunchly defend its national interests and safeguard its political security against traditional and nontraditional threats; (2) actively promote economic globalization and develop an open economy of high standards; and (3) move "toward a more just and rational new world order" by increasing China's economic power and composite strengths. In a departure from past practices, the report declared that (1) China would "move forward to center stage in the world"; and that (2) the Chinese model of "socialism with Chinese characteristics" would "offer a new option for other countries and nations who want to speed up their development while preserving their independence."

Aside from achievements and aspirations, Xi also pointed out a range of shortcomings, from the quality of development to environmental protection, from poverty alleviation to employment levels, and from education to health-care, housing, and elderly support. Other challenges cited included rural/urban, regional, and income inequalities, social tension, national security, weak governance capability and law-based governance, and many weak links in party-building. Ideological struggle would continue, he warned, and reform policies had to be followed through.

The congress announced a revised party constitution incorporating major themes such as the "two centenary goals" and the China Dream; policies such as "supply-side structural reform," a comprehensive security concept, core socialist values, and the BRI project; and pledges such as "the strictest protection of the ecological system." On the issue of the Party's "absolute leadership" over the military, the constitution for the first time inserted the notion of "Xi Jinping's thought on strengthening the military" and the "CMC chairman responsibility system" (*junwei zhuxi fuzezhi*). A fuller section on the strict governance of the Party and the persistence on anticorruption was added.[6] These revisions were the most extensive since the 1982 constitution.[7]

After the congress, the approved report became the object of a massive study campaign throughout the country. Some newly introduced social economic policies were to be implemented without further ado, whereas others that required legislation would be handled by the National People's Congress in 2018. Two days after the congress, Xi chaired a Politburo meeting and passed two resolutions. The first regulation refined and accentuated the "Eight Regulations," and the second intensified Xi's central authority by requiring Politburo members individually to submit annual written reports to Xi and the PBSC. This modified the policy, which began in 2015, of requiring only the "big five," the Standing Committee of the NPeC, the State Council, the CPPCC, the Supreme People's Court, and the Supreme People's Procuratorate, to make annual reports to the PBSC.[8] Two days after the congress Xi chaired a meeting of the new CMC. In a symbolic move to underline continuity with the past, on October 31 Xi led the new PBSC on a visit to the site of the First CCP Congress in 1921 and to the "Red Boat" located in South Lake at Jiaxing, Zhejiang, where First Congress delegates had completed their proceedings after being chased out of Shanghai by the police (see Table 9.7). On November 8 and 9, Xi received Donald Trump on a state visit.[9] On November 20, Xi chaired the first meeting of the Comprehensively Deepening Reform LSG, which passed sixteen documents.[10] Meanwhile, other normal administrative functions continued apace. For instance, in November, a Politburo meeting passed a resolution on making party affairs more transparent, preparations were made to form a Comprehensive Law-Based Governance LSG, and the first ministerial-level official, Lu Wei, deputy director of the Propaganda Department, was put under a corruption investigation.[11]

Congress Proceedings and Selection

As with the drafting process, the congress attempted to show unity and continuity in personnel changes by following long-standing processes in the nomination of CC members as well as Politburo and PBSC members. Tables 12.2 and 12.3 show the formal, parallel, but separate processes of nomination whereby the nominees were scrutinized and vetted. For the nomination to the CC, the congress Presidium appears to have had the final say, whereas for the Politburo and PBSC, the outgoing Politburo gave the final approval. The approved nominations for the CC were formally elected on October 24, whereas the new members for the Politburo and PBSC were elected at the First Plenum on October 25. Unlike the election to the CC, the numbers of nominated candidates for the PBSC and Politburo were equivalent to the number of positions, and therefore the election was simply a formal act of endorsement. Formally, the process appeared to be tightly choreographed, but behind the scenes, there was a great deal of bargaining, horse-trading, and balancing of personnel placements in bitterly fought political battles. Many opportunities existed for outgoing and retiring leaders, to varying degrees, to exert their influence to protect the interests of their families, clients, and networks. On the other hand, these struggles were to a certain extent constrained by such norms as party unity, age and term limits, and the official ban on factions. Meanwhile, two major events cast a shadow over the congress.

An "Abortive Coup" and the Purge of Sun Zhengcai

Following past succession practices, Jiang Zemin and Hu Jintao cooperated at the Eighteenth Party Congress to select and groom Hu Chunhua and Sun Zhengcai, both born in the 1960s, as potential successors to Xi and Li Keqiang, with their positions enhanced by PBSC membership. Then came a bombshell in February 2017 when a roving inspection team of the Anti-Corruption Campaign accused Sun, secretary of the Chongqing MPC, with a range of offenses.[12] In July, Sun Zhengcai suffered *shuanggui* and was expelled from the Party for a long list of crimes including corruption, nepotism, influence peddling, embezzlement, incompetence, and trading power for sex. Subsequently, he was expelled from the Party and transferred to the judiciary for prosecution.[13] As a top contender for the PBSC, Sun was the fourth sitting Politburo member and the second secretary

Table 12.2 Nomination and Election of the Nineteenth Central Committee and CCDI Members ("Two Committees")

Dates	Process and Procedure
February 2016	A PBSC meeting preparing for the Nineteenth Party Congress decides to form a cadre leading small group led by Xi to scrutinize personnel selection.
Just over a year after February 2106	Xi attends three meetings of leaders of provincial/municipality party committees and central party units. Xi makes specific demands and listens to briefings.
June 2016	The PBSC and Politburo approve a resolution on the criteria for personnel selection and composition.
July 2016	The Cadre Leading Small Group on scrutinizing Nineteenth Party Congress personnel passes a resolution on quotas, procedures, and method of nomination.
July 2016–June 2017	The Cadre LSG organizes forty-six inspection teams to scrutinize thirty-one provinces/municipalities and 124 central party and state organs, financial enterprises, and SOEs in Beijing. The CMC dispatches ten inspection teams to inspect twenty-nine major PLA units. Nominations and recommendations are based on the criteria of virtue, capability, diligence, performance, and integrity. The Cadre LSG convenes seven meetings. The PBSC convenes six meetings to be briefed by the inspection teams, one by one, and drafts a nomination list for the "two committees."
October 20, 2017	After a second meeting, the Presidium of the Nineteenth Party Congress approves the nomination list submitted by the Politburo and tables it for discussion by Congress delegates.
October 22 night and 23 morning	The third and fourth meetings of the presidium of the Nineteenth Party Congress approve the nomination list for the "two committees."
October 24 morning	The Congress delegates elect the "two committees."

Source: "Shouldering the Historical Mission and Launching the Grand Enterprise—the Birth of the First Central Committee and CCDI."
Note: A parallel process is used for the nomination of the CCDI; it and the CC together are known as the "two committees."

of the Chongqing PPC to have fallen from grace. He was alleged to have failed to clean up the mess of Bo Xilai, and his disgrace eerily resembled the fall of Bo only five years previously (for a biographical table, see Table 8.6). A subsequent court trial in May 2018 convicted him of abusing his positions between 2002 and 2017 by accepting bribes totaling ¥170 million (US$27 million). Sun was sentenced to life imprisonment, but there was no mention of any coup attempt at that time.[14]

Table 12.3 Nomination and Election of the Nineteenth Politburo and Its Standing Committee

2017	Process and Procedure
Beginning of the Year	Xi discusses with PBSC members on the selection of the top leadership
April 24	Xi chairs a PBSC meeting and passes a resolution on selecting the nominees by face-to-face conversations using a list of criteria such as loyalty, experience, skills, performance, and integrity. Xi took charge of this consultation.
Second Half of April to June	Xi takes time to interview 57 incumbent party, government, and military leaders as well as party elders to seek their input. By arrangement of the PBSC, central officials hold individual and face-to-face meetings with 258 officials at the provincial/ministerial levels. Likewise, CMC leaders seek recommendations from 32 top generals.
Second Half of May	Provincial-/ministerial-level officials are summoned to Zhongnanhai to individual meetings to make recommendations.
September 25	The PBSC decides on a list of nominees.
September 29	The Politburo examines and approves a list of nominees to be submitted to the First Plenum of the Nineteenth Party Congress for election and approval.
October 24	The Nineteenth Party Congress elects a new CC.
October 25	The new CC elects the new Politburo and PBSC.

Source: "A Strong Collective Leadership for the New Age: An Account of the Emergence of the New Central Leadership Structure of the Party."
Note: A parallel process was used for the nomination of the CMC.

The Sun case escalated further when at a sideline panel of the congress on October 18, chairman of the Chinese Securities Regulatory Commission Liu Shiyu accused Bo Xilai, Zhou Yongkang, Ling Jihua, Xu Caihou, and Guo Boxiong of a "conspiracy to usurp the Party's leadership and seize power" (*yinmou cuandang duoquan*), or, in other words, of plotting a coup back in 2012. Such terminology had not been used since the fall of the "Gang of Four" in 1976. Liu lauded Xi for having fended off a huge "hidden calamity" (*yinhuan*) and saving "the Party, military, and the country."[15] This allegation was not entirely new, but Liu seemed to have escalated previous versions. For example, at a speech at the Sixth Plenum in December, 2016 Xi had charged these heavyweights with not only greed and decadent lives, but also political ambition, subversion, faction-building, and "political conspiracy."[16] Further, a *Xinhua* article detailing the birth of the Politburo on October 26 also accused Zhou Yongkang, Ling

Jihua, and Sun Zhengcai, inter alia, of using the "recommendation" method for "ultraorganizational" activities such as lobbying and bribing for votes.[17] Later in October, a CCDI report submitted to the congress added Sun Zhengcai to the other five, accusing them of severe political and economic crimes and corruption, labeling them wildly ambitious schemers. Thanks to the timely discovery of these intrigues, the report asserted, a serious catastrophe had been avoided.[18] Official sources gave no more details even though such escalating charges derailed the official narrative of a unified leadership overseeing peaceful political successions. If in the future this official version proves to have substance, it will have interesting implications for factional analyses, since the alleged collusion was between Bo Xilai, a princeling; Zhou Yongkang, a security chief; Ling Jihua and Sun Zhengcai, both alleged to be key members of the *tuanpai*; and Xu Caihou and Guo Boxiong, senior generals in the PLA.

These official allegations gave credence to many earlier versions of events that have circulated since 2014, and the following will cite a couple of representative examples. The first is a *Voice of America* report citing such China watchers as He Ping of *Mirror Books*. This account bluntly asserts that a "new Gang of Four" comprising Zhou Yongkang, Bo Xilai, Xu Caihou, and Ling Jihua colluded with one another in "a coup of the largest scale" since the establishment of the PRC. They did so by inserting cronies in political, economic, legal, and military establishments and threatened Xi. This gang aimed to insert Bo Xilai in the PBSC to take charge of the Political and Legal Committee at the Eighteenth Party Congress and, more importantly, to overturn Xi and make Ling Jihua general secretary at the Eighteenth Party Congress. Subsequently, Xi's ACC was essentially an attempt to purge the followers of this gang from the Party and the military. A slightly different variation claims that the gang had formed an enormous organization that aimed at fomenting a coup to overturn Xi's succession.[19] A second account is a ninety-five-hundred-character Falun Gong version that claims that Zhou Yongkang launched a failed March 19 coup in 2012 to seize a key witness in the Bo Xilai case to prevent this witness from implicating Bo, and to simultaneously assassinate Wen Jiabao, who was hated by Bo and Zhou. This account further claims that Zhou had even mobilized the PAP to take control of Tiananmen and Xinhuamen, although Hu Jintao managed to transfer the Thirty-Eighth Army to stifle the uprising. Another variation of this account claims that Ling Jihua and Zhou Yongkang conspired to (1) block the news about the Ferrari incident involving Ling's son and to head off further investigation so that Ling could safely enter the PBSC, and (2) separate the Gu Kailai murder case from the Bo Xilai case. Still another variation contained in this version claims that Bo and Zhou plotted a coup to seize power from Xi *after* the Eighteenth Party Congress. This coup, it said, was masterminded by Jiang Zemin and Zeng Qinghong, attempting to use Jiang's influence in the PLA to establish another

Party Central to dispose of Xi, although the explosion of the Wang Lijun case had derailed that plot.[20] As mentioned previously, a perennial theme of Falun Gong sources is to vilify Jiang Zemin for his persecution of its members and for the organ-harvesting issue, and consequently, they refer often to Jiang's possible demise. Occasionally, they even positively evaluate Xi, entertaining the hope that Xi might eventually take down Jiang. In any case, the veracity of these versions cannot be verified at this point, and the sensationalism and drama they portray may not have anything to do with real Chinese politics. They are worth mentioning since the official narrative pointed in the same general direction. Indeed, the cases can be interpreted as Xi's cynical attempt to oust a successor not of his own choice on the pretext of corruption, and the use of a threat of a coup to exaggerate possibilities of danger and to ward off opposition.

New Procedures for the Nominations for the CC, Politburo, and PBSC

As with the drafting of the report to the congress, the protracted consultation, vetting, and inspections of the nomination processes for the CC (and consequently the Politburo/PBSC) occupied most of 2017 (see Tables 12.2 and 12.3). These nomination activities involve the interplay of many organizations and processes, methods change at each party congress, and the exact process is unknown. One constant is that the powerful COD controls the appointment of the three to four thousand members listed in the central nomenklatura (*zhongguan ganbu*) and the outgoing Politburo/PBSC essentially decides the new PBSC/Politburo, while the role played by the general secretary varies. Another constant is that the composition of the CC always corresponds with the job-slot requirement. However, as the cases of Hu Qiaomu in 1987 and Xi in 1997 show, central intentions to recruit certain members into the CC may not come to pass. For the Nineteenth Party Congress, Xi and the Politburo were determined to tightly control the process and introduce some fundamental changes. An official who had participated in past election/selection activities claims that in the past, the first step had been the convention of expanded meetings of provincial/municipal party committee conventions to "vote and recommend" candidates. But the Xi leadership group dismissed this method as mere brouhaha, claiming that it had exaggerated the weight of voting so that nominations and elections were tainted by connections, and that the selected cadres were not necessarily the best. There had been lobbying, unprincipled influence peddling, cronyism, and even bribery, according to this view. Some officials were said to have done nothing beyond putting a tick on the ballot, resulting in "arbitrary voting" and distortion of public opinion. All this, it claimed, undermined the principle that "the Party must manage the·cadres." Consequently, a revised regulation on cadre promotion in 2014 redefined the function of "democratic recommendation." Xi then repudiated the method of "large convention promotion" (*dahui haitui*) involving hundreds of people.[21] Subsequently, Beijing centralized the process by organizing a Cadre LSG led by Xi to take over the nomination work. The LSG organized forty-six inspection terms to fan out across the thirty-two provinces/municipalities, the 124 central party and state organs, financial enterprises, and SOEs to scrutinize and select nominees. Each inspection team then carried out detailed, face-to-face interviews with potential nominees to discuss a range of issues, totaling fifteen hundred cases per province. After numerous meetings the Cadre LSG, in consultation with the PBSC, drafted a nomination list for the CC and the CCDI to be approved by the congress Presidium.

At the congress, the executive committee of the Presidium consisted of long-retired leaders such as Jiang Zemin, Li Peng, Zhu Rongji, Li Ruihuan, Hu Jintao, Wen Jiabao, and He Guoqiang. It also included outgoing Politburo members who had reached age and term limits, such as Zhang Dejiang, Yu Zhengsheng, Liu Yunshan, and Wang Qishan, and even the younger ones who would be dropped from the Politburo and the CC right after the Congress. Since the number of nominees for the CC was 8 percent more than positions, and since delegates did not have to put their names on the ballot, the full outcome could not be ensured. In the past, the CC had a special work group directed by the Politburo in charge of "democratic recommendations," scrutiny, and nominations—the equivalent of "party whips." It was always expected that the nomination process would be accompanied by internal maneuvers, but tighter centralized oversight of the Nineteenth Congress might have reduced lobbying and competition and strengthened Xi's hand.

The more centralized control over the selection of CC nominees naturally applied to the selection/election of PBSC/Politburo as well, the constant being that Xi and the outgoing PBSC members essentially picked the incoming PBSC. Yet, unlike a president or prime minister who can pick her cabinets and pack the civil service with supporters and loyalists, Xi could not simply stack the PBSC because of several constraints. First, his choice was bound by the limited pool of candidates—normally PBSC members must be promoted from the Politburo (eighteen or so members) and in turn, Politburo members must be recruited from among the two hundred-odd full members of the CC, many of whom would have been disqualified because of age, lack of qualifications, or their merely symbolic representative functions. Indeed, as observed, in rare cases expediency allows parachuting into the PBSC skipping one or more rungs, but this usually raises concern about violations of principles of seniority and legitimacy. Second, in recruiting to the PBSC/Politburo, the Xi-Li leadership needed to strike a balance among leaders with different institutional and network backgrounds, including different "factions" (real or perceived), ages, skill sets, geographical regions, and the like. The interplay among these factors can only be deduced from the outcome.

In any event, Xi decided to abandon the straw-vote method used at the Seventeenth and Eighteenth Congresses originally intended to expand "intraparty democracy." As mentioned, in a December 2016 Party Life meeting, all Politburo members were obliged to self-evaluate by giving self-criticisms. This put Xi and the Politburo members on the same page regarding how to proceed with top-level personnel changes, and the process began in early 2017. From April to June, Xi met with fifty-seven incumbent and retired party and government leaders. Simultaneously, the PBSC arranged face-to-face interviews with 258 potential nominees from the provinces, ministries, and the CC. The intention was to downplay time-honored criteria such as age, seniority, and rank ("iron chairs and iron hats," *tieyi tiemao*) to privilege performance, institutional need, honesty, and integrity. This allowed flexibility to promote or demote officials (*nengshang nengxia*) so that even aspiring Politburo members could be ousted before the unofficial retirement age of sixty-eight. In some respects, this method was said to have expanded the arena of participants and deepened discussion, and, accordingly, was superior to "large convention promotion."[22] Similarly, the CMC took a parallel procedure to solicit views from the thirty-two military regions, and from departments and leaders. Such new methods of election, selection, and recruitment reflected simultaneously Xi's mistrust of spontaneity and his domineering, self-serving, and top-down approach. Official publicity touted the new procedures as a means for the Party to improve the mechanism of leadership selection. In practice, however, this showed the latitude given Xi to change and modify rules. Overall, despite the purge of a potential successor and claims of an attempted coup, the congress marked another peaceful transition of power and rejuvenation of the top leadership.

Composition of the PBSC and Politburo

The Congress elected a new CC, which, at the First Plenum (October 24), in turn elected a new Politburo and PBSC. The concomitant changes in higher-level personnel, including numerous retirements, promotions, and demotions, generated in turn an enormous reshuffle in the provinces and lower administrative levels, again producing massive political mobility, regeneration, and an infusion of a diversity of skill sets, a process that, as mentioned, may at least partially explain the strength of Chinese authoritarianism. The composition and general characteristics of the new PBSC and Politburo shed light on both power configuration and policy implications. While the power configuration is generally a variety of the dominant first-among-equals model, Xi needed the ideas and expertise of his colleagues to govern, and divisions of labor to ensure implementation of the various tasks as the head of a mammoth bureaucracy.

The Nineteenth Party Congress stressed stability and consensus, but unlike previous congresses, the outcome confounded predictions. Many persistent precongress rumors, partly informed by power maximization or faulty assumptions, did not materialize. For instance, Li Keqiang, long rumored to be axed because of assumed connections to alleged *tuanpai* leader Hu Jintao, remained in the PBSC's second spot. Li's role has been underestimated, not to mention the fact he has worked closely with Xi for a decade. Another popular prediction that did not come to pass was that Wang Qishan would remain in the PBSC by defying age limits so that Xi could stretch rules to shore up his own position. Similarly, a prediction that Xi might re-establish the chairman position to replace the general secretary did not materialize. Last, an expectation that Xi would follow the pattern of cultivating one or two top successors did not occur. He did, however, with some exceptions, observe many of the norms regarding age and progressive promotion.

The Politburo Standing Committee

The composition of the new PBSC showed both continuity and change in the application of the norms of recruitment such as retirement at age sixty-eight and promotion by seniority. (See Tables 12.4 and 12.5.) It also showed both the constraints Xi endured and the latitude that he had achieved. The new lineup of the PBSC broke with the traditional practice of inducting one or two top successors into the PBSC to groom them for at least five years before they assume the top positions. The norm of step-by-step promotion requires prior membership in the Politburo, so by applying the norm of retirement at age sixty-eight, those born in the 1940s were disqualified, leaving only twelve qualified candidates for the PBSC. Among those twelve, Xu Qiliang was disqualified because PLA generals were no longer accepted, and Sun Zhengcai was purged. Sun Chunlan as a woman fell victim to the glass ceiling that excluded women from entering the PBSC. This left a small pool of nine eligible candidates for the five vacant posts. In a break with the seniority principle that Politburo members would not be dismissed without serious cause, Li Qibao and Zhang Chunxian were demoted to the CC, and Li Yuanchao was ousted from the CC altogether. Another break with the Xi-Li dual-successor pattern saw the only putative successor, Hu Chunhua, remain in the Politburo.

Such changes bore the mark of Xi the strict disciplinarian, since on numerous occasions he had asserted that officials could go "up or down," by which he

Table 12.4 The Political Careers of PBSC Members, Nineteenth Party Congress

	Year and place of birth; year joined CCP	Family background and youth experience	Education	Early political career	Later political career				
Xi Jinping	1953, Fuping County, Shaanxi (1974)	Princeling, sent-down *zhiqing*, 1969–75; village branch secretary	PhD, part-time, Marxist theory and political education, Tsinghua University, 1998–2002; chemical engineering, Tsinghua University, 1975–79	General Office, CMC, 1979–82	Secretary, Zhengding County PC, 1983–85; executive vice mayor, Xiamen, 1985–88; secretary, Ningde Prefectural PC, 1988–90	Secretary, Fuzhou MPC, 1990–96; deputy secretary, Fujian PPC, 1995–2002; governor, Fujian, 2000–2002	Secretary, Shanghai MPC, 2007; secretary, Zhejiang PPC, 2002–7	PBSC member, vice president, 2007–12	General secretary and PBSC member, 2012–17
Li Keqiang	1955, Anhui (1976)	Sent-down *zhiqing*, 1974–76; party secretary of production brigade, 1976–78	BA in law, 1982; PhD in economics, 1994, Peking University	Various positions in the CYL, including positions in the CYL Secretariat, 1982–98	Governor of Henan, 1998–2003; deputy secretary, Henan PPC, 1998–2002	Secretary, Henan PPC, 2002–4	Secretary, Liaoning PPC, 2004–7	PBSC member, 2007–12; executive premier, 2008–13	PBSC member and premier, 2012–17

Li Zhanshu	1950, Pingshan County, Heibei (1975)	"Revolutionary family," RG2, sent-down zhiqing, 1968–72; RG3	Political studies, Hebei Normal University, 1980–83; graduate program in business economics, Chinese Academy of Social Sciences, 1996–98	Secretary, Wuji County PC, 1983–85; deputy secretary, Shijiazhuang Prefecture PC; secretary, Hebei CYL, 1986–90	Various positions, prefectural and provincial levels in Hebei, 1990–98,	Shaanxi, 1998–2003, various positions and secretary, Xian MPC, 2002–3	Deputy party secretary, Heilongjiang; vice governor, governor, Heilongjiang, 2003–10	Secretary, Guizhou PPC, 2010–12	Director, General Office, CCP, 2012–17
Wang Yang	1955, Suzhou County, Anhui (1975)	Humble family; manual laborer starting at age seventeen	Student, Central Party School, 1979–80, 1988–92; master's in management, University of Science and Technology, 1993–95	Various positions in the CYL, 1981–84	Various positions at Anhui and Tongling city, 1984–92	Vice governor, Anhui, 1993–99; member, NDRC, 1999–2003; deputy secretary general, State Council, 2003–5	Secretary, Chongqing PPC, 2005–7	Secretary, Guangdong PPC, 2007–12	Member, Politburo, 2012–17; vice premier, 2013–17
Wang Huning	1955, Shanghai (1984)		Cadre training at Shanghai Normal University, 1972–77, master's in law, Fudan University, 1981		Instructor, professor and dean, Fudan University, 1981–95		Deputy director and director, Central Policy Research Office, 1998–2017	Member, Secretariat, 2007–12	Member, Politburo, 2012–17; director, Office of the Comprehensively Deepening Reform LSG

Continued

Table 12.4 Continued

	Year and place of birth; year joined CCP	Family background and youth experience	Education	Early political career	Later political career
Zhao Leji	1957, Xining City, Qinghai (1975)	Sent-down zhiqing, 1974–75	Degree in philosophy, Peking University, 1980	Various positions in Qinghai, 1980–93	Assistant and vice governor, Qinghai, 1993–97; Governor, Qinghai, 2000–3; Secretary, Qinghai PPC, 2003–7; Secretary, Shaanxi PPC, 2007–12; Member, Politburo, 2012–17; director, COD; deputy head of both the Party Building and Inspection Work LSGs
Han Zheng	1954, Shanghai (1979)	Sent-down zhiqing, 1972–75	Master's in international economy, East China Normal University, 1994–96	Various positions in the CYL, 1990–92	Vice mayor, Shanghai, 1998–2003; deputy secretary, Shanghai PPC, 2002–12; Mayor, Shanghai, 2003–12; Member, Politburo, 201 secretary, Shanghai MPC, 2012–17

Source: Baidu baike and China Vitae.

Table 12.5 Politburo and Politburo Standing Committee Members of the Nineteenth Party Congress and Their Major Party and Government Responsibilities

	Date of birth	Age in 2017	Nineteenth Party Congress positions	Previous positions
POLITBURO STANDING COMMITTEE				
Xi Jinping 习近平	1953.06	64	General secretary, president, chair CMC	General secretary, president, chair CMC
Li Keqiang 李克强	1955.07	62	Premier	Premier
Li Zhanshu 栗战书	1950.08	67	Chair, Standing Committee, NPC	Politburo; director, Party Central Office
Wang Yang 汪洋	1955.03	62	Chair CPPCC	Politburo; vice premier
Wang Huning 王沪宁	1955.10	62	Ranking secretary, Secretariat; director, Central Committee Building Spiritual Civilization; deputy director, Comprehensively Deeping Reform LSG	Politburo; director, Central Policy Research Office; director, Office of the Comprehensively Deeping Reform LSG
Zhao Leji 赵乐际	1957.03	60	Secretary, CCDI	Politburo; Secretariat; director, COD
Han Zheng 韩正	1954.04	63	Executive vice premier	Politburo; secretary, Shanghai MPC
POLITBURO				
Ding Xuexiang 丁薛祥	1962.09	55	Secretary, Secretariat; executive director, Party Central Office; director, President's Staff Office	Executive director, Party Central Office; director, President's Staff Office
Wang Chen 王晨	1950.12	67		Vice chair and secretary general, NPC

Continued

Table 12.5 *Continued*

	Date of birth	Age in 2017	Nineteenth Party Congress positions	Previous positions
Liu He 刘鹤	1952.01	65	Vice premier	Director, Office of the Central Finance and Economic LSG; vice director, State Development and Reform Commission
Xu Qiliang 许其亮	1950.03	67	Vice chair, CMC	Politburo; vice chair, CMC
Sun Chunlan 孙春兰	1950.05	67	Vice premier	Politburo; secretary, Tianjin MPC
Li Xi 李希	1956.10	61	Secretary, Guangdong PPC	Politburo; secretary, Liaoning PPC
Li Qiang 李强	1959.07	58	Secretary, Shanghai MPC	Secretary, Jiangsu PPC
Li Hongzhong 李鸿忠	1956.08	61	Secretary, Tianjin MPC	Secretary, Tianjin MPC
Yang Jiechi 杨洁篪	1950.05	67	Vice Premier	State councilor; director, Office of Central Foreign Affairs LSG
Yang Xiaodu 杨晓渡	1953.10	64	Deputy secretary, CCDI; minister, Ministry of Supervision	Deputy secretary, CCDI; minister, Ministry of Supervision
Zhang Youxia 张又侠	1950.07	67	Vice chair CMC	Member, CMC
Chen Xi 陈希	1953.09	64	Director, COD	Deputy director, COD
Chen Quanguo 陈全国	1955.11	62	Secretary, Xinjiang ARPC	Secretary, Xinjiang ARPC
Chen Min'er 陈敏尔	1960.09	57	Secretary, Chongqing MPC	Secretary, Guizhou PPC
Hu Chunhua 胡春华	1963.04	54		Politburo; secretary, Guangdong PPC
Guo Shengkun 郭声琨	1954.10	63		State councilor; minister, minister of public security

Huang Kunming 黄坤明	1956.11	61	Director, Central Propaganda Department	Executive director, Central Propaganda Department
Cai Qi 蔡奇	1955.12	62	Secretary, Beijing MPC	Deputy secretary, Beijing MPC; mayor, Beijing

SECRETARIAT

Wang Huning 王沪宁			Concurrent, see above	
Ding Xuexiang 丁薛祥			Concurrent, see above	
Yang Xiaodu 杨晓渡			Concurrent, see above	
Chen Xi 陈希			Concurrent, see above	
Guo Shengkun 郭声琨			Concurrent, see above	
Huang Kunming 黄坤明			Concurrent, see above	
You Quan 尤权	1954.01		Secretary, Fujian PPC	Secretary, Fujian PPC

Source: "Shijiujie zhongyang zhengzhiju changwei, weiyuan, shujichu shuji mingdang ji jianli" [The Name List and Brief Biographies of Members of the PBSC, Politburo, and Secretariat], *Caixinwang*, October 25, 2017, http://china.caixin.com/2017-10-25/101160769.html.

Note: Projected state positions to be verified by the National People's Congress in early March 2018.

meant that seniority no longer guaranteed promotion. For example, in 2015, new regulations for the roving inspection teams and leadership cadres specified how officials deemed incompetent and corrupt were to be replaced.[23] In the PBSC, Xi and Li retained their positions, and the other five retired due to age. The retirees were replaced by members who had already served a five-year term in the Politburo—Li Zhanshu, Wang Yang, Wang Huning, Zhao Leji, and Han Zheng (Li and Zhao were Xi's former protégés). Turnovers in the broader Politburo were great. Among the eighteen members of the outgoing Eighteenth Politburo who were not PBSC members, six retired because of age. Five were promoted to the PBSC, two were demoted to the CC, one was ousted from the CC, and one was purged from the Party altogether. Only three members were holdovers, creating fifteen new openings. Among the twenty-five members of the broader Politburo, fifteen (or 60 percent) were newly appointed, and the ten others were regarded as Xi's protégés: Ding Xuexiang, Liu He, Li Xi, Li Qiang, Li Hongzhong, Zhang Youxia, Chen Xi, Chen Min'er, Huang Kunming, and Cai Qi. This way Xi had come to command a majority in both the PBSC and Politburo, although this hardly suggests a static situation, since the group dynamics were ever changing.

Existing factional analysis in Chinese politics tends to assume struggles among two or three distinct factions: the princelings, the Shanghai Gang, and *tuanpai*, although analysts' assessments differ as to the degree of influence of the past leaders such as Jiang Zemin and Hu Jintao.[24] According to one three-faction model, the Eighteenth Politburo and PBSC were equally divided among the three factions.[25] This pattern was repeated at the Nineteenth Party Congress, when only three members of the PBSC, Wang Qishan, Li Zhanshu, and Zhao Leji, were considered Xi allies. Consequently, Xi could not dominate. Xi's control could extend to the provincial and ministerial levels but, this theory claims, would be less so at the prefectural level, county level, and below. Another variation of the three-faction model claims that the Xi faction had been strengthened at the expense of the *tuanpai* and Shanghai Gang. The Shanghai Gang had been progressively weakened, although the *tuanpai* still provided much of the personnel, and therefore the model presumes that Xi will not fully dominate until the Twentieth Party Congress.[26]

On the other hand, according to the "one party, two coalitions" perspective, the outcome of the Nineteenth Party Congress was "paradoxical," since Xi had "compromised with competing factions." In this view, Li Zhanshu and Zhao Leji were Xi allies of the "elitist" faction. Li Keqiang and Wang Yang were protégés of Hu Jintao and therefore belong to the *tuanpai*, or "populist" group, whereas Han Zheng and Wang Huning—who advanced their careers through Shanghai—were confidants of Jiang Zemin and members of the Shanghai Gang.[27] In this two-coalition model, a "fierce" battle was carried out between Jiang Zemin's Shanghai Gang and Xi's faction, and the outcome was the elimination of Jiang and/or the Shanghai faction, since many tigers of Jiang's crew, such as Zhou Yongkang, Guo Boxiong, Xu Caihou, Ling Jihua, Su Rong, and even his supposed successor Sun Zhengcai, had been ousted. After the congress, the story goes, Xi would thoroughly clean out the Jiang faction as well as the 280 centrally administered officials who had been promoted by Jiang Zemin to undermine Hu Jintao.[28]

The factional struggle theses, as mentioned before, are based on intuition, educated guesses, or speculation, and therefore cannot be empirically verified. Consequently, the analysts using the factional thesis differ among themselves on the number of factions, their relative strength, and their membership makeup. Our exploration of policymaking during Xi's first term finds no support for the "one party, two coalitions" theory, or that the *tuanpai* is a solid bloc that propounds "populist" policy choices.

Two other interpretations of note also reject the factional interpretation. The first postulates that the PBSC comprised three main political networks: Li Zhanshu and Zhao Leji were close to Xi Jinping; Li Keqiang and Wang Yang were associated with Hu Jintao; and Han Zheng was a protégé of Jiang Zemin, although Han had also worked well with Xi at Shanghai and the Politburo. The remaining PBSC member, Wang Huning (whose career was spent almost entirely in Shanghai and who had served both Jiang Zemin and Hu Jintao) is seen as an "honest broker" providing frank policy advice regardless of who is in charge. The inclusion of people from various networks did not imply a checks-and-balances mechanism; rather, it would be Xi's "consolation prize" of recognizing the importance of various groups.[29]

A second more institutional approach postulates that membership in the Politburo and PBSC was apportioned according to institutional blocs. Therefore, members from the party apparatus bloc consisted of Wang Huning, Zhao Leji, Ding Xuexiang, Yang Xiaodu, Chen Xi, and Huang Kunming; members from the state organs bloc included Han Zheng, Wang Chen, Sun Chunlan, Yang Jiechi, Hu Chunhua, and Liu He; members from the regions' bloc included Li Xi, Li Qiang, Li Hongzhong, Chen Quanguo, Chen Min'er, and Cai Qi; and members from the military/security sector were Guo Shengkun, General Xu Qiliang, and General Zhang Youxia. As in the past, such an arrangement was intended as a kind of checks-and-balances mechanism to prevent any sector from achieving dominance, especially if it were in cahoots with the general secretary.[30]

These two analytic approaches provide sounder perspectives for further investigations, although the extent to which PBSC networks or institutional balances have any impact on policymaking after the Nineteenth Party Congress awaits more studies. In the following, I will consider the composition of the PBSC/Politburo by offering more details on the career backgrounds of selected members and attempt to explain the reasons for their rise or fall.

The Characteristics of the New Leadership

One striking feature of the Nineteenth Party Congress is that all seven PBSC members (and the majority of the Politburo), regardless of their alleged factional affiliations, were uniformly "fifth generation" leaders. The fifth generation made great strides at the Seventeenth and Eighteenth Party Congresses. Although older fifth-generation leaders such as Yu Zhengsheng and Wang Qishan had retired, Bo Xilai and Ling Jihua had been purged and Li Yuanchao sidelined, the political career of this generation reached its zenith at the Nineteenth Party Congress of 2017, and most will retire at the twentieth if the retirement age of sixty-eight holds.

As mentioned, unlike previous generations, fifth-generation leaders tend to have backgrounds in the humanities and social sciences. Their subjects of study contrast sharply with those of previous generations. From 1997 to 2007, all PBSC members had engineering backgrounds. In the Sixteenth and Seventeenth CC PBSC, eight out of nine had engineering or natural science backgrounds, and were labeled technocrats by observers. Jiang Zemin was trained as an electrical engineer, Hu Jintao as a hydraulic engineer, and Wen Jiabao as a geological engineer. This was an outcome of the drive during earlier generations to industrialize and modernize, and by a similar logic, the first-generation leaders were primarily intellectuals, peasants, and soldiers. In the Eighteenth PBSC, no one had an engineering or technocrat background except for Xi, who at first studied chemical engineering at Tsinghua as a worker/peasant/soldier student but later switched to Marxist theory and political education. The only engineer was Yu Zhengsheng who studied missile technology but took charge of ethnic minorities and religious affairs.[31]

A small number of fifth-generation leaders have studied abroad, mostly as visiting scholars but some for degrees, in a variety of countries including the UK and United States, even a few with brief stints at Harvard's Kennedy School of Government. It is plausible to argue that different educational backgrounds provide different mindsets, problem-solving skills, and decision-making styles that can impact reform and change. For instance, engineers are often thought of as technocrats because they are concerned with design, construction, machines, materials, and how to keep them intact and lasting.[32] Lawyers tend to argue from first principles and evidence, privileging procedures and rights, often in adversarial situations. Social sciences and humanities examine human behavior and thinking processes, often connecting the past and the present of human experiences to project into the future. Among the numerous areas of studies are cultures, histories, societies, and the underlying patterns that govern continuities and changes.

It is not unreasonable to assume that a more educated leadership would tackle political issues differently from one consisting primarily of peasants, workers, and soldiers, and this can be seen in differences between Maoist and post-Mao politics. And the extent to which educational backgrounds make a difference in approaches to policymaking should merit separate studies. In contemporary China, educational background probably matters less than governance experience in determining leaders' outlook and style. Most higher officials have spent decades in the bureaucracy, having chosen politics as a vocation and career choice. Further, all were deliberately recruited, cultivated, and nurtured beginning in the 1980s as "third echelon" reserve cadres. All have been rotated through various regions and administrative levels, acquiring different skill sets over three or four decades. With only one exception, secretary positions at the provincial/municipality level have been the principal springboards or perquisites to national leadership. These regional experiences covered the coastal areas (Shanghai, Guangdong, Zhejiang), northeast (Heilongjiang, Liaoning), central area (Chongqing, Henan, Inner Mongolia), and the west and southwest (Tibet, Qinghai, Guizhou). A somewhat secondary path to Politburo membership has involved mostly central organizations such as the COD, Central Office, CCDI, various LSGs, the Politics and Law Committee, and the State Security Commission. Several alleged *tuanpai* stalwarts did have actual CYL work experience for a few years in their early or middle career, but in themselves these experiences were mere stepping stones and were never enough for the very top. Our various biographical tables illustrate this fact. As mentioned before, the supposition that these experiences had fostered a lifelong loyalty and solidarity to a full-fledged "faction" is weak. Furthermore, it was not uncommon for Xi protégés, such as Li Zhanshu and Li Qiang, to have CYL experiences as well. Even Han Zheng, often presumed to be a member of the Shanghai Gang, had a stint in the CYL. So, again, the notion of "elite" and "populist" coalitions as the main policy cleavage is unlikely to be an apt representation of the new leadership, since all have had a full range of national issues to deal with and many policy options to choose from. Further, those who have been expelled from the Politburo can best be explained by factors other than an outcome of the elitist/populist struggle.

At a general level, "sixth generation" leaders refer to those who were born in the period from the end of the Great Leap through the Cultural Revolution of the late 1960s. They came of age during the era of reforms and opening and experienced rapid political-economic-social change. In contrast with their immediate predecessors, they were less indoctrinated by Maoist dogma and were not sent down to the countryside or factories for hard labor. Formal education again became important, and they were the first to seek higher education when university examinations were reintroduced in 1977. Many became highly educated, with university degrees, and the predominant science and engineering focus was replaced by social sciences and humanities. Their exposure to Western and materialistic ideas and values might have made them more liberal about new ideas. Virtually all have experienced rampant corruption because of rapid economic growth and change.[33] In their middle or early adulthood, one might add, they also experienced the Tiananmen events. In the following, we depart from these generalizations and consider the experiences and attributes of PBSC and other leaders in more detail in order to give a sense of the characteristics of the new leadership, and the reasons why some were promoted and others dismissed.

Li Keqiang (b. 1955)

Having worked directly with Xi Jinping for a full decade at the national and Politburo levels, Li's relationship with him has been cooperative and interdependent. Power and factional competition theories that persistently posit that Xi has strived to rid Li in favor of Xi's own protégés have not been borne out. Neither were the views that Li's "Likonomics" had been shunned by Xi.[34] It is misleading to label the "Xi-Li system" in the same way as the Hu Jintao–Wen Jiabao system, since the relationship has most often been formally unequal, with Xi and Li ranked as number one and two in the party hierarchy, respectively. The power distance between the two might have widened since Xi assumed a more controlling and commanding role. That said, however, Xi needed Li and the vast State Council bureaucracy to draft and implement ambitious reform. The dismissal of a premier would have incurred significant political and institutional costs. In fact, the features of what has been dubbed "Likonomics," such as reluctance to use stimulus to foster economic growth, and efforts to reduce high leveraged debt ratios and promote market-oriented reforms, were consistent with Xi's supply-side structural reforms. Li supported Xi's discipline of the party state, rule of law, economic rebalancing, and "market as the main force." Li's pronouncements over a full range of issues, such as budgetary allocation, decentralization, environment, poverty reduction, and the reduction of government red tape for businesses, were commensurate with his position as premier. Further, all important decisions were made collectively in the Politburo, and seldom did the view of one individual prevail.

Policy disagreements, competition, and conflicts are a normal part of politics, and there are always real issues within the very nature of power sharing. Previous premiers such as Zhu Rongji and Wen Jiabao seemed to enjoy more power and prominence than Li. Yet there is no evidence that the unequal status between Li and Xi has fundamentally divided the two, even though policy setbacks and reversals, such as the early snags of the Shanghai PFTZ and the market turmoil in 2015 despite repeated government interventions, begot some recriminations. As mentioned, the Xi-Li relationship resembles in some respects that of the "dual executives" of the French president and prime minister, although Xi does not enjoy the freedom of the French president with a legislative majority to pick his favorite as prime minister. French presidents regard foreign affairs and security policy as exclusively their prerogative, but Chinese premiers are also closely involved in foreign affairs as well.

As mentioned, the "one party, two coalitions" perspective assumes that Li is the head of the *tuanpai* and Xi tends to see him as a rival. Further, the power maximization approach assumes that Xi and Li would contest with one another for supreme power. Yet several accounts maintain that Li is not politically ambitious. For instance, Wang Juntao, Li's former Peking University schoolmate, a Tiananmen dissident and now an activist, claims that Li Keqiang has the sentiment of an intellectual, nonsectarian character, unwilling or unable to manipulate the levers of power.[35] He possess a less strident personality than Xi. Further, Xi and Li have worked together for a full decade as number one and two, and it is unclear why they would still stick with so-called patrons who have retired long ago. Previous chapters have demonstrated the complex and changing relationships between Xi, Li, and other top leaders, and this general theme will be pursued in the next chapter.

Li Zhanshu (b. 1950)

Li Zhanshu has had strong family and work connections with Xi and therefore is regarded as a staunch protégé. Ranked number three in the PBSC, Li hails from a family of revolutionary veterans. His grandfather Li Zaiwen and his three brothers (Zhanshu's granduncles) were revolutionaries, and Li Zaiwen later became vice governor of Shandong. Li's uncle Li Zhengtong was a revolutionary martyr killed at age twenty-six. Li Zhanshu occupied various provincial positions (deputy or below) in Hebei (where he became acquainted with Xi at Zhengding), Shaanxi, and Heilongjiang before becoming secretary of the Guizhou PPC. Like Xi, Li rose from the grassroots, occupying four key positions as secretary of a CPC, MPC, and PPC, and when he was promoted as secretary of the Guizhou PPC, he was merely an alternate member of the Seventeenth CC, a rare occurrence.[36] As director of the General Office from 2012 to 2017, Li occupied a strategic position since the office supplies the general secretary, the CC, and its various departments secretarial assistance by drafting and disseminating party regulations, policy documents, and legislation. The office also takes charge of classified documents and information and their transmission, along with the archives and the personal safety and well-being of the leadership, including healthcare and housing. Many former chiefs of the Central Office have used the position as a launching pad into the PBSC, as was the case of Wen Jiabao, who had no regional administrative experience. As Xi's chief of staff, or *mishu*, Li has accompanied Xi at virtually all important domestic and foreign meetings, and he was even sent to visit Putin all by himself. On numerous occasions, Zhao has widely expressed loyalty to Xi as the party "core" and to the Party Center itself.[37]

Zhao Leji (b. 1957)

Zhao Leji, the youngest member of the PBSC, is, like Wang Yang and Wang Huning, sufficiently young to serve two terms after 2017. As party chief of the impoverished provinces of Qinghai and Shaanxi, Zhao's experience in poverty alleviation coincided with Xi's priorities. He followed Xi's injunctions to bolster grassroots party-building by urging his subordinates to build industrial estates and internet companies. A low-profile political comer for more than a decade, Zhao held critical positions such as secretary of the Secretariat and, for more than five years, head of the COD overseeing personnel recruitment and replacement for top party-state positions. One source has claimed that it was he who had laboriously replaced hundreds of corrupt officials ousted by the ACC,[38] presumably making sure that the positions would be filled by Xi loyalists. He took over from Wang Qishan as secretary of the CCDI, since his experiences were deemed a close fit for discipline and graft-busting.[39] Zhao's power may well increase, especially with the establishment of the State Supervisory Commission.

Wang Yang (b. 1955)

Wang Yang, number four on the PBSC, was a former food factory worker who obtained a master's degree in management science (on-the-job learning) at the prestigious University of Science and Technology of China in Anhui. Wang always was presumed a staunch member of the *tuanpai* because of three-years in the CYL, even though he afterward served in more weighty positions from 2005 to 2012 as secretary of the Chongqing and Guangdong PPCs. Further, from 2013 to 2017 he was a SC vice premier in charge of the economy, agriculture, and foreign trade, especially trade with the United States. Wang has promoted Xi's priority project of poverty alleviation and has gained Xi's trust. An easygoing style and open sense of humor distinguish him from the usually dour technocrats. While provincial party chief of economic powerhouse Guangdong, Wang gained a reputation for being a liberal reformer in favor of strengthening · market reforms, innovation, the private sector, and foreign trade. Borrowing Xi's slogan "Empty the cage and let the right birds in," he attempted to transform Guangdong's cheap factory production into high-end manufacturing. Because of the advanced and globalized economy of Guangdong, Wang also attempted political reforms such as intraparty democracy and media transparency. He resolved land seizure issues at Wukan by dismissing officials, redistributing land, and encouraging village elections. Taken together, the set of policies pursued by Wang has been dubbed the Guangdong Model.[40] In 2018, Wang became the chair of the CPPCC.

Wang Huning (b. 1955)

Among all PBSC members, Wang Huning's "factional" affiliation is the most difficult to pinpoint, even though earlier studies tended to classify him as Shanghai Gang because, not only was he born, educated, and worked as a professor in Shanghai, but he was also an adviser to Jiang Zemin. Wang was a self-effacing political science professor at Fudan University with a master's in international politics and a former dean of the faculty of law. However, Hu Jintao and Xi also trusted him. The Party's preeminent theoretician and member of the "Zhongnanhai brain trust," and director of the Central Policy Research Office, his chief skills are ideology, propaganda, and party organization. In 2007, he entered the Secretariat, taking charge of the day-to-day running of the Party, and in 2012 he had already set a historical precedent by entering the Politburo as director of the Party's think tank, the Central Policy Research Office and ranking secretary in the Secretariat. In these capacities, he worked in the background assisting the general secretary, performing functions carried out by predecessors such as Hu Jintao, Zeng Qinghong, Xi, and Liu Yunshan. In 2014 he was promoted from deputy director to director of the Office for the Comprehensively Deepening Reform LSG.

Wang enjoys remarkable continuity in his career, having served and been trusted by all three general secretaries, accompanying them on inspection tours and foreign visits. He has helped draft theoretical documents since the Thirteenth Party Congress, including the draft report to the Nineteenth Party Congress. The author of many books, Wang masterminded theoretical formulations such as Jiang Zemin's "three represents," Hu Jintao's "scientific development," and even Xi's BRI project.

An intellectual by sentiment, Wang's neoauthoritarian Confucianism ideas have resonated with Jiang, Hu, and Xi. He has argued that the Chinese political system must fit with its history and culture, reforms cannot be pushed too far, and centralized decision-making and modernization are the most efficient factors in producing economic development. If central authority is weak, he has argued, the country will be divided and thrown into chaos. However, he has also stated that it is important to comply with the constitution, and that political reform will be inevitable when rapid economic growth and modernization generate conflict and greater demand for democracy.[41]

Despite his résumé, Wang's induction into the PBSC was a surprise, because hopefuls like Hu Chunhua and Chen Min'er were excluded. In addition, Wang, unlike most previous PBSC members, lacked administrative experience at the province/municipality and grassroots levels, although former premier Wen Jiabao set a precedent for having no regional experience. Since his promotion, Wang at a PBSC meeting charged thirty-six high officials to popularize the "spirit" of the Nineteenth Party Congress at various localities, and official propaganda claimed that this was quickly accomplished in ten days.[42] Wang's influence is sure to grow in Xi's second term.

Han Zheng (b. 1954)

Han Zheng has spent his career entirely in the metropolis of Shanghai, serving as deputy mayor, mayor, deputy secretary, and secretary of the Shanghai PPC. He is well connected with former patrons in Shanghai who were PBSC members, such as Huang Ju, Wu Bangguo, Zhu Rongji, Zeng Qinghong, and Yu Zhengsheng. For this he is presumed to be a member of the Shanghai Gang, although he worked with the CYL as well (see Table 12.4). Further, he also served as Xi's deputy in Shanghai in 2007 and entered the Politburo in 2012. For these reasons, the static label "Shanghai Gang," which assumes that his loyalty and policy orientation have stuck with past patron Jiang Zemin, is problematic. A seasoned administrator who has survived the many political shake-ups and scandals and gets on well with various political networks, he oversaw the Shanghai PFTZ and has special skills with finance, economics, and market-oriented reforms. He has repeatedly declared support for the Party Center with Xi as its "core."[43] As expected, Han became executive vice premier, the deputy to Premier Li Keqiang, in 2018. In 2019, Han visited Shenzhen multiple times to oversee behind the scenes the management of the Hong Kong protests.

Three Politburo Members Are Ousted

Three Politburo members were ousted at the Nineteenth Congress (see Table 12.6). The two unexpectedly demoted were Zhang Chunxian (b. 1953), former secretary of the Xinjiang Uyghur Autonomous Region and deputy director of the Party Building LSG; and Liu Qibao (b 1953), director of the Central Propaganda

Table 12.6 Political Careers of Three Ousted Politburo Members

	Date and place of birth; year joined CCP	Family background and youth experience	Education	Early political career	Later political career		
Li Yuanchao	1950.11, Jiangsu, Lianshui County (1978)	Princeling; R2G, sent-down youth, 1968–72	PhD in law, Central Party School, 1991–95; master's in economic management, Perking University, 1986; mathematics, Shanghai Normal University, 1972–74	Various positions, Fudan University CYL, 1978–82; member, CYL CC, Secretariat, 1983–90	Head, Central Bureau of Propaganda, 1990–93; deputy group leader, Central Propaganda Small Group; deputy director, Information Office of the State Council, 1993–96	Vice minister, Ministry of Culture 1996–2000; secretary, Nanjing MPC, 2001–3; secretary, Jiangsu PPC, 2001–7	Politburo; Secretariat, head, COD 2007–12	Politburo; vice president, 2012–17
Liu Qibao	1953.01, Susong, Anhui (1971)	Member, Jinba production brigade party branch; Instructor, Liuwu production team, 1968–72	Master's in economics, Jilin University, 1992; history, Anhui Normal University, 1972–74	Research staff, General Office, Anhui PPC 1974–77; secretary, Secretariat of Anhui PPC's General Office, 1977–80	Secretary, Secretariat of CYL, 1985–93; secretary, Secretariat, Anhui CYL, 1983–85; deputy director, Information Office, Anhui CYL, 1980–82	Deputy editor-in-chief, People's Daily, 1993–94	Secretary, Sichuan PPC, 2007–12; Deputy secretary and secretary, Guangxi ARC; deputy secretary general, State Council, 1994–2000	Politburo; secretary, Secretariat; Director, Central Propaganda Department 2012–17

Continued

Table 12.6 *Continued*

	Date and place of birth; year joined CCP	Family background and youth experience	Education	Early political career	Later political career		
Zhang Chunxian	1953,05 Yuzhou City, Henan (1972)	Soldier, 1970–75	Cadre, Chengguan Commune, Henan; student, Dongbei Heavy Machinery School, 1976–80	Various positions, China National Packaging Corp., 1993; director, Industrial Department Supervision Bureau, Ministry of Supervision, 1991–92	Assistant governor, People's Government, Yunnan, 1995–97	Minister, vice minister, Ministry of Transport, 1997–2005	Secretary Hunan PPC, and chair, Hunan People's Congress, 2005–10	Politburo, 2012–17; secretary, Xinjiang Uyghur ARC, 2010–16

Source: Baidu baike and China Vitae.

Department. They were driven out of the Politburo, but their retention in the CC was unprecedented. Not so lucky was Vice President Li Yuanchao, who lost his CC membership and became a mere party member. Although Zhang and Liu had not reached the age limit of sixty-eight, they were too old for provincial leadership, and their future assignments were unclear until a few months later. A perhaps too simple explanation for the ouster of Li Yuanchao and Liu Qibao is that they were associated with the CYL, Hu Jintao's alleged power base, and the *tuanpai* was not in favor with Xi. Another explanation was that the Propaganda Department under Liu Qibao had been faulted for sticking with outdated and arbitrary methods in dealing with ideology and public opinion and for mismanaging the internet by closing large numbers of WeChat accounts. Wittingly or unwittingly, Liu had turned overblown propaganda into public sarcasm and ridicule (*gajiehe*).[44]

The case of Zhang Chunxian is more complex, especially since he had no CYL connections. Once a rising star touted as the youngest ever to become a central minister, Zhang was demoted, allegedly for his unsatisfactory performance in Xinjiang, as he was deemed too soft on security issues, unable to contain the terrorist activities there, and had already been replaced as Xinjiang party chief in August 2016 by Chen Quanguo.[45] Another view, however, claims that Zhang, formerly a soldier, peasant, worker, and university student, had achieved much in his six-year sojourn in Xinjiang. Parachuted into the province during the Xinjiang crisis of 2009, Zhang was on the one hand recognized for toughness in dealing with terrorism and corruption, and on the other hand credited for such things as the reopening of the internet and microblogs, simplification of the passport application procedure, economic development, and implementation of the BRI project. One element of the last project was said to be the establishment of a train link through Kazakhstan and Turkey, shortening the transport time to Europe from forty to eighteen days.[46]

Li Yuanchao (b. 1950) was China's vice president, a former rising star, and not yet at retirement age, but his political career ended when he was expelled from both the Politburo and the CC, reducing him to a mere party member. It is rare that Politburo members are dismissed without explicit charges of wrongdoing or corruption. Although the vice president position is primarily ceremonial, as observed in chapter 7, it had been used to groom Xi by giving him domestic responsibilities and international exposure. But Li Yuanchao, as Xi's vice president, performed purely ceremonial functions with no hope of further advancement. Often presumed to be *tuanpai* because of his CYL stint in his early career, Li is also a princeling and Red Second Generation (R2G) since both his parents were revolutionaries, and his father, Li Gancheng, worked under Zeng Qinghong's father. In 1962 the elder Li served as deputy mayor of Shanghai before being imprisoned during the Cultural Revolution. Once a high-flier, Li was once considered, together with Xi and Li Keqiang, as a trio to be groomed for the highest post, although Li Yuanchao became only an alternate of the CC at the Sixteenth Party Congress in 2002, whereas Xi and Li Keqiang pulled ahead by entering the CC as full members. As party chief at Jiangsu and Nanjing, Li wrestled with developmental problems similar to those confronted by Xi in Zhejiang, and he was a proponent of the Sunan model. By most accounts he is ordinarily an amicable person, although one with an iron fist when it came to issues of bureaucracy and pollution. Like Xi, he attempted to demarcate the limits of government and introduced "service style" government as well as the direct public evaluation and scrutiny of officials. To deal with a toxic algae bloom resulting from industrial waste pollution in Lake Tai, a source of water for thirty million people west of Shanghai, in 2007 he closed thousands of small factories, although even today the results are mixed. In 2012 Li was considered a top contender for the PBSC, but allegedly some elders blamed him for ignoring their recommendations for their own men and for promoting too many of Hu Jintao's allies when he was head of the COD. Consequently, Jiang Zemin used a last-minute straw poll to block him from the PBSC, and as compensation, Li was made vice president. Although Li was deputy leader for both the Central LSG for Foreign Affairs and for Hong Kong and Macau Affairs, he was China's first vice president since 1998 who was not a PBSC member, and therefore he was not groomed, like Xi, as the successor presumptive. As vice president Li also managed mass organizations like the All-China Federation of Women and the CYL, and Xi's vehement attack on the latter did not reflect well on Li. Li's ceremonial functions saw him representing China at memorials and funerals for Nelson Mandela, Lee Kuan Yew, and Fidel Castro. During the ACC, several of Li's former associates were prosecuted, and Li was progressively marginalized.[47]

The Politburo

In the broader Politburo, Liu Yandong and Sun Chunlan were two women of the outgoing Politburo. Liu retired and Sun became the lone woman holdover. The minuscule representation of women at the very top reflected gender discrimination; no woman, including Mao Zedong's wife Jiang Qing, has ever sat in the PBSC. By tradition, the secretaries of the four municipalities also sit on the Politburo. Before the congress, in September 2016, Li Hongzhong had already replaced Huang Xingguo as secretary of the Tianjin MPC. In May 2017, Xi protégé Cai Qi replaced the retiring Guo Jinlong, a close associate of Hu Jintao, as secretary of Beijing PPC. Cai had spent twenty years in Fujian before moving to Zhejiang in 1999, serving as mayor of Quzhou and Hangzhou before entering the Zhejiang PPC. In Zhejiang, Cai was one of the high officials who exploited social media to openly discuss political issues, turning himself into a popular blogger boasting more than ten million followers.[48] In July 2017, another Xi protégé, Chen Min'er, replaced the purged Sun Zhengcai to become secretary of the Chongqing MPC. As expected, all three were inducted into the Politburo. Right after the congress, another Xi ally, Li Qiang, was made secretary of the Shanghai PPC by replacing Hang Zheng. Among these four, Cai and Yang Xiaodu were neither alternate nor full members of the CC, but they made spectacular three-step jumps into the Politburo. This reflected Xi's clout, but the fast-track promotion was also an expedient—Xi had to overcome the constraint of having small feeder pools in the CC. We will consider the political careers of selected Politburo members in the following (see Table 12.7).

Ding Xuexiang (b. 1962)

Ding Xuexiang is a low-key official whose career was spent mostly in Shanghai and who therefore, in factional parlance, belongs to the "Shanghai Gang." He was promoted to director of the Central Office and later deputy secretary general of the Shanghai MPC during Xi's seven-month stint in Shanghai to even things out after the purge of Chen Liangyu. There Ding won the confidence of Chen's successor, Yu Zhengsheng. In 2012 and 2013 Ding was quickly promoted by Xi as deputy director of the CC's General Office, serving under Li Zhanshu, a close ally of Xi, who had overhauled the personnel of the General Office since the fall of the previous director, Ling Jihua. Ding was concurrently appointed director of the President's Office and has accompanied Xi on numerous domestic and foreign trips. As Xi's personal secretary, Ding is known for his writing skills and his ability to turn Xi's remarks into official script. While the PBSC and Politburo set all major decisions and exercise general oversight, the General Office is the nerve center whereby information is filtered through to the Politburo, and decisions disseminated to all implementation agencies. This office handles paperwork, speeches, logistics, healthcare, and security for top leaders, as well as the thousands of troops of the Central Security Bureau who are dedicated to the protection of top leaders and their families. In his new posting, Ding joined a contingent of *mishu* who had built up their credentials while serving their bosses and then moved on to higher positions.[49]

Liu He (b. 1952)

Liu He, a US-educated (Seton Hall and international finance and trade at Harvard) economist, is said to be the mastermind behind the "supply-side

Table 12.7 Political Careers of Selected Politburo Members*

Date and place of birth; year joined CCP	Family background and youth experience	Education	Early political career	Later political career				Political career, 2017–
Ding Xuexiang		Research fellow, Shanghai Research Institute of Materials 1982–84; Public Administration, Fudan University; master of science, 1994–96; senior engineer;		Various positions in the Shanghai MPC, 1999–2006; only exception is deputy secretary, Zhabei Prefectural PC, 2001–4	Secretary general, Shanghai MPC, 2007–12	Secretary, Politics and Law Committee, Shanghai MPC, 2012–13	Deputy director, Party General Office; director, President's Office, 2013–17	Director, Party General Office; Director, President's Office,
1962.09 Jiangsu, Nantong City (1984)								
Liu He	Sent-down youth, 1969–70; Soldier in the Thirty-Eighth Army, 1970–73; worker, 1973–79	Degree in economics, Renmin University, 1979–83; business, Seton Hall University, 1992–93; MPA, Harvard, 1994–95	Deputy director general, Long-Term Planning and Industrial Policy Department, SPC, 1994–98; chief, Industrial Structure Section, SPC, 1991–93; deputy director, Policy Research Office, SPC 1993–94	Vice director, State Information Center, 1998–2001	Deputy director, Office of the Finance and Economics LSG, 2003–13	Deputy director, SC Policy Research Office, 2011–13	Director, Office of the Finance and Economics LSG, 2013–17; deputy director, NDRC, 2013–14	Politburo member
1952.01 Beijing (1976)								

Name	Birthdate, origin (year joined Party)							
Sun Chunlan	1950.05 Raoyang, Hebei (1973)	Worker, member of party branch, head of the CYL Committee, member of the Party Committee, Anshan Watch Factory, Liaoning, 1969–74	In-service graduate program in decision-making and management, Liaoning University, 1992–95; training course, Central Party School, 1992–93; correspondence programs in economic management, Liaoning Party School, 1989–81 and Liaoning University, 1981–84	Director, Anshan Municipal Women's Federation, Liaoning, 1988–91; various positions at the Anshan Chemical Fiber Wool Textile Factory, Liaoning, 1977–88	Deputy secretary, Liaoning PPC, 1997–2005; Secretary, Dalian MPC, 2001–5; various positions, Liaoning Provincial Federation of Trade Unions, 1991–97	Vice chair, member of the Secretariat, All-China Federation of Trade Unions, 2005–9;	Politburo member and secretary, Tianjin MPC, 2012–14; secretary, Fujian PPC, 2009–12	Head, United Front Work Department, 2014–17
Li Qiang	1959.07 Shanghai (1986)	Worker, 1976–78	Agricultural mechanization, Zhejiang Agriculture University, 1978–82	Cadre and secretary of Zhejiang CYL, 1983–84	Various positions at Zhejiang government, 1985–2002	Secretary, Wenzhou MPC, 2002–4	Secretary general and member, Zhejiang PPC, 2004–11	Governor, Zhejiang, 2013–16; deputy secretary, Zhejiang PPC, 2011–16	Secretary, Shanghai MPC

Continued

Table 12.7 *Continued*

	Date and place of birth; year joined CCP	Family background and youth experience	Education	Early political career	Later political career					Political career, 2017–
Hu Chunhua	1963.04 Hubei Wufeng County (1983)	Peasant family, Chinese Peking University	Vice chairman, All-China Youth Federation, 1997–2001; Various positions in Tibet, 1993–2001	Secretary general, Tibet Autonomous Regional Committee, 2001–7	First secretary, CYL, 2007–8		Deputy secretary, Hebei PPC, governor, acting governor, vice governor, 2008–9	Secretary, CCP Autonomous Regional Committee, Inner Mongolia, 2009–12	Chairman, Standing Committee, Inner Mongolia Regional People's Congress 2010–12; secretary, Zhejiang PPC, 2016–17	Secretary, Guangdong PPC, 2012–17
Yang Jiechi	1950.05 Shanghai (1971)	Factory worker, 1968–72	BA in international relations, Bath University; master's in economics, London School of Economics, 1973–75; PhD in history, Nanjing University 2001–6	Various positions at the Ministry of Foreign Affairs, 1987–93	Assistant minister and then vice minister, Ministry of Foreign Affairs, 1995–2000		Ambassador to United States, 2000–2004	Minister of foreign affairs, 2007–13; vice minister of foreign affairs, 2005–7	State councilor, SC, deputy director, State Climate Change and Energy Conservation LSG, 2013–	
Yang Xiaodu	1953.10 Shanghai (1973)	R2G; sent-down youth, 1970–73	Shanghai Chinese Medicine College, 1974–76	Various positions in Tibet, 1976–2001	Deputy mayor, Shanghai, 2001–6	Member, Shanghai MPC; director, United Front Work Department, 2006–12	Member, Shanghai MPC; secretary, Shanghai Discipline Inspection Committee, 2012–14	Minister of Supervision, 2016–17; deputy secretary, CCDI; minister, CCDI, 2014–16	Member, Secretariat; deputy secretary, CCDI; minister, Ministry of Supervision	Head, National Bureau of Corruption Prevention

Name	Birth / origin	Education						Current position
Chen Miner	1960.09 Zhejiang Zhuji City (1982)	Chinese language and literature, Shaoxing Normal College 1978–81; master's in law, Central Party School, 1996–98	Propaganda clerk, 1981–82	Various positions in Zhejiang, 1987–2007	Executive vice governor, Zhejiang Province, 2007–12; vice governor, Zhejiang, 2007	Deputy secretary, Guizhou PPC, 2012–15; governor, Guizhou, 2013–15	Secretary, Guizhou PPC, 2015–17	Secretary, Chongqing MPC
Guo Shengkun	1954.10 Jiangxi, Xingguo County	Student, Jiangxi Metallurgical Institute, 1977–79; PhD in management, Beijing Science and Technology University, 2003–7	Sent-down youth, 1973–77	Various positions, Ministry of Metallurgy, 1979–85; various positions, China National Nonferrous Metals Industry Corp. 1985–99	General manager and party secretary, Aluminum Corp. of China, 2001–4	Deputy secretary, Guanxi ARPC, 2004–7; secretary, Guanxi ARPC, 2007–12	Minister, Ministry of Public Security, 2012–13	State councilor, deputy secretary, Politics and Law Committee, 2013–17	Member, Secretariat; state councilor; secretary, Politics and Law Committee
Huang Kunming	1956.11 Fujian, Shanghang City	Political Education, Fujian Normal University, 1978–82; PhD, management, Tsinghua University, 2005–8	Soldier, 1974–77	Various positions at Longyan Prefecture, Fujian, 1982–99; secretary, Yongding CPC, 1995–98	Deputy secretary, Huzhou MPC, Zhejiang, 1999–2003; mayor, deputy mayor, Huzhou	Secretary, Jiaxing MPC, Zhejiang, 2003–7	Member, Zhejiang PPC, 2007–12; secretary, Hangzhou MPC, 2011–13	Deputy director, COD, 2013–14 · Executive vice director, Central Propaganda Department 2014–17	Member, Secretariat; director, Central Propaganda Department

Continued

Table 12.7 Continued

	Date and place of birth; year joined CCP	Family background and youth experience	Education	Early political career	Later political career			Political career, 2017–
Cai Qi	1953.09 Fujian, Youxi County	Sent-down youth, 1973–75	Political studies, Fujian Normal University, 1975–78; master's in economics and law, Fujian Normal University, 1994–97	Cadre, Fujian Normal University Party Committee, 1978–83; various positions, Fujian PPC, 1983–96; deputy secretary, Sanming MPC, mayor, vice mayor, 1997–1999	Secretary and Deputy Secretary, Quzhou MPC, mayor, 1999–2004; secretary, Taizhou MPC, Zhejiang, 2004–7	Deputy Secretary, Hangzhou MPC, mayor, 2007–10	Member, Zhejiang PPC, 2010–14	Vice Director, Office of the State Security Commission, 2014–16	Deputy Secretary, Beijing MPC, Acting Mayor, 2016–17	Secretary, Beijing MPC

Source: Baidu baike and China Vitae.

structural" reform. Prior to the Nineteenth Congress, he occupied a relatively modest position as the director of the Office of the Finance and Economics LSG and vice chairman of the NDRC, the top planning organ. However, as Xi's most trusted adviser on management economics, he enjoys a higher international profile than other senior economics officials because of his relationship with Xi, who has said that Liu is "very important" to him. As discussed in chapter 10, Liu was alleged to be the "authoritative person" who blasted the bureaucracy for misunderstanding and mishandling Xi's "supply-side structural reform" initiative, although this "authoritative person" was more likely a term for a group. In 2018, he was made a vice minister, despite his academic temperament and lack of administrative experience.[50] Liu distinguished himself as the chief negotiator representing Beijing during the trade war with the United States.

Hu Chunhua (b. 1960)

Precongress speculation predicting that two sixth-generation leaders, Hu Chunhua (b. 1963) and Chen Min'er would both be inducted into the PBSC as potential successors along the Xi Jinping–Li Keqiang model did not materialize. Hu Chunhua occupied a particularly awkward position after the purge of Sun Zhengcai since the two were rising stars originally tipped for the top jobs. Nicknamed "Little Hu," he has been variously described by observers as publicity shy, relaxed, unassuming, and affable. After spending two decades in Tibet before becoming governor of Hebei, then party chief of Inner Mongolia, Hu was appointed party chief of Guangdong in 2012. Hu attempted to restructure and upgrade Guangdong's economic and industrial base and ease social tension and conflicts. For Hu, like all officials at every level in Guangdong, poverty alleviation, especially in poor and remote areas in the province's northwest, was a central plank in the policy platform. As a coastal province, Guangdong, with a trade volume of 20.9 percent of the nation's total in 2016, was an early and substantial supporter of the BRI strategy. Hu led delegations to visit BRI countries such as Israel, Ireland, and the UK. Guangdong had helped Shenzhen build up its technology sector, now home to many of China's top technology companies. By 2017, Guangdong's GDP had reached US$1.16 trillion, larger than that of Indonesia, representing 10 percent of China's GDP and 28 percent of its total trade.[51]

With approximately five years' work experience in the CYL, Hu is presumed to have a close relationship with Hu Jintao, so the label *tuanpai* is often deemed a liability. But age and impeccable qualifications are also assets according to CCP standards. Further, Hu survived major scandals in his regional career, such as the Sanlu tainted milk scandal in Hebei in 2008 and ethnic protest by Mongols in 2011. In April 2017 Xi issued an instruction to Guangdong ordering it to persist on party leadership, to lead the country in reform, and to render support to the rest of the country. Later, Xi also endorsed Guangdong's (and Hu's) performance over the past five years. In reply, Hu pledged full compliance with all aspects of Xi's priorities, such as "supply-side structural reform," innovation, further opening, and accelerated socioeconomic development. He pledged loyalty to Xi as core and unleashed a campaign to study the issues.[52] Subsequently, a book was published to elaborate on the exchanges between Xi and Hu, reinforcing the general evaluation that Hu had done a good job in Guangdong.[53] After Sun's purge, Hu Chunhua joined the official chorus to support the party decision and to denounce Sun, although Hu probably also found himself in an awkward position.[54] And in spite of Xi's endorsement, Hu kept a low profile, letting his vice secretary do the talking. In contrast, Chen Min'er gave a speech with an endorsement of Xi's report.[55] Hu tread cautiously, and the expectation that he could become vice premier was fulfilled in March 2018.[56]

Chen Min'er (b. 1960)

A native of Zhejiang, Chen spent twenty-five years there before moving to Guizhou and becoming party chief. Chen worked with Xi during 2007–2012 in various positions in the Zhejiang PPC, such as head of the propaganda department and vice governor. He is said to have assisted with Xi's weekly *Zhejiang Daily* column that later was published as *New Thoughts from Zhejiang*, a summation of Xi's political/social/economic thinking. Accordingly, he was presumed to be a member of a Zhejiang "clique." As mentioned, governance experience in poor, primarily rural, and "hardship" regions such as Guizhou is considered an asset, especially when an official can demonstrate the ability to make a difference. Promising leaders are often sent there to be challenged and groomed for national leadership, as had Hu Jintao and Zhao Leji. As secretary of the Guizhou PPC, Chen used the province as a poverty-fighting testing ground. He encouraged the pooling of money, labor, and tiny, fragmented, family fields into collectives, leveraging the economics of scale in order to boost production, especially for commercial crops. Rural collectives are not by definition dysfunctional if their membership is voluntary, their management trusted and efficient, or if they are run by members of the same lineage groups still common in much of the Chinese countryside. Chen oversaw the completion of a giant radio telescope that has already discovered pulsars, although the Chinese have had difficulty attracting staff, domestic or foreign, because of its remote location. His succession to the position of secretary of the Chongqing PPC after the dramatic downfall of Sun Zhengcai in 2017 is seen to be a strategic move by Xi to groom him, even as a possible successor.[57] Chen was inducted into the Politburo, but as a mere CC member, and if "helicoptered" to the PBSC, he would have to skip one rung, defying the principle of seniority and attracting criticism. However, Chen enjoys an advantage in his relative youth, since unlike Xi's other allies, he will be able to serve two terms from 2022, when he will be sixty-two.

Yang Jiechi (b. 1950)

A former ambassador to the United States and minister of foreign affairs, Yang Jiechi was the first senior diplomat, since Qian Qichen retired in 1998, to join the Politburo in nearly two decades, reflecting the priority accorded to diplomacy at a time when foreign relations require more professional skills and tact in negotiations. A former state councilor, he was expected to exercise influence over other foreign policy players such as the Ministry of Commerce and the Party's Central Liaison Department. He would also oversee tense top-priority relations with the United States, in addition to issues involving North Korea, Taiwan, and the SCS.[58]

Yang Xiaodu (b. 1953)

Yang Xiaodu is a R2G because his father was a "red capitalist" in Shanghai who had worked underground for the CCP before 1949 and then served in Shanghai's United Front Department. A former *zhiqing*, Yang had "gone down" and spent twenty-four years in Tibet before returning to become a member of the Shanghai MPC and the Shanghai Discipline Inspection Commission, working with Xi to clean up the Chen Liangyu mess in 2007. In 2013, he oversaw the dismissal of two Shanghai high-court judges for visiting prostitutes. His career was fast-tracked by Xi, since it took only four years for him to advance from a provincial official with a deputy-ministerial rank to be a member of the Politburo.[59] As deputy secretary of the CCDI and minister of supervision, Yang was credited with leading many inspection teams for the ACC and for hunting down many "tigers." It is rare for a deputy secretary of the CCDI to enter the Politburo, but the fact that both Yang and CCDI head Zhao Leji were inducted into the Politburo underlined the perceived need to reinforce the contingent to fight corruption, especially with the departure of the formidable Wang Qishan.[60] In 2018, he was named to another concurrent post as a member of a central LSG on state supervisory work[61] and then elected as the founding director of the National Supervisory Commission.

Guo Shengkun (b. 1954)

Guo Shengkun is considered a "princeling" of R3G background since his wife's grandmother is sister to Deng Lijin, one of the twenty-seven women who took part in the Long March. Deng was mother to Zeng Qinghong, a powerful former PBSC member and a protégé of Jiang Zemin. Guo is presumed to be member of the "Jiang" faction, although there is little empirical evidence. A *zhiqing* during the Cultural Revolution, Guo accumulated more than two decades' experience in the nonferrous metal sector and managed a large SOE. After five years as Guangxi's party chief, he was called to Beijing to become minister of public security and PAP's political commissar and later deputy secretary of the Central Politics and Legal Affairs Commission (CPLAC). At the Nineteenth Party Congress, he moved up to become secretary, taking a position previously occupied for two decades by Luo Gan, Zhou Yongkang, and Meng Jianzhu respectively. Up to 2012, the CPLAC controlled the ministries of Public Security, State Security, the Procuracy, the Courts, the People's Militia, and the PAP. Increasing demands for *weiwen* enabled the power of the CPLAC and Zhou Yongkang to tremendously expand.[62] But, starting with Meng in 2012, the role of the CPLAC secretary was downgraded, and the position was no longer given PBSC membership. Apart from being a rebuke of the disgraced Zhou Yongkang, the downgrade was designed to rein in the security apparatus. As minister of public security, Guo had used Xi's ACC to shake up the ministry and weed out Zhou's remaining influence, and he repeatedly urged vigorous support of the Party's centralized leadership, with Xi as the core.[63]

The Secretariat

Xi's strong position was more evident in the Secretariat since his former associates constituted the majority in this organ (see Table 12.8). Presided over by the general secretary, the Secretariat serves the Politburo and PBSC by running and coordinating the day-to-day affairs of the Party, and its members are drawn mostly from the Politburo. Noticeably, many of these members had experience working in Zhejiang and Fujian. In the Secretariat Wang Huning is in charge of ideology; Ding Xuexiang, the Central Office; Yang Xiaodu, the CCDI; Chen Xi, the COD; Guo Shengkun, CPLAC; and Huang Kunming, the Central Propaganda Department.[64] The only non-Politburo member is You Quan, who takes charge of the United Front Work Department. Since the director of the CPLAC had not been in the Secretariat since 2002, and the director of the United Front Work Department had been absent since 1992 (except a brief stint by the disgraced Ling Jihua in 2012),[65] their reinclusion reflected an elevated

Table 12.8 Members of the Secretariat and Their Concurrent Positions

	Concurrent Positions
Wang Huning 王沪宁	Director, Central Policy Research Office; director, Central Commission on Building Spiritual Civilization
Ding Xuexiang 丁薛祥	Director, General Staff Office
Yang Xiaodu 杨晓渡	Vice director, Central Discipline Inspection Commission
Chen Xi 陈希	Director, Organization Department; principal, Central Party School
Guo Shengkun 郭声琨	Director, Central Political and Legal Affairs Commission
Huang Kunming 黄坤明	Director, Central Propaganda Department
You Quan 尤权*	Director, United Front Work Department

Source: "7 wei xinren zhongyang shujichu shuji di fengong mingxi" [The Division of Labor among the Seven New Secretaries of the Secretariat Is Now Clarified], *360doc.com*, November 7, 2017, http://www.360doc.com/content/17/1107/21/16215120_701780279.shtml.

* Only person in the Secretariat who is not a Politburo member.

importance now attached to these areas. Separately, since Secretariat member and Xi's trusted lieutenant Guo Shengkun assumed the head of the CPLAC, Xi probably felt more confident about that organization. Chen Xi, who was made principal of the Central Party School, appears to be Xi's point person for party organization and personnel. Over the years the power and functions of the Secretariat have varied, and its membership has been used to groom successors presumptive like Hu Jintao and Xi Jinping. Although Ding Xuexiang was not a designated successor, his relatively young age and his strategic position as director of the Party Central Office undoubtedly give him an advantage in a future leadership race.

Changes in the Central Committee

The anticorruption campaign had taken a toll on the CC, but that gave it the opportunity for an infusion of new blood. Before the Nineteenth Congress a record forty-three CC (twenty-six full and seventeen alternate) members had already been punished because of the anticorruption campaign. This contrasted with the previous high of four removed during the Seventeenth Party Congress, or the normal one or two at previous central committees.[66] The new CC consisted of 204 full members, 1 less than the preceding CC. One hundred and twenty-six (62 percent) were newly elected and 79 (38 percent) were re-elected. There were

38 sixth-generation members (19 percent), 10 women, and 16 minorities. Among the 172 alternates who serve as a reserve, more than 90 percent are sixth-generation officials, ministry-level officials, including more than twenty directors of state-owned financial organizations and SOEs.[67] According to the job-slot system, the CC is roughly apportioned among top leaders from provinces and municipalities, central commissions, and mass organizations. Normally, CC membership is a requisite gateway to Politburo and PBSC membership, but since the CC is designed to serve representative functions, not all CC members possess the qualifications to advance forward. Chinese leaders typically wear many hats in the functional systems of the party state, but a rough classification, according to the first-listed positions (presumably the most important) of each individual CC member, can still be made.

One source classifies the CC functional representation as the following. Affiliated with the CCP are the PBSC (2 members), Party Central (2), Central Staff Office (3), Political Research and Propaganda (7), CCDI (2), United Front (4) COD (1), Political and Legal Committee (2), and External Liaison (1). Other members are from the military (6) CMC (3), CMC departments (10), five military services (13), five military regions (10), PAP (2), military academies (2), and others (2). Also represented are the State Council (42), provinces/municipalities (65), social organizations (7), judiciary (4), NPC/CPPCC (10), and Hong Kong / Macau / Taiwan Affairs (4).[68] A simpler classification yields the following: PBSC (3), Central Party Affairs (27), military (41), State Council system (44), regional party (65), social organizations (7), judiciary (4), NPC and CPPCC (10), Hong Kong / Macau / Taiwan Affairs (4).[69]

Such classifications reflect roughly the distribution of power in the CC among the various functional constituencies. For instance, the largest group, at sixty-five, represented provincial and regional party leaders, who constituted the key power bloc and pool for future leaders. The NPeC and CPPCC with ten members and the United Front with four show that lawmaking, in conjunction with non-party consultation and support, was considered an important function. The approximately 20 percent representation for the military conformed with the norm. The relatively low status of the judiciary was reflected by the representation of only four members, which included the heads and deputy heads of the Supreme People's Procuratorate and the Supreme People's Court, despite the call for "law-based governance." Unlike the previous CC, no managers of SOEs were included, and this might reflect a downgrading of the state sector.

The average age of the CC was 57, or a margin 0.9-year increase over the previous CC. The Seventeenth CC, with an average age of 53.5, was the youngest since the establishment of the PRC. In this respect the Xi administration seemed to have sidelined Deng Xiaoping's policy of promoting young and middle-age cadres in their thirties and forties, which made it possible for Hu Jintao to become an alternate at age thirty-nine. Yet, as mentioned, Deng was facing a crisis of a gerontocracy (especially in the context of low life expectancy) and undereducated officials because of the purge of Cultural Revolution radicals who had been recruited into the CC, but under Xi, this was less an issue than the Party's ability to attract clean, capable, and loyal officials. Further, since Xi had lambasted the CYL for being "out of step with the times," bureaucratic and arrogant, and being a pool of "political aristocrats," CYL cadres had been marginalized. The CYL's former rising stars, such as its first secretary, Qin Yizhi, and Jiangsu vice governor Yang Yue, were shunned as delegates to the Nineteenth Party Congress.[70] Last, the only R2G princeling remaining on the CC was Li Xiaopeng, son of former premier Li Peng, raising the question of whether this spelled the end of the descendants of the revolutionary veterans in politics.

The Central Military Commission

Both the ACC and the PLA restructuring brought drastic changes to the CMC. An official account half-boasted that more than one hundred members at the army commander level and above, in addition to two CMC vice chairmen, had been punished for corruption, exceeding the total who were "sacrificed" since the founding of PRC.[71] In the CMC, the number of new personnel also suggests that Xi inserted loyalists, but the composition also reflected new institutions and new policy priorities. Although the chairman of the CMC is de facto commander in chief of the PLA and the PAP, Hu Jintao had essentially been a figurehead unable to exercise full control over the various bureaucratic fiefdoms and interests in these establishments.[72] Further, since most senior generals and officials had been appointed by Jiang Zemin (1997–2012), even Xi could not be assured of their loyalty. Xi was determined to change this situation and to assert his personal and party control over the PLA. Xi's anticorruption campaign in the PLA, and the purge of former CMC vice chairmen Guo Boxiong and Xu Caihou, as well as security chief Zhou Yongkang, shook up the PLA and helped consolidate Xi's power. In 2014 Xi asserted the role of the chairman of the CMC by introducing the notion of a "commission chairman responsibility system," which declared that the CMC chairman would preside over the CMC and wield the ultimate authority on all defense and military affairs.

At the First Plenum, when Xi assumed the role of chairman of the CMC, he managed to stack it with supporters who had pledged loyalty to him. The membership of the CMC was downsized from eleven to seven; and from two vice chairmen and eight members to two vice chairmen and four members (see Table 12.9). Previously, the CMC neatly represented the bureaucratic interests of the PLA, since the eight CMC members, apart from the chairmen and vice chairmen,

Table 12.9 Composition of the Central Military Commission, the Eighteenth and Nineteenth Central Committees

	Nineteenth Central Committee, 2017–2022	Eighteenth Central Committee, 2012–17
Chairman	Xi Jinping	Xi Jinping
Vice chairmen	Xu Qiliang 许其亮 1950.03 Former commander, PLA Air Force	Fan Changlong 1947.05 Former commander, Jinan Military Region
	Zhang Youxia 张又侠 1950.07 Former director, PLA General Armaments Department	Xu Qiliang 1950.03 Commander of PLA Air Force
Members	Wei Fenghe 魏凤和 1954.02 Former commander, PLA Rocket Force	Chang Wanquan 1949.01 Minister of National Defense
	Li Zuocheng 李作成 1953.10 Chief of Joint Staff	Zhang Youxia 1950.07 Director, PLA General Armaments Department
	Miao Hua 苗华 1955.11 Director, General Political Department	Fang Fenghui 1951.04 Director, PLA Staff Department
	Zhang Shengmin 张升民 1958.08 Deputy secretary, Central Commission for Discipline Inspection	Zhang Yang 1951.08 Director, PLA General Political Department
		Zhao Keshi 1947.11 Director, PLA General Logistics Department
		Ma Xiaotian 1949.08 Commander, PLA Air Force
		Wei Fenghe 1954.02 Commander, Second Artillery Corps; Commander, PLA Rocket Force (from 2015)
		Wu Shengli 1945.08 Commander, PLA Navy

Source: *Baidu* and *China Vitae*; "Xinyijie zhongyang junwei chulu, weiyuanjianban" [The Members of the New CMC Are Revealed: Membership Has Been Cut in Half], *Ifeng*, October 25, 2017, http://news.ifeng.com/a/20171025/52787431_0.shtml; "Xinyijie zhongyang junwei weiyuanhui mingdan gongbu" [The Name List of the New CMC Is Published], *Sina*, November 15, 2012, http://mil.news.sina.com.cn/2012-11-15/1329706884.html.

were the minister of defense, the heads of the four General Headquarters (General Staff Departments, General Political Department, General Logistics Department, and General Armaments Department), and the commanders of the air force, navy, and rocket force. As discussed in chapter 11, in 2016, to modernize and integrate command, the four General Headquarters were replaced by fifteen smaller functional units without decision-making powers. And the seven military regions were restructured into five theater commands. In this respect, CMC restructuring necessitated more changes. The new composition emphasized political and personnel control, and Li Zuocheng was made chief of Joint Staff, and Miao Hua director, General Political Department. The commitment to Xi's corruption-fighting priority in the PLA was reflected by the inclusion of Zhang Shengmin, deputy secretary of the Central Commission for Discipline Inspection, as a concurrent member of the CMC. Zhang was the first antigraft official to be promoted to such a high position, and it was expected that he would fight corruption in addition to his day-to-day duties in running the CMC.[73] The retention of Xu Qiliang and Wei Fenghe in the streamlined CMC suggests the prospect of greater prominence for the air force and the rocket force, the two areas they were previously associated with. Similarly, the promotion of Zhang Youxia from being a regular member to the vice chairmanship suggests more influence for the former General Armaments.

Promoted as first vice chairman, Xu Qiliang was a former Jiang Zemin confidant who had also worked with Xi in Fujian. Zhang Youxia, the new vice chairman, has close family ties with Xi since Zhang's and Xi's fathers, both natives of Shaanxi, were first-generation revolutionary founders of the PRC. Zhang Zongxun commanded the PLA's Northeast Army Corps in 1947, while Xi Zhongxun served as his political commissar. Both Xi and Zhang were born in Beijing and raised in "cadre compounds" in the same neighborhood, and when Xi was sent to Liangjiahe, Zhang Youxia joined the PLA.[74] The latter fought in China's war and clashes against Vietnam in 1979 and 1984 and rose through the ranks, but since China has not fought a war since, Zhang, together with Xu Qiliang and Li Zuocheng, was among the few senior military officials with combat experience.[75]

Among the four members of the CMC three were newly promoted, and Wei Fenghe was the only holdover. All four were promoted rapidly by Xi.[76] Before the Nineteenth Party Congress, speculation was rife that Xi would greatly expand the membership of the CMC to handle the expanded administrative load and to diffuse power by creating checks and balances, but the outcome was the opposite. One view explains that the shrinking CMC was Xi's tactic to buy time to break up factional networks and to recapture control, using anticorruption as a major weapon. This was deemed necessary since Xi's policies and initiatives had provoked fierce resistance, and he could not count on the loyalty of his generals—all officers at the rank of general and lieutenant general had been promoted during the Jiang Jemin era. Another source claims that "nearly all" senior officials, including the princelings, had bought their ranks when Xu Caihou and Guo Boxiong were in charge. Consequently, Xi needed his second term to take complete control of the PLA and to groom a new leadership.[77] In any case, the Party and the state CMC are essentially one and the same, and the membership of the CMC was automatically confirmed by the NPeC in March 2018.

The Evolving Plans and Pattern for Succession

As mentioned, because of factors such as the staggered succession and the small pool from which to draw for the top, the PBSC composition for new party congresses was readily predictable (see Table 8.1). But for the Nineteenth Party Congress, various media predictions were off. The makeup of the new PBSC showed no clear-cut successors to the post of general secretary. Xi had broken the pattern whereby a succeeding general secretary would be groomed in the PBSC for at least five years before being able to serve two five-year terms. For many, this was a clear indication that Xi was intending to stay on as general secretary for a third term or even for life. Other China watchers have variously claimed that Xi had "failed to anoint a successor," that the PBSC contained no sixth-generation leaders, and that PBSC members were all too old to continue past 2022.[78]

Yet it is remarkable that the three Politburo members born in the 1960s might be sufficiently young to serve two more terms starting in 2022. Among the three youngest members, Hu Chunhua was already a Politburo member before 2017, while Ding Xuexiang and Chen Min'er were newly inducted to the Politburo that year. Chen Min'er appeared to be Xi's favorite protégé, with Ding Xuexiang a close second. However, before the congress both were merely CC members, so induction into the PBSC meant they had to skip two rungs of the bureaucratic ladder, which posed a legitimacy issue. This presumably left a promotion gap, and the past grooming practice was now said to be history. Overall, the trends pointed to a Xi third term, but either way, there will be more uncertainty and challenges when China approaches the Twentieth Party Congress in 2022.

In this vein, a Hong Kong source claimed that in an April 2016 PBSC meeting, Xi had already abolished the existing draft proposals for PBSC membership for the Nineteenth and Twentieth Party Congresses. These proposals designated Xi, Li Keqiang, Wang Yang, Li Yuanchao, Liu Qibao, Sun Zhengcai, Zhao Leji, and Hang Zheng for the Nineteenth PBSC, and Li Keqiang, Hu Chunhua, Sun Zhengcai, Wang Yongqing, and Zhao Leji for the Twentieth. Xi reportedly rejected these proposals, citing reasons of alleged nepotism, factionalism, reliance on seniority, promotion despite failings (*daibing jinsheng*), and questionable legitimacy.[79] The reliability of this report cannot be verified, al-though later developments did show that the Xi leadership had rethought suc-cession arrangements in the PBSC. After the Third Plenum of November 2013, official propaganda began to attack matters of "transgeneration" and long-term planning. For instance, in September 2016, the Party School publication *Studies Times* published an article on succession intrigue and crisis during the Wanli reign of the Ming dynasty (1582–1660), when the emperor had to choose a crown prince. The article discussed how this had bred persistent and intense rumors, power and factional struggles, and a chaotic outcome.[80] This was eso-teric political communication, but the point was to use a historical event to show the downside of a leader picking his own successors.

To put the current situation in context, it is useful to point out that in the post-Mao period succession to general secretary evolved over time according to circumstances without a fixed pattern. There was no real tradition of a supreme leader appointing an explicit successor, although it was attempted in Mao's time. Mao's personally anointed successors, Liu Shaoqi, Lin Biao, and Hua Guofeng, all ultimately fell by the wayside. Lin Biao's anointment had even been written into the party constitution. To recap, in the reform period, succession to the top post has been achieved through collective decision-making and compromise, al-though Deng Xiaoping had greater influence than anyone else. However, Deng's protégés, Hu Yaobang and Zhao Ziyang, who had squeezed out Mao's last desig-nated successor, Hua Guofeng, were themselves purged during the Tiananmen events of 1989. Jiang Zemin was then lifted in from Shanghai as an expedient compromise choice, while Deng won the consent of the top leadership to pluck Hu Jintao (age thirty-nine) from the CC directly into the PBSC in 1992 to groom him for a decade to be his transcentury successor. Jiang served out the remainder of the Thirteenth Party Congress term and then two full terms of the Fourteenth and Fifteenth Party Congresses (thirteen years in total). Hu Jintao, commonly presumed to be the head of the *tuanpai*, succeeded Jiang as general secretary in 2002 and served two terms. Xi and Li Keqiang were inducted into the PBSC in 2007 to be implicitly groomed for five years as general secretary and premier, re-spectively. When sixth-generation leaders Sun Zhengcai and Hu Chunhua were inducted into the Politburo in 2012, it was expected that they would be promoted into the PBSC in 2017 to be groomed for five years as dual successors in 2022. However, the purge of Sun Zhengcai in 2017 and the failure of Hu Chunhua to be elected to the PBSC derailed the process. However, Chen Min'er, long regarded as Xi's trusted favorite, was not parachuted into the PBSC from the CC, as many China watchers had predicted. Four interrelated motivations/calculations for these events can be identified.

The first possibility is that Xi rethought succession arrangements with a new approach that would provide more time for potential candidates to establish themselves, acquire more experience, make connections, and prove their mettle in a bigger pool. This also gives the Party more time to scrutinize and evaluate their performance. Second, Xi might have calculated how to avoid the successor's dilemma, the perceived need for the designated successor to build up his power base, and for lower officials to ingratiate themselves with him, thereby turning the successor into a lightning rod for manipulation and attack. A third option might be that Xi intended to defy the informal retirement age of sixty-eight, and stay for a third term from 2022 to 2027, when he would be age sixty-nine to seventy-four, or even longer. Strictly speaking, the age limit has never formally applied to the general secretary position. Hu Jintao (b. 1942) began a second term at age sixty-five and retired at seventy. Jiang Zemin (b. 1926) began his second term at age seventy-one and retired at age seventy-six. The problem is that the state constitution prescribes a two-term limit for president and the chairmanship of the state CMC, and if Xi wants to keep these two positions, he needs to revise the constitution and even abolish the age limit for PBSC. The age limit was introduced in 1997 by Jiang to force Li Ruihuan to retire. Fourth, an extreme realpolitik view suggests that Xi deliberately undermined the Politburo and broke any clear succession arrangements so that he could block any challenge to his power.[81] Others have suggested that the naming of successors requires a leadership consensus, and it was not something Xi could logistically decide on his own. A variety of further scenarios are possible. For instance, Xi could give up the general secretary post and retain only the chairmanship of the CMC, or he could abolish the distinction between PBSC and Politburo.

Xi's motivations can only be surmised, but a combination of options one to three probably best explains them. Like his predecessor, Xi was also concerned with the institutional requirement of an orderly succession of "passing on, assisting, and nurturing" in cultivating top successors to ensure the survival of the party state. In any case, it should be pointed out that even Li Keqiang and new PBSC members Wang Yang, Wang Huning, and Zhao Leji will still be eligible in 2022 for one more term according to the retirement age of sixty-eight, and any two could serve as a transition team. In the rest of the Politburo, nine are likewise potentially eligible, although unlikely candidates due to various experiences. However, dark horses, surprise entries, and contingency arrangements cannot be ruled out.

The Seventh Generation Emerges

As discussed before, the CCP's and the COD's active and continuous succession planning is not limited to one or two individuals but concerns an entire echelon. The fifth-generation leaders are expected to retire en masse in 2022, but behind the scenes a whole new generation is being groomed to come to power in the 2030s. Media attention has turned to potential "seventh generation" leaders, those born in the 1970s (and currently around fifty years of age), a group of professionals who are generally well educated, as a result of the recovery and development of the Chinese educational system in the 1990s and 2000s. One source has identified approximately 250 incumbent officials in the party-state hierarchy waiting in the wings. If Xi takes on a third (2022–2027) or even a fourth (2027–2032) term, his successors will most likely be drawn from this generation. The most promising among this group are regional party leaders Liu Jie (b. 1970) and Shi Guanghui (b. 1970), members of the Guizhou PPC; and Zhuge Yujie (b. 1971), member of the Shanghai MPC. Next comes the vice governors of major provinces: Yang Jinbo (b. 1973) of Guangxi, Li Yunze (b. 1970) of Sichuan, Guo Ningning (b. 1970) of Fujian, Liu Qiang (b. 1971) of Shandong, and Fei Gaoyun (b. 1971) of Jiangsu. The last two, Zhou Liang (b. 1971) and Li Xinran (b. 1972), hail from the China Banking and Insurance Regulatory Commission.[82] Ongoing cultivation of future successors by such agents as the COD at lower levels, now under Chen Xi, continues. However, the party state is encountering new challenges to political recruitment. Various anticorruption campaigns have netted hundreds of thousands of officials, and public offices are becoming unattractive because of the discipline imposed, as well as the availability of alternative and more lucrative avenues of social mobility. Further, the CYL at both the center and the regions has been chastised by Xi for frivolity and mediocrity, raising questions whether it can continue to serve the traditional recruitment functions. Although education levels have improved tremendously over the low base of the 1980s and 1990s, the challenge of rejuvenating the party state has often been a major issue for party congresses. In early 2018, the localities published many reports on the cultivating and recruiting of reserve cadres who were born in the 1970s to the *ju* (provincial) level, those in the 1980s to the *chu* (division) level, and the 1990s to the *ke* (section) level. They asserted that a large contingent of those born in the late 1990s had already emerged, and that most of them have been sent to hardship posts at the base levels to be fortified.[83] Overall, succession at the very top remains uninstitutionalized, although recruitment and grooming below that level is still robust.

13

The Thirteenth National People's Congress, March 2018, and Administrative Reform (Age Sixty-Five)

The reforms introduced during Xi Jinping's first term, coupled with the raft of initiatives from the Nineteenth Party Congress, resulted in a sweeping revamping of the Party and government at the Thirteenth National People's Congress (NPeC, China's fused legislature and executive as in a parliamentary government) of March 2018. Normally, organizational division of labor prescribes that the party congress lays down broad policy principles, whereas the state (legislature and executive) operationalizes them with more details. The NPeC's task is to revise the state constitution, assign state positions in the State Council and ministries, and sometimes initiate administrative reforms of the state structure. Rarely does the NPeC handle the overhaul of party organs; yet the Thirteenth NPeC broke with tradition and unleashed wide-ranging restructuring plans covering the whole range of the Party, NPeC, government, CPPCC, the judiciary, and mass organizations. In both scope and depth, these changes were the most far-reaching since the 1982 constitution, and although many proposals had been discussed openly prior to the NPeC, others came as a surprise.

To varying degrees the changes conformed with Xi's tenets of regime security, "absolute" party leadership, discipline, centralization, and paternalism. They bolstered party control over the economic agenda and reasserted its domination over the state, although in some respects, there were also measures for decentralization and absorption of party agencies into state organs. Beijing reported 6.9 percent growth in 2017, and a projected per capita GDP near US$10,000 for the next five years, 2018–2023, but it anticipated tough challenges and turbulence ahead. Hence restructuring was couched in terms of raising efficiency, improving services, curbing vested interests, and enhancing coordination in the sprawling bureaucracy. All this was considered an integral part of the deepening of reforms in all areas. Simultaneously, a great many of the regime's interests, priorities, and problem-solving concerns were revealed. The NPeC put forward a crowded agenda, but the stated goals were to maintain stable and healthy economic growth, promote law-based governance and the system of socialist rule of law with Chinese characteristics, forestall and defuse major risks, carry out targeted poverty alleviation, prevent and control pollution, exercise strict governance over the Party, improve work style, promote economic, political, cultural, social, and ecological advancement and management of the Party.[1]

To achieve this, the CCP adopted a multipronged approach designed to, first, modernize and rationalize state governance; second, enhance capacity, co-ordination, and efficiency and cut red tape; third, improve services and living conditions and promote growth; fourth, boost Chinese identity, confidence, and soft power; and fifth, restructure the party state and redefine party-government relationships.

Constitutional Amendment and Removal of Term Limits

The NPeC also approved revision of the state constitution, and the process, which took about half a year, was expeditious by any standards, even compared to the drafting process for the report to the Nineteenth Party Congress. In September 2017, Xi chaired a Politburo meeting on the revision of the constitution, and Zhang Dejiang (outgoing PBSC member), Li Zhanshu, and Wang Huning took charge of drafting the document. Within four months, the regular procedures of consultation with the various party, state, and regional entities, "democratic parties," think tanks, and experts were complete, and the revised draft was duly passed by the NPeC in March 2018 (see Table 13.1). Hu Jintao's "scientific de-velopment" concept, as well as "Xi's thought for the new era of socialism with Chinese characteristics" were enshrined in the state constitution. The essence of the latter was said to encompass "innovation, coordination, green, opening up, and shared well-being." Other revisions relate to insertions or replacements of new terminology introduced by Xi. For instance, the notion of "national revival" was inserted and the phrase "strengthening of law-based governance" replaced the "strengthening of a socialist legal system." Overall, of the twenty-one sections being revised, eleven pertained to setting up the National Supervision Commission (more later),[2] although the issue receiving the most public atten-tion was the change to the presidency, since various hints were dropped in 2017. Constitutional revision removed the two-term limits for president and vice pres-ident (Article 79), although these limits were retained for premiers and vice pre-miers. Headlines outside China emphasized that this was another example of Xi's power grab that would enable him to become ruler for life, but the situation

Table 13.1 Developmental Process for the Revision of the State Constitution

Dates	Process
September 29, 2017	At a PBSC meeting, Xi decides to revise the Constitution. A Constitution revision small group is formed led by Zhang Dejiang, Li Zhanshu, and Wang Huning. Participants include representatives from Party Central, National People's Congress, State Council, Supreme People's Court, Supreme People's Procuracy.
November 13, 2017	Party Central solicits opinion from various regions and departments and receives 118 reports. Consultation with various democratic parties, the All-China Federation of Industry and nonparty personnel. A total of 2,639 proposals are presented
December 12, 2017	Party Central solicits opinions from various departments and localities and receives 118 Feedback reports and 230 revision proposals.
December 2017	Xi listens to opinions by democratic parties, the All-China Federation of Industry and nonparty personnel, and receives 10 reports.
January 2 to 3, 2018	Zhang Dejiang convenes four meetings to consult with leaders of various party committees of party and state organs and provincial/municipalities, think tanks, experts, and scholars
January 18 to 19	The Second Plenum approves the proposal for Constitutional revision. Xi and Zhang Dejiang give speeches.
January 26, 2018	Party Central presents the proposal for Constitutional revisions to the Standing Committee of the NPC.
January 29 to 30, 2018	At its 32nd Meeting, the Standing Committee of the NPC listens to an explanation by Li Zhanshu. Observing the party proposal, the NPC Law Committee draws up a draft for the revision of the Constitution to be presented to the First Session for the Thirteenth NPC for ratification.
March 11, 2018	The Third Plenary Session of the Thirteenth National People's Congress passes the resolution for the revision of the State constitution.

Source: "Wang Chen zuo guanyu Zhonghua renmin gongheguo xianfa xiuzheng caoan di shuoming" [Extracts: Wang Chen on the Draft Revision of the Constitution of the PRC], *Xinhuanet*, March 6, 2018, http://www.xinhuanet.com/2018.03/06/c_1122496003.htm.

requires a more nuanced analysis, and the change is less momentous than commonly understood. As discussed in chapter 7, the Chinese term for president translates as "state chairman" (*guojiazhuxi*), a ceremonial post with no enumerated constitutional power. Articles 80 and 81 of the constitution authorize the president to promulgate statutes, appoint or remove top leaders such as the premier and vice premiers, grant pardons, confer medals, receive diplomats, declare war, and ratify treaties according to the decisions of the Standing Committee of the NPeC. However, formally the Chinese president has no veto power over legislation, unlike the head of government in a presidential system. Previous state chairmen Mao Zedong and Liu Shaoqi had power by virtue of their party positions, whereas Li Xiannian and Yang Shangkun occupied the state chairmanship as sinecures for retired elders. In the 1990s, general secretary and chair of the CMC Jiang Zemin took on the state chairman position in order to engage in active diplomacy. Hu Jintao and Xi Jinping followed Jiang's convention of occupying all three positions, and Xi's real formal power rests with the positions of general secretary and chair of the CMC.

On the other hand, the positions of general secretary and chair of the CMC carry no term limits, and the age limit of sixty-eight has never been applied there. Party norms do not rule out a third term for Xi, and presumably he was aware of the advantages of having a figurehead who could take over the onerous ceremonial functions of the head of state. Nonetheless, he chose to follow his predecessors Jiang and Hu, making use of the position to conduct diplomacy, meet foreign leaders, and attend international conferences, especially when the term "president" is more commonly recognized internationally than the position of "general secretary." In parliamentary democracies, formal term limits do not exist for prime ministers; they and do serve multiple terms only as long as they command the confidence of their parliaments. As German chancellor and Israel's prime minister, both Angela Merkl and Benjamin Netanyahu served four terms, lasting almost sixteen years and fifteen years, respectively.

Interpretations of Xi's intentions concerning a third term coalesce along a spectrum. The benign and optimistic view suggests that a strong, stable, extended leadership is beneficial for China, and Xi has amassed enough power to push through necessary reforms that had been stalled under Hu Jintao. But Xi's numerous ambitious projects to rebalance the political economy would require time for fruition. He focused on the consolidation of power throughout his first term so that he would have more room to maneuver later. Absent a third term, he might be reluctant to force or incapable of forcing further reform and changes. On the other hand, the pessimistic and skeptical view suggests that a concentration of power under Xi for another decade could make governance less efficient, and any misstep or error could be easily magnified. Local officials might appear more compliant with central directives, but their excessive zeal could prove counterproductive over time, with the blame placed on the man at the center. The reliance on one-man rule, coupled with weak institutionalization, makes for bleak prospects on governing an enormously complicated political economy.[3]

The Vice President: The Many Models

The weak institutionalization of the Chinese system is reflected in the flexibility by which the position of the vice president (or vice chairman, *fuzhuxi*) is defined. Wang Qishan's "election" as vice president was a surprise. The Chinese constitution's brief provisions in Articles 82, 83, and 84 stipulate that the vice president may exercise functions and powers as entrusted by the president and succeeds to the presidency if that position falls vacant. In practice, however, the position has undergone five variations.[4] Wang Qishan began a new sixth model. After he retired from the PBSC upon reaching the age of sixty-eight, Wang became just an ordinary party member. One of Wang's predecessors, Rong Yiren, the tycoon head of a business family, served as vice president after the Tiananmen crackdown to signal the regime's commitment to reform, but Rong served purely ceremonial functions, and his party membership was revealed only after his death. However, Wang's party protocol ranking was officially designated number eight, just after the seven PBSC members and ahead of the Politburo members. Reportedly Wang could partake in "enlarged" PBSC meetings as a nonvoting member, but this unprecedented arrangement raised the issue of legitimacy and likely discomforted Politburo members. Meanwhile, it was expected that Wang would exert influence largely through Xi and play a major role in foreign affairs, especially with the rocky relations with the United States.[5] Subsequently, Wang was made deputy director of the new Central Foreign Affairs Commission, whereas Yang Jiechi was named director of the commission's office. The two were entrusted with a shakeup of the foreign affairs structure and raising the profile of diplomacy and China's global role. In 2019, Wang was said to have worked behind the scenes in trade talks with the United States, on calming protests in Hong Kong, and on the promotion of young leaders in their forties.[6]

Personnel Changes and Xi's Tail

The new lineup of personnel in the state apparatus reflected the leadership's orientation and priorities, as well as the characteristics of the leadership itself. It put to rest the persistent speculation about Xi's supposed desire to get rid of Li Keqiang when he was re-elected as premier. Li's importance to Xi, to the division of labor in decision-making, and to system maintenance has often been underestimated. Separately, Xi's protégé Li Zhanshu was named chair of the standing committee of the NPeC wherein he could control the legislative agenda and potentially exert influence over the State Council. Ousted Politburo member Zhang Chunxian gained the position of vice chair of the NPeC standing committee. Wang Yang was chosen head of the CPPCC, a consultative organization that is not negligible in influence, considering the size of the body (currently 2,158), its organizational structure, and the many proposals and research reports generated by its ten specialized committees.[7] The annual CPPCC and the NPeC meetings are held in March and are known as the "two sessions," and the CPPCC's counterparts at the provincial and county levels consist of a huge national bureaucracy. Membership of the CPPCC is drawn from the CCP, the eight "democratic parties,"[8] and other groups such as social luminaries, minorities, mass organizations, and overseas Chinese. The CCP lavishes attention and resources on it because the body can, to a certain extent, articulate and aggregate interests, expand political participation, co-opt opposition, and recruit nonparty elites into the Party. The high-profile CPPCC can give voice to alternative views on policymaking on a full range of political, economic, social, and cultural issues. On the flip side, the CPPCC and its hierarchy, whose memberships are eagerly sought, can be a forum for collusion between officials, VIPs, and the wealthy.[9] Judging by the large numbers of "tigers and flies" in the CPPCC convicted during the anticorruption campaign for peddling political influence, it can be deduced that this sprawling national hierarchy does carry a great deal of weight. Yet, because of the general assumption that it is mere window dressing, its operations have not been sufficiently studied. As the chair of the CPPCC, Wang took up the responsibility of promoting the Party's united-front strategy to co-opt nonparty elites. Another ousted Politburo member, Liu Qibao, became the vice chair of the CPPCC.

In the State Council, Premier Li's nomination of Han Zheng, Sun Chunlan, Hu Chunhua, and Liu He as the new vice premiers was approved, and Wei Fenghe, Wang Yong, Wang Yi, Xiao Jie, and Zhao Kezhi were endorsed as state councilors (see Table 13.2). All reported to Li Keqiang. The vice premiers assist the premier, and their responsibilities are not always fixed, depending on their qualifications and skill sets. PBSC member Han Zheng became executive vice premier charged with reform, development, and finance. Additionally, he was expected to oversee environmental protection, international trade and infrastructural development associated with the BRI initiative, and tax revenue and budgeting. Because he spent almost his entire career in Shanghai, Han is often regarded as a stalwart of the Shanghai Gang, with connections and interests limited to that metropolis and Jiang Zemin. In fact, however, Han's career and contacts are much broader, and he served under Xi when he was secretary of the Shanghai MPC in 2012. Sun Chunlan was tasked with health, education, and sports portfolios held by her predecessor, Liu Yandong, minus the portfolio of science and technology. Hu Chunhua took charge of agriculture, rural issues, and antipoverty activities like his predecessor Wang Yang, but not commerce and trade. Li He picked up commerce, trade, science, and technology, in addition to the finance portfolio.[10] In general, the long and specialized experiences of the State Council team fit their portfolios, although gender bias in Chinese politics, as elsewhere, tends to put

Table 13.2 State Positions, Thirteenth National People's Congress, March 2018

State Positions	Occupant
Chair of the NPC	Li Zhanshu
State Chairman	Xi Jinping
CMC Chair	Xi Jinping
Chair, State Supervisory Commission	Yang Xiaodu
President, Supreme People's Court	Zhou Qiang (Chief Justice)
Procurator-General, Supreme People's Procuracy	Zhang Jun (Minister of Justice)

The Cabinet	Occupant
Premier	Li Keqiang
Vice Premiers	Han Zheng, Sun Chunlan, Hu Chunhua, Liu He
State Councilors	Wei Fenghe, Wang Yong, Wang Yi, Xiao Jie, Zhao Kezhi

Source: "Shisanjie quanguo renda yici huiyi xuanju chansheng xinjijie guojia lingdaoren" [Elections of the First Session of the Thirteenth NPC Produced a New Leadership], *Xinhua*, March 17, 2018, http://www.gov.cn/xinwen/2018-03/17/content_5275007.htm#1.

women in charge of issues of health, welfare, and education. One diaspora source claims that Sun Chunlan, originally a worker (watchmaker) whose education was achieved by correspondence, was incompetent as secretary of the Tianjian MPC. Yet, as mentioned, since many Chinese leaders have had checkered backgrounds and educational experience, sexism is probably the reason for a low opinion of Sun. Since each vice premier oversees huge policy areas in the division of labor, the view that Han Zheng and Liu He were the main power beneficiaries and Sun Chunlan and Hu Chunhua were the marginalized ones is unconvincing.[11] In the military, Wei Fenghe became a member of the CMC and minister of defense; Wang Yong took charge of SOEs and emergency management. Wang Yi became minister of foreign affairs, and Zhao Kezhi minister of public security.

On the other hand, Xi's "tail," which consists of trusted supporters who have had past connections with Xi as friends (family or university) or subordinates at various stages of his career, became clear once the personnel reshuffle at the Nineteenth Party Congress and the Thirteenth NPeC was settled. Many of these former associates who had worked with Xi were promoted to the PBSC, Politburo, or other central and regional positions. Former Xi associates included (from Zhejiang) Chen Min'er, Li Qiang, Xia Baolong, Chen Yixin, Bayin Chaolu, Liu Qi, and Ying Yong; (from Shaanxi) Li Xi, Wang Dongfeng,

Zhao Leji, Wang Qishan, and Wang Zhen; (from Hebei) Li Zhanshu and Yang Zhenwu; (from Fujian) Cai Qi, Huang Kunming, and He Lifeng; and (from Shanghai) Ding Xuexiang and Xu Lin.[12] As can be seen in the biographic tables, there are similarities and differences in the social and career backgrounds of these leaders. Some were princelings or Red Second Generation (Zhang Youxia, Liu He, Li Zhanshu, Wang Qishan) and some related to the Tsinghua University (Chen Xi, Hu Heping, Chen Jining). Others had worked in the CYL. Some were born in the 1950s, whereas the ones born in the 1960s were not part of the "lost generation" traumatized by the Cultural Revolution in their formative years. Some were originally peasants, workers, or soldiers, whereas others were students/intellectuals. Their careers changed and developed over time, and virtually all had rotated many times between the regions and the center before reaching these positions. As mentioned before, the complex and crisscrossing career experiences of these leaders make static and deterministic labels such as "Shaanxi Gang," "princelings faction," or *tuanpai* problematic. The same applies to the view that certain officials constituted a self-contained Xi faction, since Xi has had long and continuous cooperative relationship with other leaders, such as Li Keqiang, Wang Huning, Han Zheng, and Wang Huning, who are not necessarily included in this "tail." It is always advisable to apply factional analysis carefully and in context.[13]

Despite being the lowest-ranking Politburo member, Liu He had worked in the background as one of the masterminds of the Thirteenth Five-Year Plan and the "supply-side structural" reform. His portfolios grew tremendously, and he was now front and center, managing finance, trade, economic affairs, and science and technology. Liu's position was reminiscent of former vice premier Zhu Rongji, who was iron-fisted in curbing overheated investments and borrowing and in fighting corruption. The only vice premier who has an overseas education, Liu was given the heavy responsibility of managing China's large economy and breaking a path toward sustainable growth. Analysts have suggested that Liu's appointment signaled that China was committed to economic globalization and was ready to seize a historical opportunity to shape the global financial order at a time when Sino-US relations were fraught and when the United States under Trump appeared to have retreated inward.[14] In an authoritative article published in February 2018 analyzing the 1929 and 2008 financial crises, Liu argued that the causes were technical innovation, unprecedented economic prosperity, and lax government regulation, as well as a large income gap, an appeal to nativism, and a prevalent mood of speculation to strike it rich. All these factors, Liu warned, were currently present in China, but he was optimistic that such crises might generate theoretical breakthroughs, redistributive effects, and transformation of the global economic order. His advice for China was to persevere, focus on development, and capitalize on the strategic opportunity to optimize benefits for China and the world.[15] In January 2018 Liu was accorded a ceremonial par with other heads of governments at the World Economic Forum, where he assured the gathering that China would implement reforms "beyond the expectations of the international community."[16] In 2018, Liu revealed his major role in party-state restructuring in an authoritative *Renmin Ribao* article explaining the reforms. The reforms were "revolutionary," he maintained, because they directly challenged entrenched power by an attempt to "integrate existing vested interests and reshape new interest patterns."[17] Both Liu He and Yang Jiechi have been Xi's point men to defuse trade tensions with the United States. As a tough chief negotiator, Liu managed to secure a limited "Phase One Deal" in 2020. However, he rejected Trump's suggestion for an early start for phase two talks and prospect of "decoupling" of the world's two largest economies.[18]

Wang Yi, foreign minister since 2013, was promoted concurrently as a state councilor, a privilege denied to his predecessor as minister, even though the position of state councilor is the highest rank a diplomat can achieve. Wang reported to Yang Jiechi, who in turn reported to Vice President Wang Qishan, who oversaw foreign and US relations. The three, together with Liu He, form a team that Beijing hoped would be sufficiently senior and powerful to mobilize resources in support of diplomacy in turbulent relations with Asian powers and especially with the United States. As state councilor, Wang Yi could raise the leverage of foreign affairs and wield more influence in coordinating other ministries (such as the Ministry of Commerce). Wang Yi's elevated status signified the new weight assigned to foreign affairs to compensate for a perceived weakening of the diplomats involved in top-level decision-making in the past. A staunch defender of China's national interests, Wang had declared that China did not intend to supplant the United States in global affairs and argued that it was a "strategic misjudgment" for the United States to brand China an adversary. He had warned Washington against interfering in Beijing's disputes in the SCS.[19] As to the other state councilors, Wei Fenghe, former commander of the Second Artillery Corps and PLA Rocket Force (from 2015), was named minister of defense and Zhao Kezhi as minister of public security. Yi Gang was appointed central bank governor.

The 2018 Restructuring and Institutional Building

Overall, this round of sweeping reforms was the outcome of an evolving process during Xi's first term (see Table 13.3). The Third Plenum of 2013 broached the notion of integrated reform of party, government, and mass organizations to rationalize their responsibilities, but it barely foreshadowed the far-reaching changes to come. The decision for such a massive organizational overhaul was

Table 13.3 Developmental Process for the March 2018 Decision to Launch Sweeping Structural Reform

Dates	Activities
November 2013	The Third Plenum (Eighteenth CC) passes a major document on comprehensive reforms, specifying integrated reforms for party, government, and mass organizations to rationalize their responsibilities
2015	Xi charges the Comprehensive Deepening Reform LSG to study reforms
July 2017	Xi gives an instruction on the deepening of organizational reform
July–August 2017	The Central Reform Office and the State Commission Office for Public Sector Reform form ten investigation groups that visit 31 provinces (municipalities) and 71 central party and government departments and listen to the proposals of 139 provincial-/ministerial-level officials; the investigation groups also send out questionnaires to 1,197 responsible officials at 657 counties and municipalities, and collect reports on regional organization reforms from 31 provinces
October 2017	Xi reports to the Nineteenth Party Congress stressing the deepening of administrative reforms and the "scientific" assignment and demarcation of power and responsibilities
December 11, 2017	Xi takes charge of the first meeting for drafting documents for the Third Plenum (Nineteenth CC) and declares that this plenum will be devoted to the deepening of administrative reform
February 1, 2018	After numerous revisions, the Party Central Office sends out a final draft document on reform to various localities and departments for comments
February 6, 2018	Xi convenes a meeting to consult with various democratic parties, the All-China Federation of Industry and Commerce and nonparty personnel
February 26–28, 2018	The Third Plenum passes two resolutions on deepening the reform of party and government organizations, one on general directions and the other on implementation specifics
March 5–20, 2018	Thirteenth National People's Congress

Source: "Xi Jinping guanyu shenhua dang he guojia jigou gaige juedinggao he gangangao shuoming" [Xi Jinping's Explanation on the Draft Decisions to Deepen the Organizational Restructuring of the Party and State], April 11, 2018, *Ifeng,* http://news.ifeng.com/a/20180411/57487759_0.shtml; "Dang he guojia jigougaige fangandanshengji" [The Birth of the Policy to Reform Party and State Structure], *Sina,* March 23, 2018, http://news.sina.com.cn/gov/xlxw/2018-03-23/doc-ifysnevk9380632.shtml.

arrived at gradually in a process of research, investigation, and discussion. Xi's pre-2017 speeches seldom focused on the issue of administrative overhaul, although Li Keqiang had repeatedly complained about the "bloated bureaucracy." In 2015, Xi charged the Comprehensively Deepening Reform LSG with studying organizational restructuring. In the summer of 2017, the Central Reform Office and the Central Office organized and sent ten study groups to thirty-two provinces and seventy-one party and government offices to examine structural reforms, sparking an extensive process of consultation and discussion.

Structural reforms were discussed at the Nineteenth Party Congress and the Central Economic Work Conference (December 18–20, 2017). In December, Xi chaired a group to draft documents for an early 2018 Third Plenum devoted to restructuring of the party state. Such a practice was a major departure from tradition because third plenums are normally held in October and November and are usually devoted to economic planning and reform. The Second Plenum (January 18–19, 2018) revised the state constitution by removing the term limits for president and vice president and discussed the new National Supervisory Commission (NSuC). Soon after, the Third Plenum (February 26–28) finalized the reform proposals to be presented to the Thirteenth NPeC.

Throughout the history of the People's Republic, administrative and structural reforms have revolved around alternating cycles of centralization (*shou*) and decentralization (*fang*), or control and relaxation. The principles and practices undergirding current rounds of reform feature continuity and change, along with the addition of new elements. In the 1980s Zhao Ziyang and his associates, with an initial nod from Deng Xiaoping, attempted to address the issues of party overdominance and the overconcentration of power. Their pragmatic concern was that these might inhibit market reforms and economic efficiencies that require flexibility, initiative, and the decentralization of power. Specifically, the Zhao Ziyang leadership argued that there were several disadvantages to the Party taking over state functions. First, it weakened the Party's leadership and its ability to focus on the big picture and party-building. Second, it immersed the Party in the minutiae of front-line implementation by running the government and enterprises. By being directly involved in the allocation of funds, resources, and the mounting of projects, it had engrossed itself in administrative details and conflicts. Third, it weakened the Party's supervisory function and its ability to control the bureaucracy if it became merely part of the bureaucracy.[20]

To address these issues Zhao Ziyang argued that political reform was essential for economic reform, and that meant the separation of the Party and the state. In his view, the Party should (1) lead by focusing on principle, ideology, organization, and goal-setting; (2) withdraw from interfering with the routines of the government, enterprises, and other social and economic organizations;

(3) de-emphasize its monist role in order to nurture limited pluralism and space for new groups to participate in the political process.

Specifically, Zhao's reforms envisioned the abolition of (1) concurrent party/state posts, as well as party organs that duplicated the same functions as state organs; (2) party core groups and committees that were embedded in party and nonparty organs such as the SOEs, universities, and mass/social organizations; and (3) party control of the military in favor of legislature and government oversight (or "nationalization," *guojiahua*). Additionally, experts and intellectuals would be given more freedom to contribute to decision-making, and there would be greater tolerance for dissent. Legal reforms would be geared toward protecting people's rights, and the Party would create new roles and institutions while still maintaining its leadership role.[21]

To preserve CCP ultimate leadership, Zhao prescribed party control over the government through the power of personnel management. The government, on the other hand, would implement policies, daily routines, and resolve social conflicts. The Party would then leave the government, people's congresses, and social and economic organizations alone so that they could develop their potentials. Zhao's notions were arrived at against the historical background of the aftermath of the Cultural Revolution, when party and government functions had been completely merged, and the Party substituted for the government, to such an extent that it monopolized and interfered excessively in daily work. Overall, dissidents and democracy activists generally supported Zhao's bold vision. They saw party-government separation as a means to democratize because separation requires the party committees to withdraw from government, legislatures, and judiciary; social, economic, and mass organizations; and local governments. Opponents, on the other hand, suspected it was a slippery slope toward the erosion of party rule, and it was also resisted by bureaucratic vested interests.

In the end, however, Zhao Ziyang's ideal of "party-government separation" was never realized. A good example was the practice of "one institution bearing two brand names." A most prominent example was the Party's and the state's military commissions, which were essentially one and the same organization. The experiment for separation followed a zigzag path,[22] and after the Tiananmen crackdown and massacre, Zhao was deposed and put under house arrest until he died in 2005. Subsequently, the CCP returned to a more traditionally orthodox approach. Concern about maintaining party rule was paramount, and Party Central restored its overall leadership over reforms. Conservative elders blamed the loosening of party control and liberalization for a regime near-collapse. Under Jiang Zemin the Party again took on state functions, a fact symbolized by Jiang's taking over the state chairmanship in addition to his positions as general secretary and chair of the CMC. Gradually, the previously separated organs were once again being merged. The

Party reinserted party core groups and party committees into all party and nonparty organs, including the NGOs. It resumed political and ideological work and reintroduced old-style ideological campaigns such as "three stresses" and "three represents" and opposed far-reaching political reforms. After the worldwide collapse of communism in the Soviet Union and other communist regimes, the CCP presumed the major cause was the downplaying of ideology and party leadership. Yet, ironically, the outcome of the various attempts at strengthening party cells and branches in organizations had been feeble.[23] Many turned into empty shells, inactive or incompetent.[24]

Such a dilemma bears some resemblance to the general Weberian principle of division of labor between politicians and bureaucrats in electoral democracies whereby the former make decisions and the latter implement policies and provide advice. Although the bureaucrats tend to defer to the politicians regardless of the latter's political stripes, tension always exists between the bureaucrats who are permanent, nonpartisan, and experienced, and politicians who are transient, politically obsessed, and lacking in expertise. For governments to function, the loyalty, expertise, and discretion of the bureaucrats are necessary, with no ambiguity regarding who is the boss.[25] Yet, as governance functions are becoming more complex, even electoral democracies are moving further away from the politician/bureaucrat distinction toward a hybrid, since politicians are now more technically competent, and bureaucrats are more politically sensitive.[26] Obviously, the Chinese case is different since the CCP does not share power or alternate in power with other parties; instead, it monopolizes power by controlling all state organizations with interlocking directorates, and by assigning most government posts to party members.

With the introduction of Xi's notions of top-level design, centralization, and unquestioned party leadership, the idea of party-state separation lost all traction. By 2017, leaders such as Wang Qishan began to argue that a strong party leadership depended on its own discipline. Dismissing the party-government separation principle, Wang argued that the Party and the government should have a division of labor rather than institutional separation. Further, he claimed, party-government separation proliferated agencies, since for every party agency there was a corresponding government agency.[27] Increasingly, the CCP was becoming ever more confident that it could directly manage the country without diluting its leadership capabilities.

The CCP of 2018 approached issues with a combined sense of challenge and confidence. It anticipated that between 2018 and 2020, it would have to fight three major battles, against financial risks, poverty, and pollution. It was also confident that strong party leadership and management would help it achieve its goals, and that the restructuring of the party state was another step. Since

1981, there have been four rounds of reform of party institutions and seven rounds of state institutions, but the revamp of party state organization of 2018 was massive and unprecedented and has required a great deal of determination. Overall, it involved changes at both the center and every other level of administration from the top to the bottom. Central party organizations were reduced by six and State Council organs by fifteen, making a total of twenty-one.[28] The Xi administration identified the following issues: first, overlap and duplication of work, excess personnel, and a bloated establishment; second, unclear demarcations of power and responsibilities; third, inefficiency, bureaucratic wrangling, and evasion of responsibility; four, officials' abuse of power, dereliction of responsibility, and arbitrary rule (the major sources of public resentment); and fifth, a sense that reforms had encountered gridlock, especially in economics and finance.

Accordingly, the goals of the latest round of restructuring were to, first, modernize China's system to improve coordination, efficiency, and law-based governance; second, transform government functions to achieve better market supervision, and management of natural resources, the environment, and public services; third, optimize the functions of party, government, and mass organizations, and raise governance capacity; fourth, clearly demarcate responsibilities so that more decision-making power could be devolved to the provinces and down, resulting in more efficient grassroot management; and fifth, raise the quality of public services such as education, healthcare, and emergency services.

This shakeup went beyond centralization and decentralization, administrative simplification, or the Party simply taking over government responsibilities. It followed the principle of "one policy area should fall under one agency." Several patterns can be identified, including rationalization by merger, reorganization, and upgrade. Some agencies were abolished, while others were strengthened or weakened. New agencies, including a couple of superstate agencies, were created, while others were left alone. Some government functions were incorporated into party agencies, whereas in other cases, party agencies were embedded in government agencies. Restructuring has affected virtually all policy areas, especially in areas such as finance and market supervision, environmental protection, transportation, and agriculture.

While the principle of strengthening and extending party control undergirded the restructuring, the Party itself also came under stricter oversight. The intention was to control vested interests and bureaucratic resistance to reforms. By dovetailing party and government functions, the various mergers were designed to effect a more rational division of labor, raise efficiency, and cut operating costs. The tremendously complex restructuring reflected the CCP's principles and future directions, and to this we turn to in the following.

Changes to the Chinese Communist Party Structure

One major change was the creation of several new party agencies to improve policy coordination and consultation, but they were embedded in existing state agencies to avoid agency proliferations.[29]

The Six New Central Commissions

All four former central LSGs that were led by Xi, the Comprehensively Deepening Reform LSG, the Internet Security and Informationization LSG, the Finance and Economic LSG, and the Foreign Affairs LSGs were upgraded into permanent commissions (see Table 13.4). Two additional new central commissions were the Central Audit Commission and the Commission for Comprehensive Law-Based Governance, the former to be headed by Xi. Headed by Politburo members, these commissions formalized the power of the LSGs, and each now had its own

Table 13.4 Officers of the Six New Central Commissions (Previously Leading Small Groups)

The Six New Central Commissions	Director	Vice Director(s)	Members	Head of Secretariat
Comprehensively Deepening Reform	Xi Jinping	Li Keqiang, Wang Huning, Han Zheng		Wang Huning (concurrent)
Finance and Economics	Xi Jinping	Li Keqiang	Wang Huning, Hang Zheng	Liu He
Foreign Affairs	Xi Jinping	Li Keqiang	Wang Qishan	Yang Jiechi
Internet Security and Informationization	Xi Jinping	Li Keqiang, Wang Huning		Xu Lin
Central Audit	Xi Jinping	Li Keqiang, Zhao Leji		
Comprehensive Governance According to Law	Xi Jinping	Li Keqiang, Li Zhanshu, Wang Huning		Guo Shengyun

Source: "Xiaozu bianshen weiyuanhui, zhongyang xinshe jigou tifa 5 ge yueqian butong" [LSGs Have Been Transformed into Commissions: The Newly Established Agencies Are Different from What Was Said Five Months Ago], *Guancha,* March 22, 2018, http://www.guancha.cn/politics/2018_03_22 _451095.shtml; *Baidu baike.*

permanent secretariat (*bangongshi*). Institutionalization of these previously informal but decision-making bodies enhanced the Party's power and is said to have facilitated Xi's policy of "top-level design." The goal was to beef up the coordination of central decision-making over key functional areas. For instance, by May 2018, the Comprehensively Deepening Reform Commission had met twice and approved dozens of regulations and reports spanning the operation of its own secretariat, the NSuC, the Shanghai Finance Court, the Pilot Free Trade Zones (Guangdong, Tianjin, and Fujian), SOE leadership and salaries, honesty in scientific research, healthcare provision, and the progress of administrative reforms in the localities.[30] The commission's seven and six meetings in 2019 and 2020, respectively, give a general reflection of its workload and priorities.[31]

The Central Foreign Affairs Commission (CFAC) replaced the Foreign Affairs LSG. It also absorbed the Safeguarding Maritime Rights LSG and transformed it into an agency of the CFAC, underlining the new priority accorded to maritime issues. The CFAC was also deemed more effective in analyzing intelligence and handling emergencies. Politburo member Yang Jiechi was named the director of the secretariat of the CFAC, a post previously occupied by state councilors, and this reflected the new priority assigned to diplomacy. In fact, Yang was made an envoy to visit North Korea in March 2018.[32]

Xi's report to the Nineteenth Party Congress proposed a new Comprehensively Law-Based Governance LSG and a Central Audit LSG, but the plan was quickly changed to two full-fledged central commissions, reflecting the urgency accorded to the two areas. As its title suggests, the responsibility of the new Commission for Comprehensive Law-Based Governance was to direct, coordinate, and promote law-based governance in both government and society. Depending on how it will operate, it may raise the priority for the rule of law, because even the heads of the Supreme People's Court and the Supreme People's Procuratorate are mere Central Committee members.

A newly created National Audit Commission (NAC) would have its business office located in the National Audit Office (NAO), a ministerial-level agency under the State Council) to oversee its work. Xi's assumption as director of this new commission raised the issue of audit to new heights. Zhao Leji, director of the CCDI, was nominated concurrently as vice director since, in the past, the CCDI and the NAO had worked hand in hand to deal with officials' violation of laws and regulations—the CCDI relied on the NAO for expertise, and the latter often turned over cases to the former. The NAO had uncovered sensitive information and netted "tigers" such as Jiang Jiemin, former chair of the state-owned Assets Supervision and Administration Commission (which supervises 102 huge state-owned conglomerates worth trillions of dollars), and head of the Ministry of Railways Liu Zhijun. Yet even though the NAO was the supreme state auditing agency, its work had often been hampered by interferences, especially in the localities. The creation of the Party's Central Audit Commission was intended to extend the scope and authority of auditing to better fight corruption and graft, especially in the many loosely supervised "blind sides." Further, since an audit office was also created under the CMC, the NAC was designed to supervise both audit offices in the State Council and in the military. Inevitably, there were overlaps of functions among the three principal supervisory agencies, but in terms of division of labor the CCDI focuses primarily on party officials, the NSuC on state employees, while the NAO provides the necessary expertise.[33] Together all three watchdogs are expected to tighten the checks on official malfeasance.

Among other important party agencies, the existing Central International Liaison Department would continue to implement the Party's foreign policies, provide research on changing global trends, present policy recommendations, liaise with foreign political parties and organizations, and manage the foreign activities of all party organizations. It would consist of eight geographical bureaus covering such regions as North America, Africa, and Western Europe. A newly formed central LSG for education would oversee the functions of the Ministry of Education to enhance political education in schools and universities, although its business office would be embedded in that ministry.

The reforms also added another layer of control. First, two separate party agencies, the Work Committee of Organizations Directly under the Central Committee and the Work Committee for Governments Organizations (Zhongyang zhishu jiguan gongzuo weiyuanhui he zhongyang guojia jiguan gongzuo weiyuanhui) were merged into the Central and Government Work Committee (Zhongyang he guojia jiguan gongzuo weiyuanhui). The functions of these two agencies had been quite similar, with the former overseeing party-building, ideology, organization, cadre education, training, and work style, with the later serving similar functions with government departments. The new work committee would supervise leadership officials, approve the nominations of secretaries and deputy secretaries of party committees and discipline committees, provide feedback for the CC, and review dismissals and disciplinary penalties. Its authority would extend over CC departments such as COD, the Central Publicity Department, the United Front Work Department, the Politics and Law Committee, the CYL, and so on.[34] Second, a new Central Party School was established by merging the existing Central Party School with the Chinese Academy of Governance. Originally, the division of labor between the two agencies was informed by a Weberian notion that party and state officials needed different political skills—the former articulate broad and diffuse interests, whereas the later mediate more narrowly focused interests of organized clienteles.[35] Hence the new CPS provided broad ideological and theoretical training for both party *and* government officials, but the Chinese Academy of Governance focused on specialized and managerial training for mainly mid- to senior-level government officials.[36] The merger reflected the end of any efforts to separate politics and administration.

The Reining in of the Security Agencies and the Party's Central Politics and Legal Affairs Commission

The 2018 reforms also attempted to rein in the power of the security agencies, whose powers had expanded tremendously under the notorious Zhou Yongkang. Two former LSGs, the Central Stability Maintenance LSG and the Preventing and Managing Religious Cults LSG (PMRCLSG, or the 610 group), in addition to the Central Committee for Comprehensive Social Management (CCCSM, known at other times as the Central Committee for the Comprehensive Management of Public Security), all notorious for their oppressive methods, were abolished. Most of their power and responsibilities were transferred to the Central Politics and Legal Affairs Commission (CPLAC). In the past, all three agencies had been powerful bureaucratic actors, especially concerning *weiwen*—the Stability Maintenance LSG wielded great power in surveillance and social control, and the PMRCLSG was established to suppress Falun Gong dissent. Nominally these were three separate entities, but their operations overlapped, and in the localities all three often shared the same office. Their control of the security *xitong* (functional system) was so pervasive that they were often dubbed a second Party Center (see Figure 13.1).

The Central Stability Maintenance LSG was formed in 1998, and its constituent units came from the CPLAC, the CCCSM, and Departments of Propaganda, Public Security, and State Broadcasting, Film, and Television. Group and deputy leaders were normally appointed by the secretary and deputy secretary of the CPLAC. On the other hand, the officials of the PMRCLSG came from the Ministry of Public Security, Central Publicity Department, and so on, and its office was set up within the CPLAC.

The abolition of the CCCSM is a good example of concerns over unwieldy bureaucratic duplication and expansion in security affairs. Formed in 1991, this organ had gradually taken on more and more responsibilities, especially with the ever-increasing social unrest in this century, when the notions of *weiwen* and "innovation in social management" gained currency. Among its fifty-one membership organs were those from the Ministry of Public Security, the procuratorates, judiciary, and even the Ministries of Foreign Affairs, Finance, and Railways. It had a broad mandate of "social management" with its own eight "specific affairs groups" (confusingly, also referred to as LSGs) on railway safety, floating populations, rehabilitation of former prisoners, juvenile delinquency

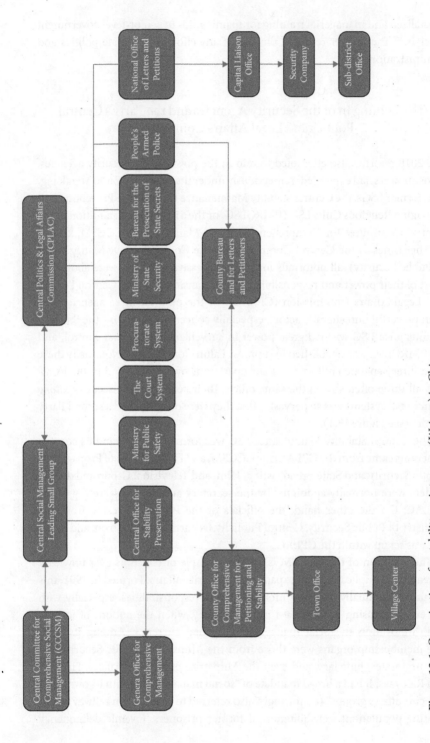

Figure 13.1 Organizations for stability maintenance (*Weiwen*) in China

Source: Adapted from "The Machinery of Stability Preservation," by *Caijing* reporters Xu Kai & Li Weiao, *Human Rights Journal*, June 8, 2011, https://www.duih uahrjournal.org/2011/06/.

prevention, schools, and their surrounding areas management. Often dubbed a "government within a government," the CCCSM had its agencies embedded in its membership organs such as ministries of railway, public security, justice, CYL, and education. Its mandate was so broad and nebulous that it simply captured any issue it desired. As a Chinese commentator said, it was just like a "wicker basket" (*kuang*) into which anything could fit. Originally, its function was law and order, dispute resolution, and "innovation in social management," but quickly the organ extended its bureaucratic reach to encompass *weiwen*, urbanization, and such issues as income distribution, grassroots party-building, and even the administration of justice. The CCCSM branches at the provincial and lower levels had eight matching "special affairs groups" like its central counterpart, but other localities had freely created even more of these groups according to their specific conditions. For instance, Yunnan had a borders management special affairs group, and its CCCSM constituents had swollen to sixty-seven![37]

The restructuring also trimmed the power of the CPLAC. Originally an LSG, it was formed in 1980 and had since been led by the notorious hardliner Luo Gan and the "security czar" Zhou Yongkang. The CPLAC was a large conglomerate that commanded huge financial, propaganda (see Figure 13.1), and power resources and oversaw all law-and-order issues, information, and intelligence relating to domestic security. It supervised all legal enforcement authorities, which included the police, procuratorates, and courts, and coordinated the handling of all mass incidents and emergencies. Since it had combined control of politics and law, national security systems, and the People's Armed Police (PAP), its budget had ballooned to be larger than the defense budget. Its power extended downward to various levels of localities, encompassing public security, procuracy, and courts. All regional and local secretaries of the politics and law committees were concurrently heads of the public security or the PAP. Because of its extensive power to interfere with the judiciary, the CPLAC became a hotbed of corruption, and the oppressive methods used by it apparently resulted in many trumped-up charges and wrongful convictions that Xi had railed against.[38] CPLAC power grew tremendously given the imperatives of *weiwen* under PBSC member Zhou Yongkang, who turned it into his power base. Bo Xilai, an ally of Zhou Yongkang, was at one time considered to be his successor as head of the CPLAC. As discussed previously, official and unofficial sources claim that Zhou tried to influence a general secretary succession outcome in favor of Bo Xilai by hatching a coup that was ultimately suppressed.

To allay concerns that a new CPLAC head might use the agency as a power base to challenge Xi as a new general secretary and even endanger his life, the Politburo picked as head Meng Jianzhu, a regular Politburo member and not a PBSC member. Since 2012, the CPLAC had been sidelined and brought more under the control of the top leadership. In 2017 Guo Shengkun was made director, and in 2018, Chen Yixin, a former Xi subordinate in Zhejiang, was named the CPLAC's secretary general.[39]

Since 2018, the CPLAC has been put in charge of coordination, supervision, proposal making, and large-scale emergency response. Its duties have been limited to research and assessment of social stability and social risks, owning the power of supervision and coordination rather than the actual operation of specific cases (Articles 18, 19, and 20). New regulations specified that the CPLAC's function is to "make proposals to the Party Center on important issues," and it is forbidden to be involved in individual cases except in foreign relations and national security.[40] Moreover, the establishment of the Commission for Comprehensive Law-Based Governance to a certain extent is designed to check the power of the CPLAC. Further, the power to command the PAP was removed from the public security system and given to the Central Military Commission. In the localities, this also broke the tradition of heads of public security bureaus taking the concurrent position of the PAP's first political commissar. And as mentioned, judicial reforms have also strengthened the vertical control over local procuracies and courts, removed their powers over personnel and resources to the provinces, and set up a circuit court system. All this has broken the previous model of the public security commanding the judiciary.[41] And as mentioned, beginning in 2013 the court system began the process of re-examining suspicious cases, exonerating many wrongfully convicted individuals. Just before the Nineteenth Party Congress, all secretaries of the political and law committees in the thirty-two provinces were replaced,[42] presumably to cleanse the lingering influence of Zhou Yongkang.

Other Central Party Agencies

The 2018 restructuring centralized more power in the already powerful agencies under the CC such as the Departments of Publicity, Organization, and United Front, making then clear winners. Many other party agencies were abolished with their power and functions merged into these conglomerates, although some of their names are retained for external purposes.

The Publicity Department
The Publicity Department (PD, *xuanchuanbu*), formerly translated as Propaganda Department (the term "propaganda" in formal Chinese usage connotes education and the spreading of knowledge with no suggestion of deception), was a winner during the restructuring. As the CCP's foremost tool of ideological and political control, however, the PD exercises tight supervision over the media, which includes television, radio, newspapers, the internet, and

mobile phones, in addition to culture, arts, education, research, and international publicity.[43] The PD's head has always been a Politburo member, reporting directly to the PBSC, and ensures that the media cleave to the party line, using methods ranging from persuasion to coercion. The PD not only commands state organs such as the Ministry of Culture, State Administration of Press, Publication, Radio, Film and Television (SAPPRFT), but also the State Press and Publication Administration, State Council Information Office, and Xinhua News Agency. In the localities, the PD's extensive networks of subsidiaries also supervise state agencies. During the reform period, the decentralization of PD functions, the social media boom, and commercialization gradually eroded the PD's power. Increasingly, the Chinese public had turned to nontraditional media sources such as satellite TV, the internet, and social-messaging systems for information and for exchanging opinions. This is especially true among the eighteen to thirty-five age group among China's eight hundred million internet users and 1.08 billion cell phone users. In contrast, all party-state agencies, including the *People's Daily*, had been required to be profitable and competitive since government subsidies and mandatory subscriptions had been curbed. The Hu Jintao administration had ordered a reduction of the number of official publications and limited mandatory subscriptions to the three principal newspapers and two magazines (which include the *People's Daily*, *Economic Daily*, and *Qiushi*). The PD's stiff propaganda has found it difficult to compete with market forces and the free flow offerings of unofficial media that cater to an increasingly complex society. It has tried to make use of commercialization to serve its functions, but its attempt to limit its remit to the political realm and leave the social realm has not been effective since the distinction cannot be easily drawn,[44] and the efficacy of recent modernizing efforts, such as the use of cartoons, popular rap songs, and video games to explain policies and positions remains to be seen. Restructuring allowed the PD to absorb the SAPPRFT and to take over its regulatory power over the press, publishing, and films. Externally, the SAPPRFT assumed the title "National Film Bureau."

The creation of two additional agencies from the SAPPRFT serving similar functions seemed to have contravened the principle of avoiding duplications. The first, the National Radio and Television Administration, which would "implement the Party's propaganda guidelines and policies" and act as the "mouthpiece" of the Party, was created directly under the State Council. The second, a Central Radio and Television Network, absorbing China Central Television, China National Radio, and China Radio International, was created under the PD. Its purposes were to guide ideology and public opinion, propagate the Party's policies, and strengthen international broadcasting competitiveness so that the Chinese "story" and viewpoints would be better represented. Externally these agencies were to be collectively named the Voice of China,[45] a nod to such nationally funded agencies as the Voice of America (United States) and Deutsche Welle (Germany).

All these were intense centralizing moves intended to bolster the regime's soft power domestically and abroad, to better shape public opinion, and to burnish China's international image. Xi has frequently argued that ideology is a major weapon for bolstering the regime's image, repeatedly urging the media "to tell the China story well." In a 2015 speech, Xi put his concern over the lack of a voice this way: "If a country falls behind, it will be beaten. . . . If it is poor, it will starve; if it loses its right to speak, it will be harangued."[46] Having tightened the supervision of news, publications, and film production, he urged all media sources to pledge loyalty to the CCP, and consequently some entertainment and social media platforms, including those who had millions of followers on WeChat, have been shut down for allegedly violating "core socialist values." With Wang Huning becoming the director of the PD, it was expected that tighter control would be effected on culture, the arts, education, and research.[47]

Changes to Other Party Central Agencies for Various Purposes

The Central Organization Department, which normally managed only the party nomenklatura, took over the functions of managing civil servants from the State Administration of Civil Service, although the title of the latter was retained for purposes of foreign exchanges. First, it would handle all policies regarding the recruitment, scrutiny, training, and welfare of all civil servants. Second, it would direct the State Commission Office for Public Sector Reform in charge of the design and setup of central agencies. The United Front Work Department (UFWD) emerged from behind the scenes to the front stage by directly taking over ethnic, religious, and overseas Chinese affairs. Its power considerably enhanced, the UFWD would henceforth control the State Ethnic Affairs Commission, which remained a State Council organ, and the State Administration of Religious Affairs, and the Overseas Chinese Affairs Office would turn into internal bureaus of the department. Historically, the "united front" tactic was used to join with the Guomindang for the resistance against Japanese aggression, and to canvass support among the "democratic parties" during the civil war (1945–1949) against the Guomindang. Mao had often referred to it, together with armed struggle and party-building, as the three "magic means"[48] for ensuring CCP victory in 1949. Since 1949 the united front has been used to mobilize support among nonparty individuals, organizations, and elites in the religious, ethnic, business, arts, and sports sectors. It oversees the co-optation of the Chinese in Taiwan, Hong Kong, and Macau, as well as other Chinese diaspora and sympathetic foreigners. Together with the CPPCC, it liaises with the eight "democratic parties" and the

All-China Federation of Industry and Commerce, as well as other nonparty social and economic elites, and cadres. And in tandem with the rise of Chinese power and influence, the UFWD increasingly operates outside of China to promote Chinese soft power. Xi, following Mao, frequently refers to it as a "magic means" for cultivating nonparty support.

The State Computer Network and Information Security Management Center, which took charge of China's "Great Firewall," was put under the Central Committee for Cyberspace Affairs, moving away from the Ministry of Industry and Information Technology. The NPeC Law Committee was renamed the NPeC Constitution and Law Committee with the avowed intent to defend and popularize the constitution and to strengthen constitutional oversight. It was empowered to reject legislation it deemed unconstitutional, and Li Fei, Beijing's top constitutional expert on Hong Kong's Basic Law, was made director.[49] Yet given that the new committee occupied a low position in the ruling hierarchy and that Li was not even an alternate member of the CC, the committee's "judicial review" functions would be a long distance from that of a constitutional court. The committee may signal the regime's commitment to judicial reform and gain it modest legitimacy, and it may be used to discipline the bureaucracy, especially in cases of local corruption and protectionism.

In other developments, Politburo and CMC members were obliged to swear allegiance to the constitution for the first time, and December 4 was declared "State Constitution Day" in 2014 to promote public awareness. This was just one symbolic baby step to promote Xi's notions of governance according to law and the strengthening of the constitution with legislative oversight.

Changes to the State/Government Structure

State Council Overhaul

The State Council overhaul of 2018 was one of the most extensive changes since the founding of the PRC. Back in 1998, the extensive reshuffle under Zhu Rongji saw forty ministries and commissions merged into twenty-nine. This time, the number of ministries and commissions was reduced by eight to twenty-six and the subministry-level organs reduced by seven. As with the party restructuring, the guiding principles were to strengthen party leadership over the running of the economy; reduce overstaffing, conflicts of interests, and bureaucratic wrangling; and raise government efficiency. All this necessitated a finer differentiation of responsibilities, divisions of labor, and changes in the regulatory regime. In some cases, entirely new ministries or agencies were formed by copying the experience of other developed countries, such as the United States.

The Formation of the National Supervisory Commission

One major institution created by the Thirteenth NPeC was the NSuC, originally envisaged in 2016. Touted as a major measure for political reform, the NSuC was intended to be an independent agency elected by the NPeC and accountable to it. In terms of status, it would be equivalent to the State Council, the Supreme People's Court, and the Supreme People's Procuratorate, what the Chinese dubbed "one council, one commission, and two yuans" (*yifu yiwei liangyuan*; see Figure 9.1),[50] and its creation required a revision of the constitution.

Inspired in part by Hong Kong's Independent Commission against Corruption and Taiwan's Control Yuan (and Dr. Sun Yat-sen's revival of the ancient notion of a censorate),[51] the NSuC is a supranational agency intended to be the head of a system of supervisory commissions spanning the provincial, municipal, and county levels. It brought together a number of formally divided control agencies under one roof and clarified the division of responsibilities. For instance, the NSuC took over the functions of the Ministry of Supervision and the State Prevention of Corruption Bureau when both were abolished. Further, the NSuC was entrusted with the power of investigation, whereas the powers to prosecute and trials were left with the Supreme People's Procuratorate and the Supreme People's Court. The new web of NSuC covered all nonparty civil servants and officials in the judiciary, SOEs, public institutions, and mass organizations, closing a major loophole by covering three times as many people as party members. Article 12.2 of the regulation governing the NPeC declares that it will tackle all who "exercise public power" and all cases of corruption, bribery, dereliction of responsibility, rent-seeking, embezzlement, and waste of state assets.[52]

Formation of such a commission was a response to concerns that the CCDI, a party organization, lacked legitimate authority to investigate and prosecute nonparty officials. Further, it was expected that the NSuC would form a powerful deterrent against corruption, replacing the campaign style of the ACC with more institutional processes. Politburo member and deputy secretary of the CCDI (since 2014) Yang Xiaodu was named founding chief.[53] The government in early 2017 announced that pilot projects were being set up in Beijing, Shanxi, and Zhejiang. Beijing was chosen to be the model for the entire country; Shanxi was chosen because of the rampant corruption syndicates there; and Zhejiang was picked because of the dominance of private enterprises in that province. Wang Qishan took charge of the drafting of the legislation during an extensive consultation process that generated heated debate.[54] In the Beijing pilot project, the number of officials being investigated expanded almost fivefold, from 210,000 to 997,000. In contrast with the old government supervisory department that could merely investigate and impose administrative penalties, the new supervisory commissions were empowered to seize suspicious assets, freeze bank accounts, and detain suspects. It would replace *shuanggui* with a new detention system (*liuzhi*) whereby the suspects could be detained for three months, the length of which could be doubled under "special circumstances."[55]

The Beijing pilot stirred controversy. In August 2017, fifty-nine lawyers petitioned citing concerns that the three-month detention without supervision by the procuracies and the lack of access to lawyers violated personal freedom. Other concerns were that the accused would have little or no recourse against official decisions. Critics argued that aggressive top-down methods to target individuals might lead to political abuse, and might be less effective than better transparency, public monitoring, and access to information such as budgeting.[56]

Xi argued that the NSuC was designed to constrain and supervise the exercise of political power, or in his parlance, "put power into the cage." The goal was to bolster the Party's unified leadership over anticorruption so that coverage extended from party members to all public officials, and as such, it was an important element of political system reform.[57]

The organization of the NSuC is known, but specifics of its responsibilities and operation will need a separate study, since its powers of search, custody, and interrogation are still being defined.[58] Yet critics are suspicious that it may turn out to be just a front for the CCDI since the two agencies share the same office. Further, Article 15 of the new legislation defines coverage to extend to state staff such as managers of SOEs, education, sports, science and research, and health institutions, but is unclear whether base-level employees such as doctors or teachers could be included since Article 15.6 states that the legislation covers all "other public officials." The extent to which the commission can perform independent and lawful functions remains to be seen.

The Curtailment of the National Development and Reform Commission

One significant development was the trimming of the power of the National Development and Reform Commission (NDRC), the biggest and most powerful macroeconomic agency under the State Council. It directed the country's development strategies, economic and social plans, macroeconomic management, and administrative control of the economy. Dubbed the "little State Council" because its power rivaled that of the State Council itself, it was a successor to the State Planning Commission, which was the core of the centrally commanded economy in charge of devising and implementing five-year plans, controlling all production targets and commodity prices. In the reform period the power of the NDRC was trimmed because of the erosion of central planning, but it still held formidable and extensive power, accounting for thirty thousand bureaucrats and twenty-six functional departments. Its formidable and wide-ranging *shenpi* approval power ranged from steel production to high-speed rail projects, from industrial policy and rural development to overseas acquisitions. It controlled prices ranging from gasoline to taxi rides, from electricity rates to drugs, and from wheat and liquor to coal. During the Hu-Wen era it dominated economic policymaking, and following the massive stimulus package introduced in 2009, it acquired even more power by controlling numerous investment projects. Possessing a mindset of strong state control, the NDRC had often been criticized for supporting overproduction and overcapacity in such areas as solar panels and subway projects. Its power of technical planning was increasingly viewed as an obstacle to Xi's notion of letting market forces play a "decisive" role in the allocation of resources. Further, because of its huge regulatory power, it was also a hotbed of corruption. A former vice chair, Liu Tienan, was given a life sentence for accepting bribes. A Chinese quip was that the NDRC is more about "development" than "reform," although the overconcentration of power in this organ was a major obstacle to reform.[59]

NDRC's successive directors had been promoted from inside, and the assignment of Ma Kai, an outsider, did little to change the mindset of bureaucratic interference. Liu He was once made a deputy director of the NDRC, but the purpose was more for him to keep an eye on it. The formation of the Comprehensively Deeping Reform LSG in 2013 and its many regional subsidiaries, it was said, had begun to circumvent the power and vested interests of the government and especially the NDRC. The latter's power was chipped away with every reduction of *shenpi*, and even its officials began to accept that as an inevitable trend.

In the latest round of reform, the NDRC lost the power to oversee the following: approval of developing zones lost to the Ministry of Natural Resources; climate change to the Ministry of Environment; agricultural investment projects to the Ministry of Agriculture and Rural Affairs; antitrust to the China Banking Regulatory Commission; "key national projects" to the NAO; pricing of medicines and healthcare services to the Health Commission.[60] The curtailment of the NDRC may represent one major move of the devolution of power from the government to the market in the long run, but it does not mean that Beijing has embraced neoliberalism and removed the state's role in the economy.[61]

Reorganization of the Regulations of Finance and Banking

A priority for the leadership has been to contain financial risks and to safeguard financial security by plugging regulatory holes. China's financial sector has expanded tremendously since it joined the World Trade Organization in 2001, and by 2016, banking sector assets had grown twelve times to reach US$35.34

trillion, whereas assets in the insurance and securities sectors also surged to US$2.36 trillion and US$68.9 billion. But the financial sector has been bedeviled by corruption, price manipulation, and rampant irregularities. The Xi-Li team had warned that China was most susceptible to a financial crisis, especially with the ever-growing debt and ballooning assets in the shadow-banking industry. After the stock market meltdown in 2015 there had been a sustained crackdown on financial irregularities and market manipulations.[62] In 2017 there was another crackdown on shadow banking, growth of wealth management products, trust products, and interbank liabilities. The People's Bank of China (PBOC) had introduced a Macro Prudential Assessment framework to gauge risks and the health of individual institutions and the entire financial system, and the China Banking Regulatory Commission (CBRC) had slapped record fines on financial institutions for concealing bad loans. Insurers, such as the giant Anbang Insurance Groups, which boosted sales by selling high-yield and short-term products and then used the earnings to buy listed companies and overseas trophy assets, were taken over by the government. In 2018, Anbang's head Wu Xiaohui was sentenced to jail for eighteen years and had US$1.7 billion confiscated from him for corruption.[63] Separately, hundreds of banking executives were punished, with ¥2.9 billion of penalties imposed on 1,877 financial institutions. Initial outcomes showed that in 2017 wealth management products grew a mere 1.7 percent, down from an average annual growth of about 50 percent between 2015 and 2016, and interbank liabilities dropped for the first time in seven years.[64]

To further reduce duplications and plug loopholes, the restructuring formed the China Banking and Insurance Regulatory Commission (CBIRC) to replace the CBRC and the China Insurance Regulatory Commission (CIRC), tasking the new agency with a crackdown on shadow banking and cross-asset financial activity. The CBIRC pushed banks to incorporate off-balance sheet assets in their balance sheets. In turn, some powers of the CBRC and CIRC were transferred to the PBOC, which was charged with the formulation of key legislation, regulations, and prudential regulation. With its power greatly enhanced, the PBOC was transformed from an adviser on monetary policy into a super-regulator to curb regulatory arbitrage and to deepen China's deleveraging campaign. The CBIRC would be the implementer overseeing US$43 trillion of banking and insurance assets.[65]

In November 2017 the State Council formed a Financial Stability and Development Commission. Headed by Ma Kai, it was tasked with exploring reforms for the financial sector, researching international and domestic situations, and coordinating regulations as well as monetary, financial, fiscal, and industrial policies.[66] The securities regulator, the China Securities Regulatory Commission (CSRC) was left untouched. This way, the new structure, dubbed "one commission [CSRC], one bank [PBOC], and two committees [CBIRC and CSRC]," set up a pyramid power structure with centralized control at the top. This replaced the former structure of "one bank [PBOC] and three commissions [CBRC, CIRC, and CSRC]," which was said to have issues with regulatory loopholes, duplication, and regulating arbitrage. Liu He, vice premier in charge of financial and economic affairs, was given control over the hierarchy. Liu touted the restructuring as an important step forward in refining the regulatory superstructure by addressing the issues of duplication, loopholes, and wrangling. Generally, Chinese officials expected that the new structure was imperfect and would present challenges and pain, and their remaining concerns would be how to address issues of balancing financial supervision with innovation and the finance of regional governments. Meanwhile, at the March NPeC session, Yin Zhongqing, deputy director of the NPeC's finance and economics committee, charged that the government's figures for local government debt (¥16.5 trillion, or US$ 2.6 trillion) and nonperforming loans (1.74 percent) were obviously underestimated and dangerous, although no short-term solutions were identified.[67] An overall public and private debt mountain of US$34 trillion continues to strike fear of an explosive disaster, and even a global financial crisis, although optimists argue that the government can manage it by growing its way out of the problem, aided by factors such as China's high saving rate and current-account surpluses.[68] Overall, Beijing continues to push forward regulations in areas of coordination between central and regional regulations, internet finance, financial holding companies, and shadow banking.[69]

The Seven New Ministries and Two New Administrations to Address Social Issues

Seven newly formed ministries that were given power and responsibilities were the following. First, the Ministry of Ecological Environment replaced the Ministry of Environment Protection and took over responsibilities previously shared by other agencies such as the NDRC (coping with climate change and emission reduction), the ministries of land and natural resources (underground water pollution), agriculture (fertilizer and pesticide pollution), and the Ocean Bureau (ocean environment). The abolished Ministry of Environment Protection was regarded as weak, its effectiveness compromised by vague overlapping responsibilities and the practice by which supervisors also acted as managers. Henceforth, the mandate of the Ministry of Ecological Environment was to beef up protection of the environment, and its augmented regulatory power reflected a stronger commitment to the formidable issues of environmental protection. For instance, Beijing has in the past closed cement and steel plants and ordered households to give up coal in favor of gas for heating, but pushbacks by heavy industries and economic planners have often impeded progress.[70]

Second, the Ministry of Natural Resources replaced the Ministry of Land and Natural Resources, to supervise and protect natural resources, which included forests, wetlands, grasslands, and maritime resources. It took over the responsibilities formally shared by the NDRC (organizational planning), Ministry of Housing and Rural/Urban Construction (rural/urban planning), and all functions of the National Administration of Surveying, Mapping and Geoinformation.

Third, a Ministry of Agriculture and Rural Affairs replaced the Ministry of Agriculture to oversee agriculture and rural development and poverty reduction, since China's poor were now located mostly in remote rural areas. The new ministry merged the responsibilities of the Central Rural Work LSG, the former Ministry of Agriculture, the Ministry of Finance's rural development projects, the Ministry of Land and Natural Resources' farmland improvement projects, and so on. It was tasked with boosting agricultural production, rural industries, e-commerce, and a more efficient use of land and technology.

Fourth, a Ministry of Veteran Affairs, like that in the United States, was formed to improve services such as welfare and retraining for some fifty-seven million demobilized and retired soldiers. This ministry merged the functions previously distributed among civil affairs and human affairs ministries, and the political works and logistics support departments of the CMC. Better management of veteran affairs was deemed a priority because widespread dissatisfaction and demonstrations by veterans constituted one source of social instability. Additionally, the entire PLA simultaneously received pay and pension increases backdated to August 2017. To placate the retrenched officers and to head off unrest, all were paid ¥1 million in addition to their pensions or at least 70 percent of their exit monthly salary for life. Such payments were funded by a defense budget that would be raised 8.1 percent to ¥1.1 trillion in 2018.[71]

Fifth, a Ministry of Emergency Management was formed to forestall and diffuse major risks and improve relief for natural disasters such as fire, flood, drought, and earthquakes. It was charged with improving safety regulations and emergency management, given that climate change had made natural disasters more frequent and severe. To cut red tape and prevent turf wars, the ministry would take over the responsibilities of the former State Administration of Work Safety as well as functions from other ministries, including firefighting (from the Ministry of Public Security); disaster relief (Ministry of Civil Affairs); geological disaster prevention (Ministry of Land and Resources); drought and flood control (Ministry of Water Resources); and prairie fire control (Ministry of Agriculture).[72]

Sixth, a Ministry of Culture and Tourism merged the former Ministry of Culture and the State Tourism Bureau, and its mandate was to enhance China's culture and soft power and to promote cultural exchanges at home and abroad.

Seventh, a National Health Commission under the State Council was formed to promote the strategy of "Healthy China" and to replace the former National Health and Family Planning Commission. The omission of the words "family planning" signified that the one-child family policy had become history. The commission's responsibilities were to formulate national health policy and reform, introduce a national prescription system, and supervise public health, medical services, and emergencies. It was also charged with overseeing family planning, helping the aging population, and providing a combination of medical care and pensions for the retired. The new commission took over functions previously performed by the National Health and Family Planning Commission, State Council LSG for Medical and Healthcare Reform, National Seniors Work Committee, and so on, signifying a shifting focus from cure to health, disease prevention, and services for the aged. Inspired by the Fujian Sanming model, which allegedly reduced the cost of medicine and medical personnel but increased income, the commission was intended to address popular complaints of inaccessible and expensive healthcare.

Finally, a National Medical Health Bureau under the State Council was established to formulate health and social insurance policies and to integrate the management of healthcare, medical insurance, and medicine. It was tasked with issues such as healthcare reform, access to quality healthcare, health emergencies, family planning, and the establishment of a national basic medicine system. It took over functions of various agencies such as the National Health and Family Planning Commission (rural cooperative healthcare), NDRC (medical services and medicine pricing), and Ministry of Civil Affairs (medical aid).

Organizations Directly under the State Council

New functions were redefined for some new or existing agencies under the State Council. First, the State Market Regulatory Administration (SMRA) gained control over the supervisory functions governing market and pricing, market entry, antimonopoly, quality control, product safety, and food safety. The China Food and Drug Administration was replaced by the State Drug Administration, which became part of the SMRA. Second, a separate State Immigration Administration was formed under the Ministry of Public Security to handle functions previously performed by the Ministry of Public Security itself. It was to serve functions akin to the US Citizenship and Immigration Services agency by looking after immigrant services such as exit and entry, customs, and immigration control. It also took charge of policies regarding immigration, citizenship services, foreigner residency, refugees, and international immigration cooperation.

Third, the State International Development Cooperation Agency was formed to coordinate, reform, and evaluate foreign aid strategy and various aid programs to serve "great power diplomacy" and the BRI project. It took over the related functions from the Ministries of Commerce and Foreign Affairs, ending their long-standing rivalry over the control of foreign aid.[73] Finally, a strengthened NAC was to independently exercise its powers of auditing key large-scale projects, fiscal supervision, and oversight of SOEs and their leaders. This office's powers were transferred from the NDRC, Ministry of Finance, and the State-owned Assets Supervision and Administration Commission, in order to remove duplications and prevent bureaucratic wrangling.[74]

The Restructuring of the People's Armed Police

As a last logical step in military reform, the NPeC also finalized the restructuring of the PAP. Officially established in 1982 after various previous incarnations, the PAP, 1.5 million strong, is a paramilitary police force in charge of internal security, law enforcement, emergency response, and maritime rights protection. Attempts have been made to professionalize the security apparatus after the muddled and high-handed military suppression of the demonstrations at Tiananmen. Originally the PAP members were drawn from the PLA's border control, security units, and fire departments, as well as Ministry of Public Security units and demobilized PLA solders. Since the PAP was put under the dual rule of the State Council and the CMC, provincial and county governments had the power to deploy PAP units, and increasingly they were used as an instrument of *weiwen* to quash mass incidents. Often, the PAP colluded with local police, officials, and other factions in a nexus of corruption. Beijing also worried that the PAP could be used to challenge its rule, especially during crisis situations. For instance, Party Central was spooked by the Wang Lijun affair, when Bo Xilai ordered the PAP to lay siege to the US consulate in Chongqing. As mentioned, the power of the CPLC expanded tremendously when Zhou Yongkang, through his control over such agencies as the Ministry of Public Security, commanded the PAP to do its bidding. In the alleged coup revealed by detailed Falun Gong sources (and sketchy official sources), Zhou was said to have ordered up a coup by using the PAP in the so-called March 19 incident.

By 2017, Xi had signaled the upcoming reform of the PAP command by asserting the principle of separating military, police, and civilian functions. Beginning in 2018, dual rule ended, and the PAP was put under the sole control of the CMC, although not under the PLA. Henceforth, local governments wishing to deploy the PAP would have to obtain permission from the CMC and its chair, Xi, forcing them to rely on the regular police to maintain social stability. The PAP's budget would be supplied by the CMC, no longer by the State Council and local governments, and heads of the Ministry of Public Security and their local counterparts were no longer allowed to serve as party secretaries for PAP units. This measure deprived the local governments of their power to mobilize the PAP without permission from the CMC.

Intended to professionalize the PAP, the reform also centralized power into both the Party and Xi's person. Presumably this would constrain powerful local opponents to Xi's reforms, including former associates of fallen leaders such as Bo Xilai and Zhou Yongkang. Similarly, it could also constrain the legions of newly minted enemies who suffered and lost out from Xi's reforms and antigraft campaigns.[75] Since Xi was the chair of the CMC, the PAP was brought under his personal control. The comprehensive powers of the National Security Commission over the PLA, the PAP, and the Ministry of Public Security was another means for Xi to ensure the safety of Party Central and even his own personal security.[76]

Of the eight corps that constituted the PAP, those whose functions were primarily civilian were transferred to the State Council: border defense and interior forces corps were turned into regular police; the firefighting corps transferred to the Ministry of Emergency Management; the forestry and mining corps to ministries of Emergency Management and Natural Resources. The hydropower corps was turned into an SOE. Only the transportation security corps remained in the PAP. However, the Coast Guard, originally managed by the State Maritime Bureau, was transferred to the PAP. It was granted powers over the policing of fisheries, maritime traffic, and customs, enabling it to oversee disputes in areas such as the SCE and the East China Sea.

Restructuring of Regional Political Organizations and Decentralization

As mentioned, local autonomy and centralized control are flip sides of the same coin, depending on the context and issue area. Xi's reforms have centralized much decision-making power in the Party, the capital, and Xi himself, although certain powers have been decentralized as noted. The 2018 round of restructuring features both centralization and decentralization, and the provinces and lower levels were given more autonomy so that they could define the specific responsibilities of various administrative agencies. This stemmed from the concern that the numerous initiatives, regulations, and campaigns emanating from Beijing and the central bureaucracies had hamstrung the local administrations and stifled their initiatives. The regional authorities had only limited capabilities to implement these central initiatives, many of them unfunded mandates, and the Chinese likened this phenomenon to "a thousand threads from above meet only one needle at the bottom." Hence, in the 2018 restructuring, the myriad of central party and government organizations, some of them mentioned previously, which had their counterparts at regions from the provinces and downward, needed reshuffling. For example, many central LSGs and ministries also had their subsidiaries or counterparts located at the provincial and lower levels. Therefore, the provinces/municipalities were allowed to restructure, to set up or abolish agencies, and to define their functions. They were empowered to test or to merge party and government organizations that served similar functions according to their own needs, if they strictly observed central quotas for the number of agencies and personnel and did not attempt to proliferate them.

Similarly, quotas were extended to all business units contracted for administrative functions. The Party Center demanded that the various "ownership systems by regions, departments, and units" be broken down to facilitate coordination. In other words, the provinces were asked to break down the traditional *tiao-kuai* vertical-horizontal demarcations of power. Regional units were urged to learn from pilot restructuring projects and from economically advanced towns, and adapt the new measures to towns and villages in order to provide more effective base-level management and better services (*bianmin*) for the public. In turn, quotas for the number of agencies for the county/cities were to be supervised by the provincial/municipality party committees. Beijing demanded all central and provincial restructuring to be quickly accomplished by the end of 2018. The restructuring below the provincial level was to be led by the provincial party committees and reported to the Party Center by the end of 2018 and accomplished by March 2019.

Overall, the ambitious and sweeping restructuring of the Chinese Leviathan in 2018 aiming to modernize leadership and governance will require stamina and determination. No major party-state institutions, including the CPPCC and mass organizations, were spared.[77] For instance, the reform of the CPPCC created a new committee for agriculture and rural affairs and renamed two committees, presumably to better utilize expert and nonparty advice in these matters. More than mere bureaucratic tinkering, the massive restructuring is the Xi leadership's initiative to significantly streamline, modernize, and reconfigure China's entire political structure. It is also an attempt to clarify the lines of authority among the maze of crisscrossing and overlapping bureaucracies to ensure long-term sustained growth and the continuation of centralized CCP leadership. According to Naughton, Xi has assembled a first-rate economic and financial team who tends to be market friendly, although he grants that the principal goal of the administrative and organizational reforms is to ensure the disciplined and efficient implementation of top-level commands.[78]

Yet all the efforts in 2018 represent only a starting point, since they involve such a huge redefinition of power and responsibilities, and numerous personnel assignments and operational measures that must be fleshed out over time. And accordingly, many laws and regulations must be revised to conform with the changes. This poses monumental challenges for further planning, communication, and coordination that exceeds the ability of one leader to control or dominate. Bureaucratic routines and stabilization will be disrupted, and resistance, foot-dragging, and conflicts will be an inevitable fact. However, habitually, some China watchers have interpreted the current reforms as another power grab, window dressing, or as conservative and retrogressive,[79] although the reality is more complex. Institution building and institutionalization is a lengthy process, and there are no silver bullets. The full effects of the reforms will take years to become clear. And the extent to which such restructuring will end up with a more efficient, service-oriented, and less corrupt system remains to be seen.

14

Conclusion

Interpreting Xi and the Rise of China

A subject as complex as that of the nature of Xi Jinping's rule, his legacy, and their broader implications for China and even the world cannot fail to excite the imagination and divide observers. The huge amount of literature on Xi exhibits a full spectrum of opinions, from the strongly approving to strongly critical. It is natural that the dramatic changes brought about by the rise of China have provoked views ranging from awe to envy, from fear to disbelief, and from disgust to panic. And as is often the case, these opinions depend on one's perspectives, assumptions, and level of analysis. To cite just a few general examples, human rights organizations tend to focus on the state's violations of the rights of its people. Foreign trade and investment interests are focused on business and commercial opportunities and returns. Western and US strategists analyze China with an eye on the extent to which China poses a threat or opportunity for their countries' perceived power and national interests, and on how to balance against an ascending China. International development agencies tend to focus on socioeconomic development. The primary concern of Falun Gong is to be able to operate in China apart from the five officially sanctioned religions, and to bring those guilty of its suppression to justice. Analysts also differ in their preferred teleological outcome and their criteria for evaluation. For instance, liberal democrats in China and abroad wish for a democratic future, greater institutionalization, and institutional constraints on power. Some China watchers evaluate changes in China in terms of whether China conforms to their own images (the "Why can't China be more like us?" syndrome). Avowed anticommunist observers tend to interpret China with what can be labeled an "inherent bad faith model."[1] Since China is construed to be a hostile enemy and an illegitimate aberration, every change and development is interpreted, regardless of the contrary evidence, to be another sign of aggressiveness or an inevitable step toward downfall. Others commit the "nirvana fallacy" by judging China to standards that no country can achieve, or assuming that there are perfect solutions to China's problems, and fault it for failing to eliminate problems such as pollution, corruption, regional inequality, and SOE inefficiency. Such a range of perspectives is reflected in academia. And as discussed, academics have analyzed China under Xi through a number of theoretical lenses. The outcome is a *Rashomon*-esque array of perspectives and interpretations, each with its merits or deficiencies. For our purpose here we may set aside those that essentially accept official discourses at face value[2] and focus on two prevalent schools of thought about the Xi "era" and how the West should respond. The first is pessimistic and ominous, and the second is optimistic and benign, although variations exist within each category. These two schools continue to echo themes articulated by analysts throughout the pre-Xi reform period on whether the Chinese system is inclined toward decay and collapse or toward resiliency and consolidation.[3] At the risk of over-simplification, I summarize this literature in the following, noting that there are varieties of views and degrees of emphasis within each large category.

Several themes in the malignant/pessimistic school can be identified. First, Xi is portrayed as an oppressive and absolutist dictator who enjoys unchecked and concentrated power at the head of the world's largest authoritarian state. Xi's main interest is said to be power aggrandizement since he has abolished term limits for president and intends to become "emperor for life." He has surrounded himself with a cult of personality and one-man rule lacking checks or balances. Second, Xi's rule has been intensely authoritarian since it has ruthlessly stifled dissent, civil society, social media, and the freedom of information. The stress on surveillance and control has never been greater, making for rule by fear. Third, Xi is inherently conservative as he has rolled back the reforms of his predecessors and has failed to initiate radical and complete reform. The outcome is political and economic stagnation, making further economic growth and development questionable. Fourth, despite talks about globalization, Xi has essentially closed China's door and rejected Western political values. He has stifled academic exchanges and civil society.

Fifth, the inexorable rise of a strong China, coupled with Xi's increasingly aggressive foreign policy is undermining liberal democracy and spreading autocracy, threatening vital US interests and the liberal global order. Xi's "Bonapartist" ambition is best reflected in China's behavior in the SCS, which threatens peace and stability in the Asia-Pacific. Progressively, Beijing is attempting to exert its sharp power overseas by buying influence with political and academic institutions, the media, and publishers, and stirring up nationalism among China's overseas students. Overall, China's muscular foreign policy will engender conflict and war and posts a danger to the world. This line of thinking tallies with the tropes of yellow peril and red menace still dominant in US public discourse.[4] Sixth and finally, one variation of this school posits a weak and vulnerable China rather than a strong one. Beset by multiple weaknesses and challenges and unwilling to accept the liberal democratic model, Xi's China will go the way of the Soviet Union and other communist countries. Social unrest, inequality, a predatory state, and economic cleavages will doom the CCP regime. The endgame is near, and Xi might be China's "last emperor." The collapse of China is imminent.[5]

Implicitly and explicitly, adherents of this school assumes that a panacea to China's ills is the adoption of US-style pluralism, checks and balances, and a balance of powers. To counter Chinese aggressiveness, many China watchers have argued that the West should act in unity to contain Beijing, check its ambition, and confront it at every turn, and even to precipitate a regime change.[6] During the coronavirus crisis of 2020, negative views of China were heightened around the world.

In contrast, the optimistic/benign school can also be summarized in a few points. First, Xi is pushing forward Deng Xiaoping's thirty-year developmental plan, which has multiplied China's GDP more than twenty times. A sterling track record saw eight hundred million Chinese escape poverty, and for the general population, "improvements in health, education, science and overall standard of living" advance at "a speed and scale that is unprecedented in human history."[7] The ambitious current plan is to boost GDP per capita by three times to US$30,000 in 2050, and to eradicate poverty and to achieve a sustainable and clean environment in two decades. China now surpasses the United States as a global engine of economic growth, and from 2013 to 2018, accounted for 28 percent of this increase.[8] Second, a string of reforms has induced structural change to the economy and created a burgeoning entrepreneurial society boasting some of the largest companies in the world. Starting from scratch, China is gradually becoming a global leader in such areas as superstructural development, high tech, big data, artificial intelligence, and mobile internet applications. Third, developments in China have been facilitated by a strong and effective developmental state at both the central and local level. The government plays a determined and resourceful role in planning and guiding industrial development, effectively combining socialism with the market economy. Promarket and proefficiency, it provides remedies for both government and market failure, smoothly achieving relative stability and legitimacy. This contradicts the view that elections and privatization are essential prerequisites to development. Fourth, the CCP is the country's political system, and despite its many flaws (which the Chinese grasp and wrestle with), it possesses an extraordinary ability to reinvent itself, accommodating change at various critical junctures of its development. A hallmark of the Chinese system is the "political meritocracy" that selects and promotes talent despite its elitist assumptions.[9] The high level of political support for the government is an outcome of its careful gauging and satisfaction of public opinion. Fifth, Beijing is advancing a new version of globalization that promotes a global community that features interconnectedness without sacrificing national sovereignty. A remarkably responsible power, Beijing's nonmilitary and nonintervention record is unique among great powers—it has not fought a war since 1979, nor has it supported proxies or armed insurgents abroad.[10] It has overturned a dominant narrative that all developing countries will modernize along the "same set of neoliberal economic and political rules and values" embraced by the West. However, Beijing has neither the wish nor capability to export the Chinese model to the outside world.[11] Hence, an appropriate strategy for the West to deal with Beijing is to engage it to resolve differences and to push back on matters of principles. Pressing global issues cannot be tackled without the cooperation of Beijing and Washington.

The two schools of thought reflect the many controversial interpretations of Chinese politics and development and their future trajectory. For instance, in interpreting the impact of the coronavirus pandemic, the malignant/pessimistic view predicts that China's weakness will accelerate the demise of the CCP, whereas the benign/optimistic view sees an opportunity for China to augment its international leadership.[12] Perhaps a third perspective that should be discussed is a more self-critical reflection on how Western observers, afflicted by arrogance and ethnocentrism, have consistently misread the Chinese experience. The key mistake, according to this view, is the assumption of convergence—a prosperous China will inevitably embrace Western values and choose capitalist democracy. As the Chinese middle class multiplies, convergence theory posits, it will seek greater political clout, and a civil society will arise, creating ever greater liberalization and leading to more and more political and economic openness. Yet this general assumption has been contradicted by the illiberal inclinations of China's elite classes, Beijing's assertive foreign behavior, and even a perceived backsliding toward Maoism.[13] Recent developments, such as the Black Lives Matter movement and the discovery of mass graves for indigenous children in the United States and Canada have obliged scholars to reexamine their assumptions in teaching and research.[14] This raises the issue of whether China can be properly understood without referring to the experiences of the West. Overall, among existing analyses, some are more sophisticated and nuanced than others. Most are informed by a healthy suspicion of unrestrained power, and they present compelling evidence and contain many elements of truth. Predictions, however, can be afflicted by self-fulfilling prophecies.

This is not the place to evaluate these views in detail. In my empirical exploration, I rejected the misleading exaggeration that China is a "frozen and closed system" under one-man rule.[15] I do not speculate about how China might collapse or evolve in the future. It is reasonable to assume the regime will last in the short run, say, for a decade or more. How China, and indeed, the world, may change in the long run in increasingly turbulent times is indeterminable.[16] The reprehensible aspects of authoritarian rule in general, and the regressive side of Xi's rule in particular, such as corruption, graft, censorship, oppression, cronyism, and restriction of personal freedom and an open press, have been widely documented. So have the risks of personalized rule. Yet China can hardly be compared with countries such as Putin's Russia, Erdoğan's Turkey, or Kim

Jong-Il's North Korea. The phenomena under consideration are so complex that they are not reducible to simple characterizations. Even history may not be a sound guide. The world has never witnessed such rapid and profound changes to 1.4 billion people under the conditions of an intertwined and interdependent global economy and threat of a nuclear apocalypse. Urgent global issues such as climate change, destructive weapons, huge inequality, poverty, environmental degradation, refugees, and pandemics are making governance in all forms of systems more turbulent. Indeed, this is not to say that historical contextualization is not the key to understanding contemporary China. Our study of Xi's governance records up to 2018 has afforded us a long historical perspective to unpack the motivations, policies, hopes and fears, as well as the constraints and opportunities of Chinese development. It throws light on China's strengths and weaknesses, and on the linkages and trade-offs in domestic and foreign policy-making. I have also analyzed the subject through a range of comparative, analytical, and theoretical lenses. A Manichaean view does little to make the Chinese experience understandable, and we will summarize the nature and implications of the Xi phenomenon in the following.

The Xi Jinping Phenomenon

Xi's unique political career among contemporary world leaders has shown that he is a survivor with an iron will to succeed. Despite a privileged childhood, his harrowing adolescent experiences were a baptism by fire. Brought up and socialized by the ethos of the Mao revolution and struggle, his thinking is reinforced by the values of populism and voluntarism. However, far from being a diehard Maoist, Xi has conversely counted the Mao period among the mishaps that China has suffered since the mid-nineteenth century, although he continues to draw on the Maoist heritage and has not denounced it in toto. His determination to climb the career ladder has a great deal in common with other "fifth generation" leaders who have made it to the apex of power, although others have slid down the greasy pole. A less-explored aspect, however, is that Xi's ascendancy was the fruition of the Party's deliberate grooming beginning in the 1980s to cultivate "third echelon" leadership successors. This unique model allows the CCP to recruit and rotate potential successors among various administrative posts for them to accumulate governance experience before they reach the capital. Consequently, despite the well-known crises, intense competitions, and occasional purges, a great deal of leadership continuity characterizes the reform period.

Before Xi became general secretary, his range of administrative experiences spanning the village, county, and provincial levels, in both inland and coastal provinces, mirrored the complex developmental trajectory of China. In Fujian, he began to establish his anticorruption and antibureaucratic credentials. As governor of economically advanced Zhejiang, he honed his skills at governance and began to consolidate his political, social, and economic views on such issues as government/market relations, poverty reduction, and pollution control. During his five-year apprenticeship as the heir apparent, he had already shown himself to be a disciplinarian in managing party work. The Eighteenth Party Congress of 2012 marked the regime's second peaceful leadership transition, and Xi ascended to the top under a leadership consensus, sloughing off a few potential conflicts over succession. Currently, the staggered sequence of succession is continuing with the cultivation of sixth-, seventh-, and eighth-generation leaders, although the efficacy of such an enterprise awaits separate studies. The Chinese economy grew exponentially during the reform period, but it was plagued by the twin issues of poverty and underdevelopment. China's nominal GDP per capita grew exponentially from a mere US$319.9 (US$987 in PPP) in 1990, US$959.4 (US$2,933 in PPP) in 2000, US$4,560.5 (US$9,333 in PPP) in 2010, to US$9976 ($17,017 in PPP) in 2018.[17] Today, Xi's former workplaces, such as Xiamen, Fuzhou, and Hangzhou, are modern metropolises crisscrossed by high-speed trains. Yet huge regional variations persist, with the incomes of the inhabitants of coastal areas three times those living inland.

As a leader in his first term, Xi has positioned himself as the most powerful and activist trailblazer since Mao at redefining the nature of collective leadership. He has completed a threefold centralization of power in the Party, the center, and himself. This has enabled him to take on ambitious goals and confront the webs of entangled vested interests that oppose reform. As argued, the power distribution at the top can best be conceptualized as "first among equals" because Xi depends on his colleagues for their expertise and the roles they play in the division of labor. In an important way, his relationship with other leaders in the PBSC and Politburo has been path-dependent and interdependent—all along he has had to work closely with other leaders who have risen, been groomed, and funneled through the party apparatus step by step. He has relied on them for their skills to make decisions and to implement the numerous ambitious reforms and policy initiatives. Actual purges of top leaders have been limited to avoid upheaval and instability. Conventional factional interpretations that place him among the princeling faction, "elite coalition," or the Shanghai Gang fail to account for his diverse experiences in the military and the provinces and his governance records spanning half a century.[18]

Xi reckons that ordinary Chinese expect their leaders to be strong and decisive. His first term in office shows that in many ways he is more coherent and strategic than his predecessors, but of course times have changed as well. China's material capabilities were much stronger than during the previous ten or even five years. However, Xi has been confronting a policy environment of accumulated domestic malaise and increasing turbulence on the world stage. At another level, if power is viewed in relational rather than absolute terms, Xi's power is constrained, considering the mammoth goals he set for himself and the pushback to his reforms. There have been many contradictions and trials and errors, and choices had to be made in the face of complex challenges. In this respect, Xi tries to foster a stable and confident environment for economic development. He acknowledges that the fate of the Party hinges on whether it can deliver, in large measure, what the people want. However, Xi's sense of paternalistic authoritarianism makes him intolerant of criticism, and he suppresses public dissent. His condoning of local governments' grotesque measures in Hong Kong are egregious examples of retrogression.

Overall, Xi's strategy and tactics are simultaneously ambitious and politically risky. The multiple chessboards he engages in show that he is determined, ambitious, and a man in a hurry. At home, he must contend with an economic model that is running out of steam and with the ever-present threat of stagnation. Xi aims to remake the economy with another paradigm, moving from manufacturing to a service-oriented and innovative economy. Instead of some idealized version of laissez-faire, he attempts to recalibrate state-market relations by strengthening both public and private sectors to serve development, and some progress is already palpable.[19] His ideal of political reform is to build institutions, tackle corruption, and institute relatively clean and lawful governance structures. Of necessity, such endeavors to reform a leviathan bred contradictions. One apt metaphor describes Xi's enterprise as an attempt to repair a motor vehicle while it is moving at two hundred kilometers an hour![20] By taking a long historical perspective, he argues that there is no time to fundamentally alter the inherited political structure, and that he has to work with the existing system to implement changes. In an important sense, China's problems are much bigger than its leadership!

As a staunch Leninist, Xi has privileged absolute party leadership, centralism, discipline, and paternalism, and his ideals are to preserve party rule to enhance regime legitimacy and to achieve a goal of a strong and powerful China by the middle of the twenty-first century. He insists on seeing leadership as a key to political-social-economic transformation by banking on the "authoritarian advantage" of a vanguard Party. Simultaneously with the upheaval of reform, he has forced discipline on the party state by attacking it with a variety of means such as anticorruption campaigns. This way, he has shaken up all the major pillars of CCP rule. Today the social composition of the CCP, a mass party with more than ninety million members, consists of the elites of a modern society, such as students, intellectuals, managers, and professionals, in addition to workers and farmers, although the West still entertains a stereotype that the CCP is a conspiratorial and revolutionary organization. In 2018, Xi effected the first sweeping restructuring of the party state since 1982 to make it more efficient. At the head of a paternalist authoritarian system, Xi assumes that he knows the interests of the nation and has pushed forward rapid economic and social development. Many reform goals announced during his first term have yet to be accomplished, although there are many tangible and decisive changes, such as the abolition of reeducation through labor and the *hukou* systems and the one-child family policy. Other major reform measures, such as the BRI and AIIB, were conceived and pushed through quickly, although the outcomes will take years to materialize. Still others, such as SOE reform, have advanced one step forward and then retreated two, although strong market forces are at work in the economy. One analyst likened the reform process to a cacophonous Beijing opera that seems to unfold at glacier pace where "every minute feels like an hour," but once the performance is over, one realizes that a remarkable story has been told.[21]

Abroad, Xi has projected a strong leader image on the world stage, conforming to the aspiration of the public. In a turbulent environment, Xi builds institutions from scratch to enmesh, to foster interdependence, and to gain a seat at the table. The BRI is a prime example of a new international institution designed to benefit China and its partners. Xi has attempted to instill pride and confidence in the Chinese people, to augment Beijing's weak soft power, and to gain international respect. Xi and his team are determined to build on their heritage and to modernize on their own terms. To borrow a quip from a China scholar, Beijing resents being perpetually treated "like a Rottweiler in the waiting room of an obedience school."[22] Simultaneously, Xi has also adopted assertive positions in the advancement of "core" national interest, as in the case of the SCS. But the rise of China and Xi's policies have spawned multiple security dilemmas with Beijing's neighbors and the United States

Yet reforms on paper are no guarantee for success. Poor policy design, faulty implementation, overreaching, and bureaucratic pushbacks and passive resistance have posed limitations to Xi's alleged supreme power. Xi has expended all his political capital and instead of heeding Deng Xiaoping's adage about "crossing the river by feeling the stones," he has bulldozed his way by pushing at all fronts, domestically and externally. There are many inherent dangers in meddling with the balance of power in an autocratic system and with alienating the political elite. The attack on the entrenched elite's wealth and privilege is dangerous for the regime since victims who have been humiliated and castigated are bent on revenge. An opposition in the elite cowed into silence can be potentially explosive, or it can be so demoralized that it reacts by passive resistance or even sabotage. As a history buff, Xi often discusses the pitfalls of the many failed reforms in Chinese history that attacked entrenched and interwoven vested interests. Keenly aware of the risks of reforms, Xi nevertheless is determined to plow ahead. Counterintuitive as it may seem, theories of revolution have shown that the decisive factors in revolutions are not popular discontent, grinding poverty, or suffering. Rather, they are the loss of nerve and confidence by the elite. Hence, Xi's attack on the elite to invigorate it is a risky proposition and a high-stakes gamble, and if he loses the confidence and support of the elite, he might provoke a crisis and undermine his own position. Another major factor for revolutions is economic prosperity and rising expectations, and the subsequent failure to satisfy them.[23] Xi likely is unfamiliar with these Western theories, but his definition of China's current principal contradiction as between "unbalanced and inadequate development" and the "people's ever-growing needs for a better life"[24] suggest he has done some thinking along this line.

Final Thoughts

First, it is a truism that the primary purpose of the CCP is to maintain power, and Xi made it a priority to consolidate his power once becoming general secretary. Analysis focusing on the primacy of power is compelling, but the exclusive focus on Xi's alleged aggrandizement of power misses a great deal of the dynamics of Chinese politics. Our consideration of the various stages of his career shows that as a leader, he has been preoccupied with the issues of governance and problem-solving, especially relating to poverty and development. Like policymakers everywhere, he has had to grapple with constraints and making choices. As top leader of a country of 1.4 billion with vast complexity, he has to make decisions under an environment of pressure, turbulence, and accelerating changes where crises and emergencies are commonplace.

Second, it would be prudent not to view Chinese domestic and foreign policies in isolation. China is now fully integrated into the liberal international order instead of on its marginalized periphery. As much as it has benefited by economic globalization, it is also subject to the challenges and competition of the ever-changing international environment that is beyond Beijing's control. This is essentially a structure-agency issue. Since China is increasingly dependent on foreign markets, resources, and energy, it is also susceptible to sudden fluctuations in foreign markets, economic shocks, and dislocations. From trade to economic growth, from technological change to cultural identity, and from corruption to pollution, Beijing's problems are intertwined with that of the rest of the world. The more Beijing perceives external pressure, the more strident its response, and the more foreign goodwill, the more its willingness to cooperate. Right from the beginning at 1949, the PRC has endured Western coercive economic measures such as containment and embargoes and is therefore wary of sanctions that may undermine its security. Further, China's interdependence with the United States is asymmetrical—China's dependence on the US market is far greater than the United States is dependent on China's. Hence, the external environment to a large extent has shaped Xi's (and his predecessors') preferences and the incentive is to minimize China's vulnerability and reliance on its rivals or competitors. The colossal BRI project, which aims at deepening economic interdependency, in addition to a muscular approach in the SCS, is but one important facet of a grand strategy to foster economic and political security. The various domestic and foreign policies minted by the Xi administration have been reactions in face of turbulence, especially under the new normal created by US president Trump.

Finally, the distinction has often been made between a "transactional" and a "transformative" leader. Transactional leaders motivate followers by appealing to their self-interests through routine transactions and bargaining. Preoccupied with the retention of power, they approach issues of rewards and punishment by manipulating their followers' base emotions of fear, greed, and hatred. They use hard power to inspire and reward. In contrast, transformative leaders resort to vision and ambitious goals to induce changes. They appeal to high ideals, moral values, and soft power to motivate and inspire. They take on unpopular causes, use conflict and crisis to raise followers' consciousness for transformation, and urge followers to transcend self-interest for higher purposes.[25] This distinction is, of course, dichotomous, and the categories are ideal types denoting two ends of a spectrum with many overlaps in the middle. A more fine-grained theorizing on leadership differentiates between "authentic" leadership that is ethical and inspiring, and a full range of "destructive" leadership that is unethical, abusive, toxic, and narcissistic. This provides promising avenues for comparative research.[26]

Another recent study on transformative leadership focuses on the neglected developing areas. It argues that the accomplished leader in these areas possesses an array of skills and a clear strategy to transform her or his vision into "economic growth, material prosperity, and human well-being." Such leaders possess emotional intelligence and core competencies in building nations and political cultures, often from scratch. Because institutions tend to be weak in the developing world, where issues are diverse and daunting, the leaders are more responsible for policy outcomes than in more developed countries. Yet a transformative leader needs not be perfect, and different transformative leaders display different attributes according to specific contexts. Hence, Nelson Mandela is a "consummate inclusionist," Seretse Khama a "resolute democrat," Lee Kuan Yew a "systematic nation-builder," and Kemal Ataturk an "uncompromising modernizer." Lee Kuan Yew, for instance, was hardly a "paragon of virtue," as he was ruthless with his adversaries. He restricted free expression and public participation, but he succeeded in realizing his goals of nation-building, rapid modernization, regime legitimacy, and the near elimination of corruption. Lee expected the polyglot Singaporean citizens to make sacrifices, but in return they would enjoy a relatively equalitarian society with extensive social services such as housing, medicine, and education. Ever a Confucian, Lee believed that good institutions were inadequate on their own—they require "good" people and talents to work and respect them, and a technocratic elite is indispensable for overseeing economic development.[27] In China, Xi certainly privileges power consolidation and self-preservation, but his inclinations for ambitious projects to transform and the courage to take on unpopular and risky policies places him nearer the transformative leader pole. Arguably, Xi's high-energy and proactive (acting in anticipation of problems) style sets him apart from more laissez-faire styles of leadership,[28] and from transactional leaders and tinpot dictators. Yet the notion of a transformative leader is an oversimplification; it does not capture the complexities of the Xi phenomenon, not least his repressive and coercive side. Xi's international reputation is so low that some China watchers have found him to be beyond redemption.[29]

In any case, Xi has set in motion great changes and reforms during his first term amid daunting domestic and international challenges. Xi's second term as general secretary will not terminate until 2022 and barring any accidents, he is posed to stay on for a third. Chinese politics has often gone through cycles of control and relaxation, but it is unsure whether the current tight reins will evolve to more moderation and liberalization. Moreover, the worldwide Covid-19 pandemic has greatly complicated China and global affairs, and the theory and practice of governance of (hyper)turbulence has become even more relevant. Accordingly, the jury is still out for Xi's entire career. In any case, the more grandiose of Xi's initiatives will take years, even decades, to come to fruition, and Xi does not accept any finality in such development. In a rhetorical flourish, the Marxist revisionist Eduard Bernstein declared, "The final goal, whatever it may be, is nothing to me; the movement is everything." Similarly, one favorite Xi quip is that "reform and opening up is an on-going process lacking a completion time,"[30] although, unlike Bernstein, his goals are defined. Currently, Xi's second term is unfolding toward the Twentieth Party Congress of 2022. For better or worse, Xi's and China's development will continue to intrigue. Now more than ever, we need an objective, realistic, and contextualized approach to get China right.

Notes

Chapter 1

1. Cited in Michael McFaul, "Xi Jinping Is Not Stalin: How a Lazy Historical Analogy Derailed Washington's China Strategy," *Foreign Affairs*, August 10, 2020, https://www.foreignaffairs.com/articles/united-states/2020-08-10/xi-jinping-not-stalin.
2. *Shibada yilai zhongyao wenxian xuanbian* [A Collection of Important Documents since the Eighteenth Party Congress] (Beijing: Zhongyang wenxian chubanshe, 2014), Vol. 1, p. 498; "Xi Jinping Is Trying to Remake the Chinese Economy," *The Economist*, August 15, 2020, https://www.economist.com/briefing/2020/08/15/xi-jinping-is-trying-to-remake-the-chinese-economy.
3. The realist concept of the security dilemma postulates that in an anarchic world where there is no one central authority to police the behavior of sovereign states, individual states that are responsible for their own security often assume a worst-case scenario. When one state augments its security either through military or economic means, regardless of its intention, other states will feel less secure. Even seemingly innocuous advancements, such as economic and technological development by this one state, can be threatening to other states because of the potential of increasing its military and other capabilities. When these other states attempt to deter the original state by developing their own capabilities, the original state will feel threatened, ending with a spiral of fear, mistrust, and insecurity. Robert Jervis, *Perceptions and Misperceptions in International Politics* (Princeton, NJ: Princeton University Press, 1976), chap. 3; Robert Jervis, "Cooperation under the Security Dilemma," *World Politics*, Vol. 30, No. 2, January 1978, pp. 167–214. Liberals and constructivists, on the other hand, tend to dismiss the concept as a self-fulfilling prophecy.
4. Graham Allison and Robert D. Blackwell, *Lee Kuan Yew* (Cambridge, MA: MIT Press, 2013), p. 17.
5. Tanner Greer, "Xi Jinping Knows Who His Enemies Are," *Foreign Policy*, November 21, 2019, https://foreignpolicy.com/2019/11/21/xi-jinping-china-communist-party-francois-bougon/; Francois Bougon, *Inside the Mind of Xi Jinping* (London: Hurst, 2017).
6. *National Security Strategy of the United States of America*, December 2017, https://www.whitehouse.gov/wp-content/uploads/2017/12/NSS-Final-12-18-2017-0905.pdf. For a criticism of this popular view, see Jessica Chen Weiss, "A World Safe for Autocracy? China's Rise and the Future of Global Politics," *Foreign Affairs*, July–August 2019, pp. 92–102.
7. Jiayang Fan et al., "Behind the Personality Cult of Xi Jinping," *Foreign Policy*, March 8, 2016, https://foreignpolicy.com/2016/03/08/the-personality-cult-of-xi-jinp

ing-china-leader-communist-party/; Christopher Johnston, "What Deng Taught Xi Jinping: Pragmatism Trumps Ideology," *East Asian Forum*, September 2013, http://www.eastasiaforum.org/2013/09/28/what-deng-taught-xi-jinping-pragmatism-tru mps-ideology/.

8. Examples of book-length studies are Elizabeth Economy, *The Third Revolution* (New York: Oxford University Press, 2018); Kerry Brown, *The World according to Xi: Everything You Need to Know about the New China* (New York: I.B. Tauris, 2018); Carl Minzner, *End of an Era* (New York: Oxford University Press, 2018); Cheng Li, *Chinese Politics in the Xi Jinping Era: Reassessing Collective Leadership* (Washington, DC: Brookings Institution Press, 2016); Willy Wo-lap Lam, *Chinese Politics in the Era of Xi Jinping: Renaissance, Reform, or Retrogression?* (New York: Routledge, 2015). Examples of edited volumes are Hoo Tiang Boon, ed., *Chinese Foreign Policy under Xi* (New York: Routledge, 2017); Robert S. Ross and Jo Inge Bekkevold, eds., *China in the Era of Xi Jinping: Domestic and Foreign Policy Challenges* (Washington, DC: Georgetown University Press, 2016); Steve Tsang and Honghua Men, eds., *China in the Xi Jinping Era* (Cham, Switzerland: Palgrave Macmillan, 2016); John Garrick and Yan Chang Bennett, eds., *China's Socialist Rule of Law Reforms under Xi Jinping* (New York: Routledge, 2016); Zheng Yongnian and Lance L. P. Gore, *China Entering the Xi Jinping Era* (New York: Routledge, 2015); Shao Binhong, ed., *China under Xi Jinping: Its Economic Challenges and Foreign Policy Initiatives* (Leiden: Brill, 2015).

9. Among the three major families of international relations theorists, realists postulate that in an anarchic world that lacks a higher authority to govern the sovereign states, states are fundamentally driven by the pursuit of power, security, and national interests. National security is essentially a matter of self-help that cannot be left to chance, and it is normal for states to hedge, to privilege their material and military power, and do more than is realistically necessary to ensure security. That is why even a neutral state like Switzerland keeps a formidable military. Realists also argue that morality is irrelevant in international relations although it is necessary for states to pay lip service to it. Similarly, they maintain that international institutions, international law, and diplomacy are of limited usefulness in the state's struggle for power, and the latter must be buttressed by military power. In contrast, liberals emphasize the interdependent and interconnected aspects among states, and privilege cooperation to further mutual interests, peace, and prosperity. They hope to rely on international organizations, law, trade, investment, and diplomacy to regulate conflicts. Finally, constructivists argue that reality, including institutions and the state, are socially constructed in a continuous process. Norms, ideas, and identities so constructed become determinants in shaping state and leader behavior, as well as global political outcomes. Other promising but nonmainstream theories include feminist, Marxist, and postmodern views and critical theory. Key works on realism, liberalism, and constructivism are Kenneth N. Waltz's *Theory of International Politics* (Reading, MA: Addison-Wesley, 1979); Robert O. Keohane's *After Hegemony: Cooperation and Discord in the World Political Economy* (Princeton, NJ: Princeton University Press, 1984); and Alexander Wendt's *Social Theory of International Politics* (Cambridge: Cambridge University Press, 1999), respectively.

A Chinese contribution to constructivism by highlighting culture and relationships is Yaqing Qin's *A Relational Theory of World Politics* (Cambridge: Cambridge University Press, 2018).

10. In explaining state behavior, patterns of their interaction, and political outcomes, system-level analysis focuses on system characteristics such as the global distribution of power (unipolar, bipolar, and multipolar configurations) and the way it limits and determines state options. State-level analysis focuses on the characteristics of states, the complex government organizations, interest groups, and public opinion that affect the making of foreign policy. Individual-level analysis concentrates on the characteristics, perceptions, and choices of individual leaders, leadership groups, and their roles in decision-making. While analytically distinct, these three levels of analysis can be combined to achieve a multifaceted exploration of international politics. See the seminal article J. D. Singer, "The Level-of-Analysis Problem in International Relations," *World Politics*, Vol. 14, No. 1, October 1961, pp. 77–92.

11. A discussion of the concept of modernization with an extensive bibliography is "Modernization," updated 2021, enecyclopedia.com, https://www.encyclopedia.com/social-sciences-and-law/political-science-and-government/military-affairs-nonnaval/modernization.

12. Christopher Ansell, Jarle Trondal, and Morten Øgård, eds., *Governance in Turbulent Times* (New York: Oxford University Press, 2017), chaps. 1 and 13; Leslie A. Pal, *Beyond Policy Analysis: Public Issue Management in Turbulent Times*, 5th ed. (Toronto: Nelson, 2014); Yehezkel Dror, *Policymaking under Adversity* (New York: Routledge, 2017).

13. Ansell, Trondal, and Øgård, *Governance in Turbulent Times*, p. 8.

14. See also Sujian Guo, ed., *Political Science and Chinese Political Studies: The State of the Field* (Heidelberg: Springer, 2013).

15. World Bank, *Governance and Development*, https://documents.worldbank.org/en/publication/documents-reports/documentdetail/604951468739447676/governance-and-development.

16. David Levi-Faur, ed., *The Oxford Handbook of Governance* (New York: Oxford University Press, 2014), p. 9 and *passim*.

17. Levi-Faur, *Oxford Handbook of Governance*, p. 9.

18. Robert I. Rotberg, *Transformative Political Leadership* (New York: Oxford University Press, 2012), chap. 5 and *passim*.

19. For a detailed discussion, see William Ascher, *Understanding the Policymaking Process in Developing Countries* (New York: Cambridge University Press, 2017), chaps. 1 and 2; Rotberg, *Transformative Political Leadership*, chap. 2.

20. Levi-Faur, *Oxford Handbook of Governance*, p. 690.

21. Kevin Rudd, "How Xi Jinping Views the World: The Core Interests That Shape China's Behavior," *Foreign Affairs*, May 10, 2018, https://www.foreignaffairs.com/articles/china/2018-05-10/how-xi-jinping-views-world.

22. Kjeld Erik Brodsgaard and Zheng Yongnian, eds., *Bringing the Party Back In* (London: Marshall Cavendish, 2004); Kjeld Erik Brosgaard and Zheng Yongnian, eds., *The Communist Party in Reform* (New York: Routledge, 2006); Yongnian Zheng and

Lance L. P. Gore, eds., *The Chinese Communist Party in Action* (New York: Routledge, 2020); Willy W. Lam, *Routledge Handbook of the Chinese Communist Party* (New York: Routledge, 2018).

23. Merilee Grindle, "Good Enough Governance Revisited," *Development Policy Review*, Vol. 25, No. 5, 2007, pp. 553–574.

24. Brian Hogwood and B. Guy Peters, *The Pathology of Public Policy* (New York: Oxford University Press, 1985).

25. Michael D. Cohen, James G. March, and Johan P. Olsen, "A Garbage Can Model of Organizational Choice," *Administrative Quarterly*, Vol. 17, No. 1, 1972, pp. 1–25.

26. Levi-Faur, *Oxford Handbook of Governance*, pp. 207–208, 217.

27. Vivienne Shue and Patricia M. Thornton, *To Govern China: Evolving Practices of Power* (Cambridge: Cambridge University Press, 2017).

28. Charles Lindblom, "Still Muddling, Not Yet Through," *Public Administration Review*, Vol. 39, No. 6, 1979, pp. 517–526; Christine Rothmayr Allison and Denis Saint-Martin, "Half a Century of 'Muddling': Are We There Yet?," *Policy and Society*, Vol. 30, No. 1, 2011, pp. 1–8.

29. "Unfavorable Views of China Reach Historic Highs in Many Countries," *Pew Research Center*, October 6, 2020, https://www.pewresearch.org/global/2020/10/06/unfavora ble-views-of-china-reach-historic-highs-in-many-countries/.

Chapter 2

1. Crane Brinton, *The Anatomy of Revolution*, rev. ed. (New York: Vintage Books, 1965). In this comparative study of the English, American, French, and Russian revolutions, Brinton identifies patterns and well-defined stages that all had gone through. Brinton argues that revolutions tend to turn more radical and violent with the presence of external counterrevolutionary threats. This is an early manifestation of linkage politics, an approach that postulates that domestic policy is often affected by external environment/policy and vice versa. For instance, intensified cultural revolution radicalism has often been attributed to the perceived foreign threat, such as the escalating Vietnam War and the impending Sino-Soviet split in the 1960s. See Chen Jian, "China's Involvement in the Vietnam War, 1964–69," *China Quarterly*, No. 142, June 1995, pp. 356–387. On the other hand, if one takes a long historical perspective, contemporary politics of the four countries studied by Brinton can also be interpreted as the continuation of the struggles among the conflicting ideals generated by their revolutions—the values of liberty, equality, and fraternity for the French Revolution, and the values of the American Constitution and the legacy of the American Civil War. For a perspective on the revolutionary heritage on contemporary Chinese political economy, see Elizabeth J. Perry, "Studying Chinese Politics: Farewell to Revolution?," *China Journal*, No. 57, January 2007, pp. 1–12.

2. Volunteerism in this context means the practice of pushing the subjective human willpower even though the requisite objective conditions are lacking, and this is still

an important strand of thinking within the CCP. For a discussion of this and the concepts of utopianism and permanent revolution, see Maurice Meisner, *Mao's China and After: A History of the People's Republic*, 3rd ed. (New York: Free Press, 1999).

3. For historical accounts, see Jack Gray, *Rebellions and Revolutions: China from the 1800s to 2000*, 2nd ed. (Oxford: Oxford University Press, 2002); Meisner, *Mao's China*; Andrew G. Walder, *China under Mao: A Revolution Derailed* (Cambridge, MA: Harvard University Press, 2015).

4. Walder, *China under Mao*, pp. 324–331. In PPP terms, the figures are US$987 in 1990 and US$2,933 in 2000.

5. Cheng Li, *China's Leaders: The New Generation* (Lanham, MD: Rowman & Littlefield, 2001), chap. 4.

6. Two detailed biographies are Xi Zhongxun zhuan bianweihui, *Xi Zhongxun Zhuan* [Biography of Xi Zhongxun], 2 vols. (Beijing: Zhongyang wenxian chubanshe, 2008, 2013); Xi Zhongxun geming shengya bianjizu, *Xi Zhongxun geming shengya* [The Revolutionary Life and Career of Xi Zhongxun] (Beijing: Zhongguo wenshi chubanshe, 2002); Mark O'Neill, "Honours for Guerilla Chief Who Became Party Leader," *South China Morning Post* (hereafter *SCMP*), June 3, 2002.

7. Jia Juchuan, "Luhuo chunqing' de Xi Zhongxun" [Xi Zhongxun's Art of Perfection], *Dangshi bolan*, No. 3, 2003, pp. 40–42; "Gaofeng liangjie Xi Zhongxun" [Xi Zhongxun's Noble Character and Unimpeachable Integrity], *Dangshi bolan*, No. 2, 2004, pp. 34–36; Shui Xinying, "Cong Shaanbei huangtudi zoujin Zhongnanhai de Xi Zhongxun" [Xi Zhongxun: From the Yellow Earth of Shaanbei to Zhongnanhai], *Dangshi wenyuan*, No. 12, 2009, pp. 13–17.

8. Mark Selden, *The Yenan Way in Revolutionary China* (Cambridge, MA: Harvard University Press, 1971); Meisner, *Mao's China*, chap. 4.

9. This metaphor was originally used by Lucian Pye.

10. Frederick Teiwes, *Politics and Purges in China: Rectification and the Decline of Party Norms, 1950–1956*, 2nd ed. (Armonk, NY: M. E. Sharpe, 1993), pp. 161–163.

11. Gao Xiao, *Ta jiang lingdao Zhongguo: Xi Jinping zhuang* [He Will Soon Lead China: A Biography of Xi Jinping] (Carle Place, NY: Mirror Books, 2010), p. 116.

12. Qi Xin, "Woyu Xi Zhongxun fengyu shuangban 55 ge chunqiu" [My Companionship with Xi Zhongxun for a Tumultuous 55 Years], *Zhongheng*, No. 1, 1999, p. 41.

13. Xi Jinping, "Woshi ruhe kuaru zhengjiedi" [How I Entered Politics], *Lingdao wencui*, November 2000, pp. 62–67. A more complete version of this interview with Yang Xiaohuai is in *Zhonghua ernu*, No. 7, 2000, reproduced in *yicai.com*, January 6, 2013, http://www.yicai.com/news/2013/01/2392583.html.

14. Qi, "My Companionship with Xi Zhongxun," p. 41.

15. Qi, "My Companionship with Xi Zhongxun," p. 42.

16. Some recently published sources tend to extol Xi and put him in a heroic light, although much information can also be collaborated by archival sources. The following, unless otherwise stated, draws mainly from Xi Jinping's own accounts as reported in the following: "Woshi huangtudi de erzi" [I Am a Son of the Yellow Earth]; the earliest but abridged version was published in *Quanguo xinshumu*, December 2002. Among the many reprints, the most detailed version is in *Xibu dakaifa*, No. 9, 2012, pp. 109–112;

Zhang Lichen, "Cong cunzhishu dao shengwei shuji" [From Village Branch Secretary to Secretary of the Provincial Party Committee], *Shenzhou*, No. 2, 2004, pp. 8–12; "Xi Jinping zeng dangliao liunian cunganbu" [Xi Jinping Has Worked as a Village Cadre for Six Years], *Lantai neiwei*, No. 6, 2011, pp. 50–52. A biographical chapter is in Wu Zhifei and Yu Wei, *Zhongguo gaoduan fangwen, 1: Ying xiang Zhongguo gaoceng juece de 18 ren* [High-Level Interviews in China, 1: The 18 Influential People in China's High-Level Decision-Making] (Shanghai: Dongfang chubanshe, 2006), pp. 129–160; Wu Zhifei, "Xi Jinping: Cong huangtugaopo dao Shanghaitan" [Xi Jinping: From the Yellow Earth High Plateau to the Bund of Shanghai], *Dangshi zongheng*, No. 5, 2007, pp. 16–21. Two interviews that directly quote Xi are "Xi Jinping mantan wangxi 30 nian" [Xi Jinping Talks Casually about His Past Thirty Years], *Dangshi wenyuan*, No. 3, 2004, pp. 52–53; "Zuo youzhiqi youzuowei deyidai: Xi Zhongxun zhizi Xi Jinping fangtanlu" [Be Part of a Generation with Courage and Achievement: An Interview with Xi Zhongxun's Son Xi Jinping], *Jiachang*, No. 2, 1997, p. 4; Xi, "How I Entered Politics"; "Wodi shangshan xiaxiang jingli" [My Experience of Going Up to the Mountains and Down to the Countryside], *Xuexi bolan*, No. 12, 2010, pp. 16–17. Xi repeated his stories in a TV interview, "Xi Jinping's Exclusive Interview with Reporters on His Experience of Joining the Production Brigade" [习近平接受记者专访 讲述自己插队经历] February, 2019]. Available on YouTube, https://www.yout ube.com/watch?v=QpBoJRhCOR8.

17. Hu Lili and Liang Jian, *Xi Jinping zhuanji* [A Biography of Xi Jinping] (Deer Park, NY: Mingjing chubanshe, 2012), p. 70.

18. Xi, "Be Part of a Generation," p. 4. At the mass "struggle meetings" the victims suffered physical and psychological violence and humiliation by mobs; they had to admit guilt for trumped-up charges, and many were killed.

19. Xi, "How I Entered Politics," p. 66.

20. Yang Ping, "Xi Zhongxun and Xi Jinping de fuzi qing" [The Father-and-Son Relationship between Xi Zhongxun and Xi Jinping], *Sohu*, January 5, 2013, http://m.sohu.com/n/556256314/?page=2&show_rest_pages=1&image_mode=f&v=2&_once_=000027_pages_leftallv2; see also Chris Buckley and Didi Kirsten Tatlow, "Cultural Revolution Shaped Xi Jinping, from Schoolboy to Survivor," *New York Times*, September 25, 2015, https://www.nytimes.com/2015/09/25/world/asia/xi-jinping-china-cultural-revolution.html.

21. Xi, "How I Entered Politics," p. 67.

22. The most detailed analysis is Liu Xiaomeng, *Zhongguo zhiqing shi: dachao* [A History of the *Zhiqing*: The Great Tide, 1966–1980] (Beijing: Dangdai Zhongguo chubanshe, 2009). In English, see Thomas P. Bernstein, *Up to the Mountains and Down to the Villages: The Transfer of Youth from Urban to Rural China* (New Haven: Yale University Press, 1977). See also Guobin Yang, "China's Zhiqing Generation: Nostalgia, Identity, and Cultural Resistance in the 1990s," *Modern China*, Vol. 29, No. 3, July 2003.

23. The *hukou* system strictly divided all Chinese into rural and urban residents. While benefits such as food quotas, subsidized housing, social security, and rights to education, employment, medical care, and retirement benefits were provided to urban

residents, they were denied to their rural counterparts. When farmers left to work and live in urban areas, they were normally denied the above-mentioned services, depending on local rules and their employment. The fear was that these migrant workers could overwhelm urban infrastructure and social services.

24. A more contemporary source is Interviews and Editorial Office of the Central Party School, *Xi Jinping de 7 nian zhiqing suiyu* [Xi Jinping's Seven Years' Experience as a *Zhiqing*] (Beijing: Zhongyang dangxiao chubanshe, 2017).

25. *Liangjiahe* (Xian: Shaanxi renmin chubanshe, 2018), pp. 64–67.

26. Xi, "Son of the Yellow Earth," p. 110; Xi, "How I Entered Politics."

27. Hu and Liang, *Biography of Xi Jinping*, p. 84.

28. *Shibada yilai zhongyao wenxian xuanbian* [A Collection of Important Documents since the Eighteenth Party Congress] (Beijing: Zhongyang wenxian chubanshe, 2014), Vol. 1, p. 659.

29. "Xinren Shanghai shiwei shuji Xi Jinping beihou de gushi" [The Background Story of the New Secretary of the Shanghai MPC], *Xinhua*, March 26, 2007, http://news.xinhuanet.com/blog/2007-03/26/content_5897527.htm.

30. Dossiers were kept on every citizen at their place of work until recently.

31. James Townsend and Brantly Womack, *Politics in China* (Boston: Little, Brown, 1986), pp. 289–294.

32. Qi, "My Companionship with Xi Zhongxun," p. 42.

33. Townsend and Womack, *Politics in China*, pp. 246, 296–297.

34. A formal appraisal entered into everyone's dossier.

35. Xi, "How I Entered Politics," p. 66.

36. Zhang, "Village Branch Secretary," p. 9.

37. "Xi Jinping yu Renmin ribao ersan wangshi" [A Few Xi Jinping Events Involving the *People's Daily*], *Dagongwang*, June 16, 2018, http://news.takungpao.com/paper/q/2018/0616/3578025.html.

38. Hu and Liang, *Biography of Xi Jinping*, p. 107; Gao, *He Will Soon Lead China*, p. 171.

39. Suzanne Pepper, "Education," in Roderick MacFarquhar and John K. Fairbank, eds., *The Cambridge History of China*, Vol. 15 (Cambridge: Cambridge University Press, 1991), pp. 571–575.

40. Hu and Liang, *Biography of Xi Jinping*, pp. 104–105.

41. Xi, "How I Entered Politics."

42. "Wang Qishan," *china.org.cn*, http://www.china.org.cn/english/chuangye/62939.htm; "Wan Qishan di zhiqings suiyu: yu Xi Jinping jiaohao tonggai yichuang beizi" [Wang Qishan's Life as a *Zhiqing*: He Shared a Blanket with His Good Friend Xi Jinping], *Ifeng*, September 8, 2013, http://news.ifeng.com/history/zhongguoxiandaishi/detail_2013_09/08/29416157_0.shtml; Xiang Jiangyu, *Xi Jinping bandi* [Xi Jinping's Background Connections] (Carle Place, NY: Mingjing chubanshe, 2011), pp. 253–270.

43. Michael Bonnin, "The 'Lost Generation': Its Definition and Its Role in Today's Chinese Elite Politics," *Social Research*, Vol. 73, No. 1, Spring 2005, pp. 245–274; Yixin Chen, "Lost in Revolution and Reform: The Socioeconomic Pains of China's Red Guards

Generation, 1966–1996," *Journal of Contemporary China*, Vol. 8, No. 21, 1999, pp. 219–239; Li, *China's Leaders*, chap. 4.

44. *Collection of Important Documents*, Vol. 1, p. 659.

45. Cheng Li, "China's Fifth Generation: Is Diversity a Source of Strength or Weakness?," in J. Patrick Boyd, L. Gordon Flake, Cheng Li, Kenneth B. Pyle, Shelley Rigger, and Richard J. Samuels, eds., *Emerging Leaders in East Asia: The Next Generation of Political Leadership in China, Japan, South Korea, and Taiwan* (Seattle: National Bureau of Asian Research, September, 2008); Michael Dillon, *China's Rulers: The Fifth Generation Takes Power, 2012–13* (London: Europe China Research and Advice Network, 2012).

46. Bonnin, "The Lost Generation," pp. 263–264; Leah Caprice, "The Lost Generation of the 17th Chinese Communist Party Politburo," *China Brief*, Vol. 8, No. 19, October 7, 2008.

47. Cheng Li, "A Biographical and Factional Analysis of the Post-2012-Politburo," *China Leadership Monitor*, No. 41, June 6, 2013, p. 8.

48. A couple of my esteemed colleagues are good examples.

49. The National People's Congress usually held in March is always shadowed by a conference held by the Chinese People's Political Consultative Conference (an organization formed by the eight "democratic parties" whose alleged function is to advise the CCP) at the same time, and they are collectively called the "Two Sessions."

50. A news clip on the visit is http://v.qq.com/cover/l/laf221fslrlnwvk.html?vid=t001 6han1bu. A news clip on the conference is http://v.qq.com/cover/l/laf221fslrlnwvk.html?vid=x0016r2d26c.

51. "Liangjiahe zaoshen yundong xinpianzhang?" [Is Liangjiahe a New Page in a Deification Movement?], *VOA*, October 20, 2015, http://www.voachinese.com/artic leprintview/3013742.html.

52. "Xi Jinping tongzhi zai zhiqing renshi shang cunzai yanzhong cuowu" [Comrade Xi Jinping's Serious Mistake in His Understanding of the *Zhiqing* Issue], *Boxun*, July 25, 2012, http://blog.boxun.com/hero/201207/sdgongl1234/9_1.shtml.

53. See, for example, "Meiti dianping Zhongguo 50 hou: zheteng chulai di yidairen" [The Media Discuss China's 1950s Generation: The Generation That Has Grown Up among Torment and Adversity], *Zhongguoxinwenwang*, April 12, 2013, http://www.chinanews.com/gn/2013/04-12/4723999.shtml.

54. *Gaoganzidi* is a term introduced during the Cultural Revolution, but modern usage refers to children of officials occupying deputy provincial, ministerial, and division posts in the Party, government, and military, respectively.

55. Xi Jinping, "Qinfen, zhencheng, tanran, jinze: Xi Jinping tan zuoguan yu zuoren" [Diligence, Truthfulness, Honesty, Accountability: Xi Jinping on How to Be an Official and a Human Being], *Shidaichao*, No. 8, 2000, p. 34.

56. Xi, "My Experience of Going Up," p. 17; Xi, "Be Part of a Generation." An attempt to explore the Xi phenomenon using a social psychological approach is Paul Nesbitt-Larking and Alfred L. Chan, "The Political Leadership of Xi Jinping: Narratives of Integrity through Transformation" (in progress).

Chapter 3

1. Information about Geng Biao's post-1949 career in English is rare—he is not even listed in *China Vitae,* https://www.chinavitae.com/. For one of the few mentions, see David Shambaugh, "China's 'Quiet Diplomacy': The International Department of the Chinese Communist Party," *China,* Vol. 5, No. 1, March 2007, pp. 38–39.

2. Geng Biao, *Geng Biao huiyilu 1909–1949* [The Memoirs of Geng Biao, 1909–1949] (Nanjing: Jiangsu renmin chubanshe, 1998); Geng, *Biao huiyilu 1949–1992* [*The Memoirs of Geng Biao, 1949–1992*] (Nanjing: Jiangsu renmin chubanshe, 1998).

3. For further discussions, see Wei Li and Lucian Pye, "The Ubiquitous Role of the *Mishu* in Chinese Politics," *China Quarterly,* Vol. 132, December, 1992, pp. 913–936; Wen-Hsuan Tsai and Nicola Dean, "Lifting the Veil of the CCP's *Mishu* System: Unrestricted Informal Politics within an Authoritarian Regime, *China Journal,* No. 73, 2015, pp. 158–185.; Xia Li Lollar and Anne Wing Hamilton, "Patronage or Prebendalism? The *Mishu/Shouzhang* Relationship and Corruption in Chinese Politics," *China Review,* Vol. 10, No. 1, Spring 2010, pp. 157–182.

4. Institutional *mishu* serve party organizations such as the Central Office of the CCP, whereas personal *mishu* (with at least four categories, political, confidential, security, and life) serve officials at the provincial/ministerial rank and above. Examples of institutional *mishu* are Xi Zhongxun, who served as general *mishu* of the State Council, and Geng Biao, who was secretary general of the CMC. Yet despite their functional differentiations, many institutional *mishu* end up essentially serving individual leaders. Tsai and Dean, "Lifting the Veil."

5. Li and Pye, "Ubiquitous Role," p. 928.

6. For lists of *mishu* who held deputy provincial-ministerial leadership rank and above as of June 2013, see Tsai and Dean, "Lifting the Veil," pp. 180–184.

7. "Dangnian gei Geng Biao dang *mishu* de qingxing" [As Secretary for Geng Biao in Those Days], *Qiyi shequ,* October 27, 2010, http://old.1237/gov.cn/n87408c109.aspx; "Xi Jinping's Meiguo zuji" [Xi Jinping's Footprints in the United States], *Nangfang zhoumu,* September 25, 2015, http://news.southcn.com/china/content/2015-09/25/content_133613785.htm.

8. Evan A. Feigenbaum, *China's Techno-warriors: National Security and Strategic Competition from the Nuclear to the Informational Age* (Stanford: Stanford University Press, 2003), pp. 132–133.

9. Robert S. Ross, ed., *China, the United States, and the Soviet Union: Tri-polarity and Policy* (Armonk, NY: M.E. Sharpe, 1993), p. 24.

10. Xi Jinping, "Woshi ruhe kuaru zhengjiedi" [How I Entered Politics], *Lingdao wencui,* November 2000; Xi, "Woshi huangtudi de erzi" [I Am a Son of the Yellow Earth], *Quanguo xinshumu,* December 2002, p. 110.

11. Yang Xiaohuai, "Xi Jinping: Woshi zheyang kuaru zhengtande" [Xi Jinping: How I Become Involved in Politics], *Baokan huicui,* No. 9, 2004, p. 14.

12. These queries are raised in Gao Xiao, *Ta jiang lingdao Zhongguo: Xi Jinping zhuang* [He Will Soon Lead China: A Biography of Xi Jinping] (Carle Place, NY: Mirror

Books, 2010), pp. 214–217; Hu Lili and Liang Jian, *Xi Jinping zhuanji* [A Biography of Xi Jinping] (Deer Park, NY: Mingjing chubanshe, 2012), pp. 138–141.

13. See, for example, Tristan Kenderdine, "How China's Poorest Province Became a Political Kingmaker," *Diplomat*, July 19, 2017, http://thediplomat.com/2017/07/how-chinas-poorest-province-became-a-political-kingmaker/.

14. Willy Wo-lap Lam, *Chinese Politics in the Era of Xi Jinping: Renaissance, Reform, or Retrogression?* (New York: Routledge, 2015), p. 43.

15. "Xi Jinping tongzhi zai Zhengding" [Comrade Xi Jinping at Zhengding], *Hebei ribao*, January 4, 2014; Zhongyang dangxiao caifang shilu bianjishi, *Xi Jinping zai Zhengding* (Beijing: Zhongyang dangxiao chubanshe, 2019.

16. See an article based on a recording of an interview with Xi Jinping. Yong Huaqi, "Xi Jinping hui Zhengding" [Xi Jinping Returns to Zhengding], *Lingdao wensui*, No. 21, 2009, p. 66.

17. Gao, *He Will Soon Lead China*, pp. 228–229.

18. "Comrade Xi Jinping at Zhengding"; "Zhengding fanshenji" [The Thorough Turnaround at Zhengding], *Renmin ribao*, June 17, 1984. This original version with twenty-one hundred words is augmented by a more detailed, or allegedly unabridged and original, version (with fifty-two hundred words) in *Zhongguo minshu bolan*, No. 2, 2015. See also "Zai Zhengding caifang" [Gathering News at Zhengding], *Lingdao wencui*, No. 8, 2015, pp. 84–87.

19. For detailed analysis of changes in other parts of China, see Daniel Kelliher, *Peasant Power in China: The Era of Rural Reform, 1979–1989* (New Haven: Yale University Press, 1992); Jean C. Oi, *State and Peasants in Contemporary China: The Political Economy of Village Government* (Berkeley: University of California Press, 1991).

20. "Thorough Turnaround at Zhengding."

21. "Comrade Xi Jinping at Zhengding."

22. "Xi Jinping di laoganbu qingjie, zhexie gushi ni yexumei" [Xi Jinping's Passion regarding the Old Cadres: Stories You Probably Do Not Know], *Meili shijiazhuang*, n.d., http://www.shijiazhuangzx.com/sjzxw/4843.html. Accessed June 7, 2018.

23. "Xi Jinping zunlao di 10 ze xiao gushi" [Ten Small Stories about Xi Jinping's Respect for the Old], *Renminwang*, February10, 2015, http://politics.people.com.cn/n/2015/0210/c1001-26542271.html.

24. "Comrade Xi Jinping at Zhengding"; Zhang Wei, "Xi Jinping zheyang zao xianwei shuji" [This Was How Xi Jinping Performed as County Party Secretary], *Shijian*, No. 5, 2015, pp. 22–23; Li Zhongzhi and Cao Yangkui, "Tong huxi caineng xinshuangyi" [Breathing Together So That Our Hearts Can Beat Together], *Hebei huabao*, No. 9, 2013; Wang Youfei, "Woyu Xi Jinping zai Zhengding de jiaowang" [My Encounters with Xi Jinping at Zhengding], *Wenshi bolan*, No. 11, 2015, pp. 46–48.

25. Yong Huaqi, "Xi Jinping hui Zhengding" [Xi Jinping Returns to Zhengding], *Lingdao wencui*, No. 21, 2009, p. 66.

26. "My Encounters with Xi Jinping."

27. "Thorough Turnaround at Zhengding."

28. For a discussion of the zigzag path of reforms in the 1980s detailing the conflicts and disputes over power, policy, and ideology, see Joseph Fewsmith, *Dilemmas of Reform in China: Political Conflict and Economic Debate* (Armonk, NY: M.E. Sharpe, 1994).

29. Ke Yunlu, *Xinxing* [New Star] (Beijing: Renmin wenxue chubanshe, 1985).

30. Gao, *He Will Soon Lead China*, pp. 228–229.

31. "80 niandai woguo disantidui jianshe di guocheng: xuanbu, peiyang, jiqi jiji zuoyong" [The Process of Building the "Third Echelon" in the 1980s: Selections, Cultivations, and Their Practical Functions], *Wenxuecheng*, December 18, 2014, http://www.lunwenstudy.com/zzzhidu/47500.html. At that time, Chinese colleagues told me that even middle-aged people could hardly put in an eight-hour day because of malnutrition.

32. "Shiyi jie sanzhong quanhui hou zhongyang xuanba nianqing ganbu neimu" [The Inside Story of How Party Central Selected Young Cadres after the Third Plenum of the Eleventh Party Congress], *Xinhuanet*, June 10, 2009, news.xinhuanet.com/theory/2009-06/10/content_11517644.htm. For more details, see also "Zhongguo tese ganbu houbei li liang: disan tidui" [Reserve Cadres' Capability with Chinese Characteristics: The "Third Echelon"], *XYNU*, numbers 1 to 9, April 2, 2015, http://znzg.xynu.edu.cn/Html/?23435.html, http://znzg.xynu.edu.cn/Html/?23434.html, http://znzg.xynu.edu.cn/Html/?23433.html, http://znzg.xynu.edu.cn/Html/?23432.html, http://znzg.xynu.edu.cn/Html/?23430.html, http://znzg.xynu.edu.cn/Html/?23429.html, http://znzg.xynu.edu.cn/Html/?23428.html, http://znzg.xynu.edu.cn/Html/?23427.html.

33. "Inside Story."

34. "Process of Building the Third Echelon."

35. Chen Yun, *Chen Yun Wenxuan* [Selected Writings from Chen Yun] (Beijing: Renmin chubanshe, 1995), Vol. 3, p. 294.

36. In Hu Yaobang's imprecise schema, the "first echelon" refers to the top decision-makers who were elders; the "second echelon" refers to those who worked at the front line of the Secretariat and the State Council.

37. CCP Central Organizational Department, Office of the Central Party Research, and Central Archives, *Materials on the Organizational History of the CCP* (Beijing: Zhonggong dangshi chubanshe, 2000), Vol. 7 (*shang*), p. 17.

38. "Disan tidu mingdan jianli qianhou: qiyong yidai xinren" [Before and after the Drawing Up of the "Third Echelon" List: the Engagement of a New Generation of People], *Zhongguo xinwen zhoukan*, September 16, 2014, http://history.sina.com.cn/bk/ds/2014-09-16/1100100211.shtml.

39. Cui Wunian, "Cong disan tidui shuoqi" [On the Third Echelon], *Sina*, June 22, 2012, http://blog.sina.com.cn/s/blog_5093ee610-10100iw.html.

40. Cui, "On the Third Echelon."

41. The practice then, which stressed decentralization of the power of personnel selection, was for the COD and central agencies to control one administrative level down, although with recentralization, the central agencies could control one or more administrative levels down.

42. From Central Committee membership to the alternate of the Politburo, then the Politburo, and then the PBSC consists of three steps.

43. Zhang Tongfang, *Cong Xi Zhongxun duo Xi Jinping* [From Xi Zhongxun to Xi Jinping] (n.p.: Caida chubanshe, 2011), p. 100.

44. For details of Xi Zhongxun's work in the Secretariat, see Xi Zhongxun zhuan bianweihui, *Xi Zhongxun Zhuan* [Biography of Xi Zhongxun], 2 vols. (Beijing: Zhongyang wenxian chubanshe, 2008, 2013), Vol. 2, chap. 23.

45. For details and regional variations in the implementations of this policy see "Before and After the Drawing Up"; "Process of Building the Third Echelon"; "Reserve Cadres' Capability"; "Zhonggong jiebanren tidui ruhe liangcheng" [How the CCP's Successors Echelons were Formed], *Caijing.com.cn*, March 29, 2012, blog.caijing. com.cn/expert_article-151453-34553.shtml.

46. "Before and after the Drawing Up."

47. "Before and after the Drawing Up."

48. Gao, *He Will Soon Lead China*, pp. 222–223.

Chapter 4

1. For more details, see Brian Hook, ed., *Fujian: Gateway to Taiwan* (New York: Oxford University Press, 1996).

2. Gong Xin, "Tantan wozhidao di zai Fujian shi di Xi Jinping" [About the Xi Jinping That I Knew in Fujian], *Boxun*, February 25, 2008, http://www.boxun.com/forum/200802/boxun2007b/420032.shtml. See also Yang Zhongmei, *Xi Jinping: zhanzai lishi shizi lukou de Zhonggong xin ling dao ren* [Xi Jinping: A New Leader at a Historical Crossroads] (Taibei Shi: Shi bao wenhua chuban qiye gufen youxian gongsi, 2011), pp. 108 and 120.

3. Hu Lili and Liang Jian, *Xi Jinping zhuanji* [A Biography of Xi Jinping] (Deer Park, NY: Mingjing chubanshe, 2012), p. 148.

4. Xi Jinping, "Qinfen, zhencheng, tanran, jinze: Xi Jinping tan zuoguan yu zuoren" [Diligence, Truthfulness, Honesty, Accountability: Xi Jinping on How to Be an Official and a Human Being], *Shidaichao*, No. 8, 2000.

5. Robert Kleinberg, *China's "Opening" to the Outside World: The Experiment with Foreign Capitalism* (Boulder, CO: Westview Press, 1990), pp. 78–84.

6. Fujiansheng renmin zhengfu, Fujian Nianjian Bianzuan Weiyunhui, ed., *Fujian nianjian* [Fujian Yearbook] (Fuzhou: Fujian renmin chubanshe, 2012), p. 41.

7. Hu and Liang, *Biography of Xi Jinping*, pp. 149–150.

8. Gao Xiao, *Ta jiang lingdao Zhongguo: Xi Jinping zhuang* [He Will Soon Lead China: A Biography of Xi Jinping] (Carle Place, NY: Mirror Books, 2010), pp. 233–234.

9. Lina Tang, Yang Zhao, Kai Yin, and Jingzhu Zhao, "City Profile: Xiamen," *Cities*, No. 31, 2013.

10. Yue-man Yeung, Jonna Lee, and Gordon Kee, "China's Special Economic Zones at 30," *Eurasian Geography and Economics*, Vol. 50, No. 2, 2009, p. 225.

11. Wu Zhifei, "Xi Jinping: Cong huangtugaopo dao shanghaitan" [Xi Jinping: From the Yellow Earth High Plateau to the Bund of Shanghai], *Dangshi zongheng*, No. 5, 2007, p. 20.

12. "Xi Jinping Sharpened His Political Skills in Fujian," *SCMP*, October 24, 2012.

13. "Xi Jinping ceng zhuchi Xiamen shetai zhanlue yanjiu" [Xi Jinping Once Took Charge of the Strategic Planning Regarding Taiwan], *Wenweipo*, December 28, 2012.

14. "Renmin qunzhong shi women liliang di yuanquan: ji Zhongyang zongshuji Xi Jinping" [The Masses and the People Are the Source of Our Strength: On CCP General Secretary Xi Jinping], *Xinhua*, December 25, 2012, http://www.xinhuanet.com/politics/2012-12/25/c_114148683_6.htm. The lengthy article is one of the most comprehensive official biographical accounts of Xi Jinping's career, and apart from the laudatory tone, most of the facts enumerated can be collaborated by existing archives. A Chinese version is in *Wenweipo*, December 24, 2012.

15. Pamphlet often translated as Liu Shaoqi, *How to Be a Good Communist* (Peking: Foreign Languages Press, 1951).

16. Often associated with Deng Xiaoping's foreign policy principle (discussed later), this ancient notion is exemplified by a historical incident. After Goujian (520–465 BC), the king of Yue, suffered a humiliating defeat by Fuchai (528–473 BC), the king of Wu, Goujian spent years devoted to recuperation and strengthening. Eventually Goujian defeated Fuchai and became the last important warlord of the Spring and Autumn period.

17. Wu Nan and Gao Xiao, *Peng Liyuan yu Xi Jinping* [Peng Liyuan and Xi Jinping] (Deer Park, NY: Haye chubanshe, 2013), pp. 189–190.

18. "Portrait of Vice President Xi Jinping: 'Ambitious Survivor' of the Cultural Revolution," *Wikileaks*, November 16, 2009, https://wikileaks.org/plusd/cables/09BE IJING3128_a.html; Ming Hong, "Xi Jinping yu Peng Liyuan de gushi" [The Story of Xi Jinping and Peng Liyuan], *Juece yu xinxi*, Nos. 1–2, 2005, p. 103.

19. Wu and Gao, *Peng Liyuan and Xi Jinping*, chap. 3; Kerry Brown, *CEO, China: The Rise of Xi Jinping* (London: I. B. Tauris, 2016), pp. 11–114; Martin Macmillan, *Together They Hold Up the Sky: The Story of China's Xi Jinping and Peng Liyuan* (Campbell, CA: FastPencil, 2012), pp. 29–31, chap. 12.

20. Zhang Lichen, "Cong cunzhishu du shengwei shuji" [From Village Branch Secretary to Secretary of the Provincial Party Committee], *Shenzhou*, Vol. 2 (2004), pp. 10–11.

21. Zhang, "Village Branch Secretary," p. 10; "Weishenme shi Xi Jinping?" [Why Xi Jinping?], *Zhaoshang zhoukan*, No. 5, 2007, p. 54.

22. Zhang, "Village Branch Secretary," p. 11.

23. "Peng Liyuan yanzhongde Xi Jinping" [Xi Jinping in the Eyes of Peng Liyuan], *Baokan huicui*, No. 4, 2004, pp. 27 and 29.

24. Zhang Jie, "Jianjue zhanzai Hu Yaobang yibian di Xi Zhongxun [Xi Zhongxun Stands Firmly on the Side of Hu Yaobang], *Hu Yaobang shiliao*, December 2012, http://www.hybsl.cn/beijingcankao/beijingfenxi/2012-12-11/32742.html.

25. Gong, "About the Xi Jinping That I Knew When I Was in Fujian."

26. Zhang, "Village Branch Secretary," pp. 10–11.

27. For an account of the pre-1949 communist movements in Fujian and Ningde see Dangdai Zhongguo congshu bianjibu, *Dangdai Zhongguo di Fujian* [Fujian in Contemporary China] (Beijing: Dangdai Zhongguo chubanshe, 1991), pp. 32–38.

28. For more details about Ningde's past and its development until 2008, see "Ningde kaikuang" [A Brief Description of Ningde], *Ningde wang*, December 10, 2008, http://www.ndwww.cn/zhengwu/ndgl/ndjs/200812/45676.html.

29. Xi Jinping, *Baituo Pinkun* [Overcoming Poverty] (Fuzhou: Fujian renmin chubanshe, 1992), hereafter, *BTPK*, pp. 59, 70, 113. Xi euphemized Mao's biased development strategy with the words "for reasons that we all knew."

30. *BTPK*, pp. 50–51.

31. "Dui Mindong jingji fazhande sikao: Zhonggong Ningde diweishuji Xi Jinping tongzhi caifanglu" [Thoughts on the Economic Development of Mindong: An Interview with CCP Ningde Prefectural Party Committee Secretary Xi Jinping], *Fujian luntan*, No. 2, 1989, pp. 46–47; *BTPK*, pp. 52, 55, and 69. Zhang, "Village Branch Secretary," pp. 10–11.

32. *BTPK*, p. 53.

33. Liang Jian, *Xi Jinping Xinzhuan* [A New Biography of Xi Jinping] (Deer Park, NY: Mirror Books, 2012), p. 172.

34. Even today, a man's wedding is often referred to as his parents' taking in of a daughter-in-law since by tradition a marriage is regarded as an affair between families rather than the individuals. A traditional belief that the groom's parents should provide a house or lodging for the newlyweds is still relatively alive, especially in the rural areas.

35. Zhang, "Village Branch Secretary," p. 11; "Xi Jinping yi Ningde fanfu" [Xi Jinping Reminiscences about Anticorruption at Ningde], *Renminwang*, October 28, 2014, http://news.ifeng.com/a/20141028/42315072_0.shtml.

36. Zhang, "Village Branch Secretary," 11; *BTPK*, p. 21.

37. *BTPK*, pp. 22–23.

38. *BTPK*, pp. 61–63.

39. *BTPK*, pp. 45–48.

40. "Masses and the People."

41. "Xi Jinping zai Fujian: yibu yibu 17 nian" [Xi Jinping at Fujian: The Many Steps that Took Seventeen Years], *Sina*, April 5, 2007, Finance.sina.com.cn/leadership/crz/20070405/01593473971.shtml.

42. Li Xiaolin et al., "Bamin daidi minzufeng: Fang Zhonggong Fujian shengwei fushuji Xi Jinping" [Fujian's Land and Folk Culture: An Interview with Xi Jinping, Deputy Secretary of the Fujian PPC], *Minzu tuanjie*, No. 1, 1991, p. 8.

43. "Xi Jinping at Fujian."

44. "Xi Jinping at Fujian."

45. Li, "Fujian's Land and Folk Culture."

46. *BTPK*, p. 160.

47. Misha Blenny, *McMafia: A Journey through the Global Criminal Underworld* (London: Vintage Books, 2008), pp. 377–379. See also Federico Varese, *Mafia on the Move: How Organized Crime Conquers New Territories* (Princeton, NJ: Princeton University Press, 2011), chaps. 6 and 7.

48. For official propaganda lauding Jin Fusheng, see Zhang Hongwei and Lin Maochun, "Jin Fusheng's de gongpu qingjie" [Jin Fung's Sentiment of a Public Servant], *Gongchan dangyuan*, No. 8, 2000, pp. 18–19; Ren Xiaogang, "Wuhui de kuaize" [Quick Choices without Regrets], *Shidaiqiao*, No. 11, 2000.

49. For the Jin Fusheng case see Liu Zheming, "Yuan Fujian shengwei xuanchuan buchang bei 'shuanggui'" [Former Propaganda Director of the Fujian's PPC Was Double Censored], *Jinri nangguo*, No. 2, 2006, pp. 46–47, http://news/qq.com/a/20051104/001545.htm; ; "Fujian Party Official Jailed for Life," *SCMP*, January 19, 2010.

50. "2017 nian Ningde shi guomin jingji he shehui fazhan tongji gongbao" [A Statistical Communiqué of Economic and Social Development in Ningde City, 2017], *Zhongguo Ningde*, March 29, 2018, http://www.ningde.gov.cn/zwgk/zjndzl/ndjj/201803/t2018 0329_242771.htm.

51. "Jianxing qunzhong luxian, tuidong Ningde fazhan" [Practice the Mass Line, Promote the Development of Ningde], *Ningdewang*, June 15, 2014, http://www.ndwww.cn/news/ndwnews/201406/470129.html; "Fujiansheng 23 ge shengji pinkunxian ji quanguo 680 ge lianpian teshu kunnan diqu fenxian mingdian" [A List of Fujian's Twenty-Three Provincial-Level Poverty-Stricken Counties and 680 National Special Hardship Regions], *Baidu wenku*, https://wenku.baidu.com/view/a24459484a35e efdc8d376eeaeaad1f347931152.html.

52. Zong Hairen, *Disidai* [The Fourth Generation] (Carle Place, NY: Mingjiang chubanshe, 2002), p. 397. A heavily condensed translation is Andrew Nathan and Bruce Gilley, *China's New Rulers: The Secret Files*, 2nd ed. (New York: New York Review of Books, 2003). The original author, Zong, is not acknowledged on the front cover of the English translation.

53. "Shigan caineng mengxiang chengzhen: Xi Jinping tongzhi zai gongzuo qijian changdao jianxing 'mashang jiuban' jishi" [Only with Hard Work Can Dreams Be Fulfilled: A Record of Xi Jinping's Promotion of the Principle "Will Do Immediately" When Working at Fuzhou], *Mishu gongzuo*, No. 2, 2015, p. 5.

54. "Only with Hard Work," pp. 12–13.

55. "Only With Hard Work," p. 5.

56. "Why Xi Jinping?," p. 54.

57. "Xi Jinping zhiding Fuzhou 3820 gongcheng: Fuzhou 20 nian fazhan licheng" [Xi Jinping Formulates Fuzhou's 3820 Project: Witnessing the Development Process of Fuzhou over Twenty Years], *Xm.ifeng*, August 1, 2014, http://xm.ifeng.com/tra vel/xiamen_2014_08/01/2694166_0.shtml; "Fuzhou shi 3820 gongcheng: hongwei de zhanlue kuayue di zuji" [The 3820 Project of Fuzhou: Grand Strategy and Transformative Heritage], *Zhongguo gongchandang xinwenwang*, October 23, 2012, http://cpc.people.com.cn/n/2012/1023/c349620-19357329.html.

58. "Only with Hard Work," p. 7.

59. "Only with Hard Work," pp. 7–9.

60. For "image projects," see Yongshun Cai, *State and Agents in China: Disciplining Government Officials* (Stanford: Stanford University Press, 2014), pp. 30–33.

61. Zhong Minyuan, "Fuzhou Changle jichang juece shiwu tiaocha" [An Investigation into the Errors of the Decision for the Changle Airport], *Nangfangchuang*, No. 2, 2004, pp. 46–48.

62. Brian Hogwood and B. Guy Peters, *The Pathology of Public Policy* (New York: Oxford University Press, 1985), 99–100.

63. Zhong Minyuan, "Fuzhou Changle jichang qisihuisheng ji" [A Tale of the Changli Airport's Resurrection from Death], *Nanfangchuang*, No. 4, 2006.

64. "Touzi Fuzhou 'sanfang qixiang' shidang hai Xi Zong beiheihuo" [The Improper Investment in Fuzhou's "Three Lanes and Seven Alleys" Turns President Xi into a Scapegoat], *Pingguo ribao*, March 16, 2018.

65. Yang, *Xi Jinping*, p. 120.

66. Xue Zhen, "Mingcheng luhai changdafeng: ji Fujianshengwei changwei, Fuzhoushiwei shuji Xi Jinping" [Famed City and Green Sea Sing a Glorious Tune: On the Secretary of the Standing Committee of Fuzhou PPC and Fuzhou MPC], *Fujian wenxue*, No. 4, 1994, p. 63.

67. "Xi Jinping zai Fujian gongzuo qijian guanxin zhichi guofang he jundui jianshe jishi" [A Chronicle on Xi Jinping's Care and Support of National Defense and Army Building When He Was Working at Fujian], *Xinhua*, August 1, 2014, http://news.xinhuanet.com/politics/2014-08/01/c_1111889481_2.htm.

68. "Famed City," p. 62.

69. "Only with Hard Work," p. 6.

70. "Top Fujian Cadres Face Sack," *SCMP*, July 17, 1992.

71. "Beidaihe huiyi rending Mei zhutai du: zhiding liangan tongyi shijianbiao buxi yu Mei yizha" [The Beidaihe Conference Affirmed That the United States Was Abetting Taiwan Independence: A Timetable for Reunification between China and Taiwan Was Set Up, Even at the Cost of a War with the United States], *Sintao ribao*, August 5, 1999.

72. Bao Pu, Renee Chiang, and Adi Ignatius, trans. and eds., *Prisoners of the State: The Secret Journal of Premier Zhou Ziyang* (New York: Simon & Schuster, 2009), pp. 199–202; Richard Baum, *Burying Mao: Chinese Politics in the Age of Deng Xiaoping* (Princeton, NJ: Princeton University Press, 1994), pp. 216–217.

73. Zong, *Disidai*, pp. 397–399.

74. "Jiang Grooms 'Fifth Wave' to Rule Country," *SCMP*, November 26, 1999.

75. *Zhongguo gongchandang lijie zhongyang weiyuan dacidian* [An Encyclopedia of the Members of the Central Committee] (Beijing: Zhonggong dangshi chubanshe, 2004), p. 1235; "Taizidang shishi" [The Princeling Gang Loses Power"], *Ming Bao*, September 19, 1997.

76. Wang Xin, "Weiguan yiren, zuofu yifang: Fujian shengzhang Xi Jinping" [Bring Benefits to Any Place You Serve as an Official: Fujian Provincial Governor Xi Jinping], *Tuozi yu hezuo*, No. 2, 2002, p. 10.

77. "Min quanli peihe zhongyang chachu" [Fujian Cooperates Fully with Central Investigation], *Wenweipo*, January 28, 2000.

78. "Son of Communist Party Elder Named Vice Governor and Acting Governor of Fujian," *SCMP*, August 10, 1999.

79. "Son of Communist."

80. Wang, "Bring Benefits," p. 10.

81. Zong, *Disidai*, pp. 399–400.

82. "Xi Jinping chang huanan ziyou maoyiqi" [Xi Jinping Proposes a South China Free Trade Zone], *Singdao ribao*, March 10, 2002.

83. "Fujian Seeking Foreign Development Expertise," *SCMP*, April 29, 1992.

84. "Fuzhou Expands Economic Cooperation with Europe," *Xinhua News Agency*, August 3, 1994.

85. Wang Nayin, "Mingang hezuo shinian: zhuaizhu jiyu, gongmou shuangying" [A Decade of Cooperation between Fujian and Hong Kong: Grasp the Opportunity and Forge a Win-Win Situation], *Kaifangchao*, Nos. 6–7, 2007, pp. 28–32.

86. "Zhengchuang xinyoushi, gengshang yicenglou, fang Fujiansheng shengzhang Xi Jinping" [Striving to Create a New Advantageous Situation and Advance One Step Further: An Interview with Fujian Governor Xi Jinping], *Taisheng zazhi*, July 2000, pp. 12–13.

87. "Striving to Create."

88. "Fujian shengzhang Xi Jinping: Fujian yao jianshe sida duitai jidi" [Fujian Provincial Governor Xi Jinping: Fujian Will Construct Four Large Bases to Deal with Taiwan], *Zhongguo jingji xinxiwang*, July 4, 2002.

89. "Su Chi Admits the '1992 Consensus' Was Made Up," *Taipei Times*, February 22, 2006, https://www.taipeitimes.com/News/taiwan/archives/2006/02/22/2003294106.

90. Shelley Rigger, "Taiwan," in William A. Joseph, ed., *Politics in China: An Introduction*, 3rd ed. (New York: Oxford University Press, 2019), p. 548.

91. See, for example, Robert Sutter, *Chinese Foreign Relations: Power and Policy since the Cold War*, 4th ed. (Lanham, MD: Rowman & Littlefield, 2016), chap. 7; Phillip Saunders, "Long-Term Trends in China-Taiwan Relations," *Asian Survey*, Vol. 45, No. 6, November–December 2005; Robert G. Sutter, "Relations with Taiwan," in chap. 8 of his *China's Rise in Asia: Promises and Perils* (Lanham, MD: Rowman & Littlefield, 2005); Andrew Scobell, "China and Taiwan: Balance of Rivalry with Weapons," in Sumit Ganguly and William Thompson, eds., *Asian Rivalries* (Stanford, CA: Stanford Security Series, 2011), chap. 2.

92. Robert Sutter, "The 1995–96 Taiwan Strait Confrontation," *International Security*, Vol. 25, No. 2, Fall 2000, p. 104.

93. For more details see Susan Shirk, *China: Fragile Superpower* (New York: Oxford University Press, 2007), chap. 8.

94. "Jiefangjun jiakuai wuli gongtai de bushu" [The PLA Accelerates the Planning for Using Force against Taiwan], *Xinbao*, August 6, 1999; "Beijing Leaders Order War Preparations," *Associated Press*, August 5, 1999.

95. "Son of Communist Party Elder Named Vice-Governor and Acting Governor of Fujian," *SCMP*, August 10, 1999; "Benbao riqian dujia baodao huozhengshi: Xi Jinping ren Mindi shengzhang" [This Newspaper's Recent Exclusive Report Has Been Confirmed: Xi Jinping Has Been Made Fujian's Deputy Governor], *Singdao ribao*, August 5, 1999.

96. "Shengzhang Xi Jinping: Fujian shunbei santong yo jiaqiang qunsheng zhanbei" [Governor Xi Jinping: Fujian Is Preparing for the Three Links as Well as the Provincial Mobilization for War], *Lianhe zaibao*, June 8, 2000.

97. "Fujian jue zhankai guofang dongyuan" [Fujian Decides on the Launching of National Defense Mobilization], *Wenweipo*, April 30, 2000.

98. "Fujian Decides"; "Nanjing zhanqu jiujin guofang dongyuan" [The Nanjing Military Region Accelerates National Defense Mobilization], *Wenweipo*, May 26, 2000.

99. "Nanjing junqu kai guofang dongyuanhui" [The Nanjing Military Region Convenes Meeting on National Defense Mobilization], *Wenweipo*, June 5, 2001.

100. "Min yubeiyi guanbing junshi yanxi" [Fujian's Reserve Officials and Soldiers Engage in Military Exercises], *Wenweipo*, November 9, 2001.

101. "Jieji yongren dong buzhu Taishang wu zhichi tadu" [The Policy of "Prudence and Patience" Cannot Hinder the Western Advance by Taiwanese Business: Fujian Urges Taiwanese Business Not to Support Taiwanese Independence], *Wenweipo*, June 7–8, 2000.

102. Feng shui is a traditional Chinese belief that harmonious surroundings can enhance the balance of energy forces that are favorable to the health and success of individuals. Since atheism is the CCP's official creed, Xi's reference to such a "superstitious" concept is rare.

103. "Zhengahishang bingrong xiangjian: Jingjishang shangjin donggu" [Political and Military Confrontation Seriously Harm Economics], *Xinbao*, August 12, 1999.

104. "Striving to Create," pp. 12–13.

105. "Policy of Prudence and Patience"; "Striving to Create," 12–13.

106. "Fujianshengzhang Xi Jinping: Yuan xiezhu shishi xiaosantong: Xiwang dasantong zaori tuidong" [Fujian Provincial Governor Xi Jinping Is Willing to Implement the Lesser Three Links, Hoping to Accelerate the Three Links], *Shibao zixun*, March 9, 2001.

107. "Fujian shengzhang: Yingti jianshe yi zhunbeihao, santongruanti jishu wenti jiudai liangan shouquan jiejue" [Fujian Provincial Governor: The Construction of the Three Links Hardware Is Complete; the Solution to Software and Technical Issues Awaits the Authorization of Both Sides of the Strait], *Lianhe zaobao*, September 11, 2000.

108. Wang Yuncai, "Fujian shengzhang tan: shanhai xiezuo, duineilianjie, duiweikaifang: goujian duiwei kaifang de zhanlue tongdao" [Fujian Governor on Land Sea Coordination, Internal Coordination, and the Opening Up to the Outside World: The Creation of a Strategy for Opening Up], *Liaowang xinwen zhoukan*, No. 41, 2002, p. 45; "Striving to Create," pp. 12–13.

109. "Fujian Reaches Out to Taiwan Business," *China Daily*, July 3, 2002.

110. Ko-lin L. Chin and Roy Godson, "Organized Crime and the Political-Criminal Nexus in China," *Trends in Organized Crime*, Vol. 9, No. 3, Spring 2006, p. 13.

111. "Dream of Better Life Abroad Feeds Chinese People-Smuggling," *Irish Times*, October 24, 2019.

112. "Xi Jinping zhichu: Fujian yidi toudu xianxiang yanzhong" [Xi Jinping Pointed Out: Human Smuggling Is Serious in Fujian], *Xianggang Zhongguo tongxunshi*, November 22, 1999; "China to Continue Combatting Illegal Emigration," *BBC Monitoring Asia Pacific*, March 13, 2002.

113. "Cockling Death Toll Really 24," *BBC News*, February 15, 2004.

114. "Xi Jinping at Fujian."

115. "Xi Jinping qiangdiao: Fujian yao jiakuai jianshe fuwuxing zhengfu" [Xi Jinping Emphasized: Fujian Should Speed Up the Construction of a Service-Oriented Government], *Zhongguo jingji xinxiwang*, February 1, 2002. The notion of "people

oriented" is a common concept, but Xi seems to be the first to have elevated it into policy usage.

116. "Xi Jinping at Fujian."

117. "Fujian feizhi yu rushi buxiangshi 294 jian guizhang" [Fujian Abolished 294 Pieces of Regulation That Contravene Requirements to Enter the World Trade Organization], *Zhongguo zixunhang*, January 9, 2002.

118. "Xi Jinping shuo Fujiansheng jiang jinyibu fangkuan waishang touzi lingyu" [Xi Jinping Said That Fujian Province Will Further Loosen the Limits for Foreign Investment], *Zhongguo zixunhang*, July 23, 2001.

119. Willy Wo-Lap Lam, *Chinese Politics in the Hu Jintao Era: New Leaders, New Challenge* (Armonk, NY: M.E. Sharpe, 2006), p. 48; "Fuwuying zhengfu" [Service-Style Governments], *Zhongguo gongchandang xinwenwang*, "Service Style Government," n.d., *Renminwang*, http://dangshi.people.com.cn/GB/221024/221 027/14907461.html.

120. Xi's interview with CCTV, August 22, 2001, http://www.cctv.com/financial/ jingji/sanji/toutiao_new/20010823/90.html; "Fujian shengzhang pishi: xiang canzhuo wuran xuanzhan" [Fujian Governor Instructs: Declare War on Food Contamination], Sohu, August 14, 2001, http://news/sohu.com/61/49/news14 6364961.shtml, accessed May 28, 2016; "Fujian zhili canzhuo wuran zouzai quanguo qianlie" [Fujian Is at the National Forefront in Ensuing Food Safety], *Zhongguo jingji xinxiwang*, September 5, 2002; "Xi Jinping zai Min changdiao shouhu shejianshang de anquan" [Xi Jinping Promotes the Protection of Food Safety at Fujian], *Ifeng*, August 1, 2014, http://xm.ifeng.com/travel/xiamen_2014_ 08/01/2694351_0.shtml.

121. "Fujian Governor Instructs; "Fujian Is at the National Forefront."

122. See, for example, "Despite Warnings, China's Regulators Failed to Stop Tainted Milk," *New York Times*, September 26, 2008; "From Milk to Peas, a Chinese Food-Safety Mess," *New York Times*, June 21, 2012.

123. A detailed official account of the Yuanhua case is provided by *Xinhua* on July 25, 2001. This is reproduced as "Yuanhua teda zousian chachu shimo" [The Beginning and End of the Investigation of the Yuanhua Smuggling Case], *Wenweipo*, July 26, 2001. See also "Chinese Tycoon Gets Life for Bribes and Smuggling," *New York Times*, May 19, 2012.

124. "Chinese Tycoon Gets Life."

125. "Fujian Leaders Face Beijing Top Brass," *SCMP*, February 18, 2000.

126. For a full list, see "Xiamen Yuanhua an bufen zhiwufanzui renyuan mingdan ji chuli jieguo" [The Outcome and Partial Name List of Indicted Officials Involved in the Yuanhua Case], *Renminwang*, February 6, 2009, http://news.sohu.com/ 20090206/n262088512.shtml; "Gonganbu yuan fubuchang Li Jizhou shou huilu beiyifa yancheng" [Former Deputy Minister of the Ministry of Public Security Li Jizhou Has Been Severely Punished by Law for Bribery], *Renmin ribao*, October 23, 2001.

127. "Life for Lai," *China Daily*, May 19, 2012; "Chinese Tycoon Gets Life for Bribes and Smuggling," *New York Times*, May 19, 2012.

128. "Xi Jinping dangxuan Fujiansheng shengzhang" [Xi Jinping Was Elected Provincial Governor], *Sina*, January 27, 2000, http: news.sina.com.cn/china/2000-1-27/57093.html.

129. Gao, *He Will Soon Lead China*, pp. 311–312.

130. Hu and Liang, *Biography of Xi Jinping*, p. 176.

131. "Zhu Confident Kingpin Will Be Extradited," *SCMP*, March 9, 2001; "Min quanli peihe zhongyang chachu" [Fujian Fully Coordinates with Central Investigations], *Wenweipo*, January 28, 2000.

132. For an early analysis of the incident, see Joseph Fewsmith, *China since Tiananmen: The Politics of Transition* (New York: Cambridge University Press, 2001), pp. 224–226.

133. "Fenghuang zhuanfang: Jia Qinglin furen yu Xiamen Yunhua zousi an wuguan" [Phoenix Interview: Mrs. Jian Qinglin Is Unrelated to the Xiamen Yuanhua Smuggling Case], *Sina*, January 27, 2001, https://news.sina.com.cn/china/2000-1-27/56997.html.

134. "Fujian Fully Coordinates."

135. "Lai Changxing fangyan Xi Jinping zhizheng wojiu huiguo du wannian" [Lai Changxing Lets It Be Known That He Would Spend His Last Years in China When Xi Jinping Takes Power], *Duowei*, July 11, 2014, https://blog.dwnews.com/post-454687.html.

136. "Factions Next Targets in Graft Crackdown," *SCMP*, January 13, 2015.

137. Fewsmith, *China since Tiananmen*, p. 226.

138. "Jiang Zemin deng jiejian Fujian lingdao: Xiamen Yuanhua an xian eryue jiean" [Jiang Zemin and Others Met with the Fujian Leadership and Ordered That the Yuanhua Case Be Adjoined by February], *Lianhe zaobao*, January 24, 2000.

139. "Min lianghui jujiao Yuanhua an" [The Two Sessions at Fujian Focus on the Yuanhua Case], *Wenweipo*, February 10, 2001; "Min zhongshi yinjin Taizi xiahua" [Fujian Is Concerned with the Decline of Taiwanese Investment], *Wenweipo*, February 17, 2001.

140. "Beginning and End."

141. Gao, *He Will Soon Lead China*, pp. 317–321.

142. Liu Zhiqin, "Qing lijie laoyidai: huainian Li Shenzhi" [Please Appreciate the Older Generations: Remembering Li Shenzhi], *Yanhuang chunqiu*, No. 6, 2008, p. 28.

143. "Xi Jinping shiyan lixing fanfu "[Xi Jinping Vows to Be Strict in Pursuing Anticorruption], *Wenweipo*, February 1, 2001.

144. "Hehong goujie anli" [Examples of Cases of Black and Red Collusions], *Wenweipo*, December 10, 2005; "Min chachu Chen Kai tuanhuoan she bairen" [Fujian's Investigation of the Case of the Chen Kai Gang Implicated One Hundred Persons], *Wenweipo*, September 15, 2005; Chin and Godson, "Organized Crime," pp. 15–17.

145. An Chen, "Secret Societies and Organized Crime in Contemporary China," *Modern Asian Studies*, Vol. 39, No. 1, 2005, pp. 77–107.

146. Chin and Godson, "Organized Crime," p. 14.

147. "Chen Kaian yinfa Fujian guanchang dadizhen: 8 da tanguan zao zhongcheng" [The Chen Kai Case Triggers an Earthquake in Fujian Officialdom: Eight Supercorrupt

Officials Received Heavy Punishments], *Sohu*, December 17, 2004, http://news. sohu.com/20041217/n223525378.shtml; "Fuzhou shoufu Chen Kai anpu guanchang heidong yingxiang chaoguo 'Yuanhua an'" [The Case of Chen Kai, Fuzhou's Richest Man, Reveals a Black Hole in Officialdom: The Impact of the Case Exceeds that of the Yuanhua Case], *Tencent*, August 18, 2004, https://news.qq.com/a/20040818/000 285.htm?edjn8; "Fujiansheng tongbao chachu Fuzhou Chen Kai fantuanhuo anjian qingkuang" [Fujiansheng Discloses the Situation on the Investigation of Fuzhou's Criminal Chen Kai Gang], http://news.xinhuanet.com/legal/2005-09/14/content_ 3491121.htm.

148. "Case of Chen Kai."

149. "Crime Boss Gets Death in Prostitution Racket," *China Daily*, January 24, 2005; "Fujiansheng Discloses the Situation." One source claims that Chen's death sentence was imposed for the main crime of running a brothel, whereas the bribery charges were relatively minor. This supports the view that the death sentence "looks suspiciously like a state-sponsored murder, designed to keep the details of the PCN firmly beyond the public domain." Blenny, *McMafia*, p. 379. My sources cite more serious punishments as listed.

150. "Chen Kai Case Triggers an Earthquake."

151. "Case of Chen Kai."

152. This source, allegedly from an official in Fujian's security department, appears in a Falun Gong site; see "Fujiansheng heie shili zai zhongyang di zonghoutai shishui?" [Who Is the Chief Backstage Supporter of the Black and Evil Forces in Fujian?], *Vision Times*, February 24, 2004, https://www.secretchina.com/news/gb/2004/02/ 24/61054.html. See also "Luo Gang shi Fujian heie guanchang di zonghoutai" [Luo Gan Is the Chief Backstage Supporter of the Black and Evil Forces in Fujian], *Vision Times*, December 25, 2005, https://www.secretchina.com/news/gb/2005/12/28/136 518.html.

153. Blenny, *McMafia*, pp. 377–378.

154. Blenny, *McMafia*, p. 378; Zhongjiwei zhuanzu yuetan shushi quanyuan Huzong lingchecha Minguanchang fubai" [The Special Team of the CCDI Interviews Scores of Officials: General Secretary Hu Jintao Orders a Thorough Investigation of Fujian's Official Corruption], *Singtao Daily*, April 21, 2004.

155. "Lai's Sentencing Marks the End of China's Great Gatsby," *Globe and Mail*, Many 18, 2012.

156. Xi Jinping, ed., *Xinshiji de xuanze* [Options for the New Millennium] (Fuzhou: Fujian jiaoyu chubanshe, 2001), pp. 1–12, 347.

157. Xi Jinping, *Zhongguo nongcun shichanghua yanjiu* [A Study on China's Agricultural Marketization], doctoral dissertation, Tsinghua University, 2001.

158. Xi, *Options for the New Millennium*, pp. 1–12, 347.

159. Xi, *China's Agricultural Marketization*, pp. 31–35, 73–74, 76.

160. Wang Yuncai, "Fujiansheng shengzhang Xi Jinping tan: Tiaozheng jingji jiegou tigao zonghe jingzhengli" [Fujian Governor's Talk on the Readjustment of the Economic Structure and the Raising of Comprehensive Competitiveness], *Liaowang xinwen zhoukan*, No. 39, 2000, pp. 25–27.

161. Zhang, "Village Branch Secretary," p. 12.

162. "East China Province Improves Business Environment," *Xinhua News Agency*, April 4, 2000.

163. For more details about the strategic plan, see "Fujian shengzhang Xi Jinping: Jiakuai jianshe santiao zhanlue tongdao" [Fujian Governor Xi Jinping: Accelerate the Building of the Three Strategic Channels], *Zhongguo jingji xinxiwang*, September 3, 2002; "Fujian jingji zai kuaisu fazhanzhong chuxian fancha xianxiang" [Retrogression Is Showing in Fujian's Rapid Economic Development], *Zhongguo jingji xinxiwang*, August 14, 2002; "Fujian goujian santiao zhanlue tongdao jiakuai fazhan bufa" [Fujian Is Constructing Three Strategic Channels to Accelerate Development], *Sina*, July 4, 2002, http://news.sina.com.cn/c/2002-07-04/0751624 786.html.

164. "Xi Jinping Proposes."

165. "Fujian: tuidong chanye jiegou youhua shengji yao qieshi zhuahao bage zhuolidian" [Fujian: To Promote the Optimization and Upgrade of the Industrial Structure, We Must Effectively Grasp the Eight Leverage Points], *Zhongguo xinxiwang*, July 4, 2002.

166. "Fujian shengzhang Xi Jinping: kuoda jiuye qudiao wanshan shehui baozhang" [Fujian Governor Xi Jinping: Expand the Channels of Employment: Perfect Social Security], *Zhongguo jingji xinxiwang*, September 10, 2002; "Fujian: Shida xizhengce jaifu xiagangren" [Fujian: Ten New Major Policies to Assist Laid-Off Workers], *Wenweipo*, September 30, 2002.

167. "Fujian shengcheng chengshi jumin zuidi shenghuo baozhang shishi banfa" [Fujian Implements the Law to Guarantee Minimum Livelihood Security for Urban Residents], *Zhongguo jixinwang*, July 18, 2001; "Fujian shengzhengfu guanyu Fujiansheng chengshi jumin zui shenghuo baozhang shishi banfa" [The Fujian Government on the Measures to Implement the Minimum Livelihood Guarantee for Urban Residents], *Zhongguo falu yu guize*, July 16, 2001.

168. "Fujian jiangyong 20 nian shijian jiancheng 'shengtaisheng'" [Fujian Will Spend Twenty Years Turning Itself into an "Ecological Province"], Zhongguo *jingji xinxi*, August 27, 2002.

169. "Xi Jinping at Fujian."

170. "Fujian Sets 20-Year Plan for "Ecological Province," *Xinhua*, August 25, 2002, http://www.china.org.cn/english/environment/40389.htm.

171. "Song Defu qiangdiao Fujian fazhan jingji buzou 'xianwuran, houzhili' luzi" [Song Defu Emphasized that Fujian Would Not Take the 'Pollute First and Clean Up Later' Route," *Zhongguo xinxiwang*, July 4, 2002.

172. "Fujian Sets 20-Year Plan"; "Xi Jinping at Fujian"; Fujian Province of China, *BRICS 2017 China*, https://www.brics2017.org/English/AboutFujian/fujian/; "Fuzhou and Xiamen among Top 10 in Air Quality," *China Daily*, January 19, 2018.

173. "Fujian Leads Nation in Ecological Preservation," *China Daily*, June 4, 2019, http://fujian.chinadaily.com.cn/2019-06/04/c_385759.htm; Fujiansheng renmin zhengfu, Fujian Nianjian Bianzuan Weiyunhui, *Fujian Yearbook, 2012*, pp. 50–51, 188–189.

174. For discussions of the Jinjiang model, see Fujian shehui kexueyuan ketizu, "Jiejian tuiguang 'Jinjiang jingyan,' chuanmian tisheng xianyu jingji fazhan shuiping" [Learn and Promote the "Jinjiang Experience"; Comprehensively Promote the Developmental Standards of the Counties), *Fujian luntan: renwen shehui kexueban*, No. 6, 2011, pp. 130–135; Zhang Junliang, Yu Wenxin, and Shen Junbin, "Gongjian gongxiang: minsheng jianshede Jinjiang jiangyan" [Build and Enjoy Together: The Jinjiang Experience and the Improvement of People's Livelihood], *Zhonggong Fujian shengwei dangxiao xuebao*, No. 10, 2012, pp. 17–27.

175. Tan Chung, *Rise of the Asian Giants: The Dragon-Elephant Tango*, ed. Patricia Uberoi (London: Anthem Press India, 2009), pp. 77–78; Kellee S. Tsai, *Back-Alley Banking: Private Entrepreneurs in China* (Ithaca: Cornell University Press, 2002), pp. 89–94.

176. "Yanjiu jiejian Jinjiang jingyan, jiakuai goujian santiao zhanlue tongdao" [Study and Emulate the Jinjiang Experience; Accelerate the Building of the Three Strategic Paths], *Xinhua*, October 5, 2002, http: fj.xinhuanet.com/zt/szqh1311/2002-10/05/c_118301751.htm.

177. Tsai, *Back-Alley Banking*, p. 94.

178. For Jinjiang model, see Chung, *Rise of the Asian Giants*, pp. 77–78; Tsai, *Back-Alley Banking*, pp. 89–94.

179. "Xi Jinping: Jinjiang tansuo he zouchu duju tese di jingji fazhan daolu" [Xi Jinping: Jinjiang Explores and Transcends a Unique Path of Economic Development], *Zhongguo wang*, December 10, 2012, http://news.china.com.cn/2012-12/10/content_27366559.htm; "Study and Emulate."

180. "Integrity Lectures for Cadres," *SCMP*, February 1, 2001.

181. "Governor's Report Avoids Fujian Scandal," *SCMP*, February 8, 2001.

182. Xi Jinping, "Youngquan jiang guande, jiaowang you yuanze" [Official Integrity Must Govern the Exercise of Power, and Principles Must Govern All Transactions], *Qiushi*, No. 19, 2004, pp. 36–38.

183. Xi was probably an honorary editor for the book, *Kexue yu aiguo: Yen Fu sixiang xintan* [Science and Patriotism: A New Exploration of the Thought of Yen Fu] (Beijing: Tsinghua daxue chubanshe, 2001). Yen Fu (1854–1921) was an eminent scholar who translated works by Thomas Huxley, Adam Smith, John Stuart Mill, and Montesquieu into Chinese.

184. *BTPK*.

185. Xi Jinping, *Zhijiang xinyu* [New Sayings from Zhejiang] (Hangzhou: Zhejiang renmin chubanshe, 2013).

186. See, for example, "Objection, Mr. Xi. Did You Earn That Law Degree?," *Sunday Times*, August 11, 2013; "Xi Jinping haipa yulun, shaoshao nadiaoliao faxue boshi" [Fearful of Public Opinion: Xi Jinping Quietly Removed PhD Title], *Radio Free Asia*, n.d., http://www.hkhkhk.com/64/messages/13530.htm.

187. A biography of Chen Xi is in *China Vitae*.

188. Xi Jinping, "Jiaru WTO yu nongcun shichanghua jianshe" [WTO Accession and the Building of Rural Marketization], *Zhonggong Fujianshengwei dangxiao xuebao*, No. 1, 2001. A near identical article with a slightly different title is "Nongcun shichanghua

jianshe yu Zhongguo jiaru WTO" [The Building of Rural Marketization and China's Accession to the WTO], *Journal of Tsinghua University* [Philosophy and Social Sciences], No. 4, 2001.

189. *BTPK*, p. 156.

190. Wei Li and Lucian Pye, "The Ubiquitous Role of the *Mishu* in Chinese Politics," *China Quarterly*, 1992, pp. 919–921.

191. For example, see Björn Alpermann, ed., *Politics and Markets in Rural China* (New York: Routledge, 2011), esp. pp. 7–10.

192. Xi, *Options for the New Millennium*.

193. "Fuzhoumeng yuzhao Zhongguomeng" [The Fuzhou Dream Presages the China Dream], *Zhengming*, No. 11, 2013, http://www.canyu.org/n81800c10.aspx.

194. "On the Xi Jinping That I Knew."

195. "Xi Jinping guanchang zhilu he qingfu mengxue" [Xi Jinping's Official Career and Mistress Mengxue], *Fanhuawang*, November 21, 2010, http://panchinese.blogpot. ca/2013/03/blog-post_833.html.

196. "Xi Jinping at Fujian."

197. "Xi Jinping at Fujian."

198. See Fujiansheng renmin zhengfu, Fujian Nianjian Bianzuan Weiyunhui *Fujian Yearbook, 2012*, pp. 41–42, 308–309, 322–324, and 402–404.

199. "Minshan Minshui yingshenqing: Xi Jinping Fujian 17 nian jishi" [Fujian's Mountains and Rivers Reflect the Deep Sentiment: A Documentary Record of Xi Jinping Seventeen Years at Fujian], *Sina*, n.d., http://fj.sina.com.cn/news/xjpfj/.

200. "Fujian baozengzhang qiangda yinqing gaoxiao yunchuan" [Fujian's Strong and Assured Growth Is an Engine for High-Efficiency Transition], *Renmin ribao*, January 16, 2009, http://paper.people.com.cn/rmrb/html/2009-01/16/content_177566.htm.

201. "Fujian Governor's Talk."

202. "Fujian Governor's Talk."

203. "Chinese President Xi Jinping: The Prince," *The Listener*, March 30, 2017, https:// www.noted.co.nz/currently/world/chinese-president-xi-jinping-the-prince/.

204. Zong, *Disidai*, pp. 400–407.

205. "Fujian chanye jiegou di bizhao shengji" [A Comparative Portrayal of Fujian's Production Structure], *xzbu.com*, n.d., http://www.xzbu.com/3/view-1739511.htm, accessed May 5, 2015.

206. Hu Ensheng, Liu Xin, and Chen Xiaolan, "Fujian sanci chanye jiegou dui jingji zengzhang gognxian de shizheng yanjiu" [An Empirical Study of the Three Sector Structure and Its Contributions to Economic Growth in Fujian], *Shicheng zhoukan*, No. 6, 2013, p. 45.

207. "Weiguan yiren, zaofu yifang: Fujian shengzhang Xi Jinping" [An Official in Duty Must Bring Benefits to His Region: Fujian Governor Xi Jinping], *Touzi yu hezuo*, No. 2, 2002, p. 10.

208. "Xi Jinping renming zhengshi gongbu" [The Appointment of Xi Jinping Is Officially Announced], *Wenweipo*, October 13, 2002.

209. "31 shengshi shuji junling jiangzhi 57" [The Average Age of 31 Secretaries of the Provinces/Municipalities Has Been Lowered to 57.9], *Wenweipo*, November 24, 2002.

Chapter 5

1. For more details see Chien-wen Kou and Xiaowei Zang, eds., *Choosing China's Leaders* (New York: Routledge, 2014).

2. "Shunli dahuanban: xinrenyuban" [Smooth Succession Transition: Half Are New Faces], *Wenweipo*, November 15, 2002.

3. Suisheng Zhao, "The New Generation of Leadership and the Direction of Political Reform after the 16th Party Congress," in Yun-han Chu, Chih-cheng Lo, and Raymon Myers, eds., *The New Chinese Leadership: Challenges and Opportunities after the Sixteenth Party Congress* (Cambridge: Cambridge University Press, 2004), p. 35.

4. Alice Miller, "China's New Party Leadership," *China Leadership Monitor*, No. 23, January 2008, p. 2.

5. For an extended discussion of factions in Chinese politics see Jonathan Unger, ed., *The Nature of Chinese Politics: From Mao to Deng* (Armonk, NY: M.E. Sharpe, 2002). A contemporary synthesis is Joseph Fewsmith, "What Is a Faction?," in Zheng Yongnian and Lance L. P. Gore, eds., *The Chinese Communist Party in Action: Consolidating Party Rule* (New York: Routledge, 2020), pp. 121–136..

6. Alice Miller, "The New Politburo Leadership," *China Leadership Monitor*, No. 40, Winter 2013, p. 6.

7. A CCP norm that refers to the obligation of seniors/superiors in any organization or enterprise to cultivate and support junior/subordinate members. According to Hu Angang, this practice is a duty of PBSC members to cultivate newcomers. See Hu Angang, *Zhongguo jiti lingdao zhidu* [China's Collective Leadership] (Beijing: Renmin daxue chubanshe, 2013), p. 84.

8. Zong Hairen, *Disidai* [The Fourth Generation] (Carle Place, NY: Mingjiang chubanshe, 2002), pp. 31, 390; Andrew Nathan and Bruce Gilley, *China's New Rulers: The Secret Files* (New York: New York Review of Books, 2003), pp. 50, 136.

9. Zong, *Disidai*, p. 390; Nathan and Gilley, *China's New Rulers*, pp. 53, 121, 145.

10. "31 shengshi shuji junling jiangzhi 57" [The Average Age of 31 Secretaries of the Provinces/Municipalities Has Been Lowered to 57.9, *Wenweipo*, November 24, 2002.

11. "Party Leaders Put Stability ahead of Rejuvenation," *SCMP*, January 12, 1998.

12. Nathan and Gilley, *China's New Rulers*, p. 51.

13. "China's Fujian Governor Flushes over Rosy Future," *Reuters*, July 3, 2002.

14. Zong, *Disidai*, p. 413; Nathan and Gilley, *China's New Rulers*, p. 137.

15. Gao Xin, "Toushi Zhonggong siqida 'dangnei minzhu xuanju'" [A Perspective on the "Democratic Inner Party Election" at the CCP's Seventeenth Party Congress], *BBC Chinese*, November 20, 2006.

16. Wu Zhifei, "Xi Jinping: Cong huangtugaopo dao shanghaitan" [Xi Jinping: From the Yellow Earth High Plateau to the Bund of Shanghai], *Dangshi zongheng*, No. 5, 2007 p. 20.

17. "Zhejiang shengwei shuji Xi Jinping: cong juece cengmian shengji Zhejiang jingyan" [Zhejiang PPC Secretary Xi Jinping: Upgrade the Zhejiang Experience from the Level of Policymaking], *Xiangkungroup*, www.xiangkungroup.com/shownews.asp?id= 2845, assessed May 6, 2017.

18. "Baba zhanle cong touyue: zhuanfang Zhejiangsheng shuji Xi Jinping" [Eight-Eight Strategy Starting from Scratch: A Special Interview with Secretary of the Zhejiang PPC, Xi Jinping], *theory.people.com*, February 9, 2006, http://theory.people.com.cn/GB/40553/4087485.html.

19. "Li Keqiang: Zhizhengzhe minsheng weizhong" [Li Keqiang: Those Who Govern Must Stress People's Livelihood], *Nanfang zhoumu*, April 4, 2008, http://www.infzm.com/content/6145; "Zai Liaoning gaizao laogongye jidi: shenmou yuanlu di zhenxing taolue" [Renovation of the Old Industrial Base in Liaoning and a Profound Revitalization Strategy], *people.cn*, March 28, 2013, http://paper.people.com.cn/hqrw/html/2013-03/26/content_1219103.htm?div=-1. See also Zong, *Disidai*, pp. 428–449; Nathan and Gilley, *China's New Rulers*, chap. 9 and p. 212.

20. Zong, *Disidai*, p. 449.

21. "Fifth Generation Star Li Keqiang Discusses Domestic Challenges, Trade Relations with Ambassador," *WikiLeaks*, March 15, 2007, https://wikileaks.org/plusd/cables/07BEIJING1760_a.html.

22. At that time, China's definition of absolute poverty was an income of ¥800 annually. "Li Keqiang: Zhizhengzhe minsheng weizhong" [Li Keqiang: Those Who Are in Positions of Power Must Give Priority to People's Livelihood], *Nanfang zhoumu* , April 4, 2008, http://www.infzm.com/content/6145; "Li Keqiang zhuzheng Liaoning shizeng fanliji panduan jumin shenghuo jingkuang" [When Li Keqiang Was in Charge of Liaoning, He Turned Over the Garbage of the Residents to Judge Their Living Conditions], *Huanqiu renwu*, March 28, 2013, http://news.sina.com.cn/c/sd/2013-03-28/103626667580.shtml; "A Few Anecdotes about Dr. Li Keqiang When He Was in Charge of Liaoning], *Ifeng*, November 15, 2012, http://news.ifeng.com/mainl and/special/zhonggong18da/dujia/detail_2012_11/15/19188705_0.shtml; "Premier Li's Second Term: From 'Likonomics' to Following Orders," *SCMP*, October 25, 2017.

23. Hong Qing, *Tajiang shi Zhongguo de guanjia: Li Keqiang* [He Will Soon Become China's Grand Housekeeper: A Biography of Li Keqiang] (Carle Place, NY: Mirror Books, 2010), pp. 335ff.

24. Zhonggong Zhejiangsheng dangshi yanjiushi, Dangdai Zhejiang yanjiusuo, *Dangdai Zhejiang Gailan* [A General Survey of Contemporary Zhejiang] (Beijing: Dangdai Zhongguo chubanshe, 2012), p. 40.

25. See "Rangren moming qimiao de chengshi Yiwu" [The Inexplicable City of Yiwu], *Jingji ribao*, August 8, 2006; http://english.caixin.com/2013-12-13/100617288.html?p1.

26. "Jiedu minying jingji dasheng: Zhejiang sheng 'daobishi' zhuanxing" [Understanding a Province with a Large Private Economy: Zhejiang's "Forced" Transformation], *Zhongguo jingji xinxiwang*, March 21, 2007.

27. The MICS is broadly defined by the World Bank to encompass all countries whose GDP per capita ranged from US$1,000 to US$12,500 in 2021.

28. Zhonggong Zhejiangsheng dangshi yanjiushi, et al., *General Survey of Contemporary Zhejiang*, pp. 120–121.

29. "Zhongguo tese shehui zhuyi zai Zhejiang shijian de zhongda lilun chengguo" [The Significant Theoretical Achievements of the Practice of Socialism with Chinese

Characteristics in Zhejiang], *theory.people.com*, April 4, 2014, http://theory.people.com.cn/n/2014/0404/c40531-24824388-4.html.

30. Zhonggong Zhejiangsheng dangshi yanjiushi, et al., *General Survey of Contemporary Zhejiang*, p. 121.

31. *Zhejiang Nianjian, 2012* [An Almanac of Zhejiang, 2012] (Hangzhou: Zhejiang nianjian she, 2012), p. 12. "The Powerhouse Province—Zhejiang Soaring," *Wordstoweb*, 2006, http://wordstoweb.com/zhejiang.htm.

32. "Zhejiangsheng jingwai touzi qiyishuo quanguo diyi" [Zhejiang's Out-of-Province Enterprise Investments Is a National First], *province data net*, n.d., http://provinced ata.mofcom.gov.cn/Statdate/disp2.asp?pid-6775, accessed January 5, 2016.

33. *IMD World Competitiveness Yearbook Scoreboard 2006*, https://www.imd.org/about/pressroom/pressreleases/upload/PR-WCY2005.pdf, accessed June 6, 2016; see also, http://www.allianceau.com/pics/advant/2006_IMD.pdf; Lowell Bennett, "The Powerhouse Province—Zhejiang Soaring," *China Pictorial*, August 2006, p. 11.

34. See Lu Lijun, Wang Zuqiang, and Yang Zhiwen, "Fazhen shehuizhuyi shichang jingji de Zhejiang moshi" [The Zhejiang Model of Developing a Socialist Market Economy], *Jingji lilun yu jingji guanli*, No. 7, 2008, pp. 18–22; "Zhejiang jingyan: Zhongguo fazhan di jingdian caifu" [The Zhejiang Experience: The Classical Richness of China's Developmental Experience], *Zhongguo jingji xinxiwang*, February 5, 2007.

35. "Significant Theoretical Achievements." For a detailed description, see "The Zhejiang Experience."

36. "Xi Jinping's Time in Zhejiang: Doing the Business," *SCMP*, October 25, 2012.

37. Zhonggong Zhejiangsheng dangshi yanjiushi, et al., *General Survey of Contemporary Zhejiang*, pp. 122–123.

38. "Xi Jinping fenxi Zhejiang 'san nong' fazhan sanyinsu [Xi Jinping Analyzes the Three Factors of the Three Agricultural Issues], *Xinhuashe jinji xinxi*, February 9, 2006.

39. "The Zhejiang Experience."

40. "Sanshi nianqian women weishime yao xuanze gaige kaifang" [Why Did We Choose to Reform and Open Up Thirty years Ago?], *Zhongguo gongchandang xinwenwang*, August 26, 2008, http//:www.cpc.people.com.cn/GB/68742/114021/13094991.html.

41. "Xi Jinping Zhejiang jingyan: licu zhuanxiang youhao youkuai" [Xi Jinping's Zhejiang Experience: Promoting a Faster and Better Transition], *Sina*, April 5, 2007, http://finance.sina.ccm.cn/leadership/crz/20070405/01593473972.shtml.

42. "Zhengshi jingji gozengchang de fuxiaoying, yifen GDP daijia fenxi de qishi" [Pay Attention to the Negative Effects of High-Speed Economic Growth: The Inspirations Provided by an Analysis of GDP Cost], *Xinhua*, December 7, 2004, http://news.xinhuanet.com/focus/2004-12/07/content_2340803.htm.

43. "Pay Attention."

44. "Pay Attention."

45. "Zhejiang 95% nengyuan ziyuan kao shengwai diaoru, dianli ziyuanjinzhang yijiu" [Zhejiang Relies on Other Provinces for 95% of Its Energy Resources: The Tight Supply of Electricity Remains Unchanged], *Xinhua*, December 8, 2004, http://news.xinhuanet.com/fortune/2004-12/08/content_2307638.htm.

46. "Zhejiang moshe: qushi yu zuli" [The Zhejiang Model: Trends and Obstacles], *Qiushi*, March 22, 2012, http://www.qstheory.cn/jj/qyjj/201203/t20120322_147240.htm.

47. "Zhejiang luoshi kexue fazhan guan quanli ezhi jingji fazhan 'sangao' zhishi" [Zhejiang Implements the Scientific Outlook on Development and Makes Every Effort to Contain the "Three Highs" Trend of Economic Development], www.gov.cn, November 16, 2005, http://www.gov.cn/jrzg/2005-11/16/content_99683.htm\; Wu, "Xi Jinping," p. 20.

48. "Zhejiang nengyuan zigou 4.5%, 95% yishang nengyuan yao huaqianmai" [Zhejiang's Energy Self-Sufficiency Rate Is 4.5%; the Other 95% Has to Be Bought], *Xinhua*, http://news.xinhuanet.com/politics/2005-11/03/content_3725024.htm; "Nengyuan liyong zhuangkuang baipishu fabu: Zhejiang nengyuan xingshi yanjun" [White Paper on Energy Utilization Released: The Situation in Zhejiang Is Grim], *Sina*, December 8, 2004, http://finance.sina.com.cn/g/20041208/05301208978.shtml.

49. "Understanding a Province."

50. "Jiang Zemin tongzhi zai dangde shiliuda shang suozuo baogao quanwen [The Full Text of the Report Made by Comrade Jiang Zemin at the Sixteenth Party Congress], *Zhongguo wang*, October 17, 2012, http://guoqing.china.com.cn/2012-10/17/conte nt_26821180.htm.

51. "Zhongguo ganbu de zhengjiguan qiaoran shanbian" [The Quiet Changes in the Outlook on Political Achievements among China's Cadres], *Xinhuashe zhongwen xinwen*, September 19, 2003.

52. "Zhongguo gongchandang lici quanguo daibu dahui shujuku" [Data Bank for the Various National Party Congresses of the Chinese Communist Party of China], *Zhongguo gongchandang xinwen*, November 8, 2002, http://cpc.people.com.cn/GB/64162/64168/64569/65444/4429125.html.

53. "Zhonghua renmin gongheguo guomin jingji he shehui fazhan di shiyige wunian guihua gangyao" [Outline of the Eleventh Five-Year Plan for Economic and Social Development], www.gov.cn, March 14, 2006, http://www.gov.cn/gongbao/content/2006/content_268766.htm.

54. Xi Jinping, *Ganzai shichu, Zozai qianlie: tuijin Zhejiang xinfazhan de sikao yu shijian* [Do Practical Work and Be at the Forefront: Thinking and Practice in Promoting New Development in Zhejiang] (Beijing: Zhonggong zhongyang dangxiao chubanshe, 2006), pp. 37 and 63. Hereafter, *GZSC.* Ma Kai, "The 11th Five-Year Plan: Targets, Paths and Policy," National Development and Reform Commission, March 23, 2006, http://en.ndrc.gov.cn/newsrelease/200603/t20060323_63813.html.

55. My study of the Great Leap Forward makes this point. Although the policy contexts are radically different in the Maoist and the post-Mao periods, the continuity in the style and substance of policymaking, including the "big push" mentality and all types of bureaucratic behaviors, is more resilient than is imagined. See Alfred L. Chan, *Mao's Crusade: Politics and Policy Implementation in China's Great Leap Forward* (New York: Oxford University Press, 2001).

56. "Hu Jintao zongshuji laidao Zhejiang daibiaotuan" [General Secretary Hu Jintao Visits with the Zhejiang Delegation], *Zheshangwang*, March 5, 2005, http://biz.zjol.com.cn/05biz/system/2005/04/11/006089788.shtml.

57. "Renzhen bawo quanmian jianshe xiaokang shehui de xingshi—yilun renzhen xuexi guanche shengwei shiyijie jiu quanhui jingshen" [Grasp the Opportunity to Build an All-Round Well-Off Society: On Earnestly Studying and Implementing the Spirit of the Ninth Plenary Session of the Eleventh Provincial Party Committee], *Zhejiang News*, November 8, 2005, http://zjnews.zjol.com.cn/05zjnews/system/2005/11/08/006359585.shtml.

58. The Chinese billion constitutes one hundred million. "Zhejiang xince: wuda baiyi gongcheng" [Zhejiang's New Policy: The Five Hundred Billion Project], *Sina*, December 23, 2003, http://news.sina.com.cn/o/2003-12-23/17381413291s.shtml.

59. *GZSC*, chap. 2, pp. 59–192; "Zhongguo tese shehuizhuyi zai Zhejiang shijian di zhongda lilun chengguo" [Major Theoretical Achievements in the Practice of Socialism with Chinese Characteristics in Zhejiang], *Zhongguo gongchandang xinwenwang*, April 4, 2014, http://theory.people.com.cn/n/2014/0404/c40531-24824 388.html; also "Baba zhanlue wei Zhejiang xiandaihua jianshe duhang" [The Double-Eight Strategy Leads the Way for Zhejiang's Modernization], *Zhejiang News*, March 1, 2013, http://zjnews.zjol.com-cn/system/2013/03/011019178382.shtml.

60. "Wen Shiyou: Xi Jinping yu Zhejiang moshe zhuanxing" [Wen Shiyou: Xi Jinping and the Transformation of the Zhejiang Model], *Sina*, October 14, 2005, http://finance.sina.com.cn/g/20051014/10262033804.shtml.

61. "Xi Jinping de Zhehu liunian" [Xi Jinping's Six Years at Zhejiang and Shanghai], *Guancha*, November 17, 2012, http://www.guancha.cn/comment/2012_11_17_110 136.shtml.

62. *GZSC*, pp. 88–92; "Xi Jinping's Time in Zhejiang."

63. "Weishenme shi Xi Jinping?" [Why Xi Jinping?], *Zhaoshang zhoukan*, No. 5, 2007; "Shanghai Zhejiang roubo shijie diyi dagang" [Shanghai and Zhejiang's Fierce Fight over the World's Number One Port], *Zhongguo jingji xingxiwang*, February 23, 2006.

64. "Shanghai Zhejiang Yangshangang guishuquan zhizheng" [The Battle between Shanghai and Zhejiang over the Ownership of the Yangshan Port], *Tencent*, August 18, 2008, http://news.qq.com/a/20080818/000376.htm; "Xi Jinping Shanghai xing: Changsanjiao yitihua buru shizhi jieduan" [Xi Jinping's Shanghai Trip: The Integration of the Shanghai Delta Enters the Realization Stage], *Sina*, April 4, 2004, http://finance.sina.com.cn/g/20030404/1149328003.shtml.

65. Zhonggong Zhejiangsheng dangshi yanjiushi, et al., *General Survey of Contemporary Zhejiang*, pp. 36–37, 92–94.

66. "Zhengfu yu shichang guanxi di Zhejiang moshi" [Government and Market Relationship in the Zhejiang Model], *Zhongguo gongchandang xinwenwang*, January 16, 2009, theory.people.com.cn/GB/49150/49152/8685664.html.

67. Joseph Fewsmith, *China since Tiananmen: The Politics of Transition*, 2nd ed. (New York: Cambridge University Press, 2008), p. 273.

68. "Zhejiang feigong qiye baiqiang shengchu: Zhizaoye qiye zhan zhudao" [Zhejiang's One Hundred Strongest Nonpublic Enterprises Are Winning: Manufacturing Enterprises Take the Lead], *Zhongguo jingji xinxiwan*, July 18, 2003.

69. "Xi Jinping: Minying jingji shi Zhejiang huoli zhi suozai" [Xi Jinping: The Private Economy Drives the Vitality of Zhejiang], *Zhongguo jingji xinxiwang*, May 14, 2003.

70. Jean-Pierre Jeannet, "Cluster Companies in China's Zhejiang Province: Strength in Numbers," *IMD*, June 2009, http://www.imd.org/research/challenges/TC033-09.cfm; see also Lu Shi and Bernard Ganne, "Understanding the Zhejiang Industrial Clusters: Questions and Re-evaluations. Asian Industrial Clusters, Global Competitiveness and New Policy Initiatives, *World Scientific*, 2009, pp. 239–266, https://halshs.archives-ouvertes.fr/halshs-00357131.

71. "Zhejiang shengwei shuji Xi Jinping: minying qiye shi Zhejiang baoguicai" [Secretary of Zhejiang PPC: Private Enterprises Are Zhejiang's Precious Treasure], *Sina*, December 13, 2003, http://news.sina.com.cn/c/2003-12-13/16181333506s.shtml; "Xi Jinping: Minying jingji shi huoli suzai" [Xi Jinping: Private Enterprises Are a Source of Vitality], *Zhonghua gongshang shibao*, January 2, 2003, http://www.china.com.cn/chinese/OP-c?255672.htm; "China's Next Boss Has Some Capitalist Cred," *Businessweek*, January 26, 2012, http://www.businessweek.com/magazine/chinas-next-boss-has-some-capitalist-cred-01262012.html. See Mo Zhang, "From Public to Private: The Newly Enacted Chinese Property Law and the Protection of Property Rights in China," *Berkeley Business Law Journal*, Vol. 5, No. 2, September 2008; "Property Rights in China: China's Next Revolution," *The Economist*, March 8, 2007.

72. Wei-chin Lee, "Yours, Mine, or Everyone's Property? China's Property Law in 2007," *Journal of Chinese Political Science*, Vol. 15, 2010.

73. "Xi Jinping's Time in Zhejiang."

74. Changhong Pei and Jianfeng Xu, eds., *Chinese Dream and Practice in Zhejiang—Economy* (Singapore: Springer Singapore Imprint, 2019), p. 12.

75. "Xi Jinping's Six Years."

76. "Xi Jinping: Xiang Jili zheyang di qiye bufuchi, huan fuchi shui" [Xi Jinping: If We Do Not Support Enterprises Like Gili, What Do We Support?], *Renminwang*, January 8, 2003, http://people.com.cn/GB/jinji/222/2174/2956/20030108/904079.html.

77. See, for example, Doug Guthrie, *China and Globalization: The Social, Economic and Political Transformation of Chinese Society*, 3rd ed. (New York: Routledge, 2012), pp. 143–149.

78. "Perverse Advantage," *The Economist*, April 27, 2013; "Geely Ranks 2nd among Zhejiang Top 100 Enterprises," *Global Times*, September 9, 2013; "China's Carmakers Are Much Weaker Than They Appear," *Automotive News*, September 10, 2012.

79. See, for example, Mark Beeson, "Developmental State in East Asia: A Comparison of the Japanese and Chinese Experiences," in his *Regionalism and Globalization in East Asia: Politics, Security and Economic Development* (New York: Palgrave Macmillan, 2007).

80. "Xi Gains Power Mixing Father's Capitalism with Mao's Marxism," *Bloomberg News*, November 6, 2012.

81. "Zhejiang Home to Most Top 500 Chinese Private Firms," *ezhejiang.gov.cn*, August 26, 2019, http://www.ezhejiang.gov.cn/2019-08/26/c_399014.htm.

82. "Zhejiang dongyong 3000 yi daikuan pojie zhongxiao qiye rongzi pingjing" [Zhejiang Allocates ¥300 Billion to Crack the Financial Bottleneck for Small and Medium Enterprises], *Wangyi caijing*, September 29, 2007, http://money.163.com/07/0929/08/3PHTV5RC002524SJ.html.

83. "Zhejiang zhongxiao minqi rongzi nanti" [The Financial Issue Confronting Zhejiang's Small and Medium Enterprises], *Renminwang*, May 29, 2014, http://finance.people.com/n/2014/0529/c383324-25082562.html; "Unable to Secure Financing, two million Zhejiang Private Enterprises Are Forced to Borrow from Loan Sharks," *Tencent*, July 21, 2008, http://news.qq.com/a/20080721/001778.htm.

84. "The Financial Issue Confronting Zhejiang's Enterprises."

85. "Zhejiang minying jingji zheng yunyu duofangmian zhongda zhidu zhuanbian" [Zhejiang's Private Economy is Gestating a Multifaceted and Major Institutional Transformation], *Zhongguo jixinhang*, February 7, 2006.

86. "400 wan ren zaiwai chuangye: qianyi zi jinzai Zhongguó youzou, Zhejiang ziben dataowang?" [Four Million People Are Starting Businesses Outside of the Province: A Billion Yuan Capital Is Flowing to China. A Great Escape of Zhejiang Capital?], *Lianhe zaobao*, November 10, 2004.

87. "Xibu da kaifa: Qianyi Zhe ji liuru sibu" [The Great Western Development: ¥100 Billion Zhejiang Capital Is Flowing to the West], *Xinhuashe jingji xinxi*, May 21, 2004.

88. "Zhejiang chanye shengji jieli shijie 500 qiang" [Zhejiang Leverages the World's Top Five Hundred to Upgrade Its Production], *Zhongguo jingji xinxiwang*, April 13, 2005.

89. "Xi Jinping huijian Lian Zhan yixing" [Xi Jinping Meets with Lien Chan and His Party], *Zhongyangshe zhongwen xinwen*, April 21, 2006.

90. For a full text, see "Anti-Secession Law Adopted by NPC," *China Daily*, March 14, 2005.

91. "Xi Jinping Meets with Lien Chan."

92. *GZSC*, pp. 235–240.

93. Claude Ake summarizes the arguments that modernization is disruptive and dis-integrative, although he maintains that the correlation does not necessarily exist. According to him, changes and disorder may be functional for states by forcing them to reform and strengthen themselves. See his "Modernization and Political Instability: A Theoretical Exploration," *World Politics*, Vol. 26, No. 4, July 1974.

94. For example, see Karita Kan, "Whither Weiwen?," *China Perspectives*, No. 1, March 2013; Chongyi Feng, "The Dilemma of Stability Preservation in China," *Journal of Current Chinese Affairs*, Vol. 42, No. 2, 2013; Xi Chan, "The Cost of Stability," *Journal of Democracy*, Vol. 24, No. 1, January 2013; Liang Wei, "Wenwen zhikun yu gongmin shehui zhi que" [The Challenge of Weiwen and the Weakness of Civil Society], *Lilun yanjiu*, No. 6, 2010.

95. David Cohen, "Decoding Social Management," *The Diplomat*, September 21, 2011, http://thediplomat.com/2011/09/decoding-social-management/.

96. See the six interviews Xi gave *Xinhua* on a range of governance issues: "Xi Jinping tan Zhejiang fanrong fazhan zhexue sheke fangmian de jingyan" [Xi Jinping on the Philosophical and Social Science Aspects of Zhejiang's Prosperous Development]; "Xi Jinping fenxi Zhejiang sannong fazhan sanyinsu" [Xi Jinping Analyzes the Three Factors Governing Zhejiang's "Three Rural" Issues]; "Xi Jinping; Jianshe pingan Zhejiang cujin shehui hexie wending" [Xi Jinping: Build a Safe Zhejiang and

Promote Social Harmony and Stability]; "Xi Jinping: Fazhan duozong suoyouzhi jingji shi Zhejiang di huoli Zhiyuan" [Xi Jinping: The Development of Various Forms of Ownership Is the Source of Zhejiang's Vitality]; "Xi Jinping; Zhejiang jingji yao tiaocha Zhejiang fazhan Zhejiang" [Xi Jinping: Zhejiang Must Jump Out of the Province to Develop]; "Xi Jinping tan Zhejiang fazhan baba zhanlue" [Xi Jinping on the Thinking of Zhejiang's Double-Eight Development Strategy], *Xinhuashe jingji xinxiwang*, February 9, 2006.

97. For studies of social protests see Xi Chen, *Social Protests and Contentious Authoritarianism in China* (New York: Cambridge University Press, 2012); Kevin J. O'Brien and Lianjiang Li, *Rightful Resistance in Rural China* (New York: Cambridge University Press, 2006); Murray Scot Tanner, "China Rethinks Unrest," *Washington Quarterly*, Vol. 27, No. 3, Summer 2004.

98. Yu Jianrong, "Zhongguo de saoluan shijian yu guanzhi weiji" [China's Incidences of Unrest and the Governance Crisis], address delivered on October 30, 2007, at the University of California, Berkeley, http://www.chinaelections.org/newsinfo. asp?newsid=118361.

99. "China Strives to Handle Mass Incidents," *China Daily*, December 9, 2006; "Weiquan lushi: mianlao yuku jingzen kaliang" [Rights Protections Lawyers Are Free from Jail: What Are Beijing's Calculations?], *Hong Kong Economic Daily*, December 23, 2006.

100. Zhong Qi, "Dangqian Zhejiang huanjing doufen ji qunti shijian yanjiu" [An Analysis of Environmental Disputes and Mass Incidents in Contemporary Zhejiang], *Tansuo yu yanjiu*, No. 2, 2012, p. 62.

101. Yu Jianrong, "Cong gangxing du renxing, bian weiwen wei chuangwen" [From the Rigid and Inflexible to the Flexible: Change Weiwen to a More Creative Form of Stability Maintenance], *Nanfang dushi bao*, April 4, 2010.

102. See Zhou Yan and Liao Xiaoyan, "Qianshi huanjing qunti shijian" [A Preliminary Analysis of Mass Incidents], *Duice yanjiu*, September 2013, p. 83; Congjie Liang and Dongping Yang, eds., *The China Environment Yearbook 1* (2005) (Boston: Brill, 2007), pp. 38–39. Another account, which claims that dozens were killed, nearly one thousand were injured, and several police vehicles were damaged, is probably exaggerated. See "Guanguo 10 da huanjing wuran daozhi di quntixing shijian yanjiu" [An Analysis of the Mass Incidents Triggered by the Ten Largest National Cases of Environment Pollution], *News.yushu*, October 30, 2009, http://news.yushu.gov.cn/ html/20091030094227.html.

103. Zhong Chi, "Dangqian Zhejiang huanjing jiufen ji quntixing shijian yanjiu" [Research on Current Environmental Conflicts and Mass Incidents in Zhejiang], *Tansuo yu yanjiu*, No. 2, 2012, pp. 62–64.

104. "Zhejiang shehui guangli mianlin tiaozhan" [Zhejiang's Innovation in Social Management Is Confronting New Challenges], *Sina*, June 1, 2005, http://news.sina. com.cn/c/sd/2012-01-06/142723757953.shtml.

105. Population figures compiled from *An Almanac of Zhejiang*, 2012, p. 12.

106. Ye Juying, "Liudong renkou de xianxiang fenxi yu sikao" [An Analysis and Consideration of the Present State of Zhejiang's Floating Population], *Zhejaing xuekan*, No. 4, 2010, pp. 218–219.

107. "Zhejiang shehui guanli chuangxin mianlin tiaozhan" [The New Challenges Confronting Social Governance in Zhejiang], *Sina*, January 6, 2012, http://news/sina.com.cn/c/sd/2012-01-06/142723757953.shtml; "Pingan Zhongguo kan Zhejiang" [Zhejiang Shows the Way for a Safe China], *Jiaxing China*, March 31, 2014, http://www.jxzz.gov.cn/NewsInfo.aspx?SiteName=jiaxing&Type=pajs%7Cjrgz&ID=10931.

108. "Zhejiang sheng fugai chengxiang de shehui baozhang tixi jiben jianli" [A Social Security System Covering Urban and Rural Areas in Zhejiang Province Has Basically Been Established], National Bureau of Statistics, February 13, 2008, http://www.stats.gov.cn/ztjc/ztfx/dfxx/200802/t20080204_33972.html.

109. "Shidian: Shehui guanli chuangxin zhuoli pojie sida nanti" [Focus: The Innovation in Social Management Strives Hard to Solve Four Major Problems], *Renmin wang*, February 24, 2011, http://politics.people.cn/GB/1026/13997544.html.

110. Wu, "Xi Jinping," p. 21; "Why Xi Jinping?" p. 55; "Zhejiang Shows the Way."

111. "Renmin qunzhong shi women liliang di yuanquan: ji Zhongyang zongshuji Xi Jinping" [The Masses and the People Are the Source of Our Strength: On CCP General Secretary Xi Jinping], *Xinhua*, December 25, 2012.

112. Xi Jinping, *Zhijiang xinyu* [New Sayings from Zhejiang] (Hangzhou: Zhejiang renmin chubanshe, 2013), pp. 64, 137–138.

113. For a comprehensive study of the subject, see Kam Wing Chan, with Fang Cai, Guanghua Wan, and Man Wang, *Urbanization with Chinese Characteristics: The Hukou System and Migration* (New York: Routledge, 2018).

114. Xi Jinping, *Zhongguo nongcun shichanghua yanjiu* [A Study on China's Agricultural Marketization], doctoral dissertation, Tsinghua University, 2001, pp. 105–106.

115. "Zhejiang chu jiejue nongmingong wenti zhengce" [Zhejiang Unveils a Policy to Solve the Problem of Rural Migrant Workers], *Zhongguo jingji xinxiwang*, February 4, 2007, http://www.people.com.cn/GB/58278/70149/4802430.html; "Zhejiang nongmingong wenti diaochabu" [An Investigative Report on Zhejiang's Rural Migrant Workers], *Xinhuanet*, June 27, 2007, http://www.zj.xinhuanet.com/zjgov/2007-06/27/content_10414096.htm.

116. "Haining quxiao nongye hukou tuixing huji guanli chengxiang yitihua gaige" [Haining Cancels Agricultural Hukou and Promotes Reform for Urban/Rural Integration], *Zhejiang ribao*, December 31, 2003, http://zjnews.zjol.com.cn/05zjnews/system/2003/12/31/002265169.shtml. See also "In Search of Equality," *Beijing Review*, Vol. 48, No. 49, December 8, 2005.

117. "Zhejaing Jiaxing jiangzai quanguo shuaixian quxiao nongye hukou" [Jiaxing in Zhejiang Will Take the National Lead in Abolishing Agricultural Hukou], *Xinhua*, September 26, 2008, http://politics.people.com.cn/GB/14562/8110895.html; "Jiaxingshi quanmian shishi huji guanli zhidu gaige" [The City of Jiaxing Implements a Comprehensive Reform of the Hukou System], *Zhejiang zaixian*, July 16, 2009, http://zjnews.zjol.com.cn/05zjnews/system/2009/07/16/015676532.shtml.

118. "Woguo shouge liudong renkou guanliju zai Zhejiang Yuhuan chengli" [Our Country's First Management Bureau for the Floating Population Is Established in Zhejiang's Yuhuan], *Xinhuawang*, September 8, 2007, http://news.sina.com.cn/c/2007-09-08/090913845595.shtml.

119. Mao Zedong, *Jianguo yilai Mao Zedong wengao* [Mao Zedong's Writings since the Founding of the State] (Beijing: Zhonggong zhongyang wenxian yanjiu shibian, 1996), Vol. 10, p. 416.

120. "Fengqiao Experience Provides Guidance for Dispute Resolutions at Grassroots Level," *Chinese Social Sciences Today*, January 20, 2014; "Dang dai Zhongguo congshu bianjibu bian ji, *Dang dai Zhongguo de Zhejiang* [Contemporary Zhejiang] (Beijing: Zhongguo shehui kexue chubanshe, Xinhua shuian jingxiao, 1989), pp. 13–15.

121. "Meiti cheng zi 2003 nian yilai meinian duyou zhongyang gaoguan dao Zhejiang Fenqiao diaoyan" [The Media Claim That Every Year since 2003 Senior Central Officials Have Conducted Research at Zhejiang's Fengqiao], *Nanfang dushibao*, October 12, 2013, http://news.ifeng.com/mainland/detail_2013_10/12/30246529_0.shtml. In 2013, the fiftieth anniversary of the *Fengqiao* experience, Xi issued an instruction for the party state to relearn the implications of the experience. This has often been cited as evidence of Xi's Maoist leaning and a revival of Maoism.

122. "Jujue wuran touzi xiangmu Zhejiang jiang hesuan luse GDP" [Rejecting Polluting Investment Projects, Zhejiang Will Factor in Green GDP], *Zhongguo jingji xinxiwan*, September 25, 2003.

123. "Zhejiang quanmian lakai shengtaisheng jianshe xumu" [Zhejiang Raises the Curtain on Building an Ecological Province], *Zhongguo jingji xinxiwang*, March 21, 2003; Xi, *New Sayings from Zhejiang*, p. 223.

124. "Zhongbu jueqi shouxian xu lixing kaifa ziyuan" [The Rise of Central China Must Prioritize the Rational Exploitation of Resources], *Zhongguo jingji xinxiwang*, May 26, 2005.

125. "Rejecting Polluting Investment Projects."

126. "Zhuanxing zhiwu kan Zhejiang: Dapo GDP chongbai rang fazhan baohan 'luse yinzi' " [Zhejiang's Transition in Curbing Pollution: Break the Worship of GDP and Let Development Be Saturated with the Green Gene], *Hebei News*, October 29, 2013, http://hebei.hebnews.cn/2013-10/29/content_3569010.htm.

127. "Rejecting Polluting Investment Projects."

128. "Zhejiang yaozai sanniannei zengqiang zhiwu nengli gaishan huanjing zhiliang" [Zhejiang Must Strengthen Its Pollution Control Capacity and Improve Its Environmental Quality within Three Years], *Zhongguo jingji xinxiwan*, October 18, 2004.

129. "Xi Jinping: Dali fazhan xunhuan jingji, tansuo kexue fazhan xinlu" [Xi Jinping: Vigorously Develop a Recycling Economy; Explore New Avenues of Scientific Development], *Zhongguo jingji xinxiwang*, July 1, 2005.

130. For instance, after a large fire killed sixteen people in the crowded and unsafe shoe-manufacturing area in Wenling, the local government there closed down more than four thousand shoe factories, many of which were tiny family businesses that were built illegally in violation of fire and health regulations. This shutdown sparked a massive riot against the government. "Zhejiang Wenling qiangzhi guanting shuqianjia xieqi" [Zhejiang's Wenling Forcefully Closed Down Several Thousand Shoe Companies], *Tencent*, February 20, 2014, http://news.qq.com/a/20140220/001148.htm.

131. "Sannian 811 xingdong Zhejiang shengtai huanjing quanguo diyi" [The 811 Action in Three Years: Zhejiang's Ecological Environment Is Number One in the Country], *Zjnews*, December 21, 2007, https://zjnews.zjol.com.cn/05zjnews/system/2007/12/20/009071541.shtml.

132. "Zhejiang Shows the Way."

133. "Zhejiang: Renmin qunzhong anquan manyishuai lianxu sinian da 92% yishang" [Zhejiang: The General Public's Satisfaction Rate on Safety Has Remained More Than 92 Percent for a Continuous Four Years], *Sohu*, September 12, 2008, http://news.sohu.com/20080912/n259522988.shtml.

134. "Zhejiang: shinian pingan jianshe dazao quanguo zui anquan shengfen" [Ten Years of Building Safety: Zhejiang Is the Safest Province Nationally], *Zhejiang zaixian*, April 11, 2014, http://zjnews.zjol.com.cn/system/2014/04/11/019962219.shtml.

135. "Zhejiang Shows the Way."

136. "The New Challenges Confronting Social Governance in Zhejiang." Presumably, "inadequate marketization" refers to the inability to allow the free play of market forces to achieve initiative and efficiency, whereas "excessive marketization" refers to the chaotic and unregulated competition that creates bubbles.

137. See Xi Jinping's discussion on socialist democracy in his *GZSC*, chap. 5 and pp. 315–326.

138. Xi, *GZSC*, pp. 319–320; Xi, *New Sayings from Zhejiang*, pp. 10, 54, 102, 131, 207, 226, 255, 260, and 272.

139. Li Fan, "Zhejiang moshe: saying jingji tuidong zhenggai" [The Zhejiang Model: Private Enterprises Promote Political Reforms], *China Digital Times*, July 9, 2012, https://www.facebook.com/permalink.php?story_fbid=479168835444673&id=116074015087492.

140. "Chinese Lighter Producers Win EU Anti-dumping Suit," *China Daily*, September 14, 2003; see also Andrew Mertha, "Society in the State: China's Non-democratic Political Pluralization," in Peter Hays Gries and Stanley Rosen, eds., *Chinese Politics: State, Society and the Market* (New York: Routledge, 2010), pp. 75ff.

141. See Ethan J. Leib and Baogang He, eds., *The Search for Deliberative Democracy in China* (New York: Palgrave Macmillan, 2010).

142. "Yuhang quanguo shouchuang cunweihui zijian haixuan" [Yuhang Creates the Country's First Village Committee and Self-Nomination Elections], *Zhejiang zaixian*, August 27, 2008, http://zjnews.zjol.com.cn/system/2008/08/27/009879278.shtml.

143. "Wuyi nanti: Xi Jinping ceng changtui cunmin jiandu cunguan zhi" [Wuyi's Problem: Xi Jinping Had Promoted the System of Villagers Supervising Village Officials], *edu.aweb.com.cn*, October 26, 2010, http://edu.aweb.com.cn/2010/10/26/5118201010261108970.html.

144. "Zhejiang Shows the Way."

145. "Xi Jinping shicha Wuyi xian Houchen cun gaodu pingjia Houchen moshe" [Xi Jinping Inspects Houchen Village at Wuyi County and Highly Lauds the Houchen Model], *jw.jindong.gov.cn*, June 24, 2005, http://jw.jindong.gov.cn/news/WDDT_9333/200562417715.aspx.

146. "Xinhuashe shouquan bofa xiugaihou de cunmin weiyuanhui zuzhifa" [Xinhua News Agency Is Authorized to Broadcast the Revised Organic Law of Villagers Committee], *Xinhua*, October 28, 2010, http://www.news.xihnuanet.com/politics/2010-10-28.

147. For the directive see "Zhonggong Wenling shiwei guanyu minzhu kongtan di ruogan guiding" [The Wenling Municipality Party Committee's Various Regulations on the Democratic Earnest Talks], *360doc*, http://www.360doc.com/content/11/0425/00/4881689_112090989.shtml; "Zhejiang Wenling shiyan xiangzhen zhili xinmoshi: minzhu cuisheng gonggong Yushan" [Zhejiang Wenling's New Experimental Model of Village and Town Management: Democracy Promotes the Public Budget], *Sina*, March 16, 2006, http:///www.news:sina.com/cn/c/2006-03-16/10529365212.shtml; "Sichuan's Electoral Democracy." See also James S. Fishkin, Baogang He, and Alice Siu, "Public Consultations through Deliberation in China: The First Chinese Deliberative Poll," and Dong Xuebing and Shi Jinchuan, "The Reconstruction of Local Power: Wenling City's 'Democratic Talk in All Sincerity,'" both in Leib and He, *Search for Deliberative Democracy*.

148. For a detailed discussion of the Wenling model and its implications, see Joseph Fewsmith, *The Logic and Limits of Political Reform in China* (Cambridge: Cambridge University Press, 2013), chap. 5.

149. Arnold J. Heidenheimer and Michael Johnson, *Political Corruption: Concepts and Contexts*, 3rd ed. (New Brunswick, NJ: Transaction Publishers, 2002); John Mukum, *Corruption in Africa: Cases, Consequences, and Cleanups* (Lanham, MD: Lexington Books, 2007), p. 95.

150. Bao Yajun, "Zhejiang sheng jiceng minzhu fazhan xianzhuang qi gaijin fangxiang" [The Current State and the Direction of Improvement for Zhejiang Base-Level Democratic Development], *Ningbo dangxiao xuebao*, No. 1, 2008, p. 26.

151. Bao, "Current State."

152. Baogang He, "How Can Deliberative Institutions be Sustainable in China?" in Zheng Yongnian and Joseph Fewsmith, eds., *China's Opening Society: The Non-state Sector and Governance* (New York: Routledge, 2008), pp. 185–195.

153. Leib and He, *Search for Deliberative Democracy*.

154. Joseph Fewsmith, "Chambers of Commerce in Wenzhou: Toward Civil Society?," in Yongnian and Fewsmith, *China's Opening Society*. Fewsmith, focusing on business associations and government relations, argues that these interactions have created social capital but not a civil society, the latter defined as an ability to bring about better and more responsible governance and as a force independent of and "perhaps" hostile to the state.

155. Xi, *New Sayings from Zhejiang*, p. 3; *GZSC*, pp. 350, 374–375, 386–387; "Integrity Lectures for Cadres," *SCMP*, February 1, 2001.

156. *GZSC*, pp. 378–379.

157. *GZSC*, pp. 390–391.

158. "Yongquan jiang guande, jiaowang you yuanze" [Apply Official Integrity When Exercising Power, Be Principled When Dealing with Other People], *Qiushi*, No. 19, 2004, pp. 36–38.

159. "Zhi Jiangping shehui guanli de Zhejiang chuangxin" [Zhi Jiangping: Zhejiang's Innovation in Social Management], *Zhejiang ribao*, June 15, 2011, http://cpc.people.com.cn/GB/64093/64099/14900136.html.

160. Ren Zhongping, "Sichuan de xuanju minzhu yu Zhejiang de xieshang minzhu" [Sichuan's Electoral Democracy and Zhejiang's Deliberative Democracy], *Aisixiang*, June 7, 2012, http://www.aisixiang.com/data/54138.html.

161. "Communique on National Economic and Social Development in Zhejiang Province in 2008," *zj.gov.cn*, February 2, 2009, https://www.zj.gov.cn/art/2009/2/2/art_1568591_26244141.html.

162. Xi, "Masses and the People."

163. Xi, "Xi Jinping Analyzes the Three Factors."

164. Eugene Bardach, *The Implementation Game: What Happens after a Bill Becomes a Law* (Cambridge, MA: MIT Press, 1977).

165. "Zhejiang's Choking Days Rise by 20 Times," *Xinhua*, December 12, 2013, China.org.ca/environment/2013-12/12/content_30874035.htm.

166. "Smog Readings in Beijing Nothing to be Concerned About," *China Daily*, February 6, 2013.

167. See works by Elizabeth Economy, especially *The Third Revolution*, chap. 6.

168. "When the U. S. and China Fight, It Is the Environment That Suffers," *New York Times*, October 12, 2020.

169. "China's Ban on Trash Imports Shifts Waste Crisis to Southeast Asia," *National Geographic*, November 16, 2018, https://www.nationalgeographic.com/environment/2018/11/china-ban-plastic-trash-imports-shifts-waste-crisis-southeast-asia-malaysia/.

170. "ZARA deng mingqi gongyinglian bei pu wuran" [The Polluting Supply Chain of ZARA and Other Well-Known Enterprises Is Exposed," *Beijing News*, April 10, 2012.

171. "Periods of Development Poses Major Threat to Marine Areas," *China Daily*, October 17, 2011.

172. "Zhejiang Shows the Way." The "rule by law" cleanup of the river at Pujiang County was said to have forced the upgrade and rapid expansion of the electronic trade within a year, out-of-towners were reduced by seventy-seven thousand, and the public sense of security shot up.

173. "Zhejiang qiye paiwu zao chufa tingchan" [Zhejiang's Polluting Enterprises Were Told to Halt Production], *Xinbao*, September 20, 2011.

174. "The Invisible Price of Nuclear," *Global Times*, January 16, 2013.

175. "Huanjing baohubu, Huaxuepin huanjing fengxian fangkong shierwu guihua" [The Environmental Protection Department: The Twelfth Five-Year Plan for the Control and Prevention of Chemical Environmental Risks], p. 11, https://www.mee.gov.cn/gkml/hbb/bwj/201302/W020130220539067366659.pdf.

176. "The Book of the Dead," *SCMP Magazine*, June 9, 2013; "Zhejiang Shaoxing yiyou duoge aichengcun: qiyi paiwu jin 20 nian wurenguan" [Zhejiang's Shaoxing Already Has Many Cancer Villages: The Enterprises Have Discharged Pollutants for Twenty Years but No One Cared], *Meijingwang*, http://www.nbd.com.cn/articles/2013-03-13/722704.html.

177. "$32,000 Offer for 20-Minute River Swim," *China Daily*, February 19, 2013.

178. "Local Officials Must Prove Cleanliness of Rivers," *China Daily*, June 27, 2014.

179. "Hangzhou Protest Tests China's Governing Capacity," *Xinhua*, May 15, 2014, http://www.china.org.cn/china/2014-05/15/content_32390637.htm.

180. "Zhejiang Haining Jingke nengyuan wuran shijian jibei Pingxi: jingfang juliu 31 ren" [Zhejiang Haining Jingke Energy Pollution Incident Basically Subsided; the Police Detained 31 People], *Xinbao*, September 20, 2011.

181. "Zhejiangsheng shixing di qianluse GDP" [Zhejiang Province Is Trying Out a Light Green GDP], *Zhongguo jingji xinxiwang*, January 30, 2007.

182. See, for example, "When Wenzhou Sneezes," *Time Magazine*, November 28, 2011, http://content.time.com/time/magazine/article/0,9171,2099675-1,00.html; "Finance, Private Business and the Wenzhou Model," *China.org.cn.*, April 9, 2012, http://www.china.org.cn/opinion/2012-04/09/content_25095523.htm; "Entrepreneurial Wenzhou Seeks New Business Model," *Global Times*, January 17, 2014, http://gbtimes.com/business/entrepreneurial-wenzhou-seeks-new-business-model.

183. "Zhejiang sheng renmin zhengfu guanyu xiada 2001 nian Zhejiang sheng guomin jingji he shehui fazhan jihua de tongzhi [Notice of the People's Government of Zhejiang Province on Issuing the National Economic and Social Development Plan of Zhejiang Province in 2011], *Zhongguo zixun xing*, February 24, 2011.

184. "How Li Qiang Cheers Zhejiang's Private Spirit," *Caixin*, December 13, 2013, http://english.caixin.com/2013-12-13/100617288.html?p1.

185. "Xi Jinping Zhang Dejiang de Zhejiang moshe" [Xi Jinping and Zhang Dejiang's Zhejiang Model], *Duowei news*, April 3, 2012, http://opinion.dwnews.com/news/2012-04-02/58686553-all.html.

186. "2006 nian Xi Jinping zuoke yangshi jiedu Zhejiang jingji" [In 2016, Xi Jinping Explains Zhejiang's Economy as Guest of CCTV], *Ifeng*, March 28, 2013, http://fiance.ifeng.com/news/people/20130328/7838630.shtml.

187. "Xi Jinping congzheng lulizhi Zhejiang shitu" [Xi Jinping's Political Career in Zhejiang], *Zhongguo gongchandang xinwenwang*, November 20, 2012, http://fj.sina.com.cn/news/m/2012-11-20/160215714_3.html.

188. "Zhejiang shengwei xuanbu zhongyang jueding Wang Dongming Xi Jinping Zhao Hongzhu jianghua" [Zhejiang's Provincial Party Committee Announces a Central Decision: Wang Dongming, Xi Jinping, and Zhao Hongzhu Gave Talks], *Zhejiang ribao*, March 26, 2007, http://360doc.com/content/12/0524/22/18056_213489615.shtml.

189. "Xi Jinping's Zhejiang Experience."

190. Zhonggong Zhejiangsheng dangshi yanjiushi, et al., *General Survey Contemporary Zhejiang*, p. 120; "Masses and the People." Per capita for Zhejiang was said to have soared to US$10,000 and US$11,000 in 2012 and 2013. See "2013 nian Zhejiang GDP zengchang 8.2% renjun GDP chao 1.1 wan meiyuan" [The GDP in Zhejiang Increased by 8.2 Percent in 2013; GDP Per Capita Has Exceeded US$11,000], *Zhejiang xinwen*, January 19, 2014, http://zjnews.zjol.com.cn/system/2014/01/19/019818802.shtml.

191. "Xi Jinping's Time in Zhejiang."
192. "Zhejiang's Slippery Slope," *Global Times*, October 14, 2012, https://www.globalti mes.cn/content/738215.shtml.
193. Statistics compiled from *An Almanac of Zhejiang*, 2012, p. 13; "Significant Theoretical Achievements"; "2013 nian Zhejiang chengxiang jumin shouru shuiping jixu weiju quanguo qianlie" [The 2013 Income Level of Urban and Rural Residents in Zhejiang Continued to Rank among the Highest in the Country], January 21, 2014, http://zjzd.stats.gov.cn/dcxx/201401/t20140121_9889.html.
194. "Princeling with a Record in Politics," *SCMP*, March 24, 2007; "Seven Men Who Rule a Billion," *SCMP*, November 16, 2012.
195. "Reformers in China Are First Port of Call for Paulson: The US Treasury Secretary Is Identifying Himself with Pro-market Outriders," *Financial Times*, September 20, 2006. For a discussion of the ideological debate, see Fewsmith, *China since Tiananmen*, 2nd ed., pp. 262ff.
196. GZSC, chaps. 1, 2, 3, and 6; "The Zhejiang Experience."
197. "The Total GDP of Zhejiang Is Comparable to That of the Netherlands," *Eastmoney. com*, January 29, 2018, http://westdollar.com/sbdm/finance/news/1355,201801 29826897568.html.
198. Greg Larson, Norman Loayza, and Michael Woolcock, "The Middle-Income Trap: Myth or Reality?," *Development Research*, No. 1, March 2016, https://papers.ssrn.com/sol3/papers.cfm?abstract_id=3249544.

Chapter 6

1. "Sanbu buzhen, sizhixiashi renshi yuenei diding" [A Three-Step Arrangement: The Personnel of Four Centrally Managed Municipalities Will Be Determined by the End of the Month], *Wenweipo*, May 2, 2007.
2. "Shanghai: Learn Lessons from Fund Scandal," *China Daily*, May 25, 2007.
3. "Weishenme shi Xi Jinping?" [Why Xi Jinping?], *Zhaoshang zhoukan*, No. 5, 2007, p. 55.
4. "Shanghai: Learn Lessons from Fund Scandal."
5. For example, see Cheng Li, "Was the Shanghai Gang Shanghaied? The Fall of Chen Liangyu and the Survival of Jiang Zemin's Faction," *China Leadership Monitor*, No. 20, 2007, p. 2.
6. Hu Lili and Liang Jian, *Xi Jinping zhuanji* [A Biography of Xi Jinping] (Deer Park, NY: Mingjing chubanshe, 2012), pp. 205–206.
7. On this point, see also Xia Fei, Yang Yun, and Bai Xiaoyun, *Taizidang he Gongqingtuan: Xi Jinping pk Li Keqiang* [The Princeling Faction and the Communist Youth League: Xi Jinping Competes with Li Keqiang] (Carle Place, NY: Mirror Books, 2007), p. 116.
8. "Shanghai: Learn Lessons from Fund Scandal."

9. At the beginning of the reform period, Shanghai party chiefs like Peng Chong, Wang Daohan, Rui Xingwen, Jiang Zemin, and Zhu Rongji were outsiders assigned by Beijing, whereas Wu Bangguo, Huang Ju, Xu Kuangdi, Chen Liangyu, and Hang Zheng were promoted within the Shanghai system. "Xi Jinping ruhe nianhao Shanghai zhebenjing" [How Did Xi Jinping Master the Shanghai Sutra?], *Dongyangjing*, April 4, 2007, http://dongyangjing.com/disp1.cgi?zno= 10003&&kno=011&&no=0061.

10. Xia et al., *Princeling Faction*.

11. Hu and Liang, *Biography of Xi Jinping*, pp. 208–209; Xia et al., *Princeling Faction*, p. 117.

12. "He Guoqiang: Zhongyang renwei Xi Jinping ren Shanghai shiwei shuji heshi" [He Guoqiang: The Center Regards the Appointment of Xi Jinping as Secretary of Shanghai MPC as Appropriate], *Sina*, March 24, 2007, http://news.sina.com.cn/c/2007-03-24/202212604342.shtml.

13. "Xinren Shanghai shiwei shuji Xi Jinping de congzheng luli" [The Political Résumé of Xi Jinping, the New Secretary of the Shanghai Municipal Party Committee], *Shenzhen xinwenwang*, March 29, 2007, http://www.sznews.com/zhuanti/content/2007-03/29/content992153.htm.

14. "Gongshangjie renshi tan Shanghai jingji yu weilai" [Members of the Industrial and Commercial Sectors on Shanghai's Economy and Its Future], *Nanfang zhoumu*, March 28, 2007, http://www.infzm.com/content/6427.

15. "Members of the Industrial and Commercial Sectors."

16. "Political Résumé of Xi Jinping."

17. "Shiqida qian defang renshi diaozheng jianjin gaochao" [Personnel Changes in the Localities Are Reaching a Climax Prior to the Seventeenth Party Congress], *Zhongguo gongchandang xinwenwamg*, March 29, 2007, http://cpc.people.com.cn/GB/64093/64099/5537740.html.

18. See "Zihao buziman, wushi bufuzao: Xi Jinping zai Zhejiang" [Proud but Not Self Satisfied, Practical, and Not Impetuous: Xi Jinping at Zhejiang], *Chinareviewnews*, March 25, 2007, http://hk.crntt.com/doc/1003/3/4/9/100334971.html?coluid= 7&kindid=0&docid=100334971.

19. "Xi Jinping ren Shanghai shiwei shuji liangyue miji diaoyan guanzhi minsheng" [Since Appointed as Secretary of the Shanghai MPC Two Months Ago, Xi Jinping Has Carried Out Intensive Research and Is Dedicated to People's Livelihood], *Renminwang*, May 23, 2007, http://politics.people.com.cn/GB/14562/5767611.html.

20. "Appointed as Secretary of the Shanghai MPC."

21. "Xi Jinping luxin yiyue sanchushou" [After Assuming Office, Xi Jinping Has in One Month Introduced Three Initiatives], *Wenweipo*, April 26, 2007.

22. Zhang Tongfang, *Cong Xi Zhongxun duo Xi Jinping* [From Xi Zhongxun to Xi Jinping] (n.p.: Caida chubanshe, 2011), pp. 251–252; Hu and Liang, *Biography of Xi Jinping*, p. 213.

23. "Zeng Qinghong ting Shanghai gonggu jingji longtou; Wen zong daohu chuxi feizhou yinhang nianhui" [Zeng Qinghong Supports Shanghai's Consolidation as an

Economic Leader; President Wen Arrives in Shanghai to Attend the Annual Meeting of the African Bank Today], *Hong Kong Economic Times*, May 16, 2007.

24. "Shanghai shiwei lingdao banzi xian sichang xinmiankong, Xu Lin zuishou guanzhu" [Among the Four New Faces of the Leadership Contingent of the Shanghai MPC, Xu Lin Receives the Most Attention], *Xinhua*, May 29, 2007, http://news.163.com/07/0529/16/3FM2EQO0000120GU.html.

25. Hu and Liang, *Biography of Xi Jinping*, pp. 210–212.

26. Hu and Liang, *Biography of Xi Jinping*, pp. 210–212.

27. "Hu Jintao zai zhongyang dangxiao fabiao zhongyao jianghua" [Hu Jintao Gives Important Speech at the Central Party School], *Xinhuawang*, June 25, 2007.

28. "Xi Jinping zhuchi Shanghai shiwei changweihui xuexi Hu Jintao de jianghua jingshen" [Xi Jinping Presides over a Meeting of the Standing Committee of the Shanghai Party Committee to Study the Spirit of Hu Jintao's Speech], *Zhongguo zhengfuwang*, June 30, 2007, http://www.gov.cn/gzdt/2007-06/30/content_668158.htm.

29. "Xi Jinping: qiangli fanfu quxin yumin" [Xi Jinping: Fight Corruption with Force and Earn the Trust of the People], *Wenweipo*, May 25, 2007; "Xi Jinping ren Shanghai shiwei shuji qiangdiao suzao shiwei xinxing" [Appointed Secretary of Shanghai Party Secretary, Xi Jinping Emphasizes the Creation of a New Image for the MPC], *Xinwenzhongxin*, May 29, 2007, http://www.jiaodong.net/news/system/2007/05/29/010024996.shtml; "Meiti cheng Xi Jinping ren Shanghai shiwei shuji tixian zhongyang liangku yongxin" [The Media Said That the Appointment of Xi Jinping as Secretary of Shanghai Municipal Party Committee Reflects the Center's Prudent Intentions], *Sina*, June 1. 2007, http://news.sina.com.cn/c/2007-06-01/185513132686.shtml.

30. "Jinding huanjie: Zhongyang erlun xunshi difang" [Keeping a Close Eye on the Transition, Party Central Twice Inspects the Localities], *Wenweipo*, May 21, 2007. These inspection groups were formally established in 2003 to act as the "eyes" and "ears" of Party Central to uncover official malfeasance and corruption at the provincial level. They were credited with disclosing the Chen Liangyu case. Reminiscent of the imperial commissioners who checked out the provinces on behalf of the emperor, these groups evolved and became a key instrument in Xi's campaign against corruption from 2013 onward.

31. "Xi ting Shanghai xin taosheng" [The Glad Tidings from Shanghai Are a Pleasure to Behold], *Renmin ribao*, September 21, 2007, http://paper.people.com.cn/rmrb/html/2007-09/21/content_20468306.htm.

32. "Glad Tidings from Shanghai."

33. Evan Osnos, "Born Red: How Xi Jinping, an Unremarkable Provincial Administrator, Became China's Most Authoritarian Leader since Mao," *New Yorker*, April 2015; Kerry Brown, *CEO, China: The Rise of Xi Jinping* (London: I.B. Tauris, 2016), pp. 4, 95.

34. Willy Wo-lap Lam, *Chinese Politics in the Era of Xi Jinping: Renaissance, Reform, or Retrogression?* (New York: Routledge, 2015), pp. 43, 45, 48, 51, 63, and *passim*.

35. "San zhengzhi xinxing bitan shiqida" [Three Rising Political Stars Are Evasive about the Seventeenth Party Congress], *Ming Bao*, March 11, 2006.

36. Shaun Breslin, "Do Leaders Matter? Chinese Politics, Leadership Transition and the 17th Party Congress," *Comparative Politics*, No. 14, Issue 2, June 2008.

37. For further discussions of the practice of step-by-step promotion see Hsin-hao Huang, "Entry into the Politburo of the CCP," in Chien-wen Kou and Xiaowei Zang, eds., *Choosing China's Leaders* (New York: Routledge, 2014), pp. 25ff.

38. Liu Siyang, Sun Chengbin, and Liu Gang, "Weiliao dang he guojia xingwang fada changzhi jiuan—dangde xinyijie zhongyang lingdao jigou chansheng jilu" [Ensuring the Long-Term Stability and Prosperity of the Party and State: How the New Leadership Came About], *Xinhuanet*, October 22, 2007, http://politics.people.com.cn/GB/1024/6422419.html.

39. Zheng Yongnian, *The Chinese Communist Party as Organizational Emperor: Culture, Reproduction and Transformation* (New York: Routledge, 2010), p. 196.

40. "Constitution of the Communist Party of China," *China.org.cn*, http://www.china.org.cn/20171105-001.pdf.

41. "Shanghai Party Boss Tipped for Higher Office," *SCMP*, September 25, 2007. See also Alice L. Miller, "The Case of Xi Jinping and the Mysterious Succession," *China Leadership Monitor*, No. 30, Fall 2009, pp. 8–9; Joseph Fewsmith, "The 17th Party Congress: Informal Politics and Formal Institutions," *China Leadership Monitor*, No. 23, Winter 2008, pp. 23.

42. See also Joseph Fewsmith, "China in 2007: The Politics of Leadership Transition," *Asian Survey*, Vol. 48, No. 1 (2008), pp. 90–91; Alice L. Miller, "China's New Party Leadership," *China Leadership Monitor*, No. 23, January 2008, pp. 7–9. See also Fewsmith, "The 17th Party Congress."

43. Kerry Dumbaugh, "China's 17th Communist Party Congress, 2007: Leadership and Policy Implications," *CRS Report for Congress*, December 5, 2007; Cheng Li, "China's 17th Party Congress: Looking Ahead to Hu Jintao's 2nd Term," presentation at the Brookings Institution, October 30, 2007, https://www.brookings.edu/wp-content/uploads/2012/04/1030china.pdf; Li Cheng, "China's 'Fifth Generation' Leaders Come of Age," *Asiatimes* (Jamestown), 2007.

44. "Huzong tuici zhizeren zhide deshi" [General Secretary Hu Promotes and Evaluates the Resignation Responsibility System], *Taiyang bao*, October 1, 2008.

45. Jia Qinglin and Huang Ju were recruited into the PBSC, while Chen Liangyu and Liu Qi were promoted into the Politburo.

46. Two steps from CC membership into Politburo and then its Standing Committee; three steps when occasionally the Politburo has an alternate member.

47. Even as party secretary of the Tibet Autonomous Region, Hu spent more time in Beijing than in Lhasa.

48. These five superministries were created to streamline administration by amalgamating the functions of various agencies and ministries in 2008. A National Energy Commission was also formed to coordinate energy policy among several ministries.

49. "Fifth Generation Star Li Keqiang discusses Domestic Challenges, Trade Relations with Ambassador," *Wikileaks*, March 15, 20017, https://wikileaks.org/plusd/cables/07BEIJING1760_a.html.

50. Li, "China's 17th Party Congress."

51. Fewsmith, "The 17th Party Congress," p. 1.

52. The following draws from Miller, "China's New Party Leadership."

53. David Shambaugh, "China's 17th Party Congress: Maintaining Delicate Balances," *Brookings Northeast Asia Commentary*, November 2007, http://www.brookings.edu/opinions/2007/11_china_shambaugh.aspx.

54. Proceedings from *Changes in China's Political Landscape: The 17th Party Congress and Beyond*, symposium, John L. Thornton China Center, Brookings Institution, Washington, DC, April 12, 2007, pp. 59–60.

55. Cheng Li, "China's Economic Decisionmakers," *China Business Review*, March–April 2008.

56. H. Lyman Miller, "Party Affairs: With Hu in Charge, Jiang's at Ease," *China Leadership Monitor*, No. 13, Winter 2005, pp. 5–7. Similarly, Alice L. Miller seems to equate institutionalization with mere established patterns and routines when she refers to "China's "institutionalization of elite politics," in her "Institutionalization and the Changing Dynamics of Chinese Leadership Politics," in Cheng Li, ed., *China's Changing Political Landscape: Prospect for Democracy* (Washington, DC: Brookings Institution, 2008). See also Miller, "China's New Party Leadership." Citing the same evidence, David Shambaugh also maintains that there was an "increased institutionalization of the party-state," in his "China's 17th Party Congress." Joseph Fewsmith, in his "The 17th Party Congress," seems to share similar ideas of institutionalization but begin to realize the limitation of such views. In noting that the records at the Seventeenth Party Congress demonstrated a mixture of institutional rules with informal politics of political contests and balancing, he also notes that the apportionment of seats for the CC, which most authors regard as an indicator of institutionalization, may limit "inner-party democracy." The imposition of Politburo age limits, Fewsmith notes, might be a political maneuver.

57. Jing Huang, "Institutionalization of Political Succession in China: Progress and Implications," in Li, *China's Changing Political Landscape*.

58. See "Comment by Larry Diamond" and "Comment by Andrew Walder," in Kenneth Lieberthal, Cheng Li, and Yu Keping, eds. *China's Political Development* (Washington, DC: Brooking Institution Press, 2014), pp. 93–100, 211–216. Hochul Lee also argues that the end stage of political development is the democratic contestation under a multiparty system. See his "Political Institutionalization as Political Development in China," *Journal of Contemporary China*, Vol. 19, No. 65, June 2010.

59. Samuel P. Huntington, *Political Order in Changing Societies* (New Haven: Yale University Press, 1968), pp. 12 and 408ff. Huntington's concepts are often mutually exclusive and difficult to operationalize. For a critique of this book, see Gabriel Ben-Dor, "Institutionalization and Political Development: A Conceptual and Theoretical Analysis," *Comparative Studies in Society and History*, Vol. 17, No. 3, July 1975.

60. Li Cheng, "China's Economic Decisionmakers," p. 21.

61. Susan Shirk, "The Delayed Institutionalization of Leadership Politics," in Jonathan Unger, ed., *The Nature of Chinese Politics* (Armonk, NY: M.E. Sharpe, 2002). On coalitions see also Li Cheng, "Will China's 'Lost Generation' Find a Path to Democracy?," in Li, *China's Changing Political Landscape*.

62. Emma L. Bernstein, "Has the U.S. Constitution Reached Its Expiration Date? A Review and Criticism of the World's Longest Lasting Constitution," *Inquiries*, Vol. 12, No. 11, 2020, http://www.inquiriesjournal.com/articles/1835/has-the-us-const itution-reached-its-expiration-date-a-review-and-criticism-of-the-worlds-longest-lasting-constitution; Alex Seitz-Wald, "The U. S. Needs a New Constitution—Here's How to Write It," *The Atlantic*, November 2, 2013, https://www.theatlantic.com/politics/archive/2013/11/the-us-needs-a-new-constitution-heres-how-to-write-it/281090/.

63. Cheng Li's 2016 restatement is in *Chinese Politics in the Xi Jinping Era: Reassessing Collective Leadership* (Washington, DC: Brookings Institution Press, 2016), chap. 7. For other articles by Li, see "One Party, Two Coalitions in China's Politics," *Brookings*, August 16, 2009, https://www.brookings.edu/opinions/one-party-two-coalitions-in-chinas-politics/.

64. Li, "China's Lost Generation," pp. 107ff; Li, "China's 17th Party Congress," p. 22.

65. Leslie Holmes, *Politics in the Communist World* (New York: Oxford University Press, 1986), p. 207.

66. Li, "China's 17th Party Congress," pp. 14ff.

67. Ai Yanghua and Chen Xiaoming, *Gongqingtuan shili* [The Power of the Communist Youth League] (Carle Place, NY: Mirror Books, 2009), pp. 67–69; "The Big League: The Communist Youth Wing Where Rising Stars Once Took Flight," *SCMP*, August 4, 2016.

68. Andrew Nathan, "Policy Oscillations in the People's Republic of China: A Critique," *China Quarterly*, Vol. 68, December 1976, p. 728.

69. "4968 hou jiangxing shanyao duitai lilian jinsheng zuizu" [The 4968 General Stars Shine: Experienced in Training against Taiwan, They Are Promoted], *Wenweipo*, October 23, 2007.

70. Leah Caprice, "The Lost Generation of the 17th Chinese Communist Party Politburo," *China Brief*, Vol. 8, No. 19, October 7, 2008. See also Joseph Fewsmith, "Generational Transition in China," *Washington Quarterly*, August 2002.

71. Fewsmith, "Generational Transition in China"; Nora Sausmikat, "Generations, Legitimacy, and Political Ideas in China: The End of Polarization or the End of Ideology?" *Asian Survey*, Vol. 43, No. 2, March–April 2003.

72. Li, "China's Lost Generation," p. 106.

73. Li, "China's Lost Generation."

74. For a comparison of the political careers of Bo Xilai and Xi Jinping, see Tables 7.2 and 12.4.

75. An informal term to denote the most influential politicians in the 1980s and 1990s. Membership of the so-called "eight senior statesmen," or "eight elders," varies according to specific times, terms of references, and usages, and often includes the following: Deng Xiaoping, Chen Yun, Li Xiannian, Peng Zhen, Yang Shangkun, Bi Yibo, Wang Zhen, Song Renqiong, Wan Li, Xi Zhongxun, and Deng Yingchao (included in this group because of her own revolutionary credentials and for being the wife of Zhou Enlai). A positive view of the group claims that it was the main pillar of post-Mao reform; a derogatory view of the so-called eight immortals sees them as

conservative hardliners who were responsible for the martial law and harsh crack-down on the Tiananmen events in 1989.

76. *China Vitae,* https://www.chinavitae.com/biography/Bo_Xilai/full.

77. Zong Hairen, *Disidai* [The Fourth Generation] (Carle Place, NY: Mingjiang chubanshe, 2002), pp. 501–508; Nathan and Gilley, *China's New Rulers,* pp. 143–145.

78. "Bo Xilai's Life in the Fast Lane," *BBC,* March 15, 2012.

79. "Bo Xilai 'Liaojun' nanxia Shenzhen zhanqia chengguo youdai luoshi" [Bo Xilai's "Liao Army" Goes South to Shenzhen, but the Results Remains to Be Seen], *Sohu,* December 18, 2001, https://news.sohu.com/43/36/news147453643.shtml.

Chapter 7

1. "Li Yuanchao shouliangxiang: guojia fuzhuxi de wuzhong moshi" [Li Yuanchao Makes His First Appearance: The Five Models by Which China's Vice State Chair Can Operate], *Duoweinews,* December 30, 2017, http://news.dwnews.com/china/news/2017-12-30/60032746.html.

2. For details, see Zheng Yongnian, *The Chinese Communist Party as Organizational Emperor: Culture, Reproduction and Transformation* (New York: Routledge, 2010), chap. 7.

3. Willy Wo-lap Lam, *Chinese Politics in the Era of Xi Jinping: Renaissance, Reform, or Retrogression?* (New York: Routledge, 2015), pp. 6 and 108.

4. For this point, see Hu Angang, *Zhongguo jiti lingdao zhidu* [China's Collective Leadership] (Beijing: Renmin daxue chubanshe, 2013), pp. 81–83.

5. Hu Lili and Liang Jian, *Xi Jinping zhuanji* [A Biography of Xi Jinping] (Deer Park, NY: Mingjing chubanshe, 2012), p. 222; Gao Xiao, *Ta jiang lingdao Zhongguo: Xi Jinping zhuang* [He Will Soon Lead China: A Biography of Xi Jinping] (Carle Place, NY: Mirror Books, 2010), pp. 403–405.

6. "Q and A: Olympics Security," *BBC,* May 5, 2004.

7. James Mulvenon, "The Party Holds the Ring: Civil-Military Relations and Olympic Security," *China Leadership Monitor,* No. 26, Fall 2008.

8. "Sichuan 2008: A Disaster on an Immense Scale," *BBC,* 9 May 2013.

9. "Peng Liyuan zhongzaiqu weiwen yanchu" [Peng Liyuan Performs in the Hardest Hit Areas], *Wenweipo,* June 25, 2008; Martin Macmillan, *Together They Hold Up the Sky: The Story of China's Xi Jinping and Peng Liyuan* (Campbell, CA: FastPencil, 2012), pp. 291–292.

10. "Security Top Priority for Olympics: China VP," *Reuters,* July 10, 2008.

11. "Security Top Priority for Olympics."

12. "Wei aoyun, Beijingren xiaokang shenghuo de bian yu bubian" [For the Olympics, Beijingers Laughed at the Changes and Inconveniences of Life], *Xinhua,* July 24, 2008.

13. "Xi Jinping: Yi pingchanxin kandai aoyun zaoyin" [Xi Jinping: Respond Calmly to the Foreign Rumbles about the Olympics], *Ifeng,* June 25, 2008, http://news.ifeng.com/mainland/200806/0625_17_615446.shtml.

14. "Ting Xi Jinping yi pingchangxin jieduao aoyun jingwai zaoyin" [Heed Xi Jinping's Calm Approach to the Foreign Rumbles about the Olympics], *Renminwang*, July 7, 2008, http://cpc.people.com.cn/GB/64093/64103/7476426.html.

15. "Aoyun anbao touru zongbingli 46,000 duo ren" [Forty-Six Thousand Soldiers Were Deployed for Olympics Security], *Sina*, April 7, 2009, http://news.sina.com.cn/c/sd/2009-04-07/153117562385_2.shtml; "Jiefangjun zongzhengbu zhuren zhuanwen jishu jundui yuanao quanguocheng" [The Director of the PLA's General Department on the Full Process of the Military's Assistance to the Olympics], *Sina*, April 7, 2009, http://news.sina.com.cn/c/sd/2009-04-07/153117562385.shtml.

16. Li Jainai, "Jundui yuanao, zairu shice de huihuang [Military Aid to the Olympics: A Glory Recorded in History], *Sina*, April 7, 2009, http://news.sina.com.cn/c/sd/2009-04-07/153117562385.shtml.

17. "Army's Olympic Figures Revealed," *China Daily*, April 8, 2009.

18. Li, "Military Aid to the Olympics."

19. "China Sees a Calendar Full of Trouble," *New York Times*, March 10, 2009. In time, the 6521 predicament was broadened to become a nickname for the *weiwen* committee. Elizabeth Perry, Challenging the Mandate of Heaven: Popular Protest in Modern China," *Critical Asian Studies*, No. 33, Issue 2, 2001, 163–180.

20. Sun Liping, "Shehui shixu shi dangxia de yanjun tiaozhan" [Social Disorder Is the Most Serious Contemporary Challenge," *eeo.com.cn*, February 28, 2011, https://www.eeo.com.cn/eobserve/Politics/by_region/2011/02/28/194539.shtml.

21. "Yingdui kuaizhunhen wansheng 8% baoweizhan" [The Speedy, Accurate, and Resolute Tactic Ensured the Accomplishment of the 8 Percent]; "Chufangliang pojilu congrong yingdui ruanezhi" [Record Breaking in Foreign Visits: Countering Soft Containment with Ease], both in *Wenweipo*, December 31, 2009; "China Plans $586 Billion Economic Stimulus," *New York Times*, November 9, 2008.

22. "Beijing to Reactivate Olympic Security Plan for Anniversary: Capital Prepares for 60th Birthday of the People's Republic," *SCMP*, August 24, 2009; "Task Forces Set Up to Keep Lid on Protests: Tighter Watch on Sources of Unrest," *SCMP*, February 28, 2009.

23. "Zhongguo lianghui anbao aoyun moshi dixian shenshou" [China Showed Off Its Flair by Adopting the Olympics Security Model to the Two Sessions], *Xianggang Zhongguo tongxunshe*, March 2, 2009; "Self-Immolators' Demands Unreasonable, Official Says," *SCMP*, March 7, 2009.

24. "Riots in Western China amid Ethnic Tension," *New York Times*, July 5, 2009; "Fatalities May Climb in Urumqi," *China Daily*, July 13, 2009.

25. "Xinjiang baoluan zhendong chaoye, Xi Jinping zhudao fangkong" [The Xinjiang Riots Shocked the Chinese Regime: Xi Jinping Is Put in Charge of Anti-terrorism," *Cenewseu*, July 7, 2009, http://www.cenews.eu/?p=15456; "Zhonggong bao wending, pingbao shengzhi zuigaoji" [Party Central Attempts to Restore Stability: Anti-terrorism Has Risen to Become Top Priority], *Xianggiang jingji ribao*, July 9, 2009.

26. "China Weaves Security Network for National Day Celebrations," *China Daily*, September 9, 2009; "China's National Day Parade: Public Barred from Celebrations," *Guardian*, September 30, 2009; "70 wanren canyu anbao" [Seven Hundred Thousand Participated in Security], *Wenweipo*, March 3, 2010.

27. Karita Kan, "Whither Weiwen?," *China Perspectives*, No. 1, March 2013; Chongyi Feng, "The Dilemma of Stability Preservation in China," *Journal of Current Chinese Affairs*, Vol. 42, No. 2, 2013; Xi Chan, "The Cost of Stability," *Journal of Democracy*, Vol. 24, No. 1, January 2013; Liang Wei, "Wenwen zhikun yu gongmin shehui zhi que" [The Challenge of Weiwen and the Weakness of Civil Society], *Lilun yanjiu*, No. 6, 2010.

28. "Catching Scent of Revolution, China Moves to Snip Jasmine," *New York Times*, May 10, 2011; "China Cracks Down after Calls for Protests," *AFP*, February 20, 2011.

29. Despite the explosion in the number of NGOs over the past decades, the CCP has always been ambivalent about NGOs, both foreign and domestic. On the one hand, the party state requires NGOs as service providers in areas such as welfare, environmental protection, poverty alleviation, and charity, and it often contracts out these services to satisfy the needs of the public. On the other hand, it worries about the potential impact of autonomous organizations, especially in politics. Hence, the operations of the NGOs are strictly regulated: they are required to register with the Civil Affairs Department and to acquire official and government or party sponsors. Domestic NGOs are often referred to as social organizations to remove any hint of dissent. Most domestic NGOs are created by the state, and many contain party branches. NGOs deemed to be more apolitical in areas such commerce, science and technology, disaster relief, and community services receive more relaxed treatment.

30. "Xi Jinping yaoqiu cong yuantou huajie shehui maodun weiwen" [Xi Jinping Demands the Resolution of the Social Conflicts from Their Sources in Order to Maintain Stability], *Sohu*, February 23, 2011, http://news.sohu.com/20110223/n27 9494186.shtml.

31. "Why Asia Turned to China during the Global Financial Crisis," *BBC*, September 13, 2018; Yongnian Zheng and Sarah Tong, eds., *China and the Global Economic Crisis* (Singapore: World Scientific, 2010).

32. Christian Goebel and Lynette H. Ong, *Social Unrest in China*, Europe China Research and Academic Network, November 2012.

33. For perceptive analysis of this issue see Alice Miller, "The Case of Xi Jinping and the Mysterious Succession," *China Leadership Monitor*, No. 30, Fall 2009, and "Splits in the Politburo Leadership?," *China Leadership Monitor*, No. 34, Winter 2011; James Mulvenon, "Xi Jinping and the Central Military Commission: Bridesmaid or Bride?," *China Leadership Monitor*, No. 34, Winter 2011.

34. Membership in these two organizations is identical. Mao used to refer to this situation as "one office, two brands."

35. Gao, *He Will Soon Lead China*, pp. 450–457; Hu and Liang, *Biography of Xi Jinping*, pp. 243–247.

36. For a summary of these theories, see Mulvenon, "Xi Jinping," p. 2.

37. Mulvenon, "Xi Jinping," p. 2.

38. Liang Jian, *Xi Jinping Xinzhuan* [A New Biography of Xi Jinping] (Deer Park, NY: Mirror Books, 2012), pp. 299–300.

39. Miller, "The Case of Xi Jinping," p. 9. Indeed, it was plausible that other contenders for the PBSC positions attempted to use this "straw vote" process to unseat Xi, but

it is unlikely that Hu Jintao intended to use this procedure to oust Xi in favor of Li Keqiang.

40. Other leaders who are not designated successors have been tasked with making explanatory speeches on major policies on ideology, party-building, and economic policy, but in the context of the grooming process described in this chapter, the role assigned to Xi at the Fourth Plenum was significant. See Miller, "Case of Xi Jinping," p. 9.

41. "Geng Ying and Geng Yan: Xi Jinping ge Geng Biao dang *mishu*" [Geng Ying and Geng Yan: When Xi Jinping Was Geng Biao's *mishu*], *Zhongguo jingji zhoukan*, No. 29, 2010, pp. 53–55.

42. Office of the Secretary of Defense, *Annual Report to Congress: Military and Security Developments Involving the People's Republic of China, 2011*, pp. 1–2.

43. Alice L. Miller, "Xi Jinping and the Party Apparatus," *China Leadership Monitor*, No. 25, Summer 2008.

44. Alice L. Miller, "Leadership Presses Party Unity in Time of Economic Stress," *China Leadership Monitor*, No. 28, Spring 2009, pp. 1–11.

45. See Joseph Fewsmith, "Promoting the Scientific Development Concept," *China Leadership Monitor*, No. 11, Summer 2004.

46. Michael Raska, "Scientific Innovation and China's Military Modernization," *The Diplomat*, September 3, 2013.

47. "Kexue fazhanguan zai junshi lingyu de yunyong he zhankai [The Application and Development of the Scientific Outlook on Development in the Military Field], December 24, 2003, *theory.people.com*, http://theory.people.com.cn/n/2013/1224/c40531-23927673.html.

48. Miller, "Leadership Presses Party Unity."

49. "Xi Jinping: Nianqing guanyuan shenfang youhuo" [Young Officials Must Beware of Temptation], *Wenweipo*, April 8, 2009; "Zhongong zhongyang guanyu jiaqiang he gaijin xinxingshi xia dangde jianshe ruogan zhongdai wenti de jueding" [Decision of the Central Committee of the Communist Party of China on Strengthening and Improving Some Major Issues concerning Party-Building under New Conditions], *Xinhua*, April 7, 2009, http://news/xinhuanet.com/politics/2009-04/07/content_1 1143776.htm.

50. "Xi Jinping: Lingdao ganbu yao aidushu duhaoshu shandushu" [Xi Jinping: Leadership Cadres Must Love to Read, Read Good Books, and Learn Well from Them], *Renminwang*, May 18, 2009, http://theory.people.com.cn/GB/49169/49171/9315765.html.

51. "Xi Jinping: Guanyu jianshe Makesi zhuyi xuexixing zhengdang di jidian xuexi tihui he renshi" [Xi Jinping: A Certain Experiential Understanding on Building a Marxist and Study-Style Party], *theory.people.com.cn*, November 17, 2009, http://theory.people.com.cn/GB/41038/10388983.html.

52. "Officials Must Improve Speeches, Xi Says," *China Daily*, May 17, 2010.

53. "Xi Jinping chuxi quanguo jiceng dangjian gongzuo shouji xinxi xitong kaitong yishi" [Xi Jinping Attends the Opening Ceremony of the Mobile Phone Information System for Grassroots Party-Building Work in China], *Xinhua*, January 5, 2010; "Xi Jinping

fadi jiceng dangjian wenhou duanxin" [Xi Jinping's Short Greeting to Grassroots Party Organizations], *360doc.com*, January 6, 2010, www.360doc.com/content/10/0106/14/547701_12803705.html.

54. "Xi Jinping Attends the Opening Ceremony."

55. Gao, *He Will Soon Lead China*, pp. 492–499.

56. "Xi Jinping qiangdao zhuoli zaojiu gaosuzhi xianwei shuj duiwu" [Xi Jinping Emphasizes the Efforts to Create a High-Quality Contingent of County Party Secretaries], *Xinhua*, December 31, 2009.

57. "Xi Jinping yaoqiu xiang Shen Hao xuexi" [Xi Jinping Demands Learning from Shen Hao], *Zhongguo gongachandang xiwenwang*, January 14, 2010.

58. "China President Xi Faces Stark Choices over Hong Kong Protests," *Wall Street Journal*, September 29, 2014.

59. Gao, *He Will Soon Lead China*, pp. 414–415.

60. "Xi Jinping qiangdiao quan zai zhongyang, wuqu gongtou zaiyin zhengyi" [Xi Jinping Stresses That Power Is Located at the Center: The Five Constituencies Public Election Again Stirs Controversy], *Radio Free Asia*, March 8, 2010, https://www.rfa.org/mandarin/yataibaodao/xjp-03082010094330.html.

61. "Does China's Next Leader Have a Soft Spot for Tibet?," *Reuters*, August 30, 2012, https://www.reuters.com/article/us-china-tibet-xi/insight-does-chinas-next-leader-have-a-soft-spot-for-tibet-idUSBRE87T1G320120830; "Xi Jinping dui Xicang wenti qiangying: huofo shuo qifu wenhe" [Xi Jinping's Harsh Attitude toward Tibet: The Living Buddha Said That Xi's Father Was Moderate], *Voice of America Chinese*, July 19, 2011, https://www.voachinese.com/a/article-20110719--chinas-heir-apparent-pledges-tough-line-on-tibet-125837403/784838.html.

62. "Tongzhan bu: Dui Xizang duli yiqian mei kai guomen jinhou yebu huikai [United Front Work Department: The Door to "Tibetan Independence" Is a Nonstarter in the Past or in the Future], *china.com.cn*, November 10, 2018, http://www.china.com.cn/news/2008-11/10/content_16739912.htm.

63. "Dalai Lama Let Slip How India Vetoed His Meeting with China's Leader in 2014," *The Guardian*, May 19, 2019.

64. "Speech of His Holiness the Dalai Lama to the European Parliament, Strasbourg," October 14, 2001, http://dalailama.com/messages/tibet/strasbourg-speech-2001.

65. "Tibetan Leader Calls on China to End Repressive Policies," *The Guardian*, June 5, 2014, https://www.theguardian.com/world/2014/jun/05/tibetan-leader-calls-on-china-end-repressive-policies; "Tibetans in Exile Re-elect Political Leader," *New York Times*, April 27, 2016, https://www.nytimes.com/2016/04/28/world/asia/harvard-research-fellow-re-elected-as-head-of-tibets-government-in-exile.html.

66. "China: End Involuntary Rehousing, Relocation of Tibetans," Human Rights Watch, June 27, 2013. See also "They Say We Should Be Grateful: Mass Rehousing and Relocation Programs in Tibetan Areas of China," Human Rights Watch, June 2013.

67. Xi's full text is in "Full Text of Speech by Xi Jinping at Tibet's Peaceful Liberation Conference," *Xinhua*, July 19, 2011, http://news.xinhuanet.com/english2010/china/2011-07/19/c_13995316.htm.

68. "Unique Celebration of His Holiness the Dalai Lama's 76th Birthday in Washington, D.C.," *dalailama.com*, July 11, 2011, https://www.dalailama.com/news/2011/unique-celebration-of-his-holiness-the-dalai-lamas-76th-birthday-in-washington-d-c.

69. "Xi Jinping's Harsh Attitude."

70. "Xi Jinping's Harsh Attitude."

71. Robert Barnett, "China's 'Liberation' of Tibet: Rules of the Game," *New York Review of Books*, August 22, 2011, https://www.nybooks.com/daily/2011/08/22/chinas-liberat ion-tibet-rules-game/.

72. "Bright Future for Xinjiang's Energy Industry," *China Daily*, May 19, 2010.

73. "Xinjiang Territory Profile—Overview," *BBC*, October 14, 2014.

74. For a Chinese version of Xinjiang's development see "White Paper on Development and Progress in Xinjiang," *China.org.cn*, September 21, 2009, http://www.china.org. cn/archive/2009-09/21/content_18566736.htm.

75. Dru C. Gladney, "Xinjiang: Bridge or Barrier to Xi Jinping's Belt and Road Initiative," *The Caravan*, September 27, 2018, https://www.hoover.org/research/xinjiang-bri dge-or-barrier-xi-jinpings-belt-and-road-initiative.

76. The following draws from the six articles collected in a special issue of *Liaowang*, No. 24, 2010. "Xinjiang nangbei jingji chajuda, gaishan shouru chengwei zuida Minxin gongcheng" [Since the Economic Exchange between North and South Xinjiang Is Large, the Improvement of Income Is Now the Largest Project to Win the Hearts of the People]; "Shizi lukou de Xinjiang" [Xinjiang at the Crossroads]; "Xinjiang gongyehua wuwang shengtaizhen" [The Industrialization of Xinjiang Must Not Overlook the Ecological Debt]; "Nanjiang dizhu" [The South Xinjiang Pillar]; and "Xin yilun yuan jiang bujiu shoulupdian" [The First Point of Departure for the New Round of Assisting Xinjiang]. "Minzu jongjiao jingce di Xinjiang xianshi" [The Realization of the National Minorities Religious Policy in Xinjiang], *News.sina*, June 12, 2010, http://sohu.com/20100612/n272754479.shtml.

77. Christopher Primiano, "China under Stress: The Xinjiang Question," *International Politics*, Vol. 50, No. 3, 2013.

78. For more details, see Michael Dillon, *Xinjiang in the Twenty-First Century: Islam, Ethnicity, and Resistance* (New York: Routledge, 2019), chaps. 6, 7, and 8 and Postscript; Michael E. Clarke, *Xinjiang and China's Rise in Central Asia: A History* (New York: Routledge, 2011), chaps. 7 and 8.

79. Angel Ryono and Matthew Galway, "Xinjiang under China: Reflections on the Multiple Dimensions of the 2009 Urumqi Uprising," *Asian Ethnicity*, Vol. 16, No. 2, 2105.

80. "Chinese Vice President Visits Xinjiang, Stressing Harmony and Stability," *Xinhuanet*, June 21, 2009.

81. "Security of Internet, Phone Top Priory in Xinjiang," *China Daily*, May 21, 2101; "Chinese Vice President."

82. "Zhongyang aidong zuida guimoduikou yuan Jiang, mingnian zijin keneng chao baiyi" [The Party Center Began the Largest Scale Assistance toward Xinjiang; The Investment for Next Year May Exceed One Hundred Yi], *Liaowang xinwen*, May 4, 2010, http:// politics.people.com.cn/GB/1026/11514545.html; "First Point of Departure."

83. "Zhonggong zhongyang guowuyuan shaokai Xinjiang gongzuo tanhui; Hu Jintao jianghua" [Hu Jintao Gave a Speech at the Work Conference on Xinjiang Convened by Party Central and the State Council], *Politics.people.com.cn*, May 21, 2010, http://politics.people.com.cn/GB/1024/11654164.html; "Xinjiang Support Package Unveiled," *China Daily*, May 21, 2010.

84. "Xinjiang Support Package Unveiled"; "Wang Lequan buzai jianren Xinjiang dangwei shuji" [Wang Lequan Will No Longer Serve Concurrently as Xinjiang's Party Secretary], *Wangyi xinwen*, April 25, 2010, http://news.163.com/10/0425/08/653RCB3Q00014AED.html.

85. "Xinjiang Support Package Unveiled."

86. "Wang Lequan Will No Longer Serve."

87. "Wang Lequan zhi Jiang shiwu nian" [Wang Lequan Governs Xinjiang for Fifteen Years], *Takungpao*, April 26, 2010; "Wang Lequan Will No Longer Serve."

88. "Employment and Labor Rights in Xinjiang," *China Daily*, September 17, 2020.

89. For Western approaches to tackle extremism, see Lorenzo Vidino and James Brandon, *Countering Radicalization in Europe* (London: International Centre for the Study of Radicalization and Political Violence, 2012); Lorenzo Vidino, *Countering Radicalization in America: Lessons from Europe* (Washington, DC: United States Institute of Peace, 2010); "How Europe Deals with Terror Offenders When They Are Freed from Jail," *BBC*, March 12, 2020.

90. Gladney, "Xinjiang: Bridge or Barrier"; Dru Gladney, "What's at Stake in Xinjiang," *China.use.edu*, May 11, 2020, https://annenberg.usc.edu/events/usc-us-china-institute/whats-stake-xinjiang.

91. "Their Goal Is to Destroy Everyone: Uighur Camp Detainees Allege Systematic Rape," *BBC*, February 2, 2021.

92. "U. S. Says China's Repression of Uighurs Is 'Genocide,'" *New York Times*, January 19, 2021.

93. "Sinister Intentions behind Xinjiang Cotton Boycott," *China Daily*, March 27, 2021.

94. Adam Dahl, *Settler Colonialism and the Foundations of Modern Democratic Thought* (Lawrence: University Press of Kansas, 2018). "Chinese President Xi Jinping: The Prince," *The Listener*, March 30, 2017, https://www.noted.co.nz/currently/world/chinese-president-xi-jinping-the-prince/.

95. Xi Jinping, "Gaige kaifang 30 nian dangde jianshe huigu yu sikao" [Retrospect and Thinking of Party Construction in the Thirty Years of Reform and Opening], December 15, 2015, *Gongchan dangyuanwang*, http://news.12371.cn/2015/12/15/ARTI1450153943918772.shtml.

96. Hu and Liang, *Biography of Xi Jinping*, pp. 240–242. People like Renmin University professor Zhou Xincheng still argue that communism equals the abolition of private ownership: "Gongchan zhuyi jiushi yao xiaomie shiyaozhi" [Communism Is about the Elimination of Private Ownership], *QSTheory.cn*, June 30, 2018, http://www.qstheory.cn/llqikan/2018-06/30/c_1123059334.htm.

97. "China Is Still in the Primary Stage of Socialism," *Theory China*, June 6, 2018, http://en.theorychina.org/xsqy_2477/201806/t20180606_365442.shtml.

98. James E. Connor, ed., *Lenin on Politics and Revolution* (New York: Pegasus, 1968), introduction and *passim*.

99. Bruce J. Dickson, *The Dictator's Dilemma: The Chinese Communist Party's Strategy for Survival* (New York: Oxford University Press, 2016), pp. 246–254; Mu Chunshan, "China's Communist Party: 3 Successes and 3 Challenges," *The Diplomat*, October 28, 2017, https://thediplomat.com/2017/10/chinas-communist-party-3-successes-and-3-challenges/.

100. "'Zhonggong zhongyang guanyu jiaqiang he gaijin xinxingshi xia dangde jianshe ruogan zhongda wenti di jueding' danshengji" [The Formulation of the CCP's Decision on the Strengthening and Improvement of Certain Major Aspects of Party Construction in the New Situation], *Renminwang*, September 29, 2009, http://cpc.people.com.cn/GB/64093/64094/10135637.html.

101. "Xi Jinping jianghua yingqi shuomingliao shenme" [What Does Xi Jinping's Tough Speech Reveal?], *BBC Chinese*, February 17, 2009, http://news.bbc.co.uk/chinese/simp/hi/newsid_7890000/newsid_7895200/7895245.stm; "China Grooms Deft Politician as the Next Leader," *New York Times*, January 24, 2011; "China's 'Next Leader' in Hardline Rant," *The Telegraph*, February 16, 2009. Theories abound about the "causes" of the 2008 financial crisis, and while Obama and Ben Bernanke blamed "fat-cat bankers" on Wall Street, others pointed fingers at China. Even Bush Treasury secretary Paulson persistently claimed that high saving rates by China and other countries were responsible for global economic imbalance. See, for example, "How China's Boom Caused the Financial Crisis and Why It Matters Today," *Foreign Policy*, January 17, 2012, https://foreignpolicy.com/2012/01/17/how-chinas-boom-caused-the-financial-crisis/.

102. Gao, *He Will Soon Lead China*, pp. 429–434.

103. "Xi Jinping wenhua zhi lu yanyi Zhongguo jiazhiguan" [Xi Jinping's Cultural Journey to Promote Chinese Values], *Ifeng*, October 14, 2009, http://news.ifeng.com/opinion/politics/200910/1014_6438_1387353.shtml.

104. Gao, *He Will Soon Lead China*, pp. 461–462. Officially, many of the retired political leaders are still being invited to policy forums, and they are regularly being consulted on policy issues. In Chinese informal politics, these retired political leaders may still carry a great deal of weight by virtue of their networks of clients who are still incumbents. Pragmatically, this can be a way for retired leaders to protect themselves, their relatives, their former subordinates, and their interests. For instance, one of Jiang Zemin's interests is said to be the protection of his two sons.

105. Willy Lam, "Xi Jinping's Chongqing Tour: Gang of Princelings Gains Clout," *China Brief*, No. 10, Issue 25, December 17, 2010, p. 4.

106. Michael J. Green, "The Democratic Party of Japan and the Future of the U.S.-Japan Alliance," *Journal of Japan Studies*, Vol. 37, No. 1, pp. 91–116.

107. "China's VP Stresses Japan Ties amid Royal Protocol Flap," *AFP*, December 15, 2009; "China Official's Royal Audience Stirs Ire in Japan," *Associated Press*, December 15, 2009.

108. "Emperor Akihito Meets China's Vice President," *Royalty in the News*, December 15, 2009.

109. Gao, *He Will Soon Lead China*, p. 467.

110. "Chinese Vice President Meets Leaders of Japanese Political Parties," *Xinhua*, December 16, 2009.

111. "Biden in China: Ties Are Key to Global Economic Stability," *Washington Post*, August 18, 2011; "China, U.S. Seek to Boost Confidence as Biden Visits," *Reuters*, August 18, 2011.

112. See, for example, US Department of State, n.d., "U.S. Officials on Biden's Trip to China, Mongolia, Japan," August 16–24, 2011, https://2009-2017.state.gov/p/eap/trvl/11/170756.htm.

113. "Zhongguo wangmin xiang Meiguo ti wuda yaoqiu Baideng fanghua zhuang shang wangluo minyi [Chinese Netizens Have Five Major Requests for the United States: Public Opinion on Biden's Visit], *Huanqiu wang*, August 16, 2011, https://world.huanqiu.com/article/9CaKrnJs2yl.

114. "Portrait of Vice President Xi Jinping: 'Ambitious Survivor' of the Cultural Revolution," American Embassy in Beijing, November 16, 2009, Reference ID 09BEIJING3128, WikiLeaks, http://www.wikileaks.org/cable/2009/11/09BEIJING3128.html.

115. "Top Leadership Dynamics Driven by Consensus, Interests, Contacts Say," American Embassy in Beijing, July 23, 2009, Reference ID 09BEIJING2112, WikiLeaks, http://www.wikileaks.org/cable/2009/07/09BEIJING2112.html.

116. Keith Richburg, "Xi Jinping, Likely China's Next Leader, Seen as Pragmatic, Low-Key," *Washington Post*, August 15, 2011.

117. 'We Must Boost Market Confidence" and "Xi, Biden Talk Business Issues in Beijing," both in *China Daily*, August 19, 2011.

118. "China, U.S. Seek to Boost Confidence."

119. "Biden Tells China U. S. Investments Safe," *Washington Post*, August 21, 2011.

120. See, for example, Keith Richburg, "Xi Jinping's U.S. Trip Plays Well in China," *Washington Post*, February 18, 2012.

121. "DreamWorks Animation Announces China Venture as Xi Visits," *Bloomberg News*, February 18, 2012.

122. "Vice President Xi Jinping Meets with U. S. Congressional Leaders," Embassy of the People's Republic of China in the United States of America, February 16, 2012, https://www.mfa.gov.cn/ce/ceus//eng/zmgxss/t906436.htm; "Xi Jinping Confronted on Human Rights in Capitol Hill Meeting," *Los Angeles Times*, February 15, 2012.

123. "DreamWorks Animation."

124. See James Mulvenon, "The Bo Xilai Affair and the PLA," *China Leadership Monitor*, Issue 38, Summer 2012; Alice L. Miller, "The Bo Xilai Affair in Central Leadership Politics," *China Leadership Monitor*, Issue 38 Summer 2012; Joseph Fewsmith, Bo Xilai and Reform: What Will Be the Impact of His Removal?," *China Leadership Monitor*, No. 38, Summer 2012; US-China Economic and Security Review Commission, *2012 Annual Report to Congress* (Washington, DC: US Government Printing Office, 2012), pp. 431–436.

125. "Bo Xilai's Downfall Tied to Wiretapping of Chinese Leaders," *New York Times*, April 25, 2012; "Bo Xilai's Officials Bugged Chinese President's Phone," *The Guardian*, April 26, 2012.

126. Robert Lawrence Kuhn, *How China's Leaders Think* (Singapore: John Wiley & Sons, 2010), p. 425.

127. "Changhong dahei budengyu Chongqing moshi" [Sing the Red and Strike the Black Is Not Equivalent to the Chongqing Model], *Xinbao*, February 29, 2012.

128. To propagate maxims means to read Maoist and Marxist works, tell stories about past struggles, and discuss Marxist maxims.

129. "Xi Jinping Chongqing diaoyan gaodu pingjia dahei" [Xi Jinping Inspects Chongqing and Lauds Highly Strike the Black], *Wenweipo*, December 9, 2010; "In China, One Man's Fall from Grace May Aid Another's Rise to Power," *New York Times*, April 27, 2012; Willy Lam, "Beijing's Post-Bo Xilai Loyalty Drive Could Blunt Calls for Reform," *China Brief*, No. 12, Issue 7, March 12, 2012; "Bo Xilai's Ouster Seen as Victory for Chinese Reformers; Populist Chongqing Party Chief's Firing Is a Defeat for Those Known as 'New Leftists,' Observers Say" *Washington Post*, March 16, 2012.

130. Willy Lam, "Hu Jintao Draws Blood with the Wang Lijun Scandal," *China Brief*, No. 12, Issue 5, March 2, 2012.

131. "As Bo Starts Prison Term His Torture Legacy Endures: Lawyers," *Agence France Presse*, September 24, 2013, https://www.ndtv.com/world-news/as-bo-xilai-starts-prison-term-his-torture-legacy-endures-lawyers-535552; "Chinese Infighting: Secrets of a Succession War," *Financial Times*, March 4, 2012, https://www.ft.com/content/36c9ffda-6456-11e1-b50e-00144feabdc0.

132. China Premier Wen Jiabao's Comments at NPC Press Conference, *Reuters*, March 14, 2012, https://www.reuters.com/article/china-npc-highlights/highlights-china-premier-wen-jiabaos-comments-at-npc-press-conference-idUSL4E8EE11K2 0120314.

133. Miller, "Bo Xilai Affair."

134. Fewsmith, "Bo Xilai and Reform."

135. Miller, "Bo Xilai Affair," p. 10.

136. Fewsmith, "Bo Xilai and Reform," p. 8.

137. Kerry Brown, "Will China's Leaders Regret Bo Xilai's Fall?," *BBC News*, September 22, 2013, https://www.bbc.com/news/world-asia-china-24019450.

138. "Bo Xilai Indicted with Bribery, Power Abuse Charges in China," *BBC*, July 25, 2013; "Bo Xilai Sentenced to Life for Bribery, Embezzlement, Abuse of Power," September 22, 2013; "Bo Xilai qiu zhongshen" [Bo Xilai Receives Life Imprisonment], *Wenweipo*, September 23, 2013.

139. "Court Upholds Life Sentence for Bo Xilai," *New York Times*, October 24, 2013.

140. "Chongqing fahuan dahie meishou caichan" [Chongqing Returns the Properties Confiscated during the Strike the Black Campaign], *Ming Pao*, October 13, 2013; "Meishou minqi zichan 4800 yi xialuo buming" [The Whereabouts of the Confiscated Private Capital Worth 4,800 Billion Are Unknown], Zhongguo *shibao*, October 14, 2013. Some reports claim that the Chongqing government repatriated

the confiscated properties of the entrepreneurs. For instance, the assets of Li Jun, which included real estate, gas stations, nightclubs, finance companies, and hotels worth ¥20 billion, were unfrozen. Li escaped overseas without being rehabilitated. The prison terms meted out for his wife, family members, and staff have not been revoked, and many are still languishing in prison. Other cases, including warrants for arrests, have not been dismissed.

Chapter 8

1. For representatives of a large amount of literature on political succession in communist states see Timothy Colton, *The Dilemma of Reform in the Soviet Union* (New York: Council on Foreign Relations, 1986); Martin McCauley and Stephen Carter, *Leadership and Succession in the Soviet Union, Eastern Europe, and China* (Houndsmills, Basingstoke, Hampshire: Macmillan, 1986); Raymond Taras, ed., *Leadership Change in Communist States* (Boston: Unwin Hyman, 1989); Anthony D'Agostino, *Soviet Succession Struggles: Kremlinology and the Russian Question from Lenin to Gorbachev* (Boston: Allen & Unwin, 1988); Myron Rush, *How Communist States Change Their Rulers* (Ithaca: Cornell University Press, 1974).

2. Leslie Holmes, *Politics in the Communist World* (New York: Oxford University Press, 1986), p. 189.

3. Frederick C. Teiwes and Warren Sun, *The Tragedy of Lin Biao: Riding the Tiger during the Cultural Revolution, 1966–1971* (London: Hurst, 1996); Stephen Uhalley Jr. and Jin Qiu, "The Lin Biao Incident: More Than Twenty Years Later," *Pacific Affairs*, Vol. 66, No. 3, Autumn 1993, pp. 386–398.

4. Holmes, *Politics in the Communist World*, pp. 190ff.

5. For further discussion, see Yijiang Ding, "Consolidation of the PRC's Leadership Succession System from Hu Jintao to Xi Jinping," *China Report*, Vol. 51, No. 1, 2015, esp. p. 52; Jinghan Zeng, "Institutionalization of the Authoritarian Leadership in China: A Power Succession System with Chinese Characteristics?," *Contemporary Politics*, Vol. 20, No. 3, 2014, pp. 294–314; Hu Angang, *Zhongguo jiti lingdao zhidu* [China's Collective Leadership] (Beijing: Renmin daxue chubanshe, 2013), chap. 4.

6. Jiang Zemin, *Jiang Zemin wenxian* [Selected Works of Jiang Zemin] (Beijing: Renmin chubanshe, 2006), Vol. 1, p. 41, Vol. 3, p. 423 (Jiang said that even murder was used to plot for positions); Hu gave similar evaluations, stressing the temptations of fame, profits, power, and sex. Hu Jintao, *Hu Jintao wenxuan* [Selected Works of Hu Jintao] (Beijing: Renmin chubanshe, 2016), Vol. 1, p. 547, Vol. 2, pp. 106–108, Vol. 3, pp. 578–581. Xi's discussion of the subject will be dealt with later. For other numerous references see, for example, "Dangde xinyijie zhongyang lingdao jigou chanshengji" [A Veritable Record of the Birth of the Central Leadership Organizations of the New Party Congress], *Xinhua*, November 15, 2012, http://news.xinhuanet.com/18cpcnc/2012-11/15/c_113700375.htm.

7. "Dangde shibada baogao danshengji" [The Birth of the Report to the Eighteenth Party Congress], *Renminwang*, November 21, 2012.

8. Hu, *China's System of Collective Leadership*, p. 85.

9. "Dangde xinyijie zhongyang lingdao jigou chanshenji [A Veritable Record of the Birth of the Central leadership Organization of the New Party Congress], *Xinhua*, October 24, 2007, " http://news.xinhuanet.com/newscenter/2007-10/24/content 6931498.htm; "Shibada changwei mingdan jiti qiaoding; Xi Jinping qiangshi tuidong quji dangnei butong shengyin" [The Member List of the Eighteenth PBSC Has Been Finalized: Xi Jinping's Forceful Advocacy Is Combined with Attention to the Different Voices within the Party], *Xinbao*, November 7, 2012; Li Cheng, *Chinese Politics in the Xi Jinping Era: Reassessing Collective Leadership* (Washington, DC: Brookings Institution Press, 2016), p. 49; Li Cheng, "Preparing for the 18th Party Congress: Procedures and Mechanisms," *China Leadership Monitor*, No. 36, Winter 2012.

10. For the first time, Hong Kong and Macau also had their own electoral districts. "Shibada daibiao shi ruhe chanshengde?" [How Were the Delegates to the Eighteenth Party Congress Put Together?], *Xinjingbao*, November 2, 2012.

11. "Chuxi Zhonggong shibada daibiao quanbu xuanchu, gong 2270 ming" [All 2,270 Delegates to the Eighteenth Party Congress Have Been Elected], *Renminwang*, August 14, 2012. Social management was a new category that refers to those who worked in the front line at the street or urban regions.

12. "Birth of the Report."

13. Delegates were supposed to be recommended by grassroots party organs and members.

14. Interview with Wang Jingqing, deputy minister of the Central Organization Department, in "Shibada daibiao xuanju dangyuan qunzhong manyidu da 97%" [97 Percent of the Public and Party Members Were Satisfied with the Election of the Representatives to the Eighteenth Party Congress], *Sina*, August 14, 2012, http://news.sina.com.cn/c/2012-08-14/111924965306.shtml.

15. "Shiba zhongwei liao xinmiankong duo" [Many New Faces in the CC Are Expected], *Wenweipo*, August 27, 2012; "Zhongguo shoufu Liang Wengen dangxuan dangdaibiao" [China's Richest Man Is Elected as a Party Delegate], *Wenweipo*, May 9, 2012.

16. "Dangde shibada zhuxituan juxing diyici huiyi" [The Presidium of the Eighteenth Party Congress Convenes Its First Meeting], *Xinhua*, November 7, 2017, http://news.xinhuanet.com/18cpcnc/2012-11/07/c_113632631.htm.

17. "Dangde shibada juxing yubei huiyi he zhuxituan diyici huiyi" [The Eighteenth Party Congress Convenes a Preparatory Meeting and a Meeting of the Congress Presidium], *Renminwang*, November 8, 2012. A full list of these "specially invited delegates" from the Thirteenth to the Seventeenth Party Congresses is in http://www.360doc.com/content/12/0221/00/7499155_188221919.shtml.

18. "All 2,270 Delegates"; "Dang daibiao jiegou bili qu youhua" [The Proportion in the Composition of Party Delegates Is Improving], *Wenweipo*, May 9, 2012.

19. "Shibada daibiao yangqi fangzhen zengyu sancheng" [Among the Delegates to the Eighteenth Party Congress, Representatives from the Centrally Owned SOEs Have Gone Up about 30 Percent], *Wenweipo*, August 28, 2012.

20. "Feigong jingji diwei tigao, minqi laoban dangdaibiao beizeng" [The Status of the Nonpublic Economy Is Rising: Party Delegates Who Are Owners of Private Enterprises Have Multiplied], *Wenweipo*, November 7, 2012.

21. "Amending the CPC Constitution Significant to Party Unity," *Xinhua*, November 18, 2012, http://www.chinadaily.com.cn/china/2012cpc/2012-11/18/content_15939 713.htm.

22. Among the many versions of events, see "Mystery of Xi Jinping's Two Weeks in Hiding," *The Independent*, November 2, 2012, http://www.independent.co.uk/news/ world/asia/mystery-of-xi-jinpings-two-weeks-in-hiding-8277816.html.

23. *Zhengming* and *Dongxiang* combined October 2017 issue, as quoted in "Gangmei pu Xi Jinping 18 da qian yinshen 2 zhou de jingren neimu" [Hong Kong Media Expose the Shocking Inside Story of Xi Jinping's Disappearance for Two Weeks before the Eighteenth National Party Congress], *Epoch Times*, http://www.epochtimes.com/gb/ 17/10/7/n9710467.htm.

24. Mao's wife Jiang Qing and Lin Biao's wife Ye Qun became Politburo members at the Ninth Party Congress in 1969.

25. The term "Propaganda Department" has recently been differently translated as the "Publicity Department," whereas in Chinese the term remains the same. The department is in charge of ideology, propaganda, censorship, and monitoring of the media. See David Shambaugh, 'China's Propaganda System: Institutions, Processes and Efficacy," *China Journal*, No. 57, January 2007. See also Anne-Marie Brady and Wang Juntao, "China's Strengthened New Order and the Role of Propaganda," *Journal of Contemporary China*, Vol. 18, No. 62, 2009.

26. For more details, see Holmes, *Politics in the Communist World*, pp. 188–191.

27. This contrasts with the view that Xi's succession was due to "extraordinary luck," and that the succession process was more "magic than political science." See Kerry Brown, *CEO, China: The Rise of Xi Jinping* (London: I.B. Tauris, 2016), pp. 79 and 92.

28. Mark Irving Lichbach and Alan S. Zuckerman, *Comparative Politics: Rationality, Culture, and Structure* (Cambridge: Cambridge University Press, 1997). An introductory text is Timothy C. Lim, *Doing Comparative Politics*, 3rd ed. (Boulder, CO: Lynne Rienner, 2016), chap. 3. For an earlier analysis that seeks to apply more theoretical approaches, see Thomas W. Robinson, "Political Succession in China," *World Politics*, Vol. 27, No. 1, October 1974.

29. Willy Wo-lap Lam, *Chinese Politics in the Era of Xi Jinping: Renaissance, Reform, or Retrogression?* (New York: Routledge, 2015), p. 58.

30. Hu Jintao's low-profile son Hu Haifeng was head of NucTech, a global company specializing in airport security technology. In 2009, NucTech was embroiled in a bribery scandal in Namibia, but young Hu was not implicated. "Investigation into NucTech Corruption Expands, the Company Formerly Headed by Hu Haifeng," *Asianews*, July 22, 2009, http://www.asianews.it/index.php?l=en&art=15849&size=. In July 2018, Hu Haifeng was named party secretary of Lishui, Zhejiang: "Hu Haifeng Moves Up

the Party Ranks," *Caixin*, July 3, 2018, https://www.caixinglobal.com/2018-07-03/hu-haifeng-moves-up-the-party-ranks-101291149.html.

31. Cheng Li, "A Biographical and Factional Analysis of the Post-2012 Politburo," *China Leadership Monitor*, No. 41, Summer 2013.

32. "Ending Congress, China Presents New Leadership Headed by Xi Jinping," *New York Times*, November 15, 2012; Joseph Fewsmith, "The 18th Party Congress: Testing the Limits of Institutionalization," *China Leadership Monitor*, No. 40, January 2013.

33. A seminal discussion of the different types of institutionalisms is Peter A. Hall and Rosemary C. R. Taylor, "Political Science and the Three New Institutionalisms," *Political Studies*, No. 44, 1996.

34. Susan Shirk, *China: Fragile Superpower* (New York: Oxford University Press, 2007), p. 48 and chap. 3.

35. Alice L. Miller, "The New Party Politburo Leadership," *China Leadership Monitor*, No. 40, Winter, 2013.

36. Miller, "New Party Politburo Leadership."

37. Miller, "New Party Politburo Leadership."

38. Miller, "New Party Politburo Leadership."

39. For instance, in an early projection Alice Miller got five out of the seven PBSC members right. See her "The 18th Central Committee Politburo: A Quixotic, Foolhardy, Rashly Speculative, but Nonetheless Ruthlessly Reasoned Projection," *China Leadership Monitor*, No. 33, Summer 2010, p. 8.

40. "Old Guards to Dominate Party's Inner Council: Conservatives Show They Still Have Sway as Reform-Minded Candidates Lost Out in the Latest Line-Up for Politburo Standing Committee," *SCMP*, November 2, 2012.

41. For a good summary of the various predictions by such media sources as *Reuters*, the *New York Times*, *SCMP*, *The Economist*, and *Nanyang shijie*, see "Pandian gemeiti shibada changwei zuixin yuce mingdan" [A Survey of the Predictions of the PBSC Name List Made by Various Media Sources], *International Business Times Headline*, November 14, 2012, http://www.ibtimes.com.cn/articles/16367/20121114/shibada-changwei.htm. For instance, the *New York Times*, November 2, 2012, also reported that the PBSC membership would be reduced from nine to seven and correctly predicted the names of the top eight contenders. The only miss was Li Yuanchao, head of the COD. True, these predictions might have benefited by last-minute intelligence, but earlier projections, such as the one made by *Mirror Books*, missed only one member.

42. Lucian Pye, *Asian Power and Politics* (Cambridge, MA: Harvard University Press, 1988); Shiping Hua, ed., *Chinese Political Culture, 1989–2000* (Armonk, NY: M.E. Sharpe, 2001); Archie Brown and Jack Gray, eds., *Political Culture and Political Change in Communist States*, 2nd ed. (New York: Holmes & Meier, 1979); Lucian Pye, *The Mandarin and the Cadre: China's Political Cultures* (Ann Arbor: Center for Chinese Studies, the University of Michigan, 1988); Peter Moody, "Political Culture and the Study of Chinese Politics," in Sujian Guo, ed. *Political Science and Chinese Political Studies: The State of the Field* (Heidelberg: Springer, 2013); Jonathan Unger, ed., *The Nature of Chinese Politics* (Armonk, NY: M.E. Sharpe, 2002).

43. Unger, *Nature of Chinese Politics*, p. 175.

44. Daniel Bell, *The China Model: Political Meritocracy and the Limits of Democracy* (Princeton, NJ: Princeton University Press, 2015).

45. For a discussion of the importance of the mass line in Chinese political culture, see Wenfang Tang, *Populist Authoritarianism: Chinese Political Culture and Regime Sustainability* (New York: Oxford University Press, 2016).

46. Miller, "New Party Politburo Leadership," pp. 2–5.

47. "Curse of Chongqing? Probe into Sun Zhengcai Evokes Memories of Bo Xilai's Dramatic Fall," *SCMP*, July 18, 2017.

48. Li, "Biographical and Factional Analysis"; "Six Politburo Standing Committee Members Are Not Technocrats," *SCMP*, November 20, 2012.

49. For an analysis of the Soviet equivalent, see Evan Mawdsley and Stephen White, *The Soviet Elite from Lenin to Gorbachev: The Central Committee and Its Members, 1917–1991* (Oxford: Oxford University Press, 2000).

50. "Zhongwei yuchae bili da 9.3%, 19 ren bei taotai" [The Rate of Elimination in the CC Reaches 9.3 Percent: Nineteen Were Eliminated], *Ta Kung Pao*, November 14, 2012.

51. Li, "Biographical and Factional Analysis," p. 2.

52. "Xinyijie zhonggong zhongyang weiyuanhui he zhonggong zhongyang jilu jiancha weiyuanhui dansheng ji" [The Birth of the New CC and CCDI], *Renminwang*, November 15, 2012; "Junxi zhongwei gaozhan ercheng 50 niandai jiangling chutou tian" [Military Representatives Occupy 20 Percent of Central Committee Posts: The Emergence of Fifth-Generation Generals], *Zhongguo shibao*, November 15, 2012; "Zhongyang weiyuanhui 61 ren ju zhiqings jingli" [Sixty-One Members of the CC Have *Zhiqing* Experience], *Xianggang jingji ribao*, November 23, 2012.

53. "Zhonggong shibajie zhongwei 90% wenfake jingying" [90 Percent of the Central Committee of the Eighteenth National Party Congress of China Consists of an Elite Who Studied the Humanities, Law, and Social Sciences], *Zhongguo shiibao*, December 3, 2012.

54. "90 Percent of the Central Committee."

55. "Junxi zhongwei gaozhan ercheng: wushi niandai jiangling chutou tian" [Military Members Make Up a New High of 20 Percent of the Central Committee: The Fifth-Generation Generals Are Now Cropping Up], *Zhongguo shibao*, November 15, 2012.

56. "90 Percent of the Central Committee."

57. See, for example, "Houbu zhongwei xinxue sizhan qisan" [New Blood Makes Up 75 Percent of CC Alternates], *Wenweipo*, November 15, 2012.

58. "Meeting Press, Party Delegates Show Their Personal Side," *Global Times*, November 14, 2012, http://www.globaltimes.cn/content/744221.shtml.

59. Miller, "New Party Politburo Leadership," pp. 10–11.

60. For an updated discussion of institutionalization and factions in China, see Joseph Fewsmith, "What Is a Faction?," in Zheng Yongnian and Lance L. P. Gore, eds., *The Chinese Communist Party in Action: Consolidating Party Rule* (New York: Routledge, 2020).

61. For more detailed discussions, see Fewsmith, "The 18th Party Congress"; and Miller, "New Party Politburo Leadership."

62. For more discussion see Hochul Lee, "Political Institutionalization as Political Development in China," *Journal of Contemporary China*, Vol. 19, No. 65, June 2010.

63. For a discussion of the EU as a young organization, see Jarle Trondal, "Governance in Turbulent Administrative Systems," in Christopher Ansell, Jarle Trondal, and Morten Øgård, eds., *Governance in Turbulent Times* (New York: Oxford University Press, 2017), chap. 7. Gabriel Ben-Dor points out that overinstitutionalization, in the Huntington sense, can subvert change. See his "Institutionalization and Political Development: A Conceptual and Theoretical Analysis," *Comparative Studies in Society and History*, Vol. 17, No. 3, July 1975 One may also add that issues arise on what kind of values have been embedded in what kind of institutions and how change is possible.

64. The Thirteenth, Fourteenth, Fifteenth, Seventeenth, and Nineteenth Party Congresses were all held in October.

Chapter 9

1. A couple of examples will suffice. Richard McGregor, "Party Man, Xi Jinping's Quest to Dominate China," *Foreign Affairs*, September–October 2019; "What Does China Really Want? To Dominate the World," *Bloomberg*, May 20, 2019, https://www.bloomberg.com/opinion/articles/2020-05-20/xi-jinping-makes-clear-that-china-s-goal-is-to-dominate-the-world. A counterpoint is Michael McFaul, "Xi Jinping Is Not Stalin: How a Lazy Historical Analogy Derailed Washington's China Strategy," *Foreign Affairs*, August 10, 2020, https://www.foreignaffairs.com/articles/united-states/2020-08-10/xi-jinping-not-stalin.

2. Sangkuk Lee, "An Institutional Analysis of Xi Jinping's Centralization of Power," *Journal of Contemporary China*, Vol. 26, No. 105, 2017.

3. Xi Jinping, *Xi Jinping tan zhiguo lizheng* [Xi Jinping on the Governance of China] (Beijing: Waiwen chubanshe, 2014), p. 35 (hereafter *Governance 1*).

4. Xi's speech in 2013 entitled "Several Problems of Upholding and Developing Socialism with Chinese Characteristics" was not published until 2019 in *Qiushi*, March 31, 2019, http://www.qstheory.cn/dukan/qs/2019-03/31/c_1124302776.htm. On many occasions Xi alluded to the fact that he and his family suffered tremendously during the Cultural Revolution, and he clearly loathed the regressive features and lost opportunities associated with it.

5. As Xi said, "Without the past, there would be no present, so we can't completely negate everything in the past."

6. See, for example, "The World Bank in China," *World Bank*, March 28, 2017, http://www.worldbank.org/en/country/china/overview.

7. Christopher Ansell, Jarle Trondal, and Morten Øgård, eds., *Governance in Turbulent Times* (New York: Oxford University Press, 2017), p. 298, chaps. 1, 4, and 13.

8. Leslie A. Pal, *Beyond Policy Analysis: Public Issue Management in Turbulent Times*, 5th ed. (Toronto: Nelson, 2014), p. 319.

9. Xi, *Governance 1*, pp. 100, 274, 348; Xi Jinping, *Xi Jinping tan zhiguo lizheng* [Xi Jinping on the Governance of China] (Beijing: Waiwen chubanshe, 2017) (hereafter *Governance 2*), pp. 81, 538.

10. Xi, *Governance 1*, pp. 98, 348.

11. For example, Aldjandro Foxley and Fernando Sossdorf argue that only a handful of countries were able to transition to advanced economies over the past fifty years. See their "Making the Transition: From Middle-Income to Advanced Economies," Carnegie Endowment for International Peace, September 2011.

12. "Quanmian jiaqiang dangjian chengjiu zongshu: zhangxian lingdao hexin zuoyong" [A Summary of the Achievements in the Comprehensive Strengthening of Party-Building: Advance the Core Function of Leadership], *Sina*, August 15, 2017, http://news.sina.com.cn/gov/2017-08-15/doc-ifyixias1032881.shtml.

13. Xi, *Governance 1*, p. 409; English version is Xi Jinping, *The Governance of China* (Beijing: Foreign Language Press, 2014), p. 457 (hereafter *Governance 1E*). The insensitive metaphor is translated in English as "drawing conclusions based on partial information."

14. For instance, the numerous policy initiatives made by the Xi administration vastly exceed the prognosis and recommendations made by foreign agencies such as the OECD's *The People's Republic of China: Avoiding the Middle-Income Trap: Policies for Sustained and Inclusive Growth*, September 2013.

15. Xi, *Governance 1*, pp. 91, 309; the updated figures are drawn from Xi's address to the American public made in 2015. The National Committee on U.S.-China Relations, "Full Text from President Xi Jinping's Speech," https://www.ncuscr.org/content/full-text-president-xi-jinpings-speech. See also Xi, *Governance 2*, p. 30.

16. Heike Holbig and Bruce Gilley, "Reclaiming Legitimacy in China," *Politics & Policy*, Vol. 38, No. 3, June 2010. See also Thomas Heberer and Gunter Schubert, *Regime Legitimacy in Contemporary China: Institutional Change and Stability* (New York: Routledge, 2009).

17. Xi, *Governance 1*, p. 409; Xi, *Governance 1E*, pp. 457–458.

18. Xi, *Governance 1*, pp. 98, 348.

19. "White Paper on China's Military Strategy," *China Daily*, May 26, 2015, http://www.chinadaily.com.cn/china/2015-05/26/content_20820628.htm.

20. "White Paper on China's Military Strategy."

21. Orville Schell and John Delury, *Wealth and Power: China's Long March to the Twenty-First Century* (New York: Random House, 2013).

22. "Ganbu bixu yongbu dongyao xinyang; geming lixiang gaoyutian" [The Ideal of the Cadres Must Never Be Shaken; Their Revolutionary Values Must Be Sky-High], *Qiushi*, November 4, 2013, http://www.chinanews.com/gn/2013/11-01/5451103.shtml.

23. Xi, *Governance 1*, pp. 200–204; "Xi Jinping's guojia anquan guan" [Xi Jinping's National Security Concept], *Zhongguo gongchandang xinwenwang*, http://news.ifeng.com/a/20170222/50720579_0.shtml; "Xi: Security of Nation a Priority," *China Daily*, February 18, 2017, http://www.chinadaily.com.cn/china/2017-02/18/content_28248812.htm.

24. Chinese historians often cite the revitalizations during the Guangwu (Han dynasty) and Jiajing (Tang dynasty) as examples of successful dynastic revivals; Shangyang (Chin dynasty) as an example of successful reform; and the Wang Anshi reforms (Song dynasty) and the Hundred Days Reform (Qing dynasty) as examples of failed reforms.

25. For more discussion, see Holbig and Gilley, "Reclaiming Legitimacy in China"; Heike Holbig, "Ideological Reform and Political Legitimacy in China: Challenges in the Post-Jiang Era," GIGA Working Paper No. 18, June 19, 2006; "Communist Party Powered by History? Why China's One-Party Rule Is Facing a Legitimacy Crisis," *SCMP*, October 10, 2015.

26. "Naner Xi Jinping" [Xi Jinping the Real Man], *DW*, January 25, 2013, http://www. dw.com/zh/%E7%94%B7%E5%84%BF%E4%B9%A0%E8%BF%91%E5%B9%B3/a-16549520?&zhongwen=simp.

27. Shannon Tiezzi, "China's National Security Strategy," *The Diplomat*, January 24, 2015, http://thediplomat.com/2015/01/chinas-national-security-strategy/.

28. Quoted in "Xi Jinping gaige zhe sannian" [The Three Years of Reform under Xi Jinping)], *Nanfang Zhoumu*, December 3, 2015, http://www.infzm.com/content/113 463. This seems to be an official lead article summarizing Xi's three years.

29. Tai Ming Cheung, "The Chinese National Security State Emerges from the Shadows to Center Stage," *China Leadership Monitor*, Issue 65, Fall 2020.

30. D. D. Wu, "Anti-espionage: A New Mass Line Campaign in China?," *The Diplomat*, April 17, 2017, http://thediplomat.com/2017/04/anti-espionage-a-new-mass-line-campaign-in-china/.

31. This formulation was first raised in 2016: "Xi Jinping zhuchi zhonggong zhongyang zhengzhi ju changweihui huiyi" [Xi Jinping Presides over a Meeting of the Standing Committee of the Politburo], *Xinhua*, January 7, 2016, http://www.xinhuanet.com/politics/2016-01/07/c_1117705534.htm.

32. For a specific example see *Xi Jinping guanyu yanming dangde jilu he guiju lunshi zhaibian* [Extracts from Xi Jinping's Discussions of the Strict Applications of the Party's Discipline and Regulations] (Beijing: Zhongguo wenxian chubanshe, 2016), pp. 36–38.

33. A familiar Chinese expression also used frequently by Dr. Sun Yat-sen to denote the alleged Chinese lack of public spirit and their inability to organize, to unite, and to observe discipline.

34. Delia Lin, *Civilizing Citizens in Post-Mao China: Understanding the Rhetoric of Suzhi* (New York: Routledge, 2017).

35. "Wang Qishan Renminribao zhuanwen: kaiqi xinshidai, tashang xinzhengcheng" [Wang Qishan's Article in the *People's Daily*: A New Era and a New Journey], *Guancha*, November 7, 2017, http://www.guancha.cn/politics/2017_11_07_433778.shtml.

36. *Extracts from Xi Jinping's Discussions*, p. 96. This collection contains Xi's harshest criticism of the Party, citing for nepotism and cronyism. He calls party members venal, unscrupulous, deceitful, and fawning.

37. *Extracts from Xi Jinping's Discussions*, p. 65.

38. For a discussion of this concept, see Kenneth G. Lieberthal and David M. Lampton, *Bureaucracy, Politics, and Decision Making in Post-Mao China* (Berkeley: University of California Press, 1992), chap. 1.

39. *Extracts from Xi Jinping's Discussions.*

40. *Extracts from Xi Jinping's Discussions*, pp. 71, 125.

41. In the Chinese government, vertical rule means that the central ministries extend control over functions such as finance, agriculture, and industry down the various administrative levels, whereas horizontal rule means that the local authorities, such as the provinces and counties, control the horizontal coordinating of *all* functions in their areas of jurisdictions.

42. China has 7.16 million civil servants. At the national level, the bureaucracy in per capita terms is small when compared with most countries in the world, but it is growing, especially at the subprovincial levels (equivalent to the OECD average). Yuen Yuen Ang, "Counting Cadres: A Comparative View of the Size of China's Public Employment," *China Quarterly*, Vol. 211, September 2012.

43. Pierre Landry, *Decentralized Authoritarianism in China: The Communist Party's Control of Local Elites in the Post-Mao Era* (New Haven: Yale University Press, 2008).

44. For an analysis of the institutional origins of the centralization of power, see Sangkuk Lee, "An Institutional Analysis of Xi Jinping's Centralization of Power," *Journal of Contemporary China*, Vol. 26, No. 105, 2017.

45. "Jianding gaige xinxin, baochi dingli he renjin" [Firm Up the Faith in Reform, Persevere with Determination and Fortitude], CCTV, August 19, 2015, http://opin ion.cntv.cn/2015/08/19/ARTI1439979953357129.shtml. Guo Ping, the pseudonym used by an official writing collective consisting of political analysts and experts, has published numerous commentaries on current events since the Eighteenth Party Congress.

46. Bruce J. Dickson, *The Dictator's Dilemma: The Chinese Communist Party's Strategy for Survival* (New York: Oxford University Press, 2016), chap. 3. See also Rory Truex, "Consultative Authoritarianism and Its Limits," *Comparative Political Studies*, Vol. 50, No. 3, June 2014.

47. Rory Truex, "Authoritarian Gridlock? Understanding Delay in the Chinese Legislative System," *Comparative Political Studies*, Vol. 53, No. 9, August 2020.

48. See David Lampton, "China Politics: The Bargaining Treadmill," in Yu-ming Shaw, ed., *Changes and Continuities in China's Communism* (New York: Routledge, 1988).

49. For Deng's governance records, see Ezra F. Vogel, *Deng Xiaoping and the Transformation of China* (Cambridge, MA: Harvard University Press, 2011), chaps. 13 to 15.

50. Eric Fish, "China's Youth Admire America Far More Than We Knew," *Foreign Policy*, February 9, 2017, http://foreignpolicy.com/2017/02/09/chinas-youth-admire-amer ica-far-more-than-we-knew-surprising-survey-results-ideological-university-crackdown/.

51. The perennial issue of how much China should incorporate Western cultural practices is represented by the notions of *ti-yong* prevalent in the mid-nineteenth century (Chinese learning for the essence, Western learning for practical use) and

the total Westernization of the May Fourth Movement of 1919. Explicit campaigns against Western influence in the post-Mao period are the campaign against Spiritual Pollution of 1983 and the campaign against Bourgeois Liberalization of 1984.

52. Samuel Barber, "Jihad vs. McWorld," *The Atlantic*, March 1992. See also his *Jihad vs. McWorld* (New York: Times Books, 1995).

53. Adam Dahl, *Settler Colonialism and the Foundations of Modern Democratic Thought* (Lawrence: University Press of Kansas, 2018). The Black Lives Matter movement represents a powerful resistance of the settler's narrative.

54. "Xi Jinping Endorses the Promotion of Confucius," *SCMP*, February 29, 2016.

55. See, for example, David Shambaugh, "China's Soft-Power Push: The Search for Respect," *Foreign Affairs*, June 2015, https://www.foreignaffairs.com/articles/china/2015-06-16/china-s-soft-power-push; Eleanor Albert, "China's Big Bet on Soft Power," Council on Foreign Relations, May 11, 2017, https://www.cfr.org/backgroun der/chinas-big-bet-soft-power.

56. The Soft Power 30: A Global Ranking of Soft Power, 2018 (n.p.: USC Center on Public Diplomacy).

57. "Dangqian woguo yishixingtai jianshe mianlin di liuda tiaozhan" [The Six Major Challenges Confronting Our Country's Ideological Construction], *Dangjian*, No. 7, 2012, pp. 22–23.

58. Xi, *Governance 1*, p. 156; Xi, *Governance 1E*, p. 175.

59. "Event Recap—Leninism Upgraded: Restoration and Innovation under Xi Jinping," *Asia Center*, April 13, 2017, https://asiacenter.harvard.edu/news/event-recap-%E2%80%93-leninism-upgraded-restoration-and-innovation-under-xi-jinping.

60. Suisheng Zhao, "China's Pragmatic Nationalism: Is It Manageable?," *Washington Quarterly*, Vol. 29, No. 1, Winter 2005–2006; Elena Barabantseva, "Nationalism," in Chris Ogden, ed., *Handbook of China's Governance and Domestic Politics* (New York: Routledge, 2013).

61. Kristin Shi-Kupfer, Mareike Ohlberg, Simon Lang, and Bertram Lang, *Ideas and Ideologies Competing for China's Political Future* (Berlin: Merics, 2017). See also Andreas Møller Mulvad, "China's Ideological Spectrum: A Two-Dimensional Model of Elite Intellectuals' Visions," *Theory and Society*, Vol. 47 (September 2018).

62. Glenn D. Hook, Julie Gilson, Christopher W. Hughes, and Hugo Dobson, *Japan's International Relations: Politics, Economics, and Security*, 3rd ed. (New York: Routledge, 2012), p. 67.

63. For further discussions of the various aspects of the rise of the Chinese middle class see Cheng Li, ed., *China's Emerging Middle Class: Beyond Economic Transformation* (Washington, DC: Brookings Institution Press, 2010).

64. For a summary discussion of these theories, see Pal, *Beyond Policy Analysis*, pp. 311ff. See also Yehezkel Dror, *Policymaking under Adversity* (New York: Routledge, 2017).

65. *Governance 2*, pp. 81–82; English translation in Xi Jinping, *The Governance of China*, Vol. 2 (Beijing: Foreign Language Press, 2017), pp. 85–86.

66. Originally, the metaphor refers to Beijing's attempts to contain financial risks., "Xi Jinping Is Biding His Time on Market Reforms, China Watcher Says," *SCMP*, June 9, 2017.

67. Two representative examples are "Will Xi Jinping's Era of One-Man Rule Bring the Progress China Desires," *SCMP*, October 31, 2017; "Xi Jinping Becomes China's Most Powerful Leader since Mao Zedong," *Time*, October 24, 2017, http://time.com/4994 618/xi-jinping-china-19th-congress-ccp-mao-zedong-constitution/.

68. Leslie Holmes, *Politics in the Communist World* (New York: Oxford University Press, 1986), pp. 183–184.

69. Many sources have indicated adversarial relations between Xi and Liu. Liu was charged with using fulsome praise to make Xi look ridiculous. "Liu Yunshan zaishi gaojihei?" [Li Yunshan Applied High-Class Black Again?], *New Tang Dynasty Television*, July 3, 2017, https://www.ntdtv.com/gb/2017/07/03/a1331722.html.

70. "Xi Stresses Joint Battle Command for Military Reform," *Xinhua*, April 20, 2016, http://news.xinhuanet.com/english/2016-04/20/c_135297662.htm.

71. For example, see "Why Xi Jinping Has No Need of Factions in the Communist Party," *SCMP*, August 8, 2016.

72. "It's Not Just the Cabinet: Trump's Transition Team May Need to Find about 4,100 Appointees," *Washington Post*, December 5, 2016.

73. For more detailed discussion of these aspects see Holmes, *Politics in the Communist World*.

74. "Dagong wang: Xi Jinping's Zhijiang xinjun" [Dagong wang: Xi Jinping's "Zhijiang New Army"], reproduced in *China Digital Times*, December 30, 2014, https://chinad igitaltimes.net/chinese/2014/12/%E5%A4%A7%E5%85%AC%E7%BD%91%EF %BD%9C%E4%B9%A0%E8%BF%91%E5%B9%B3%E7%9A%84%E4%B9%8B%E6 %B1%9F%E6%96%B0%E5%86%9B/.

75. "Xi Promotes Biggest Batch of Officers to Full General," *Strait Times*, August 5, 2016, http://www.straitstimes.com/asia/east-asia/xi-promotes-biggest-batch-of-officers-to-full-general; Bo Zhiyue, "Xi Jinping's New Generals," *The Diplomat*, August 11, 2015, https://thediplomat.com/2015/08/xi-jinpings-new-generals/.

76. "19 da qianxi Xijiajiang duoqu wujun shuaiyin paobu jiuwei" [Five Members of the "Xi Family Army" Seize the Positions of General Just before the Nineteenth Party Congress], *Voice of America*, October 13, 2017, https://www.voachinese.com/a/ xi-jinping-proteges-20171012/4068096.html; "As China's Big Leadership Revamp Nears, Xi Jinping is Carrying Out a Military Reshuffle," *Quartz*, September 1, 2017, https://qz.com/1067547/as-chinas-big-leadership-revamp-nears-xi-jinping-is-carry ing-out-a-military-reshuffle/.

77. "Xi's Nerve Centre: Chinese Politics," *The Economist*, June 10, 2017; "China's President Xi Jinping Now Has a Dozen Titles, and Counting," *Quartz*, January 23, 2017, https:// qz.com/892208/chinas-president-xi-jinping-now-has-a-dozen-titles-and-counting/ ; "Chairman of Everything," *The Economist*, April 2, 2016.

78. For more information about State Council LSGs see "Guowuyuan lingdao xiaozu you naxie ren goucheng, ruhe yunxing" [Who Occupies Positions in the State Council LSGs and How Do These Groups Function?], *Zhongguo gongchandang xinwenwang*, July 10, 2013, http://theory.people.com.cn/n/2013/0710/c40531-22143226.html.

79. This is especially the case with cohabitation, when the French president must pick the prime minister from a political party other than his own. For more details, see

Kimberly A. McQuire, "President-Prime Minister Relations, Party Systems, and Democratic Stability in Semi-presidential Regimes: Comparing the French and Russian Models," *Texas International Law Journal*, Vol. 47, 2012, pp. 433–441.

80. One rare English source is John Wong, "Interpreting Li Keqiang's Strategies of Managing the Chinese Economy and Its Reform," EAI Background Brief No. 863, October 30, 2013). Among the many Chinese-language studies of Li Keqiang are Xiang Jiangyu, *Li Keqiang bandi* [Li Keqiang's Background Connections] (Carle Place, NY: Mirror Books, 2011); Xia Fei, Yang Yun, and Bai Xiaoyun, *Taizidang he Gongqingtuan: Xi Jinping pk Li Keqiang* [The Princeling Faction and the Communist Youth League: Xi Jinping Competes with Li Keqiang] (Carle Place, NY: Mirror Books, 2007).

81. "Premier Li's Second Term: From 'Likonomics' to Following Orders," *SCMP*, October 25, 2017.

82. "Li Keqiang—China's Underrated Premier," *merics.org*, July 28, 2016, https://www. merics.org/en/blog/li-keqiang-chinas-underrated-premier.

83. *Baidu baike*, the semiofficial encyclopedia online, lists up to twenty-seven LSGs. For a discussion of the LSGs see Alice L. Miller, "More Already on the Central Committee's Leading Small Groups," *China Leadership Monitor*, No. 44, Summer 2014; Alice L. Miller, "The CCP Central Committee's Leading Small Groups," *China Leadership Monitor*, No. 26, September 2008.

84. For details, see Zhou Wang, *Zhongguo xiazu jishi yanjiu* [Research on China's Small Groups System] (Tianjin: Tianjin renmin chubanshe, 2010).

85. "The Who's Who of China's Leading Small Groups," *Mercator Institute for China Studies*, January 27, 2017, https://www.merics.org/en/merics-analysis/china-mapp ing/the-whos-who-of-chinas-leading-small-groups/.

86. Barry Naughton, "The Challenges of Economic Growth and Reform," in Robert S. Ross and Jo Inge Bekkevold, eds., *China in the Era of Xi Jinping: Domestic and Foreign Policy Challenges* (Washington, DC: Georgetown University Press, 2016), pp. 66–91.

87. "Zuigao guige lingdao xiaozu nangkuo duoshao buwei" [How Many Ministries and Commissions Are Represented in the Highest-Ranking Leading Small Groups?], *Beijing qingnianbao*, May 3, 2016, http://epaper.ynet.com/html/2016-05/03/content _195637.htm.

88. "Huigu zhongyang shengaizu zhe sinian: hangli leitai gongjian kenan dili fenjin" [A Look Back at the Central Deepening Reform Group's Four Years: The Many Courageous Battles to Advance and to Overcome Challenges], December 21, 2017, *Sina*, http://news.sina.com.cn/o/2017-12-21/doc-ifypwzxq4772446.shtml; "Xi Jinping zuozhen shengaizu, zhexie gaige zhenggai zheng gaibian nidi shenghuo" [Xi Jinping Takes Charge of the Group for Deepening Reform: Reforms Are Changing Your Lives], *Renmin ribao*, August 11, 2017, http://www.gov.cn/xinwen/2017-08/11/ content_5217145.htm.

89. On State Council LSGs see "Chaobuji jigou di guowuyuan lingdao xiaozu" [The Supraministry Organization: The State Council Leading Small Groups], *Sohu*, http:// news.sohu.com/20130722/n382222978.shtml; "Guowuyuan duoge lingdao xiaozu

yu zuzhi jigou renyuan diaozheng" [The Personnel Adjustments in the State Council Leading Small Groups and Other Organizations], *Xinhua*, July 4, 2013, http://news.xinhuanet.com/renshi/2013-07/04/c_124947684.htm.

90. "Guowuyuan lingdao xiaozu you naxieren goucheng ruhe yunxing" [How the State Council Leading Small Groups Operate and Who Staffs Them"], *Zhongguo qingnianbao*, July 10, 2013, http://theory.people.com.cn/n/2013/0710/c40531-22143226.html.

91. "Three Years of Reform"; "Gongbao qicao zu chengyuan jiemi gaige lingdao xiaozu" [A Communiqué Declassifies the Information Regarding the Membership of the Reform Leading Group], *Sina*, November 14, 2013, http://news.sina.com.cn/c/2013-11-14/105428708155.shtml.

92. "Zhongyang quanmian shenhua gaige weiyuanhui lici huiyi" [The Meetings of the Central Committee on Comprehensively Deepening Reforms], https://web.archive.org/web/20160806232638/http://xuan.news.cn/zt/shengai14.html.

93. "Zhengzhiju jueding sheli zhongyang tongzhan gongzuo lingdao xiaozu" [The Politburo Decides to Establish the Central United Front Work LSG], *Xinhuawang*, July 30, 2015, http://news.ifeng.com/a/20150730/44308867_0.shtml.

94. "Zhongyang lingdao xiaozu yu 22 ge, Xi Jinping ren 4 xiaozu zuchang" [Among the More Than Twenty-Two Central Leading Small Groups; Xi Jinping Is e Chair of Four], *Zhongguowang*, July 31, 2015, http://news.china.com.cn/2015-07/31/content_36190622.htm. There was a proliferation of LSGs beneath the county level, but they are mostly paper organizations.

95. Peter Martin and David Cohen, "Inside Xi Jinping's Reform Strategy," *National Interest*, March 20, 2014; Peter Martin, "The Humbling of the NDRC: China's National Development and Reform Commission Searches for a New Role amid Restructuring," *China Brief*, Vol. 14, No. 5, March 7, 2014.

96. See, for example, "China's Communist Party Seeks Company Control before Reform," *Financial Times*, August 14, 2017, https://www.ft.com/content/31407684-8101-11e7-a4ce-15b2513cb3ff.

97. "How the Communist Party Controls China's State-Owned Industrial Titans," *SCMP*, June 17, 2017.

98. The following draws from "Zhengzhiju 92 ci jiti xuexi muhou jiemi: Shui zai Zhongnanhai jiangke" [The Secrets of the Ninety-Two Sessions of the Politburo Study Sessions Revealed: Who Lectures at Zhongnanhai?], *Zhongguo xinwenwang*, June 3, 2014, http://www.chinanews.com/gn/2014/06-03/6236011.shtml; Phillip C. Saunders, "The Chinese Politburo Hits the Books," *China Brief*, Vol. 6, No. 15, July 19, 2006; Wen-Hsuan Tsai and Nicola Dean, "The CCP's Learning System: Thought Unification and Regime Adaptation," *China Journal*, No. 69, 2013; Alice Miller, "Politburo Processes under Xi Jinping," *China Leadership Monitor*, No. 47, Summer 2015.

99. "The CCP's Nerve Center: Xi Jinping and His Aides Hold Sway over Powerful Core Institutions," *Merics*, October 30, 2019, https://merics.org/en/short-analysis/ccps-nerve-center.

100. Joel Wuthnow, "China's Much-Heralded NSC Has Disappeared," *Foreign Policy*, June 30, 2016, http://foreignpolicy.com/2016/06/30/chinas-much-heralded-natio nal-security-council-has-disappeared-nsc-xi-jinping/.

101. Bates Gill and Martin Kleiber, "China's Space Odyssey: What the Antisatellite Test Reveals about Decision-Making in Beijing," *Foreign Affairs*, Vol. 86, No. 3, May–June 2007.

102. "Zhongguo choushe guoanwei Jiang Zemin shidai cengyou citiyi" [China Prepares for the Establishment of the National Security Commission: This Proposal Was Made in the Era of Jiang Zemin], *Takungpao*, November 12, 2013, http://news. takungpao.com/mainland/focus/2013-11/2033054.html; Yun Sun, "China's New 'State Security Committee: Questions Ahead," *PacNet*, No. 81, November 14, 2013; Ross and Bekkevold, *China in the Era of Xi Jinping*, p. 47. See also Weixing Hu, "Xi Jinping's 'Big Power Diplomacy' and China's Central Security Commission (CNSC)," *Journal of Contemporary China*, No. 25, Issue 98, 2016.

103. You Ji, "China's National Security Commission: Theory, Evolution and Operations," *Journal of Contemporary China*, No. 25, Issue 98 (2016).

104. "Zhongyang waishi gongzuo lingdao xiaozu" [The Central Foreign Affairs Leading Small Group], *Baidu baike*, http://baike.baidu.com.view/1799376.htm.

105. Pal, *Beyond Policy Analysis*, pp. 329–330.

106. Tamkin, "China's Much-Heralded NSC."

107. "Chengli sannianduo guoanwei shouci chujing" [The First Televised Exposure of the State Security Commission in the More Than Three Years since Its Inception), *Sina*, February 20, 2017, http://news.sina.com.cn/o/2017-02-20/doc-ifyarrcc8048012. shtml.

108. Wuthnow, "China's Much Heralded NSC".

109. "Xi yu Zeng Qinghong duijue: Guoanwei 20 ming gaoguan shouci chujing" [Xi Challenges Zeng Qinghong: Twenty High Officials of the State Security Commission Make Their First Appearance], *aboluowang*, February 18, 2017, http://www.aboluow ang.com/2017/0218/884178.html.

110. "Xinhua Insight: Plenary Session Offers Glimpse into CPC's Inner Workings," *Xinhua*, November 4, 2016, http://news.xinhuanet.com/english/2016-11/04/c_13 5805602.htm.

111. "Zhonggong zhongyang zhengzhiju zhaokai minzhu shenghuohui, Xi Jinping zhuchi huiyi bing fabiao zhongyao jianghua" [The Politburo of the CCP's Central Committee Convenes a Democratic Life Meeting: Xi Jinping Presided and Gave an Important Speech], December 27, 2016, http://news.xinhuanet.com/politics/2016-12/27/c_1120199912.htm. This source carries a sixteen-minute video segment of the Politburo meeting showing awkward Politburo members reading self-criticism statements and taking notes: "China's Top Party Cadres Pledge Loyalty to Xi Jinping in Mao-Style Self-Criticism Session Ahead of Reshuffle," *SCMP*, December 30, 2016.

112. "Liuzhong quanhui wenjian qicaozu chengyuan Deng Maosheng: Xi hexin yu jiti lingdao bu maodun" [Deng Maosheng, Member of the Sixth Plenum's Document Drafting Committee: The Xi Core Does Not Contradict Collective Leadership], *Zaobao*, November 1, 2016, https://www.zaobao.com.sg/special/report/politic/ cnpol/story20161101-684633.

113. For instance, "Chinese Communist Party Expands Xi Jinping's Political Power, Anointing Him 'Core' Leader," *SCMP*, October 27, 2016.

114. "The Sixth Plenum Communique Affirms the 'Xi Core' Position," *Epoch Times*, October 27, 2016, http://www.epochtimes.com/gb/16/10/27/n8436288.htm.

115. Deng Xiaoping, Deng Xiaoping Wenxuan [*Selected Works*] (Beijing: Renmin chubanshe, 1993), Vol. 3, pp. 272, 277–278, 301, and 322.

116. "10nian dangnei wu hexin, Hu Jintao ren Xi Jinping buren" [The Absence of a Core for Ten Years: Hu Jintao Put Up with It, But Not Xi), *NTDTV*, February 4, 2016, http://ca.ntdtv.com/xtr/gb/2016/02/04/a1250906.html. See also Alice L. Miller, "'Core' Leaders, 'Authoritative Persons,' and Reform Pushback," *China Leadership Monitor*, No. 50, Summer 2016.

117. Deng, *Selected Works*, Vol. 3, pp. 298 and 310.

118. "Xi hexin yu jiti lingdao bumaodun" [The Xi Core Does Not Contradict Collective Leadership], *80sd.org*, November 1, 2016, http://www.80sd.org/guonei/2016/11/01/140103.html.

119. Kerry Brown, "Another Look at China's Leaders after the 2015 Plenum," *The Diplomat*, November 3, 2015, https://thediplomat.com/2015/11/another-look-at-chinas-leaders-after-the-2015-plenum/?allpages=yes&print=yes.

120. For more discussion, see "Xi Jinping Is China's Core Leader: Here's What It Means," *New York Times*, October 31, 2017; "Why China Needs Xi Jinping as Its Core Leader," *SCMP*, November 20, 2017.

121. "Xi Jinping qinzi dianming jiebanren zui nianqing heima chuxian?" [Xi Jinping Personally Appoints; the Emergence of the Youngest Black Horse Successor?" *Kanzhongguo*, November 17, 2016, https://www.kannewyork.com/news/2016/11/17/44007.html.

122. "Three Years of Reform."

123. Xuezhi Guo argues that China, historically, philosophically, and culturally, has always demanded an all-powerful "core" leader who can serve as a sage, savior, and infallible moral model, and Xi is now trying to measure up to this ideal. See his *The Politics of the Core Leader in China: Culture, Institutions, Legitimacy and Power* (Cambridge: Cambridge University Press, 2019).

124. The concept of "inappropriate historical analogy" refers to the faulty and simplistic analogical reasoning, such as comparing compromises to appeasing Hitler at Munich. Casey Hall, "Is Xi Jinping Cultivating a Personality Cult? Or Just a Personality?," *Forbes*, April 26, 2016, http://www.forbes.com/sites/caseyhall/2016/04/26/is-xi-jinping-cultivating-a-personality-cult-or-just-a-personality/#229c335d5a13; "Beware the Cult of Xi," *Economist*, April 2, 2016.

125. Xi, *Governance 1*, pp. 423–448; Xi, *Governance 1E*, pp. 475–497.

126. "'Fans' of Xi Jinping Fawn Online over 'Pingping,' China's New Leader," *Washington Post*, December 12, 2012; "Here Are the Rare Photos of Xi Jinping Posted on a Chinese Fan Site," *Washington Post*, December 13, 2012.

127. English version on YouTube, dated October 17, 2013, is at https://www.youtube.com/watch?v=M734o_17H_A.

128. Kerry Brown, *CEO, China: The Rise of Xi Jinping* (London: I. B. Tauris, 2016), pp. 112–113.

129. "Xi Follows in Deng's Footsteps of Reform: New Party Boss Evokes Memories of Ex-Leader's 1992 Tour and Issues a Signal of His Commitment to Change by Heading to Shenzhen on First Trip," *SCMP*, December 7, 2012.

130. "Zhongyang lingdao tongzhi kanwang laotongzhi" [Central Leaders Visit Elders], *Xinhua*, February 13, 2018, http://www.xinhuanet.com/2018-02/13/c_1122415672. htm. Attempts by analysts to compare the annual lists to see which elder(s) are out of favor have not been fruitful.

131. The term "personalism" is used to denote one aspect of Japanese political culture in Frank Langdon's *Politics in Japan* (Boston: Little, Brown, 1967)is also appropriate to China.

132. Brown, *CEO, China*, chap. 3.

133. "5 Charts on Global views of China," *Factank*, October 19, 2018, https://www. pewresearch.org/fact-tank/2018/10/19/5-charts-on-global-views-of-china/; "International Publics Divided on China," *Factank*, October 1, 2018, https://www. pewresearch.org/global/2018/10/01/international-publics-divided-on-china/.

134. "Rating World Leaders: The U.S. vs Germany, China and Russia," *Gallup*, 2019, https://www.gallup.com/analytics/247040/rating-world-leaders-2019.aspx.

135. "Xi Jinping Is the World's Most Popular Leader, Says Survey," *Bloomberg*, November 18, 2014, https://www.bloomberg.com/news/articles/2014-12-18/xi-jinping-wins-the-popularity-conest; Shannon Tiezzi, "The World's Most Popular Leader: China's President Xi," *The Diplomat*, December 20, 2014, http://thediplomat.com/2014/12/the-worlds-most-popular-leader-chinas-president-xi/.

136. Chang Zhang and Ruiqin Wu, "Battlefield of Global Ranking: How Do Power Rivalries Shape Soft Power Index Building," *Global China and Media*, Vol. 4, No. 2, 2019.

137. For further discussions see Jinghan Zeng, *The Chinese Communist Party's Capacity to Rule* (Houndmills, Basingstoke, Hampshire: Palgrave Macmillan, 2016), pp. 15ff.

138. For Xi's speeches on these two occasions, see Xi, *Governance 1*, pp. 35–43.

139. "Jiang Zemin zai Zhongguo gongchandang de shiwuci quanguo daibao dahui de jianghua" [Jiang Zemin's Report to the Fifteenth Party Congress of the CCP], September 12, 1997, *Renminwang*, http://cpc.people.com.cn/GB/64162/64168/64568/65445/4526285.html.

140. "GDP Per Capita by Country, Statistics from IMF, 1980–2013," *Knoema*, n.d., https://knoema.com/pjeqzh/gdp-per-capita-by-country-statistics-from-imf-1980-2022?country=China, accessed May 9, 2016.

141. Graham Allison, *Destined for War: Can America and China Escape Thucydides's Trap?* (Boston: Houghton Mifflin Harcourt, 2017). According to Allison, Chinese officials tend to use the nominal GDP in public in order to make it look smaller and less threatening, whereas they tend to use the PPP measure in private when comparing China with the United States. Further, Allison also claims that China's 2016 GDP already doubled the 2010 level in PPP terms. See pp. 9ff.

142. Major Chinese historical revivals (*zhongxing*) and prosperous (*chengshi*) episodes that are deemed to have approximated the "relative prosperity" society ideal include

Wenjing and Guangwu in the Han dynasty, Zhenguan and Yuanhe during the Tang dynasty, and Kangxi, Yongzheng, Qianlong, and Tongguang in the Qing dynasty.

143. Zheng Wang, "The New Nationalism: 'Make My Country Great Again,'" *The Diplomat*, May 10, 2016, http://thediplomat.com/2016/05/the-new-national ism-make-my-country-great-again/; "Trump, Putin, Xi and the Rise of Nostalgic Nationalism," *Financial Times*, January 2, 2017, https://www.ft.com/content/198ef e76-ce8b-11e6-b8ce-b9c03770f8b1. For further discussion, see Robert Weatherley, *Making China Strong: The Role of Nationalism in Chinese Thinking on Democracy and Human Rights* (New York: Palgrave MacMillan, 2014).

144. "Report to the Eighteenth Party Congress," *Ministry of Foreign Affairs*, November 27, 2012, https://www.mfa.gov.cn/ce/ceus//eng/zt/18th_CPC_National_Congress_ Eng/t992917.htm secs. 3 and 6.1. These values are not necessarily new to China, since China experimented with a constitutional government right after the 1911 revolution, and since the notions of freedom and democracy were rallying cries of the May Fourth Movement of 1919. For more analysis, see "How Much Should We Read into China's New 'Core Socialist Value'?," *Council of Foreign Relations Blog*, July 6, 2016, https://www.cfr.org/blog/how-much-should-we-read-chinas-new-core-socialist-values.

145. "Xi Stresses Core Socialist Values," *Xinhua*, February 26, 2014, http://usa.chinadaily. com.cn/china/2014-02/26/content_17305163.htm.

146. "Xi Stresses Core Socialist Values"; "China's 'Core Socialist Values,' the Song and Dance Version," *New York Times*, September 1, 2016.

147. "China's Media Watchdog, Tightening Control of Content, Promote 'Core Socialist Values,'" *SCMP*, June 3, 2017.

148. "Chinese Cinemagoers Must Watch Propaganda Clips before Films," *BBC.com*, July 7, 2017, http://www.bbc.com/news/entertainment-arts-40530850.

149. "Canadian Culture in a Global World," *Global Affairs Canada*, February 1999, https://www.international.gc.ca/trade-agreements-accords-commerciaux/topics-domaines/ip-pi/canculture.aspx?lang=en.

150. "24-Word Core Socialist Values Engraved on People's Mind," *Renminwang*, March 2, 2016, http://en.people.cn/n3/2016/0302/c98649-9023926.html; Jin Kai, "Why Should China Embrace 'Universal Values'?," *The Diplomat*, June 16, 2015, http:// thediplomat.com/2015/06/why-should-china-embrace-universal-values/.

151. Steven Jackson, "China's Relations with the U.S. Pacific Rim Allies: Tensions between Trump's 'America First' and Chinese 'Sharp Power,'" in Justin Massie and Jonathan Paquin, eds., *America's Allies and the Decline of U. S. Hegemony* (New York: Routledge, 2020), pp. 64–66.

152. Brendan Taylor, *Sanctions as Grand Strategy* (Arlington, Oxon: Routledge, 2010).

153. Wenfang Tang, *Populist Authoritarianism: Chinese Political Culture and Regime Sustainability* (New York: Oxford University Press, 2016), pp. 152ff.; Dickson, *The Dictator's Dilemma*, chap. 5.

154. Dickson, The Dictator's Dilemma, chap. 6

155. Zeng, *Chinese Communist Party's Capacity to Rule*, chap. 5.

156. "New China Law Says Children 'Must Visit Parents,'" *BBC*, July 1, 2013, https://www.bbc.com/news/world-asia-china-23124345.

157. For further discussion of the China Dream, see Jonathan Sharp, ed., *The China Renaissance: The Rise of Xi Jinping and the 18th Communist Party Congress* (Singapore: World Scientific, 2013); Lawrence Kuhn, "Xi Jinping's Chinese Dream," *New York Times*, June 4, 2013, http://www.nytimes.com/2013/06/05/opinion/global/xi-jinpings-chinese-dream.html.

158. "Xi Jinping '2.19' jianghua yizhounian: Meiti gongzuozhe he xuezhe zenmekan" [The Anniversary of Xi Jinping's February 19 Speech: How Media Workers and Academics View It], *globalview.cn*, http://www.globalview.cn/html/soceities/info_16334.html.

159. "Document 9: A ChinaFile Translation," *ChinaFile*, November 8, 2013, https://www.chinafile.com/document-9-chinafile-translation. A slightly abridged Chinese version is "Guanyu dangqian yishixingtai lingyu qingkuang di tongbao; Zhonggong jiuhao wenjian quanwen" [A Circular on the Current Ideological Situation: CCP Number 9 Document"], *Bannedbook.org*, May 8, 2015, https://www.bannedbook.org/forum34/topic3971.html#p73136. Since the document has not been officially acknowledged, there is a great deal of controversy about its authenticity. Prominent dissident Bao Tong also said that the provenance of the document cannot be substantiated: "Zhu xuanlu shengji: Wubugao hou yinglai qibujiang" [The Rising Crescendo: The "Seven Unmentionables" Follow the "Five Do Nots"], *Deutsche Welle*, https://www.dw.com/zh/%E4%B8%BB%E6%97%8B%E5%BE%8B%E5%8D%87%E7%BA%A7%E4%BA%94%E4%B8%8D%E6%90%9E%E5%90%8E%E8%BF%8E%E6%9D%A5%E4%B8%83%E4%B8%8D%E8%AE%B2/a-16802727. Yet, in fact, many sources on the mainland have specifically referred to the document as well as the "seven political perils." See, for example, "Shehuizhuyi hexin jiazhi tixi yu hexin jiazhiguan chuangxin ji shidai yiyi zai renshi" [Relearning the Contemporary Significance of the System of Socialist Core Values and the Renovation of the Core Value Notion], *Hehai daixue xuebao*, April 2014, p. 7.

160. "Zhongguo gaoxiao qibujiang beiouguang yinfa reyi" [The Revelation of the "Seven Unmentionables" for the Universities Triggers a Fierce Debate), *Radio Free Asia*, May 10, 2013, https://www.rfa.org/mandarin/yataibaodao/kejiaowen/gx-05102013112922.html; "Seven Subjects Off Limits for Teaching, Chinese Universities Told," *SCMP*, May 10, 2013; September 10, 2013.

161. See also Suisheng Zhao, "Xi Jinping's Maoist Revival," *Journal of Democracy*, Vol. 27, No. 3, July 2016.

162. "Document 9."

163. Anne-Marie Brady, "'The New (Old) Normal': The CCP Propaganda System under Jiang, Hu, and Xi," in Willy Lam, ed., *Routledge Handbook of the Chinese Communist Party* (New York: Routledge, 2018), p. 174.

164. "Revelation of the Seven Unmentionables."

165. For example, see Chen Weidong, "Sifa jiguan yifa duli xingshi zhiquan yanjiu" [On the Independent Exercise of Authority by the Judicial Organs], *Zhongguo faxue*, No. 2, 2014, pp. 20–49.

166. "Chinese Universities Ordered to Ban Textbooks That Promote Western Values,"
SCMP, January 30, 2015.

167. "Xi Calls for More Thought Control on China's Campuses," *SCMP*, December
10, 2016; "Xi Jinping: Ba sixiang zhengzhi gongzuo guanchuan jiaoyu jiaoxue
quanguocheng" [Xi Jinping: Let Thinking and Political Work Run through the
Entire Process of Education and Teaching], *Xinhua*, December 6, 2016, http://news.
xinhuanet.com/politics/2016-12/08/c_1120082577.htm.

168. "Chinese Activist Hu Shigen Jailed for Subversion," *BBC*, August 3, 2016, http://
www.bbc.com/news/world-asia-china-36961431; "Zhou Shifeng: Chinese Law
Firm Founder Jailed for Subversion," *BBC*, August 4, 2016, http://www.bbc.com/
news/world-asia-china-36972206; "Chinese Activist Zhai Yanmin Found Guilty of
Subversion," *BBC*, August 2, 2016, http://www.bbc.com/news/world-asia-china-
36950011; "How Seriously Do Chinese Take 'Confession' Videos?," *BBC*, August 2,
2016, http://www.bbc.com/news/world-asia-china-36882956.

169. See also Zhang Yongnian, "How to Square Xi's Rule of Law Campaign with China's
Crackdown on Lawyers," *Huffpost*, February 16, 2016, http://www.huffingtonp
ost.com/zheng-yongnian/rule-of-law-china-crackdown-lawyers_b_9238644.
html; "'Flee at Once': China's Besieged Human Rights Lawyers," *New York Times
Magazine*, July 25, 2017, https://www.nytimes.com/2017/07/25/magazine/the-lon
ely-crusade-of-chinas-human-rights-lawyers.html.

170. "How Seriously Do Chinese Take 'Confession' Videos?"

171. "How to Understand China's Confession Videos," *Washington Post*, August 5, 2016,
https://www.washingtonpost.com/opinions/global-opinions/how-to-understand-
chinas-confession-videos/2016/08/05/1bc7a1a0-5a75-11e6-831d-0324760ca856_
story.html?utm_term=.21dd2abbbe42; "Beijing's Televised Confessions," *ChinaFile*,
January 20, 2016, http://www.chinafile.com/conversation/beijings-televised-conf
essions.

172. "China's Government Tries Again to Stop Forced Confessions through Torture,"
Reuters, October 10, 2016, http://www.reuters.com/article/us-china-rights/china-
tries-again-to-stop-confessions-through-torture-idUSKCN12A0A4.

173. Edward Wong, "China Ranks Last of 65 Nations in Internet Freedom," *New York
Times*, October 29, 2015.

174. "2018 World Press Freedom Index," Reporters Without Borders, https://rsf.org/en/
ranking/2018.

175. "U.S., British Intelligence Mining Data from Nine U.S. Internet Companies in Broad
Secret Program," *Washington Post*, June 7, 2013, https://www.washingtonpost.com/
investigations/us-intelligence-mining-data-from-nine-us-internet-companies-in-
broad-secret-program/2013/06/06/3a0c0da8-cebf-11e2-8845-d970ccb04497_st
ory.html?noredirect=on&utm_term=.33baf78bcead.

176. "China's New Cybersecurity Law Leaves Foreign Firms Guessing," *New York Times*,
May 31, 2017, https://www.nytimes.com/2017/05/31/business/china-cybersecur
ity-law.html; "Annual Report: China 2016/2017," Amnesty International, https://
www.amnesty.org/en/countries/asia-and-the-pacific/china/report-china/.

177. "New Chinese Film Law Fails to Resolve Confusion over Censorship Rules," *SCMP Magazine*, March 30, 2017; "China Passes Law to Ensure Films 'Serve the People and Socialism,'" *The Guardian*, November 8, 2016.

178. "The New Normal for Foreign NGOs in 2020," *ChinaFile*, January 3, 2020, https://www.chinafile.com/ngo/analysis/new-normal-foreign-ngos-2020.

179. "Why Foreign NGOs Are Struggling with New Chinese Law," *SCMP*, June 14, 2017; "Overseas NGOs in China: Left in Legal Limbo," *The Diplomat*, March 4, 2017, http://thediplomat.com/2017/03/overseas-ngos-in-china-left-in-legal-limbo/; "More Than 7,000 Foreign NGOs in China: Only 91 Registered So Far," *The Diplomat*, June 2, 2017, http://thediplomat.com/2017/06/more-than-7000-foreign-ngos-in-china-only-72-registered-so-far/.

180. "China Issues Regulation on Online News Service," *English.gov.cn*, May 3, 2017, http://english.gov.cn/state_council/ministries/2017/05/03/content_281475644401 426.htm; "China Updates Internet Regulations to Tighten Control over Online News," *SCMP*, May 2, 2017.

181. "China Magazine Caixin Defiant on Censorship of Article," *BBC News*, March 9, 2016. *Caixin*, respected for its financial reporting and investigative journalism, has often been a source for approved officially sensitive materials.

182. Verna Yu, "The Death of a Liberal Chinese Magazine," *The Diplomat*, July 19, 2016, http://the diplomat.com/2016/07/the-death-of-a-liberal-chinese-magazine. The many reflections of historical issues carried in *Yanhuang Chunqiu* are denigrated as "historical nihilism" since they question the official narrative.

183. "Loyal Party Members Urge Xi's Resignation," *China Digital Times*, March 16, 2016, https://chinadigitaltimes.net/2016/03/open-letter-devoted-party-members-urge-xis-resignation/.

184. "China Shutters Maoist Website Citing 'Ideological' Problems," *Radio Free Asia*, May 9, 2014.

185. "Xi Jinping: Dui wangshang shanyi de piping yao huanying" [Xi Jinping: Let's Welcome Constructive Criticism on the Internet), *Xinjingbao*, April 20, 2016, http://www.bjnews.comcn/news/2016/04/20/400708.html. "Xi Jinping Calls for Greater Tolerance of Criticism Online about China's Government," *SCMP*, April 21, 2016.

186. Cal Wong, "China Cracks Down on 'Harmful' Speech," *The Diplomat*, June 29, 2016, http://thediplomat.com/2016/06/china-cracks-down-on-harmful-speech/.

187. David Schlesinger, Anne Henochowicz, and Yaqiu Wang, "Why Xi Jinping's Media Controls Are 'Absolutely Unyielding,'" *Foreign Policy*, March 17, 2016. The views contained in the nationalistic tabloid *Global Times* do not necessarily reflect those of the Chinese leaders. On several occasions, Beijing felt the need to rein in the extreme opinions of the newspaper's editor-in-chief, Hu Xijin.

188. Gary King, Jennifer Pan, and Margaret Roberts, "How Censorship in China Allows Government Criticism but Silences Collective Expression," *American Political Science Review*, Vol. 107, No. 2, May 2013.

189. Dimitar D. Gueorguiev and Edmund J. Malesky, "Consultation and Selective Censorship in China," *Journal of Politics*, Vol. 81, No. 4, October 2019.

190. Maria Reprikova, *Media Politics in China* (New York: Cambridge University Press, 2017), chaps. 1 and 8.

191. Xi Jinping, "Woguo gudai zhuzhang lifa heshi, dezhu xingfu" [In Ancient Times, Our Country Advocated Governance According to a Combination of Ritual and Law with Morality as the Mainstay Supplemented by Punishment," *Sina*, October 13, 2014, http://news.sina.com.cn/c/2014-10-13/192030982492.shtml.

192. See Aurora Teixeira, Carlos Pimenta, António Maia, and José António Moreira, eds., *Corruption, Economic Growth and Globalization* (New York: Routledge, 2016).

193. "China Has a Message for Western Companies: Corruption Does Not Pay," *SCMP*, August 22, 2017.

194. Cited in "90 nian dai yilai waitao tanguan huoda 18000 ren xiekuan 8000 yi" [Approximately Eighteen Thousand Corrupt Officials Have Escaped Overseas since the 1990s, Absconding with ¥8 Trillion), *Zhongguo xinwen zhoukan*, October 14, 2012, http://news.qq.com/a/20121014/000453.htm.

195. "Chinese Dominate List of People and Firms Hiding Money in Tax Havens: Panama Papers Reveal," *SCMP*, May 10, 2016.

196. Yan Sun, *Corruption and Market in Contemporary China* (Ithaca: Cornell University Press, 2004).

197. Zengke He, "Corruption and Anti-corruption in Reform China," *Communist and Post-communist Studies*, Vol. 33, No. 2, 2000.

198. He, "Corruption and Anti-corruption," pp. 258–259. For a recent study on corruption in China, see Yuen Yuen Ang, *China's Gilded Age: The Paradox of Economic Boom and Vast Corruption* (Cambridge: Cambridge University Press, 2020).

199. The comparative politics literature identifies three factors—rational, structural, and cultural—that contribute to corruption. The rationality factor, which emphasizes individuals' utility maximization and calculations of costs and benefits, is universal. The structural and cultural factors, which create incentives and opportunities, are more specific to individual countries. For a classic analysis, see Mark Irving Lichbach and Alan S. Zuckerman, *Comparative Politics: Rationality, Culture, and Structure* (Cambridge: Cambridge University Press, 1997), chap. 3.

200. Xi Jinping, *Xi Jinping guanyu dangfeng lianzheng jianshe he fanfubai douzheng lunshu zhaibian* [Xi Jinping: Selections of Xi Jinping's Discussions on the Construction of a Clean Party Work Style and the Struggle against Corruption] (Beijing: Fangzheng chubanshe, 2015), p. 99. For cases of lower officials enriching themselves with poverty relief funds, see "You guanyuan jie fupin fajia; woan chuanan duobanzi quanjun fumo" [Some Officials Have Made a Fortune through "Poverty Alleviations": Many · Crime Cartels Have Been Wiped Out], *Zhongguo xinwenwang*, April 21, 2016, http://www.chinanews.com/gn/2016/04-21/7842168.shtml.

201. "Shibada yilai zhongyao wenxian xuanbian, shang" [Selections of Important Documents since the Eighteenth Party Congress] (Beijing; Zhongyang wenxian chubanshe, 2014), Vol. 1, p. 81.

202. "Zhengzhiju: Weiyuan dao jiceng diaoyan yao jianhua jiedai" [Politburo Orders: Receptions for Its Members Doing Base-Level Investigations Must Be

Simplified], *Xinhua*, December 4, 2012, http://news.sina.com.cn/c/2012-12-04/193325729695.shtml.

203. "Baxiang guiding san zhounian: quanguo chachu 104934 qi weigui wenti" [The Third Anniversary of the "Eight Regulations": Nationally 104,934 Cases of Infractions Have Been Prosecuted], December 3, 2015, *Sohu*, http://news.sohu.com/20151203/n429457403.shtml.

204. The CCDI is really the Ministry of Supervision, following the practice of two separate titles for one organization. Ross and Bekkevold, *China in the Era of Xi Jinping*, p. 55.

205. For a good discussion of Wang's career, see "Wang Qishan: China's Enforcer," *Financial Times*, July 24, 2017, https://www.ft.com/content/d82964ba-6d42-11e7-bfeb-33fe0c5b7eaa.

206. Xiang Jiangyu, *Xi Jinping bandi* [Xi Jinping's Background Connections] (Carle Place, NY: Mirror Books, 2011). For Hank Paulson's versions of the events see his *Dealing with China: An Insider Unmasks the New Economic Superpower* (New York: Twelve, 2015).

207. Deputy Secretary Steinberg's May 30, 2009, conversation with Singapore minister mentor Lee Kuan Yew, *Wikileaks*, June 4, 2009, https://wikileaks.org/plusd/cables/09SINGAPORE529_a.html.

208. "Wang Qishan di zhiqing suiyue: Yu Xi Jinping jiaohao tonggai yichuangbeizi" [Wang Qishan's Times as a *Zhiqing*: He Was a Friend of Xi Jinping and Shared the Same Blanket], *Sohu*, February 26, 2015, https://history.sohu.com/20150226/n396233263.shtml.

209. "How China Will Escalate the Anti-corruption Campaign," *Stratfor*, December 29, 2015, https://worldview.stratfor.com/analysis/how-china-will-escalate-anti-corruption-campaign.

210. "Anti-corruption Watchdog to Penetrate Communist Party Core," *SCMP*, December 12, 2014.

211. The major website for tipping-off is www.12388.gov.cn, and a CCDI complaint form can be located there.

212. "Li Keqiang: Yi jianquan xianquan cu yuantou fanfu" [Li Keqiang: Combat Corruption by Reducing and Limiting Power], *Renminwang*, March 29, 2016, http://politics.people.com.cn/n1/2016/0329/c1001-28234841.html; "Li Keqiang: Yi qingdan mingguiiju dapo xunzu fubai qianquize" [Li Keqiang: Use an Inventory List of Formal Rules to Combat the "Hidden Rules" of Rent-Seeking and Corruption], *Zhongguo zhengfuwang*, March 28, 2016, http://news.ifeng.com/a/20160328/48245009_0.shtml; "Li Keqiang: Tuidong zhengfu xitong fanfu gongzuo xiang zongshenfa" [Li Keqiang: Promote and Deepen Anticorruption Work in the Government System], *Zhongguo gaige luntanwang*, March 23, 2017, http://www.chinareform.org.cn/gov/system/Speech/201703/t20170322_262943.htm.

213. "Li Keqiang zai guowuyuan diwuci lianzheng gongzuo huiyi shang di jianghua" [Li Keqiang's Speech at the State Council's Fifth Meeting on Clean Governance], Zhongguo zhengfuwang, March 21, 2017, http://www.gov.cn/xinwen/2017-04/09/content_5184453.htm; "China Upgrades Anti-corruption Fight," *China Daily*,

April 14, 2017, http://www.chinadaily.com.cn/opinion/2017-04/14/content_28926 640.htm.

214. Yukon Huang, "The Truth about Chinese Corruption," Carnegie Endowment for International Peace, May 29, 2015, http://carnegieendowment.org/2015/05/29/truth-about-chinese-corruption-pub-60265.

215. "Anti-graft Team's Best Weapon: The One-on-One Chat," *SCMP*, June 9, 2013.

216. "The Countries Where China's Most Wanted Fugitives Are Likely Hiding," *Quartz*, April 24, 2015, https://qz.com/390637/all-the-countries-where-chinas-most-wanted-fugitives-may-be-hiding/. Pei's point is plausible, although "dirt" from allegedly high-level sources is regularly revealed in diaspora and Falun Gong media sources.

217. Official figures in "CCDI Shows Progress in Hunt for Corrupt Officials," *China Daily*, September 5, 2016, http://www.chinadaily.com.cn/china/2016-09/05/content_26697231.htm.

218. For example, see "Zhou Yongkang an shi zhonggong jianzheng yilai zuida zhengbian?" [Is the Zhou Yongkang Case the Most Significant Coup since the Establishment of the CCP Rule?], *Voice of America*, December 6, 2014, https://www.voachinese.com/a/zhouyongkang-case-20141205/2547874.html.

219. "Meiti jiemi Zhou Yongkang quanse jiaoyi: Zhishao daihuai 35 ren" [The Media Reveals Zhou Yongkang's Abuse of Power and Sex: At Least Thirty-five People Have Been Ruined], *southcn.com*, January 23, 2015, http://news.southcn.com/china/content/2015-01/23/content_116924390.htm. "Guanfang shouci ti Zhou Yongkang Bo Xilai gao feizuzhi huodong shenme yisi? [Why Do the Official Media Reveal Zhou Yongkang and Bo Xilai's Political Activities Outside of the Party?], *Guancha*, March 19, 2015, https://www.guancha.cn/politics/2015_03_19_312772.shtml.

220. See Joseph Fewsmith, "China's Political Ecology and the Fight against Corruption," *China Leadership Monitor*, No. 46, Winter, 2015, pp. 16–18.

221. "Ling Jihua beicha: shitu nizhuan zaoyoushi" [Ling Jihua Is under Investigation: His Career Reversal Has Long Been Anticipated], *Caixinwang*, December 23, 2014, http://china.caixin.com/2014-12-23/100766806_all.html; "Ling Jihua bei shuangkai bing lian zhencha" [Ling Jihua Has Been Dismissed from His Office and from the Party and Put under Prosecution], *Caixinwang*, July 25, 2015, http://china.caixin.com/2015-07-20/100830781.html.

222. "Ex-security Chief Had Ties with Other Top Graft Suspects," *China Daily*, March 17, 2015, https://www.chinadaily.com.cn/cndy/2015-03/17/content_19828411.htm.

223. "Xi Dismantles the 'New Gang of Four' with Probe of Hu's Aide," *Bloomberg*, December 23, 2014, https://www.bloomberg.com/news/articles/2014-12-23/xi-dismantles-china-s-new-gang-of-four-with-probe-of-hu-s-aide.

224. "Junzhong dahu paiying butingxie, shibada yilai yiyou 100 duoming junyishang ganbu weifa beichachu" [Nonstop Hunting of Tigers and Swatting of Flies in the Military: More Than One Hundred Guilty Cadres above the Division Level Have Already Been Prosecuted], *Sina*, August 23, 2017, http://news.sina.com.cn/c/2017-08-23/doc-ifykiurx1179343.shtml; "Gufu jianshang sankexing shibada yilai yiyou 7 wei shangjiang luoma" [Unworthy of the Three Stars on Their Shoulders, Seven Generals Have Already Been Dismissed since the Eighteenth Party Congress], *Sina*,

January 10, 2018, http://news.sina.com.cn/c/nd/2018-01-10/doc-ifyqptqv6751867. shtml.

225. "Guo Boxiong chenfu" [The Ups and Downs of Guo Boxiong], *Caixinwang*, July 30, 2015, http://china.caixin.com/2015-07-30/100834676_all.html.

226. "Biggest Numbers of Chinese Provincial-Level Corruption Suspects 'Caught in Guangdong,'" *SCMP*, July 27, 2015.

227. "Shibada yilai 67 ming dalaohu yi lingxing, 12 ren huo wuqi" [Sixty-Seven "Big Tigers" Have Been Sentenced since the Eighteenth Party Congress: Twelve Have Been Sentenced to Life Imprisonment], *Renminwang*, April 21, 2017, http://news. ifeng.com/a/20170421/50978355_0.shtml.

228. "Shanxi Acts to Clean Out Corruption," *China Daily*, March 7, 2016, http://www.chi nadaily.com.cn/kindle/2016-03/07/content_23768618.htm.

229. "Nonstop Hunting of Tigers"; "Unworthy of the Three Stars."

230. Xi, *Selections of Xi Jinping's Discussions*, pp. 24–25.

231. "Zhongjiwei: 1575 ming weiji weifa jijian jiancha ganbu bei chachu" [The CCDI: 1,575 Supervisory Cadres Were Indicted], *Xinhua*, January 7, 2015, http:// news.xinhuanet.com/legal/2015-01/07/c_127366998.htm.

232. *Selections of Important Documents*, pp. 310–312; *Selections of Xi Jinping's Discussions*.

233. *Selections of Important Documents*, pp. 135–136.

234. *Zhongguo gongchandang dangyuan* [Members of the CCP], *Baidu baike*.

235. "Xi Jinping: Dadan shiyong piping he ziwo piping youli wuqi" [Xi Jinping: Be Audacious in Using the Powerful Weapons of Criticism and Self-Criticism], *Xinhuawang*, September 27, 2013, http://www.xinhuanet.com/politics/ 2013-09/27/c_117526540_3.htm.

236. "Xi Jinping lianxidian weihe xuan Lankao" [Why Did Xi Jinping Pick Lankao as a Link?], *Zhongguo qingnianbao*, March 19, 2014, http://cpc.people.com.cn/n/2014/ 0319/c64387-24673480.html.

237. "Zhenggai luoshi bu shouchang, zhofeng jianshe zai lushang—dangde qunzhong luxian jiaoyu shijian huodong nianzhonghuimou" [The Implementation of Rectification Will Not End—the Improvement of Work Style: A Year-End Review of the Mass Line Practice Campaign], *China Daily Chinese*, December 22, 2014; "Guoji guancha, 2014: Fanfu chengwei guoji shehui guancha Zhongguo de reci" [International Observations, 2014: Anticorruption Has Become a Hot Term in the Observations of China by the International Community], *Xinhua*, December 22, 2014.

238. For instance, "China's Former Leaders Tell Xi to Halt Anti-corruption Campaign," *The Diplomat*, April 4, 2014, https://thediplomat.com/2014/04/chinas-former-lead ers-tell-xi-to-halt-anti-corruption-campaign/.

239. "China Laps Up Glossy TV Corruption Drama," *BBC*, April 8, 2017, http://www. bbc.com/news/blogs-china-blog-39524084; "China's 'House of Cards' Hits the TV Screen as Xi Jinping Whips His Cadres," *SCMP*, April 5, 2017. The TV series *In the Name of the People* is available on YouTube.

240. "Xi Jinping de 2016 bulu: Zhiyao lu zouduiliao, jiu bupa yaoyuan" [Xi Jinping's Footsteps in 2016: There Is No Fear of Distance as Long as the Path Is Right],

Renminwang, January 3, 2017, http://politics.people.com.cn/n1/2017/0103/c1001-28995158.html.

241. "China Probes 240 Centrally Administered Officials in the Past 4 Years," *Xinhuanet*, January 9, 2017, http://news.xinhuanet.com/english/2017-01/09/c_135967 749.htm.

242. "Sixty-Seven Big Tigers."

243. "Huitoukan huo 9 shengfen fanfu zaishengwen, 16 ming zhongguan ganbu luoma" [Anticorruption Is Heating Up: After "Returned Visits" to Nine Provinces, Sixteen Centrally Administered Cadres Fall], *Renminwang*, July 19, 2017, http://politics.peo ple.com.cn/n1/2017/0719/c1001-29413569.html.

244. "One of China's 'Most-Wanted' Fugitives Returns after 19 Years in U.S.," *Reuters*, July 31, 2017, https://www.reuters.com/article/us-china-corruption-usa-idUSKB N1AG14I.

245. "Factbox: Seven Facts of China's Anti-corruption Campaign," *Xinhua*, July 4, 2017, http://news.xinhuanet.com/english/2017-07/04/c_136416939.htm.

246. "China Has a Message"; "Where's China's Corruption Crackdown," *The Diplomat*, July 21, 2017, http://thediplomat.com/2017/07/where-is-chinas-corruption-crackdown/.

247. Xi Jinping Millionaire Relations Reveal Fortunes of Elite," *Bloomberg News*, June 29, 2012.

248. David Barboza, "Billions in Hidden Riches for Family of Chinese Leader," *New York Times*, October 25, 2012.

249. Originally, billionaires Zhong Shanshan was a construction worker, Qin Yinglin a pig farmer, and Jack Ma a teacher.

250. Michael Forsythe, "As China's Leader Fights Graft, His Relatives Shed Assets," *New York Times*, June 17, 2014.

251. "The Panama Papers Embarrass China's Leaders," *Economist*, April 7, 2016.

252. "Guo Wengui—about Wang Qishan," June 6, 2017, *YouTube*, https://www.youtube.com/watch?v=ZpHY0FusE58; "Xi Jinping's War on Corruption Angers China's Leaders," *Rediff News*, June 7, 2017, http://www.rediff.com/news/column/xi-jinpi ngs-war-on-corruption-angers-chinas-leaders/20170607.htm; "China's Robber Barons Take Collusion to a Whole New Level," *SCMP*, May 14, 2017.

253. For more detail, see "Guo Wengui weilie gaoguan ji: cong jiemeng dao fan" [Guo Wengui's Capture of High Officials: From Alliance to Betrayal], *Caixin*, March 25, 2015, http://china.caixin.com/2015-03-25/100794575_all.html; "Exiled Chinese Billionaire Guo Wengui Seeks US Asylum," *BBC*, September 7, 2017, http:// www.bbc.com/news/world-us-canada-41193000; "Billionaire Who Accused Top Chinese Officials of Corruption Asks U.S. for Asylum," *New York Times*, September 7, 2017.

254. "Without Corruption, Some Ask, Can the Chinese Economic System Function?," *Washington Post*, February 11, 2015.

255. Orville Schell, "Crackdown in China: Worse and Worse," *New York Review of Books*, April 21, 2016, http://www.nybooks.com/articles/2016/04/21/crackdown-in-china-worse-and-worse/.

256. "Zhonggong fanfu de sange dixia" [The Three Bottom Lines of the CCP's Anticorruption], *New York Times Chinese Web*, May 9, 2017, https://cn.nytimes.com/opinion/20170509/corruption-deng-yuwen/; "Beiji xuanzexing fanfu, Xi Jinping fanfu qiangkou zhuanxiang hongerdai" [Derided for Selective Anticorruption, Xi Jinping Turned His Gun at the Red Second Generation], *Wenxuecity*, February 7, 2015, http://www.wenxuecity.com/news/2015/02/07/4013886.html.

257. This adage highlights a dilemma similar to one attributed to Chen Yun, which reads, "Not tackling corruption will spell the end of the Party; to tackle corruption will spell the end of the state."

258. "Business Losing Out as Chinese Officials Strive to Appear Squeaky Clean," *SCMP*, August 18, 2017; "China's Corruption Clampdown Risks Policy Paralysis," *Financial Times*, May 2, 2017, https://www.ft.com/content/293d3b2a-2f1c-11e7-9555-23ef5 63ecf9a.

259. "The Political Price of Xi Jinping's Anti-corruption Campaign," *Financial Times*, January 4, 2017, https://www.ft.com/content/3f1938d6-d1cf-11e6-b06b-680c4 9b4b4c0.

260. Xi Jinping, *Guanyu yanming dangde jilu he guiju lunshu zhaibian* [Excerpts from Xi Jinping's Discussions of the Strict Applications of Party Rules and Regulations] (Beijing: Zhongyang wenxuan chubanshe, 2016), pp. 58, 64–65.

261. "Zhongjiwei zaitan jiceng fanfu, youxie cunganbu tanlan daoliao shime dibu" [The CCDI on Anticorruption at the Grassroots: What Was the Extent of Graft by Village Cadres], *Zhongqingzaixian*, July 7, 2017, http://news.cyol.com/content/2017-07/27/content_16338539.htm; "Shean yiyi, zhege cunzhishu you duo ba?" [The Case Involves ¥2 Billion: How Aggressive Has This Party Branch Secretary Been?], *Sina*, August 11, 2017, http://news.sina.com.cn/c/nd/2017-08-11/doc-ifyixcaw4251008. shtml.

262. Xi's remarks were reiterated by Xinhua in August 2016: Wang Zifei, "Qingchu zuida weixie—Xi Jinping lun fanfu" [Eliminate the "Greatest Threat": Xi Jinping on Anticorruption], *Xinhuanet*, August 12, 2016, http://news.xinhuanet.com/politics/2016-08/12/c_1119378149.htm.

263. For instance, Falun sources interpreted this to mean that Xi was signaling that former leaders such as Jiang Zemin, Jia Qinglin, and their circles might not be immune.

264. "Fanfu xingdong xieru G20 zhangxian Zhongguo fanfu juexin" [Anticorruption Has Been Acknowledged by the G20, Demonstrating China's Determination], *Renminwang*, September 7, 2016, http://cpc.people.com.cn/pinglun/n1/2016/0907/c241220-28698217.html.

265. This initiative was in part a response to the formation of a G20 anticorruption group at the G20 meeting of 2010. See "Jiemi G20 fanfu zhuitao zhuizang yanjiu zhongxin zhuyao zhineng you naxie?" [Secrets Revealed: What Are the Main Functions of the Research Center for Fugitive Repatriation and Asset Recovery?] *Yangshiwang*, September 24, 2016, http://www.chinanews.com/gn/2016/09-24/8013665.shtml.

266. Melanie Manion, "Taking China's Anticorruption Campaign Seriously," *Economic and Political Studies*, Vol. 4, No. 1, 2016. See also Christopher Carothers, "Xi's

Anticorruption Campaign: An All-Purpose Governance Tool," *China Leadership Monitor*, Issue 67, Spring 2021.

267. Transparency International, "Corruption Perceptions Index 2016," January 25, 2017, https://www.transparency.org/news/feature/corruption_perceptions_index_2016.

268. "Study: China's Corruption Doesn't Match Gilded-Age America," *Wall Street Journal*, December 12, 2012.

269. "The Party Winds Down," *Economist*, May 7, 2016, https://www.economist.com/news/international/21698239-across-world-politically-connected-tycoons-are-feeling-squeeze-party-winds; "Dealing with Murky Moguls," and "Comparing Crony Capitalism around the World, *Economist*, both May 5 2016, https://www.economist.com/blogs/graphicdetail/2016/05/daily-chart-2; https://www.economist.com/news/leaders/21698261-how-disentangle-business-government-dealing-murky-moguls.

270. Ang, *China's Gilded Age*, pp. 191–192 and *passim*.

271. A book with many case studies is Fan Wanli, *Yinxing de fubai: anli yu qishi* [Invisible Corruption: Case Examples and Insights] (Beijing: Dongfang chubanshe, 2019).

272. Cheng Li, *Chinese Politics in the Xi Jinping Era: Reassessing Collective Leadership* (Washington, DC: Brookings Institution Press, 2016), pp. 279–300.

273. "Xiangtan tuanxianwei jiti weiji: 3 nian jihu weizhaokai dangzu huiyi [The Xiangtan CYL County Committee Collectively Violated the Regulations: It Has Almost Never Convened Any Party Meetings in Three Years], *Tencent*, December 18, 2016.https://hn.qq.com/a/20161218/012441.htm.

274. "Zenyang zuohao Gongqingtuan gongzuo? Xi Jinping zhexie zhishi shouci pilu" [How to Get the CYL to Work Well? The First-Ever Revelations of Xi Jinping's Instructions], *Gongqingtuan xinwen lianbo*, September 14, 2017, http://news.cyol.com/content/2017-09/14/content_16500125.htm; *Xi Jinping guanyu qingshaonian he Gongqingtuan gongzuo lunshu zhaibian* [Selected Writings by Xi Jinping on Youth and CYL Work] (Beijing. Zhongyang wenxian chubanshe, 2017).

275. "Gongqingtuan zhongyang 2016 nian bumen yusuan jianshao 50%" [The 2016 Budget for the CYL Department Has Been Trimmed by 50%], *Ifeng*, May 1, 2016, http://news.ifeng.com/a/20160501/48651360_0.shtml.

276. "Xi Jinping guanyu shehui zhuyi zhengzhi jianshe lunshu zhaibian: Gong qing fu jue buneng chengwei guowei zhe sanlei zuzhi" [Selections from Xi Jinping's Discussion on Socialist Political Construction: Workers, Youth, and Women's Associations Cannot Imitate Their Overseas Counterparts], *Sohu*, September 22, 2017, http://www.sohu.com/a/193752029_115479.

277. For a more detailed discussion of the subject of this section, see Randall Peerenboom, "Fly High the Banner of Socialist Rule of Law with Chinese Characteristics! What Does the 4th Plenum Decision Mean for Legal Reforms in China?," *Hague Journal on the Rule of Law*, No. 7, 2015.

278. For a discussion of the mutually reinforcing relationship in the development of law, market, and economic growth in China, see Linda Yueh, "The Law and Growth Nexus in China," in John Garrick and Yan Chang Bennett, eds., *China's Socialist Rule of Law Reforms under Xi Jinping* (New York: Routledge, 2016), pp. 77–93.

279. Xi, *Governance 1*, p. 225.

280. Xi, *Governance 1*, pp. 149–159.

281. "Dangde Shibada yilai renmin fayuan sifa tizhi zhi gaige jishi" [A Real Record of the Reform of the System of People's Courts since the Party's Eighteenth Party Congress], *dtzy.chinacourt*, June 7, 2018, http://dtzy.chinacourt.org/article/detail/2018/03/id/3231687.shtml.

282. For Xi's litany of judicial abuses, see *Xi Jinping guanyu qianmian yifazhiguo lunshu zhaibian* [Xi Jinping, Selections from Xi Jinping's Discourses on Governance According to the Comprehensive Observations of the Rule of Law] (Beijing: Zhongyang wenxian chubanshe, 2015), pp. 60, 62, 68, 70–71, 72–77, 80, 96–97, 113, 118–119, 127, and *passim*; "Xi Jinping yanzhong di fazhi Zhongguo" [Chinese-Style Rule of Law in the Eyes of Xi Jinping], *Xinhua*, October 22, 2014, http://news.xinhuanet.com/politics/2014-10/22/c_1112936158.htm; "China's Xi Urges Deepening Judicial Reform," *Xinhua*, January 23, 2016, http://news.xinhua net.com/english/2016-01/23/c_135037100.htm.

283. Sections 1, 6, and 24 of *Zuigao renmin fayuan guanyu jianli jianquan fangfan xingshi yuanjiacuoan gongzuo jizhi di yijian* [The Supreme People's Court on the Building and Strengthening of a System to Prevent Trumped-Up Criminal Cases]*law-lib.com*, October 9, 2013, http://www.law-lib.com/law/law_view.asp?id=436610; "Xiaoxi cheng chu shewai dang lingyu zhengfawei jiangbuzai jieru gean shenpan" [The News Said That the Political and Legal Committee Will No Longer Be Involved in Individual Cases Except Those Relating to Foreign Countries], *21shiji jingji baodao*, November 22, 2013, https://xw.qq.com/cmsid/NEW2013112200128308.

284. This line was revealed in the CCTV's TV series *China: Governance by Law*; "Xi Jinping tan yuanjiacuoan: Zuo jiucuo di gongzuo jiushi weiliao mibu shanghai" [Xi Jinping on Trumped-Up Cases: The Correction of Mistakes Is Compensation for the Harm Inflicted], *Ifeng*, August 24, 2017, http://news.ifeng.com/a/20170824/517 47675_0.shtml.

285. "Jianding buyi tuidong sifa zeren zhi gaige quanmian kaizhan" [Firmly Promote the Comprehensive Reform of the Judicial Responsibility System], *Renminfayuanbao*, October 20, 2016, http://rmfyb.chinacourt.org/paper/html/2016-10/20/content_117480.htm?div=-1.

286. "Meng Jianzhu: Cong zhidushang fansi yuanjiacuoan yuanyin, xingxun bigong de bixu zhuize" [Meng Jianzhu: Reflect on the Causes for the False, Erroneous, and Unjust Cases from the Perspective of the System; Forced Confessions Extorted by Torture Must be Called to Account], *Pengpai*, July 20, 2016,https://www.thepaper.cn/newsDetail_forward_1501088.

287. "Communique of the 4th Plenary Session of the Eighteenth Central Committee of CPC," December 2, 2014, *China.org*, http://www.china.org.cn/china/fourth_plen ary_session/2014-12/02/content_34208801.htm; Anthony H. F. Li, "Centralization of Power in the Pursuit of Law-Based Governance: Legal Reform in China under the Xi Administration," *China Perspectives*, No. 2, 2016.

288. Ross and Bekkevold, *China in the Era of Xi Jinping*, p. 55.

289. "Chinese-Style Rule of Law."

290. "Real Record of the Reform."

291. The Supreme People's Court of the People's Republic of China, *Judicial Reform of Chinese Courts*, March 3, 2016, http://english.court.gov.cn/2016-03/03/content_237 24636_3.htm.

292. "Three Years of Reform."

293. The 2016 version is State Council Information Office of the PRC: "White Paper: New Progress in the Judicial Protection of Human rights in China," September 2016, http://www.china.org.cn/government/whitepaper/node_7241418.htm; the 2017 version is in "China Issues White Paper on Judicial Reform of Chinese Courts," *China Daily*, February 27, 2017, http://www.chinadaily.com.cn/china/2017-02/27/content_28361584.htm. See also "SPC Issues White Paper on Judicial Reform, Transparency," Supreme People's Court of the PRC, February 28, 2017, http://engl ish.court.gov.cn/2017-02/28/content_28379550.htm; "Baipishu: Zuigaofa qiantou de 18 xiang gaige, jincha yi xiang jiu wancheng" [White Paper: Among the Eighteen Reform Measures Led by the Supreme Court, Only One Item Has Not Been Completed], *Xinhuanet*, February 28, 2017, http://news.xinhuanet.com/legal/2017-02/28/c_1120539899.htm.

294. "Special Courts, Independence, Transparency Praised," *China Daily*, February 8, 2016, http://usa.chinadaily.com.cn/epaper/2016-02/08/content_23434610.htm; "Beijing Court Claims Problems with Administrative Disputes Solved," China Daily, April 27, 2017, http://www.chinadaily.com.cn/china/2017-04/27/content_29110 989.htm.

295. "Zuigao renmin fayuan baogao" [Report by the Supreme People's Court], *Zhongguo rendawang*, March 15, 2017, http://www.npc.gov.cn/npc/xinwen/2017-03/15/content_2018938.htm; "Lianghui shouquan fabu: Zuigao renmin fayuan gongzuo baogao" [Authorized Publication by the Two Sessions: Report by the Supreme People's Court], *Zhongguo rendawang*, March 20, 2016, http://news.xinhuanet.com/politics/2016lh/2016-03/20/c_1118384470.htm.

296. "Report by the Supreme People's Court"; "Authorized Publication by the Two Sessions."

297. "Full Text: China's Progress in Poverty and Human Rights," State Council, PRC, October 17, 2016, http://english.gov.cn/policies/latest_releases/2016/10/17/cont ent_281475468533275.htm.

298. Jiang Xingguang, "SPC Issues White Papers on Judicial Reform, Transparency," *English.court.gov.cn*, http://english.court.gov.cn/2017-02/28/content_28379550. htm; "China Focus: White Paper Hails China's Progress in Judicial Protection of Human Rights," *Xinhua*, http://news.xinhuanet.com/english/2016-09/12/c_135681 586.htm.

299. "China Claims Rights Progress Despite Crackdown on Dissent," *Irish Times*, September 12, 2016, http://www.irishtimes.com/news/world/asia-pacific/china-cla ims-rights-progress-despite-crackdown-on-dissent-1.2788250.

300. "Why Are Chinese Judges Resigning?," *Supreme People's Court Monitor*, August 23, 2016, https://supremepeoplescourtmonitor.com/2016/08/23/why-are-chin ese-judges-resigning/; "Hundreds of Chinese Judges Quitting over Low Pay and 'Bureaucratic Intervention,'" *SCMP*, May 31, 2015.

301. See, for example, Robert Marquand, "New for China's Courts: Trained Judges, Standard Rules," *Christian Science Monitor*, August 16, 2001, http://www.csmonitor.com/layout/set/print/2001/0816/p1s3-woap.html.

302. "Hege faguan di jiben yaoqiu" [The Basic Demands for a Qualified Judge], *Sina*, http://finance.sina.com.cn/sf/news/2016-07-27/093838743.html.

303. "Pilot Jury Program May Be Extended," *China Daily*, April 25, 2017, http://www.chinadaily.com.cn/china/2017-04/25/content_29068239.htm.

304. Zachary Keck, "4th Plenum: Rule of Law with Chinese Characteristics," *The Diplomat*, October 20, 2014, http://thediplomat.com/2014/10/4th-plenum-rule-of-law-with-chinese-characteristics/. See also Rebecca Liao, "The Law of Rule: China's Judiciary after the Fourth Plenum," *Foreign Affairs*, October 26, 2014.

305. Xi, however, argues that the practice of the "rule of law" has always been political by Western standards, and that the notion of whether the Party or the law takes precedence is a false dichotomy. See *Xi Jinping guanyu quanmian yifa zhiguo lunshu zhaibian* [Selections of Xi Jinping's Discussions on Comprehensive Law-Based Governance] (Beijing: Zhongyang wenxuan chubanshe, 2015), pp. 19, 21, 34, and 36–37.

306. "Why China Both Loves and Fears the Rule of Law," *The Diplomat*, June 25, 2016, http://thediplomat.com/2016/06/why-china-both-loves-and-fears-the-rule-of-law/.

307. Bonnie Girard, "China Is Taking Patents Seriously: The World Should Take Notice," *The Diplomat*, December 12, 2019, https://thediplomat.com/2019/12/china-is-taking-patents-seriously-the-world-should-take-notice/.

308. "Xi Jinping jiu zhengfa gongzuo zuochu zhongyao zhishi" [Xi Jinping Gives Important Instructions on Political and Legal Work], *Xinhuanet*, January 22, 2016, http://news.xinhuanet.com/politics/2016-01/22/c_1117868924.htm.

309. "China's Rights Lawyers Say Judicial White Paper 'Full of Lies,'" *Radio Free Asia*, September 13, 2016, http://www.rfa.org/english/news/china/china-judicial-09132016135020.html.

310. "Interview: Jerome Cohen," *The Diplomat*, September 1, 2016; Jerome Cohen, "A Looming Crisis for China's Legal System," *The Diplomat*, February 22, 2016, http://foreignpolicy.com/2016/02/22/a-looming-crisis-for-chinas-legal-system/.

311. Rebecca Liao, "Judicial Reform in China: How Progress Serves the Party," *Foreign Affairs*, February 2, 2017, https://www.foreignaffairs.com/articles/china/2017-02-02/judicial-reform-china.

312. Margaret Y. Woo, "Justice," in Chris Ogden, ed., *Handbook of China's Governance and Domestic Politics* (New York: Routledge, 2012), pp. 65–66. For further discussions, see Garrick and Bennett, *China's Socialist Rule of Law Reforms*.

Chapter 10

1. "The Coming Debt Bust," *The Economist*, May 6, 2016, https://www.economist.com/news/leaders/21698240-it-question-when-not-if-real-trouble-will-hit-china-coming-debt-bust; "China's Coming Debt Crisis," *Asia Sentinel*, March 27, 2017, https://

www.asiasentinel.com/econ-business/china-debt-crisis/"; "China's Debt Problem," n.d., *Thomsonreuters*, http://fingfx.thomsonreuters.com/gfx/rngs/CHINA-DEBT-GRAPHIC/0100315H2LG/, accessed October 4, 2021.

2. "Supply-Side Reform 'Needs a Big Push,'" *China Daily*, May 17, 2016.

3. Xi, *Governance 1*, pp. 335–336; Xi, *Governance 1E*, 368.

4. Xi, *Governance 1*, p. 95; Xi, *Governance 1E*, p. 106.

5. Xi, *Governance 1*, p. 117; Xi, *Governance 1E*, p. 129.

6. Xi, *Governance 1*, pp. 114, 336; Xi, *Governance 1E*, pp. 126, 369.

7. Full text of the Communiqué of the Third Plenary Session of the Eighteenth Central Committee of the CPC, in both English and Chinese, is at *Ching.org*, January 16, 2014, http://www.china.org.cn/chinese/2014-01/16/content_31213800.htm.

8. "Shibajie sanzhong quanhui baogao tongguo qianwan rengzai xiugai: Xi Jinping ren zerenren" [The Report for the Third Plenum of the Eighteenth Party Congress Was Still Being Revised the Night before Passage: Xi Jinping Takes Full Responsibility], http://www.chinanews/gn/2013/11-19/5517168_1.shtml, http://www.chinanews/gn/2013/11-19/5517168_2.shtml, http://www.chinanews/gn/2013/11-19/551716 8_3.shtml; "Jiemi quanhui wenjian qicao: Xiugai 1100 ci Jiang Jiemin bei chuming" [Disclosure: The Draft of the Third Plenum Document Was Revised Eleven Hundred Times; Jiang Jiemin's Name Was Removed], *Sina*, http://finance.sina.com.cn/china/20131123/012617410768.shtml. Article 12 of the Chinese state constitution states that "socialist public property is sacred and inviolable," even though the word "sacred" is often omitted in English translations.

9. The Fifth Plenum Communique is at http://china.org.cn/china/2010-10/19/content_21151020.htm. Full text of the Thirteenth FYP is in "Zhonggong zhongyang guanyu zhiding guomin jingji he shehui fazhan di shisange wunian guihua di jianyi" [The Thirteenth Five-Year Plan for Economic and Social Development of the PRC, 2016–2020], *Xinhuanet*, March 17, 2016, http://news.xinhuanet.com/politics/2016lh/2016-03/17/c_1118366322.htm. A summary of the plan is "Highlights of Proposals for China's Thirteenth Five-Year Plan (2016–2020)," *Xinhuanet*, November 4, 2015. Further analyses are "Thirteenth Five Year Plan Stresses Economic Restructuring," *China Business Review*, April 14, 2016; Scott Kennedy and Christopher K. Johnson, eds., *Perfecting China, Inc.: The 13th Five-Year Plan* (Lanham, MD: Rowman & Littlefield, 2016); Shannon Tiezzi, "China's Fifth Plenum: What You Need to Know," *The Diplomat*, October 29, 2015; "Prosperity for the Masses by 2020," *pwc*, 2015, http://www.pwccn.com/en/migration/pdf/prosperity-masses-2020.pdf.

10. "The Thirteenth Five-Year Plan for Economic and Social Development."

11. "Backgrounder: What Is China's Supply-Side Reform," *China Daily*, December 22, 2015, http://news.xinhuanet.com/english/2015/12/22/c_/134941783.htm; "Supply-Side Structural Reform Key to China's Growth," *China Daily*, January 22, 2016, http://www.chinadaily.com.cn/business/2016-01/22/content_23206835.htm; "China Unveils Economic Blueprint for 2016," *China Daily*, December 22, 2015, http://www.chinadaily.com.cn/china/2015-12/22/content_22769164.htm.

12. "Zhongguo gonggeice jiegouxing gaige buneng jiandian zhaoban xifang lilun" [China's Supply-Side Structural Reform Cannot Simply Copy Western Theories], *Qiushi*, April 22, 2016, http://www.qstheory.cn/dukan/hqwg/2016-04/22/c_1118710172.htm.

13. "Overcapacity a Time Bomb for China's Economy," *SCMP*, September 28, 2015.

14. "Thirteenth Five Year Plan Stresses Economic Restructuring."

15. "China's Bid to Cut Production Overcapacity in Heavy Industries 'Losing Steam,' Survey Suggests," *SCMP*, December 1, 2016.

16. "China Extends Overcapacity Fight to More Sectors in 2017—Paper," *Reuters*, December 29, 2016, http://www.reuters.com/article/china-overcapacity-idUSL4 N1EP09L.

17. "China Unveils Plans to Help Laid-Off Steel, Coal Workers," *Xinhua*, April 16, 2016, http://news.xinhuanet.com/english/2016-04/16/c_135284887.htm.

18. Nicholas R. Lardy, *The State Strikes Back* (Washington, DC: Peterson Institute for International Economics, 2019), p. 124.

19. Robert S. Ross and Jo Inge Bekkevold, eds., *China in the Era of Xi Jinping: Domestic and Foreign Policy Challenges* (Washington, DC: Georgetown University Press, 2016), pp. 70, 84.

20. Xi Jinping, "Lizhiqizhuang zuo qiang zuo you zuuda guoyou qiye" [Xi Jinping: Build Stronger, Better, and Bigger State-Owned Enterprises with Self-Assurance], *Xinhua*, http://www.xinhuanet.com//politics/2016-07/04/c_1119162333.htm.

21. "345 'Zombie' Enterprises to Be Cleaned Up," *China Daily*, May 21, 2016.

22. Ross and Bekkevold, *China in the Era of Xi Jinping*, p. 83.

23. "Syria Signs Paris Climate Agreement and Leaves US Isolated," *The Guardian*, November 7, 2017, https://www.theguardian.com/environment/2017/nov/07/syria-signs-paris-climate-agreement-and-leaves-us-isolated.

24. "Supply-Side Reform Calls for New System," *China Daily*, January 22, 2016, http://www.chinadaily.com.cn/business/2016-01/22/content_23206227.htm; "Backgrounder: What Is China's Supply-Side Reform?," *Xinhuanet*, December 22, 2015, http://news.xinhuanet.com/english/2015-12/22/c_134941783.htm.

25. "Sanzhong quanhui 60 xiang renwu zhishao yiqidong 31 xiang" [Thirty-One of the Sixty Tasks Mandated by the Third Plenum Have Started, Although Others Are Progressing Slowly Because of Vested Interests], *Xinjingbao*, February 24, 2014, http://epaper.bjnews.com.cn/html/2014-02/24/content_496462.htm.

26. "China to Carry Out Trials of Business License Reform," *English.gov.cn*, http://engl ish.gov.cn/premier/news/2015/12/16/content_281475255169997.htm; "Xi Jinping gaige zhe sannian" [The Three Years of Reform under Xi Jinping], *Nanfang Zhoumu*, December 3, 2015. http://www.infzm.com/content/113463. One source claims that "one-stop shopping" of administrative approval now took only about a month, replacing the past practice of having to go through twenty hurdles, involving eight departments and taking up to 698 days. "Li Keqiang litui de jianzheng fangquan jianshui jiangfei jiegouxing gaige huo OECD zanyu" [The Structural Reform of Simplified Administration, Power Devolution, Tax Reduction, and Lowering of Fees Promoted by Li Keqiang Was Lauded by the OECD], *Zhongguo gaigeluntan*, July 1, 2017, lunhttp://www.chinareform.org.cn/gov/system/Speech/201707/t20170701_267247.htm.

27. "China's About to Start Its Biggest Tax Overhaul in Two Decades," *Bloomberg News*, April 21, 2016, http://www.bloomberg.com/news/articles/2016-04-21/china-s-bigg est-tax-reform-in-two-decades-aims-to-boost-growth.

28. "Xi Jinping's Three Years of Reform."

29. "Fu Chengyu: Xiaoshou bankuai yewu shangshi shiji cun zhengyi" [Fu Chengyu: There Is Still Dispute Regarding the Timing for the Putting on the Market for Marketing Segments], *Caixin*, http://companies.caixin.com/2015-03-24/100794 003.html; "Xi Jinping's Three Years of Reform."

30. "Xi Jinping's Three Years of Reform."

31. "Xi Jinping's Three Years of Reform."

32. "Channeng guosheng qiye pa duandai cawu zaojia: Kui 10 yi cheng zhuan 5 qianwan" [Fearing the Loss of Financial Support, an Enterprise with Overcapacity Makes False Reports: It Claims to Have Earned ¥50 Million but in Fact It Had Lost ¥10 Billion], *Xinhuanet*, March 30, 2016, http://news.xinhuanet.com/yuqing/2016-03/30/c_12 8843842.htm.

33. "Guowuyuan pai 10 ge duchazu fu difang ducha quchanneng" [The State Council Has Dispatched Ten Inspection Groups to the Localities to Oversee the Reduction of Overcapacity], *Beijing qingnianbao*, August 20, 2016, http://epaper.ynet.com/html/2016-08/20/content_214231.htm?div=-1.

34. "Xi Jinping's Three Years of Reform."

35. "Xi Jinping's Three Years of Reform."

36. "China Accelerates Supply-Side Reform Following 'Authority' Urges," *China Daily*, May 12, 2016, http://europe.chinadaily.com.cn/business/2016-05/12/content_25239 648.htm.

37. "Welcome to Baoding, China's Most Polluted City," *The Guardian*, May 22, 2015, https://www.theguardian.com/cities/2015/may/22/baoding-china-most-polluted-city-air-pollution-beijing-hebei.

38. "Wang Yukai, Cong Xi Jinping zhiguo shiming kan quanmian shenhua gaige" [Wang Yukai: Comprehensively Deepening Reform from the Perspective of Xi Jinping's Governance Mission], *Sheke jijin zhuankan*, September 10, 2015, http://www.npo pss-cn.gov.cn/n/2015/0910/c230169-27568508.html.

39. The full text of this speech was published by the *RMRB*, May 1, 2016. "Zai shengbuji zhuyao lingdao ganbu xuexi guanche dangde shibajie wuzhong quanhui jingshen zhuanti yantaoban shang de jianghua" [Xi Jinping: Speech Delivered at the Discussion Forum with the Leading Cadres at the Provincial and Ministerial Level to Study and Implement the Spirit of the Fifth Plenum of the Eighteenth Central Committee], *RMRB*, January 18, 2016, http://paper.people.com.cn/rmrb/html/2016-05/10/nw.D110000renmrb_20160510_1-02.htm.

40. "Discord between China's Top Two Leaders Spills into the Open," *Wall Street Journal*, July 22, 2016.

41. "China's Problems Are Bigger Than Its Leadership Struggle," *Geopolitical Futures*, July 25, 2016, https://geopoliticalfutures.com/chinas-problems-are-bigger-than-its-leadership-struggle/; "China Blowing Major Bubbles in 2017," *Forbes*, December 19, 2016, https://www.forbes.com/sites/kenrapoza/2016/12/19/china-bubble-economy-2017/#4c728a564745; "How China's Latest Economic Stimulus Plan Undid Beijing's Efforts to Clean Its Air," *Washington Post*, November 22, 2016, https://www.washing tonpost.com/news/worldviews/wp/2016/11/22/how-chinas-latest-economic-stimu lus-plan-undid-beijings-efforts-to-clean-its-air/?utm_term=.47518eb0bf8d.

42. "Xi Jinping zhuchi zhaokai zhongyang caijing lingdao xiaozu di shisanci huiyi" [Xi Jinping Chaired the Thirteenth Meeting of the Central Finance and Economic Leading Small Group], *Xinhua*, May 16, 2016, http://xinhuanet.com/politics/2016-05/16/c_1118875925.htm.

43. "Supply-Side Reform Needs a Big Push."

44. "Jiji gaige ziyuan jifa chuangxin huoli gengjia fuyou chengxiao zhuo hao gaige gongzuo" [Concentrate the Resources for Reform, Stimulate the Vitality of Innovation, Do Reform Work Well with Better Efficiency], *RMRB*, June 28, 2016, http://paper.people.com.cn/rmrb/html/2016-06/28/nw.D110000renmrb_2016062 8_2-01.htm.

45. "Shenyi Zhongguo wenze tiaoli" [The Scrutiny of the Regulations on CCP Accountability], *RMRB*, June 29, 2016, http://paper.people.com.cn/rmrb/html/2016-06/29/nw.D110000renmrb_20160629_2-01.htm.

46. "Discord Between China's Top Two Leaders."

47. Alice L. Miller, "Core 'Leaders,' 'Authoritative Persons,' and Reform Pushback," *China Leadership Monitor*, No. 50, 2016, p. 4.

48. See, for example, Li Keqiang, "The World in 2016: China's Economic Blueprint," n.d., *The Economist*, https://gbr.economist.com/articles/view/564d4ca830a9cfec11b41 e98, accessed October 4, 2021; "Li Keqiang: Yao tuchu zhuahao gonggeice jiegouxing gaige" [Li Keqiang: We Must Do a Specially Good Job of Implementing Supply- Side Structural Reform], March 5, 2016, *Yangguangwang*, http://china.cnr.cn/gdgg/20160305/t20160305_521540735.shtm; "Li Keqiang: Jianchi zhiliang diyi shenhua gonggeice jiegouxing gaige" [Li Keqiang: Insist on Quality First: Deepen the Supply-Side Structural Reform], *JRJ.com*, November 8, 2017, http://finance.jrj.com.cn/2017/11/08184423358269.shtml.

49. "Zhongguo jingji zenme zou? Tamen di shengyin zhide qingting" [Whither the Chinese Economy: Their Voices Deserved to Be Heard], *Guancha*, June 4, 2016, http://www.guancha.cn/ZhangJun/2016_06_07_363210.shtml.

50. James L. Schoff and Asei Ito, *Competing with China on Technology and Innovation* (Washington, DC: Carnegie Endowment for International Peace, 2019).

51. "China's Spending on Research and Development Up 11.8 Percent to US$275 billion in 2018," *SCMP*, September 1, 2019, https://www.scmp.com/economy/china-econ omy/article/3025268/chinas-spending-research-and-development-118-cent-us275. Other sources claim that the R & D was US$496 billion.

52. "China's Record on Intellectual Property Theft Is Getting Better and Better," *Foreign Policy*, October 2019, https://foreignpolicy.com/2019/10/16/china-intellectual-property-theft-progress/.

53. "China Highlights Innovation Momentum," *People's Daily*, September 23, 2019, http://en.people.cn/n3/2019/0923/c90000-9616940.html.

54. "China Emerges as Global Tech, Innovation Leader," *deloitte.wsj.com*, October 30, 2019, https://deloitte.wsj.com/cio/2019/10/30/china-emerges-as-global-tech-inn ovation-leader/.

55. "Beijing Wants A. I. to Be Made in China by 2030," *New York Times*, July 20, 2017, https://www.nytimes.com/2017/07/20/business/china-artificial-intelligence.html.

56. Glenn D. Hook, Julie Gilson, Christopher W. Hughes, and Hugo Dobson, *Japan's International Relations: Politics, Economics, and Security*, 3rd ed. (New York: Routledge, 2012), chaps. 5, 10, and 15.

57. "The Made in China 2025 Initiative: Economic Implications for the United States," Congressional Research Services, updated April 12, 2019; Elsa Kania, "Made in China 2025, Explained," *The Diplomat*, December 28, 2018; " 'Made in China 2025' Plan Unveiled to Boost Manufacturing," *Xinhua*, May 20, 2015; "Why Does Everyone Hate Made in China 2025? *cfr.org*, March 28, 2018, https://www.cfr.org/blog/why-does-everyone-hate-made-china-2025.

58. "China Emerges."

59. "Foreign Firms Wary of 'Made in China 2025,' but It May Be China's Best Chance at Innovation," *Forbes*, March 10, 2017, https://www.forbes.com/sites/sarahsu/2017/03/10/foreign-firms-wary-of-made-in-china-2025-but-it-may-be-chinas-best-chance-at-innovation/#777a7f6524d2.

60. "Why the US Government Sees China Mobile as a National Security Threat," *SCMP*, July 4, 2018.

61. " 'Made in China 2025' Plan Unveiled to Boost Manufacture," *China Daily*, May 20, 2015, https://www.chinadaily.com.cn/bizchina/2015-05/19/content_20760528.htm; "China to Invest Big in 'Made in China 2025' Strategy," *China Daily*, October 12, 2017, https://www.chinadaily.com.cn/business/2017-10/12/content_33163772.htm.

62. "Is 'Made in China' a Threat to Global Trade?," *cfr.org*, May 13, 2019, https://www.cfr.org/backgrounder/made-china-2025-threat-global-trade; "The Made in China 2025 Initiative: Economic Implications for the United States," Congressional Research Service, April 12, 2019.

63. "Bankers' Exits and Zombie Accounts: China's Shanghai Free Trade Zone Sputters," *Reuters*, September 1, 2019, https://www.reuters.com/article/us-china-shanghai-ftz/banker-exits-zombie-accounts-chinas-shanghai-free-trade-zone-sputters-idUSKCN1VN01V.

64. China's Free Trade Zones Open Doors Wider to Foreign Investors," *China Daily*, November 29, 2019.

65. "Taking Stock of Shanghai's Free Trade Zone," *The Diplomat*, August 19, 2019.

66. "At Last, an RCEP Deal," *CSIS*, December 3, 2019, https://www.csis.org/analysis/last-rcep-deal.

67. "Why China Can Race Ahead in Digital Economy," *CGTN*, September 18, 2019, https://news.cgtn.com/news/2019-09-18/Why-China-can-race-ahead-in-digital-economy-K5P3RtrTZ6/index.html.

68. Longmei Zhang and Sally Chen, "China's Digital Economy: Opportunities and Risks, IMF Working Paper, January 2019, https://www.imf.org/en/Publications/WP/Issues/2019/01/17/Chinas-Digital-Economy-Opportunities-and-Risks-46459.

69. For more details, see *E-commerce Development: Experience from China* (Washington, DC: World Bank Group and Alibaba Group.

70. *E-commerce Development*, p. 137.

71. "One Photo Shows That China is Already in a Cashless Future," *Business Insider*, May 29, 2018, https://www.businessinsider.com/alipay-wechat-pay-china-mobile-payments-street-vendors-musicians-2018-5.

72. "One Photo Shows."

73. *E-commerce Development*, p. 1.

74. "Taobao Villages Driving 'Inclusive Growth' in Rural China," *Alizila*, November 25, 2019, https://www.alizila.com/taobao-villages-driving-inclusive-growth-rural-china/; "Stimulating Jobs Growth, Entrepreneurship, Income in Rural China through E-commerce," *worldbank.org*, November 22, 2019, https://www.worldb ank.org/en/results/2019/11/22/stimulating-jobs-growth-entrepreneurship-inc ome-in-rural-china-through-e-commerce.

75. "How Technology Saved China's Economy," *New York Times*, January 20, 2020, https://www.bloomberg.com/news/articles/2019-07-28/jack-ma-s-290-billion-loan-machine-is-changing-chinese-banking; "China's Mobile Banks Offer 1-Second Loan Decisions in Farmland," *Asia.nikkei*, August 9, 2019, https://asia.nikkei.com/ Business/Finance/China-s-mobile-banks-offer-1-second-loan-decisions-in-farmland.

76. "Yi Gang xingchang zai dishijie Lujiazui luntan shang di zhuzhi yanjiang" [Keynote Speech Given by Yi Gang, Governor of the People's Bank of China, at the Lujiazui Forum], *pbc.gov.cn*, June 14, 2018, http://www.pbc.gov.cn/goutongjiaoliu/113456/ 113469/3557760/index.html.

77. "Jack Ma's Online $290 Billion Loan Machine Is Changing China's Banking," *Bloomberg News*, July 29, 2019, https://www.bloomberg.com/news/articles/2019-07-28/jack-ma-s-290-billion-loan-CMChine-is-changing-chinese-banking; Yi, "Keynote Speech."

78. "China's Mobile Banks Offer 1-Second Loan Decisions."

79. "China Ranks 34th in E-government Online Service: UN Survey," *UN E-government Knowledgebase*, October 11, 2018, https://publicadministration.un.org/ego vkb/en-us/Resources/E-Government-Survey-in-Media/ID/1907/China-ranks-34th-in-e-government-online-service-UN-survey.

80. Zhang and Chen, "China's Digital Economy."

81. "Overview: The World Bank in China," https://www.worldbank.org/en/country/ china/overview#1. Last updated, October 12, 2021.

82. "Beijing's Supply-Side Struggle," *Wall Street Journal*, May 17, 2016, https://www.wsj. com/articles/beijings-supply-side-struggle-1463517902; "Xi Jinping's Economy Gets Stuck in Theory Stage," *Wall Street Journal*, May 17, 2016, https://www.wsj. com/articles/xis-economy-gets-stuck-in-theory-stage-1463467219.

83. "Winter 2020—the China Dashboard, Asia Society," *chinadashboard.asiasociety.org*, Winter 2020, https://chinadashboard.asiasociety.org/winter-2020/page/overview.

84. "Xi Jinping Is Trying to Remake the Chinese Economy," *The Economist*, August 15, 2020, https://www.economist.com/briefing/2020/08/15/xi-jinping-is-trying-to-remake-the-chinese-economy.

85. "OECD Technical Report on Progress on Structural Reform under the G20 ESRA," OECD, April 2017, pp. 19–20.

86. "China's Reforms and Opening-Up: Future Prospects," *china-briefing.com*, August 3, 2019, https://www.china-briefing.com/news/economic-reform-china-opening-up-future-prospects/; "Ease of Doing Business in China, 2008–2019," https://tradi ngeconomics.com/china/ease-of-doing-business, accessed October 4, 2021.

87. "Xi Jinping Is Trying to Remake the Chinese Economy."

88. "Q. and A.: Arthur R. Kroeber on 'China's Economy,'" *New York Times*, May 5, 2016, https://www.nytimes.com/2016/05/06/world/asia/china-economy-kroeber.html.

89. For discussions of various aspects of social change and development in China by Chinese academics see Li Peilin, *Chinese Society* (New York: Routledge, 2012). An earlier study is Elizabeth J. Perry and Mark Selden, eds., *Chinese Society: Change, Conflict and Resistance*, 2nd ed. (New York: RoutledgeCurzon, 2003).

90. "Xi Jinping's Three Years of Reforms."

91. "As You Wish, 5th Plenum Gives Chinese People Ten Gigantic Gift Packages," *People's Daily*, October 30, 2015, http://en.people.cn/n/2015/1030/c90000-8968 914.html.

92. "Chinese President Xi Jinping: The Prince," *The Listener*, March 30, 2017, https://www.noted.co.nz/currently/world/chinese-president-xi-jinping-the-prince/.

93. "China Has Almost Wiped Out Urban Poverty: Now It Must Tackle Inequality," *The Guardian*, August 19, 2015, https://www.theguardian.com/business/economics-blog/2015/aug/19/china-poverty-inequality-development-goals.

94. "Poverty Relief: Achievements in Five Years," *China Today*, July 3, 2017, http://www.chinatoday.com.cn/english/society/2017-07/03/content_743378.htm; "Xi Jinping shi ruhe jiang fupin kaifa tidao qiansuo weiyou gaodu di" [How Did Xi Jinping Raise the Issue of Helping the Antipoverty Development to Unprecedented Heights?], *Fenghuang zixun*, September 19, 2016, http://news.ifeng.com/a/20160919/4998813 1_0.shtml; "The Last, Toughest Mile: China's New Approach to Beating Poverty," *The Economist*, April 29, 2017, https://www.economist.com/news/china/21721393-after-decades-success-things-are-getting-harder-chinas-new-approach-beating-poverty.

95. "China Gini Coefficient," *CEIC*, https://www.ceicdata.com/en/china/resident-inc ome-distribution/gini-coefficient. In the same period, the Gini coefficient in the United States increased from 0.47 to 0.49.

96. *Clear Water Blue Skies* (Washington, DC: World Bank, 1997), https://documents1.worldbank.org/curated/en/944011468743999953/pdf/multi-page.pdf.

97. "Five Things to Know about China's Huge Anti-poverty Drive," *SCMP*, September 6, 2017.

98. See "China's Role in Efforts to Eradicate Poverty," *World Bank*, October 17, 2016, http://www.worldbank.org/en/news/opinion/2016/10/17/chinas-role-in-efforts-to-eradicate-poverty.

99. "Lankao chenggong tuopin cheng Henansheng shouge zhaimao di pinkunxian" [Lankao Is the First County in Henan to Successfully Remove Its Poverty County Label," *Xinhuawang*, March 27, 2017, http://news.xinhuanet.com/politics/2017-03/27/c_1120702673.htm.

100. "Model Village Shows Cracks in Pres. Xi Jinping's Fight to End China Poverty," *Hong Kong Free Press*, October 14, 2017, https://www.hongkongfp.com/2017/10/14/model-village-shows-cracks-pres-xi-jinpings-fight-end-china-poverty/; "Poverty & Equity Data Portal: China," World Bank, http://povertydata.worldbank.org/poverty/country/CHN; "Five Things to Know about China's Huge Anti-poverty Drive," *SCMP*, September 6, 2017. In the United States, "deep poverty" is defined

as a subsistence income at about US$12,000 annually for a family of four, and that affected 6.2 percent of the population in 2016, the most severe of which resided in the Southeast, the Mississippi Delta, Appalachia, and Native American lands. *US Department of Agriculture—Poverty Overview*, https://www.ers.usda.gov/topics/rural-economy-population/rural-poverty-well-being/poverty-overview/.

101. "Route to More Power for China's Xi Runs through Remote Guizhou," *Reuters*, March 2, 2017, https://www.reuters.com/article/us-china-politics-idUSKBN169 340; "Guizhou to Become Nation's Digital Hub," *China Daily*, June 7, 2018.

102. Cheng Li and Gary Xie, "A Brave New World," *Brookings*, April 20, 2018, https://www.brookings.edu/opinions/a-brave-new-world-xis-xiongan/; "President Xi's Dream City of Xiongan Pushes Ahead with Smart City Infrastructure Aimed at Covering All Areas," *SCMP*, September 16, 2019.

103. "China's Elderly Population Exceeds 230m," *China Daily*, August 8, 2017.

104. Spencer Sheehan, "China's Struggle with Demographic Change," *The Diplomat*, June 20, 2017, http://thediplomat.com/2017/06/chinas-struggle-with-demographic-change/.

105. "China's Birth Rate Rises but Falls Short of Governmental Estimates," *The Guardian*, January 23, 2017, https://www.theguardian.com/world/2017/jan/23/chinas-birth-rate-soars-after-relaxation-of-one-child-policy; "China's Birth Rate Falls to Near 60-Year Low," *SCMP*, January 17, 2019, https://www.scmp.com/economy/china-econ omy/article/3046481/chinas-birth-rate-falls-near-60-year-low-2019-producing.

106. See, for example, John Marshall, "China: Urbanization and Hukou Reform," *The Diplomat*, October 11, 2013, http://thediplomat.com/2013/10/china-urbanization-and-hukou-reform/.

107. Eric X. Li, "The Life of the Party the Post-democratic Future Begins in China," *Foreign Affairs*, January–February 2013, p. 43.

108. Tiejun Cheng and Mark Selden, "The Origins and Social Consequences of China's Hukou System," *China Quarterly*, No. 139, September 1994, p. 653. According to Bo Yibo, the urban population had already reached 78.3 million in 1953, a net gain of 20.6 million since 1949, and that was before collectivization began in 1955. Bo Yibo, *Ruogan Zhongda juece yu shijian de huigu* [Reminiscences on Certain Important Policies and Practices] (Beijing.: Zhonggong zhongyang dangxiao chubanshe, 1997), p. 256.

109. Peter Farrar, "China's New Generation of Urban Migrants," *The Diplomat*, June 29, 2016, http://thediplomat.com/2016/06/chinas-new-generation-of-urban-migrants/.

110. "Hukou Reform under Way in 29 Regions across China," *China Daily*, April 29, 2016.

111. "China's Urbanization Rate at 56.1%," *China Daily*, April 19, 2016.

112. Charlotte Goodburn, "The End of the Hukou System? Not Yet," China Policy Institute Policy Paper 2014 No. 2, https://kclpure.kcl.ac.uk/portal/en/publications/the-end-of-the-hukou-system-not-yet(60dca39e-2559-443c-8bd8-7107302c3993). html; Gaurav Daga, "Reforming China's Migration Barriers," *The Diplomat*, January 16, 2015, http://thediplomat.com/2015/01/reforming-chinas-migration-barriers/.

113. "Beijing Moves to Close the Urban-Rural Gap," *China Daily*, September 21, 2016.

114. "Shekeyuan baogao: Yue yiban nongmingong buxiang jincheng" [CASS Report: About Half of Rural Migrants Do Not Wish to Enter the Cities], *21 Shiji jingji baodao*, April 6, 2016, http://m.21jingji.com/article/20160406/herald/3267e c59e9eebf01cee8dc888410258b.html; "Half of Farmers Not Interested in Migrating to Urban Areas," *China Daily*, April 8, 2016; Marshall, "China: Urbanization."

115. "Beijing Moves to Close the Urban-Rural Gap."

116. Daga, "Reforming China's Migration Barriers."

117. For more details, see "Chongqing Mayor Says Rural Land Reform Pilot Has Been Just the Ticket," *Caixin Online*, September 17, 2015, http://www.caixinglobal.com/2015-09-17/101012190.html.

118. "Cultivating Prosperity," *China Daily*, April 28, 2017; Priyanka Juneja, "China's Hukou System: An Interview with Fei-ling Wang," *The Diplomat*, July 14, 2017, http://thediplomat.com/2017/07/chinas-hukou-system/.

119. "Shehui xinyong tixi jianshe guihua gangyao" [Outline of the Plan for the Construction of a Social Credit System], *gov.cn*, June 14, 2014, http://gov.cn/zhen gce/content/2014-06/27/content_8913.htm; "China's Corporate Social Credit System: What Businesses Need to Know," *China Briefing*, November 5, 2019, https://www.china-briefing.com/news/chinas-corporate-social-credit-system-how-it-works/.

120. "Discipline and Punish: The Birth of China's Social-Credit System," *The Nation*, January 23, 2019, https://www.thenation.com/article/archive/china-social-credit-system/.

121. "How China Is Using Big Data to Create a Social Credit Score," *Time*, 2019, https://time.com/collection/davos-2019/5502592/china-social-credit-score/.

122. "Outline of the Plan."

123. "Are You Ready for a Social Credit System?," *China Business Law Journal*, December 6, 2019, https://law.asia/central-government-social-credit-system/.

124. "Zhonggong tui qiyeban shehui xinping" [The CCP Launches the Social Credit System for Enterprises], September 18, 2019, *Sound of Hope*, https://www.soundofh ope.org/post/301082.

125. "Are You Ready?"

126. "The Year in Social Credit: Where Is Corporate Social Credit Going in 2020 and Beyond?," *China Business Review*, December 27, 2019, https://www.chinabusines sreview.com/the-year-in-social-credit-where-is-corporate-social-credit-going-in-2020-and-beyond/.

127. "China Bans 23m from Buying Travel Tickets as Part of 'Social Credit' System," *The Guardian*, March 1, 2019.

128. Genia Kostka, "China's Social Credit Systems and Public Opinion: Explaining High Levels of Approval," *New Media & Society*, Vol. 2, No. 7, 2019.

129. China is Waking Up to Data Protection and Privacy," *weforum.org*, November 12, 2019.

130. "China Leads Asian Neighbors on Data Privacy," *Financial Times*, May 31, 2018.

131. "How the West Got China's Social Credit System Wrong," *Wired*, July 29, 2019, https://www.wired.com/story/china-social-credit-score-system/.

132. "Uh-Oh: Silicon Valley Is Building a Chinese-Style Social Credit System," *fastcompany*, August 26, 2019, https://www.fastcompany.com/90394048/uh-oh-sili con-valley-is-building-a-chinese-style-social-credit-system; Shoshana Zuboff, *The Age of Surveillance Capitalism: The Fight for a Human Future at the New Frontier of Power* (New York: Public Affairs, 2020).

133. Glenn Greenwald, *No Place to Hide: Edward Snowden, the NSA, and the U.S. Surveillance State* (Toronto: Signal, 2015).

134. "Women xuyao yibu shimeyang di shehui xinyongfa" [What Kind of Social Credit Legislation Do We Need?], *legaldaily.com*, December 10, 2019, http://www.legalda ily.com.cn/index/content/2019-12/10/content_8069717.htm.

135. "China Leads Asian Neighbors."

136. "China to Deepen VAT Reform," *Xinhua*, September 28, 2018, http://www.xinhua net.com/english/2017-09/28/c_136646346.htm.

137. "Premier Li's Second Term: From 'Likonomics' to Following Orders," *SCMP*, October 25, 2017; "China Will Push Ahead 'Resolutely' with Financial Sector Fight, Says Li Keqiang," *SCMP*, March 20, 2018.

138. "Boom or Bust? The Big Debate Raging over China's Economic Future," *SCMP*, September 24, 2017.

139. "Overview: The World Bank in China."

140. "China," *OECD Economic Outlook*, Vol. 2017, Issue 1.

141. "China—Gini Index," https://data.worldbank.org/indicator/SI.POV.GINI?locati ons=US-CN; "China Gini Coefficient," https://www.ceicdata.com/en/china/resid ent-income-distribution/gini-coefficient, accessed September 4, 2020.

142. "Highlights of Government Work Report," *China Daily*, March 5, 2018.

143. UNDP, *Human Development Report 2019*, http://hdr.undp.org/sites/all/themes/ hdr_theme/country-notes/CHN.pdf, accessed November 5, 2020.

Chapter 11

1. For more details, see Joel Wuthnow and Phillip C. Saunders, *Chinese Military Reform in the Age of Xi Jinping: Drivers, Challenges, and Implications* (Washington, DC: National Defense University Press, March 2017); Timothy R. Heath, Kristen Gunness, and Cortez A. Cooper, *The PLA and China's Rejuvenation* (Santa Monica, CA: Rand Corporation, 2016).

2. "China Aims to Complete Military Reform by 2020," *China Daily*, May 13, 2016; White paper, "China's Military Strategy, May 2015.

3. Phillip C. Saunders and Joel Wuthnow, "China's Goldwater-Nichols? Assessing PLA Organizational Reforms," *Strategic Forum*, No. 294, April 5, 2016, http://inss. ndu.edu/Portals/68/Documents/stratforum/SF-294.pdf; Jeremy Page, "President Xi Jinping's Most Dangerous Venture Yet: Remaking China's Military," *Wall Street Journal*, April 25, 2016, https://www.wsj.com/articles/president-xi-jinpings-most-dangerous-venture-yet-remaking-chinas-military-1461608795; Wuthnow and Saunders, *Chinese Military Reform*; Peter Mattis, "China's Never-Ending Military Reforms," *The Diplomat*, No. 16, March 2016.

4. Page, "President Xi Jinping's Most Dangerous Venture."

5. Vogel claims that between 1975 and 1988, Deng had cut the size of the PLA from 6.1 million to 3.2 million. Ezra F. Vogel, *Deng Xiaoping and the Transformation of China* (Cambridge, MA: Harvard University Press, 2011), p. 526. Page, "President Xi Jinping's Most Dangerous Venture." Official sources are vague about the number of veterans. One source claims that there have been fifty-seven million retired soldiers since 1949, but apart from those who had deceased, there were still fifty-seven million in 2018. "Zhongguo xian you duoshao tuiyi junren? Tuiyi junren shiwu bu huiying" [How Many Veterans Are There in China? Department of Veterans Affairs Responds], *Sina*, July 31, 2018, http://news.sina.com.cn/o/2018-07-31/doc-ihhacrce 1716400.shtml.

6. "Jiefangjun sizongbu gaizu 15 bumen lianhe canmoubu shi zhihui guanjian" [The Four Departments of the PLA Are Reorganized into Fifteen Departments: The Joint Command Headquarters Is the Center of Command], *Takungpao*, January 12, 2016, http://news.takungpao.com/mainland/focus/2016-01/3266754.html; Ying Yu Lin, "The Implications of China's Military Reforms," *The Diplomat*, March 7, 2016, http://thediplomat.com/2016/03/the-implications-of-chinas-military-reforms/.

7. Page, "President Xi Jinping's Most Dangerous Venture Yet."

8. "Inspection Teams to Cover All of Military," *China Daily*, May 6, 2016; "China's Military Deploys Its First Corruption Inspectors," *China Daily*, May 5, 2016.

9. "Elimination of Bad Influence in PLA Continues," *Global Times*, June 28, 2017, http://www.globaltimes.cn/content/1053971.shtml; "Inspection Teams to Cover."

10. According to Shambaugh, eighty-two generals and four thousand officers were purged. See his *China's Future* (Cambridge: Polity Press, 2016), p. 123.

11. "Why Xi Is Purging the Chinese Military," *National Interest*, April 15, 2016, http://nationalinterest.org/feature/why-xi-purging-the-chinese-military-15795.

12. For more detailed discussion, see Wuthnow and Saunders, *Chinese Military Reform*, pp. 37–41; Page, "President Xi's Most Dangerous Venture"; Mattis, "China's Never-Ending Military Reforms."

13. Wuthnow and Saunders, *Chinese Military Reform*, pp. 21–22; Saunders and Wuthnow, "China's Goldwater-Nichols," pp. 3–5.

14. "Xi Jinping Xinren jiuwei liangzhi zongzhihui quanmian buju guofang jungai" [Xi Jinping Just Became Commander in Chief of the CMC Joint Command Headquarters to Comprehensively Plan for the Reform of National Defense], *Renminwang*, April 21, 2016, http://cpc.people.com.cn/xuexi/n1/2016/0421/c385474-28293613.html; "Xi Jinping Urges Stronger PLA," *China Daily*, April 21, 2016; "Xi Jinping: Jiakuai goujian juyou wojun tese de lianhe zuozhen zhihui tixi" [Xi Jinping: Accelerate the Construction of a Joint War Command System with Our Military Characteristics], *Renminwang*, April 21, 2014, http://cpc.people.com.cn/n1/2016/0421/c64094-28292 297.html; "Zhonggong sheli zhongyang junwei lianhe zuozhen zhihui zhongxing" [The Chinese Communist Party Has Established a CMC Joint War Command Center], *Fenghuang zihun*, August 5, 2014, http//news.ifeng.com/a/20140805/414 52210_0.shtml?f=hao123.

15. For more detailed discussions, see James C. Mulvenon, *Soldiers of Fortune: The Rise and Fall of the Chinese Military-Business Complex, 1978–1998* (New York: Routledge,

2001); David L. Shambaugh, *Modernizing China's Military: Progress, Problems, and Prospects* (Berkeley: University of California Press, 2003), chap. 5, "Budget and Finance."

16. "Jiji wentuo tuijin budui quanmian tingzhi youchang fuwu gongzuo" [Actively and Steadily Promote the Termination of the Armed Forces' Paid Service Work in an All-Round Way], *Renmin ribao*, March 17, 2017, http://paper.people.com.cn/rmrb/html/2017-03/17/nw.D110000renmrb_20170317_1-07.htm.

17. "Jundui he wujing budui quanmian tingzhi youchang fuwu gongzuo jihua 2018 nian wancheng" [Plans for the PLA and the PAP to Completely Cease Their Remunerated Tasks Will Be Complete by 2018], *Xinhua*, May 30, 2017, http://www.xinhuanet.com/politics/2017-05/31/c_1121063266.htm.

18. "Jundui he wujing budui quanmian tingzhi youchang fuwu gongzuo dianxing jingyan zhaideng" [A Selection of the PLA's and the PAP's Typical Experiences in Terminating Their Remunerated Services], *Zhongguo junwang*, October 16, 2017, http://www.81.cn/jwgz/2017-10/16/content_7787714_2.htm.

19. For examples of discussions on civil-military relations see Samuel Huntington, *The Soldier and the State: The Theory and Politics of Civil-Military Relations* (Cambridge, MA: Belknap Press of Harvard University Press, 1957); Samuel E. Finer, *The Man on Horseback: The Role of the Military in Politics* (Boulder, CO: Westview Press, 1988); Morris Janowitz, *The Professional Soldier: A Social and Political Portrait* (Glencoe, IL: Free Press, 1960).

20. Wuthnow and Saunders, *Chinese Military Reform*, pp. 46–47.

21. M. Taylor Fravel, *Strong Borders, Secure Nation* (Princeton, NJ: Princeton University Press, 2008).

22. Susan Shirk, *China: Fragile Superpower* (New York: Oxford University Press, 2007), chaps. 6 and 7.

23. "China: Percent of World GDP," *Global Economy.com*, https://www.theglobaleconomy.com/china/gdp_share/.

24. Huiyun Feng and Kai He, "China under Xi Jinping: Operational Code Beliefs, Foreign Policy, and the Rise of China," in Hoo Tiang Boon, ed., *Chinese Foreign Policy under Xi* (New York: Routledge, 2017), pp. 19–35.

25. See, for example, Boon, *Chinese Foreign Policy under Xi*; Jonathan Pass, *American Hegemony in the 21st Century: A Neo Neo-Gramscian Perspective* (New York: Routledge, 2019); David Shambaugh, ed., *China & the World* (New York: Oxford University Press, 2020); McKinsey Global Institute, *China and the World: Inside the Dynamics of a Changing Relationship* (n.p., 2019).

26. "China's President Is the Country's Most-Traveled Leader since Communism—and Maybe the Strongest," *Los Angeles Times*, December 25, 2015.

27. "Xi Jinping's 154 Days of Foreign Tour," *Xinhua*, December 30, 2016, http://news.xinhuanet.com/english/2016-12/30/c_135944763.htm.

28. "China's President Is the Country's Most-Travelled Leader since Communism," *Sydney Morning Herald*, December 26, 2015, http://www.smh.com.au/world/chinas-president-is-the-countrys-mosttravelled-leader-since-communism-20151226-glv49i.html.

29. "Xi Jinping, Donald Trump Oversee Signing of US$253 Billion in Trade Deals," *SCMP*, November 9, 2017.

30. Kerry Brown, "China's Globe-Trotting President," *The Diplomat*, October 21, 2015; "China's President is the Country's Most-Travelled Leader since Communism."

31. Examples of proponents of the theory of offensive realism are John Mearsheimer, *The Tragedy of Great Power Politics* (New York: Norton, 2001); "The Gathering Storm: China's Challenge to US Power in Asia," *Chinese Journal of International Politics*, Vol. 3, No. 4, 2010. An example of defensive realism theory is M. Taylor Fraval, "International Relations Theory and China's Rise: Assessing China's Potential for Territorial Expansion," *International Studies Review*, Vol. 12, No. 4, December 2010. For more discussions, including power transition and constructivist theories as applied to China, see Robert Ross and Zhu Feng, eds., *China's Ascent: Power, Security, and the Future of International Politics* (Ithaca: Cornell University Press, 2008). A critique of the neorealist and structuralist approach to China's foreign relations is Alastair Johnson, "International Structures and Chinese Foreign Policy," in Samuel S. Kim, ed., *China and the World*, 4th ed. (Boulder, CO: Westview Press, 1998).

32. "China Relies More Heavily on Mineral Imports," *Global Times*, July 11, 2018, http://www.globaltimes.cn/content/1110397.shtml; Erica Downs, "High Anxiety: The Trade War and China's Oil and Gas Supply Security," Center on Global Energy Policy, November 12, 2019, https://energypolicy.columbia.edu/research/commentary/high-anxiety-trade-war-and-china-s-oil-and-gas-supply-security.

33. Wang Yi, "Study and Implement Xi Jinping Thought on Diplomacy Conscientiously and Break New Ground in Major-Country Diplomacy with Chinese Characteristics," *Foreign Ministry of the PRC*, July 20, 2020, https://www.fmprc.gov.cn/mfa_eng/zxxx_662805/t1799305.shtml.

34. "The World Must Unite Like a 'Flock of Geese,' Says China's Xi Jinping," *The Guardian*, May 15, 2017. This notion is slightly different from Japan's hierarchical "flying geese" model, which postulates Japan's economic and technical leadership in Asia as the head goose. In catching up with the West, this concept suggests, Asian countries will leverage their different levels of comparative advantage, gradually passing on technological expertise from the most advanced to the less advanced. Glenn D. Hook, Julie Gilson, Christopher W. Hughes, and Hugo Dobson, *Japan's International Relations: Politics, Economics, and Security*, 3rd ed. (New York: Routledge, 2012), pp. 220–221.

35. "Highlights of Xi's Speech at Rally Marking PLA's 90th Anniversary," *China Daily*, August 2, 2017, https://www.chinadaily.com.cn/china/2017-08/02/content_30327309.htm.

36. This refers to what Beijing regards as core interests, illustrated by many red lines, for which there will be no compromises.

37. For further discussions of the notions of realism and security see Michael Sheehan, *International Security: An Analytical Survey* (Boulder, CO: Lynne Rienner, 2005), chap. 2 and *passim*; Alan Collins, ed., *Contemporary Security Studies* (New York: Oxford University Press, 2007).

38. Mingfu Liu and Zhongyuan Wang, *The Thoughts of Xi Jinping* (Salt Lake City, UT: American Academic Press, 2017), p. 65; Yin Fanglong: "Xin xingshi xia jianshe qiangda renmin jundui de kexue zhinan" [Yin Fanglong: A Scientific Guide to Building a Strong People's Army in the New Situation], *theory.people.com*, June 27, 2014, http://theory.people.com.cn/n/2014/0627/c40531-25207124.html.

39. Denny Roy, "'Xi Jinping Thought on Diplomacy Fails to Impress—or Reassure,'" *The Diplomat*, April 2, 2020.

40. For instance, see "How the World's Resistance to China Caught Xi Jinping Off Guard," *Washington Post*, December 21, 2018. For a critique of this view, see Jessica Chen Weiss, "A World Safe for Autocracy? China's Rise and the Future of Global Politics," *Foreign Affairs*, July–August 2019.

41. The word "solution" is used in "Speech at a Ceremony Marking the 95th Anniversary of the Founding of the Communist Party of China," *Qiushi Journal*, Vol. 8, No. 4, October–December 2016, http://english.qstheory.cn/2016-12/20/c_1120042032.htm; the word "input" is used in Yang Jiechi, "Study and Implement General Secretary Xi Jinping's Thought on Diplomacy in a Deep-Going Way and Keep Writing New Chapters of Major-Country Diplomacy with Distinctive Chinese Features," Ministry of Foreign Affairs of the PRC, July 17, 2017, https://www.fmprc.gov.cn/mfa_eng/wjbxw/t1478497.shtml.

42. "Xi Offers 'Chinese Solution' for World Economy," *Global Times*, January 19, 2017, http://www.globaltimes.cn/content/1029752.shtml.

43. Richard Rosencrance, *The Rise of the Trading State: Commerce and Conquest in the Modern World* (New York: Basic Books, 1986).

44. "Xi Offers Chinese Solution."

45. "China Finds Its Global Ambitions Humbled in Its Own Backyard," *New York Times*, May 18, 2016; Eleanor Albert, "China-Taiwan Relations," Council on Foreign Relations, May 18, 2016.

46. Sonny Lo, "The Political Cultures of Hong Kong and Mainland China: Democratization, Patrimonialism and Pluralism in the 2007 Chief Executive Election," *Asia Pacific Journal of Public Administration*, Vol. 29, No. 1, June 2007; Phillip Saunders, "Long-Term Trends in China-Taiwan Relations," *Asian Survey*, Vol. 45, No. 6, November–December 2005.

47. Bruce J. Dickson, *The Dictator's Dilemma: The Chinese Communist Party's Strategy for Survival* (New York: Oxford University Press, 2016), pp. 287ff.

48. "How Important Is Hong Kong to the Rest of China?," *Reuters*, September 4, 2019, https://www.reuters.com/article/us-hongkong-protests-markets-explainer/explainer-how-important-is-hong-kong-to-the-rest-of-china-idUSKCN1VP35H; Tianlei Huang, "Why China Still Needs Hong Kong," Peterson Institute for International Economics, July 15, 2019, https://www.piie.com/blogs/china-economic-watch/why-china-still-needs-hong-kong; Peter T. Cheung, "Who's Influencing Whom? Exploring the Influence of Hong Kong on Politics and Governance in China," *Asian Survey*, Vol. 51, No. 4, 2011.

49. "Cross-Strait Trade Down 4.5 Pct in 2016," *China Daily*, February 4, 2017.

50. "Greater Bay Area: China's Ambitious but Vague Economic Plan," *BBC*, February 26, 2019, https://www.bbc.com/news/business-47287387.

51. Ngok Ma, "The Rise of 'Anti-China' Sentiments in Hong Kong and the 2012 Legislature Council Elections," *China Review*, Vol. 15, No. 1, Spring 2015.

52. "Hong Kong and China: A Special Relationship," *Aljazeera*, March 22, 2016, http://www.aljazeera.com/indepth/opinion/2016/03/hong-kong-china-special-relationship-160320110701938.html.

53. "Smart Card, Dumb City: Is Hong Kong Laissez-Faire, or Just Lazy?," *Hong Kong Free Press*, May 22, 2018, https://www.hongkongfp.com/2018/05/22/smart-card-dumb-city-hong-kong-laissez-faire-just-lazy/; "Hong Kong's Wealth Gap Greatest in 45 Years," *SCMP*, September 27, 2018; Leo F. Goodstadt, *A City Mismanaged: Hong Kong's Struggle for Survival* (Hong Kong: Hong Kong University Press, 2018).

54. Examples are Zhen Shiyang, *Zongshuji di 8 duan qingyuan* [The General Secretary's Eight Romances] (Hong Kong: Kaiyi, 2014); Si Nuo, *Xi Jinping he tade qingrenmen* [Xi Jinping and His Many Mistresses] (Los Angeles: Xidian chubanshe, 2019). .

55. "Shenzhen-Hong Kong Stock Connect Kicks Off," *China Daily*, December 5, 2016.

56. "Hong Kong Must Always Remember That Xi Jinping Looks Beyond the City to the World Stage," *SCMP*, July 9, 2017.

57. "Why China May Call the World's Bluff on Hong Kong," *New York Times*, June 3, 2020, https://www.nytimes.com/2020/06/03/business/china-hong-kong-damage.html.

58. "The Law of the People's Republic of China on Safeguarding National Security in the Hong Kong Special Administrative Region," https://www.elegislation.gov.hk/doc/hk/a406/eng_translation_(a406)_en.pdf, accessed October 4, 2021.

59. For a comparative analysis, see Ho-fung Hung, "The Unrest of 2019, the National Security Law, and the Future of Hong Kong: A Comparative-International Perspective," *SAIS Review*, Vol. 40, No. 2, 2020.

60. Simon Shen, "The Hong Kong National Security Law Is Reshaping Political Identities," *The Diplomat*, December 31, 2020, https://thediplomat.com/2021/01/the-hong-kong-national-security-law-is-reshaping-political-identities/.

61. "Cross-Strait Trade."

62. "Xi Jinping Warns Taiwan That Unification Is the Goal and Force Is an Option," *New York Times*, January 1, 2019.

63. "Anti-Secession Law Adopted by NPC," *Xinhua*, March 15, 2005, https://www.chinadaily.com.cn/english/doc/2005-03/14/content_424643.htm.

64. "Declining Taiwanese Identity?," *Asia Dialogue*, February 8, 2019, https://theasiadialogue.com/2019/02/08/declining-taiwanese-identity/.

65. "Taiwan: Is There a Political Generation Gap?," *lowyinstitute.org*, June 9, 2017, https://www.lowyinstitute.org/the-interpreter/taiwan-there-political-generation-gap.

66. Eleanor Albert, "China-Taiwan Relations," *cfr.org*, January 22, 2020, https://www.cfr.org/backgrounder/china-taiwan-relations.

67. "Su Chi Admits the '1992 Consensus' Was Made Up," *Taipei Times*, February 22, 2006, https://www.taipeitimes.com/News/taiwan/archives/2006/02/22/2003294106.

68. Ryan Hass, "Taiwan's Tsai Ing-wen Enters Second Term with a Strong Political Mandate, but No Room for Complacency," *Brookings*, May 13, 2020, https://www.brookings.edu/blog/order-from-chaos/2020/05/13/taiwans-tsai-ing-wen-enters-second-term-with-a-strong-political-mandate-but-no-room-for-complacency/.

69. "Wang Hongguang zhongjiang: 'liuzhan yiti' wutong Taiwan" [Lieutenant General Wang Hongguang: "Six Battles in One" to Unify Taiwan with Military Force], *Global Times*, March 27, 2018, https://mil.huanqiu.com/article/9CaKrnK752t.

70. "Xi Jinping Takes Pacifying Line on Taiwan as Hawks Call for Force," *SCMP*, July 17, 2018.

71. "Beijing Advised This Is Not the Time to Take Back Taiwan," *SCMP*, May 5, 2020.

72. John Bolton, *The Room Where It Happened* (New York: Simon & Schuster, 2020), p. 313.

73. "Time May Be Ripe for China to Invade Taiwan," *Asia Times*, April 28, 2020; Eleanor Albert, "China-Taiwan Relations," *Cfr.org*, January 2020, https://www.cfr.org/backgrounder/china-taiwan-relations; "After Hong Kong: China Sets Sights on Solving 'the Taiwan Problem,'" *The Guardian*, October 2, 2020; "China Is Still Wary of Invading Taiwan," *Foreign Policy*, May 11, 2020, https://foreignpolicy.com/2020/05/11/china-taiwan-reunification-invasion-coronavirus-pandemic/.

74. For the notion of misperception, see Robert Jervis, *Perceptions and Misperceptions in International Politics* (Princeton, NJ: Princeton University Press, 1976).

75. Robert O. Keohane and Joseph S. Nye, *Power and Interdependence: World Politics in Transition* (Boston: Little, Brown, 1977), pp. 25–27, 30–32.

76. Xi Jinping, *Xi Jinping tan zhiguo lizheng* [Xi Jinping on Governance], Vol. 3 (Beijing: Waiwen chubanshe, 2020), pp. 403–410.

77. "Chinese President: Flexing Military Muscles Does Not Reflect Strength," *China Daily*, June 28, 2014, http://www.chinadaily.com.cn/china/2014-06/28/content_17621991.htm. For a similar argument see Alfred L. Chan, ed., "War against Taiwan: A Strategic Evaluation by Lieutenant General Liu Yazhou," *Chinese Law and Government*, September-October 2007.

78. "No Soul-Searching for Xi Jinping after Taiwan Rebuffs China in Election," *Japan Times*, January 13, 2020, https://www.japantimes.co.jp/news/2020/01/13/asia-pacific/xi-jinping-china-taiwan-election/#.XwqG6ud7mUk.

79. "Highlights of Xi's Speech at Taiwan Message Anniversary Event," *China Daily*, January 2, 2019.

80. "Hong Kong and China: A Special Relationship," *Aljazeera English*, March 22, 2016, http://www.aljazeera.com/indepth/opinion/2016/03/hong-kong-china-special-relationship-160320110701938.html.

81. You Ji, "China's National Security Commission: Theory, Evolution and Operations," *Journal of Contemporary China*, No. 25, Issue 98 (2016), p. 190).

82. Graham Allison, "The Thucydides's Trap," *Foreign Policy*, June 9, 2017, http://foreignpolicy.com/2017/06/09/the-thucydides-trap/; *Destined for War: Can America and China Escape Thucydides's Trap?* (Boston: Houghton Mifflin Harcourt, 2017). For power transition theory, see A. F. K. Organski, *World Politics*, 2nd ed. (New York: Knopf, 1968).

83. Brantly Womack, "Asymmetric Parity: US-China Relations in a Multi-nodal World," *International Affairs*, Vol. 92, No. 6, 2016.

84. "World Military Expenditure Grows to $1.8 Trillion in 2018," *Stockholm International Peace Research Institute,* April 29, 2019, https://www.sipri.org/media/press-release/2019/world-military-expenditure-grows-18-trillion-2018.

85. "Trends in International Arms Transfers, 2019," SIPRI Fact Sheet, March 2020, https://www.sipri.org/publications/2020/sipri-fact-sheets/trends-international-arms-transfers-2019.

86. Daniel Immerwahr, *How to Hide an Empire: A Short History of the Greater United States* (London: Bodley Head, 2019), p. 400; John Glaser, "Withdrawing from Overseas Bases," *Policy Analysis*, No. 816, July 18, 2017. On important US base is located in the Chagos islands, a British colony claimed by Mauritius.

87. Pass, *American Hegemony*, p. 191–192.

88. Andreas Xenachis, "US Foreign Policy in the Face of a 'Might Makes Right' China," *The Diplomat*, August 6, 2016. For a more pro-Chinese analysis, see Xue li and Xu Yanzhuo, "How the US Misjudged the South China Sea, Part I and II," *The Diplomat*, August 4 and August 5, 2016.

89. For further analysis, see Makau Mutua, "Savages, Victims, and Saviors: The Metaphor of Human Rights," *Harvard International Law Journal*, Vol. 42, No. 1, Winter 2001; Randall Peerenboom, *China Modernizes: Threat to the West or Model for the Rest?* (New York. Oxford University Press, 2007), chaps. 3, 4, and 5.

90. To put this in comparative perspective, the United States had, in the 1980s and 1990s, applied tremendous pressure, such as the Structural Impediments Initiative, to alter the political economy of Japan, its strategic and political ally. See Hook et al., *Japan's International Relations*, pp. 108ff and *passim*. With certain exceptions, the current trade dispute between China and the United States mirrors that between the United States and Japan.

91. "Full Text: Human Rights Record of the United States in 2018," *Xinhua*, March 14, 2019, http://www.xinhuanet.com/english/2019-03/14/c_137894730.htm.

92. See, for example, Andrew Nathan and Andrew Scobell, *China's Search for Security* (New York: Columbia Press, 2012), pp. 106–107.

93. "The People's Republic of China," U.S.-China Trade Facts, US Trade Representative, Executive Office of the President, https://ustr.gov/countries-regions/china-mongolia-taiwan/peoples-republic-china.

94. Eswar Prasad, "The U.S.-China Economic Relationship: Shifts and Twists in the Balance of Power," *Brookings*, February 25, 2010.

95. *China and the World* (n.p.: P. McKinsey Global Institute, 2019), p. 4.

96. Graham Allison, "What Xi Jinping Wants," *The Atlantic*, May 31, 2017, https://www.theatlantic.com/international/archive/2017/05/what-china-wants/528561/.

97. "Fact Sheet: President Xi Jinping's State Visit to the United States," White House, September 25, 2015, https://www.whitehouse.gov/the-press-office/2015/09/25/fact-sheet-president-xi-jinpings-state-visit-united-states.

98. "The White House Office of the Press Secretary, Remarks by President Obama and President Xi of the People's Republic of China in Joint Press Conference,"

White House, September 25, 2015, https://obamawhitehouse.archives.gov/the-press-office/2015/09/25/remarks-president-obama-and-president-xi-peoples-republic-china-joint. For a similar pronouncement during Xi's UK visit, see "Xi Jinping: There Is Only a Better, Not Best, Way, in Protecting Human Rights," *BBC Chinese*, October 21, 2015, http://www.bbc.com/zhongwen/simp/china/2015/10/151021_xi_jinping_cameron_press.

99. "China Inks Big Deals with Boeing, Cisco Systems," *USA Today*, September 24, 2015, http://www.usatoday.com/story/news/2015/09/23/china-buy-300-boeing-planes/72681578/.

100. "Trump-Taiwan Call: China Lodges Protest," *BBC*, December 3, 2016, http://www.bbc.com/news/world-asia-china-38194371.

101. "The US-China Trade War: A Timeline," *China Briefing*, February 26, 2020, https://www.china-briefing.com/news/the-us-china-trade-war-a-timeline/.

102. "Esper Marks Eventful Year as Defense Secretary," *Defense.gov.*, July 18, 2020, https://www.defense.gov/Explore/News/Article/Article/2279112/esper-marks-eventful-year-as-defense-secretary/.

103. Bolton, *Room Where It Happened*, p. 301.

104. "Hypocrisy Is a Useful Tool in Foreign Affairs: Trump is Too Crude to Play the Game," *Washington Post*, November 5, 2018, https://www.washingtonpost.com/outlook/2018/11/05/hypocrisy-is-useful-tool-foreign-affairs-trump-is-too-crude-play-game/.

105. "U. S. Is Using Taiwan as a Pressure Point in Tech Fight with China," *New York Times*, May 19, 2020; "Trump Administration Said to Be Preparing Crackdown on Huawei's Global Chip Supply," *SCMP*, March 27, 2020.

106. Feng Zhang and Richard Ned Lebow, *Taming Sino-American Rivalry* (New York: Oxford University Press, 2020).

107. Matteo Dian, "Sino-Japanese Relations in the Xi-Abe Era: Can Two Tigers Live on the Same Mountain?," in Silvio Beretta, Axel Berkofsky, and Lihong Zhang, eds., *Understanding China Today: An Exploration of Politics, Economics, Society, and International Relations* (Cham, Switzerland: Springer International Publishing, 2017), pp. 79ff; Ezra F. Vogel, *Deng Xiaoping and the Transformation of China* (Cambridge, MA: Harvard University Press, 2011).

108. Linus Hagström, "Sino-Japanese Relations: The Ice That Won't Melt," *International Journal*, Vol. 64, No. 1, Winter 2008–2009. See also Donald Gross, "Realizing Japan's Foreign Policy Goals," chap. 8 of his *The China Fallacy: How the U.S. Can Benefit from China's Rise and Avoid Another Cold War* (New York: Bloomsbury, 2013); Richard Bush, *The Perils of Proximity: China-Japan Security Relations* (Washington, DC: Brookings Institution Press, 2010).

109. JETRO Survey: *Analysis of Japan-China Trade in 2015*, February 17, 2016, https://www.jetro.go.jp/en/news/releases/2016/c52b1f3efe0aa231.html. Despite the political tensions, trade between the two countries stayed at US$330 billion in 2018, *Investopedia*, August 9, 2019, https://www.investopedia.com/articles/investing/092815/chinas-top-trading-partners.asp.

110. Fan Ying, "Growing Interdependency between China and Japan: Trade, Investment, Tourism, and Education," in Lam Penger, ed., *China-Japan Relations in the 21st Century: Antagonism Despite Interdependency* (Singapore: Palgrave Macmillan, 2017).

111. Michael Yahuda, "The Limits of Economic Interdependence," chap. 6 of Alastair Iain Johnston and Robert S. Ross, eds., *New Directions in the Study of China's Foreign Policy* (Stanford, CA: Stanford University Press, 2006); Leszek Buszynski, "Sino-Japanese Relations: Interdependence, Rivalry and Regional Security," *Contemporary Southeast Asia*, Vol. 31, No. 2, 2009; Robert G. Sutter, *Chinese Foreign Relations*, 4th ed. (Lanham, MD: Rowman & Littlefield, 2016), pp. 173–192; Ming Wan, "Japan-China Relations: Structure or Management?," in Alisa Gaunder, ed., *The Routledge Handbook of Japanese Politics* (New York: Routledge, 2011), chap. 30.

112. For a list of fighter aircraft, tanks, artillery, submarines, and aircraft carriers, see "Japan Military Strength," *Global Fire Power*, n.d., https://www.globalfirepower.com/country-military-strength-detail.asp?country_id=japan, accessed May 25, 2016. For a full discussion of the remilitarization process, see Linus Hagstrom and Jon Williamson, "'Remilitarization,' Really? Assessing Change in Japanese Foreign Security Policy," *Asian Security*, Vol. 5, No. 3, 2009; D. Bradley Gibbs, "Future Relations between the United States and Japan: Article 9 and the Remilitarization of Japan," *Houston Journal International Law*, Vol. 33,, No. 1, 2010; David Welch, "Embracing Normalcy: Toward a Japanese 'National Strategy,'" in Y. Soeya, M. Tadokoro, and D. Welch, eds., *Japan as a Normal Country? A Nation in Search of Its Place in the World* (Toronto: University of Toronto Press, 2011); Christopher Hughes, "Japan's Remilitarization," *Adelphi Papers*, Vol. 48, No. 403, 2008, pp. 11–98.

113. "Security Laws Usher in New Era for Pacifist Japan," *Japan Times*, March 29, 2016, https://www.japantimes.co.jp/news/2016/03/29/national/politics-diplomacy/japans-contentious-new-security-laws-take-effect-paving-way-collective-self-defense/#.WbcJN2aouUk. For discussions of Japan's new security approach, subsumed under the concept of "collective defense," see Joel Campbell, "Japan Steps Up Its Game: Tokyo's New Security Approach and Its Relations with Asia," *International Affairs*, Vol. 94, No. 4, 2018; Neil J. Owens, "Japan's Strategic Renaissance: Implications for US Policy in the Asia-Pacific," in D. Lai, J. F. Troxell, and F J. Gellert, eds., *Avoiding the Trap: US Strategy and Policy for Competing in the Asia-Pacific beyond the Rebalance* (2018).

114. "Japan Open for Arms Business," *East Asia Forum*, May 29, 2018, http://www.eastasiaforum.org/2018/05/29/japan-open-for-arms-business/. For more details, see Ministry of Foreign Affairs of Japan, Japan's Security, *Peace & Stability of the International Community*, May 16, 2018, https://www.mofa.go.jp/policy/security/index.html.

115. "Japan-China Tension Simmers as Xi, Abe Remain Cool on Talks in U.S.," *Japan Times*, March 30, 2016, http://www.japantimes.co.jp/news/2016/03/30/national/japan-china-tensions-simmer-xi-abe-remain-cool-talks-u-s/#.V7qU8WaV-Uk.

116. Hagstrom and Williamson, "Remilitarization"; Gibbs, "Future Relations"; Welch, "Embracing Normalcy"; Hughes, "Japan's Remilitarization."

117. "Statement by Prime Minister Abe—Pledge for Everlasting Peace," Ministry of Foreign Affairs of Japan, December 26, 2013, https://japan.kantei.go.jp/96_abe/statement/201312/1202986_7801.html.

118. Dian, "Sino-Japanese Relations."

119. "Viewpoints: China Air Zone Tensions," *BBC*, November 28, 2013, http://www.bbc.com/news/world-asia-25116119.

120. "Xi Calls on Countries to Remember War History, Pursue Peaceful Development," *Xinhua*, http://news.xinhuanet.com/english/2015-09/03/c_134586537.htm.

121. "Japan-China Tensions Simmer as Xi, Abe Remain Cool on Talks in U.S.," *Japan Times*, March 30, 2016, https://www.japantimes.co.jp/news/2016/03/30/national/japan-china-tensions-simmer-xi-abe-remain-cool-talks-u-s/#.W1DOLLgnaUk.

122. "Shinzo Abe Says Japan Is China's 'Partner,' and No Longer Its Aid Donor," *New York Times*, October 26, 2018, https://www.nytimes.com/reuters/2018/10/26/world/asia/26reuters-china-japan-speech.html.

123. "Trans-Pacific Partnership to Start in December," *Financial Times*, October 31, 2018, https://www.ft.com/content/274d411c-dc99-11e8-9f04-38d397e6661c.

124. "US Gives the Green Light to Japan's $23 B F-35 Buy," *Defense News*, July 9, 2020, https://www.defensenews.com/smr/2020/07/09/us-gives-the-green-light-to-japans-massive-23b-f-35-buy/.

125. Peter Ferdinand, "Sunset, Sunrise: China and Russia Construct a New Relationship," *International Affairs*, Vol. 83, No. 5, September 2007.

126. For a detailed analysis, see Alexander Gabuev, "Friends with Benefits? Russian-Chinese Relations after the Ukraine Crisis," Carnegie Moscow Center, June 29, 2016, http://carnegie.ru/2016/06/29/friends-with-benefits-russian-chinese-relations-after-ukraine-crisis/j2m2.

127. "China's Xi Jinping and Russia's Vladimir Putin Slam US Missile Shields," *SCMP*, June 27, 2016.

128. "Xi Jinping zhuxi yinling zhongguo tese daguo waijiao" [Chairman Xi Jinping Leads China's Special Great Power Diplomacy], *Zhongguo junwang*, August 5, 2019, http://www.81.cn/big5/jmywyl/2019-08/05/content_9580014.htm.

129. "China's Role in Syria's Endless Civil War," *SCMP*, April 7, 2017.

130. Thomas E. Kellogg, "Xi's Davos Speech: Is China the New Champion for the Liberal International Order?" *The Diplomat*, January 24, 2017, http://thediplomat.com/2017/01/xis-davos-speech-is-china-the-new-champion-for-the-liberal-international-order/.

131. Eleanor Albert, "The China–North Korea Relationship," Council on Foreign Relations, July 5, 2017, https://www.cfr.org/backgrounder/china-north-korea-relationship.

132. For a discussion of sanctions implementation, see Catherine Jones, "China's Interests, Actors, and the Implementation of Sanctions against North Korea," in Gilbert Rozman and Sergey Radchenko, eds., *International Relations and Asia's Northern Tier: Sino-Russia Relations, North Korea, and Mongolia* (Singapore: Palgrave Macmillan, 2018).

133. "U.S. Vows Tougher Action on North Korea after Missile Test," *New York Times*, July 5, 2017, https://www.nytimes.com/2017/07/05/world/asia/north-korea-war-us-icbm.html.

134. "Bad News, World: China Can't Solve the North Korea Problem," *New York Times*, September 11, 2017, https://www.nytimes.com/2017/09/06/world/asia/china-north-korea-nuclear-problem.html?mcubz=0.

135. Albert, "China–North Korea Relationship"; Jonathan Pollack, "Is Xi Jinping Rethinking Korean Unification?," *Brookings*, January 20, 2015, https://www.brookings.edu/on-the-record/is-xi-jinping-rethinking-korean-unification/.

136. "Trump Says North Korea Still 'Extraordinary Threat,'" *BBC*, June 23, 2018, https://www.bbc.com/news/world-asia-44584957?intlink_from_url=https://www.bbc.com/news/topics/cywd23g0gz5t/north-korea&link_location=live-reporting-story.

137. For example, see "Spring Release: North Korea's Economy," *The Economist*, February 28, 2015, https://www.economist.com/news/asia/21645252-tantalising-signs-change-are-emerging-whether-they-signal-more-profound-shifts-less.

138. Steven Denney, "South Korea's Economic Dependence on China," *The Diplomat*, September 4, 2015, https://thediplomat.com/2015/09/south-koreas-economic-dependence-on-china/.

139. "Beijing and South Korea Oppose North Korea Nuclear Tests," *BBC*, July 3, 2014, http://www.bbc.com/news/world-asia-28139972.

140. "Beijing and South Korea"; "Xi Jinping on Pragmatic Track with North Korea, Analysts Say," *SCMP*, June 3, 2016.

141. "South Korea's President Moon Halts Deployment of More THAAD Missile Launchers until 'Environmental Impact' Probe Is Done," *SCMP*, June 7, 2017.

142. "China, South Korea Look to Improve Ties with Beijing Summit," *Associated Press*, December 23, 2019, https://apnews.com/436720f409416bd4acce26f1744a1074.

143. "China-Europe Relations: It's Time for a Pragmatic Approach," *China Daily*, July 14, 2016.

144. Richard Maher, "The Elusive EU-China Strategic Partnership," *International Affairs*, No. 92, Issue 4, July 2016.

145. Justyna Szczudlik, "China-EU Relations: Post-summit Perspectives," Center for Security Studies, August 11, 2016, https://www.pism.pl/publications/bulletin/no-45-895.

146. "Leaked Cable Shows Fragility of EU Arms Ban on China," *Competa*, July 25, 2011, https://euobserver.com/china/32658.

147. Maher, "Elusive EU-China Strategic Partnership," p. 966.

148. Szczudlik, "China-EU Relations."

149. Shannon Tiezzi, "China's Xi Brings 'Belt and Road' to Serbia, Poland," *The Diplomat*, June 24, 2016, http://thediplomat.com/2016/06/chinas-xi-brings-belt-and-road-to-serbia-poland/.

150. "Xi Visit Raises Eastern Europe Investment Hopes," *Financial Times*, June 15, 2016, https://www.ft.com/content/db718250-32e8-11e6-bda0-04585c31b153.

151. "Greece Blocks EU Statement on China Human Rights at U.N.," *Reuters*, June 18, 2017, https://www.reuters.com/article/us-eu-un-rights/greece-blocks-eu-statement-on-china-human-rights-at-u-n-idUSKBN1990FP.

152. Maher, "Elusive EU-China Strategic Partnership."

153. "China and the EU Are Growing Sick of U.S. Financial Power," *Foreign Policy*, November 16, 2018, https://foreignpolicy.com/2018/11/16/us-eu-china-trump-sanctions/.

154. "How Much Trade Transits the South China Sea?," *China Power*, n.d., https://chinapower.csis.org/much-trade-transits-south-china-sea/, accessed October 4, 2021.

155. "How Much Trade Transits the South China Sea?"

156. "How China's Defense Industry Can Learn from Its Rival Japan: PLA Veteran," *SCMP*, March 27, 2016.

157. For a detailed analysis, see Bates Gill, Evelyn Goh, and Chin-hao Huang, *The Dynamics of US-China–Southeast Asia Relations*, United States Studies Centre, June 2016.

158. Gill et al., *Dynamics of US-China–Southeast Asia Relations*.

159. "China Vows to Step Up Air, Sea Patrols after U.S. Warship Sails Near Disputed Islands," *Washington Post*, July 3, 2017, https://www.washingtonpost.com/.../china-accuses-us...disputed-island/.../9ce7b026-5f93.

160. "Occupation and Island Building," Asia Maritime Transparency Initiative, n.d., https://amti.csis.org/island-tracker/, accessed April 7, 2021.

161. Jana Sehnalkova, "Taiwan's Policy towards the South China Sea," in Martin Riegl, Jakub Landovský, and Irina Valko, eds., *Strategic Regions in 21st Century Power Politics* (Newcastle-upon-Tyne: Cambridge Scholars, 2014), pp. 62–82.

162. "Many Myths about China Should Be Debunked for Continued Peace in S. China Sea," *Xinhua*, July 11, 2016, http://news.xinhuanet.com/english/2016-07/11/c_135505442.htm.

163. "Ruling 'Null and Void,'" *China Daily*, July 13, 2016; "Taiwan, after Rejecting South China Sea Decision, Sends Patrol Ship," *New York Times*, June 13, 2016.

164. "Duterte Aligns Philippines with China, Says U.S. Has Lost," *Reuters*, October 20, 2016, http://www.reuters.com/article/us-china-philippines-idUSKCN12K0AS; "China Visit Helps Duterte Reap Funding Deals Worth $24 Billion," *Bloomberg*, October 21, 2016, https://www.bloomberg.com/news/articles/2016-10-21/china-visit-helps-duterte-reap-funding-deals-worth-24-billion.

165. "Philippines' Duterte Seeks Alliance with China but Defense Officials Warn of Strategic Threat," *SCMP*, March 26, 2017.

166. Evelyn Goh, "Southeast Asian Perspectives on the China Challenge," *Journal of Strategic Studies*, August-October 2007, pp. 828–829.

167. Gil, et al., *Dynamics of US-China–Southeast China Relations*.

168. "South China Sea: ASEAN Avoids Mention of China Ruling," *BBC Asia Pacific*, July 25, 2016, http://www.bbc.com/news/world-asia-36878995 2016. Cambodia was staunchly supportive of the China position.

169. "Obama, ASEAN Discuss South China Sea Tensions, but No Joint Mention of China," *Reuters*, February 17, 2016, http://www.reuters.com/article/us-usa-asean-idUSKC

N0VP1F7; "US-ASEAN Summit Seeks to Counter China's Growth," *Aljazeera*, February 15, 2016, http://www.aljazeera.com/news/2016/02/asean-summit-seeks-counter-china-growth-160214080824590.html; Prashanth Parameswaran, "Why Did the US-ASEAN Sunnylands Summit Achieve?," *The Diplomat*, February 2016, http://thediplomat.com/2016/02/what-did-the-us-asean-sunnylands-summit-achieve/.

170. "China and ASEAN Agree to Draft Code of Conduct in South China Sea," *SCMP*, May 18, 2017; "China, ASEAN Approve Framework of South China Sea Code of Conduct," *Global Times*, May 18, 2017, http://www.globaltimes.cn/content/1047 662.shtml; "ASEAN and China Agree on Draft Framework for Code of Conduct in South China Sea," *Strait Times*, May 18, 2017, http://www.straitstimes.com/asia/east-asia/asean-and-china-agree-on-draft-framework-for-code-of-cond uct-in-south-china-sea.

171. J. Michael Dahm, *Introduction to South China Sea Military Capability Studies* (n.p.: John Hopkins Applied Physics Laboratory, 2020), p. 2.

172. Shiping Tang and Robin Michael Garcia, "A Radical Solution for China and the Philippines: Share the South China Sea," *National Interest*, August 22, 2016, http://nationalinterest.org/feature/radical-solution-china-the-philippi nes-share-the-south-china-17437.

173. For instance, see *The Defense of Japan 2016* (Tokyo: Japan Ministry of Defense, 2017), pp. 41, 43, and 58.

174. Jonathan Stromesth, "The Testing Ground: China's Rising Influence in Southeast Asia and Regional Responses," *Global China*, November 2019.

175. For more detailed analyses, see Kevin Cai, "The One Belt, One Road and the Asian Infrastructure Investment Bank: Beijing's New Strategy of Geoeconomics and Geopolitics," *Journal of Contemporary China*, July 2018; Hong Yu, "Motivation behind China's 'One Belt, One Road' Initiatives and Establishment of the Asia Infrastructural Investment Bank," *Journal of Contemporary China*, Vol. 26, No. 105, May, 2017; Giuseppe Gabust, "'Crossing the River by Feeling the Gold': The Asian Infrastructural Investment Bank and the Financial Support to the Belt and Road Initiative," *China and World Economy*, No. 25, Issue 5, 2017; Christian Ploberger, "One Belt, One Road—China's New Grand Strategy," *Journal of Chinese Economic and Business Studies*, No. 15, Issue 3, 2017.

176. The following draws from "Iran, China and the Silk Road Train," *The Diplomat*, March 30, 2016, http://thediplomat.com/2016/03/iran-china-and-the-silk-road-train/; "China's Xi Jinping Talks Up 'One Belt, One Road' as Keynote Project Fizzles," *Time*, August 18, 2016, http://time.com/4457044/xi-jinping-one-belt-one-road-obor-south-china-sea-economic-trade-business/; "China's Huge 'One Belt, One Road Initiative' Is Sweeping Central Asia," *National Interest*, July 27, 2016, http://nationalinterest.org/feature/chinas-huge-one-belt-one-road-initiative-sweeping-central-17150; "Our Bull Dozers, Our Rules," *The Economist*, July 2, 2016, https://www.economist.com/news/china/21701505-chinas-foreign-policy-could-reshape-good-part-world-economy-our-bulldozers-our-rules.

177. For instance, Buddhism and Islam were transmitted into China.

178. "Asia's $26tn Infrastructural Gap Threatens Growth, ABD Warns," *Financial Times*, February 27, 2017, https://www.ft.com/content/79d9e36e-fd0b-11e6-8d8e-a5e37 38f9ae4?mhq5j=el.

179. Xi, *Governance 2*, pp. 506–517.

180. For example, see Scott Cendrowski, "Inside China's Global Spending Spree," *Fortune*, December 12, 2016, http://fortune.com/china-belt-road-investment/.

181. See also "Yidai yilu guoji hezuo gaofeng luntan chengguo qingdan" [A List of the Achievements of the OBOR Summit Forum on International Cooperation], Ministry of Foreign Affairs, May 16, 2017, http://www.fmprc.gov.cn/web/zyxw/ t1461873.shtml.

182. "Yidai yilu li meibei dianming di shengfen zuoshime" [What Functions Will Provinces Not Mentioned by One Belt, One Road Perform?], *Dagongwang*, April 2, 2015, http://news.takungpao.com/mainland/focus/2015-04/2963309.html.

183. Cai, "One Belt, One Road," pp. 9–11.

184. For a good summary see Xi, *Governance 2*, pp. 506–517; Peter Ferdinand, "Westward Ho—the China Dream and 'One Belt, One Road': Chinese Foreign Policy under Xi Jinping," *International Affairs*, Vol. 92, No. 4, July 2016; François Godement, "'One Belt, One Road': China's Great Leap Outward," *European Council on Foreign Relations*, June 2015.

185. See, for example, "Yidai yilu jianshe zhong di sande tiaozhan ji yingdui: [The Three Major Challenges to the Building of the OBOR and the Remedies], *Ifeng*, June 27, 2015, http://finance.ifeng.com/a/20150627/13802234_0.shtml; "Yidai yilu shida wenti" [Ten Major Issues with the OBOR]," *Ifeng*, n.d., https://pit.ifeng.com/event/ special/yidaiyiludiaoyan/, accessed May 17, 2016.

186. "China's Xi Jinping Talks Up One Belt, One Road."

187. "Yidia yilu heyi shenxian Malaixiya zhengzhi nizhao" [Why Did the OBOR Get Stuck in the Political Tumult of Malaysia?], *Fenghuang zixun*, May 20, 2017, http:// pit.ifeng.com/a/20170520/51128101_0.shtml.

188. "China's Huge One Belt, One Road Initiative Is Sweeping Central Asia."

189. "Iran, China and the Silk Road Train," *The Diplomat*, March 30, 2016, http://thediplo mat.com/2016/03/iran-china-and-the-silk-road-train/.

190. For further analysis, see Peter Cai, *Understanding China's Belt and Road Initiative* (Sydney: Lowy Institute, 2017); Paul Stronski and Nicole Ng, *Cooperation and Competition: Russia and China in Central Asia, the Russian Far East, and the Artic*, Carnegie Endowment, February 28, 2018.

191. "2017 nian yidaiyilu zaoyu shida zhiyi Zhongguo ruhe huiying" [The Ten Major Complaints against the OBOR in 2017 and How Should China Respond?], https:// www.yidaiyilu.gov.cn/xwzx/gnxw/56930.htm, accessed January 30, 2018; "Yidaiyilu changyi cunzai naxie wenti, yinggai ruhe diaozheng" [What Are the Major Issues with the OBOR and How Can They be Dealt With?], *Sohu*, August 11, 2018, http:// www.sohu.com/a/246627413_825949.

192. "Belt and Road Helps Build Lasting Economic and Trade Relations," *China Daily*, December 12, 2019, https://global.chinadaily.com.cn/a/201912/12/WS5df18416a 310cf3e3557d903.html; "Belt and Road Reaches Out to the World," *China Daily*,

September 30, 2019, https://www.chinadaily.com.cn/a/201909/30/WS5d9160e4a
310cf3e3556e4a0.html.

193. "Success of China's Belt & Road Initiative Depends on Deep Policy Reforms, Study
Finds," *World Bank*, June 18, 2019, https://www.worldbank.org/en/news/press-rele
ase/2019/06/18/success-of-chinas-belt-road-initiative-depends-on-deep-policy-
reforms-study-finds.

194. "A Bank Too Far?," Council for Foreign Relations, March 17, 2017, https://www.
cfr.org/interview/bank-too-far; Paola Subacchi, "The AIIB Is a Threat to Global
Economic Governance," *Foreign Policy*, March 31, 2015, http://foreignpolicy.com/
2015/03/31/the-aiib-is-a-threat-to-global-economic-governance-china/.

195. Subacchi, "AIIB is a Threat."

196. For a case arguing the benefits for the United States joining the AIIB, see "Trump
Needs the AIIB to Get His American Dream on the Road," *SCMP*, March 29, 2017.
A similar argument, made before the US pullout of the TPP, is in "The AIIB and the
'One Belt, One Road," *Brookings*, January 1, 2015, https://www.brookings.edu/opini
ons/the-aiib-and-the-one-belt-one-road/.

197. Wade Shepard, "The AIIB One Year In: Not as Scary as Washington Thought,"
Forbes, January 17, 2017, https://www.forbes.com/sites/wadeshepard/2017/01/16/
the-aiib-one-year-in-not-as-scary-as-washington-thought/#40a1519b5e83.

198. Ankit Panda, "China-Led AIIB Sees Membership Expansion: What's Next?," *The
Diplomat*, March 30, 2017, http://thediplomat.com/2017/03/china-led-aiib-sees-
membership-expansion-whats-next/.

199. "A German View of the Asia Infrastructure Investment Bank," European Council
on Foreign Relations, April 27, 2017, http://www.ecfr.eu/article/commentary_a_g
erman_view_of_the_aiib_7275; "AIIB Expansion Plans Underscore China's Global
Ambitions," *Financial Times*, June 26, 2016.

200. "How the BRICS New Development Bank Serves China's Interest," *Ibtimes*, July 18,
2014, http://www.ibtimes.com/how-brics-new-development-bank-serves-chinas-
interest-1631664.

201. "NBD: A Bank with a Question Mark," *Deutsche Welle*, April 8, 2016, http://www.
dw.com/en/ndb-a-bank-with-a-question-mark/a-19172152.

202. "New Development Bank Chief Upbeat on Future," *China Daily*, November 15,
2019, https://global.chinadaily.com.cn/a/201911/15/WS5dce0f92a310cf3e35577
949.html.

203. "China Already Leads 4 of the 15 U. N. specialized Agencies—and is Aiming for
a 5th," *Washington Post*, March 3, 2020, https://www.washingtonpost.com/politics/
2020/03/03/china-already-leads-4-15-un-specialized-agencies-is-aiming-5th/.

204. Kristine Lee, "The United States Can't Quit on the UN," *Foreign Affairs*,
September 2020.

205. "China Surprises U.N. with $100 Million and Thousands of Troops for Peacekeeping,"
New York Times, September 28, 2015, http://www.nytimes.com/interactive/proje
cts/cp/reporters-notebook/xi-jinping-visit/china-surprisesu-n-with-100-million-
and-thousands-of-troops-for-peacekeeping; "China's Troop Contributions to U.N.

Peacekeeping," US Institute of Peace, July 26, 2016, https://www.usip.org/publicati ons/2016/07/chinas-troop-contributions-un-peacekeeping.

206. "China Rises to 2nd Largest Contributor to UN Budget," *Xinhua*, December 14, 2018, http://www.xinhuanet.com/english/2018-12/24/c_137696281.htm.

207. "China to Become 2nd Largest Contributor to UN Peacekeeping Budget," *China Daily*, May 30, 2016; United Nations General Assembly, Seventieth Session, *Scale of Assessments for the Apportionment of the Expenses of United Nations Peacekeeping Operations, Implementation of General Assembly Resolutions 55/235 and 55/236, Report of the Secretary-General*, 2018, https://digitallibrary.un.org/record/1657 181?ln=en.

208. "China Concludes 14-Year Peacekeeping Operation in Liberia," *Renminwang*, March 5, 2018, http://en.people.cn/n3/2018/0305/c90000-9433099.html; "China Completes Registration of 8,000 Strong UN Peacekeeping Force, Defense Ministry Says," *SCMP*, September 29, 2017.

209. "Aid, China, and Growth: Evidence from a New Global Development Finance Dataset," AIDATA, Working Paper No. 46, October 2017, http://docs.aiddata.org/ ad4/pdfs/WPS46_Aid_China_and_Growth.pdf; "China's Foreign Aid beyond the Headlines," *Fairbank Center blog*, February 12, 2018, https://medium.com/fairbank-center/chinas-foreign-aid-beyond-the-headlines-2479509d4244.

210. "Aid, China, and Growth."

211. "Zhongguo meinian hua jibaiyi gao duiwei yuanzhu zhenxiang guoren kanhou wuti toudi" [After the Chinese Found Out Why China Spends Billions for Foreign Assistance, They Are Totally Convinced by Its Wisdom], *Sohu.com*, September 15, 2017, http://www.sohu.com/a/192174990_612646.

212. "Aid, China, and Growth."

213. Figure cited in "China Has Replaced U.S. as Locomotive of Global Economy: Kemp," *Reuters*, November 5, 2019, https://www.reuters.com/article/us-economy-global-kemp-column/china-has-replaced-u-s-as-locomotive-of-global-economy-kemp-idUSKBN1XF211.

214. Aaron L. Friedberg, "Globalization and Chinese Grand Strategy," *Survival*, Vol. 60, No. 1, February–March 2018.

Chapter 12

1. "Yu 3 wan zi de shijiuda baogao chuzi shuishou" [Who Is Responsible for Composing the Report to the Nineteenth Party Congress, Which Is More Than Thirty Thousand words?], *Sina*, October 29, 2017, http://news.sina.com.cn/c/nd/2017-10-29/doc-ifynfvar4863946.shtml.

2. A much-feared interrogation method designated for party members but often applied more widely. The suspect is detained incommunicado and put under intense psychological pressure to account for alleged wrongdoings.

3. "Xin dangzhang Xi chuxian 11 ci, shaoyu Mao Deng yuan chao Jiang Hu" [Xi Appears Eleven Times in the Party Constitution, Less Than Mao and Deng but Far Exceeding Jiang and Hu], *Wangbao*, October 30, 2017.

4. "Xi Jinping shijiuda baogao quanwen" [The Full Text of Xi Jinping's Report to the Nineteenth Party Congress], *Xinhua*, October 18, 2017, http://finance.sina.com.cn/china/gncj/2017-10-18/doc-ifymvuyt4098830.shtml.

5. See also Delia Lin, *Civilizing Citizens in Post-Mao China: Understanding the Rhetoric of Suzhi* (New York: Routledge, 2017).

6. The new party constitution, with detailed annotations to the 107 revisions, is in "Dangzhang zuoliao naxie xiugai" [What Aspects of the Party Constitutions Have Been Revised?], *Sina*, October 30, 2017, http://news.sina.com.cn/c/nd/2017-10-30/doc-ifynhhay8319528.shtml.

7. "Zhonggong shijiuda Xisixiang ru dangzhang, quanli zhibi Mao Zedong, Deng Xiaoping" [Xi's Thought Is Inserted into the CCP's Constitution: Xi's Power Is Closer to That of Mao and Deng Xiaoping], *Mingbao*, October 24, 2017, https://news.mingpao.com/pns/dailynews/web_tc/article/20171025/s00013/1508868374066.

8. "Zhonggong zhongyang zhengzhiju zhaokai huiyi yanjiu bushu xuexi xuanchuan guanche dangde shujiuda jingshen" [The CCP Politburo Convenes a Meeting to Study and Arrange for the Propaganda to Implement the Spirit of the Nineteenth Party Congress], *Xinhua*, October 27, 2017, http://news.xinhuanet.com/politics/19cpcnc/2017-10/27/c_1121868508.htm; "Zhongyang zhengzhiju chengyuan yeyao shuzhi liao" [Members of the Politburo Now Have to Account for Their Work], *Sohu*, October 28, 2017, http://www.sohu.com/a/200769697_137462.

9. For a list of the numerous foreign affairs activities by senior Chinese officials after the Nineteenth Party Congress, see Policies and Activities, Ministry of Foreign Affairs of the PRC, http://www.fmprc.gov.cn/mfa_eng/wjdt_665385/wshd_665389/.

10. "Xi Jinping xinjie manyue luozi kaiju xinshidai" [Xi Jinping's New Term Is Starting a New Era after One Month], *Wenweipo*, November 28, 2017.

11. "Zhongxuanbu yuan fubuchang Lu Wei she yanzhong weiji shoucha" [Former Deputy Head of the Publicity Department Is Investigated for Serious Breach of Discipline], *Wenweipo*, November 22, December 1, 2017.

12. "Zhongyang di shiyi xunshizu xiang Chongqing shiwei fankui xunshi huitoukan qingkuang" [A Repeated Investigation of the Chongqing MPC by the Central No. 11 Roving Inspection Team], *Zhongyang jiwei jiancha wang*, February 13, 2017, https://web.archive.org/web/20170721035253/http://www.ccdi.gov.cn/yw/201702/t20170213_93903.html.

13. "Zhonggong zhongyang jueding jiyu Sun Zhengcai kaichu dangji, kaichu gongzhi chufen, jiang Sun Zhengcai shexian fanzui wenti ji xiansuo yisong sifa jiguan yifa chuli" [The CCP Party Central Decides to Discipline Sun Zhengcai by Dismissing Him from All Party and Official Positions; He and the Evidence of Misdemeanor Will Be Handed Over to the Judiciary to Be Prosecuted According to Law], September 29, 2017, *Xinhua*, http://news.xinhuanet.com/politics/2017-09/29/c_1121747644.htm.

14. "Sun Zhengcai shouhuian, yishen gongkai xuanpan bei panchu wuqi tuxing" [The Bribery Case of Sun Zhengcai: The First Intermediate Court Announces a Sentence of Life Imprisonment], *Zhongguo xinwenwang*, May 8, 2018, http://www.chinanews.com/sh/2018/05-08/8508473.shtml.

15. "Zhengjianhui zhuxi Liu Shiyu zai shijiuda jinrong xilie daibiaotuan di fayan" [Recorded Speech by the Chair of the Securities Regulation Commission, Liu Shiyu, to Representatives of the Finance Sector at the Nineteenth Party Congress], *Sina*, http://blog.sina.com.cn/s/blog_537513510102xim9.html; "Coup Plotters Foiled: Xi Jinping Fended Off Threat to 'Save Communist Party,'" *SCMP*, October 19, 2017.

16. "Xi Jinping zai dangde shibajie liuzhong quanhui dierci quanti huiyi shang di jianghua" [Extracts of the Speech Given by Xi Jinping at the Second Session of the Sixth Plenum of the Eighteenth Central Committee], *Xinhua*, January 1, 2017, http://news.xinhuanet.com/politics/2017-01/01/c_1120228200.htm.

17. "Linghang xinshidai de jianqiang lingdao jiti: Dangde xinyijie zhongyang lingdao jigou chansheng jishi" [A Strong Collective Leadership for the New Age: An Account of the Emergence of the New Central Leadership Structure of the Party], *Xinhua*, October 26, 2017, http://news.xinhuanet.com/politics/19cpcnc/2017-10/26/c_112 1860147.htm.

18. "Shibajie Zhongjiwei xiang Zhonggong shijiuda di gongzuo baogao" [The Eighteenth CCDI's Work Report to the Nineteenth Party Congress], *Xinhuawang*, October 29, 2017, https://news.qq.com/a/20171029/022008.htm.

19. "Zhou Yongkang an shi Zhonggong jianzheng yilai zuida zhengbianan? [Is the Zhou Yongkang Case the Most Far-Reaching Coup d'État since the Founding of the PRC?], *Voice of America Chinese*, December 6, 2014, https://www.voachinese.com/a/zhouy ongkang-case-20141205/2547874.html. See also "Ling Jihua luoma xinsirenbang quankua" [The Fall of Ling Jihua and the Collapse of the New Gang of Four], *Apple Daily*, December 23, 2014, https://tw.news.appledaily.com/international/daily/20141 223/36283348/; "Weixie Xi Jinping Xin sirenbang wajie, Bo Xilai, Zhou Yongkang, Xu Caihou, Ling Jihua xianhou luowang" [A Threat to Xi Jinping, the New Gang of Four Breaks Down: Bo Xilai, Zhou Yongkang, Xu Caihou, and Ling Jihua Have Been Apprehended Consecutively], *Mingbao*, December 23, 2014, http://www.mingpa ocanada.com/Tor/htm/News/20141223/taa01_r.htm; "Damaging Coup Rumors Ricochet across China," *BBC*, March 22, 2012, http://www.bbc.com/news/world-asia-china-17476760.

20. "Beijing 3.19 zhengbian, wanzhengban" [The 3.19 Coup d'État in Beijing: The Full Version], *Epochtimes*, July 4, 2015, http://www.epochtimes.com/gb/15/7/4/n4472 566.htm.

21. "Xuanren yongren bugao dahui haitui" [The Method of Election by Party Convention Will No Longer Be Used], *Wenweipo*, October 25, 2017.

22. "Dangde xinyijie zhongyang lingdao jigou chanshengji" [A Veritable Record of the Birth of the Party's New Central Leadership Organs], *Sina*, October 26, 2017, http://www.chinanews.com/gn/2017/10-26/8360984.shtml; "Three Disgraced Chinese Communist Party Officials Accused of Trying to Rig Elections," *SCMP*, October 26, 2017; "Method of Election."

23. "Zhonggong zhongyang zhengzhiju zhaokai huiyi: Shenyi Zhongguo gongchandang xunshi gongzuo tiaoli xiudinggao" [The Politburo of the CCP Convenes a Meeting to Scrutinize the CCP's Draft Revision of the Regulations on Roving Inspection Work," www.gov.cn, June 26, 2015, http://www.gov.cn/xinwen/2015-06/26/content_2885175.htm; "Guanyu tuijin lingdao ganbu nengshang nengxia de ruogan guiding shixing" [Several Trial Regulations on the Practice of Promoting and Demoting Leadership Cadres], *Xinhuanet*, June 26, 2016, http://www.xinhuanet.com/2015-06/26/c_1115737599.htm.

24. For instance, one source claims that the PBSC was neatly divided between a Jiang Zemin "faction" that consisted of Wang Huning and Han Zheng, whereas a Xi Jinping "faction" consisted of Li Zhanshu and Zhao Leji. Li Keqiang was *tuanpai*, and Wang Yang, Han Zheng, and Wang Huning were never Xi protégés. This view implies that Xi might have a harder time in pushing his policies. However, the view that the PBSC is bifurcated is interesting but unsubstantiated. "Zhonggong zhongyang xinyijie zhengzhiju wuzhang xinmiankong, Xi Jiang shili geyiban" [Five Newcomers in the New PBSC of the CCP: The Xi and Jiang Forces Each Occupy One Half], *Radio Free Asia*, October 25, 2017, https://www.rfa.org/mandarin/yataibaodao/zhengzhi/ql2-10252017101314.html. Another contradictory interpretation claims that the Jiang "faction" was totally demolished.

"Xi chenggong jiquan mijue jiu liangge zi, Jiang Zemin bimushi tandao" [Xi's Secret of Successful Centralization of Power Can Be Summarized in Two Words: Jiang Zemin Collapses at the Close of the Congress], *Aboluowang*, October 31, 2017, https://www.aboluowang.com/2017/1031/1017750.html.

25. "Xi jiajun quanmian shangwei, zhengzhiju yijia duda" [The Xi Family Army Comprehensively Advances, Solidifying Its Dominance in the Politburo], *Dongfang ribao*, October 26, 2017.

26. "Xi Family Army."

27. Cheng Li, "The Paradoxical Outcomes of China's 19th Party Congress," *Brookings*, October 26, 2017. See also "Li Cheng: Jiedu shijiuda, Zhongguo zhengzhi rengzai changgui yunzuo" [Cheng Li, the Nineteenth Party Congress: Chinese Politics Is Still Operating According to Normal Rules], *FTChinese*, November 2, 2017, http://www.ftchinese.com/story/001074892?print=y.

28. "Zhongwei mingdan yichang: Xi Jiang jizhan shijiuda" [An Unusual Central Committee List: Xi and Jiang's Fierce Fight at the Nineteenth Party Congress], *Epochtimes*, October 25, 2017, http://www.epochtimes.com/gb/17/10/25/n9767231.htm.

29. Joseph Fewsmith, "The 19th Party Congress: Ringing in Xi Jinping's New Age," *China Leadership Monitor*, No. 55, Winter 2018, p. 4.

30. Alice L. Miller, "The 19th Central Committee Politburo," *China Leadership Monitor*, No. 55, Winter 2018.

31. "Out with the Technocrats, in with China's New Breed of Politicians," *SCMP*, October 26, 2017.

32. "There Was a Lawyer, an Engineer and a Politician," *The Economist*, November 25, 2009, http://www.economist.com/node/13496638; Cheng Li, *Chinese Politics in*

the Xi Jinping Era: Reassessing Collective Leadership (Washington, DC: Brookings Institution Press, 2016), chap. 5. For a discussion of the education background of the Eighteenth CC and Politburo and the role of lawyers, see Cheng Li, "The Rise of the Legal Profession in the Chinese Leadership," *China Leadership Monitor*, No. 42, Fall 2013.

33. "Seven Rising Stars Tipped to Lead Sixth Generation of China's Leaders," *SCMP*, October 1, 2012.

34. "Premier's Li's Second Term: from 'Likonomics' to Following Orders," *SCMP*, October 25, 2017

35. Cited in Xiang Jiangyu, *Li Keqiang bandi* [Li Keqiang's Background Connections] (Carle Place, NY: Mirror Books, 2011), pp. 93–94.

36. "Li Zhanshu: Xin zhongban zhuren di duozhong lilian" [Li Zhanshu: The Multiple Trials and Tribulations of the New Director of the Central Staff Office], *Lingdao wencui*, No. 5, 2015, pp. 52–56; "Zhongbian zhuren Li Zhanshu [Li Zhanshu, Director of the Central Staff Office], *Shidai renwu*, No. 5, 2015, p. 49; Li Zhanshu, "Zhongshi jianxing wuge jiancha, zuo dangxing jianqiang de zhongbanren" [Implement Loyally the "Five Insistences," and Be a Member of the Central Office with Strong Belief in the Party], *Mishu gongzuo*, No. 9, 2014, pp. 4–17.

37. For example, "Li Zhanshu: Jianjue weihu dangzhongyang quanwei" [Li Zhanshu: Firmly Protect the Authority of Party Central], *Hongqi wengao*, No. 22, 2016; "Zijue weihuhao fuwuhao yi Xi Jinping tongzhi wei hexin di dangzhongyang" [Consciously Protect and Serve Well the Party Central as Represented by Comrade Xi Jinping], *Mishu gongzuo*, No. 1, 2017.

38. "Qishan yi fali, manghuai Zhao Leji: Zhongzuzhibu ruhe xuanbuque guanyuan" [When Qishan Exerts, Zhao Leji Gets Inundated: How the Central Organization Department Fills Vacant Official Positions," *Huanqiu renwu*, No. 25, 2014, pp. 23–25.

39. "Zhao Leji: The Younger Gun Playing Second Fiddle to Xi Jinping," *SCMP*, October 25, 2017; "Zhao Leji zhuzhang Zhongjiwei" [Zhao Leji Takes Charge of the CCDI], *Wenweipo*, October 26, 2017.

40. "Wang Yang—the 'Joker' and Reformer in Xi Jinping's New Pack," *SCMP*, October 26, 2017.

41. "Wang Huning: Hexin zhinang, xueyang shenhou" [Wang Huning, Core Brain Trust, a Profound Scholar and Man of Integrity], *Wenweipo*, October 26, 2017. "Can China's Ideology Tsar, Wang Huning, Be the Steady Hand in Sino-US Relations?," *SCMP*, November 6, 2017; "Wang Huning: The Low-Profile, Liberal Dream Weaver Who's about to Become China's Ideology Tsar," *SCMP*, October 25, 2017. See also Yi Wang, "Wang Huning: China's Antidote to Strongmen Politics," *The Diplomat*, November 22, 2017, https://thediplomat.com/2017/11/wang-huning-chinas-antidote-to-strongman-politics/; Haig Patapan and Yi Wang, "The Hidden Ruler: Wang Huning and the Making of Contemporary China," *Journal of Contemporary China*, Vol. 27, No. 109, August 2017, pp. 47–60.

42. "Wang Huning tichu de renwu 36 ming gaoguan 10 tian nei wancheng" [Thirty-Six High Officials Have Completed in Ten Days the Tasks Put Forward by Wang Huning],

Sina, November13, 2017, http://news.sina.com.cn/c/nd/2017-11-13/doc-ifynstfh 6707455.shtml.

43. See, for example, "Shanghai shijie shiwei shisici quanhui zhaokai: Han Zheng: Zuohao Shanghai de gongzuo guanjian zaidang" [At the Fourteenth Meeting of the Tenth Sessions of the Shanghai MPC, Han Zheng Declared That the Key to Doing Things Right Is the Party], *Pengpai winwen*, December 20, 2016, http://www.thepaper. cn/newsDetail_forward_1583859; "Han Zheng: Yuanyuan benben, yuanzhi yuanwei xue shijiuda jingshen, danghao xinshidai paitoubing xianxingzhe" [Han Zheng: Conscientiously and Resolutely Study the Spirit of the Nineteenth Party Congress and Become an Exceptional Vanguard and Forerunner of the New Era], *Shangguan xinwen*, October 28, 2017, http://www.cnr.cn/shanghai/tt/20171028/t201 71028_524003582.shtml.

44. "Liu Qibao tuichu zhengzhiju tuxian Zhonggong wenxuan duanban" [Liu Qibao's Removal from the Politburo Reflects the Shortcomings of the CCP's Propaganda], *Dwnews.com*, October 25, 2917, http://blog.dwnews.com/post-979525.html; "Liu Qibao zhongyao zhiwu bei tidai, quxiang zaiyin guanzhu" [The Future of Liu Qibao Arouses Interest since His Removal from His Important Position], *Duoweinews.com*, January 19, 2018, http://news.dwnews.com/china/news/2018-01-19/60036323.html; "Not Too Old, but None Too Popular: Three Senior Politicians Lose Their Seats at China's Top Table," *SCMP*, October 26, 2017.

45. "Not Too Old"; "Chujuzhe weihe yao ru zhongwei, Zhang Chunxian keneng de quxiang" [Why Someone Who Has Been Removed from the Politburo Retains His Membership in the Central Committee: The Possible Future of Zhang Chunxian], *Duoweinews.com*, November 6, 2017, http://news.dwnews.com/china/news/2017- 11-06/60021892.html.

46. "Zhang Chunxian gexinghua zhi Jiang zhe 6 nian" [The Six Years of Zhang Chunxian's Individual Governance Style in Xinjiang], *Sohu*, April 13, 2016, http://news.sohu. com/20160413/n444107347.shtml.

47. "Li Yuanchao xieqi Jiangsu xianshen: jielian luomian yin guanzhu" [Li Yuanchao Appears with His Wife at Jiangsu: His Repeated Appearances Have Attracted Attention], *Visions Times*, October 7, 2018, https://www.secretchina.com/news/gb/ 2018/10/07/873000.html.

48. "Why a Xi Jinping Protégé Came under Fire in Beijing over Mass Eviction of Migrant Workers," *SCMP*, December 22, 2017; "Cai Qi zhuzheng Beijing hanjian di ruju sanjitiao" [Cai Qi Is Put in Charge of Beijing: A Rare Three-Step Jump into the Politburo], *Duowei news*, May 27, 2017, http://news.dwnews.com/china/news/2017- 05-27/59817259.html.

49. "Xi Jinping's Allies Named as Head of Propaganda, Chief of Staff as President Tightens Grip on Power," *SCMP*, October 30, 2017.

50. "What Team Will Xi Jinping Choose to Steer the World's Second-Largest Economy into the Future?," *SCMP* December 11, 2017; "Where Will Liu He, the Mastermind of China's Economic Policies, Go Next?," *SCMP*, October 23, 2017. "How Liu He Went from Government Researcher to Xi's Right-Hand Man," *SCMP*, March 2, 2017.

51. "Guangdong Leader Strengthened in China Leadership Stakes as Rival Party Boss Ousted," *Reuters*, July 20, 2017, https://www.reuters.com/article/us-china-politics-guangdong/guangdong-leader-strengthened-in-china-leadership-stakes-as-rival-party-boss-ousted-idUSKBN1A50QG.

52. "Xi Jinping zongshuji dui Guangdong gongzuo zuochu chongyao pishi" [General Secretary Xi Jinping Issues Important Directives on the Work in Guangdong], *Nanfang ribao*, April 12, 2017, http://news.southcn.com/china/content/2017-04/12/content_168707850.htm; "Jieban Hu Chunhua jinshen dai shiji" [Hu Chunhua Is Carefully Waiting for His Chance to Take Over], *Mingbao*, October 5, 2017; "19th Party Congress: Contrasting Styles of China's Sixth Generation Leaders Chen Min'er and Hu Chunhua," *Strait Times*, October 19, 2017, http://www.straitstimes.com/asia/east-asia/19th-party-congress-contrasting-styles-of-chinas-sixth-generation-leaders-chen-miner; "The Coming-of-Age of China's Sixth Generation: A New Majority in the Party Leadership," *Brookings*, August 24, 2017, https://www.brookings.edu/opinions/the-coming-of-age-of-chinas-sixth-generation-a-new-majority-in-the-party-leadership/; "Guangdong Leader Strengthened in China Leadership Stakes as Rival Party Boss Ousted," *Reuters*, July 20, 2017, https://www.reuters.com/article/us-china-politics-guangdong/guangdong-leader-strengthened-in-china-leadership-stakes-as-rival-party-boss-ousted-idUSKBN1A50QG.

53. *Laoji zhutuo, zaichuang xinju* [Hold Fast to the Command, Create a New Situation] (Guangzhou: Nanfang renmin chubanshe, 2017).

54. Chinese 'Leader-in-Waiting' Joins Chorus of Condemnation of Former High-Flyer Sun Zhengcai," *SCMP*, October 1, 2017; "Hu Chunhua zhuchi Guangdong shengwei huiyi: jianjue yonghu shencha Sun Zhengcai" [Hu Chunhua Presides over a Meeting of the Guangdong PPC; Firmly Support the Investigation of Sun Zhengcai], *Zhongguo qingnianwang*, July 29, 2017, http://news.youth.cn/sz/201707/t20170729_10400510.htm.

55. "19th Party Congress: Contrasting Styles."

56. "Xi Jinping shifou hui ba Hu Chunhua bian wei guojia fuzhuxi" [Will Xi Jinping Demote Hu Chunhua as the Vice Chair of the PRC?], *Radio Free Asia*, December 15, 2017, http://www.rfa.org/mandarin/zhuanlan/yehuazhongnanhai/gx-12152017142632.html?searchterm:utf8:ustring=%E8%83%A1%E6%98%A5%E5%8D%8E.

57. "Xi Jinping Has Quietly Chosen His Own Successor," *Foreign Policy*, October 20, 2017, http://foreignpolicy.com/2017/10/20/xi-jinping-has-quietly-chosen-his-own-successor/.

58. "Meet the Team China Expects to Unknot Ties with the United States," *SCMP*, March 19, 2018.

59. "The Low-Profile Cadre Who Rocketed Up the Ranks to Take the Helm of China's New Anti-graft Superagency," *SCMP*, March 18, 2018.

60. "Xin jiancha buchang Yang Xiaodu: 3 nian da 13 hu fuqin zengshi Shanghai dixiadang" [Yang Xiaodu, the New Minister of the Ministry of Supervision, Hunted Thirteen Tigers in Three Years. His Father Had Worked Underground with the Party in Shanghai], *Guancha*, December 27, 2016, http://www.guancha.cn/FaZhi/2016_12_27_386274.shtml; "Low-Profile Cadre."

61. "Yang Xiaodu ren zhongyang shenhua guojia jiancha tizhi gaige shidian gongzuo lingdao xiaozu fuzuchang" [Yang Xiaodu Is Now Director of the Office for the Pilot Work for the Deepening of Reform for the State's Supervisory Work LSG], *Pengpai*, January 10, 2018, http://www.thepaper.cn/newsDetail_forward_194484.

62. Karita Kan, "Whither Weiwen?," *China Perspectives*, No. 1, March 2013.

63. See, for example, "Guo Shengkun: Jianjue weihu dangzhongyang quanwei he jizhong tongyi lingdao" [Guo Shengkun: Resolutely Uphold the Authority and the Centralized Leadership of the Party], *Renminwang*, November 24, 2017, http://cpc.people.com.cn/n1/2017/1124/c64094-29665639.html.

64. "Zhongyang shujichu renshi pandian: Minzhe Beijing shenhou" [An Analysis of the Personnel of the Central Secretariat Shows That Most Have Backgrounds in Fujian and Zhejiang], *Duoweinews*, October 25, 2017, http://news.dwnews.com/china/news/2017-10-25/60019604.html.

65. "Zhongguo gongchandang zhongyang shujichu" [The CCP's Central Secretariat], *Baidu baike*.

66. "43 ming shibajie zhongyang weiyuan houbu weiyuan bei shencha" [Forty-Three Alternate Members of the Eighteenth Central Committee Have Been Investigated], *gdifeng*, October 30, 2017, http://gd.ifeng.com/a/20171030/6103685_0.shtml. Earlier versions give the number as thirty-four. "Shibada yilai beicha dalaohu chaoguo 280 ren, luoma zhongyang weiyuan, zhongyang houbu weiyuan ge 17 ren" [More than 280 "Big Tigers" Have Been Investigated since the Eighteenth Party Congress: Among Them Seventeen Members and Seventeen Alternate Members of the CC Have Been Dismissed], *Sohu*, September 18, 2017, http://www.sohu.com/a/192711384_119707; Fewsmith, "The 19th Party Congress," p. 11.

67. "Xinjiu gengti xinjin zhongwei chao liucheng, duowei guoqi gaoguan jin houbu zhongwei" [As the New Replaces the Old: More Than 60 Percent of the CC Are Newcomers: Many Senior Managers of the SOEs Have Been Promoted Alternate Members of the CC], *Takungpao*, October 25, 2017, http://news.takungpao.com/mainland/focus/2017-10/3507055.html; "Zhongwei liucheng xinjin 60 hou da liangchang" [60 Percent of the CC Are Newcomers: Members of the Later-Sixties Generation Constitute 20 Percent], *Wenweipo*, October 25, 2017.

68. "204 ming Zhonggong shijiujie zhongyang weiyuan duiying zhiwei quanpouxi" [A Complete Analysis of the 204 Members of the Nineteenth CC and Their Corresponding Official Positions], *Hong Kong 01*, October 25, 2017, https://www.hk01.com/%E5%85%A9%E5%B2%B8/128274/-%E5%8D%81%E4%B9%9D%E5%A4%A7-204%E5%90%8D%E4%B8%AD%E5%85%B1%E5%8D%81%E4%B9%9D%E5%B1%86%E4%B8%AD%E5%A4%AE%E5%A7%94%E5%93%A1%E5%B0%8D%E6%87%89%E8%81%B7%E4%BD%8D%E5%85%A8%E5%89%96%E6%9E%90.

69. "Zhonggong shijiujie zhongyang weiyuan duiying zhiwei fenlei quanjiexi" [A Complete Examination of the Members of the Nineteenth CC and Their Corresponding Official Positions], *Duowei news*, October 24, 2017, News.dwnews.com/china/news/2017-10-24/600/940.html.

70. "Xi Jinping hanjian tongpi Gongqingtuan: Sizhi mabi, gaowei jietan" [Xi Jinping's Rare and Harsh Indictment of the CYL Claims That the Organization Is under Total

Paralysis and So Is Its Leadership], *Duowei news*, September 18, 2017, http://news. dwnews.com/china/news/2017-09-18/60013097.html.

71. "Xi Jinping: Xin shidai de lingluren" [Xi Jinping: The Leader of a New Era], *Xinhua*, November 17, 2017, http://www.gov.cn/xinwen/2017-11/17/content_5240304.htm.

72. "Hu Jintao's Weak Grip on China's Army Inspired Xi Jinping's Military Shake-Up: Sources," *SCMP*, March 11, 2015.

73. "China Confirms Anti-graft Official's Position on Military's Ruling Body as War on Corruption Heats Up," *SCMP*, March 18, 2018; "What a New PLA Promotion Says about Xi Jinping's Military Control," *The Diplomat*, November 3, 2017.

74. Li, *Chinese Politics in the Xi Jinping Era*, p. 317.

75. "Xinyijie zhongyang junwei weiyuanhui zhong 3 wei shi cong zhanhuo zouchu de jiangjun" [Three Members of the New CMC Are Generals Who Have Emerged from the Fires of War], *Sina.com*, October 27, 2017, http://news.sina.com.cn/c/nd/2017-10-27/doc-ifynfvar4607024.shtml.

76. Don Tse, "Why China's Central Military Commission Got Downsized," *The Diplomat*, November 15, 2017, https://thediplomat.com/2017/11/why-chinas-central-military-commission-got-downsized//.

77. Tse, "Why China's Central Military Commission Got Downsized"; "Xi Jinping 'Plots Shake-Up' of Men Running China's Massive Military Machine," *SCMP*, October 24, 2017.

78. "Xi Jinping Signals Intent to Remain in Power by Revealing Politburo with No Successor," *The Guardian*, October 25, 2017, https://www.theguardian.com/world/2017/oct/25/xi-jinping-signals-intent-power-successor-politburo-china; "China Congress: No Heir Apparent as Xi Reveals Top Leadership," *BBC*, October 25, 2017, https://www.bbc.co.uk/news/world-asia-china-41743804.

79. "Gangmei: Neiding jiebanren Hu Qili xu fei 'ge dai renming' he 'qi shang ba xia'" [Hong Kong Media: The Scheduled Successor, Hu Qili, Appeals for the Abolition of the Rules for the 'Transgenerational Successors' and the Retirement Age of Sixty-Eight], *www.aboluowang.com*, June 8, 2017, https://www.aboluowang.com/2017/0608/942253.html.

80. "Ming Wanli nianjian zhengzhi yaoyan luanxiang" [The Political Rumors and Chaos during the Wanli Period of the Ming Dynasty], *Xuexi shibao*, September 5, 2016, http://www.qstheory.cn/politics/2016-09/05/c_1119512517.htm.

81. "Shijiuda feichu jiebanren, Xi Jinping zaichu yizhao jiakong changwei" [The Nineteenth Party Congress Abolishes the Position of Successor: Xi Jinping Makes Another Move to Undermine the PBSC], *NTD*, October 30, 2017, http://ca.ntdtv.com/xtr/gb/2017/10/30/a1348783.html.

82. Willy Lam, "China's Seventh-Generation Leadership Emerges onto the Stage," *China Brief*, Vol. 19, Issue 7, April 9, 2019; "Rising Stars Tipped to Lead Seventh Generation of China's Leadership," *Huffington Post*, October 9, 2016, https://www.huffingtonpost.com/asiatoday/rising-stars-tipped-to-le_b_12413752.html.

83. "Linxuan 90- hou ganbu chengwei zhongdian renwu, 90 hou kaishi danren fuchu zhiwei" [The Selection of the Late-Nineties Generation Leaders Has Become a Priority Mission: These Late-Nineties Generation Leaders Are Beginning to Assume Deputy- and Division-Level Positions], *Sina*, January 8, 2017, http://news.sina.com.cn/c/nd/2018-01-08/doc-ifyqkarr7933674.shtml.

Chapter 13

1. "China Focus: 19th CPC Central Committee 3rd Plenum Issues Communique," *Xinhua*, March 1, 2018, http://www.xinhuanet.com/english/2018-03/01/c_137006 746.htm.

2. "Wang Chen zuo guanyu Zhonghua renmin gongheguo xianfa xiuzheng caoan de shuoming (zhaiyao)" [Extracts: Wang Chen on the Draft Revision of the Constitution of the PRC], *Xinhuanet*, March 6, 2018, http://www.xinhuanet.com/2018-03/06/c_ 1122496003.htm.

3. "The Way Xi Jinping Has Accumulated Power Makes It Hard to Use," *The Economist*, March 31, 2018; "The Price of Power: Xi Jinping Is Using His Growing Authority to Amass Even More," *The Economist*, March 7, 2018. "Some Economists See a Plus Side in Eliminating Term Limits for China's Xi Jinping," *National Public Radio*, March 17, 2018, https://www.npr.org/sections/parallels/2018/03/17/593841022/some-eco nomists-see-a-plus-side-in-eliminating-term-limits-for-chinas-xi-jinping.

4. "Wan Qishan chuang guojia zhuxi xinmoshi" [Wang Qishan Has Created a New Model for the Position of Vice Chair of the PRC], *Mingbao*, December 18, 2017, http://www.mingpaocanada.com/Tor/htm/News/20171218/tcab1_r.htm.

5. "Will Wang Qishan's New Job Become a Problem for the Communist Party?," *SCMP*, March 26, 2018.

6. "Xi Ally Wang Qishan behind Beijing's Selection of Young Leaders," *Nikkei*, October 27, 2019, https://asia.nikkei.com/Politics/Xi-ally-Wang-Qishan-behind-Beijing-s-selection-of-young-leaders; "Is 'Firefighter' Wang Qishan Working behind the Scenes on Trade Talks," *SCMP*, July 2, 2019.

7. The CPPCC's website at http://www.cppcc.gov.cn provides details regarding the organization's structure, news, and activities.

8. This refers to the eight political parties that supported the CCP during the Civil War (1945–1949) and still exist today.

9. See, for example, "Renda zhengxie shi tanguan fuhao laowai di julebu" [People's Congresses and People's Political Consultative Conferences Are Private Clubs for Corrupt Officials, Tycoons, and Foreigners], *China News*, November 13, 2017, http://news.creaders.net/china/2017/11/13/1889203.html.

10. "Xinren fuzongli renling xinren" [The New Vice Premier Takes Up His Position], *Wenweipo*, April 8, 2018, http://news.wenweipo.com/2018/04/08/IN1804080 027.htm.

11. "Fuzongli fengong youbian, Liu He kuoquan Sun Chunlan Hu Chunhua suoshui" [The Changing Division of Labor among the Vice Premiers: The Power of Liu He Expands, Whereas That of Sun Chunlan and Hu Chunhua Shrinks], *SecretChina. com*, April 9, 2018, https://www.secretchina.com/news/gb/2018/04/09/855226p. html; Barry Naughton, "Xi's System, Xi's Men after the March 2018 National People's Congress," *China Leadership Monitor*, No. 56, Spring 2018.

12. Guoguang Wu, "The King's Men and Others: Emerging Political Elites under Xi Jinping," *China Leadership Monitor*, No. 60, June 1, 2019; Willy Lam, "The Xi Jinping Faction Dominates Regional Appointments after the 19th Party Congress," *China*

Brief, February 13, 2018; Cheng Li, "Xi Jinping's Inner Circle: Part 1: The Shaanxi Gang," *China Leadership Monitor*, No 43, Spring 2014; Cheng Li, "Xi Jinping's Inner Circle: Part 2: Friends from Xi's Formative Years," *China Leadership Monitor*, No 44, Summer 2014.

13. Fewsmith, "What Is a Faction?"

14. "Vice Premier Liu He Set to Lead China's New Economic Team as Government Line-Up Finalized," *SCMP*, March 19, 2018.

15. "Liu He: Liangda weiji lilun: Jingji weiji shi ruhe fasheng de" [Liu He's Theory on the Two Major Crises: How Do Economic Crises Occur], *JRJ.com*, February 24, 2018, http://opinion.jrj.com.cn/2018/02/24101024145863.shtml.

16. "Liu He: China's New One-Man Debt Bomb Disposal Unit," *SCMP*, March 19, 2018.

17. "Shenhua dang he guojia jigou gaige shi yichang shenke di biange" [Deepening of the Restructuring of Party and State Organizations Is a Profound Reform], *RMRB*, March 13, 2018, http://paper.people.com.cn/rmrb/html/2018-03/13/nw.D110000renmrb_20180313_1-06.htm.

18. "China Vice Premier Liu He Rejects Trump's Suggestion of Immediate Phase Two Talks," *SCMP*, January 16, 2020.

19. "Meet the Team China Expects to Unknot Ties with the United States," *SCMP*, March 20, 2018; "China Promotes Foreign Minister Wang Yi to State Councilor, General Wei Fenghe Named Defense Minister," *SCMP*, March 19, 2018.

20. Guoguang Wu and Helen Lansdowne, eds., *Zhao Ziyang and China's Political Future* (New York: Routledge, 2008), pp. 22–24, 36–37, 169–171.

21. Wu and Lansdowne, *Zhao Ziyang*.

22. Zhao Ziyang's Speech Made at the Seven Plenum of the 12th National Party Congress, October 1987, in "Dangzheng fenkai" [The Separations of the Party and Government], *Baidu baike*; "Shisanda hou de dangzheng fenkai gaige" [The Separation of the Party and the State after the Thirteenth Party Congress], September 30, 2014, *New York Times Chinese*, https://cn.nytimes.com/china/20140930/cc30wuwei31/.

23. Tony Saich, *Governance and Politics of China* (Houndmills: Palgrave, 2001), pp. 100–106.

24. See, for example, "2016 nian dangjian gongzuo tuchu wenti, maodun, yuanyin" [The Outstanding Issues and Causes of Contradictions in Party-Building in 2016], *Meiwen daokan*, March 21, 2017, http://www.eorder.net.cn/fanwen197648/.

25. "Yes, Minister, No More: Today's Bureaucrats Have a Different Attitude," *Globe and Mail*, April 13, 2018.

26. Joel D. Aberbach, Daniel B. Mezger, and Bert A. Rockman, "Bureaucrats and Politicians: A Report on the Administrative Elites Project," *Australian Journal of Public Administration*, Vol. 50, No. 2, June 1991.

27. "Wang Qishan: Zhiyou dangzheng fengong, meiyou dangzheng fenkai" [Wang Qishan: There Is Only a Division of Labor between the Party and Government, No Formal Separation], *Xinhua*, March 6, 2017, http://www.yicai.com/news/5240260.html.

28. For the two most important documents on the reforms see "Xi Jinping guanyu shenhua dang he guojia jigou gaige juedinggao he fangangao de shuoming"

[Xi Jinping's Explanation on the Draft Decisions to Deepen the Organizational Restructuring of the Party and State], *Xinhua*, April 11, 2018, http://news.12371.cn/2018/04/11/ARTI1523454152698258.shtml; "Zhonggong zhongyang yinfa 'shenhua dang he guojia jigou gaige' fangan" [The Plan for the "Deepening of the Reform of the Party and State Structure" Published by CCP Party Central], *Xinhua*, March 21, 2018, http://www.xinhuanet.com/politics/2018-03/21/c_1122570517.htm.

29. "Xiaozu bianshen weiyuanhui, zhongyang xinshe jigou tifa 5 ge yueqian butong" [LSGs Have Been Transformed into Commissions: The Newly Established Agencies Are Different from What Was Said Five Months Ago], *Guancha*, March 22, 2018, http://www.guancha.cn/politics/2018_03_22_451095.shtml; "Zhongyang quanmian yifa zhiguo weiyuanhui: Zhuanjia, Jiang chengwei fazhi Zhongguo jianshe xinzhuashou" [An Expert Claims That the Establishment of a Central Commission on Comprehensively Governing the Country According to Law Will Be an Assurance for the Building of Rule of Law in China], *Sina*, March 21, 2018, http://news.sina.com.cn/c/2018-03-21/doc-ifysnkyv7707498.shtml.

30. "Xi Jinping zhuchi zhaokai zhongyang quanmian shenhua gaige weiyuanhui dierci huiyi" [Xi Jinping Presides Over the Second Session of the Central Comprehensively Deepening Reform Commission], *Zhongguo gongchandang xinwenwang*, May 12, 2018, http://cpc.people.com.cn/n1/2018/0512/c64094-29984190.html.

31. "Zhongyang quanmian shenhua gaige weiyuanhui huiyi" [Meetings of the Comprehensively Deepening Reform Commission], *Gongchandangyuanwang*, http://www.12371.cn/special/zyqmshggldxzhy19/.

32. "Zhongyang zhengzhiju weiyuan Yang Jiechi de xinzhiwu" [The New Responsibility of New Politburo Member Yang Jiechi], *Jingbaowang*, March 29, 2018, http://www.bjd.com.cn/sd/mrq/201803/29/t20180329_11083364.html.

33. "Guojia zhuxi zuozhen di lingdao banzi xinjiaru yiwei changwei" [A New Member of the PBSC Has Just Joined the Top Leadership Led by the State Chairman], *Shangguan xinwen*, May 26, 2018, https://web.shobserver.com/wx/detail.do?id=90812.

34. "Zhongyang zhishu jiguan gongwei zhuyao zhize" [The Main Responsibilities of the Work Committee for Organizations Directly under the CC], *Zhongzhi dangjianwang*, July 2, 2015, http://www.zzdjw.org.cn/n/2015/0702/c397012-27243378.html.

35. Joel Aberbach and Bert Rockman, "The Past and Future of Political-Administrative Relations: Research from *Bureaucrats and Politicians* to *In the Web of Politics*—and Beyond," *International Journal of Public Administration*, Vol. 29, No. 12, 2006.

36. Zheng Yongnian, *The Chinese Communist Party as Organizational Emperor: Culture, Reproduction and Transformation* (New York: Routledge, 2010), p. 165.

37. "Zongzhiwei de mingzi you gaihui quliao" [The Title of the Committee on Comprehensive Governance Is Changed Again], *Nanfang zhoumu*, October 24, 2014, http://www.infzm.com/content/104983; *Baidu baike*.

38. For a discussion of the CPLC's abuse of power under Zhou Yongkang see "Zhou Yongkang de fansi yu jianyan" [Reflections and Suggestions on the Zhou Yongkang Case], *Yanhuang chunqiu*, November 25, 2014, http://news.sohu.com/20141125/n406372113.shtml.

39. "Chan Yixin gaobie Wuhan furen zhongyang zhengfawei" [Chen Yixin Bids Farewell to Wuhan to Work for the CPLAC], *Jingbaowang*, March 26, 2018, http://www.bjd.com.cn/sd/mrq/201803/26/t20180326_11083170.html.

40. "The News Said That the Political and Legal Committee Will No Longer Be Involved in Individual Cases Except Those Relating to Foreign Countries"; "Shenpan jiandu: Yuanjiacuoan di pingfan zhidao" [The Supervision of Court Cases: The Ways to Redress Trumped Up and Wrongfully Adjudicated Cases], *Nanfengchuang*, January 23, 2018, http://www.nfcmag.com/article/7823.html.

41. "Huan Yu: Xi Jinping xiaofan buting, zhengfawei biaomian kuozhang shibei xiaoquan" [Huan Yu: Xi Jinping's Ceaseless Trimming of the Power of His Subordinate Agencies; Superficially the Power of the CPLAC Has Been Augmented but in Fact It Has Been Diminished], *ntdtv*, March 24, 2018, http://www.ntdtv.com/xtr/gb/2018/03/24/a1368699_p.html; "Kuoquan huanshi xiaoquan: Zhonggong zhengfawei buru hou Zhou Yongkang Shidai" [Has Its Power Been Expanded or Trimmed? CPLAC Advances into the Post–Zhou Yongkang Era], *Dwnews.com*, March 22, 2018, http://news.dwnews.com/china/news/2018-03-21/60047433_all.html.

42. "Liu Ning jianren Qinghai shengwei zhengfawei shuji: 31 wei zhengfa wei shuji pandian" [Liu Ning Takes Over the Concurrent Post as Secretary of the PLAC of the Qinghai PPC: An Inventory of the Thirty-One Secretaries of the PLAC], *Sina*, August 23, 2017, http://news.sina.com.cn/c/2017-08-23/doc-ifykcqaw1035818.shtml.

43. "A Look Inside China's Propaganda Bureaucracy," *Global Voice Advox*, November 12, 2017, https://advox.globalvoices.org/2017/11/12/a-look-inside-chinas-propaganda-bureaucracy/; David Shambaugh, "China's Propaganda System: Institutions, Processes and Efficacy," *China Journal*, No. 57, January 2007; Anne-Marie Brady, *Marketing Dictatorship: Propaganda and Thought Work in Contemporary China* (Lanham, MD: Rowman & Littlefield, 2008).

44. Zheng, *CCP as Organizational Emperor*, pp. 152–162.

45. "Plan for the Deepening of the Reform," sections 35 and 36.

46. "Xi Jinping zai quanguo dangxiao gongzuo huiyi shang de jianghua" [Xi Jinping's Speech at the Central Party School], *CNR*, May 1, 2016, http://news.cnr.cn/native/gd/20160501/t20160501_522037094_3.shtml.

47. "China Tightens Grip on Media with Regulator Reshuffle," *Reuters*, March 21, 2018, https://www.reuters.com/article/us-china-parliament-media/china-tightens-grip-on-media-with-regulator-reshuffle-idUSKBN1GX0JG; "Look Inside China's Propaganda Bureaucracy."

48. "Magic tools" (*fabao*) has often been translated as "magic weapons," but this misses the nuances and often causes misperception. *Fabao* is originally a Buddhist term referring to magical wisdom or a talisman that could subdue evil or monsters.

49. For a discussion of the incentives for and obstacles to the establishment of a constitutional supervision committee, see Keith J. Hand, "An Assessment of Socialist Constitutional Supervision Models and Prospects for a Constitutional Supervision Committee in China," John Garrick and Yan Chang Bennett, eds., *China's Socialist Rule of Law Reforms under Xi Jinping* (New York: Routledge, 2016), pp. 30–44.

50. The Taiwan political structure is governed by a five-power separation-of-powers principle consisting of the legislature, the executive, the judiciary, the Control Yuan (censorate), and the Examination Yuan.

51. More than a decade ago Randall Peerenboom recommended and anticipated such a censorate as a uniquely Chinese institution. See his "Globalization, Path Dependency, and the Limits of Law," in Lowell Dittmer and Guoli Liu, eds., *China's Deep Reform* (Lanham, MD: Rowman & Littlefield, 2006), p. 218.

52. The finalized legislation is in "Zhonghua renmin gongheguo jiancha fa" [The Supervisory Law of the PRC], *Zhongguo rendawang*, March 21, 2018, http://www.npc.gov.cn/npc/xinwen/2018-03/21/content_2052362.htm.

53. For more details, see "Surprise Choice for China's New Anti-graft Watchdog Signals Communist Party's Authority over the State," *SCMP*, March 18, 2018.

54. For a detailed account of the drafting process, see "Guojia jianchafa caoan shi zenyang chuludi" [How the Draft Law for State Supervision Was Forged], *Chinanews.com*, March 13, 2018, http://www.chinanews.com/gn/2018/03-13/8466179.shtml. The outcome of the pilot projects is reported in "Guojia jiancha tizhi gaige shidian qude shixiao" [The Pilot Projects for the Reform of the State Supervisory System Accomplish Substantial Results], *Renminwang*, November 6, 2017, http://politics.people.com.cn/n1/2017/1106/c1001-29627809.html.

55. "Jiancha tizhi gaige shidian chengjidan; 3 shengshi dangwei shuji pizhun liuzhi 22 renci" [Accomplishments of the Pilot Projects for the Reform of the Supervisory System; the Party Committees of the Three Provinces/Municipalities Approved Liuzhi Twenty-Two Times], *Renminwang*, November 27, 2017, http://fanfu.people.com.cn/n1/2017/1107/c64371-29630694.html; "How the Draft Law for State Supervision Was Forged."

56. "Ge Wenxiu deng 59 wei lushi lianming jiu guojia jianchafa caoan lifa xiang quanguo renda gongkai tichu sidian jianyi" [Ge Wenxiu and Fifty-Nine Lawyers Signed an Open Petition to the NPeC on the Draft State Supervisory Legislation and Make Four Proposals], *Weiquanwang*, August 13, 2017, http://wqw2010.blogspot.com/2017/08/59.html; "New Chinese Agency Could Undercut Other Anti-corruption Efforts," *Brookings*, March 6, 2018, https://www.brookings.edu/blog/order-from-chaos/2018/03/06/new-chinese-agency-could-undercut-other-anti-corruption-efforts/.

57. "Xi Jinping guanyu jigou gaige juedinggao he fangangao shuoming shouci fabu" [The Debut Publication of Xi Jinping's Explanation of the Draft Decisions on Organizational Restructuring], *Ifeng*, April 11, 2018, http://news.ifeng.com/a/20180411/57487759_0.shtml.

58. The organization chart and website of the NSuC are at http://www.ccdi.gov.cn/xxgk/zzjg/201901/t20190124_187625.html and http://www.ccdi.gov.cn/.

59. Peter Martin, "The Humbling of the NDRC: China's National Development and Reform Commission Searches for a New Role amid Restructuring," *China Brief*, Vol. 14, No. 5, March 7, 2014; "China's Economic Policy Factory: The NDRC," *Bloomberg*, June 20, 2013, https://www.bloomberg.com/news/articles/2013-06-20/chinas-economic-policy-factory-the-ndrc.

60. "Too Big and Too Powerful: Why Xi Jinping Is Reining in China's Economic Planning Agency," *SCMP*, March 14, 2018; "Zhonghua renmin gongheguo guojia fazhan he gaige weiyuanhui" [The National Development and Reform Commission in the PRC], *Baidu baike*.

61. Martin, "Humbling of the NDRC."

62. "China Will Push Ahead 'Resolutely' with Financial Sector Fight, Says Li Keqiang," *SCMP*, March 20, 2018.

63. "Former Head of China's Anbang Jailed for 18 Years," *BBC*, May 10, 2018, http://www.bbc.com/news/business-44063780.

64. "China's Central Bank Gains More Power in Xi's Regulatory Shuffle," *Bloomberg*, March 12, 2018, https://www.bloomberg.com/news/articles/2018-03-13/china-announces-plan-to-merge-banking-insurance-regulators.

65. "China to Merge Bank, Insurance Regulators," *Strait Times*, March 14, 2018, http://www.straitstimes.com/asia/east-asia/china-to-merge-bank-insurance-regulators.

66. "China Establishes Financial Stability and Development Committee," *English.gov.cn*, November 9, 2017, http://english.gov.cn/news/top_news/2017/11/08/content_2814 75936107760.htm.

67. "'One Leak and We'll All Drown': Top Chinese Lawmaker Raises Alarm over River of Local Government Debt," *SCMP*, March 14, 2018; "Chinese Local Government's US$2.4 Billion of Concealed Debt Is Uncovered by Audit Office," *SCMP*, April 21, 2018.

68. "China' Debt Bomb," *Bloomberg*, September 17, 2018.

69. "Jinrong jianguan maixiang xin geju, duoxiang xingui liao jiasu luodi" [The Supervision of Finance Is Advancing to a New State: Many New Regulations Are Being Drafted], *Xinhuanet*, April 9, 2018, http://www.xinhuanet.com/money/2018-04/09/c_129846248.htm.

70. "New Ecological Environment Ministry Is a Milestone," *China Daily*, March 17, 2018; "Tough Tasks for China's New Environment Ministry," *The Diplomat*, March 17, 2018, https://thediplomat.com/2018/03/tough-tasks-for-chinas-new-environment-minis try/; "China Has New Three-Year Plan to Clean Up Environment, Minister Says," *SCMP*, March 18, 2018.

71. "China Raises Pay, Pensions for Trimmed Down Military, Announces Plans for Veterans' Ministry," *SCMP*, March 13, 2018.

72. "New Authority Focuses on Emergency Response," *China Daily*, March 30, 2018.

73. Shannon Tiezzi, "China's Massive Government Overhaul: What You Need to Know," *The Diplomat*, March 14, 2018, https://thediplomat.com/2018/03/chinas-massive-government-overhaul-what-you-need-to-know/; Helena Legarda, "China Upgrades Diplomacy While the US Pulls Back," *The Diplomat*, March 20, 2018, https://thediplo mat.com/2018/03/china-upgrades-diplomacy-while-the-us-pulls-back/.

74. "What China's Recent Shakeup Means for the Economy," *The Diplomat*, March 23, 2018, https://thediplomat.com/2018/03/what-chinas-recent-shake-up-means-for-the-economy/.

75. For a discussion of the legions of Xi's enemies, see Kerry Brown, *CEO China: The Rise of Xi Jinping* (London: I.B. Tauris, 2016), chap. 3.

76. *Baidu baike*; "Wujing yizhu: Zhonggong weihe beijiu shi bingquan?" [The PAP Has a New Master: Why Did the CCP Remove the PLA's Power?], January 3, 2018, *Voice of America Chinese*, https://www.voachinese.com/a/voaweishi-20180103-io-china-armed-police/4190337.html; "Jundui gaige zuhou yibu? Wujing you junwei tongyi lingdao" [The Last Step in Military Reform? The PAP Has Been Put Under the Leadership of the CMC], *Duoweinews*, December 27, 2017, http://www.dw.com/zh/%E5%86%9B%E9%98%9F%E6%94%B9%E9%9D%A9%E6%9C%80%E5%90%8E%E4%B8%80%E6%AD%A5%E6%AD%A6%E8%AD%A6%E7%94%B1%E5%86%9B%E5%A7%94%E7%BB%9F%E4%B8%80%E9%A2%86%E5%AF%BC/a-41945362?&zhongwen=simp.

77. See "Plan for the "Deepening of the Reform," Article 47 and section 7.

78. Naughton, "Xi's System, Xi's Men."

79. For instance, Jean-Pierre Cabestan, "Political Changes in China since the 19th CCP Congress: Xi Jinping Is Not Weaker but More Contested," *East Asia*, No. 36, 2019.

Chapter 14

1. The notion of "inherent bad faith model" was constructed by Ole Holsti to describe John Foster Dulles's closed, negative, and selective perception of the Soviet Union, which explained away nonhostile Soviet actions and contraindicators. See Douglas Stuart and Harvey Starr, "The Inherent Bad Faith Model Reconsidered: Dulles, Kennedy, and Kissinger," *Political Psychology*, Vol. 3, Nos. 3–4, Autumn 1981–Winter 1982, pp. 1–33.

2. For example, Zhou Xinmin, *Xi Jinping's Governance and the Future of China* (New York: Skyhorse Publishing, 2017); James C. Hsiung, *The Xi Jinping Era: His Comprehensive Strategy toward the China Dream* (New York: CN Times Book, 2015); Mingfu Liu and Zhongyuan Wang, *The Thoughts of Xi Jinping* (Salt Lake City, UT: American Academic Press, 2017).

3. Pre-Xi Jinping era debates include Andrew J. Nathan, "Authoritarian Resilience," *Journal of Democracy*, Vol. 14, No. 1, January 2003; Cheng Li, "The End of the CCP's Resilient Authoritarianism? A Tripartite Assessment of Shifting Power in China," *China Quarterly*, Vol. 21, September 2012; Minxin Pei, "Is CCP Rule Fragile or Resilient?," *Journal of Democracy*, Vol. 23, No. 1, January 2012.

4. Michelle Murray Yang, *American Political Discourse on China* (New York: Routledge, 2017), introduction and conclusion.

5. A few representative examples are Richard McGregor, "Party Man: Xi Jinping's Quest to Dominate China," *Foreign Affairs*, September–October 2019; David Shambaugh, "The Coming Chinese Crack-Up," *Wall Street Journal*, March 6, 2015. See also the debate "Should the West Worry about the Threat to Liberal Values Posed by China's Rise?," *The Economist*, June 8–18, 2018 (contributions by Minxin Pei, Kishore Mahbubani, Isabel Hilton, Kerry Brown, Zhu Ning, Daniel Bell, and Fran Martin), https://debates.economist.com/; Carl Minzner, *End of an Era* (New York: Oxford University Press, 2018); Stein Ringen, *The Perfect Dictatorship* (Hong Kong: Hong Kong University

Press, 2016); Gordon Chang, "Xi Jinping: China's All-Powerful—and Possibly Last—Communist Ruler," *National Interest*, March 2018, http://nationalinterest.org/feature/xi-jinping-chinas-all-powerful%E2%80%94-possibly-last%E2%80%94communist-24711; Gordon Chang, *The Coming Collapse of China* (New York: Random House, 2001); Minxin Pei, "China's Coming Upheaval: Competition, the Coronavirus, and the Weakness of Xi Jinping," *Foreign Affairs*, May–June 2020. In Chinese, see Yu Jie, *Zhongguo jiaofu Xi Jinping* [Xi Jinping: China's Godfather] (Xianggang: Kaifang chubanshe, 2014).

6. Aaron L. Friedberg, "An Answer to Aggression: How to Push Back against Beijing," *Foreign Affairs*, September–October 2020.

7. Eric Li, "Western Media Is Still Wrong: China Will Continue to Rise," *Washington Post*, October 24, 2017.

8. "China Has Replaced U.S. as Locomotive of Global Economy: Kemp," *Reuters*, November 5, 2019, https://www.reuters.com/article/us-economy-global-kemp-column-idUSKBN1XF211.

9. Application requirements for party membership are formidable, but an often neglected fact is that China's civil service of seven million (more than ten million if other officials are included) is recruited by competitive examinations. Each year more than a million candidates apply for ten to twenty thousand vacancies, and party membership is required for a small proportion of these posts.

10. Fareed Zakaria, "The New China Scare," *Foreign Affairs*, January–February 2020, p. 56.

11. A few representative examples are Li, "Western Media Is Still Wrong"; Daniel Bell, "China's Political Meritocracy versus Western Democracy," *The Economist*, June 12, 2018; Zhu Ning, "Is China's Growth Model a Threat to Free-Market Economics," *The Economist*, June 12, 2018; Thomas Heberer, "The Chinese 'Developmental State 3.0' and the Resilience of Authoritarianism," *Journal of Chinese Governance*, Vol. 1, No. 4, November 2016; Wenfang Tang, "The 'Surprise' of Authoritarian Resilience in China," *American Affairs*, Vol. 2, No. 1, Spring 2018.

12. Pei, "China's Coming Upheaval"; Kurt M. Campbell and Rush Doshi, "The Coronavirus Could Reshape Global Order: China Is Maneuvering for International Leadership as the United States Falters," *Foreign Affairs*, March 18, 2020.

13. See, for instance, Kurt M. Campbell and Ely Ratner, "The China Reckoning: How Beijing Defied American Expectation," *Foreign Affairs*, March–April 2018 (see also comments on this article in later issues of the *Foreign Affairs*); "The West Got China Wrong: That Is No Reason to Bungle What Comes Next," *The Economist*, March 3, 2018; William Holstein, ed., *Has the American Media Misjudged China?* (n.p.: Overseas Press Club of America, 2014).

14. Robbie Shilliam, "When Did Racism Become Solely a Domestic Issue?" *Foreign Policy*, June 23, 2020, https://foreignpolicy.com/2020/06/23/racism-ir-international-relations-domestic/; Erin Blakemore, "A Century of Trauma at U. S. Boarding Schools for Native American Children," *National Geographic*, July 9, 2021, https://www.nationalgeographic.com/history/article/a-century-of-trauma-at-boarding-schools-for-native-american-children-in-the-united-states.

15. Minzner, *End of an Era*.

16. This applies to the nature of contemporary international politics. For six conflicting views, see *Foreign Affairs*, July–August 2018. For a discussion of possible trajectories of China's evolution see David Shambaugh, "Contemplating China's Future," *Journal of Chinese Political Science*, Vol. 23, No. 1, April 2017.

17. Work Bank figures, https://data.worldbank.org/indicator/NY.GDP.PCAP.CD?locati ons=CN, accessed February 4, 2021.

18. Kerry Brown, ed., *China's 19th Party Congress: Start of a New Era* (London: World Scientific, 2019), pp. 8–15.

19. "Xi Jinping Is Trying to Remake the Chinese Economy," *The Economist*, August 15, 2020, https://www.economist.com/briefing/2020/08/15/xi-jinping-is-trying-to-rem ake-the-chinese-economy.

20. "Xi Jinping Is Biding his Time on Market Reforms, China Watcher Says," *SCMP*, June 9, 2017.

21. "Hopes High for Xi's Second Term Despite Slow Pace of China Reform," *Financial Times*, March 2, 2017, https://www.ft.com/content/b7683e1a-feff-11e6-96f8-3700c 5664d30.

22. Steven I. Levine, "Sino-American Relations: Practicing Damage Control," in Samuel S. Kim, ed., *China and the World*, 4th ed. (Boulder, CO: Westview Press, 1998), p. 98.

23. A few representative works on the theories of revolutions are Crane Brinton, *The Anatomy of Revolution*, rev. ed. (New York: Vintage Books, 1965); Ted Robert Gurr, *Why Men Rebel* (Princeton, NJ: Princeton University Press, 1970); James C. Davis, "The J-Curve of Rising and Declining Satisfactions as a Cause of Revolution and Rebellion," in Hugh David Graham and Ted Robert Gurr, eds., *Violence in America* (Beverly Hills, CA: Sage, 1976); Theda Skocpol, *States and Social Revolutions* (Cambridge: Cambridge University Press, 1979); Harry Eckstein, ed., *Internal War: Problems and Approaches* (New York: Free Press of Glencoe, 1964). Chalmers Johnson has studied the Chinese revolution and postulated the formula "multiple dysfunctions exacerbated by an intransigent elite and an 'accelerator' equals revolution." See his *Revolutionary Change*, 2nd ed. (Stanford: Stanford University Press, 1982).

24. "Principal Contradiction Facing Chinese Society Has Evolved in New Era: Xi," *Xinhuanet*, October 18, 2017, http://www.xinhuanet.com/english/2017-10/18/c_13 6688132.htm.

25. James MacGregor Burns, *Leadership* (New York: Harper & Row, 1978); Joseph S. Nye, *The Power to Lead* (New York: Oxford University Press, 2008), pp. 61–69; Doris Kearns Goodwin, *Leadership in Turbulent Times* (New York: Simon & Schuster, 2018).

26. Michael G. Rumsey, ed., *The Oxford Handbook of Leadership* (New York: Oxford University Press, 2013), pp. 392–401, 439–455.

27. Robert I. Rotberg, *Transformative Political Leadership* (New York: Oxford University Press, 2012).

28. For the notion of laissez-faire or negligent leadership, see Rumsey, *Oxford Handbook of Leadership*, pp. 393–394, 448–449.

29. For example, see "George Soros Calls China's Xi Jinping 'Most Dangerous' Foe of Free Societies," *SCMP*, January 25, 2019.

30. Xi Jinping, *Xi Jinping tan zhiguo lizheng* [Xi Jinping on the Governance of China] (Beijing: Waiwen chubanshe, 2014), pp. 67–71.

Glossary

liangzhi A suspect is obliged to be present at a designated time and place to be interrogated, although he or she is not subject to detention.

gaoganzhidi Offspring of high officials.

shenpi Regulatory approval and licensing.

shangfang Visit the offices of upper-level authorities.

shuanggui A suspect is obliged to be present at designated time and place to answer charges.

tuanpai "Chinese Communist Youth League faction."

weiwen Stability maintenance.

xiafang Sent downward.

xiaokang "Relatively well off."

xinfang Letters and visits.

xitong Functional administrative system.

zhengfa Politics and law.

zhiqing Educated youth.

Zhongnanhai The vast compound in Beijing where China's central party and government offices are located.

References

Books and Articles in English

Aberbach, Joel D. and Bert A. Rockman. "The Past and Future of Political-Administrative Relations: Research from *Bureaucrats and Politicians* to *In the Web of Politics*—and Beyond." *International Journal of Public Administration*, Vol. 29, No. 12, July 2006, pp. 977–995.

"Aid, China, and Growth: Evidence from a New Global Development Finance Dataset." AIDATA, Working Paper No. 46, October 2017, pp. 1–61. http://docs.aiddata.org/ad4/pdfs/WPS46_Aid_China_and_Growth.pdf.

Ake, Claude. "Modernization and Political Instability: A Theoretical Exploration." *World Politics*, Vol. 26, No. 4, July 1974, pp. 576–591.

Albert, Eleanor. "China's Big Bet on Soft Power." Council on Foreign Relations, May 11, 2017, https://www.cfr.org/backgrounder/chinas-big-bet-soft-power#chapter-title-0-1, accessed June 11, 2017.

Allison, Christine Rothmayr and Denis Saint-Martin. "Half a Century of 'Muddling': Are We There Yet?" *Policy and Society*, Vol. 30, No. 1, 2011, pp. 1–8.

Allison, Graham. *Destined for War: Can America and China Escape Thucydides's Trap?* Boston: Houghton Mifflin Harcourt, 2017.

Allison, Graham. "The Thucydides's Trap." *Foreign Policy*, No. 224, May/June 2017, pp. 80–81.

Allison, Graham. "What Xi Jinping Wants." *The Atlantic*, May 31, 2017.

Allison, Graham and Robert D. Blackwell. *Lee Kuan Yew*. Cambridge, MA: MIT Press, 2013.

Alpermann, Björn. *Politics and Markets in Rural China*. New York: Routledge, 2011.

An Chen. "Secret Societies and Organized Crime in Contemporary China." *Modern Asian Studies*, Vol. 39, No. 1, 2005, pp. 77–107.

Ang, Yuen Yuen. *China's Gilded Age: The Paradox of Economic Boom and Vast Corruption*. Cambridge: Cambridge University Press, 2020.

Ann, Yuen Yuen. "Counting Cadres: A Comparative View of the Size of China's Public Employment." *China Quarterly*, Vol. 211, September 2012, pp. 676–696.

Ansell, Christopher, Jarle Trondal, and Morten Øgård. *Governance in Turbulent Times*. New York: Oxford University Press, 2017.

Ascher, William. *Understanding the Policymaking Process in Developing Countries*. New York: Cambridge University Press, 2017.

Bao, Pu, Renee Chiang, and Adi Ignatius, trans. and eds. *Prisoners of the State: The Secret Journal of Premier Zhou Ziyang*. New York: Simon & Schuster, 2009.

Barabantseva, Elena. "Nationalism." In Chris Ogden, ed., *Handbook of China's Governance and Domestic Politics*. New York: Routledge, 2013, pp. 153–163.

Bardach, Eugene. *The Implementation Game: What Happens after a Bill Becomes a Law*. Cambridge, MA: MIT Press, 1977.

Baum, Richard. *Burying Mao: Chinese Politics in the Age of Deng Xiaoping*. Princeton, NJ: Princeton University Press, 1994.

Beeson, Mark. "Developmental State in East Asia: A Comparison of the Japanese and Chinese Experiences." *Asian Perspectives*, Vol. 33, No. 2, 2009, pp. 5–39.

Beeson, Mark. *Regionalism and Globalization in East Asia: Politics, Security and Economic Development*. 2nd ed. New York: Palgrave Macmillan, 2014.

Bell, Daniel. *The China Model: Political Meritocracy and the Limits of Democracy*. Princeton, NJ: Princeton University Press, 2015.

Bell, Daniel. "China's Political Meritocracy versus Western Democracy." *The Economist*, June 12, 2018.

Beretta, Silvio, Axel Berkofsky, and Lihong Zhang, eds. *Understanding China Today: An Exploration of Politics, Economics, Society, and International Relations*. Cham, Switzerland: Springer International Publishing, 2017.

Bernstein, Emma L. "Has the U.S. Constitution Reached Its Expiration Date? A Review and Criticism of the World's Longest Lasting Constitution." *Inquiries*, Vol. 12, No. 11, 2020. http://www.inquiriesjournal.com/articles/1835/has-the-us-constitution-reac hed-its-expiration-date-a-review-and-criticism-of-the-worlds-longest-lasting-const itution.

Bernstein, Thomas P. *Up to the Mountains and Down to the Villages: The Transfer of Youth from Urban to Rural China*. New Haven: Yale University Press, 1977.

Blakemore, Erin. "A Century of Trauma at U. S. Boarding Schools for Native American Children." *National Geographic*, July 9, 2021. https://www.nationalgeographic.com/ history/article/a-century-of-trauma-at-boarding-schools-for-native-american-child ren-in-the-united-states, accessed August 8, 2021.

Blenny, Misha. *McMafia: A Journey through the Global Criminal Underworld*. London: Vintage Books, 2008.

Bonnin, Michael. "The 'Lost Generation': Its Definition and Its Role in Today's Chinese Elite Politics." *Social Research*, Vol. 73, No. 1, Spring 2005, pp. 245–274.

Boon, Hoo Tiang, ed. *Chinese Foreign Policy under Xi*. New York: Routledge, 2017.

Bougon, François. *Inside the Mind of Xi Jinping*. London: Hurst, 2018.

Brady, Anne-Marie. *Marketing Dictatorship: Propaganda and Thought Work in Contemporary China*. Lanham, MD: Rowman & Littlefield, 2008.

Brady, Anne-Marie and Wang Juntao. "China's Strengthened New Order and the Role of Propaganda." *Journal of Contemporary China*, Vol. 18, Issue 62, 2009, pp. 767–788.

Breslin, Shaun. "Do Leaders Matter? Chinese Politics, Leadership Transition and the 17th Party Congress." *Comparative Politics*, No. 14, Issue 2, June 2008, pp. 215–231.

Brinton, Crane. *The Anatomy of Revolution*. Rev. ed. New York: Vintage Books, 1965.

Brodsgaard, Kjeld Erik and Zheng Yongnian, eds. *Bringing the Party Back In*. London: Marshall Cavendish, 2004.

Brosgaard, Kjeld Erik and Zheng Yongnian, eds. *The Communist Party in Reform*. New York: Routledge, 2006.

Brown, Archie and Jack Gray, eds. *Political Culture and Political Change in Communist States*, 2nd ed. New York: Holmes & Meier, 1979.

Brown, Kerry. *CEO, China: The Rise of Xi Jinping*. London: I.B. Tauris, 2016.

Brown, Kerry, ed. *China's 19th Party Congress: Start of a New Era*. London: I.B. Tauris, 2019.

Brown, Kerry. *China's World: What Does China Want?* London: I.B. Tauris, 2017.

Burns, James MacGregor. *Leadership*. New York: Harper & Row, 1978.

Bush, Richard. *The Perils of Proximity: China-Japan Security Relations*. Washington, DC: Brookings Institution Press, 2010.

Buszynski, Leszek. "Sino-Japanese Relations: Interdependence, Rivalry and Regional Security." *Contemporary Southeast Asia*, Vol. 31, No. 2, 2009, pp. 143–171.

Cai, Peter. *Understanding China's Belt and Road Initiative*. Sydney: Lowy Institute, 2017.

Cai, Yongshun. *State and Agents in China: Disciplining Government Officials*. Stanford, CA: Stanford University Press, 2014.

Campbell, Kurt M. and Ely Ratner. "The China Reckoning: How Beijing Defied American Expectation." *Foreign Affairs*, March–April 2018, pp. 60–70.

Caprice, Leah. "The Lost Generation of the 17th Chinese Communist Party Politburo." *China Brief*, Vol. 8, No. 19, October 7, 2008, pp. 11–17.

Carothers, Christopher. "Xi's Anticorruption Campaign: An All-Purpose Governance Tool." *China Leadership Monitor*, Issue 67, Spring 2021, pp. 1–17.

Chan, Alfred L. "Liu Yazhou, 'A Young Turk in China's Establishment." *China Brief*, Vol. 5, No. 19, September 13, 2005, pp. 5–8.

Chan, Alfred L. *Mao's Crusade; Politics and Policy Implementation in China's Great Leap Forward*. New York: Oxford University Press, 2001.

Chan, Alfred L., ed. "War against Taiwan: A Strategic Evaluation by Lieutenant General Liu Yazhou." *Chinese Law and Government*, Vol 40, No. 5, September–October 2007, pp. 1–98.

Chan, Kam Wing, with Fang Cai, Guanghua Wan, and Man Wang. *Urbanization with Chinese Characteristics: The Hukou System and Migration*. New York: Routledge, 2018.

Chang, Gordon. *The Coming Collapse of China*. New York: Random House, 2001.

Chen, Jian. "China's Involvement in the Vietnam War, 1964–69." *China Quarterly*, No. 142, June 1995, pp. 356–387.

Chen, Xi. "The Rising Cost of Stability." *Journal of Democracy*, Vol. 24, No. 1, January 2013, pp. 57–64.

Chen, Xi. *Social Protests and Contentious Authoritarianism in China*. New York: Cambridge University Press, 2012.

Chen, Yixin. "Lost in Revolution and Reform: The Socioeconomic Pains of China's Red Guards Generation, 1966–1996." *Journal of Contemporary China*, Vol. 8, No. 21, 1999, pp. 219–239.

Cheung, Peter T. "Who's Influencing Whom? Exploring the Influence of Hong Kong on Politics and Governance in China." *Asian Survey*, Vol. 51, No. 4, 2011, pp. 713–738.

Cheung, Tai Ming. "The Chinese National Security State Emerges from the Shadows to Center Stage." *China Leadership Monitor*, Issue 65, Fall 2020, https://www.prcleader.org/cheung.

Chin, Ko-lin L. and Roy Godson. "Organized Crime and the Political-Criminal Nexus in China." *Trends in Organized Crime*, Vol. 9, No. 3, Spring 2006.

"China's Foreign Aid beyond the Headlines." *Fairbank Center blog*, February 12, 2018. https://medium.com/fairbank-center/chinas-foreign-aid-beyond-the-headlines-2479509d4244.

"China's Military Strategy." Beijing: The State Council Information Office of the People's Republic of China, May 2015, chap. 1, "National Security Situation." http://www.chinadaily.com.cn/china/2015-05/26/content_20820628.htm.

Chu, Yun-han, Chih-cheng Lo, and Ramon H. Myers. *The New Chinese Leadership: Challenges and Opportunities after the 16th Party Congress*. New York: Cambridge University Press, 2004.

Clarke, Michael E. *Xinjiang and China's Rise in Central Asia: A History*. New York: Routledge, 2011.

Clear Water Blue Skies. Washington, DC: World Bank, 1997. https://documents1.worldb ank.org/curated/en/944011468743999953/pdf/multi-page.pdf.

Cohen, Michael D., James G. March, and Johan P. Olsen, "A Garbage Can Model of Organizational Choice." *Administrative Quarterly*, Vol. 17, No. 1, 1972, pp. 1–25.

Collins, Alan, ed. *Contemporary Security Studies*. New York: Oxford University Press, 2007.

Colton, Timothy. *The Dilemma of Reform in the Soviet Union*. New York: Council on Foreign Relations, 1986.

D'Agostino, Anthony. *Soviet Succession Struggles: Kremlinology and the Russian Question from Lenin to Gorbachev*. Boston: Allen & Unwin, 1988.

Defense of Japan 2016. Tokyo: Japan Ministry of Defense, 2017.

Dillon, Michael. *China's Rulers: The Fifth Generation Takes Power, 2012–13*. London: Europe China Research and Advice Network, 2012.

Dillon, Michael. *Xinjiang in the Twenty-First Century: Islam, Ethnicity, and Resistance*. New York: Routledge, 2019.

Ding, Yijiang. "Consolidation of the PRC's Leadership Succession System from Hu Jintao to Xi Jinping." *China Report*, Vol. 51, Issue 1, 2015, pp. 49–65.

Dror, Yehezkel. *Policymaking under Adversity*. New York: Routledge, 2017.

Economy, Elizabeth. *The Third Revolution*. New York: Oxford University Press, 2018.

Edney, Kingsley, Stanley Rosen, and Ying Zhu. *Soft Power with Chinese Characteristics: China's Campaign for Hearts and Minds*. New York: Routledge, 2020.

Fan, Jiayang, et al. "Behind the Personality Cult of Xi Jinping." *Foreign Policy*, March 8, 2016, https://medium.com/fairbank-center/chinas-foreign-aid-beyond-the-headli nes-2479509d4244, accessed August 8, 2016.

Feigenbaum, Evan A. *China's Techno-warriors: National Security and Strategic Competition from the Nuclear to the Informational Age*. Stanford, CA: Stanford University Press, 2003.

Feng, Chongyi. "The Dilemma of Stability Preservation in China." *Journal of Current Chinese Affairs*, Vol. 42, No. 2, 2013, pp. 3–19.

Ferdinand, Peter. "Sunset, Sunrise: China and Russia Construct a New Relationship." *International Affairs*, Vol. 83, No. 5, September 2007, pp. 841–867.

Ferdinand, Peter. "Westward Ho—the China Dream and 'One Belt, One Road': Chinese Foreign Policy under Xi Jinping." *International Affairs*, Vol. 92, No. 4, July 2016, pp. 941–957.

Fewsmith, Joseph. "Bo Xilai and Reform: What Will Be the Impact of His Removal?" *China Leadership Monitor*, No. 38, Summer 2012, pp. 1–11.

Fewsmith, Joseph. "Chambers of Commerce in Wenzhou: Toward Civil Society?" In Zheng Yongnian and Joseph Fewsmith, eds., *China's Opening Society: The Non-state Sector and Governance*. New York: Routledge, 2008, pp.186–196.

Fewsmith, Joseph. "China in 2007: The Politics of Leadership Transition." *Asian Survey*, Vol. 48, Issue 1, 2008, pp. 90–91.

Fewsmith, Joseph. *China since Tiananmen: The Politics of Transition*. Cambridge: Cambridge University Press, 2001, 2nd ed., 2008.

Fewsmith, Joseph. "China's Political Ecology and the Fight against Corruption." *China Leadership Monitor*, No. 46, Winter 2015, pp. 1–26.

Fewsmith, Joseph. *Dilemmas of Reform in China: Political Conflict and Economic Debate.* Armonk, NY: M.E. Sharpe, 1994.

Fewsmith, Joseph. "The 18th Party Congress: Testing the Limits of Institutionalization." *China Leadership Monitor*, No. 40, January 2013, pp. 1–9.

Fewsmith, Joseph. "Generational Transition in China." *Washington Quarterly*, Vol. 25, No. 4, August 2002, pp. 23–35.

Fewsmith, Joseph. "The 19th Party Congress: Ringing in Xi Jinping's New Age." *China Leadership Monitor*, No. 55, Winter 2018, pp. 1–22.

Fewsmith, Joseph. "Promoting the Scientific Development Concept." *China Leadership Monitor*, No. 11, Summer 2004, pp. 1–10.

Fewsmith, Joseph. "The 17th Party Congress: Informal Politics and Formal Institutions." *China Leadership Monitor*, No. 23, Winter 2008, pp. 1–11.

Finer, Samuel E. *The Man on Horseback: The Role of the Military in Politics.* Boulder, CO: Westview Press, 1988.

Foster, Keith. "The Wenzhou Model for Economic Development: Impressions." *China Information*, Vol. 5, No. 3, Winter 1990–1991, pp. 53–64.

Foxley, Aldjandro and Fernando Sossdorf. "Making the Transition: From Middle-Income to Advanced Economies." Carnegie Endowment for International Peace, September 2011, pp. 1–35.

Fraval, M. Taylor. "International Relations Theory and China's Rise: Assessing China's Potential for Territorial Expansion." *International Studies Review*, Vol. 12, No. 4, December 2010, pp. 505–532.

Fravel, M. Taylor. *Strong Borders, Secure Nation.* Princeton, NJ: Princeton University Press, 2008.

Friedberg, Aaron L. *Foreign Affairs*, Vol. 99, No. 5, September–October 2020, pp. 150–164.

"Full Text: Human Rights Record of the United States in 2018." *Xinhua*, March 14, 2019, pp. 1–20. http://www.xinhuanet.com/english/2019-03/14/c_137894730.htm.

"Full Text of Hu Jintao's Report at 18th Party Congress." *Xinhua*, November 19, 2012. http://en.people.cn/90785/8024777.html.

Gabuev, Alexander. "Friends with Benefits? Russian-Chinese Relations after the Ukraine Crisis." *Carnegie Endowment for International Peace, 2016.* http://www.jstor.org/stable/resrep13017. 2016, pp. 1–50.

Garnett, Sherman W, ed. *Rapprochement or Rivalry? Russia-China Relations in a Changing Asia.* Washington, DC: Carnegie Endowment for International Peace, 2000.

Garrick, John and Yan Chang Bennett, eds. *China's Socialist Rule of Law Reforms under Xi Jinping.* New York: Routledge, 2016.

Gaunder, Alisa, ed. *The Routledge Handbook of Japanese Politics.* New York: Routledge, 2011.

Gibbs, D. Bradley. "Future Relations between the United States and Japan: Article 9 and the Remilitarization of Japan." *Houston Journal International Law*, Vol. 33, No. 1, 2010, pp. 137–136.

Gill, Bates, Evelyn Goh, and Chin-Hao Huang. *The Dynamics of US-China–Southeast Asia Relations.* Sydney: United States Studies Centre, June 2016.

Godement, François. "One Belt, One Road': China's Great Leap Outward." European Council on Foreign Relations, June 2015, pp. 1–18.

Goebel, Christian and Lynette H. Ong. *Social Unrest in China.* Europe China Research and Academic Network, November 2012.

Goh, Evelyn. "Southeast Asian Perspectives on the China Challenge." *Journal of Strategic Studies*, Vol. 30, No. 4–5, August–October 2007, pp. 809–832.

Goodwin, Doris Kearns. *Leadership in Turbulent Times*. New York: Simon & Schuster, 2018.

Gray, Jack. *Rebellions and Revolutions: China from the 1800s to 2000*. 2nd ed. Oxford: Oxford University Press, 2002.

Green, Michael J. "The Democratic Party of Japan and the Future of the U.S.-Japan Alliance." *Journal of Japan Studies*, Vol. 37, No. 1, Winter 2011, pp. 91–116.

Greenwald, Glenn. *No Place to Hide: Edward Snowden, the NSA, and the U.S. Surveillance State*. Toronto: Signal, 2015.

Grindle, Merilee. "Good Enough Governance Revisited," *Development Policy Review*, Vol. 25, No. 5, 2007, pp. 553–574.

Gross, Donald. *China Fallacy: How the U.S. Can Benefit from China's Rise and Avoid Another Cold War*. New York: Bloomsbury, 2013.

Guo, Sujian, ed. *Political Science and Chinese Political Studies: The State of the Field*. Heidelberg: Springer, 2013.

Guo, Xuezhi. *The Politics of the Core Leader in China: Culture, Institutions, Legitimacy and Power*. Cambridge: Cambridge University Press, 2019.

Guthrie, Doug. *China and Globalization: The Social, Economic and Political Transformation of Chinese Society*. 3rd ed. New York: Routledge, 2012.

Hagstrom, Linus and Jon Williamson. "'Remilitarization,' Really? Assessing Change in Japanese Foreign Security Policy." *Asian Security*, Vol. 5, No. 3, 2009, pp. 242–272.

Hall, Peter A. and Rosemary C. R. Taylor. "Political Science and the Three New Institutionalisms." *Political Studies*, Vol. 44, No. 5, pp. 936–957.

He, Baogang. "How Can Deliberative Institutions Be Sustainable in China?" In Zheng Yongnian and Joseph Fewsmith, eds., *China's Opening Society: The Non-state Sector and Governance*. New York: Routledge, 2008, pp. 197–207.

He, Zengke. "Corruption and Anti-corruption in Reform China." *Communist and Post-communist Studies*, Vol. 33, No. 2, 2000, pp. 243–270.

Health, Timothy R., Kristen Gunness, and Cortez A. Cooper. *The PLA and China's Rejuvenation*. Santa Monica, CA: Rand Corporation, 2016.

Heberer, Thomas. "The Chinese 'Developmental State 3.0' and the Resilience of Authoritarianism." *Journal of Chinese Governance*, Vol. 1, No. 4, November 2016, pp. 611–632.

Heidenheimer, Arnold J. and Michael Johnson. *Political Corruption: Concepts and Contexts*. 3rd ed. New Brunswick, NJ: Transaction Publishers, 2002.

Hogwood, Brian W. and B. Guy Peters. *The Pathology of Public Policy*. Oxford: Clarendon Press, 1985.

Holbig, Heike. "Ideological Reform and Political Legitimacy in China: Challenges in the Post-Jiang Era." In Thomas Heberer and Gunter Schubert, eds., *Regime Legitimacy in Contemporary China: Institutional Change and Stability*. New York: Routledge, 2009, pp. 27–48.

Holbig, Heike and Bruce Gilley. "Reclaiming Legitimacy in China." *Politics & Policy*, Vol. 38, No. 3, June 2010, pp. 395–422.

Holmes, Leslie. *Politics in the Communist World*. New York: Oxford University Press, 1986.

Holstein, William, ed. *Has the American Media Misjudged China?* n.p.: Overseas Press Club of America, 2014.

Hook, Brian, ed. *Fujian: Gateway to Taiwan*. New York: Oxford University Press, 1996.

Hook, Glenn D., Julie Gilson, Christopher W. Hughes, and Hugo Dobson. *Japan's International Relations: Politics, Economics, and Security*. 3rd ed. New York: Routledge, 2012.

Hsiung, James. C. *The Xi Jinping Era: His Comprehensive Strategy toward the China Dream*. New York: CN Times Book, 2015.

Hu, Weixing. "Xi Jinping's 'Big Power Diplomacy' and China's Central Security Commission (CNSC)." *Journal of Contemporary China*, No. 25, Issue 98, 2016, pp. 163–177.

Hua, Shiping, ed. *Chinese Political Culture, 1989–2000*. Armonk, NY: M.E. Sharpe, 2001.

Huang, Jing. "Institutionalization of Political Succession in China: Progress and Implications." In Cheng Li, ed., *China's Changing Political Landscape: Prospect for Democracy*. Washington, DC: Brookings Institution, 2008, pp. 80–97.

Huang, Yasheng. "Zhejiang Province: A Free-Market Success Story." *Businessweek*, October 20, 2008.

Hughes, Christopher. "Japan's Remilitarization." *Adelphi Papers*, Vol. 48, No. 403, 2008, pp. 21–34.

Hung, Ho-fung. "The Unrest of 2019, the National Security Law, and the Future of Hong Kong: A Comparative-International Perspective." *SAIS Review*, Vol. 40, No. 2, pp. 25–41.

Huntington, Samuel. *The Soldier and the State: The Theory and Politics of Civil-Military Relations*. Cambridge, MA: Belknap Press of Harvard University Press, 1957.

Janowitz, Morris. *The Professional Soldier: A Social and Political Portrait*. Glencoe, IL: Free Press, 1960.

Jervis, Robert. "Cooperation under the Security Dilemma." *World Politics*, Vol. 30, No. 2, January 1978, pp. 167–214.

Johnson, Alastair. "International Structures and Chinese Foreign Policy." In Samuel S. Kim. ed., *China and the World*. 4th ed. Boulder, CO: Westview Press, 1998, pp. 55–87.

Joseph, William. *Politics in China: An Introduction*. New York: Oxford University Press, 2019.

Karita, Kan. "Whither Weiwen?" *China Perspectives*, No. 1, March 2013, pp. 87–93.

Kelliher, Daniel. *Peasant Power in China: The Era of Rural Reform, 1979–1989*. New Haven: Yale University Press, 1992.

Keohane, Robert O. *After Hegemony: Cooperation and Discord in the World Political Economy*. Princeton, NJ: Prince University Press, 1984.

Keohane, Robert O. and Joseph S. Nye. *Power and Interdependence: World Politics in Transition*. Boston: Little, Brown, 1977.

Kleinberg, Robert. *China's "Opening" to the Outside World: The Experiment with Foreign Capitalism*. Boulder, CO: Westview Press, 1990.

Kuhn, Robert Lawrence. *How China's Leaders Think*. Singapore: John Wiley & Sons, 2010.

Lai, David, John F. Troxell, and Frederick J. Gellert. *Avoiding the Trap: U.S. Strategy and Policy for Competing in the Asia-Pacific—beyond the Rebalance*. Carlisle, PA: US Army War College Press, 2018.

Lam, Willy W. "Beijing's Post–Bo Xilai Loyalty Drive Could Blunt Calls for Reform." *China Brief*, Vol. 12, No. 7, March 12, 2012, pp. 3–5.

Lam, Willy W. "China's Seventh-Generation Leadership Emerges onto the Stage." Jamestown Foundation, Vol. 19, No. 7, April 9, 2019, pp. 5–11. https://jamestown.org/program/chinas-seventh-generation-leadership-emerges-onto-the-stage/.

Lam, Willy W. *Chinese Politics in the Era of Xi Jinping: Renaissance, Reform, or Retrogression?* New York: Routledge, 2015.

Lam, Willy W. *Chinese Politics in the Hu Jintao Era: New Leaders, New Challenges.* Armonk, NY: M.E. Sharpe, 2006.

Lam, Willy W. "Hu Jintao Draws Blood with the Wang Lijun Scandal." *China Brief*, No. 12, Issue 5, March 2, 2012, pp. 3–5.

Lam, Willy W., ed. *Routledge Handbook of the Chinese Communist Party.* New York: Routledge, 2018.

Lam, Willy W. "Xi Jinping's Chongqing Tour: Gang of Princelings Gains Clout." *China Brief*, No. 10, Issue 25, December 17, 2010, pp. 2–4.

Lampton, David. "China Politics: The Bargaining Treadmill." In Yu-ming Shaw ed., *Changes and Continuities in China's Communism.* New York: Routledge, 1988, pp. 179–204.

Landry, Pierre. *Decentralized Authoritarianism in China: The Communist Party's Control of Local Elites in the Post-Mao Era.* New Haven: Yale University Press, 2008.

Lee, Hochul. "Political Institutionalization as Political Development in China." *Journal of Contemporary China*, Vol. 19, No. 65, June 2010, pp. 559–571.

Lee, Sangkuk. "An Institutional Analysis of Xi Jinping's Centralization of Power." *Journal of Contemporary China*, Vol. 26, No. 105, 2017, pp. 325–336.

Lee, Wei-chin. "Yours, Mine, or Everyone's Property? China's Property Law in 2007." *Journal of Chinese Political Science*, Vol. 15, 2010, pp. 25–47.

Leib, Ethan J. and Baogang He, eds. *The Search for Deliberative Democracy in China.* New York: Palgrave Macmillan, 2010.

Levi-Faur, David, ed. *The Oxford Handbook of Governance.* New York: Oxford University Press, 2014.

Li, Cheng. "A Biographical and Factional Analysis of the Post-2012-Politburo." *China Leadership Monitor*, No. 41, Summer 2013, pp. 1–17.

Li, Cheng. "China's Economic Decisionmakers." *China Business Review*, Vol. 35, Issue 2, March–April 2008, pp. 20–25.

Li, Cheng. "China's Fifth Generation: Is Diversity a Source of Strength or Weakness?" In J. Patrick Boyd, L. Gordon Flake, Cheng Li, Kenneth B. Pyle, Shelley Rigger, and Richard J. Samuels, eds., *Emerging Leaders in East Asia: The Next Generation of Political Leadership in China, Japan, South Korea, and Taiwan.* National Bureau of Asian Research, September 2008, pp. 1–145.

Li, Cheng. "China's 'Fifth Generation' Leaders Come of Age." *Asiatimes* (Jamestown), 2007, http://www.atimes.com/atimes/printN.html, accessed June 2, 2009.

Li, Cheng. *China's Leaders: The New Generation.* Lanham, MD: Rowman & Littlefield, 2001.

Li, Cheng. *China's 17th Party Congress: Looking Ahead to Hu Jintao's 2nd Term.* Washington, DC: Brookings Institution, October 30, 2007.

Li, Cheng. *Chinese Politics in the Xi Jinping Era: Reassessing Collective Leadership.* Washington, DC: Brookings Institution Press, 2016.

Li, Cheng. "The End of the CCP's Resilient Authoritarianism? A Tripartite Assessment of Shifting Power in China." *China Quarterly*, Vol. 21, September 2012, pp. 595–623.

Li, Cheng. "One Party, Two Coalitions in China's Politics." *Brookings*, August 16, 2009. https://www.brookings.edu/opinions/one-party-two-coalitions-in-chinas-politics/.

Li, Cheng. "The Paradoxical Outcomes of China's 19th Party Congress." *Brookings*, October 26, 2017.

Li, Cheng. "Preparing for the 18th Party Congress: Procedures and Mechanisms." *China Leadership Monitor*, No. 36, Winter 2012, pp. 1–17.

Li, Cheng. "The Rise of the Legal Profession in the Chinese Leadership." *China Leadership Monitor*, No. 42, Fall 2013, pp. 1–26.

Li, Cheng. "Was the Shanghai Gang Shanghaied? The Fall of Chen Liangyu and the Survival of Jiang Zemin's Faction." *China Leadership Monitor*, No. 20, Winter 2007, pp. 1–17.

Li, Cheng. "Will China's 'Lost Generation' Find a Path to Democracy? In Li Cheng, ed., *China's Changing Political Landscape: Prospects for Democracy*. Washington, DC, Brooking Institutions Press, 2008, pp. 98–117.

Li, Eric X. "The Life of the Party: The Post-democratic Future Begins in China." *Foreign Affairs*, Vol. 92, No. 1, January–February 2013, pp. 34–46.

Li, Eric X. "Western Media Is Still Wrong: China Will Continue to Rise." *Washington Post*, October 24, 2017.

Li, Peilin. *Chinese Society*. New York: Routledge, 2012.

Li, Wei and Lucian Pye. "The Ubiquitous Role of the *Mishu* in Chinese Politics." *China Quarterly*, Vol. 132, No. 4, 1992, pp. 913–936.

Liang Zhang, comp., Andrew J. Nathan and Perry Link, eds. *The Tiananmen Papers*. New York: Public Affairs, 2001.

Liao, Rebecca. "The Law of Rule: China's Judiciary after the Fourth Plenum." *Foreign Affairs*, October 26, 2014, https://www.foreignaffairs.com/articles/china/2014-10-26/law-rule, accessed November 25, 2014.

Lichbach, Mark Irving and Alan S. Zuckerman. *Comparative Politics: Rationality, Culture, and Structure*. Cambridge: Cambridge University Press, 1997.

Lim, Timothy C. *Doing Comparative Politics*. Boulder, CO: Lynne Rienner, 2016.

Lin, Delia. *Civilizing Citizens in Post-Mao China: Understanding the Rhetoric of Suzhi*. New York: Routledge, 2017.

Lindblom, Charles. "Still Muddling, Not Yet Through." *Public Administration Review*, Vol. 39, No. 6, 1979, pp. 517–526.

Liu, Alan. "The 'Wenzhou Model' of Development and China's Modernization." *Asian Survey*, Vol. 32, No. 8, August 1992, pp. 696–711.

Liu, Mingfu and Zhongyuan Wang. *The Thoughts of Xi Jinping*. Salt Lake City, UT: American Academic Press, 2017.

Liu, Shaoqi. *How to Be a Good Communist*. Peking: Foreign Languages Press, 1951.

Lollar, Xia Li and Anne Wing Hamilton. "Patronage or Prebendalism? The *Mishu/Shouzhang* Relationship and Corruption in Chinese Politics." *China Review*, Vol. 10, No. 1, Spring 2010, pp. 157–182.

Ma, Ngok. "The Rise of 'Anti-China' Sentiments in Hong Kong and the 2012 Legislature Council Elections." *China Review*, Vol. 15, No. 1, Spring 2015, pp. 39–66.

MacMillan, Martin. *Together They Hold up the Sky: The Story of China's Xi Jinping and Peng Liyuan*. Campbell, CA: FastPencil, 2012.

Manion, Melanie. "Taking China's Anticorruption Campaign Seriously." *Economic and Political Studies*, Vol. 4, No. 1, 2016, pp. 3–18.

Martin, Peter. "The Humbling of the NDRC." *China Brief*, Vol. 14, Issue 5, March 7, 2014, pp. 14–18.

Martin, Peter and David Cohen. "Inside Xi Jinping's Reform Strategy." *National Interest*, March 20, 2014, https://nationalinterest.org/commentary/inside-xi-jinpings-reform-strategy-10087?page=0%2C1, accessed February 23, 2016.

Mawdsley, Evan and Stephen White. *The Soviet Elite from Lenin to Gorbachev: The Central Committee and Its Members, 1917–1991*. Oxford: Oxford University Press, 2000.

McCauley, Martin and Stephen Carter. *Leadership and Succession in the Soviet Union, Eastern Europe, and China*. Houndmills: Macmillan, 1986.

McFaul, Michael. "Xi Jinping Is Not Stalin." *Foreign Affairs*, August 10, 2020. https://www.foreignaffairs.com/articles/united-states/2020-08-10/xi-jinping-not-stalin, accessed September 5, 2020.

McGregor, Richard. "Xi Jinping's Quest to Dominate China." *Foreign Affairs*, September–October 2019, pp. 18–25.

Mearsheimer, John. *The Tragedy of Great Power Politics*. New York: Norton, 2001.

Meisner, Maurice. *Mao's China and After: A History of the People's Republic*. 3rd ed. New York: Free Press, 1999.

Mertha, Andrew. "Society in the State: China's Non-democratic Political Pluralization." In Peter Hays Gries and Stanley Rosen, eds., *Chinese Politics: State, Society and the Market*. New York: Routledge, 2010, pp. 69–84.

Miller, Alice L. "The Bo Xilai Affair in Central Leadership Politics." *China Leadership Monitor*, Issue 38, Summer 2012, pp. 1–11.

Miller, Alice L. "The Case of Xi Jinping and the Mysterious Succession." *China Leadership Monitor*, No. 30, Fall 2009, pp. 1–9.

Miller, Alice L. "The CCP Central Committee's Leading Small Groups." *China Leadership Monitor*, No. 26, September 2008, pp. 1–21.

Miller, Alice L. "China's New Party Leadership." *China Leadership Monitor*, No. 23, Winter 2008, pp. 1–10.

Miller, Alice L. "'Core' Leaders, 'Authoritative Persons,' and Reform Pushback." *China Leadership Monitor*, No. 50, Summer 2016, pp. 1–12.

Miller, Alice L. "The 18th Central Committee Politburo: A Quixotic, Foolhardy, Rashly Speculative, but Nonetheless Ruthlessly Reasoned Projection." *China Leadership Monitor*, No. 33, Summer 2010, pp. 1–10.

Miller, Alice F. "Institutionalization and the Changing Dynamics of Chinese Leadership Politics." In Cheng Li, ed., *China's Changing Political Landscape: Prospect for Democracy*. Washington, DC: Brookings Institution, pp. 61–79.

Miller, Alice L. "Leadership Presses Party Unity in Time of Economic Stress." *China Leadership Monitor*, No. 28, Spring 2009, pp. 1–11.

Miller, Alice L. "More Already on the Central Committee's Leading Small Groups." *China Leadership Monitor*, No. 44, Summer 2014, pp. 1–8.

Miller, Alice L. "The New Politburo Leadership." *China Leadership Monitor*, No. 40, Winter 2013, pp. 1–15.

Miller, Alice L. "Politburo Processes under Xi Jinping." *China Leadership Monitor*, No. 47, Summer 2015, pp. 1–13.

Miller, Alice L. "Splits in the Politburo Leadership?" *China Leadership Monitor*, No. 34, Winter 2011, pp. 1–21.

Miller, Alice L. "Xi Jinping and the Party Apparatus." *China Leadership Monitor*, No. 25, Summer 2008, pp. 1–18.

Miller, H. Lyman. "Party Affairs: With Hu in Charge, Jiang's at Ease." *China Leadership Monitor*, No. 13, Winter 2005, pp. 1–10.

Minzner, Carl. *End of an Era*. New York: Oxford University Press, 2018.

Moody, Peter. "Political Culture and the Study of Chinese Politics." In Sujian Guo, ed., *Political Science and Chinese Political Studies*. Heidelberg: Springer, 2013, pp. 32–60.

Mukum, John. *Corruption in Africa: Cases, Consequences, and Cleanups*. Lanham, MD: Lexington Books, 2007.

Mulvad, Andreas Møller. "China's Ideological Spectrum: A Two-Dimensional Model of Elite Intellectuals' Visions. *Theory and Society*, Vol. 47, September 2018, pp. 635–661.

Mulvenon, James C. "The Party Holds the Ring: Civil-Military Relations and Olympic Security." *China Leadership Monitor*, No. 26, Fall 2008, pp. 1–5.

Mulvenon, James C. *Soldiers of Fortune: The Rise and Fall of the Chinese Military-Business Complex, 1978–1998*. New York. Routledge, 2001.

Mulvenon, James C. "Xi Jinping and the Central Military Commission: Bridesmaid or Bride?" *China Leadership Monitor*, No. 34, Winter 2011, pp. 1–5.

Mutua, Makau. "Savages, Victims, and Saviors: The Metaphor of Human Rights." *Harvard International Law Journal*, Vol. 42, No. 1, Winter 2001, pp. 201–245.

Nathan, Andrew J. "Authoritarian Resilience." *Journal of Democracy*, Vol. 14, No. 1, January 2003, pp. 6–17.

Nathan, Andrew J. and Bruce Gilley. *China's New Rulers: The Secret Files*. New York: New York Review of Books, 2003.

Nathan, Andrew J. and Andrew Scobell. *China's Search for Security*. New York: Columbia University Press, 2012.

Nathan, Andres. "Policy Oscillations in the People's Republic of China: A Critique." *China Quarterly*, Vol. 68, December 1976, pp. 720–733.

Naughton, Barry. "Two Trains Running: Supply-Side Reform, SOE Reform and the Authoritative Personage." *China Leadership Monitor*, Issue 50, Summer 2016, pp. 1–10.

Naughton, Barry. "Xi's System, Xi's Men: After the March 2018 National People's Congress." *China Leadership Monitor*, No. 56, Spring 2018, pp. 1–10.

Nye, Joseph S. *The Power to Lead*. New York: Oxford University Press, 2008.

O'Brien, Kevin J. and Lianjiang Li. *Rightful Resistance in Rural China*. New York: Cambridge University Press, 2006.

Oi, Jean C. *State and Peasants in Contemporary China: The Political Economy of Village Government*. Berkeley: University of California Press, 1991.

Osnos, Evan. "Born Red: How Xi Jinping, an Unremarkable Provincial Administrator, Became China's Most Authoritarian Leader Since Mao." *New Yorker*, April 2015, https://www.newyorker.com/magazine/2015/04/06/born-red, accessed June 7, 2015.

Pal, Leslie A. *Beyond Policy Analysis: Public Issue Management in Turbulent Times*. 5th ed. Toronto: Nelson Education, 2014.

Paulson, Hank. *Dealing with China: An Insider Unmasks the New Economic Superpower*. New York: Twelve, 2015.

Peerenboom, Randall. *China Modernizes: Threat to the West or Model for the Rest?* New York: Oxford University Press, 2007.

Peerenboom, Randall. *China's Long March toward Rule of Law*. Cambridge: Cambridge University Press, 2002.

Peerenboom, Randell. "Fly High the Banner of Socialist Rule of Law with Chinese Characteristics! What Does the 4th Plenum Decision Mean for Legal Reforms in China?" *Hague Journal on the Rule of Law*, Vol. 7, No. 1, 2015, pp. 49–74.

Peerenboom, Randall. "Globalization, Path Dependency, and the Limits of Law." In Lowell Dittmer and Guoli Liu, eds., *China's Deep Reform*. Lanham, MD: Rowman & Littlefield, 2006, pp. 191–225.

Pei, Minxin. *China's Crony Capitalism*. Cambridge, MA: Harvard University Press, 2016.

Pei, Minxin. "Is CCP Rule Fragile or Resilient?" *Journal of Democracy*, Vol. 23, No. 1, January 2012, pp. 27–41.

Pepper, Suzanne. "Education." In Roderick MacFarquhar and John K. Fairbank, eds., *The Cambridge History of China*, Vol. 15. Cambridge: Cambridge University Press, 1991, pp. 540–593.

Perry, Elizabeth J. "Challenging the Mandate of Heaven: Popular Protest in Modern China." *Critical Asian Studies*, No. 33, Issue 2, 2001, 163–180.

Perry, Elizabeth J. "Studying Chinese Politics: Farewell to Revolution?" *China Journal*, No. 57, January 2007, pp. 1–22.

Perry, Elizabeth J. and Mark Selden, eds. *Chinese Society: Change, Conflict and Resistance.* Second ed. New York: RoutledgeCurzon, 2003.

Prasad, Eswar. "The U.S.-China Economic Relationship: Shifts and Twists in the Balance of Power." *Brookings*, February 25, 2010, pp. 1–20.

Primiano, Christopher. "China under Stress; the Xinjiang Question." *International Politics*, Vol. 50, No. 3, 2013, pp. 455–473.

Proceedings from Changes in China's Political Landscape: The 17th Party Congress and Beyond. Washington, DC: John L. Thornton China Center, The Brookings Institution, April 12, 2007.

Pye, Lucian. *Asian Power and Politics.* Cambridge, MA: Harvard University Press, 1988.

Pye, Lucian. *The Mandarin and the Cadre: China's Political Cultures.* Ann Arbor: Center for Chinese Studies, University of Michigan, 1988.

Qin, Yaqing. *A Relational Theory of World Politics.* Cambridge: Cambridge University Press, 2018.

Rumsey, Michael G., ed. *The Oxford Handbook of Leadership.* New York: Oxford University Press, 2013.

Reingen, Stein. *The Perfect Dictatorship.* Hong Kong: Hong Kong University Press, 2016.

Rigger, Shelley. "Taiwan." In William A. Joseph, ed., *Politics in China: An Introduction.* 3rd ed. New York: Oxford University Press, 2019, pp. 538–554.

Robinson, Thomas W. "Political Succession in China." *World Politics*, Vol. 27, No. 1, October 1974, pp. 1–38.

Rosencrance, Richard. *The Rise of the Trading State: Commerce and Conquest in the Modern World.* New York: Basic Books, 1986.

Ross, Robert S., ed. *China, the United States, and the Soviet Union: Tri-polarity and Policy.* Armonk, NY: M.E. Sharpe, 1993.

Ross, Robert S. and Jo Inge Bekkevold, eds. *China in the Era of Xi Jinping: Domestic and Foreign Policy Challenges.* Washington, DC: Georgetown University Press, 2016.

Ross, Robert S. and Zhu Feng, eds. *China's Ascent: Power, Security, and the Future of International Politics.* Ithaca: Cornell University Press, 2008.

Rotberg, Robert I. *Transformative Political Leadership: Making a Difference in the Developing World.* Chicago: University of Chicago Press, 2012.

Rumsey, Michael G., ed. *The Oxford Handbook of Leadership.* New York: Oxford University Press, 2013.

Ryono, Angel and Matthew Galway. "Xinjiang under China: Reflections on the Multiple Dimensions of the 2009 Urumqi Uprising." *Asian Ethnicity*, Vol. 16, No. 2, 2015, pp. 235–255.

Saich, Tony. *Governance and Politics of China.* Houndmills: Palgrave, 2001.

Sancton, Andrew and Chen Zhenming. *Citizen Participation at the Local Level in China and Canada.* Boca Raton: CRC Press, 2015.

Saunders, Phillip C. "The Chinese Politburo Hits the Books." *China Brief*, Vol. 6, Issue 15, July 19, 2006, pp. 7–9.

Saunders, Philip C. "Long-Term Trends in China-Taiwan Relations." *Asian Survey*, Vol. 45, No. 6, November–December 2005, pp. 970–991.

Saunders, Philip C. and Joel Wuthnow. "China's Goldwater-Nichols? Assessing PLA Organizational Reforms." *Strategic Forum 294*, April 5, 2016, pp. 68–75.

Sausmikat, Nora. "Generations, Legitimacy, and Political Ideas in China: The End of Polarization or the End of Ideology?" *Asian Survey*, Vol. 43, No. 2, March–April 2003, pp. 352–384.

Schell, Orville Schell and John Delury. *Wealth and Power: China's Long March to the Twenty-First Century*. New York: Random House, 2013.

Schlesinger, David, Anne Henochowicz, and Yaqiu Wang, "Why Xi Jinping's Media Controls Are 'Absolutely Unyielding.'" *Foreign Policy*, March 17, 2016, https://foreig npolicy.com/2016/03/17/why-xi-jinpings-media-controls-absolutely-unyielding-cen sorship-china-economy-speech/, accessed June 7, 2018.

Scobell, Andrew. "China and Taiwan: Balance of Rivalry with Weapons." In Sumit Ganguly and William Thompson, eds., *Asian Rivalries*. Stanford, CA: Stanford Security Series, 2011, pp. 26–45.

Sehnalkova, Jana. "Taiwan's Policy towards the South China Sea." In Martin Riegl, Jakub Landovský, and Irina Valko, eds. *Strategic Regions in 21st Century Power Politics*. Newcastle-upon-Tyne: Cambridge Scholars Publisher, 2014.

Seitz-Wald, Alex. "The U. S. Needs a New Constitution—Here's How to Write It." *The Atlantic*, November 2, 2013. https://www.theatlantic.com/politics/archive/2013/11/ the-us-needs-a-new-constitution-heres-how-to-write-it/281090/.

Selden, Mark. *The Yenan Way in Revolutionary China*. Cambridge, MA: Harvard University Press, 1971.

Shambaugh, David, ed. *China & the World*. New York: Oxford University Press, 2020.

Shambaugh, David. *China's Future*. Cambridge: Polity Press, 2016.

Shambaugh, David. "China's Propaganda System: Institutions, Processes and Efficacy." *China Journal*, No. 57, January 2007, pp. 25–58.

Shambaugh, David. "China's 'Quiet Diplomacy': The International Department of the Chinese Communist Party." *China: An International Journal*, Vol. 5, No. 1, March 2007, pp. 26–54.

Shambaugh, David. "China's 17th Party Congress: Maintaining Delicate Balances." *Brookings Northeast Asia Commentary*, November 2007, https://www.brookings.edu/ opinions/chinas-17th-party-congress-maintaining-delicate-balances/, accessed May 9, 2017.

Shambaugh, David. "China's Soft-Power Push: The Search for Respect." *Foreign Affairs*, June 2015, pp. 99–107.

Shambaugh, David. "Contemplating China's Future." *Journal of Chinese Political Science*, Vol. 13, Issue 1, 2017, pp. 1–7.

Shambaugh, David. *Modernizing China's Military: Progress, Problems, and Prospects*. Berkeley: University of California Press, 2003.

Shao, Binhong, ed. *China under Xi Jinping: Its Economic Challenges and Foreign Policy Initiatives*. Leiden: Brill, 2015.

Sheehan, Michael. *International Security: An Analytical Survey*. Boulder, CO: Lynne Rienner, 2005.

Shen, Simon. "The Hong Kong National Security Law Is Reshaping Political Identities." *The Diplomat*, December 31, 2020. https://thediplomat.com/2021/01/the-hong-kong-national-security-law-is-reshaping-political-identities/, accessed March 2021.

Shi-Kupfer, Kristin, Mareike Ohlberg, Simon Lang, and Bertram Lang. *Ideas and Ideologies Competing for China's Political Future*. Berlin: Merics, 2017.

Shilliam, Robbie. "When Did Racism Become Solely a Domestic Issue? " *Foreign Policy*, June 23, 2020. https://foreignpolicy.com/2020/06/23/racism-ir-international-relations-domestic/.

Shirk, Susan. *China: Fragile Superpower*. New York: Oxford University Press, 2007.

Shirk, Susan. "The Delayed Institutionalization of Leadership Politics." In Jonathan Unger, ed., *The Nature of Chinese Politics*. Armonk, NY: M.E. Sharpe, 2002, pp. 297–311.

Shue, Vivienne and Patricia M. Thornton. *To Govern China: Evolving Practices of Power*. Cambridge: Cambridge University Press, 2017.

Singer, J. D. "The Level-of-Analysis Problem in International Relations." *World Politics*, Vol. 14, No. 1, October 1961, pp. 77–92.

Stronski, Paul and Nicole Ng. Cooperation and Competition: Russia and China in Central Asia, the Russian Far East, and the Artic. Washington, DC: Carnegie Endowment for Internationl Peace, 2018.

Sutter, Robert G. *Chinese Foreign Relations: Power and Policy since the Cold War*. 4th ed. Lanham, MD: Rowman & Littlefield, 2016.

Sutter, Robert G. "Relations with Taiwan." Chap. 8 of his *China's Rise in Asia: Promises and Perils*. Lanham, MD: Rowman & Littlefield, 2005, pp. 209–230.

Tamkin, Emily. "China's Much-Heralded NSC Has Disappeared." *Foreign Policy*, June 30, 2016, https://foreignpolicy.com/2016/06/30/chinas-much-heralded-national-security-council-has-disappeared-nsc-xi-jinping/, accessed April 4, 2017.

Tang, Lina, Yang Zhao, Kai Yin, and Jingzhu Zhao. "City Profile: Xiamen." *Cities*, No. 31, 2013, pp. 615–624.

Tang, Wenfang. *Populist Authoritarianism: Chinese Political Culture and Regime Sustainability*. New York: Oxford, 2016.

Tang, Wenfang. "The 'Surprise' of Authoritarian Resilience in China." *American Affairs*, Vol. 2 No. 1, Spring 2018, pp. 101–117.

Tanner, Murray Scot. "China Rethinks Unrest." *Washington Quarterly*, Vol. 27, No. 3, Summer 2004, pp. 137–156.

Teiwes, Frederick. *Politics and Purges in China: Rectification and the Decline of Party Norms, 1950–1956*. 2nd ed. Armonk, NY: M.E. Sharpe, 1993.

Teiwes, Frederick C. and Warren Sun. *The Tragedy of Lin Biao: Riding the Tiger during the Cultural Revolution, 1966–1971*. London: Hurst, 1996.

Teixeira, Aurora, Carlos Pimenta, António Maia, and José António Moreira, eds. *Corruption, Economic Growth and Globalization*. New York: Routledge, 2016.

Transparency International. "Corruption Perceptions Index 2016." Various dates, https://www.transparency.org/news/feature/corruption_perceptions_index_2016, accessed October 9, 2017.

Townsend, James and Brantly Womack. *Politics in China*. Boston: Little, Brown, 1986.

Truex, Rory. "Consultative Authoritarianism and Its Limits." *Comparative Political Studies*, Vol. 50, No. 3, 2014, pp. 329–361.

Tsai, Kellee S. *Back-Alley Banking: Private Entrepreneurs in China*. Ithaca: Cornell University Press, 2002.

Tsai, Wen-Hsuan and Nicola Dean. "The CCP's Learning System: Thought Unification and Regime Adaptation." *China Journal*, No. 69, 2013, pp. 87–107.

Tsai, Wen-Hsuan and Nicola Dean. "Lifting the Veil of the CCP's *Mishu* System: Unrestricted Informal Politics within an Authoritarian Regime, *China Journal*, No. 73, 2015, pp. 158–185.

Tseng, Steve and Honghua Men, eds. *China in the Xi Jinping Era*. Cham, Switzerland: Palgrave Macmillan, 2016.

Uberoi, Patricia, ed. *Rise of the Asian Giants: The Dragon-Elephant Tango*. London: Anthem Press India, 2009.

Uhalley, Stephen, Jr. and Jin Qiu. "The Lin Biao Incident: More Than Twenty Years Later." *Pacific Affairs*, Vol. 66, No. 3, Autumn 1993, pp. 386–398.

Unger, Jonathan, ed. *The Nature of Chinese Politics*. Armonk, NY: M.E. Sharpe, 2002.

US-China Economic and Security Review Commission. *2012 Annual Report to Congress*. Washington, DC: US Government Printing Office, 2012.

Vidino, Lorenzo. *Countering Radicalization in America: Lessons from Europe*. Washington, DC: United States Institute of Peace, 2010.

Vidino, Lorenzo and James Brandon. *Countering Radicalization in Europe*. London: International Centre for the Study of Radicalization and Political Violence, 2012.

Vogel, Ezra. *Deng Xiaoping and the Transformation of China*. Cambridge, MA: Belknap Press of Harvard University Press, 2011.

Walder, Andrew G. *China under Mao: A Revolution Derailed*. Cambridge, MA: Harvard University Press, 2015.

Waltz, Kenneth. *Theory of International Politics*. New York: McGraw-Hill, 1979.

Wang, Zhikai. "Jiangsu-Zhejaing Model and the Nation-Wide Development of the Private Sector in China." *Frontiers of Economics in China*, Vol. 4, No. 2, June 2009, pp. 292–316.

Weatherley, Robert. *Making China Strong: The Role of Nationalism in Chinese Thinking on Democracy and Human Rights*. New York: Palgrave Macmillan, 2014.

Weiss, Jessica Chen. "A World Safe for Autocracy? China's Rise and the Future of Global Politics." *Foreign Affairs*, July–August 2019, pp. 92–97.

Welch, David. "Embracing Normalcy: Toward a Japanese 'National Strategy.'" In Y. Soeya, M. Tadokoro, and D. Welch, eds., *Japan as a Normal Country?* Toronto: University of Toronto Press, 2011, pp. 16–37.

Wendt, Alexander. *Social Theory of International Politics*. Cambridge: Cambridge University Press, 1999.

"White Paper on China's Military Strategy." *China Daily*, May 26, 2015. http://www.chinadaily.com.cn/china/2015-05/26/content_20820628.htm.

Womack, Brantly. "Asymmetric Parity: US-China Relations in a Multi-nodal World." *International Affairs*, Vol. 92, No. 6, 2016, pp. 1463–1480.

Woo, Margaret Y. "Justice." In Chris Ogden, ed., *Handbook of China's Governance and Domestic Politics*. New York: Routledge, 2012, pp. 53–66.

Wuthnow, Joel. "China's Much Heralded NSC Has Disappeared." *Foreign Policy*, June 30, 2016, https://foreignpolicy.com/2016/06/30/chinas-much-heralded-national-security-council-has-disappeared-nsc-xi-jinping/, accessed November 5, 2017.

Wuthnow, Joel and Phillip C. Saunders. *Chinese Military in the Age of Xi Jinping: Drivers, Challenges, and Implications*. Washington, DC: National Defense University Press, March 2017.

Xi, Jinping. *The Governance of China*. Beijing: Foreign Language Press, 2014.

Yahuda, Michael. "The Limits of Economic Interdependence." Chap. 6 of Alastair Iain Johnston and Robert S. Ross, eds., *New Directions in the Study of China's Foreign Policy*. Stanford, CA: Stanford University Press, 2006, pp. 162–185.

Yan Sun. *Corruption and Market in Contemporary China*. Ithaca: Cornell University Press, 2004.

Yang, Guobin. "China's Zhiqing Generation: Nostalgia, Identity, and Cultural Resistance in the 1990s." *Modern China*, Vol. 29, No. 3, July 2003, pp. 267–296.

Yang, Michelle Murray. *American Political Discourse on China*. New York: Routledge, 2017.

Yeung, Yue-man, Jonna Lee, and Gordon Kee. "China's Special Economic Zones at 30." *Eurasian Geography and Economics*, Vol. 50, No. 2, 2009, pp. 222–240.

You, Ji. "China's National Security Commission: Theory, Evolution and Operations." *Journal of Contemporary China*. Vol. 25, no. 98, 2016, pp. 178–196.

Zakaria, Fareed. "The New China Scare: Why America Shouldn't Panic about Its Latest Challenger." *Foreign Affairs*, January–February 2020, pp. 52–69.

Zeng, Jinghan. *The Chinese Communist's Party's Capacity to Rule*. New York: Palgrave Macmillan, 2016.

Zeng, Jinghan. "Institutionalization of the Authoritarian Leadership in China: A Power Succession System with Chinese Characteristics?" *Contemporary Politics*, Vol. 20, No. 3, 2014, pp. 294–314.

Zhang, Feng and Richard Ned Lebow. *Taming Sino-American Rivalry*. New York: Oxford University Press, 2020.

Zhang, Mo. "From Public to Private: The Newly Enacted Chinese Property Law and the Protection of Property Rights in China." *Berkeley Business Law Journal*, Vol. 5, Issue 2, September 2008, pp. 317–363.

Zhao, Suisheng. "The New Generation of Leadership and the Direction of Political Reform after the 16th Party Congress." In Yun-han Chu, Chih-cheng Lo, and Raymon Myers, *The New Chinese Leadership: Challenges and Opportunities after the Sixteenth Party Congress*. Cambridge: Cambridge University Press, 2004.

Zhao, Suisheng. "Xi Jinping's Maoist Revival." *Journal of Democracy*, Vol 27, No. 3, July 2016, pp. 83–97.

Zheng Yongnian. *The Chinese Communist Party as Organizational Emperor*. New York: Routledge, 2010.

Zheng, Yongnian and Lance L. P. Gore, eds. *The Chinese Communist Party in Action*. New York: Routledge, 2020.

Zheng, Yongnian and Sarah Tong, eds. *China and the Global Economic Crisis*. Singapore: World Scientific, 2010.

Zhou Xinmin. *Xi Jinping's Governance and the Future of China*. New York: Skyhorse Publishing, 2017.

Books and Articles in Chinese

"80 niandai woguo disantidui jianshe di guocheng: xuanbu, peiyang, jiqi jiji zuoyong" 80年代我国第三梯队建设的过程、选拔培养及其积极作用 [The Process of Building the '"third echelon"' in the 1980s: Selections, Cultivations, and their Practical Functions], *Wenxuecheng*, December 18, 2014. http://www.lunwenstudy.com/zzzh idu/47500.html.

Ai Yanghua and Chen Xiaoming. *Gongqingtuan shili* 共青团实力 [The Power of the Communist League]. Carle Place, NY: Mirror Books, 2009.

"Baochi dangyuan xianjinxing jiaoyu huodong di lailong qumai" [The Ins and Outs of the Educational Movement to Maintain the Advancedness of Party Members]. *China.com. cn*, January 11, 2005, www.china.com.cn/chinese/zhuanti/xjxjy/753458.htm, accessed August 9, 2017.

Bo Yibo. *Ruogan Zhongda juece yu shijian de huigu* 薄一波: 若干重大决策与事件的回顾 [Reminiscences on Certain Important Policies and Practices]. Beijing. Zhonggong zhongyang dangxiao chubanshe, 1997.

CCP Central Organizational Department, Office of the Central Party Research, and Central Archives. *Zhongguo gongchandang zuzhishi zhiliao* 中国共产党组织史资料 [Materials on the Organizational History of the CCP]. Vol. 7 (*shang*). Beijing: Zhonggong dangshi chubanshe, 2000.

Chen Yun. *Chen Yun Wenxuan* 陈云文选 [Selected Writings from Chen Yun]. Vol. 3. Beijing: Renmin chubanshe, 1995.

"Dangdai Zhongguo" congshu bianjibu bian ji. *Dangdai Zhongguo de Zhejiang* 当代中国的浙江 [Contemporary Zhejiang]. Beijing: Zhongguo shehui kexue chubanshe: Xinhua shuian jingxiao, 1989.

Fan, Wanli. *Yinxing de fubai: anli yu qishi* 隐形腐败案例与启示 [Invisible Corruption: Case Examples and Insights]. Beijing: Dongfang chubanshe, 2019.

Fujiansheng renmin zhengfu, Fujian Nianjian Bianzuan Weiyunhui, ed. *Fujian nianjian* 福建年鉴 [Fujian Yearbook]. Fuzhou: Fujian renmin chubanshe, 2012.

Gao Xiao. *Ta jiang lingdao Zhongguo: Xi Jinping zhuan* 他将领导中国：习近平传 [He Will Soon Lead China: A Biography of Xi Jinping]. Carle Place, NY: Mirror Books, 2010.

"Gaofeng liangjie Xi Zhongxun" 高风亮节习仲勋 [Xi Zhongxun's Noble Character and Unimpeachable Integrity]. *Dangshi bolan*, No. 2, 2004, pp. 34–37.

Geng Biao. *Geng Biao huiyilu 1909–1949* 耿飙回忆录 [The Memoirs of Geng Biao, 1909–1949]. Nanjing: Jiangsu renmin chubanshe, 1998.

Geng Biao. *Geng Biao huiyilu 1949–1992* 耿飙回忆录 [The Memoirs of Geng Biao, 1949–1992]. Nanjing: Jiangsu renmin chubanshe, 1998.

Hong, Qing. *Tajiang shi Zhongguo de guanjia—Li Keqiang* 他将是中国大管家—李克强传 [He Will Soon Become China's Grand Housekeeper: A Biography of Li Keqiang]. Carle Place, NY: Mirror Books, 2010.

Hu Angang. *Zhongguo jiti lingdao zhidu* 中国集体领导 [China's Collective Leadership]. Beijing: Renmin daxue chubanshe, 2013.

Hu Jintao. *Hu Jintao wenxuan* 胡锦涛文选 [Selected Works of Hu Jintao]. 3 Vols. Beijing: Renmin chubanshe, 2016.

Hu Lili and Liang Jian. *Xi Jinping zhuanji* 习近平传记 [A Biography of Xi Jinping]. Deer Park, NY: Mirror Books, 2012.

Interviews and Editorial Office of the Central Party School. *Xi Jinping de 7 nian zhiqing suiyue* 习近平的7年知青岁月 [Xi Jinping's Seven Years' Experience as a *Zhiqing*]. Beijing: Zhongyang dangxiao chubanshe, 2017.

Jia Juchuan. "Luhuo chunqing de Xi Zhongxun" 炉火纯青的习仲勋 [Xi Zhongxun's Art of Perfection]. *Dangshi bolan*, no. 3, 2003, pp. 40–42.

Jiang, Zemin. *Jiang Zemin wenxian* 江泽民文选 [Selected Works of Jiang Zemin]. 3 Vols. Beijing: Renmin chubanshe, 2006.

Jin Xiangrong. "Zhejiang moshe: qushi yu zuli" 浙江模式：趋势与阻力 [The Zhejiang Model: Trends and Obstacles]. *Shehui guancha*, March 22, 2012, pp. 44–45.

Ke Yunlu. *Xinxing* 新星 [New Star]. Beijing: Renmin wenxue chubanshe, 1985.

Laoji zhutuo, zaichuang xinju 牢记嘱托，再创新局 [Hold Fast to the Command, Create a New Situation]. Guangzhou: Nanfang renmin chubanshe, 2017.

Li Zhongzhi, and Cao Yangkui. "Tong huxi caineng xinshuangyi" [Breathing Together So That Our Hearts Can Beat Together], *Hebei huabao*, No. 9, 2013.

Liang Jian. *Xi Jinping xinzhuan* 习近平新传 [A New Biography of Xi Jinping]. Deer Park, NY: Mirror Books, 2012.

Liu Xiaomeng. *Zhongguo zhiqings shi: dachao* 中国知青史: 大潮 [A History of the *Zhiqing*: The Great Tide, 1966–1980]. Beijing: Dangdai Zhongguo chubanshe, 2009.

Lu Lei and Zhao Hong. *Guoyun: Nanfang jiahi* 国运: 南方记事 [The Fate of the Country: Records of Events from South China]. Beijing: Renmin wenxue chubanshe, 2008.

Mao Zedong. *Jianguo yilai Mao Zedong wengao* 建国以来毛泽东文稿 [Mao Zedong's Writings since the Founding of the State]. Vol. 10. Beijing: Zhonggong zhongyang wenxian yanjiu shibian, 1996.

Qi Xin. "Woyu Xi Zhongxun fengyu shuangban 55 ge chunqiu" 我与习仲勋风雨双伴55个春秋 [My Companionship with Xi Zhongxun for a Tumultuous Fifty-Five Years], *Zhongheng*, No. 1, 1999, pp. 37–44.

Shibada yilai lianzheng xinguiding 十八大以来廉政新规定 [New Regulations on Clean Government Drawn Up since the Eighteenth Party Congress]. Beijing: Renmin chubanshe, 2014.

Shibada yilai zhongyao wenxian xuanbian 十八大以来重要文献选编 [A Collection of Important Documents since the Eighteenth Party Congress]. Vol. 1. Beijing: Zhongyang wenxian chubanshe, 2014.

Shui Xinying. "Cong Shaanbei huangtudi zoujin Zhongnanhai de Xi Zhongxun 从陕北黄土地走进中南海的习仲勋 [Xi Zhongxun: From the Yellow Earth of Shaanbi to Zhongnanhai]. *Dangshi wenyuan*, No. 12, 2009, pp. 13–17.

Wang Youfei. "Woyu Xi Jinping zai Zhengding de jiaowang" [我与习近平在正定的交往]. *Wenshi bolan*, No. 11, 2015, pp. 46–48.

"Wodi shangshan xiaxiang jingli" 我的上山下乡经历 [My Experience of Going Up to the Mountains and Down to the Countryside]. *Xuexi bolan*, No. 12, 2010, pp. 16–17.

"Woshi ruhe kuaru zhengjiedi" 我是如何跨入政界的 [How I Entered Politics]. *Lingdao wencui*, November 2000, pp. 62–67.

Wu Nan and Gao Xiao. *Peng Liyuan yu Xi Jinping* 彭丽媛与习近平 [Peng Liyuan and Xi Jinping]. Deer Park, NY: Haye chubanshe, 2013.

Wu Zhifei. "Xi Jinping: Cong huangtugaopo dao shanghaitan" 习近平: 从黄土高坡到上海滩 [Xi Jinping: From the Yellow Earth High Plateau to the Bund of Shanghai], *Dangshi zongheng*, No. 5, 2007, pp. 16–21.

Wu Zhifei and Yu Wei. *Zhongguo gaoduan fangwen, 1: Ying xiang Zhongguo gaoceng juece de 18 ren* [High-Level Interviews in China, 1: The Eighteen Influential People in China's High-Level Decision-Making]. Shanghai: Dongfang chubanshe, 2006.

Xi Jinping. *Baituo pinkun* 摆脱贫困 [Overcoming Poverty]. Fuzhou: Fujian renmin chubanshe, 1992.

Xi Jinping. *Ganzai shichu, Zozai qianlie: tuijin Zhejiang xinfazhan de sihao yu shijian* 干在实处: 推进浙江新发展的思考与实践 [Do Practical Work and be at the Forefront: The Thinking and Practice in Promoting New Development in Zhejiang]. Beijing: Zhonggong zhongyang dangxiao chubanshe, 2006.

Xi Jinping. *Guanyu dangfeng lianzheng jianshe he fanfubai douzheng lunshu zhaibian* 习近平关于党风廉政建设和反腐败斗争论述摘编 [Xi Jinping: Selections of Xi Jinping's Discourses on the Construction of a Clean Party Work Style and the Struggle against Corruption]. Beijing. Fangzheng chubanshe, 2015.

Xi Jinping. *Guanyu qingshaonian he Gongqingtuan gongzuo lunshu zhaibian* 习近平关于青少年和共青团 工作论述摘编 [Selected Writings by Xi Jinping on Youth and CYL Work]. Beijing: Zhongyang wenxian chubanshe, 2017.

Xi Jinping. *Guanyu quanmian conyan zhidang lunshu zhaibian* 习近平关于全面从严治党论述摘编 [Selections from Xi Jinping's Discourses on the Strict Governance of the Party]. Beijing: Zhongyang wenxian chubanshe, 2016.

Xi Jinping. *Guanyu quanmian shenhua gaige lunshu zhaibian* 习近平关于全面深化改革论述摘编 [Selections from Xi Jinping's Discourses on the Comprehensively Deepening of Reforms]. Beijing: Zhongyang wenxian chubanshe, 2014.

Xi Jinping. *Guanyu yanming dangde jilu he guiju lunshu zhaibian* 关于严明党的纪律和规矩论述摘编 [Selections from Xi Jinping's Discourses on the Strict Enforcement of the Party's Rules and Regulations]. Beijing Zhongyang wenxian chubanshe, 2016.

Xi Jinping. *Xi Jinping guanyu quanmian yifa zhiguo lunshu zhaibian* 习近平关于全面依法治国论述摘编 [Selections of Xi Jinping's Discourses on Comprehensive Law-Based Governance]. Beijing: Zhongyang wenxuan chubanshe, 2015.

Xi Jinping. *Xi Jinping tan zhiguo lilun* 习近平谈治国理论 [Xi Jinping on Governance]. Beijing: Waiwen chubanshe, 2014.

Xi Jinping. *Xi Jinping tan zhiguo lilun* 习近平谈治国理论, 第二卷 [Xi Jinping on Governance]. Vol. 2. Beijing: Waiwen chubanshe, 2017.

Xi Jinping. *Xi Jinping tan zhiguo lizheng* 习近平谈治国理论, 第三卷 [Xi Jinping on Governance]. Vol. 3. Beijing: Waïwen chubanshe, 2020.

Xi Jinping. "Woshi huangtudi de erzi" 我是黄土地的儿子 [I Am a Son of the Yellow Earth]. The earliest but abridged version was published in *Quanguo xinshumu*, December 2002, p. 26.

Xi Jinping. "Yongquan jiang guande, jiaowang you yuanze" 用 权将官德: 交往有原则 [Official Integrity Must Govern the Exercise of Power, and Principles Must Govern All Transactions]. *Qiushi*, No. 19, 2004, pp. 36–38.

Xi Jinping. *Zhijiang xinyu* 之江新语 [New Sayings from Zhejiang]. Hangzhou: Zhejiang renmin chubanshe, 2013.

Xi Jinping. *Zhizhishen, aizhiqie* 知之深爱之切 [Learn Profoundly and Love Deeply]. Shijiazhuang: Hebei renmin chubanshe, 2015.

Xi Jinping. *Zhongguo nongcun shichanghua yanjiu* 中国农村市场化研究 [A Study on China's Marketization]. Doctoral dissertation, Tsinghua University, 2001.

"Xi Jinping ceng dangliao liunian cunganbu" 习近平曾当了六年村干部 [Xi Jinping has Worked as a Village Cadre for Six Years]. *Lantai neiwei*, No. 6, 2011, pp. 50–52.

"Xi Jinping mantan wangxi 30 nian" 习近平漫谈往昔30年 [Xi Jinping Talks Casually about His Past Thirty Years]. *Dangshi wenyuan*, No. 3, 2004, pp. 52–53.

"Xi Jinping's Exclusive Interview with Reporters on His Experience of Joining the Production Brigade" [习近平接受记者专访 讲述自己插队经历] February, 2019. Available on YouTube. https://www.youtube.com/watch?v=QpBoJRhCOR8.

"Xi Jinping zai Min changdiao shouhu shejianshang de anquan" 习近平在闽倡导守护舌尖上的安全 [Xi Jinping Promotes the Protection of Food Safety at Fujian]. *Ifeng*, August 1, 2014. http://xm.ifeng.com/travel/xiamen_2014_08/01/2694351_0.shtml, accessed April 4, 2016.

Xi Zhongxun geming shengya bianjizu. *Xi Zhongxun geming shengya* 习仲勋革命生涯 [The Revolutionary Life and Career of Xi Zhongxun]. Beijing: Zhongguo wenshi chubanshe, 2002.

Xi Zhongxun zhuan bianweihui. *Xi Zhongxun Zhuan* 习仲勋传 [Biography of Xi Zhongxun]. Beijing: Zhongyang wenxian chubanshe, Vol. 1, 2008, Vol. 2, 2013.

Xia Fei, Yang Yun, and Bai Xiaoyun. *Taizidang he Gongqingtuan: Xi Jinping pk Li Keqiang* 太子党和共青团：习近平pk 李克强 [The Princeling Faction and the Communist Youth League; Xi Jinping Competes with Li Keqiang]. Carle Place, NY: Mirror Books, 2007.

Xiang Jiangyu. *Xi Jinping bandi* 习近平班底 [Xi Jinping's Background Connections]. Carle Place, NY: Mirror Books, 2011.

Yang Zhongmei. *Xi Jinping: zhanzai lishi shizi lukou de Zhonggong xin lingdao ren* 习近平：站在历史十字路口的中国新领导人 [Xi Jinping: A New Leader at a Historical Crossroads]. Taibei Shi: Shi bao wenhua chuban qiye gufen youxian gongsi, 2011.

Yu Jianrong. "Zhongguo de saoluan shijian yu guanzhi weiji" 中国的骚乱事件与管治危机 [China's Incidences of Unrest and the Governance Crisis). Address delivered on October 30, 2007, at the University of California, Berkeley, 2007. http://www.chinaelections.org/newsinfo.asp?newsid=118361.

Yu Jie. *Zhongguo jiaofu Xi Jinping* 中国教父习近平 [Xi Jinping: China's Godfather]. Xianggang: Kaifang chubanshe, 2014.

Zhang Wei. "Xi Jinping zheyang zao xianwei shuji" [习近平这样做县委书记], *Shijian*, No. 5, 2015, pp. 22–23.

Zhang Lichen. "Cong cunzhi shu dao shengwei shuji" 从村支书到省委书记 [From Village Branch Secretary to Secretary of the Provincial Party Committee], *Shenzhou*, No. 2, 2004, pp. 8–12.

Zhang Tongfang. *From Xi Zhongxun to Xi Jinping* 从习仲勋 到 习近平. n.p.: Caida chubanshe, 2011.

Zhejiang Nianjian, 2012 [An Almanac of Zhejiang, 2012]. Hangzhou: Zhejiang nian jian she, 2012.

Zhonggong Zhejiangsheng dangshi yanjiushi, Dangdai Zhejiang yanjiusuo. *Dangdai Zhejiang gailan* 当代浙江概览 [A General Survey of Contemporary Zhejiang]. Beijing: Dangdai Zhongguo chubanshe, 2012.

Zhongguo gongchandang lijie zhongyang weiyuan dacidian 中国共产党历届中央委员大辞典 [An Encyclopedia of the Members of the Central Committee]. Beijing: Zhonggong dangshi chubanshe, 2004.

Zhou Wang. *Zhongguo xiazu jishi yanjiu* 中国"小组机制"研究 [Research on China's Small Groups System]. Tianjin: Tianjin renmin chubanshe, 2010.

Zong Hairen. *Disidai.* 第四代 [The Fourth Generation]. Carle Place, NY: Mirror Books, 2002.

"Zuo you zhiqi youzuowei diyidai: Xi Zhongxun zhizi Xi Jinping fangtanlu" 做有志气有作为的一代 [Be Part of a Generation with Courage and Achievement: An Interview with Xi Zhongxun's Son Xi Jinping]. *Jiachang*, No. 2, 1997, p. 4.

Index